Lytham Library
Tel: 736745

St. Annes Library.
Tel: 729943

trans'd to PL 2/90

spine label / label
free

IRE RS

FO REFERENCE

ONLY

a30118 006646115b

A DICTIONARY OF BRITISH SURNAMES

A
DICTIONARY
OF BRITISH
SURNAMES

by

P. H. REANEY
Litt.D., Ph.D., F.S.A.

Second edition with corrections and additions
by
R. M. WILSON
M.A.

Routledge & Kegan Paul
LONDON, BOSTON, MELBOURNE AND HENLEY

485075987

00664611

First published 1958
Second impression (with some corrections) 1961
Reprinted 1966 and 1970
Second revised edition 1976
Reprinted (with some corrections) 1977
Reprinted 1979 and 1983
by Routledge & Kegan Paul plc
39 Store Street, London WC1E 7DD,
9 Park Street, Boston, Mass 02108, U.S.A.,
464 St. Kilda Road, Melbourne,
Victoria 3004, Australia, and
Broadway House, Newham Road,
Henley-on-Thames, Oxon, RG9 1EN
Printed in Great Britain
by T. J. Press (Padstow) Ltd, Padstow, Cornwall
© University of Sheffield 1958, 1961, 1976

No part of this book may be reproduced in any form
without permission from the publisher, except for the
quotation of brief passages in criticism

ISBN 0 7100 8106 5

CONTENTS

PREFACE TO THE SECOND EDITION

SOME seven hundred names have been added to this second edition, mostly fairly common ones omitted from the original edition from considerations of space; the list of abbreviations has been rewritten; and various necessary corrections have been made. Some of the corrections, and many of the additional names, had already been included by Dr. Reaney in his own copy of the book in preparation for a new edition. In addition much of the material for the other names has been taken from Dr. Reaney's extensive files, now in the Sheffield University Library, though other sources, not at the time available to him, have also been used. The additional entries follow the pattern of those in the first edition, and it is hoped that their inclusion will make rather more comprehensive a work which has already become the standard book on the subject.

R. M. WILSON

1976

PREFACE

O F previous Dictionaries of Surnames, Lower's *Patronymica Britannica* (1860) is obviously out-of-date, Barber's *British Family Names* (1902) is a mere collection of guesses unsupported by evidence, whilst Harrison's *Surnames of the United Kingdom* (1912–18) only very occasionally gives any evidence and a large number of his etymologies are clearly based on the modern form. Still the most reliable is Bardsley, whose *Dictionary of English and Welsh Surnames*, published posthumously in 1901, firmly laid the foundations on which future study of surnames must be built. He insisted on the need for the collection of as many early examples of the surname as possible, dated and localized, on which the etymology must be based. These principles he put into practice, so far as he could, but he has suffered the inevitable fate of all pioneers. The last fifty years have seen an enormous increase in the material available in the publications of the Public Record Office, the Pipe Roll Society, county Record Societies, etc., much of it earlier than Bardsley's basic source (the late thirteenth-century Hundred Rolls), with a steadily improving standard of editing. The same period has seen, too, a marked advance in our knowledge of the English language, particularly in the history of its dialects, personal-names and place-names.

The earlier literature of surnames has been adequately discussed by Weekley, Ewen and Tengvik. Whilst subscribing to the only sound principles, Weekley, in his published works, seldom gives the evidence on which his etymologies are based, and even then, usually an undated reference to the Patent or the Close Rolls. For many names he clearly had no evidence. He fails to distinguish between Old English, Scandinavian and continental Germanic personal-names and is uncritical in his use of Searle. Ewen attempted an impossible task. Generalizations on surnames are valueless if an unimpeachable etymology has not been established. He fails to distinguish between sound and spelling, and postulates impossible forms of Old English names. Worst of all, he rejects sound etymologies which do not fit in with his preconceived theories.

The present work is based on an independent collection of material begun in 1943 to beguile the tedium of the quieter periods of fire-watching. A complete Dictionary of Surnames cannot yet be produced, partly because for many of the large number of surnames surviving material is at present scanty or lacking, partly because of the high cost of such a production. This has meant a strict economy in examples and in exposition and the elimination from the first draft of some 100,000 words and 4,000 names. All surnames included are known to survive. The great majority of those eliminated are local surnames such as Manchester, Wakefield, Essex, etc., which can easily be identified from the gazetteer. When a local surname has been traced to its source, the surname-student's task is finished. The meaning of the place-name is a problem for others and those who wish for further information should consult the *Oxford Dictionary of Place-names* or the county volumes of the English Place-name Society whose latest publication, A. H. Smith's *English Place-name Elements* (2 vols., 1956) is a comprehensive treatment of the subject.

The most valuable modern work on English surnames has been produced in Sweden. Olof von Feilitzen's book on the pre-Conquest personal-names in Domesday Book has been invaluable. Tengvik has dealt with Old English bynames, Löfvenberg with Middle English local surnames, Fransson and Thuresson with Middle English occupational-names. Ekwall, too, turning aside from English place-names, has already made valuable additions to our knowledge of surnames, particularly those of London. Here I would take the opportunity to express my appreciation of a very generous gesture which I still regard as a private act indicative of national sentiment. Shortly after the war, I mentioned casually to Dr. Gösta Langenfelt, on one of his visits to London, that all my books had been destroyed. Later I received from ten or more Swedish scholars signed copies of their books. With these constantly at hand, work on this book has been greatly facilitated. I am also indebted to the Librarian of the Royal Library, Stockholm, for depositing temporarily in the Library of the University of London certain inaccessible books; to Dr. von Feilitzen, who first suggested the transfer and has kept me informed of new Swedish publications likely to be of use; to E. H. Brandt, for access to his collection of surname material and for many useful discussions; to J. E. B. Gover, for forms from unpublished MSS; and to F. G. Emmison, of the Essex Record Office, for a copy of his unpublished transcript of the 1662 Hearth Tax Returns for Essex. To Mr. Gover and to Professor R. M. Wilson of the University of Sheffield my grateful thanks are due for the time they have spent in reading the proofs. Their comments and criticisms have been invaluable in eliminating errors and inconsistencies. For those that remain the responsibility is mine alone.

P. H. REANEY

Hildenborough
January 1958

INTRODUCTION

THE purpose of a Dictionary of Surnames is to explain the meaning of names, not to treat of genealogy and family history. The fact that Robert le Turnur lived in Staffordshire in 1199 and that there was a William de Kouintre in London in 1230 does not mean that they were the ancestors of all or any of the modern Turners or Coventrys. To establish this, a fully documented pedigree would be required and very few families can carry back their history so far. Throughout the Middle Ages surnames were constantly changing. William Tyndale was known as Huchyns when living in Gloucestershire. Oliver Cromwell was a Williams and David Livingstone was a McLeay. Even today families change their names. Blackden has become Blacktin, Hogg has been changed to Hodd and Livemore has superseded Livemore—all within living memory.

The modern form of many of our surnames is comparatively recent, often preserving a phonetic spelling found in a seventeenth- or eighteenth-century parish register. When some of the Sussex Bourers migrated to Kent in the seventeenth century they adopted the form Bowra. *Pharaoh* is a reconstructed spelling of *Faro*, originally *Farrer*, found also as *Farrey*, *Farrah* and *Farrow* in the seventeenth century. The Suffolk Deadman is a corruption of Debenham and Tudman of Tuddenham. Each surname has its pedigree which must be traced before the meaning can be discovered, and even then the true origin cannot be decided unless the family pedigree can be carried back far enough to fix definitely the original medieval form. A modern White may owe his name to an ancestor bearing the Anglo-Saxon name of *Hwīta*, or to one nicknamed 'the fair', or to an original home in the bend of a river. The original Howard may have been a ewe-herd or a hayward, or he may have borne either the French name *Huard* or the Old German name *Howard*. The modern forms often conceal rather than reveal information.

The English language lacks terms corresponding to the French *sobriquet* and *nom de famille*. Today, surname means an inherited family name; originally it meant simply an additional name and it is used in this sense in this book.[1] Only very occasionally can early medieval surnames be proved to be hereditary, and any attempt to distinguish them would end in inaccuracy and confusion.

[1] cf. *Groups*, 75.

VARIATION OF SURNAMES

Celts, Anglo-Saxons, and Scandinavians, all originally had a single name for each individual, e.g. Welsh *Llewellyn*, Gaelic *Donald*, Anglo-Saxon *Cuthbert*, Scandinavian *Gamall*. So, too, had the Normans who were ultimately of Danish descent. Already in England before the Norman Conquest we find a number of bynames, and these were increased after the Conquest by those used by Normans. In the twelfth century we have an unsettled and varied type of nomenclature, often by way of description rather than of an actual name, as in the Holme Cartulary, where we find men named by their font-name alone, or by this plus (i) their father's name in full, (ii) their father's christian name, (iii) the name of their estate or of their place of origin, or (iv) a byname, descriptive of office, occupation, or a nickname, e.g.

Odo balistarius, arbalistarius, or de Wrthstede
Osbernus decanus (de Turgetona), presbiter (de Turgertona), de Turgartona, de Tweyt, filius Griffini (de Tweyt)
Guarinus minister noster, Gwarinus dispensarius noster, Warinus dispensator, Warinus de Thoftes
Willelmus filius Hermanni, Willelmus Hermannus, Willelmus de Caletorp, Willelmus de Hobosse

Similar descriptions are found in other twelfth-century documents, the most common being a variation between the name of the father and a place-name or byname. The names of clergy varied with a change of incumbency or office, or as they rose to higher orders.
From twelfth-century Danelaw charters:

Ralph de Cheurolcurt, de Clachesbi
Johannes filius Herberti, de Orrebi
Adam filius Remigii (de Hakethorn), Wodecok
Gaufridus filius Bertranni (de Snelleslund), del Lund, de Lund, filius Bertrammi de Lund
Reginald Lequite, de Courtenay

In the thirteenth and fourteenth centuries similar but less elaborate variations are found, and here we often have real alternative surnames:

Robert Hastif, Robert de Disun 1202–3 Cur (Wa)
Ricardus filius Walteri, de Cliue 1221 AssWo
Milo de Verdun, de Creyton 1222 AssSt
Roger Waudin, Rogerus Anglicus 1243 Fees (Sa)
Adinet de Bidyk 1276 Fine, Adnettus le Taylur 1285 *Ass* (Ess)
Ralph le Verrer, Ralph Vicar 1311 ColchCt
Jordan de Newintone, Jordanus Pistor 1317 AssK

This variation of surname is sometimes implied:

Hugo de Burgo le Mazun 1257 Oseney
Johannes Gyffard dictus le Boef 1297 MinAcctCo
John Bulichromp called le Binder 1300 LLB C
Adam de Sutton, called 'Ballard', sadler 1303 LoCt
William Cros le Bole 1305 LoCt
Ralph de Eyr called Proudfot of Havering 1393 HPD (Ess)[1]

The following names of freemen of York are so entered on the roll:

Thomas le Walche, de Selby, girdeler (1329)
Alan Hare, de Acastre, carnifex (1332)
Rogerus filius Johannis de Burton, de Eton in le Clay, boucher (1343)
Johannes, filius Roberti de Gaunt, de Duffeld, mercer (1356)

With the fifteenth century such names become less common, but variation of surname continued and is found sporadically until the seventeenth century or later:

Robert Curson alias Betele 1410 AD iv (Lo)
Nichol Wigh oþerwise callyd Nicholas Ketringham oþerwise callyd John
    Segrave otherwise callyd Nicholl' Pecche 1418 LondEng
Henry Lordessone alias Henry de la Heus 1460 AD iv (Nth)
John Morys alias Rede alias Sclattere 1474 Oseney
Roger Harflete otherwise called Roger Cheker son and one of the heirs of
    Christopher Harflete otherwise called Christopher Atcheker . . . Raymond
    Harflete also called R. Atcheker 1508 ArchC 40
Richard Bishop alias Hewson of London 1671 EA (NS) iv

This variation may be merely scribal. In Domesday Book Robertus *blundus* is also called *albus*, *flauus*, *blancard*, all meaning 'fair'. The tenants of Woolfin (Devon) were Gregory *Lupus* (1222), Richard *le Low* (1303) and Walter (*le*) *Wolf* (1359 PN D 368). Here the real surname was *Wolf*, translated by the earlier scribes into Latin and French. Allard *Smyth* is identical with Alaerd *le Fevre* (1382 LoPleas).

There is, however, evidence that the surname in the document is not always that used by the man himself:

Robert le Botiler of Hertford. *Seal:* Robertus filius Willelmi (1275 AD iv)
Agnes daughter of Rogerus piscator of Coventre. *Seal:* Agnes filia Petronille
    (1299 AD v)
Thomas le Diakne of Ikelyntone. *Seal:* Thomas filius Ricardi de Fonte (1300 ib.)
Ralph de Westred. *Seal:* Radulfus filius Willelmi (13th AD iv)
Agnes de Humet. *Seal:* Agnes de Bellomonte (ib.)
Seuual de Walcfare. *Seal:* Sawale filius Petri (13th AD v)
Angerus called Humfrey of Lapworth. *Seal:* Aungerus de Bispwod (1319 ib.)
Katharine daughter of John le Jay, wife of Roger Prodhome. *Seal:* Katerina
    Franceis (14th ib.)

---

[1] For other examples, *v.* MESO 21 (1275–1533).

TRANSFER OF SURNAMES

In London, in the thirteenth and fourteenth centuries, it was quite usual for the surname of an apprentice to be replaced, either temporarily or definitely, by that of his master.[1] In most cases where sufficient material is available, the new surname displaced the old one altogether, a matter of some importance for genealogists.

Sewald, son of Sewald de Springefeld (1311 LLB B), is identical with Sewal, son of Sewal de Sprengewell, apprentice of Richard de Godesname, paternoster (1311 LLB D) and with Sewallus de Godesname (1319 SRLo). Robert Podifat (1288 LLB A) was an apprentice of Roger le Fuyster (1312 LLB D), who is also called Roger Podifat (1320 LLB E). Robert, therefore, assumed his master's nickname as his surname. Thomas de Cavendisshe, son of William atte Watre de Ewelle, late apprentice of Walter de Cavendisshe, mercer, was admitted a freeman of the city in 1311–12 (LLB D). His original surname would have been *atte Watre* or *de Ewelle*. From 1319 to 1349 he is regularly called *de Cavendish* and, in the enrolment of his will, Thomas de Cavendych, mercer or draper.

The same custom seems to have existed also at York, though less well evidenced: William Payne serviens John Payne (1323 FrY); Roger Storre, servant of Johan Storre (1379 PTY); Richard Redhode, draper, serviens Willelmi Redhode (1386 FrY); Thomas Gauke, cocus, filius Roberti Nyd servientis Simonis Gauke (1424 FrY). Here, Thomas bore the surname of his father's master which had probably been assumed earlier by his father.

CLASSIFICATION OF SURNAMES

Surnames may be divided into four groups:
1. Local Surnames
2. Surnames of Relationship
3. Surnames of Occupation or Office
4. Nicknames

Within these groups there is considerable overlapping and a full and accurate classification is impossible. In dealing with names, we are concerned with an intimate possession and with the thoughts and idiosyncrasies of those who bestowed or adopted the names. They were not concerned with rules but with satisfying an immediate need. Nicknames, in particular, were often the result of a spontaneous reaction to a particular occasion.

Local surnames may be occupational. The Panter worked *atte panetrie*. John *atte Gate* may have lived near the town-gate, or he may have been a gate-keeper or porter. Surnames of office, such as *Abbot*, *Bishop*, *Cardinal* and *King*, are often nicknames. Ralph Vicar was a glassworker, not a clergyman, and is also called *Verrer*. A single modern name may belong to more than one class. *Low* may be a French

[1] For a full discussion, v. Ekwall, *Variation* and *Two Early London Subsidy Rolls* (notes, *passim*).

nickname from the wolf, a Scandinavian nickname for a small man, a pet-name from *Laurence*, or a local surname, from *hlāw* 'hill'. *Waller* may be a nickname, 'coxcombe, spark', occupational, 'a builder of walls' or 'a salt-maker', or local, 'dweller by a wall' or 'by a stream'. *Mew* may be a patronymic, a nickname from the sea-mew, or occupational, either metonymic for *Mewer*, 'keeper of the hawks', or from a local surname, with the same occupational meaning. It is impossible to fit surnames into a strait-jacket.

LOCAL SURNAMES

Local surnames, by far the largest group, derive from a place-name, indicating where the man held land, or the place from which he had come, or where he actually lived. Richard de Tonebrige (1086 DB) was so called from his castle of Tonbridge, but he was also called Richard de Clara from the Suffolk Clare which became his chief seat and gave the family its definitive surname. Richard de Hadestoke, a London alderman c1240, had left Hadstock (Essex) and settled in London. Thomas atte Forde lived near a ford.

These local surnames derive (with occasional exceptions) from English, Scottish or French places and were originally preceded by a preposition *de, at, by, in,* etc. A certain number of Old English formations are found before the Conquest: Ælfweard æt Dentune (972), Ælfstan on Lundene (a988), Godcild of Lamburnan (c970), Leofnað in Broðortun (c1050).[1] After the Conquest the usual preposition is *de*, which is used before both English and French place-names. In French names beginning with a vowel, this *de* has often coalesced with the name: Damerell, Danvers, Daunay, Disney, Doyley, etc., and occasionally with English names, as Dash, Daysh, Delafield, Delamere. Many of the French place-names denote the seat of noble families, but many of the modern surnames merely indicate migration from a French place. There was a constant stream of merchants, workmen and others from the English provinces of France.

The earliest local surnames of French origin are chiefly from Normandy, particularly from the departments of Calvados, Eure, Seine-Inférieure and La Manche.[2] Some of the Frenchmen early acquired surnames from English places, e.g. Roger de Berchelai (1086 DB). Philip de Poswyc (c1147) was a son of Richard Basset.[3]

English local surnames may derive from the manor held (Adam de Cokefeld 1121–48 Bury); from the place of residence (Ralph de Nordstrate 1197 P, Goduy ad Westmere c1095 Bury), William Attebroc (1199 P); or from the place from which a man had come : Brihtmarus de Haverhell' (1158 P), who had moved from Suffolk to London, where his son became alderman and sheriff.[4] Occasionally we have a surname from a sign (*atte Lamb, atte Raven*), but these are usually late and less common than has been supposed. Some of the 'signs' really refer to topographical features (*Ball, Cock*).

---

[1] *v.* OEByn 31 ff, 121 ff.   [2] ibid., 59 ff.   [3] Holme 231.
[4] For the light thrown by these surnames on immigration from the provinces into thirteenth- and fourteenth-century London, *v.* Ekwall, *Two Early London Subsidy Rolls*, 49–71.

Ash, Nash, Rash; Oakes, Rook

A very large number of English local surnames derive from small places, or denote residence by a wood, in the marsh, by oaks, elms, ash, etc. These occur as *atte wode, atte fenne*, etc., and the preposition is usually lost later but is preserved in such names as *Attlee, Byfield, Uphill, Underdown*, etc. The names are from OE *æt þǣm āce, æt þǣm æsce*, etc., which became ME *atten ake, oke, atten ash; atte oke, atte ash*. The latter became *Oak, Ash*, etc.; the former became *atte noke, atte nash*, the preposition was dropped and the surnames became *Noke, Nash. Rook, Rash*, etc., derive from OE *æt þǣre āce, æt þǣre æsce*, which became ME *atter oke, atter ash; atte roke, atte rash*. In *Tash, Tesh*, ME *atte ashe, eshe* became *at tash, at tesh*.

Loss of the Preposition

The absence of the preposition in early forms of local surnames (and of the article before occupational names) has been regarded as a sign that the surname had become hereditary. Such a supposition cannot be upheld. The preposition began to disappear much earlier than has been thought and examples are too numerous to be regarded as scribal errors.

Ekwall remarks that the preposition begins to be dropped shortly after 1300, is mostly preserved through the fourteenth century, but after 1400 is usually absent. His earliest example is 1318.[1] Fransson states that in York, *de* disappears in the early fifteenth century; in Lancashire it sometimes occurs c1450; whilst in the south it is regularly dropped at the end of the fourteenth century.[2]

Tengvik has noted in 1066 in Domesday Book 163 examples of local surnames consisting of a simple place-name without a preposition.[3] There are a few also in 1086: Rogerus Blaneford (Blandford), Rogerus Povrestoch (Powerstock), Rogerus Povertone (Poorton), all in Dorset, William Tochingeuuiche (Tingewick, Bucks). A further 100 have been noted in twelfth-century documents from both English and French places, 28 in the Curia Regis Rolls (1201–21), mostly English, Alan Cheles 1219 AssL (Keal, Lincs), Richard Sulee 1221 AssWo (Sudley, Glos), and others.

In the London Subsidy Rolls for 1292 and 1319, where about half those assessed have local surnames, the preposition is always retained. In 1332 there are 23 without a preposition. In those for Sussex, local surnames without a preposition (mostly English) increase from 119 in 1296 to 319 in 1327 and 418 in 1332. In the 1327 Somerset Subsidy Roll about one-third of the surnames are local and of these 7 per cent have no preposition, a proportion very similar to that in Suffolk for the same year (6 per cent). In 1332 in Surrey about 20 per cent of the local surnames have no preposition, whilst in Lancashire in 1332 all the 1255 local surnames except 28 retain the preposition. It seems clear, therefore, that there was a definite tendency to drop the preposition from 1066; by the end of the thirteenth century the tendency was marked in Sussex and steadily increasing. In the first quarter of the fourteenth century Surrey shared this tendency, but it had not reached London. The process had

[1] *Groups*, 92.　　　[2] MESO 25.　　　[3] OEByn 125–30, 137–8.

begun in Suffolk and Somerset, was almost completely absent in Lancashire and non-existent in Yorkshire. 'The *de* before the surname is in constant use well into the reign of Henry IV.' [1]

Toponymics

A common form of local surname of which many examples survive consists of an adjective or noun denoting nationality or the country, province, county, town or district from which the individual came: English, Scott, Breton, Fleming, Angwin, Loring, Poidevin, all of which are found in Domesday Book. Later surnames are Irish, Welsh, Wallas, Gall, Norman, Brabazon, Cornish, Cornwallis, Devenish, with Norris, Surridge, Sotheran, Western, Westridge. An early example which has not survived is Wluuardus *le Doverisshe* 'of Dover' (1125 ELPN).

Toponymics formed by the addition of *-er* to some topographical term, e.g. Bridger, Brooker, etc., are particularly common in Sussex at the beginning of the fourteenth century. They are also found in the neighbouring counties of Kent and Surrey, in Essex and Hampshire, but are less common elsewhere. The meaning is 'dweller by the bridge, brook, etc.', or, occasionally, at a particular place, *Rumbridger*, from Rumbridge (Sussex).[2] The names, at times, interchange with names in *atte* and compounds of *-man*. In the Sussex Subsidy Rolls, Hugo *atte Broke* (1296) is identical with Hugo *le Broker* (1327); John *atte Combe* (1327) with John *le Coumber* (1332); John *atte Gore* (1296) with John *Gorman* (1332); William *atte Gate* (1296) and John *Gateman* (1327) both lived in Goring.

Interesting survivals of Scandinavian formations are the local surnames Sotherby, Westoby, from ON *suðr, vestr í bý* (the man who lived) 'south or west in the village', and the anglicized Dunnaby, Easterby. Similar English formations survive in Astington, Norrington, Sinton, Uppington, Westington.

SURNAMES OF RELATIONSHIP

Surnames of this class are often called patronymics, but a more comprehensive term is needed, partly because many modern surnames are formed from women's names, partly because in early sources other relationships are expressed: Alwinus *Childebroder*, Alwin' *pater Cheping'* (1066 Winton), Baldgiua *soror Osuuardi*, Lefuine *frater Toui*, Goduin *Aluuini nepos*, Wluin *Brune stepsune*, Sibbe *Ædesdohter* (c1095 Bury), Willelmus *gener Arnwi* (c1200 DC).

Such names are not uncommon in the twelfth century and are found later: Gilbert *Fathevedsteppeson* (1307 Wak), John *le Personesneve* (1324 FFEss), Richard *Hannebrothir*, Ameria *Ibbotdoghter* (1324 Wak), Amabilla *Hannewyf* (1327 ib.), William *Maisterneue* (1327 SRSf), John *Prestebruther*, Johanna *Raweswyf* (1332 SRCu), Emma *Rogerdaughter*, Robert *Prestcosyn*, Marjoria *Vicar neys* (1381 PTY), Isolda *Peersdoghter* (1430 FeuDu). The only names of this type to survive

---

[1] FrY, p. xvi.   [2] *v.* Mawer and Stenton, *Place-names of Sussex* 35, MESO 192–208.

are a few compounds of -*magh* 'brother-in-law': Hickmott, Hitchmough, Hudsmith, Watmough.

Patronymics

Names in -son

In Old English, patronymics were formed by adding -*ing* to the stem or -*sunu* to the genitive of the personal-name: *Dudding* 'son of Dudda', *Ēadrīcessunu* 'son of Ēadrīc'. The latter type was used as a patronymic adjunct: Hering Hussan sunu (603 ASC), a type found also in the eighth and ninth centuries and not uncommon in the names of the festermen of Peterborough (963–92): Godwine Ælfrices suna. This was also a common Scandinavian formation: Þurferð Rolfes sune. In his *Old English Bynames*,[1] Tengvik has collected 146 examples, of which 111 are English and 24 Scandinavian. In twelfth-century London Ekwall has noted a further eleven examples.[2]

Metronymics

Similar formations, though less common, were based on the mother's name: Eadric Wynflæde sunu (c1015 ASCh), Siwardus Leuerunessone (1066 Winton), Edric' Modheuesune (1137 ELPN).[3]

Johnson, Williamson, etc. Distribution and Origin

The frequency of names in -*son* in the North has been commonly attributed to Scandinavian influence,[4] but examples are rare or non-existent from the twelfth to the fourteenth centuries in north and south alike. The common form of both patronymics and metronymics in the twelfth and thirteenth centuries is Willelmus *filius Hugonis*, Ricardus *filius Agnetis* (1185 Templars), a form found side by side with compounds of -*sunu* in the eleventh century and, less commonly, of -*son* in the fourteenth. It is hardly conceivable that surnames like *Godricsone* (1066 DB) ceased to be used for a couple of centuries and were then suddenly revived. The formula Rogerus *filius Radulfi* may be merely a description, 'Roger son of Ralph', or it may be a translation of Roger *Fitz Ralph*, a form rare in documents. Radulfus *filius Godrici* may similarly be a translation of *Godricson*. That the formula was merely descriptive is proved by the fact that a man could be named both Willelmus *filius Hermanni* (1134–40) and Willelmus *Hermannus* (1141–9 Holme), whilst there are a few examples of the equation of a simple christian name as a surname with a compound of -*sunu*: Aluuinus *Dode*, Aluuinus *Dodesune* (1066 DB). Names like Willelmus *filius fabri* (1219 AssY), Hugo *filius clerici* (1185 Templars, Gl) are common and descriptive, 'son of the smith or the clerk'; they are found in the fourteenth century as *Smythson* and *Clerkessone* and still survive.

[1] OEByn 146–66.   [2] ELPN 127–8.   [3] OEByn 228, 232.
[4] Ewen 56, MESO 26, A. H. Smith, *Saga Book* XI (1934), 17.

In the Cumberland Subsidy Roll (1332) we find Alan *Malleson*, John *Diksson*, etc., side by side with Adam *son of Alan*, John *son of Robert* (presumably translations of *filius Alani, filius Roberti*) and Thomas *Prestson*. It would appear that the form in common use was *Diksson*, *Helewisson*, *Heliotesson*, etc., that the twelfth- and thirteenth-century scribes translated all such names by *filius Roberti*, etc., and that by the fourteenth century there was a growing tendency for the clerk to use the spoken form, particularly with the common pet-names *Dick*, *Hob*, etc. Thirteenth-century examples noted are: Adam *Saresone* 1286 LLB D, William *Marysone* 1298 ELPN (Willelmus *filius Marie* 1292 SRLo), William *Paskessone* 1293 FFC, Thomas *Wummanesone* 1297 Coram (C).

In the Sussex Subsidy Rolls there are no examples of -*son* in 1296, 4 in 1327, 13 in 1332, all metronymics. In other Subsidy Rolls we have in 1327, in Worcestershire 11 (including 4 metronymics); Somerset 8 (5 metronymics); Cambridgeshire 17 (6 metronymics); in 1332, in Surrey 6 (4 metronymics); Lancashire 23 (7 metronymics); Cumberland 22 (7 metronymics); in Yorkshire 2 in 1297, 5 in 1301, 10 in 1327, including 3 metronymics; in FrY (1272–1381) 14, all patronymics—earliest example 1323; in Suffolk (1327) 7 (3 metronymics), (1381) 12 (5 metronymics). In all these sources there are additional examples of *Reveson*, *Smithson*, etc. Occasionally the surname is based on the father's surname. In Cambridgeshire John *Brunnison* and William *Broun* occur in the same parish as do Richard and William *Lawisson* and Henry *Law*. In Cumberland, Hugh *Moserghson* was presumably the son of Thomas *de Mosergh*. *v.* also p. xliv.

The surnames in -*son* form a very small proportion of the whole and are more common in the north. In Lancashire the number assessed is only about one-fifth that in Suffolk. In the northern counties the number of individuals with no surname or described as *filius* —— is much greater than in the south where the development of surnames was more advanced. But it is clear that in the fourteenth century, when surnames in -*son* begin to appear again, they were not limited to the north. It is unlikely that in Somerset, Sussex and Surrey these names should be due to Scandinavian influence. Tengvik notes that in his Old English material examples are found at a date when 'we can hardly reckon with any important Scandinavian influence'. The local distribution of the type, too (especially in Devonshire), points to a native origin.[1]

In the north we may have to reckon with Scandinavian influence also, but the frequency of the type may be due, in part at least, to the late development there of hereditary surnames. We find such names as Henry Dicounesson de Clesnesse 1359 Pat (Nb), 'Henry, son of Dicoun de Clesnesse', Richard Jeffson Nanneson de Radford 1385 NottBR, a type found also in Yorkshire and Lancashire: Robert Tomson Watson, Robert Stevenson Malynson, Thomas Robynson Richardson 1381 PTY, John Robynson Diconson 1408 AD v (La), John Atkynson Jonson 1433 ib. (Y). It is doubtful whether the latter should be interpreted 'John, son of Atkyn, son of John' or 'John, son of Atkyn Jonson'. The occurrence together of

[1] OEByn 147.

John Prestson, Agnes ancilla Johannis Prestson and Geoffrey Jonson Prestson (1379 PTY) points clearly to a surname but that it was hereditary is doubtful. The frequency of the type and the common addition of *-wyf* (sometimes added to the christian name), *-doghter, -man, -maiden, -servant*, give a very strong impression that these were not real surnames in the modern sense but patronymic descriptions in a constant state of flux.

Font-names as Bynames

Less common in the early twelfth century than names like Symon *filius Ricardi*, but steadily increasing in number, are names of the type Johannes *Gerard*, Henricus *Bertram*, in which a font-name is added to the christian name as a byname. Tengvik has noted ten examples in the eleventh century in which, in seven instances, the byname is Scandinavian, in one, Old English, and in two, French. In Domesday Book there is a great increase in the use of French personal-names (40), as well as Old English (28) and Scandinavian (18), with three Celtic and five Latin.[1]

The general opinion is that such surnames are due to the dropping of *filius*.[2] Tengvik has noted five instances which seem to support this view: Osbern *Hauoc*, Osbern *filius Hauoc*; Rainaldus *Croc*, Rainaldus *filius Croc*, in which two of the personal names (*Hauoc* and *Dudde*) are Old English, two (*Baderon* and *Clamahoc*) Breton, and so introduced by Normans, and one (*Croc*) Scandinavian, though the christian name *Rainaldus* suggests a possible Norman origin.

It is difficult to believe in this 'dropping of *filius*' theory. A name of the type *Johannes filius Willelmi* was never used in everyday life by either Englishmen, Frenchmen or Scandinavians. It is Latin and a documentary form. Where the font-name is French, it might be a translation of Fitzwilliam, though such names are unknown in France and rare in English sources. If the font-name is English, *filius Dudde* might be a translation of *Duddesunu*, but it is unlikely that one-sixth of the Suffolk peasants of c1095 bore such names. There seems no alternative to regarding these forms as scribal descriptions. Walter Dudde was known to be the son of Dudda and he was so described in writing, in the clerk's Latin, *filius Dudde*. But in ordinary conversation, when his full name was needed, he was called Walter Dudde. Three early examples of this type have been noted by von Feilitzen: the Scandinavian Sendi Arfast (c1044), the French William Ingelram (1088) and Ieduue Ialdit (c1100–30), from OE *Ealdgȳð*.[3] Nine other examples occur in Suffolk (c1095 Bury), all English: Aldwine Ælfuine, Lemmer Brihtmer, Ordric Wihgar, etc.

The origin of surnames of this type cannot, at present, be definitely decided. The majority of such names are not, as Smith states, from personal-names of Scandinavian origin. There are numerous examples from English and French personal-names and a smaller number from Celtic. Scandinavian influence may be partly responsible, especially in the Danelaw. The type does not become common in England until after the Conquest and we may be concerned with a French custom introduced

[1] OEByn 209 ff.   [2] ibid., 209 (with references).   [3] *Namn och Bygd*, vol. 27 (1939), p. 128.

by the Normans. Similar names are found in northern France in the tenth century and in the south and south-west in the previous century.[1] The fact that similar formations from Old English personal-names are common in the south of England in the late thirteenth and the fourteenth centuries and in eleventh-century Suffolk suggests an independent formation in English. The frequency of the type may be due to all three influences, combined with its simplicity for everyday use and the analogy of similar simple attributes in the form of nicknames and occupation-names. It is noteworthy that such surnames from very common christian names like William, John, etc., are late formations.

Post-Conquest Survival of Old English Personal-names

The Norman Conquest revolutionized our personal nomenclature. The Old English name-system was gradually broken up, Old English names became less and less common and were replaced by new names from the Continent, a limited number of which gradually became more and more popular. The general trend is well known, but many of the definite statements on the relative frequency of various names are based on insufficient evidence, often from late sources which can have little or no bearing on the history of surnames. Fashions in names varied among different classes and in different parts of the country. Most of the early documents deal with the upper classes. Names of peasants are less common, rarely occur in large numbers, and have largely been ignored. Intensive work on the abundant material in manuscript and on that already printed will ultimately throw much new light on the history of our names. For the present, we must be content with a study of selected material from varied districts.

In the Holme Cartulary, some 75 per cent of the twelfth-century names are those of witnesses and grantees of charters, monks, clerics, and tenants of the abbey, and these reflect the new nomenclature introduced by the Normans. The personal-names are of French or continental Germanic origin, with Norman forms of Scandinavian names brought from Normandy. The remaining 25 per cent, the names of peasants, represent some 30 English and 35 Scandinavian names, some more than once repeated.

In the twelfth century the most popular names were William (10 per cent) and Robert (7 per cent), followed, with variation of order in different documents and counties, by Richard, Ralph, Roger, Hugo and Walter. John (3 per cent) was much less popular.[2] In a thirteenth-century collection of deeds relating to Aveley (Essex), John shares the top place with William (20 per cent) and these, with Robert, Richard, Geoffrey and Thomas, were the names of 160 out of 250 individuals. There were 41 other French names in use, including the Breton Alan, Hervey and Wygan, shared by 86 persons. In addition, 28 persons shared 16 English names, including an un-recorded *Weorðing*.[3] In the fourteenth century Old English names were fewer and much smaller in proportion, 7 persons sharing 5 names. Some 460 persons shared

[1] OEByn 210–11.   [2] Reaney, *Essex Review*, vol. 61, pp. 135–8.   [3] ibid., pp. 142, 202–4, 209–11.

35 French names. John (34 per cent) was now much more popular than William (18 per cent). Then came Thomas (9 per cent), Richard and Robert (6 per cent), Henry, Roger and Geoffrey, these 8 names being boᵣᵢe by 375 persons. The remaining 32 names were shared by 85 persons.

Unrecorded Old English personal-names are found in Middle English documents. Most of these conform to the traditional *Wulfstan*-type. Some contain elements not noted before (*Geongwine, Weorðgifu*), others elements rare in OE names (*Mǣðwynn, Wudubeorht*). Some, especially the original bynames, may have been formed in the Middle English period. Many of these names were those of peasants, among whom the native habits of name-giving survived longer than among the upper classes.[1] A number of personal-names which are not recorded in Old English after the eighth or ninth centuries reappear in Middle English. Some of these names are evidenced only by their occurrence as surnames, others by their first record in the eleventh, twelfth or thirteenth century. Five (including *Uhtrīc, v.* Outridge) are not found before the fourteenth century and one (*Cwēnrǣd*) only in the fifteenth. Some survive as surnames: *Cwēnhild* (1086) in Quennell; *Ēadwacer* (1066) in Edicker; *Wæcerhild* (c1130) in Wackrell. Others are of importance in confirming the existence of personal-names postulated to explain place-names. *Pacchild* noted in Essex in 1166 must be a compound of OE *Pæcc(i)* and the common theme *-hild*. No example of *Pæcc(i)* is known, but it has been assumed as the base of Patching (Essex, Sussex), Patcham, Pashley (Sussex) and other related place-names. Similarly *Wlanchild*, recorded only as the name of a peasant-woman in 1206 in Cambridgeshire, and reappearing as a surname in Suffolk (Warin *Wlankild* 1277 *Ely*), is a compound of *-hild* with OE *wlanc* 'proud', postulated as a personal-name to explain Longslow (Salop).[2]

This vitality of Old English names is confirmed by the number of fourteenth-century surnames formed from Old English personal-names no longer then in use. We can only suppose that these personal-names had continued in use long after the Conquest and that the surnames had already become hereditary. In the 1327 Subsidy Roll for Somerset, 66 per cent of those assessed were named: John (23 per cent), William (16 per cent), Robert (8 per cent), Richard (7 per cent), Walter (6 per cent) or Thomas (6 per cent). The rest shared 95 different names of which 8 were English and 5 Scandinavian. But there were some 200 surnames formed from English or Scandinavian personal-names no longer in use, e.g. Thomas Ailmer, Richard Leverich, John Sefoghel, William Serich, Robert Outright, Philip Thorbarn, Edith Thurkyld.

The rate at which this change from English to Norman christian names proceeded varied from class to class and among different families of the same class. It was slowest among the peasantry. In 1115, at Winchester, two out of six English fathers gave their children English names. In 1148 all the children named bore

---

[1] von Feilitzen, *Namn och Bygd*, vol. 33, pp. 69–98 (1945).
[2] *v.* Reaney, *Survival of OE Personal Names in ME* (Studier i modern språkvetenskap, vol. 18, pp. 84–112), 1953; *Pedigrees of Villeins and Freemen* (NQ, vol. 197, pp. 222–5), 1952; *Three Unrecorded OE Personal Names of a late type* (Modern Language Review, vol. 47, p. 374), 1952.

French names whether their fathers had English, Scandinavian or French names. At King's Lynn in 1166 the process was less advanced. Of 17 fathers with Scandinavian names and 18 with English names, only half followed the new fashion.

Occasional pedigrees put forward to support or resist a claim that a man was a villein shed some light on the names used by peasants. In one from Lincolnshire which must take us back to 1100 or beyond (1200 Cur), a man with the English name of Elric had a daughter Oise or Osse and two sons Agge and Siuuerd, all probably bearing Scandinavian names. *Oise* may be ODa *Ása* (f), *Agge* is ODa *Aggi; Siuuerd* may be ODa *Sigwarth* or OE *Sigweard*. Siward had a son Uhtred (OE) and Agge a son named Elric after his grandfather and a daughter with the French name Beatrice who married a Walter and named her son (living in 1200) after his father. Oise had a son William Belle and two grandsons Roger and Robert Belle. Here the change to French names seems to have been due to women.

A similar Suffolk pedigree (1200 Cur) takes us back a generation farther. Godwin named his three children from three different languages: Turgod (Scandinavian), Goda (English) and Watcelina (French). Goda gave his son the French name of Robert and his daughter Agatha married a man named Thomas. Watcelina named her daughers Einilda (OG *Aginildis*) and Langiva (OE **Langgifu*). Turgod named both his sons in English, Godwin and Edric, the latter continuing the English tradition in Alfridus (probably OE *Ælfrǣd*, possibly *Æðelfrið*), whose son (alive in 1200) was Osbert (OE *Ōsbeorht*). Thus Godwin's descendants in the male line kept to the native tradition in names for five generations to 1200.

From a number of similar pedigrees going back for two to four generations from 1200 it would appear that among the peasants at the beginning of the thirteenth century Old English personal-names were being replaced by names of French origin, but some families were more conservative than others. The variety of personal-names used, both English and French, is noteworthy, as well as the general absence of bynames. The vitality of the Old English name-system is revealed by the evidence of the persistence of the repetition of either the first or second theme in names of the same family and by the existence of names otherwise unrecorded.[1] Both English and Scandinavian personal-names were still common on the Suffolk manors of the Bishop of Ely in 1277.

OE Personal-names surviving in Modern Surnames

Monothematic

Bada (Bade), **Beald* (Bald), **Becca* (Beck), *Bēda* (Beade), *Beorn* (Barne), *Bil* (Bill), *Bisceop* (Bishop), **Blīða* (Bly), *Boda* (Bode), *Botta* (Bott), *Brūn* (Brown), *Budda* (Budd), **Butt(a)* (Butt), *Bynni* (Binns), *Cada* (Cadd, Cade), *Cana* (Cane), *Ceadda* (Chadd), **Cēne*, **Cyne* (Keen), *Cniht* (Knight), **Cocc(a)* (Cock), **Codd(a)* (Codd), *Cola* (Cole), *Creoda* (Creed), *Cyng* (King), **Cyppe* (Kipps), **Dæcca* (Dack), *Dēora* (Dear), *Dodd(a)*, *Dudd(a)* (Dodd), **Ducc* (Ducket, Duxon), **Dylla*, **Dylli*

---

[1] For details, *v.* Reaney, *Pedigrees of Villeins and Freemen.*

(Dill), *Flint* (Flint), *Fugol* (Fowl), **Glæd* (Glade), **Glēaw* (Glew), *Goda* (m), *Gode* (f) (Good), *Golda* (m), *Golde* (f) (Gold), **Grante*, **Grente* (Grant), **Grēne* (Green), **Hand* (Hand), *Heafoc* (Hawk), *Hēaha* (Hay), **Heard* (Hard), *Hunna* (Hunn), *Hwīta* (White), **Lemma* (Lemm), *Lēof* (Leaf), *Lēofa* (m), *Lēofe* (f) (Leaves), **Leppe* (Lipp), **Lutta* (Lutt), *Mann* (Man), *Mawa*, **Mēawa* (Maw), **Mēaw* (Mew), **Milde* (f) (Millsom), **Modd* (Mudd), *Odda* (Odd), *Pæga* (Pay), *Pymma* (Pim), *Scot* (Scott), **Sida* (Seed), *Snel* (Snell), **Sprott* (Sprott), *Swan* (Swan), *Swēt(a)* (m), *Swēte* (f) (Sweet), *Swift* (Swift), **Tæppa* (Tapp), **Tāt* (Tate), **Tetta* (Tett), *Tunna* (Tunn), **Þeōda* (m), **Þeōde* (f) (Theed), **Ucca* (Huck), **Ugga* (Hug), *Wada* (Wade), *Wine* (Winn)

Derivatives in -ing

*Bealding (Balding), *Billing* (Billing), **Botting* (Botting), *Brūning* (Browning), **Budding* (Budding), **Cypping* (Kipping), *Dēoring*, *Dȳring* (Dearing), *Dēorling*, *Dȳrling* (Darling), *Dūning* (Downing), *Dunning* (Dunning), **Dylling* (Delling, Dilling), **Fugeling* (Fowling), **Glæding* (Gladden), *Goding* (Gooding), *Golding* (Golding), *Hearding* (Harding), **Hræfning* (Ravening), *Hunning* (Hunning), **Hwætling* (Whatlin), *Hwīting* (Whiting), **Lēofecing* (Lucking), *Lēofing*, *Lȳfing* (Levinge), **Lēofring* (Lovering), *Manning* (Manning), **Munding* (Munnings), **Pening* (Penney), *Snelling* (Snelling), *Swēting* (Sweeting), **Tæpping* (Tappin), **Tipping* (Tipping), **Tylling* (Tilling), **Utting* (Utting), **Wealding* (Walding), **Weorðing* (Worthing), **Wihtling*, **Hwītling* (Whitling), **Wilding* (Wilding), **Wulfing* (Woolving)

Dithematic

*Ācmann (Oakman)

Ælfflæd (f) (Alflatt), *Ælfgār* (Algar), *Ælfhēah* (Alphege), *Ælfhere* (Alvar), **Ælfmann* (Elfman), *Ælfnōð* (Allnatt), *Ælfrǣd* (Alfred, Averay), *Ælfrīc* (Aldrich), *Ælfsige* (Elsey), *Ælfstān* (Allston), *Ælfweald* (Eliot, Ellwood), *Ælfweard* (Allward), *Ælfwīg* (Alaway, Allvey), *Ælfwine* (Alven, Alwin)

Æscwine (Ashwin)

Æðelbeorht (Albright), **Æðeldæg* (f) (Allday), *Æðelflæd* (f) (Alflatt), *Æðelfrið* (m), **Æðelfrīð* (f) (Alfrey), *Æðelgār* (Algar), *Æðelgēat*, *Æðelgȳð* (f) (Aylett), *Æðelgifu* (f) (Ayliff), *Æðelheard* (Adlard), *Æðelmǣr* (Aylmer), *Æðelnōð* (Allnatt), *Æðelrǣd* (Aldred, Allred), *Æðelrīc* (Aldrich, Allright, Etheredge), *Æðelstān* (Allston, Aston, Athelstan), *Æðelðrȳð* (f) (Audrey), *Æðelweard* (Allward, Aylward), *Æðelwīg* (Alaway), *Æðelwine* (Alven, Alwin, Aylwin)

Beadurīc (Badrick), **Bealdgȳð* (f) (Baldey), **Bealdrīc* (Baldree), **Bealdmann* (Balman), **Bealdstān* (Balston)

Beorhtgifu (f) (Berriff, Brightiff), *Beorhtsige* (Brixey), *Beorhtmann* (Brightman), *Beorhtmǣr* (Brightmore), *Beorhtwīg* (Brighty), *Beorhtwine*, *Beorhtwynn* (f) (Brightween)

*Bīedlufu (f) (Bedloe)

Blæchere (Blacker), *Blæcmann* (Blackman), *Blæcstān* (Blackston)

Brūngār (Brunger), *Brūnstān* (Brunsdon), **Brūnsunu* (Brownson), *Brūnwine* (Brunwin)

Burgheard (Burchard, Burrard), *Burgrǣd* (Burrett), *Burgrīc* (Burridge), *Burgstān*, **Bucstān* (Buxton), *Burgweald* (Burall), *Burgweard* (Burward)

*Cēnweard (Kenward), **Cēnwīg* (Kenway), *Cēolmund*, **Cildmann* (Chillman)

Cūðbeald (Cobbald), *Cūðbeorht* (Cuthbert), *Cūðrīc* (Cutteridge), *Cūðwulf* (Culf)

Cwēnhild (f) (Quenell)

Cynebeald (Kemble), *Cynemǣr* (Kenmare), *Cynemann* (Kinman), *Cynerīc* (Kerrich), *Cyneweard* (Kenward), *Cynewīg* (Kenway)

*Dægmǣr (Daymer), **Dægmann* (Dayman), **Denebeald* (Denbow), *Dēormann* (Dearman), *Dēorwine* (Darwin), *Dudemann* (Dodman), *Dūnstān* (Dunstan)

Ēadgār (Edgar), *Ēadhūn* (Eaden), *Ēadmǣr* (Admer), **Ēadmann* (Edman), *Ēadmund* (Edmond), *Ēadrǣd* (Errett), *Ēadrīc* (Edrich), *Ēadstān* (Aston, Easton), *Ēadwacer* (Edicker), *Ēadweard* (Edward, Ewart), *Ēadwīg* (Eddy), *Ēadwine* (Edwin), *Ēadwulf* (Eddols)

Ealdgār (Algar), **Ealdnōð* (Allnatt), *Ealdrǣd* (Aldred, Allred), **Ealdstān* (Allston, Elston), *Ealdwīg* (Alaway, Aldway), *Ealdwine* (Alden, Alwin)

Ealhhere (Alger, Alker), *Ealhstān* (Allston, Elston), *Ealhðrȳð* (f) (Audrey)

Earnwīg (Arneway), *Ēastmǣr* (Eastmure), *Ēastmund* (Eastman)

Ecgbeorht (Egbert), *Ecgwulf* (Edgell)

Eoforwacer (Earwaker), *Eoforwine* (Erwin)

Forðrǣd (Fordred), *Frēobeorn* (Freeborn), *Friðulāf* (Freelove)

Gārmund (Garman), *Gārwīg* (Garraway), *Gārwulf* (Gorrell), **Geongwine* (Yonwin), **Glædmann* (Gladman), **Glædwine* (Gladwin)

Godgifu (f) (Goodeve), *Godhere* (Gooder), *Godlamb* (Goodlamb), *Godlēof*, **Godlēofu* (f) (Goodliffe), *Godmǣr* (Gummer), *Godmann* (Goodman), *Godrīc* (Goodrich), *Godsunu* (Godson), *Godweard* (Godward), *Godwīg* (Goodway), *Godwine* (Godwin, Goodwin)

*Goldbeorht (Goldbard), **Goldburg* (f) (Goldburg), **Goldheafoc* (Goldhawk), **Goldhere* (Golder), **Goldmann* (Goldman), *Goldstān* (Goldston), **Goldwīg* (Goldway), *Goldwine* (Goldwin)

*Gūðbeald (Gubell), *Gūðlāc* (Goodlake), **Gūðmǣr* (Gummer), *Gūðmund* (Godman)

*Heardmann (Hardman), *Heaðuwīg* (Hathaway), *Hereweald* (Harold), *Hereweard* (Hereward), **Holdbeorht* (Holbert), **Hūngār* (Hunger), **Huntmann* (Huntman), *Hūnwine* (Unwin), *Hwætmann* (Whatman), **Hwītheard* (Whittard), **Hwītmann* (Whiteman), **Hygemann* (Human)

Landbeorht (Lambrick), *Lēodmǣr* (Lemmer)

Lēofdæg (Loveday), *Lēofeca* (Levick, Livick, Leffek), *Lēofgār* (Loveguard), *Lēofgēat* (Levet), *Lēofgōd* (Lovegood), *Lēofmǣr* (Lemmer), *Lēofmann* (Loveman), *Lēofrǣd* (Leverett), *Lēofrīc* (Leverage), *Lēofsige* (Lewsey), *Lēofsunu* (Leveson), *Lēofweald* (Leavold), *Lēofweard* (Livard), *Lēofwīg* (Leavey), *Lēofwine* (Lewin)

*Leohtwine (Litwin), **Lȳtelmann* (Lilleyman)

Mǣrgēat (Merrett), *Mildburh* (f) (Milborrow), *Norðmann* (Norman)

Ordgār (Orgar), *Ordrīc* (Orrick), *Ordwīg* (Ordway)

Ōsgār (Hosker), *Ōsmǣr* (Osmer), *Ōsweald* (Oswald), *Ōswine* (Oswin)

Pīcstān (Pickstone), *Rǣdwīg* (Redway), *Rǣdwine* (Readwin), *Rimhild* (f) (Rimell)

Sǣbeorht (Seabert), *Sǣbeorn* (Seaborn), *Sǣburh* (Seaber), *Sǣfaru* (f) (Seavers), *Sǣfrið* (Saffery), *Sǣgār* (Sagar), *Sǣgēat* (Sait), *Sǣgōd* (Seagood), *Sǣlēofu* (f) (Sealeaf), *Sǣlida* (Sallitt), *Sǣlwīg* (Salway), *Sǣmǣr* (Seamer), *Sǣmann* (Seaman), *Sǣrīc* (Search), *Sǣweald* (Sewell), *Sǣweard* (Seward), *Sǣwulf* (Self)

Sidumann (Seedman)

Sigeflǣd (f) (Siffleet), *Sigegār* (Siggers), *Sigemǣg* (Simey), *Sigenōð* (Sinnatt), *Sigerǣd* (Sired), *Sigerīc* (Search), *Sigeweald* (Sewell), *Sigeweard* (Seward)

Smēawine (Smewing), *Snelgār* (Snelgar), *Spearheafoc* (Sparrowhawk)

Stānburg (f) (Stanberry), *Stānheard* (Stannard), *Stānhild* (f) (Stanhill), *Stānmǣr* (Stammer)

Stubheard (Stubbert), *Sunnmann* (Sunman)

Swētlufu (f) (Sweetlove), *Swētmann* (Sweetman), *Swētrīc* (Swatridge)

Trumbeald (Trumble), *Tūnheard* (Tunnard), *Tūnhild* (f) (Tunnell)

Þēodbeorht (Tebrich)

Unwine (Unwin), *Uhtrǣd* (Oughtred), *Uhtrīc* (Outridge)

Wæcerhild (f) (Wackrill), *Wǣrmund* (Warman), *Wealdwine* (Walwin)

Wīgbeorht (Wyberd), *Wīgbeorn* (Wyborn), *Wīgburh* (f) (Wyber), *Wīgheard* (Wyard), *Wīgmǣr* (Wymer), *Wīgmund* (Wyman)

Wihtgār (Widger), *Wihtheard* (Whittard), *Wihtlāc* (Whitelock), *Wihtmann* (Wightman), *Wihtrīc* (Whitteridge)

Wilbeorht (Wilbert), *Wilrīc* (Wildridge)

Winebeald (Winbolt), *Winegār* (Wingar), *Winemann* (Winman)

Wudufugol (Woodfull), *Wuduheard* (Huddart, Woodard), *Wudulāc* (Woodlake)

Wulfbeald (Wolbold), *Wulffrīð* (Woolfrey), *Wulfgār* (Woolgar), *Wulfgēat* (Woolvett), *Wulfgifu* (f) (Wolvey), *Wulfmǣr* (Woolmer), *Wulfnōð* (Woolner), *Wulfrǣd* (Orred), *Wulfrīc* (Woolrich, Hurry), *Wulfsige* (Woolsey), *Wulfstān* (Woolston), *Wulfweard* (Woollard), *Wulfwīg* (Woolway), *Wulfwine* (Woolven)

Wynrīc (Windridge)

Scandinavian Personal-names

The vitality of the Scandinavian name-system in the Danelaw has been discussed and illustrated by Sir Frank Stenton.[1] In addition to Scandinavian names like Thorald, Swain, Haldan, etc., which might appear in southern texts, there are characteristic northern names like Gamel, Gille, Ketel, and others of characteristic rarity, as Ketelbern, Airic, Ailof, etc. Particularly noteworthy are such diminutive

---

[1] Stenton, *Danelaw Charters*, pp. cxii ff.

forms as *Hasti* or *Asti*, a colloquial diminutive of ON *Ásketell*, surviving in *Hastie*, *Steinki*, a short form of compounds of *Stein*, *Anke*, a diminutive of names in *Arn-*, the source of *Hanks*.

Though less extensive than in Lincolnshire, Scandinavian influence was not negligible in East Anglia. Some 8 per cent of the peasants of the Bury manors c1095 bore Scandinavian names of which *Lute* and *Challi* are not recorded elsewhere in England.[1] The vitality of these names is shown by the formation of such Anglo-Scandinavian compounds as *Lefchetel*, *Ketelbert* and *þurwif*, recorded in 962 and reappearing in Yorkshire in 1166 (P), and by the survival in *Kilvert*, *Ketteridge* and *Tureff* of the unrecorded hybrids *Cylferð*, *Cytelrīc* and *þorgifu* (f). The pet-form *Suarche*, from Anglo-Scandinavian *Swartcol*, has its parallel in the otherwise unknown *Samke*, still found in the rare surname *Sank*. Other noteworthy survivals are *Goodhew* from the previously unknown *Guðhugi*, a parallel to the *Illhugi* found at Thorney and the Suffolk *Tovell* from ON *Tófa-Hildr*, a rare type of compound, 'Hildr the daughter of Tofi'.[2]

Scandinavian Personal-names surviving in Modern Surnames

Aggi (ODa) (Agg), *Aki* (ODa) (Okey), *Álfgeirr* (Alger), *Algot* (ODa) (Allgood), *Álfgrímr* (Allgrim), *Alli* (ODa) (Alley), *Arnkell* (Arkell), *Ásbiǫrn* (Osborn), *Ásgautr* (Osgood), *Ásketill* (Ashkettle), *Áskell* (Askell), *Áslákr* (Haslock), *Ásvaldr* (Oswald), *Auti* (ODa) (Autie)

Bjǫrn (Barne), *Bóndi* (Bond), *Bóthildr* (f) (Bottle), *Brandr* (Brand), *Bróðir* (Brothers)

Dólgfinnr (Dolphin), *Dreng* (Dring), *Drómundr* (Drummond)

Elaf (ODa) (Ayloffe), *Eiléfr*, ODa *Elef* (Ayliffe), *Eiríkr* (Herrick)

Farmann (Farman), *Farðegn* (Farthing), *Fastúlfr* (Fastolf), *Fathir* (ODa) (Fathers), *Finnr* (Finn), *Fótr* (Foot)

Gamall (Gambell), *Gauki* (Gookey), *Geiri* (Garey), *Gilli* (Gill), *Greifi* (Grave, Greavey), *Grímr* (Grime), *Grímhildr* (f) (Grimmet), *Gunnr* (Gunn), *Gunnildr* (f) (Gunnell), *Gunvor* (f) (Gunner), **Guð(h)ugi* (Goodhew), *Guðmundr* (Goodman), *Guðrøðr* (Goodread)

Hafleikr (Havelock), *Haghni* (ODa) (Hagan), *Haki* (Hake), *Hákun* (Hacon), *Hálfdan* (Haldane), *Hámundr* (Oman), *Haraldr* (Harold), *Hasteinn* (Hasting), *Hávarðr* (Haward), *Hemmingr* (Hemming), *Hrafn* (Raven), *Hrafnhildr* (f) (Ravenhall), *Hrafnkell* (Rankill), *Hróaldr* (Rowat), *Hrólfr* (Rolf)

Ingialdr (Ingall), *Ingiriðr*, ODa *Ingrith* (f) (Ingrey, Ingley), *Ingólfr* (Ingell), *Ingvar* (ODa) (Ingar), *Ívarr* (Ivor)

Karl(i) (Carl), *Karman* (Carman), *Kaupmaðr* (Copeman), *Kel* (Kell), *Ketilbiǫrn* (Kettleburn), *Ketill* (Kettle), *Knútr* (Knott), *Kolbein* (Colban), *Kolbrandr* (Colbran),

[1] v. Douglas, *Feudal Documents . . . of Bury St Edmunds*, cxvii–cxx.
[2] v. also Whitelock, *Scandinavian Personal Names in the Liber Vitae of Thorney Abbey* (Saga Book, vol. 12 (1940), pp. 127–53), and, for Norfolk, West, *St Benet of Holme*, vol. 2, pp. 258–60.

Koli (Cole), *Kalman* (Coleman), *Kollr* (Coll), *Kollungr* (Colling), *Kouse* (Couse), *Kupsi* (Copsey)

Lag(h)man (ODa) (Lawman), *Langabein* (Langbain), *Lax* (Lax)

Magnus (Magnus), *Móðir* (Mothers)

Oddr (Odd), *Óleifr* (Olliff), *Ormr* (Orme), *Ottár* (Otter)

Rannulfr (Randolph)

*Samke (Sank), **Sandi* (Sandey), *Segrim* (ODa) (Seagrim), *Sigarr* (Siggers), *Sigga* (f) (Siggs), *Sighvatr* (Suett), *Sigmundr* (Simmonds), *Sigríðr* (f) (Sired), *Snari* (Snarey), *Sǫrli* (Sarl), *Steinn* (Stein), *Stígandr* (Stigand, Styan), *Stóri* (Storey), *Sumarliðr* (Summerlad), *Svanhildr* (f) (Swannell), *Sveinn* (Swain)

Þóraldr (Thorold), *Þorbiǫrn* (Thurban), *Þorfinnr* (Turpin), **Þorfrøðr* (Tollfree), *Þorgautr* (Thurgood), *Þorgeirr* (Thurgar), *Þorgils* (Sturge), *Þórhildr* (f) (Turrill), *Þórir* (Thory), *Þorkell* (Thurkell), *Þormundr* (Thurman), *Þorsteinn* (Thurston)

*Tófa-Hildr (f) (Tovell), *Tófi* (Tovee), *Tóki* (Took, Tookey), *Tóli* (Tooley), *Topi* (Toop), *Tubbi* (Tubb), *Tunni* (ODa) (Tunney), **Turk* (Turk)

Úlfr (Ulph), *Úlfketel*, *Úlfkell* (Uncle)

Vestmaðr (Westman), *Vígarr* (Wigger), *Vigot* (ODa) (Wiggett), *Víkingr* (Wicking), *Víðarr* (Wither)

Anglo-Scandinavian Survivals

*Cytelferð (Kilvert), **Cytelrīc* (Ketteridge), *Healfdene* (Alden), **Sǣfugol* (Saffell), **Spracaling* (Sprackling), **Þorbert*, **Þurbert* (Turbard), **Þorgifu* (f) (Turreff), *Þurcytel* (Thurkettle), **Toll* (Toll), **Tukka* (Tuck), *Walþēof* (Waddilove, Wallett, Walthew)

Norman Names

Scandinavian names were used by Normans in France where ON *Ás-* occurs as *An-* which survives in *Anketel, Ankin, Antin, Angood, Angold*. Norman diminutives are found in *Asketin* and *Turkentine*. Norman *Turstin* (for *Thorstein*) survives as *Tustin, Tutin, Dusting*. Initial *T* for *Th* may also represent a Norman pronunciation in England, especially of names not found in Normandy, e.g. *Tory* for *Thory*.

Personal-names in Medieval London

Ekwall's discussion of early London personal-names (ELPN) is an outstanding example of what can be achieved by a detailed study of the names of a particular locality, and a perpetual challenge to others to do the same for other areas. In the early twelfth century, Old English personal-names were still in living use in London, but gradually grow rarer and after 1200 are found only occasionally, apart from a few names which lived on and are still in use. Particularly common were such names as Ailward and Ailwin, Brichtmar, Godric and Godwin, Leofric and Leofwin,

Wulfric, Wulfweard and Wulfwine. The only Old English woman's name at all common was Edith. Rare in Old English were Eadwacer and Smeawine, and the feminine Eastorhild, whilst a few such as Godleofu and Wacerhild, both feminine, are unrecorded in Old English. We find a number of compounds in -*ing*: Bruning, Hearding, Sweting, and the unrecorded Funding and Sperling. Short forms were rare but we have Golde (f), Milde (f), Hunna, But and Werth.

Some Scandinavian names from late Old English times must have been current in twelfth-century London. Some may have been introduced direct from Normandy. Such names as *Turgis* are Norman in form. It is noteworthy that few of the Scandinavian names recorded in Domesday Book are found in London sources, but some 30 personal-names (e.g. *Askill*, *Esger*, *Ketel*) are probably Scandinavian rather than Norman in origin. Names like *Thurstan*, *Thorold*, when spelled *Tursten*, *Torold*, may be Norman in origin.

There is reason to believe that Old English names survived longer in the provinces than in the capital, where the fashion set by Normans would be followed more quickly. Old English names in London were often those of immigrants from the provinces. The old names were superseded by names introduced by the Normans and many of those with French names in the first two or three decades of the twelfth century must have been Normans by birth. Those with English names at the same period were as a rule of English descent, as, probably, were those with English names later in the century. But it does not follow that a French name necessarily denotes French descent. As early as c1100 it was quite common for English people to give French names to their children whilst there are only a few examples of sons or daughters of parents with French names being given English names. The earliest instances are found among the upper classes, both the clergy and patrician families. Some Englishmen with French names must have been born c1090 or earlier. After 1100 it became a fashion for English families to give French names to their children. Some families were more conservative than others and continued to use the old names. Some gave French names to one or more of their children and English names to another or others. Thus, in a very few generations the Old English christian names were altogether disused in London, apart from a few special names, Alfred, Edmund, Edward and Godwin. Edmund is frequent in London between 1250 and 1350 but Edward occurs only occasionally. Edward I does not seem to have been popular in London and the few Edwards were probably named after the saint, Edward the Confessor. It is unlikely, therefore, that the popularity of Edmund was due mainly to Edmund, son of Henry III. Some, at least, of the London Edmunds came from East Anglia: Edmund de Suffolk 1309, Edmund de Bery 1346 (Bury St Edmunds), and others from places in Norfolk. These Edmunds were, no doubt, named after St Edmund, the martyr-king of East Anglia and founder of the monastery of St Edmundsbury, to whom a London church was dedicated.

The Norman-French names given by apparently English people to their children were generally the names most commonly used by the Normans and the names still most frequent in England: Geoffrey, Gilbert, Henry, Robert, Peter, John, etc., and the women's names Agnes, Alice and Maud. The personal-nomenclature of twelfth-century London was well on its way to the modern stage which was, in the main, reached in the thirteenth century.

The Breton Element

The large Breton contingent which fought at Hastings was rewarded with lands in England. At their head was Earl Alan of Richmond, a cadet of the ducal house, with a fee of the first importance in Lincolnshire, East Anglia and neighbouring counties. In the south-west, Judhael of Totnes had a fief which in the twelfth century owed service of 70 knights. In thirteenth-century Suffolk was a 'Breton soke'. 'There is, in fact, hardly a county in which this Breton element is not found, and in some counties its influence was deep and permanent ... the Breton colony founded by Earl Alan of Richmond can still be traced, late in the twelfth century, by the personal-names which give a highly individual character to records relating to the country round Boston, itself a town of Breton creation, and Louth. In these districts, as also in the North Riding of York, the Breton settlers of the eleventh and twelfth centuries preserved their ancient personal nomenclature with a conservatism resembling that of the Anglo-Scandinavian peasants among whom they lived ... it was something more than the establishment of a few score knights and sergeants in military tenancies. It must have had the character of a genuine migration, though a migration upon a small scale.'[1]

In twelfth-century Lincolnshire Alan was as common a name as Simon and more popular than Henry and Adam. Other common Breton names were Brian, Conan, Constantine (with its short form Coste), Jarnegon, Justin (with its pet-form Just), Mengi, Samson, and Tengi, all surviving as modern surnames. The christian name of Judhael de Totnes is still found as a surname in Devonshire as Jewell, and elsewhere as Jekyll and Joel. In Essex, Helion Bumpstead, and in Devon, Upton Helions, owe their attributes to Tihel de Herion, their Domesday lord who came from Helléan in Morbihan. His christian name survived in Essex until the thirteenth century and is found as a surname at Barking in 1206 (Roger *Tihell*), whilst his surname, though rare, still lives on in Essex and Suffolk, in Devon and Somerset (*v.* Elion). Wiggens Green in Helion Bumpstead owes its name to the family of John *Wygayn* whose eponymous ancestor may well have been an actual follower of Tihel the Breton. Bretts in Aveley owes its name to John le Bret 'the Breton'. In Aveley is a field, Bumpstead Mead, the last relic of a Bumpsted Hall named from Gilbert de Bumsted ad Turrim who seems to have been accompanied to Aveley by Bumpstead men of Breton descent whose names are found in the district in the thirteenth century (*Wygan, Hervey, Alan, Bryce*).[2] In Essex, too, we find a twelfth-century, *Mingghi*. This Breton influence has left no small mark on our modern surnames.

[1] Stenton, *English Feudalism*, 24–6.　　　[2] *Essex Review*, vol. 61, p. 140.

The Celtic Element

Although Welsh surnames, as distinct from characteristic Welsh patronymic descriptions, were very late formations, the not inconsiderable number of immigrants from Wales into the border counties found their personal-names treated exactly like English names in the formation of surnames. Thus surnames were formed from Welsh personal-names and became hereditary in England long before hereditary surnames were known in Wales. e.g. Kemble (1185), Meredith (1191), Morgan (1221), Owen (1221), Cadogan (1273), Maddock (1274), etc.

About 890-3 a body of Norwegians from Ireland entered Yorkshire and were followed by a greater number, probably between 919 and 952. These Norwegians had been settled in Ireland sufficiently long to become partly Celticized and they have left their mark on the modern map of Cumberland and North Yorkshire in a series of place-names containing Irish loan-words and in inversion compounds in which the defining element comes last: Aspatria, Kirkoswald, Kirkbride. They had also adopted Goidelic personal-names some of which survive both in place-names and modern surnames. e.g. Coleman, Duncan, Gill, Murdoch, Neal, Patrick, Troyte.[1] Some of these surnames are more common in Scotland where they originated independently.

The Final -s in Jones, Parsons, Stocks, etc.

Weekley has remarked [2] that 'the majority of monosyllabic, and many dissyllabic, local names are commonly found with -s, originally due to analogy with *Wills, Jones*, etc., where -s is the sign of the genitive. It will be found that this addition of -s in local names generally takes place whenever it does not involve an extra syllable or any exertion in pronunciation, e.g. *Birks* but *Birch*, *Noakes* but *Nash*, *Marks* but *March*, *Meadows* but *Field*, *Sykes* but *Sich*. The only important exception to this phonetic rule is *Bridges*, which is usually derived, not from *bridge*, but from Bruges, once commonly called Bridges in English. This -s is also added to specific place-names, e.g. *Cheales* from Cheal (Linc.),[3] *Tarbox* from Tarbock (Lanc.), *Burls* from some spot in Essex formerly called Berle,[4] *Rhymes* from Ryme (Dors.), etc.' Elsewhere he asks, 'but why always *Summers* or *Somers* with s and *Winter* without?' [5]

Generalizations on surnames are always dangerous. Both *Summer* and *Winters* survive, as does *Fields*. The final -s was formerly found in such names as (Ralph) *Saches* Hy 2 DC, (Richard) *Ryches* 1296 SRSx, (Alice) *la Gegges* 1310 ColchCt, and survives in *Hedges* and *Latches*.[6] In a number of local surnames, plurals are

---

[1] v. Ekwall, *Scandinavians and Celts*: A. H. Smith, *Irish Influence in Yorkshire* (Revue Celtique, vol. 44, pp. 34–58), *Danes and Norwegians in Yorkshire* (Saga Book, vol. 10); Armstrong, Mawer, Stenton and Dickins, *Place-names of Cumberland*, vol. 3, pp. xxii–xxv.

[2] *Surnames*, p. 71, n. 1.   [3] Keal occurs as *Keles* 12th DC.

[4] There was never any such place in Essex. *Berle* is probably Barley (Herts).

[5] *Romance of Names*, 90.   [6] And, from personal-names, in *Hitches, Hodges, Riches*.

found quite early: *Hales* (1180), *Coates* (1190), *Howes* (1212), *Holmes* (1219). The final -*s* of surnames from French place-names is retained or dropped quite arbitrarily, the variation, perhaps, being due to the difference between the English and French pronunciation: Caliss (Calais), Gamage (Gamaches), Danvers (Anvers), Amyas (Amiens), Challen (Chalons), Sessions (Soissons).

The final -*s* in surnames like *Williams, Parsons, Carters*, is a different problem. It cannot be a sign of the plural. For *Parsons, Vicars*, etc., there are two origins:

(i) Alicia *le Parsones* 1327 SRWo, Margery *le Vikers* 1332 SRWa, Ralph *le Prestes* 1327 SRWo, where we have an elliptic genitive, 'the parson's (servant)', etc. cf. Henricus *homo Vicarii* 1297 SRY. Malyna *la Roperes* (1311 ColchCt), described as a servant, was either the servant of the roper or of a man named Roper. Surnames like John *Alysaundresman* 1297 Coram (Bk), Robert *Nicholesman* 1309 AssSt, with others in -*knave*, -*sergeant*, etc., are not uncommon, so that, whilst Gilbert *le Potteres*, Richard *le Cokes* (1327 SRWo) may mean 'son of the potter or of the cook', they might also denote his servant. But Philip *le Redes* (ib.) must be 'servant of a man named *Rede*'. Thus, too, John *Pastons* (1327 SRWo), John *Byltons* (1327 SRC), where the surname is local, 'servant of Paston or of Bylton'.

(ii) William *atte Personnes* 1327 SRSf, again elliptic, '(servant) at the parson's (house)', etc. Similarly Beadles, Stevens, etc. (Margaret *ate Budeles*, Sibilla *ate Stevenes* 1332 SRSo) may also mean 'servant at the beadle's (house)' and 'servant at Steven's'.

No satisfactory explanation has been given of this final -*s* in surnames formed from personal-names. Fransson's examples are late (1310). He regards them as elliptic genitives. As all his examples but one (Roger *le Persones*) are women, he must take all four to mean 'servant of Robert, the parson, etc.'.[1]

Ewen's account is confused.[2] He cites Willelmus *Johannis* (1159–60) and three similar forms of 1229–35 as examples of 'inflected genitives' due to '*filius* and *filia* having fallen into disuse'. But surnames of the type Willelmus *filius* Johannis are common long after 1235. He notes also two undated metronymics, Johanna *Mariote* and Willelmus *Margarete*, adding 'but the English nominative form, as Henry Maynard or John Rogers was also used, and the genitive ending (*es, is, ys*, or *s*) also begins to be noticeable, and at first most frequently in the names of women, thus Robertus filius Radulfi became Robertus Rolle (Raoul), but Matilda filia Radulfi was written Matilda Rolles . . . There was no precise rule, many surnames of women are without the final sibilant, which is occasionally found added to the second names of men.'[3] He does not explain why *filius Radulfi* becomes *Rolle* when the name is a man's, but *Rolles* when it is that of a woman. He repeats the argument later: 'John, Robin's son, would be called John Robin, but Margaret, Robin's (daughter), would be known as Margaret Robines.'[4] That in the early instances (his earliest example is 1230) the terminal *s* was due to the influence of the French nominative singular ending, seen in names like Jacques, Gilles, Jules, etc.,[5] is most unlikely. Such forms are rare in English and would not be employed for surnames

---

[1] MESO 27.   [2] *History of Surnames*, 120, 246-8.

[3] ibid., 120.   [4] ibid., 247.   [5] ibid., 247.

which his own Latin examples prove were in the genitive. Nor can it be accepted that *Driveres* and *Smithes* 'may possibly exhibit the feminine agential suffix'.[1]

Tengvik cites four much earlier examples of surnames like Ulmer *Æltredes*, where an Old English (or Scandinavian) personal-name is in the genitive, and two in Latin, Ælfuine *Goduini*, all from Bury (c 1095), and regards them as due to the omission of OE *suna* and Latin *filius* respectively.[2] Twenty other examples of this type in -*es* have been noted between 1100 and 1230, all names of men, formed usually from Old English or Scandinavian masculine names: Walter *Ricaldes* c1100 MedEA (Nf), Ranulph *Godes* 1186–1210 Holme, Edricus *Keteles* 1188 BuryS (Sf). Two are Old French: Eudo *Luueles* 12th DC (L), Stephen *Paynes* 1230 Pat, one Welsh, Robert *Howeles* 1210 Cur (Nth), and three from women's names, two English, Æilric *Osuuennes* c1095 Bury (Sf), Segarus *Aileves* 1188 BuryS (Sf), and one French, Walter *Auices* 1186–1210 Holme (Nf).

The Latin type is more common than Tengvik and Ewen would lead us to think. Over 50 examples have been noted between 1130 and 1240, all except one (Emma *Philippi* 1240 Rams, Nf), names of men, usually from French personal-names: Hugo *Oillardi* 1130 P (Sr), Willelmus *Walkelini* 12th DC (Lei), Willelmus *Luce* 1185 Templars (K), Johannes *Jeremie* 1196 P (Y); occasionally from Old English or Scandinavian names: Willelmus *Ailrici* 12th DC (L), Robertus *Edwini* 1229 Pat (So), Alanus *Torberti* 1212 Cur (Ha). Three are formed from names of women: Arnaldus *Mabilie* 1185 Templars (Ess), Robertus *Margerie* 1195 P (Gl). These names can only mean 'John, son of Jeremiah', 'Arnold, son of Mabel', etc., literal translations of the vernacular, just as the clerk translated 'Edward of Salisbury' by Edwardus *Saresberiae* 1100–35 Rams (Hu).

The English forms are early examples of the elliptic genitive, Edricus *Keteles* 'Edric Ketel's (son)', parallel to *Personnes, Prestes* above. That this interpretation is correct is proved by the following. In 1281 we have mention of Robert de Rokesle junior who is twice called Robert Dobes in 1305. His father was Robert de Rokesle senior who must often have been called by his pet-name *Dob*. Hence his son's surname *Dobes* which must mean 'son of Dob', i.e. of Robert.[3]

Toward the end of the thirteenth century, this type of name becomes more common and steadily increases in the fourteenth, but there is a marked difference in its frequency in different counties. In the Worcestershire Subsidy Roll for 1275 there are only 7 examples, 5 being names of women; in that for 1327 we find 138 men and 30 women so named. In Somerset in 1327: 128 men, 73 women; in Warwickshire (1332), 161 men, 20 women; in Suffolk (1327), 27 men, 1 woman; in Surrey (1332), 5 men, 11 women. In other Subsidy Rolls the number is negligible: Sussex (1296), 6; (1327) 2; (1332) 3; Cambridgeshire 4; Lancashire 2; Cumberland 2; Yorkshire (1297) 6; (1301) 3; (1327) 3, all men. In Essex there are 5 men in 1295 ParlR, a number in the Colchester Court Rolls (1311–45) and about 12 (all women) in the 1349 Fingrith Hall Court Rolls. The surnames are usually the common christian names in use, often pet-forms, rarely Old English and almost invariably masculine. Some few are nicknames or occupational-names (these sometimes preceded

---

[1] ibid., 252.   [2] OEByn 207–9.   [3] *Variation*, 44.

by *le*, occasionally *la*): Ysabella *Barones* 1275 SRWo, Hugh *Rabuckes* 1301 SRY, Claricia *le Parkeres* 1327 SRSo, Juliana *la Kinges* 1285 *Ass* (Ess), Amiscia *la Wrihtes* 1333 ColchCt. Occasionally we have a place-name: John *Dounes* 1327 SRWo.

The interpretation of these surnames is more difficult than one would expect. It is clear that in the twelfth century Segarus *Aileves* meant 'son of Aileve' and that is probably the meaning in the fourteenth century in the names of men. But John *le Cokes* (1327 SRWo) may well have been the cook's servant or assistant and names like William *Hogges* may have lost the article and have a similar meaning. So with women's names. Claricia *le Parkeres* may have been the servant of the parker and Isabella *la Chancelers* 'the servant of (a man named) Chanceler'. But such an interpretation is unsatisfactory for Avice *la Schepherdes* (1311 ColchCt) and Juliana *le Smithes* (1279 RH), for shepherds and blacksmiths were unlikely to have servants. Where the surname is a place-name, 'servant of a man named Bylton', etc., is probable.

In the Colchester Court Rolls (1311 ff.), large numbers of women were regularly fined at court after court for selling ale at too high a price. They were usually described as 'the wife of John Carpenter', etc., but a certain number are mentioned by name, which almost invariably ends in -*es* (Joan *la Warneres*, Alice *Sayheres*). It is a reasonable presumption that they were widows and that this type of women's surname denoted either a widow or a married woman. Matilda *Candeles* (1327 SRSx) was probably the wife of Ralph *Candel*, for in 1332 she is described as 'Matilda relicta Candel'. Margery *la Mazones* was the wife of Walter *le Mazoun* (1311 ColchCt). Agnes *Rickemannes* (1329 Husting) was probably the widow of *Rickeman* le Chaumberleng (1292 SRLo) and if so, we have to reckon with the fact that some of these women's names denote the christian name and not the surname of their husbands. It is not uncommon in these documents to find pairs of names like Nicholas *le Knyt* and Cecilia *Knyctes* (1297 MinAcctCo), who, we may fairly assume, were husband and wife. Amisia *Hugines* (1327 SRWo) was probably the wife of William *Hugyns* and here the surname means 'son of Hugyn'. Thus, a surname like *Stevens* may mean 'son of Stephen', 'servant of Stephen', or 'servant at Stephen's house', or it may be a metronymic derived from a form *Stevenes* 'Stephen's wife'. The only certainty is that *atte Stevenes* means 'servant at Stephen's house'. The -*s* of local surnames may be a plural inflexion (or a sign of French origin), but more often falls into one or other of the above classes. Sometimes, in late additions, it may be a dialectal pronunciation, with excrescent *s*.[1]

Pet-names

Already in Old English we find pet-names in use: *Tuma* for *Trumwine* in the seventh century and *Ælle* for *Ælfwine* in the tenth, and such forms as *Wine* and *Wulfa* for *Winefrið* and *Wulfwine*.[2] Names of this type continued to be formed and

---

[1] For a similar genitival formation in -*en*, v. Geffen.
[2] Stenton, *Personal Names in Place-names*, in Mawer and Stenton, *Introduction to the Survey of English Place-names*, 169-70.

a number still survive in surnames, some otherwise unrecorded. But most of the pet-names in modern surnames are of post-Conquest formation and some are difficult to identify. Examples are found in the twelfth century; they become more numerous in the middle of the thirteenth and in the fourteenth are common. They are found among all classes and are derived from Old English, Scandinavian and French personal-names alike. *Cudd* (1358) and *Cutt* (1279) are from OE *Cūðbeorht*, *Ugga* (1212) from *Uhtrǽd*; *Asti* (1203) is a pet-form of ON *Ásketill*; *Lamb* (1161) is for *Lambert*, *Gibbe* (1179) for *Gilbert*, *Lina* (1181) for *Adelina* or *Emelina*, whilst the Breton *Sanson*, *Samson* has given *Sanne* (1260) and *Samme* (1275). Not all pet-names are so easy to identify. *Hudd* (1177) and *Hulle* (1227) are undoubtedly for *Hugh*, but *Hudd* is also used for *Richard*. *Pelle* (1274) is a pet-name for *Peter*. *Hann* is undoubtedly for *John* (from *Jehan*), but is just as certainly for *Hanry* (Henry) and is said to have been used also for *Randolph*.

Some of these forms follow normal phonetic laws of assimilation: *Judd* from *Jurd* (Jordan); *Fippe* from *Philip*, *Bette* from *Bertin* and *Bertelmeu* (Bartholomew), *Penne*, a shortening of *Pennel*, from *Pernel*, *Cuss* from *Cust* (Custance, Constance), *Ibb* for *Isabel*. In others, the name begins by anticipating the following medial consonant: *Dande* (1246) for *Andrew*, *Biby* (1240) for *Isabel*. Some pet-names are formed from the second syllable of the full name: *Pot* (1115) from *Philipot*, itself a diminutive of *Philip*; *Coll* (1247) from *Nichol*, *Belle* (1279) from *Isabel*; *Sander* (1248) from *Alexander*. Voiced and voiceless consonants were used indiscriminately: *Dicke*, *Digge*; *Hikke*, *Higge*; *Gepp*, *Gebbe*; *Judde*, *Jutte*. Vowels were unrounded: *Rob*, *Rab*; *Dobb*, *Dabb*; or rounded: *Malle*, *Molle* (Mary); *Magge*, *Mogge* (Margaret), whilst the changes were rung on the consonants: *Robb* (1196), *Hobbe* (1176), *Dobbe* (1202), *Nabbe* (1298), all for *Robert*. In some names we find a combination of more than one of these features: *Libbe* (Elizabeth), *Pogge* (Margaret).

The clue to the explanation of these pet-names is given by Napier and Stevenson when they suggest that OE names such as *Lilla*, *Bubba* and *Nunna* are due to 'regressive assimilation' and have their origin in the speech of children.[1] Scandinavian scholars call them 'Lall-names'. According to this theory, *Lilla* is a short form of some compound of the stem *Bil-*, such names as *Bilheard* or *Bilnoth*. Stenton is disinclined to accept this on the ground that it implies the contemporaneous existence of two sharply contrasted conceptions of nomenclature. 'The state of mind which produced the compound names with their far-fetched significance is hardly compatible with one which allowed infantile attempts at expressing a name to pass into permanent use.' He admits, however, that this theory has 'the great merit of proposing an intelligible connection between these meaningless names and compounds of the normal Germanic type. Its chief weakness is the remoteness of the sound-association between the original compound name and the suggested simple derivative'.[2]

Children are children and parents are parents, whether we are concerned with the eighth or the twentieth century. The process of learning to speak is the same—trial and error by imitation of sounds heard and there are innumerable examples of

---

[1] *Crawford Charters* 51.   [2] Stenton, op. cit., 174.

common words which have been corrupted in form through misdivision, mispronunciation and misunderstanding. When an Anglo-Saxon named Æðel*stan* and his wife *Wulf*gifu deliberately named their son, the future Bishop of Worcester, *Wulfstan,* a combination of the first theme of the mother's name and the second of the father's, they were not concerned with the meaning of the compound—'wolfstone', any more than were those who named their children *Friþuwulf* 'peace-wolf' or *Wīgfrið* 'war-peace'. Names had become names and their meaning was a matter of no concern. Association—here, a perpetuation of themes common to the two families—is more important than meaning.

Detailed studies of the early speech-habits of children would throw much light on the eccentric forms of many pet-names. A wreath sent recently by the Queen was from *Lilibet,* the name by which Her Majesty is known in the family circle, a deliberate perpetuation of her early attempts to pronounce her own name. My own daughter still answers to the name of *Titt,* a shortening of *Titter,* her first attempts at *sister.* A newly-wedded wife of my acquaintance regularly addressed her young husband as *sweetheart,* which gradually became *weetheart, sweetie, weetie* and finally *weet,* a pet-name used for many years. There must be many similar petnames confined to a particular family and never seen in print. With such developments, it is not difficult to realize that a pet-name may have more than one origin, and that a single name may give rise to a variety of pet-names.

Diminutives

A few diminutives in *-uc* of OE origin survive (*Haddock, Whittock, Willock*), but most are derivatives of French names. The most common suffixes are *-ot, -et, -un, -in, -el*: Philpot, Ibbott; Hewett, Jowett; Paton, Dickens; Rankin, Higgins; Pannel, Pottell.

Double diminutives are formed from these suffixes:

-el-in: Hamlin, Hewlins, Jacklin
-el-ot: Giblett, Roblett
-in-ot: Adnett, Rabnott
-et-in (rare): Turkentine

The variety of surnames resulting from these different forms of pet-names may be seen from the following (varieties of spelling ignored):

Richard (pronounced *Rich-ard* and *Rick-ard*):
Rich, Richings, Ritchie; Hitch, Hitchcock, Hitchen, Hitchman, Hitchmough
Ricard, Rick, Ricky; Hick, Hicken, Hicklin, Hickman, Hickmott, Hickox; Higgett, Higgins, Higgs; Dick, Dickels, Dicken, Dickin, Dicketts, Dickie; Digg, Diggen
Robert: Rabb, Rabbets, Rabjohn, Rablen, Rabnott; Robb, Robbie, Ropkins, Robins, Robjant, Roblett, Roblin; Dabbs, Dabin, Dabinett; Dobb, Dobbie,

Dobbin; Hob, Hobbins, Hobday, Hobgen, Hoblin, Hopkin; Nabb, Nap, Nobbs, Nopp

Hugh: Hugo, Hue, Hew, How; Hewell, Hewett, Hewlett, Hewlins; Houchen, Howett, Howlett, Howlin(g); Hudd, Hudden, Huddle, Hudman, Hudsmith; Huelin, Huett, Huot; Huggett, Huggin, Huggon, Huglin; Hukin, Hewkin, Howkins; Hull, Hullett, Hullot; Hutchin

William: Will, Wilkin, Wilcock, Willet, Willott; Willmott, Wellemin, Wellerman, Willmin, Willament

Gill(h)am, Gilliam, Gillet, Gillman, Guillerman, Gelman

v. also Henry, Jack, John, Maud, Paul, Philip.

The Suffixes -cock and -kin

These two suffixes are used to form diminutives of the more common names and are very frequently used as personal-names, sometimes to distinguish son from father, sometimes as pet-names. John and Jankin, William and Wilkin, are both used as names of the same man. Compounds of *-cock* are less common and later than those of *-kin*, which are found already in the twelfth century: *Potechin* 1166, *Hardekin* 1175, *Lambekyn* 1178, *Wilekin* 1180, *Adekin* 1191; *Hellecoc* 1202, *Alecoc* 1204, *Adecok*, *Wilcok* 1246. Occasionally they are compounded with women's names: *Edekin* 1279, *Malkyn* 1297, *Marekyn* 1390; *Becok*, *Geuecok* 1332.

Such names become more common from the middle of the thirteenth century and are very frequent in the fourteenth, particularly among the lower classes. The earliest examples of *-kin* are names of Flemings: *Derechin* (1158, Essex). *Wilechin* (1166, Newcastle) was the son of a moneyer who may have been a foreigner. This supports the common view that the suffix was brought from the Netherlands but there seems to be no concentration in the east, whilst *-kin* names were common in Cheshire at the end of the thirteenth century.

SURNAMES OF OCCUPATION AND OFFICE

In early post-Conquest documents, the innumerable surnames of this type—almost invariably in Latin—refer to actual holders of the office, whether of church or of state: Abbot, Prior, Chancellor, Chamberlain, Steward (dapifer), or to ecclesiastical or manorial status: Monk, Dean, Reeve, Sergeant. Among the Normans some offices of state such as steward, constable, marshal, etc., became hereditary and gave rise to hereditary surnames, but the terms were also commonly used of lesser offices, whilst *marshal* was a common term for a farrier and such names frequently denoted the actual occupation. Abbots, priors, monks and nuns were bound by vows of celibacy and thus could not found families. As medieval surnames, these must be nicknames, 'lordly as an abbot', 'meek as a nun', often, too, bestowed on one of most unpriestly habits.

Occupational surnames originally denoted the actual occupation followed by the individual. At what period they became hereditary is a difficult problem. It has often been held that the absence of the article points to a hereditary surname, a supposition which cannot be upheld for early in the twelfth century the article is frequently omitted and the same man is called both Richard *turnur* and *le turnur* (12th DC). It is unlikely that, as Fransson suggests, trade-names were used as nicknames and that a man might be called 'the shoemaker' because he mended his own boots. But it is difficult to account satisfactorily for names like Mower, Ripper (reaper), Sawer (sower), which must have been only seasonal occupations.

A marked feature is the surprising variety and specialized nature of medieval occupations, particularly in the cloth industry where Fransson (p. 30) has noted 165 different surnames, whilst the metal trades provide 108, and provision dealers 107 different names. Many of these were clumsy and have disappeared but other surnames still recall occupations or occupational-terms long decayed: Arkwright, Ashburner, Barker (tanner), Billeter (bell-founder), Chaucer (shoe-maker), Cheesewright (cheese-maker), Deathridge (tinder-maker), Harbisher (maker of hauberks), Lister (dyer), Slaymaker (shuttle-maker), Thrower (silk-winder), Whittier (white leather-dresser), etc.

Many of the occupation-names were descriptive and could be varied. A worker in metal could be called both *Seintier* or *Bellyeter* from the bells he cast, or simply *Sporoner* from the spurs he made, or 'moneyer' if he made coins. William *le Pinour* 'maker of combs' was also called *le Horner* from the horn he used. Adam *le Marbrer* who paved part of St Paul's and Peter the *Pavier* who paved St Stephen's Chapel, Westminster, both followed the same occupation. William *Founder* cast both bells and cannon.

Surnames of occupation are more common than the modern forms suggest. Many surnames, previously regarded as nicknames difficult to explain, are really occupational. Apart from mere shortening by which *Cofferer* and *Coverer* became *Coffer* and *Cover*, the name of the article made or the commodity dealt in was used by metonymy for the maker or dealer. Modern *Garlick* represents not only medieval *Garlek* but also *Garleker* and *Garlekmonger*. *Cheese* is found as a surname in the twelfth century but, whilst *Cheser* has disappeared, both *Cheeseman* and *Cheesewright* survive. Of *Cheverell*, *Chevereller* and *Cheverelmonger*, only the metonymic *Cheverell* still exists. This frequent use of metonymy gives a satisfactory explanation of such names as *Death*, *Meal*, *Pouch*, etc. So, too, the man in charge of the colts or the palfreys was called not only *Colter* or *Coltman*, *Palfreyer* or *Palfreyman*, but also *Colt* or *Palfrey*. Thus, *Bull* and *Lamb* (sometimes from a personal-name) are not always nicknames. They may be metonymic for *bull-herd* and *lamb-herd*.

Brooker and *Brook* (*atte Broke*) are undoubtedly local surnames, 'dweller by the brook'. *Bridge*, *Bridger* and *Bridgeman* may similarly be local, but as the keeper of the bridge, especially where tolls had to be collected, also lived near the bridge, the surnames may be occupational also. But names like *Kitchen* (*atte Kechene*), *Kitchener*, *Pantry*, *Buttery*, etc., must be occupational. The man worked in or had charge of the kitchen or the pantry or the buttery, but he certainly did not live in them. Similarly, *Hall*, *Haller*, *Hallman*, probably denote a servant at the hall, where he also may have lived. But the owner—probably the lord of the manor—would have a different surname, one commemorating his possessions or an ancestor.

NICKNAMES

That many modern surnames were originally nicknames is proved conclusively by the material in the following pages. No full and satisfactory classification can be attempted. Some are unintelligible; the meaning of many is doubtful. Nicknames arise spontaneously from some fortuitous chance. The schoolboy's 'Tiny' is usually a hefty giant in the first eleven, but 'Tubby' is more often an accurate description. In my schooldays, 'Feet' was the nickname of a tall, lanky individual, with heavy boots on large feet which caused havoc in the unorthodox football played during breaks. The chemistry master rejoiced in the name of 'Bublum Squeaks', a corruption of 'Bubble and Squeak'. He was excitable, no disciplinarian, with a voice which rose higher and higher to a shrill squeak as he vainly tried to make himself heard above the uproar in the laboratory. But why a colleague of his was known as 'Joe Plug' no one ever knew. His christian name was Arthur and his surname Watson. Even when the origin of a nickname is known, it is difficult to see why it should stick. A schoolboy, called on to translate a Latin Unseen about Polyphemus, was thenceforth 'Polly' to his friends. Why should one schoolmaster be called 'Wally' and another 'Mike', names impossible to associate with either christian name or surname? 'Kip' had an interesting history. Originally 'Skipper'—Why, nobody knew—it quickly became 'Kipper', later shortened to 'Kip'. It is not surprising, therefore, if we frequently fail to get behind the mentality of the thirteenth and fourteenth centuries and cannot interpret their nicknames.

Many medieval nicknames—some cruel and indescribably coarse—have disappeared. Some are simple and obvious, describing physical attributes or peculiarities: Head, Neck, Mouth, Leg, Foot, Shanks, and, with attributes, Broadhead, Redhead, Coxhead, Ramshead, Barefoot, Cruickshanks, Sheepshanks, Goosey, Hawkey, Pauncefote 'arched belly', Vidler 'wolf-face', Chaffin 'bald', Hurren 'shaggy-haired', Garnham 'moustache', Grelley 'pock-marked', etc.

Mental and moral characteristics are often particularized: Good, Moody 'bold', Sharp, Wise, Root 'cheerful'; Daft 'foolish', Grim 'fierce', Musard 'stupid', Sturdy 'reckless', Proud, Prowse 'doughty', Vaisey 'playful', Gulliver 'glutton'; abstract nouns, as Comfort, Greed, Lawty 'loyalty', Sollas, Verity, Wisdom. Here, too, belong such names as Gutsell 'good soul', Thoroughgood, Goodenough, Careless, Pennyfather 'miser', Girling 'lion-heart', Gaine 'trickery', Fairweather, Milsopp.

Names of animals may be nicknames, descriptive of appearance or disposition. *Lamb* may denote meekness, *Bull* strength or a headstrong nature, *Colt* a lively, frisky individual, but they may often be used of a keeper of these animals. Bird-names are not always easy to interpret: Raven 'black', Heron, Stork 'long legs', Nightingale and Thrush 'songsters', Kite 'ravenous'. Plant-names may refer to a grower or seller, but may be nicknames: Cardon 'thistle', obstinate, stubborn, Pinnell 'tall and upright as a young pine'.

Names derived from dress and equipment are often occupational: Cottle 'cutler', Hood, Capp, Mantell, probably makers of these, but some are nicknames from a partiality for a particular type of dress: Greenhead 'green hood', Hussey 'booted', Gildersleeve 'golden sleeves', Shorthouse or Shorthose 'short boot'.

Many names, originally nicknames, were undoubtedly used as occupation-names: Besant 'banker', Blampin 'white-bread', a baker, Collop 'ham and eggs', a cook-house keeper, Drinkwater, sometimes a taverner, Goodale 'beer-seller'.

Particularly interesting are what have been called 'phrase-names', a term not entirely satisfactory, as there are two distinct types, the first consisting chiefly, but not entirely, of oath-names, the second of 'imperative-names', again an unsatisfactory term, as the verb may be merely the verbal stem. Oath-names are chiefly French: Debney 'God bless you', Dugard 'God protect you', Pardew, Purday, Purefoy, Pepperday. Of English origin are: Godbehere, Godsave 'for God's sake', and, sometimes, Mothersole. From habitual expressions: Goodday, Goodenday, Goodyear, Drinkale, Bonnally, and the French Bonger 'bon jour'.

'Imperative-names' consist of a verb plus a noun or an adverb. A few examples are found in Domesday Book but they are not common until the thirteenth and fourteenth centuries. Most are of French origin but the majority of those surviving are English, with some translations of the French: Crakebone (Brisbane), Cutbush (Tallboys), and a few hybrids: Bindloss, Pritlove, Shakesby 'draw sword'. Many of these nicknames are more or less derogatory occupation-names: Bendbow (archer), Copestake (wood-cutter), Knatchbull (butcher), Waghorn (trumpeter), Wagstaff (beadle), Catchpole (constable), Fettiplace (usher). Others indicate some quality or characteristic: Scattergood (spendthrift), Sherwin (speed), Makepeace, Turnbull (strength or bravery), Bevin (drinker), Crawcour (break-heart), Dolittle, Hakluyt (lazy), Parlabean (good-speaker), Standfast, Standalone, etc.[1]

HEREDITY OF SURNAMES

The rise of surnames, according to the accepted theory, was due to the Norman Conquest when Old English personal-names were rapidly superseded by the new christian names introduced by the Normans. Of these, only a few were really popular and in the twelfth century this scarcity of christian names led to the increasing use of surnames to distinguish the numerous individuals of the same name.[2] This is an oversimplification. Bynames—both English and Scandinavian—are found in England before the Conquest. Some Normans had hereditary surnames before they came to England. Evidence is accumulating that the OE personal-names lived on longer than has been supposed, a fact confirmed by the large number of modern surnames to which they have given rise and which must have been in living use after the Conquest. The new French personal-names, too, were more varied than is

---

[1] v. also Passmore, Perceval, Gotobed, and, for similar obsolete names, Weekley, *Surnames* 270–7.
[2] ODCN xxviii, OEByn 8–9.

commonly believed. A few, William, Robert, Richard and John, certainly became much more popular than the rest, but it was not from these that the earliest patronymic surnames were formed. It is often assumed that men 'adopted' their surnames. Some certainly did, but the individual himself had no need for a label to distinguish him from his fellows. The development of the feudal system made it essential that the king should know exactly what service each knight owed. Payments to and by the exchequer required that debtors and creditors should be particularized. The lawyers saw to it that the parties to transfers of land or those concerned in criminal proceedings could be definitely identified. Monasteries drew up surveys and extents with details of tenants of all classes and their services. And later the net was thrown wider in the long lists of those assessed in the subsidy rolls. It was the official who required exact identification of the individual. His early efforts often consisted of long-winded descriptions attached to a personal-name. Any description which definitely identified the man was satisfactory—his father's name, the name of his land, or a nickname known to be his. The upper classes—mostly illiterate—were those with whom the officials were chiefly concerned and among them surnames first became numerous and hereditary. It is noteworthy that in London, with its organized government and elaborate records, surnames became fixed early among the patrician classes.

There is evidence that surnames would have developed in England even had there been no Norman Conquest. Towards the end of the Old English period, a limited number of personal-names were becoming particularly popular. In the Suffolk Domesday the names of 217 freemen in the Hundred of Colneis are given, only four having bynames. In nine villages there were two or more men of the same name and the clerk was driven to occasional descriptions such as *alter Vluric* 'and a second Wulfric'. In Burgate 4 out of 15 men were named *Godric*, of whom one had a nickname *Godric long*. In Burgh, of 16 persons, two were named *Almer* and three *Godric*. At Micklegate, *Goda*, at Trimley, *Derstan*, each occurs twice in four names. The inevitable result of this state of affairs can be seen from a list of names of Suffolk peasants (c1095).[1] Of 660, more than half (359) had a single name only; 104 were described by their father's name (Ailuuard Goduini filius); 163 had bynames of the various types (Brihtmer Haiuuard, Aluric Godhand, Lemmer Brihtmer, Ulfuine de Laueshel)—a clear indication of the rise of surnames among peasants of English ancestry and name.

The only serious discussion of the heredity of surnames is that of Fransson.[2] His material is late and some of it inconclusive. His general conclusions are sound but require some modification: 'Hereditary surnames existed among the Norman noblemen already in the early 12th century. Among people in general they began to come into use in the following century, and by the end of this they were fairly frequent (especially local surnames and nicknames). This custom increased rapidly in the course of the fourteenth century, and by the end of it practically all people were provided with hereditary surnames.'

[1] Bury 25–44.   [2] MESO 33–41.

His suggestion that one reason for the rise of surnames was that a need was felt to unite the members of a family by means of a common surname is unlikely. It assumes that surnames were adopted and not given and would hardly apply to nicknames. Nor does it explain the varied surnames found in the twelfth century for different members of the same family. Whether local surnames, because of their frequency, had any influence on the fixing of surnames is doubtful. For barons and important land-holders to derive their surnames from their fiefs or manors was natural, but these form only a small proportion of the whole. When surnames like Nash, Wood, etc., became hereditary is a problem for which material is seldom available. In London, local surnames indicated the place from which the man had come, and became hereditary early.

Surnames of various types found in Domesday Book became hereditary at once: Bruce, Glanville, Montgomery, Percy (from French fiefs), Giffard, Peverell (patronymics), Basset and Gernon (nicknames).[1] Robert de Stafford, a brother of Ralph de Toeni (a surname surviving into the fourteenth century), took his surname from the head of his English barony. The fact that father and son bore the same surname is not always, as assumed by Tengvik and Fransson, a proof that the surname was hereditary. Robertus *Balistarius* held Worstead (Norfolk) in 1086 by serjeanty of performing the duties of *arbalistarius*. His son, Odo *arbalistarius*, inherited the office and the lands (c1140 Holme) and owed his surname either to inheritance or to his office. He is also called Odo *de Wrthesteda* (c1150 Crawford) and his son Richard and his grandson Robert were both called *de Worsted* (1166, 1210 Holme).

Throughout the twelfth and thirteenth centuries surnames of the type Johannes *filius Hugonis* are common, side by side with Johannes *Hugo*, where the son has his father's christian name as his surname. Such names indicate the beginning of a hereditary surname, but proof that it became established is often lacking:

Hugo filius Wisman, Hugo Wisman 1166–7 P (Nf)
Walterus filius Abelot, Walter Abelot 1195–6 P (Sa)
John le fiz michel 1292 SRLo, John Michel 1301 LoCt
Paganus le Cachepol, father of William Payn 1285 *Ass* (Ess)
John Gerveis son of Gervase de Pelsedun 1299 AD vi (K)

Such names as the following are probably already hereditary:

Reginald Ridel son of Hugh Ridel 1156–80 Bury (Nth)
Ralph Belet son of William Belet 1176 P (Sr)
William Brese son of Roger Brese 1210 P (Nf)
Gote Ketel, brother of Peter Ketel; Thomas Ketel son of Peter Ketel c1200, 1218–22 StP (Lo)

Clear evidence of heredity:

A charter of 1153 of Agnes de Sibbeford, wife of Ralph Clement, is witnessed

---

[1] For other examples, *v.* OEByn 14 ff.

by Hugo Clement and William, son of Ralph Clement, who is later called Willelmus
Clemens, with a brother Robertus Clemens (1155 Templars).

Thomas Noel, founder of Ronton Priory, is so called in 1182–5. His father
was Robert Noel (ib.), who is called Robertus Noelli filius (c1150 StCh).

Probably hereditary:

William Shepescank, Gilbert his brother, John Sepesank' 1224 Cur (Nf)
John Caritas, Simon Caritas, brothers 1265 FrLeic
William Lefthand, Ralph Lefthand 1268 FrLeic
Peter Wedercok son of Symon Wedircok 1302 Miller (C)

The twelfth century was also a period of vacillation and change in surnames:

Ralph, son of Robert Puintel de Walsham, had two brothers, William de
Criketot and Ralph Cangard (12th Holme). He is also called Ralph de Crichetot
(1141–9 ib.), with a son Hubert de Criketot (1163–6 ib.).

Philip de Powyk (1147–54 Holme) was a brother of Geoffrey Ridel (1153–68
ib.), a son of Richard Basset, and is called Philip Basset in 1185 (RotDom).

Stigand the priest (1126–7 Holme) had three sons: Thurbern the dean (1126–7),
Simond de Ludham (1153–66) and Robert de Ludham or de Ling (1141–9). Simon's
son and grandson were Thomas and Stephen de Walton (1175–86).

Griffin de Tweyt (1153–68 Holme) had a son Osbern de Thurgerton (1140–53)
who married Cecilia, daughter of Roger de Curcun. Their son was Robert de
Thweyt (1153–6) or de Curcun or Robert de Curcun de Thweyt (1186–1210). His
son was Robert the Clerk.

In London, surnames of all kinds, patronymics, local, occupational and nicknames, became hereditary among the patrician classes in the twelfth century. They
steadily increase in number and are frequent by the end of the thirteenth century.[1]
At the same time, there are many later examples which are not hereditary, especially
among the lower classes:

Luke le Ayler father of Walter le Mazerer 1278 LLB A, 1306 LLB B
Henry called Cros, son of William le Hornere 1303 LLB C
Amiel de Honesdon, late chandler, or Amiel le Chaundeller had two daughters:
Johanna Amyel and Cristina la Chaundeller 1349 Husting
Bartholomew Guidonis (1357 LLB G) or Castiloun (1369 ib.) was father of
John Chaungeour (1384 ib.)

Definite information on the development of surnames among the common folk
is difficult to find. Their names mostly occur in isolation, with little or no indication
of relationship. Fransson has suggested several methods by which heredity can be
inferred when relationship is not given. When two men of the same name are distinguished by the addition of *senior* and *junior*, it is a fair assumption that they
were father and son.[2] Such examples are fairly common in the subsidy rolls and
later.

---

[1] ELPN 119, 124, 130, 178.   [2] MESO 36 ff.

Further, he notes that in the subsidy rolls it is not uncommon to find several men of the same name assessed in the same village and suggests, very plausibly, that where the surname is a nickname, it has become hereditary. The same might be said of patronymics. Local surnames are not safe instances. There is no proof that the man did not actually live at the place. Similarly, an occupational-name may well mean that the man followed that particular occupation. But when a trade-name, different from the surname, follows it, we may safely assume that the surname was hereditary. His caution that a man might have had two trades or that a trade-name might be a nickname seems unnecessary. Examples are found in London in the thirteenth century and elsewhere later, though they are rare where they would be most valuable—in the subsidy rolls: John le Spencer, spicer 1306 LoCt; John Pistor, Taillour 1319 SRLo; John Mariner, hatter 1327 Pinchbeck (Sf); John le Fyssher, pistor, Robert Muleward, carpentarius 1353 Putnam (W).

Where material is available, a further test is to compare different documents of different periods relating to the same village. For Suffolk we have two surveys of the manors of the Bishop of Ely for 1221 and 1277, full of names. Many of these peasants had no surname and most bore English or Scandinavian names. In 15 parishes, we find the same surname in 1221 and 1277 as in the subsidy of 1327 and these can safely be regarded as hereditary. Only two or three parallels are found, as a rule, in any one parish, but in Glemsford, 6 surnames occur in both 1221 and 1277, 2 in 1277 and 1327, and one (*Curteis*) in all three years. In Rattlesden, 7 surnames occur both in 1221 and 1327, *Haliday* twice in each year, *Barun* twice in 1221, *Hardheved* twice in 1327.

For the Bury manors we have a subsidy of 1283 for Blackburn Hundred, unfortunately damaged, with the loss of many names, and surveys of the Hundreds of Thedwestrey, Thingoe, Blackburn, Cosford and Babergh c1188–90. These surveys are much less detailed than those of the Ely manors and contain many fewer names. In 27 parishes we find some of the surnames of 1327 also in one or both the earlier documents, cumulative evidence that surnames were becoming hereditary throughout the county. In Stanton, N. *Wluric* of 1283 probably owed his surname to *Wuluricus* filius fabri of 1188. *Cat* is found in all three documents, *Hubert* and *Kenne* in 1283 and 1327, *Cauel* and *Brunston* in 1188 and 1327. In Hopton, Honington and Troston six, in Walsham five, and in Culford, Rickinghall and Ixworth Thorpe four surnames occur in both 1283 and 1327.

A noteworthy feature of the southern subsidy rolls is the large number of surnames formed from OE personal-names no longer in use in the county: Worcestershire (1275) 203, Somerset (1327) 208, Suffolk (1327) 441, Surrey (1332) 85; Yorkshire (1297) 17, Lancashire (1332) 1. The complete disappearance of these personal-names proves that the surnames must have become hereditary. There is also evidence of a marked difference between north and south and a hint of a variation in the rate of development in the southern counties themselves.

Much detailed work remains to be done before the full facts can be known. But it appears that surnames among the common people became hereditary later than those of the upper classes. They are found in the thirteenth century and are well established in the south by the middle of the fourteenth. But there is clear proof that many men still had no surname and that many were still not hereditary. In 1381 SRSf, whilst 5 men followed a trade different from that indicated by their surname, there were 20 whose surname denoted their occupation (John Soutere, soutere; Walter Webb, webber). Later examples of the instability of surnames are: William Saukyn *alias* Archer (1442), Philip Daunce *alias* Defford (1473); John Walworth, called Mundis (1502), John Bullok *alias* Byde (1527), Richard Bolle *alias* Bronde (1568 ER 61); Richard Johnson *alias* Jackeson, whose daughters were Margaret Richardson and Elizabeth Richardson 1568 AD v (Ch); Richard son of Geoffrey *Reynald* of Edmascote otherwise called Richard *Ryvelle*, otherwise Richard son of Joan, daughter of William *Ryvell* 1408 Cl. Another example of a surname from a mother's name is: John *Organ* of Treworian, son of *Organa*, wife of Ives de Treworian 1327 AD v.

Yorkshire Names

The editor of *Freemen of York*[1] notes that surnames were chiefly from place-names or trade-names. In the earlier years, patronymics were non-existent except as 'Thomas filius Johannis de Wistow' (1295), or, 'Thomas filius Johannis praepositi de Wistow' (1295). Names such as 'Johannes filius Davidis, pulter' (1277) were exceptional. The earliest name in *-son* is 1323. 'It is still later [than the reign of Henry IV] before we find the son invariably taking his father's name; one of the last, if not the last instance to the contrary, occurs in [1431] when we find Robertus de Lynby, fil. Thomae Johnson.' Derogatory nicknames survived late: Henry Scrapetrough, molendinarius 1293; William Whitebrow, plasterer 1333; John Nevergelt, goldsmyth 1431; William Heteblack, baker 1460.

A tenement in Nawton was acquired by a certain Abraham and passed to his son Robert and so to John Abraham grandfather of William Abraham who held it in 1298.[2] This surname goes back, therefore, to 1200 or earlier. In the thirteenth century, William Samson owed his surname to his great grandfather Sansom de Alreton (Kirkstall). There is some evidence of heredity of surnames, too, in York where a number of freemen followed occupations different from those denoted by their surnames: Richard le warner, carnifex 1319; Richard le sauser, pelter, son of John le Sauser 1331; Thomas le hosteler, mariner 1331; Adam Fetheler, mercer 1360. But there is much evidence to the contrary: William Belle, son of Andrew le taillour 1316; William Candler, son of Robert de Stoke 1324; Thomas le parchemyner, son of John le hatter 1334; Johannes filius Willelmi filii Ricardi de Carleton, draper 1339; William Whitehals son of Henry de Marston, webster 1369; John Byller, baxter, son of Henry Holtbyman, milner 1427.

The Yorkshire Subsidy Rolls confirm the impression that surnames were transient and ephemeral. There are only occasional hints of heredity. Most surnames were local, occupational or nicknames. In 1297 (3,160 names) 17 per cent had

[1] p. xvi.   [2] 1327 SRY, p. 50, n. 2.

names of the *filius*-type; in 1301 (8,400 names) 21 per cent; in 1327 (4,500 names) 13 per cent; christian name plus christian name (e.g. Robert Reyner) accounted for 6 per cent in 1297, 3 per cent in 1301 and 1327. Names like Johnson were very rare: 2 in 1297, 5 in 1301, 12 in 1327.

The West Riding Poll-tax of 1379 (19,600 names) provides material quite unlike that found in the south and paralleled only by the East Riding Poll-tax of 1381. The *filius*-type of name is much less common than in 1327; that in *-son* much more common. What is noticeable is the frequency of names in *-wyf*, and *-doghter* and those of servants in *-man*, *-servant*, *-woman*, *-mayden*, besides names indicating other relationships in *-brother*, *-cosyn*, *-syster*, *-stepson*:

Matilda Hanwyfe, Elena Hobsonwyf, Beatrice Clerkwyf, Alice Caresonewyf, Dionisia Raulynwyf, Johanna Jackewyf

Matilda ffoxdoghter, Isabella Shephirddoghter, Johanna Rosedoghter, Johanna Malkyndoghter, Magota Stevendoghter, Johanna Robyndoghter

In two instances we have a man's surname: Robertus ffelisdoghter et Cecilia vxor ejus; Richard Wryghtdoghter

John Websterman, Thomas Masonman. Husband and wife were at times servants of the same man: William Mathewman, Magota Mathewwoman; Adam Parsonman, Emma Parsonwoman

Richard Hogeservant, Johanna Vikarservant, Elena Houchounservant

Isabella Vikerwoman, Johanna Prestewoman, Margareta Hallewoman

Matilda Marschalmaydyn, Alice Gibmayden, Elisot' Milessonmayden, Alice Martynmayden

Robert Parsonbrother, Henry Parsoncosyn, Agnes Vikercister, Alice Prest-syster servant, John Robertstepson

In these names, the suffix was often added to the surname and the master, etc., may be named separately:

John Odson, Alice Odsonwyf; William de Bilton, Roger Biltonman; Robert de Wallerthwayte, Margareta Wallerthwaytdoghter; Emma Hurle, Johanna Hurle-mayden; Ellota de Helagh, Agnes Helaghmayden; John Whitebred, Adam Wyt-bredman, John Adamson Whitebredman

Similarly, names in *-son* were also based on the surname:

John Payg, John Paygson; Richard Parlebene, Robert Parlebeneson; Matilda Millot', Roger Millotson; John Websterson; Adam Souterson. cf. also Roger Taylourson, Agnes Taylourdoghter; William Saunderson, Alice Saunderdoghter; William Milnerson, Agnes Milnerwyf. The wife of Roger *Wright* was Elena *Wright-wyf*; his son, John *Wrightson*.

The sons of William Jonson are named William Willeson Johanson and Benedict Willeson Johnson; that of Robert Hudson was William Robynson Hud-son. Wives were similarly named: Margareta Wilkynwyf Raulynson, Agnes Dycounwyfdowson.

It is abundantly clear that in the north surnames became hereditary much later than in the south. There is a fair amount of evidence that a number of occupation-names had become hereditary, but many certainly had not. In his *Memoirs of the Wilsons of Bromhead*,[1] Joseph Hunter demolishes the earlier pedigrees by proving errors of heralds and forging of documents. The family descended ultimately from William, father of John de Hunshelf or de Waldershelf (b. c1320) but owed their surname, not to this William, but to William (1369–87), father of John Wilson de Bromhead who is called John son of William son of John de Waldershelf in 1398. Hunter notes that John Dyson de Langeside derived his surname from his mother Dionysia de Langside (1369) and that a Thomas Richardson was the son of Richard de Schagh (1409). 'This (1380)', he concludes, 'was the age at which that class of surnames, which end in -son, began to be assumed', a conclusion not inconsistent with the evidence above.

WELSH SURNAMES

Hereditary surnames in Wales are a post-sixteenth century development. Many of the modern surnames derived from old Welsh personal-names arose in England where they became hereditary in the fourteenth century or earlier, long before such surnames were known in Wales; some, in the eastern counties, derive from Breton immigrants. The normal type of Welsh name was a patronymic: Madog ap Jevan ap Jorwerth, 'Madoc, son of Evan, son of Yorwerth', a type which resulted ultimately in such names as Pumfrey, Benian, Bevan, etc. In 1292, 48 per cent of Welsh names were patronymics of this kind (in some parishes, over 70 per cent); others included nicknames, occupation-names and some local surnames. The great majority of the surnames in the Extent of Chirk (1392–3) were of this patronymic type, with occasional nicknames (Jevan Gough, Ithel Lloit, Grono Vachann), rare occupational-names (Madog Taillour), and a few simple personal-names (Jevan Annwyl, Jevan Gethin), none of which were hereditary.

In later Chirk documents these patronymics are still the normal form. In 1538, all the thirteen men of a jury had names like: *John ap Madog ap Gryffyd ap Res junior*. There is evidence that a change had begun. Edward *ap Richard* and Edward *ap Robert* point to the future preponderance of the Welsh Jones, Williams and Roberts. In 1536 we find one such name already hereditary: John Edwards son of William Edwards. It was only in the reign of Henry VIII that surnames began to be hereditary among the gentry of Wales and the custom spread only slowly among the common people. Even in the nineteenth century, in Merionethshire, it was still not uncommon for a man to take his father's christian name as his surname: e.g. William Roberts son of Robert Williams. The three sons of Evan Thomas and Gwen Jones were known as Howal Thomas, Hugh Evans and Owen Jones, surnames derived (i) from the father's surname, (ii) from his christian name, (iii) from the mother's surname. In the nineteenth century, the frequency of Jones, Williams, etc., brought a need for further distinction and a tendency developed to create double surnames by prefixing the name of a house, parish or the mother's surname, as Cynddylan Jones, Rhondda Williams, etc.[2] In the following generation a hyphen was often introduced, hence Nash-Williams, etc.

---

[1] *Yorkshire Archaeological Journal*, vol. 5 (1879), pp. 63–125.   [2] Ewen 208, 387.

SCOTTISH SURNAMES

The earliest surnames in Scotland, found in the reign of David I (1124–53), were those of Normans: Robert de Brus, Robert de Umfraville, Gervase Ridel, etc., surnames which had already become hereditary in England and were later to be reinforced by such names as Balliol, Cumin, etc. In the towns, the burgesses bore English or continental personal-names, with trade-names or occasional nick-names.

In Scotland, early material for the study of surnames is much later than in England. Many names are undocumented before the fifteenth or sixteenth centuries, a period so late that definite etymologies are often impossible. 'The largest and most authentic enumeration now extant of the nobility, barons, landowners and burgesses as well as of the clergy of Scotland, prior to the fourteenth century,' is the Ragman Roll[1] which records the deeds of homage made to Edward I in 1296—an English official document. 'No part of the public records of Scotland prior to that era has been preserved from which any detailed information of the kind might have been derived.'[2] The surnames in the Ragman Roll are, for the most part, of the same type as those found in English sources of the same period—local, patronymic, occupational and nicknames. A number of local surnames derive from places in Scotland. Gaelic surnames occur, but form a distinct minority: e.g. Fergus Mac Dowilt, Macrath ap Molegan, Huwe Kenedy, Dovenal Galbrathe.

In 1382, of 56 tenants of Fermartyne excommunicated by the Bishop of Aberdeen,[3] 23 had names like Robertus filius Abraam. Celtic personal-names were rare. The solitary Gaelic surname is Adam Kerde (Caird 'craftsman'). Of the 23 surnames, 4 are patronymics from OE personal-names, *Bronnyng*, with three examples of *Freluf* (*v.* Browning, Freelove); 12 are local; one is Scandinavian, John Grefe (*v.* Grave); 3 are occupational (Cissor, Barkar, Faber); 2 are nicknames (Gray, Mykyl).

The surnames of 50 members of the Guild of Ayr (c1431)[4] have all the appearance of modern surnames: 16 patronymics (Neil Neilsoun, Patrik McMartyn, Patrik Ahar, Patoun Dugald); 6 local; 12 occupational (Listar, Walkar) and 5 nicknames (Petit, Cambell, Broun, Lang).

The paucity of Gaelic names in these sources is noteworthy. They are from the Lowlands, from Ayr and from Aberdeen, which 'was already predominantly English-speaking in the twelfth century'.[5] The Lowland Scots dialects derive from Northern English, though they have developed their own pronunciations and characteristic vocabularies, and Lowland surnames developed on the same lines as those in England, though they were slower to become hereditary. At the end of the fifteenth century and later we find clear evidence that surnames were not generally fixed. In 1473 the son of Thomas Souter was named David Thomson and in 1481

[1] *Cal. Docs. Scotland*, vol. 2, pp. 193–214.
[2] T. Thomson, *Instrumenta Publica* (Bannatyne Club), p. xiv.
[3] List printed by Black, *Surnames of Scotland*, p. xxiii.   [4] ibid., p. xxiv.
[5] F. C. Diack, *Scottish Gaelic Studies*, vol. i, p. 92.

Alexander Donaldson was the son of Donald Symonson. The frequent patronymics were not permanent. They changed with each succeeding generation and in the Highlands it was not until the eighteenth century that this custom was abandoned.

It was a common practice in Scotland for a laird to take his name from the estate, which itself was often named from its owner. The lands of Hugh de Paduinan (1165–73) were called from him *villa Hugonis* or *Huwitston* 'the estate of *Hewitt*', a pet-form of *Hugh*. His descendants took hence their surname, Fynlawe *de Hustone* (1296 CalSc), now *Houston*. Similarly, the modern *Symington* derives from *Symoundestone* (now Symington, Lanarkshire), the barony once held by *Symon* Locard (c1160). Owing to the frequency of such territorial names, lairds and farmers were often called by the name of their estate or farm and signed their letters and documents by their farm-names. In the seventeenth century an Act was passed forbidding any except noblemen and clerics of high office so to sign themselves but such estate-names long persisted in speech.

In the Highlands, hereditary surnames developed late. The clan system resulted in large numbers of people with the same name, but no specific surname of their own. The desire for protection in unsettled times caused men to attach themselves to a powerful clan and to assume its name. Chiefs of clans and heads of landed families increased the number of their followers by conciliation or coercion, and all took the name of the clan. In the sixteenth and seventeenth centuries the rapid increase in the Clan Mackenzie was due to the inclusion of the old native tenants on lands acquired from time to time by the chiefs. 'Frasers of the boll of meal' were poor Bissets who had changed their name to Fraser for a bribe. Oppressed people from the neighbouring districts sought the protection of Gilbert Cumin who adopted them as clansmen by baptizing them in the stone hen-trough at his castle door. Henceforth they were 'Cumins of the hen-trough' to distinguish them from Cumins of the true blood.[1]

In 1603 an Act was passed ordering the McGregors to renounce their name under pain of death. Some took the names of Johnestoun, Doyle, Menzies or Ramsay. For loyalty to Charles II the Act was repealed in 1661 but revived in 1693.[2] In 1695 'Evan, formerly called M'Grigor' was granted permission to resume his surname of McGregor for life, but only on condition that he gave his children a different surname, for which he chose *Evanson*.[3]

After the Battle of Culloden (1746), Gaelic names began to creep into the Lowlands and were often anglicized to overcome Lowland hostility. English or Lowland surnames were adopted. Names were translated, Johnson for Maciain, Livingstone for MacLevy, Cochrane for Maceachrain. Macdonald became Donald or was translated Donaldson. In the years after 1820, began a steady influx of Irishmen into south-west Scotland, especially into Lanarkshire, Renfrewshire, Ayrshire and Galloway, with further corruption of Gaelic names: Doyle for O'Toole, Swan for McSweeney, Graham for McGrimes and Cuming for McSkimming.[4]

The modern bearer of a clan-surname, therefore, is not necessarily a member

---

[1] *v.* Black, pp. xxxvii–xxxviii.   [2] Ewen 421–2.   [3] ibid., 423.
[4] *v.* Black, pp. xl, xlv.

of the clan by blood or heredity. Nor does a Gaelic or English surname prove descent. A Celtic surname may be borne by one with very little Celtic blood in his veins, whilst a man with an Anglo-Saxon name may be almost a pure Celt.[1]

Clan-names

The varied origins of Scottish surnames is well illustrated by the names of the clans.

From Scottish places: Baird, Brodie, Buchanan, Chisholm, Cunningham, Douglas, Drummond, Erskine, Forbes, Gordon, Innes, Keith, Leslie, Livingstone, Murray, Ogilvie, Ramsay, Ross, Skene, Sutherland, Urquhart

Gaelic: Cameron, Campbell, Clan Chattan, Duncan, Farquharson, Ferguson, Gow, Kennedy, Maclennan, Macalpine, Macarthur, Macbean, Maccallum, Maccoll, Macdonald, Macdonnell, Macdougall, Macduff, Macewen, Macfarlane, Macfie, MacGillivray, Macinnes, Macintosh, Macintyre, Mackay, Mackenzie, Mackinnon, Maclaren, Maclean, Maclaine, Macmillan, Macnab, Macnaughton, Macneill, Macpherson, Macquarrie, Macqueen, Macrae, Malcolm, Matheson, Munro, Rob Roy, Shaw

French: Anderson, Bruce, Cumin, Davidson, Fletcher, Fraser, Grant, Hay, Henderson, Johnston, Macalister, MacGregor, MacNicol, Menzies, Montgomery, Morrison, Napier, Oliphant, Robertson, Sinclair

English: Armstrong, Barclay, Elliot, Graham, Hamilton, Lindsay, Scott, Stewart, Wallace

Scandinavian: Gunn, Kerr, Lamont, Macaulay, MacIvarr, MacLachlan, MacLeod

IRISH SURNAMES

Surnames appear in Ireland in the middle of the tenth century. These were patronymics formed by prefixing *O* or *Ua* to the grandfather's name or *Mac* to the father's, whether a personal- or an occupation-name. Of these, the *Mac*-names are the later. It has been claimed that these surnames became hereditary by an ordinance of Brian Boru (1002–14) but neither Brian himself nor his sons had hereditary surnames. It was only in the time of his grandsons that O'Brien first came into existence. The development of such surnames was slow and spread over several centuries. Definite evidence is lacking and patronymics have been confused with hereditary family names. Woulfe considers that by the end of the twelfth century surnames were universal in Ireland but admits that they were not at first of a lasting character, and in some instances were laid aside after a generation or two in favour of new surnames taken from less remote ancestors. He admits, too, that some surnames are not older than the thirteenth or fourteenth centuries, whilst a few originated in the sixteenth century.[2]

---

[1] *v.* Black, pp. xlii–xliii.   [2] Woulfe, *Sloinnte Gaedheal is Gall*, pp. xviii, xix.

The Anglo-Norman invasion of Ireland had a similar effect to that of the Norman Conquest in England. New personal-names were introduced, and a new type of surname. Some Normans took names from Irish places: John de Athy, Adam de Trim, both now rare surnames in Ireland. Burke, Birmingham and London derive from Anglo-Normans, as do Bassett, Bissett, Savage; Hammond, Hewlett, Sampson.

A list of about 1,500 Dublin surnames of the end of the twelfth century contains very few that could not appear in an English list of the same period. The personal-names are mostly French, with a fair sprinkling of English and Scandinavian (Godwin, Ailward, Cristraid, Edwacer; Torsten, Swein, Toki, Turchetel). Of the few Celtic names, Bricius, Samsun and Cradok are found in England. Only Padin, Cullin and Gillamorus are pure Irish. So, too, with the surnames: local names from Colchester, Leominster and Worcester; common occupational-names, *lorimer*, *turnur*, etc.; nicknames as Holega, Litalprud, le Crespe, le Gentil, Prudfot, Unred, Philip Unnithing, etc. Walter palmer was the son of David de Tokesburi. There is no hint of hereditary surnames. Two similar lists of some 550 free citizens (1225–50) and of about 200 members of the Dublin Guild Merchant (1256–7) are similar in nature.[1] The names are Anglo-Norman names established in Ireland.

At Limerick and Cork, in 1295, surnames were Irish:[2] O'Kynnedy, Ofechan, Omoriharthy, Maccloni, Maccarthen. Irishmen were beginning to use French christian names: Reginald, Maurice, Thomas, Walter.

One result of the Anglo-Norman settlement was that names acquired two forms, one Irish, one English. Some English settlers adopted Irish names. The Birminghams took the surname of MacFeeter from Peter de Bermingham and the Stauntons that of Mac an Mhíliadha (MacEvilly) from Milo de Staunton. After the murder of William de Burgo, third earl of Ulster, in 1333 and the lessening of English power in Ireland, many Anglo-Norman families in Connaught and Munster adopted the Irish language and assumed Irish surnames (MacWilliam, MacGibbin, etc.) and became so thoroughly hibernicized that in 1366 an Act was passed ordering that 'every Englishman use the English language, and be named by an English name, leaving off entirely the manner of naming by the Irish'.[3] In 1465 an attempt was made to stamp out the use of Irish names among the Irish themselves. Every Irishman living in the counties of Dublin, Meath, Louth, and Kildare was ordered to assume 'an English surname of a town, as Sutton, Chester, Trim, Skreen, Cork, Kinsale; or a colour, as White, Black, Brown; or an art, as Smith or Carpenter; or an office, as Cook, Butler'. The name so selected was to be used also by his issue under penalty for failure so to do.[4]

After the revolution of 1688 the change of Irish into English names increased. This process of anglicization followed very much the same course as in Scotland. Ó Cobhthaigh became Coffey, Cowie or Cowhey, whilst Coffey may represent Ó Cobhthaigh, Ó Cathbhadha, Ó Cathbhuadhaigh or Ó Cathmhogha. *O'* and *Mac* were frequently dropped. Ryan may be for O'Mulryan. Names might be translated

[1] Gilbert, *Historic and Municipal Documents of Ireland*, pp. 3–48; 112–23; 136–40.
[2] Lists printed by Ewen, p. 129.   [3] ibid., 425.   [4] ibid., 426.

(Badger for Ó Bruic; Johnson for MacSeáin); or attracted to a better-known sur-name (Ó Blathmhaic, anglicized as Blawick and attracted to Blake), or assimilated to a foreign name (Summerville for Ó Somacháin; De Moleyns for Ó Maoláin; Harrington for Ó hArrachtáin); or by substitution (Clifford for Ó Clumháin; Loftus for O Lachtnáin).[1] Such surnames were carried by Irish immigrants to England, Scotland and America where they were often further corrupted in pro-nunciation and spelling, thus adding endless complications to the difficulties of tracing their origin.

MANX SURNAMES

Manx surnames reflect the history of the island. Orosius tells us that in the fifth century both Ireland and the Isle of Man were inhabited by *Scoti*—Gaels, of the same name as those from whom Scotland derived its name. In the ninth century Norsemen subdued the island which was mainly ruled by Norwegians from Dublin. In 1266 Norway ceded Man to Scotland who held it about a hundred years, though it was frequently in the hands of the English. The Scandinavian settlers, already partly celticized, intermarried with the native Gaels and added Norse to the Celtic personal-names in common use. Patronymics were formed by prefixing *Mac* to the father's name. The Irish *O'* never took root.

Of modern surnames, Moore estimates that 68 per cent are pure Celtic, 9 per cent pure Scandinavian, 6 per cent Celtic-Scandinavian, 5·4 per cent pure English, 3·3 per cent English-Celtic and 1·3 per cent English-Scandinavian.[2] Early in the sixteenth century the prefix *Mac* was almost universal; a hundred years later it had almost disappeared.[3] In pronunciation, the *Mac* was unstressed and the final consonant tended to coalesce with the first consonant of the following personal-name and became the initial consonant of the surname when the *Mac* was lost. Hence the characteristic Manx surnames beginning with C, K, or Q: Caine (Mac-Cathain), Curphey (MacMurchadha), Kay (MacAedha), Kermode (MacDermot), Kneen (MacCianain), Quine (MacCuinn); Corkhill (MacThorketill), Cowley (MacAmhlaibh, Macaulay, from ON *Óláfr*), Crennell (Macraghnaill, ON *Rögn-valdr*). Some names of this type are from Anglo-Norman personal-names: Clucas (MacLucas), Costain (MacAustin), Kissack (MacIsaac), Quail (MacPhail, Paul), Qualtrough (MacWalter), Quilliam (MacWilliam).

---

[1] *v.* Woulfe, 36–39.   [2] Moore, *Surnames and Place-names of the Isle of Man*, 11.
[3] ibid., 9.

ABBREVIATIONS

a	*ante*
Abbr	*Placitorum . . . abbreviatio*, London, 1811
AC	J. H. Round, *Ancient Charters* (Pipe Roll Soc. 10, 1888)
Acc	H. M. Colvin, *Building Accounts of King Henry III*, Oxford, 1971
AccM	S. Challenger, *Accounts for Works on the Royal Mills and Castle at Marlborough, 1237–8 and 1238–9* (Wilts Arch. Soc. 12, 1956)
AD	*A Descriptive Catalogue of Ancient Deeds* (in progress)
Add	BM., Additional MSS.
AddCh	BM., Additional Charters
AFr	Anglo-French
ANF	L. C. Loyd, *The Origins of some Anglo-Norman Families* (Harleian Soc. 103, 1951)
ArchC	*Archaeologia Cantiana* (in progress)
ASC	*Anglo-Saxon Chronicle*
ASCh	A. J. Robertson, *Anglo-Saxon Charters*, Cambridge, 1939
Ass	Assize Rolls (unpublished)
Ass	Assize Rolls: Beds (Beds Hist. Rec. Soc. 1, 3, 1913–16); Bucks (Bucks Rec. Soc. 6, 1945); Cambs (W. M. Palmer, *The Assizes held at Cambridge A.D. 1260*, Linton, 1930; Cambs Antiq. Soc. 55, 1942); Ches (Salt Arch. Soc. (OS) 15, 1894; Chetham Soc. 84, 1925); Durham (Surtees Soc. 127, 1916); Essex (Essex Arch. Soc. 1953); Glos (Selden Soc. 59, 1940); Kent (Kent Rec. Soc. 13, 1933); Lancs (Lancs and Ches Rec. Soc. 47, 49, 1904–5); Lincs (Lincs Rec. Soc. 22, 30, 36, 49, 56, 65, 1926–71; Selden Soc. 53, 1934); London (London Rec. Soc. 1, 1965); Northants (Northants Rec. Soc. 5, 11, 1930–40); Northumb (Surtees Soc. 88, 1891); Som (Som Rec. Soc. 11, 36, 41, 44, 1897–1929); Staffs (Salt Arch. Soc. (OS) 3–7, 1882–6; Selden Soc. 59, 1940); Warwicks (Dugdale Soc. 16, 1939; Selden Soc. 59, 1940); Wilts (Wilts Arch. Soc. 16, 26, 1961–71); Worcs (Selden Soc. 53, 1934); Yorks (Yorks Arch. Soc. 44, 100, 1911–39; Selden Soc. 56, 1937)
ASWills	D. Whitelock, *Anglo-Saxon Wills*, Cambridge, 1930
ASWrits	F. E. Harmer, *Anglo-Saxon Writs*, Manchester, 1952
Bacon	*The Annalls of Ipswiche 1654*, ed. W. H. Richardson, Ipswich, 1884
Balliol	*The Oxford Deeds of Balliol College* (Oxford Hist. Soc. 64, 1913)
BarkingAS	*Transactions of the Barking Antiquarian Society* (in progress)
Barnwell	*Liber Memorandorum Ecclesie de Bernewelle*, ed. J. W. Clark, Cambridge, 1907
Bart	N. Moore, *The History of St. Bartholomew's Hospital*, 2 vols, London, 1918
Battle	*Custumals of Battle Abbey* (Camden Soc. (NS) 41, 1887)
BCS	W. G. de G. Birch, *Cartularium Saxonicum*, 3 vols, London, 1885–99
Bec	*Select Documents of the English Lands of the Abbey of Bec* (Camden Soc. 3rd Ser. 73, 1951)
Beds	Bedfordshire
Berks	Berkshire

Binham	BM. Cott. Claudius D xiii
BishamPR	*The Register of Bisham, co. Berks*, London, 1898
Bk	Buckinghamshire
Black	G. F. Black, *The Surnames of Scotland*, New York, 1946
BM	*Index to the Charters and Rolls in the . . . British Museum*, 2 vols, London, 1902
Boldon	*Boldon Book* (DB vol. iv; Surtees Soc. 25, 1852)
Bosville	T. W. Hall, *A Descriptive Catalogue of . . . the Bosville and the Lindsay Collections*, Sheffield, 1930
Building	L. F. Salzman, *Building in England down to 1540*, Oxford, 1952
Burton	*Abstract of the Contents of the Burton Chartulary* (Salt Arch. Soc. (OS) 5, 1884)
Bury	D. C. Douglas, *Feudal Documents from the Abbey of Bury St. Edmunds*, London, 1932
BuryS	*The Kalendar of Abbot Samson of Bury St. Edmunds and related documents* (Camden Soc. 3rd Ser. 84, 1954)
BuryW	*Wills and Inventories from . . . Bury St. Edmunds* (Camden Soc. (OS) 49, 1850)
Butley	A. G. Dickens, *The Register or Chronicle of Butley Priory, Suffolk, 1510–1535*, Winchester, 1951
Buxhall	W. A. Copinger, *History of the Parish of Buxhall*, London, 1902
c	*circa*
C	Cambridgeshire
Caen	Cartulary of Holy Trinity Abbey, Caen (Paris, Bib. Nat., MS lat. 5650)
CalSc	*Calendar of Documents relating to Scotland*, 4 vols, London, 1881–8
Calv	*The Calverley Charters* (Thoresby Soc. 6, 1904)
CantW	*Index of Wills and Administrations . . . in the Probate Registry at Canterbury, 1396–1558 and 1640–1650* (Index Library 50, 1920)
CAPr	*Proceedings of the Cambridge Antiquarian Society* (in progress)
CarshCt	*Court Rolls of the Manor of Carshalton* (Surrey Rec. Soc. 2, 1916)
CartAntiq	*Cartae Antiquae Rolls* (Pipe Roll Soc. (NS) 17, 33, 1939–60)
CathAngl	*Catholicon Anglicum*, ed. J. H. Herrtage (EETS (OS) 75, 1881)
Ch	Cheshire
Ch	*Calendar of the Charter Rolls*, 6 vols, London, 1903–27
ChambAcctCh	*Accounts of the Chamberlains . . . of the County of Chester, 1301–1360* (Lancs and Ches Rec. Soc. 59, 1910)
ChertseyCt	*Chertsey Abbey Court Rolls* (Surrey Rec. Soc. 38, 48, 1937–54)
Chirk	G. P. Jones, *The Extent of Chirkland, 1391–1393*, London, 1933
ChR	*Rotuli Chartarum*, London, 1837
ChW	*An Index of the Wills . . . at the Diocesan Registry, Chester* (Lancs and Ches Rec. Soc. 33, 1875)
ChwWo	*The Churchwardens' Accounts of St Michael's in Bedwardine, Worcester* (Worcs Hist. Soc., 1896)
Cl	*Calendar of the Close Rolls* (in progress)
Clerkenwell	*Cartulary of St. Mary, Clerkenwell* (Camden Soc. 3rd Ser. 71, 1949)
ClR	*Rotuli litterarum clausarum*, 2 vols, London, 1833
Co	Cornwall
Cockersand	*The Chartulary of Cockersand Abbey* (Chetham Soc. 38–40, 43, 56, 57, 64, 1898–1909)
Colch	*Cartularium Monasterii S. Joh. Bapt. de Colecestria*, Roxburghe Club, 2 vols, 1897
ColchCt	*Court Rolls of the Borough of Colchester*, 3 vols, Colchester, 1921–41
Combermere	*The Book of the Abbot of Combermere* (Lancs and Ches Rec. Soc. 31, 1896)
Copinger	W. A. Copinger, *Materials for the History of Suffolk*, 5 vols, London, 1904
Cor	Coroners' Rolls (PRO) (unpublished)

Cor	Coroners' Rolls: (Selden Soc. 9, 1896); London (R. R. Sharpe, *Calendar of Coroners' Rolls of the City of London A.D. 1300–1378*, London, 1913); Notts (Thoroton Soc. 25, 1969)
Coram	Coram Rege Rolls (PRO) (unpublished)
Coram	*Placita coram domino Rege . . . 1297* (British Rec. Soc. 19, 1898)
CoWills	*Calendar of Wills . . . relating to the counties of Cornwall and Devon* (Index Library 56, 59, 1929–32)
CPR	*Cambridgeshire Parish Registers*, 8 vols, ed. W. P. W. Phillimore, London, 1907–27
CR	Pipe Roll, Chancellor's Copy
Crispin	J. A. Robinson, *Gilbert Crispin, Abbot of Westminister*, Cambridge, 1911
Crowland	F. M. Page, *The Estates of Crowland Abbey*, Cambridge, 1934
Ct	Court Rolls (unpublished)
CtH	B. Farr, *The Rolls of Highworth Hundred 1275–1287* (Wilts Arch. Soc. 21, 22, 1966–7)
CtSt	*Alrewas Court Rolls* (Salt Arch. Soc. (NS) 10, 1907, 3rd Ser. 1, 1910)
CtW	R. E. Latham and C. A. F. Meekings, *The Veredictum of Chippenham Hundred, 1281* (Wilts Arch. Soc. 12, 1956); R. B. Pugh, *Court Rolls of the Wiltshire Manors of Adam de Stratton* (Wilts Arch. Soc. 24, 1970)
Cu	Cumberland
Cullum	J. Cullum, *The History and Antiquities of Hawsted*, London, 1784
Cur	*Curia Regis Rolls* (in progress; Pipe Roll Soc. 14, 1891)
CurR	*Rotuli Curiae Regis*, 2 vols, London, 1835
Cust	T. J. Hunt, *The Medieval Customs of the manors of Taunton and Bradford on Tone* (Som Rec. Soc. 66, 1962)
CWAS	*Transactions of the Cumberland and Westmorland Antiquarian Society* (in progress)
D	Devonshire
Db	Derbyshire
DB	Domesday Book
DbAS	*Journal of the Derbyshire Archaeological and Natural History Society* (in progress)
DbCh	I. H. Jeayes, *Descriptive Catalogue of Derbyshire Charters*, London, 1906
DBStP	*The Domesday of St Paul's of the year 1222* (Camden Soc. (OS) 69, 1858)
DC	F. M. Stenton, *Documents illustrative of the Social and Economic History of the Danelaw*, London, 1920
DenhamPR	*Denham Parish Registers* (Suffolk Green Books 8, 1904)
DEPN	E. Ekwall, *The Concise Oxford Dictionary of English Place-Names*, Oxford, 1960
Dickin	E. P. Dickin, *A History of Brightlingsea*, Brightlingsea, 1939
DKR	*The Forty-First Annual Report of the Deputy Keeper of the Public Records*, London, 1880
DM	D. C. Douglas, *The Domesday Monachorum of Christ Church, Canterbury*, London, 1944
Do	Dorset
Du	Durham
Dublin	J. T. Gilbert, *Historic and Municipal Documents of Ireland, A.D. 1172–1320* (Rolls Series 53, 1870)
Dugd	W. Dugdale, *Monasticon Anglicanum*, London, 1817–30
DWills	*Calendar of Wills and Administrations in Devon and Cornwall* (Index Library 35, 1908)
e	early
EA	*The East Anglian*, 17 vols, 1858–1910
EAS	*Transactions of the Essex Archaeological Society* (in progress)
EChCh	*Facsimiles of Early Cheshire Charters* (Lancs and Ches Rec. Soc, 1957)

Edmunds	T. W. Hall, *Descriptive Calendar of the Edmunds Collection*, Sheffield, 1924
Ek	E. Ekwall, 'Some Early London Bynames and Surnames' (*English Studies* 46 (1965), 113–18)
ELPN	E. Ekwall, *Early London Personal Names*, Lund, 1947
Ely	BM. Cott. Claudius C xi
ElyA	BM. Cott. Tiberius B ii
ElyCouch	Liber R (Ely Diocesan Registry)
EME	Early Middle English
EngFeud	F. M. Stenton, *The First Century of English Feudalism, 1066–1166*, Oxford, 1932
EngLife	L. F. Salzman, *English Life in the Middle Ages*, Oxford, 1950
ER	*The Essex Review* (in progress)
ERO	Unpublished documents in the Essex Record Office, Chelmsford
Ess	Essex
Ewen	C. L. Ewen, *A History of Surnames of the British Isles*, London, 1931
EwenG	C. L. Ewen, *A Guide to the Origin of British Surnames*, London, 1938
Ewing	G. Ewing, *A History of Cowden*, Tunbridge Wells, 1926
Exon	Exeter version of DB
Eynsham	*Eynsham Cartulary* (Oxford Hist. Soc. 49, 51, 1907–8)
FA	*Inquisitions and Assessments relating to Feudal Aids*, 6 vols, London, 1899–1921
Fanshawe	H. C. Fanshawe, *The History of the Fanshawe Family*, Newcastle upon Tyne, 1927
Fees	*Liber Feodorum*, 3 vols, London, 1920–31
FeuDu	*Feodarium Prioratus Dunelmensis* (Surtees Soc. 58, 1872)
FF	Feet of Fines (unpublished)
FF	Feet of Fines: (Pipe Roll Soc. 17, 20, 23, 24, 1894–1900); Bucks (Bucks Rec. Soc. 4, 1942); Cambs (Cambs Antiq. Soc. 26, 1891); Essex (Essex Arch. Soc., 4 vols, 1899–1964); Hunts (Cambs Antiq. Soc. 37, 1913); Kent (Archaeologia Cantiana 11–15, 18, 20, 1877–93; Kent Rec. Soc. 15, 1956); Lancs (Lancs and Ches Rec. Soc. 39, 46, 50, 60, 1899–1910); Lincs (Lincs Rec. Soc. 17, 1920; Pipe Roll Soc. (NS) 29, 1954); Norfolk (Pipe Roll Soc. (NS) 27, 32, 1952–8); Oxford (Oxford Rec. Soc. 12, 1930); Som (Som Rec. Soc. 6, 12, 17, 22, 1892–1906); Staffs (Salt Arch. Soc. (OS) 3, 4, 11, 12, (NS) 10, 1882–1907); Suffolk (Pipe Roll Soc. (NS) 32, 1958; Cambs Antiq. Soc. 1900); Surrey (Surrey Arch. Soc. 1894); Sussex (Sussex Rec. Soc. 2, 7, 23, 1903–16); Warwicks (Dugdale Soc. 11, 15, 18, 1932–43); Yorks (Yorks Arch. Soc. 2, 5, 7, 8, 42, 52, 62, 67, 82, 121, 127, 1887–1965)
Finchale	*The Charters . . . of the Priory of Finchale* (Surtees Soc. 6, 1837)
Fine	*Calendar of the Fine Rolls*, 22 vols, London, 1911–62
FineR	*Rotuli de Oblatis et Finibus . . . tempore regis Johannis*, London, 1835
For	Pleas of the Forest (PRO) (unpublished)
For	*Select Pleas of the Forest* (Selden Soc. 13, 1901)
Forssner	T. Forssner, *Continental-Germanic Personal Names in England*, Uppsala, 1916
ForSt	*Staffordshire Forest Pleas* (Salt Arch. Soc. (OS) 5, 1884)
France	J. H. Round, *Calendar of Documents preserved in France*, London, 1899
FrC	S. L. Thrupp, *The Earliest Canterbury Freemen's Rolls 1298–1363* (Kent Rec. Soc. 18, 1964)
FrLeic	H. Hartopp, *Register of the Freemen of Leicester, 1196–1770*, Leicester, 1927
FrNorw	J. L'Estrange, *Calendar of the Freemen of Norwich from 1317 to 1603*, ed. W. Rye, London, 1888
FrY	*Register of the Freemen of the City of York* (Surtees Soc. 96, 102, 1897–9)
FrYar	*A Calendar of the Freemen of Great Yarmouth* (Norfolk and Norwich Arch. Soc. 1910)
Gage	J. Gage, *The History and Antiquities of Suffolk. Thingoe Hundred*, Bury St. Edmunds, 1838

Gardner	T. Gardner, *An Historical Account of Dunwich*, London, 1754
Gascon	*The Gascon Calendar of 1322* (Camden Soc. 3rd Ser. 70, 1949)
GeldR	The Geld Roll of 1084 (in DB)
Gilb	*Transcripts of Charters relating to the Gilbertine Houses* (Lincs Rec. Soc. 18, 1922)
GildC	*The Register of the Guild of the Holy Trinity . . . of Coventry* (Dugdale Soc. 13, 19, 1935–44)
GildY	*Register of the Guild of the Corpus Christi in the City of York* (Surtees Soc. 57, 1872)
Gl	Gloucestershire
Glam	Glamorganshire
Glast	*The Great Chartulary of Glastonbury* (Som Rec. Soc. 59, 63, 64, 1947–56)
Goring	*A Collection of Charters relating to Goring, Streatley, and the Neighbourhood* (Oxford Rec. Soc. 13, 14, 1931–2)
GreenwichPR	*Greenwich Parish Registers, 1615–1637* (Trans. Greenwich and Lewisham Ant. Soc. 2, 1920)
Groups	E. Ekwall, *Studies on the Genitive of Groups in English*, Lund, 1943
Guisb	*Cartularium prioratus de Gyseburne* (Surtees Soc. 86, 89, 1889–94)
Ha	Hampshire
Hartland	*The Register of Baptisms, Marriages and Burials of the Parish of Hartland, Devon, 1558–1837* (Devon and Cornwall Rec. Soc. 1930–4)
He	Herefordshire
HeCh	*Charters of the Earldom of Hereford 1095–1201* (Camden Soc. 4th Ser. 1, 1964)
Herts	Hertfordshire
Holme	*St. Benet of Holme, 1020–1240* (Norfolk Rec. Soc. 2, 3, 1932)
HorringerPR	*Horringer Parish Registers* (Suffolk Green Books 4, 1900)
Hoskins	W. G. Hoskins and H. P. Finberg, *Devonshire Studies*, London, 1952
HPD	H. F. Westlake, *Hornchurch Priory. A Kalendar of Documents in the Possession of the Warden and Fellows of New College, Oxford*, London, 1923
HTEss	Essex Hearth Tax Returns, 1662, transcribed by F. G. Emmison (unpublished)
HT	Hearth Tax Returns: Oxford (Oxford Rec. Soc. 21, 1940); Suffolk (Suffolk Green Books 11, 1905); Yorks (Thoresby Soc. 2, 1891)
Hu	Huntingdonshire
Husting	R. R. Sharpe, *Calendar of Wills . . . in the Court of Husting*, London, AD. 1258–AD. 1688, 2 vols, London, 1889–90
ICC	*Inquisitio Comitatus Cantabrigiensis . . . Subjicitur Inquisitio Eliensis*, ed. N. E. S. A. Hamilton, London, 1876
IckworthPR	*Ickworth Parish Registers* (Suffolk Green Books 3, 1894)
InqAug	A. Ballard, *An Eleventh-Century Inquisition of St. Augustine's, Canterbury*, London, 1920
InqEl	*Inquisitio Eliensis*. v. ICC
InqLa	*Lancashire Inquests, Extents, and Feudal Aids* (Lancs and Ches Rec. Soc. 48, 54, 1903–7)
Ipm	*Inquisitiones post mortem* (unpublished)
Ipm	*Calendar of Inquisitiones post mortem* (in progress); Glos (Index Library 30, 40, 47, 1903–14); Lancs (Chetham Soc. 95, 1875); Notts (Thoroton Soc. 6, 12, 1939–52); Wilts (Index Library 37. 48, 1908–14); Yorks (Yorks Arch. Soc. 12, 23, 31, 37, 59, 1892–1918)
IPN	A. Mawer and F. M. Stenton, *Introduction to the Survey of English Place-Names*, Cambridge, 1923
Ipsw	*Historical Manuscripts Commission, Report IX*, Appendix, pp. 221–61
Ir	Irish
Jackson	K. Jackson, *Language and History in Early Britain*, Edinburgh, 1953
JMac	J. B. Johnston, *The Scottish Macs*, Paisley, 1922

K	Kent
KCD	J. M. Kemble, *Codex diplomaticus aevi Saxonici*, 6 vols, London, 1839–48
KentW	*Testamenta Cantiana* (Kent Arch. Soc., 1906–7)
Kirk	*Kirkstall Abbey Rent Roll 1459* (Thoresby Soc. 2, 1891)
Kirkstall	*The Coucher Book of the Cistercian Abbey of Kirkstall* (Thoresby Soc. 8, 1904)
KPN	J. K. Wallenberg, *Kentish Place-Names*, Uppsala, 1931
Kris	G. Kristensson, 'Studies on Middle English Local Surnames containing Elements of French Origin' (*English Studies* 50 (1969), 465–86)
L	Lincolnshire
La	Lancashire
LaCt	*Some Court Rolls . . . of Thomas, Earl of Lancaster* (Lancs and Ches Rec. Soc. 41, 1901)
Lacy	*Two 'Compoti' of . . . Henry de Lacy* (Chetham Soc. (OS) 112, 1884)
Landwade	W. M. Palmer, *Landwade and the Cotton Family* (Cambs Antiq. Soc. 38, 1939)
LaPleas	*Pleadings and Depositions in the Duchy Court of Lancashire* (Lancs and Ches Rec. Soc. 32, 35, 40, 1896–9)
LaWills	*A List of the Lancashire Wills proved within the Archdeaconry of Richmond* (Lancs and Ches Rec. Soc. 10, 1884)
Layer	W. M. Palmer, *John Layer (1586–1640) of Shepreth, Cambridgeshire* (Cambs Antiq. Soc. 53, 1935)
LedburyPR	*The Registers of Ledbury, co. Hereford* (Parish Reg. Soc. 1899)
Lei	Leicestershire
LeiAS	*Transactions of the Leicestershire Archaeological Society* (in progress)
LeicBR	M. Bateson, *Records of the Borough of Leicester*, 3 vols, London, 1895–1905
Lewes	*Lewes Chartulary* (Sussex Rec. Soc. 38, 40, 1933–5; Norfolk Rec. Soc. 12, 1939; J. H. Bullock and W. M. Palmer, *The Cambridgeshire Portion of the Chartulary of St. Pancras of Lewes*, Cambridge, 1938)
LewishamPR	*The Register of . . . St. Mary's, Lewisham, 1558–1750* (Lewisham Antiq. Soc., 1891)
LibEl	*Liber Eliensis*, ed. E. O. Blake (Camden Soc. 3rd Ser. 92, 1962)
Lichfield	*Catalogue of the Muniments . . . of the Dean and Chapter of Lichfield* (Salt Arch. Soc. (OS) 6, 1886)
LitSaxhamPR	*Little Saxham Parish Registers* (Suffolk Green Books 5, 1901)
LLB	*Calendar of Letter Books . . . of the City of London*, 11 vols, London, 1899–1912
Lo	London
LoCt	*Calendar of Early Mayor's Court Rolls*, ed. A. H. Thomas, Cambridge, 1924
LondEng	R. W. Chambers and M. Daunt, *A Book of London English*, Oxford, 1931
LoPleas	*Calendar of Plea and Memoranda Rolls preserved among the Archives of the . . . City of London*, ed. A. H. Thomas, 3 vols, Cambridge, 1926–32
Loth	J. Loth, *Chrestomathie bretonne*, Paris, 1890
LP	*Letters and Papers, Foreign and Domestic, of the reign of Henry VIII*, 23 vols, London, 1862–1932
LVD	*Liber Vitæ Ecclesiæ Dunelmensis* (Surtees Soc. 136, 1923)
LWills	*Calendars of Lincoln Wills* (Index Library 28, 1902)
Malmesbury	*Registrum Malmesburiense* (Rolls Ser. 72, 1879–80)
ME	Middle English
MED	*Middle English Dictionary*, ed. H. Kurath, S. M. Kuhn, and J. Reidy, Ann Arbor, 1954– (in progress)
MedEA	D. C. Douglas, *The Social Structure of Mediaeval East Anglia*, Oxford, 1927
MedInd	L. F. Salzman, *English Industries in the Middle Ages*, Oxford, 1923
MELS	M. T. Löfvenberg, *Studies on Middle English Local Surnames*, Lund, 1942
MemR	*Memoranda Roll* (Pipe Roll Soc. (NS) 11, 21, 1933–43)

MEOT	B. Thuresson, *Middle English Occupational Terms*, Lund, 1950
Merton	*Merton Muniments* (Oxford Hist. Soc. 86, 1928)
MESO	G. Fransson, *Middle English Surnames of Occupation, 1100–1350*, Lund, 1935
METrade	L. F. Salzman, *English Trade in the Middle Ages*, Oxford, 1931
Miller	E. Miller, *The Abbey and Bishopric of Ely*, Cambridge, 1951
MinAcctCo	*Ministers' Accounts of the Earldom of Cornwall* (Camden Soc. 3rd Ser. 66, 68, 1942–5)
MLWL	*Revised Medieval Latin Word List from British and Irish Sources*, ed. R. E. Latham, London, 1965
Misc	*Calendar of Inquisitions Miscellaneous* (in progress)
Mon	Monmouthshire
Moore	A. W. Moore, *Manx Names*, London, 1903
Morris	T. E. Morris, 'Welsh Surnames in the Border Counties of Wales' (*Y Cymmrodor* 43 (1932), 93–173)
Moulton	H. R. Moulton, *Palæography, Genealogy and Topography*, London, 1930
MScots	Middle Scottish
Musters	Muster Rolls: Norfolk (Norfolk Rec. Soc. 6, 7, 1935–6); Surrey (Surrey Rec. Soc. 3, 1914–19)
MW	Middle Welsh
Mx	Middlesex
Nb	Northumberland
NED	*A New English Dictionary*, Oxford, 1888–1933
Nf	Norfolk
NI	*Nonarum Inquisitiones*, London, 1807
NIWo	*Nonarum Inquisitiones 1340 for the County of Worcester* (Worcs Hist. Soc., 1899)
NLC	*Newington Longeville Charters* (Oxford Rec. Soc. 3, 1921)
NME	Northern Middle English
NoB	*Namn och Bygd* (in progress)
NorwDeeds	*A Short Calendar of the Deeds relating to Norwich, 1285–1306; A Calendar of Norwich Deeds . . . 1307–1341* (Norfolk and Norwich Arch. Soc., 1903, 1915)
NorwDep	*Depositions taken before the Mayor and Aldermen of Norwich, 1549–67* (Norfolk and Norwich Arch. Soc. 1905)
NorwLt	*Leet Jurisdiction in the City of Norwich during the XIIIth and XIVth Centuries* (Selden Soc. 5, 1891)
NorwW	*Index to Wills proved in the Consistory Court of Norwich* (Index Library 69, 73, 1945–50)
NottBR	*Records of the Borough of Nottingham*, vol. I, Nottingham, 1882
NQ	*Notes and Queries* (in progress)
NS	New Series
Nt	Nottinghamshire
Nth	Northamptonshire
NthCh	*Facsimiles of Early Charters from Northamptonshire Collections* (Northants Rec. Soc. 4, 1930)
O	Oxfordshire
OBret	Old Breton
OC	Old Cornish
ODa	Old Danish
ODCN	E. G. Withycombe, *The Oxford Dictionary of English Christian Names*, Oxford, 1950
OE	Old English
OEByn	G. Tengvik, *Old English Bynames*, Uppsala, 1938
OFr	Old French

OFris	Old Frisian
OG	Old German
OI	Old Irish
ON	Old Norse
ONFr	Old Norman French
Oriel	*Oriel College Records* (Oxford Hist. Soc. 85, 1926)
Orig	*Rotulorum originalium . . . abbreviatio*, 2 vols, London, 1805–10
OS	Original Series
Oseney	*Cartulary of Oseney Abbey* (Oxford Hist. Soc. 89–91, 97, 98, 101, 1929–35)
OSw	Old Swedish
OW	Old Welsh
Oxon	*Register of the University of Oxford* (Oxford Hist. Soc. 1, 10–12, 14, 1885–9)
p	post
P	Pipe Rolls: Record Commission, 3 vols, London, 1833–44; Pipe Roll Soc. (in progress); *The Great Roll of the Pipe for the twenty-sixth year of Henry the Third*, ed. H. L. Cannon, Yale Hist. Pub., 1918
ParlR	*Rotuli Parliamentorum*, 7 vols, London, 1767–1833
ParlWrits	*The Parliamentary Writs*, 2 vols, London, 1827–34
Past	*Paston Letters and Papers of the Fifteenth Century, vol. 1*, ed. N. Davis, Oxford, 1971
Pat	*Calendar of the Patent Rolls* (in progress)
PatR	*Rotuli Litterarum Patentium*, London, 1835
PCC	*Index of Wills proved in the Prerogative Court of Canterbury* (Index Library, 12 vols, 1893–1960)
Percy	*The Percy Chartulary* (Surtees Soc. 117, 1911)
Petre	Petre Documents in *ERO*. Calendared by C. J. Kuypers
Pinchbeck	*The Pinchbeck Register*, ed. Lord Francis Hervey, 2 vols, Oxford, 1925
Pl	*Pleas before the King or his Justices 1198–1202* (Selden Soc. 67, 68, 1952–3); *1198–1212* (Selden Soc. 83, 84, 1966–7)
PN	*Place-Names of* (PN Bk, *Place-Names of Buckinghamshire*, etc., English Place-Name Society)
PNDB	O. von Feilitzen, *The Preconquest Personal Names of Domesday Book*, Uppsala, 1937
PN K	J. K. Wallenberg, *The Place-names of Kent*, Uppsala, 1934
PN La	E. Ekwall, *The Place-names of Lancashire*, Manchester, 1922
PN NbDu	A. Mawer, *The Place-names of Northumberland and Durham*, Cambridge, 1920
PN Wt	H. Kökeritz, *The Place-names of the Isle of Wight*, Uppsala, 1940
PR	Parish Register(s) (of the specified place)
Praes	*Praestita Roll 14–18 John* (Pipe Roll Soc. (NS) 37, 1964)
PrD	Protestation Returns for Devon (through the courtesy of Mr A. J. Howard)
PrGR	*The Rolls of Burgesses at the Guilds Merchant of the Borough of Preston* (Lancs and Ches Rec. Soc. 9, 1884)
PromptParv	*Promptorium Parvulorum* (Camden Soc. (OS) 25, 54, 89, 1843–65)
PTW	*Clerical Poll-Taxes in the Diocese of Salisbury 1377–81* (Wilts Arch. Soc. 12, 1956)
PTY	*Yorkshire Poll Tax Returns* (Yorks Arch. Journal 5–7, 9, 20, 1879–1909; Trans. East Riding Antiq. Soc. 30)
Putnam	B. H. Putnam, *The Enforcement of the Statutes of Labourers, 1349–1359*, New York, 1908
PWi	N. R. Holt, *The Pipe Roll of the Bishopric of Winchester, 1210–11*, Manchester, 1964
QW	*Placita de Quo Warranto*, London, 1818
R	Rutland
Rad	*The Priory of Saint Radegund, Cambridge* (Cambs Antiq. Soc. 31, 1898)
Rams	*Cartularium monasterii de Rameseia* (Rolls Series 79, 3 vols, 1884–94)

RamsCt	W. O. Ault, *Court Rolls of the Abbey of Ramsey and of the Honor of Clare*, Yale University Press, 1928
RBE	*The Red Book of the Exchequer* (Rolls Series 99, 3 vols, 1896)
RBWo	*The Red Book of Worcester* (Worcs Hist. Soc., 1934–50)
Redin	M. Redin, *Studies on Uncompounded Personal Names in Old English*, Uppsala, 1919
RegAntiquiss	*Registrum Antiquissimum* (Lincs Rec. Soc., 10 vols, 1931–68)
Req	Court of Requests (PRO)
RH	*Rotuli Hundredorum*, 2 vols, London, 1812–18
Riev	*Cartularium Abbathiæ de Rievalle* (Surtees Soc. 83, 1889)
RochW	*Index of Wills proved in the Rochester Consistory Court* (Kent Rec. Soc. 9, 1924)
Ronton	*The Chartulary of Ronton Priory* (Salt Arch. Soc. (OS) 4, 1883)
RotDom	*Rotuli de Dominabus* (Pipe Roll Soc. 35, 1913)
RothwellPR	*The Registers of the Parish Church of Rothwell* (Yorks Parish Reg. Soc. 27, 34, 51, 1906–14)
RushbrookPR	*Rushbrook Parish Registers* (Suffolk Green Books 6, 1903)
Rydware	*The Rydeware Chartulary* (Salt Arch. Soc. (OS) 16, 1895)
Sa	Shropshire
SaAS	*Transactions of the Shropshire Archaeological and Natural History Society* (in progress)
SaG	*The Merchants' Guild of Shrewsbury. The Two Earliest Rolls* (Trans. Shrops Arch. and Nat. Hist. Soc. 2nd Series 8, 1896)
Saga Bk	*Saga-Book of the Viking Society* (in progress)
SaltAS	*Transactions of the William Salt Archaeological Society* (in progress)
Seals	L. C. Loyd and D. M. Stenton, *Sir Christopher Hatton's Book of Seals*, Oxford, 1950
Selden Soc.	Publications of the Selden Society
Selt	B. Seltén, 'Some Notes on Middle English By-names in Independent Use' (*English Studies* 46 (1965), 165–81)
Sf	Suffolk
SfPR	*Suffolk Parish Registers. Marriages*, ed. W. P. W. Phillimore, 3 vols, London, 1910–16
Shef	T. W. Hall and A. H. Thomas, *Descriptive Catalogue of Charters . . . forming the Jackson Collection at the Sheffield Public Reference Library*, Sheffield, 1914
ShefA	T. W. Hall, *Sheffield, Hallamshire: A Descriptive Catalogue of Sheffield Manorial Records*, 3 vols, Sheffield, 1926–34
ShotleyPR	*Shotley Parish Registers, 1571–1850* (Suffolk Green Books 16, 1894)
SIA	*Proceedings of the Suffolk Institute of Archaeology* (in progress)
So	Somerset
Sol	*Liber Henrici de Soliaco, Abbatis Glaston.*, ed. J. H. Jackson, Roxburghe Club, 1882
SPD	*Calendar of State Papers Domestic*, 48 vols, London, 1856–86
SPl	*Select Pleas of the Crown* (Selden Soc. 1, 1888); *Select Civil Pleas* (Selden Soc. 3, 1890)
Sr	Surrey
SR	Subsidy Rolls (unpublished)
SR	Subsidy Rolls: Beds (Suffolk Green Books 18, 1925); Cambs (C. H. Evelyn White, *Lay Subsidy for the Year 1327*, n.d.); Cumb (J. P. Steel, *Cumberland Lay Subsidy . . . 6th Edward III*, Kendal, 1912); Derbyshire (Journal of the Derbyshire Arch. and Nat. Hist. Soc. 24, 30, 44, 1902–22); Dorset (Dorset Rec. Soc. 4, 1971); Kent (Arch. Cant. 12); Lancs (Lancs and Ches Rec. Soc. 27, 31, 1893–6); Leics (Associated Architectural Societies: Reports and Papers 19.2, 20.1, 1888–9); London (G. Unwin, *Finance and Trade under Edward III*, Manchester, 1918; E. Ekwall, *Two Early London Subsidy Rolls*, Lund, 1951); Northumb (Archaeologia Aeliana 3rd Ser. 13, 1916); Shropshire (Trans. Shropshire Arch.

and Nat. Hist. Soc. 2nd Ser. 1, 4, 5, 8, 10, 11, 3rd Ser. 5–7); Som (Som Rec. Soc. 3, 1889); Staffs (Salt Arch. Soc. (OS) 7, 10, 1886–89); Suffolk (E. Powell, *The Rising in East Anglia in 1381*, Cambridge, 1896; *A Suffolk Hundred in 1283*, Cambridge, 1910; Suffolk Green Books 9, 10, 12, 1906–10); Surrey (Surrey Rec. Soc. 18, 33, 1922–32); Sussex (Sussex Rec. Soc. 10, 56, 1910–56); Warwicks (Dugdale Soc. 6, 1926); Wilts (Wilts Arch. Soc. 10, 1954); Worcs (Worcs Hist. Soc., 4 vols, 1893–1900); Yorks (Thoresby Soc. 2, 1891; Yorks Arch. Soc. 16, 21, 74, 1894–1929)

St	Staffordshire
StaplehurstPR	*The Old Register of Staplehurst, 1538–1558*, Canterbury, 1907
StarChSt	*Staffordshire Suits in the Court of Star Chamber* (Salt Arch. Soc. (NS) 10, 1907)
StCh	*The Staffordshire Chartulary* (Salt Arch. Soc. (OS) 2, 3, 1881–2)
StGreg	*Cartulary of the Priory of St. Gregory, Canterbury* (Camden Soc. 3rd Ser. 88, 1956)
StJohn	BM. Cott. Nero E vi
Stoke	BM. Cott. Appendix xxi
Stone	*The Stone Chartulary* (Salt Arch. Soc. (OS) 6, 1885)
StP	*Early Charters of the Cathedral Church of St. Paul London* (Camden Soc. 3rd Ser. 58, 1939)
Str	*Accounts and Surveys of the Wiltshire Lands of Adam de Stratton* (Wilts Arch. Soc. 14, 1959)
StThomas	*A Chartulary of the Priory of St. Thomas, the Martyr, near Stafford* (Salt Arch. Soc. (OS) 8, 1887)
StudNP	*Studia Neophilologica* (in progress)
Suckling	A. I. Suckling, *The History and Antiquities of the County of Suffolk*, London, 1846–8
Surnames	E. Weekley, *Surnames*, London, 1936
Sx	Sussex
SxAS	*Sussex Archaeological Collections* (in progress)
SxWills	*Sussex Wills* (Sussex Rec. Soc. 41, 43, 45, 1935–41)
Templars	B. A. Lees, *Records of the Templars in England in the Twelfth Century*, London, 1935
Trentham	*A Chartulary of the Augustine Priory of Trentham* (Salt Arch. Soc. (OS) 11, 1890)
Variation	E. Ekwall, *Variation in Surnames in Medieval London*, Lund, 1945
W	Wiltshire
Wa	Warwickshire
Wak	*Court Rolls of the Manor of Wakefield* (Yorks Arch. Soc. 29, 36, 57, 78, 1901–45)
WBCinque	F. Hull, *A Calendar of the White and Black Books of the Cinque Ports, 1432–1955*, London, 1966
We	Westmorland
Wenlok	*Documents illustrating the Rule of Walter de Wenlok, Abbot of Westminster, 1283–1307* (Camden Soc. 4th Ser. 2, 1965)
WhC	*The Coucher Book or Chartulary of Whalley Abbey* (Chetham Soc. 10, 11, 16, 20, 1847–9)
Wheat	T. W. Hall, *Descriptive Catalogue of charters . . . of the Wheat Collection at the Public Reference Library*, Sheffield, 1920
Whitby	*Cartularium Abbathiæ de Whiteby* (Surtees Soc. 69, 72, 1879–81)
Winton	*Liber Wintoniensis* (in DB, vol. iv)
Wo	Worcestershire
WordwellPR	*Wordwell Parish Registers, 1580–1850* (Suffolk Green Books 7, 1903)
Works	C. T. Flower, *Public Works in Mediaeval Law* (Selden Soc. 32, 40, 1915–23)
WStowPR	*West Stow Parish Registers, 1558–1850* (Suffolk Green Books 7, 1903)
W'stowW	G. S. Fry, *Abstracts of Wills relating to Walthamstow* (Walthamstow Antiq. Soc., 1921)

Wt	Isle of Wight
Y	Yorkshire
YAJ	*Yorkshire Archaeological Journal* (in progress)
YCh	W. Farrer and C. T. Clay, *Early Yorkshire Charters*, 12 vols, 1914–65
YDeeds	*Yorkshire Deeds* (Yorks Arch. Soc. 39, 50, 1909–15)
YWills	*Yorkshire Wills* (Yorks Arch. Soc. 73, 93, 1928–37)
*	a postulated form

OTHER WORKS CONSULTED

Bain, R.	*The Clans and Tartans of Scotland*, London, 1953
Bardsley, C. W.	*A Dictionary of English and Welsh Surnames*, London, 1901
Björkman, E.	*Nordische Personnamen in England*, Halle, 1910
	Zur englischen Namenkunde, Halle, 1912
Boehler, M.	*Die altenglischen Frauennamen*, Berlin, 1930
Carnoy, A.	*Origine des noms de familles en Belgique*, Louvain, 1953
Cottle, A. B.	*The Penguin Dictionary of Surnames*, Harmondsworth, 1967
Dauzat, A.	*Dictionnaire étymologique des noms de familles et prénoms de France*, Paris, 1951
	Les noms de famille de France, Paris, 1945
	Les noms de personnes, Paris, 1946
Davies, T. R.	*A Book of Welsh Names*, London, 1952
Ekwall, E.	*Scandinavians and Celts*, Lund, 1918
	Street-Names of the City of London, Oxford, 1954
Fabricius, A.	*Danske Minder i Normandiet*, Copenhagen, 1897
Feilitzen, O. von	'Notes on Old English Bynames' (*Namn och Bygd* 27 (1939), 116–30)
	'Some Unrecorded Old and Middle English Personal Names' (*Namn och Bygd* 33 (1945), 69–98)
	'Some Continental Germanic Personal Names in England' (in *Early English and Norse Studies*, ed. A. Brown and P. Foote, London, 1963, pp. 46–61)
	'Notes on some Scandinavian Personal Names in English 12th-Century Records, (*Personnamns Studier: Anthroponymica Suecana* 6 (1964), 62–8)
	'Some Old English Uncompounded Personal Names and Bynames' (*Studia Neophilologica* 40 (1968), 5–16)
Forssner, T.	*Beiträge zum Studium der neuenglischen Familiennamen*, Göttingen, 1920
	De l'influence française sur les noms propres anglais, Skövde, 1920
	Deutsche und englische Imperativnamen, Östersund, 1922
	Imitative Alterations in Modern English Personal Nomenclature, Skövde, 1920
Förstemann, E.	*Altdeutsches Namenbuch*, Bonn, 1900–16
Förster, M.	'Keltisches Wortgut im Englischen' (in *Festgabe für F. Liebermann*, Halle, 1921)
Gautries, J. A. des	*Les Noms de personnes Scandinaves en Normandie de 911 à 1066*, Lund, 1954
Godefroy, F.	*Dictionnaire de l'ancienne langue française*, Paris, 1881–1902
Guppy, H. B.	*Homes of Family Names in Great Britain*, London, 1890
Harrison, H.	*Surnames of the United Kingdom*, London, 1912–18
Lebel, P.	*Les Noms de personnes en France*, Paris, 1946
Loth, J.	*Les Noms de saints bretons*, Paris, 1910
Lower, M. A.	*Patronymica Britannica*, London, 1860
MacLysaght, E.	*The Surnames of Ireland*, Dublin, 1969
Matthews, C. M.	*English Surnames*, London, 1966
Michaëlsson, K.	*Etudes sur les noms de personne français d'après les roles de taille parisiens*, Uppsala, 1927. 1936

Moisy, H.   *Noms de famille normands*, Paris, 1875

Nicholson, E. W. B.   *The Pedigree of 'Jack' and of various allied names*, London, 1892

Reaney, P. H.   'Notes on Christian Names' (NQ 196 (1951), 199–200)

'Onomasticon Essexiense' (*Essex Review* 61 (1952), 133–42, 202–15)

'Pedigrees of Villeins and Freemen' (NQ 197 (1952), 222–5)

'Three Unrecorded Old English Personal Names of a Late Type' (*Modern Language Review* 47 (1952), 374)

'The Survival of Old English Personal Names in Middle English' (*Studier i modern språkvetenskap* 18 (1953), 84–112)

Ritchie, R. L. G.   *The Normans in Scotland*, Edinburgh, 1954

Searle, W. G.   *Onomasticon Anglo-Saxonicum*, Cambridge, 1897

Seltén, B.   *The Anglo-Saxon Heritage in Middle English Personal Names: East Anglia 1100–1399*, Lund, 1972

Smith, A. H.   'Some Aspects of Irish Influence on Yorkshire' (*Revue Celtique* 44 (1927), 34–58)

'Danes and Norwegians in Yorkshire' (*Saga Bk* 10 (1929), 188–215)

'Early Northern Nick-names and Surnames' (*Saga Bk* 11 (1934), 30–60)

English Place-Name Elements (English Place-Name Society 25, 26), Cambridge, 1956

Smith, E. C.   *American Surnames*, New York, 1969

Ström, H.   *Old English Personal Names in Bede's History*, Lund, 1939

Sundby, B.   'Some Middle English Occupational Terms' (*English Studies* 33 (1952), 18–19)

Wagner, A. R.   *English Genealogy*, Oxford, 1960

Weekley, E.   *Jack and Jill*, London, 1948

Romance of Names, London, 1922

Whitelock, D.   'Scandinavian Personal Names in the Liber Vitae of Thorney Abbey' (*Saga Bk* 12 (1940), 127–153)

Woulfe, P.   *Sloinnte Gaedheal is Gall*, Dublin, 1923

A DICTIONARY

OF BRITISH

SURNAMES

A

Abadam, Badams, Baddams, Badham: Hoel *ab Adam* 1255 RH (Sa); John *Apadam, Ab Adham* 1308, 1310 ParlWrits (Gl); Mary *Baddam* 1597 Bardsley. 'Son of *Adam*', Welsh *ab, ap*. cf. BOWEN.

Abba, Abbay, Abbey, Abbie, Abby, Labey: (i) Ralph *le Abbe* 1177 P (Lo); Geoffrey *Labbe* Hy 2 DC (Lei); John *Abby* 1297 MinAcctCo. OFr *abe, abet* 'abbot'. v. ABBATT. The Scottish *Abbie* (*Abbe* 1178–80, *del Abbeye* 1370) derives from the office of lay-abbot of a monastery which was hereditary in the leading family of the district (Black). (ii) William *del Abbay* 1283 FrY; Adam *dil Abbeye* 1327 SRSf. From employment at an abbey.

Abbatt, Abbett, Abbitt, Abbot, Abbots, Abbott, Abbotts, Labbet: Walter *Abbot* 12th DC (L); Walter *Abat* 1219 AssY; Peter *le Abbot* 1237 HPD (Ess); Ralph *Abbod* 1272 AssSo. OE *abbod*, late OE *abbat, abbot* 'abbot'. Early Latin examples such as Alfwoldus *abbas* 1111–17 Holme (Nf) are names of actual holders of the office of abbot and can hardly have given rise to surnames. Later examples are nicknames.

Abbey, Abbie: v. ABBA

Abdey, Abdie: Robert *del Abdy* 1379 PTY. 'One employed at an abbey', ME *abbodie*, Lat *abbatia* which meant both 'abbacy' and 'abbey'.

Abear, A'Bear: John *atte Bere* 1332 SRSr; John *Abere* 1517 PCC (K). 'At the swine-pasture', probably 'swineherd'. v. BEAR.

Abel, Abell, Abele, Abeles, Able, Abelson, Ableson: *Abellus* Hy 2 DC (Lei); *Abel* de Etton' 1221 AssWa; William *Abel* 1197 P (Ess); Thomas *Abelle* 1301 SRY; Richard *Abelson* 1623 Bardsley. Hebrew *Abel*, probably 'son', a common 13th-century christian name.

Abercrombie, Abercromby: William, John *de Abercromby* 1296, 1305 Black (Fife). From the barony of Abercromby (Fife).

Abethell: v. BITHELL

Ablett, Ablitt, Ablott: *Abelota* loue 1277 *Ely* (Sf); *Abelot* 1279 RH (C); William *Abelot* 1279 RH (C); William *Ablot* 1335 FrY. *Abel-ot*, a diminutive of *Abel*, sometimes used as a woman's name.

Ablewhite: v. APPLEWHAITE

Aborn: Robert *Abourne* 1379 LLB G; Jamys *A Bourne* 1467 ArchC xi. For *atte borne*. v. BOURNE.

Abraham, Abrahams, Abram, Abrams, Abrahamson, Abramson: *Abraham* de Strattuna 1170–5 DC (L); John *Abraham* 1193 P (Nth)· Robert *Abram* 1252 Rams (Hu). Hebrew *Abram* 'high father', changed to *Abraham* 'father of a multitude'. *Abraham*, the name of a priest in DB (1086), was not confined to Jews.

Abraham, Abram, Adburgham: John *de Abburgham* 1246 AssLa; Gilbert *de Abram* Hy 4 Bardsley. From Abram (Lancs), *Adburgham* a1199 DEPN.

A'Brook: Roger *Attebrok*' 1297 MinAcctCo; John *A'Brooke* 1542 SxWills. v. BROOK.

Absalom, Absolem, Absolom, Absolon, Aspenlon, Aspland, Asplen, Asplin, Aspling, Ashplant: *Absolon filius Apsolon* 1199 FFC; *Aspelon* 1252 Rams (Hu); Johannes *filius Asplom* 1302 SRY; Stephen *Abselon* 1208 Cur (O); John *Asplon'* 1279 RH (Hu); Thomas *Absolon, Aspelon* 1281, 1297 LLB B; William *Aspland, Aspline* 1684, 1690 CPR iii. *Absalom*, from Hebrew *Abshálóm* 'father of peace'. Used as a nickname by Chaucer for a man with a fine head of hair: 'Crul was his heer and as the gold it shoon'.

Aburn: John *Aburne* 1572 FFHu. v. BOURNE.

Ace, Aze: *Azo* 1086 DB; *Asce* Halvecniht 1213 Cur (Ha); Benedict, John *Ace* 1230 Cl (Ha), 1246–89 Bart (Lo); Geoffrey *Aze* 1296 SRSx. OFr *Ace, Asse*, OG *Azo, Atso*, hypocoristics of compounds in *Adal-*.

Achard, Ackert, Ashard, Hatchard: *Acardus* de Lincolnia c1150 DC (L); *Achardus* de Sproxton' 1207 Cur (Lei); William *Achard* 1160 P (Berks); William *Achart* 1177 P (Ha); Willelmus *Achardi* 1190 P (Berks); William *Hachard* 1279 RH (C); Thomas *Acard* 1401 Shef (Y). OFr *Achart, Aquart*, probably from OG *Agihard, Akihart*.

Acheson, Aicheson, Aitcheson, Aitchison, Atcheson, Atchison: Scottish and border forms of *Atkinson* found in Cumberland as *Attchison* in 1596 (CWAS viii) and in Scotland as *Atzinson* 1475, *Achesoun* 1497, *Atyesoun* 1540, and *Aicheson* 1590 (Black). The *z* was pronounced *y* and *Atyeson* became *Acheson* as the colloquial 'got yer' became 'gotcha'.

Ackary, Ackery: *Acharias, Accarisius filius Copsi* 1155, Hy 1 FeuDu; *Achari* Hy 1 Rams (Hu); Robert *Akari* 1199 CurR (Hu). Hebrew *Zacharias* 'Jehovah has remembered', surviving also as *Zachary*. Roger son of *Zacharias* de Burdun (1217 FeuDu) is also called Rogerus *filius Acharisiae, Akariae, Acris, Akaris* (c1200 ib.).

Ackerman, Acraman, Acreman, Akerman: William *Acreman* Hy 1 Rams (Hu); Robert *le*

1

Akerman 1233 HPD (Ess). OE *æcermann* 'farmer', a husbandman or ploughman.

Ackers: *v.* ACRES

Ackert: *v.* ACHARD

Ackery: *v.* ACKARY

Acket, Acketts: *v.* HACKETT

Ackland, Acland: The Devonshire Acklands are said to owe their surname to a grove of oaks near their seat of Acland Barton in Landkey (Devon). Here lived in 1275 William *de Ackelane* (RH). The real meaning of Acland is 'Acca's lane', which is only some four miles from Accott in Swimbridge, 'Acca's cottage' (PN D 342, 351). Robert *de Acland* 1257 Oseney (O) took his surname from land on which oaks grew (OE *āc, land*).

Ackling: *v.* HACKLING

Ackroyd, Acroyd, Akeroyd, Akroyd, Aykroyd, Ackred, Akred, Ecroyd: Hugo *Aikroide* 1612 FrY; Henry *Ackroyd* 1645 ib.; Henry *Akeroyd* 1648 ib.; Christopher *Acred* 1721 ib. 'Dweller by the oak-clearing' (OE *āc, rod*), a Yorkshire name, preserving the dialectal pronunciation *royd*.

Acraman, Acreman: *v.* ACKERMAN

Acres, Ackers, Acors, Akers, Akess, Akker: William *del Acr'* 1214 Cur (Sx); Adam *de Acres* 1346 LLB F. 'Dweller by the plot of arable land' (OE *æcer*). Or from Castle, South or West Acre (Norfolk).

Acton: Hugh *de Acton'* 1194 P (Sa); Warin *de Aketon* 1202–3 FFEss; John *de Acton* 1327 SRWo; Richard *Acton* 1421–2 FFWa. From one of the many places of this name.

Adam, Adames, Adams, Addams, Adem, Adhams: *Adam* Warenarius 1146–53 DC (L); Alianor *Adam* 1281 AssCh; William *Adames* 1327 SRWo. Hebrew *Adam* 'red', found in DB, and common thereafter, with diminutives *Adcock, Adkin, Adnett*.

Adamson: John *Adamsone* 1296 Black, 1327 SRDb; Richard *Adamessone* 13th AD i (Nf). 'Son of *Adam*.'

Adburgham: *v.* ABRAHAM

Adcock, Adcocks, Atcock, Hadcock: *Adecok* Kay 1246 AssLa; Richard *Hadecoc* 1226 FrLeic; Robert *Adekok* 1275 SRWo; John *Atkoc* 1327 SRSt. *Adecoc*, a pet-form of *Adam*.

Addams: *v.* ADAM

Addekin: *v.* ADKIN

Addey, Addie, Addy, Addess, Addis, Adds, Haddy: *Addy* 1290 AssCh; *Addy* de Beuerlay 1297 SRY; John *Haddy* 1279 RH (Beds); Richard *Addy* 1301 SRY; John *Adies* 1327 SRWo; William *Addes* 1379 PTY. A pet-form of *Adam*.

Addington: William *de Adinton* 1176 P (Bk); Hugh *de Adinton'* 1202 AssNth; Gilbert *de Adintun'* 1226 Cur (Sr). From Addington (Bucks, Kent, Northants, Surrey).

Addison: John *Addisone* 1308 Pat (Y); Robert *Addeson* 1498 GildY. 'Son of *Addy*.'

Addlestone: *v.* ATHELSTAN

Adds, Addy: *v.* ADDEY

Addyman: *Adiman* 1204 P (Y); John *Addeman* 1379 PTY. 'Servant of *Addy*.'

Ade, Ades, Adeson: Thomas *Ade* 1327 SRSx;

William *Adeson'* 1379 PTY. A pet-form of *Adam*.

Adeane, A'Deane: John *Adene* 1484 RochW; Thomas *a Dene* 1516 KentW. From *atte dene*. *v.* DEAN.

Adeline: *Adelina* joculatrix 1086 DB (Ha); William *Adeline* 1260 AssC. OG *Adalina, Adelina*. The seal of *Adaleide*, wife of William Peverel (1107–13 NthCh), bears the legend: SIGNVM ADELINE, which was thus used as a pet-form of OG *Adelhaid*, in ME usually *Adeliz, Alesia, Aalis*. *v.* also ALIS, EDLIN.

Adem: *v.* ADAM

Adey, Adie, Ady, Adye: Thomas *Ady* 1327 SRWo; William *Adee* 1524 SRSf. A pet-form of *Ade* (Adam).

Adger: *v.* EDGAR

Adhams: *v.* ADAM

Adkin, Adkins, Addekin, Atkin, Atkins, Atkyns, Attkins, Hadkins: *Adekin* filius Turst' 1191 P (Nf); John *Adekyn* 1296 Crowland (C); William *Atkyns* 1327 SRWo; John *Adekynes* 1332 SRWa; William *Atkyn* 1441 ShefA. *Ade-kin*, a pet-form of *Adam*.

Adlam: *Adelelmus* 1066 DB (K); Walterus *filius Adelam* 1191 P (Sa); Robertus *Adelelmus* 1130 P (Ess); Roger *Adalem* 1260 AssC. From c940 onwards OE *Æðelhelm* regularly appears as *Æðelm* and occurs in DB as *Ailm* (PNDB). Hence the above forms are probably all from OG *Adalhelm, Adelelm* 'noble protector'.

Adlard, Allard, Allarde, Allart, Allars, Aylard, Ellard, Ellert, Hallard, Hallett: *Ailardus, Ælard* 1066 DB (D, Sx); *Adelardus* Hornewitesinne 1125 (c1425) LLB C; *Aeilardus* 1143–7 DC (L); *Halardus* de Weres a1150 ib.; *Elard* de Beisebi 1161 P (L); Walterus *filius Eilardi* 1205 Cur (W); Rogerus *filius Alardi, Adelard'*, *Athelardi* 1212, 1242 Fees (L); Roger *Aillard* 1205 P (Gl); Richard *Alard'* 1209 P (Gl); Nicholas *Adelard* 1275 SRWo; Stephen *Eyllard* 1296 SRSx; Richard, William *Athelard* 1327 SRC, SRSx; John *Adhelard, Allard* 1327, 1332 SRSx; John *Allerd* 1327 SRC. The DB forms are probably from OE *Æðelheard* 'noble-hard', but may be for OG *Adelard* or *Agilard*. *Adel-* is usually continental in origin, *Ayl-* usually from OE *Æðel-*, but may occasionally be for OG *Adel-* or *Agil-*. Both the native and the continental names are represented but cannot be safely distinguished except that *Ellard* and *Ellert* are probably of English origin. *Alard* the Fleming (1198 P), whose name is certainly of continental origin, also occurs as *Ayllard* (1193 ChR) and *Adthelard* (Ric 1 (1279) RH). *Alard* de Cotekyn of Zeeland (1311 Pat) was also a Fleming. Both personal-names may later have become *Aylett, Allatt*.

Admans: *v.* EDMAN

Admer: Lefstan *filius Ædmeri* c1095 Bury (Sf); *Admerus* le Burgeis 1203 Cur (Sx); Walter *Edmer* 1275 SRWo. OE *Ēadmǣr* 'prosperity-famous'. The surname is also local in origin: Reginald *de Addemere* 1296 SRSx, Nicholas *de Admare* 1344 FrY.

Adnet, Adnitt: *Adenet* le Wayder 1293 MESO

(Nf); *Adinet del Forest* 1379 PTY; Robert *Adynet*, *Adinot* 1366 AD ii (Lei), 1428 FA (Sr). OFr *Adenet, Adenot*, diminutives of *Adam. Adam* de Bidyk (1286 ChancW) is also called *Adinet* (1276 Fine).

Adrain, Adrian, Adrien: *Adrianus* janitor 1186–1210 Holme (Nf); Walter *Adran'*, *Adrian* c1232 Clerkenwell (Lo); Ralph *Adrien* 1277 LLB A. Lat *Hadrianus* 'of the Adriatic', the name of a Roman emperor and several popes, including Nicholas Brakespear, the only English pope (d. 1159).

Ady(e): *v.* ADEY

Aers: *v.* AYER

Affery, Affray: *v.* ALFREY

Agar, Agars, Ager: *v.* ALGAR, EDGAR

Agass, Aggas, Aggass, Aggis, Aggiss, Aggus, Aguss: *Robertus filius Agacie* 1279 RH (C); Roger *Agace* 1275 SRWo; Thomas *Agas* 1480 AD iii (Sx); Matthew *Agess*, Thomas *Aggis* 1674 HTSf. OFr *Agace* (f), the vernacular form of the learned *Agatha*, from Greek ἀγαθός 'good'.

Agate, Agates: John *a gate, atte Gate* 1296, 1327 SRSx. From residence near a gate.

Agg, Aggs: Simon *filius Agge* 1195 P (L); William *Agge* 1275 RH (L). ODa *Aggi*.

Agget, Aggett, Agott: Gilbert *Agote* 1301 ParlR (Ess). A diminutive of *Agg*, a pet-form of *Agnes*, or *Agace* (Agatha).

Agnes, Agness: *Agnes* de Papewurda 1160 P (C); Hugo *Agneis* 1219 AssL; Robert *Agnes* 1230 P (L). Fr *Agnes*, from Greek ἀγνός 'pure, chaste', the learned form of the vernacular *Anes, Anneis.* *v.* ANNAS.

Agnew: (i) Mabel *de Aignaus, de Agniws* 1208–9 Pl; Robert *de Ayneaus* 1227 Cur (Sf); Robert *de Aygnel* 1249 AssW. From Agneaux (La Manche). (ii) Thomas *Agnel* 1201–12 RBE (Sf); Susanna *Agniel* 1206 Cur (Bk); Lawrence, John *Agnel* 1254, 1284 IpmW. A nickname from Fr. *agneau, agnelle* 'lamb'.

Aguila, Aguilar: Henry *Laguillier* 1188 P (Ha); Godfrey *Aigillier* 1206 P (Sr); Robert *le Aguiller* 1221 AssSa. OFr *aiguillier, agullier* 'a maker of needles'.

Aguss: *v.* AGASS

Aicheson: *v.* ACHESON

Aiers: *v.* AYER

Aiken(s), Aikin, Aickin: *v.* AITKEN

Aikett: *v.* AKED

Ailward: *v.* AYLWARD

Ailwyn: *v.* AYLWIN

Aimer(s): *v.* AYMER

Ainger: *v.* ANGER

Ainsley, Ainslee, Ainslie, Aynsley: William *de Anslee* c1220 Black (Glasgow); Adam *de Aynesleye*, Thomas *de Ainslay* 1357 ib. (Roxburgh), Putnam (Db); Adam *Aynesley* 1652 RothwellPR (Y). From Annesley (Notts), or Ansley (Warwicks).

Air(e)s: *v.* AYER

Airey, Airy, Ary: Robert *de Hayra* 1301 IpmLa (We); John *Ary* 1617 FrY; Christopher *Airy* 1647 ib. Robert *de Ayrawe* 1332 SRCu, assessed in Threlkeld (Cumb), must have owed his name to

Aira Beck or Aira Force (Ullswater), *Arey* 1522, with a surname *de Ayraw* 1301 (PN Cu 254). Airy's Bridge in Borrowdale is named from Christopher *Arraye* 1603 and Jane *Araye* 1634 (ib. 352), whilst Airygill Lane in Great Strickland (PN We ii, 150), *John Airey Gill* 1838, commemorates the local family of *Airy* (*Arey, Arraye, Arra* 1586–1731). From 1508 to 1774 the surname is usually spelt *Airy*, with variants *Ayraie, Ayree, Arye, Aery*, etc., and occasionally *Eyrye, Eyree.* The persistent *Ai-* and the final *-ay, -ey* dissociate the name from the suggested ON *erg* 'shieling'. It is probably 'dweller by the gravel-bank', cf. ON *eyrará* 'gravel-bank river', or from Aira Force or some similarly named place.

Aish: *v.* ASH

Aishford: *v.* ASHFORD

Aitcheson, Aitchison: *v.* ACHESON

Aitken, Aitkens, Aitkin, Aitkins, Aiken, Aikens, Aickin, Aikin: *Atkyn* de Barr 1340 Black; *Aitkane* of Dunsleson 1482 ib.; Andrew *Atkin* 1469 ib.; William *Ackin* 1476 ib.; Robert *Aykkyne* 1539 ib.; Robert *Aitkins* 1674 HTSf; James *Aitkine* 1685 Black. Scottish forms of *Atkin*.

Aiton: *v.* AYTON

Aizlewood: *v.* HAZELWOOD

Aked, Akett, Akitt, Aikett: Richard *de Aykeheved* 1280 Riev (Y). 'Dweller by the oak-covered headland' (OE *āc, hēafod*).

Akerman: *v.* ACKERMAN

Akeroyd: *v.* ACKROYD

Akers, Akess: *v.* ACRES

Akett, Akitt: *v.* AKED

Akker: *v.* ACRES

Akred, Akroyd: *v.* ACKROYD

Alabastar, Alabaster, Albisser, Arblaster: Geoffrey *Arbalister* 1198 Cur (Ess); Richard *le Arbelaster* 1198 P (R); Ralph *Alebaster* c1200 HPD (Ess); Peter *le Arblaster* 1278 FFSf. AFr *alblaster, arblaster*, OFr *arbalestier, arbelestier* 'a soldier armed with a crossbow, a crossbowman' (c1325 MED). *v.* also BALLASTER. The surname is also due to office. Robertus *Arbalistarius, Balistarius* (1086 DB) and his son Odo *albalistarius* (c1140 Holme) held their land of the king by serjeanty of performing the duties of *arbalistarius*. Others of the same surname held their land by serving at Wallingford Castle with an arbalest, by guarding Exeter gaol, or by providing two arbalests. As London *arblasters* are stated to have had apprentices, the surname may also mean 'maker of cross-bows'.

Alabone: *v.* ALBAN

Alais: *v.* ALIS

Alan: *v.* ALLAIN

Alaway, Alway, Allaway, Alleway, Alloway, Allawy, Allway, Allways, Elloway, Hallaway, Halloway, Hallway: (i) *Ailwi, Aluui* 1066 DB; Willelmus *filius Ailwi* 1206 P (Nth); Godfrey *Ailwi* 1188 BuryS (Sf); Peter *Athelwy* 1302 SRf. OE *Æðelwīg* 'noble war'. (ii) *Æluui, Eluui* 1066 DB; Willelmus *filius Alewi* 1185 P (Bk); *Aleway* Pote 1297 SRY; Roger *Alewy* 1200 P (Mx). 1221 AssWo; Henry *Alwi* 1221 ElyA (Sf); Richard

Alawy, Halewy 1260, 1264 Eynsham (O); William *Halawey* 1279 RH (Hu); John *Always* 1301 SRY; Henry *Halloway* 1674 HTSf. The DB forms may stand for OE *Æðelwīg*, 'noble-war', *Ælfwīg* 'elf-war' or *Ealdwīg* 'old war' (rare). *v.* also ALDWY, ALLVEY.

Alban, Albon, Albone, Allbon, Allbones, Alabone, Allebone, Alliban, Allibon, Allibone, Aubon: *Albanus* filius Willelmi 1212 Cur (Y); Walter *Alban* 1250 Fees (Bk); Adam *Albon* 1275 SRWo; Hugh *Alybon* 1297 Coram (Db); William *Albon, Albone* 1376 LLB G; William *Albanes* 1379 PTY; William *Alybone* 1397 FrY. Latin *Albanus* 'of Alba', the name of the first British martyr. St Albans is recorded as *Seynt Albones* in 1421 (PN Herts 87).

Albert, Alberts, Aubert: *Albertus* 1066 DB (Beds); Philippus *filius Alberti, Auberti* 1211 Cur (Do); Robert *Alberd, Albert* 1221 AssWa; Isabella *Aubert* 1327 SRSf. OG *Albert* (Fr *Aubert*), from OG *Adalbert*. The cognate OE *Æðelbeorht* 'noble bright' occurs in DB in 1066 as *Ailbertus, Ailbriht* and once as *Albrict*. The *Ailbertus* of 1066 InqEl (C) appears in DB as *Albertus*. Thus *Albert* may sometimes be identical with *Albright*.

Albin, Albinson, Aubin, Obin: *Albinus* 1148–53 Bury (Sf), Hy 2 Gilb (L); *Obin* Kinel 1202 AssL; Roger *Albin* 1194 P (Wo); Gilbert *Aubin* 1210 Cur (Nf); John *Obin*, James *Aubyn* 1275 SRWo. OFr *Albin, Aubin*, Lat *Albinus*, a derivative of *albus* 'white'.

Albisser: *v.* ALABASTAR
Albon(e): *v.* ALBAN

Albright, Allbright: *Ailbricd* c1160 DC (L); *Ailbrict* 1202 FFC; Alexander *filius Ailbriht* 1205 Cur (Sr); William *Albrich'* 1275 SRWo; Eusebius *Ailbrit, Ailbric* 1279 RH (Hu); Herrieservant *Albryght* ('servant of Harry Albryght') 1378 Pat (Beds). OE *Æðelbriht*, a metathesized form of *Æðelbeorht*. *v.* ALBERT.

Albutt: *v.* ALLBUT

Alcock, Alecock, Allcock, Aucock, Awcock: *Alekoc, Alecoc* 1204 Cur (Nt), P (Y); *Awcok* de Leuer 1246 AssLa; *Alkok* 1332 SRCu; Alexander *Alecoc* 1275 SRWo; John *Alekok, Auecoc* 1296, 1327 SRSx. A pet-form of some short name in *Al-*.

Alcoe: Probably for *Alcock*. Cf. the pronunciation *Coeburn* for *Cockburn* and *Coeshot* for *Cockshott*.

Alcott, Allcott, Allcoat, Aucott, Aucutt: Philip *de Allecote* 1255 RH (Sa); Thomas *de Aldecote, de Alecote* 1275 SRWo. 'Dweller at the old cottage' (OE *eald, cot(e)*). Often, no doubt, confused with *Alcock*. John *Alkot* 1290 AssCh may be a misreading of *Alkoc*.

Alden, Aldin, Aldine, Aldins, Allden, Auden, Olden: (i) *Aldanus, Alden(e)* 1066 DB; Gamel *filius Alden* 1196 P (We); Walterus *filius Aldan, Aldein, Haldein* 1218–19 AssL; Alexander *Aldeyn* 1279 RH (O); John *Alden* 1524 SRSf. Anglo-Scand *Healfdene*. *v.* HALDANE. (ii) Ælfwine *Aldine* c1095 Bury (Sf); Osgotus *Aldwinus* 1196 P (Berks); Reginald *Aldyne* 1275 RH (Nf). OE *Ealdwine*. *v.*

ALWIN. cf. *Aldenesawe, Aldwynshawe* c1200 DEPN for Audenshaw.

Alder, Alders, Allder, Nalder, Nolder, Nolda, Older: Ralph *de Alre* 1221 Cur (Berks); William *atte Nalre, atte Naldhres* 1277 AssSo, 1313 FFEss; John *atte Alre* 1327 SRSo; Richard *atten Alre* 1332 MELS (So); Alexander *Aldres* 1332 SRWa. 'Dweller by the alder(s)' (OE *alor*).

Alderman: Adam *le alderman* 12th DC (L); John *Alderman* 1175 P (Sx). OE *ealdormann* 'alderman', also headman, governor of a guild.

Aldhous(e): *v.* ALDIS
Aldin(s): *v.* ALDEN

Aldis, Aldiss, Alldis, Aldhous, Aldhouse, Aldous, Aldus, Audas, Audiss, Audus, Oldis: Radulfus *filius Alduse* 1168 P (Y); Willelmus *filius Aldus* 1202 AssL; *Aldusa* filia Cristine 1219 AssY; Peter, Robert *Aldus* 1230 P (Nf), 1301 SRY; Peter *Aldous* 1327 SRSf; Robert *Aldhous*, William *Aldowes* 1524 SRSf; Francis *Aldhowse* 1647 Shef (Y); Goody *Aldis* 1674 HTSf. *Aldus* (f), a pet-form of some woman's name in *Ald-*, e.g. *Ealdgȳð*. *v.* EDIS. The Scottish *Aldis* is from Auldhous in Eastwood (Renfrewshire): Reginald *de Aldhous* 1265 Black.

Aldred, Alldread, Alldred, Alldritt, Audritt, Eldred, Eldrett, Eldrid, Elldred: (i) *Ældred, Ældret, Aldret, Eldred, Eldret* 1066 DB; *Aldret* de Windegate c1145–65 Seals (Nb); *Eldredus* 1161–77 Rams (Herts); Roger *Aldredus* 1207 P (D); Golding *Aldred* a1224 Clerkenwell (Mx); William *Aldret* 1275 SRWo. OE *Ealdrǣd* 'old counsel'. Forms in *Alred* may also belong here. (ii) *Eilredus* de Mannest' 1198 Cur (K); William *Eyldred* 1317 AssK; Maud *Aildred* 1327 *SR* (Ess). OE *Æðelrǣd* 'noble counsel', which appears in DB as *Ailred, Alret, Aldret*, and in InqAug (11th) as *Elred*. Forms in both *Alred* and *Aldred* may, therefore, also belong here. *v.* also ALDRITT and ALLRED.

Aldren: Thomas *in the Aldren*, Henry *in the Alren* 1327 SRSo. From residence among the alders (OE *alor*).

Aldrich, Aldrick, Aldridge, Alldridge, Allderidge, Elderidge, Eldridge, Elrick, Oldridge: These surnames may be local in origin, but usually derive from OE *Ælfrīc* 'elf-ruler' or *Æðelrīc* 'noble ruler'. Both survived the Conquest, by which time the first element had often been reduced to *Al-* or *El-* and consequently cannot be distinguished. A common post-Conquest form of *Æðelric* was *Ailric* or *Eilric*. *v.* ALLRIGHT. (i) From OE *Ælfrīc*: *Ælfric, Alfric, Aluric* 1066 DB; Hugo *Ælurici filius* c1095 Bury (Sf); Ricardus *Alurici* 1209 P (W); William *Alfric* 1212 Cur (Berks); William *Alfrich* 1296 SRSx; John *Alfryg* 1327 SRSo. (ii) From OE *Æðelrīc*: *Adelric, Agelricus, Egelric, Ailric, Aelricus, Alricus, Aluric* 1066 DB; *Ailricus, Ældricus* de Burc 1066 DB (Sf); *Aldrich* (*Ailrich*) 1220 Cur (Sr); William *Ailric* 1209 P (W); Henry *Aldric*, Geoffrey *Aldrich* 1275 SRWo; Robert *Aylrich, Alrych* 1279 RH (Hu); William *Eldrich* 1336 AD ii (Sr); James *Aldridge* 1674 HTSf. (iii) From OE *Ælfrīc* or *Æðelrīc*: *Ælric, Alric, Alrich, Elric* 1066 DB; *Elricus* filius Leppe Hy 2 DC (L); Roger

Elrich 1279 Barnwell (C); Robert *Alriche* 1327 SRC; Seman *Olrich* 1327 SRSf; Amicia *Alric* 1346 FFC; Alexander *Elrick* 1510 Black; Peter *Oldryk* 1527 SRSf. (iv) Local. From Aldridge (Staffs): Drogo *de Alrewic* 1201 P (St); from Aldridge Grove (Bucks), *Eldrigge* 1227 PN Bk 151; or from an unidentified place in or near Worcester: Hugo *Elrugge* 1327 SRWo.

Aldritt, Alldritt, Eldrett, Eldritt, Naldrett, Neldrett: Robert *atte Nalrette* 1305 FFSx; Robert *atte Aldratte*, Walter *ate Naldratte*, Gilbert *ate Nelrette* 1327 SRSx; John *atte Alrette* 1332 SRSx. OE **alrett, *elrett* 'alder-grove', a derivative of OE *alor* 'alder'. Common in Sussex, usually as *Naldrett(s)* and in Nalderswood Fm (PN Sr 298). *v.* also ARLET. *Aldritt* and *Eldrett* may also derive from OE *Ealdrǣd*. *v.* ALDRED.

Aldwy: *Aldui* 1066 DB (So); Geoffrey *Aldwi* 1221 ElyA (Sf); William *Aldwy* 1279 RH (O). OE *Ealdwīg* 'old-war'. *v.* also ALAWAY.

Alecock. *v.* ALCOCK

Alefounder: Walter *le Alefondere* 1275 Cl; John *Alefondere* 1381 FFEss; Widow *Alefounder* 1674 HTSf. 'Inspector of ale', one appointed by the Court Leet to examine it as it was poured out (Lat *fundere* 'to pour out'). The name still survives in Essex and Norfolk.

Alexander: *Alexander* c1150–60 DC (L); Thomas *Alexander* 1283 SRSf. Greek 'Αλέξανδρος 'defender of men'. *v.* SANDARS.

Alflat, Alflatt, Allflat, Elfleet, Elflitt: *Elfled* 1222 Cur (Sf); Adam *Ailflet* 1221 ElyA (Sf); Thomas *Alfled* 1279 RH (C). *Æfled, Alfled, Alfleta* (1066 DB) may stand for either OE *Ælfflǣd* 'elf-beauty' or *Æðelflǣd* (f) 'noble beauty'. The latter is also *Ædelflete* in DB and *Ailflet* is certainly from this. *Alf-* or *Elf-* may be from either.

Alfred, Alfreds, Allured, Alured: *Alured* 1066 DB; *Elfredus pelliparius* Hy 2 Gilb (L); *Alfredus Folkeredus* 1204 Cur (Sr); Alexander *filius Alvredi* 1206 Cur (Nf); Walter *Alured* 1260 AssC; Thomas *Alfred* 1294 RamsCt (Beds). OE *Ælfrǣd* 'elf-counsel'. This personal name is not so rare after the Conquest as has been suggested. Michaëlsson has shown that in the *Roman de Rou* the name of Alfred the Great appears as *Alured, Aluered, Auuered, Alvere,* and *Auuere* and that between 1292 and 1313 the French form *Auveré* is found in Paris both as a personal name and a surname. This pronunciation was also used by Normans in England. *Alfred* is probably concealed in many examples of the Latin *Alvredus*, though this certainly includes examples of *Avery*. The father of Normannus *filius Alfredi* (1242 Fees) is also called *Averay* (1236 ib.). cf. also Hugo *filius Alfredi, Aufrey, Alveredi* (1242 ib.). *Alvredus* is usually spelled *Aluredus* which, curiously enough, survives as *Al(l)ured*. *v.* ALFREY and AVERAY.

Alfrey, Alfry, Allfree, Allfrey, Affery, Affray, Elvery: Ricardus *filius Aufridi* 1212 Fees (L); Richard *Aufrey* 1275 RH (Wo), 1277 Ipm (Nth); John *Aufred* 1279 RH (Hu); Robert *Alfray* 1296 SRSx; Gilbert *Alfrey* 1317 AssK; John *Alfreth*

1327 *SR* (Ess); Adam *Alfrid* 1327 SRSo; William *Alfred, Alfreth, Alfride* 1327 *SR* (Ess). The Lincs *Aufridus* and the Somerset and Essex *Alfrid(e)* suggest that we are not always concerned with *Alfred*, but rather with a name ending in *-frith*, perhaps OE *Æðelfrið* (m), DB *Elfridus*, or **Æðelfrið* (f), DB *Egelfride*, both rare after the Conquest; or, possibly, OG *Adalfrith. Alfred* may also belong here, the *-frey* being due to analogical influence from compounds in *-frið*.

Algar, Alger, Algore, Augar, Augur, Agar, Elger: (i) *Ailgarus filius Lucie* 1151–3 DC (L); *Ailgarus, Agare* (abbot of Faversham) 1193–9, 1200–4 StGreg (K); *Eylgar de Berwe* 1273 RH (Sx); *Elgarus, Ailgarus King* c1232 Clerkenwell (K); Robert *Elger* 1271 AD iv (Nf); Walter *Eylgar, Elgar* 1317 AssK. OE *Æðelgār* 'noble spear' which occurs in DB only as *Algar*. (ii) *Alfgerus, Ælger, Algerus* 1066 DB (L, Nf, Sf); *Ælfger de Brademere, Alger* c1095 Bury (Sf); *Algerus faber* 1150 DC (L); Simon, Thomas *Alger* 1221 ElyA (Sf), 1297 MinAcctCo (Y). ON *Álfgeirr*, ODa *Alger*. Some of these forms may be from OE *Ælfgār* or *Ealhhere*, but all are from counties where Scandinavian influence was strong. (iii) *Algar* c1095 Bury (Sf); *Algarus Dalling* 1210 Cur (C); William *Algar* 1221 AssWo; Walter *Elgar* 1234 FFSf; Thomas *Algor* 1260 AssC. OE *Ælfgār* 'elf-spear' occurs once in DB as *Alfgarus* or *Elgar*, otherwise as *Ælgar, Algar*. OE *Ealdgār* 'old spear' is DB *Ealgarus. Ælfgār* is much the more common name and both appear later almost regularly as *Algar*. These surnames may derive from either or from *Æðelgār*.

Algate: Edricus *de Alegat'* 1219 Cur (Mx). From Aldgate (London).

Alger, Aljer, Auger: *Alcher (Alg(h)erus* Exon) 1066 DB (D); *Alcherus Venator* 1166 P (Ess); *Auchere filius Henrici* 1327 SRC; Willelmus *filius Auger* 1346 SRWo; Ailwin *Alher, Alcher* 1180, c1216 Bart (Lo); Walter *Alger* 1275 SRWo; Henry *Auger* 1279 RH (Hu); John *Aucher* 1428 FA (W); William *Awger* 1498 FrY. OE *Ealhhere* 'temple-army', which, through Anglo-Norman vocalization of *l*, became *Aucher, Auger*. cf. AYER. *Alger* (with a hard *g*) is from ON *Álfgeirr. v.* ALGAR.

Algore: *v.* ALGAR
Aliman: *v.* ALLMAN

Alis, Alise, Allies, Allis, Alliss, Allish, Alais, Hallis: *Adeliz de Raimes* Hy 2 DC (Nth); *Aliz Martel* ib. (L); *Ahelis, Ahelissa* 1188 BuryS (Sf); Willelmus *filius Alis* 1214 Cur (Beds); *Alicia filia Engrami* 1219 AssY; *Atheleisia, Aelesia, Aeleis* (identical) 1219–20 Cur (Nf); Roger *Alys* 1221 AssWa; William *Aliz* 1297 MinAcctCo. OFr *Aalis, Aliz*, OG *Adalhaidis* 'noble kind, sort', modern *Alice.*

Alison, Allison, Alleeson, Hallison: (i) *Alison* c1386 Chaucer; *Alison Home* 1524 Black (Berwick); William *Alisun* c1248 Bec (Bk); John *Allison* 1332 SRCu. OFr *Alison, Alizon*, a pet-name for *Alice*, common both in England and in Scotland from the 13th to the 17th centuries.

In Scotland, it became *Elison*: *Elison* Dalrymple 1514; *Alysone* or *Helysoune* Rouche 1535 (Black). *v.* ELLISON. (ii) Patrick *Alissone* 1296 Black (Berwick); John *Aliceson* 1324 Wak (Y); William *Aleissone* 1381 SRSt. 'Son of *Aleis* or *Alice*'. Also a late form of *Allanson. v.* also DALLINSON.

Alister, Allister: Hugo *de Alencestr*' 1221 AssWo; Adam *de Alicestr*' 1275 SRWo. From Alcester (Warwicks). Also for MACALASTER.

Alker: (i) William *de Altekar* 1341 LLB F; William *Alker* 1630 Bardsley. From Altcar (Lancs). (ii) William *Alker* 1212 Cur (Nf). This cannot be local in origin and is from OE *Ealhhere. v.* ALGER.

Alkin, Allkins, Aukin: *Alkin* the Jonge 1296 AssCh; John *Alkyn* 1307 ParlWrits (He). Probably a pet-form of *Allan* or *Alexander, Al-* plus *-kin.* cf. ALCOCK.

Allain, Allan, Allans, Allen, Alleyn, Alleyne, Allin, Allon, Alan, Alen, FitzAlan: *Alanus* 1066 DB (Sf), c1150 (Lei); *Alain* 1183 DC (L); Geoffrey *Alein* 1234 FFC; Roger *Alain* c1246 Calv (Y); Richard *Aleyns* 1309 AssSt; John *Fitz Alan* 1416 FrY; Richard *Alen* 1544 FFHu; Matthias *Allyn* 1593 ib. OFr *Alain, Alein*, OBret *Alan*, the name of a Welsh and Breton saint, which was popular with the Bretons who came over with the Conqueror, particularly in Lincolnshire, where it ranked eighth in popularity in the 12th century, level with Simon and more numerous than Henry. From 1139 it was common in Scotland where the surnames also derive from Gaelic *Ailéne, Ailin*, from *ail* 'rock'.

Allaker: *v.* ELLERKER

Allamand: *v.* ALLMAND

Allanby, Allenby, Allonby, Allamby, Allemby: Adam *de Aleynby* 1332 SRCu; John *Alomby* 1522 FrY. From Allonby (Cumb), *Aleynby* 1285, *Alanby* 1306, *Allonby* 1576.

Allanson, Allenson, Allinson, Allison: Henry *Aleyson* 1332 SRWa; Nicholas *Aleynesson* 1383 AssC; John *Alanson* 1395 Whitby (Y); Thomas *Alynson* 1401 AD i (Db); Allison *Allasoune* 1554 Black (Glasgow). 'Son of *Alain* or *Alan*.' *v.* ALLAIN. Occasionally 'Son of *Alwin*': Otho *Alwinessune* 1130 P (Lo). *v.* ALWIN and DALLINSON.

Allard: *v.* ADLARD

Allars, Allart: *v.* ADLARD

Allason: Giles *Alardson* 1421 LLB I. 'Son of *Alard*'. *v.* ADLARD. It may also derive from *Allanson* or *Allatson*.

Allatson: *v.* ALLETSON

Allatt: *v.* ADLARD, AYLETT

Allaway, Allawy: *v.* ALAWAY

Allbon, Allbones: *v.* ALBAN

Allbright: *v.* ALBRIGHT

Allbut, Allbutt, Albut, Albutt: *Albodo* 1114–20 Rams; *Ailbodus* c1155 DC (L); John *Albot* 1275 RH (D); Symon *Albod* 1275 SRWo. OG *Albod, Albot, Adelbodo*.

Allcoat: *v.* ALCOTT

Allcock: *v.* ALCOCK

Allcott: *v.* ALCOTT

Allday: Nicholas *Alday* 1327 SR (Ess); John

Aldaye 1455 ArchC 34; Thomas *Aldy* 1534 ib. 37. From OG *Aildag* or possibly OE *Æðeldæg. cf. *Aildeig* 1066 DB (Nf). Here, too, probably belong: John,, William *Aldeth* 1524 SRSf, from OE *Ealdgȳð* (f), 'old combat', found in DB in 1066 as *Ældiet, Ældit, Aldgid, Aldid*, and still in use in the 13th century: *Aldeth* Fin 1190 BuryS (Sf); *Alditha de Pelham* 1212 Cur (Herts). For the development to *-ey*, cf. ALFREY.

Allden: *v.* ALDEN

Allder: *v.* ALDER

Allderidge: *v.* ALDRICH

Alldis: *v.* ALDIS

Alldread, Alldred, Alldritt: *v.* ALDRED

Alldridge: *v.* ALDRICH

Allebone: *v.* ALBAN

Alleeson: *v.* ALISON

Allemby, Allonby: *v.* ALLANBY

Allen: *v.* ALLAIN

Allenson: *v.* ALLANSON

Alletson, Allatson: Adam *Allotesone* 1301 SRY; Agnes *Aletson* 1516 GildY. 'Son of *Allott*'. Also, perhaps, 'son of *Aylett*'.

Allett: *v.* AYLETT

Alleway: *v.* ALAWAY

Alley, Ally: Johannes *filius Alli* 1205 Cur (Nf); Hugo son of *Ally* 1332 SRCu; Alice, Richard *Ally* 1275 SRWo, 1352 FrY; Walter *Alleye* 1279 RH (O). ODa *Alli*, OSw *Alle*, found as *Alli* in DB (1066) in Bucks. Beds, Northants and Staffs.

Alleyn(e): *v.* ALLAIN

Allfield: *v.* OLDFIELD

Allflatt: *v.* ALFLAT

Allfree, Allfrey. *v.* ALFREY

Allgood, Augood: *Algod* 1066 DB (Nt); Iordanus *filius Algodi* c1174 Clerkenwell (Lo); *Algotus de Banneberi* 1178 P (O); Philip *Halgot* 1190 Oseney (O); Ralph *Alegod, Halgot, Halegod* 1200 ib.; Thomas *Algod* 1225 Pat; Robert *Algood* 1327 SRSf. ODa, OSw *Algot, Algut*.

Allgrim: *Algrim* 1066 DB (Y); *Algrim de Frisemareis* 1195 P (Y); John *Algrym* 1402 YWills. ON *Álfgrímr. The modern form may also be a corruption of *Allgroom*. cf. Richard *Aldegrom* 1198 P (K), 'the old servant', ME *grom*.

Alliban, Allibon(e): *v.* ALBAN

Allies: *v.* ALIS

Alliker: *v.* ELLERKER

Allimant: *v.* ALLMAND

Allin: *v.* ALLAIN

Allinson: *v.* ALLANSON

Alliott *v.* AYLETT

Allis, Allish: *v.* ALIS

Allison: *v.* ALISON, ALLANSON

Allister: *v.* ALISTER

Allitt: *v.* AYLETT

Allkins: *v.* ALKIN

Allman, Allmann, Allmen, Aliman, Alman, Almon, Almond: (i) *Alemannus* 1101–25, 1125 Holme (Nf); Henricus *filius Aleman* 1219 AssY. As there is no known OE personal name from which this can be derived, it is probably OFr *aleman* 'German' used as a personal-name. (ii)

John *Aleman* 1199 MemR (Nb); Walter *le Aleman* 1200 Cur (Y); Roger *Alemon* 1275 SRWo; Robert *Alman* 1327 SRC. OFr *aleman*, modFr *allemand* 'German'. With an excrescent *d* (as in modern French), this would become *Almond*. cf. Bardsley's 'Hanekin *Almond* and John *de Almann*, valets of the countess of Surrey' in 1358, and 'the almond leap', a German dance (1611 NED). (iii) Thomas *de Alemayne* 1320 LLB E; Inglebright *de Alman* 1332 FrY. 'The man from Germany', commonly called *Almeyne* in the 14th century. This, too, would become *Almond*.

Allmand, Almand, Alment, Almond, Allamand, Allimant: Terricus *le Alemaund* 1276 RH (Bk); John *le Alemaund* 1284 LLB A. OFr *alemaund* 'German'.

Allmark, Almack, Awmack, Hallmark: Robert *Alfmarck* 1279 RH (Hu); Adam *Halfmark* 1296 Wak (Y); Emma *Halmark* 1324 LaCt; John *Awmack* 1722 YWills. 'Half-a-mark', a nickname from the money of account.

Allnatt, Allnutt, Allner, Alner, Elnaugh, Elnough: *Ælnod, Alnoth, Alnot, Alnod, Elnoc, Elnod* 1066 DB; *Alnoduſ* (*Ailnoð*) ingeniator 1177 P (Mx); *Alnotus* Papillun 1197 FF (Nth); *Ailnothus* Peni 1204 Cur (Sr); William *Aylnoth, Alnoth* 13th Lewes (Nf); Gilbert *Elnod* 1312 FFK; Richard *Eylnoth* 1317 AssK; Thomas *Alnowe* 1427 FFEss. The DB forms may be for OE *Ælfnōð, Æðelnōð, *Ealdnōð* or *Ealhnōð*, but the surname is chiefly, if not solely, derived from OE *Æðelnōð* 'noble daring'. cf. WOOLNER.

Allon: *v.* ALLAIN

Allonby: *v.* ALLANBY

Allott: *Alote* c1191 BuryS (Sf); Adam *filius Alot* 1203 P (L); William *Allot* 1275 SRWo; Walter *Alote* 1296 SRSx. *Allot* (OFr *Aalot*), a hypocoristic of *Alis*.

Allred, Alred: *Alret* 1066 DB (K); Godardus *filius Ailred*' 1205 P (Lo); *Alredus de Wicham* 1206 Cur (K); Robert *Alred* 1198 P (K); Walter *Ailred*, Martin *Alred* 1279 RH (Hu). OE *Æðelræd*. *v.* ALDRED. Possibly also from OE *Ealdræd*.

Allright, Allwright, Oldwright: William *Ailricht, Ailriht* 1250 Fees (Beds), 1279 RH (C); Roger *Alright* 1457 LLB K; Elizabeth *Aldwright* 1720 Bardsley. OE *Æðelrīc*. *v.* ALDRICH.

Allsep, Allsepp, Allsop, Allsopp, Allsup, Allsupp, Alsop, Alsopp, Elsip, Elsop: Gamel *de Haleshoppe* 1175 P (Db); Philip *Alsope* 1279 RH (C). From Alsop en le Dale (Derby), *Elleshope* DB.

Allston, Alston, Alstone: (i) Ælfuine *filius Ælstani* c1095 Bury (Sf); Hugo *filius Alstani* 1209 P (Lei); Henry *Alston* 1279 RH (C); William *Alstan* 1283 SRSf. OE *Æðelstān* appears in DB as *Alestan*. *v.* ATHELSTAN. The DB *Alstan* may also be derived from OE *Ælfstān* 'elf stone', *Ealdstān* 'old stone' or *Ealhstān* 'temple stone', all of which may have contributed to these surnames: cf. Thomas son of *Aldeston* 1332 SRCu, Richard *Aldston* 1185 Templars (Herts). *v.* also ELSTON. (ii) These surnames may also be local in origin: Roger *de Alleston* 1246 AssLa, from Alston

in Ribchester (Lancs); John *de Alnethestan* 1230 P (D), from Alston in Holberton (Devon); William *de Alsiston*' 1221 AssWo, Richard *de Alston*' 1275 SRWo, from Alstone (Glos); Richard *de Aluredeston*' 1194 P (St), from Alstone in Hill Chorlton (Staffs); and possibly also from Alston (Cumb, Som).

Allured: *v.* ALFRED

Allvey, Alvey, Alvy, Elvey, Elvy, Elphee: Godric *filius Ælfuuii* c1095 Bury (Sf); *Alfwy* 1212 Fees (Berks); Swein, William *Alvi* 1212 Cur (O); Thomas *Alfy* 1279 RH (C); Simon *Elphey* 1279 RH (D); Adam *Alfwy* 1296 SRSx; John, Agnes *Aluy* 1327 SRSx; Edward *Eluy* 1327 SRSx. OE *Ælfwīg* 'elf war'. *v.* ALAWAY, ELVEY.

Allward, Alward, Elward: *Aluardus, Alfwardus* pistor 1182-6, 1200-11 BuryS (Sf); Willelmus *filius Eluard, Ælfwardi* 1191, 1192 P (Nf); Robert *Elward* 1275 RH (Sf); Gilbert *Allward* 1279 RH (C). The DB *Æluuard, Aluuard, Eluuardus* may represent OE *Ælfweard* 'elf guard' which is clearly represented above or OE *Æðelweard* 'noble guard' which survives as *Aylward* and also appears as *Alward*. In the 12th century the two names were confused. *Ailwardus grossus* and *Ælward judex* occur also as *Alfward* and *Ailward* respectively (c1116 ELPN).

Allway: *v.* ALAWAY

Allweather: Robert *Alwether* 1500 NorwW. cf. FAIRWEATHER.

Allwood: *v.* ELLWOOD

Allwork: Robert *de Aldwerc*' 1275 RH (L). From Aldwark (Derby, NRYorks, WRYorks).

Allwright: *v.* ALLRIGHT

Ally: *v.* ALLEY

Almack: *v.* ALLMARK

Alman, Almon: *v.* ALLMAN

Almand: *v.* ALLMAND

Almond: *Ælmund, Almund, Æilmundus, Ailmundus* 1066 DB; Alward *filius Elmund* 1086 DB (Sa); *Eilmund* Sperie 1224 Cur (Ess); Thomas *Ailmun* 1279 RH (C); Thomas *Awmond* 1562 FrY; Laurence *Almond* 1564 LaWills. OE *Æðelmund* 'noble protector' or *Ealhmund* 'temple-protector'.

Alner: *v.* ALLNATT

Alp, Alpe, Alps: Matilda *Alpe* 1275 RH (Nf); James *Alpes* 1664 FrY. A nickname from the bullfinch, ME *alp(e)* (c1400 NED).

Alphege, Elfick, Elphick, Elphicke, Elvidge: *Ælfec* (Ha), *Ælfech* (Sx), *Ælfhag* (Nt), *Alfeg* (Co), *Alfah* (Nf), *Elfeg* (Db), *Elfac* (Sa) 1066 DB; *Alfegus* 1137 ELPN; *Elfegus* de Ernington 1166 P (Gl); *Elphegus* a1216 StGreg (K); *Alfeg*' ater Legh 1296 SRSx; John *Elpheg*' 1297 Coram (K); William *Alfegh* 1318 AD vi (K); Robert *Elfegh* 1526 KentW; William *Elphike* 1549 RochW; Margaret *Elvishe* 1609 YWills. OE *Ælfhēah* 'elf-high'. *Alphege* is a Norman form.

Alpin, Alpine, Elfin: *Elphin* or *Elpin* c1225 Black; *Alpinus* 1287, *Alpin* mac Donald 1295 ib. GalloLat *Alpinus*, Welsh *Elffin*, the name of two or three Pictish kings.

Alshioner: *v.* ELESENDER

Alsop(p): v. ALLSEP
Alstead: v. HALSTEAD
Alston(e): v. ALLSTON
Altham: Adam *de Eluetham* 1246 AssLa; Symon *de Aluetham* 1304 WhC; John *Altham* 1372 LaPleas. From Altham in Whalley (Lancs), *Elvetham* c1150.
Alton: Simon *de Altun* c1141–54 RegAntiquiss; John *de Alton'* 1219 AssL; Peter *de Alton* 1325 IpmNt; Thomas *Alton* 1508 CorNt. From one or other of the many places of this name.
Alty: v. AUTIE
Alured: v. ALFRED
Alvar, Elvar, Elver: *Ælfere* (Nf), *Alfer* (K, Sx), *Elfer* (Sx) 1066 DB; *Alfare de Neteltuna* Hy 2 Gilb (L); Godwinus (*filius*) *Elfare* 1221 ElyA (Nf); Thomas *Elvare* 1499 ArchC 37. OE *Ælfhere* 'elf-army'. The surnames are rare.
Alven, Alvin, Elven, Elvin, Elvins: Hugo *filius Elfwin* 1193 P (He); *Eilwinus, Elfinus de Benindenne* 1214 StGreg (K); John *Alvene* 1279 RH (C); Richard *Elvene* 1296 SRSx; Thomas *Eluyn* 1327 SRWo; Thomas *Aluene, Alwyne* 1351 AssEss, 1357 FFEss. OE *Ælfwine* 'elf-friend' or *Æðelwine* 'noble-friend'. v. AYLWIN, ALWIN. cf. WOOLVEN from *Wulfwine*.
Alv(e)y: v. ALLVEY
Alway: v. ALAWAY
Alwin, Alwen, Alwyn, Allwyn, Elwin, Elwyn: (i) *Alduin, Elduinus* 1066 DB; Walter *filius Heldewin* 1191 P (L); *Aldwinus de Vivario* 1207 Cur (Ess); Osegod *Aldwini* 1195 P (Berks); Cristina *Aldwyne* 1275 SRWo; William *Aldwen* 1327 SRC. OE *Ealdwine* 'old friend'. (ii) *Æluuinus* (*Eiluuinus* Exon) 1066 DB (D); Robertus *filius Ailwini, Alwini* 1213–14 Cur (Ess). OE *Æðelwine* 'noble friend', which survives as *Aylwin*, appears in DB as *Aluuine, Eluuinus* and such forms as *Alwin, Elwin* infra may derive from this. (iii) *Æluuin, Alfuuinus, Aluuinus, Eluuin* 1066 DB; Goduine *Ælfuini filius* c1095 Bury (Sf); *Elfwinus de Bekeringe* 1165 DC (L). OE *Ælfwine* 'elf friend'. From this, too, may derive *Alwin, Elwin*. There was early confusion between *Ælfwine* and *Æðelwine*, both of which are found as *Alwine*: *Ælfwin Finche* is probably identical with *Ailwinus, Alwinus Finch* 1168, 1173, and *Alfwinus filius Leofstani* with *Ailwin* son of Leofstan (ELPN 12). cf. also Robertus *filius Ailwini, Ailfwini* 1214 Cur (Nth). (iv) *Æluuin, Aluuin(e), Eluuin(e)* 1066 DB; *Elwine Ecses* 1101–7 Holme (Nf); *Ælwine presbiter* 1127–34 ib.; *Alwinus Blundus* 1207 Cur (Sx); John *Allewin* 1219 AssY; Thomas *Alwine* 1260 AssC; Geoffrey *Elwyne* 1274 RH (Nf); William *Helewyn,* Thomas *Alwyn* 1296 SRSx. All these may derive from OE *Ealdwine, Æðelwine,* or, least common, *Ælfwine.* v. also ALVEN.
Amand, Aman, Amann, Amans, Ament, Ammann: Magister *Amandus* 1199 Cur (Lei); *Amanda filia Johannis* 1221 AssWa; *Amanus de Preston'* 1221 AssSa; Richard *Amand* 1279 RH (C); Robert *Amant* 1332 SRSx; Simon *Ament* 1674 HTSf. OFr *Amand, Amant,* Lat *amandus* 'meet to be

loved', the name of a 5th-century Bishop of Bordeaux and of four saints. Also used as a woman's name.
Amar: v. AYMER
Ambler: (i) William *le Amayler* 1303 LoCt; Simon *le Amelour* 1344 MESO (So); Robert *Ambeler* 1375 LoPleas. OFr *esmailleur* 'enameller', with intrusive *b.* (ii) Thomas *le Amblur* 1276 RH (L); Nicholas *le Aumbleour* 1307 Wak (Y); Alexander *Ambler* 1474 FrY. NED has *amblere* c1386 in the sense 'an ambling horse or mule', a derivative of *amble.* The surname may mean 'keeper of the stable' or be a nickname for one with an ambling gait or a facetious nickname for a fuller. cf. John *Ambeler,* walker 1440 FrY.
Amblin: v. EMBLEM
Ambrose, Ambrus: *Ambrosius* 1168–75 Holme (Nf); Henry *Ambreis* 1279 RH (O); William *Ambroys* 1332 SRSx. Lat *Ambrosius,* Fr *Ambroise,* from Gk ἀμβρόσιος 'divine, immortal'.
Amelot, Amlot: *Emelot Minne* 12th NthCh (Nth); Ricardus *filius Amelot* 1275 RH (D); Robert *Emelot* 1183 P (Lo); Nicholas *Amelot* 1275 RH (W). OFr *Amelot, Emelot,* a hypocoristic of *Ameline.* v. EMBLEM.
Amery, Amori, Amory, Emary, Emery, Emory, Embery, Emberry, Embrey, Embry, Embury, Emeric, Emerick, Emerig, Imbery, Imbrey, Imbrie, Imery, Imray, Imrie, Hemery, Hembrey, Hembreye, Hembry: *Amalricus* 1086 DB; *Ymerus filius Reineri* c1160 DC (L); *Haimeri* 1170 P (St); *Haimericus filius Gidhe* c1190–5 DC (L); *Eimericus uinitor* 1191 P (Wa); Robertus *filius Amalrici, Almarici, Aumarici* 1207–14 Cur (Nt); *Amauricus, Amaricus, Ailmarus, Almarus, Aumaricus, Almaricus de Sancto Amando* 1221 Cur; *Hemericus, Eymericus, Heimericus Buche* 1222 Cur (Do); *Emeric Orchard* 1241 AssSo; *Emery de Roche Chaward* 1269 AssSo; *Aymery de Rupe Cawardi* 1278 AssSo; Roger *Hemeri* a1182 Clerkenwell (Ess); Robert *Amalri* 1207 Cur (O); Richard *Aumauri* 1221 Cur (Do); Robert *Emeri* 1223 Pat (Lei); Robert *Heymeri* 1240 Rams (C); Simon *Amarik* 1260 AssY; William *Emeric* 1276 LLB A; Robert *Amary, Amory* 1279 RH (Bk); Walter *Ymery* 1513 Black; John *Imbrie* 1611 ib. OFr *Amauri, Emaurri,* from OG *Amalric* 'work-rule'.
Ames, Amess, Amies, Amis, Amiss, Amys, Amos, Amoss: Robert *Amis* 1221 ElyA (Sf); Joan *Amice* 1279 RH (O); John *Amize, Amys* 1309–10 LLB D; Gregory *Amys* or *Amisse* 1525 Oxon. Fr *Amis* (m) or *Amice* (f). *Amis* cas-sujet, *Ami* cas-régime, is from Lat *amicus* 'friend', used in late Latin as a name for the lower classes, especially for slaves. There were also derivatives of this, *Amicius* (m) and *Amicia* (f). Both were in use in England: *Amisius* 1200 Cur (D), 1213 ib. (Sr), *Amisius de Hospitali* 1211 Cur (Herts); *Amicia* 1189 DC (L), 1207 Cur (Ess), 1210 ib. (Wa). *Amos(s)* is due to the influence of the Biblical name which was not used in England before the Reformation. v. AMIAS, AMIET. Occasionally the surname is from the cas-sujet of the noun: William *le Amiz* 1275 SRWo.

Amey, Amy, L'Amie, Lamey: (i) William *Amy* 1219 AssY; William *Lamy* 1275 RH (Lo); William *le Amy* 1282 LLB A. Fr *ami* 'friend'. (ii) William *Ame* 1248 Ass (Ess). Fr *Amé*, from Lat *amatus* 'beloved'. (iii) *Amia cameraria* 1193 P (L); Martinus *filius Amye* 1297 SRY. The Latin form of OFr *Amée*, from *Amata*, the feminine of *Amé*. Occasionally we may have the masculine *Ami*, casrégime of *Amis*. cf. Rogerus *filius Ami* c1250 Rams (Nf) and *v.* AMES.

Amias, Amyas: Richard *Amias* 1185 Templars (Wa); Willard *de Amiens* 1193 P (Y); Roger *de Amias* 1276 LLB A; John *Amyas* 1296 SRSx. From Amiens. cf. 'merchants of *Amias*' 1326 LLB E. In the 16th century the surname was confused with *Ames*. Thomas *Amyas* of Wethersfield (1521) was, no doubt, of the same family as Robert *Amys*, *Amyse*, *Amyce*, *Ameys* (1462–78 ER 61).

Amiel: Alicia *Amyel* 1327 SRSf; Joan *Amyel*, daughter of *Amiel* de Honesdon 1349 Husting. A diminutive of *Ami* or *Amia*. cf. AMIET.

Amies: *v.* AMES

Amiet, Amiot, Amyot: William *Amiot* 1195 P (Gl), 1279 RH (O); Stephen *Amyot* 1317 AssK. *Ami* (m) or (f), plus *-ot*. *Amiot* de Wudestoch' 1191 P (Berks) is identical with *Amisius* filius Amisii de Wodestoke 1250 Eynsham (O), a clear case of the pet-form of the masculine *Amis* or *Ami*. *v.* AMES, AMEY.

Amis, Amiss: *v.* AMES

Amison, Amson: John *Amysone* 1358 Putnam (Nth); John *Amysson* 1384 Cl; Matthew *Amson* 1568 Bardsley. 'Son of *Amice*, *Amis* or *Ami*'. *v.* AMES, AMEY.

Amlot: *v.* AMELOT

Ammann: *v.* AMAND

Ammon, Ammonds, Amon, Amond: *Agemund*, *Aghemundus* 1066 DB; *Hagemundus* c1150 DC (L); *Agmundus* de Gutario 12th DC (L); *Amund* de Cotes Hy 2 DC (L); Alexander, Ralph *Aghemond* 1327 SRSx; Margeria *Awomond* 1327 SRSo; Henry *Amond* 1380 AssC; James *Amon*, Charles *Amons* 1674 HTSf. ON *Qgmundr*, OSw *Aghmund*.

Amoore: John *of Moore* 1467 BuryW; William *A moore* 1479 SIA xii. 'Dweller by the marsh'. *v.* MOOR.

Amor, Amour: Adam *Amour* 1327 SRSf. OFr *amo(u)r* 'love'.

Amori, Amory: *v.* AMERY

Amos(s): *v.* AMES

Amy: *v.* AMEY

Ancell: *v.* ANSELL

Ancliff(e): *v.* ANTCLIFF

Anders: *v.* ANDRE

Anderson, Enderson: Henry *Androsoun* c1443 Black; John *Andrewson* 1444 ib.; Robert *Androwson*, *Androson* 1455, 1482 GildY; Thomas *Anderson* 1471 FrY; Thomas *Enderson* 1674 HTSf. 'Son of *Andrew*'.

Andison: Geoffrey *Andisone* 1376 Black. 'Son of *Andie* or *Andy*', a pet-form of *Andrew*.

Andre, Andrea, Andree, Andrey, Andress, Andriss, Anders: Josep *Andree* 1229 Cl; Geoffrey *Andre* 1279 RH (C); John *Andres* 1326 LoPleas. Michaëlsson notes that in the Paris tax-rolls of 1292–1313 the common form of *Andrew* is *Andri* whilst *Andriu* is rare. *Andri* he explains as influenced by the Germanic *Andrik* or the Græco-Latin *Andricus*. In England and Scotland all early forms of the christian name are in the learned form *Andreas*. In surnames we find both *Andre* and *Andreu* at the beginning of the 13th century. *Andre* is, no doubt, this French *Andri* with a lowering of *i* to *e*. The modern *Andre* often appears as *André*, sometimes a recent introduction from France, though one suspects that the accent is not always original.

Andrew, Andrewes, Andrews, Andros, Andrus; *Andreas* 1086 DB, a1242 Black (Moray); *Andreas* filius Hugonis 1147–53 DC (Nt); William *Andreu* 1237 Fees (Bk); Moricius *Andrewys* 1275 SRWo; Richard *Andrew* 1317 AssK; William *Andro* 1399 Black (Aberdeen); John *Andrus* 1510 NorwW; Humfrey *Andros* 1552 FrY; Anthony *Androwes* 1543 FFHu. Greek Ἀνδρέας from ἀνδρεῖος 'manly', was latinized as *Andraeus*, *Andreus*, whence Fr *Andrieu*, English *Andrew*. *v.* ANDRE.

Angear: *v.* ANGER

Angel, Angell: Warinus *Angelus* 1193 P (K); Ralph *Angel* 1221 *ElyA* (Sf). A nickname, from OFr *angele*, Lat *angelus* 'messenger, angel'.

Anger, Angear, Angier, Aunger, Ainger: *Ansgarus*, *Anser*, *Angarus*, *Angerus* 1066 DB; *Angerus* de Middelton 1191 P (Sf); *Aunger* the Pheliper 1277 LLB A; Lefuine *Anger* c1095 Bury (Sf); Willelmus *Angeri* 1197 P (Wa); John *Aunger*, *Anger* 1279–80 AssSo. A continental personal name, either a Norman form of ON *Ásgeirr*, or Fr *Angier* from OG *Anser*.

Angers, Aungiers: Hugo *de Angiers*, *de Angers* 1207–8 Cur (W). From Angers (Maine-et-Loire).

Angle, Angles, Nangle: William *del Angle* 1208 P (Gl); Richard *in the Angle* 1327 SRWo; Peter *Nangle* 1571 Oxon. 'Dweller in the nook or outlying spot', ME, OFr *angle*.

Angless, Angliss, English: Nicolaus *Angleis* c1200 StP (Lo). Fr. *anglais* 'Englishman'. *v.* ENGLISH.

Angold: Alice *Angold* 1326 Wak (Y); Stephyn *Angold* 1568 SRSf. There is no second element *-gold* in OE or ON personal-names. This surname is identical with *Angood*, with a change of *-god* to *-gold* on the analogy of such ME names as *Alwold*. *Albold*, etc. *v.* OSGOOD.

Angood: *v.* OSGOOD

Angove: George *Angove* 1591 CoWills. Cornish *an* 'the' and OC *gof* 'smith'.

Anguish: Margaret *Anguisshe* 1530, Erl of *Anguyshe* 1563 Bardsley. For ANGUS.

Angus: Gael, Irish *Aonghus* 'unique choice'. The surname is also local, from Angus: Serlo *de Anegus* 1229, Andrew *Anguis* 1573 Black.

Angwin: (i) William *Angeuin* 1150 Oseney (O); Reginald *Langeuin* 1194 P (K); Godfrey *Aungewin* 1247 AssSt. 'The Angevin', the man from Anjou. (ii) Also a Cornish name, with the article *an* and *gwynn* 'the white'.

Anker, Ankers, Ankier, Anchor, Annacker, Annercaw: *Anker* de Fressenvill' 1208 Cur (Nth); Alice *Anker* 1395 NottBR. OFr *Anchier*.

Anketell, Ankettle, Anquetil, Ankill, Antell, Antill: *Anketillus* c1155 DC (Lei), 1207 Cur (L); Elyas *filius Ankil* 1210 P (So); Geoffrey *Anketil* 1209 P (Nf); John *Antell* 1524 SRSf. A Norman form of ON *Ásketill*. *v.* ASHKETTLE, ASKELL.

Ankin: *v.* ANTIN

Ankrett, Ankritt: *Angharad* 1207 Cur (He); *Anachorita* 1221 *ElyA* (Sf); *Angaret* 1246 AssLa; *Ankharet* 1322 AD vi (Ch); *Ancreta* Dibney 1571 ER 62; Gylbart *Ancret* 1580 ChwWo. A Welsh woman's name, *Angharad*, from *an* 'much' and *cariad* 'loved one', recorded in Wales in 877.

Annable, Anable, Annible: *Amabilis* c1150–60 DC (L), 1197 FFEss; *Amable* de Creuequer Hy 2 DC (L); *Amabilia*, predicta *Mabilia* 1185 RotDom (Ess); *Amabilla* (*Amable*), *Mabillia* (*Amabilis*) 1200 Cur (Db); *Anabel* de Nostrefeld 1204 AssY; *Annabel* 1260 AssC, (*Anilla*) 1374 Ipm (La); *Anabilia* 1284 FFHu; *Anabilla* 1305 FFEss; *Anabella* c1308 Calv (Y); *Anabel, Amabel* 1312, 1313 AssSt (identical); *Walterus Amabilis* 1166 P (Nf); Robert, John *Anable* 1259 CtSt, 1282 Pat (Gl); John *Amable* 1275 RH (C). Lat *amabilis* 'lovable'. *Amable* was shortened to *Mabel* (*v.* MABLE) and also, apparently by a process of dissimilation, became *Anabel*. Occasionally the surname may be local in origin, from Amble (Northumb), *Anebell* 1256, *Anebelle* 1292: Henry de *Anebelle* 1256 AssNb. *v.* HUNNABLE.

Annacker: *v.* ANKER

Annakin, Annikin: *v.* ANTIN

Annand: *Anundus, Anunt dacus, Anand, Anant* 1066 DB (Sf, Ess, Nf); *Anund* 1101–7 Holme (Nf); Godefridus *filius Anandi* 1182 P (Sf); Roger *Anant* 1275 RH (Nf). ODa, OSw *Anund*.

Annas, Anness, Annis, Anniss: *Annes* 1170–76 YCh; *Agnes, Anneis* (identical) Hy 2 DC (L); *Annas* de Preston 1194 P (La); Adam *Anice* 1275 SRWo; John *Anneys* 1296 SRSx. OFr *Anés*, the vernacular form of *Agnes*.

Annatt, Annett, Annetts, Annott: *Annote* Resthanbe 1297 Wak (Y); Thomas *filius Anot* 1357 ShefA; Robert *Anot* 1275 Wak (Y); John *Annot* 1327 SRC. *Ann-ot*, a diminutive of *Ann*, a pet-form of *Annes* (Agnes).

Anne: Ralph de *Anne* 1200 P (Ha). From Ann (Hants).

Annercaw: *v.* ANKER

Anness: *v.* ANNAS

Annett, Annetts: *v.* ANNATT

Annis, Anniss: *v.* ANNAS

Annison: (i) William *Anyssone* 1332 SRSt. 'Son of *Annis*'. (ii) Roger *Annotson* 1430 FeuDu; Thomas *Annetson* 1547 FrY. 'Son of *Annot*'. *v.* ANNATT.

Annott: *v.* ANNATT

Anquetil: *v.* ANKETELL

Ansell, Anshell, Ansill, Ancell, Hancell, Hansel, Hansell, Hansill; *Anse(l)lmus archiepiscopus* 1094–

5, 1108 StP; *Anselmus, Ansellus* de Ixew(o)rth' 1182–1211 BuryS (Sf), 1208 Cur (Nf); *Ansel, Anselmus* Candau' 1161 P (Ess); *Ancelmus* de Montegni 1166–89 Bec; *Anselmus* de Shelton', *Aunsell'* de Sheldon', *Ansellus* de Seldon' 1221–2 AssWa; *Ancell, Anselm* de Gornay 1269 AssSo; *Aunsel* le Furbur 1296 LLB A, *Ánselm* forbisor 1300 ib. B; Petrus *Anselmus* 1192 P (Sx); Roger *Aunsel* 1271 AssSt; William *Ansel* 1279 RH (C); John *Auncel* 1327 SRSx; William *Hansell* 1495 FrY. *Anselm*, a Lombard name, from OG *Ansehelm* 'god-helmet', found in France as *Ansellus*, where, as in England, *Anselm* and *Ansell* were used of the same man.

Anslyn: William *Hanselyn* 1379 PTY. OFr *Anselin*, a diminutive of *Ansell*.

Anstee, Anstey, Anstie: Richard de *Anesti* 1164 P (Ess). From Anstey (Devon, Dorset, Hants, Herts, Wilts) or Ansty (Warwicks).

Ansteys, Anstice, Anstis, Anstiss: *Anstasius* de Schirbec 1188 P (L); *Anastasia* 1221 Cur (Herts); *Anstice* 1602 Bardsley; Osegod, William *Anastasie* 1222 FFBk; Ralph *Anstayse* 1327 SRSo. The first surname above certainly derives from the feminine *Anastasia*, though the masculine *Anastasius* also existed. Both are from adjectives from Greek ἀνάστασις 'resurrection'.

Antcliff, Antcliffe, Antliff, Ancliff, Ancliffe: Thomas de *Arnecliv'* 1207 Cur (Y); Luke *Antcliff* 1748 Bardsley. From Arncliff, Ingleby Arncliffe (NRYorks) or Arncliffe (WRYorks).

Antell, Antill: *v.* ANKETELL

Anthoney, Anthonies, Anthony, Antoney, Antony: *Antonius* Hy 1 Rams (Hu), 1149 NthCh (Nth), 1214 Cur (D); John, Richard *Antoyne* 1275 SRWo; William *Antony* 1306 FFSf. Lat *Antonius*, Fr *Antoine*.

Antin, Ankin, Annakin, Annikin: *Hanchetin* de paruo Stepinge Hy 2 DC (L); *Anketin* 1219 AssY; Roger *Anketin* 1209 P (Nf). A Norman form of ON *Áskell*. *v.* ASKELL. *Hanccetin* de Lud Hy 2 DC (L) is also called *Asketillus*. Annakin and Annikin, rare Yorks names, are probably for *Ankin*. cf. *Ankill* and *Antill* from *Anketell*.

Antliff: *v.* ANTCLIFF

Anyan, Anyon: *v.* ENNION

Aplin, Applin, Appling: Thomas *Abelyn* 1275 RH (K); John *Applyn* 1547 FrY. *Ab-el-in*, a double diminutive of *Ab*, a pet-form of *Abel*.

Appelbe(e): *v.* APPLEBY

Apperley, Apperly: Richard de *Apperlee* 1221 AssGl; Thomas de *Apperleye* c1280 SRWo; Walter *Appurlee* 1372 IpmGl. From Apperley (Glos, Northumb, Som), or Apperley Bridge (WRYorks).

Appleby, Applebe, Applebee, Applebey, Appelbe, Appelbee: Vlf de *Appelbi* 1163 P; Hugh de *Apelby* 1204 Pl (Y); Thomas *Appelby* 1366 AssLo. From Appleby (Leics, Lincs, Westmorland).

Applegarth, Applegath, Applegate: William de *Apelgart* c1115 Bury (Sf); Robert *Appelgarth* 1279 Ipm (Y); Richard *del Appelgarthe* 1297 MinAcctCo (Y). From Applegarth (NRYorks, ERYorks, Cumb), or from residence near an apple-orchard (ON *apaldr(s)garðr*) in a Scandinavian county.

Appleton, Napleton: Hemeri *de Lepeltone* c1182 RBWo; Tomas *de Appleton'* 1196 P (Y); Thomas *ate Napeltone, ate Apiltone* 1317 AssK. From Appleton (Cheshire, Kent, Yorkshire, etc.), or from residence near an orchard (OE *æppeltūn*), or at a homestead where apples are grown.

Applewhaite, Applewhite, Ablewhite: Stephen *Appeltheit* 1327 SRSf; Robert *Apylweyte* 1524 SRSf; George *Applewhite* 1674 HTSf; Sarah *Applewhait* 1678 SfPR; Henry *Ablewhite* 1797 ib. From Applethwaite (Cumb, Westmorland), or a lost place in Suffolk.

Appleyard: Elias *del Apelyerd* 1275 Wak (Y); John *del Apelyard* 1315 ib. From Appleyard (WRYorks) or from residence near an orchard, OE *æppel* 'apple' and *geard* 'enclosure'.

Applin(g): *v.* APLIN

Apps, Aps, Asp, Epps, Happs, Hesp, Hespe: John *de Apse* 1214 Cur (Sr); Robert *atte Hepse* 1296 SRSx; Robert *atte Apse* 1327 SRSx. 'Dweller by the aspen', OE *æpse*, a metathesized form of *æspe*.

April, Averill, Avril: Thomas *Averel* 1275 SRWo; Robert *Aprill'* 1301 SRY; Richard *Averil* 1322 AssSt; John *Aueril* 1327 SRSx. According to ODCN, *Averil* is to be associated with *Everild*, a christian name not uncommon in the Middle Ages, from OE *Eoforhild* or OG *Eburhilt*. These, however, would become *Everil*. Bardsley has no example of the surname before 1626 and confuses the name with *Avenell*. Harrison, without evidence, explains the surname as 'dweller at the wild-boar hill', which would also become *Everil*. There can be no doubt that here we are concerned with the name of the month, OFr *avrill*, Lat *aprīlis*, which appears in English as *aueril* in 1297 and as *averylle* c1450 (NED). The word was refashioned after the Latin and is found as *apprile* in 1377. There is no evidence for its use as a christian name and the surname must be regarded as a nickname, perhaps with reference to the changeable weather of the month, 'changeable, vacillating', or with reference to spring or youth. Dauzat explains the French *Avril, Abril* thus, with an alternative 'child found in April'. It might denote one born in that month. The modern christian name *Avril* is of recent origin.

Arber: *v.* HARBER

Arblaster: *v.* ALABASTER

Arborn, Arbon, Arboune: *Erneber, Ernebernus, Gernebern* 1066 DB (Y, L, Db); *Arbernus* 1190–5 DC (L); Roger *Arborn* 1279 RH (C); William *Arbon* 1329 Rams (Nth). ON *Arnbiǫrn*, ODa, OSw *Arnbiorn*.

Arbuckle, Hornbuckle: John *Arnbukle, Arbukile* 1499, 1511 Black. From Arbuckle (Lanarkshire).

Archambault, Archanbault, Archbald, Archbell, Archbold, Archbould, Archbutt, Archibald, Archibold, Archibould: *Archembold* Wiverun 1130 P; Robert *Archenbold* 1210 P (Gl); William *Erchebaud* 1239 FFSf; Thomas *Herchebaud* 1302 SRY; Agnes *Archebald* 1327 SRSf; Seath *Archbutt* 1616 FrY.

OFr *Archamboult*, from OG *Ercanbald* 'precious-bold', found in DB (1086) as *Erchenbaldus, Arcenbaldus* and *Arcebaldus*.

Archdeacon, Arcedeckne: Walter *le Ercedekene, le Ercedeiakene, le Archedekene* 1268–71 AssSo; Roger *le Arcedekne* 1297 MinAcctCo. OE *arce-, erçediacon*, OFr *arc(h)ediacne* 'the chief deacon, chief of the attendants on a bishop'.

Archer, Larcher, L'Archer: Edward *Archier*, Robert *Larchier* 1166 P (Ha, W); Hugh *le Archer* 1199 FFC. ME *archere*, AFr *archer*, OFr *archier* 'bowman' (c1300 MED).

Archibald, Archibold, Archibould: *v.* ARCHAM-BAULT

Arckoll: *v.* ARKELL

Arding: *v.* HARDING

Argent, Hargent, Largent: Geoffrey *Argent* 1180 P (Nth); John *Largeant* 1524 SRSf. OFr *argent* 'silver', probably for one with silvery-white hair.

Aries, Aris, Ariss: *v.* ARRAS

Arkell, Arkill, Arkle, Arckoll, Arkcoll: *Arnketel* 1019 Rams (Nf); *Archetel, Archel, Archil* 1066 DB; *Archil de Corebr'* 1159 P (Nb); Richard *Arkill* 1256 AssNb; Roger *Arketyl* 1279 RH (Hu); William *Harkill, Arkel* 1316, 1331 Wak (Y); John *Arcle* 1455 FrY. ON *Arnkell*, ODa *Arnketil*, OSw *Arkil*.

Arkus, Arkush: *v.* HARCUS

Arkwright, Artrick, Hartwright, Hartrick, Hattrick: Gilbert *de* (sic) *Arkewright* 1246 AssLa; John *de* (sic) *Arcwryt* Hy 3 DbCh; Thomas *the Arkewrytte* 1286 AssCh; George *Arkewright* 1450 FrY; William *Hartwright* 1494 GildY; George *Arthwright* 1582 PrGR; Thomas *Artwright* 1649 LaWills; Alice *Arthricke* 1670 ib.; Christopher *Arkrick* 1673 ib. OE *arc* 'ark' and *wyrhta*, 'a maker of arks, chests, etc.'.

Arles: *v.* ARLISS

Arlet, Arlett: Thomas *Attenerlette* 1276 MELS (Sx); Philip *atte Arlette*, Robert *aten Erlette* 1296 SRSx. A metathesized form of OE **alrett, *elrett*, 'alder-grove'. *v.* ALDRITT.

Arling: *v.* HURLIN

Arliss, Arles, Harliss: Henry *Earles* 1295 Barnwell (C). OE *ēare* and *lēas* 'ear-less'.

Arlott, Arlotte: Geoffrey *Herlot* 1193 P (Nf); Ralph *le Harlot* 1246 AssLa; John *le Harlet* 1276 RH (C); Muriel *Arlot* 1279 RH (C). OFr *herlot, harlot, arlot* 'lad, young fellow', found in English as a masculine noun in the 13th century in the sense 'vagabond, beggar, rogue' (c1230 MED). It was used by Chaucer both as a term of derision 'ye false harlot', and also playfully for a good fellow, 'he was a gentil harlot and a kynde'. In the 14th century it was used of an itinerant jester, buffoon or juggler, and also of a male servant, attendant, menial. The modern sense is not found before the 15th century.

Arlow: *v.* HARLOW

Armatage, Armatys: *v.* HERMITAGE

Armer, Armor, Armour, Larmer, Larmor, Larmour: Gwydo *le Armerer* 1279 RH (O); Simon *Larmourer* 1334 LLB E; John *Armar* 1519 Black.

AFr *armurer*, OFr *armurier* 'armourer, maker of arms'.

Armett: *v.* HERMITTE

Armiger, Arminger: William *Armiger* 1279 RH (O); Thomas *Arminger* 1674 HTSf. Lat *armiger* 'armour-bearer, squire'.

Armin, Ermen: *Ermyn* Donetoun 1327 SRC; Hervicus *Ermin* 1279 RH (O); Thomas *Armyn* 1481 FrY. *Ermin*, a hypocoristic of names in *Ermen-, Ermin-*, such as OG *Ermenald, Ermingaud*.

Arminson, Armison, Armson: Robert *Armison* 1669 FrY; Mary *Armson* 1749 Bardsley. 'Son of *Ermin*.'

Armistead, Armitstead, Armstead: Laurence *del Armetsted* 1379 PTY; William *Armistead* 1642 PrGR. 'Dweller by or at the hermitage,' OFr *ermite*. and OE *stede* 'place'.

Armit(t): *v.* HERMITTE

Armitage: *v.* HERMITAGE

Armour: *v.* ARMER

Armson: *v.* ARMINSON

Armstead: *v.* ARMISTEAD

Armstrong: Adam, William *Arm(e)strang* 1250 CalSc (Cu), 1279 AssNb. OE *earm, strang* 'strong in the arm', a well-known Border name.

Armytage: *v.* HERMITAGE

Arnald, Arnall, Arnatt, Arnaud, Arnell, Arnhold, Arnold, Arnoll, Arnot, Arnott, Arnould, Arnout, Arnull, Harnett, Harnott: (i) *Ernold*, Rogerus *filius Ernaldi* 1066 DB; *Arnoldus, Hernaldus* de Bolonia 1212 RBE; Puntius *Arnaldi* 1196 P (D); William *Arnold* 1277 FFSf; John *Arnoud* 1279 RH (C). OFr *Arnaut, Ernaut, Hernaut*, from OG *Arnald, Arnold, Arnolt* 'eagle-power'. (ii) Richard *de Ærnhale* 1191 P (Y), from Arnold (ERYorks); Roger *de Arnhal'* 1212 Fees (Nt), from Arnold (Notts).

Arnason: *v.* ARNISON

Arndell: *v.* ARUNDALE

Arneway: *Ernui, Erneuui, Arnui* 1066 DB; *Ernwi*, c1150 DC (Nt); *Arnwi* Hy 2 ib. (L); Peter *Ernewy* 1243 AssSo; Richard *Arnwy* c1272 HPD (Ess); Hugo *Ernawey*, Walter *Ernowey* 1279 RH (Bk). OE *Earnwīg* 'eagle-warrior'.

Arnhold: *v.* ARNALD

Arnison, Arnason, Arnson: William *Arnaldson* 1460 FrY; Matthew *Arnison* 1680 ib. 'Son of *Arnald*.'

Arnold, Arnoll: *v.* ARNALD

Arnot, Arnott: Michael *de Arnoth* 1284 Black. From Arnot in Portmoak (Kinross-shire). *v.* also ARNALD.

Arnould, Arnout. *v.* ARNALD

Arnson: *v.* ARNISON

Arnull: *v.* ARNALD

Arpin: *v.* HARPIN

Arrandale: *v.* ARUNDALE

Arras, Arres: John *de Aroz* 1296; Adam *de Airwis* 1328; Adam *de la Arus* 1333; John *Arres* 1525 Black. Probably, as suggested by Black, from Airhouse in Channelkirk (Berwicks), *Aras* 1655, *Arreis* 1630.

Arras, Aries, Aris, Ariss: (i) Simon *de Araz*

1202 P (L); Robert *de Arras* 1281 LLB A. From Arras (France). (ii) Hugo *de Erghes* 1347 FrY; John *Aras* 1421 FrY. From Arras (ERYorks), *Herges* 1156. For *Aries*, cf. 'One bede coveringe of *aries* (i.e. *arras*) worke' 1562 Bardsley.

Arrowsmith, Arsmith, Harrismith, Harrowsmith: Roger *le Aruesmuth* 1278 AssSt; William *le Arwesmyth* 1324 FFEss; Richard *Arsmith* Eliz Bardsley. OE *arwe* 'arrow' and *smith*. A smith who makes arrows, especially iron arrow-heads (1278 MED). *Harrismith* and *Harrowsmith* are rare but exist side by side with *Arrowsmith* in Yorks and Lancs.

Arscott: (i) William *de Ardescote* 1255 RH (Sa). From Arscott (Salop). (ii) John *Aryscote, Adescote, Addyscote, Adescote* or *Addyscoote* 1513 LP (D); John *Arscot* 1523 ib. From Addyscote in South Tawton (Devon), *Arscott* alias *Addiscott* 1656, with a surname *Atherscote* in 1297 (PN D 448). (iii) William *de Hassecote* 1201 Pl (Co); Alnet *Arscot* 1642 PrD. From Arscott in Ashwater or Arscott in Holsworthy (Devon).

Arsnell: *v.* HORSNAIL

Arson: *v.* HARSANT

Arter: *v.* ARTHUR

Arthington: Peter, Serlo *de Ardington'* 1175–94 YCh; William *de Arthyngton* 1283 FrY; Robert *Arthington* 1459 Kirk. From Arthington (WRYorks).

Arthur, Arthurs, Arthars, Arter: *Erturus* 1130 P (Ha); Henricus *filius Arturi, Artur* 1187 P, 1212 Cur (Cu); *Ærturus* 1192 P (Y); Normannus *filius Arcturi* 1196 P (Y); Geoffrey *Artur* 1135 Oseney (O); Robertus *Arcturi* 1197 P (He); Adam *Arthur* 1246 AssLa. The DB forms *Artor, Azer, Azor*, given by ODCN, are wrongly assigned. They are for ON *Arnþórr*, ODa *Azur* respectively. *Artur(us)* 1086 DB (Ess, Wo) is probably for *Arthur*, the well-known Celtic name, of disputed etymology.

Artis, Artiss, Artist, Artois, Artus: William *Artoys* 1327 SRSf; John *Artes* 1524 SRSf; Thomas *Arteis* 1568 SRSf; Robert *Artis* 1674 HTSf; Abraham *Artus* 1724 FrY. Man from Artois.

Artrick: *v.* ARKWRIGHT

Arundale, Arundel, Arundell, Arondel, Arrandale, Arrundale, Arndell: (i) Rogerius *Arundel, Harundel* 1086 DB (Do, So); Robert, Roger *Arundel* 1130, 1159 P (Do, So); Osbert *Arundel, Harundel* 1154 Riev (Y). (ii) Roger *de Arundelle* 1148 Eynsham (O); Thomas *Arundel (de Arundel)* 1178 P (Y); John *de Arundel* c1198 Bart (Lo); Roger *Arundel (de Arundel)* 1204 AssY; Nicholas *(de) Arundel*, Roger *de Arundel* 1225, 1268 AssSo; Robert *Arundel*, Robert *de Arundell* 1327, 1332 SRSx; Richard *Arrandell, Arrendale* 1631, 1638 RothwellPR (Y). The most usual source of these surnames must be Arundel (Sussex), *Harundel* 1086 DB, *Arundell'* 1087 France, *Arndle* 1788, locally pronounced *Arndell*. The earliest bearer of the name, Roger *Arundel*, the Domesday tenant-in-chief, has left his name in Sampford Arundel (Som) which he held in 1086. His byname cannot derive from the Sussex place but must be a nickname from OFr *arondel* 'little swallow'. So, too, with Osbert *Arundel*. Though they were, presumably, the respective ancestors of the Somerset and Yorkshire families, the later *de* introduced into their name suggests a Sussex origin. The problem is further complicated by the fact that Arundel itself early lost its initial *H*, whilst the nickname equally early acquired an inorganic initial *H*. The influence of Arundel with its castle was probably too strong for the nickname, the meaning of which was soon forgotten.

Ary: *v.* AIREY

Asch: *v.* ASH

Ascham: *v.* ASKAM

Ascough: *v.* ASKEW

Ascroft: *v.* ASHCROFT

Ash, Ashe, Asch, Asche, Dash, Daish, Daysh, Nash, Rasch, Rash, Tasch, Tash, Esh, Tesche, Tesh, Aish, Aysh, Naish, Nayshe: Richard *del Eshe* 1221 AssWo; Ralph *de Asche* 1296 SRSx; Alice *aten Eysse* ib.; William *atte Nasche* ib.; John *ater Aysse* ib.; Henry *Aten Assche* 1301 MELS (Wo); Richard *Dasche, de Ayssh* 1320 LLB E, 1327 LoPleas; Roger *ate Assh* 1327 SRSx; Alan *Tassh* 1327 SRSf; John *atte Naysshe* 1349 LLB F; William *Rash* 1381 SRSf; William *Teshe* 1599 FrY. From a place called Ash or Nash or 'dweller by the ash-tree' (OE *æsc*). *v.* Introd., p. xiv and NESS. *Dash* retains the French *de*.

Ashard. *v.* ACHARD

Ashbee, Ashbey: *v.* ASHBY

Ashbolt, Ashpool, Ashpole: Robert *Archpoole* 1523 RochW (K); Edward *Archepoll, Archepole* 1591, 1595 ChwWo; Nicholas *Archepoll, Archebold* 1591, 1593 ib. *Ashbolt* is probably a corruption of *Archbolt*, i.e. *Archibald*, through *Archpoll*, which also became *Ashpole*.

Ashburner: Robert, William *le Askebrenner* 1278 AssLa, 1308 Wak (Y); Robert *Askbrinner* 1332 SRCu; Thomas *Asborner* 1332 SRSx; Edward *Ascheburner* 1532 FrY. ON *aska* 'ashes' plus a derivative of ON *brenna* or OE *brinnan* 'to burn', 'a burner of ashes' or maker of potash from the ashes of wood, bushes, straw, etc. In Sussex we have the native OE *æsc* plus a derivative of OE *beornan*, which had replaced the Scandinavian word in York by the 16th century.

Ashby, Ashbee, Ashbey: Robert *de Aschebi* 1200 Pl (Nf); Alexander *de Assheby* 1309-10 FFWa; Richard *Assheby* 1332 SRSx; William *Ashbee* 1633, *Eashbee* 1637, *Eshbee* 1639 LeiAS xxiii. From one or other of the many places of this name, or from Asby (Cumb, Westmorland).

Ashcroft, Ascroft: Margar' *de Asecroft* 1275 RH (Nf). 'Dweller at a croft with an ash-tree.'

Ashfold, Ashfull: Richard *de Asshefold* 1305 FFSx. 'Dweller by a fold near an ash', OE *æsc, falod.*

Ashford, Ashforth, Aishford, Ayshford: Reginald *de Asford'* 1221 AssSa. From Ashford (Devon, Derby, Salop) or Ayshford (Devon).

Ashken: *v.* ASKIN

Ashkettle: *Asketillus* de Kedham 1101-25

Holme (Nf); *Aschetillus* Bardel 1158 P (Ess); Robert *Asketill'* 1200 P (Ha); Alexander *Asketell'* 1205 Cur (Nf); Sarah *Ashkettle* 1785 SfPR. ON *Ásketill*, common before the Conquest and found in DB as *Aschil*. It survives as ASKELL. *Ash-* is a late dialectal development. *v.* also AXTELL.

Ashley, Ashlee, Ashleigh: Walter *de Esselega* 1162 P (Gl); Robert *de Ashley* 1281 CtW; Thomas *Assheley* 1401 AssLa. From one or other of the many places of this name.

Ashlin, Ashling: *v.* ASLIN

Ashman, Ashment, Asman: *Assemanus* 1066 DB (Sf); *Asseman, Asman* 13th Rams (Hu); Robert *Asheman* 1275 RH (Sf); Roger *Asman* 1279 RH (C); John *Essheman* 1317 AssK. OE *Æscmann*, perhaps an original byname from OE *æscmann* 'shipman, sailor, pirate'. As the surname is found at Gorleston and in Rochford Hundred (Essex), it may sometimes be an occupation-name.

Ashplant: *v.* ABSALOM

Ashpole, Ashpool: *v.* ASHBOLT

Ashton: John *de Essheton* 1306 IpmY; John *de Ashtone* 1323, 1326 CorNth; Thomas *Assheton* 1431 FFEss. From one or other of the many places of this name, or from Aston (Glos, Hereford, Salop).

Ashwin: William *Ashwyne* 1332 SRSr. OE *Æscwine* 'ash-, spear-friend', the name of a King of Wessex (674-6). It was not common in OE but clearly survived the Conquest.

Askam, Askem, Askham, Ascham: Conan *de Ascham* 1201 P (Y); Richard *de Ascum* 1204 AssY; John *de Askham* 1290 FrY. From Askham (Notts, WRYorks. Westmorland).

Askell, Astell, Astil, Astill, Eskell, Haskel, Haskell: *Aschil, Osketel, Anschil* 1066 DB; Robertus *filius Askel* 1180 P (Y); Alanus *filius Askil* 1186-1211 BuryS (Nf); *Astillus* 1202 AssL; Ricardus *filius Eskill'* 1219 AssY; William *Astil* 1227 AssBeds; Thomas *Askil* c1248 Bec (O); Robert *Astel* 1260 AssC; Hugo *Astyl pro Asketyl* Ed 1 Battle (Sx). ON *Áskell*, ODa *Eskil*, OSw *Æskil*, a contracted form of *Ásketill* (*v.* ASHKETTLE), common both before and after the Conquest. The name was also popular in Normandy in the forms *Anschetill* and *Anketill* (*v.* ANKETELL) and elsewhere in northern France as *Anquetin* and *Asketin* (*v.* ASKIN). The various forms are often used of the same man in England. In the Whitby cartulary *Aschetillus* de Houkesgard (c1155) is also called *Aschetinus* (c1145), *Astillus* (c1170) and *Astinus* (12th). In DC (Lei), in the late 12th century, *Anketinus persona* de Prestwalda appears also as *Asketinus* filius Hugonis de Prestewalda and as *Anketillus* de Prestwalda. Cf. also *Aschetillus, Ancatillus, Anquetillus* Malore(i) Hy 2 DC (Lei). The name is found in Scotland as MACASGILL and in the Isle of Man as CASTELL. *v.* also AXCELL.

Askew, Haskew, Ascough, Haskow, Ayscough, Askey, Askie, Haskey: William *de Aykescoghe* 1366 SRLa; Robert *Ascowe* 1390 LLB H; Simon *Ascogh* 1488 FrY; John *Ascow*, William *Askew*

1488 GildY; Richard *Askoo* 1533 FrY; Amy *Askie* 1618 Bardsley; William *Ayscough* 1675 FrY; John *Ashkey* 1674 HTSf. From Aiskew (NR Yorks).

Askham: *v.* ASKAM

Askin, Askins, Astin, Astins, Ashken, Haskin, Haskins, Hasking, Haskings, Hastin, Hastins: *Asketinus filius* Od 1163 DC (L); *Robertus filius Astin* 1219 AssY; *Hastinus* caretarius 1223 Pat (Y); John *Astin* 1230 P (D); Hugh *Astyn* 1297 AssY; John *Asketyn*, William *Hastin* 1317 AssK; John *Haskyn* 1524 SRSf; John *Askin* 1674 HTSf. A Norman form of ON *Ásketill*. *v.* ASHKETTLE, ASKELL.

Aslam, Aslen: *v.* HASLAM

Aslet, Aslett, Astlett: *Rogerus filius Aselot'* Ric 1 Cur (L); *Johannes filius Ascelot* 1221 Cur (O); Hugh *Asselote* 1327 SRSf; William *Asselot* 1327 SRSx. OFr *Ascelot* (m), a double diminutive of OG *Azo*. *v.* ACE and ASLIN.

Aslin, Asling, Ashlin, Ashling, Astling: *Ascelinus* de Wudecroft 1162 P (Nth); *Acelina* de Stanfelde 1195 P (Nf); *Walterus filius Acelini, Ascelini* 1206 Cur (Nth); *Ascelina* 1214 Cur (Mx); *Henricus Ascelinus* 1204 P (W); Nicholaus *Asceline* 1255 Rams (Hu); Richard *Asselyn* 1279 RH (Bk); Henry *Asshelyn* 1374 LLB G. OFr *Acelin, Ascelin* (m), from OG *Azilin*, a double diminutive of *Azo*. cf. ASLET. There was also a feminine *A(s)celine*. The surname survives in Ashlyns and Ashlings in High Ongar which occur as *Astelyns* 1456–9, *Astlynge* 1568 (PN Ess 72).

Asman: *v.* ASHMAN

Asp: *v.* APPS

Aspenlon: *v.* ABSALOM

Aspinal, Aspinall, Aspinell, Aspinwall, Haspineall: Henry *de Aspenewell* 1246 AssLa; Miles *Haspinall* 1578 YWills; Edmond *Aspenall* 1599 FrY. From Aspinwall (Lancs).

Aspland, Asplen, Asplin, Aspling: *v.* ABSALOM

Aspole: For *Aspall* or ASHBOLT.

Asquith, Askwith: Ulf' *de Askwith'* 1219 AssY; Adam *de Askequid* 1297 SRY. From Askwith (WRYorks).

Assan: *v.* HARSANT

Assard: *v.* HAZARD

Astall: Walter *de Astalle, de Estalle* 1279 RH (O). From Asthall (Oxon).

Astbury: William *de Astbury* 1287 AssCh. From Astbury (Ches).

Astell, Astill, Astle, Astles: Simon *de Astell* c1225 Lichfield (St); Richard *de Asthul* (*Astell*) 1349 FrY. From Astle (Ches) or from residence near the east hill (OE *ēast, hyll*). *v.* also ASKELL.

Astin: *v.* ASKIN

Astington: *v.* SINTON

Astle(s): *v.* ASTELL

Astlett: *v.* ASLET

Astling: *v.* ASLIN

Astman: *v.* EASTMAN

Aston: (i) *Asthone* de Sancto Luca c1140 DC (L); Tomas *filius Adestan* 1187 P (Y); *Astanus* de Hune 1190 P (Y); Lewin *Adstan* 1221 ElyA (Nf);

Thomas *Astan* 1276 RH (L). *Adestan* may be from OE *Æðelstān*. *v.* ATHELSTAN and ALLSTON. Robertus *filius Adestani* and Walterus *filius Alstan* 1206 Cur (Sf), both mentioned in the same document relating to the same parish were both probably sons of *Æðelstan*. Or we may occasionally have the less common OE *Ēadstān* 'prosperity-stone', DB *Edstan*. The DB *Æstanus, Estan* may represent either name. (ii) Very often, this surname is local in origin, from one of the numerous places named Aston. cf. Richard *de Aston'* 1206 Cur (Gl). (iii) William *Stone, Astone* 1494, 1500 WBCinque; Thomas *A Stone* 1525 SRSx; Thomas *A Stone*, John *a stone* 1569 Musters (Sr). This is probably for *atte stone* 'dweller by the stone', cf. AMOORE, AVANN, AGATE.

Atack: *v.* ATTACK

Atberry: John *Ateburi* 1279 (O); Hugh *ate Bery* 1327 SRC. 'Dweller or servant at the manor-house' (OE *burh*).

Atcheson, Atchison: *v.* ACHESON

Atcock: *v.* ADCOCK

Atfield, Attfield: Stephen *Attefeld* 1262 FFEss. 'Dweller by the open field' (OE *feld*).

Atheis: Thomas *atte Heye* 1327 SRSo. 'Dweller at the enclosures', containing the plural of OE *(ge)hæg*.

Athell: *v.* ATHILL

Athelstan, Addlestone, Edleston: *Adelstanus* 1195 P (K); Hugo *filius Athelstan, Adelstan'* 1218, 1219 AssL; Herbertus *filius Edelstani* 1240 Rams (Nf); William *Athelston* c1198 Bart (Lo); Geoffrey *Athelstan* 1219 AssL. OE *Æðelstān* 'noble stone'. *v.* ALLSTON and ASTON.

Atherden: William *ater Dene*, Peter *in ther Dene* 1296 SRX; William *Atherdonne*, Ruben *Atherton* 1568 SRSf. 'Dweller in the valley', OE *denu*.

Atherfold: cf. John *atte Fold* 1327 SRWo. 'Dweller or worker at the fold', preserving the variant ME *at ther folde*.

Atherley: Alfeg' *ater Legh* 1296 SRSx; John *Atherlee* 1419 LLB I. A variant of ATLAY.

Athersmith: John *atter Smythe* (1330 PN D 386) lived at the smithy (OE *smiþþe*) and was presumably a blacksmith. The surname might also derive from ME *at ther smethe* 'dweller at the smooth, level place' (OE *smēðe*). cf. William *del Smethe* 1327 SRSf.

Atherstone: Adam *de Atherston'* 1275 SRWo. From Atherstone (Warwicks).

Athersuch, Athersych, Athersytch: The obvious derivation of the last two names would be from ME *at ther siche* 'dweller by the brook or drain'. As *Athersytch* is found in Sheffield, where *siche* occurs as *Sykes*, all the names are probably dialectal pronunciations of *Hathersage*, a Derbyshire village some ten miles distant. cf. HATHERSICH.

Atherton: Henry *de Athertone* 1332 SRLa; William *de Atherton* 1384 IpmLa; Humphrey *Addertone* alias *Athurton* 1470 Combermere (Ch). From Atherton (Lancs), *Aderton* 1212.

Athey, Athy: Lecia *Ateheye* 1279 RH (C). 'Dweller at the enclosure', OE *(ge)hæg*.

Athill, Atthill, Athell: Richard *Athill* 1255 RH (Sa); Ralph *atte Helle* 1319 *SR* (Ess). 'Dweller by the hill', OE *hyll*.

Athoke: John *atte Hok* 1254 *Ass* (Ess). 'Dweller by the bend', OE *hōc* 'hook'.

Athol, Atholl: Robert *atte Hole* 1296 SRSx. 'Dweller in the hollow', OE *holh*. The Scottish *Atholl* derives from Atholl in Perthshire.

Athorn, Athorne: William *atte Horne* 1332 SRSx. 'Dweller by the spit of land', OE *horn*. Or 'dweller by the thorn-bush': Emma *Attethorn*' 1297 MinAcctCo.

Athowe, Atthowe: John *ate How* 1296 SRSx. 'Dweller by the ridge', OE *hōh*. *v.* HOW.

Athridge: *v.* ETHEREDGE

Athy: *v.* ATHEY

Atkey: William *atte Keye* 1370 LoPleas. 'Dweller or worker at the quay'. *v.* KAY.

Atkin, Atkins, Atkyns: *v.* ADKIN

Atkinson, Ackenson: John *Adkynsone* 1381 SRSt; John *Atkinson* 1402 FA (We). 'Son of *Adkin*.'

Atlay, Atlee, Atley, Attle, Attlee: Robert *Atte lee* 1275 SRWo; John *Attele* 1276 RH (Berks); William *atte Leye* 1296 SRSx; Thomas *Attlee* 1327 Pinchbeck (Sf). 'Dweller by the wood or clearing', OE *lēah*. cf. ATHERLEY.

Atmeare, Atmer, Attmere: Cecil' *Atemer*' 1279 RH (C); John *Atmer* 1524 SRSf; Edmund *Attmear* 1568 SRSf. 'Dweller by the mere or pool' (OE *mere*) or near the boundary (OE *(ge)mǣre*).

Atmore: Jordan *Attemore* 1276 LLB A. 'Dweller near the marsh', OE *mōr*.

Atread, Attread, Attreed: Robert *atte Reed* c1295 MELS (Sx). 'Dweller in a clearing.' *v.* READ.

Atrill: *v.* ATTRILL

Attack, Attoc, Attock, Atack: Geoffrey *atte Ock* 1296 SRSx; Thomas *Atack* 1709 Bardsley. 'Dweller by the oak' (OE *āc*).

Attale: Robert *Attehal*' 1212 Cur (L); William *atte Hale* 1235 *Ass* (Ess). 'Dweller by a nook or in a remote valley' in the South and Midlands, or by flat, alluvial land near a river in the North (OE *healh*). *v.* HALE.

Attaway: John *ate Wey* 1279 RH (C). 'Dweller by the road' (OE *weg*) or at a place called *Atteweye*, the name in 1306 of Way in Thorverton (Devon), or at Attway (Devon). *v.* PN D 573, 468.

Attawell: *v.* ATTWELL

Attenbarrow, Attenborough, Attenborrow, Attenbrough, Attenbrow, Attenburrow: These surnames can hardly derive from Attenborough (Notts), earlier *Adinburcha*, which was not a village in the Middle Ages, the name being that of a church only. They are probably all from ME *atten* plus the dative of OE *bearu* 'a grove' or *beorg* 'hill, mound'. The second element was, as often, changed to *borough* through association with *burh*. Hence 'dweller by the grove, hill or mound'.

Atter: Edguinus *atre*, Edwin *Atter* 1111, c1130 ELPN. A nickname from OE *ātor*, ME *atter* 'poison, venom; gall, bitterness'.

Atteridge: John *atte Rygge* 1333 PN D 567. 'Dweller by the ridge', OE *hrycg*. *v.* also MELS 173 and ETHEREDGE.

Atterwill: For ME *at ther wille* 'dweller by the spring or stream'. cf. John *ater Welle* 1296 SRSx. *Will* is a south-western form of *well*. *v.* ATTWELL.

Attewell, Attewill, Attiwill: *v.* ATTWELL

Attick: *v.* ATTWICK

Attle, Attlee: *v.* ATLAY

Atto, Attoe: Roger *Atteho* 1236 FFSx. 'Dweller at the ridge', OE *hōh*. *v.* HOW.

Attoc, Attock: *v.* ATTACK

Attom: Adam *de la Homme* 1275 SRWo. 'Dweller by the water-meadow.' *v.* HAM.

Attree, Attrie, Attrey: Thomas *Attere* 1272 PN C 15; Walter *at Reghe* 1287 PN Sr 330; Thomas *Atry* 1320 FFHu; Matthew *atte Ry* 1389 PN Ess 387; Richard *Atre* 1545 SxWills. 'Dweller by the stream (OE *ēa*) or low-lying land (OE *ēg*).' *v.* REA. Also 'dweller by the enclosure' (OE *(ge)hæg*), Simon *ater Hegh* 1296 SRSx; or 'by the tree' (OE *trēo*), John *A'Tree* 1558 SxWills. *v.* TREE.

Attrell: *v.* ATTRILL

Attride, Attryde: John *at Ride* (1446) and Henry *at Ryde* (1524) took their name from a clearing (OE **rīed, *rȳd*), but Thomas *at Ride* (1524) and John *Attryde* (1588) owed theirs to a streamlet (OE *rīþ, rīðe*). *v.* PN Sr 242, 148.

Attridge: *v.* ETHEREDGE

Attrill, Attrell, Atrill: Walter *atter Hille* 1330 PN D 477; John *at Ryll* 1524 ib. 562. 'Dweller by the hill', a not uncommon Devon development, surviving in place-names as both Rill and Rull.

Attru: Hugo *de la Truwe* 1250 Fees (So); Agnes *atte Trewe* 1333 PN D 595. 'Dweller by the tree', OE *trēow*. *v.* TRUE. Also from OE *rǣw* 'row, hedgerow', used also of a row of houses, a street or hamlet: Maurice *atte Rewe* 1333 PN D 464.

Attryde: *v.* ATTRIDE

Attwater, Atwater: William *Atewatr*' 1198 CurR (Herts); Marye *Atwaters* 1660 ArchC xxx. 'Dweller by the water', OE *wæter*.

Attwell, Attwill, Attwool, Attwooll, Atwell, Atwill, Atwool, Attawell, Attewell, Attewill, Attiwill: Gilbert *Attewell* 1274 RH (Ess); Richard *atte Wille* 1333 PN D 450. 'Dweller by the stream or spring', OE *wiella*. *Atwill* is a Devon and Somerset form, *Attwool* a Dorset one. *v.* WOOLL.

Attwick, Attick: Walter *ate Wyk* 1327 SRSx. 'Dweller or worker at the dairy-farm', OE *wīc*. *Attwick* still survives in Sussex.

Attwood, Atwood: Thomas *Attewode* 1243 AssSo; Robert *Atwode* 1457 Oseney (O). 'Dweller by the wood', OE *wudu*.

Atty: John *atte Tye* 1327 *SR* (Ess); Thomas *Attye* 1568 SRSf. 'Dweller by the enclosure, close or common pasture', OE *tēag*. Also from OE *(ge)hæg* 'enclosure': Geoffrey *Atteheg* 1327 SRDb.

Atyeo: Roger *atte Yo* 1333 PN D 263. 'Dweller by the river.' *v.* YEA.

Aubert: *v.* ALBERT

Aubin: *v.* ALBIN

Aubon: *v.* ALBAN

Aubray, Aubrey, Aubry, Aubery, Aubury, Awbery, Obray: (i) Walterus *filius Alberici, Albrici, Alberi* 1086 DB (Sf); *Albricus* de Capella 1214 Cur (C); *Aubri* Bunt 1279 RH (C); John *Aubri* ib.; Robert *Aubri* 1308 FFSf; Adam *Albry* 1327 SRSf; Geoffrey *Aubry* 1380 AssC. OFr *Aubri, Auberi*, OG *Albericus* 'elf-ruler'. (ii) Osbertus *filius Alberade* 1115 Winton (Ha); *Albreda* 1198 Cur (Herts), 1205 Cur (Wa); Ricardus *filius Albrei* 1199 FrLeic; *Aubreda* 1219 AssY; *Albreda, Albree* de Jarpenvill' 1221 Cur (Bk); Johannes *filius Aubre* 1279 RH (O); *Albray, Aubray* 1379 PTY; John *Albre* 1243 AssSo; Robert *Aubrey* 1279 RH (Bk); William *Aubray* 1324 Wak (Y); John *Aubery, Awberry, Aubry* 1460 Bardsley (Nf). OFr *Albree, Aubree, Auberee*, OG *Alb(e)rada* 'elf-counsel' (f).

Aucock: *v.* ALCOCK

Aucott, Aucutt: *v.* ALCOTT

Audas, Audiss: *v.* ALDIS

Auden: *v.* ALDEN

Audrey, Awdrey, Awdry: *Aldreda* 1066 DB (Nf), 1219 AssY; Robert *Audrey* 1279 RH (O). The DB personal-name may be for OE *Ælfðrȳð, Æðelðrȳð* or *Ealhðrȳð*, all feminine. Of these the most common was the second, 'noble strength', popular through the reputation of St Etheldreda, Queen of Northumbria and foundress of the convent at Ely. This became *Audrey* and is found in the 14th century in Essex and Suffolk as *Etheldreda* (1304 AD i (Ess), 1381 SRSf).

Audritt: *v.* ALDRED

Audus: *v.* ALDIS

Augar, Auger, Augur: *v.* ALGAR, ALGER

Augood: *v.* ALLGOOD

Augustin: *Augustinus* cantor 1153–68 Holme (Nf); Nicholas *Augustin* 1275 SRWo. Lat *Augustinus*, from *augustus* 'venerable'. The christian name is very common, usually in the Latin form, but as a surname is rare, both in ME and today. The medieval surname is common in the vernacular form *Austin. v.* AUSTEN.

Auker: *v.* ALKER

Aukin: *v.* ALKIN

Auld, Aulds, Ault, Awde: John *Alde* 1284 Black (Perth); Johannes *dictus Ald* 1302 ib.; John *Auld* 1488 ib. A Scottish form of OLD, from Northern English *ald*.

Aungier(s): *v.* ANGER, ANGERS

Austen, Austin, Austing, Austins, Auston: *Austinus* de Bernardeston 1224 FFSf; *Austinus* de Beston' 1230 P (Nf); *Ostin* atte Putte 1327 SRSo; Henry *Austin*, Edith *Austines* 1275 SRWo; Avice *Augstyn* (*Austynes*) 1327 SR (Ess). OFr *Aoustin*, the vernacular form of *Augustine. v.* AUGUSTIN.

Autie, Auty, Awty, Alty: *Auti, Alti, Outi* 1066 DB; *Outi* de Lincol' 1166 P (Nf); Walterus *filius Aulti* 1177 P (L); Willelmus *filius Auti* 1200 P (Y); John *Oty* 1251 Rams (Hu); John *Awty* 1524 AD vi (Sf). ODa *Auti*.

Avann: John *Avanne* 1527 SxWills. 'Dweller by the fen.' *v.* FANN.

Avel: *Auel* de Wappeham 1176 P (Nth); Peter *Auel* 1296 SRSx. A diminutive of OG *Avo*.

Aveline, Aveling: *Auelina* 1175–86 Holme (Nf), 1327 SRC; Henry *Avelin* 1279 RH (C); Reginald *Auelyn* 1296 SRSx. OFr *Aveline*, OG *Avelina* (f), a double diminutive of OG *Avo*.

Avenall, Avenel, Avenell: *Avenel* 1086 DB (Sa), 1166 RBE (Ess); *Auenellus* 1190 P (Y), 1196 Eynsham (O); Robert, Paganus *Auenel* 1139 Templars (O), 1195 P (He). A double diminutive of OG *Avo*. Both christian name and surname are common.

Avent: *Avenant* de Twipp' 1204 Cur (D); Osbert, Ralph *Auenant* 1156–80 Bury (Sf), 1198 FFNf. OFr *auenant*, pres. part. of *avenir* 'to arrive, happen, befit, become'; 'suitable' (1300 NED), 'handsome, comely' (1340). Used also as a personal-name.

Averay, Avery, Avory, Averies: Rogerus *filius Alvredi* 1166 RBE (Y); Hugo *filius Auveray* 1275 RH (Nt); Willelmus *filius Averay* 1275 SRWo; *Alvrei* venator 1294 Ch (Y); Nicholas *Auverey* 1273 RH (Wo); William *Auure* 1275 RH (W); Walter *Averay* 1275 SRWo; Cust *Alvere* 1279 RH (C); Edmund *Avered* 1279 RH (C); Walter *Averey* 1279 RH (O); Richard *Avore* 1428 FA (Sx). A French pronunciation of ALFRED.

Averill: *v.* APRIL

Aves, Aveson: Willelmus *filius Aue* 1198 FFNf; Elizabethe *Aves* 1568 SRSf. OG *Avo*.

Aveston: William *de Alueston* 1190 P (Wa). From Alveston (Glos, Warwicks).

Avins: *Avina* 1221 Cur (Nt); *Avin'* de Eyton' 1255 RH (Sa). *Avina*, wife of Robert de Turuill' (1221 AssGl) was also called *Auicia*. *Avina* is therefore probably a hypocoristic of *Avis*.

Avis, Aviss, Avison: *Auicia* c1175–86 Holme (Nf), 12th DC (Nt), 1199 FFEss; *Auizia* Hy 2 DC (Lei); Ricardus *filius Avice* 1332 SRSt; Walter *Auices* 1186–1210 Holme (Nf); Thomas *Avyce* 1220 Fees (Berks); Thomas *Avis* 1524 SRSf; Ralph *Avyson* 1674 FrY. OFr *Avice*, sometimes derived from OG *Aveza* but Michaëlsson (ii. 79–82) has shown that it probably derives from Lat *Avitia* which, with the masculine *Avitius*, was used in Gaul. cf. *Amis* s.n. AMES.

Avner: Roger, Alexander *le Avener* 1230 P (Ha), 1231 Pat (Lo). OFr *avenier, avener* 'oat-merchant'. Used also of the chief officer of the stable who had charge of the provender for the horses (1282 NED).

Avril: *v.* APRIL

Awbery: *v.* AUBRAY

Awcock: *v.* ALCOCK

Awdas: *v.* ALDIS

Awde: *v.* AULD

Awdrey, Awdry: *v.* AUDREY

Awmack: *v.* ALLMARK

Awty: *v.* AUTIE

Axbey: *Aksby*, a metathesized form of *Askby* from some place Ashby. Castle Ashby (Northants) is *Axeby* in 1235 (PN Nth 142).

Axcell, Axel, Axell: Probably metathesized

forms of *Askell* through the series *Askell, Aksell, Axell*. cf. AXTELL.

Axleby, Exelby, Eshelby, Hasselby: John *de Eskelby* 1327 SRY; Richard *Exilby* 1490 FrY; Thomas *Eshleby* 1672 FrY. From Exelby (NR Yorks), a metathesized form of *Eskelby*. A similar metathesis of the DB *Aschilebi* would become *Axleby*. Both surnames might also derive from Asselby (ERYorks) which is found as *Askelby* 1282, *Eskilby* 1199 and *Axilbye* 1551. *v.* PN ERY 248, PN NRY 226.

Axon: Thomas *Acson* 1561, Thomas *Axon* 1635, John *Ackson* 1641 Bardsley (Ch). This might be 'son of *Acke*', OE *Acca*. But forms are late and we may equally well have a metathesis of *Askin*, giving *Aksin, Akson. v.* also AXTEN.

Axtell: Elizabeth *Axtell*, John *Axstell*, Richard *Axtill* 1683–90 Bardsley. These forms, though late, are almost certainly from ON *Ásketill*, with loss of the unstressed medial vowel to *Asktill*, and metathesis to *Akstill, Akstell. v.* ASHKETTLE.

Axten, Axtens, Axton: Agnes *Axton* 1524 SRSf, Laurence *Axton, Axon* 1561 Bardsley. It is impossible to decide whether *Axton* is from *Axon* (a metathesis of *Askin*), with intrusive t, or whether *Axon* is a simplified form of *Axton*. An original *Axton* would be a metathesized form of *Ashton*. The Northants Ashton is *Axton* in 1253 (PN Nth 229).

Ayer, Ayers, Ayr, Ayre, Ayres, Ayris, Aiers, Air, Aires, Airs, Aers, Eayrs, Eayres, Eyer, Eyers, Eyre, Eyres, Hair, Haire, Hayer, Heyer, Hoyer: (i) Ralph *le Eir* 1208 FFEss; Robertus *Heres* 1220 Cur (C); Robert *leyre* 1245 FFC; Richard *le Heyer* 1274 RH (Gl); Henry *Ayer, le Eyer* 1275 RH (L, O); Adam *le Hayre* 1275 Wak (Y); Robert *le Heir* 1281 Eynsham (O); Robert *Air* 1281, John *Ayr* 1296 Black; William *Hoyre* 1302 SRSf; Francis *Eyre* alias *Eare* alias *Aire* 1724 DKR 41 (Co). ME *eir, eyr*, etc., OFr *eir, heir*, CentFr *oir, hoir*, AFr *heyr*, Lat *heres* 'heir' (c1275 NED). *leyre* is one source of LAYER. (ii) Occasionally we may have a personal name: Robertus *filius Aier* 1166 RBE, *filius Aer, Aier* 1180, 1196 P (Sa), the latter being identical with Robert *Aier* 1201 P (Sa). cf. Aston Eyre (Salop), held in 1212 by Robert, grandson of *Aer*, a name which Ekwall suggests may be derived from that of the DB tenant *Alcher*, i.e. OE *Ealhhere. v.* ALGER. *v.* also HAIR. (iii) Reginald *of Ayr* 1287 Black (Ayr); Albinus *de Are* 1315–21 ib. From the royal burgh of Ayr.

Aykroyd: *v.* ACKROYD

Aylard: *v.* ADLARD

Aylen: *v.* AYLING

Ayler: Luke *le Ayler, le Ayeler* 'peverer' (i.e. 'pepperer') 1287, 1304 LLB B. OFr *aillier, -iere* 'garlic-seller'.

Aylett, Aylott, Allatt, Allett, Allitt, Alliott, Ellyatt, Eliot: Galfridus *filius Ailghieti* a1176 Colch (Ess); *Ailletus* 1180–1207 Rams (Nf); Simon *filius Alet* 1199 P (L); *Ailleth, Ailed* (f) 1198 FF (Nf); *Æliot* Grim 1202 AssL; *Ailhiet* (f) 1202 FF (Nf); Gilebertus *filius Aillith* 1204 P (C); *Ailith*,

Ailleth filia Godwini 1207 Cur (Sf); *Alettus* Prepositus 1212 Cur (Nth); Simon *filius Aileda* 1279 RH (C); *Alyott* de Symondston 1311 Lacy (La); Boydin *Ailet* 1212 Fees (Ess); Walter *Aliot, Aylet*, Thomas *Ailot*, John *Ayllyth* 1279 RH (C); Ralph *Alyet* 1286 Pinchbeck (Sf). In DB *Ailiet* and *Aliet* are found for both the common OE *Æðelgȳð* (f) 'noble combat' and OE **Æðelgēat* (m) 'noble Geat', which is not recorded before the Conquest but was certainly in use later, and it is impossible to distinguish between them when the sex of the bearer is unknown. The confusion is increased by the variety of forms found for both themes of each name, but it is clear that all the above surnames may derive from either of these personal names. In DB *Æðelgȳð* is *Adelid, Ailiet, Ailith, Ailid, Ailad, Alith,* and *Alid*, all except the first referring to *Æðelgȳð* wife of Þurstan. *Æðelgēat* is found as *Ailiet, Ailet, Ælget, Aliet, Elget* and *Eliet*, all of which might stand for *Æðelgȳð* where the gender is doubtful. The last two forms make it clear that these OE names have contributed to the frequency of ELIOT in its various spellings. *v.* ADLARD.

Ayliff, Ayliffe, Ayloff, Ellif: (i) *Ailef* de Palestun 1175 P (Nb); Willelmus *filius Eilaf* 1191 P (Nth); Robertus *filius Egelof* 1196 P (L); *Egelaf* 12th MedEA (Sf); Ricardus *filius Ailof* 1203 Cur (Nth); Nicholas *Eiluf, Ailof* 1221 AssWa; Julian' *Aylif* 1279 RH (O); Geoffrey *Ayllef*, John *Aylofh* 1327 SRSf. The DB *Eilaf* (*Egilaf, Ailaf* Exon), *Ailof, Elaf* are probably from ODa, OSw *Elaf* (hence *Ayloffe*), but they may also represent ON *Eileifr*, ODa, OSw *Elef* or ON *Eilifr*, ODa, OSw *Elif* with substitution of OE or EScand *-lāf* for *-lef, -lif* (hence *Ayliff, Ellif*). *v.* also ILIFF. (ii) *Eilieua* de Kerletona Hy 2 DC (Lei); Edwardus *filius Eileve* 1206 Cur (Sx); Rogerus *filius Aelive* 1214 Cur (C); Segarus *filius Aileves* 1188 BuryS (Sf); Robert *Aylgive* 1275 SRWo; Edelina *Ayleve* 1279 RH (Hu). OE *Æðelgifu* (f) 'noble gift', which appears in DB as *Æileua, Eileua, Aileua* and *Eleua*. For *-iff* from *-gifu*, cf. BRIGHTIFF, here, perhaps, influenced also by *Ailiff*. Ayloffe can only be included here by assuming influence from the Scandinavian name. cf. Richard *Aylyaue* 1332 SRWa.

Ayling, Aylin, Aylen: Eadmund *Æðeling* 1006 KCD 1302 (Do); Æðwardus *Aðeling* 1176 P (K); Gilbert *Ædeling* 1177 P (Y); Reginald *Aylyng* 1296 SRSx. OE *æðeling* 'noble, prince of the royal blood', used occasionally as a personal-name: *Ailligg'* (*Eiling*) buttarius 1230 P (Nf). Edgarus *Adeling* 1086 DB (Herts) is also called Eadgar *Cild. v.* CHILD.

Aylmer, Aylmore, Elmar, Elmer, Elmers: *Ailmar Æilmar, Eilmerus, Aimar, Almer, Elmar, Elmer* 1066 DB; Godwinus filius *Elmari* 1115 Winton (Ha); *Hælmerus* Hy 2 DC (L); *Ailmerus* le Bercher 1212 Cur (Herts), quidam *Ailmerus* villanus ib. (Y); Henry *Ailmer'* 1208 Cur (Berks); Roger *Ailmar* 1221 AssWa; William *Elmer* 1316 FA (Sx). OE *Æðelmær* 'noble famous'. *Elmer* is also local in origin. *v.* also AYMER.

Aylward, Ailward: Godric *filius Æilwardi*

c1095 Bury (Sf); *Egelwardus* 1126-7 Holme (Nf); *Ailwardus* presbiter 1153-68 ib.; Robert *Ailward'* 1201 P (Ha); Robertus *Ailwardi* 1229 Cl (Gl); Nicholas *Eylward* 1243 AssSo. OE *Æðelweard* 'noble protector', DB. *Aegelward, Ailuuard*. *v*. also ALLWARD.

Aylwin, Aylwen, Ailwyn: *Adelwinus, Ailwinus, Aluuin(e), Eluuinus* 1066 DB; *Ailwinus* Neht Hy 2 DC (L); *Eilwinus* de la Berne 1211 Cur (Sr); Hubert *egelwin* 1194 Cur (Bk); Walter *Athelwin* 1205 P (Gl); Simon *Aylwyn* 1230 P (Beds); Alice *Eylwyn* 1297 MinAcctCo. OE *Æðelwine* 'noble friend'. *v*. also ALWIN, ALVEN.

Aymer, Aimer, Aimers, Amar: *Eymer* Thurberd 1260 AssC; *Aymar* de Valence 1298 Gascon; Philip *Aimer* 1180 P (Ess). In DB *Aimar* is one of the forms for OE *Æðelmǣr*. *v*. AYLMER. Here we have also a continental personal-name either OG *Agimar* or OG *Hadamar, Adamar*.

Aynsley: *v*. AINSLEY
Ayre(s): *v*. AYER
Ayscough: *v*. ASKEW
Aysh: *v*. ASH
Ayshford: *v*. ASHFORD
Ayton, Aytoun, Aiton: (i) Helias *de eitun* c1166 Black (Dunbar); William *de Eytone* 1296 ib. (Berwick); John *de Aytoun* 1300 ib. From the lands of Ayton in Berwick. (ii) William *de Atune* c1174 YCh; John *de Aiton'* 1219 AssY; John *de Ayton'* 1300 FFY. From Ayton (NRYorks), *Aton* DB. *v*. also EYTON.

Aze: *v*. ACE

B

Babb, Babbs: Alwinus, Richard *Babbe* 1198 FF (Sf), 1230 P (D); Ralph, Walter *le Babb(e)* 1199 MemR (W), 1327 SRSx. A pet-form of *Barbara*. cf. Margery *Babel*, Nicholas *Babelot* 1279 RH (C) and BABOT. *le Babbe* is a nickname from *babe* (c1230 MED) 'infant, young child'.

Babot: Geoffrey *Babeth* 1279 RH(C). A diminutive of *Bab* (Barbara).

Baccas, Bacchus: *v.* BACKHOUSE

Bach, Bache, Batch: Reiner *de Bache* 1212 Cur (L); Ralph *de la Bache* 1252 Rydware (St); William *atte Bache* 1327 SRWo. 'Dweller near a stream', OE *bæce*. *v.* BASH.

Bachelor, Bachellier, Batchelar, Batcheler, Batchellor, Batchelor, Batchelour, Batchlor, Batchelder, Batcheldor: Roger *Bachelere* c1165 StCh; Stephen *le bachilier* 1203 FFSf; Walter *le Bachelor* 1248 FFSf; Thomas *Batcheller*, Widow *Bachelder* 1674 HTSf. ME, OFr *bacheler* 'a young knight, a novice in arms' (1297 NED). *v.* also BACKLER.

Bacher: Philip *Bacher* 1255 RH (Bk); William *le Bachiere* 1280 MESO (Ha). 'Dweller by a stream.' cf. BACH.

Bachus: *v.* BACKHOUSE

Back, Backes, Bax: Godwine *Bace* c1055 OEByn (So); Godwin the clerk, called *Bak* 12th ELPN; Richard *Bac* 1182 P (Co); Richard *Backe* 1277 *Ely* (Sf); Henry *le Bak* 1297 Coram (K). Tengvik explains the OE example as from OE *Bacca* or as a nickname from OE *bæc*, in the sense of one with a prominent chin or back or one of a fat, rotund appearance. Ekwall takes the London example as perhaps from OE *bæc* 'back'. We may have a personal-name. OE *Bacca* was in use in Suffolk after the Conquest (*Baccce* (dat.) c1189–1200 BuryS). The nickname is probably, as suggested by Weekley, ME *bakke* 'a bat', either 'blind as a bat' or with reference to their nocturnal habits; retiring by day to dark recesses, 'they hate the day and love the night'. Also local: Joan *atte Back* 1327 SRSo, 'dweller by the ridge' (OE *bæc*).

Backer: *v.* BAKER

Backhouse, Baccas, Bacchus, Bachus, Backus: Walter *de Bakhous* 1306 LLB E; Richard *del Bakhous* 1332 SRLa; Thomas *Bachous* 1334 LLB E; Charles *Baccus* 1544 AD v (Y); Edward *Bacchus* 1725 DKR 41 (Beds). 'One employed at a bakery', from OE **bæchūs* 'bakery, bakehouse' (a1300 MED).

Backler: John *de* (sic) *Bakalur* 1196 Cur (D); Nicholas *le Bakelere* 1320 Cl (Sa); Edmund *Bacler* 1524 SRSf. Identical with *Bachelor*, with dissimilation of *chl* to *kl*.

Backman: Walter *Bakman* 1279 RH (C); John *Bakeman* 1327 *SR* (Ess). OE *(ge)bæc* 'bakemeats', and *mann*, a maker or seller of pastries, pies, etc. cf. Walter *le Bakmonger* 1314 MEOT (Herts).

Backner: *v.* BACON

Backshall, Backshaw, Backshell: Philip *de Bacselve* 1296 SRSx; John *Bakshelue* 1327 ib.; Henry *Backshyll* 1525 ib.; John *Backshell*, Mary *Backshall* 1591, 1713 Sx Rec. Soc. ix. These are probably forms of Backshells in Billingshurst (Sussex). For the development of the forms with *-shall* and *-shaw*, cf. Gomshall (Surrey), *Gomeselve* 1154, *Gunshal* 1675, and Bashall Eaves in Great Mitton (WRYorks), *Bacscshelf* DB, *Basshall* 1562, *Bashawe* 1591.

Bacon, Bakon: William, Richard *Bacun* c1150 StCh, DC (L); Nicholas *Bachun* 1226 Burton (St); Geoffrey *Bacon* 1296 SRSx. OFr, ME *bacon*, *bacun* 'buttock, ham, side of bacon' is not recorded in England before c1330 (MED), though it may well be older. It refers usually to the cured flesh, occasionally to fresh pork, but is seldom used of the live pig. Hence a nickname must be metonymic and refer to a pork-butcher, as does the Fr *Baconnier* and probably the English *Backner*, though no early forms have been found. The surname is common and early, used of Norman knights, and is probably the accusative of OG *Bacco*, the nominative of which occurs as *Bacus* c1113 Burton (St).

Badams, Baddams, Badham: *v.* ABADAM

Badcock, Batcock: *Batecok* 1288 AssCh; *Badekoc* Korneys 1296 SRSx; Edrich' *Bathecoc* 1221 AssWo; Richard *Batcok* 1285 AssCh; William *Badecok* 1297 MinAcctCo (Do), 1327 SRDb. Both names are usually explained as a compound of *Bat(e)*, a pet-name for *Bartholomew*, and *cock*, but as both occur frequently side by side, the *d* of *Badecok* may well be original. In 'de catellis *Badde*' (1230 P) we have probably a survival of OE *Bada* (cf. BADE) which may also be the source of the surnames of William *Badde* 1221 AssWo and John *Badde, Bade* 1317 AssK. Though the forms are late, OE *Baduca* probably survives in *Baddock*, whilst an unrecorded OE **Badding* occurs as a surname in Robert *Badding* 1197–1221

AD i (Mx) and William *Bading* 1275 SRWo. A formation *Badecoc* is, therefore, not impossible.

Badcoe: Probably for *Badcock*. cf. ALCOE.

Badder: *v.* BATHA

Baddick, Baddock, Badock: William *Baddoke* 1534 FrY. OE *Baduca*. *v.* BADCOCK.

Bade: *Bado* 1066 DB (Db); Bictricus *Bade* 1066 Winton (Ha). OE *Bada*. cf. BADCOCK.

Badger, Badgers, Bagger: (i) Ivo, Richard *le Bagger* 1246 AssLa, 1297 Wak (Y); Adam *Badger* 1324 Wak (Y); Ralph *Baghere* 1348 DbAS 36. The interpretation of *Bagger* is uncertain. It may stand for *Bagger* or *Badger*. The former would be a derivative of ME *bagge* 'bag, small sack', hence *bagger* 'a maker of bags'. *Badger*, not recorded before 1467–8 in MED and of doubtful origin, means 'a hawker, huckster'. Fransson's arguments in favour of a change in pronunciation from *bagger* to *badger*, partly on the grounds that there is no modern surname *Bagger*, cannot be accepted. Though very rare, *Bagger* is still found in Sevenoaks. As often, the metonymic *Bagg(s)* is more common. (ii) William *de Beggeshour'* 1221 AssSa. From Badger (Salop).

Badham: *v.* ABADAM

Badman: Simon, John *Bademan* 1279 RH (C), 1375 LoPleas. OE **Beadumann*, a late compound of the common theme *Beadu-* and *-mann*.

Badock: *v.* BADDICK

Badrick, Badrock, Batrick, Battrick, Betteridge, Bettridge, Betteriss: Robert *Baderich'* 1275 SRWo; William *Betrich* 1279 RH (C); John *Betryche, Betrich* 1296, 1327 SRSx. OE *Beaduric* 'battlepowerful', a personal name found in Battersea (Surrey) and Bethersden (Kent), but very rare in independent use.

Bagehot: *v.* BAGGETT

Bagenal: *v.* BAGNALL

Bagg, Bagge, Baggs: William, Nicholas *Bagge* 1166 P (Nf), 1214 Cur (Wa). Although no examples of its independent use have been noted, this may be the cas-sujet of OG *Bago* (*Baco*) surviving in the French *Bague* with its diminutive *Baguelin, Baglin*, which is found also in England: William *Bagelin* 1327 SRSo. *v.* also BAGGETT. The surname was common in ME and may also be metonymic for *Bagger*, 'a maker of bags', from ME *bagge* 'bag, pack, bundle'. It might also have been used for a beggar. cf. 'Hit is beggares rihte uorte beren bagge on bac & burgeises for to beren purses' (c1230 NED).

Baggallay, Baggalley, Baggally, Baggarley: *v.* BAGLEY

Bagger: *v.* BADGER

Baggett, Baggott, Bagot, Bagott, Bagehot: (i) *Bagot* c1125 StCh; Herueius *filius Bagot* 1130–2 Seals (St); Hereveus *Bagod* c1159 StCh; Ingeram *Bagot* Hy 2 DC (L); Hereficus *Bachot* 1195 Cur (Wa); Simon *Baghot* 1198 FFSt; Walter *Bagot* 1201 Cur (Y). A diminutive of OG *Bago*. cf. BAGG. (ii) Robert *Baggard* 1191 P (Sf); Geoffrey, Richard *Bagard* 1275 SRWo, 1279 AssSo. OG *Bago* plus the suffix *-(h)ard*.

Bagley, Baguley, Baggallay, Baggalley, Baggally, Baggarley, Bagguley: Peter *de Baggeleg'* 1260 AssCh; Thomas *de Baggeleghe* 1327 SRSo; Walthev *de Baglay* c1345 Calv; John *Baguley* 1527 CorNt. From Bagley (Bucks, Salop, Som, WRYorks), or Baguley (Ches).

Bagnall, Bagnell, Bagnold, Bagenal: William *de Bagenholt* 1299 AssSt; John *Bagenelle* 1379 LLB H; Ralph *Bagnall, Bagnold, Bagenall* alias *Bagnald* 1561 Pat. From Bagnall (Staffs).

Bagster: *v.* BAXTER

Baiker: *v.* BAKER

Bail, Baile, Bailes, Bails, Bale, Bales, Bayles: Richard *del Baille* c1190 Bart (Lo); Eudo *del Bayle* 1301 SRY; John *Bayl* 1382 FFSx; Thomas *Bale* 1524 SRSf; William *a Bales* 1537 FFHu; Zacarias *Bailes* 1629 FrY. OFr, ME *bail(e)* 'the wall of the outer court of a feudal castle', later used of the courts themselves (a1200 MED). The surname is probably identical with *Bailward*, 'the guardian of the courts or bailey'. The London examples refer to the Old Bailey.

Baileff, Bailiff, Bayliff, Bayliffe, Baylyff: Richard *le Baillif* 1242 Fees (He); Gilbert *le Balif* 1280 AssSo; John *Bayllif, Baylly* 1296 SRSx. OFr *bailif*, cas-régime of *baillis*, originally 'carrier', later 'manager, administrator'. Used of the public administrator of a district, the chief officer of a Hundred (1297 NED) or of an officer of justice under a sheriff, a warrant officer, pursuivant, a catchpoll (1377 NED). This form of the name is much less common than *Bailey*. *v.* BAYLIS.

Bailess: *v.* BAYLIS

Bailey, Bailie, Baillie, Baily, Baly, Baylay, Bayley, Baylie, Bayly: (i) Roger *le baylly* 1230 P (Sf); John *Baly* 1274 Wak (Y); Thomas *le Baly* 1327 SRSx; Thomas *Bailie* 1327 SRSf. OFr *bailli*, a later form of *baillis, baillif*. *v.* BAILEFF. The term *baillie*, now obsolete in England, is still the common form in Scotland, where it was used of the chief magistrate of a barony or part of a county, a sheriff. (ii) John *ate Baylie* 1317 AssK. A ME variant of *bayle* (a1200 MED). *v.* BAIL. Dyonisya *en la baillye* owned houses and shops in the Old Bailey, London (1319 SRLo). The earliest examples of the Scottish *Baillie*, William *de Bailli* 1311–12 (Black), seem to belong here rather than to the noun above. (iii) Ralph *de Baylegh* 1246 AssLa. From Bailey (Lancs).

Bailhache: *Baylehache* marescallus 1154 EngFeud (Sf); John *Baillehache* 1418 DKR 41. OFr *baille hache* 'give axe', a name for an executioner.

Bailward: *v.* BAIL

Bain, Baine, Baines, Bains, Baynes, Bayns: (i) William *Banes* 1246 AssLa; Hewerard *Ban*, Cristiana *Bane* 1279 RH (C, O); Thomas *Baynes* 1446 FrY; Alexander *Banys* 1541 Black; Andrew *Baines* 1676 ib. OE *bān* 'bone' in the North and in Scotland became ME *bān* and later *bain;* in the Midlands and the South it became ME *bōn*, modern *bone* and survives as BONES. A nickname, probably usually plural. (ii) Richard *Beine* 1279 RH (C); John *Bayne* 1301 SRY; William *Bayn*

1323 AssSt. ME *beyn, bayn*, ON *beinn* 'straight, direct', also 'ready to serve, hospitable'. Always singular. (iii) Thomas *Ban* 1324 Black (Perth); David *Bane* or *Bayn* 1456–60 ib.; Ewir *Bayne* alias *Quhyte* 1623 ib. Gael *bàn* 'fair, white'. Always singular. (iv) Serlo *Baynes* 1219 AssY; John *de Bayns* 1275 RH (L); Roger *Bayns* 1277 AssLa; Thomas *de Bainnes* 1333 FrY. ME *bayne*, Fr *bain* 'bath'. Probably 'attendant at the public baths'. The forms without a preposition are too early to be regarded as northern forms of *bān* 'bone'.

Bainbridge, Bainbrigge: Matilda *de Baynbrigg'* 1301 SRY; Robert *Baynbryg'* 1379 PTY. From Bainbridge (WRYorks).

Bairnsfather, Barnfather, Banfather: William *Barnefader* 1246 AssLa, 1260 AssY; Henry *Barnefathir* 1392 Shef (Y); Adam *Barnisfader* 1502 Black. OE *bearn* 'child' and *fæder* 'father'. cf. ON *barnfaðir* 'a child's alleged father', which might well be the direct source of the second form.

Bairstow, Barstow Baistow, Bastow: Ralph *de Bayrestowe* 1277 Wak (Y); Thomas *de Barstowe* 1348 DbAS 36. From Bairstow (WRYorks).

Baisbrown, Bisbrown: William *Basbroun* 1332 SRCu; Christopher *Baysbrown* 1494 FrY; Laurence *Besbrowne* 1595 LaWills; Hugh *Bisbrowne* 1667 ib. From Baisbrowne (Westmorland).

Baish: *v.* BASH

Baiss: *v.* BASS

Baister: *v.* BASTER

Baitson: *v.* BATESON

Baker, Baiker, Backer: William *le Bakere* 1177 P (Nf); Robert *Bakere* 1246 AssLa; Walter *le Backere* 1280 MESO (Ha). OE *bæcere* 'baker'. cf. BAXTER.

Bakon: *v.* BACON

Balaam, Ballaam (i) Hamelinus *de Baalon* 1176 P (D); John *Balum* 1212 Cur (W); Rosa *Balam* 1275 SRWo. From Baalon in Meuse. (ii) John *Balam* 1568 SRSf; Eliza *Baalam* 1830 LitWelnethamPR (Sf); Sophia *Baylham* 1834 ib. From Baylham (Suffolk).

Balch: *v.* BELCH

Bald, Bauld: (i) Simon *le Bald'* 1178 P (Ess); Hugo *Calvus* 1198 FF (Herts); John *Balde* 1221 AssWo; William *le Ballede* c1248 Bec (W). ME *ballede*, used first of rotundity or corpulence (1287 NED), later, of baldness (c1386 ib.). cf. Madoc *le Balled* 14th AD vi (Ch), whose seal was inscribed s. MADOCI CAL[VI], and *v.* BALLARD. (ii) *Balde* c1150 DC (L), 1191 P (Lo), 1198 P (Beds); *Bald' filius Bald'* 1199 P (Herts); *Boold* 1332 SRLa. A short form of the common OG *Baldwin* or *Baldric* or of OE **Beald*. *Balt* 1066 DB (Y) may be OE or continental. cf. BALDING. Survives occasionally as BOLD.

Balder: *Balder'* Martell' 1160–2 Clerkenwell (Do); Thomas *Balder* 1524 SRSf. A rare surname from the not common OE *Bealdhere* 'bold army'.

Balderson, Bolderson, Boldison: Probably assimilated forms of *Balderston* and *Bolderston* rather than from the rare *Balder*.

Balderston, Balderstone, Bolderston, Boulderstone: William *de Baldreston* 1292 WhC (La). From Balderston (Lancs) or Balderstone (Lancs).

Baldery: *v.* BALDREE

Baldey, Baldie, Baldy, Boldy: William *Baldith* 1204 P (Gl); Simon, John *Baldy* 1274 RH (Sf), 1332 SRSx. OE **Bealdgýð* (f) 'bold combat', a woman's name not recorded before the Conquest but noted once in *Baldith* uxor c1170 Rams (Hu) and, possibly, in a corrupt form in *Baldethiva* 13th AD iv (Wa). In Suffolk, we may have ON *Baldi*. In Scotland, *Baldie* is a pet-form of *Archibald* or *Baldwin* and, as a surname, late: Thomas *Baldy* 1540 Black.

Baldick, Baldock: Hugh *de Baldoca* 1185 Templars (Beds); Thomas *Baldac* c1280 SRWo; Robert *Baldec* 1331 IpmW; William *Baldocke* 1460 IpmNt. From Baldock (Herts), a town founded in the 12th century by the Knights Templar, and given the name of Baghdad in its OFr form.

Balding, Belding, Bolding, Boulding: Joscius *filius Balding'* Ric 1 Cur (L); Gilebertus *filius Balding* 1212 Cur (L); William, Joan *Bolding* 1255 RH (Sa), 1327 SRSf; Alice, John *Baldyng* 1327 SRSx; Robert *Beldyng* 1332 SRSx. OE **Bealding*, a derivative of *Beald*, not recorded before the Conquest. In 1674 HTSf Anthony *Baldin* and Bartholomew *Baldinge* occur side by side with *Baldwin*, so that *Balding* is sometimes a late development of *Baldwin*. A possible earlier example is Alexander *Baldyne* 1251 Rams (Hu).

Baldree, Baldrey, Baldry, Baldrick, Baudrey, Baudry, Baldery, Boldero, Bolderoe, Boldra, Boldry: *Baldric* 1066, 1086 DB; *Baldricus* 1127–54 Holme (Nf); *Baldri* de Grendal Hy 2 DC (L); *Baudricus* de Lawdecote 1208 Cur (Sr); William *Baldri* 1185 Templars (Herts); Aluredus *Baltriht* 1197 P (W); Henry *Belrich* 1203 P (O); Alexander *Baudri* 1205 Cur (Sf); Richard *Balrich* 1238 Oseney (O); Walter *Baldrich* 1275 SRWo; Robert *Baldrik*, Henry *Baudrik* 1327 *SR* (Ess); Francis *Baldry*, *Boldery*, James *Baldery* 1674 HTSf; Mrs *Balderoe*, Stephen *Bolderowe* ib.; Martin *Boldroe*, Widow *Boldery*, *Boldry* ib. OG *Baldric* 'bold rule', common in the French forms *Baldri, Baudri*. The cognate OE **Bealdrīc* is unrecorded but such forms as *Belrich, Balrich* and *Baldrich* suggest that it did exist and was used after the Conquest.

Baldwin, Balwin: *Baldewinus* c1095 Bury (Sf); Randulfus *filius Balduini* Hy 2 DC (L); Stephen *Baldewin* 1200 P (Ha); John *Baudewin* 1260 AssC. OG *Baldwin* 'bold friend', a popular Flemish name, common in England both before and after the Conquest.

Baldy: *v.* BALDEY

Bale, Bales: *v.* BAIL

Balfour: John, William *de Balfure* 1304, 1331–5 Black; Michael *de Balfoure* 1365 ib. From the barony of Balfour (Fife).

Ball, Balle, Balls, Le Ball: (i) Godwin *Balle* 1137 ELPN; Norman *Balle* 1183 P (Nth). *Balle* is here disyllabic and may be from *Balle*, an ODa personal-name found in Scandinavian place-names in England and possibly surviving as *Balla* 1250 Fees (Ha). If a nickname, it might be OFr *balle* or OE **bealla* 'ball', or an adjective *ball* might have developed from *ball* 'a bald place', *balle* being the weak form. In later examples, *balle* became monosyllabic and is a form of *bal*. (ii) Robert, Matilda *le Bal* 1296, 1327 SRSx. Either ME *bal, ball(e)* 'the rotund one' or an adjective *ball* in the sense 'bald' from *ball* 'a white streak, a bald place'. *v.* NED s.v. *ball* and ELPN 137. (iii) Alfwin' *attebal* 1166 P (Nf); Henry *atte Balle* 1327 SRSo. From residence near a *ball*, 'a knoll', 'a rounded hill' (1166 MED). *v.* MELS 5–6, PN W 422.

Ballaam: *v.* BALAAM

Ballance, Ballans: Roger *Balance, Balaunce* 1196 FF (Wa), 1221 AssWa. Metonymic for 'balancer' from AFr *balancer*, OFr *balancier* 'one who weighs with a balance'. cf. Thomas *le Balauncer* 1283 LLB A.

Ballard: Peter, Adam *Ballard* 1196 Cur (Nth), 1210 Cur (C). ME *ball* plus *-ard*, 'a bald-headed man'. Where Wyclif has 'Stye up, ballard!', Coverdale translates, 'Come vp here thou balde heade'. Cf. Robert *Balheved* 1316 FFEss, Thomas *Balhefd* 1402 FA (Sf).

Ballaster, Ballester, Ballister, Balster: William *le Balister* 1293 AssCh. OFr *balestier* 'cross-bowman' (c1450 MED). *v.* ALABASTAR.

Baller: Alan *le Baller* 1243 AssSo; Geoffrey *Ballar* 13th Rams (C). A derivative of ME *ball*, either 'maker of balls' or 'dweller by a rounded hill'. *v.* BALL.

Ballon, Balon: *Baloun, Balun* 1276 RH (Lei); John *le Balun* 1275 RH (He); John *Ballon* 1297 MinAcctCo; Thomas *le Balon* 1327 SRWo; Walter *Ballun, Ballom* 1296, 1327 SRSx. OFr *Ballon*, casrégime of OG *Ballo*. The *le* proves we have also a noun, OFr *balon* 'little ball or pack' (Cotgrave), 'package', which may be metonymic for 'a packer' or a nickname for a little man of rotund form.

Balman: *Baldeman* filius Fabri 1188 BuryS (Sf); Nicolaus *filius Baldeman* ib.; Adam *Baleman* 1332 SRSx; Richard *Balman* 1415 LLB I. OE **Bealdmann*.

Balmer: Richard *le Baumere* 1305 LoCt. A derivative of ME *balme, bawme*, an aromatic substance prized for its medicinal qualities; a spicedealer or seller of ointments.

Balster: *v.* BALLASTER

Balston, Balstone: Robert *Balston* 1327 SRSf. Probably OE **Bealdstān* 'bold stone'.

Balwin: *v.* BALDWIN

Baly: *v.* BAILEY

Bamford, Bamforth, Bampford, Bampforth: William, Thomas de *Bamford* 1228 Cur (Sf), 1312 WhC; Christopher *Bamfurth* 1539 CorNt. From Bamford (Derby, Lancs).

Bane(s): *v.* BAIN

Baney, Boney: John, William *Bani* 1279 RH (Bk); Agnes, Alice *Bonye* ib. (O). Early examples of *bony* (a1515 NED), from ME *bān, bŏn* 'bone'. cf. BAIN, BONES.

Banfather: *v.* BAIRNSFATHER

Banister: *v..* BANNISTER

Banker: Albrice *le Baunker* 1245 FFC; Thomas *Bankar* 1358 Putnam (Nth). 'Dweller by a bank.'

Bankes, Banks: Walter *del Banck'* 1297 SRY; Matthew *Banke* 1327 SRSf. 'Dweller by a slope, bank, hillside' (ME *banke*). The plural form may conceal an original *-hous:* William *Bankhous* 1482 FrY; Robert *Bancus* 1513 GildY.

Bannerman: Dovinaldus *Banerman* 1368 Black. A Scottish name, 'standard-bearer, ensign' (1450 MED).

Bannister, Bannester, Banister: Turstan, Richard *Banastre* 1149–53 EngFeud (L), 1186 Eynsham (O); Richard *Banester* 1459 AD vi (St); John *Banyster* 1554 FrY. OFr *banastre* 'basket'. Metonymic for a basket-maker.

Banyard, Bunyard: Ralph *Baignard, Bangiard, Baniardus* 1086 DB (Herts); Robert *Baniard, Bainard* 1207, 1208 Cur (Nf); William *Banyard* 1346 FA (Sf). A variant of *Baynard*, due to the Englishman's difficulty in pronouncing the French *n* mouillé. cf. the English *onion* from the French *oignon*.

Barbe: Bernardus *Barb* 1086 DB (Ha); William *Barbe* 1229 Pat (K). A pet-form of *Barbara*, or OFr *barbe* 'beard'. *v.* BEARD.

Barber, Barbour: Alan, John *le Barbur* 1221 AssWa, 1248 FFEss; Thomas, Richard *le Barber* 1281 LLB A, 1298 LoCt; Seykin, Robert *le Barbier* 1299 LLB C. *Barbour* is from AFr *barbour*, OFr *barbeor* (c1320 NED), *Barber* from OFr *barbier* 'barber'. The barber was formerly a regular practitioner in surgery and dentistry.

Barchard: *v.* BURCHARD

Barclay, Berkeley, Berkley: Roger *de Berchelai, de Bercleia* 1086 DB (Gl, So); Henry *de Barcley* 1327 SRDb; Helewys' *de Berkele* 1327 SRSx. From Berkeley (Glos), Berkley (Som), or Barklye in Heathfield (Sussex). William *de Berchelai*, Chamberlain of Scotland in 1165, and the Scottish Barclays probably came from Berkeley (Glos).

Bardolph: *Bardolfus* de Fotipoi 12th DC (Nt); Hugo *Bardulfus, Bardol* 1142–53 DC (L); Thomas *Bardolf* 1184 Gilb (L); William *Bardoul* 1418 DKR 41. OG *Bartholf*.

Bardwell, Beardwell: Tedricus *de Berdewelle* 1190 P (Sf). From Bardwell (Suffolk).

Bare: John, Roger *Bare* 1274 RH (Sf), 1327 SRSf. OE *bær* 'bare' in one of its early senses, 'unarmed, defenceless, deserted, indigent'.

Barefoot, Barfoot: Robert *barefot* c1160 Eng Feud (Nth); Reginald *Berfot* 1203 P (Cu); John *Barfot* 1317 AssK. OE *bær* and *fōt* 'with bare feet', 'barefooted', used of friars, pilgrims and those doing penance. cf. Simon *Barleg* 1297 Min AcctCo, Emeloth *Baresanke* 1221 ElyA (Nf) 'barelegged'.

Barff: *v.* BARGH

Bargate: Adam *de la Bargate* 1275 SRWo. 'Dweller by the gate that bars entry into the town.' The surname may also refer to the keeper of the Bargate.

Barge: Peter *del Barge*, mariner 1359 FrY. 'Bargeman, seaman.' OFr *barge* was originally used of a small sea-going vessel with sails.

Bargh, Barff, Barugh: Robert *de Bargh* 1310 FFSf; John *de Bergh* 1365 FrY. The modern northern form of BARROW, ME *bergh*, OE *beorh*. 'Dweller by the hill' as at Barff Hill (ERYorks) and Barugh, pronounced *Barf* (NRYorks).

Barkas: *v.* BARKHOUSE

Barker, Berker: (i) Ralph *Berker* 1185 Templars (Y); Aluredus *le berkier* 1193 P (L); John *le Bercher* 1212 Cur (Ha). OFr *berchier, bercher, berkier, berker* 'shepherd'. OFr also had the form *barcher* which may well be represented below. Later, when ME *-er* had become *-ar*, *barker* 'shepherd' would be indistinguishable in form from *barker* 'tanner'. (ii) Jordan *le Barkere* 1255 Ass (Ess); John *le Barker* 1260 AssC. A derivative of ME *bark* 'to tan', a tanner.

Barkhouse, Barkas, Barkis: Thomas *del Barkhous* 1379 PTY. 'A barkhouse' (1463 DbCh, 1483 NED) was a tannery. In 1383 Hugh *de Barkhowse* (*del Barkhous* 1384 DbCh) granted all his goods and chattels in his tannery at Beauchief to Ralph de Dore. The surname is thus occupational, 'a tanner'.

Barkshire: *v.* BERKSHIRE

Barlett: Willelmus *filius Berlet'* 1219 AssY; Robert *Berlet* 1206 P (Nt); John *Barlet* 1242 Fees (W); Adam *Berilot* 1327 FrY. *Ber-el-ot*, a double diminutive of *Ber-*, from OG *Berard*.

Barley, Barlee: (i) Jordan *Barlie* 1221 AssWa; John *Barlich*, Reur' *Barliche* 1279 RH (O, C). OE *bærlīc*, ME *barlich, barli* 'barley', used for BARLEY-MAN or by metonymy for a maker or seller of barley-bread or cakes. cf. Josce *Barlibred* 1185 P (Nf) (c1320 NED), Roger *Barliwastel* 1210 FFL. (ii) Leofric *de Berle* c975 OEByn (Herts); Henry *de Berel'* 1219 AssY. From Barley (Herts, Lancs, WRYorks). *v.* also BARLOW.

Barleycorn: William, Godfrey *Barlicorn* 1233 Cl (L), 1279 RH (C). *Barleycorn* (1382 NED) was used of both the plant and the grain. The surname may refer to a grower of or dealer in barley. cf. GRANDAGE.

Barleyman: Peter *Barlyman* 1332 MEOT (L). A dealer in barley.

Barlow: Thomas *de Barlowe* 1260 AssLa; John *de Berlowe* 1379 PTY; Margery *Barley* or *Barlowe*, William *Barlee* or *Barlowe* 1509 LP (Db, Ess). From Barlow (Derby, Lancs, WRYorks), but there seems also to have been some confusion with BARLEY.

Barlthrop, Barltrop: *v.* BARTHORP

Barman, Bearman, Berman: Alsi, Gilbert *Berman* 1137 ELPN, 1222 Cur (Sr); Ralph *Bareman* 1275 RH (Beds); Simon *le Berman* 1281 MEOT (L); Geoffrey *le Barman* 1301 SRY. OE *bærmann* 'bearer, porter'. *Berman*, without the article, may also be personal in origin. Walterus *filius Bereman* 1198 P (K) may have been the son of a porter, but his father may have borne the name of *Beornmann*, unrecorded in OE, but of a type common in the 11th and 12th centuries. Occasionally we may have

the rare OE *Beornmund*. cf. Adam *Beremund* 1204 P (Lo); William *Beremund* 1272 Ass (Ha).

Barnabé, Barnaby, Barneby: (i) Roger *Barnabe* 1327 SRC; Roger *Barnaby* 1331 FFC. The English form of *Barnabas*, not common in the records, but found in the 14th century (ODCN) and surviving until the 19th century as in Dickens's *Barnaby Rudge*. (ii) Richard *de Bernaldeby* 1160 Guisb (Y). From Barnaby in Skelton (NRYorks).

Barnacle, Barnacal, Barnikel, Burnikell: Richard *Bernikel* 1344 Cl (K); Richard *Barnakyll* 1514 Oxon; John *Barnacle* 1545 Bardsley. Barnacle (Warwicks), DB *Bernhangre*, did not reach its modern form before 1547. We are, therefore, clearly concerned with a nickname from ME *bernacle, barnakyll*, a diminutive of ME *bernak*, OFr *bernac* 'a kind of powerful bit or twitch for the mouth of a horse or an ass', used to restrain a restive animal, also used as an instrument of torture. The nickname might have been applied to an expert in taming horses or to a torturer or it might have been given to a man of savage, un-restrained temper who needed such restraint. A further possibility is a nickname from the barnacle goose, ME *barnakyll*, a species of wild goose (cf. WILDGOOSE).

Barnaclough: *v.* BARRACLOUGH

Barnard, Barnet, Barnett, Bernard: *Bernardus* 1066 DB (Hu), 1101–16 Holme (Nf); Ricardus *filius Bernardi* 1205 Cur (So); Hugo *Bernard'* 1130 P (L); Thomas *Bernhard* 1260 AssC; Robert *Barnard* 1446 FrY. OFr *Bernart*, OG *Bernard* 'bear-brave'.

Barne: (i) Siuuard *Barn* 1066 DB (Wa), *Bearn, Barn* 1071, 1072 ASC D, E; Gamell' *Barn* 1166 P (Y); Adam *le Barn* 1212 Cur (Y); William *le Barne* 1232 Pat (L). ON *barn* 'child'. Used in DB as a byname of men of the upper classes, it might also have had the meaning 'a young man of a prominent family'. cf. the English CHILD. (ii) *Beornus* 1066 DB (Sf); *Bern* 1066 DB (Do); Tomas *filius Bern'* 1177 P (St); Þirne *Beorn* c1050 YCh; William, Simon *Bern* 1190 P (Wo), 1202 AssL. In Yorks, Lincs, Staffs and Suffolk we have the Scandinavian personal-name *Biǫrn*, anglicized as *Beorn*. In Dorset and Worcs we may have OE *Beorn*. The source may occasionally be OE *beorn* 'warrior'. (iii) Eilwin *de la Berne* 1211 Cur (Sr); Richard *atte Berne* 1275 SRWo; Peter *del Barne* 1316 Wak (Y). From residence near or employment at a barn (OE *bere-ærn*). *v.* BARNES.

Barnes, Barns: Philip *de Bernes* temp. John Seals (Sr); Peter *del Bernes* 1327 SRDb; William *Bernes* 1380 AssC; Joan *Barnes* 1450 Rad (C). From Barnes (Surrey) or residence near or employ-ment at the barns. cf. BARNE.

Barnet, Barnett, Barnitt: Brictnod *de la Bernet* c1200 MELS (Sx); William *atte Bernette* 1296 SRSx; Jordan *atte Barnette* 1310 LLB D. From residence near land cleared by burning (OE *bærnet* 'burning') or from Barnet (Herts, Middlesex), or Barnett Fm in Wonersh (Surrey).

Barnfather: *v.* BAIRNSFATHER

Barnikel: *v.* BARNACLE

Baron, Barron: Lefuine *Barun* c1095 Bury (Sf); Geoffrey *le Barun* 1236 *Ass* (Ha); John *Baron* 1296 SRSx. EME *barun*, OFr *barun, -on* 'baron', sometimes, no doubt, denoting title or rank, but more often, especially when applied to peasants, a nickname, proud or haughty as a baron. The term was anciently applied to freemen of the cities of London and York who were homagers of the king and also to the freemen of the Cinque Ports who had the feudal service of bearing the canopy over the head of the sovereign on the day of coronation. Gervase *le Cordewaner* or *camerarius* was also called Gervase *Baronn*, no doubt because he was alderman of Aldgate Ward 1250-6 (ELPN 137). This was an old surname in Angus where it originated from the small baronies attached to the Abbey of Coupar-Angus. The tenant of the barony of Glenisla became Robert *Barrone*, tenant of Glennylay (1508), etc. Elsewhere in Scotland 'barons' were land-owners who had a certain amount of jurisdiction over the population of their lands (Black).

Barr, Barrs, Le Barr: (i) Anger *de la Barra* c1216-17 Clerkenwell (Lo); Peter *de Bar* 13th Lewes (Nf); John *ate Barre* 1283 Battle (Sx). OFr, ME *barre* 'barrier, gateway' (c1220 NED). cf. Temple Bar and *v.* BARRER. In the fens *bar* was used of an obstruction (perhaps a weir) in a stream. The Scottish Barrs derive from Barr in Ayrshire or Barr in Renfrewshire. Atkyn *de Barr* was baillie of Ayr in 1340 (Black). (ii) Edricius *de la Barre* 1170 P (St); William *de Barre* 1199 AssSt. From Great Barr (Staffs). This is from Welsh *bar* 'top, summit' and refers to Barr Beacon. (iii) Richard *de Barra* 1086 DB (So). From Barre-en-Ouche (Eure), or, perhaps, from Barre-de-Semilly (La Manche). (iv) Hugo *Barre* 1155 DC (L); Alexander *Barre* 12th Riev (Y). OFr *barre* 'a piece of any material long in proportion to its thickness or width', a bar or stake, used as a nickname for a tall, thin man, Or metonymic for a maker of bars. cf. Robert *Barremakere* 1347 LLB F.

Barraclough, Barrowclough, Barrowcliff, Barrow-cliffe, Barnaclough, Berecloth, Berrecloth, Berry-cloth: Peter *del Baricloughe, de Barneclogh* 1315, 1316 Wak (Y); Robert *Bereclough* 1493 GildY; Henry *Barrayclught* 1561 RothwellPR (Y); Thomas *Baraclough* 1588 ib.; Anne *Beraclough* 1606 ib.; Francis *Baroclough, Barrowclough* 1612, 1631 ib.; Elizabeth *Barraclue* 1627 Bardsley; Edward *Barra-cliff* 1765 ib. From an unidentified place, probably near Wakefield (WRYorks). The pronunciation is *Barracluff,* in London *Barraclow* or *Barraclue.*

Barrat, Barratt, Barrett, Barritt, Barrott: Matthew *Baret* c1150-5 DC (L); Robert *Barate* 1165 P (Nt); Jordan *Barat* 1185 Templars (Herts); Seman *Barette* 1207 P (Ha); William *Barrette* (*Barat*) 1327 *SR* (Ess). This is a difficult name. There seems no evidence for a derivation from OG *Beroald,* OFr *Beraud,* as has been suggested. ON *Bárðr* is found in Yorks and Lincs in DB as *Bared, Baret,* but there is no proof of its continued use. The commonest form is *Barat* and this must be from OFr *barat,* ME *bar(r)at, bar(r)et(te),* which accounts for all the forms. The original sense in Romanic seems to have been 'traffic, commerce, dealing' and in ME 'trouble, distress' (c1230); 'deception, fraud' (1292); 'contention, strife' (c1300), from any of which a nickname could arise. Occasionally we may have OFr *barrette* 'a cap, bonnet', as an occupation name, 'a maker of caps'.

Barrell: Turstin *Baril* 1166 P (Nf); William *Baril* 1185 P (Wo). OFr *baril* 'a barrel, cask'. Perhaps chiefly for a maker of barrels, a cooper. cf. Stephen *le Bariller* 1224 Pat. It may also have been used as a nickname for a man with a well-rounded belly. cf. 'the ydell and *barrell bealies* of monkes' (1561 NED), *barrel-belly'd* (1697 ib.); or, perhaps, of a man with the capacity of a cask. cf. 'olde barel ful of lies' (1386 ib.), 'to drinke a barelle fulle of gode berkyne' (1436 ib.), *barrel-fever,* a disease caused by immoderate drinking. Also a late form of BARWELL: John and Susan *Barrell, Barwell* 1688, 1691 Bardsley.

Barrer, Barrere: Gilbert (*le*) *Barrer* 1221-2 Cur (D, Do), 1229 Cl (Sx); William *Barrer* 1332 SRSx (in the town of Arundel). Equivalent to *atte Barre* 'dweller by a town or castle gate'. *v.* BARR. Gilbert *le Barrier* 1210 P (Sx) is probably identical with Gilbert *Barre* 1221 Cur (K) and Walter *atte Barre* 1296 SRSx with Walter *le Barrer'* 1327 ib.

Barrick: *v.* BERWICK

Barrie: *v.* BARRY

Barrow, Barrows, Berrow: Adam *de Barewe* 1192 P (L); John *de la Berewe* 1242 Fees (Wo); William *del Berwe* 1260 AssC; John *atte Barwe* 1327 SRSo. Either 'dweller by the grove', OE *bearu,* dative *bearwe,* giving modern *Barrow,* or 'dweller by the hill', OE *beorg,* ME dative *berwe, barwe,* modern *Berrow, Barrow.*

Barrowclough, Barrowcliff: *v.* BARRACLOUGH

Barrowman: *v.* BORROWMAN

Barry, Barrie: (i) Nest *de Barri* 1185 P (Sx); Richard *Barri* 1195 FFSf. Though most examples are without a preposition, the surname must, in the absence of any evidence for a personal-name or any suitable attribute, be local in origin. It was probably brought over from France where it survives as *Barry* and *Dubarry,* from OFr *barri* 'rampart', later applied to the suburb below the rampart, hence 'dweller in the suburb' (Dauzat). The Irish Barry is also chiefly Anglo-Norman, deriving from Philip *de Barry* (1179). It is also for *Ó Báire* 'descendant of *Báire'*, short for *Fionnbharr* 'fair-head' or for *Ó Beargha* 'descendant of *Beargha'* 'spear-like'. (ii) William *de Barry* 1360 Black. The Scottish surname derives from Barry in Angus.

Barryman: *v.* BORROWMAN

Barsham, Basham, Bassham: Henry *de Barsham* 1198 FFNf; Martin *Barsham, Bassham* 1367 ColchCt. From Barsham (Norfolk, Suffolk).

Barson: Hugo *Bertson* 1332 SRCu. 'Son of *Bert',* a short form of *Bertelmeu* 'Bartholomew'. *v.* BART.

Barstow: v. BAIRSTOW

Bart: Award *Bart* 1246 AssLa; William *Barte* 1420 LLB I. A short form of *Bartelmew* (Bartholomew).

Bartholomew, Berthelemy: *Bartholomeus* canonicus 12th DC (Nt); Robert *Bartelmeu* 1273 RH (Hu); Nicholas *Bertelmev* 1296 SRSx; Walter *Berthelmeu* 1334 LLB E. *Bartholomew*, Hebrew 'son of Talmai' ('abounding in furrows'), a common medieval name, with numerous diminutives.

Barthorp, Barthorpe, Bartrap, Bartrip, Bartrop, Bartropp, Bartrup, Bartrupt, Bartup, Bathrup, Barlthrop, Barltrop; William *de Baretorp* 1200 P (L); William *de Barkentorp'* 1219 AssY; Walter *Berthrop* 1327 SRWo; John, William *Baltrip* 1341 LLB F, 1351 AssEss; Bartholomew *Balthroppe* 1586 DenhamPR (Sf); Jonathan *Barthrope* 1673 Shef (Y); Hester *Bartrap* 1687 Bardsley; Christopher *Barthrup* 1706 FrY. From Barthorpe Bottoms (ERYorks).

Bartie: v. BARTY

Bartin: v. BERTIN

Bartindale: John *Bartendale* 1424 FrY. From Bartin Dale, a depopulated place in Hunmanby (ERYorks).

Bartlet, Bartlett, Bartleet, Barttelot, Bertalot: Godricus, Walter *Bertelot* c1157 Holme (Nf), 1296 SRSx; Thomas *Bartelot* 1294 FFC, 1327 SRSx; Thomas *Bartlot* 1379 PTY. *Bart-el-ot*, *Bert-el-ot*, double diminutives of *Bart-*, *Bert-*, from *Bartelmew*, *Bertelmew* (Bartholomew).

Barton, Barten: Ælfric *æt Bertune* 1015 OEByn; Paganus *de Barton* 1163 P; John *de Barton'* 1300 FFY; Thomas *Barten*, *Bartyn* 1586, 1609 Shef. From one or other of the many places of this name.

Bartram, Bartrum, Barttrum, Bertram, Bertrand, Batram, Batrim, Batterham, Battram, Borthram, Buttrum: *Bertrannus* 1086 DB; *Bertram* c1150–60 DC (L), identical with *Bertrannus* a1183 ib.; William *Bertram* 1086 DB (Ha); Henry *Bertran* c1155 DC (L); John *Bartram* 1278 LLB A; John *Bartrem* 1332 SRSt; Mariota *Berteram* 1332 SRSx; Nycolas *Bartrum* 1524 SRSf; William *Battram*, George *Bartrom*, *Bateram* 1674 HTSf. OFr *Bertran(t)*, OG *Bertram*, *Bertran(d)* 'bright raven'.

Bartrap, Bartrip, Bartrop, Bartropp, Bartrup, Bartrupt: v. BARTHORP

Barttelot: v. BARTLET

Bartup: v. BARTHORP

Barty, Bartie: Robert *Barty* 1552 Black (Dundee); John *Bairty* 1587 ib. (Edinburgh). A Scottish diminutive of *Bartholomew*.

Barugh: v. BARGH

Barwell: Elyas *de Barewelle* 12th DC (Lei). From Barwell (Leics). v. also BARRELL.

Barwick: v. BERWICK

Base: v. BASS

Baseley, Basley, Bazeley, Bazley, Basil, Bassil, Bassill, Bazell, Bazelle: *Basilia* 1134 40 Holme (Nf), Hy 2 DC (L); Willelmus *filius Basilie* 1219 AssY; *Basill'* Vidua 1296 SRSx; Ralph *Basille*

1251 Rams (Hu); John *Basyly* 1252 Rams (Hu); Walter *Basely* 1275 SRWo; Thomas *Bazill* 1674 HTSf. OFr *Basile*, *Bazile*, *Basyle*, *Basille* (f), from Lat *Basilia*, feminine of *Basilius*, from Greek βασίλειος 'kingly'. The English form was *Basil* or *Bassilly*. The masculine *Basil* is found occasionally: Ricardus *filius Basilii* 1252 Rams (Hu).

Bash, Baish: Robert *de Basche* 1199 AssSt. For *Bach*, with a change of *sh* for *ch*.

Basham: v. BARSHAM

Basil: v. BASELEY

Bask: Henry, Roger *Baske* 1332 SRSt; 1357 AssSt. ME *baisk*, *bask*, ON *beiskr* 'bitter, acrid', 'ungrateful or irritating to the senses'.

Baskerville, Baskerfield, Basketfield, Baskeyfield, Basterfield, Baskwell, Paskerful, Pasterfield, Pesterfield: Roger *de Bascheruilla* 1127 AC (Gl); James *Baskerfield*, *Baskervyle* 1530 StarChSt. From Boscherville (Eure).

Baskett: (i) William, Henry *Basket* 1191 P (Sr), 1198 CurR (Ess). ME *basket*, here used of a basket-maker. cf. BASKETTER. Or used for one who carried the *baskettes* full of stones to the lime-kiln (Building 151). (ii) Basilia *de Besecot'* 1221 AssWa; Adam *de Baskote* 1373 Oriel (O). From Bascote (Warwicks). (iii) Margeria *atte Bascat* 1319 SRLo; Thomas Kent *atte Basket* beside Billyngesgate 1424 LondEng 184. One who lived or worked at the sign of the Basket. Probably a basketmaker.

Basketter: cf. William *Basketwricte* 1229 Pat (L). 'A maker of baskets.' *Basketter* is ME *basket* plus *-er*.

Baskwell: v. BASKERVILLE

Basley: v. BASELEY

Bason: v. BATESON

Bass, Base, Baiss: (i) Aelizia *Bass'* 1180 P (Wa); Dauid *le Bas* 1205 P (Gl); Geoffrey *Base* 1274 RH (L). OFr *bas*, *basse*, ME *bass* 1393, *bace* c1440, *base* 1425 'low, of small height'. A man with short legs. cf. BASSETT. (ii) Osbert *Bars* 1207 P (Gl); Richard *le Bars* 1327 SRSx. OE *bærs*, now *bass*, a fish; cf. *Bace*, fysche c1440 PromptParv.

Basset, Bassett: Ralph *Basset* 1086 DB (Herts, Beds), 1115 Winton (Ha); Milo *Basseth* 1139 Templars (O); Philip *le Basset* 1260 LLB B. OFr *basset* 'of low stature', a diminutive of *bas* 'low'; 'a dwarf or very low man' (Cotgrave). According to Ordericus Vitalis, Ralph Basset was raised by Henry II from an ignoble stock and from the very dust, 'de ignobili stirpe ac de pulvere'.

Bassham: v. BARSHAM

Bassick: v. BASTICK

Bassil(l): v. BASELEY

Bassingthwaighte, Bassingthwait: John *Bassyngewhytt* 1568 SRSf. From Bassenthwaite (Cumb).

Bastable: Richard *de Bardestapel* 1219 FFEss; Ralph *Barstaple* 1327 SRSo. From Barstable Hall (Essex) or Barnstaple (Devon).

Bastard: Robert *Bastard* 1086 DB (D); William *le Bastard* 1201 AssSo. OFr *bastard* (1297 NED). Not always regarded as a stigma. The Conqueror himself is described as 'William the Bastard' in state documents.

Basten: *v.* BASTIAN

Baster, Baister: Baldwynus, Peter *le bastere* 1230 P (D); 1327 SRSt. OFr *bastier* 'saddler'.

Basterfield: *v.* BASKERVILLE

Bastian, Bastien, Basten, Bastin: *Bastianus* a1200 Dublin, 1221 AssWo; Colin *Bastin* 1225 Pat; John *Bastian* 1317 AssK. A pet-form of *Sebastian*, from Lat *Sebastianus* 'man of Sebastia', a city in Pontus.

Bastick, Bassick: Geoffrey *de Bastwyke* 1335 AssC. From Bastwick (Norfolk).

Baston, Bastone: (i) Ernaldus, Richard *Bastun* 1191 P (Sf), 1203 AssNth; Nicholas *Baston* 1279 RH (O). A nickname from OFr *bastun* 'a stick', used as a personal-name in the first element of Bassenthwaite (Cumb). (ii) Turstan *de Baston* 1191 P (L). From Baston (Lincs).

Bastow: *v.* BAIRSTOW

Batch: *v.* BACH

Batchelar, Batchelder, Batchlor: *v.* BACHELOR

Batcock: *v.* BADCOCK

Bate, Bates: (i) *Bate* 1275, 1286 Wak (Y); Rogerus *filius Bate* 1327 SRDb; Roger *Bate* 1275 SRWo; Richard *Bates* 1297 MinAcctCo (Y); John *Bat, Bate* 1394, 1396 LLB H. A pet-form of *Bartholomew*, found also as *Batt*. For the variation between *Bat* and *Bate*, cf. *Add* and *Ade* for *Adam*, and *Pat* and *Pate* for *Patrick*. (ii) Thomas *del Bate* 1270 Ipm (Nb); William *of Ye Bate* 1297 SRY. This might be OE *bāt*, Northern ME *bat* 'boat', used for a boatman. More probably we have ON *bati* 'dweller by the fat pasture'. *v.* BATT. It can have no connexion with the common Northern *bait* 'food', etc., which always appears as *bayt*, *beyt*.

Bateman, Baitman, Batman, Battman: *Bathemanus* de Staunford' 1222 Cur (R); *Bateman* le Keu 1267 Pat; *Batman* d'Appleton 1313 FrY; Alexander *Bateman* 1260 AssC; William *Batemon* 1275 SRWo; John *Baytman* 1553 FrY. *Bateman* 'servant of Bartholomew' is a type of surname formerly common in Yorkshire. cf. ADDYMAN, HARRIMAN, etc. Here it is used early and often as a christian name, perhaps on the analogy of such names of *Blæcmann*, *Dēormann*, etc. *Pateman* was similarly used in Scotland in the 15th century as an alternative for the christian name *Paton* (Patrick).

Bater: Edmund, Robert *le batur* 1199 P (Gl), 1210 P (Ha). OFr *bateor* 'one who beats' has been taken to mean a beater of cloth or fuller, or as a short form of *orbatour*, a beater of metals. It probably means 'a coppersmith or dealer in *baterie*, i.e. beaten copper or brassware' (LoCt). Stephen *le Coperbeter* (1286) was identical with Stephen *le Batur* (1292 LLB A). *v.* BEATER.

Bateson, Baitson, Batson, Battson, Bason: John *Batessone* 1327 SRDb; Richard *Bateson* 1327 Wak (Y); John *Battson* 1467 GildY; William *Baitson* 1662 PrGR. 'Son of *Bate* or *Batt*'. *v.* also BEATSON.

Batey, Batie, Baty: William *Baty* 1277 AssSo; Hugo *Baty* 1301 SRY. A pet-form of *Bate* (Bartholomew). cf. BEATY.

Batha, Bathe, Batho, Bather, Badder: *Atha ap Atha*, William *ap Atha* 1327 SRSa; *Atha Gogh* 1332 Chirk; Jevan *ap Atha, ap Adda* 1391 ib.; John *Bathowe* 1537 Morris (Haverfordwest); Jevan ap John ap Gryffyd *Batto* 1538 Chirk; Humffrey *Bathowe*, John *Batowe* 1538 SaAS 3/viii; Richard *Bathaw* 1574 Bardsley (Ch); William *Batha*, Adam *Batho* 1610, 1613 ib.; Elizabeth, Hannah *Bather* 1683, 1782 ib. Morris (155) gives *Batha, Batho, Bather* as Shropshire and Cheshire variants of *Batha*, i.e. *ap Atha* 'son of *Atha*', probably correctly, since the Welsh personal name was common in Shropshire and Chirkland in the 14th century. *Badder* may be from the by-form *ap Adda*, and the variation in the unstressed final syllable can be paralleled in other names.

Bathrup: *v.* BARTHORP

Bathurst: William *de Batherst* 1296 SRSx; Geoffrey *de Bathurst* 1327 SRSx; Katherine *Batherst* 1392 CtH. From Bathurst in Warbleton (Sussex).

Batisson: Remiger *Batisson* 1332 SRCu. 'Son of *Bate* or *Batey*.'

Batkin: *Batekyn* clericus 1274 RH (Ess); Thomas *Batekyn* 1325 FFEss; Hugh *Batkyn* 1332 SRSt. A diminutive of *Bate* (Bartholomew).

Batman: *v.* BATEMAN

Baton: *v.* BATTEN

Batram, Batrim: *v.* BARTRAM

Batrick: *v.* BADRICK

Batsford, Battisford: Richard *de Batesford* 1182–1211 BuryS (Sf); Everard *de Bateford', de Batesford'* 1202 FFSf; John *de Batesford* 1300 Eynsham. From Batsford (Glos), Batsford in Warbleton (Sussex), or Battisford (Suffolk).

Batson, Battson: *v.* BATESON

Batt, Batte, Batts: (i) Reginald, Richard *le Bat* 1275 RH (Y), 1296 SRSx. A nickname from the bat, a form first found c1575 and replacing an earlier *bakke*. *v.* BACK. (ii) William, Herbert *Bat* 1170–87 ELPN, 1182 P (Sa); Matilda *Battes* 1279 RH (C); John *Bate* or *Batt* 1570 Oxon. Without the article, the surname is common and may be a nickname 'the bat' or a pet-name of Bartholomew. Both Gascoigne and Gabriel Harvey addressed their friend Bartholomew Withypoll as *Batt(e)*. We have also to take into account the byname of a Winchester monk: Ælfricus qui *Bata* cognominabatur (c1051 OEByn). This has given rise to various conjectures, none wholly satisfactory. Tengvik suggests a nickname from OE *batt* 'a cudgel', as does Ekwall for the first form above. Tengvik considers the reference is to a person of stout heavy appearance. For the byname *Bata* Ekwall suggests a personal name OE *Bata which he finds as the first element in Batcombe (Dorset, Som), and other place-names, but, in view of the triple occurrence of Batcombe, he suggests also the possibility of a common noun *bata*, corresponding to ON *bati*, OFris *bata* 'profit, gain', in some transferred sense such as 'fat pasture' (*v.* below), or even 'good husbandman'. With this surname we must also take BATTOCK. This is clearly a diminutive, either OE **Batuc*, from **Bata*, or a noun **batuc* 'the little good husbandman'. OE **Battoc* is the source of Battisborough (Devon). (iii) Walter *atte Batte* 1327 SRSo. This form seems to confirm Ekwall's derivation of Batcombe (Som) from a topographical term. 'Dweller by the fat pasture'.

Battell: *v.* BATTLE

Batten, Battin, Batting, Baton: *Batin* Bythemore, *Bathon* Mayster 1327 SRSo; Walter *Batun* 1248 FFEss; Robert *Batin* 1261 AssSo; William *Baton* 1275 SRWo; John *Batten* 1327 SRSt. Diminutives in *-in*, *-un* of *Bat* (Bartholomew).

Batterham: *v.* BARTRAM

Batterson, Batteson, Battison, Battisson: Andrew *Batenson* 1561 Bardsley (Du); Abraham *Battison* 1699 FrY; George *Battison* alias *Pattison*, son of John *Pattison* 1758 FrY. 'Son of *Batten*', later confused with *Patterson*. Also, no doubt, 'Son of *Batty*'.

Battiscombe: John *Battiscombe* 1440 AD ii (Do). From Bettiscombe (Dorset).

Battle, Battell, Battyll: Hubert *Bataile* c1140 AD i (Ess); William *de la Bataille* 1196 Cur (Nth); John *de Labatil* c1245 Black (Inchaffray); Simon *le Batel* 1327 SRSx. OFr *de la bataile* '(man) of the battle-array, warrior'.

Battman: *v.* BATEMAN

Battock: Turchil *Batoc* 1066 DB (Wa); Thomas, John *Battok* 1327 SRSf, 1362 Shef (Sf). *v.* BATT.

Battram: *v.* BARTRAM

Battrick: *v.* BADRICK

Battrum: *v.* BARTRAM

Battson: *v.* BATESON

Batty, Battye, Battey, Battie: Johannes *filius Batti* 1332 SRLa; John *Batty*, William *Batti* 1308, 1316 Wak (Y). A pet-form of *Batt* (Bartholomew).

Battyll: *v.* BATTLE

Baty: *v.* BATEY

Baucutt: *v.* BAWCOCK

Baud: Simon, Reginald *le Baud* 1219 Cur (Nth), 1239 FFC. OFr *baud* 'gay, sprightly' (c1400 NED).

Baudr(e)y: *v.* BALDREE

Baugh: Madog, Jevan *Bach* 1391 Chirk; Madog Lloit *Bach* 1391–3 ib.; Geoffrey *Bagh'* 1450 SaG; Rychard *Bawgh* 1545 SRW. Probably Welsh *bach* 'little'.

Baulch: *v.* BELCH

Bavridge: *v.* BEVERIDGE

Bawcock, Bawcutt, Baucutt, Bowcock, Bowcott, Bocock, Boocock: Geoffrey *Balcok* 1276 RH (Y); Alan *Balkok* 1279 RH (Hu); Walter *Boucok* 1297 MinAcctCo; Ibbot *Bolkok* 1379 PTY; Sara *Bawcoke* 1627 Bardsley; William *Bo(o)cocke* 1627, 1641 RothwellPR (Y). *Bald*, a short form of *Baldwin* or *Baldric* (*v.* BALD, BALDREE) and the diminutive suffix *-cock*.

Bax: *v.* BACK

Baxter, Bagster: Liueger *se Bacestere* a1093 OEByn (D); Hanne *Bakestre* 1260 AssCh; William *le Baxtere* 1333 FFSf. OE *bæcestre*, fem. of *bæcere* 'baker'. *Baxter* is found mainly in the Anglian counties and is used chiefly of men. Only two examples have been noted with a woman's christian name. Fransson found only four.

Bayard: Ralph *baird* (*baiart*) 1086 InqEl (Herts); Godfrey *Baiart, Baiard* 1161–2 P (Y); Simon *Bai(h)ard* 1203, 1206 Cur (Herts). OFr *baiart, baiard* 'bay-coloured', used generally of a bay horse, but in particular of the bright-bay-coloured magic steed given by Charlemagne to Renaud and hence as a mock-heroic allusive name for any horse. Cf. Chaucer's 'proud Bayard'. Later, 'Bayard' was taken as the type of blindness or blind recklessness. As a surname, this may be used of reddish-brown hair or complexion, but more probably of a proud, haughty or reckless disposition. Cf. 'Þay blustered as blynde as bayard' (c1325 NED); 'But as Bayard the blinde stede ... He goth there no man will him bidde' (1393 ib.). The surname may also be occupational in origin, from OFr *bayard, baiart* 'a hand-barrow used for heavy loads' (1642 NED), used by metonymy for OFr, AFr *baïardeur* 'a mason's labourer'. NED doubts the use of this in England. *Bayardours*, however, is found in 1359 (Building 439) and *baiard* 'hand-barrow' in 1278 (ib. 243). In the Vale Royal accounts of 1278 the *bayarders* or *bairdores* are defined as 'men carrying with barrows large stones to be carved into the workshop and out' (Building 353).

Baylay, Bayley, Baylie: *v.* BAILEY

Bayles: *v.* BAIL

Bayliff(e): *v.* BAILEFF

Baylis, Bayliss, Bayless, Bailess: Thomas *Baillis* 1547 FrY; Samuel *Baylles* 1635 ib. OFr *baillis*, nominative of *bailliff*.

Baynard: Rotbert' homo *bainardi* 1086 InqEl (Sf); Ralph *baignart, bainard* 1086 DB (Ess), InqEl (Nf); Robert *Bainard* 1182 Guisb (Y); John *Baynard, Beynard* 1317 AssK. OG *Beinhard, -hart*, probably compounded of ON *beinn* 'ready, willing' and OG *hart* 'hart'. *v.* also BANYARD.

Bayne(s): *v.* BAIN

Baynham: *v.* BEYNON

Baz(e)ley, Bazell(e): *v.* BASELEY

Beach: *v.* BEECH

Beacham, Beachamp: *v.* BEAUCHAMP

Beacock: Henricus *filius Becok* 1332 SRLa; Stephen *Becoc* 1279 RH (O); John *Becokson* 1366 SRLa. *Be*, a pet-form of *Beton* or *Beatrice*, plus the diminutive suffix *-coc*.

Beade, Beed: Alanus *filius Bede* de Swainton' 1230 P (Y); Raymond *Bede* 1260 AssC; Robert *Beda* 1275 RH (W). OE *Bēda*. The name of the Venerable Bede remained in use, though rare, until the 13th century, long enough to become a surname.

Beadel, Beadell, Beadle, Beadles, Beddall, Bedell, Bedells, Bedle, Beedell, Beedle, Biddell, Biddle, Biddles, Buddell, Buddle, Buddles: Brun *Bydel* 11th KCD 1353 (So); Brictmarus *Bedel* 1066 DB (Sf); Erneis *bedel*, Luinus, Richard *budel* 1148 Winton

(Ha); Ailsi *le Bedell'* 1175 P (Lei); Robert *le Budel* 1327 SRSt; Margaret *ate Budeles* 1332 SRSr; Richard *Bedle* 1541 RochW; Richard *Byddell* 1559 FFHu; John *Biddle* 1655 FrY; William *Beadle*, John *Beddall* 1674 HTSf; Adam *Buddle* 1676 EA (OS) iv. OE *bydel* 'beadle'. OE *y*, in ME dialects, became *i*, *e* or *u*, all of which have survived. Some examples of *bedel* are from OFr *bedel* (Lat *bedellus*), especially in counties such as Hants where OE *y* became *u*. These surnames may also be late forms of BEDWELL. For *Buddle*, *v.* also BOODLE.

Beadman: William *Bedman* 1327 SRSo; William *Bedemon* 1381 SRSt. ME *bedeman* 'a man of prayer', one who prays for the soul of a benefactor.

Beal, Beale, Beales, Beals, Beall, Beel, Beels: (i) *Bele* 1194 Cur (Sx); Alexander *filius Bele* 1203 P (L); *Bella, Bele* Coty 1275 RH (L); Thomas *Bele* 1206 Cur (Ess); John *Bele* 1275 SRWo; Ralph *le Bele* 1279 RH (C); Joan *Beles* 1327 SRSo; William *Beall* 1379 PTY. OFr *bele* 'beautiful', used also as a woman's name. (ii) Simon *de Beel* 1275 SRWo; Thomas *de Behil* 1382 Bardsley (Nb); John *Bele* 1517 ib. (Nb). From Beal (Northumberland), earlier *Behill*, or Beal (WRYorks), *Begale* DB.

Beaman, Beamand, Beament, Beamont: *v.* BEAUMONT

Beamer: *v.* BEEMER

Beames, Beamish, Beamiss, Beams: William *Baumis, de Beaumis* Hy 2 DC (L); Richard *de Beames, de Belmes.* 1191–2 P (Sa); Robert *de Beaumeis* 1208 FFHu. From Beaumais-sur-Dive (Calvados). *v.* ANF.

Bean, Beane, Been: (i) Robertus *filius Biene* 1168 P (Cu); Ricardus *filius Bene* 1278 AssLa; Gerard, Ailwardus *Bene* 1166 P (Nf), 1180 P (Lo); Juliana *Bean* 1301 SRY. *Bene* is an original nickname from ME *bēne* 'pleasant, genial, kindly' (a1200 NED) which itself is also used as a nickname. We have also OE *bēan* 'bean', used like *Barley*, of a grower or seller of beans. cf. John *le Bener* 1282 LLB A. Also a nickname. The bean was regarded as typical of things of small value. cf. 'Al nas wurth a bene' c1325 MED. cf. Adam *Benecod* 1221 *ElyA* (Nf). Or we may have reference to the Twelfth-night custom when the man in whose portion of the cake the bean was found was appointed King of the Company. (ii) The Scottish *Bean* is from Gael *beathán*, a diminutive of *betha, beatha* 'life'.

Bear, Beara, Beare, Beer, Beers, Bere, De La Bere: (i) Ordric *de Bera* 1168 P (D); William *de la Bera* 1168 P (Ha); Nicholas *Attebere* 1247 AssSo; Henry *del Beer* 1327 SRDb. Walter *de la Bere* lived in 1263 at Beare Green in Capel (Surrey) and owed his name to his residence near a swinepasture (OE *bǣr*). *v.* PN Sr 267. But the real home of this name is in the south-west. In Devon there are 18 places called Beare or Beara and 17 named Beer, Beera or Beere, from most of which surnames were derived, usually in the form (Robert) *atte Beare* (1330). These are from OE *bearu* 'grove', the normal dative of which (*bearwe*) would

become *barrow*. In Devon and the neighbouring counties of Somerset and Dorset, it had a dative *beara*, ME *bere*. (ii) Tedric' *Vrs*' 1130 P (O); Theodoricus *le Bere* 1166 Oseney (O); Ralph *Bere* 1177 P (Nf); Nicholas *le Urs* 1219 AssSt; Robert *le Beer* 1296 SRSx. OE *bera* 'bear' (translated by Lat *ursus*, OFr *urs*).

Beard: (i) *Ælfsige mid þam berde* c1100–30 OEByn (D); Hugo *AlaBarbe, Barbatus* 1086 DB (Ha); Baldeuuinus *cum barba* 1086 ICC (C); Alsi *berd* 1086 InqEl (C); Alwine *bierd* 1148 Winton (Ha); Alfwin' *berd* 1155 P (Herts); Robert *a la barbe* 1178 P (Bk); Thomas *Ouelabarbe* 1280 AssSo; William *od la Barbe* 1311 LLB D. OE *beard*, frequently translated by Fr *barbe*, and often in a prepositional form, '(the man) with the beard'. *v.* BARBE. (ii) Adam *de Berd* 1327 SRDb. From Beard (Derby).

Beardwell: *v.* BARDWELL

Bearryman: *v.* BERRIMAN

Beasley: *v.* BEESLEY

Beaston: *v.* BEESTON

Beat: *v.* BEET

Beater, Better: Richard *Batere* 1166 P (Berks); Jordan *le Bettere* 1200 Cur (L); John *le Betere* 1275 RH (W). OE *bēatere* 'beater, fighter, champion'. cf. CHAMPION. It may also be a short form of the common *Coperbeter, Flaxbeter, Goldbeter, Ledbeter, Wodebeter, Wolbeter.*

Beatey: *v.* BEATY

Beaton: *v.* BEETON

Beatson: John *Batisoun* 1458 Black; William *Beatisoun* 1627 ib.; Thomas *Beatson* 1691 FrY. A Scottish form of BATESON, found also as *Battison*.

Beaty, Beatey, Beattie, Beatty: *Baty* Flessor c1340 Black; David *filius Bety* 1342 ib.; John *Bety* 1558 ib.; Hew *Batie* 1569 ib. A Scottish form of BATEY.

Beauchamp, Beachamp, Beacham, Beachem, Beecham: Hugo *de Belcamp* 1086 DB (Herts); William *de Bello Campo* 1161 Templars (Lo); Robert *de Beauchamp* 1203 FFEss; John *Bechaumpe* 1376 LLB H; Oliver *Beacham* 1674 HTSf. The DB family came from Beauchamps (La Manche). Others may have come from other French places named Beauchamp.

Beaufoy, Boffee, Boffey, Boffy, Buffey: Ralph *de Bellafago, de Belfago* 1086 DB (Nf, Sf); William *Belfou, de Belfou* ib. (Herts, W); Nicholas *de Bealfo* 1114–16 Holme (Nf); Thomas *de Beaufow* 1185 RotDom (R); Robert *de Biaufey* 1210 Cur (Db); Emma *de Beaufey, de Beaufo* 1212, 1236 Fees (Nt); Thomas *Buffy* 1276 RH (O); William *Bouffaye* 1544 FFHu; Anne *Boffey* 1793 Bardsley. The DB tenants came from Beaufour (Calvados), *Belfou, Beaufou* 1100, *Bellefai* c1160 OEByn.

Beauman: *v.* BEAUMONT, BOWMAN

Beaumont, Beaument, Beumant, Beaman, Beamand, Beament, Beamont, Beauman, Bemand, Belmont, Bemment: Rogerius *de Belmont, de Bellomonte* 1086 DB (Do, Gl); Ralph *de Belmunt* 1187 P (O); *John Bemund* 1274 RH (Sf); Godfrey *de Beumund* 1275 RH (Nf); William *Beumound*, *Beumon* 1279 RH (O); John *Bomund* 1300 FFSf; Robert *Beaumond* 1332 SRSx; Laurence *Beamond* 1369 LLB G; Wedow *Beament*, Mrs *Beamonte* 1568 SRSf; Mrs *Bemant*, Peter *Beaman*, Widow *Bomant* 1674 HTSf. From one of the five places in Normandy named Beaumont. The DB family came from Beaumont-le-Roger (Eure).

Beausire, Bellsyer, Bowser: Geoffrey *Beusire* 1226 Cur (Ess); John *Belsire* 1274 RH (K); Gregory *Bousyre* 1314–16 SRSt; Alexander *Belsier*, *Belshyre* 1542 Oseney. OFr *bel*, *beu* and *sire* 'fair sir', a term of address (cf. GOODSIR, SWEETSER), confused in the 16th century with BELCHER.

Beavan, Beaven, Beavon: *v.* BEVAN

Beaver, Beavers, Beavors, Beever, Beevers, Beevor, Beevors, Bevar, Bever, Bevers, Bevir, Biever: (i) Ralph *de Belueeir* 1170 P (Y); John *de Beauveir* 1204 AssY; William *Bever*, *de Beuver* 1207–8 Cur (Lei, Do). From Belvoir (Leics), pronounced *Beever*. (ii) Godwyn *Beure* 1084 (c1300) ELPN; Adam *Bever* 1274 RH (So); Thomas *le Bevere* 1327 SRSx. A nickname from the beaver (OE *beofor*).

Beaves, Beavis, Beevis, Beves, Bevis, Beviss, Bovis: (i) Goisbert *de Beluaco* 1086 DB (Herts); Thomas *Beueys* 1317 AssK; Philip *de Beauveys* 1321 QW (La); Robert *de Beueys* 1327 SRC. From Beauvais (Oise). (ii) Odo *Belfiz* 1176 P (Ha); William *Beaufiz*, *Biaufiz* 1208 Cur (Gl); Hugo *Beaufiz*, *Beauuiz* 1221 AssWa. OFr *bel*, *biau*, *beau* 'fine' and AFr *fiz* 'son'. *Bel* was often used as a term of affection, hence 'dear son'.

Beavill: *v.* BEVILL

Beavin: *v.* BEVIN

Beazley: *v.* BEESLEY

Bec: *v.* BECK

Bech: *v.* BEECH

Becher: *v.* BEECHER

Beck, Becke, Bec: (i) Walter *Bec* 1086 DB (Bk); Geoffrey *de Bech* ib. (Do); Robert *de Becco* 1199 AssSt. The DB under-tenants probably came from Bec-Hellouin (Eure). Others may have come from one of the numerous places in France named Bec. (ii) Adam *del Bec* 1207 Cur (L); Henry *Delebec*, Ralph *del Bek* (his son) 1263 Ipm (Ess); Robert *Attebek* 1297 SRY. 'Dweller by the brook', ME *bekke*, ON *bekkr*, common in the North, the Danelaw, and in Scotland. (iii) Æluuin *Becce filius*, Brun *Becce filius* c1095 Bury (Sf); Robertus *filius Beck'* 1297 MinAcctCo (Y). OE **Becca*, from *becca* 'pick-axe', or OE *Beocca*. (iv) Osbert *Becche* c1140 ELPN; Terricus *Becce* c1166 ib.; Robert *Becke* 1296 SRSx. Either from the personal-name above or from OE *becca* 'mattock', metonymic for a maker, seller or user of mattocks. (iv) Henry *Bec* 1196 P (L); Bartholomew *Beck* 1297 MinAcctCo (W). OFr *bec* 'beak, bill of a bird'. According to Suetonius, Antonius Primus, as a boy, had a nickname *Beccus*, 'id valet, *gallinacei rostrum*', a nose like a cock's beak. cf. also *Naso adunco*, a beake-nose 1598 Florio.

Becket, Beckett, Beckitt: William *Bechet*, *Beckett* c1155 DC (L); Robert *Beket* 1176 FF (Berks); Robert *Becket* 1379 PTY. This surname, common in the 12th and 13th centuries as *Beket*, without article or preposition, must be a diminutive of OFr *bec*, 'little beak or mouth' (Moisy). *v.* BECK (iv). The only evidence noted that this might possibly be 'at the beck-head' is: Elezabeth *Becked* 1549 RothwellPR (Y). It may occasionally be local, from Beckett (Berks): John *de Beckcote* 1279 RH (O); or from Beckett (Devon), from a 1333 surname *Bykecote* (PN D 179).

Beckwith: John *Bekwyth'* 1379 PTY; Richard *Bekwyth* 1415 IpmY; Adam *Bekwith* 1423 FrY. From Beckwith (WRYorks).

Beddall: *v.* BEADEL

Beddard: *v.* BEDWARD

Beddoe, Beddoes, Beddow, Beddowes, Beddows: *Bedo ap* Richard 1493 SaAS 2/xi; Johanna *Bedowe* 1577 Bardsley; John *Beddoe* 1641 SaAS 3/iv. From *Bedo*, a pet-form of *Meredith*.

Bedell, Bedle: *v.* BEADEL

Bedloe: William *Bedeluue*, *Biedeluue* 1191–3 P (C). OE **Bīedlufu*, an otherwise unknown woman's name, from OE *bēodan* 'to command' and *-lufu* 'love'.

Bedser: Alice *de Bedesore*, John *Badesore* 1296, 1327 SRSx. From a lost place, possibly near Bexhill (Sussex).

Bedward, Beddard: Dafydd *ap Edward ap* Hoell 1498 Chirk; John *Bedhard* 1643 FrY. Welsh *ap* 'son' of *Edward*. cf. BOWEN.

Bedwell, Bidwell, Biddwell, Bidewell: Stephen *de Bedewell'* 1229 Cl (Ess). 'Dweller by the spring or stream in a shallow valley' (OE **bydewelle*), as at Bedwell (Essex, Herts), Bedlar's Green (Essex), Bidwell (Northants, Beds, Devon, Som), or Biddles Fm (Bucks). *v.* PN Nth 222. Bedwellhay in Ely is *Bedelhey* 1576, *Beddlehay* 1615 PN C 127. Later forms have been confused with BEADEL.

Bee: Walter *le Be* 1195 Oseney (O); Robert *Be* 1198 CurR (Y); William *le Beo* 1243 AssSo. OE *bēo* 'bee', used, no doubt, of a busy, industrious person.

Beech, Beach, Bech: John *de la Beche* 1236 Fees (Wo); Idonea *de Beche* 1240 FFEss; Jacob' *atte Beche* 1296 SRSx; William *de la Beche* 1340 FFSt. *Beche* may be for OE *bece* 'stream', *bēce* 'beech', or from OE *bæce* 'stream', and without further evidence it is impossible to distinguish these in ME. In Worcs and Staffs, where *bæce* normally survives as *Bach(e)*, *beche* is probably a variant of this. Robert *de Beche* (1327 SRC) came from either Landbeach or Waterbeach, both earlier *Beche* 'stream, valley'. Elias *ater Beche* (1296 SRSx) probably lived at Beech Fm in Battle. 'Dweller by the stream or the beech-tree.'

Beecham: *v.* BEAUCHAMP

Beecher, Becher: John *Becher(e)* 1279 RH (C), 1428 FA (Sx). 'Dweller by the beech-tree' (OE *bēce*). *v.* BEECHMAN.

Beechey: Thomas *de la Bechey* 1279 RH (O) 'Dweller by the beech-enclosure', OE *bēce*, *(ge)hæg*.

Beechman: John *Becheman* 1332 SRSr. Identical with BEECHER.

Beedell, Beedle: *v.* BEADEL

Beel(s): *v.* BEAL

Beeman, Beman, Beaman: R. *Beman* 1283 SRSf; William *le Bemon* 1324 LaCt. OE *bēo* 'bee' and *mann*, 'bee-keeper'. The modern forms may also be for BEAUMONT.

Beemaster: *v.* BEMISTER

Beemer, Beamer: Normannus *Bemere* 1160–5 ELPN. OE *bīemere* 'trumpeter'.

Been: *v.* BEAN

Beer(e): *v.* BEAR

Beesley, Beasley, Beazleigh, Beazley, Beisley, Bezley: Thomas *de Besleg* 1246 AssLa. From Beesley (Lancs).

Beeston, Beaston, Beeson: (i) William *de Beston(e)* 1153–66 Holme (Nf), 1205 P (Nt). From Beeston (Notts), pronounced *Beeson*, or one of the other Beestons, explained as *Bēostun* 'tūn where bent-grass grew' (DEPN). (ii) Andrew *de Bieston* 1203 P (Y); Herbert *de Beston* 1219 AssY; Richard *de Bestayn* 1297 MinAcctCo (Y). From Beeston (WRYorks), *Bestayn* 1297 MinAcctCo, a place called 'by the stone', OE *bī*, *be* and ON *steinn*, alternating with OE *stān*. (iii) Ralph *de Bestune* 1279 RH (C). Ralph came from The Beesons in Sutton (Cambs), *Estounesende* 1302, *Beestoun* 1348 '(the place) to the east of the hamlet', in contrast to *Westounesende* de Sutton (PN C 239). (iv) William *Besteton*, Ralph *Biesteton* c1248 Bec (Ha); Ralph *Byeston* 1256 RamsCt (Hu). '(The man who lived) to the east of the hamlet', OE *bī ēastan tūne*.

Beet, Beat: Adam *Bete* 1298 DbCh, 1332 SRLa. *Bete* is a pet-form of *Beton* (Beatrice).

Beeton, Beaton: *Beton* de Wath 1379 PTY; *Bete* or *Betune* (Betryse) c1440 PromptParv; John *Betoun* 1311 ColchCt; Richard *Beton* 1327 SRDb. *Beton*, a diminutive of *Bete* (Beatrice), still used as a christian name in Cornwall in 1630 (Bardsley).

Beevens: *v.* BEVAN

Beever(s): *v.* BEAVER

Beevis: *v.* BEAVES

Beilby: *v.* BIELBY

Beisley: *v.* BEESLEY

Belch, Belk, Balch, Baulch, Boalch: William *Belch* 1185 Templars (O); William *le Belch* 1295 ParlR (Ess); Robert *Balch* 1327 SRSo; Richard *le Balch* 1332 SRSx. ME *balche, belche, belke*, from OE *bælc* (*bælce*), (i) a belch, *eructatio*, (ii) stomach, pride, arrogance. From this latter sense a surname could arise. cf. PRIDE. The word probably had also in ME the same meaning as OE *balca* 'balk, beam, bank, ridge', and *le Balch*, *le Belch* may have meant 'the beam', used metaphorically for a man of stout, heavy build. *Belk* was also used as a topographical term: Henry *del Belk* 1252 Ipm (Nt), probably 'dweller by the bank or ridge'.

Belcham, Belchem, Belsham, Belshem, Bellsham: These Essex surnames preserve the correct *-ham* and the local pronunciation (*Belsham*) of Belchamp Otton, St Paul's and Walter (Essex).

Belchambers: *v.* BELLCHAMBER

Belcher, Belsher, Belshaw, Beuscher, Beushaw, Bewshire, Bewshaw, Bewshea, Beaushaw, Bowsher: Thomas *Belcher* 1219 AssY; Richard *Belecher* 1274 RH (Gl); Alexander *Belcher* 1453 FFEss; Margaret *Bewcher* 1530 SIA (Sf); William *Bewshawe* 1539 FrY; Henry *Bowschere* 1575 Oxon; Henry *Belsher* 1662 HTEss. OFr *bel(e)*, *beu* and *chiere*, originally 'fair face', later 'fair look', one of a cheerful, pleasant demeanour. The surname was often confused with BEAUSIRE, and in the York Plays is used as a term of address, often derogatory: Herod addresses a messenger, 'Bewcher! wele ye be', and when Annas orders a boy who has been bound to be brought in, the soldier announces, 'Lo, here is the belschere broght that ye bad bring'. cf. GOACHER, GOODFAR.

Beldam, Beldan, Beldham, Beldom: Godfrey, Richard *Beledame* 1296, 1332 SRSx. AFr *beledame* 'fine lady', a derogatory nickname. ME *beldam* 'grandmother' is not recorded before c1440 and the sense 'aged woman, hag' not until the 16th century.

Belding: *v.* BALDING

Belenger: *v.* BERRINGER

Belfrage: John *Belverage* 1685, Thomas *Belfrage* or *Beveridge* 1690 Black. A Scottish form of BEVERIDGE, with intrusive *l* as in *Calmeron* for Cameron and *Chalmers* for Chambers. In Fife, the name also occurs as BERRIDGE: John *Berrage*, *Berrige* 1675, 1711 Black.

Belgian, Belgion, Belgions: William *Belegambe* 1185 Templars (So); Nicholas *Belejaumbe* 1221 AssWo; John *Belgeam* 1492 Black. AFr *bele jambe* 'fine leg'.

Belham, Belhomme: *v.* BELLHAM

Belk: *v.* BELCH

Bell: (i) Ailuuardus *filius Belli* 1086 DB (Sf); Ricardus *filius Bell* 1279 RH (Hu); Osbertus *filius Belle* 1297 SRY. *Bell* may be a pet-form of *Isabel*. *Bella* is probably a latinization of *Bele*, OFr *belle* 'beautiful'. *v.* BEAL. *Bellus* is a Latin form of OFr *Bel* 'beautiful', otherwise unknown as a personal-name. (ii) Seaman *Belle* 1181–7 ELPN; Serlo *Belle* 1190 P (Y). OE *belle* 'bell', probably metonymic for BELLMAN or BELLRINGER. (iii) Hugo *bel* 1148 Winton (Ha); Robertus *bellus* ib.; Robert *le bel* 1186–1200 Holme (Nf). OFr *bel* 'beautiful, fair'. (iv) Roger *del Bel* 1209 P (Nf); Robert *de la Belle* 1222 DBStP; John *atte Belle* 1332 SRLo. The last example denotes one who lives at the sign of the Bell. This type of name is not so common as has been suggested and the other examples are unusually early. They may denote a dweller by the church or town bell or bellhouse or be metonymic for the bellman or bellringer.

Bellam: *v.* BELLHAM

Bellamy: Walter *Belami* 1185 Templars (Y); Ralph *Belamy* 1214 Cur (Nf). OFr *bel ami* 'fair friend'.

Bellanger: *v.* BERRINGER

Bellas: *v.* BELLHOUSE

Bellchamber, Bellchambers, Belchambers: Thomas *Belchambre* 1369 LLB G. This surname has been regarded as a corruption of *Bellencombre*. The family of William *Belencumbre* (1235 *Ass*) settled in Essex and has long been extinct. Their name survives in Belcumber Hall in Finchingfield and there is no evidence that the name ever took the form of *Belchamber*. The solitary example above (nearly 500 years earlier than the first example in NED) was earlier *atte Belchambre*. The bellhouse was originally a detached structure. The belfry (c1440 NED) was generally attached to the church and later (1549) was used of the room or storey where the bells were hung. This must also have been called the bellchamber. A man could hardly live in this and if he lived by the bellchamber, a more natural name would have been *atte church*. Hence, the surname probably refers to the keeper of the bellchamber or the ringer of the bells, often, no doubt, the same man.

Bellenger: *v.* BERRINGER

Beller: Richard *le Beller* 1281 MEOT (L); Henry *Beller* 1332 SRCu. A derivative of OE *belle* 'bell', a bell-founder.

Bellett, Bellot, Bellott, Bellotte: *Belet* 1188 BuryS (Sf); William *Belet, Belot* 1086 DB (Do); Herueus *belet* 1130 P (O); Adam *Belot* 1279 RH (Hu). *Belet*, which was very common, may be a nickname from a diminutive of OFr *bel* 'beautiful'. Both *Belet* and *Belot* are diminutives of *Bel*, a pet-form of *Isabel*.

Bellham, Belham, Bellam, Belhomme: Reginald *Belhume, Belhome* 1179, 1180 P (C, Sx); William *Belhom* 1279 RH (C). OFr *bel* 'beautiful, fair' and *homme* 'man'.

Bellhanger: *v.* BERRINGER

Bellhouse, Bellas: Ernald *Belhus* 1167 P (Nf); Richard *de Bellus, de Bellehus* 1206 P (Y), 1230 P (Ess); Walter *atte Belhous* 1266 LLB C; Richard *Bellus* 1572 RothwellPR (Y); William *Bellas* 1653 FrY. From residence near a detached bell-house or tower, OE *bell-hūs*.

Bellinger: *v.* BERRINGER

Bellis, Belliss: (i) John *ap Elys* 1513 Chirk; John *Bellis* 1747 Bardsley (Ch). 'Son of Ellis.' cf. BOWEN. (ii) For BELLOWS, of which the regular form was *bellies* until the 16th century, whilst *bellis, bellice* are still found in the dialects (NED). cf. Ursula *Bellies* 1610 Bardsley.

Bellmaine: Nicholas *Belesmains* 1210 Cur (Herts); John *Belemeins* 1237 Colch (Herts). OFr *belle* and *mains* 'beautiful hands'.

Bellman, Belman: William *Belman* 1300 Crowland (C); Katerina *Beleman* 1327 SRC; Gilbert *Belman* 1398 Black. OE *belle* and *mann* 'bellman', in York and Scotland, used of the town-crier. *Beleman* may mean 'servant of *Bele*' (*v.* BEAL) or it might be a hybrid, OF *bele* 'beautiful, fair' and ME *man*. cf. FAIRMAN, BELLHAM. In the Denham Parish Register (Suffolk) the surname appears as *Beleman, Belleman, Belliman* (1585–1606), *Billeman* (1776), *Billyman* (1784) and in that of Rushbrook as *Billeman* and *Billerman* (1760, 1791). The per-

sistent medial vowel suggests that this is for ME *beli-man*, from ME *beli* 'bellows', 'bellows-blower'. cf. BELLOW.

Bellot(t): *v.* BELLETT

Bellow, Bellows, Beloe, Billows: William *Beli* 1178 P (Wa); Ralph *Belewe* 1253 Oseney (O); John *Below* 1379 PTY; John *Byllow, Below, Bellow* 1464–79 Oseney (O). ME *beli, belu, below*, from OE (*blæst)bel(i)ʒ* 'bellows', used only as a singular until 1400; here, metonymic for a bellows-blower. cf. William *Belymuð* 1275 RH (Nf), 'bellows-mouth'.

Bellringer: Richard *Belringer* 1216–72 MFOT (Sr). 'Bell-ringer' (1543 NED).

Bellsham: *v.* BELCHAM

Bellson, Belson: (i) Thomas *Beleson* 1317 AssK; John *Belessone, Bellesson* 1339, 1341 Crowland (C). 'Son of *Bele*' (*v.* BEAL) or of *Bell* (Isabel). (ii) *Belsante, Belsant* 1185, 1190 Oseney (O); William *Belsent, Belesent* 1327, 1332 SRSx. OFr *Belisant, Belisent* (f), OG *Belissendis.*

Bellsyer: *v.* BEAUSIRE

Belmont: *v.* BEAUMONT

Beloe: *v.* BELLOW

Belsham, Belshem: *v.* BELCHAM

Belshaw, Belsher: *v.* BELCHER

Belson: *v.* BELLSON

Belt: Arnold, Robert *Belt(e)* 1203 FFEss, 1327 SRC. OE *belt*, used of a belt-maker. cf. Benedict *le beleter* 1295 FrY.

Beman: *v.* BEEMAN

Bemand: *v.* BEAUMONT

Bemister, Beemaster: The local pronunciation of Beaminster (Dorset).

Bemment: *v.* BEAUMONT

Benbow, Benbough: William *Bendebowe* 1349 LLB F; John *Benbowe* 1545 FFHu. 'Bend bow', a nickname for an archer.

Bence: Ernisius *filius Bence* 1175 P (Y); Ærnulfus *filius Benze* 1178 P (Nb); Osmund *Benz* 1066, 1086 DB (Db); William *Bence* 1279 RH (O). OG *Benzo*. A diminutive *Benzelinus* occurs in DB (O, W) and gave rise to a surname in Suffolk (Seman *Bencelyn* 1327 SRSf), side by side with *Bence* (Roger *Bence* 1327 SRSf), whilst the feminine *Bencelina* is found in Kent (1207 Cur).

Bench: Robert *Benche* 1279 RH (C); Thomas *atte Bench* 1327 SRSo. 'Dweller by the terrace, bank, river-bank', from OE *benc* 'bench'. cf. Roger *le Bencher* 1279 RH (O).

Bendall, Bendell: *v.* BENTALL

Bender: Robert *le Bendare* 1327 SRSx. A derivative of OE *bendan* 'to bend' (the bow). Perhaps synonymous with BENBOW.

Bendle: *v.* BENTALL

Benedict, Bennedik: Geoffrey *Benedicite* 1221 AssWa; William *Benedicite* 1322 AssSt. Lat *benedicite* 'bless (you)', a nickname, no doubt from a favourite saying.

Benger: *v.* BERRINGER

Benian: *v.* BEYNON

Benjamin, Benjaman: *Beniamin* 12th MedEA (Nf); Roger *Beniamin* 1166 P (Nf). Hebrew

Benjamin 'son of the south', interpreted in Genesis 'son of the right hand', much less frequent than *Adam*. The surname is also found in Berkshire, Cambridgeshire and Wiltshire before 1250.

Benn, Bennis, Benns: *Benne* de Ecclesille 1246 AssLa; John son of *Benne* 1306 Wak (Y); Leuuinus *Benne* 1066 DB (Sf); Siuard *Benne* c1190 Gilb (L); Thomas *Ben* 1275 SRWo; Thomas *Bennes* 1524 SRSf. Whether the later Suffolk surname (1327, 1381 SRSf) is identical with the DB *Benne* is doubtful. This Tengvik explains as a nickname 'the plump, lumpish one', or from OE *Bynna* or *Beonna* for the post-Conquest use of which there is no clear evidence. The 13th-century *Benne* is more likely to be a pet-name of some common christian name, of *Bennet* rather than of *Benjamin*.

Bennedik: *v.* BENEDICT

Bennet, Bennett, Bennette, Bennetts, Bennitt, Bennitts: *Beneit* Kernet 12th DC (Nt); *Beneit, Benedictus* Kepeherm 1193, 1200 Oseney (O); Robertus *filius Benite* 1301 SRY; Robert *Beneyt* Hy 2 Gilb (L); William *Benet* 1208 ChR (Du); Robert *Benyt* 1327 SRC; Thomas *Benetes* 1327 SRSt. OFr *Beneit, Beneoit*, Lat *Benedictus* 'blessed', a common christian name from the 12th century.

Benninger: *v.* BERRINGER

Bennion: *v.* BEYNON

Bennison: John *Benettesson* 1396 FrY; Robert *Benyson* 1517 GildY. 'Son of *Bennet*.'

Benson: (i) John *Benneson*, Adam *Bensome* 1326 Wak (Y); Alan *Benson* 1332 SRCu; John *Benesson* 1393 FrY. 'Son of *Benn* (Bennet)'. (ii) Peter *de Bensinton* 1208 Cur (O); Henry *de Benson* 1269 Oseney (O). From Benson or Bensington (Oxon).

Bent: Nicholas *Bent* 1256 AssNb; Henry, Adam *del Bent* 1327, 1332 SRSt. 'Dweller by the grassy plain, heath', ME *bent*, from OE *beonet* 'stiff grass'.

Bentall, Benthall, Bendall, Bendell, Bendle: Robert *de Benethal'* 1221 AssSa; Philip *de Benedhal* 1255 RH (Sa). From Benthall (Salop).

Bentley, Bently, Bintley: William *de Benetlega* 1176 P (Db); William *de Benteley* 1316–17 FFWa; John *Benteley* 1388–9 FFSr. From one or other of the many places of this name.

Benyon: *v.* BEYNON

Berard: *Berardus* c1125 Bury (Sf), 1143–7 DC (L); Reginaldus *filius Berard'* 1221 AssGl; William, Ralph *Berard* 1208–12 Cur (Y). OFr *Berart*, OG *Berard* 'bear-strong'.

Berecloth: *v.* BARRACLOUGH

Bergh: Rogert *de le Bergh'* 1221 AssWo. 'Dweller by the hill', OE *beorg*.

Beriman: *v.* BERRIMAN

Beringer: *v.* BERRINGER

Berk(e)ley: *v.* BARCLAY

Berkenshaw: *v.* BIRKENSHAW

Berker: *v.* BARKER

Berkshire, Barkshire: William *Berksir* 1249 AssW; William *de Barkescire* 1317 AssK; John *Barksher* 1525 SRSx. 'The man from Berkshire.'

Berman: *v.* BARMAN

Bernard: *v.* BARNARD

Berner: Tetbaldus *filius Bernerii* 1086 DB (D); *Bernerus* 1211 Cur (Bk); William *Berner* 1150–60 DC (L); Robert *le berner, le Bernier* 1190–1 (L); Walter *Berner*, Nicholas *le Berner* 1219 AssY. (i) OFr *Bernier*, OG *Berner* 'bear-army'; (ii) OFr *berner, bernier* 'keeper of the hounds'; (iii) A derivative of OE *beornan* 'to burn', a limeburner or charcoal burner. cf. ASHBURNER; (iv) A toponymic, equivalent to *atte berne*. *v.* BARNE. *v.* also BRENNER, BOURNER.

Berners: Hugo *de Berneres* 1086 DB (Mx, Ess); Goda *de Berners* 1185 Templars (Lo). From Bernières (Calvados).

Berney, Burney, Burnie: Ralph *de Bernai* 1086 DB (He, Wo, Sf); Henry *de Berney* 1268 Bardsley (Nf); Walter *Berneye* 1362 LLB G; Roger, Thomas *Burney* 1451 Bardsley (Nf), 1524 SRSf. From Bernay (Eure) or Berney (Norfolk).

Berrecloth: *v.* BARRACLOUGH

Berrey: *v.* BERRY

Berrick: *v.* BERWICK

Berridge: *v.* BELFRAGE

Berrie: *v.* BERRY

Berriff: *v.* BRIGHTIFF

Berriman, Berryman, Beriman, Bearryman: Edricus *Buriman* 1148 Winton (Ha); Alexander *Beriman* 1176 P (Bk). 'Servant at the manor-house', from ME *buri*, the manorial use of OE *burh*.

Berringer, Beringer, Bellenger, Belenger, Bellinger, Bellanger, Bellhanger, Benninger, Benger: *Berengerus* 1086 DB (Nf); Robertus *filius Berengarii* c1150 EngFeud (L); *Bengerus* 1203 Cur (Beds); *Belingar'* 1207 ChR (Do); *Berenger* faber 1219 AssY; Hugo *Berengeri* Ric 1 DC (L); Walter *Beneger* 1208 Cur (Gl); Reginald *Beringer* c1260 Lewes (C); John *Berenger* alias *Beniger* 1271 Ipm (W); John *Belinger* 1275 SRWo. OFr *Berengier*, OG *Beringar* 'bear-spear', the name of one of the paladins in the Charlemagne romances and fairly common in England in the 12th and 13th centuries. The various forms are due to the common Anglo-Norman interchange or loss of liquids in names containing *l, n* and *r. Berenger* became *Belenger* or *Benenger*, and in the latter the second *n* was lost, giving *Beneger*, later shortened to *Benger*.

Berriwin: *v.* BERWIN

Berrow: *v.* BARROW

Berry, Berrey, Berrie, Bury: Gilbert *de la Beri* 1202 P (Co); Adam *Biry* 1257 Ipm (Y); Roger *Bury* 1260 AssC; Hubert *Bery* 1268 FFSf; Walter *del Bury* 1275 SRWo; William *ate Bery* 1327 SRSx. OE *byrig*, dative of *burh* 'fort', surviving in Berry Pomeroy (Devon), Bury St Edmunds (Suffolk) and Bury (Hunts, Lancs). ME *beri, biri, buri* was used of a manor-house and the surname must often mean 'servant at the manor-house'. Occasionally *Bury* may be 'dweller by an enclosure near the bower' (OE *būr*) or the fort (OE *burh*): Hugo *de Burhey*.

Berrycloth: *v.* BARRACLOUGH

Berryman: *v.* BERRIMAN

Bert: *Berta* 1101–21 Holme (Nf), 1143–7 DC

(L); Robertus *vir Berte* 1196 P (Sx); Richard, John *Berte* 1327 SRSf, 1332 SRSx. OFr *Berte* (f), OG *Berhta, Berta*.

Bertalot: *v*. BARTLET

Bertenshaw: *v*. BIRKENSHAW

Bertin, Bertim, Bartin: *Bertinus* 1112 Bury (Sf), 1203 Cur (Sx); *Bertinus* Ruffyn 1322 FFK; *Bartyn de Rankesley* 1441 ShefA (Y); Peter *Bertin* 1204 ChR; John *Bertyn* 1296 SRSx. OFr *Bertin*, OG *Bertin*, a diminutive of names in *Berht-*. Michaëlsson notes its use as a hypocoristic of *Bertrand*.

Bertram, Bertrand: *v*. BARTRAM

Bertwistle: *v*. BIRTWHISTLE

Berwick, Berrick, Barwick, Barrick: Laurence *de Berewyke* 1278 RH (O); Edward *Barwyk* 1463 FrY; John *Barycke* 1547 EA (NS) ii. 'Dweller at an outlying grange', OE *berewīc* 'barley-farm', as at Berwick (Dorset, Northumb, etc.), Berrick (Oxon), Barwick (Norfolk, WRYorks) and Barricks in High Easter (Essex).

Berwin, Berwyn, Berriwin: Goscelinus *Beruinus* 1086 DB (D); Matthew *Berewynson* 1428 FrY. OG *Bernwin*.

Besant, Bessant, Bessent, Beszant, Bezant, Bezzant: Lefwin *besant* 1147–68 Bart (Lo); Robert *Besant* 1186–92 Clerkenwell (Lo), 1195 P (Lo). ME *besant, besand*, OFr *besan*, pl. *besanz*, Lat *byzantius (nummus)*, a gold coin first minted at Byzantium (c1200 NED). *bizantia* is first recorded in MLWL in 1187. cf. *unam bisanciam* c1179 Bart. Lefwin *Besant* was a moneyer (1168 P).

Bessemer: Ingulf *besmere* 1148 Winton (Ha); John *le Besmere* 1263 MESO (Sx); William *Besemere* 1279 RH (O). A derivative of OE *besma* 'besom', a maker of besoms.

Best, Beste: William *Best* 1201 AssSo; Wilkin *le Best* 1260 AssCh. ME, OFr *beste* 'beast', used of a brutal, savage man, in earlier examples often connoting stupidity or folly. Also metonymic for BESTER.

Bestar, Bester: J. *le Bestere* 1279 RH (Hu); R. *Bestare* 1311 ColchCt. A derivative of ME *beste*, a herdsman.

Bestman: John *Besteman* 1327 *SR* (Ess). ME *beste* 'beast' and *man*. Equivalent to BESTER.

Bethel, Bethell: Amicia, Walter *Bethel* 1279 RH (O). The surname is often for ABETHELL, but these forms are too early for such a development. They must be diminutives of *Beth* (Elizabeth). cf. *Betha de Bureswelles* 1176–9 Clerkenwell (Ch).

Bethson: 'Son of *Beth*'. *v*. BETHEL.

Bethune, Betton, Beaton, Beeton: Baldwinus *de Betton, de Betun* 1195–7 P (Berks); William *de Bettoyne, de Betton* 1282–8 LLB A. From Béthune (Pas-de-Calais).

Betson: Richard *Bettessone* 1329 AD i (Hu); William *Bettesone* 1332 SRSt. 'Son of *Bett*.'

Bett, Bette, Betts: Reginald *filius Bette* 1197 FF (Bk); *Betta* Caperun 1247 FrLeic; Terri *Bette* Hy 2 Bart (Lo); Richard *Bette* 1175 P (Nt); Emma *Bettes* 1279 RH (O). Usually explained as a petform of *Beatrice*, which is possible. cf. BEET. There is, however, evidence that *Bette* was at times, at least, masculine: 'Bettinus Beaumond and *Bette*

his brother' 1289 LLB A. '*Bette* the bocher' in *Piers Plowman* was also, presumably, a man. This was a pet-name for *Bertram* or *Bertelmew* (Bartholomew). cf. Robert *Bet* son of *Bartholomew Bette* 1312 LLB D, where the surname may be due to a family partiality for the christian name *Bertelmew*. The form *Bettes* is more frequent than usual and is probably often a toponymic with loss of the preposition. cf. John *del Bettis* 1379 NottBR, from OE *bytt* 'butt, cask, flagon, womb', used topographically like OE *byden* 'butt' (cf. BEDWELL) and *trog* 'trough'. Hence, probably, 'dweller by the hollows'.

Bettenson: *v*. BETTINSON

Better: *v*. BEATER

Betteridge: *v*. BADRICK

Bettinson, Bettenson, Bettison: Adam *le fit Betun* 1285 FFEss; Roger *Betonessone* 1316 ib.; Roger *Betissone* 1327 SRSf. 'Son of *Beton*.' *v*. BEETON.

Betton: *v*. BETHUNE

Bettridge: *v*. BADRICK

Beumant: *v*. BEAUMONT

Beuscher, Beushaw: *v*. BELCHER

Bevan, Bevans, Beven, Bevens, Beavan, Beaven, Beavon, Beevens: Edenevet *ap Ieuan* 1287 AssCh; Howel *ap Evan* c1300 Bardsley; Thomas *Bevans* 1680 ib. 'Son of *Evan*.' cf. BOWEN.

Bevar, Bever: *v*. BEAVER

Beveridge, Bavridge: Wido, William *Beverage* 1212 Cur (Bk), 1230 P (Sr); Richard *Bevereche* c1240 Rams (Hu); William *Bauerich* 1280 AssSo; William *Beuerege* 1297 MinAcctCo; Robert *Beuerich* 1315 FFHu. ME *beuerage*, OFr *bevrege buverage* 'drink, liquor for consumption' (1275 MED), also used of a drink or beverage which binds a bargain. Bailey in 1721 has '*To pay Beverage*, to give a treat upon the first wearing of a new Suit of Cloths' and Dr Johnson in 1755 '*Beverage*, a treat at first coming into a prison, called also *garnish*'. These must be survivals of a much older custom. cf. 'Bargeyns and beuerages bigonne to aryse' (Langland 1362). At Whitby in 1199 the purchaser of land paid by custom 4*d*. for seisin and 1*d*. to the burgesses *ad beuerage* (ChR i, 14). At a court of the Abbot of Ramsey in 1275, Thomas de Welles complained that Adam Garsoppe unjustly detained a copper he had previously bought from him for 6*d*., of which he had paid Adam 2*d*. 'et beuerech' and a drink in advance. Later he went and offered to pay the rest but Adam refused to take it and kept the copper 'to his damage and dishonour 2*s*.'. Adam was fined 6*d*. and pledged his overcoat (Selden i, 138). The nickname may well have been bestowed on a man who made a practice of getting free drinks for clinching bargains he had no intention of keeping. This custom of *beverage* was an old one on the continent where it was called *vin du marché* (Du Cange). *v*. BELFRAGE.

Beverley: Albert *de Beuerli* 1145–52 YCh; John *de Beverlay* 1204 AssY; John *Beverlee* 1327 *SR* (Ess); William *Beverlay* 1401 IpmY. From Beverley (ERYorks).

Beves: v. BEAVES

Bevill, Beville, Beavill: Robert (*de*) *Beyville, de Beville* c1225 Rams (Hu). From Beuville (Calvados) or Bouville (Seine-Inférieure). v. BOVILL.

Bevin, Beavin, Bivins: Simon *Beivin* 1203 FFEss; William *Bevin* 1236 Fees (Do); Nicholas *Boyvin* 1243 AssSo. OFr *bei vin, boi vin* 'drink wine'. cf. DRINKWATER.

Bevir: v. BEAVER

Bevis: v. BEAVES

Bew: Robert *le Beu, le Bel* 1242 AssSo; John *le Beu* (*Bew*) 1327 *SR* (Ess). OFr *bel, beu* 'beautiful, fair'.

Bewes, Bews: John *de Baiocis* 1212 Fees (L); William *Baiues* 1235 Fees (Bk); Henry *de Beause, de Beuse* 1242 ib. From Bayeux (Calvados).

Bewick, Bewicke, Bowick, Buick: John *de Bewic'* 1219 AssY. From Bewick (ERYorks, Northumb), the latter being *Bowich* 1167 P.

Bewshaw, Bewshea, Bewshire: v. BELCHER

Beynon, Baynham, Benian, Benians, Bennion, Benyon, Binnion, Binyon, Pinion, Pinnion, Pinyon, Pinyoun: Cadugan *ap Eynon* 1285 Ch (Radnor); Iorworth *ap Egnon* 1287 AssCh; David *Abeinon* 1313 ParlWrits; John *Baynham* 1455 AD i (Wo); John *Beynon* 1507 Oxon; Daniel *Benion* 1610 FrY; George *Benyon* 1621 Bardsley. Welsh *ap Einion, ap Eynon* 'son of *Einion*'. v. ENNION. *Pinnion*, etc., preserve the *p* of Welsh *ap* 'son', *Beynon*, etc., the *b* of later *ab*. In spite of appearance, *Baynham* is not local in origin.

Bezley: v. BEESLEY

Biart: v. BYARD

Bibbey, Bibby: *Biby* de Knolle 1240 AssLa; Dobbe son of *Bibby* ib.; William *Bibbe* 1196 P (Sa); William *Bibbi* 1228 AssSt; Robert *Bybby* 1284 Wak (Y). A diminutive of *Bibb*, a pet-name of *Isabel*.

Bible: *Bibele* 1200 Oseney (O); Godwin, Robert *Bibel* Ric 1 Cur (Sf), 1283 SRSf. *Bib-el*, a diminutive of *Bibb* (Isabel).

Bicker, Bickers, Bikker: (i) Robert *le Biker* 1176 P (St); Reginald *le Bikere* 1207 P (Sf); Jordan *the Bekere* 1286 AssCh; John *Bickers* 1721 FrY. OE *bēocere*, Anglian *bīocere* (ME *bīker*) 'beekeeper'. (ii) Richard *Bicre* 1185 Templars (L); Roger *de Bikere* 1193 P (L). From Bicker (Lincs).

Bickerstaff, Bickerstaffe, Bickersteth, Biggerstaff: Alan *de Birkestad, de Bikerstath* 1246 AssLa; Henry *Bekerstaff* 1397 IpmNt; Robert *Byggerstafe, Beckerstaffe* 1539, 1557 ArchC xxxiv. From Bickerstaffe (Lancs), *Bickerstath* 1226.

Bicknell, Bignell, Bignall, Bignold: Thomas *de Bikenhulle* 1214 Cur (Wa); John *de Bikenhull, Walter Bykenhulle* 1327 SRSo; Nicholas *Bicknell* 1642 PrD. From Bickenhall (Som), or Bickenhill (Warwicks). v. also BIGNAL.

Bidaway: v. BYTHEWAY

Biddell, Biddle: v. BEADEL

Biddlecombe: Galopin *de Bitelescumba* 1180 P (So). From Bittiscombe (Som).

Biddolph, Biddulph: Thomas *de Bidulf* 1199 AssSt; Roger *de Bydoulf* 1285 FA (St); John *de Bydulfe* 1332–3 SRSt. From Biddulph (Staffs).

Biddwell: v. BEDWELL

Bielby, Beilby: Walter, John *de Beleby* 1202 AssL, 1372 FFY; Sicillia *Beilby* 1464 FrY. From Beelby (Lincs), or Bielby (ERYorks).

Bier(s): v. BYARS

Biever: v. BEAVER

Bifield: v. BYFIELD

Bigg, Bigge, Biggs: Ægelric *Bigga* c1036 OEByn (K); Walter, Henry *Bigge* 1177, 1195 P (Sf, Gl). ME *bigge* 'large, strong, stout' (c1300 MED). A topographical origin is also possible, though the meaning is obscure: William *de Bigges* 1327 SRC; Laurentia *atte Bigge* 1327 SRSo.

Biggar: Baldwin *de Bigre* p1170 Black (Lanark); Henry *de Bygar* 1330 ib. From Biggar (Lanarkshire).

Bigger, Biggers: John *le Biggere* 1307 MEOT (Herts); Richard *Bygor* 1321 FFEss. A derivative of OE *bycgan* 'to buy', a buyer, purchaser. Hollinshed's 'He came here as a bier, not as a begger' implies a play on the pronunciations *bigger* and *begger*.

Biggerstaff: v. BICKERSTAFF

Biggin, Biggins: Thomas *del Biggyng* 1391 FrY; William *atte Byggyngge* 1397 PN C 191. ME *bigging* 'dwelling-place, home', used also of an outbuilding as distinct from a house.

Bignal, Bignall, Bignell, Bignold: William *de Bigenhull* 1279 RH (O); William *Bignolle*, John *Bygnold* 1525 SRSx; Thomas *Bignell* 1727 Bardsley; Robert *Bignall* 1758 FrY. From Bignell in Bicester (Oxon), *Bigenhull* 1220, *Bikenhulle* 1285. Without early forms it is impossible to derive *Bignal* and *Bicknell* with any certainty. v. also BICKNELL.

Bigrave: v. BYGRAVE

Bikker: v. BICKER

Biles, Byles: Walter, Nicholas *Bile* 1185 Templars (Gl), 1176 P (St); Robert *atte Byle*, Walter *atte Bille* 1275, 1327 SRWo. OE *bile* 'bill, beak of a bird' used both as a nickname (cf. BECK) and as a topographical term 'dweller at the beak-like projection, promontory, hill'. v. MELS 13.

Bill, Billes, Bills: Willelmus *filius Bille* 1301 SRY; Griffin, William *Bil* 1188, 1194 P (Wa, Nf); Sewinus *Bille* 1221 AssWa. OE *Bil*, from OE *bil(l)* 'sword', or, possibly, ON *Bildr*, but more commonly metonymic for BILLER.

Biller: John *Billere* 1275 RH (Sf); Henry *le Billere* 1279 RH (C). A derivative of OE *bil* 'a bill', a maker of bills (halberds or billhooks). cf. Thomas *Bilhouk* 1327 SRSo.

Billing, Billings, Billins: (i) Osebertus *Billing* 1188 BuryS (Sf); Geoffrey *Billyng* Hy 3 Gilb (L); Thomas *Billinge* 1282 Oseney (O). Probably OE *Billing*, though rare in OE and not noted in independent use after the Conquest. (ii) Osbertus *de Parua Billing'* 1201 P (Nth). From Billing (Northants). He is probably not identical with the Suffolk sokeman above.

Billinge: Mary *de Billinge* Edw 1 Bardsley (La). From Billinge (Lancs).

Billiter: William *le Belyotar'* 1247 Oseney (O); Robert *le Bellegeter* 1283 FrY; Alexander *le Belleyeter* 1377 AD vi (Ch); John *Bellitour* 1534 LP. OE *belle* and *gēotere* 'bell-founder' (1440 NED). The corresponding French term survives as SENTER which Stahlschmidt confuses with *ceinturier* 'girdler'. Salzman, however, notes a 13th-century Worcester family called indifferently *Ceynturer* and *Belleyeter*. 'The demand for bells could hardly have been large enough to enable a craftsman to specialize entirely in that branch; a bell-maker would always have been primarily a founder, and according as the main portion of his trade lay in casting buckles and other fittings for belts, or pots, or bells, he would be known as a girdler, a potter, or a bell-founder.' Most of the known London bell-founders used the title 'potter'. Ekwall notes that Ædmund *Seintier* 1168 (ELPN) is called a moneyer. Most moneyers were goldsmiths, but occasionally other metal-workers had a die in the mint, and a bell-founder may have acted as a moneyer. Several bells were cast for Westminster Abbey by Edward FitzOdo, the famous goldsmith of Henry III. William *Founder* cast both bells and cannon. His trade stamp, bearing his name and a representation of two birds and a conventionalized tree, appears on a number of bells and hints at his real surname—clearly *Woodward*. In two successive entries in 1385 he is called William *the founder* and William *Wodeward* and in 1417 cannon were supplied by William *Wodeward, founder*. At Exeter c1285, Bishop Peter de Quivil assured the proper care of the bells of the cathedral by granting a small property in Paignton to Robert *le Bellyetere* as a retaining fee, Robert and his heirs being bound to make or repair, when necessary, the bells, organ and clock of the cathedral, the chapter paying all expenses, including the food and drink oı the workmen, and these obligations were duly fulfilled for at least three generations. In 1454 a Norwich bell-founder was called Richard *Brasier*. v. MedInd 145–54.

Billows: v. BELLOW

Bilton: Robert *de Bileton'* 1190 P (Y); John *de Bilton* 1297 SRY; John *Bilton* 1340–1450 GildC. From Bilton (Northumb, Warwicks, ER, NRYorks).

Binder: Hugh *le binder* 1219 AssY; Richard *le Byndere* 1278 LLB B. OE *bindere* 'binder', probably of books. cf. William *le Bokbynder'* 1323 MESO (Ha).

Bindloes, Bindloss, Bindless, Binless: Alan *Byndlowes* 1301 SRY; John *Byndeloue* 1327 SRSf; Robert *Byndlowys* 1379 PTY; Christopher *Byndelase* 1461 PN Ess 641, *Bindlos* 1582 Oxon. 'Bind wolves', a hybrid from OE *bindan* and OFr *lou*. Probably a wolf-trapper. cf. TRUSLOVE.

Bingham: William *de Bingeham* 1175 P (Nt, Db); William *de Bingham* 1257 FFL; William *Byngham* 1433 AssLo. From Bingham (Notts).

Bingley: Aliz *de Bingeleia* 1185 Templars;

William *de Byngeleye* 1339 CorLo; Richard *Bingley* 1541 CorNt. From Bingley (WRYorks).

Binks: Robert *de Benkys*, Thomas *del Binkys* 1297, 1301 SRY; Simon *at the benk* 1327 Pinchbeck (Sf). 'Dweller by the banks.' ME *benk*, a northern form of *bench*, now *bink*. cf. BENCH.

Binless: v. BINDLOES

Binne, Binnes, Binns: Robert *Binns* 1275 RH (L); Missa *Binne* 1279 RH (O); Robert *Byn* 1327 SRSx. OE *binn* 'manger, bin', metonymic for BINNER. Also used topographically: William *de Bynns* 1279 AssSo. 'Dweller by the hollows.'

Binner: Walter *le Bynere* 1296 SRSx; Thomas *Binere* 1373 ColchCt. 'Maker of bins' (for corn, meal, bread, etc.). v. BINNE.

Binney, Binnie, Binny: (i) Ricardus *filius Bini* 1220 Cur (L); Robert, William *Bynny* 1297 SRY, 1379 PTY. From a personal name, probably OE *Bynni*. (ii) Robert *de Binay* 1210 P (C); Ralph *de Bynne* 1317 AssK. 'Dweller on land enclosed by a stream', OE *binnan ēa* 'within the stream', as at Binney Fm in Hoo All Hallows or Binny Cottages in Tonge (Kent). (iii) William *de Binin* 1243 Black; Simon *de Bynninge*, *de Beny* 1396, 1399 ib.; John *Binnie* 1574 ib. From Binney in Uphall (West Lothian). The older form BINNING also survives.

Binning: v. BINNEY

Binnion: v. BEYNON

Bintley: v. BENTLEY

Biram: v. BYROM

Birch, Burch, Byrch: Walter *de la Birche* c1182 MELS (Wo); Richard *de Birches* 1246 AssLa; Ralph *atte Birche*, Richard *del Birche* 1275 SRWo; Robert *Birch* 1275 RH (Sf); William *de la Burch* 1275 MELS (So); John *Burch* 1309 RamsCt (Sf); William *in le Byrchez* 1332 SRSt. 'Dweller by the birch(es)', OE *birce, byrce*.

Birchett, Burchett: (i) Ralph *atte Birchett* c1280 PN Sr 139; William *atte Burchett'* 1296 SRSx; Adam *Byrchet* ib. 'Dweller by the birch-grove', OE **bircett, *byrcett*, very common in minor names in Sussex and found also in Kent, Surrey and Essex. (ii) Henry *Burrcheued* 1204 P (L); Thomas *de Bircheued* 1327 SRDb (Norton); Robert *Birchehed* 1447 Shef (Y); Catharine *Birchett* of Birchett Hall (Norton) 1622 Fanshawe. 'Dweller by the birch-covered headland', OE *birce* and *hēafod*.

Bircumshaw: v. BIRKENSHAW

Bird, Birds, Byrd, Byrde, Bride: Ernald, William *Brid* 1193 P (Y), 1221 *ElyA* (Sf); Ralph, Robert *le Brid(d)* 1235 FFEss, 1243 AssSo; Richard *Bird* 1260 AssC; John *Bride* 1332 SRCu; Richard *Bride* alias *Birde* 1568 SRSf. OE *bridd* 'bird', a nickname. Sometimes, no doubt, metonymic for *birdclever*: Robert *Birdclever* 1427 Calv (Y), William *Burdclever* 1495 FrY, 'bird-catcher'.

Birkenshaw, Birkinshaw, Bircumshaw, Birtenshaw, Berkenshaw, Bertenshaw, Burkenshaw, Burkinshaw, Burkinshear, Burkimsher, Burtinshaw, Burtonshaw, Buttanshaw, Buttenshaw, Buttonshaw, Brigenshaw, Briggenshaw, Briginshaw, Brigginshaw,

Brockenshaw, Brokenshaw, Brokenshire, Bruck-
shaw: William *del Birkenschawe* 1274 Wak (Y);
Roger *Birchynshawe* 1408 LLB I; Richard *Brekyn-
shawe*, *Burtenshaw* 1500, 1637 PN Sx 314; Leonard
Byrkenshay, *Byrtynschaw*, *Byrkynshay* 1542–58
RothwellPR (Y); Thomas *Birkenshire* 1739 FrY.
From Birkenshaw (WRYorks).

Birkett, Birkhead, Brickett: John *de Birkhaved*
1301 SRY; John *Birkehede* 1442 FrY; Henry
Brikket, *Byrkett* 1524 SRSf. 'Dweller by the birch-
covered headland', OE *bi(e)rce*, *hēafod*, surviving
as *Birkett* in late minor names in Cumberland and
Lancashire.

Birks, Burks: Richard *del Birkes* 1275 Wak (Y).
'Dweller by the birches', from the northern form
of OE *birce*.

Birn: *v.* BYRNE
Biron: *v.* BYRON
Birtenshaw: *v.* BIRKENSHAW
Birtwhistle, Birtwisle, Bertwistle, Burtwistle:
John *de Briddestwysill* 1285 AssLa; Adam *de
Briddestwyssle* 1329 Kirkstall (Y); John *Brittwis-
sill* 1397 PrGR; Thomas *Birtwisill* 1460 FrY;
Thomas *Burtwisle* 1618 RothwellPR (Y). From a
lost *Birtwisle* in Padiham (Lancs), Briestwistle in
Thornhill (WRYorks), *Brerethwisel* 1243 PN
WRY ii, 211, or a lost *Breretwisel* in Wath-on-
Dearne (1253 ib. i, 120).

Bisacre, Bisiker, Bisseker: Ralph *de Beseacra*
1182 P (Y); Robert *Bysacle* 1382 FrY. From
Bessacar (WRYorks).

Bisbrown: *v.* BAISBROWN
Bisgood: *v.* PEASCOD
Bish, Bysh: John *de Labisse* 12th MELS (Sr);
John *Bische* 1316 FA (Sx); Ralph *ate Byshe* 1327
SRSx. 'Dweller by a thicket', from OE **(ge)bysce*,
surviving in Bish Wood (Sussex) and Bysshe
Court (Surrey).

Bishell: *v.* BUSHELL
Bishop, Bishopp, Bisshopp: *Biscop* 1066 DB
(Nth); *Bissop* 1195 P (Nf); *Bissop* atte Combe
1327 SRSo; Algar *se Bisceop* c1100–30 OEByn(D);
Lefwinus *Bissop* 1166 P (Nt); Thurstan *le Byssop*
1240 FFEss; Thomas *le Byscop* 1297 MinAcctCo.
OE *Bisc(e)op*, or a nickname for one with the ap-
pearance or bearing of a bishop, or a pageant-
name from the custom of electing a boy-bishop on
St Nicholas's Day.

Bisiker: *v.* BISACRE
Bisler: *v.* BUSHELL
Bismire: William *Bysmere* 1407 LLB I, *Bysmare*
1412 ib. OE *bīsmer*, *bīsmor*. Originally 'shame, disgrace', it developed the sense of 'a person worthy
of scorn; a lewd person, a pander or bawd'.

Biss: Stephen, William *Bys* 1327 SRC, SRSf.
OFr, ME *bis* 'brownish or dark grey', of complexion or dress. cf. BISSETT.

Bisseker: *v.* BISACRE
Bissell, Bissill: *v.* BUSHELL
Bissett: Manasser, Ernulf *Biset* 1155–8 Bury
(Sf), 1176 P (Bk). OFr *biset* 'dark', a diminutive of
bis. cf. BISS.

Bisshopp: *v.* BISHOP

Bithell, Abethell: Lewlyn *ap Ithel* 1325 Parl-
Writs (Radnor), 'Son of *Ithel*'. *v.* ITHELL, BOWEN.

Bittleston, Bittlestone: Robert *de Bitlesden*' 1220
Cur (Berks). From Biddlesden (Bucks).

Bivins: *v.* BEVIN
Black, Blacke: Wulfhun *pes Blaca* 901 OEByn
(So); Wulfsie *se blaca* 964 ib. (K); Willelmus *Blac*,
Niger 1086 DB (Herts, D); Godebertus *leblac*
1130 P (Caermarthen); Thomas *Blac* 1198 Cur (Nf);
Edericke *le Blacke* 1275 RH (L). OE *blæc* 'black',
dark-complexioned. Wlfricus *Niger* (c1080 OEByn)
is said to have received this nickname because he
once went unrecognized among his foes as he had
blackened his face with charcoal. The inflected
form OE *blaca* became ME *blāke* which was often
confused with ME *blāk(e)* from OE *blāc* 'bright,
shining; pale, wan', so that the exact meaning of
Blake is doubtful. *Black-* and *Blake-* frequently
interchange in place-names and other surnames. *v.*
BLATCH.

Blackadder, Blacketer, Blaketter: Adam *of
Blacathathir* 1477 Black; Robert *Blackader* 15th
ib.; Charles *Blakater* 1486 ib. From Blackadder
(Berwickshire).

Blackah: Alice *Blaca* 1475 GildY. From Blacker
(WRYorks).

Blackale, Blackall: *v.* BLACKHALL
Blackaller, Blackler: John *Blakaller* 1431 AD i
(D); John *Blackaller* alias *Blacklawe* 1693 DWills;
Agnes *Blacklar* 1715 ib. From Blackler (Devon)
where the surname occurs as *Blakalre* in 1333
(PN D 521).

Blackbird: Brunstanus *Blachebiert* 1066 Winton
(Ha); William *Blacberd* 1206 AssL; Thomas
Blakeberd 1275 SRWo; William *Blakebird* 1279
AssSo. OE *blæc*, *beard* 'black beard'. cf. William
Brouneberd 1379 PTY.

Blackborn, Blackborne, Blackbourn, Black-
bourne, Blackburn, Blackburne: Henry *de Blake-
burn*' 1206 Cur (La). From Blackburn (Lancs).

Blackboro, Blackborough, Blackborow, Black-
brough, Blagbrough, Blakeborough, Blakebrough:
Robert *de Blakeberg*' 1201 P (Gl); Simon *de
Blakeberwe* 1275 RH (Sf). From Blackborough
(Devon, Norfolk).

Blackden, Blagden, Blagdon: Roger *de Blakeden*'
1275 SRWo; John *Blakedowne* 1327 ib.; Walter
de Blakedon 1327 SRSo; Sarah *Blacdon*, *Blagden*
1688–9 Bardsley. 'Dweller in the dark valley' as at
Blackden (Ches) or at Blagdon (Northumb), or
by the black hill as at Blagdon (Devon, Som) or
at Blagden Fm in Hempstead (Essex).

Blackell: Gilbert *ate Blakehulle* 1327 SRSx;
Robert *de Blakhill* 1347 FrY; Thomas *Blakell*
1456 ib. 'Dweller by the black hill.'

Blacker, Blaker: *Blakere* 1047–64 Holme (Nf);
Roger *Blacker* 1246 AssLa; Ralph *le blaker*' 1291
MESO (Ess); William *Blaker* 1296 SRSx; Roger
le Blackere 1312 ParlWrits. (i) OE *Blæckere* 'black-
army'; (ii) A derivative of ME *blāken*, OE *blæcan*
'to bleach', bleacher. cf. BLATCHER. Fransson
explains this as 'one who blacks', from *blæc*, but
does not specify the occupation.

Blacketer: v. BLACKADDER

Blackett: (i) Thomas *Blakeheuede* 1301 SRY; Adam *Blakhed* 1332 SRLa; 'Black head' or 'fair head'. cf. BLACK. (ii) Ralph *Blachod* 1327 SRSf; Robert *Blakhod* 1327 Pinchbeck (Sf). 'Black hood'. (iii) Ralph, Robert *Blachet* 1208 Cur (C), 1274 RH (So); William *Blaket* 1275 RH (Herts), 1332 SRCu. This, the most common form, cannot be from *Blakeheved*, whether as a nickname or a place-name. It must be a diminutive of *Black*, with the French suffix *-et*.

Blackford: Robert *de Blakeford*' 1211 Cur (Ha); Roger *de Blakeforde* 1296 SRSx; Richard *atte Blakeforde* 1314 MELS (Wo). 'Dweller by the black ford', as at Blackford (Som).

Blackhall, Blackale, Blackall: Robert *de Blakehall* 1221 AssWo; Ralph *de Blackhale* 1332 SRCu. 'Dweller by the dark nook', ME *hale*, with the common confusion with *hall*.

Blackham: Benedictus *de Blakeham* 1135–48 Bury (Sf). From Blakenham (Suffolk).

Blackhurst: Robert *atte Blakhurst, de Blakehurst* 1296 SRSx. 'Dweller by the black wooded hill', OE *hyrst*.

Blackie: (i) Henry *Blackeye* 1275 RH (Nf); Roger *Blakheye* 1327 SRSf. A nickname, 'black eye', unless these are from place-names where the preposition has been lost. If so, 'dweller by the black low-lying land or enclosure', OE *ēg* or *(ge)hæg*. (ii) John *Blakye* 1506 Black. A Scottish diminutive of BLACK.

Blackiston: v. BLACKSTON

Blackledge, Blacklidge: John *del Blakelache* 1332 SRLa; Richard *Blacklach* 1473 DbAS 30; Evan *Blaklidge* 1662 PrGR. 'Dweller by the dark stream', OE *læcc* 'a stream flowing through boggy land'.

Blackler: v. BLACKALLER

Blackley, Blacklee, Blaikley, Blakeley, Blakely, Blakly: William *de la Blekelegh* 1301 ParlWrits (St); Robert *atte Blakeley* 1337 AssSt; John *Blaklay* 1543 FrY; Mungo *Blaikley* 1687 Black. 'Dweller by the black wood or clearing', as at Blackley (Lancs), pronounced *Blakeley*.

Blacklock, Blaiklock, Blakelock: Peter *Blacloke* 1275 RH (W); Adam *Blakelok* 1332 SRCu; Robert *Blaykelok* 1431 FrY. Though *Blayke-* might mean either 'black' or 'fair' (cf. BLACK), all are probably for 'black lock', OE *blæc, locc*, the man with black hair, as distinct from WHITELOCK.

Blackman, Blakeman: *Blacheman filius Ædwardi* 1166 P (Nf); Jordanus *filius Blakeman* 1188 P (Ha); John *Blakeman* 1206 P (Sr); Henry *Blacman* 1279 RH (O). OE *Blæcmann* 'dark man', a personal name fairly common until the 13th century.

Blackoe, Blacoe, Blacow: John *Blakow* 1542 PrGR; John *Blacoll* 1562 ib. From Blackhall (Lancs), pronounced *Blackow*.

Blackstock: William *de la Blakestok* 1296 SRSx; Adam *Blakstok* 1332 SRCu. 'Dweller by the black stock or stump', OE *stocc*.

Blackston, Blackstone, Blackiston, Blakeston, Blakiston, Blaxton: (i) *Blackstan* 1086 DB (Ess); William *Blacston*', *Blakeston*', *Blackstan* 1235–42

Fees (Bk). OE *Blæcstān* 'black stone'. (ii) Philip *Atteblakeston*' 1275 SRWo; William *de Blakstan* 1316 FFK. 'Dweller by the black stone', as at Blackstone Edge (Lancs) or Blaxton (WRYorks).

Blacktin: About two generations ago, two branches of a family of Greystones (Sheffield) adopted different forms of their surname, originally *Blackden*: (i) *Blagden*, (ii) *Blacktin*.

Blackwall: For BLACKWELL. v. WALL.

Blackwell: Leofric *æt Blacewellan* 1012 OEByn (Wo); Mauricius *de Blacwella* 1175 P (Db); Benedictus *de Blakewelle* 1243 AssDu; Robert *atte Blakewell* 1296 SRSx. From Blackwell (Derby, Durham, Worcs) or from residence near a dark well or stream.

Blackwood: William *de Blacwode* 1327 SRSt; Robert *Blakwode* 1384 Black. 'Dweller by the dark wood', as at Blackwood (ERYorks, WRYorks, Dumfries, Lanarks).

Blader: Andrew *le Blader* 1305 LoCt. A derivative of OE *blæd* 'blade', a maker of blades, a bladesmith. cf. Nicholas *Bladsmith* 1357 FrY.

Blades, Blaydes: Jacke *Blade* 1297 Wak (Y); Robert *Blades* 1460 FrY; James *Blaydes* 1506 ib. Metonymic for *Blader* or *Bladesmith*. Also topographical in origin, from some unidentified place: Alan, Hugh *de Bladis* 1230 P (Lei), 1258 AssSt; William *de Blades* 1301 SRY.

Blagbrough: v. BLACKBORO

Blagden, Blagdon: v. BLACKDEN

Blaikie: Patrick *Blaikie* 1660 Black. A Scottish diminutive of BLAKE.

Blaikley: v. BLACKLEY

Blaiklock: v. BLACKLOCK

Blake: Walter *le Blake* 1167 P (D); Adam *Blake* 1219 AssY. v. BLACK.

Blakeley: v. BLACKLEY

Blaker: v. BLACKER

Blakesley, Blaksley, Blaxley: William *de Blakesle* 1199 AssSt. From Blakesley (Northants).

Blaketter: v. BLACKADDER

Blakeway: Hugo *de Blakewey* 1221 AssSa. 'Dweller by the dark road.'

Blakiston: v. BLACKSTON

Blakley: v. BLACKLEY

Blaksley: v. BLAKESLEY

Blamire, Blamires, Blamore, Blaymire: William *de Blamyre* 1250 CalSc (Cu). 'Dweller by the dark, swampy place' (ON *blá(r), mýrr*), as at Blamires (WRYorks).

Blampey, Blampied: Richard *Blancpie* 1198 P (Nf). 'White foot', OFr *blanc, pied*.

Blamphin, Plampin: Nigellus *Blanpein* 1184 Oseney (O); Henry *Blancpain* 1191 P (Nth); Thomas *Plampeyn* 1496 SIA xii; John *Plampen* 1564 EA (OS) i (Sf); Robert *Plampin* 1568 SRSf; Thomas *Blampyn* 1662 DWills. OFr *blanc pain* 'white bread', a nickname for a baker.

Blampied: v. BLAMPEY

Blanc, Blanck, Blank, Blanks: Nigellus *Blanke* 1196 Cur (Lei); John *Blaunk* 1293 LLB C. OFr *blanc* 'white, fair', with reference to hair or complexion.

Blanchard, Blanshard: *Blanchard* de Morba 1180 P (D); Rotbertus *blancard*, Rotbertus quippe *blancard* 1086 InqEl (Sf); Richard *Blanchard'* 1177 P (L); William *Blanchart* 1198 P (L); Thomas *Blansherde* 1552 FrY. OFr *Blancart, Blanchart,* OG *Blankard, Blanchard.* The 1086 example is, however, certainly a nickname, probably identical with Robertus *Blancardus* (1086 DB, Nf), who is probably identical with Robertus *Blundus, Albus, Flavus.* OFr *blanchart* 'whitish', probably with reference to the hair. Only one example of the personal name has been noted.

Blanchet, Blanchett, Blanket, Blankett, Branchett: (i) Robert, John *Blanket* 1275 SRWo, 1365 LLB G. OFr *blankete,* ME *blankett* 'white or undyed woollen stuff used for clothing', first recorded in MED c1300, but much older. cf. 'ix ulnis de blanchet' 1182 P. A nickname for a maker or seller of this white cloth. (ii) Jocelin *Blancheved* 1203 Cur (L). A hybrid from OFr *blanc* and OE *hēafod* 'white head'. Rare.

Blanchflower, Branchflower: Cecilia *Blaunchflur* 1228 Cl (He); John *Blanchflur'* 1275 SRWo; Jeffrey *Branchflower* 1654 SfPR. OFr *blanche flour* 'white, fair flower', a suitable nickname for a woman. Applied to a man, it was probably derogatory, fair as a woman, of effeminate appearance.

Blancowe: *v.* BLENCOWE

Bland: John *de Bland'* 1297 SRY; John *Bland* 1447 FrY. From Bland (WRYorks).

Blandamore: Christiana *Pleynamur* 1275 RH (Sf); Richard *Playndeamours* 1284 AssLa. OFr *pleyn d'amour* 'full of love'. cf. FULLALOVE.

Blank(s): *v.* BLANC

Blankau, Blanko: *v.* BLENCOWE

Blankett: *v.* BLANCHET

Blankley: Simon *de Blankeneia* 1202 AssL. From Blankney (Lincs).

Blanshard: *v.* BLANCHARD

Blatch: Geoffrey (*le*) *Blache* 1164–5 P (Nf); Roll' *Blecch'* 1200 P (Nf); Richard *Blatche* Ed 2 FFEss. OE *blæc.* A palatal form of BLACK.

Blatcher: Robert *le Blacchere* 1305 MESO (So); Roger *le Blakkere, le Blecchere* 1313 ParlWrits (W). A variant of BLEACHER. cf. BLACKER.

Blaxall, Blaxill, Blacksell: Adam *de Blakesale* 1308 LLB C; Roger *de Blaxhale* 1324 FFEss; John *Blaksell* 1674 HTSf. From Blaxhall (Suffolk).

Blaxley: *v.* BLAKESLEY

Blaxter: William *de* (sic) *Blakestere* 1199 AssSt; Richard *le Blakestare* 1275 SRWo; John *Blakestre* ib. The feminine form of ME *blaker* 'bleacher', but applied to men. *v.* BLACKER, BLATCHER.

Blaxton: *v.* BLACKSTON

Blaydes: *v.* BLADES

Blaymire: *v.* BLAMIRE

Bleacher: Robert *le Blechere* 1327 MESO (Ha). A derivative of OE *blǣcan* 'to bleach', a bleacher.

Blench: Rogert *Blenc* 1153–68 Holme (Nf); Thomas, Richard *Blench* 1178 P (Y), 1214 Cur (Ess). OE **blenc* 'a trick, stratagem' (a1250 NED).

Blencowe, Blenko, Blinco, Blincoe, Blincko, Blincow, Blancowe, Blankau, Blanko: Adam *de*

Blencow 1332 SRCu; Thomas *Blincoe* 1623 *ERO.* From Blencow (Cumb).

Blenkarn, Blenkarne, Blenkhorn, Blenkiron, Blinkhorn: William *Blenkarn* 1429 FrY; Robert *Blynkarne* 1547 FFHu; William *Blinkhorne* 1664 FrY. From Blencarn (Cumb).

Blenkin: John *Blenkynson* 1553 FrY. The etymology of *Blenkinsop* is obscure. The first element may be a personal name which these names suggest continued in use.

Blenkinsop, Blenkinship: Symon *de Blanchainesop, de Blencaneshop, de Blenkensope* 13th Riev (Y). From Blenkinsopp (Northumb).

Blenko: *v.* BLENCOWE

Blennerhasset, Blennerhassett: John *Blenerhasset,* Raff *Blaundrehasset* 1473 Past; Henry *Blanerhasset* 1495 FrY; Thomas *Blenayrhasset* 1524 SRSf. From Blennerhassett (Cumb).

Blessed, Blest, Blissett: Alicia *Iblessed* 1297 MinAcctCo; John *le Blessed* 1327 SRSt; John *le Blest* 1332 SRSx; Thomas *Blesset* 1380 SRSt. ME *iblescede,* past participle of OE *blētsian* 'to make sacred', in the sense 'happy, fortunate' (c1175 NED). From 1300 onwards the word occurs as *blisced, blissed,* a form surviving, no doubt, in *Blissett,* which may also derive from a woman's name: *Blissot* atte Pole 1327 SRSo.

Bletcher: Either for BLATCHER or for BLEACHER, with a shortening of the vowel.

Blethyn, Blevin, Blevins, Pleaden, Pleavin, Pleven, Plevin, Plevins: *Bleþgent* 1063 ASC D; *Bledienus* filius Keneweret' 1173 P(Sa); Madoc son of *Bledena* 1246 AssLa; Hugh son of *Bleuin* ib.; *Blethin* ap Maddoc 1287 AssCh; Robert *Blevyn* 1275 RH (Nf); Llewellyn *ap Bledyn* 1313 ParlWrits; William *Blethyn* 1366 SRLa; Dauid *ap Plethyn* 1391 Chirk; Hugh *Plethen* 1524 SRSf; William *Plevin* 1685 Bardsley (Ch). OW *Bledgint,* MW *Blethyn.* Ap *Blethyn* was assimilated to *ap Plethyn.*

Blewett, Blewitt, Blouet, Bluett: Ralph *Bloiet, Blouet, Bloet* 1086 DB (Ha, So); Tedbald *Blauet* 1185 Templars (Herts); Walter *Blohet* ib. (So); William *le Blut* ib. (L); Robert *Bluet* 1196 Cur (W); Geoffrey *le Bleuit* 1327 SRC. OFr *bleuet, blouet* 'bluish', a diminutive of *bleu* 'blue'.

Bligh, Blight: *v.* BLY

Blincko, Blinco(e), Blincow: *v.* BLENCOWE

Blind: Edricus *Cecus* 1066, 1086 DB (Sf); Angnes *Blinde* 1221 ElyA (Sf); Ralph *le Blinde* 1274 RH (Nf). OE *blind,* Lat *caecus* 'blind'. cf. BORN.

Blindell: *Blindel* Hy 2 Gilb (L) is identical with *Blundel* (ib.). cf. Alured *Blindel* (*Blundel*) 1221 AssGl. *v.* BLONDEL.

Blinkhorn: *v.* BLENKARN

Bliss: William *Blisse* 1240 Rams (Hu); Thomas *Blysse* 1260 AssY. OE *blīðs,* ME *blisse* 'gladness, joy'. Also occasionally from Blay (Normandy): Hugo *de Blez* 1275 SRWo. cf. Stoke Bliss (Worcs).

Blissett: *v.* BLESSED

Block: Robert *Bloc* 1199 Cur (W); Benedict *Blok* 1327 SRSf. Probably metonymic for *blocker:* Henry *le Blocker* 1212 Cur (Y); Deodatus *le*

Blokkere 1275 RH (Nf); one who blocks, especially in shoemaking and bookbinding.

Biocksidge: v. BLOXIDGE

Blomefield, Blomfield, Bloomfield, Blumfield: William *de Blunuill'* 1207 Cur (Sf); Thomas *de Blumuill'* 1230 P (Nf); John *Blumfeilde* 1582 EA (NS) i (Nf). From Blonville-sur-Mer (Calvados).

Blomer: v. BLOOMER

Blondel, Blondell, Blundal, Blundell: *Blundel* 1115 Winton (Ha), c1150 DC (Nt); Walterus *filius Blundelli* 1203 Cur (L); John *Blundel* c1140 StCh; John *Blondel* 1297 MinAcctCo. OFr *blondel*, a diminutive of *blond* 'fair', of hair or complexion. cf. BLUNT. Also used as a personal name.

Blood: William, John *Blod* 1256 AssNb, 1328 LLB E. OE *blōd* 'blood', used as a term of address in Chaucer: 'Now beth nought wroth, my blode, my nece'; also 'child, near relative', 'one dear as one's own offspring'. Also metonymic for a bloodletter: Uluric, Walter *Blodletere* c1095 Bury (Sf), 1221 ElyA (Nf), OE *blōdlætere*; or for *blooder*: Adam *Blodyr* 1441 GildY, from ME *blōden* 'to let blood'. In Ireland, for *ab Lloyd* 'son of Lloyd'.

Bloom: Anselm, Walter *Blome* 1177, 1198 P (Sx, Lo). Metonymic for BLOOMER.

Bloomer, Blomer, Blumer: William *Blomere* 1202 P (Db); Robert *le Blomere* 1279 AssSt. A derivative of OE *blōma* 'an ingot of iron', hence 'maker of blooms, iron-worker'.

Bloomfield: v. BLOMEFIELD

Blossom: Walter *Blosme* 1195 P (Wa); Peter *Blostme* 1297 MinAcctCo. OE *blōstm(a)*, *blōsma* 'blossom', used in the 15th century of one lovely and full of promise.

Blouet: v. BLEWETT

Blount: v. BLUNT

Blower, Blowers: William *le Blowerre* 1199 P (Sr), *Blouer* 1219 AssY; Lucia *Blowere* 1317 AssK; Reginald *le Blawere* 1327 *SR* (Ess). OE *blāwere* 'blower' of the horn or bellows. cf. Gilbert *Blouhorn* 1275 RH (L).

Bloxam, Bloxham, Bloxsom, Bloxsome: Robert *de Bloxeham* 1130 P (L); William *de Blokesham*, Alexander *de Bloxam* 1279 RH (O). From Bloxham (Oxon) or Bloxholm (Lincs).

Bloxidge, Bloxsidge, Blocksidge: Clement *de Bloxwych* 1332 SRSt. From Bloxwich (Staffs).

Bluett: v. BLEWETT

Blumer: v. BLOOMER

Blumfield: v. BLOMEFIELD

Blumsom, Blumson: Thomas *Blumsome* 1661 Bardsley. For BLUNSOM or BLUNSEN.

Blundal, Blundell: v. BLONDEL

Blundstone, Blunstone: Robert *de Blundeston* 1327 SRSf; Nicholas *Bluneston* 1593 FFHu. From Blundeston (Suffolk).

Blunsden, Blunsdon: Brian *de Bluntesdon'* 1255 RH (W). From Blunsdon (Wilts).

Blunsen, Blunson: For BLUNDSTONE or BLUNSDEN.

Blunsom, Blunsum: John *de Bluntisham* 1229 FFHu; John *Bluntsham* 1406 Bardsley; John

Blonsham 1734 ib. From Bluntisham (Hunts). Also a possible late form of *Blunsen*.

Blunt, Blount: Rodbertus *Blon, Blondus, Blundus* 1086 DB; Robert *se Blund* c1100–30 OEByn (D); Ralph *le Blund* Hy 2 DC (Lei); John *le blunt* c1194 StCh; Hamelin *Blund* 1201 AssSo; Richard *le Blount* 1279 RH (O). OFr *blund, blond* (Lat *blondus*) 'blond, fair, yellow-haired', used also of complexion (1481 NED). cf. BLONDEL and Joce *Blonthefed* 1195 P (L) 'fair head'. In DB, Robert *Blundus* is also called *Albus, flauus* and *blancard*.

Bly, Blyde, Blyth, Blythe, Bligh, Blight: (i) William *de Bliða* 1177 P (Ess); Gilbert *de Blie* 1200 P (Nt). From Blyth (Northumb, Notts) or Blythe (Warwicks). *Bly* is due to Anglo-Norman loss of *th*. (ii) *Blide* 1101–7 Holme (Nf); Willelmus *filius Blie* 1188 P (La); *Blithe* de Ryseford 1276 RH (Y); Robert *Blithe* 1221 ElyA (Nf); John *Blythe* 1296 SRSx. Either a nickname from OE *blīðe* 'gentle, merry' or from an unrecorded personal name, OE **Blīða*, derived from this. The adjective is found as *bliht* and *bligh* in the 13th century (NED).

Boalch: v. BELCH

Boaler: v. BOWLER

Boar, Boor, Bor, Bore: Æilmar *Bar* c1095 Bury (Sf); Godwin *bar* 1148 Winton (Ha); Walter *Bor* 1255 Rams (Hu); Robert *le Bor* 1287 Ipm (Bk); John *le Boor* 1312 AD iv (D). OE *bār* 'boar'.

Board, Boord: Nicholas, William *Borde* 1230 P (Do), 1296 SRSx. Metonymic for BOARDER.

Boarder, Border, Borders, Bordier: Thomas *le Border* 1201 AssSo; Robert *le Bordere* 1296 SRSx. Bardsley and Thuresson derive this from OFr *bordier* 'bordar, cottager', a word found only in the medieval Latin form *bordarius* in DB and, as an English word, only in modern historians (1776 NED). The surname may be a derivative of OE *bord* 'board, plank, ? table', ME **border* 'maker of boards or tables'. Cf. Robert *Bordmakere* 1356 LLB G, William *le Bordhewere* 1327 MESO, Richard *Bordwreghte* 1332 SRSx. Or it may be from ME *bourd(e)our*, AFr *bourd(e)our*, OFr *bordeor* 'a jester, joker, buffoon' (1330 NED), though we should have expected some examples of *bourder*. cf. Bordyoure, or pleyare. *Lusor, joculator* c1440 PromptParv (*bordere* 1499).

Boarer: v. BOWRA

Boast, Bost: Walter *Bost* 1279 RH (O); Walterus *dictus Bost* c1300 Balliol (O); Ralph *Boste* 1327 SRSf; Walter *Boost* 1327 SRSx. ME *bōst* 'vaunt, brag, "tall talk"; vain-glory'.

Boater: John *Botere* 1279 RH (Hu), 1317 AssK, *le Botere* 1301 LLB C. A derivative of OE *bāt* 'boat', a boatman (1605 NED).

Boatman, Bottman: Thomas *Bootman* 1225 Gardner (Sf); Thomas *Botman* 1378 MEOT (So). OE *bāt* and *mann* 'boatman' (1513 NED).

Boatswain, Boeson: Wicing *Batswegen* 1050–71 OEByn (D); Peter *Botsweyn, le Botsweyn* 1327, 1332 *SR* (Ess). Late OE *bātswegen*, from ON *bátsveinn* 'boatman' (1450 NED). Used also as a personal name: *Batsuen* 1055 DB (Sa), *Walterus filius Batsuein* 1190 P (L).

Boatte: Alice, William *atte Bote* 1327, 1332 SRSx. Richard *Beselin atte Bote* MELS (Sx) had to 'ferry the Bishop and his carriages and all the men in his service and all avers coming from Busshopestone Manor', thus owing his attribute to the services due from his holding. The surname might also be occupational, 'boatman', 'ferryman'.

Boatwright, Botwright: John *Botwright* 1469 SIA xii; John *Botewrighte* 1524 SRSf. OE *bāt* 'boat' and *wyrhta* 'wright', a maker of boats. Common in Suffolk.

Boayer: v. BOWYER
Boby: v. BOOTHBY
Bock: v. BUCK
Bockett: v. BURCHARD
Bocock: v. BAWCOCK

Bode: *Boda* 1066, 1086 DB (Ha); *Bode* 1066 ib. (W); Hugo *filius Bode* 12th Rams (Nf); Walter *Bode* 1220 Fees (Berks); Robert *Bode* 1221 ElyA (Nf); William *le Bode* 1296 SRSx. OE *boda* 'herald, messenger'. Also used as a personal name (Redin).

Boder: Andrew *le Bodere* 1296 SRSx; Bartholomew *Bodyr* 1327 SRC. OE *bodere* 'announcer, messenger'. Ralph *le Bodere* 1212 Fees (Ess) is called *le Criur* 1227 ib. cf. CRIER.

Bodfish: Joane *Botfishe*, John *Botefyshe*, Alice *Bootefishe* 1523–41 ArchC 41. ME *butte* (c1300 MED), cognate with Sw *butta* 'turbot', Du *bot* 'flounder', flatfish, as sole, fluke, plaice, turbot, etc. cf. But, *fysche*, *Pecten* PromptParv, Butte *fysshe*, *plye* Palsgrave. It would appear that *butfish* was used as a generic term and the surname probably denotes a seller of flatfish. cf. *butt-woman* 'a fishwife' 1620 NED.

Bodin, Boyden: *Bodin* 1066 DB (St); *Bodin* prior de Parco, prior *Boydin* de Parco Hy 2 DC (L); *Bodinus* or *Boydinus* 1156–80 Bury (Sf); Turstan, Robert *Bodin* 12th DC (L), 1200 P (O); Mainard *Boidin* 1208 Cur (Sx); John *Boydon* 1401 FrY. OFr *Bodin, OG *Baudin*.

Bodman: Ralph, Thomas *Bodeman* 13th Guisb, 1316 Wak (Y). OE *boda* 'messenger' or OE *(ge)bod* 'message' and *mann*. 'Servant of the messenger' or equivalent to BODER.

Body, Bodey, Boddy: Hugh *Body* 1219 AssY; Richard *Body* 1277 FFEss; Roger *Body* 1340 AssSt. A nickname from OE *bodig* 'trunk, frame, bodily presence'. cf. GOODBODY, TRUEBODY.

Boeson: v. BOATSWAIN

Boff, Leboff: Robert *le Buef* 1169 P (L); Walter *Beof*, *le Boef'*, *le Bof'* 1219 Cur (K). OFr *boef* 'bullock', a nickname for a big, powerful man, a great lubberly fellow.

Boffee, Boffey: v. BEAUFOY

Bogg: (i) Giles *Bog* 1327 *SR* (Ess); Robert *Bogge* 1504 FrY. Probably early examples of *bog*, adj., 'bold, proud, saucy' (1592 NED). (ii) John *atte Bogge* 1327 SRSo. 'Dweller by the bog' (a1450 MED).

Boggers, Boggis, Boggs: Elyas, John *Bogeys* 1260 AssY, 1327 *SR* (Ess); John *Bogays* 1301 SRY, 1327 SRSf; William *Bogace* 1309 Wak (Y); William *Bogges* 1327 SRSf; Richard *Bogas* 1366 FrY. ME *bogeys* 'inclined to bluster or brag, puffed up, bold'; cf. 'bogeysliche as a boy' a1375 MED.

Boice: v. BOYES

Bold, Boud, Bould, Boulde, Bowld: (i) Richard *Bolde* 1206 P (La); Henry *Bolde*, *le Bolde* 1317 AssK, 1327 SRSx; William *Boulde* 1428 FrY; Robert *Bowde* 1563 FrY. ME *bold*, OE *bald* (WS *beald*) 'stout-hearted, courageous'. v. also BALD. (ii) Heremer *de la Bolde* 1176 P (St); Geoffrey *de Bold* 1199 AssSt; Herbert *de la Boude* 1200 Cur (Sa); Robert *Attebolde* 1332 SRSt. OE *bold* 'dwelling-house'. From Bold (Lancs), The Bold (Salop), or local. 'At the house' is not particularly distinctive. It might refer to residence at a small farm or to employment at the manor-house.

Boldero, Bolderoe: v. BALDREE
Bolderson: v. BALDERSON
Bolderston: v. BALDERSTON
Bolding: v. BALDING
Boldison: v. BALDERSON
Boldra, Boldry: v. BALDREE
Boldron, Bowran, Bowron: Robert *de Bolroun* 1332 SRLa. From Boldron (NRYorks).
Boldy: v. BALDEY
Bole, Boles: v. BULL
Boler: v. BOWLER
Bolgar, Bolger: v. BOULGER
Bolland, Bollands, Boland: John *de Bolland* 1237 HPD; John *de Boughland* 1351 FrY; William *de Bowland* 1370 FrY; John *Bolland* 1482 FFEss. From Bolland (Devon), Bowland (Lancs, WRYorks), or Bowlands (ERYorks).
Bollen: v. BULLEN
Bollett: v. BULLETT
Bolley: v. BULLEY
Bolt, Bolte, Boult: *Godinc Bolt* 1066 ICC (C); Walter, Roger *Bolt* 1202 Cur (Sr), c1248 Bec (W). OE *bolt* 'bolt, bar'. For the first example, Tengvik compares the ON nickname *Boltr*, which might have been applied to a short, heavy person. Later instances are probably metonymic for BOLTER, a maker of bolts. cf. John *Boltsmith* 1346 MESO.
Bolter, Boulter: Roger *le Buleter*, *le Buletor*, *le Bolter* 1246, 1248, 1253 Oseney (O); Roger *le Boletere* 1261 Oriel (O); Geoffrey *le Bolter* 1276 RH (Berks). OFr *buleteor* 'a sifter of meal'. *Bolter*, which is the most common form, is probably often a derivative of OE *bolt*, 'a maker of bolts'. cf. BOLT.
Bolton, Boulton: Robert *de Boulton'* a1191 YCh; Thomas *de Bolton* 1262–3 FFWa; Robert *Bolton* 1371 AssL. From one or other of the many places of this name, or from Boulton (Derby).
Boman: v. BOWMAN
Bomfield: v. BONFIELD
Bompas, Bompus, Bumpus: William *Bonpas* 1175 P (Gl); Anne *Bompase* 1616 Bardsley; James *Bumpus* 1670 ib. OFr *bon pas* 'good pace'. cf. LIGHTFOOT, GOLIGHTLY.

Bomphrey: *v.* BOUMPHREY

Bonafont: *v.* BONIFANT

Bonally, Bonallo, Bonella, Bonello, Bonnalie, Bonnella: William *Bonaylay* c1570 Black; Robert *Bonalay* 1637 ib.; David *Bonallo* 1818 ib. Black derives these surnames from Bonaly (Midlothian) or a lost Banaley (Fife). They are probably a Scottish equivalent of the English *Drinkale*, from MScots *bonalai*, *bonnaillie*, from Fr *bon* 'good' and *aller* 'to go, going', 'good speed, farewell!' as in 'to drink one's bonallie' (c1470 NED).

Bonamy: *v.* BONNAMY

Bonar: *v.* BONNAIRE

Bonas: *v.* BOWNAS

Bond, Bondi, Bonds, Bondy, Bound, Bounds, Boundy, Bunday, Bundey, Bundy: *Bonde*, *Bondi*, *Bunde*, *Bundi* 1086 DB; Albertus *filius Bund'*, *Bonde* 1199, 1202 FFNf; Norman *le Bonde* 1180 P (Wa); William *Bonde* 1185 Templars (Wa); Robert *Bunde* 1198 P (Beds); Henry *le Bounde* 1297 MinAcctCo (Herts). *le Bonde* is clearly from OE *bŏnda*, *būnda*, ON *bónde*, *bóndi* 'husbandman, peasant, churl', later 'unfree tenant, serf'. The simple *Bonde* may be from the same source or from ON *Bóndi*, ODa *Bondi*, *Bundi*, OSw *Bonde*.

Bondfield: *v.* BONFIELD

Bone, Bonn, Bonne, Bunn: Edward *le Bon* 1204 Cur (O); Rocelin *le Bun* 1255 RH (W); Walter *le Bone* 1296 SRSx; Thomas *Bonne* 1379 LLB H. OFr *bon* 'good'. For *Bone*, *v.* also BOON.

Bonella, Bonello: *v.* BONALLY

Boner: *v.* BONNAIRE

Bones: Alicia *Bones* 1327 SRSf. *v.* BAIN.

Boness: *v.* BOWNAS

Boneter, Bonetta: 'A maker of bonnets.' *v.* BONNET.

Boney: *v.* BANEY

Bonfellow: *v.* BOUTFLOUR

Bonfield, Bondfield, Bomfield: Richard *de Bondauilla* 1131 FeuDu; Robert *de Boneville* 1197 P (Y). From Bonneville (Normandy) where there are three places of the name, two near Rouen.

Bonger, Bongers, Bonjour: Osbert *Bonior* 1199 FF (Nth); Roger *Boniur* 1275 RH (Sf); Alice *Bonjour* 1327 SRSx. OFr *bon jour* 'good day!'. cf. GOODDAY.

Bonham, Bonhomme, Bonome: *Bonhom* Luscus 1177 P (Lei); *Bonhom fullo* 1219 AssY; Randulfus *bonus homo* 1148 Winton (Ha); Nigel *Bonhume* 1247 AssBeds; William *Bonum* (*Bonhom*) 1327 SR (Ess). OFr *bon homme* 'good man'. cf. GODMAN. This may also occasionally be local in origin: William *de Bonham* 1225, 1269 AssSo.

Boniface, Bonifas, Bonniface: *Bonefacius* uinitor 1193 P (Y); *Bonifacius* 1208 Cur (Ha); Tomas *Boniface* 1190 P (Y); Alis *Boneface* 1200 P (Ha). Contrary to the common opinion, this name derives not from Latin *bonifacius* 'well-doer', but from *bonifatius*, from *bonum* 'good' and *fatum* 'fate'. The change to *Bonifacius* was due to the pronunciation and from this was deduced a false etymology. *Bonifatius* is frequent on Latin inscriptions. *Bonifacius* is found only twice and these late

(*Thesaurus*). In Latin the name was given chiefly to ecclesiastics, rarely to men of the lower orders. In ME the form was *Boniface*, but the name was never very popular in England, though it had enough vitality to produce a surname.

Bonifant, Bonafont, Bullivant: William *Bonenfant*, *Bonenfand* 1207–8 Cur (O); Henry *Bonefant* 1279 RH (Bk); John *Bon Effaunt* 1332 SRSx; Roger *Bonyfaunt* 1472 LLB L; Henry *Bolyvaunt* 1524 SRSf; William *Bonyvant* 1540 RochW; Elizabeth *Bullivant* 1707 SfPR. Fr *bon enfant*, identical in meaning with GOODCHILD.

Bonjour: *v.* BONGER

Bonn, Bonne: *v.* BONE

Bonnaire, Bonnar, Bonner, Bonnor, Bonar, Boner: John *Boneyre* 13th Rams (Hu); Thomas *Boner* 1281 Black (Aberdeen); Walter *Boneyre* 1297 FFEss; Robert *Boner* 1332 SRSx; Alexander *Bonour* 1413 FrY; William *Bonare*, *Bonere*, *Bonour* 1451–3 Black (St Andrews); Walter *Bonnar* 1527 ib. ME *boner(e)*, *bonour*, OFr *bonnaire* 'gentle, courteous', shortened from *debonnaire* (c1300 MED).

Bonnalie: *v.* BONALLY

Bonnamy, Bonamy: William *bon ami* c1162 DC (L); William *Bonami* 1203 AssL. OFr *bon ami* 'good friend'.

Bonnan: Peter *Bonhand* 1327 *SR* (Ess). OFr *bon* 'good' and OE *hand* 'hand'. 'Good hand.'

Bonnar: *v.* BONNAIRE

Bonnard: Walter *Bonard* 1327 SRSx. OFr *bon* 'good' with the intensive suffix *-ard*.

Bonnella: *v.* BONALLY

Bonner: *v.* BONNAIRE

Bonnet, Bonnett: Isabella *Bonet* 1201 AssSo; John *Bonet* 1212 Cur (W), 1219 AssL, 1230 P (Sa). ME, OFr *bonet*, used for a maker of bonnets. cf. BONETER.

Bonnick: *v.* BONWICK

Bonniface: *v.* BONIFACE

Bonnor: *v.* BONNAIRE

Bonome: *v.* BONHAM

Bonser, Bonsier, Bonsor: Roger *bonsire* 1246 Bart (Lo); Robert *Bonsir* 1332 SRSx. OFr *bon sire* 'good sir'.

Bonwick, Bonnick: Walter *Bonwyk*, William *de Bonwyk* 1296, 1332 SRSx; John *de Bonnewyk'* 1363 AssY. From Bonwick (ERYorks). Walter probably gave his name to Bonwicks Place in Ifield (Sussex).

Boocock: *v.* BAWCOCK

Boodle, Buddle: Robert, John *atte Bothele* 1327 MELS (So), 1330 PN D 484. From Buddle Oak in Halse (Som), Buddle in Fordingbridge (Hants), Buddle in Niton (Isle of Wight) or Budleigh in Moretonhampstead (Devon), all from OE *bŏðl*, cognate with OE *botl*, *bold*. cf. BOLD. *bŏðl* 'dwelling-house' probably denoted a homestead of some size.

Booker: (i) William *le Bocer* 1255 RH (Sa), 1296 SRSx; John *Boker* 1275 RH (Nf). OE *bōcere* 'writer of books, scribe'. (ii) Robert *le Bukere* 1229 FFSx; William *le Buker* 1246 AssLa; Elias *le*

Boukere 1296 SRSx. A derivative of ME *bouken* 'to steep in lye, to bleach' (1377 NED), a bleacher.

Bool(s): *v.* BULL

Boon, Boone, Bone, Bown, Bowne: Hunfridus *de Bohum* 1086 DB (Nf); Wnfridus *de Bowhun* 1120–3 EngFeud; William *de Boun* 1119 Colch (Ess); Matildis *de Bohun* Hy 2 DC (L); John *de Bown* 1275 RH (Sx); Reginald *Boon'* 1279 RH (C). From Bohon (La Manche). Bohun's Hall (Essex) is *Boneshall* 1540, *Bowneshall* 1604 (PN Ess 305) and is now pronounced *Boon's* Hall.

Boor: *v.* BOAR

Boord: *v.* BOARD

Boorer: *v.* BOWRA

Boorman: *v.* BOWERMAN

Boosey: Richard, Roger *Bosy* 1327 *SR* (Ess), 1376 FrY. Late forms, probably for *atte Bosy* 'at the ox- or cow-stall', OE *bōsig*. 'A cowman.'

Boosie, Bousie, Bowsie: John *Bousie, Bowsie* 1566, 1580 Black. From Balhousie (Fife) 17th *Bowsie*, and still so pronounced.

Boot, Boote: Hugh, William *Bote* 1186 P (Wa), 1279 RH (C); Adam *Boot* 1345 AD i (K). OFr, ME *bote* 'boot', a maker or seller of boots.

Booth, Boothe: Gilbert *Bothe, del Both'* 1274, 1297 Wak (Y); John *de la Bouthe* 1287 AssCh; William *atte Bothe* 1297 Coram (Nf). ME *bōþ(e)*, from ODa *bōth* 'cow-house, herdsman's hut'. An occupational name for a cowman or herdsman, identical with BOOTHMAN.

Boothby, Boby: Hugo *de Boebi, de Bothebi* 1190, 1205 P (L). From one of the three places named Boothby in Lincs.

Boothman: Roger *Bothman* 1279 RH (Hu); Nicholas *the Bouthman* 1287 AssCh. ME *bōþ(e)* and *man. v.* BOOTH.

Boothroyd: John *del Botherode*, Adam *de Buderude* 1274, 1296 Wak; Richard *Buthroid* 1627 RothwellPR (Y). From Boothroyd (WRYorks).

Borar: *v.* BOWRA

Border(s): *v.* BOARDER

Bore: *v.* BOAR

Borel: *v.* BURREL

Borer: Robert *le Boriere* 1318 LLB B; Hugo *le Borer* 1332 MESO (L). A derivative of OE *borian* 'to bore', one who bores or pierces. cf. Adam Cok *borer* 1366 MESO (Lei). *v.* also BOWRA.

Borger: *v.* BURGER

Borges: *v.* BURGES

Borgonon, Burgin: Robert *Burguignon* 1160 P; John *(le) Burguinun* 1173 P (Lo); John *le Burguinn* 1214 P (Mx); John *le Burgenun* 1259 Acc; John *Burgoynoun* 1330 Trentham (St). OFr *Bourguignon, Bourgoin* 'the Burgundian'. *v.* BURGOIN.

Borkett, Borkwood: *v.* BURCHARD

Borman: *v.* BOWERMAN

Born, Borne: William, Walter *le Borne* 1164, 1185 P (Nf, Do); Simon *Monoculus* 1212 Cur (Berks). OFr *borgne* 'one-eyed, squint-eyed'.

Borner: *v.* BOURNER

Borodale, Borradaile, Borrodell, Borrowdale: John *Borowdale, Borowdall* 1433, 1483 FrY. From Borrowdale (Cumb, Westmorland).

Borrell, Borrill: *v.* BURREL

Borrett, Borritt: *v.* BURRARD, BURRETT

Borrow(s): *v.* BURROUGH(ES)

Borrowman, Borroman, Burkman, Burman, Barrowman, Barryman: John *Burgman* de Eboraco 1219 AssY; William *Burman* (*Burghman*) 1221 AssGl; Robert *le Borekman* 1279 RH (Bk); John *Burgman, Burkman* 1281, c1284 NottBR; Geoffrey *Borughman* 1309 ib.; Thomas *Burghman* 1314 FFK; William *Borovman* 1437 Black (Montrose); Alexander *Burowman* 1468 ib. (Edinburgh); Lokky *Barrowman* 1570 ib. (Aberdeen). OE *burhmann* 'townsman, citizen, burgess', in some Yorkshire boroughs 'a burgage tenant'. Both meanings are found in Scotland. Black explains *Barrowman*, also found as *Barraman*, as 'one who helps to carry a handbarrow', but, apart from his first example which is found as *Baroumane* and *Borrowman* in two different MSS, his earliest evidence is in 1570, whilst the first example in NED is c1675. There can be no doubt that this is a late variant of *Burowman*. *v.* also BOWERMAN.

Borshell: Walter *de Borselle* 1296 SRSx. From Boarzell in Ticehurst (Sussex).

Borthram: *v.* BARTRAM

Borton: *v.* BURTON

Bosanquet: John and David Bosanquet of Lunel in Languedoc came to England as Huguenot refugees in 1685. Their surname is probably the Languedoc *Bouzanguet* 'dwarf'.

Bosence: *v.* BOSSOM

Boshell: *v.* BUSHELL

Bosher, Boshere, Boshier, Busher: William *Boschier* 1205 P (Do); Henry *Boscher* 1221 AssWa; Robert *le Buscher* 1276 LLB A. OFr *buschier* 'woodmonger'.

Boskin: *v.* BUSKENS

Boss: *Bosse* filius Edrici 1196 P (Sx); Radulfus *filius Bosse* 1210 P (Nf); Hugo, Walter, William *Bosse* 1179 P (C), 1191 P (Y), 1227 AssBeds. A common surname in the 12th and 13th centuries, with more than one origin. The personal name is OG *Boso* 'wicked', Fr *Bos, Boson*. (ii) A nickname from ME *boce, bos*, OFr *boce* 'protuberance, swelling'; 'a hunch or hump on the back', metonymic for a hunch-back. cf. 'crumpled knees and boce on bak' a1300 NED. (iii) In 1333 a vessel called *bos* was used for carrying mortar at Westminster. cf. 'a boket called *le bosse*' (1423 Building 338, 353). This must be *boss* sb. 4, 'a plasterer's tray or hod' (1542 NED), for a maker or a user of these.

Bossel: *v.* BUSHELL

Bossey, Bossy: Simon, Robert *le Bocu* 1196 P (C), 1202 FFK; Robert *le Bossu* 1275 RH (Do). OFr *bocu* 'hunch-backed'.

Bossiney: Walter *de Boscinny* 1297 MinAcctCo. From Bossiney in Tintagel (Cornwall).

Bossom, Bosson, Bossons, Bosence: John *Botswayne*, Armand *Bosome*, John *Bottswaine* 1639, 1644 EA (OS) iii, 53, 118 (all in Beccles). A late development of BOATSWAIN. The Sussex *Bossom* is from Bosham (Sussex).

Bost: v. BOAST

Bostel, Bostle: Martin *de Borstall'* 1198 P (K); Robert *atte Borstalle* 1296 SRSx. OE *borgsteall* 'place of refuge', later 'pathway up a steep hill', common in Kent: Borstal, Bostall Wood, Borstal Hall, Borstalhill Fm; also at Bostal Road in Poynings (Sussex), Boarstall (Bucks) and Boshill (Devon).

Boswall, Boswell: William *de Boesavilla* c1130 StCh; Michael *de Bosevill'* 1176 P (Ess); Hugo *de Beseuilla* 1199 FF (Sx); William *Bosevyll* 1362 Shef (Ravenfield); John *Boswell* 1379 PTY. From Beuzeville-la-Giffard (Seine-Inférieure), *Boesevilla, Bosavilla* 12th ANF.

Bosworth: Richard *de Baresworth'* 1206 Cur (Nth); William *de Boreswurth'* 1230 Cur (Lei); Alexander *de Boseworth'* 1298 AssL; Henry *Boseworth* 1327 SRWa. From Bosworth (Leics), *Baresworde* DB.

Botham: v. BOTTOM

Bothamley: v. BOTTOMLEY

Botler: Sarra *le Bottler* 1332 SRWa; Johan *Bottler* 1351 AssEss. A derivative of ME *botel*, OFr *bouteille* 'bottle', a maker of leather bottles. cf. Stephen, Thomas *Botelmaker* 1346 ColchCt, 1420 LLB I.

Bott: *Botte* Buny 1222 AssWa; Aldred *Bot, Alrebot* 1066, 1086 DB (K); Walter, William, Richard *Botte* 1189 P (O), 1214 Cur (Wa), 1225 Lewes (Nf); Richard *Bot* 1212 Fees (Ha); Walter *le Botte* 1279 RH (O). Tengvick takes the DB name to be OE **Butt*, a nickname, but it should, no doubt, be taken with the other forms. We have clearly a nickname from OFr *bot* 'toad' and are also concerned with a personal name, probably OE *Botta*, found in Botley (Bucks) and in BOTTING.

Bottams: v. BOTTOM

Bottell: v. BOTTLE

Botten: v. BUTTON

Botterell, Botterill, Bottrell, Bottrill, Butteris, Butteriss, Buttress, Buttriss: (i) Hamo, Rannulf *Boterel* c1155 DC (L), 1198 P (Nf); Reginald *Boterell* 1193 P (Y); (ii) Emma *des Boterell'*, *des Boteraus* 1197 P (D), 1211 Cur (So); William *de Botereus* 1277 AssSo; Thomas *Buttris* 1639 YWills. These surnames are difficult and complicated. We seem to have a nickname from OFr *boterel* 'toad' but Peter *Boterel* 1127–47 Bec (W) is also called *Boter* (1107–33 ib.). He was one of the family of *Butery*, tenants of Ogbourne (Wilts), other members of which were Geoffrey *Boter* (1107–33), William *Boterel* (1122–47), James *Butery* and William *Buteri* (c1248). The various forms of the surname must have the same meaning. *Buteri* is for *atte buteri* 'keeper of the buttery', from OFr *boterie*, lateLat *botaria*, from *bota*, a variant of *butta* (OFr *botte*) 'cask, bottle'. cf. BUTTERY. *Boter* is a derivative of *bota*, one in charge of the casks or bottles. The diminutive *Boterel* is curious but we may compare Fr *Pasturel* from *Pasture* 'shepherd or owner of the pasture' and *Peverell*, a diminutive of *peivre* 'pepper'. Bos-

castle (Cornwall) is *Boterelescastel* in 1302 and was then held by William *de Botereus* whose family presumably took its name from Les Bottereaux in Normandy (DEPN). The place-name means 'Boterel's castle' and is, no doubt, to be associated with William *boterel* 1130 P (Co). One would take this to be a nickname from the toad were he not called *de* or *as Boterell'* in 1178 (P). Aston Botterell (Salop) was held in 1203 by William *Botterell* whose surname is taken as the nickname in DEPN. He is probably identical with William *des Boterels, des Botereals* 1197–8 P (Sa) and of the same family as Albreda *Boterell'*, *de Botereus, de Boterell'* 1221 AssSa, *de Botereaus, de Boterels* 1226, 1242 Fees. Here we seem to have early examples of the loss of the preposition and the substitution of the singular *Boterel* for the plural form of the place-name which appears to mean 'the toads'. The modern surnames may represent all these varieties. *Buttress, Buttriss*, and *Butteriss* are certainly from Les Bottereaux.

Botting: John *Bottyng* 1277 AssSo; William *Botting* 1327 SRSx. OE **Botting* 'son of *Botta*'. v. BOTT.

Bottle, Bottell: Godwinus *filius Botild* 1188 BuryS (Sf); Johannes *filius Botill'* 1219 AssY; Adam *Botild'* 1221 AssGl; Richard *Botyld* 1296 SRSx; Cuthbert *Bottyll* 1565 Oxon. ON *Bóthildr*, ODa, OSw *Bothild* (f). Also, probably, metonymic for BOTLER.

Bottlerell: A curious corruption of BOTTERELL.

Bottman: v. BOATMAN

Bottom, Bottome, Bottoms, Bottams, Botham, Bothams: Dowe *de Bothemes* 1246 AssLa; Richard *del Bothom* 1307 Wak (Y). 'Dweller in the dell or hollow(s)', OE *botm* 'bottom, lowest part of a valley'.

Bottomley, Bothamley: Hanne *de Bothemley* 1277 Wak (Y); Peter *Botumley* 1524 SRSf. From Bottomley near Halifax (WRYorks).

Bottrell, Bottrill: v. BOTTERELL

Bouch, Buche, Budge: Ralph *Buche* 1160–70 Templars (Y); Fegga *Buche, Bucca, Bugga* 1165–7 P (L); Hugo *Buche, Bucca* 1199, 13th Guisb (Y); Alexander *Buche, Bugge* 1221 AssWo; Michael *od la Buche* 1225 Pat; Geoffrey *Bouche* 1226 FFBk; John *Bouge*, Walter *Bugge* 1327 SRSf; John *Bougge* 1327 SR (Ess). OFr *bouche* 'mouth', a nickname. In ME this also became *bouge* and later *budge*, especially in the sense 'an allowance of victuals granted by a king or nobleman to his household or attendants on a military expedition' (c1440 MED). This sense may be older and may account for some of the alternatives above. *Buche* is common. The form *Bugge*, also common, is ambiguous. It may be for ME *bouge*, OFr *bouge*, also *boulge, buche* (Godefroy) 'a small leather bag or wallet, a skin-bottle' and denote a maker of these. Or it may be for BUGG, where doubtful forms are given.

Bouchard: v. BURCHARD

Boucher: v. BUTCHER

Boud: v. BOLD

Bouffler: James *Beauflour* 1313 Cl (Beds), 1322 ParlWrits (Lo). OFr *beau flour* 'fair flower'.

Bough: *v.* BOW

Boughtflower: *v.* BOUTFLOUR

Bould(s): *v.* BOLD

Boulding: *v.* BALDING

Boulderstone: *v.* BALDERSTON

Boule: *v.* BOWL

Boulger, Boulsher, Bolgar, Bolger, Bulger: John *Bulgere* 1300 MESO (Wo). OFr *boulgier* 'maker of leather wallets or bags', from OFr *boulge*, ME *bulge* 'leathern bag'.

Boullen, Boullin: *v.* BULLEN

Bouller: *v.* BOWLER

Boulsher: *v.* BOULGER

Boult: *v.* BOLT

Boulter: *v.* BOLTER

Boumphrey, Bomphrey, Bumphries: Roger *Bomfrey* 1633 Bardsley. Welsh *ab Humphrey* 'son of *Humphrey*'. *v.* PUMFREY.

Bound(s), Boundy: *v.* BOND

Bourdon: *v.* BURDEN

Bourgein, Bourgoin: *v.* BURGOIN

Bourke: *v.* BURK

Bourne, Born, Borne, Burn, Burne: Godric *æt Burnan* 1044 OEByn (K); Almarus *de Brunna* 1066 ICC (C); Basilia *de la Burne* 1219 FFEss; William *Atteburn* 1256 AssNb; Richard *Atteburne* 1261 AssSo; Adam *de Burne* c1280 Black (Ayr); Richard *atte Bourne* 1327 SRSx; Robert *del Burn* 1332 SRCu. The first reference above is to Bishopsbourne (K), OE *burna* 'stream', the second to Bourn (Cambs), ON *brunnr* 'stream'. In the North and Scotland *burn* is still the living word for a stream. In the rest of England it was early replaced by *brōc* 'brook' and in the south *bourn* came to be used of a stream which flows only in winter or at long intervals, a meaning still found in the dialects of Kent, Surrey and Wilts. Here, in surnames, the reference is usually to an old stream called *burna*, a name often surviving as that of a farm, etc. Bourne (Surrey) is named from an intermittent stream. *v.* BORN.

Bourner, Borner, Burner: Walter *Bournere* 1318 LLB E. 'Dweller by a stream', equivalent to *atte burne*. *v.* BOURNE.

Bourton: *v.* BURTON

Bousie: *v.* BOOSIE

Boutall, Boutell: *v.* BULTEEL

Boutcher: *v.* BUTCHER

Boutflour, Boughtflower, Bonfellow: John *Bult(e)-flour* 1303 Surnames 258, 1430 FrY; Adam *Bonteflour* 1332 Sundby; Helen *Bonfela* 1438 NorwW (Sf); John *Bownflower* 1505 ArchC 41; John, Thomas *Boutflower* 1511 ib.; William *Buntflowre* ib.; Robert *Bonfelow*, *Bunfellow* 1521 NorwW (Nf); Ralph *Bultflower* 1568 SRSf. ME *bulte* 'to sift' and *flour* 'flour', 'sift flour', a nick-name for a miller. cf. BOLTER. *Buntflowre*, pronounced *Bunfler, Bunfeler*, was reconstructed as *Bonfellow*.

Bovill, Boville, Bovell: William *de Bu uilla*, *de Boe uilla*, *de Bee uilla*, *de Boeuilla*, Humphrey *de*

Buivile, Sahala *de Bou uilla* 1086 DB (Sf); William *de Bouilla*, *de Buiuilla* c1150 DC (L); William *de Bowile* 1179 Clerkenwell (Ess); John *de Bouilla* 1182 Eynsham (O). Probably from Bouville (Seine-Inférieure). Early forms of two places named Beuville in Calvados make these less certain identifications (OEByn). Four places in Essex preserve this surname: Bovill's Hall (2), Uplands and Marsh, the latter occurring as *Bowelles* (temp. Henry VIII), so that the surname may also have become BOWELL. *v.* BOWLES.

Bovis: *v.* BEAVES

Bow, Bowe, Bough: Henry *atte Bowe*, *atte Bogh* 1298, 1304 PN D 513; Richard *atte Bowe* 1306 LLB B; Nicholas *atte Boghe* 1327 SRSo. From Bow (Devon, Middlesex) or from minor places of the same name. 'Dweller near a bridge', from OE *boga* 'bow, arch, vault', here 'an arched bridge'.

Bowbrick: Wigor *Buuebroc* 1221 ElyA (Sf); John *Abovebrok* 1279 RH (Hu); John *Bowebroke* 1453 SRSr. 'Dweller above the brook', OE *būfan brōce*.

Bowcher: *v.* BUTCHER

Bowcock, Bowcott: *v.* BAWCOCK

Bowden, Bowdon: *Bowden* is frequent but often represents an older *Bowdon*. (i) John *de Boghedon* 1333 PN D 205. There are 17 places called Bowden in Devon and one Bowdin, all 'curved hill'; Bowden Edge (Derby) has the same origin: (ii) Thomas *Bovedon'* 1279 RH (O); OE *būfan dūne* '(dweller) above the hill', as at Bowden (Wilts); (iii) also from Great Bowden (Leics) or Bowdon (Ches), earlier *Bugge-*, *Bogedone*; (iv) from Bowden (Roxburghshire): Richard *de Boulden* 1200–40 Black.

Bowell: Peter *de Boelles* Hy 3 HPD (Ess); Ralph *de Bueles* 1249 FFEss; Walter *de Bowell* 1275 RH (Herts). In 1086 Shellow Bowells (Essex) was held by Lambert *de Buella* who probably came from Bouelles (Seine-Inférieure). *v.* also BOVILL.

Bowen: Madocus *ap Oweyn* 1292 QW (Sa); John *Bowen* 1305 FrY; Riseus *Abowen* alias *apowen* 1558 AD v (Gl). Welsh *ab Owein* 'son of Owen'.

Bower, Bowers, Bour: (i) Matthew *de Labur'* 1194 Cur (Sr); Mayfflin *Attebur'* 1280 AssSo; Henry *del Boure* 1287 AssCh; Gilbert *atte Boure* 1296 SRSx; Lorence *atte Bure* 1296 Black (Peebles); Peter *ate Boures* 1327 SRC. From minor places called Bower (Som, Sussex, Peeblesshire, etc.) or equivalent to CHAMBERS 'chamber-servant', from OE *būr* 'cottage, chamber'. (ii) Teodricus *Bouer* 1187 P (He); Peter *le Bouer* 1296 SRSx; John *Bour* 'bowyer' 1325 Pat; Robert *le Bowyere*, *le Bower'* 1327, 1332 SRSt. A form of ME *bowyere*, identical with BOWYER.

Bowering: *v.* BOWRING

Bowerman, Boorman, Borman, Burman: William *Bureman* 1204 P (Y); Robert *Boreman* 1279 RH (O); William *Bourman* 1327 SRSx; Walter *Burman* 1327 SRC. OE *būr* and *mann* 'a servant at the bower'. Identical in meaning with *atte Boure*. *v.* BOWER and BOWRA. cf. Alice *Bourwyman* 1301 SRY, Marion *Bourswain* 13th AD i (Sx), Alice *Bourgrom* 1327 SRSo. *v.* also BORROWMAN.

Bowes, Bows: Gerard *de Bowes* 1269 AssNb; John *de Boughes* 1341 FrY; John *Bowys* 1423–4 FFWa. From Bowes (NRYorks), or 'dweller at the arches or bridge', OE *boga*.

Bowgen, Budgen, Budgeon: Robert *Bonjohan* 1297 MinAcctCo; Thomas *Bowgeon* 1454 Fr Norw; John *Bowgyn* 1524 SRSf. Fr *bon Johan* 'good John', perhaps 'the good servant'.

Bowie, Buie, Buy, Buye: John *Boye* alias *Bowy* alias *Boee* 1481 Black; Donald *Buy* 1671 ib. Gael *buidhe* 'yellow or fair haired'.

Bowker: *v.* BUTCHER

Bowl, Bowle, Boule: John *le Boul* 1296 SRSx; James *Boule* 1297 MinAcctCo. OFr *boule* 'round'. cf. BULLETT. Probably also metonymic for *Bowler*.

Bowler, Bouller, Boaler, Boler: John *le Bouller* 1316 FFSo; Robert *le Bollere* 1332 SRSt. A derivative of OE *bolla* 'bowl', a maker or seller of bowls. Also 'one who continues at the bowl, a tippler' (c1320 NED).

Bowles: John *de Boweles* 1292 FFHu; Thomas *Bowles* 1553 ib. *v.* BOWELL.

Bowman, Bowmen, Boman, Beauman: Adam *Bogheman* 1223 Cur (We); Thomas *Bouman* 1279 AssNb; Nicholas *the Bowemon, the Bouman* 1286–7 AssCh. OE *boga* 'bow' and *mann*, a bowman, a fighting man armed with a bow (1297 NED).

Bown: *v.* BOON

Bownas, Bownass, Bowness, Bonas, Bonass, Boness: William *Bownus* 1592 FrY; Matthew *Bownas* 1633 ib.; Richard *Bowness* 1758 ib. From Bowness (Cumb).

Bowra, Bowrah, Boarer, Boorer, Borer, Burra: Hugo *le Burer* 1218 AssL; Alice *Burrer* 1279 RH (C); William *le Bourere* 1332 SRSr; John *Bourere* 1375 FFSx; John *Bowrer* 1498 AD vi (Sr); William *Bowrar* 1535 SxWills; John *Bowra* 1683 ArchC 53; Thomas *Borer* 1697 DKR 41 (Sx). The name of Thomas *atte Boure*, MP for Horsham in 1320, eventually took the form of *Bourer* or *Borer*, whence the family of William *Borrer*, High Sheriff of Sussex (SxAS viii, 274). The meaning is identical with that of *Bower* and *Bowerman* 'dweller or servant at the bower' (OE *būr*). *Bowra* is a specifically Kentish form. Thomas *Bowra*, surgeon, of Sevenoaks, who was born at East Grinstead, Sussex, abandoned the earlier forms of his name, *Boorer* or *Bowrer*, after migrating to Kent during the Commonwealth. The relatives he left behind in Sussex continued to use various older forms, *Borrer, Boreer, Boorer, Borar, Borra* (ArchC 58, 77).

Bowran, Bowron: *v.* BOLDRON

Bowrick: John *le Boghewrichgte* 1292 MESO (La); Robert *Bowwright* 1332 SRCu. OE *boga* and *wyrhta* 'bow-maker'. cf. ARTRICK for ARKWRIGHT.

Bowring, Bowering: Henry *Bouryng* 1302 DbCh; Walter *Bowryng* 1327 SRSo. OE **būring*, a derivative of *būr* 'bower', probably synonymous with BOWRA and BOWERMAN.

Bowser: *v.* BEAUSIRE
Bowsie: *v.* BOOSIE
Bowtell, Bowtle: *v.* BULTEEL

Bowton, Bufton: Robert *Buveton'* 1222 Cur (Beds); Roger *Abovetoun*, John *Aboventoun* c1240 Rams (Hu). '(Dweller) above the village' (OE *(on) būfan tūne*).

Bowyer, Boyer, Boayer: Ailwardus *le Bogiere* 1183 P (Lo); William *le Boghier*. *le Bowiere* 1275 RH (Lo); William *Boyer* 1279 RH (Hu); Henry *le Bowyere* 1296 FFSf. ME *bowyere* 'maker of or trader in bows' (c1300 MED), from OE *boga* 'a bow'. *v.* BOWER.

Box: (i) Adam *Box* 1276 LLB A, 1317 AssK; John *Box* 1327 SRC. OE *box* 'box-tree', 'box-wood' was used in ME of colour, or of teeth yellow as box, and associated with jaundice. (ii) From Box (Glos), William *Box* 1181 P (Gl); Box Hall (Herts), Alan *de Boxe* 1198 P (Herts); or Box (Wilts), Ebrard *de La Boxe* 1182 P (W). Or from residence near a box-tree: Thomas *atteboxe* 1263 PN Sr 270.

Boxer: Apparently from a lost place in Oxfordshire: Alice *de Boxore* 1279 RH (O), 'box-tree bank'.

Boyce: *v.* BOYES

Boycott, Boykett: Gerard, William *de Boycote* 1256 FFK, 1278 RH (Bk); John, Adam *de Boycote* 1334–5 SRK. From Boycott (Bucks, Salop).

Boyd, Boyde: (i) John *Boyde* 1301 SRY. Gael, Ir *buidhe* 'yellow'. The Manx name is from *Mac Giolla Buidhe* 'the yellow-haired youth's son': Conn *Mac Gillabhuidhe* 1100, *McOboy, McBooy* 1511, *Boid* 1617 Moore. (ii) In Scotland and Ireland, from Bute (Gael *Bod*): Robert *de Boyd* 1205 Black; Walter *de Boht* c1272 ib.

Boyden: *v.* BODIN
Boyer: *v.* BOWYER

Boyes, Boys, Boyse, Boice, Boyce: (i) Nicholas *del Bois* 1201 P (L); Thomas *Boys* 1296 SRSx; Roger *du Boys* 1327 SRSf; John *Boyse* 1396 FrY. Fr *bois* 'wood'; equivalent to *atte Wode*. *v.* WOOD. (ii) Godui *Boie filius* c1095 Bury (Sf); Stephanus *filius Boie* 1202 P (Nth); Aluuinus *Boi* 1066 DB (Sr); William *Boie* 1166 P (Nf); Ivo *le Boye* 1232 Pat (L). The personal-name may be OG *Boio* or OE **Boia*, derived from the ancestor of *boy* which is not recorded before 1300. This is common in place-names and is probably of native origin. In ME it meant 'young man' or 'servant' (c1300 MED). *Boie* was the name of a 'border' 1221–26 AD iv (So). cf. LADD. It may also have been used as a nickname, 'knave, rogue, wretch' c1300 MED.

Boyman: Geoffrey, Robert *Boyman* 1268 AssSo, 1357 Black. 'Bowman.' cf. BOWYER.

Boys(e): *v.* BOYES

Braban, Brabant, Braben, Brabin, Brabon, Brabyn, Brabban, Brabben, Brabbins, Brabham: Richard *Braban* 1260 AssC; Heliseus *de Brabayn* 1275 RH (L); Raban *de Braban* 1281 LLB A; John *le Braban* 1283 LLB A; John *Brabon* 1296 SRSx; Richard *Brabyn* 1549 FrY. Flemish *Brabant* 'a native of Brabant' (Flanders), alternating with the name of the Duchy.

Brabazon, Brobson: Thomas *le Brabacum* c1200

Gilb (L); Thomas *Brabezon* 1276 RH (Y); Thomas *le Brabazun* 1294 AssSt; Roger *le Brabanzon* 1301 LLB C; Adam *Brabson* 1381 AssWa; Geoffrey *Brabysson, Brabbesson* 1472 NorwW (Sf); Richard *Bropson* 1531 KentW. AFr *Brabançon* 'a native of Brabant'. cf. BRABAN. In the 13th century, *les brabançons* were companies of adventurers of various nationalities who devastated several French provinces.

Brabban, Brabben, Brabbins, Brabham: *v.* BRABAN

Brabiner, Brabner, Brebner: Peter *Brabaner, Brabaynner* 1379 PTY. 'A native of Brabant', an English formation by the addition of *-er* to the name of the Duchy.

Bracegirdle: John *Brachgyrdyll* or *Brecchegirdle* 1544 Oxon; Roger *Brachegirdle* or *Brasgirdell* 1556 ib.; John *Bretchgirdle* 1561 Pat (Wa); Timothy *Brasegirdell* 1620 Bardsley; Roger *Bracegirdle* 1649 ChW. Metonymic for 'a maker of breech-girdles', cf. William *Brigerdler* 1281 LLB B. ME *brēc*, OFr *braie* 'breeches' and OE *gyrdel*.

Bracer: *v.* BRASSEUR

Brach, Breach, Brech, Britch: Peter *de la Breche* 1221 AssSa; Peter *de la Brach* 1248–52 AD iii (Sr); Philip *atte Breche* 1296 SRSx; Rose *atte Brache* 1309 SRBeds. From residence near a piece of newly cultivated land (OE *brēc*), as at Breach in Maulden and Brache in Luton (Beds).

Bracher, Bratcher, Breacher, Brecher, Britcher: Robert, William *le Brechere* 1245 Oseney (O), 1297 MinAcctCo. Identical in meaning with *atte brache*. *v.* BRACH.

Brachett, Brackett: Ralph, Richard *Brachet* 1214 Cur (C), 1327 *SR* (Ess); William *Braket* 1524 SRSf. OFr *brachet*, a diminutive of *brach*, from which *braket* was also formed. *v.* BRACK.

Brack: Relicta *le Brak* 1296 SRSx; William *Brak* 1327 SRSx; Thomas *Brakke, Braxez, Brax* 1484, 1496, 1532 FrY. ME *braches* plur. is probably OFr *brachés*, plur. of *brachet*. From this plural was apparently educed an English singular *brache* 'a hound which hunts by scent' (c1340 NED). *braches* occurs as *brackes* in 1490.

Brackenridge, Braikenridge, Breckenridge, Brekonridge: Nicholas *de Bracanrig* 1332 SRCu; John *Brakanryg, Breckinrig* 1454, 1634 Black; William *Braikinrig* 1629 ib. 'Dweller by the bracken-covered ridge.' There are five places named Brackenrigg in Cumberland and one in Lanarkshire.

Brackett: *v.* BRACHETT

Brackner: Walter *le Brakener* 1309 RamsCt (Ess). OFr *braconier* 'a keeper of hounds', from OFr *bracon* 'hound' (1490 NED).

Bradbrook: William *de Bradebrok* 1327 SRSf. 'Dweller by the broad brook'.

Bradbury, Bradbery, Bradberry: William, Richard *de Bradbury* 1288 AssCh, 1327 SRDb; Robert *Bradbury* 1401 AssLo. From Bradbury (Ches, Durham).

Bradd: Robert, Stephen *Bradde* 1275 RH (Sf), 1332 SRCu. A shortening of OE *brād* 'broad'.

Braddle: *v.* BRADWELL

Braddock: Geoffrey *Brodhok* 1275 RH (K); Thomas *del Brodok* 1282 AssSt; Thomas *Broddock* 1341 NI (Ess). 'Dweller by the broad oak', OE *brād, āc*.

Brade: *v.* BROAD

Brader: Robert *le Bredere* 1286 MESO (Nf); John *le Brayder* 1324 ib. (La); William *Brader* 1382 FrY. A derivative of OE *breʒdan* 'to braid, plait'. cf. William *le Lacebreyder'* 1329 MESO (Nf), 'a maker of cords', from ME *lace* 'cord', and Neet Breydare PromptParv.

Bradfer: Matthew, William *Braz de fer* 1205 P (Gl), 1230 P (Berks); Matthew *Bradefer* 1212 Rams (Hu). Fr *bras de fer* 'Iron arm'. Now largely absorbed by *Bradford*.

Bradford, Bradforth, Braidford: Alexander, Brun *de Bradeford'* 1206 Cur (D), 1219 AssY; Thomas *de Bradforth* 1358 FrY. From one of the numerous Bradfords.

Bradgate: *v.* BROADGATE

Bradie, Brady, Broady: Roger *Bradeie, Bradege, Brodege* 1170, 1184, 1200 Oseney (O); Geoffrey *Bradege* 1188 P (K); Walter *Bradeye* 1243 AssDu; Simon *Brodhegh* 1247 AssBeds; Robert *Brody* 1275 RH (Nt); William *Brodeie* 1279 RH (C); Agatha *de Brodheghe*, Peter *Brodeye* 1327 SRSf; Richard *Brady* 1430 Black (Dundee). Clearly a nickname, 'broad eye', OE *brād, ēage;* also 'dweller by the broad island' (OE *ēg*), or the broad enclosure (OE *(ge)hæg*). Bradie is Scottish. cf. BROAD.

Bradlaugh: Robert *de Bradlawe* 1275 RH (Db); Godfrey *Bradlaugh* alias Jacob, William Jacobo alias *Brodleye* 1568 SRSf. From Bradley (Derby).

Bradley, Bradly, Bratley, Broadley, Brodley: William *de Bradelai* 1170 P (L); William *Brodelegh* 1379 PTY. From Bradley (Lincs, WRYorks, etc.). *v.* BRADLAUGH.

Bradman, Braidman: William *Bradman* 1275 RH (Nf). 'Broad man.'

Bradmore, Breadmore: Ælfger *de Brademere* c1095 Bury (Sf); Aluredus *de Brademor* 1185 Templars (Wa). From Bradmore (Notts) or residence near a broad lake (OE *mere*).

Bradnam, Bradnum: Suift *de Bradenham* 1177 P (Nf); Francis *Bradnam, Bradnum* 1612, 1628 WStowPR (Sf). From Bradenham (Norfolk).

Bradney: Simon *de Bradneghe* 1327 SRSo; William *de Bradeny* 1296 SRSx. From Bradney (Som) or Bradness Wood (Sussex).

Bradridge, Broadridge: Hugo *de Braderugg'* 1275 SRWo. 'Dweller by the broad ridge', OE *brād, hrycg*.

Bradshaw: William *de Bradesaghe* 1246 AssLa; Simon *de Bradeshaghe* 1303 FFY; Roger *Bradschawe* 1418 IpmNt; Wylliam *Bradsha* 1554 DbAS xxiv; Robert *Bradshey* 1646 RothwellPR (Y). From Bradshaw (Derby, Lancs, WRYorks).

Bradstock, Brastock: Simon *de Bradestoke* 1279 RH (O). From Bradenstoke (Oxon).

Bradstreet: Roger *de Bradestret* 1327 SRSf. 'Dweller in the broad street', OE *brād, strǣt*.

Bradwell, Braddle: Walter *de Bradewelle* 1275 SRWo; John *Braddell* 1622 PrGR. 'Dweller by the broad stream' (OE *brād, wella*), or from Bradwell.

Brady: *v.* BRADIE

Bragg, Bragge: Walter *Bragge* 1243 AssSo; Henry *Brag* 1260 AssC, 1275 RH (W). ME *brag(ge)* 'brisk, lively, mettlesome' (c1325 MED).

Braham, Brahame, Braime, Brame, Bramham, Bramman, Brayham, Bream, Breem: Eustace *de Braham* 1189–99 Colch (Ess); Matthew *de Bramham, de Braham* 1219 AssY; Agnes *de Brame* 1379 PTY; Elizabetha *Bramam* 1628 RothwellPR (Y). From Bramham (WRYorks), Braham (ib.), *Bram* DB, *Braham* 1242 Fees, Braham Fm in Ely (C) or, occasionally, from Brantham (Suffolk), *Braham* 1200 Cur *et freq*. Braham Hall (Essex) is *Braham* 1314, *Brames* 1429, *Bream* 1777, and Bream's Fm (Essex) is *Braham* 1314, *Braeme* 1540, *Breame's farm* 1680 (PN Ess 333, 257). For the development, cf. GRAHAM.

Braid, Braide, Bread: (i) Henry *de Brade* 12th Black; Helen *Braid* 1638 ib. From Braid Hills near Edinburgh. In Fife and Perthshire, this is now Bread. (ii) Geoffrey *Braid'* 1198 FFNf; William *Breyd* 1275 RH (L). These forms are too early to be regarded as forms of BRADE 'broad'. We must have OE *brægd* 'a sudden jerk', used in 1530 for 'a plait, braid', a sense which must have developed much earlier as in the verb. Metonymic for BRADER.

Braidford: *v.* BRADFORD
Braidman: *v.* BRADMAN
Braikenridge: *v.* BRACKENRIDGE
Brailsford, Brellisford, Brelsford: Henry *de Brailesford* 12th DbCh; Jeffray *Brelsforth* 1624 Shef. From Brailesford (Derby).

Braime: *v.* BRAHAM

Braithewaite, Braithwaite, Breathwaite: Reginald *de Braidewad* 1185 P (Y); Adam *de Braythwayt* 1301 SRY; Peter *Braytwayt* 1364 AssY; Robert *Braithwaite* 1642 PrD. From Braithwaite (Cumb, ER, NR, WRYorks).

Braizier: *v.* BRASIER

Brake: Alan *de la Brake* 1176 P (L); John *de Brake* 1275 RH (Nf); Robert *Brake* 1279 RH (Hu). 'Dweller by the copse or thicket', OE *bræc*, ME *brake*.

Brakefield: David *de Brakefeld* 1275 RH (Nf). 'Dweller by the bracken-covered open land', ME *brake*, corresponding to the northern *bracken*.

Brakspear, Braksper: *v.* BREAKSPEAR

Bramah, Bramald, Bramall, Bramalt, Brameld, Bramhall, Brammall, Brammer: Robert *de Bramhal'* 1221 AssWo; Thomas *Bramall, Brammall* 1543, 1566 ShefA. 'Dweller by the broom-covered nook', OE *brōm*, shortened to *bram*, and *healh*, as at Bramhall (Ches). In Sheffield, where there is a Bramall Lane, *Bramah, Bramall* and *Brammer* are common.

Brame: *v.* BRAHAM
Brameld, Bramhall: *v.* BRAMAH
Bramham: *v.* BRAHAM

Brammall: *v.* BRAMAH
Bramman: *v.* BRAHAM
Brammer: *v.* BRAMAH
Bramson, Bramston: *v.* BRANSTON

Branaghan, Branigan: For Irish *Ó Branagáin* 'descendant of *Branagán*', a diminutive of *bran* 'raven'.

Branchett: *v.* BLANCHET
Branchflower: *v.* BLANCHFLOWER

Brand, Brandt, Brant, Braund, Braun, Brauns, Bront: *Brand* 1193 P (Lo); Jacobus *filius Brand* 1206 AssL; William *Brant* 1086 DB (Nf); Ralph *Brand* 1184 P (Lo); Hamo *Brand, Brant, Braund* 1203–4 P, StP (Lo), 1219 Cur (Beds); Richard *Brawne* 1661 Bardsley. ON *Brandr*, ODa *Brand*, 'fire-brand, sword', found also in Normandy.

Brandom, Brandon: Leofric *de Brandune* c975 LibEl (Nf/Sf). From Brandon (Durham, Norfolk, Suffolk, Warwicks) or Brundon (Essex).

Brangwin, Brangwyn: *Brangwayna* 1250 FFSf; Adam *Brangwyne* 1283 SRSf; Robert *Brangwayn* 1300 LoCt. Welsh *Branwen, Brangwain* (f), from *bran* 'raven' and *(g)wen* 'fair'. Branwen, daughter of Llyr, is one of the legendary heroines of Wales. In the Tristan legend Brangwain the Fair was the handmaid and companion of Queen Isolde.

Branigan: *v.* BRANAGHAN

Brann: *Bran* 1154–86 Black (Galloway); Philip *Bran* 1275 RH (Sf); William *Bran* 1275 SRWo, 1629 Black. Gael, Ir, Welsh *bran* 'raven'. The name was also used in Brittany, hence, probably, the Suffolk surname.

Branston, Branson, Bransom, Bramston, Bramson: Gilbert *de Branteston'* 1200 P (Sf); Haim *de Branzton'* 1202 FFL; Helte *de Brandeston'* 1210 P (Sf); Richard *de Braunteston'* 1221 AssSa (St); Robert *Braunston*, William *Branston*, Adam *Branson*, Roger *Bramston* 1568 SRSf. From Branston (Leics, Lincs, Staffs), Brandeston (Suffolk), Brandiston (Norfolk), or Braunston (Leics, Northants). *v.* also BRIMSON.

Brant: *v.* BRAND

Branthwaite, Branwhite: Alan *de Braunthwait* 1332 SRCu; Simon *Branthwite* 1523 FrY; Bloss *Branwhite* 1764 Bardsley. From Branthwaite (Cumb).

Branton, Brantown, Brantom, Braunton: Ralph *de Branton'* 1162 P (Nth). From Branton (WRYorks) or Braunton (Devon).

Brashaw: *v.* BRAYSHAW
Brashour: *v.* BRASSEUR

Brasier, Brasher, Braizier, Brazier: William *Brasier'* 1327 SR (Ess); Thomas *Brasyer* 1381 AssC. A derivative of OE *brasian* 'to make of brass', a worker in brass (a1425 MED). cf. Thomas *le Brasgetere* 1333 MESO (So), 'brass-founder'.

Brassett: Richard *Brassehevede* 1301 SRY. OE *bræs* 'brass', used as a type of hardness, insensibility (c1330 MED) and *hēafod* 'head'. cf. *brassehead buls* 1613 NED. cf. Roger *Brasenhed* 1434 FrNorw.

Brasseur, Le Brasseur, Bracer, Brasher: Azo *le Brascur* 1168 P (K); Richard *le Brazur* 1199 FFEss;

Ralph *Bracur'* 1202 Cur (Sr); German *le Brassur* 1296 SRSx. OFr *braceor, brasseur* 'brewer'.

Brastock: *v.* BRADSTOCK
Bratcher: *v.* BRACHER
Bratley: *v.* BRADLEY
Braun, Braund: *v.* BRAND
Braunton: *v.* BRANTON
Brawn: *v.* BRAND

Bray, Braye: (i) Alnod *de Braio* 1084 GeldR (D); Richard *de Brai* 1135 Eynsham (O); Ralph *de Bray* 1225 Cur (D); Daniel *de Bray* 1297 MinAcctCo. From Bray (Berks), High Bray (Devon), or some unidentified place in Cornwall. (ii) Roger *le Bray* 1202 AssNth; Hugh, William *le Brey* 1275 RH (C), c1304 Glast (So); John, Henry *le Bray* 1327 SRC, SRSf. Cornish *bregh* 'fine, brave'. The great home of the Brays is Cornwall; in the eastern counties the name is of Breton origin. (iii) There was also a woman's name *Braya*, which may derive from the Cornish nickname, cf. *Braya*, daughter of William a Istetone of West Angmering 1316 AD i (Sx), and Peter *Braya* of Ist Angmerynge 1324 ib. was probably of the same family. (iv) Godfrey *de Bra* 1400 Black (Aberdeen); Thomas *de Bra* 1438–48 ib. (Dunfermline); Agnes *Bray* 1617 ib. From one of the many places in Scotland called Brae. (v) In Ireland, either a toponymic, *de Bré*, or Ir *Ó Breaghdha*, a native of Bregia, a territory in Meath (Mac-Lysaght).

Brayer: William *Braier'* 1198 P (K); Godfrey *le Brayer* 1279 RH (O); Walter *le Broyer* 1301 SRY; John *Broyer* 1327 SRC. 'A maker or seller of pestles', from OFr *breie, broie*.

Brayham: *v.* BRAHAM

Brayshaw, Brayshay, Brashaw: Elizabeth *Brawshawe* 1571 RothwellPR (Y); Henry *Brashay, Brayshawe, Brayshay* 1602–17 ib. Local pronunciations of the Yorkshire *Bradshaw*.

Brazier: *v.* BRASIER
Breach: *v.* BRACH
Breacher: *v.* BRACHER
Bread: *v.* BRAID
Breadmore: *v.* BRADMORE

Breakspear, Brakspear, Braksper: Alexander *Brekespere* 1199 CurR (L); Geoffrey *Brekespere* 1206 Cur (Sr); Thomas *Brekaspere* 1227 AssBeds. 'Break spear', which, as Bardsley remarks, 'would be cheerfully accepted as a nickname by the successful candidate in the tournament'. It could also have reference to achievement in actual battle. cf. Stephen *Bruselaunce* 1308 RamsCt (Sf); Martin *Briselaunce* 1312 LLB D; Richard *Brekeswerd* 1195 P (L) 'break sword', and *v.* SHAKESPEAR.

Bream, Breem, Brim, Brims, Brimm: *Breme* 1066 DB (Sf); Hugo *Brem* 1221 AssWa; Symon *Brim* 1279 RH (C); Agatha *Breme* 1327 SRC; Robert *Brymme* 1327 SRSx. OE *brēme*, ME *brem(e), brim(me)* 'vigorous, fierce', earlier 'famous, noble', or OE *Brēme. v.* also BRAHAM.

Brear, Breare: Walter, Richard *le Brer* 1255 RH (Sa), 1279 RH (O); William *Brere* 1346 FrY. OE *brǣr* 'prickly thorn-bush', modern *briar*, used as a nickname. cf. 'sharp as brere' (Chaucer). *v.* BRIAR.

Brearley: *v.* BRIERLEY

Brearton, Breerton, Brereton: Richard *de Brertona* 1176 YCh; Alexander *de Breretone* 1242 AssDu; William *de Brereton* 1356 FFY. From Brereton (Ches. Staffs), Brierton (Durham), or Brearton (WRYorks).

Breathwaite: *v.* BRAITHEWAITE
Brebner: *v.* BRABINER
Brech: *v.* BRACH
Brecher: *v.* BRACHER
Breckenridge: *v.* BRACKENRIDGE

Brede, Breed, Breede, Breeds: Brian *de Brede* 1195 FFNf; William *de Bredes*, John *de Brede* 1296 SRSx; Elena *atte Brede* 1317 AssK; Marjery *Brede* 1352 ColchCt. 'Dweller by the plain or flat expanse' as at Brede (Sussex). OE *brǣdu* 'breadth', used topographically in ME of a broad strip of land.

Breeder: Equivalent to *atte Brede. v.* BREDE.

Breem: *v.* BRAHAM, BREAM

Breese, Breeze: Roger *Brese* 1210 P (Nf); William *Brese* 1275 Wak (Y). Usually explained as *ab Rees* 'son of *Rees*'. This may be the origin of Robert *Breese* 1666 Bardsley (Ch), but the above forms are too early for this development. They are nicknames from OE *brēosa* 'a gadfly'.

Breffitt: *v.* BREVETOR
Brekonridge: *v.* BRACKENRIDGE
Brellisford, Brelsford: *v.* BRAILSFORD

Bremner, Brimner, Brymner: Walter *Brabounare* 1418–26 Black (Ayrshire); Agnus *Brebner* 1489 ib. (Elgin); Finlay *Brembner* 1649 ib.; James *Brimner* 1630 ib. cf. BRABINER. Artisans and traders from Brabant settled early at Aberdeen and on the east coast of Scotland. *Bremner* is still at times pronounced *Brembner* in Caithness.

Brend, Brent, Brind: (i) Gilbert *Brende* 1273 RH (St); Adam *Brend*, John *Brent* 1327 SRWo; Hugo *le Brent* 1279 RH (O); Geoffrey *le Brende* 1327 SRSf. *Brend, brent* and *brind* are ME forms of the past participle of OE *beornan* 'to burn'. 'The burnt', a nickname for a criminal who had been branded. cf. Henry *Brendcheke* 1279 AssNb, Cutte *Brendhers* 1279 RH (C). cf. BRENNAN. (ii) Symon *del Brend* 1318 FrY. Here *brend* is used topographically of 'burnt land', hence 'dweller by the burnt land' as at Brind (ERYorks), *Brende* 1188 P. *v.* also BRENT.

Brennan, Brennans, Brennand, Brennen, Burnand: Reginald *Brennehand'* 12th DC (L); Walter *Brenhand* 1229 Whitby (Y); William *Brennand* 1277 Ipm (Nt); Joan *Byrnand* 1475 GildY; Anna *Burnand* 1512 ib. 'Burn hand', a nickname for the official who carried out the harsh punishment of medieval law. Matilda *Brendhand* 1295 Barnwell (C), whose surname would also become modern *Brennan*, had suffered this punishment. *Brennan* may also be for Irish *Ó Braondáin* 'descendant of *Braonán*', a diminutive of *braon* 'sadness'.

Brenner: Jordan, John *le Brenner* 1280 AssSt, 1327 SRSf; John *le Brynner* 1327 Pat. OFr *brenier* 'keeper of the hounds', or a derivative of ON *brenna* 'to burn', 'burner' of lime, bricks or charcoal. cf. BERNER.

Brenson: *v.* BRIMSON

Brent: Robert *de Brente* 1269 AssSo. From South Brent (Devon) or East Brent (Som). *v.* also BREND.

Brereton: *v.* BREARTON

Bret, Brett, Britt, Britts: Edward *Brit* 1066 DB (D); Tihellus *Brito* 1086 DB (Ess); Walter *Bret* 1164 StCh; Alan *le Bret* 1177 P (C); William *le Brit, le Brut* 1230, 1256 Oseney (O); Matthew *le Brut* 1242 Fees (He); Henry *Brit* 1275 SRWo; Ralph *le Brut* 1296 SRSx. The most frequent form of these common surnames is *Bret* which is usually from OFr *Bret*, nominative of *Breton* 'a Breton'. The variation between *e*, *i* and *u* points to OE *Brit, Bryt, Bret*, which meant 'a Briton' and continued to be applied to the Strathclyde Britons until c1300. In the Welsh border counties it may have been used of the Welsh as *Waleys* was of the Strathclyde Britons. *v.* WALLIS.

Breton, Le Breton, Bretton, Briton, Britton, Brutton: Geoffrey (*le*) *Bretun, le Briton* 1164–9 P (Ess, Y); Lowis *le Briton* 1166 RBE (Ess); Ralph *Bretun* 1166 Oseney (O); William, John *le Bruton'* 1248 Fees (Ess), 1279 AssSo. *Bretun*, the most common form, is the cas-régime of OFr *Bret* 'a Breton'. For the variation between *Breton, Briton* and *Bruton*, cf. BRET.

Brettel, Brettell, Brettle, Bretelle: *Bretel* 1066 DB (Co); *Bretellus, Britellus* 1086 DB (D, Do, So); *Bretellus* de Amber' 1130 P (Ha); Reginald *Bretel* 1169 P (Hu); John *Brutel* 1235 Oseney (O); Richard *Britel* 1243 AssSo. OCornish *Brytthael*, OBret *Brithael*: Godwine *Brytæl* 1035 OEByn (Do).

Bretton: Osbert *de Bretton'* 1193 P (Y). From Bretton (Derby, WRYorks).

Brettoner, Britnor, Britner, Bruttner: John *Bretener* 1379 PTY. ME *Bretoner, Brutiner* 'a Breton', used as a term of reproach. cf. 'A Brutiner, a Braggere, a-bosted him also' (a1376 MED).

Brevetor, Brevitt, Breffit, Breffitt: Alexander *Brevetur* 1221 ElyA (C); Adam *le Breuetor'* 1275 SRWo; Walter *le Brefeter* 1285 Ass (Ess); Joan *Breftour* 1327 SR (Ess); John *Breuet* 1357 ColchCt. A derivative of OFr, ME *brevet*, a diminutive of OFr, ME *bref*, 'an official or authoritative message in writing', especially Papal indulgences, used also by metonymy for a bearer of these (1275 NED).

Brew: A purely Manx name from *MacVriw* 'son of the judge', now the Deemster: *McBrow* 1408, *McBrewe* 1417, *Brew* 1616 Moore.

Brewer, Brewers, Brouwer, Brower: (i) Richard *Briwerra* 1192 AC (Ha); William *Bruwere* (*Briwere*) 1148 Winton (Ha); John *Browere* 1201–12 RBE (Sf); Henry *le Brewere* 1278 AssSo. ME *brewere*, a derivative of OE *brēowan* 'to brew', a brewer (a1300 NED). *v.* BREWSTER. (ii) Ralph *de Brueria* 1086 DB (D); Nicholas *de la Bruiere* 1195 P (Gl); Thomas *de la Bruera* 1221 FFSt. The DB undertenant may have come from Bruyère (Calvados), from OFr *bruière* 'heath', a term used also in

England: Temple Bruer (Lincs), *la Bruere* Hy 2. Bruera (Ches) is a translation of OE *hæð, Heeth* 12th, *Bruera* c1190.

Brewis, Brewse, Browse, Bruce: (i) William *de Briouze* a1080 France; William *de Braiose* 1086 DB (Sx, Sr, Ha, Berks, W); William *de Breosa* 1154 Templars (Sx), *de Braiuse* 1169 P (Sx), *de Braosa, de Breusa, de Breuse, de Breiuse* 1206 Cur (He, Sr), *de Brews'* 1212 Fees (Sx); Reginald *de Brause, de Brawose* 1206 Cur (Sx), *de Brause* 1212 Fees (D), *de Breus', de Breius, de Breuis* 1219 Cur (Sx), *de Breaus'* 1226 Fees (He); Maria *de Brewes* 1296 SRSx; Robert *Brous* 1327 SRSx. From the time of Domesday the family of Briouze were lords of the rape of Bramber (Sussex). They came from Briouze (Orne) and their surname survives in Manningford Bruce (Wilts) and Wickhambreux (Kent). Its later forms are inextricably confused with those of BRUCE. (ii) Hugh *del Breuhous* 1302 FrY; Robert *del Brewhus* 1332 SRCu; Richard *del Bruhous* 1401 FrY. 'Worker at the brew-house', a brewer.

Brewitt, Browett: Robert *Bruet* 1207 Cur (W); John *Brouet* 1268 Pat (Wa); John *Brewett* 1524 SRSf. OFr *brouet, broet* 'soup made of flesh broth', a diminutive of OFr *breu*, earlier *bro*, ME *browet, bruet* (1399 NED). Used for a maker or seller of broth.

Brewster, Broster, Bruster: Roger *Breuestere* 1221 ElyA (Sf); Emma *le Breustere* 1279 RH (Bk); Geoffrey *Brouster* 1283 SRSf; John *Browster*, Margaret *Brewster* 1381 SRSf; Henry *Bruster* 1383 FrY. ME *brewestere, browestere* 'a woman brewer' (1308) NED. cf. BREWER. Three-quarters of the examples are names of men. cf. BAXTER. *Broster* may sometimes be from *broudester* 'a female embroiderer', from ME *broudin* from OFr *brouder* 'to embroider' (1450 NED): Gelisius *Browdester* 1377 FrY; Nicholas *Broudester* 1381 PTY.

Brian, Briance, Briand, Briant, Brien, Brient, Bryan, Bryand, Bryans, Bryant, O'Brian, O'Brien: Radulfus *filius Brien* 1086 DB (Ess); *Briendus* de Scal' 1086 ICC (C); *Brien* 1088 StCh, 1114–19 Bury (Sf); *Brient* 1130 P (W); *Brianus* filius Radulfi, Alani 1207 Cur (Sr, Y); Ralph *Brien* 1160 Bury (Sf); Ralph *Brian'* 1205 P (Y); Bennet *Briant* 1524 SRSf. A Breton name introduced into England by the Normans. In the north, it is OIr *Brian*, brought by Norsemen from Ireland (where the name was common) to Cumberland and across the Pennines into Yorkshire. It is found in ON as *Brján*.

Briar, Briars, Brier, Briers, Bryar, Bryars, Bryer, Bryers: John *in le Breres* 1279 RH (Hu). 'Dweller among the brambles', OE *brēr* 'prickly thorn-bush', formerly including the bramble.

Brice, Bryce: *Bricius* de Kyrkebi 12th DC (L); *Bricius* judex c1189–99 Black (Abernethy); *Brice* 1208 Cur (Y); William, Roger *Brice* 1240 FFEss, 1277 Ely (Sf). The name of St *Britius* or *Brice*, successor of St Martin as Bishop of Tours, was popular in England and Scotland in the 12th and 13th centuries. It is probably Celtic in origin.

Brickett: v. BIRKETT

Brickstock: v. BRIGSTOCKE

Briddock, Brideoke: *Bridoc* c1190 Black; Joan *Brydok* 1379 PTY. Gaelic *Brideoc*, a diminutive of *Bride*, Ir, MScots *Brighid*.

Bride: v. BIRD. In Scotland, for MCBRIDE.

Bridell: v. BRIDLE

Bridewell: Walter *de Bridewill'* 1297 MinAcctCo (Co). 'Dweller by a well dedicated to St Bride or near a spring or stream frequented by birds' (OE *bridd*). There can be no reference to Bridewell as a prison. The London Bridewell was a 'lodging' built by Henry VIII near St Bride's Well and later given by Edward VI as a hospital. The modern meaning arose later, when the hospital was converted into a house of correction.

Bridge, Delbridge, Dellbridge, Dealbridge: Gilbert *atte Brigge* 1272 PN Sr 143; Nicholas *de la Brugge* 1275 SRWo; William *ater Bregg* 1296 SRSx; Roger *dil Brigge* 1327 SRSf. 'Dweller near or keeper of the bridge', OE *brycg*. v. BRIDGEMAN.

Bridgeland, Bridgland: Robert *Bregelonde* 1296 SRSx; Henry *de Bregelonde* 1317 AssK. 'Dweller by the land near the bridge.'

Bridgeman, Bridgman: John *Brygeman* 1296 SRSx; John *Bregman* 1310 PN Ess 217; John *Bruggemon* 1332 SRWa. 'Dweller by or keeper of the bridge' (1648 NED). William *Breggeman* is identical with William *atte Bregge* (1332-3 ERO). v. BRIDGER, PONTER.

Bridgen, Bridgens, Bruggen: Aylward *Attarebrughend'* 1239 MELS (So); John *At Brugeende* 1279 RH (O); John *Attebriggende* 1280 AssSt; Richard *atte Bruggende* of Kingston 1377 LoPleas; Thomas *Bridgin* 1640 SaltAS xv. 'Dweller at the end of the bridge.' Occasionally, 'man from Bruges': Alexander *Brugeyn* 1260 AssC.

Bridger, Brugger: Walter *le Briggere* 1327 SRSo; Walter *Bregger* 1327 SRSx; John *Bruger* 1332 SRSr. A derivative of OE *brycg* 'bridge', with the same meaning as BRIDGEMAN. John *le Bruggere*, also called John *de Ponte* (1294) lived at Bridge End in Ockham (Surrey). v. PN Nth xlvi.

Bridges, Brydges: William *de Bruges, de Brieges* 1205 Cur (O). From Bruges (Belgium).

Bridgstock: v. BRIGSTOCKE

Bridle, Bridel, Bridell: Walter *Bridel* 1196 FrLeic; Richard *Brydel* 1266 FFEss. OE *brīdel* 'bridle', as an occupation name. cf. *bridelsmyth* 1321-4 Pat, 'Bridle-Cutters . . . and all other Makers, Dressers, or Workers in Leather' (1697 NED).

Bridson, Brydson: *Giolla Brighde* 1146, *McGilbrid* 1511, *Bridson* 1609 Moore. A Manx name, originally *Mac Giolla Brighde* 'Bridget's servant's son', from St Bridget. Pronounced *Brideson*. cf. Irish KILBRIDE, Gaelic MCBRIDE.

Brier: v. BRIAR

Brierley, Brierly, Brearley: Ivetta *de Brerelay* 1248 AssSt; Roger *de Brerley* 1275 Wak (Y). From Brierley (Staffs) or Brierly (WRYorks).

Brigenshaw, Briginshaw: v. BIRKENSHAW

Brigg, Briggs: Robert *del Brig* 1275 Wak (Y);

Alexander *del Brigg* 1332 SRCu; Robert *atte Brig* 1379 PTY. 'Dweller by the bridge', ME *brig(g)*, ON *bryggia*, the northern and Scottish word for bridge.

Bright: John *Briht* 1252 Rams (Hu); William *le Brythe* 1278 AssSo; Herveus *Brite* 1279 RH (C); Adam *Bright* 1296 SRSx. OE *beorht* 'bright, beautiful, fair'.

Brighten: v. BRIGHTON

Brightiff, Beriff: *Bricteva, Britheue* 1066 DB; Godric *Brihteue filius* c1095 Bury (Sf); *Birghiva* 1208 Cur (Herts); Angerus *filius Brihtiue* 1219 AssL; Adam *Brightyeue*, Thomas *Brytheue* 1326, 1327 FFSf; Edmund *Brightyeve* or *Britiff* 1467 Bardsley (Nf); John *Beriffe* 1496 Dickin (Ess); Richard *Brygthewe, Brighteve* 1479 SIA xii, 1508 NorwW (Nf); Thomas *Bereve* 1522 SIA xii; John *Brightif* 1559 Bardsley (Nf). *Berriff* is from OE *Beorhtgifu* 'fair gift'; *Brightiff* is from the metathesized form *Brihtgifu*, a woman's name still in use in the 13th century. v. BRIGHTY.

Brightley, Brightly: Peter *de Brihtleg'* 1199 P (D). From Brightley (Devon).

Brightman: *Brihtmanus* 1066 DB (Sf); Robert *Brightman* (*Brithman*) 1327 SR (Ess). OE *Brihtmann, Beorhtmann* 'fair man'.

Brightmore, Brimmer, Burkmar: *Brihtmarus, Britmar* 1066 DB; Ædmer *Brihtmari filius* c1095 Bury (Sf); *Brichmerus filius Hunne* 1193 P (Nf); Lemmer *Brihtmer* c1095 Bury (Sf); John *Brictmer* 1221 AssWo; John *Britmar* 1309 SRBeds; William *Brightmer* 1332 SRSx; Robert *Brykemare* 1568 SRSf. OE *Beorhtmær, Brihtmær* 'fair-famous', a personal-name common in DB and throughout the 12th century. *Britmer* became *Brimmer* and *Brykemare* became, through metathesis, *Byrkmar, Burkmar*.

Brighton, Brighten: Richard *de Brighton* 1328 FrY; Adam *de Bryghton* 1341 Pat (Cu); Nicholas *de Brighton* 1342 Cl (Nt). From Breighton (ERYorks), *Bristun* DB, *Bryghton* 1298-1567, *Breighton* 1636 (PN ERY 239). The surname can have no connexion with the Sussex Brighton, earlier *Brightelmeston*. This occurs as *Brighton* in deeds of the reign of Charles I but did not come into common use until the early nineteenth century (PN Sx 291).

Brightween, Brightwen: *Brictuinus, Brithuinus* 1066 DB; *Brithwen uidua* 1066 Winton (Ha); *Brictwen* 1148 ib.; *Brihtwinus de Ixwrthe* 12th MedEA (Sf); *Brichtwenne* 1222 DBStP (Ess); Bartholomew *Bryctwyne* 1296 SRSx; John *Bryghtwyne* 1332 ib. The surname forms are from OE *Beorhtwine* (m) 'fair friend'; the modern forms point rather to OE *Beorhtwynn* (f) 'bright joy'.

Brighty: *Brictui* 1066 DB (Do); *Brichwi* 1188 BuryS (Sf); *Berdwi faber* 1192 P (K); Osbertus *filius Britwi* 1221 ElyA (Ess); Alexander *Brictwi* 1210 Cur (C); Agnes *Britwy* 1277 Ely (Sf); Thomas *Brightwy* 1327 SRSx. OE *Beorhtwīg, Brihtwīg* 'bright war'. The surname may also be for BRIGHTIFF, from the 1479 *Brygthewe*.

Brigstocke, Brickstock, Bridgstock: Walter

Brigestok 1275 RH (L). From Brigstock (Northants).

Brim: *v.* BREAM

Brimblecombe, Brimacombe, Brimicombe, Brimmacombe, Brimmicombe, Brinicombe: From Brimblecombe (Devon), where the surname was *Brumelcome* in 1281 and *Bremylcomb* in 1330 (PN D 343).

Brimmer: *v.* BRIGHTMORE

Brimner: *v.* BREMNER

Brimson, Brinson, Brenston: John *de Brinzun* 1240 FFEss; Joan *de Bryaunesoun* 1297 ib.; Bartholomew *Brinsun* 1274 RH (Ess). This family came from Briençun (Normandy) and has left its name in Brimstone Hill in Little Wakering (Essex), *Breaunsons* 1419, *Bremsons, Bramsons* 1549, *Brendston* 1553. New Hall in Purleigh was formerly called from them; *Brymshams* 1527, *Bremstones* 1537, *Brempsons* 1554 (PN Ess 204, 223). The surname may also have contributed to *Bramson, Branson, Branston*.

Brind: *v.* BREND

Brinicombe: *v.* BRIMBLECOMBE

Brinkler: *v.* BRINKLOW

Brinklow, Brinkler: William *de Brinkelawa* 1190 P (Y). From Brinklow (Warwicks).

Brinson: *v.* BRIMSON

Brisbane, Brisbourne: Ralph *Briseban* 1275 AD i (Mx); John *Brusebon* 1297 MinAcctCo; William *Brisbone* 1298 Black. A hybrid, from OFr *brise* 'break' and OE *bān* 'bone', 'break bone'. *Brisbourne* is due to the common pronunciation of *-bourne* as *-bone*. cf. CRAKEBONE.

Brisco, Briscoe, Brisker, Briskey: Robert *de Briscaw* 1332 SRCu. From Briscoe (Cumb, NRYorks, WRYorks).

Bristol, Bristoll: John *de Brystall* 1392 FrY. From Burstall (ERYorks), *Bristall* 1160–2, or Birstal (WRYorks), *Bristal* 1292. The modern form has been influenced by that of the better known Bristol.

Bristow, Bristowe, Bristo, Brister: Lia *de Bristou* 1191 P (Gl); Peter *de Bristo* 1195 P (O). From Bristol (Glos), originally *Brycgstow*, DB *Bristou*. The form in common use until at least the 16th century was *Bristow*. The modern *Bristol* is scribes' Latin. Occasionally the source may be Burstow (Surrey), *Brystowe* from 1486, or Bristow Fm in Frimley (Surrey), *Brister* 1765. *v.* PN Sr 286, 127.

Britain, Brittain, Brittan, Britten, Brittin, Brittian, Brittney: John *de Bretagne* 1291 AssSt; Thomas *de Brytannia* 1297 MinAcctCo; John *de Bretayne* 1327 SRC. From Brittany, OFr *Bretagne*. Some of the modern forms are from the ME *Brytane, Brittan* 'Breton'.

Britch: *v.* BRACH

Britcher: *v.* BRACHER

Britner, Britnor: *v.* BRETTONER

Briton, Britton: *v.* BRETON

Britt: *v.* BRET

Brittney: *v.* BRITAIN

Brixey, Brixhe: Alsi *filius Brixi* 1066 DB (Ha); Godric *filius Brichsii* c1095 Bury (Sf); Alanus

filius Brixi 1209 P (Nf); Stephen, Roger *Brixy* 1275, 1276 RH (Nf, Beds). OE *Beorhtsige, Brihtsige* 'bright victory'.

Broad, Brade, Braid, Braide: John *le Brade* 1212 Cur (K); Gilbert *le Brode* 1235 FFEss. OE *brād*, ME *brod(e)* 'broad'. In the north and Scotland, the *ā* remained in ME, later spelled *ai*, giving modern *Brade, Braid*.

Broadbelt: Adam *Bradbelt* 1379 PTY; Richard *Broadbelt* 1682 FrY. 'Broad belt', one who wore a broad belt, a nickname for a stout man. cf. William *Brodgirdel* 1275 RH (Nt).

Broadbent: Robert *Brodebent* 1513 FrY; William *Brodbent* 1528 KentW. 'Dweller by the broad grassy plain.' *v.* BENT.

Broadfoot: Turgis *Bradfot* 1157 P (Cu); Roger *Brodfot* 1247 AssBeds. OE *brād* and *fōt* 'broad foot', a common early nickname.

Broadgate, Bradgate: Ralph *de Bradgate* 1275 RH (Lei); Nicholas *atte Brodegate* 1344 LLB F. 'Dweller by the broad gate' (ME *gate*) as at Bradgate (Leics).

Broadhead: (i) Thomas *Bradheuid* 1243 AssDu; John *Brodheved* 1281 Rams (Hu); Daniel *Broadhead* 1664 FrY. 'Broad head', OE *brād, hēafod*. William *Brodhod* 1327 SRDb may have borne the same nickname, with ON *hǫfuð*, Da *hoved* for OE *hēafod;* or he may have worn a broad hood (OE *hōd*). cf. GREENHEAD. (ii) Henry *de Bradeheved* 1272 AssSt; Alan *del Brodeheued* 1332 SRLa; Robert *de Bradehed* 1332 SRSt. 'Dweller by the broad headland.'

Broadhouse, Broadis: Richard *de Bradhus* 1214 Cur (L). 'Dweller at the large house', OE *brād* 'broad, extensive' and *hūs*.

Broadhurst, Brodhurst: Roger *de Brodhurst* 1281 AssLa. 'Dweller by the broad wood', OE *hyrst*.

Broadis: *v.* BROADHOUSE

Broadley: *v.* BRADLEY

Broadmead: Roger *atte Brodmed* 1327 SRSo. 'Dweller by the broad meadow.'

Broadribb, Brodribb: Peter *Brodribbe* 1327 SRSo; Richard *Brawdrib* 1533 RochW. Clearly a nickname, 'broad rib'.

Broadridge: *v.* BRADRIDGE

Broadwood: Walter *de Brodwode* 1274 RH (So). 'Dweller by the broad wood', OE *brād* and *wudu*.

Broady: *v.* BRADIE

Broatch: *v.* BROOCH

Brobson: *v.* BRABAZON

Brobyn: *v.* PROBIN

Brock, Brocks: (i) Ralph *Broc* 1119 Colch (Ess); Joel *le Broc* 1222 Pat (D); Richard *Brock* 1275 SRWo. OE *brocc* 'badger'. From c1400 *brock* is often used with the epithet *stinking* and in the 16th century meant 'a stinking or dirty fellow' (ELPN). Or from OFr *broque, brocke* 'a young stag'. *v.* BROCKET. (ii) Laurence *del Brock* 1267 Abbr (So); Nigel *de Brocke* 1285 FA (Sx); Robert *de la Brockes* 1286 Ipm (Wo); Alma *ate Brock'*, Imeyna *du Brock'* 1297 MinAcctCo. OE *brōc* 'brook, stream'. For the short vowel, cf. the river-name Brock (Lancs). In Kent and Sussex, *brook* still means 'water-meadow' and in the plural 'low marshy ground'. Hence 'one who lives by a stream or by the water-meadow(s)'. *v.* MELS and BROOK.

Brockbank: *v.* BROOKSBANK

Brockenshaw: *v.* BIRKENSHAW

Brocket, Brockett: (i) Osbert *Brochard* 1175 P (Ha); John *Brocard* 1327 SRC. (ii) Henry *Broket* 1279 RH (O); John *Broket* 1297 MinAcctCo. OFr *brocart, brocquart* from OFr *broque, brocke,* from which was formed ME *broket, brocket* 'a stag in its second year with its first horns' (c1410 MED).

Brockhouse, Brockis: *v.* BROOKHOUSE

Brockhurst, Brockherst: Richard *de Brocherst'* 1201 Pl; Robert, William *de Brokhurst* 1296 SRSx; Thomas *Brokhurst* 1381 AssWa. From Brockhurst (Hants, Sussex, Warwicks).

Brockless, Brockliss: *Broclos, Brocles* 1066 DB (L); Roger *Broclaus* Ric 1 Gilb (L). ON *bróklauss* 'breech-less, without breeches', a nickname used also as a personal name which is the first element of Brocklesby (Lincs). cf. Robert *Brekeles* 1276 RH (Y), the English equivalent.

Brockman: *v.* BROOKMAN

Brockway: Walter *de Brokweye* 1255 RH (W). 'Dweller by the road near the brook.'

Brodhurst: *v.* BROADHURST

Brodie: Michael *de Brothie* 1311 Black. From Brodie (Moray). *v.* also BRADIE.

Brodley: *v.* BRADLEY

Brodribb: *v.* BROADRIBB

Broke: *v.* BROOK

Brokenshaw, Brokenshire: *v.* BIRKENSHAW

Brokus: *v.* BROOKHOUSE

Bromage: *v.* BROMWICH

Broman: *v.* BROOMAN

Brome: *v.* BROOM

Bromehead, Bromet: *v.* BROOMHEAD

Bromfield: *v.* BROOMFIELD

Bromhall: *v.* BROOMHALL

Bromhead: *v.* BROOMHEAD

Bromige: *v.* BROMWICH

Bromley, Bromly, Brumbley: Hubert *de Brumle* 1194 StCh; Edward *de Bromleghe* c1200 ArchC vi. From Bromley (Essex, Herts, Kent, Staffs).

Brommage: *v.* BROMWICH

Brompton, Brumpton: Geoffrey *de Brunton'* 1205 P (Y); William *de Bromptone* 1312 LLP. D. From Brompton (Middlesex, Salop, ERYorks, NRYorks).

Bromwich, Bromage, Bromige, Brommage: Adam *de Bromwiz* 1221 AssWa; William *de Bromwic* 1225 AssSt; Thomas *Bromidge* 1581 Bardsley; John *Bromage* 1583 ib. From West Bromwich (Staffs) or Castle and Little Bromwich (Warwicks).

Bron: *v.* BROWN

Bronsdon, Bronson: Chanaan *de Bronteston'* 1176 P (St). From Branson (Staffs).

Bront: *v.* BRAND

Brooch, Broatch: Metonymic for *Brocher.* cf. Ralph *Brocher* 1222 FFSf; John *Brocher,* Roger *le Brochere* 1281 LLB B. ME, OFr *broche* 'a tapering, pointed instrument or thing, a lance, spear, bodkin, etc.', also 'a brooch'. Hence, a maker of

broaches (lances, spears, etc.) or of brooches. cf. William *Bruchemaker* 1381 PTY and William *ploghbrocher* 1281 MESO (L), probably a maker of ploughshares.

Brook, Brooke, Brookes, Brooks, Broke, Bruck: Eustace *delbroc* 1130 P (Nth); Rand' *de Broc* 1157 P (Ha); William *de la Broke* 1208 Cur (Sr); Emma *de Brokes* 1220 Cur (Sf); Peter *Attebroke* 1262 For (Ess); William *aboventhebroc* 1276 MELS (Wo); William *atte Brouk* 1296 SRSx; William *in le Broke, Ithebroke* 1317 AssK; Sarra *Bithebrok* 1327 SRSo; William *atte Bruck* 1327 SRC; William *del Brokes* 1332 SRLa; John *Bethebrokes* 1332 SRWo. From Brook (Kent, Rutland), Brooke (Norfolk), or from residence near a stream or by the water-meadow(s). *v.* BROCK.

Brookbank(s): *v.* BROOKSBANK

Brooker, Brucker: William *Brokere,* John *le Broker* 1296 SRSx; John *le Brouker* 1327 ib. 'Dweller by the brook.' William *le Broker* (1332 ib.) was probably a descendant of Anger *atte Broke* (1296 ib.).

Brookfield: Thomas *de Brokefeld'* 1199 MemR (O); Adam *del Brokefeld* 1332 SRLa. 'Dweller by the field near the brook', OE *brōc, feld.*

Brookhouse, Brockhouse, Brockis, Brokus: Ralph *del Brokhouses* 1297 SRY; Hugh *de Brokehous'* 1379 PTY; William *Brokkus* 1562 Black. 'Dweller at the house by the brook.'

Brookman, Brockman: Stephen *Brokman* 1296 SRSx; John *Brookman* 1372 ColchCt. Equivalent to BROOKER.

Brooksbank, Brookbank, Brookbanks, Brockbank: Thomas *Brokesbank'* 1379 PTY; John *Brockbank* 1700 FrY; Charles *Brookbank* 1758 ib. 'Dweller by the bank of the brook.'

Broom, Broome, Brome: Robert *de Brome* 1193 P (Lei); Alexander *Brom'* 1221 AssWa; Eustace *de la Brome* 1275 RH (K); Richard *atte Brome* 1285 *Ass* (Ess); Richard *del Brom* 1297 SRY. From Broom (Beds, Durham, Worcs), Broome (Norfolk, Salop, Warwicks) or Brome (Suffolk), or from residence near a place where broom (OE *brōm*) grew.

Brooman, Broman: *Bruman(nus)* 1066 DB (K, Bk); *Brummanus* 1140–53 Holme (Nf); Gilebertus *filius Brunman* 1211 Cur (Cu); Brihtmar *Bruman, Brunman* 1199, 1200 P (Nf); Ralph *Broneman* 1296 SRSx; John *Bromman* 1327 ib.; Alexander *Brounman* 1327 *SR* (Ess); John *Broman* 1372 ColchCt. OE *Brūnmann.*

Broomer: Thomas *de Brommor,* John *Brommor* 1296 SRSx; Robert *Bromere, Bromor* 1327, 1332 ib. All probably came from Bramber Fm, Bremere Rife or Broomer Fm in Birdham (Sussex). *v.* PN Sx 73, 80.

Broomfield, Bromfield, Brumfield: Hamo *de Bromfeld* 1275 RH (K); William *atte Bromfeld* 1296 SRSx; John *de Bromfeld* 1327 SRSf. From Broomfield (Essex, Kent, Som), Bromfield (Cumb, Salop) or from residence near broom-covered open-land (OE *brōm, feld*).

Broomhall, Bromhall: Matthew *de Bromhale*

1182 P (Ch); Godwin *de Bromhal'* 1182–1200 BuryS (Sf). From Broomhall (Ches, WRYorks), Bromhall (Berks) or residence by a broom-covered nook (OE *healh*).

Broomhead, Bromehead, Bromhead, Bromet, Brumhead, Brummitt: Henry *de Bromeheuede* 1290 ShefA; John *Bromehed* 1440 ib.; Mary *Brummett* 1717 Bardsley. From Broomhead in Hallamshire (Sheffield).

Broster: *v.* BREWSTER

Brothers: *Broder* (St, Sf), *Brodor* (St), *Brodre* (D) 1066 DB; Willelmus *filius Brother* 1202 AssL; John *Brother* 1272 AD i (Mx); Nicholas *le Bruthre* 1279 AssSo; Adam (*le*) *Brother* 1280 ib.; John *Brothers* 1621 Bardsley. ON *Brôðir*, ODa *Brothir* or OE *brôðor* 'brother', used in ME of a kinsman (1382) and a fellow-member of a guild or corporation (1362).

Brough, Brugh, Bruff: Daniel *de Burg'* 1219 AssY; William *de Bruggh* 1275 RH (Nf); Arthur *Browghe* 1567 Bardsley. From Brough (Derby, Notts, Westmorland, ERYorks, NRYorks), all ancient camps (OE *burg*), usually Roman, and pronounced *Bruff* or *Broof*.

Brougham: Simon, Richard *de Broham* t John SP1 (Y), 1244 AssLo; Robert *de Brouham* 1332 SRCu. From Brougham (Westmorland), *Broham* 1176.

Broughton: Gerald *de Broctun* 1189 CartAntiq; Richard *de Broghtone* 1247 FFO; William *Broghton* 1332 SRSx. From one or other of the many places of this name.

Brouncker: *v.* BRUNGER

Broune: *v.* BROWN

Brounfield: *v.* BROWNFIELD

Breuwer, Brower: *v.* BREWER

Browett: *v.* BREWITT

Brown, Browne, Broun, Broune, Bron: *Brun, Brunus* 1066 DB; *Brun* 1185 Templars (Wa); Conan *filius Brun* 1209 AssL; Richard *Brun, le Brun* le mercer 1111–38, c1140 ELPN; William *le Brun* 1169 P (Nth); William *Brun* 1182–1205 BuryS (Sf); Hugh *Bron* 1274 RH (Sa); Agnes *Broun* 1296 SRSx; John *le Browne* 1318 FFC. Occasionally we may have a personal name, OE *Brūn* or, possibly, ON *Brúnn*, but neither was common after the Conquest. Usually we have a nickname, OE *brūn*, or, perhaps occasionally, OFr *brun* 'brown', of hair or complexion.

Brownett, Brunet: Richard *Brunote, Brounnhote* (*Brounote*) 1310 LLB D, 1327 *SR* (Ess); Robert *Brunet*, John *Brownet* 1674 HTSf. *Brun-ot, Brun-et*, diminutives of OFr *brun* 'brown'.

Brownfield, Brounfield: Ralph *de Brounfeld* 1309 LLB D; Henry *Brounfeld* 1384 ib. H. A variant of BROOMFIELD. The Essex Broomfield is *Brounfeld* 1349 Ipm.

Browning, Brownings: *Bruning'* de Cestretona 1086 InqEl (C); Robertus *filius Bruning* 1203 AssSt; *Brunyng* Dypres, *Brounyng* Otelond 1296, 1327 SRSx; Hugo, Robert *Bruning'* 1198, 1199 P (Nf, Sf); William *Brouning* 1291 FFC; Richard *Brownyng* 1522 FrY. OE *Brūning*, a derivative of

Brūn, not uncommon after the Conquest, surviving in use until the 14th century.

Brownjohn: John *Browneion* 1349 *ERO*. 'Brown John'. cf. *Brun Edrith* (i.e. Edrich) 1255 RH (Sa), Adam *Brounadam* 1329 ColchCt, and *v.* DUNBABIN, HORRABIN.

Brownnutt, Brownutt: Alexander, Robert *Brunenote* 1279, 1294 RamsCt (Hu). 'Brown nut', for the more common NUTBROWN.

Brownsmith: Thomas *le Brounesmyth* 1296 Wak (Y); William *Brounsmyth* 1327 SRSo. OE *brūn* and *smið* 'brown smith', 'a worker in copper and brass'.

Brownson, Brunson: *Brunesune* 1066 DB (K); Alric *Brunesune* 1066 InqEl (C); Alstan *Brunesune* c1095 Bury (Sf); William *Brounsone* 1297 MinAcctCo (Y); Arnulph *Brounessone* 1318 FFEss; John *Brunnisson* 1327 SRC; Hugh *Brouneson* 1327 SRDb. *Brune sune* is 'son of OE *Brūna* or of ON *Brúni*', and has probably not contributed to the surname. The InqEl form is OE **Brūnsunu* 'brown son', a personal name not recorded before the Conquest and rare thereafter. *Brounessone* is 'son of *Broun*'. The later forms with a single *s* may be from the personal name but more probably mean 'son of a man named Brown'.

Brownutt: *v.* BROWNNUTT

Broxton: William *de Broxton'* 1230 P (Nf). From Browston (Suffolk), *Brockestuna* DB.

Bruce: Robert *de Bruis* 1086 DB (Y), 1185 Templars (L); Robert *de Brus* c1110 Whitby (Y), 1152 Clerkenwell (Mx); John *de Briwes, de Brues* 1225, 1277 AssSo; Richard *le Brewys* 1275 SRWo; Robert *le Brus*, Richard *de Brus* 1274–5 RH (Ess). This is usually derived from Brix (La Manche), a derivation accepted without reserve by the *Complete Peerage*. There are certainly some remains of an old castle but no early forms of the place-name have been found. L. C. Loyd cancelled his entry for Brus and discarded the derivation from Brix as the evidence 'hardly seems sufficient' (ANF viii). Tengvik called attention to Le Brus (Calvados), early forms of which (*Bruis* 1177, *Bruix* 1234) fit in with the DB form, though nothing is known of the early history of the place. The son of the Domesday baron, a friend of David I, king of Scotland, was granted by him in 1124 the Lordship of Annandale and his second son Robert became the founder of the Scottish house of Bruce. Later forms of the name have become inextricably confused with BREWIS.

Bruck: *v.* BROOK

Brucker: *v.* BROOKER

Bruff: *v.* BROUGH

Bruggen: *v.* BRIDGEN

Brugger: *v.* BRIDGER

Brugh: *v.* BROUGH

Bruin: William *Bruin* 1209 Pl (Nf); Patrick *le Bruin* 1269 AssNb; William, Maurice *Bruyn* 1330 IpmW, 1425 FFEss. The name suggests connexion with Dutch *bruin* 'bear', but it may simply show attempts to indicate the pronunciation of Fr *brun* 'brown'.

Brumbley: *v.* BROMLEY

Brumfield: v. BROOMFIELD

Brummer: *Brumarus, Brumerus* 1066 DB(Sf); Ulmerus *Brumari filius* c1095 Bury (Sf); Robert *Brommer* 1510 Butley (Sf). OE *Brūnmǣr* 'brown-fame', of which the above are the only examples known.

Brummitt: v. BROOMHEAD

Brumpton: v. BROMPTON

Brunell: v. BURNEL

Brunet: v. BROWNETT

Brunger, Brunker, Brouncker: *Brungar(us)* 1066 DB (Do), 1111–38 ELPN; *Brunger* atte Yate 1327 SRSo; Thomas, William *Brunger* 1275 RH (Nf), SRWo; Robeit, Simon *Brungor* 1311 ELPN, 1327 SRSf; William *Brunker* 1572 PN W 127. OE *Brūngār* 'brown spear'. *Brunger* may be from OG *Brunger*.

Brunham: Geoffrey (*de*) *Brunham* Hy 2 Gilb (L). From Burnham (Lincs, Norfolk), both with early forms *Brunham*.

Brunning: William *Brunning* 1260 AssC; John *Brunnyng* 1317 AssK. OE *Brūning*, with shortening of the vowel. v. BROWNING.

Brunsdon, Brunsden: *Brunstanus* blachebiert 1066 Winton (Ha); *Brunstan(us)* c1095, 1121–48 Bury (Sf); Ralph *Brunston* 13th Rams (Hu); Roger *Brunstan* 1230 P (Nf). OE *Brūnstān* 'brown stone', recorded before the Conquest only in the 11th century as the name of a lay brother of Hyde and of a moneyer.

Brunwin: *Brunwinus, Brunnuinus* 1066 DB (Sf); Laurence, Richard *Brunwyn* 1247 AssBeds, 1276 RH (L); William *Brounwyne*, Geoffrey *Bronwyne* 1327 SRSf. OE *Brūnwine* 'brown friend', a late and rare OE name.

Bruton: William *de Briweton* 1271 AssSo. From Bruton (Som). v. also BRETON.

Bryan, Bryand, Bryant: v. BRIAN

Bryar(s): v. BRIAR

Bryce: v. BRICE

Bryceson, Bryson: John *Briceson* 1332 SRCu; Thomas *Bryson* 1524 SRSf. 'Son of *Brice*'.

Brydson: v. BRIDSON

Bryer(s): v. BRIAR

Brymner: v. BREMNER

Bryson: v. BRYCESON

Buchan: (i) Mariedoc *Bohhan*, Lewelin *Bochan* 1160, 1198 P (Sa). Welsh *bychan* 'small'. (ii) Richard *de Buchan* 1207–8 Black (Aberdeen). From Buchan (Aberdeenshire).

Buchanan: Alan *de Buchanan* c1270 Black; Walter *de Buchanan* 1373 ib.; George *Buchanan* 1506–82 ib. From Buchanan (Stirling).

Buchard: v. BURCHARD

Buche: v. BOUCH

Bucher: v. BUTCHER

Buck, Bucke: (i) Godwig *se Bucca* c1055 OEByn (So); Herbert *Bucke* 1195 P (Sx); Robert *Buc* 1200 P (Sf); Walter *le Buk* 1243 AssSo. A nickname, OE *bucca* 'he-goat', 'as wild as a buck', or *bucc* 'a male deer', perhaps denoting speed. The surnames may also be metonymic for longer occupational names: Roger *le Bucmanger'* 1221 AssWa, a dealer in bucks or venison; Walter *Bucswayn*

1327 SRSo, perhaps a goat-herd. (ii) Hugo (*del*) *Buc* 1221 *ElyA* (Nf); Peter *atte Buk* 1327 SRSf. 'Dweller by the beech-tree', OE *bōc*.

Buckell: v. BUCKLE

Buckett: Ralph *Bukat* 1275 RH (Herts); Godfrey *Bucket* 1279 RH (C); John *Boket* 1327 SRWo. These forms are too early to be derived from *Burchard*. They may be identical with Fr *Bouquet*, *Bouquerel*, which Dauzat explains as diminutives of *bouc* 'he-goat' in the sense 'lecherous, wanton'. *Buckerel* is also found in England: Gaufridus *bucherellus* 1130 P (Lo); Andrew *Bukerel* 1174 ib.; William *Bukerel* 1276 LLB A; and these London merchants may well have borne occupationalnames. ME *buk* means both 'he-goat' and 'deer' and both *Bukerel* and *Bucket* may be synonymous with *Buckskin* (v. BUSKENS), a worker or dealer in buck-skin or leather-goods. cf. CHEVERALL.

Buckhurst: Richard *de Buchurst* 1200 P (Bk); John *de Bocherst* 1296 SRSx; Cecilia *de Boukhurst* 1332 SRSx. From Buckhurst (Essex, Sussex).

Buckland: Ælfgyð *of Boclande* c 970 BCS (D); Hugh *de Boclanda* 1169 P (Berks); William *de Bocland* 1219 FFO; Thomas *de Boukeland* 1362 IpmW; Richard *Buklond* 1427–8 FFWa. From one or other of the many places of this name which, apart from a single example in Lincs, is found only in the south.

Buckle, Buckell, Buckels: John *Bokele* 1296 SRSx; Wymark *Bokel* 1327 SRSf; John *Bukle* 1524 SRSf. ME *bokel* 'buckle', metonymic for *Buckler*.

Buckler: Anschetil *buclar'* 1148 Winton (Ha); Peter *le Bucler* 1203 Cur (Y); William *Bokeler* 1317 AssK. OFr. *bouclier* 'maker of buckles'. cf. John *Bokelsmyth(e)* 1384 LLB H. Perhaps also metonymic for *bokeler-player* 'fencer' (1339 MED). cf. Nicholas *Bokelereplayere* and Ralph *Bokelerpleyer* 1379, 1381 AssWa.

Buckley, Bucklee, Buckleigh: Alan *de Buckeleg'* 1235–6 FFWa; William *de Bockeleye* 1332 SRWa; John *Buckley* 1545 SRW. A common minor placename, cf. Buckleigh in Abbotsham (Devon), Buckley Heath (Sussex), Buckley Green (Warwicks), etc.

Buckman: (i) Roger *Bukkeman* 1278 Ewen (Cu). OE *bucca* 'goat' and *mann*, 'goat-keeper'. (ii) Alan *Bokeman* 1279 RH (O); Adam *Bocman* 1294 AD ii (Sf). OE *bōc* 'book' and *mann*, 'a scholar, student' (1583 NED). Perhaps also 'a copier of books, a bookbinder'. cf. William *le Bokmakere* 1293 MESO (Y).

Buckmaster: Adam *de Bucemenistre* 1180 P (Lei); John *Buckmuster* 1623 Bardsley; William *Buckmaster* 1629 ib. From Buckminster (Leics).

Buckston: v. BUXTON

Budd, Budds: Brihtmerus *Budde* c1025 OEByn (C); Leofwinus *Budda* 1135 Oseney (O); Ralph *Budde* 1170 P (Ha). OE *Budda*, from OE *budda* 'beetle', is not recorded in independent use after the Conquest, but may have been used. BUDDING may well be an OE derivative 'son of *Budda*' and BUDDY is probably 'servant of *Budda*'. We have also Simon *Budecok* 1275 RH (Nf) and William *Budekin* 1279 RH (C), both surnames regularly formed diminutives of a personal name, though *-kin* is also added to common nouns. *Beetle* is a frequent school-boy nickname. The root meaning of *budda* is 'to swell', as in *bud*, and the nickname might also denote a fat, corpulent individual. The first example above is glossed *pro densitate sic cognominatus* 'so called because of his thickness'.

Buddell: *v.* BEADEL

Budding: Ralph *Budding* 1225 AssSo; Julian' *Buddyyng* 1296 SRSx. *v.* BUDD.

Buddle(s): *v.* BEADEL, BOODLE

Buddy: Andrew *Budday* 1279 RH (C). 'Servant of *Budd*', OE *dǣge*.

Budge: *v.* BOUCH, BUGG

Budgen, Budgeon: *v.* BOWGEN

Budgett: *v.* BURCHARD

Budgey, Buggey, Buggy: William *Buggi* 1242 Fees (W); Thomas *Buggy* 1275 SRWo; John *Bogi*, 1327 SRSx. The ON byname *Buggi*, with hard *g* cannot be the source of this surname, pronounced with a *j*-sound, all the early examples of which are from the south. We have ME *bugee*, *bug(g)e*, *buggye*, a dissyllable, of obscure origin, 'a kind of fur, lamb's skin with the wool dressed outwards' (1382 NED *s.v.* budge sb. 1). cf. 'gounes . . . furryd with bogey' (1465 ib.). The surname probably denotes a maker of *bugee*. BUGGE may also sometimes belong here. cf. BOUCH, BUGG.

Buffard: Richard, Reginald *Buffard* 1221 AssSa, 1274 RH (Sa). OFr *bouffard* 'often puffing, much blowing, swelling vp, strouting out; also swelling with anger' (Cotgrave), c1430 NED.

Buffey: *v.* BEAUFOY

Bufton: *v.* BOWTON

Bugden: William *de Buggeden'* 1195 P (L); Claricia *de Buggeden'* 1219 AssY. From Buckden (Hunts, WRYorks).

Bugg, Bugge, Buggs: Walter *Bugge* 1169 P (L); Osbert *le Bugge* 1327 *SR* (Ess). ME *bugge*, *bugg* 'hobgoblin, bogy, scarecrow' (1388 NED). *v.* also BOUCH.

Buggey: *v.* BUDGEY

Buick: *v.* BEWICK

Buie: *v.* BOWIE

Bulbeck, Bulbick: Hugo *de Bolebec*, Hugo *Bolebec* 1086 DB (Beds); Ralph *de Bolebec* 1197 P (Y). From Bolbec (Seine-Inférieure).

Bulcock: Edwin *Bulecoc* 1221 AssWo; John *Bulekock* 1301 SRY. A compound of *bull* and the diminutive suffix *cock*.

Bulger: *v.* BOULGER

Bulgin: Walter *Bulekin* 1200 P (Sx). A diminutive of *Bull*. cf. BULCOCK, BULLOCK.

Bulkeley, Bulkley: Robert *de Bulkelegh* 1259 AssCh; Richard *de Bulkele* 1339 CorLo; Thomas *Bulkley* 1489 FFEss. From Bulkeley (Essex).

Bull, Bulle, Bool, Boole, Bools: Wulfwin *Bule* 1170 P (Ha); Hulle *le Bule* 1201 P (St); William *le Bole* 1214 Cur (Sr); William *Bull* Hy 3 Gilb (L); Ralph *le Bulle* 1288 Ipm (Nth); Robert *le Bool* 1327 SRSx; Robert *Boole*, *Bull* 1524 SRSf.

OE *bula* 'bull'. Occasionally from a sign: Simon *atte Bole* 1377 LLB H.

Bullan, Bullant, Bullent: *v.* BULLEN

Bullar, Buller: Thomas *le Bulur* 1203 AssSt; John *Bolur*, *Bolour*, *le Bulur* 1296, 1327, 1332 SRSx; Philip *Boler* 1348 DbAS 36; Hugh *Bullour* 1354 FrY. OFr *bouleur*, ME *bullere* 'a publisher of false bulls, a deceiver, cheat' (a1300 NED). *v.* BULLARD.

Bullard: Henry *Buliard* 1198 FFSf; Fulco *Bulard* 1275 RH (K); Geoffrey *Bolhard* 1275 RH (W); Marke *Buller*, *Bullard* 1653, 1672 FrY. These forms can have no connection with *bull-herd* as commonly explained. That word developed into *bullard* very late (1825 NED). The surname might occasionally be from *bull-ward* (1614 NED): John *Bulward* 1524 SRSf. The early forms are probably from OFr *boul(e)*, *bole*, ME *bole* 'fraud, deceit' (c1300 MED) with the addition of the suffix *-(h)ard* and may be a synonym for BULLAR, a common early surname. NED records the verb *bul* and *bulling* 'fraudulent scheming' in 1532. Or we may have a similar derivative of OFr *boule* 'round, rotund'. cf. BULLETT.

Bullas, Bullass, Bullus: John *de la Bulehuse* 1224 Pat (Ha); Henry *de Bolus* 1327 SRDb; William *Bolehouse* 1327 SRSo; Thomas *Bulluse*, John *Bolouse* 1478 ShefA (Y); William *Bullos*, Thomas *Bullus* 1502, 1564 ib.; Robert *Bullas* 1673 ib. 'One employed at the bull-house' (1807 NED).

Bulled, Bulleid: Robert *Buleheued* 1195 P (Sx); Richard *Bolehead* 1317 AssK. OE *bula* 'bull' and *hēafod* 'head', a nickname for one noted for his bull-headed impetuosity.

Bullen, Bullent, Bulleyn, Bullin, Bullon, Bollen, Boullin, Boullen, Bullan, Bullant: Helias *de Bolonia* 1121–48 Bury (Sf); William *Bulein* 1204 P (L); Richard *de Boloygne* 1255 FFEss; Thomas *de Bolenne* 1289 AssCh; John *Boleyn*, Robert *Bolen*, Thomas *Bollyng*, Rychard *Bullyng* 1524 SRSf. From Boulogne, the English pronunciation of which was *Bullen* or *Bullin*.

Bullett, Bollett: Robert *le Bulet* 1194 CurR (Sr), *le Bolete* 1290 SRSr; Robert *Bullet* 1268 AssSo. Whilst this may occasionally be a late development of BULLED 'bull-head', as regularly explained, the main source is clearly different. We have probably a diminutive of OFr *boule* 'round' found in the French surnames *Boule*, *Boulle*, *Boulot*, *Boulet*, *Boullot* and *Boullet* which Dauzat explains as 'un individu gros, arrondi'. The noun *bullet* is from Fr *boulet*, a diminutive of *boule* 'ball' (1557 NED). cf. BOWL, BULLARD and ROUND.

Bulley, Bully: (i) Gilbert *de Buili* 1086 DB (Wa); John *de Bulli*, *de Builli* 1208 Fees (Y, L). Gilbert *de Buili* may have come from Bouillé (La Manche) or perhaps, from Bouillé (Maine-et-Loire, Mayenne). Roger *de Busli* 1086 DB (Wa) may have come from Bully-en-Brai (Seine-Inférieure). *v.* OEByn. (ii) Reginald *Bulega* 1185 P (Wo); Roger *(de) Bullege* 1197 FFK; Wyot *de Bulleye* 1275 SRWo; Maurice *Boleye* 1275 RH (L); Thomas *de Bolleye* 1327 SRWo. The surname is from a place-name;

e.g. Bulley (Glos) or Bulleigh Barton in Ipplepen (Devon). As it means 'bull-clearing', it was probably common. There was land called *Buleia* in Worcestershire in 1204 (P). Mainfenin *de Buleheia* 1201 P (Herts) and Nicholas *de Buleheye* 1218 Cur (Bk) took their names from unidentified places meaning 'bull-enclosure'. They may have lived near-by or worked there as bull-herds.

Bullfinch: Ralph *Bulvinch* 1218–19 FFK; Robert *Bolefynch* 1332 SRSx. A nickname from the bird.

Bullick: Henry *de Bolewic* 1198 FFNf. From Bolwick (Nf) or Bulwick (Northants), pronounced *Bullick*.

Bullinger, Pullinger, Pillinger: Terricus *le Bulenger* 1180 P (Sx); William *Pullenger* 1553–74 ArchC 49. OFr *bolonger, boulengier* 'baker'.

Bullivant: v. BONIFANT

Bullman, Bulman: Ailward *Buleman* 1209 P (Nf); John *Boleman* 1279 RH (C). OE *bula* 'bull' and *mann*, a bull-keeper or bull-herd.

Bullock, Bullocke: Walter *Bulluc* c1170 Moulton (Ha); Robert, William *Bulloc* 1195 FF, 1225 AssSo. OE *bulluc* 'a bull calf'. Perhaps also occupational: cf. Richard *le Bollocherde* 1281 Eynsham (O); Roger *Bullokman* 1332 SRCu.

Bullus: v. BULLAS

Bulman: v. BULLMAN

Bulpin: John *de Bulepenne* 1274 RH (So). 'Worker at the bull-pen', OE *pen(n)* 'pen, enclosure'. cf. Robert *at Bulryng* 1381 PTY.

Bulstrode: Richard, Ralph *de Bulestrod'* 1205 Cur (Sr), 1221 AssGl; John *Bulstrode* 1407 AssLo. From Bulstrode (Bucks).

Bulteel, Boutall, Boutell, Boutle, Bouttell, Bouttle, Bowtell, Bowtle: Ralph *Buletell'* 1205 Cur (L); Richard *Bultel* 1280 LLB A; John *Bultell* 1524 SRSf; John *Buttell, Boultell, Bowtyle* 1568 SRSf. OFr **buletel*, earlier *buretel* 'a meal-sieve'. In ME *buletel* was used of a kind of cloth specially prepared for sifting. The surname is synonymous with BOULTER. The Bulteels were reinforced by Huguenots. James *Bulteel* of Tournai came to London in 1634 and a family of this name became prominent at Plymouth.

Bumphries: v. BOUMPHREY

Bumpus: v. BOMPAS

Bunce: v. BONE

Bunch: Geoffrey *Bunch* 1195 P (Nth); William *Bunche* 1327 SRC. Perhaps ME *bunche* 'a protuberance, a hump on the back' (c1325 NED). cf. *bunch-back* 1618 ib.

Bunclarke: William *Bonclerk* 1327 SRSf. 'Good clerk', OFr *bon, clerc*.

Buncombe: Richard *de Bouncombe* 1327 SRSo. 'Dweller in the reed-valley', OE *bune* 'reed'.

Bund(e)y: v. BOND

Bunker: Reginald *Bonquer* 1229 Cur (Sr); William, John *Bonquer* 1257–8 FFK, 1298 AssL; Peter *Bonkere* 1381 SRSt. OFr *bon quer* 'good heart'. Bunker's Hill in Charlestown, Mass., first mentioned as *Bunker Hill*, was land assigned to George *Bunker* of Charlestown (1634) who came

originally from Odell near Bedford.

Bunn: v. BONE

Bunney, Bunny: Botte *Buny* 1222 AssWa; Richard *Bunny* 1309 Wak (Y). Perhaps OFr *bugne, beugne* 'a swelling'. cf. 'Bony or grete knobbe . . . *gibbus*' c1440 NED; 'bownche or bunnye, *gibba*' 1552 ib. v. BUNCH, BUNYAN.

Bunyan, Bunyon: Henry *Buniun* 1204 Cur (Beds); Simon *Boynon* 1309 SRBeds. As Roger and John *Buignon* were sons of John *Buignon*, the surname, which has been noted only in Beds, was already hereditary in 1227 (AssBeds), when it appears as *Buingon, Buinon, Buignon* and *Bungnon* in the neighbourhood of Ampthill and Bedford. John *Bunyan* was baptized in 1628 as 'sonne of Thomas *Bonnioun*' who was himself baptized as *Bunyon* in 1603. John signed his name *Bunyan* in 1653 and *Bunyon* in 1672 and was twice called *Bunnion* in the general pardon granting him release from Newgate Gaol. Of the numerous spellings noted, only three, and those late, have no *u*: *Bynyon, Binyan, Binnyan*. Bardsley, retracting his earlier etymology *Bonjean* 'Good John', adopted that of Lower, from Welsh *ab Enion, Benyon*, and was followed by Harrison, Ewen and Weekley, although Dr. J. Brown in his *Life of John Bunyan* (1885) had solved the problem. Adducing the 1219 form *Buignon*, he equated it with OFr *beignet* 'fritter' and cited from Godefroy 'Et bone char et granz buignons' with the comment: 'The word signifies a little raised pattie with fruit in the middle'. His only error was to regard this as the original instead of a derived meaning. OFr *bugnon* is a diminutive of *bugne* 'a bile, blane' (*v.* BUNNEY) and came to be applied to any round knob or bunch, and later to a raised pattie and also to a bunion, first recorded in NED c1718. The simple *bugne* is probably the origin of *bun*. The existence of this sense in OFr can now be assumed from that of *bugnon*. cf. also: '*bugnets*, little round loaves, or lumpes made of fine meale, oyle or butter, and reasons; bunnes, Lenten loaves'. The surname might be a nickname for one disfigured by a knob, lump or hump, or it might be occupational, a pastry-cook, though the latter hardly fits in with the activities of the 1227 Bunyans.

Bunyard: v. BANYARD

Burall: (i) Robertus *filius Burewoldi* 1184 Oseney (O); Gilebertus *filius Buroldi* 1198 ib.; Hugh *Burewald* 1200 ib.; Lambert *Borewald* 1279 RH (O). OE *Burgweald* 'fortress-power', first recorded in the 11th century. (ii) William *de la Burhalle* 1275 RH (L). 'Dweller or servant at the bower-hall', OE *būr* and *heall*.

Burbage, Burbidge, Burbudge: Ralph *de Burebeche* 1172 P (Db); William *de Burbache* 1200 Cl (Ha); John *Burbache, Burbage* 1340–1450 GildC; Helene *Burbadge* 1576 SRW. From Burbage (Derby, Leics, Wilts).

Burch: v. BIRCH

Burchard, Burchatt, Burghard, Burckitt, Burkart, Burkett, Burkitt, Buchard, Butchard, Buckett, Budgett, Bockett, Borkett, Borkwood, Bouchard,

Barchard: Gaufridus *nepos Bocardi* c1150 DC (L); *Burekardus* de Burewelle Hy 2 DC (L); *Buchardus* 1196 P (Du); Reginaldus *filius Burchardi* 1220 Cur (Sf); *Burchardus, Burcardus* 1222 Cur (Do); Robert *Bocard'* 1207 Cur (Sf); Ralph *Bochard'* 1219 Cur (Nth); Thomas *Burchart* c1248 Bec (Sf); Walter *Buchard* 1255 RH (W); Warin *Burchard*, Robert *Burghard* 1275 RH (Sf); Richard *Burkett* 1524 SRSf; Peter *Barchard* 1702 FrY. The frequency of these surnames and the variety of their forms are due to two names, both ultimately of Germanic origin. OE *Burgheard* 'fortress-hard' is found in DB as *Burchardus, Burkart, Burchart*, and *Bucardus*. The cognate OG *Burghard, Burcard* became OFr *Bouchart* and was brought across the Channel by the Normans.

Burchett: *v.* BIRCHETT

Burckitt: *v.* BURCHARD

Burd, Burds: William *Burde* 1275 RH (Sx), 1285 *Ass* (Ess). ME *burde* 'young lady, maiden', probably a derogatory nickname.

Burdas, Burdass, Birdis, Burdus: Alan *de Burdeus* 1297 SRY; Christopher *Burdus* 1519 GildY; John *Burdas* 1662 FrY. From Bordeaux.

Burdekin: John *Burdycane, Burdekin* 1597, 1636 Shef (Y). A diminutive of *burde* 'little young lady', undoubtedly derogatory.

Burden, Burdon, Burdoun, Bourdon: (i) Ralph *Burdun* 1128–9 Holme (Nf); Ilger *Burdun* 1166 P (Y). (ii) Arnulf *Burdin* 1115 Winton (Ha); Bruni *Burdin* 1180 P (Bk). With these forms we must include BURDETT. All may be diminutives of OG *Burdo*, introduced from France or, possibly, of Lat *burdo* 'mule'. *Burdonus* and other derivatives of the Celtic *Burdo* are found in France, but in view of the rarity of this name, Michaëlsson prefers to derive the French surname from OFr *bourdon* 'a pilgrim's staff'. The personal name does occur in England, but is very rare: Hamo *filius Burdun* 1166 RBE (Nf). Only two examples of *Burdin* have been noted. *Burdon* is very common in early English sources and in Paris c1300. *Burdet* is equally frequent in England. (iii) Zacharias *de Burdun* 1217 FeuDu. From Great Burdon (Durham) or from Burdon Head (WRYorks) or Burden near Harewood (WRYorks). (iv) Ælfsige *Burðen* 968 BCS 1212 (K); Hugelyn *Bourþeyn*, Hugelinus *cubicularius* 1052–65 Rams (Hu); Nicholas *Burþein, Burdon* 1242 Fees (W). OE *burðegn* 'bower-servant', 'chamberlain'. This is probably the least common source.

Burdett, Burditt: Robert *Burdet, Burdel*, Hugo *Burdet* 1066 DB (Lei); Ralph *Burdet* c1160 DC (Lei); George *Burditt* 1690 FrY. *v.* BURDEN.

Burdge: *v.* BURGE

Burfitt, Burfoot: Stephen *Burford* of Cowden (Kent) signed his name *Burfoot* in 1673 (Ewing 83).

Burford: Clement *de Bureford* 1186 P (O); John *de Burreford* 1327 SRSx. From Burford (Devon, Oxon, Salop) or Burford Bridge (Surrey).

Burge, Burdge: Robert *de la Burge* 1200 P (Ha); Roger *Burge* 1479 AD vi (Ess). William *atte Brugge*

lived at Burge End (Herts) in 1302 (PN Herts 21). This metathesis of *r* in OE *brycg* 'bridge' has also been noted in Bucks, Cambridge, Northants, Notts, Oxford, Somerset, Wilts and Warwicks. *v.* PN Nth xxxii.

Burger, Burgher, Burker, Borger: Henry *le Burger* 1275 RH (Lo); Robert *Burger* 1327 SRSf. ME *burger* 'inhabitant of a borough', 'a citizen' (1568 NED).

Burges, Burgess, Burgis, Burgiss, Borges: Geoffrey *burgeis* 1115 Winton (Ha); Ralph *le Burgeis* 1195 P (Sx); Philip *Burgis* 1199 FrLeic; Philip *Burges, Burgeis* 1220, 1234 Oseney (O); Walter *le Borgeys* 1296 SRSx. OFr *burgeis* 'inhabitant of a borough', strictly one possessing full municipal rights, 'a freeman of a borough' (c1230 MED).

Burgett, Burgot: Absalon *de Burgate* 1198 P (K); Ralph *atte Burgate* 1260 AssC; Robert *de Burhtʒete* 1274 RH (Gl); Ingram *atte Burghʒete* 1333 MESO (So). From Burgate (Hants, Suffolk, Surrey) or 'dweller by the castle or city gate'. OE *burggeat* (Burgett), ME *burgate* (Burgot).

Burgh: Ailricus *de Burg* 1066 DB (Sf); Ralph *de Burc* 1177 P (Nf). From one of the many places named Burgh.

Burghard, Burkart: *v.* BURCHARD

Burgin: *v.* BORGONON, BURGOIN

Burglin, Burlin, Burling, Burlong: John *Burgelun* Ric I Bart; William *le Burguillun* 1243 AssSt; William *Burgelun* 1275 RH (Nf); John *Burgoillioun* 1327 SRSf; Widow *Burling* 1674 HTSf. 'The Burgundian', probably a variant of OFr *Bourguignon*. *v.* BORGONON.

Burgoin, Burgoine, Burgoyne, Burgon, Burgin, Burgwin, Bourgein, Bourgoin: Walter *Burgoin* 1086 DB (D); Simon *Burgunie* 1210 Cur (C); Adam *de Burgoigne* 1319 SRLo; Elizabeth *de Burgon* 1379 PTY; John *Burgin* 1638 Bardsley. 'The man from Burgundy', Fr *Bourgogne*. Various forms were used of the same man: John *le Burgoyn* 1301 LLB B, *le Borgiloun* 1310 ib., *de Burgoyne* 1319 SRLo; Ralph *le Burginon* 1314, *Burgillon* 1323 AssSt, *le Burgoynon* 1330 FFSt. Nicholas *Burgoin* was the son of John *Burgoin* and both are also called *Burgwine*, while the seal of Felicia, wife of Nicholas *Burgelun*, bears the legend S. FELICIA BURGUNUNG 1212–23 Bart. *v.* also BURGLIN, BORGONON.

Burk, Burke, Bourke: Ailricus *de Burc* 1066 DB (Sf); John *de Burk* 1274 RH (So). The first example refers to Burgh (Suffolk). *Burk* is an Anglo-Norman pronunciation of *Burgh* (which survives as BURGH) and it is doubtful whether the Norman pronunciation took root in England. *Burke* is a very common Irish name which derives from the family of *de Burgh*. William *de Burgo* went to Ireland in 1171 with Henry II and later became Earl of Ulster.

Burkenshaw: *v.* BIRKENSHAW

Burker: *v.* BURGER

Burkett, Burkitt: *v.* BURCHARD

Burkimsher, Burkinshaw, Burkinshear: *v.* BIRKENSHAW

Burkman: *v.* BORROWMAN

Burkmar: v. BRIGHTMORE

Burks: v. BIRKS

Burle, Burles, Burls: John *Byrle* 1327 *SR* (Ess). OE *byrele*, *byrle* 'cup-bearer, butler'.

Burler: James *Burler* 1369 FFEss. A derivative of ME *burle* 'to burl', from ME *burle*, OFr *bourle* 'flock of wool'; a burler, one who dresses cloth by removing knots and extraneous particles (c1475 MED). v. also BURREL.

Burlin, Burling, Burlong: v. BURGLIN

Burlington: Martin *de Breddelington* 1204 AssY. From Bridlington (ERYorks), pronounced locally *Burlington*.

Burman: v. BORROWMAN, BOWERMAN

Burn: v. BOURNE

Burnard: *Burnardus* 1211 Cur (Nf); Rogerus *burnardus* 1130 P (Beds); Odo *Burnard* 1192 P (Ess); Richard *Burnhard* 1279 RH (Beds). *Burnhard*, a compound of OFr *brun* and *-hard*, with the same metathesis as in *Burnel* and *Burnet*. A nickname for one of brownish, dark hair or complexion, used occasionally, like *Burnel*, as a personal name.

Burnel, Burnell, Brunell: *Burnellus* de Aumeivill 1200 Cur (Y); Robertus *burnellus* 1130 P (O); Roger, William *Burnel* Hy 2 DC (L), 1197 FF (Sa). ME *burnel*, a metathesized form of OFr *brunel*, a diminutive of OFr *brun* 'brown'. A nickname for one of brownish complexion, used also as a personal name. *Brunell* is probably recent, Fr *Brunel*.

Burner: v. BOURNER

Burnes, Burness, Burns: (i) Robert, Gervase *Brenhus* 1208 P (Y), 1275 RH (Nf). A nickname, 'burn house'. cf. BRENNAN. (ii) David *Burnis* 1526 Black. The forefathers of Robert Burns migrated from Burnhouse in Taynuilt to Forfarshire where they were called Campbells of Burnhouse, and later *Burness* or *Burns* (MacBain, *Inverness Names*). The stress in *Burness* was on the first syllable and as the name was pronounced in Ayrshire as if written *Burns*, Robert and his brother agreed to drop *Burness* and to assume *Burns* in April 1786 (Black).

Burnet, Burnett, Burnitt: Robert *Burnet* 1219 AssY; Richard *Bornet* 1279 RH (Bk); Cristina *Burnete* 1365 LoPleas. OFr *burnete*, *brunette*, a diminutive of *brun* 'brown', 'dark brown' (c1200 NED), used like *Burnell* of complexion. *Burnete* was also used of a wool-dyed cloth of superior quality, originally of dark-brown colour (1284 NED). cf. 'pro . . . caligis *de burneta*; caligas *de burneto*' 1200 Oseney i, 64, 66 'hose of burnet or coloured cloth' (Ed.). The surname might denote a maker or seller of this.

Burney, Burnie: v. BERNEY

Burnham: Geoffrey, Roger *de Burnham* 1193 P (Nf), 1262 FFO; Thomas *Burnham* 1446 IpmNt. From Burnham (Bucks, Essex, Lincs, Norfolk, Som).

Burnikell: v. BARNACLE

Burns: v. BURNES

Burr: Hugo, Samson *Burre* 1185 Templars

(Y), 1206 Cur (C). ME *burre* 'a bur' (c1330 MED), used by Shakespeare of one who sticks like a bur, a person difficult to 'shake off'. This sense may well be older.

Burra: v. BOWRA

Burrage: v. BURRIDGE

Burrard: Robert *Borard'* 1219 AssY; Simon *Borhard, Borart* 1235, 1242 Fees (Lei); Nicholas *Burhard* 1327 SRSf. OE *Burgheard*. v. BURCHARD. This may also have become *Borrett, Burrett*, etc.

Burrel, Burrell, Burrells, Borel, Borell: Roger, William *Burel* 1194, 1196 P (W, L); Simon *Borel* 1296 SRSx. ME *borel*, OFr *burel* 'reddish-brown', used of a coarse woollen cloth of this colour (a1325 MED). The surname might refer to dress or complexion, or it may denote a maker of *borel*, a *bureller*. cf. Alfred *le Bureller* 1277 LLB A; John *Burelman* 1311 LLB D. *Borel* had also in ME the meaning 'belonging to the laity' (c1390 MED), 'unlearned, rude' (1513 NED). It was also used as a personal name, perhaps an original nickname in the sense 'dark': Johannes *filius Borelli* 1205 Cur (R); *Burellus* de Rathesnese 1274 RH (Nf).

Burrett, Borrett, Borritt, Boret: (i) *Burredus* 1114–18, *Burret* 1161–77 Rams (Hu); Hugo *filius Buret* 1199 FF (R); Koleman *Burred* 1133–60 Rams (Hu); Nicholas *Bured* 1275 SRWo. OE *Burgrǣd* 'fortress-counsel', found in DB as *Burghered, Burgret, Burred, Burret, Borgered, Borred* and *Borret*. (ii) John *Bureheued* 1219 AssY; William *Burreheud* 1308 Wak (Y); Agnes *Borheued* 1327 SRSf; William, Robert *Borhed, Borrett* 1403, 1577 Shef (Y); Robert *Borhed*, Herry *Boret* 1524 SRSf. OFr *bourre* 'rough hair, flock of wool' and OE *hēafod* 'head', a nickname for one with rough, shaggy hair.

Burridge, Burrage: *Burcheric, Burchricus, Burricus, Buric* 1066 DB; *Burrich* de Bradefeld 1203 AssNth (Sf); William *Burrich* 1327 SRSf; Henry *Borrich* 1327 SRSo; John *Burrage* 1568 SRSf; William *Burrydge* 1587 FFHu. OE *Burgrīc* 'fortress-powerful'.

Burrough, Burrow, Borrow: John *atte Boroghe*, Thomas *Burewe* 1327 SRSo; Henry *Borowe* 1527 FrY. 'Dweller by the hill' (OE *beorg*), as at Burrow (Devon, Som), or from Burrow (Leics, Lancs), OE *burg* 'fort'.

Burroughes, Burrows, Burrus, Burris, Burriss, Borrows: John *de Burhus* 1440 ShefA; Margaret *Burrous* 1564 ib.; William *Burrowes* 1585 ib.; William *Burrosse* 1572 ib.; William *Burroughs* 1742 Bardsley. 'Dweller at the bower-house', or one employed there, OE *būr, hūs*. cf. *Bourhouse* Edw 4 EA (OS) i, a manor of Waltham Abbey.

Bursey, Bersey: (i) Serlo *de Burci* 1084 GeldR (W); Serlo *Borci* 1086 DB (So); Hugo *de Burci* 1185 Templars (So). From Burcy (Calvados), (ii) Rannulf *Bursi* 1195 P (He); Hugh *Bursey* 1275 RH (Nf). These forms are from OE *Beorhtsige*, found as *Birhsie* in Devon (BCS 1248). v. BRIXEY.

Burton, Bourton, Borton: Ioluard *in Burhtun*

c1150 YCh; Gerard *de Burton* 1178 P (Wa, Lei); William *de Borton'* 1275–6 RegAntiquiss; William *Burton* 1327 SRSx; John *Borton* 1332 SRWo. From one or other of the many places called Burton or Bourton.

Burtonshaw: *v.* BIRKENSHAW

Burtwistle: *v.* BIRTWHISTLE

Burward: *Burewardus* 1206 P (Sf); Ralph *Borgward* 1299 LLB E; Robert *Boreward* 1327 SRSf; William *Burghward*, Austen *Burward* 1524 SRSf. OE *Burgweard* 'fortress-guard'.

Bury: *v.* BERRY

Bush, Bushe, Busk: Richard *de la Busce* 1181 P (Y); Henry *del Busk* 1275 RH (Nf); Roger *atte Buske, del Bushe* 1305 SIA iii; Richard *Bussh* 1309 FFSf; Roland *atte Bushe* 1384 LoPleas. 'Dweller by the bush', ME *busk, busche.* Bush is from OE **busc* (*v.* MELS), *Busk* (less common), from ON *buskr.*

Bushell, Bushill, Bussell, Boshell, Bossel, Bishell, Bissell, Bissill: Roger *Buissel* 1086 DB (So); Alan *Buscel* c1140 YCh; Richard *Bussell* 1200 P (Beds); Richard *Buschel* 1243 AssSo. ME *buyscel, busshel, bysshell,* OFr *boissell, buissiel* 'bushel', probably for one who measured out corn, etc., in bushels, or for a maker of bushel-vessels. cf. Stephen *Busselman* 1327 SRSo, Robert *le Busselar* 1243 AssSo, Peter *Boseler* 1305 MESO (L), OFr *boisselier* 'maker of vessels (baskets) holding a bushel'. This may survive in the very rare BISLER. *Bussell* may also be from OFr *bucel* 'small barrel', for a maker of these.

Busher: *v.* BOSHER

Buskens, Buskin, Boskin: (i) Nicholas *atte Busken, atte Bosken* 1329–30 PN D 140. From Buskin (Devon) or 'dweller by the bushes', from the dative plural of OE **busc.* (ii) Roger *Buckeskyn* 1281 FFEss; Walter *Buskyn* 1281 Cl; Katharine *Bukeskyn* 1295 Ipm (Nf). 'Buck-skin', skin of a buck, used particularly of 'breeches made of buckskin' (1481–90 NED), and as a surname, for a maker of these or for a worker in buckskin or leather. Richard de Gravele called *Bokskyn* was an apprentice of Walter Polyt *fuyster* 1311 LLB D. *v.* FEWSTER. *Buckskin* would inevitably come to be pronounced *Buskin.*

Busky: Remig' *de Buskeheye* 1296 SRSx. 'Dweller by the bush-enclosure', OE **busc-(ge)hæg.*

Buss, Busse: Walter, Richard *Busse* 1195 P (Nf), 1220 Cur (Berks). OFr *busse* 'cask'. cf. BARRELL.

Bussell: *v.* BUSHELL

Bussey, Bussy: Robert *de Buci, de Boci* 1086 DB (Nth); Robert *Buscy* 1208 Cur (Sx); William *Bussy* 1310 EAS xx. The DB under-tenant came from Bouce (Orne). *v.* ANF. Others may have come from Boucey (La Manche) or Bucy-le-Long (Aisne).

Buszard: *v.* BUZZARD

Butchard: *v.* BURCHARD

Butcher, Butchers, Bucher, Boucher, Boutcher, Bowcher, Bowker: Ailwardus *le Bochere* 1184 P (Lo); Richard *le Bucher* 1240 FFEss; William *Bochier*, Alan *le Boucher* 1327 SRSx; Thomas *le Bouker* 1332 SRLa. AFr *bocher, boucher*, OFr *bochier, bouchier* 'butcher'.

Butler, Buttler: Hugo *Buteiller* 1055 France; Alexander *le butiller* 1174–84 Seals (Hu); Baldwin *le Buteilier* 1200 P (K); William *le Boteller* 1260 AssC; Henry *le Butler* 1327 SRWo. AFr *butuiller*, OFr *bouteillier* 'servant in charge of the wine-cellar', usually the head servant (c1250 NED). In some early examples, an officer of high rank nominally connected with the supply and importation of wine (1297 NED). Forms like *Boteller* may occasionally be for BOTLER.

Butlin, Bucklin: Robert *Butevilain* 1130 P (Nf); Robertus *Buteuillanus* archidiaconus 1147–53 DC (Nt); Ernis *Buteuilein* 1205 P (D); William *Butveleyn* 1429 Pat (Nth). OFr *boute-vilain* 'hustle the churl'.

Butner: Henry, Geoffrey *le Botoner* 1274 RH (Lo), 1282 LLB A. OFr *botonier* 'maker of buttons'.

Butt, Butts: (i) *But* (a moneyer) Wm 2; his son was Robertus *filius But'* 1137 ELPN; Godlambus filius *But* 1133–60 Rams (Nf); *But* 1170 P (Ha); Walter, Hubert *But* 1114–30 Rams (Nf), c1150 ELPN; Leuricus *Butte* 1185 Templars (Beds); Robert, William *le But* 1198 P (Sx), 1214 ELPN; Margery *Buttes* 1275 SRWo. OE **Butt* is found in Butsash (Hants) and **Butta* in Butley (Ches, Suffolk), a personal name which, though unrecorded in OE, was in use in the 12th century. It is one source of the surname, particularly of the early examples without the article. cf. Richard *Buttyng* 1327 SRSo 'son of Butt'. We have also clearly a nickname from ME *butt* 'thicker end, stump', probably used of a thickset person. (ii) William *de Butte* 1200 Oseney (O); Henry *atte Buttys* 1380 NorwW (Nf). ME *butt*, OFr *but* 'a goal; mark for shooting'. One who lived near the archery butts or, perhaps, an archer. cf. FURLONG.

Buttanshaw, Buttenshaw: *v.* BIRKENSHAW

Butter, Butters, Buttar: (i) Henry *Butor* 1169 P (Y); Henry *le Butor* Cur (D). ME *botor*, OFr *butor* 'bittern', noted for its 'boom' in the breeding season and called 'bull of the bog', hence, perhaps, the nickname. (ii) William *le Buter* 1243 AssSo; John *le Buttare* 1275 SRWo; William *le Buttere* 14th AD v (Wa). 'Keeper of the buttery.' *v.* BOTTERELL. (iii) Turchetillus, William *Butere* 1130 P (Do), 1198 FF (Nth); Geoffrey *Butter* 1327 SRWo; John *Buttere* 1327 SR (Ess). OE *butere* 'butter', metonymic for a maker or seller of butter. cf. William *le Buterar'* 1327 SRSx, John *Butercharl* c1192 HPD (Ess), Thomas *Butterman* 1302 SRY, Henry *Botreman* 1327 Pinchbeck (Sf), Margaret *le Buttermonggere* 1306 LoCt. Forms for (ii) and (iii) cannot always be distinguished.

Butterfield, Butterfill: Hugh *de Buteresfeld'* 1199 Pl (Bk); Philip, Adam *de Butterfeld'* 1231 Cur (Bk), 1379 PTY; William *Boterfeld* 1423 LLB K. From Butterfield (WRYorks), or from other minor places of the name.

Butteris(s): v. BOTTERELL

Buttery, Buttrey: William *Buteri* 1177 P (Bk); Reginald *Boteri* 1211 Cur (He); William *de Buteri* 1219 Cur (Sf); John *de la Boterye* 1334 FFSt. OFr *boterie*, originally 'place for storing liquor', but early used of a 'room where provisions were laid up' (1384 MED). 'Keeper of the buttery.' v. also BOTTERELL.

Buttler: v. BUTLER

Button, Botten: William, Robert *Boton* 1296 SRSx, 1317 AssK; Stephen *Botun* 1327 SRSx. OFr *boton* 'button', metonymic for BUTNER.

Buttonshaw: v. BIRKENSHAW

Buttress, Buttriss: v. BOTTERELL

Buttrey: v. BUTTERY

Buttrum: v. BARTRAM

Buxton, Buckston: (i) Henry *de Bucstanes* 1230 P (Db). From Buxton (Derby). William *Buckeston* 1279 RH (Hu). Probably from Buxton (Norfolk), DB *Bukestuna*. (ii) Ailricus *Bucstan* 1170 P (L); John *Bucstan* 1221 AssWa; Richard *Bocston* (*Bokston*) 1327 *SR* (Ess); John *Bucstone* 1377 LLB H. The distribution and the frequency of this name, regularly in the singular and without sign of a preposition, suggest a personal-name otherwise unknown, perhaps OE *Bucstān*, a combination of OE *Bucca* and the common theme *-stān*. cf. PICKSTONE. Or we may have an OE *Burgstān*, with early loss of *r* as in *Burgheard*. cf. BURCHARD.

Buy(e): v. BOWIE, BY

Buyers: v. BYARS

Buzzard, Buszard: Robert *Boszart* 1177 P (He); William *Bozard* 1258 AD vi (W); Peter *Busard* 1274 RH (Sf). OFr *busart*, ME *busard, bosard* 'buzzard', an inferior kind of hawk, useless for falconry, used also of a worthless, stupid, ignorant person (1377 NED).

By, Bye, Buy, Buye: Hugh *de la Bye* 1243 AssSo; Alicia *de By* 1250–70 Black (Berwick); John *ate Bey* 1279 RH (C); William *in the By* 1327 SRSo; John *Bye* 1327 SRC. 'Dweller in the bend', OE *byge*. We are also occasionally concerned with a personal name of obscure origin: Thomas, Henricus *filius Bye* 1279 RH (C).

Byam: v. BYHAM

Byard, Byart, Biart: Thomas *Byerd* 1296 SRSx. 'Dweller by the enclosure', ME *bi yerd*.

Byars, Byers, Byre, Byres, Bier, Biers, Buyers: Elias *de la Byare* 1275 RH (D); Willelmus *del Byre* 1301 SRY; John *de Byres* 1309 Black (Newbottle); John *Buyres* 1327 SRSo. 'One employed at the cow-house' (OE *bȳre*), cow-man, or from Byers Green (Durham) or the old barony of Byres (East Lothian).

Byas, Byass: Adam *de Byus* 1275 RH (L); John *de Bayhus* ib. (Beds); John *Byas* 1699 FrY. 'Dweller at the house in the bend', OE *byge, hūs*.

Byatt, Byatte, Byott, Bygate: Nicholas *Byate* 1297 MinAcctCo; Ralph *Bytheyate* 1379 PTY. 'Dweller by the gate', OE *geat*, ME *yat, gate*.

Byfield, Bifield: Nigel *de Bifeld* 1202 FFNf; Robert *de Byfeld* 1314–16 AssNth; Adam *Byfelde* 1367 IpmGl. From Byfield (Northants), or 'dweller by the open country'.

Bygrave, Bygraves, Bigrave, Bygreaves, Bygrove: Leommær æt *Biggrafan* c1015 ASWills (Herts); William *Bygrave* 1312 LLB D. From Bygrave (Herts) or residence near a grove. v. GREAVES, GROVE.

Byham, Byam: William *de Biham* 1202 P (Y). Probably from Bytham (Lincs), *Biham* c1100 DEPN.

Byles: v. BILES

Byott: v. BYATT

Byrch: v. BIRCH

Byrde: v. BIRD

Byre(s): v. BYARS

Byrne, Byrnes, Birn: Ir *Ó Birn* 'descendant of *Biorn*' (ON *Bjǫrn*) or *Ó Broin* 'descendant of *Bran*' (raven).

Byrom, Byram, Biram: Roger *de Birum* 1240 FFY; John, Simon *de Byrom* 1342 FFY, 1401 AssLa. From Byram (WRYorks), *Birum* c1170, *Byrun* 1268, or 'dweller at the cowsheds'.

Byron, Byran, Biron: William *de Byrun* 1240 FFY; Richard *de Birune* 1242 AssDu; John *de Byron* 1294–5 IpmY; Richard *Byron* 1401 AssLa. A variant of BYROM. The forms give no support to Harrison's derivation from Fr *bu(i)ron*.

Bysh: v. BISH

Bysouth: Henry *Bisuthe* 1221 AssWo; Maurice *Bi Suthe* 1279 RH (O). One who lived 'to the south'.

Bythesea: William *Bythesee* 1336 MESO (So); John *Bethesee, Bitheseo* 1363–4 ib. 'Dweller by the watercourse or drain', OE *sēoh*, a Somerset term, referring to inland places near Bridgwater and to Sea near Ilminster. In Robert *Bythse* 1333 ib. (So), the reference is again to an inland place, OE *sæ*, 'dweller by the lake or pool'. The surname might also refer to residence near the sea. v. MELS.

Bytheseashore: An interesting surname, both because of its survival and for its pronunciation, *Bitherseyshore*, with stress as in Battersea.

Bytheway, Bythway, Byway, Bidaway: Richard *Bithewaye* 1243 AssSo. 'Dweller by the road.' Gervase *Bethewy* 1244 Rams (Hu) is also called *de la Rode*.

Bywater, Bywaters: Thomas *Bithewater* 1219 AssY; Elyas *Biþewatere* 1279 RH (O); John *Beyewatyr* 1327 SRC. 'Dweller by the water.'

Bywood: Edward *Bythewode* 1275 RH (Do). 'Dweller by the wood.'

C

Cadd, Cade: Wigan *filius Cade* c1155 DC (L); Thomas *filius Kade* 1219 AssY; William, Eustace *Cade* c1140 ArchC iv, 1186 P (L); William *le Cade* 1327 SRSx; Richard *Cadde* 1327 SRWo. Some of these examples point to the survival of OE *Cada* but *le Cade* is clearly a byname, found also in (Wulfwine cognomeno) *Cada* (a1050 OEByn) which Tengvik derives from a Germanic root meaning 'something lumpy or protruding', hence 'a stout lumpish person'. *Cade* may be identical with *cade* (sb. 2, MED) 'a young animal cast or left by its mother and brought up by hand as a domestic pet', 'a pet lamb': or it may be ME, OFr *cade* 'cask, barrel' (1337 MED), either a nickname for one round as a barrel or metonymic for a maker of casks.

Caddell: *v.* CALDWELL, CAUDELL

Caddick, Caddock: Richard *Caddok* 1260 AssC; William *Caddouc'* 1327 SRSx. OFr *caduc* 'infirm, decrepit, frail', used by Trevisa of 'men that haue the fallyng euyll', epileptics.

Caddow: John, Richard *Caddo* 1327 SRC. ME *cad(d)aw, cad(d)owe* 'jackdaw' (1440 MED).

Cade: *v.* CADD

Cadel, Cadle: *v.* CAUDELL

Cadge: *v.* CAGE

Cadman: Robert *Cademan* 1279 RH (C); Geoffrey *Cademon* 1327 SRDb. Either 'servant of *Cade*' or 'maker of casks'. There is no evidence for the post-Conquest use of OE *Cædmon*.

Cadogan: *Caducan* 1161 P (Wo); *Cadegan de Middelton'* 1191 P (Sa); Jevan *ap Cadugon* 1287 AssCh; Richard *Cadigan* 1273 RH (Wa). OW *Cadwugaun*.

Cadwall, Cadwell, Kadwell, Kadwill: (i) Nicholas *de Cattedale* 1202 AssL. From Cadwell (Lincs). (ii) Robert *de Cadewelle* 1279 RH (O). From Cadwell (Devon, Herts, Oxon). *v.* also CALDWELL.

Caesar: *Cesar clericus* 1185 Templars (Y); *Cesar Walpole* d. 1613 ODCN; Henry *Sesare* 1334 SRK; John, Harriet *Caesar* 1705, 1748 Bardsley. In ME this is a pageant name, *v.* CAYZER, and though rare is found occasionally both as a first name and as a surname, cf. also *Caesaria*, sister of the wife of William de la Rode 13th Rams (Hu). The chief family of the name, still with modern descendants, was that of Sir Julius *Caesar* (1558–1636), of Italian extraction. His grandfather, Pietro Marie *Adelmare*, married Paola, daughter of Giovanni Pietro *Caesarini*, and one of his sons, Cesare *Adelmare*, emigrated to England c1550 and became physician to Queen Mary and to Queen Elizabeth. He died in 1569 and his children adopted *Caesar* as their surname (DNB).

Caff: *v.* CHAFF

Caffery, Caffray, Caffrey: For MacCAFFRAY.

Caffin, Caffyn: *v.* CHAFFIN

Cage, Cadge: (i) Gervase, Matilda *Cage* 1211 FrLeic, 1279 RH (C); Richard *Cagge* 1275 SRWo; Robert *Cadge* 1524 SRSf. ME, OFr *cage* 'cage', either metonymic for CAGER or equivalent to *atte Cage* below. (ii) Jacobus *dil Cage* 1327 SRSf; John *atte Cage* 1327 SRSo. *Cage* was used of 'a prison for petty malefactors' c1500 (NED), but the metaphorical meaning of confinement was much earlier (1300 ib.). 'Dweller near, or keeper of the Cage.'

Cager, Caiger: William, Geoffrey *Cager* 1319, 1327 *SR* (Ess). OFr *cagier* 'a maker or seller of cages' or equivalent to *atte Cage* above.

Cain, Caine, Kain, Kaine, Kayne, O'Kane, Cane, Kane: (i) *Keina mater Berte* 1202 AssL; Godfrey *Kein* 1198–1200 BuryS (Sf); Thomas *Kayne* 1260 AssC. *Keina* is a woman's name, perhaps a short form of such Welsh names as *Ceindrych, Ceinlys, Ceinwen*, all feminine, from Welsh *cain* 'beautiful'. cf. St Keyne (Cornwall). The Manx name is a contraction of *Mac Cathain* 'son of *Cathan*', from *cath* 'a battle', 'a warrior': *McKane* 1408, *MacCann* 1430, *MacCane* 1511, *Cain* 1586 Moore. Irish *Ó Catháin* 'descendant of *Cathán*'. (ii) Geoffrey *de Chain* Hy 2 DC (L); Richard *de Kain* 1275 RH (Nf). From Caen (Calvados). cf. CANE, CAM.

Caines, Cains, Kaines, Keynes: William *de Cahaignes, de Cahanges* 1086 DB (C, Bk, Nth, Sx); Willaim *de Caynes* 1222 Cur (Nth). From Cahaignes (Eure) or Cahagnes (Calvados).

Caird: Gilfolan *Kerd* 1275, John *Caird* 1613 Black. Gael, Ir *ceard* 'craftsman, smith, tinker'.

Cake, Cakes: Alured *Cake* 1210 P (Nf); Gilbert *Kake* 13th NthCh. ME *kake, cake*, a comparatively small flattened sort of bread, originally round or oval, usually baked hard on both sides by being turned in the process (c1225 MED). Metonymic for a cake-maker: John *le Kakier* 1292 SRLo, Symon *Cakyer* 1332 SRSx.

Cakebread: Ædwinus *Cacabred* 1109–31 Miller (C); Richard *Cakebred* 1327 SRSf. Metonymic for a maker of *cakebrede*, bread made in flattened cakes, or of the finer and more dainty quality of cake (1377 NED).

Calcott: *v.* CALDECOT

Calcraft, Chalcraft, Chalcroft, Choldcroft: William *Caldcroft* 1441 FrY. 'Dweller at the cold croft', OE *ceald, croft. v.* also CHALCRAFT.

Caldecot, Caldecott, Caldecourt, Caldicot, Caldicott, Callicott, Calcott, Calcut, Calcutt, Callcott, Caulcutt, Caulkett, Cawcutt, Corcut, Corkett, Corkitt, Coldicott, Colicot, Collacot, Collacott, Collecott, Collicutt, Colcott, Colcutt, Collcott, Collcutt, Colkett, Colocott, Chaldecott, Chalcot: Simon *de Caldecot* 1195 P (C); Geoffrey *de Caudecot* 1206 Cur (K); William *de Cheldecot* 1225 PN W 210; Edmund *de Caldicote* 1275 RH (Bk); Richard *de Coldecote* 1275 SRWo; John *Caldekote* 1296 SRSx; John *Calicot* 1524 SRSf. From a common place-name 'cold huts', OE *ceald, cote*, such as Chaldicotes Fm (Wilts), Chalcot(s) (Wilts, Middlesex), and Chollacott (Devon, Wilts). The northern and midland *cald* survives in the common Caldecote, Caldecott, and in Calcot (Berks), Calcutt (Warwicks), Caulcott (Oxon) and Coldcotes (WRYorks). In Calcutt (Wilts) and Collacotts (Devon) we have 'Cola's hut': Thomas *de Colecote* 1275 RH (D).

Calder, Caulder: (i) Adam, Thomas *de Calder* 1246 AssLa, 1332 SRCu. From Calder (Cumb). (ii) Hugh *de Kaledouer* c1178–89 Black; Donald *of Calder* 1419 ib.; Farchard *de Caldor* 1461 ib. From Calder or Cawdor (Caithness).

Calderon, Cauldron, Cawdron, Coldron: Stephen *Caldron* 1289 FrY. AFr *caud(e)ron* 'cauldron'. For a maker of cauldrons, OFr *chalderonnier, cauderonnier:* Roger *le calaroner* 1299 FrY.

Caldwell, Calwell, Cauldwell, Caudell, Caudle, Cawdell, Caddell, Cadel, Cadle, Cadwell, Cardwell, Coldwell, Couldwell, Chadwell, Cholwell: Adam *de Caldewella* 1195 P (Db); Richard *de Coldewell* 1379 PTY; Richard *Cauldwell* 1381 PTY; John *Cawdewelle* 1524 SRSf. 'Cold spring or stream', OE *ceald, wielle*, surviving as Caldwell (Warwicks, NRYorks), Caldwall (Worcs), Cauldwell (Beds, Derby, Notts), Caudle Green (Glos), Caudle Ditch and Cawdle Fen (Cambs), *Cadewell* 1417, *Cadle* 1591, Chadwell (Essex, Herts, Leics, Wilts), Chardwell (Essex) and Chardle Ditch (Cambs), *Kadewelle* 13th, *Cadwel* 14th. For forms, cf. CALDECOT. *v.* also CADWALL, CADWELL. In Scotland *Caldwell* and *Coldwell*, formerly pronounced *Carwall*, are from Caldwell (Renfrewshire).

Cale: David, Walter *Cale* 1275 SRWo. OFr *cale* 'a woman's head-dress' (1588 NED). *v.* CALL.

Calendar: *v.* CALLANDER

Caley, Calley, Callie, Cayley, Kaley, Kayley: (i) William *Cailgi, de Cailgi, de Calgi* 1086 DB (Berks), *de Caillei, de Callei* 1086 ICC; William *de Kailli, de Caly* 1210 Cur (Nf); Adam *de Caly, de Kally* 1212 Cur (Wa). From Cailly (Seine-Inférieure). Walter *de Cayeley* 1332 SRSt probably came from Cayley in Winwick parish (Lancs). (ii) Caley, a common Manx name, is contracted

from *Mac Caolaidhe* 'son of *Caoladh*', a personal name from Gael *caol*, Ir *cael* 'slender': *McCaley* 1511, *Cally* 1605, *Caley* 1642 Moore.

Calf, Callf: Robert *Calf* 1163 DC (L); Ailwin *Calf* 1176 P (Bk). OE *cealf*, Anglian *calf* 'calf'.

Call, Caules: Swanus *Calle* 1275 RH (W); John *Calle* 1279 RH (C). ME *calle*, Fr *cale* 'a close fitting cap worn by women' (1327 NED), metonymic for CALLER. cf. CALE. cf. also Walter *atte Calle* 1307 LLB C, from ME *calle* 'sheepfold' (1483 NED), hence 'shepherd'.

Callan, Callen in Scotland is from *Macallan*. In Ireland, *Callan* is for *Ó Cathaláin* 'descendant of *Cathalán*', a diminutive of *cathgal* 'battle-mighty'. *v.* CALLIN.

Callander, Callendar, Callender, Calendar: (i) Bartholomew *le Calendrer* 1311 LLB B; Paganel, Walter *le Kalendrer* ib. OFr *calendrier, calendreur* 'one who calenders cloth', i.e. passes it through rollers for smoothing (1495 NED). (ii) Alwyn *de Calyntyr* c1248 Black; George *Kallender* 1631 ib. From Callander (Perthshire).

Callaway, Calloway, Calway, Kellaway, Kelleway, Kelway: Philip *de Chailewai* 1165 P (Gl); Thomas *de Kaillewey* 1242 Fees (W); William *Calleweye* 1242 Fees (D). This surname is the source of Kellaways (Wilts) and may derive from Caillouet (Eure). *v.* DEPN, PN W 99.

Calicott: *v.* CALDECOT

Callender: *v.* CALLANDER

Caller, Callear, Callier: Walter *Calyer* 1275 RH (K); Henry *le Callere* 1281 LLB B. A derivative of ME *calle*, from Fr *cale* 'a kind of cap', 'a maker of cauls or coifs for the head'. cf. CALL.

Calley, Callie: *v.* CALEY

Callicott: *v.* CALDECOT

Callin: A Manx name from *MacCathalain* 'son of *Cathalan*', from Gael *cathal* 'valour'. *v.* CALLAN. Occasionally from *Mac Allen*: *McAleyn* 1511, *Callin* 1623 Moore.

Callis: William *de Caleio* 1086 InqEl; Richard *de Caliz* 1190 P (Gl). From Calais.

Callister, Collister: A Manx name for *Mac Alister* 'son of Alexander': *Mac Alisandre* 1417, *Mac Alexander* 1429, *Callister* 1606, *Collister* 1799 Moore.

Callow, Calow: Brichric *se Calewa* 1070 OEByn (So); Philip *Calewe* 1260 AssC; Simon *Calu*, John *le Calue* 1296 SRSx. OE *calu (calewa)* 'bald'. cf. CHAFF.

Calloway: *v.* CALLAWAY

Calpin: a contraction of *MacAlpin*.

Calver: David *de Caluenore, de Caluoure* 1200 P (Db); John *aKarffer* 1560 RothwellPR (Y); Jonathan and Mary *Carver, Calver* 1702, 1705 ShotleyPR (Sf). From Calver (Derby). Indistinguishable in pronunciation from CARVER.

Calvert, Calverd, Calvard: Warin *le Calfhirde* 1269 FFY; William *Calvehird'* 1297 SRY; John *Calverde* of York 1309 LLB D; James *Calvart* 1596 FrY; William *Calvert* 1620 FrY. OE (Anglian) *calf* and *hierde* 'the calf-herd'. cf. John

Calueknave 1284 RamsCt (Hu) and William *Caluerknave* 1327 SRSf.

Calway: *v*. CALLAWAY

Calwell: *v*. CALDWELL

Cam, Camm: (i) William *de Cada, de Cadam, de Cadomo* 1086 DB (Sf); Ralph *de Caham, de Cadomo* c1162 DC (L); Walter *de Cam* (*Cadam'* CR) 1205 P (Y). From Caen (Calvados): *Cadum* 1040, *Cadomum* 1080. William *Cam* 1205 P (Ha) probably belongs here. cf. William *de Cadumo* 1148 Winton (Ha); Fabian *de Cam'* 1184 P (Ha). cf. also CANE. Winterborne Came (Dorset) belonged to the Abbey of Caen in 1086. (ii) Hugh, William *de Camme* 1221 AssGl, 1214 Cur (So). From Cam (Glos). (iii) Walter *le Camm* 1260 AssY; Richard *le Kam* 1282 Oseney (O); Hector *Cam* 1541 Black (Skye). Gael *cam* 'crooked, deformed, one-eyed, cross-eyed'.

Camb: *v*. CAMBER

Camber, Cammer, Comber, Comer, Le Comber, Lecomber, Camb: Ralph (*le*) *Cambere* 1201–2 P (L); Reginald *Combere* (*le Camber*) 1220 Cur (Herts); Ralph *le Combere*, William *le Comere* 1286 MESO (Nf); John *Camere, Camber, Comber* 1359–60 ColchCt. A derivative of OE *camb, comb* 'comb', a maker of combs. CAMB is metonymic. Outr. *Cambmaker* is also called *Camber* (1373, 1379 ColchCt). cf. Thomas *Kambesmyth* 1381 PTY, Alice *Comsmyth* 1590 RothwellPR (Y). *v*. also COMBER.

Camble: *v*. CAMPBELL

Cambray, Cambrey, Gambray, Kembery: Godefridus *de Cambrai* 1086 DB (Lei); Simon *Camberay, Cambrey* 1296 SRSx. From one of three places called Cambrai (Calvados) or from Cambrai (Nord).

Cambridge: Richard *de Cambrige* 1182 P (St) and Alan *de Cambrigge* 1227 AssSt must have come from Cambridge (Glos), *Cambrigga* 1200–10. Picot *de Grantebrige* 1086 DB (C) and William *de Cantebregge* 1338 LLB F certainly owed their names to the University town, but it was not until late in the 14th century that the form *Cambrigge* became common: Stephen *de Caumbrigge* 1348 Works (C), John *Caumbrigge* 1376 LLB H.

Camden, Cambden: Ebrard *de Campeden'* 1190 P (C); John *de Campeden* 1260 AssCh. From Broad, Chipping Campden (Glos).

Camel, Camell, Cammell: (i) Robert *de Camel* 12th Seals (So); Richard *de Cammel* 1319 FFC. From Queen or West Camel (Som). (ii) Walter, Ivo *Camel* 1200 P (D), 1220 Cur (W); John *le Camule* 1332 SRSx. The last form is clearly a nickname, perhaps in the sense 'a great, awkward, hulking fellow' as used by Shakespeare: 'A Dray-man, a Porter, a very Camell.' *v*. CAMPBELL.

Cameron: The Highland clan name is Gael *camshrón* 'wry or hook nose'. The Lowland name is from Cameron (Fife): Adam *de Kamerum* 1214–49, Hugh *Cambrun* 1219, John *de Cameron* 1421 Black.

Camidge, Cammidge: *v*. GAMAGE

Cammell: *v*. CAMEL

Cammer: *v*. CAMBER

Cammis, Camis, Cammish, Camous, Camoys, Camus, Keemish: (i) Adam *le Camhus* 1256 AssNb.; Robert *Cambysshe* 1455 FrY; William *Cammas* 1620 ib.; George *Camisse* 1632 ib. ME *cammus, camois*, OFr *camus* 'having a short, flat nose, pug-nosed' (c1380 MED). (ii) Bartholomew *le Camisur* 1282 LLB B. A derivative of ONFr *camise, kemise*, OFr *chemise*, MedLat *camisia*, an undergarment worn by both men and women, a shirt; used also of a priest's surplice, a herald's robe. Metonymic for a maker of shirts, etc. (iii) Stephen *de Cameis* 1200 P (Nth); Matillis *de Camois* 1205 Cur (Sr). Perhaps from Campeaux (Calvados).

Camp, Campe: Alricus *campe* (*cemp*) 1066 ICC (C); Robert *Campe* 1195 P (Wa); Tomas *le Campe* 1200 P (Ha); John *Campe* (*Kempe*) 1205 P (Do). OE *cempa* 'warrior'. *v*. KEMP. *Camp* may be due to the influence of OE *camp* 'battle', *campian* 'to fight'.

Campaign, Campain, Campen, Campin, Camping: Gilbert *de Campania, de Champanie* Hy 2 DC (L); Graves *de la Campaine* ib.; Roger *de Campen* ib. (Lei); William *Campaignes* 1180 P (Do). From one of the places named Campagne (Pas-de-Calais (several), Oise), or a Norman form of Champaigne.

Campbell, Camble: (i) Colin *Campbell* 1282 Black; Neel *Cambel* 1296 CalSc; Duncan *le Cambell* 1447 Black. Gael *caimbeul* 'wry or crooked mouth'. The surname occurs as *Camille* (1451), *Cammell* (1473), *Camble* (1513). (ii) Thomas *Campell* 1524 SRSf; John *Camell* 1612 FrY. John *Camell* (1667 FrY) or *Cambell* (1697 ib.) was a son of Michael *Camell* and father of Michael *Campbell* and Daniel *Camell* is also called Daniel *Campbell* (1691, 1719 ib.). Their real surname was probably *Cammell*.

Campion: *v*. CHAMPION

Camplin, Campling: Stephen *Camelyn* 1230 Cl; William *Campelin'* 1275 RH (Nf); James *Camplen* 1664 FrY; Daniel *Camplin*, John *Camplinge* 1674 HTSf. OFr *camelin*, a kind of stuff made (or supposed to be made) of camel's hair (c1400 NED). Either a maker or a wearer of cameline.

Camwell: Richard *de Camuilla, de Canuilla* 1148 Eynsham (O), c1155 Holme (Nf); Thomas *Camuille* 1327 SRSx; Samuel *Camwell* 1713 FrY. From Canville-les-Deux-Eglises (Seine-Inférieure). *v*. ANF.

Canaan: *Chanaan* de Bronteston' 1176 P (St); William *Canaan* 1203 AssSt. *v*. CANNAN (ii).

Cancellor: *v*. CHANCELLOR

Candish: *v*. CAVENDISH

Candle: (i) Ailuuin *Candela* c1095 Bury (Sf); Adam *Chandeille* 1196 P (Sr); Samson *Candeille, Candel* 1197, 1207 P (W). OE *candel*, Lat *candela*, or ONFr *candeile*, OFr *chandeile* 'candle', metonymic for a maker or seller of candles. (ii) Ralph *de Candel* 1176 P (So). From Caundel (Dorset).

Candler: *v*. CHANDLER

Cane, Kane: (i) *Cana, Cane, Cano* 1066 DB (Sr, Sx); *Cane* 1160–70 MedEA (Nf); Willelmus *filius Cane* c1213 Fees (Berks); Leofwine *Kana*

11th OEByn; Leouuinus *Chane* 1066 Winton (Ha); Herueus *Cane* 1177 P (Sf); Hugo *Kane* 1210 P (He); William *le Cane* 1332 SRSx. The personal-name is probably OE *Cana*. *v.* also CAIN. The nickname is ME, OFr *cane* 'cane, reed', used, probably, for a man tall and slender as a reed. (ii) Alan *de Cane* 1230 P (Y). From Caen (Calvados). cf. CAIN, CAM. Kirby Cane (Norfolk) was held in 1205 by Walter *de Cadamo* and in 1242 by Maria *de Cham* (DEPN).

Canham: Henry *de Cauenham* 1327 SRSf. From Cavenham (Suffolk).

Cann: (i) Bartholomew *Canne* 1327 SRSf; Richard *Can* 1327 *SR* (Ess). OE *canne* 'can'. Metonymic for CANNER. (ii) Richard *de Canne* 1276 RH (O). From Cann (Dorset).

Cannan, Cannon: (i) The Manx name is *Mac-Cannon* 1511, *Cannan* 1638, from Ir *Mac Canna-nain* 'son of *Cannanan*' (*Ceann-fhionn* 'white head'), recorded in 950 (Moore). (ii) *Canan* 1296 CalSc; Fergus *Acannane* 1562 Black; David *Cannane* 1624 ib. Ir *O'Canáin*, descendant of *Canán*, a diminutive of *Cano* 'wolf-cub'.

Cannel, Cannell: Simon, John *Canel* 1314 LLB D, 1327 SRC; Richard *Cannell* 1428 FA (Wa). ME, OFr *canele* 'cinnamon'. A seller of cinnamon, a spicer.

Cannell (Manx): *Mac Connell* 1511, *Cannell* 1606. From *Mac Conaill* 'Conall's son' (Moore).

Canner: John *le Kannere* 1305 MESO (Ha); William *le Cannere* 1327 SRSt. A derivative of OE *canne* 'can', a maker or seller of cans.

Cannon, Cannons, Canon, Channon: Aluric *se Canonica* 11th OEByn (D); Reginald *Canun* 1177 P (C); Nicholas *le Chanone* 1332 SRSt; William *Canons* 1401 FrY. The first example is from OE *canonic*, the later ones from ME *canun*, ONFr *canonie*, later *canoine;* ME *chanun*, central OFr *chanoine* 'a clergyman living with others in a clergy house' (c1205 NED). *v.* CANNAN.

Cant, Caunt, Chant: Richard *Cante* 1327 SRSf, *Caunt* 1357 FFHu. ONFr *cant*, OFr *chant* 'singing, song', metonymic for CANTER, CHANTER.

Cantellow, Cantelo, Cantelo, Cantlow: Waterus (*sic*) *de Cantelupo* c1135 DC (L); Roger *de Cantelo* 1185 Templars (So); William *de Cante-lowe* 1320 Eynsham (O); William *Cantlowe* 1448 LLB K. One family came from Canteleu (Seine-Inférieure), another from Canteloup (Calvados). *v.* ANF 24.

Canter, Cantor, Caunter, Kanter: Augustinus *cantor, precentor* 1153–68, 1186–1210 Holme (Nf); Walter *le Canter* 1230 Eynsham (O). The early examples are all from Latin *cantor* and refer to precentors in cathedrals or monasteries. The last is from AFr *caunter, cauntour* 'singer, one who leads the singing'. cf. CHANTER.

Cantes: *v.* KENTISH

Cantrell: Robert *de Canterhulle* 1330 PN D 284. From Cantrell (Devon). *v.* also CHANTRELL.

Cape, Cope: Ailward, Walter *Cape* 1190 P (K), 1221 AssGl; Walter, Maud *Cope* 1275 RH (Lo), SRWo. OE **cāpe*, ME *cope* 'a long cloak or cape'

(a1225 MED). *Cope* is the normal development, *Cape* the early form retained in the north.

Capel, Capell, Capelle, Caple, Cappel, Cappell: Jacob *de Capel* 1193 P (He); Ralph, Philip *Capel* 1214 Cur (Nth), 1285 *Ass* (Ess); Robert *atte Capele* 1296 SRSx. From Capel or Capel Le Ferne (Kent), Capel St Andrew or St Mary (Suffolk), Capel (Surrey) or How or King's Caple (Hereford), or from residence near or service at a chapel (ME *capel*, ONFr *capele*). Occasionally also from ME *capel, capul* 'a nag': Rogerus *Caballus* 1230 ArchC 6. *v.* CAPPLEMAN.

Capelen, Capelin, Capeling: *v.* CHAPLAIN

Capers: William, Thomas *Caper* 1200–50 Seals (Sf), 1327 SRWo. A derivative of ME *cape*, 'a maker of capes or copes'. *v.* CAPE.

Caplan, Caplen, Caplin: *v.* CHAPLAIN

Capon, Cappon: Simon *Capun* 1227 FFC; Thomas *Capoun* 1382 LLB H. OE *capun* 'a castrated cock', metonymic for a seller of capons.

Caporn, Capern: *v.* CAPRON

Capp, Capps: William *Cappa* 1111–38 ELPN; Alward *Cappe* 1178 P (K); Roger *Caps* 1327 SRSo. OE *cæppe* 'cap', metonymic for CAPPER.

Capper, Kapper: Nicholas *le Capyare* 1275 SRWo; Symon *le Cappere* 1276 RH (O); William *Capier* 1285 *Ass* (Ess). A derivative of OE *cæppe* 'cap', a maker of caps (1389 NED).

Cappleman: Walter *Capelman* 1327 SRSx. Either from ME *capel, capul* 'horse', one who looks after horses (cf. PALFREYMAN), or one who lives near or is employed at a chapel. *v.* CAPEL, CHAPPEL and cf. TEMPLEMAN.

Cappon: *v.* CAPON

Capron, Capuron, Capern, Caporn: *Caperun* 1130–32 ELPN, 1148 Winton (Ha), 1185 Templars (L); Robert *Caperun* 1130 P (Berks); Roger *Caperun, Chaperon* camerarius Henrici regis 1154–64, 1173–83 Bury (Sf); William *Capron* 13th Gilb (L); John *Capurne* 1503 NorwW (C). ONFr *capron*, OFr *chaperon* 'hood or cap worn by nobles' (c1380 NED). Roger Chaperon was the royal chamberlain whose duties included those of Master of the Robes. cf. 'As hys chamberleyn hym broȝte vorto . . . werye, a peyre hose of say' (1297 NED) and 'Hys (the king's) chaumberlayn hym wrappyd warm' (c1325 ib.). *Caperun* may be a name of office, 'the robe-master', but its chief meaning is, no doubt, 'a maker of hoods'. cf. William *Caper-oner* 1327 SRSo. The modern meaning of 'chaperon' is not found before the 18th century.

Capstack, Capstick: *v.* COPESTAKE

Carass: *v.* CARUS

Carbonell, Charbonell: *Carbunel(lus)* 1086 DB (He); Durandus *Carbonellus* 1130 P (O); Robertus *Charbonellus* c1145 DC (L); William *Carbonel* 1175 P (D). OFr *carbon, charbon* 'charcoal', probably an affectionate diminutive for one with a swarthy complexion or hair black as coal, the essential characteristic of charcoal. The name was sometimes confused with CARDINAL and became CARNALL. cf. Cardinal's Fm (PN Ess 429): *Car-bonels* 1381, *Cardynals* 1577, *Carnals* 1777.

Carbott: William *Carbott* 1412 FrY; Matthew *Garbutt* son of Robert *Carbutt* 1672 ib. For GARBUTT.

Card, Carde: Arnald, Laurence *Carde* 1221 AssSa, 1297 MinAcctCo. OFr *carde* 'teasel-head, wool-card'. Metonymic for CARDER or for *Cardmaker:* Richard *Cardemakere.* 1346 FrNorw.

Carden, Cardon, Carding: William *Cardon, Cardun* 1086 DB, InqEl (Ess); Richard *Cardun* 1121–48 Bury (Sf). OFr *cardon* 'thistle', used perhaps for one of an obstinate, stubborn character. *Carden* is very common and must sometimes derive from Carden (Ches).

Carder: John *le carder* 1332 FrY. 'One who cards wool' (c1450 NED).

Cardew, Cardy, Carthew: John *de Carthew* 1332 SRCu; Richard *Cardew* 1376 FrY. From Cardew (Cumb).

Cardinal, Cardinall, Cardnell: Ingelrannus *Cardinal'* 1190 P (Y); Geofffrey *Cardinell', Cardinal* 1208 Cur (Y), 1327 SRC. OFr *cardinal* 'cardinal', a pageant-name or a nickname for one like (or unlike) a cardinal or with a partiality for dressing in red. *v.* CARBONELL.

Carding, Cardon: *v.* CARDEN

Cardis, Cardus: *v.* CARRUTHERS

Cardwell: *v.* CALDWELL

Cardy: *v.* CARDEW

Care: *v.* KEAR

Careless: *v.* CARLESS

Caress, Cariss: *v.* CARUS

Carey: *v.* CARY

Carker, Charker: Wulgor *le Carkere* 1166 P (Ha). ME *cark(e)*, AFr *kark(e)*, a northern French form of *carche, charche* 'a load, a weight of three or four hundredweights' (a1300 NED), a kark of pepper, ginger, etc. (c1502). Probably 'carrier'. *Karck* is metonymic.

Carl, Carle, Karl, Karle: Godric *filius Carle, Carli,* Godric *Carlesone* 1066 DB (K); Edmundus *filius Carle* 1205 Cur (Sf); Robert *le Karl* 1202 AssL; William *Carl* 1296 SRSx. The personal name may be ON, ODa *Karli,* ODa *Karl* or OG *Karl.* A more common source is probably ME *carl,* ON *karl* 'man', used in ME with various meanings at different times: man of the common people, a countryman, husbandman; a free peasant; by 1300 it meant 'bondman, villain' and also 'a fellow of low birth or rude manners, a churl'.

Carless, Careless, Carloss, Carlos: Richard, Reginald *Carles* 1141 ELPN, 1200 P (Gl); Alan *Karelees,* Margaret *Kareles* 1260 AssC. OE *carlēas* 'free from care', or more likely 'unconcerned, careless'.

Carlisle, Carlile, Carlill, Carlyle: Odard *de Carlyle* 1158–64 Black; Thomas *de Karlisle* 1310–11 LLB D; Adam *Carlelle, Carlille* 1363, 1370 ib. G. From Carlisle (Cumb).

Carlos: *v.* CARLESS

Carlyle: *v.* CARLISLE

Carman: Simon *nepos Kareman* 1196 Cur (Nth); Hamo *filius Karlman* 1201 Cur (K); Robert *Kareman* 1184 P (Lei); Henry *Carman* 1275 RH (Sf);

Robert *Carleman, Karleman* 1279 RH (C). ON *karmann,* a variant of *karlmann* (nom. *karmaðr*) 'male, man, an adult male', used as a personal name. *v.* CHARMAN.

Carnall, Carnell, Carnelley, Crenel, Crennell: William *de la Kernel, de la Karnaile* 1244, c1250 Rams (C); Hugo *de la Karnell* 1247 FFHu. ONFr *carnel,* a variant of *kernel,* OFr *crenel* 'battlement, embrasure'. The reference is, no doubt, to arbalesters whose post was on the battlements. *v.* also CARBONELL, CARDINAL.

Carothers: *v.* CARRUTHERS

Carpenter: Godwin *carpentar'* 1121–48 Bury (Sf); Ralph *carpenter'* 1175 P (Y); Robert *le carpenter* 1212 Cur (Sf). AFr *carpenter* 'carpenter' (c1325 NED).

Carr, Ker, Kerr: Osbert *de Ker* c1200 Riev (Y); Robert *Ker* 1231 Pat (Nb); William *Carre* 1279 RH (O); John *del Car* 1332 SRLa; John *Atteker* 1375 NorwW (Nf). 'Dweller by the marsh or fenny copse', ME *kerr,* ON *kjarr* 'brushwood, wet ground'.

Carradice: *v.* CARRUTHERS

Carran, Carine, Karran: *Mac Ciarain* 1136, *McCarrane* 1430, *Carran* 1648, *Carine* 1729. Manx names from *Mac Ciarain* 'son of Ciaran', one of the twelve great saints of Ireland, from *ciar* 'mouse-coloured' (Moore).

Carras: *v.* CARUS

Carriage: *v.* KERRICH

Carrier, Carryer: Robert *de* (sic) *Carier* 1332 SRCu; Roger *le Cariour* 1332 SRLa. ONFr *carier* 'carrier, porter'.

Carrington: (i) Thomas *de Karington* 1219 AssLa; John *de Carrington* 1294 AssCh; Richard *Carington* 1523 CorNt. From Carrington (Ches). (ii) Wautier *de Keringtone* 1296 Black; William *Keringtoun* 1506 ib. From Carrington (East Lothian).

Carris(s): *v.* CARUS

Carruthers, Carrothers, Carothers, Carradice, Carrodus, Cardis, Cardus, Crothers, Crowdace, Cruddace, Cruddas: John *de Carutherys* c1320 Black; William *of Carruderys* 1460 ib.; William *Corrodas* 1625 RothwellPR (Y); Bertha *Cruddas* 1888 Bardsley. From Carruthers (Dumfriesshire), pronounced *Cridders.*

Carsey: *v.* KERSEY

Carslake, Caslake, Karslake, Kerslake, Keslake: Ranulph *de Carselak'* 1279 AssSo. 'Dweller by the cress-stream', OE *cærse, lacu.*

Carslaw, Carsley: *v.* KEARSLEY

Carswell, Casewell, Casswall, Casswell, Caswall, Caswell, Caswill, Crasswell, Craswell, Cressall, Cressell, Cresswell, Creswell, Crisswell, Criswell, Crissell, Kerswell, Kerswill: Basilia *de Caswella* 1165 P (D); Tomas *de Cressewella* 1190 P (St); Reginald *de Kersewell'* 1212 Cur (O); William *de Kereswell'* 1221 AssWo; Richard *de Carswall,* William *de Karswille* 1275 RH (D); Robert *de Carswell* 1327 SRSo; John and Alice *Cresshills, Creswell* 1816, 1822 ShotleyPR (Sf). 'Dweller by the water-cress-stream', OE *cærse, wiella,* surviving in Carswell (Berks, Devon), Carsewell (Renfrew), Caswell

(Dorset, Northants, Som), Crasswall (Hereford), Cresswell (Derby, Staffs), Kerswell (Devon, Worcs) and Kerswill (Devon).

Carter, Cartter, Charter: (i) Fulco *carettarius* 1177 P (C); Rannulfus *carettator* 1191 P (Hu). (ii) Rannulf *carettier, le caretier* 1192–3 P (Hu); Odo *le careter* 1210 Cur (Nth). (iii) Hugh *Karter* 1225 Lewes (Nf); Robert *le Carter* 1240 FFEss, 1275 SRWo. (iv) Henry *le Chareter* 1222 Cur (So), 1225 AssSo (*le careter* 1225 ib.); William *le Chareter*, John *le Charetter, le Charter*, Walter *le Charettier* 1275 SRWo. NED derives *carter* from ME *cart(e)*, of native or Scandinavian origin, plus *-er* (a1250). The history of the name is more elaborate. Of the above forms, (i) is MedLat (*carettarius* 1213 in MLWL, which does not contain *carettator*); (ii) is ONFr *caretier*, not in NED, but surviving in the modern French surnames *Carratier, Carretier* and *Cartier* of Norman and Picard origin; (iii) as in NED; (iv) OFr *charetier* 'charioteer' (c1340 NED), but clearly used in English for 'carter'.

Carters: Margerie *le Carteres* c1275 St Thomas (St). *v.* CARTER and pp. xxix–xxxii.

Carthew: *v.* CARDEW

Cartledge, Cartlidge: Richard *de Cartelache* 1290 AssCh; Richard *de Cartlege* 1435 DbCh; Thomas *Cartlidge* 1641 Shef. From Cartledge in Holmesfield (Derby).

Cartwright, Kortwright: John *le Cartwereste* 1275 SRWo; Richard *the Cartwrytte* 1290 AssCh; William *le Cartewryght* 13th Guisb (Y). OE *cræt* or ON *kartr* 'cart' and OE *wyrhta* 'wright', a maker of carts.

Carus, Carass, Caress, Cariss, Carras, Carris, Carriss: Robert *del Karhouses* 1332 SRLa; Thomas *de Carrehous* 1379 PTY; James *Carous* 1555 FrY; William *Caras* 1619 ib.; Robert *Carus* 1709 ib. 'Dweller at the marsh-house.' cf. CARR, and 'road from Balby to *Carhouse*' 1638 Shef.

Carver: (i) Peter *le caruier* 1203 P (Nt); Gerard *le Carver* 1209 FFEss. OFr *charuier, caruier* 'ploughman'. (ii) Richard *le Kerver(e)* 1275 RH (L), 1277 FFC; William *Keruer* 1327 SRSx. A derivative of OE *ceorfan* 'to cut, carve', one who carves, usually in wood, sometimes in stone; 'wood-carver, sculptor' (c1385 MED). This would later become *Carver*.

Carvill, Carville: Walter *de Careuilla* 1195 P (W). From Carville (Calvados, Seine-Inférieure).

Carwardine: Richard *de Carwardyn* 1302 Chamb-AcctCh. From Carden (Ches).

Cary, Carey, Carye: Hamo *de Kari* 1205 Pl (So); Richard *de Kary* 1242 Fees (D); Robert *Karye* 1296 SRSx; Thomas *Cary* 1375 AssLo. From Carey Barton (Devon), Castle, Lytes Cary, Cary Fitzpaine, or Babcary (Som).

Casbolt: Stephen *Casebolt* 1327 SRC. ME *casbalde* 'bald-head', a term of reproach: cf. 'Go home, casbalde, with þi clowte' (c1440 *York Plays*).

Casborne, Casburn, Casbon, Caseborne, Case- bourne: John *de Caseburn* 1275 RH (K). From Casebourne Wood in Hythe (Kent).

Case: William, Richard *Case* 1274 RH (Sf), 1327 SRC. Metonymic for 'a maker of boxes, chests, or receptacles', ONFr *casse*, cf. Clais *Casemaker* 1367 MEOT. *v.* also CASS.

Caselaw, Caseley: *v.* KEARSLEY

Casement: Mac *Casmonde* 1429, *Casymound, Casmyn* 1540, *Casement* 1612. From *Mac Ásmundr*, from Celtic *Mac* 'son' and ON *Ásmundr* 'god protector' (Moore).

Casewell: *v.* CARSWELL

Cashen, Cashin, Cassin: Ir, Gael *Caisín*, a diminutive of *cas* 'crooked'. The Manx name is a contraction of *Mac Caisin*: McCashen 1511, *Cashen* 1641, *Cassin* 1687 Moore.

Caskie, Casky: For MACASKIE.

Caslake: *v.* CARSLAKE

Casley, de Casley: *v.* KEARSLEY

Cason: Wolfren *Cawson*, Ro. *Caston, Cason*, Stephen *Corson* 1674 HTSf; Elizabeth *Casen, Cawston* 1788, 1793 LitWelnethamPR (Sf). A local pronunciation of Cawston (Norfolk).

Cass: *Casse* Rumpe 1279 RH (C); John, William *Casse* 1170 P (Y), 1200 P (Ess). A pet-form of *Cassandra*, a common 13th-century woman's name: *Cassandra* 1182–1211 BuryS (C), 1208 Cur (Y), 1275 RH (Nf).

Cassin: *v.* CASHEN

Cassingham: William *de Casinghamme* 1275 RH (K). From Kensham Green in Benenden (Kent).

Cassler: *v.* CASTLEHOW

Cassley: *v.* KEARSLEY

Casson: William *Casson* 1601 FrY. (i) Ralph *Cattessone* 1115 Winton (Ha), John *Catesone* 1366 FFSf. 'Son of *Catt*.' (ii) Robert *Casseson* 1327 SRC. 'Son of *Cass*.'

Casswell: *v.* CARSWELL

Castell, Caistell: *MacAskel* 1311, *MacCaskel, Caskell* 1511, *Caistil* 1669, *Castell* 1750 Moore. For *MacAskell* (Manx). cf. ASKELL. *v.* also CASTLE.

Castellan, Castellain, Castelein, Castling, Chatelain: (i) Hugh *le Chastelein* 1235 FFEss; Osbert *Casteleyn* c1240 ArchC viii; Walter *Castelyn* 1255 Ass (Ess); Warin *Castellan* 1311 ColchCt. ME, ONFr *castelain*, OFr *chastelain* 'governor or constable of a castle', also 'warden of a prison'. (ii) William *de Castellon* 1086 DB (Bk); Hugo *de Castelliun* 1206 Cur (Bk); Robert *de Chastellun* 1220 Cur (Lo). From Castellion (Eure).

Castle, Castles, Castell, Castells: Richard, Robert *Castel* 1148–54 Bec (Sx), 1201 P (Lei); John *del Castel* 1307 Wak (Y); William *ate Castele* 1317 AssK. ME, ONFr *castel* 'castle'. One who lived near or was employed at a castle. Sometimes from services or rent due to a castle. Henry *de Castell* (1260 AssC) owed rent to Cambridge Castle.

Castlehow, Castlehowe, Castello, Castelly, Castley, Castlo, Cassler: John *Castlehow* 1667 Bampton-PR (We); Elizabeth, Mary *Castley* 1683, 1685 ib. There are seven places of the name in Westmorland, usually recorded very late, the earliest being Castle

Howe in Kendal (1577) and Castlehow Scar in Crosby Ravensworth (1629). *de Castello*, not infrequent in medieval sources, is probably a latinization of CASTLE, but may have contributed to these names.

Castleman: Ralph *Castelman* 1327 SRSo. One employed at a castle. cf. TEMPLEMAN.

Castling: *v.* CASTELLAN

Caswall, Caswell, Caswill: *v.* CARSWELL

Catanach, Catnach, Cattanach, Cattenach: Thomas *Kethirnathie* 1407 Black; Arthur *Catanache* 1623 ib. Gael *Catanach* 'belonging to (Clan) Chattan' which claims descent from *Gillacatain* 'servant of (St) *Catan*', 'little cat'.

Catch: Godfrey *Cacch*' 1225 AssSo; Margery *Cach* 1326 SRC. ME *cache* 'the act of catching', from AFr *cachier* 'to chase', in the sense of 'chase, pursuit', metonymic for *Catcher*

Catcher, Ketcher: (i) Richard *Kaccher* 1200 P (L); Jordan *Cachere* 1221 AssWa. ME *cachere* 'one who chases or drives', 'a huntsman' (c1340 NED). It is probably also used in the same sense as the diminutive *cacherel* which is common both as a name of office and as a surname in Norfolk in 1275 (RH): Alexander *le Cacherel*, Hugh *le Chacherel*, Adam *Kacherel*, Richard *Wyche*, *cacherel*. The *cacherels* were the bailiffs of the hundred and had an unpleasant reputation for extortion and oppression. (ii) William *Kacchehare* 1204 P (C); Edhiva *Cachehare* 1240 Rams (Hu). 'Catch hare', perhaps 'speedy as a hare', cf. CATCHPOLE and TURNER.

Catchlove: Bernard *Cachelu* 1189 Oseney (O); William *Cacheluve* 1208 Cur (Y). ONFr *cachelove*, *cacheleu* 'chase wolf', 'wolf-hunter'. cf. CATCHPOLE.

Catchpole, Catchpoll, Catchpool, Catchpoole, Catchpoule: Aluricus *Chacepol* 1086 DB (Mx); Robert *le Chachepol* Hy 2 AD i (Mx); Hugo *le Cachepol* 1221 AssSa. ME *caccepol*, *cachpol*, OFr (central) *chacepol*, ONFr *cachepol* 'chase fowl', 'a collector of poultry in default of money'; 'a taxgatherer' (a1050); 'a petty officer of justice, a sheriff's officer or sergeant, especially a warrant officer who arrests for debt' (1377 NED). cf. CATCHLOVE and Geoffrey *Cacemoine* 1198 Cur (Y) 'chase monk', Robert *Kachevache* 1221 *ElyA* (Sf) 'chase cow', Walter *Chacefreins* 1195 P (D), Emma *Cachefrensh* 1327 SRSx 'get hold of the reins', Robert *Chacecapel* 1201 P (D) 'chase nag', Peter *Cachefis* 1279 RH (C), 'catch fish'.

Cater, Cator, Chater, Chaters, Chaytor: William *le Chatur*, identical with William *Emptor* 1220 Cur (Beds); Robert *le Achatour* 1229 Rams (C); Amicia *Lakature*, Elias *le Katur* 1271 RamsCt (C); William *le Catour*, *le Chatur*, *le Katour* 1310 Balliol (O); John *Chayter* 1667 FrY. AFr *acatour*, early OFr *acateor*, central OFr *achatour* 'buyer' (c1386 NED), ME *catour*, aphetic form of *acatour*, *acater* 'buyer of provisions for a large household' (c1400 NED). *Cator* is also local, from Cator (Devon): Laua *de Cadatrea* 1167 P (D).

Caterer: William *Katerer* 1279 RH (Hu).

Cater (sb. or vb.) plus *-er*. 'One who caters or purveys provisions for a household' (1469 MED).

Cates, Kates: Thurstan *Cati* c1095 Bury (Sf); Osbert *Kate* 1183 Boldon (Du); Geoffrey *Cates* 1332 SRSx. ON *Káti* (nickname) 'the merry one', or, less likely, ODa *Kati*, OSw *Kate* (pers. names).

Cathcart: Reginald *de Cathekert* c1200 Black; William *de Kathkerte* 1296 ib.; Adam *Cathcart* 1622 ib. From Cathcart (Renfrew).

Catherall, Cathrall: *v.* CATTERALL

Catlin, Catling, Cattlin: *Katelina* de Walcote 13th Rams (Hu); *Katerina, Katelina* de Sauston 1275 RH (Hu); Gervase, Robert *Caterin* Hy 2 Seals (Sr), 1247 AssBeds; William *Catelin, Katelin* 1198 FFNf; Robert *Catyln* 1441 ShefA; Richard *Catlyng* 1653 EA (OS) iv (C). OFr *Caterine, Cateline*, the French form of *Catharine*, introduced into England in the 12th century when it became popular, usually in the form *Catelin(e)*.

Catnach: *v.* CATANACH

Caton: Richard *Caton* 1279 RH (C); Peter *Catoun* 1327 SRSf. *Cat-un*, a diminutive of *Cat*, a pet-form of *Catelin*. cf. KATIN.

Catt, Katte, Chatt: *Lufmancat* 1066 DB (Ha); Robert *le Cat* 1167 P (Nf); Geoffrey *Chat* 1190–1200 Seals (Sf); Margaret *Kat* 1202 AssL; Adam *le Chat* 1203 P (W). A common nickname from the cat (OE *catt*, ONFr *cat*, OFr *chat*). *Catt* is probably also a pet-form of *Catelin*, from which were formed the diminutives *Catell, Caton, Katin*.

Cattanach: *v.* CATANACH

Cattel, Cattell, Catell, Cattle: *Cattle* Bagge 1279 RH (C); Hervey, Geoffrey *Catel* 1275, 1279 RH (Nf, Hu); John *Cattle* 1653 FrY; John *Cattell, Cattall* 1683, 1707 ib. A diminutive of *Cat*, a short form of *Catelin*. cf. CATON, KATIN and Fr *Catelet*.

Catterall, Catterell, Catterill, Catteroll, Cattrall, Cattrell, Cattroll, Catherall, Cathrall: Robert *de Caterell*' 1222 Cur (Ha); John *de Caterhale* 1332 SRLa; Lawrence *Cattrall* 1462 Calv (Y); Richard *Caterall* 1500 FrY. From Catterall (Lancs) and, apparently, also from a place in Hants with a second element *-hill*. William *Katerel* 1203 AssSt suggests also a pet-form of *Caterin*.

Caudell, Caudle, Cawdell, Cadel, Caddell, Cadle: Godfrey, John *Cadel* 1187 P (Gl), 1276 RH (O); Walter, William *Caudel* 1198 FFNf, 1279 RH (C); William *Kaldel* 1277 LLB B. ME *caudel (cadel)*, ONFr *caudel*, MedLat *caldellum* 'a hot drink', a thin gruel, mixed with wine or ale, sweetened and spiced, given chiefly to sick people, especially to women in childbed; also to their visitors (c1325 MED). Probably a derogatory nickname given to a man who could not hold his drink and so should stick to this invalid beverage, or, conversely, for a toper who scorned anything but a man's drink. *v.* also CALDWELL.

Caudwell: *v.* CALDWELL

Caulcutt: *v.* CALDECOT

Cauldron: *v.* CALDERON

Cauldwell: *v.* CALDWELL

Caules: v. CALL
Caulkett: v. CALDECOT
Caunt: v. CANT
Caunter: v. CANTER
Causey, Cawsey: (i) Robert *le Cauceis, le Calceis* 1166 RBE, 1166–73 ANF (L); William *le Cauceis* 1212 Cur (Nt); Robert *Causeys, Causay* 1327, 1332 SRSx. A man from the pays de Caux (Seine-Inférieure). cf. Fr *Cauchois* and v. CAW. (ii) Robert *de Calceto* 1202 AssL; Henry *atte Cauce* 1356 Putnam (So); Nycolas *Cawsey* 1524 SRSf. 'Dweller by a causeway', ME *cauce.*
Causton: v. CAWSTON
Cave, Kave: Nigel *de Caua* 1185 Templars (Y); Hugh *Cave,* William *de Cave* 1212 Cur (L). From Cave (ERYorks). v. also CHAFF.
Cavell: Roger *Caluel, Chauuel* 1190, 1195 P (K); Enger' *Cauuel'* 1199–1227 Seals (W); Adam *Cavel* 1275 SRWo. A diminutive of OFr *chauf, cauf* 'bald'.
Cavendish, Candish: Simon *de Cauendis* 1201 Pl (Sf); Richard *de Cavendish* 1344 FFEss; William *Caundyssh* 1416 FFEss. From Cavendish (Suffolk).
Cavill: Tomas *de Kauill', de Cauill'* 1190, 1194 P (Y). From Cavil (ERYorks).
Caw, Caws, Cawse: Robert *de Chauz* 1166 RBE (Nt), *de Calz, de Cauz* 1206 Cur (Sx). From the pays de Caux (Seine-Inférieure). cf. CAUSEY.
Cawcutt: v. CALDECOT
Cawdell: v. CALDWELL, CAUDELL
Cawdron: v. CALDERON
Cawker: v. CHALKER
Cawsey: v. CAUSEY
Cawston, Causton: Heroldus *de Caustuna* 1066 DB (Sf); William *de Causton'* c1125 MedEA (Nf). From Cawston (Norfolk).
Cawthorn, Cawthorne, Cawthron: William *de Calthorn* 1175 P (Y), 1357 Calv; Robert *de Cauthorne* 1379 PTY. From Cawthorn (NRYorks), *Calthorn* 1175, or Cawthorne (WRYorks), *Calthorn* c1125.
Cayley: v. CALEY
Cayzer, Kayser, Kayzer, Keyser, Keysor, Keyzor: Henry *le Caisere* 1172 P (Wa); William *le Keiser* 1195 Oseney (O). ME *caisere,* ultimately from Lat *Caesar* 'emperor'. A pageant name.
Cecil, Saycell: *Saissil* 1066 DB (He); *Seisil* 1188 P (Sa); William *Seisil, Seysel* 1205 P (He), 1275 SRWo; Sir Thomas *Cecill* 1591 Bardsley (Nf). OW *Seisill,* said to derive from Lat *Caecilius.*
Cedervall: v. SIRDIFIELD
Ceeley, Ceely, Cely, Ceiley: v. SEALEY
Center, Senter: Agnes *la Ceintere,* John *le Ceinture,* Henry *le Ceynter, le Seynter* 1275 SRWo. girdle' (1595 NED). Metonymic for CENTURY. v. also SENTER.
Century: John *le Ceinturer* 1275 MESO (Wo); Robert *le Ceinturer* 1298 LoCt. OFr *ceinturier, sainturier* 'maker of waist-belts'. This may also have become SENTRY.
Chace: v. CHASE
Chadd: *Cedda de Alrewys* 1275 RH (St); *Chad*

Maryon 1524 SRSf; Hugo, Henry *Chadde* 1190 P (Wa), 1247 AssBeds; Ralph *Chad* 1219 AssY; Henry *Ced* 1379 PTY; Joan *Chedde,* William *Shedde* 1524 SRSf. OE *Ceadd(a),* which, though the evidence is slight, seems to have remained long in use.
Chadwell: v. CALDWELL
Chadwick, Chadwyck, Chaddock, Shaddick, Shaddock, Shadwick, Chattock: Richard *de Chadeleswic'* 1221 AssWa; Andrew *de Chadewyke* 1328 WhC; Pers *Chadick* 1553 WhC; John *Chadwikke* alias *Chaddokke* 1554 CorNt; Thomas *Chadeck* 1704 FrY. From Chadwick (Lancs, Warwicks, Worcs), or Chadwich (Worcs), *Chadeleswik* 1212.
Chafen: v. CHAFFIN
Chafer: John *del Chaufeur* 1301 SRY. OFr *chauffour* 'limekiln', hence 'worker at a limekiln'. cf. William *le Limbrenner* 1305 MESO (L), 'limeburner'. The surname may also survive as CHAFFER.
Chaff, Chaffe, Chave, Caff, Cave, Kave: Roger *le Chauf, le Cauf, Calvus* 1214, 1220 Cur (Co); William *Caff* 1214 Cur (L); William *le Cave* 1280 AssSo; Richard *Chafe* 1649 Bardsley. OFr *chauf, cauf,* Lat *calvus* 'bald'.
Chaffer: John *Chaffar* 1327 SRC, 1359 FrY. OE **cēapfaru,* ME *chaffere (chaffar)* 'traffic, trade', also 'merchandise, wares', used by metonymy for a dealer, merchant. cf. *chafferer* 'dealer' (1382 NED). v. also CHAFER.
Chaffin, Chafen, Chauvin, Caffin, Caffyn: Richard *Chaufin* 1273 RH (Nt); Richard *Caffyn* 1327 SRSx; Thomas *Chafyn* 1505 Oxon. A diminutive of OFr *chauf, cauf* 'bald'.
Chainey: v. CHEYNEY
Chalcot: v. CALDECOT
Chalcraft, Chalcroft, Calcraft: Thomas *de Chalvecroft* 1272 Ass (Ha); John *de Chalfcroft* 1296 SRSx; Robert *de Calvecrofth* 1327 SRSf. From Chalcroft in South Stoneham (Hants) or 'dweller by the calves' croft', OE *cealf.* v. also CALCRAFT.
Chaldecott: v. CALDECOT
Chalice: v. CHALLIS
Chalk, Chalke, Chaulk: Walter *de Chelka* 1177 P (W); Ralph *de Chalke* 1268 ArchC 5; William *atte Chalke* 1296 SRSx. From Bower or Broad Chalke (Wilts) or Chalk (Kent), or from residence near a chalk down. OE *cealc* 'chalk', here 'chalky soil' or an OE **cealce* 'chalk down'. v. MELS.
Chalker, Kalker, Cawker: Robert *Calchier* 1195–1215 StP (Lo); Thomas *le Chalker* 1275 RH (W); Nicholas *le Calkere* 1327 SRSf. A derivative of OE *(ge)cealcian* 'to whiten', 'whitewasher'. But in Wilts and Kent this might also mean 'dweller on the chalk'.
Challen, Challens, Challin: Peter *de Chalun, de Chaluns* 1194–5 P (D); Godfrey *Challon* 1275 RH (D); Robert *Chalons* 1428 FA (W). From Chalon-sur-Saône or Châlons-sur-Marne. Or metonymic for CHALLENER.
Challener, Challender, Challenor, Challinor, Chaloner, Chawner, Channer: John *le Chaloner*

1213 Cur (Sr); Ralph *le Chaluner* 1224 FFSf; Thomas *Chalander* 1485 RochW; Thomas *Chauner* 1583 AD vi (St). A derivative of ME *chaloun* 'blanket', from its place of manufacture, Châlons-sur-Marne, 'maker of or dealer in *chalons*, blankets or coverlets' (1372 NED). 'Chalons of Guildford' were bought for the king's use at Winchester Fair in 1252 (MedInd).

Challenger: Philip *le Chalengur* 1202 AssL. A derivative of ME *chalangen*, OFr *chalonger* 'to challenge', 'an accuser, plaintiff, claimant' (1382 NED).

Challis, Challiss, Challice, Chalice, Challes: Henry *de Scalers, de Scalariis* 1086 DB; Henry *de Shallers* 1153–85 Templars (Herts); Geoffrey *de Chaliers* 1203 FFC; Thomas *de Chalers* 1340 AssC; Thomas *Chales* 1524 SRSf; William *Challice* 1642 PrD. From Eschalles (Pas-de-Calais). *v.* OEByn 87.

Chalmers is a Scottish form of CHAMBERS: *chalmer* 1375 NED. The *mb* was assimilated to *mm;* the *l* was purely graphic, indicating that the preceding *a* was long, and did not affect the pronunciation: Robert *de la Chaumbre* 1296 Black (Lanarks); Alexander *Chaumir* 1475 ib. (Aberdeen); Robert *Chamer* 1472 ib. (Angus); John *Chalmyr* 1555 ib. (Glasgow). We also find *Chalmer* in Suffolk and Worcester in the 13th century: Roger *le Chalmere* 1255 FFSf; Ralph *le Chalmer* 1275 SRWo. This is probably for *Challoner*, with dissimilation of *ln* to *lm* in *Chalner*.

Chaloner: *v.* CHALLENER

Cham: Semar *Chamme* 1181 P (D); Werreis *de Cham, de Cam* 1204, 1207 P (Sf). From Caen (Calvados).

Chamberlain, Chamberlaine, Chamberlayne, Chamberlen, Chamberlin, Champerlen: Henry *le canberlain* Hy 2 DC (L); Geoffrey *le Chaumberleng* 1194 Cur (W); Robert *canberlenc* 1195 FF; Thomas *Chamberleng'* *seruiens Regis* 1196 P (C); Martin *le Chamberleyn* 1232 FFC; Thomas *le Chaumberlyn* 1293 AssSt. OFr *chamberlain, -len, -lanc, -lenc* 'officer charged with the management of the private chambers of a sovereign or nobleman' (a1225 NED).

Chambers: Nicholas *de Chambres* 1219 Cur (Db); Stephen *de la Chambre* 1240 FFEss. ME *chaumbre*, OFr *chambre* 'room (in a house)', 'reception room in a palace' (a1225 NED). Originally official, identical with *Chamberlain*. To pay *in cameram* was to pay into the exchequer of which the *camerarius* was in charge. The surname also applies to those employed there. cf. Nicholas *atte Chambre dictus Clerk* 1351 AssEss. It was later used of a chamber-attendant, 'chamber-man, chambermaid'

Chambley: *v.* CHOLMONDELEY

Champain: Peter *de Champaigne* 1195 P (L). From the French province of Champagne. cf. CHAMPNESS.

Champerlen: *v.* CHAMBERLAIN

Champernowne: Jordan *de Campo Arnulfi* 1172 RBE; Richard *de Cambernof* 1189–99 France; Geoffrey *de Chaumbernun* 1230 P (D). From Cambernon (La Manche).

Champion, Campion: Herbert *campion* 1148 Winton (Ha); Geoffrey *Champiun* 1154–69 NthCh (Nth); Roger *le Campion* 1197 P (O); William *le Champiun* 1220 Cur (Sf). ONFr *campiun, campion*, central OFr *champiun, champion* 'a combatant in the campus or arena', 'one who "does battle" for another in wager of battle', 'a champion' (a1225 NED). In the ordeal by battle, in criminal cases, the accuser and the accused took the field themselves, but in disputes about the ownership of land, the actual parties to the suit were represented by 'champions', in theory their free tenants, but in practice, hired men, professional champions, and very well paid. In 1294 the Dean and Chapter of Southwell incurred a prospective liability of about £750 in modern money in hiring a champion to fight a duel to settle a law-suit about the advowson of a church. A *pugil* or champion was a regular member of the household of more than one medieval bishop, Thomas Cantilupe, Bishop of Hereford (1275–82), paying his champion, Thomas de Bruges, a salary of half a mark a year. *Champion* may sometimes be a corruption of CHAMPAIN (cf. also CHAMPNESS). Champion Wood (PN K 287) owes its name to a family variously called *de Chaumpayne* or *Champeyneys* (1278) and *de Campayne* (1332).

Champness, Champney, Champneys, Champniss: William *le Champeneys* 1219 Cur (Nf); John *Champenay* 1333 FrY; John *Champness* 1520 ArchC 33. AFr *le champeneis* 'the man from Champagne'.

Chance: Robert, Ralph *Chance* 1209 P (Ess), 1310 FFEss. ME *chea(u)nce*, OFr *cheance* in one of its senses, 'fortune, accident, mischance, luck' (c1300 MED). Perhaps used of a gambler. cf. HAZARD.

Chancellor, Cancellor: Reinbald *Canceler* 1066 DB (He); Richard *le Chaunceler* 1214 Cur (Berks). ME, AFr *canceler, chanceler*, 'usher of a lawcourt', 'custodian of records', 'secretary'.

Chandler, Chantler, Candler: Matthew *le Candeler* 1274 RH (Lo); William *le Chandeler* 1285 Ass (Ess). AFr *chandeler*, OFr *chandelier, candelier* 'maker or seller of candles' (1389 MED). Both *Chandler* and *Candler* are used of the same man in 1756 and 1759 in IckworthPR (Sf). cf. William *Candleman* 1268 AD ii (Sf).

Chandos: Roger *de Candos* 1086 DB (Sf); Walter *de Chandos* c1148 EngFeud (He). From Candos (Eure). *v.* ANF.

Chaney: *v.* CHEYNEY
Channer: *v.* CHALLENER
Channon: *v.* CANNON
Chant: *v.* CANT

Chanter: Hugh *le Chantur* 1235 Fees (Lei); Walter *le Chauntur* 1285 FFC. ME, AFr *chantour*, OFr *chanteor* 'enchanter, magician' (c1300 MED), 'singer, chorister, precentor' (a1387 ib.). cf. CANTER.

Chantler: *v.* CHANDLER

Chantrell, Chantrill, Cantrell, Cantrill: Walterus *Canterellus* (*Chanterel*) 1177 P (Sa); Philip *Canterel* 1203 AssSt; Robert *Chanterel* 1221 AssWa; John *Cantrel* 1297 MinAcctCo. Perhaps OFr *chanterelle* 'a small bell', 'the treble in singing, a treble string or bell' (Cotgrave), probably used of a bellman. Or a diminutive of CANTER, CHANTER.

Chantrey, Chantry: John *del Chauntre* 1379 PTY; Thomas *off the Chantery* 1524 SRSf. OFr *chanterie*, originally 'singing or chanting of the mass', then applied successively to the endowment of a priest to sing mass, the priests so endowed, and finally to the chapel where they officiated. The surname might refer to the chantry-priest, but more probably to his servant.

Chaplain, Chaplin, Chapling, Chaperlin, Chaperling, Caplan, Caplen, Caplin, Capelen, Capelin, Capeling, Kaplan, Kaplin: William *Capelein* 1203 Cur (Ha); Thomas *le Chapelyn* 1241 FFC; Nicholas *le Chapelain* 1260 AssC. ONFr *capelain*, OFr *chapelain* 'priest, clergyman, chantry-priest'.

Chapman, Chipman: Hugh *Chapman* 1206 Cur (Y); Alice *Chepman* 1207 P (Db); Thomas *le Chapman* 1266 AssSt; Nicholas *le Chipman* 1320 MESO (So); Henry *le Chupman* 1327 ib. (Ha). OE *cēapmann*, *cȳp(e)mann*, *cēpemann* 'merchant, trader'. *Chapman* is a general form, *Chipman* is West Saxon.

Chapp: Reginald *Chape* 1297 MinAcctCo. OFr *chape* 'a churchman's cope'. cf. Thomas *le chapemaker* 1351 FrY.

Chappel, Chappell, Chappelle, Chappele, Chappill, Chapple, Chapell: John *Chapel* 1202 P (Nf); Richard *de la Chapele* 1296 SRSx; Eymer *atte Chapele* 1312 LLB D; William *del Chapell* 1380 FrY. From residence near or service at a chapel, ME, OFr *chapele*. cf. CAPEL.

Chapper, Cheeper, Chipper: John *Chaper* 1200 Cur (Sr); Geoffrey *Chipere* 1254 ELPN; William *le Chappere* 1327 MESO (Ha); Ralph *Chiper* 1327 SRC. A derivative of OE *cēapian* 'to bargain, trade, buy'. The early examples of *Chiper* are rather from OE *cīepan*, *cīpan* 'to sell'. In both cases, the meaning is 'barterer, trader'.

Charbonneau, Charbonnel: *v.* CARBONELL

Charity: Herluin *Caritet* 1148–54 Bec (Sx); Geoffrey *de Caritate*, *de la Carite* 1185–7 P (Ha); Turstan *Charite* 1195–7 P (Nf); John *de la Charite* 1203 Cur (Ha); Richard *Charite*, *Karite* Hy 3 Gilb (L); Robert *Karitas* 1236 FrLeic. ONFr *caritedh*, *caritet*, later *carité*, OFr *chariet*, *charité*, Lat *cāritātem*, found in ME in various senses: 'almsgiving, hospitality' (a1160 MED), 'man's love for God' (a1225), 'Christian love' (c1200), from which a nickname could easily arise. The local origin is from ONFr *carité*, OFr *charité* 'hospice, refuge'.

Charker: *v.* CARKER

Charles: (i) *Carolus*, *Karolus* 1208 Cur (Sf, Nf); *Karolus* filius Gerberge 1210 Cur (Nf); *Carolus* filius Willelmi 1212 Cur (Nf); Colina, Nicolas *Charles* 1250 Fees (Sf), 1253 Bart; Robert *son of Charles*, Thomas and Joan *Charles* 1274 FFSf. OFr *Charles*, from a latinization *Carolus* of OG

Karl 'man', introduced into England by the Normans, but never common until the Stuart period. (ii) Osbert *Cherle* 1193 P (Wa); Freþesant *Cherl* 1221 ElyA (C); John *Charl* 1296 SRSx. OE *ceorl*, originally 'a freeman of the lowest rank'; in ME 'a tenant in pure villeinage, serf, bondman'; also 'countryman, peasant'. *Charl* would later be inevitably assimilated to the personal name.

Charlton: Jordan, Robert *de Cherleton* 1193 P (Gl), 1230 Cur (Beds); Hugh *de Charleton* 1333 IpmNt; Robert *Charletone* 1372 CorLo. From one or other of the many places of this name.

Charman: William *le Charman* 1293 AssSt; Adam *le Charman* 1310 LLB B. OFr *char*, *car*, 'car, cart' and OE *mann*, 'carter, carrier'. *Carman*, which is not uncommon, may belong here as well as to CARMAN, to which occasional early examples of *Charman* belong: Robert *Chareman* (*Careman*) 1183 P (Wa).

Charnell: Gilbert *de Charneles* 1170–5 DC (Lei); Hugh *de Charnell* 1246 FFC; Maud *de Cimiterio* 14th Rad (C). ME, OFr *charnel*, 'burial-place, mortuary chapel, cemetery', denoting one in charge of this.

Charsley, Chartesley, Cheasley: Geoffrey *de Chardesle* 1279 RH (O). From Chearsley (Bucks).

Chart: Richard *de Chert* c1200 ArchC vi; John *de la Chert* 1241 PN Sr 306; Ralph *Atte Chert* 1290 MELS. From residence near a rough common (OE *cert*, *ceart*), as at Chart (Kent, Surrey) or Churt (Surrey).

Charter: *v.* CARTER

Charteris, Charters, Chartres, Chatteris, Chatters: (i) Alcher *de Chartris* 1179 P (Sx); Robert *de Chartres* 1296 (Black); James *Charterhouse* 1556 ib.; John *Charters* 1790 ib. From Chartres (Eure-et-Loire). (ii) Ralph *de Chateriz* 1259 FFC; Alan *de Chartres*, *de Chartris* 1279 RH (Hu), 1293 Ipm (Hu); John *Charteres* 1417 FFHu; John *Chateryse* 1445 NorwW. From Chatteris (Cambs), earlier *Chateriz*, *Chatriz* 1086, *Chartriz* 1200 (PN C 247–8). cf. Abbatissa *de Charters* 1279 RH (Hu).

Chase, Chace: Robert *Chace* 1327 SR (Ess); John *Chase* 1393 FrY. Probably metonymic for *chaser*, from OFr *chaceur*, *chaceour* 'hunter'. cf. Stephen *le Chacur* 1204 Cur (Nt), Walter *Chacere* 1327 SRSf.

Chasey: Simon *de Caucy* 1205 Cur (L); Geoffrey *de Chausi* 1206 Cur (O). From Chaussy (Seine-et-Oise) which may also have become CAUSEY. cf. Chazey Fm in Mapledurham (Oxon), from Walter *de Chauseia* c1180. Chazey Wood is *Causies Wood* 1658 (PN O 60).

Chasteney, Chasney, Chastney: *v.* CHEYNEY

Chaster: *v.* CHESTER

Chaston: Adam *Chasteyn*, Robert *Chasten* 1279 RH (C); John *Chasteyn* 1327 SRSf. ME *chastein*, OFr *chastaigne* 'chestnut-tree'. 'Dweller by the chestnut-tree', originally *atte chastein*.

Chatelain: *v.* CASTELLAN

Chater: *v.* CATER

Chatt: *v.* CATT

Chatteris, Chatters: *v.* CHARTERIS

Chatto: William *de Chetue* c1198–1214 Black; Alexander *de Chatthou* c1225 ib.; Eustace *of Chattow* 1358 ib. From the lands of Chatto (Roxburgh).

Chattock: *v.* CHADWICK

Chaucer, Chauser: Ralph *le Chaucer* 1220 Cur (Lo); Robert *le Chauser* 1256 AssNb. OFr *chaucier* 'maker of *chausses*', from OFr *chauces* 'clothing for the legs, breeches, pantaloons, hose'. In 1484 these were 'chauces of yron or legge harneys' (NED), but ME *chawce* was a general term for anything worn on the feet, boots, shoes, etc. As Baldwin *le Chaucer* (1307 LLB B) was of Cordwanerstrete, the early chaucer was probably a worker in leather, a maker of leather breeches, boots, etc.

Chaumont: Hugo *de Chaumont* 1200 P (Y). From Chaumont (Orne).

Chave: *v.* CHAFF

Chawner: *v.* CHALLENER

Chaytor: *v.* CATER

Cheal, Cheale, Cheales, Cheel: (i) Gilbert *de Chele*(s) 1275 RH (L). From Cheal (Lincs). (ii) William, Robert *Chele* 1275 SRWo, 1327 SRSx. OE *cele, ciele* (sb.) 'cold, coldness', ME *chile, chele* 'cold (of the weather), frost'. cf. FROST.

Cheasley: *v.* CHARSLEY

Cheater, Chetter: John *Chetour* 1327 SRSf. ME *chetour*, an aphetic form of *eschetour* 'escheator, an officer appointed to look after the king's escheats' (c1330 MED).

Checker, Chequer: Laurence *de le Eschekere* 1256 *Ass* (Ha); Roger *de la Checker* 1279 RH (C); Gilbert *le Cheker* 1316 Wak (Y); Roger *Cheker*, son of Christopher *Atcheker* 1508 ArchC 40. ME *cheker*, an aphetic form of ME, AFr *escheker*, originally a chess-board, later the table which gave name to the king's exchequer; a table for accounts; the Court of Exchequer. Laurence *de Scaccario* (1279 RH), who has left his name in Chequers (Bucks), was, no doubt, one of the leading officials of the Exchequer. As a surname, the name probably meant, as a rule, a clerk in the exchequer.

Cheek, Cheeke, Cheke: Æluric *Chec* c1095 Bury (Sf); Adam, Walter *Cheke* 1202 P (W), 1243 AssSo. OE *cēace, cēce* 'jaw-bone', a nickname for one with a prominent jaw. *v.* CHICK.

Cheel: *v.* CHEAL

Cheeld: *v.* CHILD

Cheese, Chiese: Ailwin *chese* Hy 2 Bart (Lo); Willelmus *cum frumento* 1176 P (Y); John *Chese*, William *Chuse* 1279 RH (Hu, O); Robert *Chuse*, Michael *Chouse* 1332 SRSx. OE *cēse* (Anglian), WSaxon *cȳse* 'cheese', used of a maker or seller of cheese. cf. John de Hugat, *cheser* 1316 FrY, Walter *le cheser* 1366 AD i (He).

Cheeseman, Cheasman, Cheesman, Cheseman, Chesman, Chessman, Chiesman, Chisman, Chismon: Henry *le Cheseman* 1260 AssC; William *le Chesman* 1311 Battle (Sx); Thomas *Chesman, le Chusman* 1327 SRSx; Adam *le Chisman*, Alice *Chisman* 1327 SRSo. 'Maker or seller of cheese.' cf. Robert

le Chesemaker 1275 RH (L), Baldwin *le Chesemangere* 1186 P (K).

Cheeseright, Cheesewright, Cheeswright, Cheswright, Chesswright: Richard *Chesewricte* 1228 Pat (L); Augustin *le Chesewryghte* 1293 MESO (Y); John *Cheswright* 1478 LLB L; Margaret *Chestwright* 1795 SfPR. OE *cȳswyrhte* (f) 'cheesemaker', perhaps also OE **cēsewyrhta* (m).

Cheetham, Cheetam: Geoffrey *de Chetham* 1246 AssLa, 13th WhC; Thomas *de Cheteham* 1394 IpmLa. From Cheetham (Lancs).

Cheever, Cheevers, Chevers, Chivers: William *Cheure, Capra* 1086 DB (D, W); Hamelin *Chieure* 1186 P (L); Nicholas *le Chiuer* 1327 SRSx. AFr *chivere, chevre*, OFr *chievre*, Lat *capra* 'she-goat' (1491 NED), probably denoting agility.

Cheke: *v.* CHEEK

Chene, Cheney: *v.* CHEYNEY

Chequer: *v.* CHECKER

Cherrett, Cherritt: A Suffolk pronunciation of CHEESERIGHT: Nicholas and Jane *Cheswright, Cherit, Cheritt* 1655, 1656, 1660 DenhamPR (Sf), Nicholas *Cherit* 1674 HTSf.

Cherry, Cherriman, Cherryman: Robert *Chyry* 1284 AssLa; Hugh *Chirie*, Richard *Chery* 1524 SRSf. ME *chirie, cherye* 'cherry'. Probably 'grower or seller of cherries'. cf. PERRY, PERRIMAN.

Chesham, Chessam, Chessum: Burchard *de Cestresham* 1200 P (Bk); William *de Chesham* 1297 MinAcctCo (W); William *Chessam* 1525 SRSx; John *Chessum* 1728 Bardsley. From Chesham (Bucks), *Cestreham* DB, or Chestham Park in Henfield (Sussex), *Chesham* 1657.

Cheshire, Chesher, Cheshir, Chesshire, Chesshyre, Chesser, Chessor: Richard *de Cestersir'* 1219 AssY; Agnes *Chessyr* 1442 GildY; Nicholas *Chesshyre* 1575 SfPR. From Cheshire.

Chesnay, Chesney: *v.* CHEYNEY

Chessex: *v.* CHISWICK

Chessman: *v.* CHEESEMAN

Chester, Chesters, Chaster: Richard *de Cestre* 1200 P (L); John, William *de Chester* 1332 SRWa; John *Chestre* 1366–7 FFWa; Barbara *Chesters* 1611 RothwellPR (Y). Usually from Chester (Ches), but occasionally from Little Chester (Derby), Chester le Street (Durham), or Chesters (Northumb).

Chesterton: Bruning *de Cestretona* 1086 InqEl (C); Robert *de Chesterton'* 1227 Cur (O); Edward *Chestreton* 1416–17 FFWa. From Chesterton (Cambs, Glos, Hunts, Oxon, Staffs, Warwicks).

Chestney: *v.* CHEYNEY

Cheswick: *v.* CHISWICK

Chetter: *v.* CHEATER

Cheverall, Cheverell, Cheverill, Chiverall, Chiverrell, Chivrall: (i) William *Cheuerel*(*l*) 1195–6 P (Berks); Tristram *le Cheverer, le Cheverell* 1278, 1289 LLB A, *le Cheverel*(*l*)*er* 1291–2 ib. C. ME *chevrelle*, OFr *chevrele, chevrelle* 'kid' (a1400 NED), but in ME always used in the sense of the full *cheverel-leather* 'kid-leather'. The earliest example may be a nickname from the kid, but *cheverel* was certainly sometimes used for *cheverell-*

er, 'a maker or seller of kid-leather goods'. cf. Ralph *le Cheverelmongere* 1310 LLB B. (ii) Simon *de Chiverell'* 1200 Cur (W); John *Chiverel* 1275 RH (W). From Great or Little Cheverell (Wilts).

Chevers: *v.* CHEEVER

Cheverton, Chiverton: Ralph *de Chevereston* 1275 RH (D). From Chiverstone Fm in Kenton (Devon).

Chevins, Chevis: Margaret *Chyuin* 1295 Barnwell (C); Simon *Cheuyn* 1327 SRC. OFr *chevesne*, Fr *chevin*, a fish, the chub (c1450 NED). 'The cheuyn is a stately fish' (1496). 'Chevins and Millers thumbs are a kind of jolt-headed Gudgeons' (1655).

Chew, Chue: (i) Randal *de Chiw* 1201 AssSo. From Chew (Som). (ii) Geoffrey *Chiue* 1203 Cur (C). OE *cīo, cēo* (not found in ME), a bird of the crow family, a name applied to all the smaller chattering species, especially the jackdaw.

Cheyney, Cheyne, Chainey, Chaney, Cheeney, Chene, Cheney, Chasney, Chasteney, Chastney, Chesnay, Chesney, Chestney: Radulfus *de Caisned* 1086 DB (Sx); Hugh *de Chaisnei, de Cheisnei* 1140, 1166 Eynsham (O); Robert *de Cheinnei* a1183 DC (L); Hugh *de Chennei* 12th ib.; William *de Chesnei* 1205 Cur (L); Bartholomew *del Chennay* 1212 Fees (Sr); William *de Cheny* 1235 Fees (Sf); Roger *del Chesne* 1236 FFEss; Alexander *de Cheyny* 1242 Fees (Beds); Alexander *de Cheyne* 1296 SRSx; John *de Chene* 1317 AssK. The DB under-tenant came from Le Quesnay (Seine-Inférieure). *v.* ANF. Others may have come from Quesnay (Calvados, La Manche) or Quesnay-Guesnon (Calvados). All derive ultimately from MedLat *casnetum* (OFr *chesnai*) 'oak-grove' and the surname may also denote an immigrant from France who lived by an oak-grove or came from a place Chenay, Chenoy, or Chesnoy.

Chichester: James *de Cicestrie* 1225 Cur (Sx); Walter *de Chichestre* 1301 CorLo; William *Chichestre* 1382 AssLa. From Chichester (Sussex).

Chick: Richard *Chike* 1198 P (Do); Richard *le Chike* 1317 AssK. ME *chike* 'chicken' (c1320 NED), used as a term of endearment. *Chike* occasionally becomes *Cheke*, which would become CHEEK: William *Chike, Cheke* 1278 PN K 269. Cheek's Fm in Bentley (Hants), *Cheakes* c1550 *Req*, owes its name to William *Chike* (1333 *SR*).

Chicken: Amindus, Roger *Chiken* 1210, 1212 Cur (Sf, Berks). OE *cicen* 'chicken'. cf. Alexander *Chikehed* 1301 SRY, John *Chykenmouth* 1327 Pinchbeck (Sf).

Chiese: *v.* CHEESE

Child, Childe, Childs, Chiles, Chill, Chilles, Cheeld: (i) Ægelmerus *Cyld*, Æluricus *Cyld*, quod intelligitur *puer* c975 LibEl (Herts); Aluric *Cild, Cilt* 1066 DB (Ess, C); Rodbertus *Puer* 1086 DB (Do); Gode *Cild* c1095 Bury (Sf); Iuinus *child* 1148 Winton (Ha); Willelmus *Infans* 1159 P (Ess); Roger *le Child* 1204 Cur (Berks). OE *cild* 'child'. In the earliest examples it probably denotes one comparable in status to the drengs of the northern Danelaw, the sergeants of Norman times.

Ekwall has shown that Robert *Child* (1202 ELPN) may have been called by the pet-name of *Child* because he was the youngest child or a minor at the time of his parents' death. cf. *puer* and *Infans* supra. In the 13th and 14th centuries *child* appears to have been applied to a young noble awaiting knighthood (MED). It may also mean 'childish, immature' (c1200 MED), 'a page attendant' (1382 ib.). (ii) Peter *de la Child* 1262 ArchC iii; Richard *Attechilde* 1267 FFK. From residence near a spring, OE *celde*.

Childerhouse, Childers: Hemericus *de Childerhus* 1230 Cl (Nf); William *atte Childerhous* 1275 RH (Nf); Philip *del Childirhus* 1295 AssCh; John *Chyldirhous, Childurous* 1415, 1450 AD iv, v (Sf); Thomas *Childers* 1675 Shef. From an unrecorded OE **cildra-hūs* 'children's house, orphanage'. cf. *childermas* and CHILDREN.

Children: John *atte Children* 1267 Pat (K); Daniel *Chyltren, de Chiltren* 1298, 1300 LoCt; Peter *ate Children* 1317 AssK; Thomas *Children* 1477 RochW; Robert *Achildren* 1560 ib. Identical in formation and meaning with CHILDERHOUSE, from an unrecorded OE **cildra-ærn* 'children's house, orphanage'.

Chiles, Chill: *v.* CHILD

Chillman, Chilman: (i) *Chilmannus* Lenner, *Chilleman* Dilly 1327 SRC; Nicholas *Childman* 1239 FFC; William *Childeman* 1253 AssSt; William *le Childesman* 1276 AssSo; Walter *Chileman* 1311 ColchCt. *Childesman* is 'the servant or attendant of the young noble'. cf. CHILD. *Childman* may have the same meaning, or it may be from an unrecorded OE personal name **Cildmann*, one of the late OE personal names compounded with *-mann*. Nicholas *Childman* was the son of *Childman* 1279 RH (C). (ii) William, Henry *Chilemound(e)* 1327 SRSo; John *Chylemonde* ib.; Agnes *Chilmon* 1580 Bardsley. This must be OE *Cēolmund*, 'shipguardian', common in the 8th and 9th centuries and recorded once later, c1050, in Herts. It must have continued in use after the Conquest, at least in Somerset. For *-man* from *-mund*, cf. OSMAN.

Chilton: William *de Chilton* 1195 P (Nb). A common surname from one of the many places named Chilton. Editha *de Childton', de Childhamton'* 1297 MinAcctCo (W) came from Chilhampton (Wilts), a development of the name not hitherto noted.

Chin, Chinn: Stephen *Chinne* 1243 AssSo; John *Chynne* 1276 RH (Hu). OE *cin* 'chin'. The nickname may be for one with a prominent or long chin or for one with a beard. cf. 'Swor bi his chinne þat he wuste Merlin' (c1205 NED); 'Forked fair þe chine he bare' (a1300 ib.).

Chine: Richard *Chyne* 1275 SRWo; Henry *de Chine* 1279 RH (C); Ryner *Attechine* 1298 LLB B. OE *cinu* 'fissure, cleft, chasm'; in Hants 'a deep narrow ravine'. 'Dweller by the ravine.'

Chippendale, Chippindale, Chippindall: Dyke *de Chipendale* 1246 AssLa; Richard *Chipyndale* 1379 PTY; John *Chippendale* 1434 FrY. From Chippingdale (Lancs).

Chipper: v. CHAPPER

Chipping: William *Chipping* 1178 P (Wa); Adam *atte Chepingg* 1327 *SR* (Ess). 'Dweller near, or trader in the market', OE *cēping, cī(e)ping*.

Chisman, Chismon: v. CHEESEMAN

Chiswick, Chissick, Cheswick, Chessex: Henry *Chesewic* 1170-87 AD i (Lo); John *de Cheswyk* 1275 RH (Ess). From Chiswick (Essex, Middlesex) or Cheswick (Northumb), all 'cheese-farm'.

Chittleburg, Chittleburgh: (i) Matthew *de Chytelesber'* 1275 RH (D). From Chittleburn (Devon), where *-burn* is, as not uncommonly, for earlier *-burgh*. (ii) Matthew *Chettleborowe* 1653 EA (NS) ii (Sf); Thomas *Chittleborough*, Henry *Chetleburgh*, Robert *Chickleborowe* 1674 HTSf. From Kettleburgh (Suffolk), *Chetelbiria, Kettleberga* DB, 'Ketil's hill' or possibly a Scandinavianized form of an OE **cetel-beorg* 'hill by a narrow valley' (DEPN). The persistence of the *Ch-* in the local pronunciation suggests that the latter is the correct etymology.

Chittock: Roger, Henry *Chittok* 1279 RH (Hu), 1327 SRSf. *Chitt-ok*, a diminutive of ME *chitte* 'young of a beast, cub, kitten' (a1382 MED).

Chiverrell: v. CHEVERALL

Chivers: v. CHEEVER

Chiverton: v. CHEVERTON

Cholmondeley, Cholmeley, Chumley, Chumbley, Chambley: Hugh *de Chelmundeleg'* 1288 AssCh; Thomas *Cholmeley* 1567 Bardsley; William *Chombley* 1666 ib.; Susanna *Chumbly* 1689 ib.; John *Chumley* 1726 ib. From Cholmondeley (Ches). Roger *Chomley* (1493 GildY) was a son of Richard *Chamley* (1502 ib.) or Sir Richard *Cholmley* (Ed.).

Chopin, Choppen, Choppin, Chopping: Walter *Chopin* 1219 Cur (D); Henry *Choppin* 1280 AssSo. OFr *chopine*, an old measure (1275 NED). '*Chopine* a chopine; or the Parisien halfe pint; almost as big as our whole one' (Cotgrave). cf. Fr *chopiner* 'to tipple'. A nickname for a tippler.

Crichton: v. CRICHTON

Chrippes, Chrisp: v. CRISP

Chrispin: v. CRISPIN

Christal: v. CHRYSTAL

Christian: *Christiana* 1154 Bury (Sf), 12th DC (L); *Cristianus* 1201 Cur (Berks); Thomas *filius Cristian* 1228 FFEss; Robert *Crestien* 1163-9 Miller (C); Philip *Cristian* temp. John HPD (Ess). *Cristian*, Lat *Christianus*, was common in Brittany. In England the masculine name was less frequent than the feminine, which was also common as *Cristina*, the native form. v. CHRISTIN.

Christie, Christey, Christy: Thomas *Crysty* 1412 FFY; John *Chrysty* 1457 Black (Aberdeen). A Scottish and Northern English pet-form of *Christian* or *Christine*. cf. *Cristine* or *Cristy de Carvan(t)* 1296 Black.

Christin, Christine: *Cristina* 1219 AssY; *Cristina de Burlingeham* 1221 AssGl; Peter *Cristyn* 1296 SRSx; Thomas *Crystyn* 1332 SRSt. *Cristin* is the English form (from OE *cristen* 'christian') of *Cristiana*. v. CHRISTIAN.

Christison: John *Cristenesone* 1312 FFSf; Robert *Cristianson* 1324 Wak (Y); Henry *Cristeson* 1412 Black (Stirling); Alexander *Cristisone* 1446 ib.; John *Cristerson* 1514 FrY. 'Son of Christian or Christine'.

Christman: William *Cristeman'* 1202 Cur (Ha); Walter *Cristesmon* 1275 SRWo. 'Servant of Christ', probably a pet-form of *Christian, Christine* or *Christopher*. cf. John *Crist* 1309 SRBeds.

Christmas, Chrismas: Ralph *Cristemesse* 1185 RotDom (Ess); Roger *Cristemasse* 1191 P (Sf); Richard *Cristesmesse* 1308 LLB C. A frequent surname for one born at Christmas. cf. Matilda *Candelmes* 1379 PTY.

Christopher, Christophers: *Christoforus* 1209 P (Hu); *Cristoferus* Murdac 1221 AssWa; Roger *Cristofore* 1379 PTY; Laurence *Cristofore* 1396 AssWa. Gk Χριστοφόρος, Lat *Christopherus* 'Christbearing'. The christian name does not appear to have been common and examples of the surname are late. The earliest noted denotes residence: Thomas *Cristofre* (1319 SRLo), son of William *de Sancto cristoforo* (1292 ib.), also called William *Cristofre* (1317 Husting), who left his son a tenement in St Christopher (St Christopher le Stocks, London).

Christopherson: John *Cristovirson* 1514 GildY. 'Son of Christopher.'

Christy: v. CHRISTIE

Chrystal, Chrystall, Christal, Crystal, Crystall, Crystol, Kristall: *Cristall* Knowis 1549 Black; *Christall* Murray 1561 ib.; William *Cristole* 1470 ib.; John *Cristall* 1491 ib. A Scots diminutive of *Christopher*.

Chubb: Richard, Gilbert *Chubbe* 1180 P (D), 1202 AssL; William *Chubbe, Chuppe* 1230 P (Lo). ME *chubbe*, a fish, 'chub' (c1450 MED), was also used of a 'lazy spiritless fellow; a rustic, simpleton; dolt, fool' (1558), whilst Bailey has '*Chub*, a Jolthead, a great-headed, full-cheeked Fellow', a description reminiscent of that of the chevin, another name for the chub. v. CHEVINS. Thus the nickname may have meant either 'short and thick, dumpy like a chub' or 'of the nature of a chub, dull and clownish'.

Chuck: v. SUCH

Chue: v. CHEW

Chum(b)ley: v. CHOLMONDELEY

Church: Thomas *Attechirche* 1275 SRWo; Henry *atte Churche* 1296 SRSx; Henry *of the Chirche* 1368 FrY. Usually 'dweller near the church', but *of the Chirche* suggests an official, verger, sexton, etc., rather than residence near the church. John *Atte-cherch*, rector of Metton, Norfolk, in 1338 (Bardsley), can hardly have owed his surname to his residence. As rector, his attribute would have been *Parson*. *Attecherch* is here probably a hereditary surname.

Churchard, Churchyard: John *atte Chircheyerde* 1298 AssSt; Henry *del Churcheyard* 1332 SRWa. This can hardly mean 'dweller by the churchyard'. The natural expression would be 'at the church'. It probably denotes one responsible for the upkeep of the churchyard. Richard *de la Chirchard* (1291 MELS) is identical with Richard *atte Church* (1289 ib.), both surnames being occupational. Similarly, Reginald *atte Churchedoor* (1300 Bardsley) was the church door-keeper.

Churchers, Churches, Churchouse, Churchus: Iuo *de Cherchous* 1327 SRSf; William *del Chyrchehous* 1332 SRSt. The church-house was formerly a house adjoining the church where church-ales, etc., were held, a parish-room. Again probably occupational, 'care-taker of the parish-room', though he may also have lived there.

Churchill: John *de Chirchehul* 1221 AssWa; Matilda *de Chirchull'* 1275 SRWo. From Churchill (Devon, Som, Worcs, Warwicks). The name may also denote residence on the church-hill. William *atte Churchull'* 1333 MELS (So) lived near the church-stile and was also called William *Churchestyele* (1327 ib.).

Churchman: Ælfled *Cerceman* c1095 Bury (Sf); Ralph *Chircheman* 1259 RamsCt (Hu); Ouse *le Chercheman* 1279 RH (C); John *Churcheman* 1307 RamsCt (Hu). OE *cyriceman* 'custodian or keeper of a church'. The meanings 'ecclesiastic, clergyman' (a1400 MED) and 'churchwarden' (1523) are much later.

Churchward: Oscetel *Circwærd* 949 BCS 882 (Gl); Ælfnoð *Cyrceweard* 11th OEByn; William *le Chirchewart* 1275 SRWo. OE *ciricweard* 'custodian of a church (building)'.

Churchyard: *v.* CHURCHARD

Circuitt, Cirket, Serkitt, Sirkett, Surkett: John *de Suthcote* 1297 MinAcctCo (Herts). The rare Bedfordshire *Cirket*, formerly *Surcot, Surcoate*, etc., derives from Southcott in Linslade (Bk), *Surcote* 1826, now pronounced *Cirket*, or from a lost Southcott in Stone (*Sircotes* 1511 PN Bk 80, 165). The Berkshire Southcot occurs as *Circuit* c1728 (NQ 196). The surname may also be a nickname from the surcoat: John *Surcote* 1327 SRSf.

Clack: *Clac* de Fugelburne c975 LibEl (C); Godwinus *Clec* 1086 DB (W); Godricius *Clacca* 1169 P (Berks); Simon *Clac* 1327 SRSo. OE *Clacc* or ODa *Klak* surviving as *Clak* in Lincolnshire temp. Hy 2 (Gilb), 1193 FF (L). The surname must sometimes be metonymic for *Clacker*: Walter *le Clackere* Ed 1 Malmesbury, Roger *Clackere* c1250 AD iv (W). This may be a nickname 'chatterer', from ME *clacken* (a1250 MED), or for a miller, from the clack or clatter of his mill, or for a bell-ringer, though these senses are not recorded until much later. cf. William *Clacyere* 'belleyetere' (c1425 Building 327), bell-founder.

Clackett, Claget, Claggitt: *v.* CLAYGATE

Clague: *MacLiag* 1014, *Gilla Macliag* 1173, *MacClewage* 1511, *Cloage* 1601, *Claige* 1622, *Clague* 1655 Moore. Ir and Manx *MacLiaigh* 'son of the leech' (*liagh*).

Clanfield: Richard *de Clanefeld* 1279 RH (O). From Clanfield (Hants). *v.* GLANDFIELD.

Clapham: Alexander *de Clapehamme* 1204 AssY; William *de Clapham* 1331 FFY; Richard *Clapham* 1416–17 IpmNt. From Clapham (Beds, Surrey, Sussex, WRYorks).

Clapp: Simon *Clapp'*, *Cloppe* 1206 Cur (O); Adam, Godard, William *le Clop* 1219 AssY, 1222 Cur (C), 1227 AssBeds; Laurence *Clappe* 1230 P (O); John *Clap* 1327 SR (Ess). There is no evidence for the post-Conquest use of OE *Clappa* which has been suggested as the source of this name. *le Clop* is a nickname, identical with OE **clop* 'lump, hillock, hill' which, Ekwall has shown, is found in the common place-names Clapham, Clapton and Clopton. In some of these, *Clop-* had become *Clap-* early in the 13th century. The surname means 'bulky, heavily-built'.

Clapper: John *atte Clapere* 1332 SRSx. 'Dweller by the clapper bridge', a rough or natural bridge across a stream. Matilda *de la Claper'* (1330 PN D 359) lived at Clapper Bridge. Ingram *Clapere* 1267 Pat may be an early example with loss of the preposition, or a nickname from ME *clappe* 'chatter' (c1230 MED), 'chatterer'.

Clapton: Turstan *de Cloptuna* 1154 Bury; Alan *de Clapeton* c1185–1210 YCh; Robert *de Cloptun* 1228 FFEss; Roger *de Clapton* 1298 AssL. From Clapton (Berks, Cambs, Glos, Middlesex, Northants, Som), or Clopton (Glos, Suffolk, Warwicks, Worcs), both names having OE *clop* 'rock, hill' as the first element.

Clarabut: *v.* CLARINGBOLD

Clarage, Claridge: Robert *de Claurugge* 1327 SRSx; John *Claridge* 1665 HTO. From Clearhedge Wood in Waldron (Sussex), *Clavregge* 1288, *Claregge* 1429.

Clare: (i) *Clara* 1210 Cur (Hu); Robertus *filius Clarae* 1240, 1255 Rams (Nf, Hu); Goditha, Richard *Clare* 1317 AssK, 1327 SRSo. Fr *Claire*, Lat *Clara*, 'bright, fair', a woman's name, common, probably, owing to the popularity of St Clare of Assisi. (ii) Richard *de Clara* 1086 DB (Sf). From Clare (Suffolk). (iii) Simon *le Clayere* 1279 RH (C); Richard *le Cleyere* 1305 Pinchbeck (Sf). A derivative of OE *clæg* 'clay'. The clayer was engaged in plastering with mud in wattle and daub work, called *torching* in 1278, *plastering* in 1368 and *claying* in 1486 (Building 189).

Clarges: Richard (*le*) *Clergis* 1279 RH (Beds); Nicholas, Richard *Clergys* 1309 SRBeds. In ME *clergy* was used as a singular, with a plural *clergis* 'clergymen'. cf. A clerge, *clerus, clerimonia* Cath-Angl. The surname is probably a parallel to *Parsons* and *Vickers*, 'the clergyman's servant'.

Claringbold, Claringbould, Claringbull, Clarabut: *Clarumbald medicus* a1116 ELPN; *Clarebaldus* c1150 DC (L); *Clarenbaldus pincerna* 1177 P (Sf); *Clerebaud del Aune* 1200 Cur (Sf); Roger *Clerenbald* 1223 FFSf; Nicholas *Clarebold* 1274 AD i (Ha); William *Cleribaud* 1275 RH (K); John *Claringbold* 1485 KentW; Pascall *Clarebote* 1565 Bardsley; Elizabeth *Clarabutt, Claringbull* 1735–6 Bardsley. OFr *Clarembald, Clarebald, Clarembaut*, from OG *Clarembald*, a hybrid from Lat *clarus* 'famous' and OG *-bald* 'bold'.

Claris: *Claricia* 1150–60 DC (L); *Clericia* 1175–

86 Holme (Nf); *Clarice* (nom.) 1191 P (Mx); Rogerus *Claritia* Hy 3 Colch (Sf); Walter *Clarice* 1275 SRWo; Richard *Clarisse* 1279 RH (O). *Clarice*, a well-established woman's name. It has been regarded as a derivative of *Clara*, but the formation is difficult. It may be from an abstract noun *claritia*, based on Lat *clarus* 'bright, shining', used as a personal name on the analogy of *Lettice*, from *laetitia* 'joy, gladness'.

Clark, Clarke, Clerk, Clerke: Richerius *clericus* 1086 DB (Ha); Willelm *ðe Clerec* c1100 OEByn (So); Reginald *Clerc* 1205 Cur (R); John *le Clerk* 1272 Gilb (L). OE *clerec*, *clerc* (Lat *clericus*), OFr *clerc* 'clerk'. The original sense was 'a man in a religious order, cleric, clergyman'. As all writing and secretarial work in the Middle Ages was done by the clergy, the term came to mean 'scholar, secretary, recorder or penman'. As a surname, it was particularly common for one who had taken only minor orders. *Clerk(e)* is now rare.

Clarkson: Alan *le Clerkissone* 1306 FFSf; William *Clerksone* 1332 SRCu; Ralph *Clarkson* 1491 GildY. 'Son of the clerk.' *v.* CLARSON.

Clarson: (i) Johannes *filius Clarae* 1240 Rams (Nf); John *Clareson* 1326 Wak (Y). 'Son of *Clara*'. (ii) William *Clariceson* 1327 SRSo; Thomas *Cleryson* 1467 Shef. 'Son of *Clarice*.' (iii) Thomas *Clerson* 1431 FrY; John *Clarson* 1553 RothwellPR (Y); Margaret *Clarsome* wife of Francis *Clarsom* 1588 ShotleyPR (Sf); Francis *Clarkson* husband of Margaret *Clarkson* 1608 ib. Identical with CLARKSON.

Clarvis: Michael *de Clervaus, de Clereuals* 1208 FFHu, 1209 P (Hu); John *Clervaus* 1320 FFHu; Margaret *Clarevas* 1446 GildY; Henry *Clerves* 1524 SRSf. From Clairvaux (Aube, Jura).

Clater: John *Clatere* 1327 SRWo. ME *clater* 'noisy talk, gabble', metonymic for *claterer* 'babbler, tattler' (c1390 MED).

Clay, Claye: Ralph *de Clai* 1172 P (Sf); Reginald *de la Claie* 1200 P (Ess); William *Cley* 1221 ElyA (C); Richard *atte Cley* 1296 SRSx; Nicholas *del Clay* 1302 SRY. 'Dweller on the clay' (OE *clæg*). As this would not be distinctive in a county like Essex, the surname may sometimes be occupational, for a worker in a claypit. *v.* CLAYMAN, CLARE.

Claygate, Clackett, Claget, Claggitt, Cleggett: Roger *de la Claigate* 1198 FFK; Robert *de Cleygate* 1215 Wenlok; Gilbert *atte Claygate* 1317 AssK; Joane *Cleget* wife of William *Clegget* 1660 ArchC xxx. From Claygate (Surrey), or from some similarly named minor place, cf. Claygate Farm in Buxted (Sussex), Clacket in Tabsfield (Surrey), Clackett's Place in Ryarsh (Kent), etc.

Clayman: John, Thomas *Clayman* 1327 *SR* (Ess), 1365 AD ii (Mx). 'One who prepares clay for use in brickmaking' (NED). PromptParv equates *cleymann* with *dauber*. *v.* CLAY, CLARE.

Clayton: Jordan *de Claiton* a1191 YCh; Walter *de Clayton* 1332 SRSx; Richard *Clayton* 1452 FFEss. From Clayton (Lancs, Staffs, Sussex, WRYorks).

Clear, Cleare, Clere: (i) Gilbert *filius Cler'* 1279 RH (O); William, Geoffrey *Clere* 1279 RH (Hu), 1296 SRSx. *Clere* was the French popular form of *Clare*. *v.* CLARE. (ii) Ralph *de Clere* 1319 SRLo. From Clere (Hants).

Cleatherow: *v.* CLITHEROE

Cleave: *v.* CLIFF

Cleaver, Cleever: Richard, John *le Cleuar* 1332 SRSx. A derivative of OE *clēofan* 'to cleave, split', one who split boards with wedges instead of sawing. These were called *clouenbord* 1345, *clofbord* temp. Edward III (Building 243). The surname may also mean 'dweller by the cliff'. *v.* CLIFF.

Clee: (i) William *de Clee* 1359 LLB G; John *Clee*, Richard *Cle* 1327 SRSf. From Clee (Lincs, Salop), from OE *clǣg*. The Suffolk name is for *atte cley*. (ii) John *atte Cleo* 1332 SRWo; William *atte Clee* 1349 MELS (Wo). 'Dweller by the river-fork or fork in a road', from OE (Anglian) *cleo* 'claw, cloven hoof'. *v.* MELS.

Cleef: *v.* CLIFF

Cleever: *v.* CLEAVER

Cleft: *v.* CLIFF

Cleggett: *v.* CLAYGATE

Clem, Clemm, Clemans, Clemence, Clemens, Clement, Clements, Clemons, Clemas, Climance, Climas, Clemmans, Clemmens: *Clemens* monachus 1153–68 Holme (Nf); *Clementia* 1162 DC (L); *Clemencia* 1210 Cur (Herts); *Clemens* filius *Clementis* 1212 Cur (Ess); William, Richard *Clement* 1153 Templars (O), 1202 AssL; Robertus *Clemens* 1155 Templars (O); William *Clement, Climent* 1275 RH (Nf); Richard *Clemence* 1279 RH (Hu); Robert *Clymant* 1327 SRSx. Fr *Clement*, Lat *Clemens* 'mild, merciful', the name of several popes, was popular in England from the middle of the 12th century and the corresponding woman's name *Clemence*, Lat *Clementia* 'mildness' from about 1200. Both have contributed to the surnames. *Clem* is a pet-form found in 1273 (RH). *Clim* is not much later: John *Climme* 1327 SRC. *v.* also CLEMO, CLEMMEY.

Clementson, Cleminson, Clemerson, Clemetson, Clempson, Clemson, Climenson, Climpson: Peter *Clementson* 1379 PTY; John *Clementesson* 1392 FrY; Roger *Clempson* Eliz Bardsley; John *Clympson* 1577 ib. 'Son of *Clement*.'

Clemmey, Climie: *Clemie* Croser 1581 Bardsley (Cu); George *Clemy* 1553 Black (Glasgow); William *Climay* 1652 ib. A Scottish pet-name for *Clement*.

Clemo, Clemow, Clemmow, Climo, Clyma, Clymo: John *Clemmowe* 1544 Bardsley; Morice *Clymow* 1630 DWills (Co); Ots *Clemow* 1634 ib. A Cornish form of *Clement*.

Clench, Clinch: Hugh *Clinche* 1223 Cur (L); Richard, Robert *Clench(e)* 1275 RH (Sf), 1327 SRSf; John *de la Clenche* 1275 RH (W); Isabell *atte Clenche* 1332 SRSx. 'Dweller by the hill' as at Clinch Green (Sussex) or on elevated (dry) land in a fen as at Clenchwarton (Norfolk), from OE **clenc* 'lump, mass', found in several minor place-names. *v.* MELS. *v.* also CLINK.

Clendenin, Clendennen: v. GLENDENING
Clere: v. CLEAR
Cleugh: v. CLOUGH
Cleve: v. CLIFF
Clew, Clew(e)s: v. CLOUGH
Cliff, Cliffe, Clive, Cleave, Cleaves, Cleef, Cleeve, Cleeves, Cleve, Clift, Cleft: Gislebertus de Cliua 1084 GeldR (W); Alecok del Clif 1274 Wak (Y); John Clif 1279 RH (O); Adam del Clef 1290 AssCh; John del Clyfes 1315 Wak (Y); William Undertheclif 1327 SRDb; Walter atte Cliue 1327 SRSx; John ate Clif 1327 SRC; John de Cleue 1327 SRSf; Richard Clyft 1524 SRSf; Mary Cleft, Clift 1755, 1757 DenhamPR (Sf). OE clif 'cliff, rock, steep descent' is found in numerous place-names as Cliff(e), Cleeve, Cleve and Clive, any of which may have given rise to a surname. Its most common meaning seems to be 'slope' (not necessarily a steep one) or 'bank of a river' and many of the surnames are due to residence near such a slope or bank. John atte Clyve or atte Cleve 1361 ColchCt is called Clever in 1365 (ib.). His descendants may have been called Clive, Cleeve or Cleaver and his name proves that CLEAVER may mean 'dweller by the slope'.

Clifford, Clifforth: Fulk, Roger de Clifford 1182 P (Wa, Lei), 1269 IpmW; John Clifford 1387–8 FFSr. From Clifford (Devon, Glos, Hereford, WRYorks), or 'dweller at the ford by the steep bank'.

Climance, Climas: v. CLEM
Climenson: v. CLEMENTSON
Climie: v. CLEMMEY
Climo: v. CLEMO
Climpson: Ælfled of Clymestune c970 OEByn (D); Arthenbaldus de Climeston' 1207 P (Co). From Climson (Cornwall). v. also CLEMENTSON.

Clinch: v. CLENCH
Clindening: v. GLENDENING
Cline: v. CLYNES
Clink, Clinker: Martin Clink, Roger Ctynk 1327 SRSf. In the 14th century, clinch and clench were used of door-nails secured by clinching or riveting. In 1323 Richard Spark, clenchar', was paid 4½d. per day for clinching and riveting great nails. cf. also clencher, clenchours 1363, clencheres 1375 (Building 309). The ME verb clenchen, from OE clenc(e)an is found from 1250 and the corresponding northern form clink from 1440. Clink, and also CLENCH and CLINCH, are metonymic for 'clincher, riveter'.

Clitheroe, Clitherow, Cleatherow, Cluderay: Thomas de Cliderhou 1176 P (Y); Robert Cletherowe 1439 FrY; Richard Cludre, Clydero 1526, 1541 GildY. From Clitheroe (Lancs).

Clive: v. CLIFF
Clodd: Achi, Adam Clod 1166 P (Nf), 1275 RH (Sf). ME clodde 'clod of earth', vb., 'to free land from clods by harrowing, rolling, etc.' (c1440 MED). 'Harrower.' cf. William le Clodder' 1221 AssWo.

Clogg: Symond Clogg, Joan Clog 1524 SRSf. ME clog(ge) 'a wooden-soled shoe' (1390 MED),

used for a maker of clogs: cf. Matthew Clogmaker 1367 ColchCt.

Close, Closs: (i) Nicholas de Clos 1296 SRSx; Thomas del Close 1327 SRY. ME clos(e), OFr clos 'enclosure' (a1325 MED), 'farm-yard' (1386). 'Dweller by the enclosed place' or, possibly, 'worker in the farm-yard'. (ii) William le Clos 1214 Cur (C); John Cloos 1409 LoPleas. ME clos (adj.) 'practising secrecy, reserved, reticent' (c1400 NED).

Clothier: Robert le Clother 1286 MESO (Nf). A derivative of OE clāþ 'cloth', maker or seller of cloth. cf. Richard le Clothmongere 1296 Oseney (O), Thomas Clothman 1416 LLB I.

Cloude: Wimarc' de la Clude 1199 P (So); Robert atte Cloude 1327 SRSo. 'Dweller by the rock or hill' (OE clūd 'mass of rock, hill'), as at Temple Cloud (Som), Cloud Bridge (Warwicks), Clouds Wood (Herts).

Clough, Cleugh, Cluff, Clow, Clew, Clewes, Clews, Clue, Clues: Alan Bouenthecloue 1261 AssLa; Richard Clowe 1275 SRWo; Roger Clough 1279 RH (O); John del Clogh 1298 Wak (Y); Richard Clewe 1327 SRSf; Robert del Clough 1327 SRDb; Richard Cluff 1428 FA (St); Esabell Clughe 1555 RothwellPR (Y). 'Dweller in a ravine or steep-sided valley', OE *clōh. Cleugh is a Scottish form. For the development, cf. enough and enow, dough and (plum)duff.

Clout, Cloutt: Enial Clut 1175 P (He); Walter Clut 1207 P (Gl). OE clūt 'patch'. v. CLOUTER.

Clouter: Adam le Clutere 1286 MESO (Nf); Robert (le) Clutere 1301 LLB C; Adam Clouter 1307 Wak (Y). A derivative of OE clūt 'patch', patcher, cobbler. cf. Robert le Cloutkeruer 1327 Pinchbeck (Sf) 'patch-cutter'. Also, possibly, but less likely, from OFr cloutier 'nail-smith'.

Clouting, Cloughting: William Cloutyng 1327 SRSf; William Clowting 1524 SRSf; John Cloughting 1568 SRSf; John Cloutinge, Henry Clouton, Thomas Clouten 1674 HTSf. ME clouting 'the action of patching, mending, etc.' (1382 NED). Synonymous with CLOUTER.

Cloutman: An alternative for CLOUTER.

Clover: Robert le Clovier 1300 LoCt; Alen Clover, John Clovier, William Clovyer 1524 SRSf. A variant of CLEAVER, from OE clēofan 'to split', with change of stress to cleófan, cloven, whence Clover.

Clow: v. CLOUGH
Clower: William le Cloer, le Cloier 1201 P (So). A derivative of OFr clou 'nail', hence 'nailer'. Stephen le cloer 1292 SRLo is identical with Stephen le Naylere 1300 LoCt.

Clowes, Cluse: Nicholas de Cluse 1275 SRWo; Thomas atte Cluse 1332 SRSx. 'Dweller at the enclosure' or 'keeper of the mill-dam or sluice', OE clūse, ME cluse, clowse 'enclosure, narrow-passage', 'dam for water, sluice or floodgate'.

Clowser: Rychard Closer 1526 SxWills; John Clouser 1549 ib.; Moulde Clowser 1546 ib. These three, with Thomas atte Cluse above, all lived in

Warnham (Sussex), and their surnames are identical in meaning. *v.* CLOWES.

Club, Clubb: William, Gilbert *Clobbe* 1166 P (C), 1202 Cur (Sf); Stephen, Walter *Clubbe* 1204 P (C), 1279 RH (Hu). ME *clubbe, clobbe* 'club', metonymic for *clubber* 'maker of clubs': Richard *clobbere* 1222 DBStP; Walter *le Clubbere* 1260 AssC. In 1198–1212 (Bart i, 267), Robert *clobbere* of the text witnesses as Robert *clobbe*. By the Assize of Arms, every adult man had to be provided with at least a knife and a staff or club.

Clucas: *MacLucas* 1511, *Clucas* 1643 Moore. From *MacLucais* 'son of *Lucas*'.

Cluderay: *v.* CLITHEROE

Clue, Cluff: *v.* CLOUGH

Clunie, Cluney, Cluny: (i) Ralph *de Cluneia* 1086 InqEl; William *de Cluini* 1195 P (D). From Cluny (Saône-et-Loire). (ii) William *de Cluny* of Perthshire 1296 Black. Probably from Clunie in Stormont (Perthshire).

Cluse: *v.* CLOWES

Clyma, Clymo: *v.* CLEMO

Clynes, Clyne, Cline: (i) Adam *de Cleynes* c1280 SRWo; John *Clynes* 1327 IpmGl; Benjamin *Cline* 1664 HTSo. From North Claines (Worcs), *Cleynes* 1234, *Clynes* 1293. (ii) William *de Clyn* 1375 Black; Malcolm *de Clyne* 1390 ib. From Clyne (Sutherland).

Coad(e): *v.* CODE

Coales: *v.* COLE

Coard: *v.* CORDES

Coate(s): *v.* COTE

Coatman: *v.* COTMAN

Cobb, Cobbe: *Cobba* 1201 Pl (Co); Leuric *Cobbe* 1066 DB; Walter *Cobbe* 1234–5 FFEss; John *Cobbe* 1327 SRSo. OE **Cobba* 'big, leading man', an original nickname, unrecorded in OE but not uncommon from the 12th century onwards, *v.* OEByn 305. In the eastern counties it may represent ON *Kobbi*, while a shortened form of *Jacob* is a further possibility.

Cobbald, Cobbold, Cutbill: *Cotebaldus* de Wigornia a1200 Dublin; Aluuinus *Cubold* 1066 DB (Nth); Ricardus *Cubaldus* 1174 P (He); John *Cubald* 1219 AssL; Thomas *Cutebold*', William *Cotebold* 1292, 1332–57 PN K 492; John *Cobald* 1309 FFSf. OE *Cūðbeald* 'famous-bold'.

Cobbe: *v.* COBB

Cobham, Cobbam: Robert, Nicholas *de Cobeham* 1199–1200 FFK, 1332 SRSx; Thomas *Cobham* 1400 AssLo. From Cobham (Kent, Surrey, Sussex).

Cochran, Cochrane, Cochren, Colqueran: Waldeve *de Coueran* 1262 Black; William *de Coughran* 1296 ib.; Robert *de Cochrane* c1360 ib. From Cochrane (Renfrewshire).

Cock, Cocke, Cocks, Cox: (i) *Coc* de domo Abraham 1192 P (Lo); *Koc* filius Pertuin 1230 P (L); *Cock le Botiller* 1281 LLB C; *Koc* Forester, *Kok* de mari 1296 SRSx; Aluuinus *Coc* 1066 DB (C); Osbern *Cocc* 1175–95 Seals (Db); Aki *Coc* 1177 P (Nf); Nicholas *Cock* 1297 MinAcctCo; Petronilla *Cockes* 1327 SRWo; John *Cocks* 1332

SRCu; Walter *Cocks, Cox* 1515 Oxon. The first example is the name of a Jew and is probably a diminutive of *Isaac* in its Hebrew form (Jacobs). *Cock*, a common personal name still in use about 1500, may partly be from OE *Cocc* or *Cocca*, found in place-names, although not on independent record. But as *cock* became a common term for a boy, it may also have been used affectionately as a personal name. (ii) William, Godard *le Cock* 1271 ForSt, 1281 LLB A; Thomas *le Cok* 1285 *Ass* (Ess); John *le Cockes* 1327 SRWo. OE *cocc* 'cock', a nickname for one who strutted like a cock. This became a common term for a pert boy and was used of scullions, apprentices, servants, etc., and came to be attached to christian names as a pet diminutive (*Simcock, Wilcock*, etc.). Forms without the article may belong here; *cok* is ambiguous and may be for *Cook*. The surname may also mean 'watchman, leader' and, according to Welsh writers, may also be from Welsh, Cornish *coch* 'red'. (iii) Hugh *ate Cocke, ate Coke* 1319 SRLo, 1320 LLB E; William *dil Cok* 1327 SRSf; Thomas *atte Cok* 1380 FFSf. 'Dweller by the hill', OE *cocc* 'haycock, heap, hillock'. In London it probably derived from the sign of a house or inn. Sometimes we may have ME *cock* 'small ship's boat' (1319 MED), name for a boatman. cf. BARGE.

Cockayne: William *Cokein, Cocaine* 1193 P (Wa), 1221 Cur (Bk); Hawisa *de Cokaingne* 1219 AssY; Geoffrey *de Cokaygne* 1228 FFEss; John *Cokkayn* 1332 SRCu. ME *cokaygne*, OFr *coquaigne*, the name of an imaginary country, the abode of luxury and idleness. Cocken (Lancs), pronounced *Cockin*, is said to have been named in jest as the land there was cleared by the monks of Furness Abbey. The surname was probably given to one whose habits and manner of life suggested he had come from the fabulous land of Cockaigne. It has also become COCKIN and COCKING.

Cockcroft, Cockroft: Richard *de Cocckecroft* 1296 Wak (Y). 'Dweller at the cockcroft.'

Cockell, Cockill, Cockle: Simon, Thomas *Cockel* 1198 P (Nth), 1202 P (K); Richard *le Cokel* 1279 RH (O); William *Cockyl* 1327 SRSf; Ralph *Kokyl* 1327 SRC. Various explanations are possible: OE *coccul, coccel* 'çockle', a weed particularly common in cornfields. For the *taris* of Wyclif's 1388 version, that of 1382 has *dernel* or *cokil*, and the Rheims and Authorized Versions have *cockle*. cf. DARNELL. Or ME, OFr *cokille* 'a shell', also 'cockle', the bivalve. cf. William *le Cokeler* 1281 MESO (L), which Fransson takes as OFr *coquillier* 'fabricant de coquilles' (Godefroy) a maker of head-coverings for women. Thuresson explains (William) *Cokeler* 1332 MEOT (L) as a gatherer of cockles. cf. MULLET. The Fr *Coquille* Dauzat takes to be a surname applied to pilgrims to the shrine of St James of Compostella who sewed shells on their clothes as a sign of their pilgrimage. cf. *cockle-hat* (1834 NED), a hat with a cockle or scallop-shell stuck into it, worn for the same reason.

Cocker: Henry *Cokere* 1198 P (K); Geoffrey, Alexander *Cokkere* 1237 Fees (Bk), 1327 SRSf; Adam *le Kockere* 1327 SRSt. Either a derivative of ME *cocken* 'to fight', a fighter, wrangler, or of ME *coke* 'to put up hay in cocks', haymaker.

Cockerell, Cockerill, Cockarill, Cockrell, Cockrill: Stephen *Cokerel* 1166 P (Y); Adam *Cokerell* 1200 P (Sf). *Cockerell* 'a young cock' is not recorded in MED before 1440, though that is not an insuperable objection to its appearance as a surname much earlier. The surname is common and early and is often, no doubt, from OFr *cocherel*, *cokerel* 'cock-seller', 'poultry-dealer'.

Cockerham, Cockram, Cockrem, Cockran, Cockren: John *de Kokerham* 1349 FrY; Thomas *Cokeram* 1450 ArchC vii; Thomas *Cockrom* 1596 RothwellPR (Y); Nathaniel *Cockerum* 1674 HTSf; William *Cockran* 1756 FrY. From Cockerham (Lancs).

Cockett: *v.* COCKIN

Cockin, Cockett, Cockitt: Henry, John *Cokin* 1207 Cur (Ess), 1273 RH (Nt); Richard *Cochet* 1170 P (Ess); John *Coket* 1221 AssWa. These two surnames are metonymic for bakers. cf. Ralph *Cocunbred* 1209 FrLeic, Adam, Ralph *Cokinbred* 1265, 1299 ib. *Cockin-bread* is presumably the same as *cocket-bread*, a leavened bread or loaf slightly inferior in quality to the wastell or finest bread (1266 MED). It has been suggested (without evidence) that the bread was stamped with a seal or cocket. This was a seal (AFr *cokette*) belonging to the King's Custom House (1293 NED) and might have been used by metonymy as a surname for a sealer or a customs' house officer. *v.* also COCKAYNE.

Cocking, Cockings: (i) William *Cocking*' 1327 SRSx. From Cocking (Sussex). (ii) William *Coccing* 1266 LeiBR. Probably OE *Coccing* 'son of *Cocc*'. *v.* also COCKAYNE.

Cockle: *v.* COCKELL

Cocklin, Cockling: *Kokelinus* carectarius 1295 Barnwell (C); Ralph *Cokelin* 1279 RH (C); Reginald *Kokelin* 1284 FFHu. A double diminutive of *Cocc*. *v.* COCK.

Cockman, Cookman: William, Reynballus *Cokeman* 1276 AssSo, 1297 MinAcctCo; John *Cookman* 1374 ColchCt. Either 'servant of Cook' or 'the cook's servant'. *Cockman* is from *cōkman*, with shortening of the vowel before OE *cōc* became ME *couk, cook*.

Cockram, Cockran: *v.* COCKERHAM

Cockrell, Cockrill: *v.* COCKERELL

Cockroft: *v.* COCKCROFT

Cockshed, Coxhead: Roger *Kockesheued* 1227 AssBeds. 'Cock's head', a nickname. cf. William *Cokkesbrayn* 1275 RH (Sx), Henry *Cockeshank* 1323 Wak (Y).

Cockshot, Cockshott, Cockshoot, Cockshut, Cockshutt: Symon *de Cokshute* 1296 SRSx; John *Cokschote* 1312 ColchCt; Alice *atte Cocshete* 1327 SRSx; John *Cocke Shoute* 1562 AD vi (Berks). Sometimes pronounced *Coeshot*. OE *coccscÿte*, 'a place where nets were stretched to catch wood-

cock' as at Cockshoot Fm (Worcs), Cockshot (Kent), Cockshut (Lancs), etc.

Cockson: *v.* COXON

Codd: Alanus *filius Chod* 1150–5 DC (L); Osbert *cod* 1148 Winton (Ha); John *Lecod* 1219 AssY. *Chod* may be an example of OE **Codda*, unrecorded, but found in place-names, or an original nickname. The surname was usually a nickname but the exact meaning is obscure. It may be OE *cod(d)* 'bag, scrip', used a1250 of the belly or stomach, hence, perhaps, for a man with a belly like a bag. Or we may have ME *codd(e)* 'cod'. cf. John *le Codherte* 1297 MinAcctCo 'cod-heart', Robert *Codbody* 1332 SRSx, either 'with a body like a cod' or with one like a well-filled bag, and Robert *Codhorn* 1202 P (Y), where the meaning is not clear. cf. also *cod's-head* 'a stupid fellow' 1566 NED. In the 16th century *codder* denoted a worker in leather, a saddler or a peltmonger so that the surname may, perhaps, also be metonymic for a maker of leather bags or a saddler.

Code, Coad, Coade: Robert *Chode* 1182 P (L); Nicholas *Code* 1275 SRWo. ME *code* 'pitch, cobbler's wax', a name for a cobbler.

Codlin, Codling, Quadling, Quodling, Girling, Gurling: (i) John *Kodling* 1208 Cur (Y); Robert *Codling* 1275 RH (L); Emma *Codelingg*' 1297 SRY. ME *codling* 'a young or small cod' (1289 MED), either a seller of these fish, or, perhaps, as the only examples noted are from Yorkshire and Lincolnshire, for a fisherman, or used as an affectionate diminutive. This would survive only as *Codlin* or *Codling*. (ii) Richard *Querdeleon* 1247 AssBeds; Adam *Girdelyon, Girdelion* 1296–7 Wak (Y); William *Gerlyn* 1296 SRSx; William *Querdelion* 1304 LLB C; John *Qwerdeling* 1327 SRSf; Robert *Gerling* 1327 SRC; Thomas *Querdelyng* 1365 LoPleas; John *Kodlyng*, George *Codlyng* 1524 SRSf; Wyllyam *Gyrlinge* 1547 EA (NS) ii (Sf). Fr *cœur-de-lion* 'lion-heart'. cf. the development of *codling* 'a hard kind of apple' (sound to the core), *querdlynge* c1440, *codlyng* 1530, *quodlinge* 1586, *quadlin* 1625 NED. *Girdelion* would become *Girdling* and then *Girling*. *Codling* is common in Yorkshire (North and East Ridings), *Quodling* and *Quadling* are Norfolk and Suffolk names, whilst *Girling*, particularly common in Suffolk, is frequent also in Essex and Norfolk.

Codman: William *Codeman* 1327 SRC; Robert *Codman* 1524 SRSf. An occupational name, either a worker in leather, a saddler, a catcher or seller of codfish, or a cobbler. *v.* CODD, CODE.

Codner: *v.* CORDNER

Coe, Coo: Osbert *Ka* 1188 P (L); John *Co* 1221 AssWa; Gilbert *le Co* 1252 Rams (Hu); Beatrice *le Coe* 1274 RH (L); Roger *le Coo* 1327 SRC. ME *co, coo*, the midland form corresponding to northern *ka*, ON *ká* 'jackdaw' (c1325 MED). *v.* also KAY.

Coey: *v.* COY

Coffer: Thomas *le Coffer* 1298 LoCt; John *Coffere* 1299 LLB B. OFr *cof(f)re* 'box, chest' (c1250 MED), here used for OFr *coffrier* 'maker of coffers' (1402 MED), also 'treasurer' (a1338 MED); John *le Cofrer* 1275 AssSo, John *le Cofferer* 1290 LLB A.

Cogan, Coggan, Coggin, Coggins: (i) William *de Cogan* 1185 P (Glam); Richard *Cogayn* 1271 AssSo; Peter *Coggane* 1642 PrD. From Cogan (Glamorgan). (ii) In Ireland also for *MacCogan*, Ir *Mac Cogadhain* 'son of the hound of war'.

Cogger: Arnaldus *coggorius, coggarius* 1191–2 P (L); Osbert (*le*) *Coggere* 1195–7 P (Do). The Latin forms are derivatives of MedLat *coga, cogo* 'boat' (c1200, 13th MLWL), for ME *cogge*, OFr *cogue* 'small ship, cock-boat', used by Chaucer of the ships in which Jason and Hercules sailed. A *cogger* (c1450 NED) may have been a builder of cogs but was more probably a sailor or master of the cog. Roger *le Cogere* and John *le Cogger* were bailiffs of Dunwich in 1218 and 1219 respectively (Gardner). The only examples that do not come from coastal counties are from Cambridgeshire, Herts and Surrey where the Cam, the Lea and the Thames were important waterways, so that Thuresson's alternative suggestion 'maker of cogs for wheels', is an unlikely origin.

Coggeshall, Coxall: William *de Choggeshala* 1181 P (Ess); Wlfgarus *de Cokesale* 1232 Colch (Ess). From Coggeshall (Essex).

Cogman: Benjamin *Cogman* 1647 Bardsley (Nf). Identical in meaning with COGGER.

Coke: *v.* COOK.

Colban: *Colben* 1066 DB (Ch); Richard *Colbain* 1170 P (D); William *Colbeyn* 1235 Fees (Nth). ON *Kolbeinn*, ODa, OSw *Kolben*.

Colbeck: *v.* COLDBECK

Colbert: *Colbert* 1066 DB (D, Ch, L); John *Colbert* 1205 P (D). OG *Colbert*.

Colborn, Colborne, Colbourn, Colbourne, Colburn, Colburne, Colbon, Colbond: Geoffrey *de Colebrunn'* 1208 Pl (Y); William *de Colburn* 1386 FrY; John *Colborne* 1642 PrD. From Colburn (NRYorks), or Colesborne (Glos). Occasionally a personal name may be involved, ON *Kolbrún, Kolbiorn*, cf. Robert *filius Colbern* 1185 P (D).

Colbran, Colbron, Colbrun, Coalbran: *Colbrand, Colebran* 1066 DB (D, Wa); *Colebrandus* c1200 DC (L); Malger *Colebrond* 1275 RH (Sx); Walter *Colebrand* 1297 MinAcctCo. ON *Kolbrandr*, OSw *Kolbrand*.

Colby, Colbey, Coleby: Ralph *de Colebi* 1192–1218 YCh; William *de Colby* 1332 IpmNt; William *Colbe* 1525 SRSx. From Colby (Norfolk, Westmorland), Coleby (Lincs), or Coulby (NRYorks).

Colcock: Peter *Colcock* 1379 LLB H. *Col*, a petname for *Nicholas*, and *cock*, an affectionate diminutive. *v.* COCK.

Colcott, Colcutt: *v.* CALDECOT

Coldbeck, Colbeck, Colebeck, Coulbeck: Thomas *de Caldebek* 1321 FrY. From Caldbeck (Cumb).

Coldicott: *v.* CALDECOT

Coldron: *v.* CALDERON

Coldwell: *v.* CALDWELL

Cole, Coles, Coales: *Cola, Cole* 1066 DB; *Cole, Cola* filius Lanterii c1145 EngFeud (K); Robertus

filius Cole 1206 AssL; Geoffrey, Richard *Cole* 1148 Winton (Ha), 1185 Templars (Wa); George *Coles* 1555 FrY. The personal name may be ON, ODa *Koli*, a short form of names in *Kol-*, but the distribution in DB suggests that it is more often OE *Cola*, an original byname from OE *col* 'coal' in the sense 'coal-black, swarthy'. The surname may also be a nickname with the same meaning: John *le Col* 1321 FFEss.

Colebrook, Colebrooke: Alexander *de Colebroc* 1160 P (D); Fucherus *de la Colebrok* 1241 MELS (Sx). From Colebrook (Devon), or 'dweller by the cool brook' (OE *cōl, brōc*).

Coleman, Colman, Collman, Coulman: *Coleman* 1066 DB; *Colemannus* de Eston' 1176 P (Bk); Hervicus, Richard *Coleman* 1166 RBE (Y), 1176 P (Sr). The surname is early, frequent and widely distributed. In the north it is usually from OIr *Colmán*, earlier *Columbán*, adopted by Scandinavians as ON *Kalman*, and introduced into Cumberland, Westmorland and Yorkshire by Norwegians from Ireland. In DB the personal name is southern and south-eastern and is probably OG *Col(e)man*. In the Sussex Subsidy Rolls, where both *Coleman* and *Collier* are frequent surnames, both probably mean 'charcoal-burner'.

Coleson, Colson, Coulson, Coulsen: (i) Algarus *Colessune* 1138–60 ELPN. 'Son of *Col*', probably ODa *Kol*, or possibly, ODa *Koli*. (ii) Ælstan *Cole sune* c1095 Bury (Sf); Bruning *Cola suna* 1100–30 OEByn (D); William *Colesone* 1332 SRSt; John *Colson* 1379 PTY. The first two examples are from either ON *Koli* or OE *Cola. v.* COLE. Later examples may have the same origin or may belong below. (iii) John *Collesson'* 1339 Crowland (C), 1379 PTY; John *Colleson* 1386 FFSf; John *Colleson, Colson* 1401, 1408 FrY. 'Son of *Coll*', a petform of *Nicholas*.

Colfox: John *Colfox* 1221 AssWa; Richard *Colvox* 1274 RH (Sa). ME *colfox*, from OE *col* 'coal' and *fox*', 'coal-fox', the brant-fox, a variety of fox distinguished by a greater admixture of black in its fur. According to Chaucer, the tail and both ears were tipped with black, unlike the rest of his hairs. A nickname. cf. 'a colfox, ful of sly iniquitee' (c1390 MED).

Colicot, Colkett: *v.* CALDECOT

Colin: *v.* COLLIN

Coling: *v.* COLLING

Colkin: Hamo *Colekyn* 1242 Fees (K); Roger *Colkyng* 1296 SRSx; Robert *Colkyn* 1327 ib. A diminutive of *Cole* or *Coll*.

Coll, Colle, Colls, Coull, Coule, Coules, Cowl, Cowle, Cowles: (i) *Col* 1066 DB (L); *Colle* serviens Henrici 1204 Cur (Y); *Colle* Rikmai 1247 AssBeds; Robert *Cholle* 1166 P (Nf); Osbert, William *Colle* 1196 P (L), 1200 P (Wo); Thomas *Colles* 1327 SRSf; Robert *Coule* 1341 FrY; Thomas *Cowles* 1568 SRSf. The DB *Col* is ON *Kollr*, OSw *Koll*, or ON *Kolr*, ODa, OSw *Kol*. *Colle* may have the same origin or it may be for ON, ODa *Kolli*, but, especially in later examples, it is a pet-form of *Colin*, found from the beginning of the 13th century as a diminutive of *Nicholas*. (ii) Robert *atte Cole* 1275 SRWo; Adam *atte Colle* ib. Probably 'dweller by the hill', from OE **coll* 'hill'. *v.* MELS.

Collacot(t): *v.* CALDECOT

Collar, Coller, Colla: John *Coller* 1362 Crowland (C); William *Coler* 1377 LLB H. A form of COLLIER (a1375 MED).

Collard: *Colard* le Fauconer 1264 *Ipm* (Ess); *Colard* Hariel 1275 RH (Gl); Richard *Colard* 1332 SRSx. A pet-form of *Nicholas, Col*, plus the French suffix *-ard*.

Collcott, Collecott: *v.* CALDECOT

Colledd: John *Colhod* 1327 SRSf. 'Wearer of a black hood', OE *col* 'coal, coal-black' and *hōd* 'hood'.

Colledge, Collidge: Brian *de Colewich* 1210 Cur (Nt). From Colwich (Staffs) or Colwick (Notts).

Collet, Collett, Collete: *Colet* 1202 AssNth; Richard, Robert *Colet* 1213 Lewes (Nf), 1243 AssSo; Adam *Collette* 1332 SRSt. *Col-et*, a diminutive of *Col* (Nicholas) plus *-et*. There was also a feminine form: *Collette* 1379 PTY. Occasionally the surname is an apheptic form of *acolyte:* Simon *Colyte* 1294 RamsCt (Beds).

Colley, Collie: Hugh *Coly* 1212 Cur (Y); Dande *Colly* 1219 AssY; Philip *Coli* 1275 SRWo. OE **colig* 'coaly, coal-black'. The original short vowel is retained in the 16th century *colly* 'dirtied with coal and soot'. cf. 'a colie colour' (1565), colley sheep (with black faces and legs) 1793, and *colley* the Somerset dialect name for a blackbird. The surname probably meant 'swarthy', or, perhaps, black-haired.

Collick: Reginald *de Colewic* 1202 P (Nt). From Colwick (Notts).

Collicutt: *v.* CALDECOT

Collidge: *v.* COLLEDGE

Collier, Colliar, Colliard, Colleer, Collyear, Collyer, Colyer: Ranulf *colier* a1150 DC (L); Bernard *le coliere* 1172 P (So). A derivative of OE *col* 'coal', a maker or seller of charcoal (a1375 MED).

Collin, Collins, Collen, Collens, Collyns, Colin: *Colinus* de Andresia 1191 P (Berks); *Colinus* 1196 FrLeic; John *Collin* 1221 Cur (D); William *Colin* 1246 AssLa; Roger *Colynes* 1327 SRSo. *Col-in*, a diminutive of *Col*, a pet form of *Nicholas*. *Colinus* Harrengod 1207 Cur (Sf) is identical with *Nicholaus* Harengot (1206 ib.). There was also a feminine form: *Colina* Charles 1250 Fees (Sf).

Colling, Collinge, Collings, Coling, Cowling: *Collinc* 1066 DB (Sa, Db); Gerardus *filius Colling* 1185 P (Y); Aluuardus *Colling, Collinc* 1066, 1086 DB (W); Griffin *Collingus* c1114 Burton (St); Roger *Kolling* c1125 MedEA (Nf); John *Collynges* 1376 AD iv (Sa). ON *Kollungr*. The distribution does not support Tengvik's opinion that the name is of native origin. Scandinavian personal names are found in the south by 1066. *Colling(s)* may also be a late development of *Collin(s)*.

Collingwood, Collingworth, Collinwood: Richard *de Calangwode, de Chalaungwode* 1323 AssSt, 1327 SRSt; John *atte Calengewode* 1349 DbCh; Ralph *Colyngwood* 1516 ib.; William *Colynwod* 1512

GildY. From Collingwood (Staffs) 'the wood of disputed ownership'.

Collinson, Collison: Thomas, John *Colynson* 1349 Whitby (Y), 1382 FFHu; John *Colisson* 1381 SRSf; Clement *Collyngson* 1524 SRSf; Thomas *Collison* 1622 RothwellPR (Y). 'Son of Colin'. *Colisson* is 'son of *Coll*' or, possibly, of *Cole*.

Collishaw: *v.* COWLISHAW

Collister: *v.* CALLISTER

Collman: *v.* COLEMAN

Collop: John *Collop* 1279 RH (C); Henry *Colhoppe* 1290 FFEss. ME *colhope, col(l)op* 'an egg fried on bacon; fried ham and eggs' (1362 NED). Probably a name for a cook-house keeper.

Collyns: *v.* COLLIN

Colman: *v.* COLEMAN

Colocott: *v.* CALDECOT

Colqueran: *v.* COCHRAN

Colson: *v.* COLESON

Colston, Coulston: (i) Reginald *filius Colstan* 1190 P (L); *Colstan* 1213 Cur (Do); Roger *Colstayn* 1297 SRY; Adam *Colstan* 1332 SRCu. OE *Colstān*, ON *Kolstein*. (ii) Roger *de Coleston* 1208 FFY; Robert *de Colstone* 1352 LLB G; John *Colston* 1426 FrY. From Colston Basset, Carcolston (Notts), or Coulston (Wilts).

Colt, Coult: Godric, Anselm *Colt* 1017 OEByn, 1188 BuryS (Sf); Henry *le Colt* 1227 AssSt. OE *colt* 'colt', either a nickname 'frisky, lively', or metonymic for COLTER, COLTMAN.

Coltard, Coltart, Colthard, Colthart, Coulthard, Coulthart: Peter *Coltehird* 1301 SRY; John *Coltart* 1627 Black (Dumfries); John *Coultart* 1679 FrY. OE *colt* and *hierde* 'keeper of colts'. In Scotland, often pronounced *Cowtart*.

Colter: Robert *le Coltier* 1285 MEOT (O); John *le Coltere* 1327 SRSf. A derivative of OE *colt*. 'A keeper of colts.'

Coltman: Anote *Coltman* 1332 SRCu; John *le Coltmon* 1365 DbCh. OE *colt* and *mann*. cf. COLTER.

Colton, Coulton: Thomas, Pagan *de Colton* 1176 P (St), 1214 P (Y); Roger *Colton* 1371 AssL. From Colton (Lancs, Norfolk, Som, Staffs, WRYorks).

Colvill, Colville: William *de Colevil(e)* 1086 DB (Y); Gilbert *de Colauilla* ib. (Sf); William *Coleuille* 1142–53 DC (L). From Colleville (Seine-Inférieure).

Colvin: *Coluinus* 1066 DB (D); Godwyne *Colwynes suna* 1100–30 OEByn (D); Wlfwinus *Colewin* 1210 Cur (Db); Ralph *Coluin* 1296 SRSx. OW *Coluin, Colwin*.

Colyer: *v.* COLLIER

Combe, Combes, Coom, Coombes, Coombs: Richard *de la Cumbe* 1194 FF (Sx); Alan *in la Cumbe* 1269 AssSo; Robert *atte Cumbe* 1296 SRSx; Thomas *de Combe* 1317 AssK; John *ate Combe* ib. From one of the many places named Comb, Combe or Coombe, or from residence in a small valley (OE *cumb*).

Comber, Coomber, Coomer, Cumber, Cumbers: William *le Combere* 1260 AssC; Roger *le Coumber* 1276 RH (Berks); John *Comber* 1296 SRSx;

Walter *Cumbar'* 1332 SRSx. 'Dweller in a valley.' *v.* COMBE and also CAMBER.

Comer: *v.* CAMBER.

Comfort, Comport: William, Richard *Cumfort* 1269 AssSo, 1279 RH (O); Richard *Counfort* 1375 LoPleas. ME *cumfort, comfort,* OFr *cunfort, confort* 'strengthening, encouragement, aid, succour, support', used of 'one who strengthens or supports, a source of strength' (1455 NED). *Comport* seems to be a late development in Kent where both forms are still found. Bardsley notes Edward *Comport* alias *Comfort* of Chislehurst.

Comings, Comins, Comyns: *v.* CUMING

Commander: Roger *le cumandur de templo* 1176–85 Templars (C); William *le Comandur* 1274 RH (So), 1297 MinAcctCo (W). ME *comander, comando(u)r* 'one who commands, ruler, leader' (1300 NED), sometimes 'officer in charge of a commandery' e.g. of the Knights Templars (OFr *comandeor*).

Commin(s), Commings: *v.* CUMING

Compain: Odo *Compyn,* William *Compayn* 1327 SR (Ess). OFr *compain,* originally the nominative of *compagnon* 'chum' (1643 NED). A very rare surname. cf. Ralph *Cumpainun* 1221 AssWo.

Comper: Elyas *Cumper* 1224 Cur (So); Walter *Compere, le Compeyre* 1332 SRSx. ME, OFr *comper* 'companion, associate, comrade'.

Comport: *v.* COMFORT

Compton, Cumpton: Gladwin *de Cumtuna* 1167–c1175 YCh; William *de Compton'* 1212 Pl; Nicholas *de Cumpton* 1263 FFL; Richard *Compton* 1376 FFEss. From one or other of the many places of this name.

Conan, Conant, Conen: *Conanus dux Britanniae et comes Richemundie* a1155 DC (L); Henricus *filius Conani, Cunani* 1196 P (Nth), 1208 Cur (Y); *Connand, Conian Gossipe* 1479–86 FrY; Gilbert, Thomas *Conan* c1198 Bart (Lo), 1297 MinAcctCo (Y); Robert *Connand,* Adam *Conand* 1379 PTY. OBret *Conan,* the name of Breton chiefs, kings and of a saint; one of the Breton names introduced at the Conquest and common among tenants of the Richmond fee in Lincs and Yorks.

Conder, Condor: Robert *de Conedour'* 1221 AssSa; William *Conder* 1275 SRWo. From Condover (Salop).

Condict: *v.* CONDUIT

Condie, Condy, Cundey, Cundy: Roger *de Cundi* c1150 Riev (Y), *de Condeio* Hy 2 DC (L); Aliz *de Condi* 1185 Templars (L); Nicholas *Cundy* 1200 P (L). From Condé (Nord, Oise, Orne, etc). *v.* also CONDUIT.

Conduit, Condict, Condy, Cundick, Cundict, Cunditt, Cundy: Robert *atte Conduyt* 1334 LLB F; William *atte Conduit* 1340 AssC; Walter *atte Condut* 1342 LLB F. ME *conduit, condit, cundit,* OFr *conduit,* originally an artificial channel or pipe for conveying water, later a structure from which water was distributed, a fountain or pump. The surname probably refers to the latter. *v.* also CONDIE.

Coney, Conie, Cony: Richard *le Cony* 1296 SRSx; Robert *Cony* 1327 SRC. ME *conig, cony* 'rabbit', a nickname. cf. CONNING. The fact that Thomas *Cony* (1323 FrY) was a pelter suggests that the surname may also have denoted a dealer in rabbit-skins, perhaps also a furrier.

Congrave, Congreave, Congreve: Alan *de Cungrave* 1203 AssSt; Robert *Cungreve* 1381 SRSt; Thomas *Congreve* 1466 FFEss. From Congreve (Staffs).

Coningham, Conyngham: *v.* CUNNINGHAM

Conner, Connah: Robert *le Conner* 1297 LLB A; Geoffrey *le Conner* 1327 SRSf. OE *cunnere* 'examiner, inspector', especially an ale-conner.

Conning: Geoffrey *Conyng,* Ralph *Konyng* 1296 SRSx. ME, AFr *coning* 'rabbit'. cf. CONEY.

Consell: *v.* COUNCEL

Considine: *v.* CONSTERDINE

Constable: Richard *Conestabl'* 1130 P (C); Alice *Cunestabl'* 1200 P (L), *la Konestabl', Constabl* 1202–3 AssL. ME, OFr *cunestable, conestable,* representing late Lat *comes stabuli* 'count or officer of the stable'. 'Chief officer of the household, court' (1240), 'governor of a royal fortress' (1297), 'military officer' (c1300), 'parish constable' (1328 NED).

Constance, Custance: (i) *Custancia, Constancia* Ric 1 Gilb (L); *Custans* 1379 PTY; Robert *Custance* 1207 P (C); John *Custaunce* 1279 RH (C). Fr *Constance,* from Lat *constantia* 'constancy', a common woman's name, usually anglicized as *Custance.* *v.* also CUST. Occasionally we may have the masculine form: Hugo *filius Constantii* 1086 DB (Wa), Willelmus *filius Custancii* 1196 Cur (Lei). (ii) William *de Constenciis* c1150 DC (L); Walter *de Constanc', Walterus *Custancie* 1173–80, 1181 Bury (Sf); William *de Custanc'* 1206 Cur (O). From Coutances (La Manche). A less common source.

Constant: Robert *le Costent'* 1194, 1197 P (L), *le Constent'* 1196 ib. Probably from OFr *constant,* Lat *constans* 'steadfast, resolute' (c1386 NED).

Constantine, Cossentine: (i) Willelmus *filius Constantini* 1086 DB (Bk); *Constantin (Costetin CR) filius Godric* 1166 P (Nf); Willelmus *Constantinus* c1150 Riev (Y); Geoffrey, Richard *Costentin* 1195 P (W), 1221 AssWo; Henry *Constantin* 1272 FFSf. OFr *Constantin, Costantin,* from Lat *Constantinus,* a derivative of *constans* 'steadfast'. The real pronunciation is represented by COSTINS, COSTAIN, and the pet-form COSTE. *Cossentine* is due to assimilation of *st* to *ss* in *Costentin.* (ii) Geoffrey *de Costentin* 1153 StCh, *de Constantin'* 1156–80 Bury (Sf); Henry *Costentin, de Costentin* 1166, 1180 Oseney (O). From the Cotentin (La Manche). A less common source. *v.* OEByn, ANF.

Consterdine, Considine: From *Constantine* through the forms *Constentin, Consterterdine* and *Constetin, Consetin, Considine.*

Conte: Walter, Robert *Conte* 1296 SRSx, 1297 MinAcctCo. OFr *cun ·, conte* 'count', in AFr in the sense 'earl'.

Convent: Gabriel *Couent* 1327 SRSx. For *atte couent,* servant at the convent, probably a monastery, but possibly a nunnery (ME, AFr *covent*, OFr *convent*).

Converse: Hugo *conuersus* Hy 2 DC (L); Emma *la Converse* 1214 Cur (Ha); Peter *le conuers* 1219 AssY. OFr *convers*, Lat *conversus*, adj 'converted' (a1300 NED), sb 'a convert' (1388), used of one converted from secular to religious life in adult age, 'a lay member of a convent' (14..), a sense much older. The Cistercian and Augustinian *conversi* were men living according to a rule less strict than that of the monks or canons, engaged chiefly in manual work, with their own living quarters and their own part of the church. They were numerous among the Cistercians in the 12th and 13th centuries, often outnumbering the monks and were, by rule, illiterate. These lay-brothers were employed on the monastic manors and granges where they were liable to fall into the sin of owning private property. They acquired a reputation for violence and misbehaviour—at Neath in 1269 they locked the abbot in his bedroom and stole his horses—and they were gradually replaced by more manageable paid servants.

Conway: (i) John *de Conweye* 1268 Glast (So); David *Coneway* 1340–1450 GildC. From Conway (Caernarvon). (ii) In Ireland an anglicization of various Celtic names, e.g. *Mac Connmhaigh* 'head smashing', *Mac Conmidhe* 'hound of Meath', or *Ó Conbhuidhe* 'yellow hound', v. MacLysaght.

Cony: v. CONEY

Conyer: John *le Conyare* 1327 SRSx; Henry *Coyner* 1327 SRSf. A derivative of OFr *coignier* 'to stamp money, to mint', a coiner of money, minter. Common from 1202 as *Coner, Cuner*. v. MESO.

Conyers: Roger *de Coyners* c1170 Riev (Y), *de Coisneres, de Coisnieres* 1196 P (Y); William *de Coniers* 1208 Cur (Nb). From Coignières (Seine-et-Oise) or Cogners (Sarthe).

Coo: v. COE

Cooch: v. COUCH

Cooil: v. COOLE

Cook, Cooke, Cookes, Coke: Ælfsige *ðene Coc* c950 ASWills; Galter *Coc* 1086 DB (Ess); Walter *le Kuc* 1260 AssC; Richard *Cok* 1269 AssSt; Henry *Coke* 1279 AssSo; Ralph *le Cook* 1296 SRSx; Joan *Cokes* ib.; Robert *le Couk* 1327 SRSx; Roger *le Kokes* 1332 SRSt. OE *cōc* 'cook', often, no doubt, a seller of cooked-meats, etc. v. also KEW.

Cookman: v. COCKMAN

Cookson, Cuckson, Cuxon, Cuxson: Hugo *filius Coci* 1208 Cur (Sf); Gilbert *le Fiz Kew, Fiz le Keu* 1279 AssNb; Agnes *Cukeson* 1511 GildY. 'Son of the cook.'

Coole, Cooil: *McCoil, McCole* 1511, *Coole* 1666, *Cooile* 1711 Moore. Manx *MacCumhail* 'son of *Cumhall*', from *comhal* 'courageous'.

Coom: v. COMBE

Coomber: v. COMBER

Coomb(e)s: v. COMBE

Coomer: v. COMBER

Cooper, Coopper, Copper, Couper, Cowper, Cup- per: Robert (*le*) *Cupere* 1176–7 P (Sr); Selide *le Copere, le Cupere* 1181–2 P (Nf); William *le Coupere* 1296 SRSx; Geoffrey *Cowper* 1377 FrY; Walter *Cuppere, Couper* 1378, 1391 LLB H; John *Copper* 1424 FrY. ME *couper* 'maker or repairer of wooden casks, buckets or tubs' (c1400 MED). v. also COPPER.

Coopman: v. COPEMAN

Coot, Coote, Cootes, Coots: Reginald, John *Cote* 1201 P (L), 1219 AssY; William *le Coot* 1327 SRC. ME *cote, coote* 'a coot' (c1300 MED), originally the name of various swimming or diving birds, especially the Guillemot, later restricted to the Bald Coot, whose appearance and traditional stupidity ('as bald (or as stupid) as a coot') would readily give rise to a nickname. 'The mad coote, With a balde face to toot' (a1529 Skelton).

Cope: v. CAPE

Copeland, Copland, Coopland, Coupland, Cowpland: Samson *de Copland* 1204 Pl (Nth, R); William *de Coupeland, de Copeland* 1256 AssNb; Thomas *Coupeland* 1376 FFEss. From Copeland (Cumb), or Coupland (Northumb).

Copeman, Coopman, Coupman: *Copmannus Clokersuo* 1141–6 Holme (Nf); Johannes *filius Copeman* 1256 AssNb; John *Copman* 1205 P (Nf); Eustace *Coupman* 1230 P (Nf). ON *kaupmaðr* 'chapman, merchant', used also as a personal name.

Copestake, Copestick, Capstack, Capstick: Geoffrey *Coupstak* 1295 FrY; Henry *Coupestack'* 1301 SRY; John *Copestake* 1474 FrY. A hybrid from OFr *couper* 'to cut' and OE *staca* 'a stake'. 'Cut-stake', a name for a wood-cutter.

Copner: Robert, Richard *le Copener* 1242 Fees (D). OE *copenere* 'paramour, lover'.

Copp: (i) Eduinus *coppa* 1148 Winton (Ha); Robert, Geoffrey *Coppe* 1192 P (St), 1212 Cur (Sr). OE *cop, copp* 'top, summit', used of the head: 'Sire Simond de Montfort hath suore by ys cop' c1264 NED. (ii) Roger *de la Coppe* 1221 AssWa; John *atte Coppe* 1332 SRWa. 'Dweller at the top of the hill.'

Coppard, Coppeard: William *Copard* 1327 SRSx. OE *cop* 'top, head' plus OFr *-ard*. cf. TESTAR.

Coppell: v. CUPPLES

Copper: Juliana *la Copper* 1275 SRWo; Bartholomew, John *le Copper(e)* 1327 SRSf; William *le Copperer* ib. In the 12th century, *copere* is certainly a variant of *cupere* 'cooper', found late as *copper*, but it may sometimes be from OE *coper* 'copper'. The short vowel is clearly evidenced in *Copper* above, 'a worker in copper' used by metonymy for *copperer*. cf. COPPERSMITH, COOPER.

Coppersmith: Richard *Copersmid* 1212–23 Bart (Lo); Robert *copersmith* eHy 3 ib.; John *le copersmyth* 1305 LoCt. 'Maker of copper utensils' (1327 MED). cf. Hugo *Coperman* 1202 P (We), Stephen *le Coperbeter* 1286 LLB A.

Coppin, Coppins, Coppen: *Copin* 1188 P (L); *Copin de Sancto Ædmundo* 1188 P (Nf); Nicholas *Copin* 1243 AssSo; William *Copyn* 1275 SRWo.

Copin is a pet diminutive of *Jacob*. *Jacpb* de Troye (1273 RH) is identical with *Copyn* de Troys 1275 LLB A.

Copping: Gilbert *Copping* 1188 BuryS (Sf); Henry *Copping* 1202 AssL. Apparently a derivative of OE *copp* 'top, summit', the exact meaning of which is obscure. For similar formations, cf. Robert *Badding* 1187–1221 ELPN, William *Fatting*' 1297 ib., from the adjectives *bad* and *fat*.

Copple: *v.* CUPPLES

Copsey: *Cofsi, Copsi* 1066 DB (Y); Acharias filius *Copsi* 1155 FeuDu; *Copsi* 1177 P (Nf); Hugo, Robert *Copsi* 1170 P (Wa), 1182 P (St). ON *Kupsi*, OSw *Kofse*.

Corb: Angot *le Corb* 1206–7 Cur (Bk) is identical with Angod' *le Corf* ib. OFr. *corb, corp, corf* 'raven'. *v.* CORBET, CORBIN, CORFE.

Corbell, Corble: (i) Richard *Corbeille, Corbell*' 1180, 1197 P (K); John *Curbeyle* 1327 SRC. OFr *corbeille* 'basket' (1706 NED). cf. Robert *Corbiller* 1225 MESO 171, from OFr *corbeillier* 'basket-maker'. (ii) Eudo *Corbel* 1198 P (Y). This might be identical with the above, but might also be from OFr *corbel*, now *corbeau* 'raven'. cf. CORBET, CORBIN.

Corbet, Corbett, Corbitt: Rogerius filius *Corbet* 1086 DB (Sa); Roger *Corbet* ib., 1158 P (Sa), 1221 AssWo; Thomas *le Corbet* 1323 Eynsham (O). OFr *corbet* 'raven' (c1384 NED), probably a nickname for one with dark hair or complexion. *v.* CORB, CORBELL, CORBIN, CORFE.

Corbin, Corben, Corbyn: (i) *Corbin(us)* 1086 DB (Wa, K); Roger *Corbin* 1201 AssSo; Walter *Corbyn* 1219 AssY. OFr *corbin* from *corb* 'raven' (a1225 NED). (ii) William *Corbun* 1086 DB (Ess); Hugo *de Corbun* ib. (Nf, Sf). From Corbon (Calvados) or, possibly, Corbon (Orne). The Essex example is probably due to early loss of the preposition, but might, possibly, be an early example of ME *corbun* 'raven' (a1300 NED). cf. CORBET.

Corcoran, Corkan: Cathasach *Ua Corcrain* 1045, Donagh *Mac Corcrane* 1576, *Corkan* 1611 Moore. *Mac Corcráin* 'son of *Corcrán*', the red-complexioned.

Cordell, Cordall, Cordle: Hugo *Cordel* 12th NthCh (Nth); Margery *Cordel* 1213 Cur (Nf). OFr *cordele*, a diminutive of *corde* 'cord'. The diminutive is not found in ME, but cf. ME *cordilere* (c1430) 'a Franciscan friar of the strict rule', so called from the knotted cord round his waist (OFr *cordelier*).

Corden, Cordon, Cordwent, Corwin: Robert *Corduan* 1221 AssWo; Walter *Kordewan* 1296 SRSx; William *Cordiwant* 1327 SRSo. ME *corduan, cordewan*, OFr *cordoan* 'Spanish leather made originally at Cordova', much used for shoes. Metonymic for CORDNER. For forms, cf. *corden* a1400, *corwen* 1483, *cordiwin* 1593 NED.

Corder, Cordier: Ralph *Corder* 1207 FineR (Ha); Osbert *le Corder* 1227 FrLeic. OFr *cordier* 'maker of cords'. cf. Augustinus *Cordemaker* 1199 Cur (Sf).

Corderey, Corderoy, Cordurey, Cordeary, Cor- dero, **Cordery, Cordray, Cordrey:** Rober *de Querderai* c1200 Riev (Y); Hugh *Queor de Rey* 1246 AssLa; Thomas *le Cordrey* 1275 SRWo; Richard *Cordray* 1287 Fees (Wt); William *Corderei* 1327 SRWo; Peter *Kerderey* 1332 SRSr; Robert *Querderey* 1347 WhC (La). *Corderoy* corresponds to Fr *cœur-de-roi* '(with the) heart of a king'; the early forms have AFr *rei* 'king' which survives as *-ray, -r(e)y. Corder(e)y, Cordray* and *Cordrey* may also derive from OFr *corderie* 'rope-walk': John *de la Corderie* 1292 Bardsley, a worker at the ropery.

Cordes, Cords, Coard: Walter, Osmer *Corde* 1182–1211 BuryS (Sf), 1185 P (Co). OFr *corde* 'string' (c1300 MED). Metonymic for CORDER.

Cordle: *v.* CORDELL

Cordner, Codner: (i) Randolf *se Cordewan*' 1100–30 OEByn (D); Richard *Cordewaner* 1170 P (St); Walter *Lecordewaner* 1173 P (Gl); Maurice *le corduaner* 1221 AssWo; Bartholomew *le Cordenewaner* 1281 MESO (L). AFr *cordewaner*, OFr *cordoanier* 'cordwainer, shoemaker'. *Corduaner*, no doubt, became *Cord(e)ner*. (ii) Peres, Stephen *le Cordener* 1292 SRLo, 1312 Gardner (Sf). A derivative of OFr *cordon* 'cord, ribbon'. *v.* CORDER.

Cordon: Robert *Cordon* 1327 SRSf. OFr *cordon* 'cord'. Metonymic for *cordoner*. *v.* CORDNER.

Cordray, Cordrey: *v.* CORDEREY

Cordwell: John *de Caldewell* 1327 SRDb. From Cordwell in Holmsfield (Derby).

Cordwent: *v.* CORDEN

Corey: *v.* CORY

Corfe: (i) Alard *de Corf* 1195 P (Gl). From Corfe Castle or Corfe Mullen (Dorset), or Corfe (Som). (ii) Angod' *le Corf* 1208 Cur (Bk). OFr *corf* 'raven'. *v.* CORB.

Cork, Corke, Corck: Geoffrey *Cork* 1278 LLB B. ME *cork* 'cork', metonymic for CORKER.

Corkan: *v.* CORCORAN

Corker: Adam, Geoffrey *le Corker* 1297 Wak (Y), 1338 MESO (La). A derivative of ME *cork* 'a purple or red dye-stuff', one who sells purple dye; or synonymous with (William) *le Corklittster* 1279 MESO (Y), a dyer of cloth with 'cork'.

Corkett: *v.* CALDECOT

Corkhill, Corkill: Donald *MacCorkyll* 1408, Edward *Corkhill* 1532 Moore. A Manx contraction of *Mac Þorketill, MacÞorkill.* cf. the Gaelic MCCORQUODALE, MCCORKELL, and *v.* THURKETTLE, THURKELL.

Corlett: *Corlett* 1504, *MacCorleot* 1511 Moore. A Manx contraction of *MacÞorliótr*, from ON *Þorliótr* 'Thor-people'.

Cormack, Cormick: Irish *Ó Cormaic* 'descendant of *Cormac*'. 'Son of the chariot.'

Cormade: A variant of Manx KERMODE.

Cormell: Gozelin, Anfrid *de Cormelies, de Cormeliis, de Cormel* 1086 DB (Ha, He); Ralph *de Cormeilles* 1197 P (Gl); Roger *de Cormell*' 1222 Cur (Ess). The DB tenants derive from Cormeilles (Eure) but other families may have come later from Cormeilles-en-Vexin. *v.* ANF.

Cornah, Cornall, Cornell, Corney, all common in Lancs, derive from a lost place in Lancs. cf.

William *de Cornay* 1332 SRLa; John *Cornall* of Cornall (1672), Adam *Corney* (1666), Richard *Corney* of Greenhall (1571), Richard *Cornah* of Greenall (1737 LaWills).

Cornell: A weakened form of CORNALL, CORN-HILL, CORNWALL or CORNWELL. Cornhill (Nb) is *Cornhale* 12th, *Cornelle* 1539 FeuDu. Henry *de Cornell'* (1229–31 StP) took his name from Corn-hill (London). Thomas *Cornell* (1722 HorringerPR) is also called *Cornwall* (1736), *Cornwell* (1740) and *Cornhill* (1766). A further source is Fr *corneille* 'rook, crow', a nickname for a chatterer: Herbert *corneilla* 1148 Winton (Ha); William *Corneille* 1206 Cur.

Corner, Cornner: (i) John *de Cornera* 1204 P (Ess); Dyonisia *Attecornere* 1297 MinAcctCo; Agnes *de la Cornere* in Bredstrate 1299 LoCt. AFr, ME *corner* 'angle, corner' (a1300 NED), 'place where two streets meet' (1382). 'One who lived near the corner', as, no doubt, did Roger *Cornirer* 1218–22 StP (Lo). cf. BRIDGER. Alys or Agnes *Acorner* gave a close called *Cornerwong* to the Abbey of Shelford a1483 (NottBR). (ii) Hereu-eus *Cornur* 1179 P (Sf); William *le Cornur* 1185 RotDom (L); Agnes *le cornier* 1209 P (Nt); Augustine *le corner* 1230 P (Db). AFr *cornier*, OFr *corneor* 'hornblower', from OFr *corn* 'a musical instrument, horn' (c1477 NED).

Cornes: *v.* CORNISH

Cornet: Durand, Alured *cornet* 1148 Winton (Ha), 1195 P (Co). OFr *cornet* 'a wind instrument made of horn or resembling a horn' (a1400 NED), a diminutive of *corn*. cf. CORNER (ii). 'A player of the cornet.'

Corney: Benedict *de Corneye* 1260 AssC; Robert *Cornay* 1301 SRY. From Corney (Herts, Cumb). *v.* CORNAH.

Cornford, Cornforth: Thomas *de Corneford* 1242 AssDu; Michael *de Cornford* 1339 CorLo; William *Cornefurth* 1469 FrY; Richard *Corneforth* 1514 FFEss. From Cornford (Durham).

Cornhill: Geruase *de Cornhill'* 1179 P (K); William *Cornhel* 1214 Cur (Y); Henry *de Cornhell'* 1229–31 StP (Lo); Bartholomew *ate Cornhell* 1311 ColchCt. From Cornhill (London) or one of the many places of that name, some of which are no longer remembered. This often becomes CORNELL and has been confused with CORNALL, CORNWALL and CORNWELL.

Cornish, Cornes: Badekoc *Korneys* 1296 SRSx; John *Corneys* 1327 SRSf; Henry *Cornysh* 1375 LoPleas. *Cornish* 'a Cornish man' is first recorded in NED in 1547. There must have been a ME *Cornish* formed on the analogy of *English* which was usually Normanized as *Corneys*. Adam *Cornys* (1300 LoCt) is probably identical with Adam *le Cornwalais* 1275 RH. *v.* CORNWALLIS.

Cornwall: William *de Cornewale*, *de Cornewayle* 1305 LoCt, LLB B. From Cornwall.

Cornwallis: Henry *le Cornwaleys* 1256 Ass (Ha); Stephen *le Cornewalleys* 1260 AssC; Walter *le Corn-wallis* 1280 LLB A. A Normanizing of an un-recorded ME *Cornwalish*. Walter *le Cornewaleys*,

sheriff of London in 1277 (LLB A), is also called Walter *de Cornwall* in 1280 and Walter *le Engleys* in 1277. As Ekwall notes, his real name must have been *English* (*Engleys*) which was changed to *Corn-waleys* or *Cornwall* after his removal to London.

Cornwell: Roger *de Cornwelle* 1161 Eynsham. From Cornwell (Oxon). *v.* CORNELL.

Corp, Corpe: Walter, William *le Corp* 1177 P (Y), 1231 Oseney (O); James *Corp* 1297 Min-AcctCo (Sf). In Yorks and Suffolk, the source is ON *korpr* 'raven', in Oxfordshire, probably OFr *corp* 'raven'.

Corran, Corrin: *M'Corrane* 1422, *M'Corrin*, *Cor-rin* 1504 Moore. A Manx contraction of *Mac Oran* from *Mac Odhrain* 'son of *Odhran*' pale-faced, Ir *Odar*. St Odhran was St Patrick's charioteer.

Corser: Anketill *le Corser* 1227 AssSt. ME *corser* 'jobber, horse-dealer' (c1383 MED).

Corson: *v.* CURZON

Corte: *v.* COURT

Corteen: Ceallach *Mac Curtin* 1376, *Cortin* 1652, *Corteen* 1659 Moore. A Manx contraction of *Mac Cruitin* 'son of *Cruitin*' (hunch-backed), meta-thesized to *Mac Curtin*.

Cortes, Cortis: *v.* CURTIS

Corwin: *v.* CORDEN

Cory, Corey: Robert *Cori* 1266 FFEss; Henry *Cory* 1297 MinAcctCo (W), 1327 SRC. This might be ON *Kori*, the first element of Corby (Lincs, Northants), or ON *Kári*. cf. *Cari* 1066 DB (Lei), Walter *Cari* 1200 P (Sf), and Corton (Suffolk), DB *Karetun*, 1266 *Corton*.

Cosens, Cosin, Cosyns: *v.* COUSEN

Cosh, Coyish, Coysh: Lucas *de la Kosche* 1248 Ass (Ess); Roger *de Coyssh* 1296 SRSx; Robert *Cosh* Ed 1 AD ii (Lei); Philip *atte Cossh* 1327 SR (Ess). ME *cosche*, *cosshe* 'small cottage, hut, hovel' (c1490 NED).

Cossar, Cosser: Ralph *le Kosser'* 1299 MESO (Ess); John *Cosser*, *Cossier* 1392 LLB H. ME *cosser* 'dealer, broker', 'horse-corser' (1300 MED).

Cossentine: *v.* CONSTANTINE

Cossins: *v.* COUSEN

Costain, Costean, Costen: *Costane*, *Costan* 1583 ODCN (Y); *Costaine* or *Constantine* 1586 ib. (Y); Hen *Costen*, *Costein* 1182, 1197 P (Lei); Alex *Cos-tein* 1219 Cur (Lei). *Costein* is from *Costetin* by dissimilatory loss of *t*. cf. CONSTANTINE. In the Isle of Man, the surname is a contraction of *Mac Austeyn*, from *Mac Augustin* 'son of Augustin': *Costeane* 1507, *Mac Coisten*, *Mac Costen*, *Coisten*, *Costen* 1511, *Costain* 1715 Moore.

Coste: *Coste* de Widkale 1175 P (L); *Costus* Falconarius 1180 P (Nt); Osbert, Hugo *Coste* 1218 AssL, 1317 AssK. A short form of *Constantine*, common as *Costantin*, *Costetin*. *v.* CONSTANTINE, COSTINS.

Costean, Costen: *v.* COSTAIN

Costins, Costons, Costings: Herbert *filius Con-stantini*, *Costin* 1207 Cur (Nf); *Costinus* 1221 ElyA (Sf); William *Costin* ib. (Nf); Elycia *Costan-tyn*, *Costyn* 1311, 1329 ColchCt. A short form of CONSTANTINE. *v.* also COSTAIN.

Cote, Cotes, Coat, Coate, Coates, Coatts, Cottis, Dallicoat, Dallicott, Delicate: William *de Cotes* 1190 P (L); Walter *de la Cote* 1210 Cur (O); Godfrey *Cote* 1214 Cur (K); Roger *atte Kote* 1296 SRSx. From Coat (Som), Cote (Oxon), Coates (Lincs), Cotes (Leic), or one of the numerous similarly named places, all from OE *cot, cote* 'cottage', also 'shelter', sometimes 'a woodman's hut'. In ME, when the term was common, the surname may denote a dweller at the cottage(s) or, as it was used especially of a sheep-cote, one employed in the care of animals, a shepherd.

Cotgrave, Cotgreave, Cotgrove: Robert *de Cotegraue* 1202 FFL; Thomas *de Cotegrave* 1259 AssCh; Richard *Cotgrave* 1458 IpmNt. From Cotgrave (Notts), or Cotgreave in Mapperley (Derby).

Cotherill: *v.* COTTEREL

Cotman, Coatman: Ulkillus *cotmannus* 1183 Boldon (Du); William *Cotman, Coteman, Mercator* 1206–8 P (Sx); William *Coteman* 1275 RH (Nf). OE *cot* 'cottage' and *mann* 'a cottager', 'cotset', 'coterell', in Scotland 'a cottar' (*cotmannus* DB, *cotman* 1559 NED), corresponding to Med-Lat *bordarius*. cf. COTTER, COTTEREL. The equation with *Mercator* points to an alternative origin. OFr, ME *cote* 'outer-garment, coat' (c1300 NED), 'seller of coats'. cf. *Capman* 'maker or seller of caps' MESO 116.

Coton, Cottam, Cottom, Cotten, Cotton: Randulf *de Cotton* 1185 P (Wo); Ralph *de Cottum* 1212 Cur (Y); Stephen *de Coten*' 1297 MinAcctCo (L); John *de Cotome* 1310 LLB B; John *de Cotun* 1325 ib. D; Brian *Cotham, Cotam* 1569, 1596 FrY. OE *æt cotum* (dweller) 'at the cottages', as at Coton (Cambs), Cotton (Ches), Coatham (Durham, NRYorks), Cotham (Notts), Cottam (Notts, ERYorks). The *-um* is preserved only in Durham, Lancs, Notts and Yorks; *Cot(t)on* is found in the midlands, in Cambs, Ches, Derby, Leic, Lincs, Northants, Salop, Staffs, Oxon, Warwicks. cf. COTE.

Cottel, Cottell, Cottle, Cuttell, Cuttill, Cuttles: Beringarius *Cotel* 1084 GeldR (W); Adam *Cotella* 1167 P (Do); Eilwinus *Kutel, Cutel* 1185 Templars (Ess); Walter *Cotel* 1206 Cur (O). The first form is probably, as suggested by Tengvik, OFr *cotel* 'coat of mail'. The later examples may also derive from OFr *cotel, coutel* 'a short knife or dagger' and are probably metonymic for a cutler.

Cotter, Cottier: Robert *le Cotier* 1198 P (Sx); William *le Coter(e)* 1270 HPD (Ess), 1297 MinAcctCo. OFr *cotier* 'cottager' (1386 NED), DB *cotarius* 'villein who held a cot by labour-service'. *v.* COTMAN, COTTEREL. Both names are found in Isle of Man, pronounced *Cotchier* (MacCotter, MacCottier 1504, *Cottier* 1616, *Cotter* 1625 Moore), from *Mac Ottar*, 'son of Ottar' (ON *Óttarr*).

Cotterel, Cotterell, Cotterill, Cotherill, Cottrell, Cottrill: William, Gerard *Coterel* 1130, 1170 P (Lo, Berks); Honde *Cotrell* 1288 AssCh. OFr *coterel*, a diminutive of OFr *cotier* 'cottager' (1393 NED), DB *coterellus*. cf. COTTER.

Cottis: *v.* COTE
Cottle: *v.* COTTEL
Cottom, Cotton: *v.* COTON
Cottrell, Cottrill: *v.* COTTEREL
Coubrough: David *Cowbratht* 1515 Black, Euphame *Cubrughe* 1669 ib. For MACCOUBRIE.

Couch, Cooch, Cough: Geruerd *Coh* 1160 P (Sa); John *Coh* 1167 P (He); Meriaduc *Choch* 1170 P (Sa); Thomas *Cuche* 1305 AssSt. Welsh *coch* 'red'.

Couch, Couche: Simon, John *Couche* 1279 RH (O), 1386 LoPleas. ME, OFr *couch* 'couch, bed'. Metonymic for COUCHER.

Coucher, Coucha, Cowcher: Stephen *Cuchur* Ed 1 Battle (Sx); Nicholas *le Couchur* 1295 MESO (Wo). AFr *coucheour* 'maker of couches, upholsterer'.

Couchman: Thomas *Cocheman* 1374 Ct (Ha); William *Cowcheman* 1500 KentW. Identical in meaning with COUCHER.

Coudray: *v.* COWDRAY
Cough: *v.* COUCH
Coulbeck: *v.* COLDBECK
Couldwell: *v.* CALDWELL
Couling, Coulling: *v.* COWLING
Coulman: *v.* COLEMAN
Coulsen, Coulson: *v.* COLESON
Coulston: *v.* COLSTON
Coult: *v.* COLT

Coultar, Coulter, Culter: Alexander *de Cultre* c1248 Black; John *Coulter* 1686 ib. From Coulter (Lanarkshire, Aberdeenshire).

Coultard, Coultart: *v.* COLTARD
Coultas, Coultass, Coultous, Coultish, Cowtas: William *Cowthus* 1562 FrY; John *Coultas, Coultus, Cowtus* 1657, 1671, 1691, 1733 FrY. 'Worker at the colt-house', colt-keeper.

Coulthard: *v.* COLTARD
Coulton: *v.* COLTON
Councel, Councell, Council, Counsel, Counsell, Consell: William *Cunseil* 1208 P (Berks), *Consell* 1208 Cur (Bk); John *Counseil* 1310 LLB D. AFr *counseil*, OFr *conseil, cunseil* 'consultation, deliberation' (c1290 NED).

Count, Le Count, Lecount: Ralph *le Cunte* 1196 P (Du); Walterus *Comes, le Conte* 1204–5 Cur (Sf); William *Counte* 1225 AssSo. AFr *counte*, OFr *conte, cunte*, Lat *comitem* 'count' (1553 NED).

Counter: Matthew *Cunter* 1250 Fees (Ha); John *le Cuntur, le Cunter, le Counter* 1289, 1301 AssSt. AFr *countour*, OFr *conteor* 'one who counts, reckons', 'accountant, treasurer' (1297 NED).

Countess: Agnes *Cuntasce* 1279 RH (C); John *Cuntesse* 1279 RH (Beds); John *le Contesse* 1327 SRSf. OFr *contesse* 'countess', when applied to a woman, probably 'proud, haughty as a countess'; applied to a man as a nickname for an effeminate dandy.

Couper: *v.* COOPER
Coupland: *v.* COPELAND
Courage: (i) Walter, William *Curage* 1254, 1260 FFEss. ME *corage*, OFr *corage, curage*, used as an adjective, 'stout' of body. cf. Corage or Craske,

Crassus, coragiosus c1440 PromptParv. (ii) John *de Courugge* 1309 SRBeds. From Cowridge End in Luton (Beds) which came to be pronounced *Courage* and is now pronounced *Scourge End*. *v.* also KERRICH.

Coursey: *v.* DECOURCY

Court, Courts, Corte, Curt: (i) William *de la Curt, de la Cort* 1242 Ipm (Sa); Richard *atte Curt*, William *de la Court* 1296 SRSx. From residence or employment at a large house or manor-house, castle, from OFr *cort, curt*, ME *curt, courte* (1297 NED). cf. COURTMAN. (ii) Reginald *Corte* 1181 P (Sf); Richard *le Curt* 1199 FF (Sr); Richard *le Cort* 1279 RH (O). OFr *curt* 'short, small'.

Courtald, Courtauld: A Huguenot name which Dauzat explains as a diminutive of *court* 'short, small'.

Courtenay, Courteney: Reginald *de Curtenay, de Courtenay* 1164–9 Bury, c1182 Gilb (L). From Courtenay (Loiret, Isère).

Courthope: William *de Curtehope* 1296 SRSx. Cf. Courtup Fm, *Curtehope* (1310 PN Sx 231), but, as the well-known Sussex family is commonly found in East Sussex, it derived, perhaps, from an unidentified *Curting(e)hope* in the eastern part of the county.

Courtice, Courtis: *v.* CURTIS

Courtier: Nicholas *le Curter* 1279 RH (O). A derivative of ME *curt*, identical in meaning with COURT and COURTMAN, rather than the common *courtier* (ME *courteour, courtyer*), which has influenced the spelling.

Courtman: Adam, Robert *Curtman* 1275 RH (C), 1296 SRSx; John *Courtman* 1327 ib. 'Dweller near or one employed at a castle or manor-house.' *v.* COURT, COURTIER.

Courtney: *v.* COURTENAY

Cousans: *v.* COUSEN

Couse: Robertus *filius Cous* 1297 MinAcctCo (R); Robert, William *Couse* 1185 P, 1211 Cur (L). ON *Kouse, Kause*, corresponding to ON *Kausi*, a nickname meaning 'tom-cat', the first element of Cowesby (NRYorks).

Cousen, Cousens, Cousans, Cousin, Cousins, Couzens, Cosens, Cosin, Cosyns, Cossins, Cossons, Cozens, Cozins, Cozins, Cusins, Cussen, Cussins, Cussons, Cuzen: Æthelstano *chusin*, id est, cognato suo (i.e. of Wlfstan) c977 (c1200) LibEl (C); Sumerda, Roger *Cusin* 1166, 1169 P (Nf, L); Simon *Cosyn* 1260 AssC; Thomas *Cossin* 1275 RH (Lo); Agnes *Cousseyns* 1327 SRSf. OFr. *cusin, cosin*, in ME 'a kinsman or kinswoman', 'cousin' (c1290 NED). *v.* CUSSEN.

Coventry: Alan *de Couintre* 1194 P (Nth); Henry *de Coventre* 1262–3 FFEss; John *Coventre* 1366 IpmW. From Coventry (Warwicks).

Cover: (i) Robert *le Cuver* 1210 FrLeic; Richard *Couer* 1219 AssY. A derivative of ME, OFr *cuve* 'cask, vat', or OFr **cuvier* 'cooper'. (ii) Walter *le Cuverur* 1200 Cur (Sr); Hamund *le Coverur* 1262 For (Ess). OFr *couvreor, covreor* 'one who covers or roofs buildings' (1393 NED). This would inevitably become *Cover*.

Coverdale: Reginald *de Coverdall* 1245 FFL; Thomas *de Coverdale* 1297 SRY; John *Couerdale* 1379 PTY. From Coverdale (ER, NR, WRYorks).

Cowan: *v.* MacOWEN

Coward, Cowherd: Thomas *le Cuherde* 1255 MEOT (Ess); John *Kuhirde* 1274 RH (Hu); Adam *le Couherd* 1317 AssK; John *Cowherde* 1327 SRWo; John *Coward* 1540 Whitby (Y). OE *cūhyrde* 'cow-herd'. A rare variant is evidenced in the forename of *Cuward* de Blakepet 1198 FF (Bk). OE **cū-weard* 'cow-guard'. *Cowherd* is uncommon.

Cowcher: *v.* COUCHER

Cowdray, Cowdrey, Cowdry, Cowdroy, Cowderoy, Cowdery, Coudray: Engelram *de Coudrai* c1170 Riev (Y); Richard *de Coudrey* 1220 Cur (Ha); Henry *de la Coudrey* 1279 AssSt. OFr *coudraie* 'hazel-copse'. The earliest bearers of the name came from France, e.g. Coudrai (Seine-Inférieure), Coudray (Eure), etc. As Cowdray (Sussex), which has replaced the earlier English name of *Sengle*, is found as *la Codray* in 1285 (PN Sx 17), the French *coudraie* was also used in England and the surname may derive from the Sussex place or denote residence near a hazel-copse. Later forms show confusion with CORDEREY.

Cowell, Cowwell: (i) Henry *de Cuwell* 1196 MemR (Nth); Thomas *de Cuhull'* 1221 AssGl; John *Cowell* 1401 AssLa. From Cowhill (Lancs, Glos), or Cowleigh Park (Worcs). (ii) In Manx for *Mac Cathmaoil* 'son of *Cathmaol*', Cionaidh *Ua Cathmhaoil* 967, Conor *Mac Cawel* 1252, *McCowle, McCowell, Cowle* 1511, *Cowell* 1690 Moore.

Cowherd: *v.* COWARD

Cowler, Cowlman: Richard *le Coulare* 1333 MEOT (So). A derivative of OE *cug(e)le, cūle* 'a garment worn by monks, a cowl', a maker of cowls.

Cowley: Osbert *de Couela* 1167 P (O); Juliana *de Kulega* 1199 AssSt; John *de Couele* 1230 P (Mx); William *de Coule* 1314 LLB E; William *de Colley* 1327 SRDb. From Cowley (Bucks, Devon, Oxon, Staffs; Derby, Lancs; Glos, Middlesex), of varied origins.

Cowley, Kewley: Flann *MacAulay* 1178, *Mac-Cowley* 1504, *Cowley* 1587, *Kewley* 1611 Moore. A Manx contraction of MACAULAY.

Cowling, Cowlin, Couling, Coulling: Mathew *de Couling* 1260 AssC; William *Cowlyng* 1520 FrY. From Cowling (WRYorks). *v.* also COLLING.

Cowlishaw, Coleyshaw, Collishaw: William *Colishaw* 1680 DbAS 36; Sarah *Cowlishaw* 1704 ib. From Cowlishaw (Lancs, Derby).

Cowlman: *v.* COWLER

Cowper: *v.* COOPER

Cowpland: *v.* COPELAND

Cowtas: *v.* COULTAS

Cowwell: *v.* COWELL

Cox: *v.* COCK

Coxall: *v.* COGGESHALL

Coxeter: Adam *le Cocsetere* 1260 AssCh. 'One who sets the cocks in a cock-fight' (1828 NED).

Coxhead: Thomas *Cokkeshed* 1424 LondEng. 'Cock's head', a nickname.

Coxon, Coxen, Cockson: Godui *Coccesune* c1095 Bury (Sf); Roger *Cokson* 1332 SRCu; John *Coxson* 1539 FeuDu; William *Coxon* 1631 FrY. 'Son of *Cock*', an original nickname from OE *coc(c)* 'cock'.

Coy, Coey: Walter *le Coi* 1203 AssNth; Walter *le Coy* 1296 SRSx; William *Coye* 1301 SRY. Fr *coi*, earlier *quei* 'quiet, still', 'shy, coy' (c1330 NED).

Coyish: *v.* COSH

Coyne: Allan *Coigne* 13th Ronton (St); John *Coyne* 1242 FFSt; John *Coyn* 1327 SRC. ME *coyn, coigne*, AFr *coigne*, Fr *coin* 'a die for stamping money' (1362 NED), 'a piece of money' (c1386). Metonymic for coiner, minter, a common occupation-name: William *le Coiner* 1327 SRSo. cf. CONYER.

Coysh: *v.* COSH

Cozens, Cozins: *v.* COUSEN

Crabb, Crabbe, Krabbe: Walter, Steffanus *Crabbe* 1188 P (Do), 1217 Pat. OE *crabba* 'crab', either for one who walked like a crab (cf. *Crabeleg* 1148 Winton) or, as in German and East Frisian, for a cross-grained, fractious person; or ME *crabbe* 'wild apple' (c1420 NED), of persons 'crabbed, cross-grained, ill-tempered' (1580).

Crabtree: John *atte Crabbetrywe* 1301 ParlR (Ess). 'Dweller by the wild apple-tree' (c1425 NED).

Crace: *v.* CRASS

Crackel: Alan *de Crachale* 1204 AssY; Thomas *Crakall* 1414 FrY. From Crakehall or Crakehill (NRYorks).

Cracknall, Cracknell: Elias *de Crackenhal'* 1220 Cur (Y); Robert *Craknell* 1524 SRSf. Crakehall and Crakehill (NRYorks) are explained by Smith as 'Craca's nook'. This would be OE *Cracanhale*, a form which has survived in the surname although not evidenced in the place-name forms. cf. CRACKEL.

Craddock, Cradduck, Cradock, Cradick: *Cradoc* (*Caradoch'*) 1177 P (He), 1185 P (Glam); *Craddoc* Arcuarius 1187 P (Sa); William, Philip *Craddoc* 1205 P (Wo), 1296 SRSx; Robert *Cradock* 1301 SRY. Welsh *Caradawc, Cradawc, Caradoc, Caradog*, an old and famous name, familiar in its Latin form *Caractacus* for *Caratācos* who was taken as prisoner to Rome c. 51 A.D.

Craft, Crafts: (i) Aluric *Craft* 1185 Templars (Ess); Basil *Craft* 1283 SRSf. OE *cræft* 'skill, art', especially 'guile, cunning'. (ii) Roger *de Craft* 1213 Cur (Wa), *de Croft* (*Craft*) 1214 ib.; Robert *de Craft* 1222 AssWa. From Croft (Lei), earlier *Craft*. Probably also local. *v.* CROFT.

Cragg, Craggs: Henry *Crag* 1204 AssY; Hudde *del Crag* 1260 AssLa; Peter *del Kragg*, John *Cragges* 1301 SRY. 'Dweller by the steep or precipitous rugged rock(s)' (ME *crag*).

Craig John *del Crag* 1143–1214 Black; John *of the Craig* 1335 ib. A Scottish form of CRAGG.

Craigie: Brice *de Cragy* 1317 Black; John *de Craigie* 1371 ib. From Craigie (Ayrshire, West Lothian, Angus, Perthshire).

Craik, Crake, Creyk: Henry *de Crake* (Dumfries), James *de Crake* (Selkirk) 1296 CalSc; Andrew *Craik* 1453 Black. Scottish Lowland surnames from Crayke (NRYorks).

Crain, Craine: *McCroyn* 1408, *McCraine* 1422, *MacCarrane* 1422, *Craine* 1586 Moore. A Manx contraction of *Mac Ciarain* 'son of *Ciaran*'.

Craise: For CRASS.

Crake: Ralph, Henry *Crake* 1276, 1279 RH (Y, C). ME *crake* 'crow or raven'.

Crakebone: Simon, Walter *Crakebon* 1279 RH (C), 1327 *SR* (Ess). 'Crack bone', 'break bone', a nickname for the official who inflicted the cruel punishment of medieval law. cf. 'Quikliche cam a cacchepol and craked a-two here legges' (Langland). cf. BRISBANE.

Craker: *v.* CRAWCOUR

Cramp: Walter *Crampe* 1200 Oseney (O); William *Crampe*, Richard *le Crompe* 1275 SRWo. A variant of CRUMP. cf. OHG *chrampf*, Ger *krampf* 'curved, a hook'.

Cran: *v.* CRANE

Crane, Cran: Osbert *Crane* 1177 P (C); Jordan *Cran* 1219 Cur (Ess); William *le Crane* 1235 FFEss; Thomas *le Cran* 1243 AssSo. OE *cran* 'crane', no doubt 'long-legged'.

Crank, Cronk: Godric *Cranc'* 1121–48 Bury (Sf). ME *cranke* 'lusty, vigorous', 'in high spirits', 'merry' (1398 NED).

Crankshaw, Cranshaw: *v.* CRONKSHAW

Crapper: *v.* CROPPER

Craske: Godith *Crasc* 1197 P (Nf); Ralph *Craske* 1207 Cur (Nf). 'The fat, lusty'. cf. c1440 PromptParv 'craske, or fryke of fatte (K. crask, or lusty). *crassus*'.

Crass, Crace, Craise, Craze: Normannus *Crassus* 1086 DB (L); Hervey *le Cras* 1130–2 Seals (St); Rogerus *Crassus*, Roger *le Cras* 1203 Cur (L); Robert *Krase* 1277 *Ely* (Sf). OFr *cras* 'fat, big', Lat *crassus*. *v.* also GRACE and GROSS with which this name was early confused: Rogerus *Crossus*, *Crassus*, *Grassus* 1202 AssL; Hugo *Grassus*, *Crassus* 1211–12 Cur (W).

Crasswell: *v.* CARSWELL

Crassweller: John *Cressweller* 1558 SxWills. 'Man from Cresswell.' *v.* CARSWELL.

Crauford, Craufurd, Crawford, Crawforth, Crawfurd: John *de Crauford* 1147–60 (Black). From Crawford (Lanark). The surname appears early in England: Nicolaus *de Crauford* 1205 P (So).

Craven: Torfin, John *de Crauene* 1166 Cur (Y), 1242 AssDu; John, Agnes *Craven* 1332 SRCu. From the district of Craven (WRYorks).

Crawcour, Craker, Croaker, Croker, Crocker, Creegor, Cregor: Helias *de Creuequor* 1158 P (Sf); Robert (*de*) *Creuequoer* 1195 P (K); Robert *de Crouequoer* 1200 P (K); Rainald, Alexander *de Creuker* 1212 Fees (L); Robert *de Crequer* 1284 FA (C). From Crèvecœur (Calvados, Oise, Nord). The baronial family came from Calvados. Occasional examples with *le* suggest the possibility also of a nickname, Fr *crève-cœur* 'break heart, heart-breaker'. cf. Richard *Brekehert* 1327 SRSo.

The surname has probably been partly absorbed by *Craker, Croaker, Croker* and *Crocker*. Hamo *de Creueker* has left his name in Crockers (Sussex) and The Creakers in Great Barford (Beds), *Crewkers* 1539, *Crecors* 17th, *Crakers* 1766 (PN Sx 524, PN BedsHu 52).

Crawley, Crowley: Pagan *de Craweleia* 1130 P (Bk); Thomas *de Crowele* c1280 SRWo; William *Craweley* 1397 IpmGl. From Crawley (Bucks, Essex, Hants, Oxon, Sussex), or Crawley in Membury (Devon).

Crawshaw, Crawshay, Croshaw, Crowsher: John *de Crouschagh* 1308 Wak (Y); Adam *de Craweshaghe* 1332 SRLa; Ralph *de Croshawe* 1379 PTY; Susanna *Crawshay* 1760 Bardsley. From Crawshaw Booth (Lancs).

Craze: *v.* CRASS

Crearer: *v.* CRERAR

Crease, Crees, Creese: Cenric *Cres* c1095 Bury (Sf); Richard *le Cres* 1275 RH (Nf); Hugh *Crees* 1316 Wak (Y). OE *crēas* 'fine, elegant'.

Crebbin: *v.* CRIBBIN

Crecy, Cressy: Hugo *de Creissi* 1171 P (La); Alexander *de Crecy, de Cressi* c1182 Gilb, 1185 Templars (L); Beatrix *Cressy* Hy 3 Gilb (L). From Cressy (Seine-Inférieure). *v.* ANF.

Creech: (i) John *ate Creche* 1327 SRSx; Robert *Creche* 1327 SRSf. 'Dweller by the creek'; OE **cricc*, ME *crich(e)*, with lengthening of *i* in the open syllable became *crēche*. *v.* PN C 254–6. (ii) Peter *de Cryche* 1327 SRSo. From Creech (Dorset, Som). (iii) Douenaldus *de Creych* 1204–41 Black. From Creich (Fifeshire).

Creed (i) *Creda* 1198 FFNf; *Crede* 1279 Barnwell (C); Wadin *Crede* 1191 P (Wa); Theynewin *Crede* 1242 AssSo. OE *Creoda* (Redin). (ii) John *de Crede* 1370 LoPleas. From Creed Fm in Bosham (Sussex).

Cre(e)gor: *v.* CRAWCOUR

Crees(e): *v.* CREASE

Creighton: John *de Creghton* 1327 SRDb. From Creighton (Staffs). *v.* CRICHTON.

Crellin: A metathesized form of *Crennell*, a Manx name from *MacRaghnaill* 'son of *Raghnall*', from ON *Rǫgnvaldr* 'ruler of the gods', the name of several kings of Man: Godfrey *MacMicRagnaill*, king of Dublin, 1075, *MacReynylt* 1511, *Crenilt* 1627, *Crennil* 1646, *Crellin* 1610 Moore.

Crenell, Crennell: *v.* CARNALL, CRELLIN

Crepin: *v.* CRISPIN

Crerar, Crerer, Crearer: John *McAchrerar* 1541 Black; William *Crerar* 1554 ib. Gael *criathrar* (miller's) 'sifter' or 'sievewright'.

Cressall, Cressell, Cresswell: *v.* CARSWELL

Cressy: *v.* CRECY

Crew(e)s: *v.* CRUISE

Crewther: *v.* CROWTHER

Cribb, Cribbes: Hugo, Osbert *Cribbe* 1195, 1200 P (So). OE *crib(b)* originally 'a barred receptacle for fodder in cow-sheds' (used of the manger of Christ c1000), 'a stall or cabin of an ox' (a1340 NED). cf. dial *crib* 'cattle-fold'. The surname is metonymic for a cow-man.

Cribbin, Crebbin, Gribbin, Gribbon: *MacRobyn* 1511, *Crebbin* 1640, *Cribbin* 1666 Moore. Ir *MacRoibin* 'Robin's son'. *Crebbin* is Manx.

Crichton, Crighton, Chrichton, Creighton: Turstan *de Crectune* c1128 (Black); Thomas *de Creitton* c1200 ib.; William *de Crichton* c1248 ib.; Alisaundre *de Creightone* 1296 ib.; Margaret *Chrightone* 1685 ib. From Crichton (Midlothian).

Crier, Cryer: Geoffrey, Ralph *le Criur* 1221 Cur (Herts), 1221 AssWo; Robert *le Crieur* 1269 AssNb. ME *criere*, OFr *criere*, nominative of *crieur* 'crier', 'officer of the court of justice who makes public announcements' (1292 NED), 'common or town crier' (1387 NED).

Crighton: *v.* CRICHTON

Crippen, Crippin: *v.* CRISPIN

Cripps: *v.* CRISP

Crisp, Crispe, Chrisp, Cripps, Crips, Chrippes, Scripps: Benedictus *Crispus* c1030 OEByn; Henry *le Cresp* c1200 ELPN; Walter *Crips* 1273 RH (Hu); Richard *Crysp* 1275 SRWo; Richard *Crispe, Crips* 1289 AssCh; Joan *le Crypse* 1297 MinAcctCo; Gilbert *le Crispe* 1311 Battle (Sx); John *Chrispe* 1589 SfPR. OE *crisp, cryps*, Lat *crispus* 'curly, curly-haired' or OFr *crespe* 'curled'. *Crisp* may also be a short form of *Crispin*. cf. Odin *Crispi filius* c1095 Bury (Sf), Roger *filius Crispi* c1150–60 DC (L). *Scripps* is for *Cripps*, with inorganic initial *S* as in STURGE.

Crispin, Chrispin, Crepin, Crippen, Crippin: Stanmer *Crispini filius* c1095 Bury (Sf); *Crespinus* 1207 Cur (L); Willelmus *filius Crispian* 1273 RH (O); *Creppinus le Seller* 1319 SRLo, *Crispin la Seeler* 1336 LLB E; Milo *Crispinus* 1086 DB; Turstin' *Crispin* 1166 P (Y); Ralph *Crespin* 1169 P (D); Ralph *Crispun* 1208 Cur (Y); Elias *Crepun* 1208 P (W); Roger *le Crespin* 1268 AssSo; Edmund, Walter *Crepyn* 1312, 1317 FFC. *Crispinus*, a Roman cognomen from Lat *crispus* 'curly', was the name of the patron saint of the shoemakers who was martyred at Soissons c285 along with *Crispinianus*, in French, SS. *Crépin* and *Crépinien*. The former survives as *Crepin* or *Crippin* which may also be nicknames from OFr *crespin*, a derivative of *crespe* 'curly'. cf. Ralph de Alegate called *Crepyn*, Ralph *Crepyn* called de Alegate 1306 LLB B. *Crispun* and *Crepun* are hypocoristics of *Crispin, Crepin* and cannot be associated with OFr *crespon*, Fr *crépon* 'crape', a material with a crisped or minutely wrinkled surface which is unknown before the 16th century. The surnames may derive from the saint or from a nickname 'curly-haired'. According to Lanfranc (d. 1089), Gilbert Crispin was the first man to receive this nickname and two of his sons adopted it as their surname. His grandson Gilbert Crispin was abbot of Westminster.

Crissell, Crisswell, Criswell: *v.* CARSWELL

Croaker: *v.* CRAWCOUR

Croasdale, Croasdell: *v.* CROSSDALE

Crocker, Croker: John *le Crockare* 1275 SRWo; Simon *le Crockere* 1279 RH (O); Henry *le Crokere* 1288 MESO (Sx). A derivative of OE *croc(c)*, *crocca* 'an earthen pot', hence 'potter' (a1333 MED). The surname might also be identical with CRAWCOUR.

Crockford: Richard *de Crocford* 1214 P (Sr); William *de Crockford* 1332 SRSr; Thomas *Crockford* 1576 SRW. From Crockford Bridge in Chertsey (Surrey).

Croft, Crofts, Cruft: Hugo *de Croft* 1162 P (He); Richard *de la Croft* 1230 P (Ha); William *del Croft* 1288 AssCh; Robert *del Croftes* 1332 SRSt; Richard *atte Crofte*, William *Craft, Cruft* 1353 ColchCt; John *Craft, Croft* 1361, 1367 ib. From Croft (Hereford, Lincs, NRYorks) or 'dweller by the croft(s),' OE *croft*. In ColchCt, *Craft* is the almost invariable form. It must often be for *Croft*, but sometimes, probably, for CRAFT.

Crofter: For *atte Croft*. cf. Matill *Croftman* 1327 SRSx.

Croker: *v.* CRAWCOUR, CROCKER

Crole, Croll: *v.* CROWL, CURL

Cromb, Crome, Croom, Croome, Croombes, Croombs, Crumb: (i) Robert *le Crumbe* 1199 AssSt; Maud *le Crombe*, John *Croume* 1275 SRWo; Simon *Crumbe* 1296 SRSx; Luke *Croom* 1309 FFEss; Geoffrey *Crombe* 1327 SRSx. OE *crumb* 'bent, crooked, stooping' or OE **cramb, *cromb*, ME *crome, cromb* 'a hook, crook', also in the forms *croumbe, cromp*. As we also find Richard *le Crombere* 1327 SRSf, the surname may be either a nickname 'bent, stooping' or occupational 'maker of hooks or crooks'. (ii) Adam *de Crumbe* 1199 MemR (Wo); Simon *de Crombe* 1275 SRWo; Stephen *de Crome* 1275 RH (W); John *de Crome* 1349 FrY. From Croom (ERYorks) or Croome (Worcs).

Crombie, Cromie, Crumbie, Crummay, Crummey, Crummie, Crummy: Patrick *of Cromby* 1423 Black; Robert *Crumby* 1450 ib.; David *Crommy* 1516 ib. From Crombie (Aberdeenshire), in which the *b* is not pronounced.

Crompton, Crumpton: Richard *de Crompton* 1246 AssLa; Thomas, Widdow *Crompton* 1592 AssLa, 1672 HTY. From Crompton (Lancs).

Cromwell: Ralph *de Cromwella, de Crumwella* 1177, 1195 P (Nt); John *de Crombewelle* 1310 LLB D; Ralph *Cromwell* 1454 IpmNt. From Cromwell (Notts).

Cronk: *v.* CRANK

Cronkshaw, Cronshaw, Cronshey, Crankshaw, Cranshaw: William *de Crounkeshawe* 1412 WhC (La). From Cronkshaw (Lancs), *Cronkshay* 1507 PN La.

Crook, Crooke, Krook: (i) Rainald *filius Croc*, Rainald *Croc* 1086 DB (Ha); *Crocus venator* Wm 2 (1235) Ch (Ha); Lefwin *Croc* 1066 DB (Sf); Walter *Chroc* c1130 EngFeud (W); Matthew *Croc* 1158 P (Ha); John *le Cruk* 1269 AssSo; Philip *le Crok* 1288 Pat. ON *Krókr*, ODa *Krōk*, which may have been introduced into England from Denmark or Normandy, or the ON nickname *Krókr* 'hook, something crooked', referring to crook-backed or sly and cunning persons. The surname may also derive from the common noun *krókr*, a

Scandinavian loan-word in English, in the latter sense. (ii) John, William *del Crok* 1310–33 InqLa, 1332 SRLa. 'Dweller at a nook or bend', ME *crok*, ON *krókr*.

Crooker: 'Dweller at a bend.' cf. CROOK.

Crookes, Crooks: Robert *de Crokis* 1297 SRY. From Crookes in Sheffield (Yorks).

Crookshank(s): *v.* CRUICKSHANK

Crookson: 'Son of *Crook*.' *v.* CROOK.

Croom(e), Croomb(e)s: *v.* CROMB

Cropper, Crapper: Roger *le Croppere* 1221 AssWo; John *Crapere* 1275 RH (Nf); William *Croper* 1276 RH (Y); Alice *le Crappere* 1315 Wak (Y). A derivative of ME *croppen* 'to crop, pluck', a cropper, reaper. cf. A cropper, *decimator* CathAngl. For the unrounding of *a* in *Crapper*, cf. CRAFT and CROFT.

Crosby, Crosbie, Crossbee: (i) Gillemichel *de Crossebi* 1176 P (We); Adam *de Crosseby* 1227 Cur (L); Henry *Crosseby* 1383 AssWa. From Crosby (Cumb, Lancs, Lincs, Westmorland, NRYorks). (ii) Iuo *de Crosseby* 1178–80 Black; Richard *de Crossebi* c1249 ib.; Robert *de Crosby* 1347 ib. From Crosbie or Corsbie (Ayr, Kirkcudbright, Berwick).

Croshaw: *v.* CRAWSHAW

Crosier, Crozier, Croser: William *le Croyser* 1264 Eynsham (O); William *le Crocer* 1305 MEOT (Sf); Thomas *Croser* 1393 FFEss. OFr *crosier, crocier, crosser* 'crosier', the bearer of a bishop's crook or pastoral staff, or of the cross at a monastery. The name might also denote a seller of crosses or a dweller by a cross. *Croyser* is the common early form.

Cross, Crosse, du Cros: Richard *del Crosse* 1285 AssLa; William *atte Cros* 1327 SRSf; Robert *Cros* 1354 ColchCt. 'Dweller by the cross.'

Crossdale, Croasdale, Croasdell, Croysdill: John *de Crosdale* 1379 PTY; John *Crosedill* 1688 FrY. From Crossdale (Cumb).

Crossland, Crosseland, Crosland: Christiana *de Crosseland* 1308 Wak; George *Crosland*, William *Crosselonde* 1536, 1538 CorNt. From Crosland (WRYorks).

Crossman: Philip *Crosman* 1327 SRSo. 'Dweller by the cross.'

Crosthwaite, Crosswaite, Crostwight: Henry *de Crostweyt* 1242 Fees (Nf); John *de Crosthuaite* 1332 SRCu. From Crostwight, Crostwick (Norfolk) or Crosthwaite (Cumb, Westmorland, NRYorks).

Crotch: *v.* CROUCH

Crother: *v.* CROWTHER

Crothers: *v.* CARRUTHERS

Crouch, Crowch, Crotch, Crutch: Gilbert *Cruche* 1221 Cur (D); William *Attecruche* 1290 *Ass* (Ess); Laurence *atte Crouch* 1327 SRSx; Thomas *Crouch* 1327 *SR* (Ess). 'One who lives near a cross', from OE *crūc*. cf. CROUCHER, CROUCHMAN.

Croucher, Crutcher: Dauid *Crucher* 1220 Cur (So); Christina *le Crochere* 1297 MinAcctCo (Beds); John *Crouchere* 1383 AssC. 'Dweller by the cross.' *v.* CROUCH, CROUCHMAN.

Crouchman: Richard *Crucheman* 1255 *Ass* (Ess);

Ralph *Crocheman* 1260 AssC; John *Croucheman* 1327 SRSx. 'Dweller near the cross.' *v.* CROUCH, CROUCHER.

Croudace: *v.* CARRUTHERS

Crouse: *v.* CRUISE

Crow, Crowe: Ailwin *Crawe* 1180 P (Wa); Nicholas *Crowe* 1187 P (Nf); John *le Crowe* 1332 SRSx. OE *crāwe* 'crow'. In Ireland and the Isle of Man *Crow(e)* is a translation of *Mac Fiachain* 'son of *Fiachan*', 'the crow'.

Crowdace: *v.* CARRUTHERS

Crowhurst, Crowest: Roger *de Croherst* c1200 ArchC vi (K); William *de Crouherst* 1296 SRSx. From Crowhurst (Surrey, Sussex).

Crowl, Crowle, Crole: Walter *de Crul* 1201 P (L); Hugo *de Croul'* 1221 AssWo; Richard *de Crol*, Richard *Croll* 1275–6 RH (L). From Crowle (Lincs, Worcs). *v.* also CURL.

Crowley: *v.* CRAWLEY

Crowsher: *v.* CRAWSHAW

Crowther, Crowder, Crother, Crewther: Richard *le Cruder* 1275 RH (K); Hugo *le Crouder* 1278 FrLeic; Kenwrick *le Cruther* 1289 AssCh; Adam *le Crouther* 1296 Wak (Y). A derivative of ME *crouth, croude* 'fiddle', a fiddler.

Croyle: *v.* KERRELL

Croysdill: *v.* CROSSDALE

Crozier: *v.* CROSIER

Cruddace, Cruddas: *v.* CARRUTHERS

Cruft: *v.* CRAFT, CROFT

Cruickshank, Cruickshanks, Cruikshank, Crookshank, Crookshanks: John *Crokeshanks* 1296 CalSc (Haddington); Christin *Crukschank* 1334 Black (Aberdeen). A Scottish name, from ON *krókr* 'hook, something bent', and OE *sceanca* 'shank, leg', 'crooked leg', in early forms always singular.

Cruise, Cruse, Crewes, Crews, Cruwys, Crouse: (i) Nicholas *le Criuse* 1213 Cur (Beds), *le Cruse* 1279 RH (Beds); Robert *Creuse* ib. ME *crus(e)*, northern *crous(e)* 'bold, fierce'. (ii) Richard *de Crues* 1214 Cur (D). Perhaps from Cruys-Straëte (Nord).

Crumb: *v.* CROMB

Crumbie: *v.* CROMBIE

Crummack, Crummock, Cromack: John *de Crumbok* 1379 PTY. 'Dweller by the twisted oak', OE *crumb* 'crooked' and *āc* 'oak'.

Crummay, Crummey, Crummie, Crummy: *v.* CROMBIE

Crump: Peter *Crumpe* 1176 P (Berks); Adam *le Crumpe* 1203 AssSt. OE *crump* 'bent, crooked'.

Crumpton: *v.* CROMPTON

Crundall, Crundle: Robert *ate Crundle* 1279 RH (O); Thomas *de la Crundle* 1280 AssSo. From Crondall (Hants), Crundale (Kent) or from residence near a chalk-pit or hollow (OE *crundel*).

Cruse: *v.* CRUISE

Crust: Herveus *Cruste* 1109 Rams (C); Robert *Crust* 1208 FFL; Nicholas *Crouste* 1275 SRWo. OF *crouste* 'crust of bread', used by metonymy of one hard as crust, obstinate, stubborn.

Crutch: *v.* CROUCH

Crutcher: *v.* CROUCHER

Cruttenden: William *Crotynden* 1451 Pat (K). A Kent and Sussex name from a lost place *Cruttenden* in Headcorn (Kent).

Cruwys: *v.* CRUISE

Cryer: *v.* CRIER

Crystal, Crystol: *v.* CHRYSTAL

Cubbin, Cubbon: *Gybone* 1429, *M'Cubbon* 1430, *MacGibbon* 1511, *Cubbon* 1605, *Cubbin* 1645 Moore. Manx contractions of MCCUBBIN, MC-GIBBON.

Cuckow: Warin *Kuku* 1195 P (Y); Gilbert *cuccu* 1195 P (L). ME *cuccou, cuckkow*, OFr *coucou* 'cuckoo'.

Cuckson: *v.* COOKSON

Cudbird: *v.* CUTHBERT

Cudd: *Cudde* Robson 1587 Bardsley (Nb); John *Cudde* 1358 AssSt. A pet-form of *Cuthbert*.

Culf: *Cudulf, Codolf, Cuulf, Coolf* 1066 DB; Thomas *Couthulf* 1275 SRWo; William *Cuttwlf* 1299 Ipm (L); Richard *Culfe* 1327 SRWo. OE *Cūðwulf* 'famous wolf'.

Cullen, Cullin, Cullon: Bertram *de Coloigne* 1307 LLB D; John *de Coline* 1340 ib. F; John *de Culayn* 1447 FrY; John *Cullan* 1487 ib.; John *Cullen* 1524 SRSf. From Cologne. The Scottish *Cullen* is from Cullen (Banffshire): Henry *de Culane* 1340 Black. In Ayrshire and Galloway it is probably Irish *MacCullen*.

Culling: *Culling* 1086 DB, 1198 P (Nb); Warner *Culling* 1196 P (W); Tresmund *Culling'* 1207 ChR (Do). A personal name not recorded before 1086, perhaps to be identified with *Colling*.

Culpepper: Walter *Colpeper* 1313 AD vi (K); John *Coulpeper* 1332 SRSx. 'Cull (gather) pepper', a name for a spicer.

Culter: *v.* COULTAR

Culverhouse: Richard *Attekulverhuse* 1266 FFEss; Adam *Colverhous* 1309 SRBeds. OE *culfrehūs* 'dove-cote', for the man in charge.

Cumber(s): *v.* COMBER

Cumberland: William *de Cumb'land*, *de Cumberlande* 1191 P (Cu), 1301 SRY; Thomas, John *Comerlond* 1524 SRSf. 'The man from Cumberland'.

Cuming, Cumings, Cumine, Cummin, Cummins, Cummine, Cumming, Cummings, Comings, Comins, Comyns, Commin, Commins, Commings: Godwinus *filius Cumine* 1173 P (Nf); Eustachius *filius Cumini* 1219 AssL; Petrus filius *Kymine* 1301 SRY; William *Comyn* 1133 Black; Hugh *Coufnini* 1157 France; Walter *Cumin* 1158 P (Wa); John *Comin* 1175–9 DC (L); William *Cumyn* 1230 P (Ha). These forms lend no support to the common derivation from Comines given by the *Scots Peerage*, the *Dictionary of National Biography* and Freeman. This derivation must be based on the form of the name in Ordericus Vitalis, Rodbertus *de Cuminis*, the only form noted with the preposition apart from Balduinus *de Comminis* (1197 France), who may have been of a different family. Robert (d. 1069), one of the companions of the Conqueror and ancestor of the Scottish Comyns, is elsewhere named Rod bearde eorle (ASC D *s.a.* 1068) and Robertus *cognomento* (*cognomine*) *Cumin* (Symeon of Durham). Comines (Nord) is near the Belgian border. Le Prevost's suggestion that the family came from Bosc-Benard-Commin (Eure) is probably correct. The place is just south of the Seine, on the edge of the Forêt de Rouvray, near Rouen, where Hugh Coumini (1157) and Bernard Comin (1175) held land (France), in the heart of the district from which came numerous Domesday barons. The surname is clearly from a personal-name which, surviving in Norfolk, Lincolnshire and Yorkshire in the 12th and 13th centuries, may be of Breton origin. cf. OBret *Cunmin* (895 Loth). There was a 7th-century abbot of Iona named *Cumin*, whilst Woulfe derives the Irish *Comyn*, *Cummin(g)* from *Ó Coimín* or *Ó Cuimín* 'descendant of *Coimín* or *Cuimín*', diminutives of *cam* 'bent, crooked'. The Scottish Comyns may have owed their name ultimately to a Breton ancestor. cf. MALLET for evidence of Breton influence in Rouen.

Cumpton: *v.* COMPTON

Cundey, Cundick, Cundict, Cunditt: *v.* CONDIE, CONDUIT

Cunningham, Cunninghame, Cuningham, Cuninghame, Cunynghame, Coningham, Conyngham: Richard *de Cunningham* 1210–33 Black. From Cunningham (Ayrshire).

Cunnington: Pagan, Richard *de Cuninton'* 1193 P (Lei), 1210 Cur (C). From Conington (Cambs, Hunts).

Cupper: *v.* COOPER

Cupples, Coppell, Copple: (i) Walter *Curtpeil* 1200 Cur (Sf); Roger *Curpeil* 1210 Cur (Nf); John *Curpel* (*Curtpail*, *Curpeil*) 1221 Cur (Herts); William *Corpoyl* 1275 SRWo; Robert *Coppayl* 1381 SR (Ess). OFr *curt peil* 'short hair'. cf. Coupals Fm from a family of this name (PN Ess 462). (ii) John *de Cophull* 1243 InqLa; Robert *de Cuphull* 1275 SRWo. 'Dweller by the peaked hill' (OE *copp* and *hyll*) as at Coppul (Lancs).

Curl, Croll: Burewoldus *Crul* 1066 Winton (Ha); Ralph *Crul* 1191 P (Nf); William *Curle* 1202 AssL; Roger *Crolle* 1221 AssSa. ME *crull(e)*, *curl(e)*, 'curly (hair)'. *v.* also CROWL.

Curling: Robert *Crullyng* 1296 SRSx; John *Crollyng* 1327 SRSx. ME *crulling* 'the curly one.'

Curphey: *McCurghey* 1422, *Courghey* 1601, *Curphey* 1643 Moore. A Manx contraction of *Mac Murchadha* 'son of *Murchad*', the sea-warrior.

Curr: William *le Curre* 1180 P (Ess); Hugo *le Cur* 1212 Cur (L); Richerus *Canis* 1212 Cur (Herts). ME *curre* 'cur, dog'.

Currant: William *Curaunt* c1180 Lichfield (St); John *Corant* 1260 FFHu. Present participle of OFr *courir*, 'running'. For Fr *Courant*, Dauzat assumes an ellipse for *chien courant*, a name for a hunter.

Currey, Currie, Curry: (i) Dodda *æt Curi* c1075 OEByn (So); Richard *de Cury* 1212 Fees (So). From Curry (Som). (ii) Robert *atte Curie* 1327 SRSx, *atte Corye* 1332 ib.; William *Curry* ib. OFr *curie* 'kitchen'. cf. Curry (PN Ess 210), Petty Cury (PN C 47). (iii) Philip *de Curry* 1179 Black. From Currie (Midlothian).

Currier, Curryer: Thurstan *conreor* c1220 Bart (Lo); Richard *le Curur* 1256 AssNb; Henry *le Coureer* 1281 LLB B; Maurice *le couraour* 1293 FrY; William *le Coureour* 1314 LLB D; William *Curreyour*, Robert *Curreour*, John *Curreior* 1375–6 ColchCt; Andrew *Curier* 1400 FrY; Robert *Curryar* 1546 FFHu. Fr *couraieur* (16th cent), OFr *conreeur* 'currier' (1286 MED), a leather-dresser.

Curror: Nicol *Corour* 1296 CalSc (Berwicks); Thomas *Corour*, *Currour* 1331, 1430 FeuDu. OFr *coreor* 'runner, courier'.

Cursham: John *Cursom*, Robert *Cursumme* 1524 SRSf. For CURZON, with the frequent change of final *n* to *m*.

Curson: *v.* CURZON

Curt: *v.* COURT

Curtin: Robert *le Curten* 1275 RH (Nf); Robert *Curtyn* 1311 ColchCt. A diminutive of OFr *curt* 'short'. Also for *MacCurtin*, a metathesized form of *MacCruitin* 'son of *Cruitin*', the hunch-backed.

Curtis, Curtiss, Curteis, Curtice, Curties, Curthoys, Curtois, Cortès, Cortis, Courtice, Courtis, Kertess: *Curteis* de Capella 1130 P (Wa); *Curteis* de Cantebr' 1200 Cur (C); Richard *Curteis* 1166 P (Beds); Robert *le Curteis* 1168 P (D); Ralph *le Curtoys* 1230 P (L); John *le Korteys* 1238 Kirkstall (Y); Henry *Courteys* 1297 MinAcctCo; John *Corties* 1327 SRSx; William *Curtes* 1542 ChwWo; John *Curthoise*, Edmund *Curtice*, *Curtis* 1674 HTSf. OFr *corteis*, *curteis*, later *cortois*, *courtois* 'courteous' (a1300 MED), in feudal society denoting a man of good education. Used also as a personal name.

Curtler, Kirtler: Geoffrey *le Cultelier* 1186 P (Ess); William *le Curtillier* 1199 P (W); Ralph *Curtiler* 1296 SRSx; William, Roger (*le*) *Corteler* 1327 SRSf. OFr *cortiller*, *courtillier*, *cultilier* 'gardener'; or a derivative of ME *curtil* 'kirtle', a maker of kirtles. cf. Alicia *Curtle* 1231 Cl (D).

Curwen: Gilbert *de Culewen* 1262 Black; William *de Colven* 1298 CalSc (Dumfries); Gilbert *de Colwenn* 1332 SRCu; Robert *Curwen* 1379 PTY; William *de Curwen* 1388 FrY. From *Culewen*, now Colvend (Kirkcudbrightshire). The family was early established in Cumberland.

Curzon, Curson, Cursons, Corson: (i) Robert *de Curcon* 1086 DB (Nf)); Ralph *de Curtesun* (*Curcun*) 1127–34 Holme (Nf); William (*de*) *Cursun* 1198 Cur (Nf). From Notre-Dame-de-Courson (Calvados). *v.* ANF. (ii) Robert *le Curezun* 12th Gilb (L); Richard *Cursun* c1180 DC (L); William *le Curcun* 1202 FFNf; Katherine *la Curzoun* 1316 FFEss; Thomas *le Curson* 1332 FFSf. There has been some confusion in early forms between *le* and *de*, but the name was also clearly a nickname from OFr *courson*, a diminutive of *curt* 'short'. cf. *courçon*, *courchon* 'a piece of land shorter than the others' (Godefroy). Weekley's alternative suggestion from 'a cursen man', i.e. christian as opposed to heathen, is unlikely as this form is not found before the 16th century.

Cush, Cuss, Cusse: *v.* KISS

Cushing, Cushion, Cushen, Cusheon: Emme

Cusschon, Cusshoun 1507 NorwW (Nf); Mr. *Cushinge* 1674 HTSf. A dialectal form of CUSSEN or COUSEN.

Cushworth: *v.* CUSWORTH

Cusins: *v.* COUSEN

Cuss: *v.* CUST

Cussen, Cusson, Cussons: (i) Robert *Custson* 1332 SRCu; William *Custeson,* Richard *Cusson* 1379 PTY. 'Son of *Cust*', i.e. Constance. (ii) Henry *Cuttesone* 1329 ColchCt. 'Son of *Cutt*', i.e. Cuthbert.

Cust, Cuss: *Custe* filia Willelmi 1219 AssY; *Cus* nepta Johannis Frost 1279 RH (C); *Cuss* Balla ib. (Hu); *Custa* atte Halle 1296 SRSx; Richard *Cust* 1279 RH (O). Short forms of *Custance* or *Constance.* cf. *Cussata (Constancia)* 1230 P (D).

Custance: *v.* CONSTANCE

Custer: Sibilla *la Custere* 1254 AssSt. OFr *coustier* (m), *coustiere* (f) 'a maker of feather-beds or cushions'.

Custerson: Adam *Custanson* 1379 PTY. 'Son of *Custance.*' cf. *Dickinson* and *Dickerson, Stevenson* and *Steverson.*

Cusworth, Cushworth: Robert *de Cusworth* 1358 FrY. From Cusworth (WRYorks).

Cutbill: *v.* COBBALD

Cutbush: Henry *Cutbussh* 1450 ArchC vii. 'Cut bush.' cf. TALLBOY.

Cuthbert, Cudbird: Austinus *filius Cudberti* 1202 P (Y); Laurencius *filius Cutberti* 1207 FFHu; William *Cutbright, Cudbriht* 1260 AssC, 1276 RH (C); John *Cutbert* 1279 RH (Hu); Robert *Cudbert* 1301 SRY; John *Cutberd* 1327 SRC; William

Cuthbert 1469 FrY. OE *Cūðbeorht* 'famous-bright', a common OE name and popular after the Conquest in the north and the Scottish Lowlands.

Cuthbertson: John *Cutberdson* 1410 FrY. 'Son of *Cuthbert.*'

Cutlack: *v.* GOODLAKE

Cutler, Cuttler: Ralph *le Cuteiller* 1212–23 Bart (Lo); Peter *le Cutelir* c1216 Clerkenwell (Lo); Dauid *le Cutiller* 1219 AssY. OFr *coutelier, cotelier* 'cutler', 'maker, repairer or seller of knives, etc.' (c1400 MED).

Cutt, Cutts: *Cutte* Brendhers 1279 RH (C); *Cuttie* or *Cuthbert* Armorer 1589 Black; John, Robert *Cut* 1185, 1188 P (He, Db). A pet-form of *Cuthbert.*

Cuttell, Cuttill, Cuttles: *v.* COTTEL

Cutteridge, Cuttridge, Cutress, Cuttriss, Gutteridge, Gutridge: Ailric *Cuterich* 1176 P (O); Joan *Cudrich* 1279 RH (O); William *Cutrich* 1327 SRSf; Hugh *Coterich* 1327 SRSo; William *Gutheridge* 1597 PN Herts 49; Arthur *Gutterich, Cutterice* 1606, 1611 IckworthPR (Sf); William *Cutteridge,* Widow *Cutteris* 1674 HTSf; Marten *Gutteridge,* Henry *Guttrage* ib. OE *Cūðrīc* 'famous ruler', a rare OE personal name. *Gut(ter)idge* is due to late confusion with *Goodrich.*

Cutting: Herlewin, William *Cutting* 1221 ElyA (Nf); Richard *Cutting* 1235 FFEss; William *Cutton, Cutting* 1767, 1775 ShotleyPR (Sf). OE *Cutting* 'son of *Cutt*', a pet-form of *Cūðbeorht* or *Cūðbeald.* cf. CUTHBERT, COBBALD.

Cuxon, Cuxson: *v.* COOKSON

Cuzen: *v.* COUSEN

D

Dabbs: John *Dabbe* 1524 SRSf. *Dobb* (Robert), with unrounded vowel.

Daber: *v.* DAUBER

D'Abernon: Roger *de Abernon* 1086 DB (Sr); Jordan *Dabernun* 1197 P (Wa). From Abenon (Calvados).

Dabinett: Walter *Dobinet* 1301 SRY. *Dob-in-et*, a double diminutive of *Dob*. *v.* DABBS.

Dabney: *v.* DAUBENEY

Dabson: For DOBSON. cf. DABBS.

Dack, Dax: *Dacke* 1250 AssSt; Alexander *Dacke* 1275 RH (Nf). Perhaps OE **Dæcca*, the first element of Dagenham (Essex), surviving in Hugo *filius Decche* 12th (L). *v.* IPN 186.

Dadds: William *Dad* 1279 RH (C). *v.* DOD, with vowel unrounded.

Dade: *v.* DEED

D'Aeth: *v.* DEATH

Daft: John, Robert *Daft* c1230 NottBR, 1242 Fees (Nt). OE *gedæft* 'gentle, meek', ME *daffte* 'foolish, stupid'.

Dafter, Dafters, Daftors: *v.* DAUGHTERS

Dagg: Robert *Dag* 1275 SRWo; Ralph *Dagg* 1327 *SR* (Ess). OFr *dague* 'dagger', an ellipse for one who carried a dagger.

Daggar, Dagger, Daggers, Daggett: Henry *Daget* 1219 AssY; Peter *Dagard* 1279 RH (C). *Daget* is a diminutive of OFr *dague* 'dagger'. *v.* DAGG. cf. Richard *Dagun* 1203 P (Y), John *Dagenet* 1185 Templars (Herts), William *Dagenet*, *Dagunet* 1210 Cur, 1221 AssWa and the French surnames *Dagon, Dagot, Daguet, Dagonet, Dague-riet*, all 'carrier of a dagger' (Dauzat). The ultimate origin of *dagger* is unsettled. It occurs as *daggere* a1375, *daggardus* 15th, *dagard* 1535. If the last form could be regarded as original, the word would be OFr *dague* plus *-ard* (NED). The 1279 form above suggests that this may be the origin.

Dagleas, Dagless, Daglish: *v.* DALGLEISH

Daile: *v.* DALE

Dailey, Dailley: *v.* DOYLEY

Dain, Daine, Daines, Dayne, Daynes, Deyns, Dines, Doyne, Dyne: Robert *le Dine* 1201 P (Sr); Richard *le Digne* 1222 Cur (Sr); Gilbert *le Dyne*, *Dynes* 1275, 1284 Wak (Y); Nicholas *Dain* 1275 SRWo; Matilda *Deine* 1279 RH (O); John *le Dyen* 1296 SRSx; William *Dien* 1297 MinAcctCo; William *le Deyne* 1327 SRSx; Richard, Walter *Doyn* 1327 SRSx; John *Deynes* 1327 SRC. (i) ME *digne*, *deyn(e)*, Fr *digne* (11th), perhaps OFr **dein*

'worthy, honourable' (1297 NED); (ii) ME *dain(e)*, OFr **deigne*, Burgundian *doigne*, Fr *digne* 'haughty, reserved' (c1500 NED); (iii) OFr *deien*, *dien*, modFr *doyen* 'dean'. cf. DEAN. The forms are inextricably confused.

Dainteth, Daintith, Dentith: Agnes *Deynteth* 1379 NottBR; Thomas *Dentithe* 1591 SfPR. OFr *daintiet, deintiet*, from Lat *dignität-em*, ME *deinteth*, an archaic form of DAINTY.

Daintree, Daintrey, Daintry, Daventry: Philip *de Dauintrie* 1162 P (K); Gilbert *Dantre* 1369 LLB G; Thomas *Daintree* 1637 Fen DraytonPR (C). From Daventry (Northants), the correct local pronunciation of which is *Daintree*.

Dainty, Denty: Osbert *Deintie* 1199 P (Nth); Henry, William *Deinte* 1227 AssBk, c1248 Bec (O). ME *deinte*, OFr *deintié, daintié, dainté*, sb. 'pleasure, tit-bit' (a1225 NED), adj., 'fine, handsome, pleasant' (c1340 NED). *v.* DAINTETH.

Dairson: *v.* DEARSON

Daish: *v.* ASH.

Dakers: *v.* ACRES

Dakin: *v.* DAYKIN

Dalby, Daulby, D'Aulby: Matthew *de Dalbi* Hy 2 DC (L). From Dalby (Leics, Lincs, NR Yorks).

Dale, Dales, Daile: Ralph *de la Dale* 1275 RH (Sf); William *en le Dale* 1318 ShefA (Y); John *atte Dale* 1327 SRSx; Nicholas *Daile* 1481 FrY. 'Dweller in the dale', OE *dæl*.

Dalgleish, Dalgliesh, Dalglish, Dagleas, Dagless, Daglish: Symon *de Dalgles* 1407 Black; Adam *Dalgleisch*, Andrew *Dawgles* 1507–10 ib. From Dalgleish (Selkirkshire).

Dallamore: *v.* DELAMAR

Dallas: (i) Roger *del Dalhous* 1301 SRY; William *de Dalhous* 1327 SRY. 'Dweller at the house in the dale.' (ii) Archibald *de Doleys* 1262 Black; John *de Dolas* 1429 ib.; Henry *Dallas* 1513 ib. From the old barony of Dallas (Moray).

Dallicoat: *v.* COTE

Dallimore: *v.* DELAMAR

Dalling, Dallin, Dallyn: Turoldus *de Dallenges* 1108 MedEA (Nf). From Dalling (Norfolk).

Dallinson, Dallison: Bernard *de Alencon* 1086 DB (Sf); John *de Alecon* 1189 Whitby (Y); Alexander *Dalencun*, William *Dalizun* 13th Lewes (Nf); Nicholas *Dalasson* 1378 LLB H. From Alençon (Orne). The surname has also contributed to ALLANSON and ALISON.

Dallman, Dalman: Thomas, Hugh *Daleman* 1327 *SR* (Ess), SRC. 'Dweller in the dale' (OE *dæl*).

Dalton, Daulton, Daughton, Dawton: William *de Daltone* 1155 FeuDu; William *Dawton* 1518 FrY. From Dalton (Durham, Lancs, Northumb, Westmorland, ER, NR and WRYorks).

Daltry: *v.* DAWTREY

Dalyell, Dalyiel, Dalzell, Dalziel: Hugh *de Dalyhel* 1288 Black; James *Deell* 1684 ib.; James *Dyell* 1689 ib. From the old barony of Dalziel (Lanarkshire). Also spelled *Deyell, De Yell*. Pronounced *Diyell* or DL, sometimes *Dal-yell* and now also *Dalzeel, Dalzell*. The old form *Dalʒel* was printed *Dalzel*, hence the incorrect pronunciation with *z* instead of *y*.

Damary, D'Amery, Dammery, Damry, Amori, Amory: William *de Dalmari, de Dalmereio, de Almereio* 1086 DB (Do); Richard *de Ameri, Dameri* 1159, 1166 P (Beds, L); Roger *Damery, Dammary, Daimary, de Ammary, de Aumary* 1280 AssSo; Roger *de Amory, Damori* 1274 RH (Bk, O). From Daumeray (Maine-et-Loire). The initial *D* was often regarded as a preposition and the name wrongly divided as *De Aumari*. This preposition was then lost, hence *Amori, Amory*. The name was probably then confused with AMERY.

Dame: Henry *Dame* 1279 RH (O); Agnes *Dame* 1327 SRSf. Fr *dame* 'lady'. Perhaps an ironical attribute.

Damer: *v.* DAYMAR

Damerell, Damiral, Dammarell, Damrel, Damrell: Robert *de Alba Marula, de Albemarle* 1086 DB (D); Reginald *de Aumarle* 1243 AssSo; Bernullus *de Aumeryl* 13th WhC (La); Thomas *Damarell* 1568 SRSf. From Aumale (Seine-Inférieure), earlier *Alba Margila*. The fuller form is preserved in the title of the Duke of Albemarle. Hinton Admiral (Hants) preserves the surname without the preposition.

Dammery: *v.* DAMARY

Dampier, Damper: William *de Damper* 1225 Pat; William *Damper* 1229 ib. (Y). From Dampierre, the name of numerous places in France, two of which are in Normandy.

Damrell: *v.* DAMERELL

Damry: *v.* DAMARY

Dams, Damms: Peter *del Dam* 1221 ElyA (Nf); Thomas *ate Dam* 1327 SRC; Alice *Dam* 1327 SRSf. 'Dweller near a dam', from OE **damm* 'dam' (a1400 MED).

Damsell: Ralph *Damisel, Dameisele* 1191, 1204 P (Y); Henry *Damisel* 1204 P (Gl); Roger *Damisele* 1214 Cur (Bk). OFr *dameisele, damisele* (f) 'a maiden', originally of noble birth and OFr *dameisel* (m) 'a young squire, page'. Both seem to be represented, the former, probably, in the sense 'effeminate'.

Damson: Geoffrey *Dammessune* 1186 P (Nth); Henry *Dameson* 1276 AssSo. OFr *dame*, earlier *damme*, 'the dame's son'.

Damyon: *Damianus* 1199 MemR (Nf), 1206 Cur (Mx); William, John *Damyen* 1294 FFEss, 1327 SRSf. St *Damianus* was martyred in Cilicia in 303 under Diocletian. His name, perhaps to be associated with the goddess Damia, was not common in England.

Danby: Rand *de Danbi* 1189 P (L); Robert *de Danebi* 1212 P (Y); John *Danby* 1392 IpmNt. From Danby (NRYorks).

Dance: William, Robert *Daunce* 1247 AssBeds, 1301 SRY. ME, OFr *dance* (c1300 NED), metonymic for a dancer or *dawnceledere* (c1440). Robert *de la Daunce* 1305 LoCt was probably a professional dancer, chief of 'a dancing party', a meaning recorded c1385 NED.

Dancer: Godwin *Dancere* 1130 P (Herts); Ralph (*le*) *Dancere* 1240 Rams (Nf), *le Dauncer* 1327 SRSx. A derivative of ME *dancen* 'to dance', 'a dancer, especially a professional dancer in public'.

Dancey, Dancy, Dansey, Dansie, Dauncey: William *de Anesi* 1086 Winton (Ha); Milo *de Dantesia* 1177 P (W), *de Andesie, de Dantesie, de Dantesia* 1208 Cur (W); Richard *Danesi* 1210 Cur (K), *de Anesye* 1236 Fees (W), *de Danteseia* 1242 ib., *de Anesy* alias *Daneseye* 1249 Ipm (W); Thomas *de Aunteseye* 1269 AssNb. From Anisy (Calvados). *de Anesi* became *Danesi* and, with an intrusive *t*, *Dantesi*. This was identical in form with the DB and later forms of Dauntsey (Wilts) where Roger *Dantesie* held ¼ of a fee in 1242 (Fees). The surname was often thought to derive from the Wiltshire place and an additional *de* inserted (*de Dantesie*). The confusion was increased as the family also left its name in Winterbourne Dauntsey in the same county. The modern surname may derive independently from Dauntsey.

Dand, Dandie, Dandy, Dandison: *Dande* de Hale, de Leuer 1246 AssLa; *Dandi* ballivus 1275 RH (L); Richard *Dande* 1279 RH (Hu); Adam *Dandy* 1312 FrY; Thomas *Dandisone* 1332 SRLa. *Dand* and *Dandie*, pet forms of *Andrew*, are generally regarded as Scottish, but the English examples are much earlier than Black's earliest: *Dand* or Andrew Kerr (1499), Andrew alias *Dandie* Cranston (1514).

Dando, Daddow, Daunay, Dauney, Dawnay, Dawney, Delaney, Delany, de Launay, Delauney, De Launey: William *de Alno* 1086 DB (Sf); John *de Alnai* 1150–60 DC (L); Robert *del Aunei* Hy 2 Gilb (L); Henry *de Launei* 1159–85 Templars (Lo); Helias *de Aunou* 1201 AssSo; William *del Alnei* 1206 P (Nf), *del Aune* 1212 Cur (Ess); Geoffrey *de Alno, de Alneto, Dauno* 1225–54 AssSo; Jordan *del Aunney* 1225 AssSo; Reginald *de Auney* 1242 Fees (D); Mathew *Dauney* 1251 Whitby (Y); Alexander, Richard *Dando* 1274 RH (So), 1296 SRSx. The Somerset family came from Aunou (Orne) and has left its name in Compton Dando (Som). The surname may also derive from Aunay (Calvados, Eure-et-Loir, Seine-et-Oise, etc.) or Laulne (La Manche), from Lat *alnetum*, Fr *aunaie* 'alder-grove'

Dandy: *v.* DAND

Dane, Danes: Henry *Bithedane* Edw 1 Battle (Sx); William *de la Dane* 1275 RH (K); William *atte Dane* 1327 SR (Ess). OE *denu* 'valley', found as *dane* in place-names in Essex, Herts, Beds, Kent and Sussex. Roger *ate Dene* (1294) and Walter *ate Dane* (1296) both lived at Dane End (PN Herts 79). *v.* DEAN.

Danecourt: *v.* d'EYNCOURT

Danell, Danels: *v.* DANIEL

Danford, Danforth: Nicholas *de Darneford* 1279 RH (C); Robert *de Derneforde* 1327 SRSf; James *Danford* 1568 SRSf; Robert *Danforth* 1524 SRSf. From Darnford (Suffolk) or Dernford Fm in Sawston (Cambs); or for DURNFORD.

Dangar, Danger: Alric *Dangier* c1200 ELPN; Reginald *Danger* 1223–5 ib.; Alexander *Daunger* 1246 AssLa. OFr *dangier, danger* in one of its early senses: 'power, dominion' or 'hesitation, reluctance, coyness'. cf. Gerard *Daungerous* 1275 RH (L).

Dangerfield: William *de Angeruill'* 1205 P (Do); Foulke *Dangerfeild* 1659 Bardsley. From one of the places named Angerville in Normandy.

Daniel, Daniels, Daniell, Daniells, Danniel, Danell, Danels, Dannel, Dennell, Denial: Eudo *filius Daniel* 1121–48 Bury (Sf); Roger *Daniel* 1086 DB (Sx); Walter *Danyel* 1268 FFSf; Cecilia *Denyel* 1279 RH (C); John *Danyeles* 1319 SRLo; Matthew *Danel* 1327 SRSx. Hebrew *Daniel* 'God has judged'. *Denial* is pronounced *Denyel*.

Dann: Geoffrey *atte Danne* 1327 SRSx; Simon *Dann* 1332 SRSx. 'Dweller in the valley.' *v.* DANE.

Dannel, Danniel: *v.* DANIEL

Dansey, Dansie: *v.* DANCEY

Danson: Robert *Dandeson* 1332 SRCu; John *Dandsone* 1363 FrY; Robert *Danson* 1381 PTY. 'Son of *Dand*' or Andrew. Perhaps also 'son of *Dan*'.

Danvers: Ralph *de Anuers, Danuers* 1230 P, MemR (Berks). From Anvers (Antwerp).

Darben: Gilbert *Derebarn* 1277 FrY. ME *derebarne* 'dear child'. cf. Alicia *Derechild* 1275 SRWo.

Darby, Darbey, Derby: Roger *de Derby* 1160–82 RegAntiquiss; Edelota *Darby* 1278 RH (O); Simon *Derby* 1377 AssEss. From Derby.

Darbyshire, Darbishire, Derbyshire: Geoffrey *de Derbesire* 1203 AssSt; Henry, Richard *de Derbyshire* 1307 AssSt, 1394–5 IpmLa. 'The man from Derbyshire'.

Darcey, Darcy, D'Arcy: Norman *de Adreci, de Areci* 1086 DB (L); William *Daresci* 1166 P (L); Roger *Arsi* 1173–82 DC (L); Thomas *Darcy* 1276 Gilb (L). From Arcy (La Manche). The Irish Darcy derives from John *d'Arcy* (14th) but is also an anglicizing of *Ó Dorchaidhe* 'descendant of the dark man'.

Dark, Darke, Darkes, Durk: Robert *Derck* 1221 AssWa; Richard *Durk* 1229 Pat (So); Godewynus *Derc* 1230 P (Ess); John *Darke* 1362 LLB G. OE *deorc* 'dark' of complexion.

Darker: John *le Darkere* 1349 AD i (Wa); John *Darker* 1524 SRSf. This must be an occupational name, 'one who darkens'. cf. BLACKER, WHITER, and 'Every coriar shall well and sufficiently corie and blacke the said Lether tanned' (1532–3 NED),

'*Noircisseur*, a blacker . . . darkener, obscurer' 1611 Cotgrave.

Darknell: *v.* DURTNALL

Darley: Warin *de Derleg'* 1200 P (Ess); William *de Derlay* 1379 PTY; John *Darley* 1541 CorNt. From Darley (Derby).

Darling, Dearling, Dorling, Durling: Oter *Dirlinges sunu* 1100–30 OEByn (D); *Derling* 1133–60 Rams (Beds), 1177 P (D); *Derling* de Arfdift a1177 Black (Berwick); *Durling* atte Forde 1330 PN D 433; *Ælmær Deorlingc, Dyrling* 1016 ASC E, D; William *Dierling, Derling* 1195–6 P (D); Henry *Durling* 1242 Fees (W); Emma *Derlyng* 1244 Rams (Beds); Ralph *Durlyng* 1327 SRSo; Richard *Dorling, Dorlynges* 1327 SRWo; Adam *Darlyng* 1379 PTY. OE *Dīerling, Dȳrling, Dēorling*, from OE *dēorling* 'darling', 'one dearly loved', both as a personal name and as an attribute.

Darnell: Goduine *Dernel* c1095 Bury (Sf); Godwin *Darnel* 1177 P (Sf); Tomas *Darnele* 1193 P (Nf). OFr *darnel* 'darnel' (c1384 MED), a plant formerly believed to produce intoxication (Weekley). Occasionally also local, from Darnall in Sheffield (Yorks): William *de Darnale* 13th Shef.

Darree, Darry, Denre, Denry, Derry: William *Darri, Derri* 1200 Cur (Nth); Nicholas *Darre* 1288 FFSf; Robert *Darre*, John *Dary*, John *Deree* 1327 SRSf. AFr *darree*, OFr *denree* 'penny-worth'. cf. Fr *Danré, Danrée* 'surnom probable de marchand' (Dauzat).

Darrell: *v.* DAYRAL

Darter: *v.* DAUGHTERS

Dartnall, Dartnell: *v.* DURTNALL

Darwen, Darwent, Derwent: Syward *de Derewent* 1246 AssLa. From Darwen (Lancs), on the river Derwent.

Darwin: *Derwen* 1170 P (Ess); *Derewinus* Purs 1176 P (Bk); John *Derewin* 1219 Fees (Ess); William *Derwyne* c1248 Bec (Bk). OE *Dēorwine* 'dear-friend', recorded in the 10th century, but rare. In 1225 (AssSo) Mabel, daughter of *Derwin'*, had as pledges William, Nicholas, Henry and Hugh *Derwin'*, probably her brothers, who owed their surname to their father.

Darwood: *v.* DURWARD

Dash: *v.* ASH

Dashfield: For *De Ashfield*. cf. DASH.

Dashper, Disper: Henry *Duzepers* 1203 P (Nth); Alb(e)ricus *Duzepers, Duzeper* 1221 Cur (Nth), 1221 AssGl; William *Duzeper* 1279 RH (O); Roger *Dozeper* 1293 Fees (D). OFr *doce, duze pers* 'twelve equals, twelve peers' (*dyssypers* 1503, *duchepers* a1400 NED, of which *Dashper* is a corruption). The reference is to the twelve peers or paladins of Charlemagne, said to be attached to his person as being the bravest of his knights. Later, the term was applied to other illustrious nobles or knights (c1330 MED) and a singular was formed some 200 years before the earliest example in MED (c1380).

Dashwood: Zachary *Dashwood* 1693 DWills. For *De Ashwood*.

Daubeney, Daubeny, Daubney, D'Aubney, Dabney, Dobney: Nigel *de Albengi, de Al-*

bingi de Albinie, de Albinio 1086 DB (Beds, Berks, Bk); Willelmus *Brito* 1086 DB (Hu), William *de Albinneio* 1115 Winton (Ha), Willelmus *Albineius Brito* 1116–20 France; Nigel *de Albuniaco* 1100–23 Rams (Hu), *de Albeni* 1114–23 ib.; William *de Aubeneio* 1124–30 Rams (Beds), *de Aubini, de Aubeni* 1199 MemR (Ha, Bk); William *Daubenny* 1212 Fees (Berks); Ralf *de Dabeney* 1269 AssSo; Thomas *Dabeney* 1524 SRSf. William, founder of the line of Aubigni, earls of Arundel, and Nigel of that of Cainhoe (Beds) came from Saint-Martin d'Aubigny (La Manche). The family of Aubigny (Brito) of Belvoir came from Saint-Aubin d'Aubigny (Ille-et-Vilaine). *v.* ANF. There is also another Aubigny in Calvados, of identical origin, which may have contributed to the surname.

Dauber, Dawber, Daber, Dober, Doberer: Hugo *Daubur* 1219 AssY; Robert *le Daubur* 1221 Cur (Berks); Nicholas *le Doubur* 1260 AssLa; Walter *Dobere, le Daubere* 1319, 1327 SR (Ess); Peter, Roger *le Daber* 1332 SRSx; Joseph *Dauber, Douber* 1346 ColchCt. AFr *daubour*, OFr **daubier* 'whitewasher, plasterer'. In the Middle Ages walls of 'wattle and daub' were extremely common. Wattling consisted of a row of upright stakes the spaces between which were more or less filled by interweaving small branches, hazel rods, osiers, reeds, etc. On one side, or more usually on both sides of this foundation, earth or clay was daubed and thrust well into the interstices, the surfaces being smoothed and usually treated with plaster or at least a coat of whitewash. Closely allied to daubing was pargetting or rough-casting in which mortar or a coarse form of plaster was used instead of clay or loam. At Corfe in 1285 there is a reference to 'Stephen the Dauber who pargetted the long chamber' and it is not always possible to decide whether the daubers were really daubing or whitewashing (Building 188, 190, 191). cf. PARGETER.

Daugherty: *v.* DOUGHARTY

Daughters, Dauter, Darter, Dafter, Dafters, Daftors, Doctor: Katheryn *Doctor* 1570 ChwWo is, no doubt, from OE *dohtor* 'daughter'. The surname is ill-documented, the modern forms chiefly colloquial spellings or dialectal pronunciations, and the reference may be to a sole heiress who would ultimately inherit her father's land. Early examples clearly indicate an actual relationship: Joan *Tomdoutter*, Rose *Anotdoghter*, Alice *Wilkynsondoghter* 1379 PTY, but these were not likely to survive though they were used as men's surnames, cf. Richard *Wryghtdoghter*, Robert *ffelisdoghter* 1379 PTY.

Daughtery, Daughtry: *v.* DAWTREY
Daughton: *v.* DALTON
Daukes: *v.* DAWKES
Daulby, D'Aulby: *v.* DALBY
Daulton: *v.* DALTON
Daultrey: *v.* DAWTREY
Dauncey: *v.* DANCEY
Dauney: *v.* DANDO
Davage: *v.* DAVIDGE

Davall, Davolls, Deavall, Deaville, Devall, De Vile, Devill, Deville, De Ville, de Ville, Divall, Divell, Evill: (i) Walter *de Davidisvilla* 1107 ANF; Robert *de Aiuilla, de Daiuill'* 1175, 1195 P (Y); Walter *Daiville* 1184 Templars (L), *de Daeuill'* 1190 P (R); Roger *de Divill'* 1198 Cur (Nf); Hugh *Davilla* c1200 Riev (Y); Roger *Deyvill* 1251 AssY; John *de Eyvill* 1260 AssY; Robert *de Hevill', de Heyvill', de Deyvill', de Aivill'* 1235, 1242 Fevs (Lei, Nt); Richard *Divill* 1553 WhC (La); Francis *Devall* 1571 FrY. From Déville (Seine-Inférieure). The correct form was *de Daiville*. When the preposition was omitted, *Daiville* was taken to be for *de Aiville*. Hence *Evill*, from *de (H)eville*. John *le Deyvile*, an alternative name for John *Devile* (1305 SIA) is probably an error for *de Deyvile*. For *Devall, Davall*, cf. Cotes de Val (Leics), *Cotesdeyvill* 1285 FA, held by a family from Déville. All the modern forms may be of topographical origin but some of them are also undoubtedly due to a desire to dissociate the name from *devil* which was certainly used as a nickname. (ii) Aluuinus *Deule* 1066 DB (Beds, Hu); Roger *le Diable* 1230 P (Ess); Laurencius dictus *diabolus* alias Stanford 13th *St John* (Ess); Robert *Dyvel* 1301 SRY; William *Deuel* 1310 ColchCt; John *le Deuyle* 1327 SRSf; John *Deuile* 1327 SRC. OE *dēofol* 'devil', which may be a nickname or a pageant name.

Davenport: Richard *de Deveneport* 1162–73 P (Ch); Richard *de Taueneport, de Daveneport* 1203 AssSt; Thomas *Davenport* 1642 PrD. From Davenport (Ches).

Daventry: *v.* DAINTREE

Davers: Robert *de Alvers* 1086 DB (Nth); Ralph *de Auuers* 1205 P (Berks); Geoffrey *Dauuers* 1209 Fees (O); Ralph *de Avers* 1235 Fees (Mx). From Auvers (La Manche) or Auvers-le-Hamon (Sarthe).

Daves: *v.* DAVIES

Davey, Davie, Davy: *Daui* Capriht 1292 SRLo; Walter *dauy* 1198–1212 Bart (Lo); Richard *Davy* 1275 SRWo. In Scotland, *Davie* is a pet-form of *David*. Here it is rather the French popular form which still survives as *Davy* and was common in England from the 13th century.

David, Davitt: *Dauid clericus* 1150–60 DC (L); *Davit Burre* 1278 RH (C); Thomas *Davit* 1275 RH (Nf); Robert *David* 1276 RH (Lei). Hebrew *David* 'darling, friend', a name common in both England and Scotland from the 12th century and in Wales much earlier.

Davidge, Davage are for *David's* (son): Richard *Davydge* 1591 SPD.

Davidson, Davison, Davisson, Davson: Thomas *Davyson* 1327 SRY; John *Davideson* 1350 AD vi (Wa); William *Daveson* 1500 FrY. 'Son of David.'

Davies, Davis, Daviss, Daves, Davys: John *Dauisse* 1327 SRC; Richard *Davys* 1402 FrY. 'Son of Davy', i.e. David.

Davill: *v.* DAVALL
Davison: *v.* DAVIDSON
Davitt: *v.* DAVID
Davolls: *v.* DAVALL
Davy: *v.* DAVEY

Daw, Dawe, Dawes, Daws: *Dawe* 1212 Fees (La), 1219 AssY; Ralph *Dawe* 1211 Cur (Wo), 1275 RH (D); Lovekin *Dawes* 1279 RH (O). *Dawe* is a pet-name for *David* which shares this common surname with OE **dawe*, ME *dawe* 'jack-daw' (1432 NED).

Dawber: *v.* DAUBER

Dawkes, Daukes, Daux: Simon *Dawkes* 1431 FA (Wo). A contracted form of *Dawkins*. cf. JENKS.

Dawkins: Willelmus filius *Daukyn* 1332 SRLa; William *Daukyn* 13th WhC (La); Richard *Daukyns* 1354 AssSt; Magister Doctor *Dawkyns* 1534 GildY, identical with John *Dakyn*, LL.D., vicar-general of York. 'Little David', from *Dawe* plus *kin*. *v.* DAW, DAYKIN.

Dawn: Roger *Dawen* 1332 SRWa. *v.* DAW, GEFFEN.

Dawnay, Dawney: *v.* DANDO

Dawson: Thomas *Daweson* 1326 Wak (Y); Richard *Dauewesone* 1332 SRWa. 'Son of *Dawe*', i.e. David, or of David himself: Roger *Daudeson* 1372 DbCh.

Dawton: *v.* DALTON

Dawtrey, Dawtry, Daughtery, Daughtrey, Daughtry, Daltry, Daltrey, Daultrey, Dealtry, Doughtery, Dowtry, Hawtrey, Hatry: William *de Alta ripa* 1166 P (Y); Robert *de Halteripa* c1155 DC (L); Philip *de Hauteriue* 12th DC (L); Philip *de Alteriva* c1200 Riev (Y); Nicholas, Walter *Dautre* 1379 PTY, 1386 LLB A; Robert *Hawtry* 1524 SRSf; George *Daltry*, *Dealtry* 1671, 1679 FrY. From Hauterive (Orne), Lat *Alta ripa* 'high bank'.

Day, Daye, Dey, D'Eye, Deyes: Leofgife *ða Dægean* c1055 OEByn (So); Godiua *Daia* c1095 Bury (Sf); Aluric *Dai* 1196 P (Bk); Ralph *Deie* 1211 FrLeic; Gunild' *daiam domini episcopi* 1221 AssWo; Walter *le Daye* 1269 AssSo; Thomas *le Deye* 1277 Ely (Sf). OE *dǣge* (fem), ME *day(e)*, *dey(e)* 'kneader of bread, bread-baker', later 'dairy-maid', 'female-servant' (cf. the 1221 example). Originally used only of women, it was later used of men (1271 MED, but clearly much earlier). Women's christian names are rare. The first two early examples are, no doubt, used in the original sense. According to Bardsley, *Day* is also a pet-name for *David*. cf. Roger filius *Daye* 1300 Guisb (Y). *D'Eye* is, no doubt, an affected spelling for *Deye*, rather than for *de Eye*.

Daybell: Thomas *Daybell* 1435 Shef. cf. 'Thei daunsyd all the nyʒt, till the son con ryse; The clerke rang the day-bell, as it was his gise' (15.. NED). Probably a nickname for one who turned night into day.

Daykin, Dakin: *Daykenus judaeus* 1275 RH (R); *Daykin* de Wich 1290 AssCh; Richard *Deykin* 1344 AD vi (Sa); Thomas *Dakyn* 1551 AD vi (Sr). *Day-kin* 'Little David'. cf. DAWKINS.

Dayley: *v.* DOYLEY

Dayman: *Dayman* Buntyng 1221 ElyA (C); Stephen *Deyman* 1224 Cur (Bk); Richard *le Deymon* 1332 SRSt. Bardsley notes that in 1363 *deyes* were coupled with cow-herds, shepherds, swine-

herds and other keepers of live stock. Hence, *Dayman* probably meant herdsman or, possibly, dairy-man. This was also used as a personal name like *Flotmann* 'sailor' and *Glīwmann* 'ministrel' (DB).

Daymar, Damer: *Daimer* de Rodinton' 1203 Cur (Sa). An unrecorded OE **Dægmǣr* 'day-fame'. cf. OE *Dæghēah, Dæghelm*.

Dayne(s): *v.* DAIN

Dayral, Dayrell, Darell, Darrell: Thomas *de Arel* 1166 Cur (Y); Marmaduc *Darel* 1182 P (Y); Ralph *Darel(l)*, *Dairel(l)* 1204–5 Cur (Mx); Henry *de Ayrel*, *Dayrel* 1235 Fees (Bk). From Airelle (Calvados).

Daysh: *v.* ASH

Dayson, Deason: Henry *Deyesone* 1366 Eynsham (O); John *Deyesone* 1381 SRSt. 'Son of *Day*' (David) or, possibly, of the herdsman.

Deacon, Deakan, Deakin, Deakins: Richard *le Diakne* 1212 Cur (Sf); Richard *le Deken(e)* 1247 AssBeds, 1256 AssNb; John *Dekne* 1327 SRSx; William *le Dekon* 1332 SRSt. OE *diacon, dēacon*, ME *deakne*, OFr, ME *diacne* 'deacon' (*v.* NED).

Deadman: *v.* DEBENHAM

Deakes: *v.* DEEKES, DITCH

Deal: Roger *de le Dele*, John *Dele* 1275 RH (Nf); John, Hubert *de Dele* 1317 AssK, 1327 SRSf. From Deal (Kent) or from residence in a valley (OE *dæl*).

Dealbridge: *v.* BRIDGE

Dealtry: *v.* DAWTREY

Deamer: *v.* DEEMER

Dean, Deane, Deanes, Deans, Deen, Dene: (i) Ralph *de Dene* 1086 DB (Sx); William *de la Dena* 1193 P (Sr); Simon *in la Dene* 1271 AssSo; Robert *ater Dene*, Peter *in ther Dene*, William *atte Dene* 1296 SRSx; Thomas *del Denes* 1297 MinAcctCo; John *Dene* 1366 ColchCt. Very common, from East or West Dean (Sussex), Deane (Hants), etc., from minor places as Dean Fm (Sussex), Deans (Essex), Dene Fm (Surrey), etc., or from residence in or near a valley (OE *denu*). *v.* MELS 49. cf. DANE. (ii) Dauid *Decanus* 1160 P (Nf); Reiner *Dene* 1177 P (Nf); Geoffrey *le Dean* quondam persona (de Whalleye) 1278 WhC (Y); Robert *le Deen* 1279 RH (C); Richard *Dien* 1327 SRWo. ME *deen*, OFr *deien, dien*, modFr *doyen* 'dean' (c1330 MED). *v.* DAIN. Willelmus filius *Dene* 1301 SRY is, no doubt, parallel to Thomas filius *Decani* 1210 Cur (O), 'the dean's son'. *v.* DENSON.

Deaner: Henry *Deaner'* 1279 RH (C). 'Dweller in the valley.' *v.* DEAN.

Dear, Deare, Deares, Deer, Deere, Deerr: Goduine *Dere* filius c1095 Bury (Sf); Rogerus filius *Dere* 1221 ElyA (Nf); Goduui *dere* 1066, 1086 DB (Beds); Matthew *Dere* 1196 FrLeic; Robert *le Dere* 1279 RH (O). The personal-name may be OE *Dēora*, a short form of names in *Dēor-*, or an original nickname from OE *dēore* 'beloved' or OE *dēor* 'brave, bold'. The surname may be from any of these or from OE *dēor* 'wild animal', 'deer', probably 'the swift'. *v.* DEARSON.

Dearing, Deering, Dering, Doring: *Derinc* 1066

DB (K); *Diering*(*us*) 1185 Templars (K); Willelmus *filius Derinch* 1190–4 Seals (Bk); Ælfsige *Dyring* 955 BCS 917 (W); Richard *Dering* c1250 Rams (Nf); John *Dyring'* 1275 SRWo; Henry *During* 1327 SRSo. OE *Dēoring*, *Dȳring*, patronymics of OE *Dēor*, *Dȳre*.

Dearling: *v.* DARLING

Dearman, Dorman, Durman: *Derman* 1066 DB (Wa); *Dermannus* clanewatere c1130 AC (Lo); William, Robert *Derman* 1201 Cur (Y), 1300 LoCt. OE *Dēormann* from OE *Dēor* (*v.* DEAR) and *mann*.

Dearsley, Dearsly: Alan *de Deresle* 1279 RH (C). From Derisley Fm in Woodditton (Cambs).

Dearson, Dairson: William *Dereson* 1327 SRC. 'Son of *Dēor*(*a*).' *v.* DEAR.

Deason: *v.* DAYSON

Death, Deeth, Dearth, D'Eath, D'Eathe, De Ath, De'Ath, D'Aeth: Robert *Deth* 1196 P (Beds); Roger *Deth* 1221 ElyA (C), 1327 SRSf; Robert *Death* Ed 1 Battle (Sx); Gilbert *Deth* 1272 AssSo; Alice *Deth* (*Ded*), William *Deth* (*Det*), Geoffrey *Deth* (*Deet*) 1327 *SR* (Ess); Richard *Deeth* 1346 Pat (Sf). The common explanation that this surname derives from *Ath* (Belgium) is just possible. One example has been noted: Gerardus *de Athia* 1208 Cur (Gl), but the numerous other examples are certainly not topographical in origin. *De Ath*, *D'Eath*, etc., must be regarded as affected spellings designed to dissociate the name from *death*, OE *dēaþ*, ME *deeth*, *deth*, which fits the above forms. The pronunciation is *Deeth*, the normal development of *dēaþ*. As Weekley has suggested, the name may be derived from the pageants. Death was personified in the Chester plays. cf. *Mort* and the French *Lamort*. Fransson has noted a rare occupational name, John *le Dethewright'*, *le Dede-writhe*, *le Dedewrighte* in Essex in 1299 and 1327 (MESO), from OE *dȳð* 'fuel, tinder'. This survives as *Deathridge* and *Deth*(*e*)*ridge*. *Death*, a medieval and modern surname common in Essex and East Anglia, where *dȳð* would occur in ME as *deeth*, is probably metonymic for a maker of tinder, an etymology confirmed by the survival of *Deether* and *Deetman*, which must be synonymous with *Deathridge*. Bardsley's topographical examples are errors for *Deche*. *v.* DEEKES.

Deathridge: *v.* DEATH

Deavall, Deaville: *v.* DAVALL

Deave, Deaves, Deeves: Rogerus *Surdus* 1196 Cur (Nth); Ralph *le Deue* 1251 Oseney (O); Sarra *le Deaue* (*la Deafe*) 1317 AssK. OE *dēaf* 'deaf'; *deave* is from the inflected forms *deafum*, *deafe*.

Deavin: *v.* DEVIN

Debbage: William *Debeche*, Robert *Debedge* 1568 SRSf. From Debach (Suffolk), pronounced *Debbidge*.

Debell, Deeble: William *Debel* 1197 P (Y); Alexander *le Deble* 1221 AssSa; Mary *Deeble* 1699 DWills. Fr *debile*, Lat *dēbil-is* 'weak, feeble' (1536 NED).

Debenham, Debnam, Deadman, Dedman: John *de Debenham* 1279 RH (Hu); Robert *Debenham*, *Debnam* 1674 HTSf; Francis *Debnam*, *Deadman* ib.; John *Deadman*, *Debingham* ib.; Stephen *Dedman*, Thomas *Dednum* ib. From Debenham (Suffolk).

Debney: Robert *deulebeneie* 1162 P (Nb); Laurence *Deubeneye* 1328 LLB E; Ralph *Dieubeneye* 1341 LLB F; Widow *Debny* 1674 HTSf. A French phrase-name 'God bless (him)'. cf. Olive *Goadebles* 1269 Pat.

Debutt: For TEBBUTT, with voicing of initial *T*. *v.* THEOBALD, DIBBLE.

Decker: *v.* DICKER

Decoursy, de Courcy, de Courcey, Coursey: Richard *de Curci* 1086 DB (O); Thomas *de Curci* c1150–60 DC (L). From Courcy (Calvados).

Dede: *v.* DEED

Dedman: *v.* DEBENHAM

Deeble: *v.* DEBELL

Deed, Deedes, Dede, Dade: Richard *Ded* 1195 P (Bk); Hugo *Dede* 1210 P (D); Thomas *Dade*, Adam *Ded* 1275, 1285 Wak (Y); Roger *Dade* 1275 RH (L). OE *dǣd* 'deed, exploit'.

Deeker: *v.* DEEKES, DICKER

Deekes, Deeks, Deex, Deakes: (i) *Dike* Marescallus 1212 Cur (Y); *Dyke* de Chypendale 1246 AssLa; Richard, John *Dike* 1195 P (Sf), 1279 RH (Hu); Robert *Dykes* 1327 SRWo; John *Deke* 1332 SRSx; Thomas *Deeke* 1568 SRSf. *Dick* often appears as *Dike* which, with a lowering and lengthening of the *i*, would become *Deke*, *Deek*. *Dickins* is found as *Deekins* in 1728 (Bardsley). (ii) Similarly, OE *dīc* 'ditch, dike' occurs both as *dīke* and *dēke* in ME. cf. *Dekeleye* (1377) for Dickley (PN Ess 344) and Henry and Alice *de Deche* 1279 RH (C). This is printed *Dethe*, but they undoubtedly lived near the Devil's Dyke. *Atte Deke* would become *Deek* and correspond to *Deeker* 'the dweller by the dike'. *v.* DITCH.

Deem, Deam: Gilbert, Richard *Deme* 1279 RH (O). OE *dēma* 'judge'. cf. DOME.

Deemer, Deamer, Demer, Demers: Leuric *Demere* c1095 Bury (Sf); Alan *Demur* 1250 Trentham (St); Richard *le Demor*, *le Demur* 1301, 1357 ib. OE *dēmere* 'deemer, judge', one who pronounces the verdict or doom. cf. '*Demar*, Iudicator' PromptParv, and *v.* DEEMING, DEMPSTER, DOMAN.

Deeming, Demings: Reginald *Demung* 1246 Seals (W); John *Domyng* 1351 AssEss. OE **dēmung* 'judging, judgement', from OE *dēma* 'judge'. *Domyng* may be an error for *Demyng*, otherwise from OE **dōmung* 'judgement', from OE *dōm* 'doom, judgement'. The surname is identical in meaning with DEEMER and DOMAN.

Deen: *v.* DEAN

Deer, Deere, Deerr: *v.* DEAR

Deering: *v.* DEARING

Deetch: *v.* DITCH

Deetcher: *v.* DICKER

Deeth, Deether, Deetman: *v.* DEATH

Deeves: *v.* DEAVE

Deex: *v.* DICK, DITCH

de Fraine, de Freyne: *v.* FRAIN

Deeves: *v.* DEAVE

Deex: v. DEEKES, DICK, DITCH

de Fraine, de Freyne: v. PRAIN

Deighton: Thomas, Henry *de Dicton* 1204 AssY, 1259 IpmY; Richard *de Dyghton* 1327 FFY; John *Dyghton* 1419 IpmY. From Deighton (ER, NR, WRYorks).

Delafield, de la Feld: v. FIELD

Delahaye, De La Haye, de la Hey, Delhay: Ranulf *de Lahaia* 1119 Colch (Ess); John *del Haye* 1275 RH (Nth); Richard *del Heye* 1275 SRWo. Robert *de Haia* (1123), founder of Boxgrove Priory (Sussex), came from Haye-du-Puits (La Manche). v. ANF. The surname is commonly English in origin, 'dweller by the enclosure'. v. HAY.

Delahooke: v. HOOK

Delamar, Delamare, de la Mare, Delamere, Delamore, Dallamore, Dallimore, Dillamore, Dolamore, Dollamore, Dollemore, Dolleymore, Dollimore, Dollymore: Henry *de Lamara* 1130 P (O); Coleman *de Lamora* 1135–85 Seals (Nth); Robert *de la Mare* 1190 BuryS (Sf); William *de la Mere* 1260 FFEss; Henry *Dalamare* 1385 FrY; Thomas *Dallamour* 1732 FrY; John *Dallamore* 1733 FrY. Early bearers of the name came from one of the numerous French places named La Mare 'pool'. Many later names are of English origin, 'dweller by the mere, lake, marsh or moor', OE *mere*, *mōr*, with common confusion of these words. v. MOOR. Dollyman's Fm in Rawreth (Essex), *Dallamers* alias *Dalymers* in 1600, owes its name to John *de la Mare* (1342 PN Ess 193).

Delaney, Delany, de Launay, Delauney: v. DANDO

Delbridge: v. BRIDGE

Delf, Delph, Delve, Delves: Richard *de la Delphe* 1295 MELS (Sx); Mabel *de la Delue*, John *atte Delue* 1296 SRSx; John *Delves* 1376 AD vi (St). 'Dweller by the ditch(es), quarry or quarries', OE (*ge*)*delf* 'digging, excavation'. Sometimes metonymic for 'excavator, quarrier' (OE *delfere*): William *le Deluer* 1230 P (So). Lettice *atte Delue* (1357 ColchCt) is probably to be associated with John *Delvere* (1359 ib.).

Delhay: v. DELAHAYE

Delicate: v. COTE

De Lisle, De L'Isle, de Lyle: v. LISLE

Dell: William, Robert *atte Delle* 1296 SRSx, 1309 LLB D. 'Dweller in the dell' (OE *dell*). v. also DIL.

Delland: Philip *Deneland* 1275 RH (D); Roger *Denlond* 1296 SRSx. 'Dweller by the valley-estate' (OE *denu*, *land*).

Dellar, Deller: Ralph, John *Dellere* 1275 RH (Nf), 1347 AD iii (Sr). 'Dweller in the dell.' cf. DELL.

Dellbridge: v. BRIDGE

Delleman: Equivalent to DELLAR.

Dellew: Henry, John *del Ewe* 1250 Oseney (O), 1274 RH (Sa). 'Dweller by the water' (Fr *eau*).

Delling: Henry, Jordan *Dellyng* 1296 SRSx, 1327 SRSo. v. DILLING.

Dello, Dellow: (i) Walter *Delho* 1275 RH

(Herts); William *Delhou* 1279 RH (O). (ii) William *Dellowe* 1275 RH (W). 'Dweller by the ridge or hill' (OE *hōh*, *hlāw*). v. HOW, LOW. *Dell*, rare in place-names, is apparently unknown as a first element.

Delph, Delve(s): v. DELF

Deman, Demant: v. DIAMANT

Demers: v. DEEMER

Demings: v. DEEMING

Demmar: William *le Demmere* 1296 SRSx. A derivative of OE **demman* 'to dam, obstruct the course of water'. A maker of dams.

de Montmorency: Herueus *de Munmoreci* 1177 P (Sx). From Montmorency (Seine-et-Oise, Aube).

Dempsey, Dempsy: James *Dempse* 1526 GildY. Irish *Ó Díomasaigh* 'descendant of *Díomasach*' (proud).

Dempster: Haldan *Deemester* 1296 Black (Perth); Walter *Demester* 1313 MEOT (La); Andrew *Dempstar* 1360 Black (Brechin). A feminine form of *Deemer*, like *Baxter*, etc., used of men. A northern and Manx term for 'judge', common in Scotland for the judge of the Parliament, shire or baron-bailie. Until 1747 every laird of a barony had power to hold courts for the trial by his dempster of certain offenders within his barony.

Denbow: Eudo, Philip, William *Denebaud* 1214 Cur (So), 1276 RH (D), 1298 Ipm (Do); John *Dembel* 1338 FFSf. OE **Denebeald*, an unrecorded compound of *Dene-*.

Dence, Denns, Dench: Thomas *Dench* 1327 SRWo. OE *denisc*, ME *denshe*, *dench*, Scottish *Dence, Dens* 'Danish'.

Denham, Denholm, Denholme: Richard *de Deneham* 1176 P (Bk); John *de Deneholme* 1332 SRLa; John *Denham* 1466–7 FFSr. From Denham (Bucks, Suffolk), Denholme (WRYorks), or 'dweller at the farm in the valley'.

Denholm, Denholme: John *de Deneholme* 1332 SRLa. 'Dweller by the holm in the valley.' v. HOLME

Denial: v. DANIEL

Denis, Denise, Dennis, Denniss, Dennys, Dennes, Denness, Dinnis: (i) *Dionisius* de Chotum Hy 2 DC (L); *Dionisia* Hy 2 DC (L); *Denis* de Sixlea 1176 P (L); *Deonisia* 1212 Cur (Y); *Denise* 1321 FFEss; *Deonis* 1327 SRSo; *Dionis* ate Brome 1332 SRSr; *Denes* Lister 1379 PTY; Walter *Denys* 1272 AssSt; Walter *Dyonis* 1297 MinAcctCo; Ralph *Denys, Dynis* 1308 EAS xviii; Robert *Deonis'* 1317 AssK. Lat *Dionysius*, Gk Διονύσιος, 'of Dionysos', the name of several saints, common in England after the 12th century. The feminine *Dionysia, Denise* was equally popular and both are represented in the surnames. Robert *Denys* was the son of *Dionisius* de Grauntebrigge (1321 Cor). (ii) Radulfus *Dacus* 1176 P (Ha); Robertus *Danus* 1193 P (Nf); Rannulf *le Daneis* 1193 P (Wa); William *le Daneys, le Deneys* 1232, 1241 FFHu. ME *danais*, OFr *daneis* 'Danish', 'the Dane', with the vowel influenced by that of ME *denshe*, OE *denisc*. cf. DENCE.

Denison, Dennison: (i) Roger *Deneyson* 13th

Binham (Nf); Adam *Deynissone* 1381 SRSf;
Henry *Dennesson* 1450 Rad. 'Son of *Denis*.' (ii)
Walter *Denizen* 1275 RH (Ess). AFr *deinzein*, a
burgess who enjoyed the privileges of those living
deinz la cité 'within the city'.

Denleigh, Denley, Denly: Thomas *de Denley*
1279 RH (O). 'Dweller by the valley-clearing'
(OE *denu, lēah*).

Denman: William *Deneman* 1314 FFEss; Adam
Deneman 1332 SRSr. 'Dweller in the valley.'

Denmer, Denmore: Alan *Denmere* 1296 SRSx.
'Dweller by the valley-lake' (OE *denu, mere*).

Denn, Denne: (i) Thomas *de Denne* c1160 ArchC
5; Baldwin *de la Denne* 1275 RH (K); John *atte
Denn* 1296 SRSx. A swineherd, one who worked
in the woodland or swine-pasture (OE *denn*). (ii)
William *Denn* 1296 SRSx. This may be for *atte
Denne*, but, as *Denis* had a diminutive *Denet*, a
pet-name *Den* must have existed side by side with
Din.

Dennell: *v.* DANIEL

Denner: 'Dweller in the valley.' cf. DENMAN.

Dennes: *v.* DENIS

Dennet, Dennett, Dennitts: Alice *Denet* 1279
RH (Beds); Richard *Dynot* 1279 RH (O); John
Denot 1332 SRSx. Diminutives of *Den*, a pet-
form of *Denis*. In *Piers Plowman*, *Denote* is a
woman's name, from *Denise*.

Dennis, Dennys, Denness, Denniss: *v.* DENIS
Dennish: for DENIS or DEVENISH.

Dennison: *v.* DENISON

Denns: *v.* DENCE, DENN

Denre, Denry: *v.* DARREE

Denson, Densum: Henry *le Deneson* 1295 AssSt;
Adam *Densone* 1362 FrY. 'Son of the dean.'

Dent: Waltheef *de Dent* 1131 FeuDu; William,
John *de Dent* c1200 Riev, 1356 FFY; John *Dent*
1403–4 IpmY. From Dent (WRYorks).

Dentith: *v.* DAINTETH

Denton: Ælfweard *æt Dentune* 972 BCS (Nth);
William *de Denton* 1271 FFL; Richard *Denton*
1403 IpmNt. From one or other of the many places
of this name.

Denty: *v.* DAINTY

Derby, Derbyshire: *v.* DARBY, DARBYSHIRE

Dering: *v.* DEARING

Dermott: *Dermot* an Irishman 1243 AssSo. *v.*
MACDERMOT.

Derry: *v.* DARREE

Detheridge, Dethridge: *v.* DEATH

Deuters, Dewters: Martin *Dutere* 1191–1212
Bart; Christopher *Dewtris, Dewtrice* 1671, 1682
FrY. Perhaps a derivative of ME *duten, douten*,
OFr *duter, douter* 'to hesitate', used of one who is
timid, wavering in opinion, one who dilly-dallies.

Devall: *v.* DAVALL

Devenish, Devonish: Robert *le Deueneis* 1205 P
(L); William *le Deveneys* 1243 AssSo; John *le
Devenisshe* 1337 LLB F. OE *defenisc* 'the man
from Devon'.

**Deveraux, Devereaux, Devereu, Devereux, Deve-
roux, Deverose, Everix, Everiss, Everest, Everist:**
Roger *de Ebrois* 1086 DB (Nf); Walter *de Eureus*

1159 P (He); Stephen *de Euereus* 1199 MemR
(Wo); Osmund *de Deuereals* ib. (W); Eustace *de
Deueraus* 1204 P (So); Thomas *de Euereus,
Deuereus* 1279 AssSo; John *de Ebroicis* 1297 AssSt;
John *Deveros* 1385 LLB H; Robert *Everis* 1495
GildY. From Evreux (Eure), from the Celtic
tribal name *Eburovices* 'dwellers on the Ebura or
Eure River'.

De Vile, Deville, De Ville, de Ville: *v.* DAVALL

Devin, Devine, Devinn, Deavin, Divine: Nicholas
le Deuin, le Diuin 1187–8 P (He). ME *devin, divin*,
OFr *devin* 'divine', used of persons 'of more than
ordinary excellence' (c1374 NED). The Irish
Devin(e) is for *Ó Daimhín* or *Ó Duibhín* 'descendant of *Daimhín* or of *Duibhín*', diminutives of
damh 'ox, stag' and *dubh* 'black'.

Devlin: Adam *de Divelyn* 1256 AssNb; William
Develyn 1380 LoPleas. From Dublin. The Irish
Devlin is *Ó Dobhailein* or *Ó Doibhilin* 'descendant
of *Dobhailen*'.

Devon, Devons: Adam *de Devoun* 1275 RH (Nf).
From Devon.

Devonish: *v.* DEVENISH

Dewar: (i) Gael *Deoir, Deoireach* 'pilgrim,
sojourner'. The medieval *deoradh* had custody of
the relics of a saint. *v.* MACINDEOR. (ii) Thomas
de Deware 1296 CalSc (Edinburgh). From Dewar
(Midlothian).

Dewhirst, Dewhurst, Jewhurst: Roger *de le
Dewyhurst* c1300 WhC (La). From Dewhurst
(Lancs).

**Dewsbury, Duesbury, Jewesbury, Jewsbury, Joes-
bury:** Tomas *de Dewesberi* 1204 P (Y). From
Dewsbury (WRYorks). *Jews-* is a common colloquial pronunciation of *Dews-*. cf. *Chuesday* for
Tuesday.

Dexter: John, Ralph *le Dextere* 1262 FrLeic,
1327 SRSf; Roger, Simon *le Dykestre* 1305 SIA;
William *Dexter* 1378 AssWa. A form of *Dyster*,
noted in Essex, Leicester, Suffolk and Warwicks
(14.. NED).

Dey, Deyes. *v.* DAY

Deykes: *v.* DITCH

d'Eyncourt, Danecourt: Walter *de Aincurt* 1086
DB (Nth, Db, L, Y); Ralph *Daincurt* c1157 Gilb
(L); Oliver *Deyncourt, de Aincurt, de Eyncurt* 1243
AssSo. From Aincurt (Seine-et-Oise).

Deyns: *v.* DAIN

**Diamant, Diamond, Deman, Demant, Diment,
Dimond, Dimont, Dyment, Dymond:** *Diamant* and
Diamond may occasionally derive from *Diamanda*
1221 Cur (Mx), 1349 Husting, one of the fanciful
names given to women in the Middle Ages. Hence,
probably, William *Dyamond* 1332 SRD, who gave
his name to Dymond's Bridge in Whitestone
(Devon). But these examples will hardly explain
Thomas *Dymande* 1332 SRSr; Robert *Dymond'*
1379 PTY; William *Demaunde, Dymaunde* 1391,
1392 CarshCt (Sr), or the numerous and varied
forms in the HartlandPR (D): Edmund, Joanna
Demon 1564, 1566; Thomas *Deymon* 1581;
Joanna, Samuel *Dymon* 1582, 1826; John *Deman*
1632; Elizabeth *Daymand* 1685; Charles, Ann

Daymond 1686, 1688; Grace *Dyamond* 1753; Joannah *Dyman*, Mr Wm *Dayman's* wife 1765; Margaret *Daimant* 1801; Humphrey *Dyment* 1817; Susan *Dayment* 1833. cf. also John *Deyman* alias *Dymond* 1698 DKR (D), while Daymond's Hill in Tiverton (Devon) owes its name to John *Dayman* 1589 SRD. The excrescent *t* or *d* is not common before the 17th century, and all probably derive from *Dayman*, a personal and occupational name 'herdsman'. *v.* DAYMAN.

Diaper: *v.* DIPPER

Dibb, Dibbs: John *del Dybbe* 1469 FrY. 'Dweller by the hollow', from *dib*, a northern dialect form of *dip*, a small hollow in the ground (1847–78 NED). The surname may also be from *Dibb*, a short form of *Dibble*.

Dibble, Dible, Diboll, Dybald, Dyball, Dybell, Dyble, Dipple: William *Dibel* 1275 RH (Lo); Walter *Dipel* ib. (Sf); Ralph *Dibald* 1276 RH (Y); William *Dybald* 1277 AssLa; William *Dybel* 1277 LLB B; William *Dypel* 1327 SRWo; Edmund *Dyboll* 1524 SRSf; Sarah *Dipple*, *Dibble* 1678, 1680 SaltAS (OS) x. *Dibald* is from *Tibald* (*Theobald*), with a voicing of the initial consonant. *Dibel* is a diminutive of *Dibb*, a pet-name for *Theobald*. For *Dipple*, cf. TIPPELL.

Dice, Dyce: Richard *Dyse* 1327 SRSf; John *Dyce*, *Dys* 1412, 1418 LLB B, I. ME *dyse*, *dyce* 'dice', both singular and plural; also 'chance, luck', a nickname for a gambler. cf. HAZARD.

Dick, Dicke, Dicks, Dix: *Dicke* Smith 1220 Cur (L); *Dik* 1260 AssCh; *Dik de Hyde* 1286 ib.; Richard *Dike* Hy 3 Colch (Ess); William *Dik* 1356 LLB G; William *Dyckes* 1362 AD iii (Nf). A pet-form of *Richard*, found also as *Dike*, *v.* DEEKES.

Dickason: *v.* DICKENSON

Dickels: *v.* DIGGLE

Dicken, Dickens, Dickin, Dickins, Dickings, Dickons, Dykins, Dekin, Dekiss: *Dicun* Malebiss' 1207 Cur (Y); Richard *Dicun* 1203 AssSt, 1230 P (Beds); John *Dycon* 1327 SRSt; Maud *Dyconnis*, David *Dyccons* 1327 SRWo; Robert *Dekoun* 1327 SRC. A diminutive of *Dick*, *Dic-un*. Other diminutives were *Dic-el*, *Dic-el-in*, *Dic-et*. *v.* DIGGEN, DEEKES. *Dekoun* would become *Deekon*, *Deekin*. *Dekiss* is from *Deakins*, cf. HODGKINS and HODGKISS.

Dickenson, Dickinson, Dickerson, Dickeson, Dickison, Dickason: William *Dykounson* 1366 SRLa; John *Dykonesson* 1388 FrY; Henry *Dicason* 1518 GildY; Gilbert *Dyckenson* 1585 ShefA; Nicholas *Dikersone* 1598 AD vi (Nf). 'Son of *Dicun*.' John and Henry '*Dicounesson de Clesnesse*' were sons of *Richard*, son of Henry de Clesnesse 1359 Pat (Nb).

Dicker, Dikkers, Decker, Deeker, Ditcher, Deetcher: (i) John *Dicher* 1210 Cur (Ess); Simon *le Dykere* 1296 SRSx; Hugh *le Dykere* (*Dikkere*) 1327 *SR* (Ess); Agnes *le Dycher* 1354 Putnam (Ch). OE *dīcere* 'one who digs ditches, ditcher', or 'one who lives by a dike'. cf. DICKMAN, DEEKES. (ii) Henry *ater Dykere* 1296 SRSx; John *atte Diker*

1327 ib. *Dicker*, still surviving in Sussex, may also derive from The Dicker (PN Sx 439, MELS 51).

Dicketts: John, Robert *Dyket* 1296 SRSx, 1329 ColchCt. A diminutive of *Dick*.

Dickie, Dickey: Robert *Dikky* 1504 Black (Glasgow). A Scottish diminutive of *Dick*.

Dickin(son): *v.* DICKEN(SON)

Dickman, Digman: (i) Richard, John *Dikeman* 1206 Cur (L), 1227 AssSt; Thomas *Dekeman* 1327 SRC. OE *dīc* 'ditch, dike' and *mann*, 'one who lives near, or works in a ditch or dike'. cf. DICKER. *Dekeman* would become *Deekman*. cf. DEEKER. (ii) Robertus *serviens Ricardi*, Thomas *Dikman*, *Richardman* 1379 PTY. 'Servant of *Dick*.'

Dicksee: *v.* DIXEY

Dickson, Dixon, Dixson: Thom *Dicson* 1307 Black (Castle Douglas); John *Diksson*, *Dikson* 1332 SRCu; Nicholas *Dyxon* 1425 FFEss; Robert *Dixson* 1429 LLB K. 'Dick's son.'

Dieppe: Saladinus *de Depe* 1224 Pat. From Dieppe.

Difford: Hugh *de Difford* 1276 RH (Y). 'Dweller by the deep ford', OE *dēop*, *ford*.

Digan: *v.* DIGGEN

Digby: Roger *de Digby* c1160–5 RegAntiquiss; Geoffrey *de Dyggeby* 1250 FFL; Simon *Digby* 1497 FFWa. From Digby (Lincs).

Digg, Digges: William *Dyg* 1296 SRSx; Thomas *Dygge* 1327 SRSf; John *le Digge* 1327 SRSx; Christina *Dygges* 1335 AD i (Do). ME *digge* 'a duck' (c1450 MED). Also from a voiced form of *Dick*: *Digge de Torot* 1246 AssLa.

Diggan: *v.* DIGGEN

Diggatt: William *Diggard* 1209 P (Nf); Henry *Digard* 1275 RH (Nf). OFr *digard* (Normandy) 'a spur', hence 'a maker or seller of spurs'.

Diggen, Diggens, Diggines, Diggins, Digings, Digan, Diggan, Digance, Diggon: John, Richard *Digun* 1227 AssBk, 1247 AssBeds; Richard *Digon* 1273 RH (Lo); Richard *Digoun*, *Dicoun* 1375–6 LLB H; Fr. *Diggins* 1674 HTSf. *Digun*, a common variant of *Dicun*. *v.* DICKEN.

Diggle, Diggles, Dickels: Agnes *Diggell'* 1219 AssY. *Dikel*, *Digel*, diminutives of *Dick*. cf. *Dikelin* 1275 RH (Nf). This double diminutive survived as a surname until the 17th century when Thomas *Diglin* gave name to Diglin's Drove in Parson Drove (Cambs), called *Diggles* and *Diglings* Drove in 1864 (PN C 279).

Diggon: *v.* DIGGEN

Dightham: A Leeds and Bradford name, for *Dighton*.

Dighton: William *de Dicton'* 1207 P (Y). From Deighton (ER, NR, WRYorks).

Digman: *v.* DICKMAN

Dil, Dill, Diller, Dilcock, Dilling, Dulcken: Johannes *filius Dulle* 1279 RH (C); Godwin *Dul* 1185 P (Ha); William *Delle* 1195 Cur (Nf); Roger, Godfrey *Dulle* 1202 FF (Nf), 1232 Pat (L); Robert *Dille* 1279 RH (Bk); Alice *le Dul* ib. (C); Warin, Geoffrey *Dylle* 1283 Battle (Sx), 1327 SRSo; William *Del* 1297 MinAcctCo; John *Dyl* 1301 SRY; Thomas *dictus Dyll* c1360 Black (Inverness); Marjorie dicta *Dyll* 1361 ib. A difficult group of names. An OE **Dulla*, postulated to explain Dullingham (Cambs), seems to be confirmed by the 13th-century *Dulle* in the same county, possibly surviving in *Dulson*. A mutated form of this, OE **Dylli* or **Dylla* is found in Dillington (Hunts) and Dilton (Wilts). This would give ME *Delle, Dille, Dulle*, which may account for some of the surnames *Dell* and *Dill*. An unrecorded compound **Dylwine* appears to have existed in Norfolk (Philip, Mariot *Dylewyne* 1275 RH), where we also find *Delle* and *Dulle*. Harrison derives *Dilnott* from **Dilnōð*, a possible but unrecorded form. *Dilcock, Dolcok* (Robert, Roger *Dolcok* 1327 SRWo) and *Dulcken* (from *Dulekin*) are pet-forms in which the suffixes are usually added to short forms of personal names. It may be, too, that *Dilke* is a contracted form of an OE **Dylluc*. ME *dull* 'dull, foolish' is found once in the 13th century, but is not usual before 1350; *dill* is found in the same sense from 1200 to 1440 and the two forms point to an original OE **dyl, *dylle* (MED) which would give ME *dell, dill, dull*, thus accounting for *Dell, Dill* and the obsolete *Dull*. The nickname certainly occurred in 1279 as *le Dul* in Cambridgeshire where *Dulle* is also found as a personal-name side by side with *Dill, Dilke* and *Dilcock*. The plant *dill* was commonly cultivated in the Middle Ages for its carminated fruits or seeds and OE *dile, dyle* is the first element of Dilham (Norfolk), Dilicar (Westmorland) and Dilworth (Lancs). This might well be one source of *Dill*, an occupation name for a grower or seller of dill, metonymic for *Diller*, found in 14th-century Somerset where both then and today we find *Dill* and where OE **Dylle, *dylle* would become *Dulle* as in (Robert, Roger) *Dolcok* (1327 SRSo). *Dilnott*, of which no examples have been found, is probably ME *dilnote* (a1400 MED), an old name for the Earth-nut, used in the herbals for cyclamen. *Dilling*, noted in 14th-century Yorkshire by the side of *Dill* and *Dilcock*, and *Delling*, found in Sussex in 1296, may be for **Dylling* 'son of *Dylla*' or **dylling* 'the dull one'.

Dilcock: Geoffrey *Dilcok* 1327 SRC, Adam *Dilkoc* 1379 PTY. *v.* DIL.

Dilger: Stannard *Dilker* 1275 RH (Nf). Perhaps 'dill-field'. cf. Dilicar (Westmorland).

Dilke, Dilkes, Dilks: Adam *Dylke* 1278 AssSo; Nicholas *Dilkes* 1279 RH (C). *v.* DIL.

Dillamore: *v.* DELAMAR

Diller: Robert *Dyler* 1301 SRY; Thomas *Diller* 1327 SRSo. *v.* DIL.

Dilling: John *Dillyng* 1275 RH (K); Henry *Dyllyng* 1379 PTY. *v.* DIL.

Dillon, Dyllon: (i) Geoffrey *Dilun* 1203 SP1 (Sa); Richard *Dylon* 1332 SRWa. Perhaps OG *Dillo* with the diminutive *-on*. (ii) Robert, John *de Dilun* 1203 P1 (Sa), 1247 FFO. From Dilwyn (Hereford), *Dilun* 1138.

Dilnot, Dilnott, Dilnutt: *v.* DIL

Dimblebee, Dimbleby, Dimbledee: Eustace *de*

Denbelby c1190 Gilb (L). From Dembleby (Lincs). *Dimbledee* is a Welsh corruption.

Diment, Dimond, Dimont: *v.* DIAMANT

Dimmack, Dimmick, Dimmock, Dimock, Dymick, Dymock, Dymoke: Nicholas *de Dimmoch* 1169 P (Gl). From Dymock (Glos).

Dimmer: *v.* DISMORE

Din, Dinn: *Dyn* Hunte 1296 SRSx. A pet-name of *Dinis* (*Denis*).

Dinan: Rolland *de Dinan* c1155 DC (L); Josce *de Dinant* 1158 P (Berks). From Dinan (Côtes-du-Nord).

Dines: *v.* DAIN

Dingain: *v.* GAIN

Dingle: Richard *Dingyl* 1246 AssLa; Hugh *de la Dingle* 1275 SRWo; John *ate Dyngle* 1299 MELS (Wo). 'Dweller in the deep dell or hollow', ME *dingle*. cf. Dingle (Lancs).

Dinn: *v.* DIN

Dinnis: *v.* DENIS

Diplock, Duplock: John *Depelak* 1327 SRSx; Samuel *Deeplocke* 1674 HTSf. Found as *Diplock, Duplake, Deeplake* (16th PN Sx 438). 'Dweller by the deep stream' (OE *dēop, lacu*).

Dipper, Diaper: (i) William *de Ipra* 1140–1 Seals (L), *dipre* 1185 Templars (Beds); Geoffrey *de Ipres* 1243 AssSo; Bruning *Dypres* 1296 SRSx. From Ypres (Belgium). (ii) Geoffrey *Dipere* t John Seals (Sr); William *le dipere* 1227 AssBeds; Davy *Dipper* 1520 ChwWo; Rose *Diaper* 1687 Buxhall (Sf). ME *dipper* 'a diving bird, water ousel, kingfisher' (1388 NED). cf. DIVER.

Dipple: *v.* DIBBLE

Disher: Roger *le Disser* 1273 RH (Wa); Richard *Dysser* 1301 SRY; John, Robert *le Disshere* 1304–47 LLB C, E, F. 'Maker or seller of dishes' from OE *disc* 'dish' (1304 NED). In London dishers were makers of wooden measures for wine and ale who had to have each a mark of his own placed on the bottom of each measure, samples of the marks to be submitted to the Chamberlain. They were also called *turnours* (John, Thomas *le Turnour*) 1347 LLB F 160.

Dismore, Dimmer: Robert *Dimars* 1220 Fees (Berks); Roger *Dismars* 1225 FrLeic. OFr *dix mars* 'ten marks'. cf. Alan *de duabus marcis* 1202 AssL, Robert *Deumars* 1280 LLB A, Bartholomew *Dewmars* 1334 ib., E, from *deux*, 'two marks', which may have been absorbed by *Dimmer*.

Disney: William *de Ysini* c1150 DC (L), *de Yseigni* 1177 P (L); Adam *Dyseni* 1202 AssL; Anthony *Dysney* 1552 AD vi (W). From Isigny (Calvados).

Disper: *v.* DASHPER

Ditch, Deetch, Deykes, Dyke, Dykes: Joc. *de la Dike* c1250 MELS (Sx); John *attedich* 1260 AssC; Matilda *in Dich* 1279 RH (C); Roger *de la Diche* ib (O); John *del Dike* 1297 SRY; William *del Dikes* 1332 SRCu. 'Dweller by the ditch(es) or the dike(s)', OE *dīc. v.* also DICK, DEEKES.

Ditcham, Ditchum: Walter *de Decheham* 1296 SRSx; Thomas *Ditcham* 1674 HTSf. From Ditcham in Buriton (Hants), half-a-mile from the Sussex boundary.

Ditcher: v. DICKER

Diter, Dyter: Helewisa *Ditur* 1327 SRSx. OFr, ME *ditour* 'author', used of a composer, public crier; summoner, indicter (1303 NED).

Divall, Divell: v. DAVALL

Diver, Divers, Divver: Robert *Dyvere* 1252 Rams (Hu); Gunnilda *Divere* 1279 RH (C); Richard *Diverse* 1597 RothwellPR (Y). A derivative of *dive*, 'a diving bird', 'a diver' (c1510 NED).

Dives: Boselinus *de Diue* 1086 DB (C); William *de Dyves*, *de Dyve* 1242 Fees (O). From Dives (Calvados), earlier *Diva*.

Divine: v. DEVIN

Dix: v. DICK

Dixey, Dixcee, Dixcey, Dixie, Dicksee: Laurence *Dixi* 1279 RH (C); Robert *Dysci* 1301 FFHu; Alice *Dixi* 1379 PTY. Lat *dixi* 'I have spoken', like the French *Dixi*, a name for a chorister derived from the beginning of a psalm (Dauzat). *Dysci*, by metathesis, for *Dycsi*.

Dixon: v. DICKSON

Doag: v. DOIG

Doak: v. DOIG, DUCK

Dobb, Dobbe, Dobbs: *Dobbe* filius Iuonis 1202 AssL; *Dobbe* de Denêby 1219 AssY; Reginald, William *Dobbe* 1275 SRWo, 1275 RH (Nf); Robert *Dobes* 1279 RH (O). A pet-form of *Robert*, very common in the 13th century in Yorks, Lancs, Cheshire and Staffs. *Dobbe* de Whitemore (1307 AssSt) is identical with *Robert* de Whitemore (1318 ib.). Richardus *filius Dobbe* was the same man as Richard *Dobbe* (1297 MinAcctCo).

Dobbie, Dobby, Dobbie, Dobey, Doby: *Dobbei* 1212 Cur (Y); *Dobi* Spendluf 1457 Black (Peebles); John *Doby* 1275 RH (L); Walter *Dobby* 1327 SRWo; Thomas *Doby* 1471 Black (Peebles). A pet-form of *Dobb*. Common in Scotland.

Dobbin, Dobbins, Dobbing, Dobbings, Dobbyn, Dobing: *Dobin* de Hatton 1203 AssSt; *Dobin* Cusin 1221 Cur (D); Hugo, Robert *Dobin* 1207 Cur (He), 1227 AssBk; Thomas *Dobinge* 1539 FeuDu; Samuel *Dobbins* 1674 HTSf. A common diminutive of *Dobb* (Robert).

Dobbinson, Dobbison, Dobinson: John *Dobynson* 1379 PTY; Robert *Dobyson* 1507 FrY. 'Son of *Dobbin*.'

Dobel, Dobell, Doble, Doubell, Double, Doubble: Richard *dublel* 1115 Winton (Ha); Robert *Dub-(b)le* 1191-6 P (Sf); Adam *le Dobel* 1296 SRSx; Richard *Double* 1336 LLB E. OFr *doublel* 'a twin', used as a nickname in OFr. cf. French *Jumeau* and v. GEMMELL.

Dobey, Dobie: v. DOBBIE

Dobieson: John *Dobysoun* 1429 Black (Lanarks). 'Son of *Dobie*.'

Dobinson: v. DOBBINSON

Dobney: v. DAUBENEY

Dobson, Dopson: Henry *Dobbesone* 1327 SRWo; Roger *Dobbessone* 1356 Putnam (Ch). 'Son of *Dobbe*.'

Doby: v. DOBBIE

Docharty, Docherty, Dockerty: v. DOUGHARTY

Dock: Wulfric' *Doc* 1177 P (Nf); Richard *Docke* 1221 Cur (Mx). Perhaps for DUCK, or from OE *Docca*. v. DOGGETT.

Dockeray, Dockery, Dockray, Dockree, Docwra: John *de Dokwra* 1332 SRCu. From Dockray (Cumb).

Dockett: John *Dockeeved'* 1212 Cur (Y). A nickname 'duck-head'. v. also DOGGETT, DUCKET.

Docksey: v. DOXEY

Doctor: v. DAUGHTERS

Dod, Dodd, Dodds, Dods: Brictricus *filius Doddi* 1066 DB (Wo); Balterus *filius Dudde*, Walterus *Dudde* 11th OEByn (Wo); *Dodde* de Lismanoch 1194 P (D); Johannes *filius Dode* 1332 SRLa; Ælfweard *Dudd* c1030 OEByn (Ha); Aluric *Dod* 1066 DB (Do); Aluinus *Dode*, *Dodeson* ib. (Herts); Æluric *Doddes* c1095 Bury (Sf); Gamel *Dod* 1175 P (Y); Ailricus *Dodde* 1176 P (Herts). Tengvik regards the OE bynames as nicknames from a Germanic root *dudd-* (*dodd-*) 'something rounded', denoting a rounded, lumpish man or a stupid person, or from the root of OE *dydrian* 'to deceive', 'deceiver, rascal', or, possibly, 'the hairless, close-cropped one' from *dod* 'to make bare, lop, cut off'. This is possible and may be supported by the solitary Thomas *le Dode* (1327 SRSx). But we have also clear evidence of derivation from a personal name, OE *Dodd(a)*, *Dudd(a)*, which was in use from Lincolnshire to Devonshire and from Essex to Lancashire until the 14th century and is probably the usual source.

Dodding: *Dodding* 1201 P (L); *Doding'* 1208 Cur (Gl); William *Doding* 1251 ElyCouch (C), 1268 AssSo; Andrew *Doddyng* 1296 SRSx. OE *Dodding* 'son of *Dodda*'. v. DOD.

Doddrell: a variant of DOTTRELL

Dodell, Duddell, Duddle: Simon *Dodul* 1275 SRWo; John *le Doudel*, William *Dudel* 1296 SRSx; Richard *Dodel* 1310 ColchCt. OE *Duddel*, a diminutive of *Dudda*, or a diminutive of the *dod*, *dud* discussed *s.n.* DOD, perhaps early examples of the 17th-century *doddle*, *doodle* 'foolish fellow'.

Dodge: *Doge* filius Arnaldi 1196 P (Y); Wigot *filius Doge* 1214 Cur (L); *Dogge* 1246 AssLa; Robert, Nicholas *Dogge* 1206 Cur (Gl), 1279 RH (O). A pet-name for *Roger*, rhymed on *Rodge* and *Hodge*.

Dodgen, Dodgeon, Dodgin, Dudgeon: *Dogynus* de Sourhulle 1327 SRSo; Thomas *Doioun* 1327 *SR* (Ess); John *Dugeoun* 1536 Black. *Dogg-in*, *Dogg-un*, diminutives of *Dodge*. Bardsley notes that *Dodgson* and *Hodgson* were pronounced *Dodgin* and *Hodgin* in north Lancashire.

Dodgson, Dodgshon, Dodgshun, Dodson, Dudson: Henry *Doggeson* 1332 SRLa; Robert *Dogesson* 1385 FrY; John *Dogeson*, *Dodshon* 1489, 1530 GildY; William *Dodggson* 1642 FrY; William *Dodgshon* 1713 FrY; John *Dodson* 1720 FrY. 'Son of *Dodge*.' There appears to be no post-Conquest trace of the DB *Dodeson;* the modern

Dodson is due to a simplification of the medial *dgs* of *Dodgson*.

Dodman, Dudman: Goduine *filius Dudeman* 1066 DB (K); Goduine *Dudumanni filius* c1095 Bury (Sf); *Dudeman* 1206 P (Co), 14th AD vi (Sx); Thomas, Walter, John *Dudeman* c1179 Bart (Lo), 1199 FrLeic, 1221 AssSa (Wa); Gilbert *Dodemon* 1275 SRWo; Simon *Dodeman, Dudeman* 1296, 1297 Wak (Y); Andrew *Dodeman, Dudeman* 1327, 1332 SRSx. OE *Dudemann*, recorded in the 9th century, and then not until the 11th.

Dodson: v. DODGSON

Doe: (i) Robert *le Do*(*e*) 1188–90 P (Sf); William *Do* 1220 Cur (Ess); Henry *le Daa* 1332 SRLa. OE *dā* 'doe'. (ii) Occasionally, perhaps, local. cf. Willingale Doe (PN Ess 500), from Hugh de *Ou, D'eu* t Hy 2. From Eu (Seine-Inférieure).

Dogerty: v. DOUGHARTY

Doggett, Dockett: *Dogget* 1199 P (Hu); *Doget* 1203 Cur (Herts); William *Doget* 1206 AssL; John *Doget, Doket* 1212, 1219 Fees (Y); Roger *Doket* 1225 AssSo. *Doket*, a diminutive of OE *Docca*, with voicing of the medial consonant to *Doget*, which may also be a diminutive of *dog*. cf. Roger *le Doge* 1296 SRSx, Rogerus *Canis* 1200 Cur (C), and v. CURR. *Doggett* may also be a late development of (Syward) *Dogheafd* 1177–95 Seals (Db) 'doghead'. cf. Matthew *Doggenecce* 1275 RH (L), Symon *Doggeschanke* c1246 Calv (Y), and Lucas *Dogge*(*s*)*tayl* 1279–80 PN Wt 10.

Doggrell: Nicholas, William *Doggerel* 1249 AssW, 1277 AssSo; Alice *Dogerel* 1321 EwenG (Beds). These names carry the word back over 100 years, but lack of context forbids a definite explanation or etymology though the form suggests comparison with COCKERELL, PICKERELL, and PUTTERILL. The root is probably the word for 'dog' and the nickname may refer to some characteristic of the puppy, later applied derisively to wretched poetry, its irregular rhythm perhaps suggesting the clumsy antics of the puppy.

Doherty: v. DOUGHARTY

Doidge, Doige: Richard *Doegson*, Alice *Doegewyf*, John *Doegeman* 1379 PTY. A northern form of *Dodge*. cf. William *Doide* 1469 Black (for *Dod*).

Doig, Doag, Doeg, Doak: Alexander *Dog* 1491 Black; David *Dogg* or *Doig* 1653–67 ib. *Dog*, for *Gille Dog* 'St Cadoc's servant'.

Doke: v. DUCK

Dolamore: v. DELAMAR

Dole, Dool: William *de la Dole* 1279 RH (C). OE *dāl*, ME *dole* 'portion or share of land', especially in the common field; also used of a boundary-mark and as a unit of area. Perhaps 'dweller by the boundary-mark'.

Doley: v. DOYLEY

Dolittle, Doolittle, Dollittle: Hugo *Dolitel* 1204 P (R), 1230 Pat (Nb); Walter *Dolitle* 1219 AssY; John *Do Littel* 1275 SRWo; Juliana *Dolutel, Dolute* Ed 1 Malms. A nickname for an idler. For *Dolute*, cf. HAKLUYT. One Molly *Dolitle* (b. c1900) deliberately changed her name to *De Little*.

Doll: Lewingus *Dol* 1066 Winton; Robert *Dol*

1198 P (Bk); Letitia *Dolle* 1279 RH (C). OE *dol* 'foolish'.

Dollamore, Dollemore, Dolleymore, Dollimore: v. DELAMAR

Dollar: Matthew *de Doler* 1316 Black. From Dollar (Clackmannanshire).

Dolley: v. DOYLEY

Dolling, Dowling: William *Dolling* 1243 AssSo; Peter *Dollyng* 1275 SRWo; Edmund *Dowlinge* 1674 HTSf. OE *dolling* 'the dull one'. v. DOLL. Also from a late assimilation of *rl* to *ll* in DORLING: Samuel *Dorling, Dolling* 1770, 1782 WStowPR (Sf).

Dollman, Dolman: William *Dolman* 1260 AssC; Richard *Doleman* 1279 RH (O). 'Dweller by the boundary-mark' (cf. DOLE) or 'dull, foolish man': Richard *Dolle* (1280 AssSo) is regularly called *Dolleman* in another roll. cf. DOLL, DOLLING.

Dolph: Thomas *Dolf* 1275 SRWo. A variant of DELF.

Dolphin, Duffin: *Dolfin de Cluttun'* 1193 P (Y); Adam *filius Dolfin* 1256 AssNb; Geoffrey, Richard *Dolfin* 1171, 1182 P (Ha, Herts); William *Duffin* 1279 RH (Hu), 1674 HTSf; Robert *Dolphin, Dewfine* 1606, 1609 Bardsley (La). ON *Dólgfinnr*, a common name in 11th-century northern England. *Duffin* may also be from ON *Dufan*, a loan from OIr *Dubán*: William *Duffane* 1379 PTY.

Doman, Dooman: John *Doman* 1327 SRSf. OE *dōm* and *mann* 'doom-man', 'judge'. cf. Roger *Dememan* 1246 Seals (W), William *Deman* 1285 AssLa, from OE *dēma* 'judge'. cf. DEEMER.

Dome: Henry *Dome* 1275 RH (Lo). OE *dōm* 'judgement', metonymic for DEEM 'judge'.

Domesday, Dumsday: Reginald *Domesday* 1297 Coram (Nf); John *Domisday* 1327 SRC; John *Demysday* 1479 NorwW (Nf). 'Servant of the judge', OE *dēma* and *dæge*. *Dome* occurs once in ME for 'judge'. This NED considers perhaps an error of transcription for *deme* but there seems to have been a tendency to substitute *dome* for *deme*. v. DEEMING, DOMAN. cf. Hugh *Domesman* 1155–75 Barnwell (C), William *Domesman* 1260 AssC 'man of judgement, judge'.

Domm, Domb: Thomas *Domme* 1297 MinAcctCo; Robert *le Doumbe* 1309 SRBeds. OE *dumb*, ME *domm*(*e*) 'mute, speechless'.

Dommett: v. DUMMETT

Domvil(l)e: v. DUMVILLE

Don: v. DUNN

Donaghie, Donaghy, Donahue: v. O'DONOGHUE

Donald: Haket *Donald* 1328 Black (Kinross). Gael *Domhnall*, OIr *Domnall* (pronounced *Dovnall*), PrCeltic *Dubno-valos* 'world-mighty', found in 13th-century Scotland as *Dofnald, Douenald, Dufenald* and in 1376: Willelmus *filius Donaldi*. v. Black.

Donaldson: Henry *Donaldson* 1339–40 Black. 'Son of Donald.'

Donat, Donnet, Donnett, Donnay: Geoffrey *Doneth*, Roger *Donet* 1296 SRSx; Nicholas, Bernard *Donat* 1362 LoPleas, 1364 FFSf. Lat *donatus*, Fr *donat* 'given', the name of several saints which has given rise to the French surnames *Donat, Donnat, Donnet, Donné, Donnay.* 'Nom mystique ou affectif, donné' (Dauzat). The name has, no doubt, the same meaning as the fuller *Deodatus, Deodonatus.*

Donbavand: *v.* DUNBABIN

Doncaster: Laurence *de Doncastrie* 1183–99 YCh; William *de Danecastre* 1259 FFL; John *Doncastre* 1379 PTY. From Doncaster (WRYorks).

Dongate: *v.* DUNGATE

Donkin: *v.* DUNCAN

Donley: Alfridus *de Donnleye* 1327 SRWo. From Dunley (Worcs).

Donn(e): *v.* DUNN

Donnelly: Irish *Ó Donnghaile* 'descendant of *Donnghál*' (brown-valour).

Donnet: *v.* DONAT

Donovan: Irish *Ó Donnabháin* 'descendant of *Donndubhán*' (dark-brown).

Dooks: *v.* DUCK

Dool: *v.* DOLE, DOYLE

Doolan: Irish *Ó Dubhláin* 'descendant of *Dubhfhlán*' (black-defiance).

Dooley, Dowley: Irish *Ó Dubhlaoich* 'descendant of *Dubhlaoch*' (black-hero).

Dooman: *v.* DOMAN

Dopson: *v.* DOBSON

Doran, Dorran: Martha *Dorrane* 1685 Black (Kirkcudbright). Ir *Ó Deoradháin*, a diminutive of *deorádh* 'exile, stranger'.

Dorant: *v.* DURRAND

Doring: *v.* DEARING

Dorling: *v.* DARLING

Dorman, Dormand: *v.* DEARMAN

Dormer: Geoffrey *Dormour* 1327 SRSf. Fr *dormeur* 'sleeper, sluggard'.

Dornford: *v.* DURNFORD

Dorran: *v.* DORAN

Dorrance, Dorrins: *v.* DURRAND

Dorrett: *v.* DURWARD

Dorset, Dorsett, Dossett: Alexander *de Dorset* 1225 AssSo; Ralph *Dossett* 1602 FrY. From Dorset.

Dorward, Dorwood: *v.* DURWARD

Dosi: Walter, William *Dosy* c1200 Colch (Sf), 1327 SRSx. ME *dosye*, an obsolete by-form of *dizzy* (OE *dysig*) 'foolish, stupid'.

Dossett: *v.* DORSET

Dossetter, Dossettor: Robert *de Dorkecestre, de Dorceste* 1297 MinAcctCo; John *Dossetyr* 1524 SRSf; William *Dorcetor* alias *Dossytor* 1568 FFHu. From Dorchester (Oxon).

Dottrell: William, Roger *Doterel* 1182–1211 BuryS (Sf), 1292 Burton (St); Ralph *Dotrell* 1301 SRY. ME *dotterel, dottrel* 'a species of plover', also 'a silly person' (1440 MED), cf. 'Dottrelle, fowle, *idem quod* Dotarde', c1440 PromptParv. A derogatory diminutive 'little dotard' (cf. ME *doten* 'to be foolish') from the plover, 'a very foolish bird, easily caught'.

Doubell, Double: *v.* DOBEL

Doubleday, Douberday: William, Robert *Dubelday* 1219 AssY. 1223 Pat (Y); William *Dubilday* 14th AD iii (Lei); John *Dubbelday* 1388 AD ii (Nf). Probably 'the servant of *Do(u)bel*' 'the twin'. cf. DOBEL, DAY and Nicholas *Dob(b)eday* 1294, 1305 RamsCt (Hu), 'servant of *Dobbe*' (Robert).

Doubler: William *Dubler, Dublier* 1191, 1192 P (L); Adam *le dubblier* 1207 P (Ha); Ralph *Doublere* 1334 SRK. AFr *dobler, dubler*, OFr *doblier, doublier* 'a kind of dish'. Metonymic for a maker of plates or dishes. cf. Adam *le Dublerwrite* 1249 AssW, Hugh *le dublerwrith* 14th YDeeds I.

Doublet, Doublett: Alexander *Dublet* 1192 P (Berks); John *Doublet* 1297 MinAcctCo. ME *dobbelet*, OFr *doublet* 'doublet' (1326 NED), a maker or seller of doublets.

Douce, Dowse, Duce: *Duze* filia Rannulfi fabri 1219 AssY; *Dulcia* Vidua 1275 SRWo; Hugo *Duce, le Duz, Dulcis* 1200 Oseney (O); Geoffrey *Duz* 1200 P (L); Gilbert *le Dus*, Godfrey *le Douz* 1296 SRSx; Walter *Dous, Douce* 1327 SRWo. ME *douce, dowce*, OFr *dolz, dous*, later *doux* 'sweet, pleasant' (c1325 MED). Often used as a woman's name and occasionally of a man: *Douce* de Moster 1274 RH (Ess), *Douce* of Chedle 1307 AssSt.

Doucet: *v.* DOWSETT

Dougal, Dougall, Dougill: *Dufgal* filius Mocche c1128 Black; *Duuegall* 1208–14 ib.; *Dugall* 1261 ib.; Edward *Dougall* c1552 ib. Gael, OIr *Dubhghall* 'black stranger', a name originally applied by the Irish to Norwegians, now chiefly a Scottish Highland name.

Dougan: *v.* DUGAN

Dougharty, Dougherty, Doherty, Docharty, Docherty, Dockerty, Dogerty, Daugherty: Donnall *O' Dochartaigh* 1119, *Daugherdy* 1630, *Dougherty* 1666 Moore. Originally *O'Dochartaigh* 'descendant of *Dochartach*' 'the stern'. Very common in Ireland but now rare in the Isle of Man.

Doughty, Douty, Dowty, Dufty: William *Douti* 1247 AssBeds; William *Doughty* 1300 FrLeic; John *Dughti* 1314 FrY; Han. *Doubty* 1674 HTSf. OE *dohtig, dyhtig* 'valiant, strong'.

Douglas, Douglass: William *de Duglas* 1175–99 Black (Kelso), *de Duglasse* 1256 AssNb. From Douglas (Lanarkshire), 'the black water' (Gael *dubh, glas*).

Doull: *Doull* Macgilleduf 1502 Black; James *Doull* 1623 ib. For *Domhnall.* *v.* DONALD.

Doust: *v.* DUST

Douthwaite, Dowthwaite, Douthet: John *de Doventhuayt* 1332 SRCu; John *Dowthwayt* 1540 Whitby. From Dowthwaite (Cumb) or Dowthwaite Hall (NRYorks).

Dove: *Duua* Hy 2 DC (L), 1175–86 Holme (Nf); Robertus *filius Duue, Doue* 1166 P (Y), 1195 P (Nt); Ralph, William *Duue* 1197 P (Nf), 1289 Barnwell (C); Nicholas *le Duv* 1322 ParlWrits (D). OE **Dūfe* (f), from OE *dūfe* 'dove', occasionally from ON *dúfa* 'dove', used also as a byname for one gentle as a dove. In Suffolk *Dove* is pronounced *Dow*. In Scotland *Dove* is also a variant of *Dow*.

Dover: Theoloneus *de Doure* 1086 DB; John

de Dover 1223–4 FFK; Walter *Douer* 1332 IpmW. From Dover (Kent).

Dow, Dowe: (i) *Dowe* de Bothemes 1246 AssLa; *Dow* 1332 SRCu; William *Dowe* 1194 P (Nth); Laurence *Dow* 1254 AssSo. A pet-form of *David*. cf. DAW. (ii) Ede *Douw* 1366 Black. Gael *dubh* 'black'. Angus son of John *Dubh* Macallister is called Angus John *Dowisoun* (1516 Black). *v.* also DOVE.

Dowall, Dowell: Symon *Dowele* 1408 Black. For DOUGAL.

Dowcett: *v.* DOWSETT

Dowd: *Doude* (1290 AssCh) is a variant of the more common *Daud* 'David': *Daud* Jonson, William *Daud* 1379 PTY. cf. DAW, DOW. *v.* also O'DOWD.

Dowell: *v.* DOYLE

Dower, Dowers: Richard, John *le Douar*' 1332 SRSx; William *le Doghere* 1333 SRSr. A derivative of OE *dāh* (gen. *dāges*) 'dough'. 'A maker of dough, baker' 1483 (MED).

Dowey, Douie: Walter *de Doai, de Duuai, de Duaco* 1086 DB; Roger *Dowai* Hy 2 DC (L). From Douai (Nord).

Dowle: Thurstan, William *le Doul* 1247–8 FFSr, c1280 SRWo; Michael *Doul* 1334–5 SRK. ME *dul* 'stupid', cf. Dowles Farm (PN K 426) from Alan *le Dul* 1254, *le Doul* 1257. *v.* DULLARD.

Dowler: John *le Doulare*, Roger *le Douler* 1275 SRWo; William *Dowler* 1431 FA (Wo). A derivative of ME *dowle, doule* 'dowel', 'maker of dowels' (headless pins, pegs or bolts).

Dowley: *v.* DOOLEY

Dowling: *v.* DOLLING

Dowman: Adam *Douman, Doweman* 1332 SRCu, 1379 PTY. 'Servant of *Dow*' or David. *v.* DOW.

Down, Downe, Downes, Downs: Thomas *da la Duna* c1170 MELS (Sx); John *atte Doune* 1296 SRSx; William *Bythedoune* 1327 SRSo; John *Dun*, Emylyna *Doun* 1332 SRSx; Reginald *del Downes* 1407 Bardsley (Ch). 'Dweller by the down(s)' (OE *dūn*). We may also be concerned with a personal name: Ricardus *filius Dune* 1220 Cur (L), OE *Dūn*.

Downer: Ralph *le Douner*, Stephen *le Downar* 1327 SRSx. 'Dweller by the down.' cf. DOWN, DOWNMAN.

Downham: Siverth, Humphrey *de Dunham* c975 LibEl, c1115 Bury (Sf); John *de Downham* 1327 SRWo; Hugh *Downam* 1382 IpmNt. From Downham (Cambs, Essex, Lancs, Northumb, Norfolk, Suffolk).

Downing: Richard *Duning* 1197 FF (O); Geoffrey *Dounyng* 1311 ColchCt; Alice *Downyng* 1379 PTY; OE *Dūning* 'son of *Dūn*'. Later confused with DUNNING: John *Dunning* or *Downing* 1432 Bardsley (Nf).

Downman, Dunman: Geoffrey, William *Dunman* 1199 P, 1279 RH (O). 'Dweller by the down.' *v.* DOWNER. Also a late corruption of DOWNHAM: Robert *Downnam* or *Doneman* or *Downeman* 1579 Oxon. cf. DEADMAN.

Downton: *v.* DUNTON

Dowse: *v.* DOUCE

Dowsett, Dowcett, Doucet: John *Dousot* 1315 FFHu; John *Dousete* 1376 LLB H; William *Doucet* 1411 LoPleas. ME *doucet, dowcet, dulcette*, AFr *doucet*, a diminutive of *doux* 'sweet to eye or ear, pleasing, agreeable' (c1425 MED).

Dowsing: Robert *Dusing* 1199 P (Nf); Wido *Dusing* 1202 AssL; William *Dowsyng* 1376 AD ii (Nf). This cannot, as suggested by Bardsley, be an *-in* diminutive of *Douce*. His sole evidence is Nicholas *Doussin* (1669) in London. This is clearly the Fr *Doucin, Doussin*, which could not have become *Dusing* in England by 1199. Nicholas may have been a Huguenot. The modern surname is common in Norfolk and Suffolk and was particularly common in Norfolk in the 13th century. It seems to have arisen especially in the eastern counties where Scandinavian influence was strong and is probably an *-ing* derivative of ODa *Dūsi* which forms the first element of Dowsby (Lincs). '*Dūsi*'s son.' It was later confused with DOWSON: John *Dowsyng* 1584 IckworthPR (Sf), *Dowsen* 1589 ib.

Dowson: (i) Henry *Doucesone* 1320 AssSt; William *Douceson* 1327 SR (Ess); Thomas *Dousone* 1376 AD vi (St). 'Son of *Douce*.' (ii) John *Dowson* 1349 Whitby (Y); Robert *Doweson* 1379 PTY. 'Son of *Dow*.' *v.* DAVID, DAW, DOWMAN.

Dowthwaite: *v.* DOUTHWAITE

Dowtry: *v.* DAWTREY

Dowty: *v.* DOUGHTY

Doxey, Doxsey, Docksey: Richard *de Dokeseye* 1298 AssSt. From Doxey (Staffs).

Doyle, Dowell, Doole: Irish *Ó Dubhghaill* 'descendant of *Dubhghall*' (black stranger, Dane).

Doyley, D'Oyley, Doley, Dolley, Duley, Duly, Dailey, Dailley, Dayley, Olley, Ollie: Robert *Oilgi, Olgi, de Oilgi, de Olgi, de Oilli* 1086 DB; Robert *de Olleyo, de Oili* 1135 Oseney, 1140 Eynsham (O); Henry *de Olli, Doilli* 1156, 1163 ib.; Henry *de Oly, Dolly* 1212 Cur (O); Reginald, Thomas *Duly* ib. (Y), 1297 MinAcctCo (L); John *Dolye* 1272 AssSt; Henry *Dayly* 1279 RH (O); Robert *de Doley* ib.; John *Deyli* 1293 AssSt; Thomas *Duly, Doyllye* 1327, 1332 SRSx; Robert *Oylly, de Oylly* 1378 Oseney (O). There are five Ouillys in Calvados. The DB tenant probably came from Ouilly-le-Basset, or, possibly, from Ouilly-le-Vicomte. The name may also derive from Ouilly-du-Houlley, Ouilly-la-Ribaude or Ouilly-le-Tesson. *v.* OEByn.

Doyne: *v.* DAIN

Drabble: Matthew, Geoffrey *Drabel* 1273, 1279 RH (Wa, C); Robert *Drabel* 1293 AssSt; Ralph *Drabelle* 1302 SRY. OE *Drabba*, recorded as the name of a Peterborough festerman in 963–92 (ASCh), may survive in the surnames of Robert *Drabe* 1161 P (L) and Walter *Drabbe* 1327 SRSf, and the modern surnames may be from a diminutive of this, **Drabbel*. But we may also have early examples of *drab* 'a dirty, untidy woman' and a diminutive of this. *Drab*, not recorded before the 16th century, is of uncertain derivation and has been associated with Gael *drabag*, Irish *drabog* 'slattern' and also with LG *drabbe* 'dirt, mire'.

Dragon: Walter *Dragun* 1166 P (Y); Walter *Dragon* 1221 FrLeic, *le Dragon* 1275 RH (Sx). Occasionally a nickname, but usually metonymic for *dragoner*: Adam *le Dragoner* 1338 LLB F, John *Dragenir* 1343 AD ii (Wt). OFr *dragonier* 'a standard-bearer'. Standards were often emblazoned with a dragon and were carried not only in battle but in pageants and processions. cf. (at Westminster) 'Hym that beryth the Dragon on Easter Evyn' (c1540 NED). Occasionally also from a sign: William Strode called *atte Dragon*, brewer 1374 AD ii (Mx).

Drake, Drakes, Drakers: Leuing *Drache* 1066 Winton (Ha); Robert, David *Drake* 1185, 1190 P (Nt, Wa); Wimund *le Drake* 1205 ChR (Do); Geoffrey *le Drak'* 1225 AssSo. OE *draca* 'dragon', like OFr *dragon*, was used in ME of a battle-standard as well as of a serpent or a water-monster. The surname is clearly sometimes a nickname and is also metonymic for *Draker* 'standard-bearer': Godman *the Drakere* 1260 AssC. cf. also the ODa nickname *Draki* 'dragon' which may sometimes occur in the Scandinavian counties. The surname may also be from ME *drake* 'male of the duck' (c1300 MED).

Drane, Dron: Roger *Drane* 1276 RH (Y); Adam *le Dron* 1275 SRWo; Walter *le Dran* 1285 *Ass* (Ess). OE *drān* 'drone', a nickname, 'the lazy'.

Drape: OFr *drap* 'cloth'. For DRAPER.

Draper, Drapier, Drapper: Hugo *drapier*, Walter *draper* 1148 Winton (Ha); Robert *(le) Drapier* 1181–2 P (L). OFr *drapier*, AFr *draper* 'maker or seller of woollen cloth, draper' (c1376 MED).

Drawater, Drawwater: Richard *Drawater* 1279 RH (Hu). 'A drawer of water.'

Drawer: Sayhere *Draghere* 1327 *SR* (Ess); John *Drahere* 1327 SRSf; John *le Drawere* 1332 SRLo. A derivative of OE *dragan* 'to draw'. 'One who draws' in various senses. cf. Richard *le Pakke-drawere* 1332 SRLo, a drawer or carrier of packs of wool. He was employed at the woolwharf in Tower Ward; David *Tothedrawer* 1422 LoPleas, Elias *Wyndrawer* 1373 ib., Roger le *wirdragher* 1313 FrY, Alan de Wifestow, *mukdragher* 1340 FrY, a leader of dung, or, perhaps, a scavenger.

Dreng, Dring: *Dreng* de Calualea 1161 P (Nb); Roger, William *Dreng* 1155 FeuDu, 1201 P (L); Roger de Brunham *le dreng* Hy 3 Seals (L); Robert *Dring* 1379 PTY. Occasionally we may have the ON personal name *Drengr*, found in DB, but usually the surname is OE *dreng*, from ON *drengr* 'young man', used of a free tenant, especially in ancient Northumbria, holding by a tenure partly military, partly servile.

Dresser: Robert *le Dressour* 1324 LaCt; Adam *Dressur* 1332 MEOT (Y). A derivative of ME *dressen*, OFr *dresser* 'to arrange' in various special and technical senses. Perhaps 'a dresser of textile fabrics', a finisher who gives them a nap, smooth surface. cf. 'Shermen, dressers, carders and spynners' (1520 NED).

Dreux: *v.* DRUCE

Drew, Drewe, Dru: (i) *Drogo* 1086 DB; Radulfus *filius Drogonis* 1159 P (L); *Driu* filius Radulfi Hy 2 DC (R); Radulfus *filius Dru* 1185 Templars (L); Anschet' *driue* 1130 P (Caermarthen); Ralph *Dreu* 1188 BuryS (Sf); William *Dryw* 1275 SRWo; John *Drew* 1327 SRC. OG *Drogo*, the name of a son of Charlemagne, probably of Frankish origin (OSax *(gi)drog* 'ghost, phantom'), became OFr *Dreus, Drues* (nom.) and *Dru, Driu, Dreu* (acc.). *Drew* was also used as a pet-name of *Andrew* which was confused with the French *Drew*. In 1400 Drew Barentyn appealed to the Council to correct his christian name to *Drew* in the list of freemen of the City where it had been entered as *Andrew* (Riley). (ii) Henry *le Dru* 1255 RH (W); John *le Drew* 1279 RH (O); Henry *le Druie*, William *Dru* 1275 SRWo. OFr *dru* 'sturdy', later 'lover' and in this sense common as a surname.

Drewell: William *Drewel* 1176 P (Beds); Baldwin *Druell'* 1196 Cur (Bk); William *Druel* (v.l. *Druett*) 1221 Cur (Beds). A diminutive of OFr *Dru, Drewel* interchanging with *Drewet*. *v.* DREW, DREWETT.

Drewery, Drewry, Druery, Drury: Alexander *Druri* 1200 Cur (Sf); Robert *Druerie* 1204 P (La). OFr *druirie, druerie* 'love, friendship', 'love-token' (c1225 MED), 'sweetheart' (a1393 ib.).

Drewes: *v.* DRUCE

Drewett, Dreweatt, Drewitt, Drouet, Druett, Druitt: *Druet* 1206 Cur (Sf); Walter *Druet* 1185 Templars (O); William *Drauet* 1198 P (K); Walter *Drywet* 1309 AD v (Sx). A diminutive of OFr *Dru*. *Druettus* Malerbe 1273 RH (Nth) is elsewhere called *Drogo*. In Mabila *Druet* c1248 Bec (Mx), we may have a diminutive of *dru*, 'little sweetheart'. *v.* DREW.

Dreyer: *v.* DRYER

Driffield, Driffill: Stephen, William *de Driffeld* 1192–1218 YCh, 1271–7 Str; John *Dryffeld* 1366 AssLo. From Driffield (Glos, ERYorks).

Dring: *v.* DRENG

Dringer: Richard *Drenger* 1256 AssSo; Richard *le Drynkere* 1296 SRSx; Walter *le Drynkar* 1327 SRWo. OE *drincere* 'drinker'. Used of a tippler a1225 (MED).

Drinkale, Drinkald, Drinkall, Drinkhall: *Drinc hala* 1200 Caen (Ess); Thomas *Drinkhale* 1281 LLB B; Henry *Drinkale* 1301 SRY; John *Drynkall* 1509 GildY; William *Drynkell* 1559 FrY; Nicholas *Drinkeld* 1677 LaWills. A nickname from the customary courteous reply to a pledge in drinking, *drinc hail* 'drink good health or good luck'. *hala* probably points to OE *hæl*, an anglicizing of ON *heill* 'good luck'. As ale was the usual drink, there was no point in a nickname *drink-ale*. *v.* DRINKWATER.

Drinkwater: John *Drinkewater* 1274 RH (Sa); Thomas *Dreinkewater, Drynkewater* 1300, 1310 LLB B. 'Ale for an Englysshe man is a naturall drynke.' It was drunk at all times, taking the place not only of tea, coffee, etc., but also of water. A 13th-century writer describing the extreme poverty of the Franciscans when they first settled in London (1224) writes: 'I have seen the brothers drink ale so sour that some would have preferred to drink water' (MedInd 286). The surname was perhaps applied to a man so poor that he could not afford to drink ale even when it was four gallons a penny. It was also used ironically of a tavern-keeper and, perhaps, of a tippler: Margery *Drynke-water*, wife of Philip le Taverner (1324 LLB E), Thomas *Drinkewater*, of Drinkewaterestaverne (1328 Husting). cf. Adam *Drinckmilke* 1674 HTSf.

Drinkwell: William *Drinkwell* 1309 SRBeds. A nickname. cf. Henry *Drink al up* 1282 FFEss, Fulredus, William *Drinkepin* 1206 ChR, 1207 Rams 'one who drinks a peg' (pegs were fixed on the inside of large drinking vessels), William *Drinkepani* 1224–46 Bart, 'drink-penny' (cf. BEVERIDGE).

Driscoll: Irish *Ó hEidersceoil* 'descendant of *Eidirsceól*' (interpreter).

Driver, Drivers: Alice *le Driveres* 1279 RH (C); Gilbert *le Drivere* 1283 SRSf. A derivative of *drive*, 'driver' (14.. NED).

Dron: *v.* DRANE

Droop: Adam *Drope* 1177 P (Nf); Edric *Drup* 1197 P (Gl); Robert *Drop* 1202 AssL. ME *drup* 'dejected, sad, gloomy', a rare adjective. *v.* MED. The surname may also be local: William *atte Thrope* lived at Drupe Fm in 1330 (*Droope* 1679 PN D 587).

Drouet: *v.* DREWETT

Drover: Hugh *Drouere* 1294 MEOT (Herts); Henry *le Drovere* 1327 SRSt. A derivative of OE *dráf* 'drove, herd', a drover.

Druce, Drewes: (i) Herman *de Dreuues* 1086 DB (W); Hugo *le Droeis* 1225 Pat (W); Robert *de Dreus* 1230 P (O); William *Drueys, Drois, le Droys, le Droes* 1242 Fees (W). From Dreux (Eure-et-Loir); alternating with the toponymic. (ii) Elias *de Ruwes, de Riueus, Driues, de Ripariis, Droeys* 1235, 1242 Fees (Bk). From some French place Rieux 'streams'.

Druery: *v.* DREWERY

Druett, Druitt: *v.* DREWETT

Drummond: (i) Agge *Dromund* 1221 ElyA (C); John *Drommund* 1327 SRC. ON *Drómundr*. (ii) Gilbert *de Drummyn* c1199 Black; Malcolm *de Drummond* or *Drumman* 1270–90 ib. From the barony of Drummond, probably identical with the parish of Drymen (Stirling).

Drury: *v.* DREWERY

Dryer, Dreyer: Roger *le Dreyere* 1318 Oseney (O). A derivative of OE *drȳgean* 'to dry', perhaps a drier of cloth. 'The cloth, having been fulled, had to be stretched on tenters to dry' (MedInd 224). The feminine form, used also of men, seems to have been more frequent: Alice *le Dreyster'* 1292 MESO (La), Adam *Dreyster* 1301 SRY.

Drysdale: Gawine *Dryfesdale* 1499 Black; Thomas *Dryisdaill* 1619 ib. From Dryfesdale (Annandale), pronounced *Drysdale*.

Dubber: Godwin *Ladubur* 1168 P (Lo); Salamon *Leadubur* 1204 P (Lo); William *le Dubbere* 1210 FrLeic; Paganus *le Dubbour* 1226 NED. Bardsley

notes the Company of Dubbers of York and suggests that they embellished dresses with gold lace, etc. Halliwell suggests they were trimmers or binders of books. OFr *adubeour, adubur* 'repairer', renovator of old clothes, perhaps also used of a polisher of arms or harness, ME *dubber* 'fripperer'.

Ducat: Wolveva, Alice, William *Dukat* 1314 FFSf. OFr *ducat*, It *ducato* 'a gold coin', late Lat *ducatus* 'duchy', so called because, when first coined c1140 in the Duchy of Apulia, they bore the legend: 'sit tibi, Christe, datus, quem tu regis, iste *ducatus*'. *Ducat* is a 'restored form', spelled *duket* by Chaucer and *ducket* by Shakespeare. The surname has been confused with DUCKET.

Duce: *v.* DOUCE

Duck, Duckes, Doak, Doke, Dooks: Robert *Ducke* 1260 AssCh; Hugo *Doke* 1279 RH (C); Richard *Duck, Dooke, Doke* 1510 Oxon. ME *duk(ke), duck, doke, dook* 'duck'. *v.* DUCKET.

Duckels: John *Dukel*, Richard *le Dukel* 1296 SRSx. A diminutive of *duk* 'duck'. cf. John *Duklyng* 1483 LLB L.

Ducker, Duker: Philip *Duker* 1365 FrY. ME *dokare, douker* 'a bather' or 'a diving bird'. cf. DIVER.

Duckers: *v.* DUCKHOUSE

Ducket, Duckett, Duckit, Duckitt: Rannulf *Duchet* 1130 P (Ha); Herbert *Duket* 1176 P (Herts). The surname is common, usually as *Duket*, and the persistent *-et* dissociates it from DUCAT. *Duchet* 1148 Winton is probably identical with Ralph *Duchet* (ib.) but we seem to have a clear example of a personal name in *Duchet* 1185 Templars (K), *Duket* 1198 P (K). This is probably a diminutive of OE **Ducc(a)* found in Duxford (Cambs), and Duckington (Ches), with a diminutive **Duccel* in Ducklington (Oxon) and a compound **Ducemann* in Duckmanton (Derby). Willelmus *filius Duket* (1301 SRY) and *Doket Flasby* (1379 PTY) are probably diminutives of *Marmaduke*, a purely northern name, from a pet form, *Duke* Shillito 1634 Bardsley, with a shortened vowel in *Ducke* Duy 1246 AssLa. This is the source of the Yorkshire surname Agnes *Duket* (1301 SRY), John *Doket* (1379 PTY). But in general the surname is either an unrecorded diminutive of *duck* or OFr *ducquet*, a diminutive of *duc* 'leader, guide', one of the names of the owl, so called because thought to serve as guide to certain birds (Littré). *v.* DOCKETT.

Duckhouse, Duckers: Richard *Duckhouse* 1553 WhC (La), a name for one in charge of the ducks (1699 NED).

Duddell, Duddle: *v.* DODELL

Duddin: *Dodin* 1153–65 Black; *Dudyn* de Broughtune c1190 ib.; Alexander *Dudyn* 1296 ib. OFr *Dodin*, a diminutive of *Dode* (OG *Dodo*).

Dudding: Andrew *Doddyng* 1296 SRSx; Thomas *Duddyng* 1514 FrY. OE *Dudding* 'son of *Dudd(a)*'. cf. DOD.

Duddy: Robert, Reginald *Dudehay* 1332 SRSx. From some lost place in Sussex, 'Dudda's enclosure'.

Dudgeon: v. DODGEN

Dudley: Gladewin *de Duddeleia* 1176 P (St); Herbert *de Dudeleg'* 1225 Cur (St. Wo); William *Dudely* 1379 PTY. From Dudley (Worcs).

Dudman: v. DODMAN

Dudson: v. DODGSON

Duesbury: v. DEWSBURY

Duff: Duncan *Duff* c1275 Black. In Scotland 'The family name Duff is merely the adjective *dubh* "black" used epithetically' (Macbain). v. also DOVE. In Ireland, also for *Ó Duibh* and *Mac Giolla Dhuibh* 'son of the black youth', the latter surviving also as *MacIlduff, Gilduff, Kilduff.*

Duffes: v. DUFFUS

Duffet, Duffett, Duffitt: Richard *Dovefote* 1301 SRY; William *Dowfhed* 1355 FrY. A nickname, either 'dove-foot' or 'dove-head'.

Duffey, Duffie, Duffy: v. MCFEE, O'DUFFY

Duffield, Duffell, Duffill: Roger *de Duffeld'* 1190 P (Y); Geoffrey *de Duffeld* 1276 LLB A; William *Duffeld'* 1383 AssL. From Duffield (Derby, ERYorks).

Duffin: v. DOLPHIN

Duffus, Duffes: Robert *del Dufhus* 1275 RH (Sf). 'Keeper of the dovehouse.' In Scotland, from Duffus (Moray): Arkembaldus *de Duffus* 1222 Black; Agnes *Duffers* 1586 ib.; James *Duffes* 1633 ib.

Dufty: v. DOUGHTY

Dugan, Dougan: John *Dugan* 1413 Black; Adam *Dougane* 1665 ib. Irish *Ó Dubhagáin* 'descendant of *Dubhagán*', a diminutive of *dubh* 'black'.

Dugard: Richard *Deugard* 1322 AD vi (D); William *Dugard* 1327 *SR* (Ess). A phrase-name, Fr *Dieu (te) garde* 'God guard (you)'. cf. Fr *Dieutegard.*

Duggan, Duggon: *Ó Dubhagain* 1372, *Dogan* 1540, *Duggan* 1723 Moore. A Manx name for *O'Dubhagáin.* v. DUGAN.

Duguid: John *Dogude* 1379 Black; Robert *Dugoude* 1536 ib.; Francis *Duiguid* 1675 ib. A nickname 'do good'. Black's other examples, *Doget, Dowcat,* etc., cannot belong here.

Duke, Dukes: Herbert *le Duc* 1185 Templars (Sa); Adam *Duke* 1198 P (Bk); Henry *Dukes* 1214 Cur (Wa); Osbert *le Duk* 1230 P (D). ME *duc, duk(e), douk, doke,* OFr *duc* 'leader of an army, captain', often, no doubt, a nickname. ME forms cannot always be distinguished from those of DUCK. In Yorkshire, this may be a pet-form of Marmaduke. v. DUCKET, DUXON.

Duker: v. DUCKER

Dulcken: John *Dolekyn, Dulekyn* 1301 ParlR (Ess), 1311–12 ColchCt. ME *Dul-kin,* a diminutive of OE **Dylla.* v. DIL.

Duley, Duly: John *Deu Le* (*del Le*) 1230 P (La); John *Dulay* 1279 RH (Hu); *John du Lay* 1327 SRSf. 'Dweller by the clearing', Fr *del, du* and OE *lēah.* cf. LEA. v. also DOYLEY.

Dullard: Richard *Dullard, Dollard* 1231 Cl, 1329 ColchCt. ME *dull* plus *-ard* 'a dull or stupid person' (c1440 MED).

Dulson: v. DIL

Dumbell, Dumbill, Dumble: (i) Thomas *Dumbel* 1273 RH (Wa); William *Dumbulle* 1367 LLB G. A diminutive of *dumb.* cf. 'A Dumel, *stupidus* . . . A Dummel, *mutus*' 1570 NED, *dummil,* a slow jade (Halliwell) and Hants dialectal *dummell* 'slow to comprehend', *dumble* 'stupid'. *Dumbulle* may be for *dunn bull.* cf. DUNCALF. (ii) The Liverpool *Dumbell, Dumbill* are probably Cheshire corruptions of *Dumville:* James *Domvile* 1521, James *Dowmbill* 1522, Elizabeth *Dombell* 1568, Hannah *Dumbell* 1660 (Bardsley).

Dumjohn: v. DUNJOHN

Dummer, Dummere, Dumper: Henry *de Dumera, de Dommere* 1115 Winton (Ha). From Dummer (Hants).

Dummett, Dommett: Gerald *de Domnomedardo* c1150 Seals (Nth); Aliz *de Dunmart, de Dummart* 1200–1 P (Wa). From Dumart-en-Ponthieu (Somme).

Dumsday: v. DOMESDAY

Dumville, Dunville, Domvile, Domville, Dunfield: Hugh *de Donvil* 1274 RH (Sa). From Donville (Calvados). v. also DUMBELL.

Dunbabin, Dunbobbin, Dunbavin, Dunbavand, Dunbebin, Dunbevand, Donbavand: All these surnames are found in Liverpool and Manchester. Bardsley notes Ralph and Anthony *Dunbabin* of Warrington (1597–8) where he found *Dunbobbin* and *Dunbobin* also surviving. *Dunbabin* is a variant of *Dunbobbin, Dunrobin,* with unrounding of the vowel. 'Dun (dark) Bobbin or Babbin.' cf. *Bob* and *Rab* for *Robert, Broun Robin* 1309 Wak (Y), *Robert* called *Brounerobyn* 1311 ColchCt and v. HORRABIN and BROWNJOHN. The other surnames are colloquial pronunciations of an uncommon, unintelligible name.

Duncalf, Duncalfe, Duncuff: Adam *Duncalf* 1354 Putnam (Ch); John *Doncalfe* 1449 DbCh. 'The dun calf', a nickname. cf. Robert *Dunnebrid* 1183 P (Y), Thomas *Dunfugell* 1291 AssCh 'dun bird'.

Duncan, Dunkin, Donkin: *Donecan* 1086 DB (So); *Dunecan'* 1130 P (W), c1135 Black, 1181 P (Y); *Donchadus* c1150 Black; Hugh *Dunkan, Dunken* 1275–6 RH (L); Ralf *Donekan* 1280 AssSo; John *Dunkan* 1327 SRSt, 1367 Black (Berwick); Richard *Donykyn* 1327 SRSo; William *Donekyn* 1332 SRSx; Richard *Donkin* 1674 HTSf. *Dunecan,* from OIr, OGael *Donnchad* 'brown warrior'. This common Scottish name is found in Yorkshire and Cumberland in the 12th century. Here it was probably introduced from Ireland as in Somerset where the name occurs in 1086 and had become a surname in the 13th century. In 1327 (SRSo) there are several men named *le Ireys* and one *Irlonde.*

Duncanson, Dunkinson: Nicholas *Donecandonesoune* 1296 CalSc (Dunbar); John *Dunkanson* 1367 ib. (Berwick); John *Dunkysoun* 1603 Black. 'Son of *Duncan.*'

Dunce, Duns, Dunse: William *le Duns* 1327 SRSx; William *Douns,* Cristina *le Douns* 1332 SRSx. *Dunce* is not recorded in NED before 1527. It is derived from the name of John *Duns* Scotus, the scholastic theologian, and in the 16th century was used of a disciple or follower of his, a school-man, a subtle, sophistical reasoner, and, when his system was attacked and ridiculed by the humanists and reformers, of a 'blockhead incapable of learn-ing or scholarship', 'a dull pedant', 'a dullard'. The surname, found so soon after the death of the 'Subtle Doctor' in 1308, cannot have any dero-gatory meaning. It must be equivalent to *Duns man* or schoolman, scholar. The Scottish *Duns(e)* is from Duns (Berwick): Hugh *de Duns* c1150 Black. It may be that John *Duns* Scotus came from here.

Duncuff: *v.* DUNCALF

Dunfield: *v.* DUMVILLE

Dungate, Dongate: Geoffrey *de Doungate* 1275 SRWo; Richard *ate Dungate* 1296 SRSx. 'Dweller by the gap in the hill', OE *dūn, geat.*

Dunger: Roger *Dunger* 1221 AssWo; William *Donger* 1327 MEOT (L). A derivative of ME *dun-gen* 'to dung', one who manures the ground.

Dungworth: John *de Dungeworth* 1440 ShefA. From Dungworth in Bradfield (Sheffield).

Dunham: Richard, William *de Dunham* 1190 P (Nf), 1221 AssWa; William *Dunham* 1332 SRSx. From Dunham (Ches, Norfolk, Notts), or Dun-holme (Lincs).

Dunicliffe: *v.* TUNNICLIFF

Dunjohn, Dumjohn: Laurence *de (del) Duniun, de Dungun* 1204, 1208 P (Ha, K); Ralph *Dungun* 1255 RH (Bk). From employment at 'the chief tower of a castle' (OFr *donjon*), probably 'jailer'. cf. Dungeon Fm, pronounced 'Don Johns', from Peter *Dungun* (1272 PN Ess 436).

Dunkin: *v.* DUNCAN

Dunkinson: *v.* DUNCANSON

Dunman: *v.* DOWNMAN

Dunn, Dunne, Don, Donn, Donne: William *Dun* 1180 P (Gl); John *le Dunn* 1198 FF (Herts); Jobin *Don* 1271 ForSt; Adam *le Don, le Dun* 1275 SRWo, 1308 AssSt. OE *dunn* 'dull brown', 'dark, swarthy'.

Dunnaby: Semon *Donyby* 1381 PTY. *Dūne i bý* (the man who lived) 'down in the village'. A partly anglicized form (OE *dūne* 'down') of a Scandina-vian phrase. cf. WESTOBY.

Dunnage: Walter *de Dunewic* 1182–1200 BuryS (Sf); Jasper *Dunwich*, Thomas *Dunage* 1674 HTSf. From Dunwich (Suffolk).

Dunnet, Dunnett: Walter *Dunheued, de Dune-heued* 1201, 1208 P (So); John *de Dunheued* 1246 Seals (W); Jeffery *Dunnett*, Robert *Dunnit* 1674 HTSf. From Downhead (Som) or Donhead (Wilts).

Dunnicliff(e): *v.* TUNNICLIFF

Dunning: (i) *Dunning, Dunninc, Donninc* 1066 DB; *Dunning* 1086 (Ch, Gl); Gilbertus *filius Dunning* 1166 P (C); *Dunnigus (Dunningus)* 1205 P (Gl); Æluuard *Dunning* 1086 DB (Sa); Roger, Nicholas *Dunning* 1166 P (C), 1201 P (So); Symon *Donnyng* 1332 SRSx. OE *Dunning* 'son of *Dunn*' or 'the dark, swarthy one'. (ii) Gillemichel *de Dunin* c1208 Black; John *Donnung* 1321 ib. From Dunning in Lower Strathearn (Perthshire).

Dunrobin: *v.* DUNBABIN

Duns(e): *v.* DUNCE

Dunstall: *v.* TUNSTALL

Dunstan, Dunston, Dunstone: (i) *Dun(e)stan, Donestan* 1086 DB; *Dunstan de Berstede* 1275 RH (K); William *Dunestan* 1212 Cur (Db); Thomas, Margaret *Dunstan* 1275 RH (K), 1327 SRSf. OE *Dūnstān* 'hill-stone'. (ii) Alexander *de Duneston'* 1190 P (L); Hugo *de Dunestun'* 1202 FF (Nf); Reyner *de Dunstan* 1242 Fees (Nb). From Dunstan (Northumb), Dunston (Derby, Lincs, Norfolk), or Dunstone (Devon).

Dunsterville: Adeliz *de Dunstanuilla* 1130 P (Lei); Walter *de Dunstervill'* 1235 Fees (Co). From Dénestanville (Seine-Inférieure).

Dunton, Downton: Richard *de la Duntun'* 1275 SRWo; Ralph *de Dunton* 1296 SRSx. From one of the Duntons or 'dweller at the homestead on the hill' (OE *dūn, tūn*).

Dunville: *v.* DUMVILLE

Duplock: *v.* DIPLOCK

Duran, Durand, Durant: *v.* DURRAND

Durden, Durdin: William, Roger *Duredent* 1148–54 Bec (Sx), 1176 P (St); William *Durdent* 1272 FFSt; Nicholas *Durdon* 1428 FA (W). OFr *dur, dent* 'hard-tooth'.

Durham, Durram: Osbert *de Dunelm'* 1163 P; William *de Durham* 1236–7 FFEss; Adam *de Duram* 1327 SRSx; Lawrence *Durham* 1400 AssLo. From Durham.

Durk: *v.* DARK

Durling: *v.* DARLING

Durman: *v.* DEARMAN

Durnford, Dornford: Roger *de Derneford'* 1190 P (W); William *de Durneford* 1255 RH (W). From Durnford (Wilts). cf. DANFORD.

Durrad: *v.* DURWARD

Durrand, Durrant, Durran, Durrans, Durrance, Duran, Durand, Durant, Doran, Dorant, Dorran, Dorrance, Dorrins: *Durandus* 1066 Winton (Ha); Robertus *filius Durand* 1115 ib.; *Durant stabula-rius* Hy 2 DC (L); *Doraunt de Moreby* 1312 FrY; Walter *Durand'* 1196 MemR (We); Robert *Duraund* 1221 AssWa; John *Durant* 1222 Cur (Sr); Robert *Duran* 1275 SRWo; William *Doraunt* 1285 FrY; Gabriel *Durance* 1676 Bardsley. OFr *Durant*, perhaps 'obstinate'.

Durtnall, Durtnal, Durtnell, Dutnall, Dartnall, Dartnell, Darknell: Robert *Darkynhole*, William *Durkynghole* 1435, 1453 Streatfeild MSS; William *Darknold* 1505 KentW; William *Derkynhole* 1512 EdenbridgePR; Robert *Darkenhole* 1539 LP (Lo); Robert *Darknoll* 1540 LP (K); John *Dartnoll* 1551, *Durtenall* 1554, Alice *Darknall* 1555, John *Dyrknall* 1556 StaplehurstPR (K); Robert *Darknall, Darken-all, Darkenoll* 1553 Pat (K). A west Kent and Sussex name, found as *de Durkinghol'* in 1240, from a lost place in Penshurst, now perhaps Doubleton's Farm, *v.* PN K 89–90.

Durward, Dorward, Dorwood, Darwood, Durrad, Dorrett: Reiner *Dureward'* 1208 Cur (Nf); William *Doreward* 1230 P (Ha); Richard *le Doreward* 1255 FFEss; Thomas *Durart* 1620 Black; George *Durrat* 1724 ib.; John *Dorrat* 1753 ib. OE *duru-*

weard 'door-keeper, porter'. In Scotland the office of door-ward to the king, *Hostiarius regis*, was hereditary. Alan *Durward* (*Ostiarius, le Usher*), justiciar of Scotland (d. 1268), was the son of Thomas *Ostiarius*. *Dorward*, still common around Arbroath, is probably from the office of door-ward of the Abbey. Others, both in Scotland and England, derive from a less exalted office.

Dust, Doust: Ulf *Dust* c1030 OEByn; Walter *Dust* 1203 P (Y); Robert *le Doust* 1316 FFK. OE *dūst* 'dust', with reference to a dust-coloured complexion or hair, or to a person of little worth, or to a workman (cf. Dusty Miller). cf. Thomas *Dustiberd* 1229 Pat (So), William *Dustifot*' 1221 AssWo, a term used later (a1400) of a wayfarer, especially a travelling pedlar. We may also have an unexplained topographical term: Richard *del Doustes* 1332 SRLa.

Dusting: *v.* THURSTAN

Dutch: John *Duch(e)* 1360 ColchCt, 1427 FFEss. 'Dutch', a name given to immigrant Dutch weavers.

Dutchman: Henry, John *Duch(e)man* 1354 FrY, 1366 ColchCt. *v.* DUTCH. Also applied in the 15th century to Flemish brick-makers (Building 142).

Dutnall: *v.* DURTNALL

Duxon, Duxson: (i) Sawi *Duchessune* 1168 P (W). 'Son of Ducc', OE *Ducc. v.* DUCKET. (ii) John *Dokeson* 1379 PTY; Thomas *Duckesson* 1586 Bardsley. 'Son of *Duke*' or Marmaduke.

Dwelley, Dwelly: Robert *Dweyle* 1255 RH (W); Richard *Dwelie* 1275 RH (W); Robert *Dwole*, Walter *Dwelie* 1327 SRSo; John *le Dwole*, Richard *le Dwele*, Alice *Duolie* 1332 SRSr. OE **dweollīc* 'foolish, erring, heretical', a variant of *dwollīc*, recorded in the same sense, from *dwelian, dweolian, dwolian* 'to err'. cf. *dweola* 'error, heresy', *dwolung* 'dotage'. This surname explains Dwelly Fm in Lingfield (Surrey) where all the early forms are from surnames. In PN Sr 328 the name has

wrongly been taken as a compound of *lēah*. The name is manorial, 'Dwelly's Fm'.

Dyason, Dyerson: John *Dyosone* 1332 SRSt; William *Dyotson* 1381 PTY; Richard *Dyatson* 1520 FrY. 'Son of *Dyott*.'

Dybald, Dyball, Dybell, Dyble: *v.* DIBBLE

Dyce: *v.* DICE

Dye: *Dye* 1301 SRY, 1316 Wak (Y); Walter *Dye*. 1316 Wak (Y). A pet-form of *Dionisia*.

Dyer, Dyers: Henry *le Deghar* 1260 MESO (So); Robert *le Deyare* 1275 SRWo; Alexander *Dyghere* 1296 SRSx; Henry *le Dyer* 1327 SRDb. OE *dēagere* 'dyer'.

Dyerson: *v.* DYASON

Dyett, Dyott: *Diota* 1296 Wak (Y); *Dyota* 1319 SRLo; *Dyot* 1332 SRCu; William *Dyot* 1348 DbAS 36; Robert *Diotte* 1396 AD v (Y). A diminutive of *Dye*, a pet-form of *Dionisia*.

Dyke(s): *v.* DITCH

Dykins: *v.* DICKEN

Dyllon: *v.* DILLON

Dyment, Dymond: *v.* DIAMANT

Dymick, Dymock, Dymoke: *v.* DIMMOCK

Dymott: Adam *Dyemogh* 1332 SRLa. Probably 'relative of *Dye*', a pet-form of *Dyonisia. v.* DYE and cf. HICKMOTT.

Dyne: *v.* DAIN

Dyson: Richard *Dysun* 1275 RH (Lo); Ralph *Dyson* 1296 SRSx; John *Dysone, Dyesson* 1327 SRWo, 1387 FrY. 'Son of *Dye*.' John *son of Dionysia* de Langside is also called John *Dyson* de Langside 1369 YAJ v, 76. cf. also Robert *Dyotson* 1379 PTY.

Dyster: Henry *le Deystere* 1280 MESO (Wo); Eua *Dygestre* 1296 SRSx; William *le Deyghester* 1325 AssSt; Robert *le Deyster, le Dyster* 1332 SRWa; Thomas *Diestere* 1355 AD iii (O). OE **deaʒestre, *deʒ(e)stre* 'dyer' (f), but used also of men. cf. DEXTER, DYER.

Dyter: *v.* DITER

E

Eacersall: *v.* ECCLESHALL

Ead, Eade, Eades, Eads, Ede, Edes: *Eda* Hy 2 DC (L), 1194 P (Wo); Roger, William *Ede* 1275 SRWo, RH (Nf); Gilbert *Eadis* 1279 RH (O). *Eda*, always feminine, is rather a pet-form of *Edith* (OE *Ēadgӯð*) than a survival of OE *Ēda*.

Eaden, Eadon, Eden, Edens, Edon: (i) Tomas *filius Edon'* 1203 P (O); Edon *le Poleter* 1270 FFSf; Roger *Edun* 1327 SRC; Stephen *Edoun* 1327 SRSf. OE *Ēadhūn*. (ii) Nicholas *de Edune* 1178 P (Nb); William *de Eden* 1256 AssNb. From Castle Eden or Eden Burn (Durham).

Eadington, Eadmeades: *v.* EDDINGTON, EDMEAD

Eagar, Eager, Eagers, Egar, Egarr, Eger: *v.* EDGAR

Eagland: *v.* EGLIN

Eagle, Eagles, Eagell: (i) Ralph *Egle* 1230 P (Y); Robert *le Egle* 1297 Coram. A nickname from the bird. (ii) Gilbertus *de Aquila* 1196 P (Y); Richer *del Egle* 1210 Cur (Nth). From Laigle (Orne).

Eaglen, Eagling: *v.* EGLIN

Eakin: *v.* EDKINS

Ealey: *v.* ELY

Eames, Heams, Hemes: Andrew *le Em* 1274 RH (Nf); John *Eame* 1280 Bart (Lo); Hugo *Eem* 1281 Rams (Hu); Robert *Heme* 1524 SRSf; William *Eames* 1540 Whitby (Y). OE *ēam*, ME *eme* 'uncle'. Ralph *Heam* (c1200 ELPN) is identical with Radulfus *auunculus*.

Earl, Earle, Harle, Hearl, Hearle, Hurl, Hurle, Hurles, Hurll: Lefuin *Eorl* c1095 Bury (Sf); Ernald, William *Hurl* 1182 P (Do), 1221 AssWa; Hervicus *Herl* 1210 Cur (C); William *Erl* 1230 P (Ha); Hugh *le Erl* 1255 FFSf; Emma *le Heorl*, Thomas *le Erl*, Margeria *la Horl* 1275 SRWo. OE *eorl* 'earl'. Leofric *Eorl* and Harold *Eorl* (1038–44 OEByn) bore titles of rank; the surnames above are nicknames or pageant-names.

Earley, Early, Erleigh, Erley, Erly: John *de Erlea* 1162 P (So); William *de Erlega* 1190 P (Sx); John *de Erley* 1230 P (Berks). From Earley (Berks), Earnley (Sussex), Arley (Ches, Lancs, Warwicks, Worcs), all 'eagle-wood'. Occasionally a nickname: Geoffrey *le Urrly* 1275 RH (Nf). OE *eorlīc* 'manly'.

Earnshaw: Richard *de Erneschaghe* 1316 Wak (Y). 'Dweller by the eagle-wood', OE *earn*, *sceaga*.

Earwaker, Earwicker, Erricker: *Euerwacer de Gepeswic* 1130 P (Sf); Edmundus *Erwak'* 1230 P (Do); Richard *Herewaker* 1247 AssBeds; Hamo, John *Euerwaker* 1327 SRSf. OE *Eoforwacer* 'boar-watchman', recorded in 1061. *Earwicker* is pronounced *Erricker*.

Easdale: *v.* ESDAILE

Easman: *v.* HEASEMAN

Eason, Easom, Easun, Easson, Esson: *Aythe filius* Thome c1360 Black; *Aye* Jonson 1395 ib.; John *Ayson'* 1392 ib.; John *Asson* or *Easson* 1681 ib. 'Son of Adam', Gael *Adamh*. Common in Angus.

East, Eastes, Este: Ralph *del Est* 1196–1237 Colch (Ess); Walter *Est* c1220 Gilb (L); Osbert *Upest* c1240 Fees (Beds). 'Man from the east' or 'dweller to the east' of the village.

Eastabrook: *v.* EASTBROOK

Eastaff: cf. Simon *de Essetoft* 1331 FrY. From Eastoft (WRYorks).

Eastall, Eastell, Estall, Estell: Walter *de Easthalle, de Estalle* 1279 RH (O); Jonathan *Eastall* 1674 HTSf. 'Dweller at the East Hall.'

Eastaugh, Easto, Eastoe, Estaugh: John *de Esthawe*, Geoffrey *de Esthagh* 1327 SRSf. 'Dweller at the east enclosure', OE *ēast*, *haga*.

Eastbrook, Eastabrook, Easterbrook, Esterbrook: William *Bestebroke* 1296 SRSx; Alan *bi Estebrouk*, Matilda *Estbrok* 1327 SRSx. OE *be ēastan brōce* '(one who lives) to the east of the brook'. Or from residence at a placed called Eastbrook. William *de Estbrok* (1254 Ass) lived at Eastbrook Fm in Dagenham (Essex).

Eastcott, Eastcourt, Escot, Escott, Estcourt: Gundwinus *de Estcota* 1190 P (Beds). From Eastcott (Middlesex, Wilts), Eastcotts (Beds) or Eastcourt (Wilts). Robert *atte Estcote* (1327 SRSx) lived at the east cottage, now Eastcourt, near Estcot's Fm in East Grinstead (Sussex).

Eastell: *v.* EASTALL

Easterbrook: *v.* EASTBROOK

Easterby: Peter *Austebi* 1204 P (Y); Robert *Oustinby* 1297 SRY; Martin *Oustiby* ib.; William *Estyby* ib.; Hugh *Estinby* ib.; Richard *Esterby* 1474 GildY. ON *austr í bý*, influenced by OE *ēast*, (one who lives) 'east in the village'. cf. WESTOBY.

Eastgate: Walter *de Estgat'* 1200 P (Nf). From residence near the east gate of some town or castle.

Easthope, Eastop: John *de Esthop'* 1275 RH (Sa); William *Estoppe* 1327 SRSx. From Easthope (Salop) or 'dweller in the eastern valley' (OE *hop*).

Eastland: Simon *de Estlande* 1198 P (K). From

residence near one of the many minor places so called.

Eastman, Eastment, Astman, Esmond, Esmonde: *Estmunt* 1066 DB (Sf); Ricardus *filius Estmund* 1195 P (Ess); *Esmond* 1313–14 ODCN; Stephen *Estmund* 1227 AssBk; Geoffrey *Astmund* 1275 SRWo; John *Eastmunde* 1277 AssSo; Alan *Esmund* 1285 FFEss. OE *Ēastmund* 'grace or favour-protection'.

Eastmure: Alicia *filia Eastmer* 1212 Cur (Bk); *Estmar* le Carbonier 13th AD ii (Mx); Walter *Estmer* 1221 AssWo; Robert *Eastmer* 1309 FFK; William *Estmor* 1311 Rams (Nf); John *Estmar* 1312 LLB B. OE *Ēastmǣr* 'grace or favour-famous', recorded only as the names of moneyers *temp.* Edward the Confessor to William I.

Easto, Eastoe: *v.* EASTAUGH

Easton: (i) John *de Eston* 1299 LoCt. From one of the many Eastons. (ii) Philip *atte Estone* 1327 SRSo. 'Dweller at the eastern homestead.' (iii) William *Byestone* 1297 MinAcctCo. OE *be ēastan tūne* (one who lived) 'to the east of the village'. cf. EASTBROOK. (iv) William, John *Anesteton* 1296 SRSx. OE *on ēastan tūne* (dweller) 'on the east of the village'. (v) *Edstan, Estan* 1066 DB (Nf, L); Roger, Robert *Estan* 1275 RH (Nf, Sf). OE *Ēadstān* 'prosperity-stone'.

Eastop: *v.* EASTHOPE

Eastwood: Adam *de Estwde* 1221 ElyA (C). From a place named Eastwood or from residence east of a wood (John *Byestewode* 1339 PN D 98). Also 'dweller to the eastward': Hugh *Enesteward* 1279 RH (O).

Eatwell: Hugo *de Hetewelle* 1187 P (Db). From Etwall (Derby).

Eaves, Eavis, Eves, Reeves: John *atte Euese* 1275 SRWo; John *atte Reuese* 1327 ib. (identical); Robert *del Eves* 1332 SRLa. 'Dweller by the border or edge' of a wood or hill (OE *efes*). *v.* also EVE, REEVES.

Eayres, Eayrs: *v.* AYER

Ebbatson: John *Ebotson* 1485 GildY. 'Son of *Ebbot*.' *v.* EBBETTS.

Ebbetts, Ebbitt, Ebbutt: *Ebbot* (f), *Ebota* 1379 PTY; *Ebete* (f) 1381 SRSf; Simon *Ebet* 1195 P (Nf); Adam *Ebboth* 1327 SRSo; Ralph *Ebottys* 1534 FrNorw; John *Ebitt* 1675 FrY. *Ebbot* and *Ebbet*, as women's names, are diminutives of *Ebb* for *Ibb*, a pet-name for *Isabel*. Occasionally they may be masculine, from *Ebbi*. *v.* EBBS.

Ebblewhite: *v.* HEBBLETHWAITE

Ebbs: Alicia *Relicta Ebbe* 1296 SRSx; Robert, John *Ebbys* 1524 SRSf, 1528 FrNorw. *Ebbe* must be the pet-form of *Isabel* from which *Ebbot* was formed. It is not clear whether *Ebbe* above is the surname or the christian name of Alice's husband. If the latter, it must be masculine and is a pet-form of *Herbert*. cf. *Ebbi* le Estreis 1218 AssL, where *Ebbi* is an interlineation for the cancelled *Herebertus*.

Eccersley: *v.* ECKERSLEY

Eccles, Ekless: Adam, Warin *de Eccles* c1170 Black, 1212 Cur (K); Peter *Ekeles* 1378 AssLo.

From Eccles (Kent, Lancs, Norfolk, Berwick, Dumfries).

Eccleshall, Eckersall, Eacersall: William *de Eccleshull* 1246 AssLa; Robert *de Eccleshale* 1251 AssY, *de Ekilsale* 1297 SRY. From Ecclesall (WRYorks), Eccleshall (St), Eccleshill (Lancs, WRYorks).

Eckersley, Eccersley: Henry *de Ecclesleye* 1301 QW (Y); Jane *Eckersley* 1603 Bardsley (La). From a lost place in Lancashire. *v.* PN La 101.

Eckhard, Eckart, Eckert, Eckett: Simon *filius Echardi* 1219 Cur (L); Adam *Ecard* 1275 RH (Nf). OG *Eckhard, Eckard* 'edge-hard'.

Ecroyd: *v.* ACKROYD

Edden: Robert *Edden* 1332 SRWa. *v.* EDDS, GEFFEN.

Eddington, Edington, Eadington: Jordan *de Edingeton'* 1201 Pl (Wa); Gilbert *de Edington* 1327 SRSo; Thomas *Edyngton* 1448 IpmNt. From Eddington (Berks), or Edington (Northumb, Som, Wilts).

Eddis: *v.* EDIS

Eddison: *v.* EDESON

Eddolls: Robertus *filius Edolfi* 1206 Cur (Nb); *Edulfus* 1214 Cur (Ess); *Edolf'* 1219 AssY; Ralph *Edolf* 1276 RH (Berks); Simon *Edulf* 1327 SR (Ess). OE *Ēadwulf* 'prosperity-wolf', a common OE name.

Eddowes: *v.* EDIS

Edds: *Edde* 1279 RH (O); John *Edde* 1524 SRSf. Perhaps a pet-form of *Edwin* or *Edward*, both surviving in use in the 14th century. cf. *Edda* rusticus (968) and *Edwine qui et Eda* dictus est (801 Redin). Or for EAD: *Edda* mater Johannis 1379 PTY.

Eddy, Eddie: *Edwy* Morwy 1221 AssWo; Willelmus *filius Edwy* 1250 Fees (Sr); John, Robert *Edwy* 1254 ArchC xii, 1275 SRWo; Adam *Eadwy, Edwy* 1275 RH (Nf), 1327 SRSf. OE *Ēadwīg* 'prosperity-war', a common OE name. The surname is fairly common in ME and has probably become *Eddy*.

Ede(s): *v.* EAD

Eden(s) *v.* EADEN

Edenborough: *v.* EDINBOROUGH

Edeson, Eddison, Edson: William *Eddesone* 1314 AssSt; Geoffrey *Edessone* 1328 AD i (Hu); William *Edison* 1394 DbCh. 'Son of *Ead*' or of *Edd*.

Edgar, Edgars, Edger, Eagar, Eager, Eagers, Eagger, Egar, Egarr, Eger, Eggar, Egger, Eggers, Adger, Agar, Agars, Ager: *Edgar* 1066 DB (Hu), 1148–67 AD i (Lo); *Ædgar* c1095 Bury (Sf); *Adger* 1182–8 BuryS (Sf); Walter *Eadgar* 1250 FFSf; Thomas *Edgar* 1250 Fees (Sr); John *Adger* 1309 LLB D; William *Agar* 1521 FrY; Richard *Egger* 1563 Black; John *Egor* 1664 RothwellPR (Y). OE *Ēadgār* 'prosperity-spear'. *Eager* is a Northern Irish, *Egarr* a Dumfries form. cf. *Aeggar* King of Scots a1189 Black.

Edge: Henry *del Egge* 1221 AssWo, *sub Egge* 1290 ShefA (Y); John *de Egge* 1260 AssCh, *atte Egge* 1327 SRWo. 'Dweller near or below some prominent edge, ridge, steep hill or hill-side' (OE *ecg*).

Edgeley, Edgley: John *de Eggelye* 1296 SRSx; William *de Eddesleye* 1348 AssSt; Henry *Edgly* 1674 HTSf. From Edgeley (Ches), or Edgeley (Salop), *Edesleye* 1327.

Edgell: Roger *Eggolf* 1275 SRWo; William, Richard *Eggel(l)*' 1278 FFEss, 1327 *SR* (Ess); Robert *Eggolfe*, William *Eggculf* 1327 SRWo. OE *Ecgwulf* 'sword-wolf', a common OE name. *Eggell* is from OE **Ecgel*, a diminutive of *Ecg-*.

Edgeworth, Edgworth: Peter *de Egewurth*' 1221 AssGl; Stephen *de Eggeworth* 1352 AssSt; Robert *Egeworthe* 1524 FFEss. From Edgeworth (Glos, Lancs).

Edhouse: *v.* EDIS

Edicker: *Edwacre* 1066 Winton (Ha); *Eduuacher* 1111–38 ELPN; *Edwaker* 1200 FFK; Godwinus *filius Edwacher* 1135 Oseney (O); Adam, Thomas *Edwaker* 1279 RH (O). OE *Ēadwacer* 'prosperity-watchman' or, perhaps, OE *ēadwacer* 'watchman of property' used as a personal name; a late name, recorded only twice before the Conquest.

Edinborough, Edenborough, Edingborough, Edinbry, Edynbry: Alexander *de Edynburgh*, *de Edenburg* 1233–55 Black; Thomas *of Edynburgh* 1396 ib. From Edinburgh.

Edis, Ediss, Edhouse, Eddis, Eddowes: *Eddusa* 1196 P (Wo); *Edus* 1197 ib., 1227 AssBk; *Edusa* 1196 P (Y), 1211 Cur (Gl), 1219 AssL; John *Edus* 1277 Ely (Sf); William *Eddows, Edhouse* 1744, 1749 WStowPR (Sf); Thomas *Eddis* 1744 Bardsley. This is one of a difficult series of names ending in *-us* or *-usa*, including *Sigus, Hacus* and *Ingus*, the last taken by Smith as a short form of ON *Ingiríðr* (PN NRY 261). All are feminine, as is *Aldus* (*Aldous*) which is taken in ODCN as masculine from OG *Aldo* 'old'. The only example given is *Aldus* (RH) which is certainly feminine for in RH we find also Hugo *filius Aldus* (not *Aldi*), and Hugo *filius Alduse*, i.e. 'son of *Aldusa* (f)'. cf. *Aldusa* Vidua 'the widow' 1212 Cur (L). Smith notes that one *Edus* is also called *Ēadgifu*. *Edusa soror Erenburge* 1198 Cur (Sf) is identical with *Ediz*, with alternative readings *Editha, Edit* (1200 Cur). cf. Ricardus *filius Eddiz* 1207 Cur (Nf). *Edus* is therefore a short form of a woman's name in *Ēad-*, either OE *Ēadgifu* or *Ēadgyð* and *Aldus* similarly of a feminine name in *Eald-*, e.g. OE *Ealdgyð*.

Edkins, Eakin, Ekins: *Edekin* Gomey 1279 RH (O); Joan *Edekin* ib.; Elena *Edkynes* 1327 SRSo; Mary *Eakyn* 1598 Bardsley. *Edekin*, a diminutive of *Eda*. *v.* EAD.

Edleston: Peter *de Edelauston* 1288 AssCh. From Edlaston (Derby) or Edleston (Ches). *v.* also ATHELSTAN.

Edlin, Edling: *Edelina* 1214 Cur (K); *Athelina* or *Edelina* 1221 AssWa; John *Edelin*' 1239 Rams (Nf); Thomas *Edling* 1660 FrY. OG *Adelina* (Rom). *Edelina* (f) is due to the influence of OE names in *Æðel-* which became *Adel-, Edel-* in ME.

Edman, Edmans, Edmands, Admans: *Ediman* Cumin, Canun (*sic*) 1295–7 P (Nth); William *Edemon, Edeman* 1275 SRWo, 1298 LoCt; William

Edmon 1332 SRWa; William *Adman* 1644 FrY OE **Ēadmann* 'prosperity-man'.

Edmead, Edmed, Edmett, Edmott, Edmeades, Edmeads, Eadmeades, Eadmeads: Gervase *Eadmede*, Roger *Edemede* 1334 SRK; John *Edmed* 1485 CantW; William *Edmete*, Robert *Edmets* 1577, 1604 StaplehurstPR; John *Edmeads* c1700 ArchC xlix. OE *ēadmēde* 'humble'.

Edmond, Edmonds, Edmons, Edmund, Edmunds: *Ædmundus* presbyter, *Edmund(us)* 1066 DB; *Edmund* Wedertihand Hy 2 DC (L); Nicholaus *Edmundus* 1210 Cur (C); John *Edmond*, Sibil *Edmund* 1275 SRWo; William *Admond* 1349 Crowland (C). OE *Ēadmund* 'prosperity-protector'.

Edmondson, Edmundson, Edmenson, Edminson: Robert *Edmondson* 1379 PTY; John *Edmundson* 1414 FrY; Richard *Edmonson* alias Jonson 1558 Shef (Y). 'Son of *Edmund*.'

Edon: *v.* EADEN

Edrich, Edridge: *Ædricus, Edric(us)* 1066 DB; *Edrich* Buck 1275 RH (Nf); *Edericke* le Blacke 1275 RH (L); Thomas *Hedricus* 1185 Templars (Gl); Robert *Edrich*' 1200 P (Ha); Robert *Eadric* 1221 Oseney (O); William *Ederyge* 1332 SRSt; Edmund *Edryk* 1381 SRSf. OE *Ēadrīc* 'prosperity-powerful'.

Edrupt: *Hettrop* Crestien c1166 NthCh (Sa); *Aitrop, Attropus* de Merc 1178 P (Ess); *Eutropius* Alanus 1193 P (Gl); Richard *Edrop* 1332 SRLo. A rare surname from an uncommon personal name of Greek origin, Εὐτρόπιος, from εὔτροπος 'probatis moribus', one of proved character. Aythorpe Roding (Essex), *Aydroprothyng* 1351 PN Ess 491, owes its attribute to a 12th-century benefactor of the parish, *Aeitrop* or *Eutropius* son of Hugh, also named *Eitropus, Autropus, Eydrop, Eiltrop* (1206–20 Cur).

Edsall, Edsell, Edscer, Edser: William *de Egeshawe* 1332 SRSr; Robert *Eggyshaw* 1372 FFSr; John *Edsawe*, Thomas *Edsall* 1583 Musters (Sr); Robert *Edsurs* 1684 ib. From High Edser in Ewhurst (Surrey). *v.* PN Sr 239.

Edson: *v.* EDESON

Edward, Edwardes, Edwards: *Eaduuardus, Eduuard(us), Æduuardus* 1066 DB; *Edwardus* serviens 1206 Cur (Co); William *Edward*' 1219 Cur (Sf); Cristina *Edwardis* 1279 RH (Hu); John *Edwards* 1498 Chirk. OE *Ēadweard* 'prosperity-guard'.

Edwardson: William *Edwardson* 1518 KentW. 'Son of *Edward*.'

Edwin, Edwing, Edwyn: *Edwin*' Wridel 1066 Winton (Ha); Adam *filius Edwini* 1206 Cur (Nf); William *Edwin*' 1221 AssWa; Stephen *Edwyn* 1252 Rams (Beds). OE *Ēadwine* 'prosperity-friend'.

Edynbry: *v.* EDINBOROUGH

Eeley: *v.* ELY

Effemy, Effeney, Effeny: *Eufemia* 1188 BuryS (Sf), 1206 Cur (Gl); *Eufemmia* de Neville 1275 RH (L); Katerina *Eufemme* 1275 RH (Nf); Michael *Effemme* 1327 SRSf. Gk Εὐφημία 'auspicious speech', the name of a 4th-century Bithynian martyr who was canonized.

Egbert: *Egbert* 1086 DB; Martin *Egebrith* 1279

RH (C). OE *Ecgbeorht* 'sword-bright'. A rare surname.

Eggar, Egger(s): v. EDGAR

Eggerton, Egerton: David *Eggerton* 1282 AssCh; Joan *de Egerton*' 1327 SRSa; Ralph *Eggerton* 1662 PrGR. From Egerton (Ches, Kent), Egerton in Scammonden, or Edgerton in Huddersfield (WRYorks).

Eggleston, Egglestone, Egleston: Roger *de Egleston*' 1196 P (Du); Ralph *de Egliston* 1260 AssLa; John *Egleston, Eggleston* 1530, 1545 CorNt. From Eggleston (Durham), or Egglestone (NRYorks).

Eglin, Eglen, Eaglen, Eagland, Eagling: *Egelina de Curtenay* 1207 Cur (O); Alexander *Egelin* 1185 P (Sf); Peter *Eglyn* 1369 LLB G. *Egelina* (f) is probably a Norman form of OG *Agilina.

Eisdale, Eisdell: v. ESDAILE

Ekins: v. EDKINS

Ekless: v. ECCLES

Elce: v. ELL

Elcock, Elcocks, Elcoux, Ellcock, Ellicock: *Elecocc* (son of Elias) 1246 AssLa; *Elkoc Habraham* 1297 Wak (Y); Roger *Hellecok* 1275 RH (Gl); Richard *Elcok* 1379 PTY. *Eli-coc*, a diminutive of *Elie* (Elias or Ellis). v. HELLCAT.

Elcy: v. ELSEY

Elder, Elders: Hugo *le Heldere* 1212 Cur (Herts); Ricardus *ye Elder* 1379 PTY. 'The elder. senior.'

Elderidge: v. ALDRICH

Elderton: v. ELLERTON

Eldred, Eldrid: v. ALDRED

Eldrett: v. ALDRED, ALDRITT

Eldridge: v. ALDRICH

Elen: v. ELLEN

Elesender, Elshenar, Elshener, Elshender, Alshioner: Roger *Elysandre* 1327 SRSo; John *Alshenour* 1596 Black; Katherine *Elshenour* 1597 ib.; Archibald *Alexshunder* or *Alschunder* 1596 ib.; Deacon *Elshender* 1840 ib. Scottish forms of *Alexander*.

Eley: v. ELY

Elfick: v. ALPHEGE

Elgar, Elger: v. ALGAR

Elgood: *Helgot* 1086 DB (Bk, D, St); *Helgod* ib. (Sa); Philippus *filius Helgot* 1185 P (St); John *Elgood* 1524 SRSf. OFr *Helgot*, OG *Helgaud*, from OG *Hildegaud* or OFr *Eligaud*.

Elias, Eliasson: v. ELLIS

Elin: v. ELION, ELLEN

Elinson: Richard *Eleyneson* 1327 SRWo; Thomas *Elenessone* 1359 AssCh; John *Elynson* 1379 PTY. 'Son of *Ellen*.' v. also ELLISON.

Elion, Elin, Helin, Hellen, Hellin, Hellins, Helling, Hellings, Hellon, Hillen, Hilling, Hillings: Robert *de Helion* 1190 P (Ess); William *de Elyon* 1200 P (D); John *Heline* 1251 Rams (Hu); Robert *de Helun*' 13th Seals (Sf); John *Helon* 1524 SRSf; Edward *Hellynge* 1568 SRSf. Helion Bumpstead (Essex), recorded as *Bumpstede Elyns* (1544), *Heleyns* (1554), *Hellyn* (1570) and locally known as *Helen's* Bumpstead, was held in 1086 (DB) by Tihel *de Herion*, called also Tihel *Brito* 'the Breton',

who came from Helléan (Morbihan). The family also had land in Haverhill (Suffolk) where Andrew *de Helin*' held a fee in 1275 (RH) and John *Elioun* half a fee in 1346 (FA). Bumpstead and Haverhill are near the Essex–Suffolk boundary. *Elin, Elion* and *Hillen* are rare surnames still found in Essex and Suffolk. *Helin*, also rare, survives in London. The same family has also left its name in Upton Hellions (Devon) where the attribute occurs as *Hyliun* (1270), *Hylon* (1385) and *Helling* (1557). *Hellings, Hellins* and *Hilling*, all rare, found today in Somerset. v. PN Ess 508–9, PN D 419. Some of these surnames have alternative origins. v. ELLEN, HELLING, HILLING.

Eliot, Eliott, Elliot, Elliott: (i) *Heliot de Slohebi* 12th DC (L); *Elyot* 1188 BuryS (Sf); William *Elyot* 1257 AssSo; William *Eliot* 1327 SRSx. A diminutive of *Elias*, from OFr *Élie* and *-ot*. The frequency of these surnames is due partly to the absorption of OE *Æðelgēat* (m) and *Æðelgȳð* (f). v. AYLETT. (ii) According to Black, the Scottish *Eliot*, with the same four modern spellings, appears regularly as *Elwald* or *Elwold* until the end of the 15th century. This is from OE *Ælfweald* 'elf-ruler'. cf. *Elewald* 1279 CalSc (Cu). From the 16th century, there is a bewildering variety of forms, some of which are difficult to account for. The development, in general, seems to have been: *Elwaud, Elwat, Eluat, Eluott, Elioat, Eliot*, with variants surviving as ELLWAND, ELLWOOD.

Elis: v. ELLIS

Elkin, Elkins: *Elekin* 1279 RH (O); John *Elekyn* 1310 FFEss; Thomas *Elkyns* 1447 Balliol (O). *Eli-kin*, a diminutive of *Elie* (Elias), or of *Ela* (Ellen).

Ell, Ells, Else, Elce: *Ala* 1208 Cur (Sx); *Ela* 1208 Cur (Ess), 1214 ib. (Nf); Roger, William *Elle* 1221 ElyA, 1327 SRSo. *Ala* is a variant of *Ela*, both forms being used of the same woman: *Ala* or *Ela de Eching(e)ham* 1207 Cur (Sx); *Ela de Marci* (1207, 1210 Cur) is identical with *Ala* de Saukevill', widow of William de Marcy (1207 ib.). *Ela* is a variant reading of *Elena*, widow of Edwin de Tuggel' 1221 Cur (Sr) whilst *Elena*, wife of the Earl of Salisbury, is also called *Ela* and once *Eda*, the latter being indexed as *Ela* (1212–22 Cur). *Ela* is thus a short form of *Elena* and possibly also for *Eleanor*, the less common *Ala* being due to the influence of *Alienora*.

Ellard: v. ADLARD

Ellcock: v. ELCOCK

Elldred: v. ALDRED

Ellen, Ellens, Elleyne, Ellin, Ellins, Ellings, Elen, Elin, Hellen, Hellens, Hellin: (i) *Elena ostiaria* 1204 P (So); *Elena . . . ipsam Helenam* 1219 AssY; *Helena de Sutton* 1210 Cur (Nth); Roger *Heleyne* 13th StJohn (Ess); Robert *Helene* 1275 SRWo; Walter *Eleyn* 1279 RH (O); Ralph *Elene* 1314 FFEss; Robert *Elyn* 1327 SRSf; William *Helyns* 1332 SRWo. Ellen (f) is the earlier English form of *Helen*, Greek Ἑλένη, feminine of Ἕλενος 'the bright one'. The popularity of the name is due to St Helena, mother of the Emperor Constantine, said to have been the daughter of a British king. (ii) Nicholas *in the Ellene* 1327 SRSo; Robert *atte Hellene, atte Ellene* 1327, 1332 SRSx. 'Dweller by the alder(s)', OE *ellen*.

Ellenor, Ellinor: *Alienor* c1202 NthCh (Nth), 1211 Cur (Beds); Richard *Elyanor* 1327 SRSf; Richard *Elynoreson* 1375 AD vi (Lei); Elizabeth *Ellener* 1674 HTSf. Provençal *Aliénor*, a form of *Helen*, introduced into England by *Eleanor* of Aquitaine (1122–1204), wife of Henry II.

Elleray: *v.* HILLARY

Ellerker, Elliker, Allaker, Alliker: Denis *de Elreker* 1204 AssY. From Ellerker (ERYorks), *Allerker* 1180–95 PN ERY 222.

Ellerman: *v.* ELLIMAN

Ellert: *v.* ADLARD

Ellerton, Elderton: Ralph *de Elreton* 1204 AssY; Roger *de Ethelartone* 1307 Ronton (St). From Ellerton (ERYorks, Salop).

Ellery: *v.* HILLARY

Elles: *v.* ELL, ELLIS

Elletson: John *Elotson* 1332 SRCu. 'Son of *Elot*.' *v.* ELLETT.

Ellett: *Ellot* 1332 SRLa, SRCu; *Ellota* 1379 PTY; William *Elot* 1323 AssSt; Thomas *Elote* 1327 SRSf; Rychard *Ellet* 1568 SRSf. A diminutive of *Ellen*.

Elleyne: *v.* ELLEN

Ellice: *v.* ELLIS

Ellick: *v.* ELWICK

Ellicock: *v.* ELCOCK

Elliff: *v.* AYLIFF

Elliker: *v.* ELLERKER

Elliman, Ellerman, Elman: Thomas *Elyman* 1377 MESO (Lei); Etheldreda *Elyman* 1381 SRSf. OE *æle* 'oil' and *mann*, 'oil-man', seller of oil. cf. Roger *le Elymaker* 1344 MESO (So).

Ellin, Ellings, Ellins: *v.* ELLEN

Ellington, Elington: William *de Elinton'* 1206 Pl (Hu); John *de Ellington* 1274 RH (L); John *Elyngton* 1576 SRW. From Ellington (Hunts, Kent, Northumb, NRYorks).

Elliot: *v.* ELIOT

Ellis, Elliss, Ellice, Elles, Elis, Elys, Heelis, Helis, Hellis, Elias: *Helias* scriptor c1150 DC (L); *Elyas* de Westone c1160 ib.; *Heliseus* de Brunne c1175 ib., *Helyas, Elyas* de Brunna Hy 2 ib; Willelmus *filius Helis* 1212 Cur (So); *Elis* de Adham 1220 Cur (Mx); *Elice* de Cheindue 1224 AssSt; William *Elyas* 1200 P (Y); William *Elis* 1202 P (L); Roger *Elys, Helys* Hy 3 HPD (Ess); Andrew *Elice* 1309 SRBeds. ME *Elis* 'Elias', the Greek form of the Hebrew *Elijah*. John *Elys* was the son of *Elias* de Bampton (1318, 1331 Husting). *Elias* is not common as a surname. *v.* also ELY. *Ellice* may also be a pet-name for Elizabeth. *v.* 1319 SRLo 278.

Ellison: (i) Rogier *Elyssone* 1296 Black (Berwick); Adam *Elisson* 1379 PTY; John *Ellyson* 1487 FrY. 'Son of *Ellis*.' *v.* also ALISON. (ii) Adam *filius Elysant* 1190 P (He); *Helisent* de Twining' 1221 AssGl; Henry *Elesant* (*Elesand*) 1327 SR (Ess). OFr *Elissent, Elisant* (f), OG *Elisind* (f).

Elloway: *v.* ALAWAY

Ellston: *v.* ELSTON

Ellwand: *Elwand* is found in 1502 and later for *Elwald*, now the Scottish ELIOT.

Ellwood, Elwood, Allwood: *Aluuoldus* episcopus 1066 DB (Do); *Aluuolt* (*Alfuuold*) 1066 InqEl (Sf); Arkillus *filius Aluoldi* 1131 FeuDu; *Alfwold* presbiter 1212 Fees (Berks); Robert *Elwald, Elwaud* 1469, 1579 FrY; William *Elwold* 1524 SRSf; Thomas *Elwod* 1572 FrY. OE *Ælfweald* 'elf-ruler'. In Scotland this has become ELIOT.

Ellyatt: *v.* AYLETT

Elm, Elmes, Elms, Nelmes, Nelms: John *atte Elme* 1316 Ipm (Wo); Stephen *ate Nelme* 1317 AssK; John *atte Elmes* 1322 MELS (Sr); Thomas *Elm* 1327 SRSf; Semannus *atte Nelmes* 1339 Cl (Ess); William *ate Thelmes* 1356 HPD (Ess). 'Dweller by the elm(s).' *v.* also HELM.

Elman: *v.* ELLIMAN

Elmar, Elmer, Elmers: *v.* AYLMER

Elnaugh, Elnough: *v.* ALLNATT

Elphee: *v.* ALLVEY

Elphick: *v.* ALPHEGE, ELVEY

Elphinston, Elphinstone: John *de Elphinstone, de Elphinston* c1250, a1340 Black; Alexander, William *Elphynston* 1486 ib. From the lands of Elphinstone in Tranent (Midlothian).

Elray: *v.* HILLARY

Elrick: *v.* ALDRICH

Else: *v.* ELL

Elsey, Elsie, Elcy: *Alfsi* 1066 DB (Sf); *Alsi* ib. (Ha); Robertus *filius Elfsi* 1191 P (K); *Elsy* faber 1230 P (L); Reginald, John *Elsi* 1155–77 Templars (Y), 1275 RH (Nf). OE *Ælfsige* 'elf-victory'.

Elshenar, Elshener, Elshender: *v.* ELESENDER

Elsip: *v.* ALLSEP

Elsley: John *de Eltesley* 1310 LLB D; William *Elsley* 1674 FrY. From Eltisley (Cambs).

Elsop: *v.* ALLSEP

Elston, Elstone, Ellston: (i) Galfridus *filius Elstan* 1193 P (Nf); Warinus *filius Elstani* 1230 P (Nb); Henry *Elstan* 1279 RH (O); John *Elston* 1411 FrY. OE **Ealdstān* or *Ealhstān*. cf. ALLSTON. (ii) William *de Ethelistone* 1332 SRLa. From Elston (Notts, Lancs, Wilts).

Elton: Thomas *de Eleton* 1230 P (Berks); William *de Elton'* 1327 SRLei; James *Elton* 1434–5 IpmNt. From Elton (Berks, Ches, Derby, Durham, Hereford, Hunts, Lancs, Notts).

Elvar, Elver: *v.* ALVAR

Elven: *v.* ALVEN

Elverson: Probably 'Ælfred's son'. cf. William *Elvered* alias *Elluerd* 1696 DKR 41 (W).

Elvery: *v.* ALFREY

Elvey, Elvy: *Elviva* 1325 NorwDeeds; Richard *Elvy* 1338 FFY; John *Elphy* 1450 ArchC v; Thomas *Elveve*, John *Elvew* 1488, 1518 CantW. OE *Ælfgifu* (f) 'elf-gift'. *v.* also ALLVEY.

Elvidge: *v.* ALPHEGE

Elvin(s): *v.* ALVEN

Elward: *v.* ALLWARD

Elwes, Elwess: *Helewis* 1086 DB (Nf); *Heilewisa Extranea* 1160 P (Gl); *Elewisa uidua* 1221 *ElyA*

(Sf); John *Helewis* 1274 RH (Ess); William *Helewys* 1297 MinAcctCo; Thomas *Ellwes* 1625 FrY. OFr *Heluïs*, *Heloïs*, from OG *Heilwidis*, *Helewidis* (f) 'hale or sound-wide'.

Elwick, Ellick: Ralph *Elwyke* 1512 FrY; John *Ellyk* 1569 ib. From Elwick (Durham, Northumb).

Elwin, Elwyn: *v.* ALWIN

Elwood: *v.* ELLWOOD

Ely, Ealey, Eeley, Eley, Hely, Heley: (i) *Hely* de Amandeuilla 1150–60 Gilb (L); Philippus *filius Helie* 1213 Cur (So); William *Heli* Hy 2 DC (Nt); John *Elye* 1327 SRC. OFr *Elie* 'Elijah'. *v.* ELLIS. (ii) Huna *de Ely* 1086 ICC (C); Geoffrey *de heli* 1133 Bart (Lo). From Ely (Cambs).

Elys: *v.* ELLIS

Emans: *v.* EMENEY

Emberson: *v.* EMMERSON

Embery, Embra, Hembrow, Hembra, Hembry, Hembury: These Somerset surnames may all derive from Emborough (Som): William *de Enneberg* 1258 AssSo. Or from Hembury (Devon) or Henbury (Dorset): John *Hembury* 1491 PCC (D/Do). *v.* also AMERY.

Emblem, Emblin, Embling, Emeline, Emlyn, Amblin: Anschitil *filius Ameline* 1066 DB (Do); Godefridus *filius Emeline* 1115 Winton (Ha); *Emmelina* Hy 2 DC (L); *Emelina* ib. (Db), 1221 Cur (O); *Amelina* 1221 AssSa; John *Emelin* 1208 ChR (Sf); Geoffrey *Amelyn* 1296 SRSx. OFr *Ameline*, *Emmeline*, a hypocoristic formation of OG names in *Adal-*.

Embley: *v.* EMLEY

Embra, Embr(e)y, Embury: *v.* AMERY, EMBERY

Emeline: *v.* EMBLEM

Emeney, Emeny, Emmony, Emney, Emmans, Emmence, Emmens, Emmins, Emmons, Emans, Emons, Immink: *Ysmeine* de Cherchefeld 1199 P (R); *Ismenia, Ysmeina, Hismena* 1206–12 Cur (Sf, Nt); Rogerus *filius Immine* 1219 AssY; *Emoni* Turberd 1275 RH (Y); Hugh *Imayn* 1276 RH (Lei); John *Ymanie* 1279 RH (K); *Imanie* Springold 1279 RH (C); *Hemin'* uxor Bercarii ib.; *Imaigne* de Rothynge 1319 SRLo; Roger *Emaygne* 1352 ColchCt; Nicholas *Eman* 1524 SRSf; William *Immings* 1658 Bardsley; Francis *Immynes* 1707 ib.; William *Emmines* 1717 ib.; Ann *Emens* 1783 ib. *Isemeine* (1227 AssBk) is also called *Isemay* but the two names can hardly be identical. *Ismaine, Ismenia*, a common woman's name, found as *Emonie, Emeny* until the end of the 18th century, is a difficult name. In ODCN a Celtic origin is suggested. It may be that we have an OG compound *Ismagin 'iron-strength'; both elements are common though *-magin* is not known as a second element and *Ismeine* seems to be unknown in France.

Emeric(k), Emerig: *v.* AMERY

Emerley: *v.* EMLEY

Emerson: *v.* EMMERSON

Emery: *v.* AMERY

Emes: *v.* EAMES

Emett: *v.* EMMATT

Eminson: *v.* EMMISON

Emley, Emly, Embley, Emerley: John *de Emlay* 1304 FrY. From Emley (WRYorks).

Emlyn: *v.* EMBLEM

Emm, Emms: *Ema* c1160 DC (Lei); *Emma* 1187 DC (L), 1219 AssY; *Emm* in the Hurn 1327 SRSo; William *Emms* 1274 RH (Sa); John *Emme* 1279 RH (O). *Emm* was the English form of the popular Norman *Emma* (OG *Emma, Imma*). *v.* EMMATT.

Emmans: *v.* EMENEY, EMMINGS

Emmatt, Emmet, Emmett, Emmitt, Emmott, Emmert, Emett, Hemmett: *Emmote* 1279 RH (Bk); *Emmota* 1327 SRSo, SRY; *Emmete* de Fur' 1279 RH (C); John *Emote* 1327 SRWo; Ranulph *Emmot*, William *Emmoten* 1332 SRWa. *Emmot* was a very common pet-name for *Emma*. The names were interchangeable: *Emma* wife of Adam faber is called also *Emmota* 1353 AD vi (Mx); *Emma* alias *Emmote* Bochere 1413 AD iii (K). *Emmott* may also be from Emmot (Lancs): William *de Emot* 1324 LaCt.

Emmerig: *v.* AMERY

Emmerson, Emberson, Emerson: William *Emeryson* 1411 Finchale; Cuthbert *Emerson* 1498 FrY. 'Son of *Emery*.' *v.* AMERY, EMPSON.

Emmert: *v.* EMMATT

Emmings: Thomas *Emmyng*, John *Hemmyng* 1296 SRSx; John *Emings* 1674 HTSf. 'Son of *Hemming*', and in later examples sometimes for *Emans*, etc. *v.* HEMMING.

Emmison: William *Emmotson* 1381 PRY; Robert *Emmysson* 1479 NorwW (Nf); John *Emyson* 1489 FrY. 'Son of *Emmott*.' Also 'Son of *Eman* or *Emeny*': Robert *Emanson* 1594 SPD, surviving as EMINSON; and for EMMERSON. *v.* EMPSON.

Emney: *v.* EMENEY

Emonson: Christopher *Emondson* 1507 FrY. Probably for *Edmondson*.

Emory: *v.* AMERY

Empson: Richard *Empson* 1498 Chirk, 1510 Butley (Sf). For EMSON. Also for EMMERSON: Richard *Emryson, Emereson, Empson* 1490–5 Bardsley.

Emson, Hemson: Richard *Emmeson* 1327 SRSx; Robert *Emson* 1381 PTY. 'Son of *Emma*.' Also for *Emmerson*, an intermediate stage between *Emereson* and *Empson*.

Enderby: Robert *de Enderbi* 1170–98 P (L); Thomas *de Enderby* 1298 AssL; Robert *Enderby* 1384 AssWa. From Enderby (Leics, Lincs).

Enderson: *v.* ANDERSON

Enderwick: *v.* INDERWICK

Enfield, Envill: William *de Enefeld'* 1190 P (Lo). From Enfield (Middlesex).

Engeham: *v.* GAIN

Engelbert: *v.* INGLEBRIGHT

England: Nicholas *de Engelond* 1260 AssC; William *de Engelond* 1295 AssCh; John *Ingelond* (*Engelond*) 1327 SR (Ess). There is no authority for the *ing-land* 'meadowland' of Bardsley and Weekley. The reference must be to the name of the country, a surname which appears curiously out-of-place in England. *v.* ENGLISH.

English, Inglis, Inglish: Gillebertus *Anglicus* 1171 P (He); Robert *le Engleis* 12th DC (Lei); Adam *le Englis* 1194–1211 Black (Cumb); William *le Engles* 1205 Oseney (O); Gilbert *Engleis* 1208 Cur (Ess); Nicholas *le Engleys* 1269 AssNb; John (*le*) *Englisshe* 1317 AssK; Willelmus dictus *Ingles* a1321 Black (Moffat); John *Inglis* 1402 ib. (Aberdeen); Alexander *Inglyssh* 1478 ib. OE *Englisc* 'English', originally referring to Angles as distinct from Saxons, a meaning not to be considered for the surname. *Inglis* is a Scottish form denoting an Englishman as opposed to the Scottish borderer or the Celtic Scot, whilst the northern *English* probably referred to an Englishman living among Strathclyde Welsh. But the name was not confined to this district. In the Welsh border counties the name would be given to an Englishman in a preponderatingly Welsh community, in the Danelaw to a newcomer who did not share the common Danish origin with its flourishing Danish customs and names. For some generations after the Conquest an official distinction was made between *Angli* and *Franci*, the native, defeated English and the conquering Normans, and this may account for the name in Essex, Kent and Sussex, where it was probably at first derogatory. At the end of the 13th century *l'Englois* is found as a surname in Paris and this, given by Frenchmen in France, may well have been retained when the emigrant returned home. Baudet *le Engleis* (1311 LLB D) was the valet of John Hauekyn, merchant of St Quentin. *v.* also INGLIS.

Ennion, Enion, Eynon, Inions, Anyan, Anyon, Onians, Onion, Onions, O'Nions, Onyon, Hennion: *Ennian* filius Gieruerð 1159 P (Sa); *Ennion* de Caple 1205 Cur (He); *Eynon, Eynun* 1221 AssSa; *Eignon* 1287 AssCh; *Anian* bishop of Bangor 1284 Ch; Gruffydd ap Madog *Vnyon* 1392 Chirk; Gode *heynon* 1221 ElyA (Sf); William *Anyun* 1279 RH (Bk); Andrew *Heizhnon* 1327 *SR* (Ess); John *Eynon* 1327 SRWo; Richard *Anyon* 1512 AD iii (Ch); Robert *Onnyon* 1568 SRSf; William *Ineon* 1593 Bardsley; Hugh *Inniones* 1622 ib. OW *Enniaun*, an old Welsh name, ultimately from Lat *Anniānus*, also associated with Welsh *einion* 'anvil' for 'stability, fortitude' and, doubtfully, with *uniawn* 'upright, just'.

Ensoll: *v.* INSALL

Ensom, Ensum: Robert *de Eygnesham* 1260 Oseney (O). From Eynsham (Oxon).

Ensor: Adam *de Ednesovere* 1247 AssSt. From Edensor (Derby).

Enticknap: John *de Anekecnappe* 13th, Thomas *de Anteknappe* 1332 PN Sr 235; George *Enticknap* 1696 DKR 41. From Enticknaps Copse (Surrey).

Entwistle, Entwisle, Entwhistle: Elias, Roger *de Ennetwysel* 1276 AssLa, Misc (La); John *Entwisell* 1332 SRLa. From Entwisle (Lancs).

Envill: *v.* ENFIELD

Erett: *v.* ERRETT

Erleigh, Erley: *v.* EARLEY

Ermen: *v.* ARMIN

Ernest, Harness: (i) Hamo *filius Erneis* 1115 Win-

ton (Ha); *Herneis* c1127 AC (Gl); *Hernis* de Neuella, *Arnisius* de Neuille 1154–72 Gilb (L); *Ernis* de Besebia 12th DC (L); Geoffrey *Ernis* 1207 P (Ha); Roger *Arneis* 1235 FFEss; Robert *Herneys* 13th WhC (La); Charles *Earnest* 1758 FrY. OG *Arn(e)gis*, OFr *Erneïs, Ernaïs Hernaïs, Hernays.* (ii) Philip *Harneis* 1285 FFEss; John *Harneys* 1310 FFSf. OFr *harneis*, ME *harnais* 'harness', for a maker of harness or suits of mail. cf. William *le Hernesemaker* 1300 LoCt, William *Duble Harneys*, saddler 1276 LLB A.

Errett, Erett: Gamel *filius Edredi* 1131 FeuDu; *Edredus* Cuperius 1220 Fees (Berks); Maurice *Edred* 1226 Pat; Thomas *Edret* 1276 RH (Berks). OE *Ēadrǣd* 'prosperity-counsel'.

Erricker: *v.* EARWACKER

Ervin(g): *v.* IRVIN

Erwin, Everwin, Irwin, Irwine, Irwing, Urwin: *Eueruinus* 1066 Winton (Ha), 1086 DB (Nf); Gilchrist *filius Eruini* 1124–65 Black; Willelmus *filius Irwine* 1185 Templars (Ess); Augustinus *filius Erwin'* 1255 RH (Sa); Eustace *Everwyn* 1310 LLB D; Thomas *Erwyn* 1459 FrY. OE *Eoforwine* 'boar-friend'. There has been confusion with IRVIN.

Escott: *v.* EASTCOTT

Escreet, Escritt, Eskriett: William *de Escrik* 1307 FrY. From Escrick (ERYorks).

Escuyer: *v.* SQUIRE

Esdaile, Esdale, Easdale, Eisdal, Eisdell, Isdale, Isdell: John *de Esdale* 1413 Black; Margaret *Eskdale* 1472 ib.; James *Esdaill* 1493 ib.; John *Aisdaill* 1599 ib.; John *Isdaill* 1669 ib. From Eskdale (Dumfriesshire).

Eshelby: *v.* AXLEBY

Esherwood: *v.* ISHERWOOD

Eskell: *v.* ASKELL

Eskriett: *v.* ESCREET

Esmond(e): *v.* EASTMAN

Essex: Suein *de Essexa* 1114–16 CartAntiq; William *de Essex* 1246–7 FFWa; John *Essex* 1340–1450 GildC. 'The man from Essex.'

Esson: Sometimes for EASTON. *v.* EASON.

Estall, Estell: *v.* EASTALL

Estaugh: *v.* EASTAUGH

Estcourt: *v.* EASTCOTT

Esterbrook: *v.* EASTBROOK

Estridge: Peter *Estreis* 1148 Winton (Ha); Henry *le Estreis* 1185 P (Cu). OFr *estreis* 'eastern'. In 13th-century London a name applied to Germans, Easterlings: Hereman *le Estreys* was appointed attorney to receive money on behalf of Bartholomew de Hamburk (1282 LLB A). But the name must also have been used of a newcomer from the east. cf. NORRIS, SURRIDGE, WESTRICH.

Etchells, Neachell: Richard *de Echeles* 1269 AssSt; William *Attecheles* 1299 ib.; Richard *Atte Echeles* 1332 SRSt. 'Dweller on a piece of land added to an estate' (OE *ēcels*), frequently found in Warwickshire as the name of small farms and hamlets, e.g. Echills Wood, Nechells; also in Nechells and Neachill (Staffs), in Hitchells (Yorks), and occasionally in Derbyshire and Cheshire. *v.* PN Wa 30.

Etheredge, Etheridge, Ethridge, Etteridge, Etridge, Ettridge, Athridge, Ateridge, Attridge: *Aethericus* 1066 DB; Jacobus *Atteriche* 1276 RH (Berks); John *Etherych* 1524 SRSf; Henry *Etheridge*, William *Etteredge* 1674 HTSf. *Aethericus* is for OE *Æðelrīc*. *v.* also ALDRICH.

Eubanks: *v.* EWBANK

Eustace, Eustice: *Eustachius* 1066 Winton (Ha); *Eustacius* camerarius 1166–75 DC (L); Richard *Eustas(e)* 1275 SRWo, 1279 RH (C); Margery *Eustace* 1297 MinAcctCo. Lat *Eustachius*, *Eustacius*, of Greek origin, probably from εὐσταχος 'fruitful'. Occasionally, perhaps, from the feminine *Eustachia* 1214, 1222 Cur (Sr, Wa). *v.* also STACEY.

Evans, Evens, Evins, Heaven, Heavens: John *Evens*, *Evans* 1568 SRSf, 1679 FrY; James *Hevens* 1674 HTSf. *Evan* is the Welsh form of *John*, dating from about 1500.

Evason, Everson, Evison: William *Evoteson* 1325 Wak (Y); Thomas *Eversome* 1634 Buxhall (Sf); Edward *Everson*, *Eversham* 1639, 1644 ib. 'Son of *Evot*.' cf. IBBERSON.

Evatt, Evett, Evetts, Evitt, Evitts: *Evot* 1314 Wak (Y); *Euota* 1317 AssK; *Evette* 1420 Shef; William, Walter *Euote* 1295 Barnwell (C), 1327 SRY; William *Evett* 1555 Pat; John *Evatts* 1624 Oriel (O). *Evot* or *Evet*, diminutives of *Eve*.

Eve: *Eva* Hy 2 DC (L), 1206, 1211 Cur (Sr, Lei); Gregory *Eve* 1279 RH (C). *Eve* (Lat *Eva*) of Hebrew origin.

Evening: Walter *Evenyng* 1275 RH (Sx); Walter *Evening* 1302 FA (Sx). ME *evening* 'an equal, a match', a neighbour in the scriptural sense.

Everard, Everatt, Evered, Everett, Everid, Everitt: *Ebrard, Eurardus* 1086 DB; *Eurardus* de Langetona 12th DC (L); *Eborardus* 1222 Cur (C); *Everedus* c1250 Rams (C); Richard, William *Everard* 1204 Cur (Beds), 1225 AssSo; William *Euerrad* 1230 P (Lei); Symon *Eborard* 1275 RH (Nf); Geofffrey *Everad* 1300 Rams (Nf): Mary *Everet* 1725, *Everard* 1728, *Evered* 1732, *Everrad* 1734 IckworthPR. This might occasionally be from OE *Eoforheard* but many of the bearers of this name were undoubtedly from the Continent and the surname is usually from the cognate OG *Eburhard, Everhard* 'boar-hard'.

Everest, Everiss, Everix: *v.* DEVERAUX

Everson: *v.* EVASON

Everton: Alured *de Euerton*' 1212 P (C, Hu); William *de Everton* 1348 IpmW; Robert *Everton* 1474 FFEss. From Everton (Beds, Lancs, Notts).

Everwin: *v.* ERWIN

Eves: *v.* EAVES

Eveson: John *Evessone* 13th Rams (C); Hugh *Eveson* 1373 ColchCt. 'Son of *Eve*.'

Evill: *v.* DAVALL

Evins: *v.* EVANS

Evitt: *v.* EVATT

Ewan, Ewen, Ewens, Ewing, Ewings, Ewin, Ewins, Hewin, Hewins, Uwins, Yewen, Youens, Youings: *Ewen, Ewein* Brit(t)o 1086 DB (He); *Ewain* 1164 Black (Scone); *Ywein* Ladde 1177 P (Nf); *Eugene* c1178 Black (Moray); *Ywanus* surdus 1181 P (L);

Ewanus filius Walteri 1192 P (L); Robertus *filius Ywein* 1200 P (Wa); *Yowayne* de Bulling 1246 AssLa; *Ewyn, Iwin* de Salt 1271 AssSt; Dovenaldus *Ewain* a1165 Black; Walter *Ywain* 1202 P (Wa); Robert *Ywein* c1248 Bec (Berks); John *Iuuen* 1297 MinAcctCo; John *Youn* 1346 LLB F; Lucia *Iwynes* 1359 Putnam (Co); Bartholomew *Ewinge* 1555 Black (Glasgow); Richard *Ewyns, Ewens, Ewinges* 1605, 1639, 1681 FrY; George *Yewing* 1664 Black; David *Yewine* 1717 ib. *Ewen* and *Owen* have been regarded as different names and varied etymologies have been advanced for each. The post-Conquest forms suggest we have only one name, ultimately from Greek εὐγενής 'well-born', Gael *Eòghann*, MGael *Eogan*, OIr *Eogán*, OW *Eugein, Ougein*, MW *Ewein, Ywein, Oue(i)n*. In Scotland, Ireland and Wales the name was frequently Latinized as *Eugenius*. It occurs in Scotland as *Eugene* in 1178 and Macewen is *M'Eogan* in 1355. The form *Ewen* is not confined to Scotland, whilst both *Ewein* and *Ywein* appear side by side along the Welsh border. In the eastern counties the name was introduced from Brittany where it occurred as *Even* and has given modern Fr *Ivain*, Breton *Yven, Ivin*. cf. *Ivo* or *Iwein* Titneshoue 1243 Fees (St); already in 1086 we find *Ewen* the Breton in Hereford. *v.* also OWEN.

Ewart, Yeoward, Yeowart, Youatt: (i) *Ewart* aurifaber 1084 ELPN; *Eward* filius Gaufridi 1189–1200 BuryS (Sf); Hugo *filius Esward* 1199 ChR; Gillemichel *filius Eward* 1212 Fees (La); Thomas *Eward* 1279 RH (C); John *Ewarde* 1512 RochW. *Ewart*, a French form of *Edward*. The first example is probably identical with *Eadward*, a moneyer of William I. (ii) Adam *Yowehirde* 1297 SRY; John *Ewehird* 1379 PTY; Robert *Yowarde* 1381 PTY; William *Yeoward* 1607 RothwellPR (Y). OE *ēowu* and *hierde*, 'ewe-herd', keeper of the dairy-farm. Ewes were kept for their milk from which cheese was made. (iii) Robert *de Ewrth*' 1242 Fees (Nb). From Ewart (Northumb).

Ewbank, Eubanks, Ubank: Waldef *de Yuebanc* c1258 PN Cu 453; William *Hughbank* 1464 FrY; Robert *Hewbank* 1475 GildY; Oswald *Ewbanke* 1592 FrY. 'Dweller by the yew-bank' (OE *īw*), as at Yew Bank in Whitehaven (Cumb).

Ewen(s): *v.* EWAN

Ewer, Ewers, Lewer, Lower: Richard *le Ewer* 1185 Templars (Wa); Richard *Lewer* 1219 Fees (Sr); Alexander *Euer* 1309 SRBeds; Robert *Lower* 1513 FrY. OFr *ewer* 'servant who supplied guests at a table with water to wash their hands' (1361 NED).

Ewin(s): *v.* EWAN

Exall, Excell, Exell: Richard *de Ecleshal*' 1221 AssWa; Robert *Exall*' 1542 FFHu. From Exhall near Coventry or near Alcester (Warwicks).

Exelby: *v.* AXLEBY

Eye, D'Eye: Peitevin *de Eya* 1191 P (Sf); Peter *Ege* ib.; John *de la Eye* 1327 SRWo; Thomas *ate Eye* 1341 NI (Sx). From Eye (Hereford, Northants, Suffolk) or from residence near low-lying land (OE *ēg*). *v.* RAY, REA, RYE, NYE, YEA.

Eyer(s), Eyre(s): *v.* AYER
Eynon: *v.* ENNION
Eyton: Robert *de Eiton'* 1185 P (Sa); John *de Eyton'* 1280 FFY; John *Eiton* 1384 IpmGl; William *Eyton, Eton* or *Heyton* 1509 LP (Nth). From Eyton (Salop), Eaton (Ches, Leics, Staffs), *Eyton* 1313, 1236, 1293, Eaton Bray (Beds), *Eitona* 1130, Cold, Eaton (Derby), *Coldeyton* 1323, *Long Eyton* 1288.

Ezard: *v.* ISSARD

F

Faber: Aluricus *filius Fabri* 1066 DB (Sf); Godui *faber* c1095 Bury (Sf); Henry *Fabers* 1279 RH (C). Lat *faber* 'smith', usually occupational, but also used as a personal name: *Faber* de Suterton 1177 P (Y).

Fabian, Fabien: *Fabianus* de Cam 1184 P (Ha), de Hulmo 1191 P (Nf); Willelmus *filius Fabiani*, identical with William *Fabian* 1220 Cur (Ess); William *Fabien* 1231–53 Rams (Nf). Lat *Fabianus* 'of Fabius', probably from *faba* 'a bean'.

Facey: *v.* VAISEY

Fadder: *v.* FATHERS

Faers: *v.* FAIR

Fage: John *Fage* 1327 SRSo, 1388 FFC. ME *fage* 'the action of coaxing or deceiving' (c1421 MED); the verb 'to coax, flatter' is found c1400. cf. *fagere*, 'flatterer' (1435).

Fagg, Fagge, Vagg, Vaggs: Daniel, William *Fag* 1202 FFK, 1269 AssSo; Richard *le Vag* 1286 PNW 144; Ivelo *Vag'* 1317 AssK. cf. Peter *Clanvagg'* baker (1268 ELPN) which Ekwall explains as 'clean loaf', a name for a baker who sold clean bread, from OE *facg*, recorded only in the sense 'a flat fish, plaice', but probably used also of a 'flat loaf'. cf. early Mod *fadge* 'a large flat loaf or bannock'. The nickname may be metonymic for fishmonger or a baker.

Faggeter, Faggetter: Simon *le fagotter* 1279 MEOT (Sr). A derivative of ME, OFr *fagot* 'a bundle of sticks', hence a maker or seller of faggots.

Faiers: *v.* FAIR

Fainer, Feiner: Roger *le Fener* 1271 MEOT (Sx); Gilbert *le Feyner* 1299 LLB C. OFr *fenier*, 'haymonger'.

Fair, Faire, Faires, Fairs, Faiers, Faers, Fayer, Fayers, Fayre, Feyer, Fyers, Phair, Phayre: Edeua *Faira* 1066 DB, *Pulchra* 1086 ib., *Bella* 1086 ICC; Robert *faier* 1191 FF (Sf); Henry *le Vayre* 1297 MinAcctCo; Thomas *le Fayre* 1332 SRSx. OE *fæger* 'fair, beautiful', used occasionally as a personal name: Johannes *filius Fair* 1203 Cur (C).

Fairall: *v.* FAIRHALL

Fairbain: John *ffairban* 1332 SRCu. 'Fair bone' (OE *bān*), one with fine limbs.

Fairbairn, Fairbairns, Fairbarns: Augustin, Robert *Fayr(e)barn(e)* 1297 SRY, 1379 PTY. 'Beautiful child' (OE *bearn*).

Fairbank, Fairbanks: Robert *Fairebank* son of Richard *Farebank* 1583 FrY. 'Dweller by the fair bank(s).'

Fairbard, Fairbeard: Thomas *Fairberd* 1331 Wak (Y); Thomas *Fayrebeard* 1590 Oxon. 'Fair beard' (OE *beard*).

Fairbourn, Fairbourne, Fairburn, Fairburne: Simon *de Fareburne* 1185 Templars (Y); Margery *de Fareburn* 1274 RH (K); John *de Farburn'* 1351 AssL. From Fairbourne (Kent), or Fairburn (WRYorks).

Fairbrass: *v.* FIREBRACE

Fairbrother, Farebrother, Farbrother, Fayerbrother: John *Fayerbrother* 1524 SRSf. Perhaps 'brother of *Fair*'. cf. p. xliv.

Fairchild: Lefui *Fæger Cild* c1095 Bury (Sf); Stephen *Veirchill'* 1214 Cur (Ess); Robert *Fairchild* 1250 Fees (Sr). 'Beautiful child' (OE *cild*). cf. CHILD.

Fairclough, Faircloth, Fairtlough, Faircliff, Faircliffe: Simon *de ffairclogh* 1332 SRLa; William *Fayercliffe*, Robert *Fayreclought* 1568 SRSf; John *Fayercloth* 1629 LitSaxhamPR (Sf); Samuel *Fear Cloth* 1655 Bardsley; Allfabell *Farcloe* 1669 ib. 'Dweller in the fair hollow' (ME *clo(u)gh*).

Fairer, Fayrer: Henry *Fayrher* 1279 RH (C); Gervas' *Vayr Hyer* 1296 SRSx; Robert *Fairer*, William *Farher* 1327 ib.; William *Feyrere* 1375 ColchCt. OE *fæger* 'fair' and *hær* 'hair', 'one with fair hair'.

Fairest: *v.* FAIRHURST.

Fairey, Fairrie, Fairy, Farey: (i) Lifwine *Feireage* 1050 KCD 1338 (K); Thomas *Feireie* 1231 Pat (O); Ralph *Feyrighe* 1275 RH (W). OE *fæger* 'fair' and *ēage* 'eye'. (ii) Also local, from residence near or employment at some small place such as Fairyhall in Felsted or Fairy Fm in Wethersfield, 'ox or pig enclosure' (PN Ess 422, 467).

Fairfax: Nicholas *Faierfax* 1195 P (Y); William *Fairfax*, *Fayrfex* 1208 Cur (Y), 1219 AssY. OE *fæger* 'fair' and *feax* 'hair'. cf. FAIRER.

Fairfield, Fearfield: Ralph *de Feirfeld* 1327 SRDb; Edmund *de ffeyrefeld'* 1331 FFK. 'Dweller by the fair field.'

Fairfoot, Farfort: Gundwi *de Faierford* 1203 P (Gl); Beatrix *de Faierford* 1209 P (L). From Fairford (Glos) or Farforth (Lincs). Also a nickname, 'fair foot': Adam *Fairefot* 1328 WhC (La).

Fairfoul, Fairfoull, Fairfull: John *Fayrfowel* 1277 AssSo. 'Fair bird' (OE *fugol* 'fowl').

Fairhall, Fairall: Thomas *atte Fayrehale* 1332 SRSx. 'Dweller in the fair nook' (OE *healh*).

Fairham: v. FAIRHOLME

Fairhead: (i) William *Fairhevid* 1279 RH (Hu); John *Feyrhed* 1332 SRWa. 'Fair head' (OE *fæger, hēafod*). (ii) John *Fairhod, Fayrhode* 1299–1311 LLB C, D. A nickname for one noted for his beautiful hood (OE *hōd*). cf. GREENHEAD.

Fairholme, Fairham: Richard *Fairhome* 1379 PTY. 'Dweller by the fair island' (ON *holmr*).

Fairhurst, Fairest: Henry *de Fairhurst* 1260 AssLa. 'Dweller by the fair wood or wooded hill' (OE *hyrst*).

Fairlamb, Fairlem: Found in Manchester, this surname is probably for FARLAM, but a nickname is possible. cf. WHITELAM.

Fairlaw: v. FARLOW

Fairman, Fayerman, Fierman, Fireman: Nicholas *Fairman* 1201 Cur (Sf); Reginald *Feierman, Fareman* 1208 ib. (Nf); Henry *Fayrman* 1297 Min-AcctCo. OE *fæger* 'fair' and *mann* 'man'. As *Fareman* clearly occurs for both *Fayerman* and *Farmann*, it cannot be definitely assigned to either. Robert *Farman* or *Fareman*, 1222 Cur (So), was known also as Robertus *Senex* and Robert *le Bel*, so that *Farman* may be a translation of *le Bel* 'the fair'. v. FARMAN.

Fairrie: v. FAIREY

Fairs: v. FAIR

Fairtlough: v. FAIRCLOUGH

Fairweather, Fareweather: Agnes *Fairweder, Farrweder* c1248 Bec (Nf); Hugh *Fairweder* 1274 RH (L); John *Fayrewether* 1477 AD vi (D); William *Farewedder* 1547 FrY. ME *fair weder* 'weather not wet or stormy', probably 'one with a bright and sunny disposition'. cf. FOUWEATHER, *Manyweathers*, MERRYWEATHER, and John *Cold-wedre* 1327 SRC, Alexander *Starkweder*, William *Skoneweder* 1327 SRSf, Alexander *Ilwedyr* 1316 Wak (Y).

Fairy: v. FAIREY

Faith: William *Feythe* 1389 FrNorw. Probably for *Faithfull*, now fairly common.

Faizey: v. VAISEY

Fake, Falck, Falco: v. FAWKE

Falcon, Faucon, Facon: Reginald *Falcun* 1187 P (Nf); Martin *Faukun* 1318 FFSf; Walter *Fakoun, Faucoun* 1346 FA (Sf). ME *faucon, faukun*, OFr *faucon, falcun* 'falcon'. A nickname from the bird or metonymic for *Falconer*.

Falconer, Falconar, Falkner, Faulconer, Faulkener, Faulkner, Fawckner: Henry *Falkenar* 1194 Cur (W); Richard *facuner* 12th DC (Lei); Henry *le fauconer'* 1219 AssY. OFr *fau(l)connier* 'one who hunts with falcons or follows hawking as a sport'; also 'keeper and trainer of hawks' (1424 MED). The name may also be from a rent. Colard *le ffauconer* in 1264 paid one falcon's hood and 1*d*. yearly for 26 acres of land at Walthamstow (*Ipm*). The surname may also mean 'worker of a crane'. *Faukonarii* worked at Caernarvon Castle in 1282 at 6*d*. per day in summer and 5*d*. in winter. In 1257 a carpenter was paid for making a *faucon*,

a kind of crane or windlass, which the *falconarii* worked (Building 70, 324).

Falgate: v. FOLGATE

Falk: v. FAWKE

Falkner: v. FALCONER

Falkous, Falkus: v. FAWKE

Fall, Falle, Falls, Faull, Fawle: William *de Fall* 1255 RH (O); Gilbert *de la Falle* 1263 AssLa; Geoffrey *del Falles* 1297 SRY; Richard *Fawle* 1579 FrY. 'Dweller by the fall' (ME *falle*), the slope(s) or waterfall(s).

Fallas, Fallis: (i) William *de Faleise, de Falisia* 1086 DB (W). From Falaise (Calvados). v. OEByn. (ii) Isabella *atte Faleise* 1327 SRSx; John *de la Faleyse* of Dunwich 1300 FFSf; Augustine *de la Faleys* of Westleton 1316 FA (Sf); William *Faleys* 1337 ColchCt. Fr *falaise* 'cliff' seems to have been adopted into ME and the surname is also local; the above individuals, like Edmund *de la Klyf* of Brampton, 1346 FA (Sf), lived on the cliffs of Sussex or Suffolk.

Fallover: cf. Joan *Falladun* 1279 RH (O).

Fallow, Fallows: Ralph *de la Falewe* 1272 Ass (Ha); Henry *de Falg(h)* 1327, 1332 SRSx; Thomas *del Falghes* 1376 Bardsley (Ch); Rendul *Fallowes* 1563 ib. 'Dweller by the newly cultivated land', OE *fealg*, ME *falwe*.

Fallowell, Fallwell: John *Falinthewol* 1301 SRY; Henry *ffalliwolle* 1327 SRC; John *Falleinthewall, Falleinthewelle* 1332 SRSt, 1343 AssSt. 'Fall in the well', an interesting nickname.

Fane, Fayne, Faynes, Vaines, Vane, Vanes, Vayne: William *le Vain* 1242 Fees (W); Robert *Fane* 1279 RH (C); Richard *le Feyn* 1378 FFC. OE *fægen*, ME *fein, fayn, fane* 'glad, well-disposed', proverbially opposed to fools: 'Fayne promys makyth folys fayne' (1471 NED). Also used as a personal name: Ivo *filius Fane* 1208 FFL.

Fann, Van, Vann, Vanne, Vanns, Vance: John *del Fan* 1199 MemR (Ess); Richard *ate Fanne* 1297 MinAcctCo (Beds); John *in the Vanne* 1327 SR (Ess); Henry *atte Vanne* 1341 NI (Sx). A form of OE *fenn* 'marsh, fen', common in Essex, Herts and Surrey, and noted also in Beds, Cambs, Suffolk, Middlesex, Kent and Sussex. v. FENN.

Fanner, Vanner, Vannah: (i) William *le Fanner* 1285 *Ass, le Vannere* 1319 *SR* (Ess); John *le Fannere, le Vannere* 1294, 1307 PN Sr. In the southeastern counties, often a derivative of ME *fann* meaning 'dweller by the marsh'. *Fanner* is East Saxon, *Vanner* the southern form of this. In the Sussex Subsidy Roll, Ralph *le Fanner* of 1327 is called Ralph *atte Fanne* in 1332. John *Vanner* (1373 ColchCt) is probably identical with John *Fanner* (1377 ib.) and may be of the same family as John *atte Vanne* (1310 ib.) who is identical with John *Vanneman* (1336 ib.). It seems clear that *Vanner, atte Vanne* and *Vanneman* are synonymous terms for a marsh-dweller. But examples of (ii) may also be found in these counties. (ii) Walter *Fannere* 1279 RH (Bk); John, Walter *le Vanner(e)* ib. (O); Thomas *le vannere* 1297 MinAcctCo (Do); William *le Fanner* 1332 SRWa. In these counties, *fenn* does not become *fann*, hence we have a derivative of OE *fannian* 'to fan, winnow', one who fans, a winnower (c1515 NED), or more probably of OE *fann* 'maker of fans or winnowing-baskets'. cf. John *Fanwryghte, Vanwrighte* 1379 AssEss. In the south *Fanner* was pronounced *Vanner*, which might also be from OFr *vannier* 'basket-maker'. (iii) Roger *le Vanur* 1275 SRWo. A clear example of 'basket-maker' from Fr *vanneur*.

Fanshaw, Fanshawe: John *ffawnchall, Fanshawe,* 1490, 1566 DbAS 30. From Fanshaw Gate in Holmesfield (Derby).

Fant, Fantes, Faunt, Font, Vant: Thomas *Lenfaunt* 1230 P (Sa); William *le Faunt* 1271 ForSt; John *Faunt* 1277 LLB A; Walter *le Font* 1327 SRSx; Alan *Fant* 1327 SRSf. Fr *enfant* 'child'. *Le enfant* became *Lenfant*; this, with dissimilatory loss of the first *n*, became *Lefant*, which was re-divided as *le Fant* and the new article was finally dropped. *Vant* is due to the southern retention of the voiced sound of OE initial *f*. cf. FENN and VENN. Here, it is irregular as French initial *f* was retained. The origin of the shortened *Fant* was forgotten and the word treated as English.

Faragher, Fargher, Faraker: *Farker* 1504, *MacFargher* 1511, *Faragher* 1649 Moore. A Manx equivalent to Gaelic FARQUHAR.

Farbrace: *v.* FIREBRACE

Farbrother: *v.* FAIRBROTHER

Fare, Phare: Peter *ate Fare* 1341 MELS (Sx). 'Dweller by the track or road' (OE *fær*).

Farebrother: *v.* FAIRBROTHER

Fareweather: *v.* FAIRWEATHER

Farewell, Farwell, Varwell: Bartholomew *de Faierwelle* 1180 P (Y); Stephen *Farwel* 1224 Cur (C); Richard *Farewel* 1275 RH (Sf). The first example may derive from Farewell (Staffs) or from a Yorkshire place. *Farewell* appears frequently in Suffolk from 1275 to 1417, always without a preposition, and is, no doubt, a phrase-name, 'Fare well!'.

Farey: *v.* FAIREY

Farfort: *v.* FAIRFOOT

Fargher: *v.* FARAGHER

Farindon, Farenden, Farringdon: Elsi *de Ferendone* 1066 DB; John *de Faringdon'* 1278 RH (O); Roger *Faryndon* 1327 SRSo. From Faringdon (Berks, Dorset, Hants, Oxon), or Farringdon (Devon).

Farlam: Richard *de ffarlham* 1332 SRCu. From Farlam (Cumb).

Farley, Farleigh: William *de Ferlecheia* 1189 Sol; Richard *de Farlegh'* 1222 Acc; John *Farleye* 1332 SRWo. From one or other of the many places of these names.

Farlow, Varlow, Fairlaw: Philip *de Farlawe* 1255 RH (Sa); Richard *Farelowe* alias *Farely* 1706 DKR 41 (Y). From Farlow (Salop) or Fairley (Salop).

Farman: *Farmannus* 1066 Winton (Ha), 1086 ICC (C); *Fareman* 1168 P (So); Richard *Fareman* 1086 ICC (C); Roger *Fareman, Farman* 1260 AssY. ON *Farmann,* ODa, OSw *Farman. v.* also FAIRMAN.

Farmar, Farmer, Fermer, Fermor: William *le Fermer* 1238 FFEss; William *le Farmere* 1279 RH

(C); Richard *Fermor* 1293 Fees (D). AFr *fermer,* OFr *fermier,* MedLat *firmārius* 'one who undertakes the collection of taxes, revenues, etc., paying a fixed sum for the proceeds' (c1385 NED), or, perhaps more frequently, 'one who cultivates land for the owner; a bailiff, steward' (1382 NED).

Farmery: William *del enfermerie* 12th FeuDu; Robert *de la Fermeria* 1203 P (Lei); William *del Fermere* 1301 SRY; Geoffrey *ate Fermerie* 1327 SRSx; Robert *Firmarie* 1366 LLB H. 'Worker at the (monastic) infirmary' (OFr *enfermerie*).

Farn, Farnes: *v.* FERN

Farnall, Farnell, Farnill, Farnhill, Fearnall, Varnals, Vernall: Richard *de Farenhull'* 1214 Cur (Berks); William *de Fernhulle* 1263 Ct (Ha); Hugh *de la Fernhull'* 1275 SRWo; John *de Farnhull* 1275 RH (W); William *atte Farnhulle* 1298 PN Sr 286; Alexander *Farnell* 1414 LLB I; Francis *Fearnall* 1679 Bardsley (Ch). 'Dweller by the fern-covered hill' (OE *fearn, hyll*), as at Farnhill (WRYorks), Fernhill (Ches), Farnell Wood (Kent), Farnell Copse (Wilts), or Vernal in Tichborne (Hants).

Farncombe, Vearncombe: Robert *de Ferncumb* 1296 SRSx. From Farncombe (Surrey).

Farndale, Farndell, Varndell: John *de Farnedale, de Farndall, Fernedill* 1363, 1397, 1409 FrY. From Farndale (NRYorks). *Varndell* must be from some southern place of the same name.

Farnell, Farnill: *v.* FARNALL

Farnfield: William *atte Fernefeld* 1327 SRSo. 'Dweller by the fern-covered land.'

Farnham, Varnham, Varnam: Richard *de Farenham* 1205 P (Sr); Robert *de Farnham* 1219 AssY; John *de Farnam* 1323 FrY; Stephen *Varneham* 1674 HTSf. From Farnham (Bucks, Dorset, Essex, Suffolk, Surrey, WRYorks).

Farnhill: *v.* FARNALL

Farnorth, Farnsworth, Farnworth: Leising' *de Farnewurd'* 1185 P (Ch). From Farnworth (Lancs).

Farquhar, Farquar: *Ferchart* a1178 Black; *Farquhar* Macintosh 1382 ib.; Andro *Farchare* 1450 ib. Gael *Fearchar* 'very dear one'.

Farquharson: David *Farcharsoun* 1440 Black. 'Son of *Fearchar*.'

Faro: *v.* FARRAR

Farr: Nicolas *le ferre* Hy 2 Bart (Lo); Simon *Farre* 1381 ArchC iii. OE *fearr* 'bull'.

Farra, Farrah: *v.* FARRAR

Farraker: *v.* FARAGHER

Farrand, Farrant, Farrants, Farrance, Farran, Farren, Ferrand, Ferran, Ferrans, Ferens, Ference: *Ferrandus* clericus 1190 P (Ess); Herebertus filius *Feran* 1198 FF (Herts); *Ferant* Arblastarius 1249 Fees (Ha); Gilbert, Peter *Ferrant* 1188 P (Wa), 1202 AssL; John *Farrant* 1573 RothwellPR (Y); Roger *ffarrand* 1642 PrGR (La); George *Farrance* 1674 HTSf. OFr *Fer(r)ant* (Ferdinand), or OFr *ferrant* 'iron-grey'.

Farrar, Farrer, Farrah, Farra, Farrey, Farrow, Faro, Pharaoh, Pharro: Hugo *Farrour* 1379 PTY; Roger *Farrer* 1613 FrY; William *Farrar* 1675 ib.; Magister doctor *Pharor,* identical with Dom. Will. *Farar* 1517–18 GildY; James *Farro* 1525 FrY;

William *Farrowe* 1528 GildY; Alys *Farray* 1559 RothwellPR (Y); John *Farry* 1674 HTSf; Tristram *Farrey, Farrer, Farrah* 1632, 1641, 1679 RothwellPR (Y); William *Pharrow*, Fr. *Pharoe* 1674 HTSf; Elizabeth *Pharao* 1702 Bardsley; Giles *Pharaoh* 1760 ib. All these names are variations of FERRER. The unstressed *-er* was slurred in pronunciation and variously spelled *-ey, -ah, -a*, giving *Farrey, Farrah* and *Farra*. This was regarded as an incorrect dialectal pronunciation and the name was re-spelled *Farrow* on the analogy of *barrow*. At Hoxne (Suffolk) in 1835, Dinah *Farrer* signed the marriage register *Farrow* (SfPR). Initial *Ph-* for *F-* is common and *Pharrow, Pharoe* were associated with the biblical *Pharaoh*, which, however, may occasionally be a pageant name or a nickname. cf. Rogero *Pharaone* (abl.) c1158 EngFeud (Nth). *v.* also VARROW.

Farren, Farrin, Varran: John *Farhyn* 1297 MinAcctCo; William *Varyn* 1332 SRSx; Nathaniel *Farren* 1674 HTSf. The second element is ME *hine* 'servant'. *v.* HINE. The first may be OE *fæger* 'fair', found in the 13th century as *Far(e)-* (cf. FARSON), or OE *fearr* 'bull'. Probably 'fair servant', possibly 'bull-herd'.

Farringdon: *v.* FARINDON

Farrow: *v.* FARRAR

Farson: Richard *ffayrson* 1327 SRC; Adam *ffarson* 1332 SRCu. 'Fair son.'

Farthing: (i) *Fardein, Fardan* 1066 DB (Nth, Y); Willelmus *filius Fardain, Fardein* 1163–6 DC (L), William *Farthain* 12th ib. (identical); Reinfrid *filius Farthein* 1166 P (So); Þurlac *Ferðeng* 972–92 OEByn (Nth); Robert *Fardenc* 1086 DB (Sf); Hugo *Ferðing* 1176 P (Y); William *Farding* 1219 AssY. ON *Farðegn*, ODa *Farthin*. This should give *Far-* but as it became late OE *Færðegn*, it might appear as *Far-, Fer-*. *Ferthing* cannot be distinguished from OE *fēorðing* 'a fourth part', 'a farthing'. Both John *Ferthinge* and Margery *Halpeny* were assessed in Pershore in 1327 SRWo. cf. HALFPENNY. In ColchCt, both *Ferthing* 1312–52 and *Farthing* 1334–52 are common. The first example of *farthing* in MED is 1442. (ii) Robert *de la Ferthing* 1279 PN Sx; John *atte fferthynge* 1333 MELS (So). OE *fēorðing* 'a fourth part', used as a measure of land, *ferdin* in Exon, see MED. The meaning was probably 'homestead consisting of a *fēorðing*'. The term survives frequently in minor place-names in Devon, Essex, Surrey and Sussex.

Farwell: *v.* FAREWELL

Fasset: *v.* FAWCETT

Fastolf: *Fastolf* 1066 DB (L); Alexander, William *Fastolf* 1291 FFSf, 1295 AD iv (Nf); Henry *Forstalff* 1451 Rad (C). ON *Fastúlfr*, ODa, OSw *Fastolf*.

Fates, Laffeaty, Laffitte, Lafitte: William *Affaitied* c1162 BM, *Lafeite* 1180 P (Lo); Henry *la Faitie* 1189–99 AD i (Lo); Thomas *Fayte* c1239 Bart (Ess); William *la Feyte* 1262 *For* (Ess); Robert *le Affete* 1276 LLB B; Simon *la Affayte* 1277 FFEss; John *ffaiti* 1319 SRLo; Walter *Laffete*

1327 *SR* (Ess); William *Fayt* 1359 FrY. OFr *afaitié* 'affected, skilful, prudent'. For *Fate*, instead of *Fatey*, cf. PETCH and PETCHEY.

Fathers, Fadder: *Fader* 1066 DB (Nf, Sf) c1095 Bury (Sf); Roger, Alan *Fader* c1095 Bury (Sf), 1167 P (Ha); Robert, Walter *le Fader* 1201 AssSo, 1244 Rams (Hu); John *Father* 1327 SRSx; Juliana *le Faderes* 1332 SRSr. ODa *Fathir*, OSw *Fadhir* is certainly the source of some of the names, but *le Fader* is clearly from OE *fæder* 'father', used in ME of one who exercises protecting care like that of a father, and also of a religious teacher or a confessor.

Fatt: Æðestan *Fætta* 1049–58 OEByn (Wo); Richard *Fatt* 1260 AssC; Hugh *le Fatte* 1327 SRSo. OE *fætt* 'fat'.

Faucett: *v.* FAWCETT

Faucon: *v.* FALCON

Faugh: Hugh *Faluo, Faue, le Fauue* 1222–42 Oseney (O). OE *fealu* 'of a pale brownish or reddish yellow colour', probably of the hair. *Fauue* may be OFr *fauve*. cf. FAVEL.

Faulconer: *v.* FALCONER

Faulder: *v.* FOLDER

Faulds: *v.* FOLD

Faulkener, Faulkner: *v.* FALCONER

Faulk(e)s: *v.* FAWKE

Faull: *v.* FALL

Faun, Faunce, Fawn, Fawns, Fownes: William *filius Faun'* 1230 P (Ha); John *Foun* 1180 P (Nt); Richard *le Foun* 1299 AssSt; Robert *Faun* 1390 LLB H. OFr *faon, foun*, ME *faun, foun* 'a young animal, cub', 'a young fallow deer' (a1382 MED), used, probably, of a lively, frisky youth. Also used as a personal name. The Scottish *Fawns* is from the lands of Fans or Faunes (Berwicks): Richard *de Fawnes* c1150–90 Black.

Faux: *v.* FAWKE

Favel, Favell, Favelle, Favill: Eudo *Faluel* 1160–76 Seals (Y); Rannulf *fauuel'* 1195 P (He); William *Fauel* 1346 AD ii (Wt). OFr *fauvel* 'fallow-coloured, tawny', perhaps with reference to the hair, but also used as a symbol of cunning, duplicity or hypocrisy (c1325 NED).

Fawcett, Fawcitt, Fawssett, Faucett, Fausset, Faussett, Fasset, Fossett, Fossitt: Alan *de Fausyde* 1238 Black; Elias *de ffagheside* 1332 SRLa; John *del ffawside* 1332 SRCu; Richard *Fascet* 1398 FrY; Henry *Fauset, Faucet* 1457, 1481 ib.; Robert *Fawsett* 1548 ib.; Robert *Faucit* 1591 RothwellPR (Y); William *Faucett*, John *Fasset*, Thomas *Fossett* 1674 HTSf. From Fawsyde (East Lothian), Fawcett (Westmorland) or Facit (Lancs). Some of the numerous Yorkshire Fawcetts probably derive from Forcett (NRYorks) which is indistinguishable in pronunciation from *Fawcett* and would naturally become *Fossett*: Thomas *de Forset* 1327 SRY.

Fawckner: *v.* FALCONER

Fawcus: *v.* FAWKE

Fawell: John *Fawvell* 1412 FrY; Richard *Fawell* 1530 ib. For FAVEL.

Fawke, Fawkes, Fawcus, Faux, Falck, Falco,

Falk, Falkous, Falkus, Faulkes, Faulks, Fake, Fakes: *Falco* le Taverner 1274 RH (Lo); *Falc'* de Fonte 1296 SRSx; Tomas *Falch* 1182 P (Wo); Walter *Falc* 1221 AssWo; Geoffrey *Faukes* Hy 3 Gilb (L); William *Faukus* 1251 Rams (Hu); John *Falk* 1275 SRWo; Richard *Fauke* 1305 SIA iii; John *Fakes, Faukys* 1327 *SR* (Ess); Robert *Faukes, Faucous* 1327, 1332 SRSx; Roger *Faux* 1443 Oseney (O). OFr *Fauque, Fauques* (nom.), *Faucon* (acc.), OG *Falco* 'falcon'. *Faucon* may sometimes be the source of FALCON which is usually from the name of the bird. The personal name is best known from the famous (or infamous) Falkes de Breauté whose name occurs as *Falco* 1219 Fees, *Falk* Hy 3 Ipm, *Falkesius* 1219 Cur, *Falkasius* 1222 ib., *Falkes* 1233 Cl and survives in Vauxhall (Surrey). The modern VAUX may thus also derive from this personal name which has also contributed to FOX: Foxhall Fm in Steeple (Essex) owes its name to one John *ffaukes* (1319 PN Ess 228). The name has also been confused with FOLK: Folkes in Cranham (Essex) is named from Thomas *ffakys, ffaukes* (1463, 1473 ib. 125).

Fawle: *v.* FALL

Fay, Faye, Fey: (i) Ralph *de Faia* 1194 P (Sx); Richard *de Fay, de Fago* 1242 Fees (He). From a French place named *Fay* (OFr *fay*, Lat *fagus* 'beech'). (ii) Margaret *le Fey* 1332 SRSr. OFr *fae* 'fairy'.

Fayerbrother: *v.* FAIRBROTHER

Fayerman: *v.* FAIRMAN

Fayers: *v.* FAIR

Fayle: *McFalle* 1408, *Fail* 1511 Moore. Manx for *Mac Giolla Phoil* 'son of Paul's servant'. cf. QUAYLE.

Fayne: *v.* FANE

Fayrer: *v.* FAIRER

Fayter: *v.* FETTERS

Fazackerley, Fazakerley, Phizackerley, Phizackerly, Phizakarley, Phizaclea: Henry *de Fasakerlegh* 1276 AssLa; Lawrence *Phezackerley* 1792 Bardsley. From Fazakerley (Lancs).

Feacey: *v.* VAISEY

Feakes: *v.* FICK

Feakins: *v.* FICKEN

Fear, Feare, Phear: Walter *Fere* 1279 RH (O); Roger *le Feer* 1327 *SR* (Ess). ME *fere* (*feare, feer*) 'companion, comrade' or ME *fere, feer,* OFr *f(i)er* 'fierce, bold, proud'. In some instances we must have the noun *fear:* cf. Rogerus *Timor* 1200 Cur (Bk).

Fearenside: *v.* FEARNSIDE

Fearfield: *v.* FAIRFIELD

Fearman: *v.* FAIRMAN

Fearn(e): *v.* FERN

Fearnall: *v.* FARNALL

Fearnehough, Fearnyhough, Fearnyough: *v.* FERNEYHOUGH

Fearnside, Fearnsides, Fearenside: Nicholas *del ffernyside* 1324 LaCt; Edward *Fearnesyde* 1587 RothwellPR (Y). 'Dweller on the ferny slope' (OE *side* 'side').

Fearon, Feron: Walter *le ferrun* c1179 Bart (Lo); Hervey *le Feron* 1277 AD ii (Mx). OFr *ferron, feron* 'ironmonger, smith'.

Feasey: *v.* VAISEY

Feather, Fedder: Juliana *la Fethere* 1296 SRSx; Adam *ffethir* 1332 SRCu; Antony *Fedder* 1544 RothwellPR (Y). OE *feðer* 'feather', metonymic for a buyer or seller of feathers. cf. Richard *Fethermongere* 1282 LLB A, William *le fetherman* 1275 MESO (Nf), Robert *Le Feþerbycger* 1304 ib. (Ess). But also clearly a nickname for one light as a feather.

Featherby: Ralph *de Fecherbi* 1185 Templars (Y). From Fearby (NRYorks).

Featherston, Featherstone, Fetherston: William *de Federestan* 1187 P (St). From Featherstone (Staffs, WRYorks).

Featherstonehaugh, Featherstonhaugh, Fetherstonhaugh: Elias *de Fetherestanehalg'* 1204 Cur (Nb). From Featherstone (Northumb). The surname preserves the full original form of the place-name.

Feaver, Feavers, Feaviour, Fever, Fevers, Lefeaver, Lefever, Le Fever, Lefevre, Le Fevre, Le Feuvre: Roger *le Fevere* 1243 AssSo; Abraham *le Fevre* 1248 FFEss. OFr *fevere, fevre*, Lat *faber* 'smith'.

Feaveryear, Feavearyear, Feaviour, Feveyear, Fevyer: John *Feveryer*, Robert *Feveryere* 1524 SRSf; Edmonde *Feueryeare* 1568 SRSf; Zimri *Fevier* 1813 SfPR; John *Fevyear* 1826 ib.; Robert *Feaviour* 1829 ib. ME forms of *February. v.* FEVEREL.

Fedder: *v.* FEATHER

Feehally: Thomas *Fitz Harry* 1449 FFEss. A Liverpool form of Irish *Feeharry* 'son of Harry'.

Feek(s): *v.* FICK

Feesey: *v.* VAISEY

Feiling: William *de Fieling* 1203 P (Y). From Fitling (ERYorks).

Feiner: *v.* FAINER

Feirn: *v.* FERN

Felbridge: Roger *de Felebrig'* 1232 Fees (Nf). From Felbrigg (Norfolk).

Feldwick, Feldwicke, Fieldwick: Roger *de Feldwyke* (1296 SRSx) lived at *Feldwycks*, now Old House in West Hoathly (Sussex). *v.* PN Sx 273.

Felgate: *v.* FIELDGATE

Felice, Fillis: *Felicia* 1194 P (Wo), 1207 Cur (Wa), 1218 FFEss; *Felis* 1381 SRSf; Gilbert *Felice* 1279 RH (C); Margaret *ffelys* 1469 SIA xii. *Felis, Phelis* was the English form of Fr *Felise* (f), from Lat *Felicia*, feminine of *Felix*.

Felix: *Felix* monachus 1122 AC (Sx); *Felix* filius Hamonis, Hamo *Felix* 1229 Pat (K); Richard *Felix* 1352 ColchCt. Lat *Felix* 'happy', less common than *Felicia* and also *Felis* in the vernacular, so that the surname may have partly coalesced with *Felice*.

Fell, Fells: (i) Roger *del Fel* 1318 AD iv (Cu); Robert *of the Fell* 1421 FrY. 'Dweller on the fell', ON *fell, fjall* 'fell, mountain'. (ii) William *Fel* 1275 RH (Nb), 1279 ib. (O). Black notes that *Fell* was an old surname in Dundee where Finlay Fell, butcher, passed on his trade and his name to his descendants for over a century from 1533. The surname is metonymic for *fell-monger*, a dealer in hides or skins: Mabel *Felmonger* 1332 SRSr. The Northumbrian example might be for (i) with early loss of the preposition, but that from Oxford certainly belongs here.

Feller, Fella: Robert le *Felur* 1275 SRWo. Either a derivative of OE *fell* 'skin, hide', a fell-monger, or of the verb 'to fell', a feller of timber.

Fellgate: v. FIELDGATE

Fellowes, Fellows: Richard *Felawe* 12th Lichfield (St); Walter *Felagh* 1256 AssNb; Robert le *Felagh* 1327 SRSx. Late OE *fēolaga*, ON *félagi* 'partner, co-worker, companion'. v. FIELDHOUSE.

Fellowship: William *Feliship* 1449 GildY. *Fellowship*, originally 'companionship', came to mean 'membership of a society', perhaps of a guild.

Felt: Metonymic for FELTERS.

Felters: Roger *Feltere* 1220 FrLeic; Robert, John le *Feltere* 1275 RH (L), 1280 AssSo. A derivative of OE *felt* 'felt'. A maker of felt.

Felton: Adam *de Felton'* 1208–9 Pl (Nf); Richard *de Felton* 1301–2 FFSr; Ranulph *Feltone* 1413 CorSt. From Felton (Hereford, Northumb, Salop, Som).

Femister, Fimister, Phemister, Phimester, Phimister: Alexander *Feemaister* 1458 Black; Christian *Phemister* 1595 ib.; James *Fimister* 1684 ib.; Robert *Phimister* 1737 ib. 'The fee-master', one in charge of the flocks and herds.

Fenby: William *de Fenneby* 1274 RH (L); William, Robert *de Fenby* 1381, 1383 AssL. From Fenby (Lincs).

Fendall: Aibrond *de Fendhale* 1191 P (Nf). From Fenhale (Norfolk).

Fender: Robert le *Fendur* 1267 FFHu; Thomas le *Fendour* 1301 SRY. A derivative of *fend*, a shortened form of *defend*, 'defender'.

Fendick: Adam *de Fendyk* 1375 FrY. 'Dweller by the fen-dike.'

Fenemore, Fenimore, Fennemore: v. FINNEMORE

Fenn, Venn: Godwin *de la Fenna* 1176 P (D); Thomas *attefenne* 1185 Templars (Wa); Ralph *de Fenne* 1190 P (L); Herveus *del Fen* 1190 BuryS (Sf); John *atte Venne* 1327 SRSo; Walter *en la Fenne* 1340 SRWo. OE *fenn* 'marsh, fen'. From Fen (Lincs), one of the Devon places called Venn, or from residence near a marsh. cf. FANN.

Fennel, Fennell: (i) William *Fenigle* 1327 SRSx; Henry *atte Fenegle* 1332 SRSx. 'Grower of fennel', a plant cultivated for its use in sauces. OE *finugl*, *fenol*. (ii) William, Cristiana *Fenel* 1327 SRC, SRSo. ME *fenel* used metonymically. (iii) A development of *FitzNeal*. Fennells Wood (PN Bk 201), *Fenelgrove* 1391, is named from Robert *FitzNeel* (1283); Fitznells (PN Sr 75), *Fenelles* 1450–3, derives from Robert le *Fitz Nel* (1332).

Fenner: v. VENNER

Fenton: (i) Walter, Adam *de Fenton'* 1199 Pl (Y), 1230 Cur (Db); William *Fenton* 1382 AssL. From Fenton (Cumb, Lincs, Northumb, Notts, Staffs), Church Fenton (WRYorks), or Venton (Devon).

(ii) John *de Fenton* 1261 Black (Forfar); Alexander *de Fentoun* c1330 ib. From the barony of Fenton (East Lothian).

Fenwick, Finnick, Vinick: Robert *de ffenwic* c1220 Black (Kelso); Walter *del Feneweke* 1275 RH (L); Thomas *de Fenwyk* 1279 AssNb; Nichol *of Fynnyk* c1431 Black (Ayr). From Fenwick (Northumb, WRYorks, Ayrshire) or 'dweller at the dairy-farm in the fen'. *Vinick* is Southern.

Ference, Ferens: v. FARRAND

Fergus: Gillebertus *filius Fergusi* 1180 P (Cu); *Fergus filius Suein* 1188 P (Y); Gilbert *Feregus* 1199 P (Cu); John *Fergus* 1251 AssY. Gael *Fearghus*, OIr *Fergus* 'man-choice'.

Ferguson, Fergyson: John *Fergusson* 1466 Black. 'Son of *Fergus*.'

Fermer, Fermor: v. FARMAR

Ferminger: v. FIRMINGER

Fern, Ferne, Ferns, Fearn, Fearne, Feirn, Farn, Farnes, Fairn, Varnes, Varns, Vern, Verne: John *de la Ferne*, Henry *atte Verne* 1275 SRWo; Joceus *de Ferne* 1296 SRSx. OE *fearn*, used collectively in the singular. 'Dweller among the ferns.' *Verne* is the southern form.

Ferneyhough, Fernihough, Fernyhough, Fearnehough, Fearnyhough, Fearnyough: Adam *de Fernyhough* 1332 SRSt. 'Dweller in the ferny hollow' (OE *holh*).

Feron: v FEARON

Ferrand, Ferran(s): v. FARRAND

Ferrer, Ferrar, Farrer: Henry le *Ferrur* 1196 Cur (Lei); Picot le *Ferur* 1200 P (L, Ha); Hugo, Thomas *Farrour* 1379 PTY. OFr *ferreor*, *ferour* 'worker in iron, smith' (c1400 MED). v. also FARRAR, FAIRER.

Ferrers: Henry *de Feireres, de Fereres, de Ferrariis*, 1086 DB; Henry *Ferreres, Ferrieres* ib.; Hugo *de Ferrers* 1222 Cur (He). The Ferrers, earls of Derby, came from Ferrières-Saint-Hilaire (Eure) and the Ferrers of Bere and Newton Ferrers (Devon) from Ferrières (La Manche). v. ANF.

Ferret: Walter *Feret* 1296 SRSx; John *Furet* 1327 SR (Ess). ME *fyrette, ferette*, OFr *fuiret, furet* 'ferret', lit. 'little pilferer' (c1350 MED).

Ferreter: Walter le *Furettour* 1318 Cl. A derivative of the verb 'to ferret', 'one who searches for rabbits, etc., with a ferret', also 'one who searches closely, a rummager' (1601 NED).

Ferrier, Ferrior: Sibyll le *Feryere* 1279 RH (Hu); John *Feryour* 1390 LoPleas. A derivative of *ferry* 'one who keeps or looks after a ferry' (c1440 NED).

Ferriman, Ferryman: Robert *ferriman* 1192 P (Berks); Richard le *Feriman* 1246 AssLa. ME *feri* and *man*, identical in meaning with FERRIER (1464 MED).

Ferry, Ferrie, Ferri, Ferrey: Walter *de Ferie* 1217 FeuDu; John *del Fery* 1379 PTY. From Ferrybridge (WRYorks), DB *Ferie*, or from residence near a ferry, ME *feri* (c1425 NED), or 'ferryman'.

Fetherston: v. FEATHERSTON

Fetherstonhaugh: v. FEATHERSTONEHAUGH

Fetters, Fayter: Walter *le Faytour* 1255 Rams (Beds); Adam *le Feytur* 1272 FFSt; Ysabella *le Feter* 1279 RH (C). ME, AFr *faitour* 'doer, maker', in the special sense 'impostor, cheat'.

Fettiplace: Thomas *Faiteplace* 1210 Oseney (O); Robert *Fetesplace* 1227 AssBeds; Adam *Feteplace, Fetteplace* 1259–60 Oseney (O); Peter *Fetiplace* 1427 AD vi (O). AFr *fete place* 'make room', probably a name for an usher. A specifically Oxford name, borne by a 14th-century mayor.

Fever: *v.* FEAVER

Feverel: Roger *Feuerelle* 1153–85 Templars (Herts); Robert *Feuerel* 1286 FFEss; Simon *Feverel* 1334 LLB E. ME *feoverel, feverel* (a1225 MED) is a form of *February*, apparently of English origin. 'February is paynted as an olde man sittynge by the fyre' (1389 Trevisa) suggests a possible origin for the nickname. cf. FEAVERYEAR.

Feveyear, Fevyer: *v.* FEAVERYEAR

Fewster, Foister, Foyster, Fuster: Durand, Walter *le fuster* c1179 Bart (Lo), 1272 AD ii (Mx); William *Fuyster* 1557 FrY; William *Fuister*, son of Nicholas *Fewster* 1627 ib. AFr *fuster, fuyster*, OFr *fustier, fuyster, fustrier* 'saddle-tree maker' (1309 NED). *v.* also FORSTER, FOSTER.

Fey: *v.* FAY

Fick, Ficke, Feakes, Feaks, Feek, Feeks: *Ficka* 14th AD vi (St); Semann' *Fike* 1197 P (Nf); Stephen *Fykke*, Walter *Feke* 1332 SRSx, SRSt. *v.* FITCH. *Feek* is from *Fēke*, with lowering and lengthening of the vowel of *Fike*.

Ficken, Feakins: Richard *Ficun, Fycun* 1219 AssY. A diminutive of FICK.

Ficker: William *Fikere* 1230 P (K), John *ffeker* 1327 SRC. *v.* FITCH, FITCHER.

Fickett: Alexander *Fiket* 1206 P (Sr); Richard *Fyket* 1284 FFSf. *v.* FITCH.

Fiddes: Edmund *de Fotheis* 1200–7 Black; Walter *de Fothes* 1328–9 ib.; William *Fudes*, Elizabeth *Fiddes* 1524, 1600 ib. From the barony of Fiddes in Foveran (Kincardine).

Fiddian: *v.* VIVIAN

Fiddy, Fido, Fidoe: John, Walter *Fizdeu, fideu* 1327 Pinchbeck (Sf). Fr *fitz deu* 'son of God'. *v.* FITHIE.

Fidge: Richard, William *Fige* 1198 P (Sx), 1230 P (Lo). *v.* FITCH.

Fidgeon, Fidgen: *v.* VIVIAN. Also for *FitzJohn*. Fidgeons Croft in High Easter is named from Peter *ffitz John* 1403 PN Ess 638. Other Essex farms named Fitzjohns occur as *Figeons* alias *Fitzjohns* 1630, *Phigons* 1776, *Phidgeons* 1777.

Fidgett: *v.* FITCH

Fidkin, Fitkin: Philip *Fidekyn* 1324 Wak (Y). A diminutive of *Fidd*, probably a pet-form of *Vivian*.

Fidler, Fiddler, Vidler: (i) John *le Fithelare* 1275 SRWo, *le ffithelere* 1285 FF (Ess); Simon *Le Vythelar*' 1327 SRWo; John *Fydeler* 1379 PTY. OE *fiðelere* 'fiddler', 'one who plays on the fiddle', especially for hire. *Vidler* is the southern pronunciation. (ii) Hunfridus *Uis de leuu* 1086 DB (Berks), *Vis de lupo* ib. (Ha); Walchelinus *Visus lupi* 1130 P (O), *Videlu* 1198 FF (Sf); William *Visdelou*

1160 P (Sf). OFr *vis de leuu* 'wolf's face', from OFr *vis* (Lat *visus*) 'face' and *leuu* (Lat *lupus*, 'wolf'). *Videlu* would become *Vidloe* and *Vidler*, then be confused with *fiddler*, now the usual form in place-names.

Fidling, Fidlin: Geoffrey *de Fiteling, Fitling* 1193, 1230 P (Y). From Fitling (ERYorks), DB *Fidlinge*.

Fido(e): *v.* FIDDY

Field, Fields, Feild, de la Feld, Delafield: Robert *de Felde* 1185 Templars (Gl); Hugo *de la Felde* 1188 P (Beds); John *del Feld* 1190 BuryS (Sf); James *atte Felde* 1296 SRSx; William *othe felde* 1327 SRWo; John *in theffelde* 1333 MELS; Baldwin *Felde* 1428 FA (Wo). OE *feld*, but, here, probably, with reference to cultivated land or the open fields.

Fielden, Feilden, Velden: William *de la Felden* 1286 Ipm (Wo). The dative plural of OE *feld*, 'one who lives in the fields'.

Fielder: Geoffrey *le Felder* 1327 SRSx. 'Dweller by the field', equivalent to *atte felde* (cf. BRIDGER) or 'worker in the field': *Felders* is an alternative reading for *sowers* in *Piers Plowman* (1393 NED).

Fielders: *v.* FIELDHOUSE

Fieldgate, Felgate, Fellgate, Fellgett, Filgate: Godwin *de Feldegat*' 1203 P (Nf); Elias *de Felgate* 1327 SRWo. From residence near a field-gate, OE *geat* 'gate' (cf. Felgate PN Wo 241), or by a road leading to a field (ON *gata* 'road').

Fieldhouse, Fielders: Thomas *de Feldeshous*, Henry *de Felhouse* 1332 SRSt. 'Dweller at the house in the fields' cf. WOODHOUSE. *Felhouse* may have become *Fellowes*.

Fielding: Ralph *Felding* 1279 RH (Hu); Roger *Fylding* 1327 SRDb; Richard *Feildeinge* 1630 RothwellPR (Y). OE **felding* 'dweller in the open country'.

Fieldsend: John *attefeldesende* 1270 MELS (Wo). 'Dweller at the end of the field.'

Fieldwick: *v.* FELDWICK

Fiennes, Fynes: Sibilla *de Fiednes* 1199 MemR (Berks): William *de Fiennes, de Fiesnes* 1212, 1216 ChR; John *de Fienes* 1332 SRSx. From Fiennes (Pas-de-Calais).

Fierman: *v.* FAIRMAN

Fifehead, Fifefield, Fifield, Fifett, Fifoot: Richard *de Fifhida* 1170 P (Berks); William *de Fiffide* 1236 Fees (W); Richard *Fiffede* 1317 AssK. From Fifehead (Dorset), Fivehead, Fitzhead (Som), Fifield (Oxon, Wilts) or Fyfield (Berks, Essex, Glos, Hants, Wilts), all 'five hides'.

Figg, Figge: John *le Figge* 1327 SRSx; Simon *Figge* 1381 LLB H. *v.* FITCH.

Figgess, Figgis: Thomas *le Fykes, Fykeis* 1281 LLB B, William *Fykays* 1317 AssK. A Norman-French form of OFr *ficheis* 'faithful'.

Figgett, Figgitt: *v.* FITCH.

Figgins: Robert *Fygen*, John *Fygyn* 1545 SxWills. *v.* FITCH.

Filby, Filbee, Filbey, Philby, Philbey: Nicholas *de Filebi* 1202 FFNf; Adam *de Phyleby* 1287 Wenlok; Simon *de Filby* 1310 LLB D. From Filby (Norfolk).

Fildes: Dike *del Filde* 1281 AssLa. From The Fylde (Lancs).

Filer: John *le Filur* 1275 SRWo; John *le Fyler* 1309 SRBeds. OFr *fileur* 'spinner', from *fil* 'thread' or a derivative of ME *filen* 'to file', one who files, smooths, polishes, or of OE *fēol*, *fīl* 'file', a maker of files.

Filgate: *v.* FIELDGATE

Filkin, Filkins: (i) Geoffrey *de Filking* 1185 Templars (O); John *Filekins, Philekinge* 1257–68 Oseney (O). From Filkins (Oxon). (ii) Philip *Filkyn* 1373 AD vi (Ch). A diminutive of *Phil* (Philip). cf. German *Filcoke* 1298 Wak (Y).

Fill, Fills, Filson, Philson: John son of *Fylle* 1344 AD vi (Sa); William *Fille, Phille* 1317 AssK; William *Filleson* 1327 SRWo. *Phill, Fill*, a short form of *Philip*.

Fillary, Fillery: Richard *fiz le Rey* 1245 FFEss; Henry *Filleray, Fyleray, Fiz le Rey* 13th Percy (Sx); William *Fylderay* 1332 SRSx. 'The king's son', AFr *fiz, fil le (de) rei*, with variation in the forms between *fiz* from *fils* from Lat *filius* and *fil* from *filium*. cf. Fitzleroi Fm and Philderayes (PN Sx 127, 177).

Finch, Fink, Vinck, Vink: Godric *Finc* 1049–58 OEByn; Ælfwin *Finche*, Allwin *Finke* 1148–67 ELPN; Gilbert *le Finch* 1205 Cur (Nf); Walter *le Vinch* 1275 SRWo; John *Vynk* 1373 ColchCt. OE *finc* 'finch', as a nickname, perhaps 'simpleton'. *Vinch, Vynk* are southern forms. *Fink* may sometimes be of recent German origin, but is often certainly old. Ælfwin (Aylwin) *Finche, Finke* was of the family which gave name to Finch Lane and St Benet Fink (London), *Finkeslane* in parochia *Sancti Benedicti Finke* 1231 Clerkenwell.

Findlater, Finlator, Finlater: Geoffrey *de Fynleter* 1342 Black. From Findlater (Banffshire).

Findlay, Findley, Findlow: *v.* FINLAY

Fine, Fines: *Fina* 1293 FFEss, 1327 SR (Ess); Richard *Fine* 1196 P (Wa). OFr *fin* 'delicate, tender', or a woman's name *Fina*.

Finer, Finar: Walter *Finor* 1189 FFC; Ralph *le finur* 1218 AssL. OFr *fineur* 'refiner of gold, silver, etc.' (1489 NED).

Finesilver: Hugh *Findsilver* 1279 RH (C). cf. William *Findegold* 1202 FFL. Both may be nicknames or both may be occupational, 'refiner of silver, gold', with intrusive *d*.

Fingard: Robert *Finegod* 1279 RH (Beds); John *fyngod* 1332 SRCu. The earliest example is *Finde-, ffyn(d)godeshurne* 1232, 1285 PN Ess 159. The nickname may be a parallel to *Gathergood* and the opposite of *Scattergood* but the *d* appears to be intrusive and we may have 'fine goods', a nickname for a seller of choice merchandise.

Fink: *v.* FINCH

Finlater: *v.* FINDLATER

Finlay, Finley, Findlay, Findley, Findlow, Finlow: *Fionnlaoich, Findlaech* c1070 Black; *Fynlayus clericus* 1246 ib.; Andrew *Fyndelai* 1526 ib.; Robert *Finlaw* 1567 ib.; John *Findlo* 1639 ib. Gael *Fionnlagh* 'fair hero'.

Finlayson, Finlaison, Finlason: Brice *Fynlawesone* 1296 Black; John *Finlason* 1511 ib. 'Son of *Finlay*.'

Finn, Fynn, Phin, Phinn: *Fin, Phin danus* 1066 DB; *Fin de Haltun* 1143–7 DC (L); Aldeth, Norman *Fin* 1190 BuryS (Sf), 1202 AssL. ON *Finnr*, ODa, OSw *Fin*. Hugo *filius Fin* is identical with Hugo *Fin* 1178–9 P (Y). In Ireland, for *Ó Finn* 'descendant of *Fionn*' (fair).

Finnemore: Richard, William *Finamur* 1204 Cur (D), 1237 FF (Ha). OFr *fin amour* 'dear love'.

Finnick: *v.* FENWICK

Firbank, Furbank: Henry *Firthbank* 1470 FrY; Richard *ffirbanck* 1657 EA (OS) iv. 27 (Sf). 'Dweller by the wooded slope' (OE *(ge)fyrhþe*).

Firebrace, Fairbrass, Farbrace: John *Fierebrache* 1190 P (O); John *Fierbrace* 1196 P (Ess); Robert *Ferbraz* 1221 Pat (Bk); Walter *Firbras* 1280 LLB A; John *Farbrace* 1533 KentW; Charles *Firebrace* 1723 DKR 41 (Sf). OFr *fer, fier*, ME *feer, fere* 'bold, fierce, proud' and Fr *bras* 'arm'.

Fireman: *v.* FAIRMAN

Firk(s): *v.* FRITH

Firmage(r): *v.* FIRMINGER, FURMAGE

Firmin, Firman, Furman: *Firmin' lifget* 1086 ICC (C); Alexander *filius Firmin* 1214–32 AD i (Mx); Richard *Fermin* 1200 Cur (Sf); Stephen *Furmin* 1219 AssY; William *ffyrman* 1522 SIA xii. OFr *Firmin* from Lat *Firminus*, a diminutive of *firmus* 'firm, strong'.

Firminger, Ferminger, Furmenger, Furminger, Firmager: Henry *Furmagier* 1198 P (K); William *le Furmager* 1219 AssY; John *Furmonger* 1490–1508 ArchC 49. OFr *fromagier, formagier* 'maker or seller of cheese'. cf. MESSENGER from *Messager*. *v. also* FURMAGE.

Firth, Frith, Frid, Fridd, Fryd, Freeth, Freed, Vreede, Frift, Thrift, Fright, Freak, Freake, Freke, Firk, Firks: All these surnames derive from various developments of OE *firhþe, (ge)fyrhþe, ferhþe* 'frith, wood, woodland'. (i) The combination *-rhþ-* was difficult to pronounce. The medial *h* was dropped, *firhþe* became ME *firthe, ferthe*: Robert *atte Verthe* 1295 MELS (Sx); Nicholas *atte Ferthe* 1296 SRSx. *Firth* is common in Lancashire and Yorkshire. Vert Wood (Sussex) preserves the southern initial *V*. (ii) By metathesis, ME *firthe* became *frithe, frethe, frid, frede*, and later, dialectal *freeth* and *vreath* (Devon, Glos, Som): Ralph *delfrid* 1176 P (Sr); Wlmar *de Frith* 1195 P (K); John *del Frith* 1201 P (Nf); William *in le Frith* 1276 For (Ess); Nicholas *atte Frithe* 1275 SRWo; Edith *Ythefrithe* 1300 MELS (Wo); Denis *Frede* 1327 SR (Ess); Thomas *atte Vrythe* 1333 MELS (So); Richard *atte Frethe* 1377 FFSx. *Frith* is frequent in Essex, Herts, Sussex, Kent, Wilts; cf. Frid Fm and Wood (Kent), Freath Fm (Wilts), Frieth (Bucks). *Thrift* is a common late development, not so far noted before the 18th century. (iii) If the *h* was preserved, *-hþ-* became *-ht-*: *firhþe* became *friht*, later *fright*, especially in Kent where the surname is common: Serlo, John *del Friht* 1197, 1203 P (K, Nf); Henry *de fricht* c1248 Bec (Bk); John *atte Frizte* 1327 SRSx. cf. Fright Fm (Sussex). (iv) Or, *-hþ-*

became *-kþ-: fyrhþe* became *fyrkþe*, ME *ferkthe*, and, by metathesis, *frekthe, freek:* Alexander *de la Frike* 1275 SRWo; Robert *atte Ferghe* 1327 SRSx; John *atte Ferkche* 1332 ib. cf. Freek's Fm and Frag Barrow (PN Sx 260, 301) and *v.* MELS 72–3.

Fish, Fysh, Fisk, Fiske: Ernis *Fish* 1202 AssL; Daniel *Fisc* 1208 ChR (Sf); Robert *Fisk'* 1230 P (Nt); Robert *le Fysch* 1297 MinAcctCo. OE *fisc* 'fish', a nickname. *Fisc* occurs as a personal name in DB (Nf) and is probably ON *fiskr* 'fish' used as a byname.

Fishbourn, Fishbourne, Fishburn, Fishburne: Richard *de Fisseburn'* 1206 Cur (Lei); Ranulf *de Fissheburne* c1250 FeuDu; William *Fysshebourn* 1332·SRSx. From Fishbourne (Sussex), or Fishburn (Durham).

Fisher: (i) Richard *le Fischer* 1263 FFEss. OE *fiscere* 'fisherman', the common source of this surname. (ii) Ralph *de Fisshar'* 1296 SRSx; Martin *atte Fisshar* ib. 'Dweller by an enclosure for catching fish', OE **fiscgear. v.* Fisher (PN Sx 74) and MELS 65.

Fishlock: Simon *de Fislake* 1204 AssY; William *Fysshlak* 1274 SIA xiii. From Fishlake (WR Yorks). John *Fischlake* (1366 ColchCt) is called *Fisshlaker* in 1367, 'dweller by the fish-stream'. cf. BRIDGER.

Fishman: Randolph *Fissheman* 1474 MEOT (Sx). 'Fisherman, or seller of fish.'

Fishwick: Henry *de Fiswich* 1203 P (La); Robert *de Fisshewyk* 1327 SRY; Roger *Fysshewyk* 1431 FFEss. From Fishwick (Devon, Lancs).

Fisk(e): *v.* FISH

Fitch, Fitchell, Fitchen, Fitchet, Fitchett: Hugh, Roger, William *Fiche* 1243 AssSo, 1297 SRY, 1327 SRSf; *Fichet* 1201 Cur (K); Hugh, Robert, Walter *Fichet* 1176, 1183 P (Do, Nth), 1194 Cur (He). The common derivation of *Fitch* and *Fitchet* from the polecat is untenable. This word is from OFr *fissell*, plural *fissiaulx*, later *fissau*, with forms *fitchewes* 1394, *fycheux* 1418, *fechets* 1535, *fichat* 1653 (NED). This late development of *-et* cannot account for the 12th century *Fichet*. We may compare the French *Fiche, Fichet, Fichot*, which Dauzat derives from OFr *fiche* 'an iron point', from *ficher* 'to fix, plant'. ·*Fitch* is thus 'an iron-pointed implement', used by metonymy for *Fitcher*, the workman who uses this, and *Fitchen* and *Fitchet* are diminutives. As Hugh *Malet* is said to have abandoned for a time his nickname 'little hammer' in favour of *Fichet* (*v.* MALLET), *fiche* must have been used of a pointed weapon, a spear or lance, and *Fitch* and *Fitchett* of a spearman or a knight famous for his exploits with the lance. By the side of these, French has the Norman *Fiquet*, whence the English *Fickett*, the simple *Fick*, with *Feakes* and *Feek(s)*, the diminutive *Ficken*, the occupative *Ficker* and the apparently obsolete Ædredus *Fikeman* 1180 P (Wo), Nicholas *Fekeman* 1327 SRSf. Richard *fikberd* (1277 Ely) probably wore a pointed beard. With these names must be taken *Figg, Figgett, Figgitt*, and *Figgins*, with the non-surviving diminutive Alfwinus *Figgel* 1166 P

(K), Richard *Figel* 1279 RH (Beds), where we have the voicing of *k* to *g* as in *Picot* and *Piggott*. Here, too, must belong *Fidge*, and *Fidgett*, with a similar voicing of *ch* to *dg*. No early examples of *Fidgett* have been found. It cannot be associated with the common *fidget* which occurs too late to have given a surname, apart from the difficulty of derivation. *Fitch*, like *Fick* and *Fichet*, may have been used as a personal name. cf. also *Fechel* de Fercalahn 1225–50 Dublin. This would account for the diminutives. *Fitcher, Ficker* and *Fikeman* must be occupational.

Fitcher: Roger *Fychere*, Richard *Fichere* 1327 SRSf. *v.* FITCH.

Fitchew, Fitchie: *v.* FITHIE

Fithie, Fithye: (i) Alice *Feithew* (widow of Henry, lord *Fitzhugh*) 1473 GildY; Edward *Fythewe, Fitzhugh* 1492, 1497 ib.; John *Fyddie* 1609 FrY. A colloquial pronunciation of *FitzHugh* 'son of Hugh'. This probably also became *Fitchew* and *Fitchie*. (ii) In Scotland, from Fithie in Farnell (Angus): Henry *of Fythie, de Fethy* c1328 Black.

Fitkin: *v.* FIDKIN

Fitter: Geoffrey, Hugh *le Fittere* 1195 P (Wa), 1231 Cl (Gl). 'A fitter.' Bardsley suggests 'carpenter'. In northern dialect the term meant one 'who vends and loads coals, fitting ships with cargoes' (Halliwell).

Fitton: (i) Richard *ffyton* 1188 WhC (La); Richard *Fitun* 1195 P (Wa). In ME *fitten* was a common term for lying, deceit. (ii) Alan *de Fittun* c1213 Fees (C). From Fitton Hall in Leverington (Cambs).

Fitz, Fitze: Reginald *le Fiz* 1193 P (Wa); Robertus *Filius*, Robert *Fiz* 1212 Cur (Y); Bartholomew Burghassh *le Fitz* 1346 FA (Sf). AFr *fiz* 'son'. The last example perhaps gives a clue to the meaning. It is apparently used to distinguish the son from the father. Names like *Fitzalan, Fitzwilliam*, etc., have acquired an aristocratic flavour. Early examples are rare. Osbertus *le fiz Fulco* 12th EngFeud (Y), etc., usually appear in documents as Osbertus *filius Fulconis* and at this period were descriptions rather than surnames. This Latin form has often been translated into French by historians and genealogists, and, unfortunately, sometimes by editors of documents who have thus created families of FitzOdo, Fitz-Thomas, etc., at a time when the family had no fixed surname. In colloquial speech, the *fitz* was liable to various forms of assimilation to the following consonant, thus giving *Fithie* and *Fitchew* for *FitzHugh, Fidgeon* for *Fitzjohn, Filleray* for *FitzRoy, Fennell* for *FitzNeal, Feehally* for *Fitz-Harry*. For FITZGERALD, FITZPAYN, etc., *v.* GERALD, PAYN, etc.

FitzAlan: *v.* ALLAIN

FitzAucher: *v.* ALGER

FitzHugh: *v.* FITHIE, HUGH

FitzNeal: *v.* FENNEL, NEAL

Fitzroy: Henry *fis le Rey* 1296 SRSx. cf. FILLARY.

Fitzwater: *v.* WALTER, WATER

Fladgate: *v.* FLOODGATE

Flagg: Peter *de la Flagge* c1280 SRWo; Henry *del Flagg* 1327 SRDb. ON *flaga* 'a flagstone', or ON *flag* 'a turf, sod'. Hence 'dweller at a place where turfs were cut or flagstones obtained', as at Flagg (Derby), or Flags (Notts).

Flaherty: *v.* O'FLAHERTY

Flamank: *v.* FLEMING

Flambard, Flambert: Robert *Flambard* 1158 CartAntiq; John, Matthew *Flambard* 1218, 1303 FFEss. OFr *flambard* 'a flaming torch'. The earliest and best known of the name was Ranulf Flambard, bishop of Durham 1099–1128. He appears as *Ranulfus capellanus* 1087–99 StP, but his original nickname appears to have been *Passeflambard*, cf. Randulf *Passeflambard* of Dunholme 1128 ASC E, Radulfus *Passeflambard*, Randulfus *Basseflambard* 12th LibEl. This is a phrase-name 'pass on the flaming torch'.

Flanagan: Ir *Ó Flannagáin* 'descendant of *Flannagán*' (red).

Flanders, Flinders: Euerdai *de Flandria* a1191 DC (L); Thomas *Flaundres* 1327 SRSo. From Flanders.

Flann: *v.* FLAWN

Flanner: Richard *le Flauner* 1211 FrLeic; Reginald *Flawner* 1222–32 Seals (Herts); Walter *le flaoner* 1246–89 Bart (Lo); Simon *le Flanner* 1260 AssC. OFr *flaonnier*, *flaunier* 'maker of flawns', a kind of custard or pancake. *v.* FLAWN.

Flash, Flasher, Flashman: Felicia *Flasche* 1279 RH (C); Habram *de Flaskes* 1301 SRY; William *del Flosche* 1314 Wak (Y). 'Dweller by the pool or marshy spot', ME *flasshe*, *flask*.

Flatman: Thomas *Flatman* 1568 SRSf. *v.* FLATT.

Flatt: Geoffrey *del Flate* 1327 SRDb; Thomas *del Flat* 1349 FrY. 'Dweller on the level ground.' ON *flatr*.

Flawn, Flann: Elena *fflaun* 1327 SRC; John *Flaoun* 1357 LLB G. OFr *flaon*, ME *flaun*. Metonymic for FLANNER.

Flaxman, Flexman: William *Flexman* 1279 RH (Hu); Nicholas *Flaxman* 1332 MESO (Nf). *v.* FLEXER and cf. Cristina *Flexwyf* 1378 LLB H; Crispin *Flaxbeter*' 1219 AssY; Richard *le flexmongere* 1294 RamsCt (Hu); John *Flax* 1327 SRY.

Fleeman: *v.* FLEMING

Fleet: (i) Richard *de Flet* c1158 Gilb (L); Simon *ate Flete* 1297 MinAcctCo; Alicia *del Flete* 1327 SRSf. From Fleet (Lincs) or 'dweller by the estuary or stream', OE *flēot*. (ii) John *le Fleet*, *le Fleot* 1327 SRSo. ME *flete* 'swift'. cf. OE *flēotig*.

Fleming, Flemming, Flemons, Flemyng, Fleeming, Fleeman, Flamank, Flament, Flement, Le Fleming: Serlo *le Flemyng* c1150 Gilb (L); William *le Flamanc, Flandrensis, Flamanc* 1219 AssY; Adam *Flemyng* 1296 SRSx; Thomas *Flemin* 1644 FrY; Richard *Fleaming* 1648 ib.; Isaac *Fleeming* 1674 ib.; David *Fleemen* 1697 ib. AN *fleming*, OFr *flamanc* 'a Fleming' (c1430 NED). cf. FLANDERS.

Flesher: (i) Richard *le Fleshewere* 1268 MESO (Y); Albred *le Flesshewere* 1311 FFC; Richard *Flesseure* 1374 AD ii (Bk); Thomas *Flesshour, Flesshuer* 1453, 1455 GildY. OE *flǣsc* 'flesh' and a

derivative of *hēawan* 'to cut', 'a butcher'. (ii) Adam, John *Flescher* 1379 PTY; Richard *Flescher* 1410 GildY. A derivative of *flesh*, with the same meaning, 'butcher'. The surname has been confused with *Fletcher*, Fletcher Gate at Nottingham was formerly Flesher Gate (PN Nt 17).

Fletcher: Robert *le Flecher* 1203 AssSt; William *Flecher*' 1203 Cur (La); Peter *le flechier* 1227 AssBeds. OFr *flechier, flecher* 'maker or seller of arrows' (c1330 MED).

Fleury, Florey, Flory, Flury: (i) Ranulf *de Flury* 1201 AssSo; Hugh *de Flori*, Giles *Florey* 1286, 1295 FFEss. From Fleury, a common northern French place-name. (ii) *Fluri* 1192 P (Ha); *Floria* 1193 P (Lo), 1221 AssWa; Gilbert *Fluri* Hy 2 DC (L); John *Flory* 1230 P (Nf). A woman's name, ultimately from Lat *flos* 'flower'. There was a Spanish saint Floria, martyred in the 9th century.

Flewett, Flewitt, Flowitt: Hubert *flohardus* 1130 P (Lei). A rare name, probably OG *Hlodhard* 'glory-strong', surviving in France as *Floutard*. For the loss of *d*, cf. *Floheld, Fluold* (Forssner 90).

Flexer: Richard *Le Flexere* 1316 MESO (Ess); Roger *Flaxer* 1329 ib. (Nf). A derivative of OE *fleax, flex*, 'dresser or seller of flax'. cf. Robert *Flexhewer* 1367 AD i (Lo).

Flexman: *v.* FLAXMAN

Flinders: *v.* FLANDERS

Flinn: *v.* O'FLINN

Flint, Flindt: (i) *Flint* 1066 DB (Sf); John, William *Flint* c1248 Bec (O), 1250 Fees (Bk). OE **Flint*, an original nickname from OE *flint* 'rock', or a nickname, 'hard as a rock'. (ii) William *del, de Flynt* 1291–2 AssCh; John *del Flynt* 1345 FrY. From Flint or 'dweller by the rock'.

Flitter: Robert *le Flittere* 1196 FF (Nf). OE *flītere* 'a disputer', later 'a scold', from OE *flītan* 'to contend, wrangle'.

Float, Floate, Flote: Ralph *Flot* 1155–8 Holme (Nf); Roger *Flote* 1166 P (Y). OE *flota* 'boat, ship', metonymic for FLOATER, FLODMAN.

Floater: William *le Flotyere* 1249 MEOT (Sx); Ralph *le Floter* 1281 ib. (L). A derivative of OE *flota* 'ship', a sailor.

Flodman: Walter, John *Floteman* 1215 Oseney (O), 1524 SRSf. OE *flotmann* 'sailor'.

Flood, Floud, Flude: Wigot *de la Flode* 1198 P (Berks); Roger *flod* c1200 DC (L); Adam *del Flod* 1244 Rams (Beds); Thomas *atte Floud* 1327 SRSx. 'Dweller by the stream (OE *flōd*) or channel, gutter (OE *flōde*)'.

Floodgate, Fladgate: Walter *atte Flodgate* 1327 SRSo. 'Dweller by (or keeper of) the flood-gate' (OE **flōdgeat*).

Florence: (i) *Florentius* 1130–2 Seals (St); *Florentius de Grotene* 1201 Cur (Sf); *Florentia, Florencia* 1207–8 Cur (Sr, W); Richard *Florenz* 1220 Oseney (O); Gilbert *Florence* 1250 FFSf. *Florence*, both masculine and feminine, Lat *Florentius, Florentia*, from *florens* 'blooming'. (ii) Bartholomew *de Florence* 1273 RH (Y), Skelmynius *de Florentia* 1334 FrY. From Florence (Italy).

Florey: *v.* FLEURY

Flote: v. FLOAT

Floud: v. FLOOD

Flower, Flowers: (i) William *Floere*, John *le Floer* 1275 RH (D). ME *flöer*, a derivative of ME *flö*, OE *flā* 'arrow', an arrow-maker. (ii) William *Flur* 1203 P (Y); Edmund *Flour* 1313 FFEss; John *Flower* 1517 FrY. ME *flur, flour*, OFr *flur* 'flower', used already in the 13th century of persons, usually with the epithet 'sweet', and as a woman's name: *Flur', Flour'* 1297 MinAcctCo. cf. Robert *Flouressone* 1325 AssSt. The same forms were used for *flour*, the 'flower' of the meal and the surnames may denote a maker of flour: Robert *le fflourmakere* 1332 SRLo, who may be identical with Robert *Flourman* 1338 LoPleas, though this latter surname may also mean 'servant of Flower'. cf. Walter *Floureman* or *Floureknave* 1309 RamsCt (Ess).

Flowitt: v. FLEWETT

Floyd, Floyde, Floyed, Flude: Richard, John *Floyd* 1509, 1532 LP; Griffin *Floyde* 1544 Musters (Sr); William *Floyd* alias *Flowde* 1560 Pat (Lo). A form of LLOYD.

Flude: v. FLOOD

Flury: v. FLEURY

Flute: Metonymic for *fluter*. v. FLUTTER.

Flutter: Arnulf *Flouter* 1224 Pat (Db); William *the Floutere* 1268 FFY. A derivative of ME *floute* 'to play on the flute', flute-player.

Foad, Foat, Food: Elfred *fode* 1221 *ElyA* (Nf); Richard *Food, Vod, Wod, le Vod* 1237 HPD (Ess); Thomas *Vood, le Fod* 1251, 1262 ib.; Hugo *le Vode, le Wode* 1317 AssK. OE *föda* 'food', later 'that which is fed', 'a child' (a1225 MED). *Vod* shows the southern pronunciation, *Wod*(e) early examples of the dialectal change of initial *V* to *W*. This has probably contributed to the frequency of *Wood*.

Foakes: v. FOLK

Foale: Robert, Reginald *Fole* 1193 P (Wa), 1279 RH (Hu). OE *fola* 'foal', perhaps a nickname, 'frisky', but in the 14th century used of persons in the sense 'ragged: rough, shaggy'.

Foard: v. FORD

Foat: v. FOAD

Focke: v. FOLK

Fodor: Roger *le Fodere* 1327 SRSf; Walter *Fodere, Fodier* 1327, 1332 SRSx. A derivative of ME *födien* 'to feed', a feeder of cattle.

Foers: v. FOWER

Fogarty, Fogerty, Fogaty, Foggarty: Ir *Ó Fógartaigh* 'descendant of *Fógartach*' (banished).

Foister: v. FEWSTER

Foker: v. FULCHER

Fokes: v. FOLK

Fold, Foldes, Folds, Fould, Fouldes, Foulds, Fowlds, Faulds: Hugh *del Foldis* 1275 Wak (Y); Adam *in le Fold* 1327 SRDb; John *atte Fold* 1327 SRSo; Adam *de Falde* 1332 SRSt; John *del ffald* 1332 SRCu. 'Worker at the fold(s) or cattle-pen(s)', OE *falod*, later *fäld*, ME *fold*.

Folder, Faulder: Iuo *faulder* 1332 SRCu. v. FOLD.

Folgate, Falgate: Peter *de le Falgate*, Richard *de Faldgate* 1275 RH (Nf). 'Dweller by the foldgate', OE *falod, geat*.

Folger: v. FULCHER

Foljambe, Fulljames: William *Foleiambe* 1172 P (Db); Tomas *Folegambe* 1206 P (Nth); John *Fulgeam* 1533 Bardsley; Godfrey *Fuljambe* 1588 Shef (Y). OFr *fol* 'foolish, silly' and *jambe* 'leg', probably, as suggested by Lower, for a useless, maimed leg, the opposite of BELGIAN. In OFr *fol* was used of something useless or of little value: *farine folle* 'mill-dust', *figue folle* 'a good-for-nothing fig'.

Folk, Folke, Folkes, Folks, ffoulkes, Foulkes, Foulks, Fulk, Fulkes, Fulks, Fewkes, Foakes, Fokes, Fookes, Fooks, Foukx, Foux, Fowke, Fowkes, Fuke, Voak, Vokes, Volk, Volke, Volkes, Volks: *Folco, Fulco* 1086 DB; *Folche* Ribalt c1155 Gilb (L); *Folc'* filius *Folc'* 1156–80 Bury (Sf); Alan *filius Fuke* 1166–95 Seals (Lei); Willelmus *filius Fulk* 1177 P (L); Ricardus *filius Fuc* 1196 Cur (He); *Folco, Fulko picus* 12th DC (L); *Fouke de Coudrey* 1255 RH (Bk); *Folkes* 1279 RH (C); *Foke* Odell 1503 ParlR (Nth); *Fooke* Edmonds 1611 Bardsley; Peter *Fulch'* 1198 FF (So); Richard *Fulc* t John HPD (Ess); Robert *Fuke* 1209 P (Nf); Richard *Foke* 1221 AssWo; Robert *Fulco* 1227 AssSt; Hugo *Fouke* 1275 SRWo; Robert *Folke*, Juliana *Folkes* 1279 RH (C); John *Fukes* 1296 SRSx; Richard *Foulk* 1297 MinAcctCo; Alice *Fouke, Foukes* 1307, 1314 Balliol (O); Walter *Fowke* 1311 ColchCt; John *Fokes* 1317 AssK; William *Fulke* 1333 ERO (Ess); Blanch *Fokes*, James *Fooxe*, John *Foockes*, Raphe *Fookes* 1564 SRSf; Thomas *Foakes* 1796 Bardsley. OFr *Fulco, Fouques*, OG *Fulco, Folco* 'people'.

Folkard, Folkerts, Foucard: *Fulcardus sacerdos* 1101–25 Holme (Nf); *Folcardus presbiter* 1121–48 Bury (Sf); *Fucard (Fulcardus)* filius Johannis 1198 FF (Sf); Rogerus *filius Folkart* 1219 AssY; Rau *Folkard* c1100 OEByn (D); John, Richard *Folkard* 1327 SRSf. OG *Fulcard* 'people-brave'.

Folker: v. FULCHER

Folkson, Foxon, Foxen: Roger *Folkesune* Ed 1 NottBR. 'Son of Folk.'

Foll: William *le fol* 1202 AssL; Robert *Folle* 1202 P (L); Simon *le Fu* 1273 Ipm. OFr *fol*, modFr *fou* 'foolish, silly'.

Follenfant: Hugo *Folenfant* 12th DC (Nt); John *Folenfant, Fol Enfant, Foleinfant* 1200–12 Cur (Ess). OFr *fol* 'foolish' and *enfant* 'child'.

Follet, Follett, Follit, Follitt: William *Folet* 1086 DB (K); Roger *Folet* 1158 P (K). OFr *folet*, a diminutive of *fol* 'foolish'.

Folley, Folly: Richard *de la Folia* 1176 P (W); Thomas *de la Folie* 1214 Cur (Nf). *Folly*, common in minor place-names, especially in Warwicks and Wilts, originally had reference to some example of human folly, amusement or pleasure, but occasionally is used of a small plantation, a usage difficult to explain. The above examples are clearly from Fr *folie* 'foolishness' and are earlier than any previously noted (1228). The first example probably refers to one of the places called Folly in Wilts. *v.* PN Wa 382–5, PN W 451, PN C 353.

Follick: *v.* FULLICK

Fontaine: *v.* FOUNTAIN

Food: *v.* FOAD

Fook(e)s: *v.* FOLK

Foord: *v.* FORD

Foort: *v.* FORT

Foot, Foote: Seild filia *Fot* 1212 Cur (Ha); Ernui, Goduin *Fot* 1066 DB (Ch, K); Robert *Fot* 1166 P (Y); Gregorious *cum pede* 1271 FrLeic; Henricus *Pes* 1290 ShefA. Either the ON nickname *Fótr* 'foot' or OE *fōt* 'foot', translated by the Lat *pes*.

Footman: Thomas *Fotman* 1327 Pinchbeck (Sf), 1332 SRCu. OE *fōt* and *mann*, 'footman', probably 'foot-soldier' (c1325 MED).

Forber: *v.* FURBER

Forbes: Duncan *de Forbeys* c1272 Black. From Forbes (Aberdeenshire).

Forcer: Ralph *le forcier, le Forcer* 1210 P, 1221 AssWa; William *le Forcir* 1228 Fees (Sa). A derivative of *force*, from OFr *forcer* 'to clip or shear wool', from *forces* 'clipping-shears'; 'one who forces wool'. cf. 'Sheer-men and Dyers, Forcers of Wools, Casters of Wools and Sorters of Wools' (1533 NED).

Ford, Forde, fforde, Foard, Foord, Forth: Bruman' *de la forda* 1066 Winton (Ha); Eadric *æt Fordan* 1100–30 OEByn (So); Reginald *de la Forthe* 1273 RH (Sf); Geoffrey *atte Forde* 1296 SRSx; William *Foorde* 1418 LLB I. 'Dweller by the ford' (OE *ford*) or from Ford (Som, etc.).

Forder: William *Forder* 1327 SRSx. 'Dweller by the ford.'

Fordred: *Fordretus* 1084 Exon (So); Ivo *Fordred* 1275 RH (K). OE *Forðrǣd* 'forth-counsel', common in the 9th century, but rare thereafter.

Fordyce: John *Fordise* 1460 Black; William *Fordyce* 1567 ib. From Fordyce (Banff).

Foreman, Forman, Fourman: Robert, Cristina *Foreman* 1296 Black, 1301 SRY; Alan *Forman*, Robert *Fourman* 1327 SRY. OE *fōr* 'pig' and *mann*, 'swineherd'. The surname may also have absorbed *Fordman*: Robert *Fordman* 1327 *SR* (Ess), 'dweller by the ford'.

Foresight: *v.* FORSYTH

Forester, Forestier, Forrester, Forrestor: John *Forester* 1183 P (Sr); Richard *le Forester* 1240 FFEss; Robert *le Forestier* 1322 LLB E. OFr *forestier*, ME *forester* 'officer in charge of a forest' (c1325 MED), also used of one employed in a forest. At Pulham (Norfolk) in 1222 a free tenant held 20 acres *per servicium forestare*. In 1277, at Hitcham (Suffolk), Robertus *forestarius*, a free tenant, paid 4*s.* 8*d.* and suit of court for 17 acres. He had to guard all the woods of his lord, the Bishop of Ely, and had various forest privileges including one log for his fire at Christmas, all trees and branches in the woods blown down in a storm, and the right to keep his pigs in the wood (*ElyA*). *v.* also FORSTER, FOSTER.

Forfeitt: Sexi *Forfot* 1137 ELPN. OE *fōr* and *fōt* 'pig-foot'.

Forge: Ralph *del Forge* 1297 Coram (Y). 'Worker at a forge', blacksmith.

Forley, Fortly: Stephen *Forle* 1279 RH (Hu). From Fordley (Suffolk).

Forman: *v.* FOREMAN

Former: Simon *le Formur* 1219 AssY. ME *former* 'maker, fashioner' (c1340 NED), 'Brycke former or maker' (1552 ib).

Forrest: Hugh *de Foresta* 1204 Cur (Ha); Adam *ate Forest* 1300 Ipm (K); Anabilla *del fforest* 1354 Kirkstall (Y). 'Dweller or worker in the forest.' *v.* FORESTER.

Forrester, Forrestor: *v.* FORESTER

Forsbrook: *v.* FOSBROOKE

Forsdick, Forsdike, Forsdyke: *v.* FOSDIKE

Forse: *v.* FOSS

Forsey: *v.* FURSEY

Forst: *v.* FROST

Forster: John *Forster* 1315 AssC; William *le Forster* 1341 AD iv (L); Richard *Forstier* 1381 AD ii (Mx). Various origins are possible: (i) A shortened form of FORESTER (*forster* c1320 NED): Walter *Forster, Forester* 1356 LLB G. (ii) Equivalent to FEWSTER: Warin *le forstere* 1199 Bart (Lo) may have been a forester, in which case we have a very early example of this development, but more probably he followed the same occupation as Durand *le fuster* (1179), 'the saddle-tree maker'; OFr *fustrier* could, by metathesis, become *furster* or *forster*; cf. Gilbert *Le Furstare* or *le Fuster* 1305 MESO (Wo); John *Forstar* 1202 Cur (Y); Walter *le Forster* 1275 SRWo; Robert, Adam *Forster*, Robert *Foster* 1327 ib. (iii) OFr *forcetier* 'maker of scissors, shearer, cutler': Richard *le Forseter, le Forceter* 1311 ColchCt. cf. AFr *forcettes* 'scissors', a diminutive of *forces* (1474 NED). *v.* FORCER. *Foster* is common in ColchCt, *Forester* rare. cf. William *Forset* 1214 Cur (Bk), 1441 FrY from *forcettes*, 'a maker of scissors'. This does not seem to have survived. It has probably been absorbed by *Fawcett*.

Forsyth, Forsaith, Forseith, Foresight, Forsyde: (i) Osbert *filius Forsyth* c1308 Black (Stirling); *Fersith, Forsyth* 1364 ib.; *Fersithi* mag Uibne 1464 Black; Robert *Fersith* 1420 ib. (Stirling); James *Fersith, Forsithe* 1446 ib. Gaelic *Fearsithe* 'man of peace'. (ii) William *de Fersith* 1365 Black (Edinburgh); Robert, Thomas *de Forsith* 1426, 1487 ib. From an unidentified place of this name.

Fort, Forte, Foort, Lefort: Fegge *Fort* 1200 Cur (L); Isabel *le Fort* 1268 AssSo. AFr, OFr *fort* 'strong'.

Fortescue, Foskew: Richard *Fort Escu, Fortescu* 1177, 1185 P (D); Oliver *Fortescue* 1212 Cur (Co). OFr *fort escu* 'strong shield'.

Fortey, Forty, Fortye: William *de Forteye*, Thomas *de la Fortheye* 1275 SRWo; John *ate Fortheye* 1297 MinAcctCo (Berks); John *de la Forteye* 1318 Cl (Berks). OE **forþ-ēg* 'forth-island', land standing well out from surrounding marsh or fen, or, possibly, OE **forþ-tēag*, from *tēag* 'enclosure', a paddock in front of or near the farm-house. Cf. Forty Green (Essex, Worcs), The Forty (Wilts),

Forty Hill (Middlesex) and *v.* PN Wo 202, PN Ess 23, MELS 69–70.

Forth: *v.* FORD

Fortly: *v.* FORLEY

Fortman: William *Fortesmains* 1219 AssY. 'Strong hands.'

Fortnam, Fortnum: Nicholas *Fortanon* 1279 RH (O). OFr *fort anon* 'strong young ass'.

Forty: *v.* FORTEY

Forward, Forwood: Bartholomew *Forward, Forreward* 1279 RH (C); Florence *Forewardes* 1327 *SR* (Ess). OE *fōr* 'pig, hog' and *weard* 'guard, watchman', 'swineherd'. cf. Thomas *Blleward* 1319 *SR* (Ess), from *bull* and *v.* COWARD.

Fosbrooke, Forsbrook: Osbert *de Fotesbroc* c1190 StCh. From Forsbrook (Staffs).

Fosdike, Fosdyke, Forsdick, Forsdike, Forsdyke: Walter *de Fotesdik* 1202 AssL; John *Fosdyke* 1524 SRSf. From Fosdyke (Lincs). cf. FOSBROOKE.

Foskew: *v.* FORTESCUE

Foss, Forse, Vos, Voss: John *del Fosse* 1199 MemR (Sx); John *atte, de la Fosse* 1295, 1330 MELS (So). 'Dweller by the ditch' (OE **foss*). In Somerset the surname is recorded from Doulting and Shepton Mallet, on each side of the Fosse Way, along which lie three farms named *Fosse* in Wilts, four in Warwicks and two in Notts. The initial *V* in *Voss* is southern. cf. Voss (Robert *atte Fosse* 1330 PN D 254).

Fossey: Arnold *de la Fossie* 1282 LLB A; John *del Fossey* 1297 SRY; Richard *Fossey* 1279 RH (O). 'Dweller by the low-lying land near the dike', OE **foss, ēg*. The Ampthill *Fossey* is from a lost place *Fotsey* in Aspley Guise, *Foteseige* 969 PN BedsHu 114.

Foster: John *Foster* 1373 ColchCt; Edward *Foster* 1381 AssC. This may be ME *foster* 'foster-parent, nurse' (a1225 MED), found once in the compound OE *cild-fōstre*. But it may also be: (i) a development of FORESTER (1386 NED) or FORSTER 'forester'. The seal of Walter *Forestier* (1371 AD v, Lo) bore the legend: SIGILLVM. WALTERI. LE. FOSTER. (ii) from *Forseter* 'shearer', which would inevitably become *Forster* and then *Foster*, which is common in the ColchCt. (iii) equivalent to FEWSTER, OFr *fustrier* becoming *furster, forster* by metathesis, and then *foster*. *v.* FORSTER.

Fothergill: Henry *Fodyrgyll* 1514 CorNt; William *Futhergill*, John *Fothergill* 1583, 1611 FrY. From Fothergill Well (WRYorks), or from other minor places of the name.

Foucar: *v.* FULCHER

Foucard: *v.* FOLKARD

Foukx: *v.* FOLK

Foulcher, Foulger, Foulker: *v.* FULCHER

Fould(e)s: *v.* FOLD

Foulkes: *v.* FOLK

Foulser: *v.* FULCHER

Foulston, Foulstone, Fowlestone, Fowlston, Fullstone: Robert *de Fugeleston* 1197 FFK; Robert *de Foweleston* 1251 AssY. From Fulston Manor in Sittingbourne (Kent) or Fulstone (WRYorks).

Fountain, Fountaine, Fontaine: Hugo *de Funteines* 1202 P (K); John *de Funtayne* 1270 FFEss; John *de la Funtayne* 1275 AssSo; John *Fowntens* 1426 FA (Sr). 'Dweller near the spring(s)', OFr *fontaine*, ME *fontayne* (a1450 MED). Probably from a French place named Fontaine, Fonteyne or Lafontaine.

Fouracre, Fouracres, Foweraker: William *Fourakre* 1327 SRSo; William *Foweracres* 1682 DWills. 'Occupier of a holding of four acres.'

Fourman: *v.* FOREMAN

Fournel: *v.* FURNELL

Fourniss: *v.* FURNACE

Fouweather, Foweather, Fowweather: John *Fulweder* 1284 FFHu; William *Foulweder* 1342 Rams (Hu). ME *foul wedir* (c1380 NED) 'wet and stormy', the opposite of FAIRWEATHER.

Foux: *v.* FOLK

Fowell(s): *v.* FOWLE

Fower, Foers: Ansger' *Focarius, Fouuer* 1084 GeldR, 1086 DB (So); Turkillus *le foer* 1190 P (Wa); Hugo *(le) Fuer* 1219 AssY; Ralph *Four* 1219 AssL; Roger *le Fower* 1279 RH (Nth). OFr *fouuer*, Lat *focarius* 'hearth-keeper'. Occasionally in the form: Hugh *de la Four* 1275 RH (Nth).

Foweraker: *v.* FOURACRE

Fowke(s): *v.* FOLK

Fowlds: *v.* FOLD

Fowle, Fowles, Fowell, Fowells, Fowls, Fuggle, Fuggles, Voules, Vowell, Vowells, Vowels, Vowles: *Fugel* 1066 Winton (Ha); *Fugel de Hoilanda* 1177 P (Y); Wuluard' *Fugel* 1166 P (K); Robert *(le) Fugel* 1186–7 P (So); William *le Foul* 1271 FFC; Agnes *Foweles*, Nicholas *le Fowel* 1275 SRWo; Roger *Fogel* 1296 SRSx; Nicholas *Vogel* 1327 SRSo; William *Vouell* 1578 Oxon; Thomas *Fuggill* 1632 YWills; William *Fugghill* 1685 ib. OE *Fugel*, from OE *fugol* 'fowl, bird', used both as a personal-name and a nickname. The southern form survives in Vuggles Fm (Sussex).

Fowler, Fugler, Vowler: Richard *Fugelere* 1218 AssL; Roger *le Fugler* 1227 Pat (Nf); John *þe Fogelere* 1275 RH (W); Ralph *Vouler* 1279 RH (Bk); Edward *le Vowelar* 1327 SRSo; Ralph *le Foweler* 1329 ColchCt. OE *fugelere* 'hunter of wild birds, fowler'.

Fowl(e)ston(e): *v.* FOULSTON

Fowling: Alan, Elpher *Fogheling, Fughelyng* 1327–32 SRSx. OE **Fugeling* 'son of *Fugel*'. *v.* FOWLE.

Fownes: *v.* FAUN

Fowweather: *v.* FOUWEATHER

Fox: Toue *fox* Hy 2 DC (L); Hugo *le Fox* 1297 MinAcctCo. A nickname.

Foyle: (i) Henry *de Foyle* 1249 AssW; John *atte Foyle* 1311 Battle. From Foyle Farm in Oxted (Surrey), or 'dweller by the pit', OFr *fouille* 'excavation'. (ii) Howel *Voyle* 1285 Morris; Ralph *Foil* 1327 SRSo; Samuel *Foyle* 1642 PrD. Welsh *moel* 'bald'.

Frail, Freel: Richard *Fresle* 1086 DB (Nt); Robert *Fresle* 1115 Winton (Ha); Robert *Frelle*

1130 P (Ha). ME *freil, frele, frelle*, OFr *fresle* (*fraisle*) 'frail, weak' (a1340 NED).

Frain, Frane, Frayn, Frayne, Frean, Freen, Freyne, de Fraine, de Freyne: William *de Fraisn'* 1156 P (Sf); Thomas *del Freisne* 1206 Cur (He); Peter *de Frane* 1228 Cl (Lo); Richard *del Frene* 1271 ForSt; Cristina *Freen* 1275 SRWo; William *a la Freyne* 1279 RH (O); John *del Freyn* 1280 AssSo. OFr *fraisne, fresne* 'ash-tree'. 'Dweller by an ash-tree.' cf. FRANEY.

Frais, Frose: Geoffrey *Freys, Frois* 1275 RH (Lo); Richard *Froyse, Frose* 1403, 1467 FrY. OFr *freis* (m), *fresche* (f) 'full of vigour, active' (c1385 MED), 'blooming, looking healthy or youthful' (c1385 ib.).

Frances, Francies, Francis, Franses: Robertus *filius Franceis* 1207 Cur (Sx); *Francais de Irtona* c1230 Whitby (Y); Hugo *Francus, Franceis* 1135, 1166 Oseney (O); Robert *le Franceis* 1169 P (D); Roger *Franceis* 1177 P (Ha); Robertus *Francigena, Franciscus* 1199 P (Wo, Nf); Adam *le Francess* 1201 AssSo. OFr *Franceis*, modFr *François*, the popular form of *Franciscus*, originally 'a Frank', though later used to denote a Frenchman. The surname is usually from the adj. *Franceis* 'Frenchman'.

Francke: *v.* FRANK
Franckeiss: *v.* FRANKIS
Francklin, Francklyn: *v.* FRANKLIN
Francom, Francombe: *v.* FRANKHAM
Frane: *v.* FRAIN
Franey, Freeney, Freney: William *de Freisneto, de Fraisneto* 1170, 1176 P (Cu, R); Ingelrammus *del Freisnei* 1204 P (He); Alicia *de Fresnei* 1205 P (R); Ingelram *del Freidnei, del Frednei* 1205 P (He); William *de Freiney* 1207 Cur (C); Reginald *de Freney* 1244 Fees (R). From residence near an ash-wood, OFr *fraisnaie, fresnay*, or from one of the French villages so called. cf. FRAIN.

Frank, Franks, Franck, Francke: *Franco, Francus* 1086 DB (Sa, Y, Nf, Sr); Ricardus *filius Franc, filius Franke* 1172 DC, 1188 P (L); *Franke de Cnihteton'* 1221 AssWo; Ricardus *Franc'* 1201 Cur (Ess); Walter *le Franc* 1221 Cur (C); Richard *le Fraunc* Hy 3 HPD (Ess); Thomas *Frank* 1270 AssSo; Geruas' *le Fraunk*, Adam *le Fronk* 1296 SRSx. OG *Franco* 'a Frank' was not uncommon from the 11th to the 14th centuries. The surname is, perhaps, more commonly descriptive, from ME, OFr *franc* 'free', not a serf or slave (c1325 MED).

Frankham, Frankom, Frankcombe, Frankum, Francom, Francomb, Francombe: Thomas *le Franchume* 1234 FFC; Robert *Frankeham* 1243 AssSo; Robert *Frankhom* 1260 AssC. OFr *franc* 'free' and *homme* 'man', equivalent to FREEMAN.

Frankis, Frankiss, Frankish, Franckeiss: Roð ðe *Frenccisce* c1100-30 OEByn (So); William *Franckeche* 1240 Fees (K); William *le Frenkisse* 1289 AssCh; Richard *Frankis* 1297 SRY; Henry *Frankissh* c1310 Calv (Y). OE *frencisc* 'French(man)', ME *frankys* (a1325 MED).

Franklin, Franklyn, Franklen, Francklin, Francklyn, Frankling: Ralph *Frankelein* 1195 P (Y); Luke

le Franckeleyn 1234 FFC; Roger *le Franklyn* 1274 RH (D); John *ffranklyng* 1522 ArchC 33. AFr *fraunclein*, ME *frankeleyn* 'a freeman', 'a landowner of free but not noble birth' (c1300 MED).

Frankum: *v.* FRANKHAM
Franses: *v.* FRANCES
Fransham, Frensham, Frenchum: Agnes *de Franesham'* 1198 FFNf. From Fransham (Norfolk).

Frary: *v.* FREDERICK
Frater: Richard *del Fraytour* 1301 SRY. 'One in charge of the refectory of a monastery', OFr *fraitur*.

Frayne: *v.* FRAIN
Freake(s): *v.* FIRTH
Freaker: Equivalent to *atte freke.* *v.* FIRTH.
Frean: *v.* FRAIN
Frear, Freear, Freer, Frere, Friar, Frier, Fryer: Robert (*le*) *Frere* 1196-7 P (Y); Roger *le Frier* 1243 AssSo. OFr *frere* 'friar'.

Frears: William *del Freres* 1314 FrY. 'Servant at the friars'.'

Frearson: John *le Frereson* 1335 AD vi (St). 'The friar's son.'

Frecheville, Freshfield: Cardo *de Frescheuill'* 1204 P (Nf); John *de Fressefeld* 1296 SRSx; Ralph *de Frechefeld* 1327 SRSx. From one of the French places named Frècheville.

Frederick, Fredericks, Frederic, Frary: *Frederic* (K), *Fredri* (Sx) 1066 DB; *Frethericus, Fredricus, Fedricus* 1086 DB (Nf); *Frari filius Willelmi* 1198 FF (Nf); *Fredericus, Fraricus, Frarius, Frarinus de Bisshopesdon'* 1221 AssWa, AssGl; Walter *Frethryk* 1275 RH (Sf); John *Frereric* 1279 RH (C); Ralph *Fretherik* 1315 FFSf; John, William *Frary* 1372 FrNorw, 1378 AssEss. OG *Frideric, Frederic* 'peace-rule', not a common medieval name in England, found chiefly in the eastern counties.

Free: Walter *le Free* 1255 RH (W); Adam *le Fre* 1282 LLB B. OE *frēo*, ME *fre* 'free'. cf. FRY.

Freebairn: William, Maurice *Frebarn(e)* 1248 FFEss, 1318 LLB E. OE *frēo, bearn* 'free child'.

Freebody: William *Frebodi* 1275 SRWo; Henry *Frybody* 1296 SRSx. OE *frēo, frīo* 'free' and *bodig* 'body', used in ME of a person, 'a free man'.

Freeborn, Freeborne, Freeberne, Freeburn: (i) *Frebern* c1095 Bury (Sf), 1211 Cur (Berks); *Frebern de Eshcot'* 1221 AssWa; Robert, William *Frebern* 1163 P (Nb), 1193 P (Berks). OE *Frēobeorn*, 'free-man'. (ii) John *Freborn'* 1256 AssNb; Robert *ffreborn* 1327 SRC. OE *frēo* 'free' and *boren* 'born', 'one born free, inheriting liberty'.

Freed: *v.* FIRTH
Freeder: Equivalent to *atte frede.* *v.* FIRTH.
Freel: *v.* FRAIL
Freeland: Walter *Freland'* 1198 FF (Nf); Ralph *Frieland* 1202 FFC; Richard *de la Fryelonde* 1296 SRSx; Richard *atte Frilonde* 1317 AssK. A holder of 'land held without obligation of rent or service' OE **frēoland, *frigland*.

Freelove: *Frelof* Pollard 1235 Ch (Nf); Nicholas,

Joanna *Frelove* 1279 RH (Beds), 1568 SfPR. OE *Friðulāf* 'peace-survivor', recorded twice in the 10th century.

Freeman, Friman, Fryman: *Freman* Sceil 1188 P (Ess); William *Freman* 1196 FFNf; Reginald *le Freman* 1221 AssWo; Osbert *Friman* 1240 Fees (Beds). OE *frēomann, frīgmann* 'freeman', 'free-born man', used also as a personal name.

Freemantle, Fremantle: Reginald *Freitmantel* 1190 Oseney; Gamel *Freimantell* 1212 Cur (Y); Robert, John *Fremantel* 1360–2 FrC, 1396–7 FFSr. The name is borrowed from France where *Fromentel* 'cold cloak', a common place-name, was also the name of a forest. As a nickname it probably meant 'poorly clad, ragged, cold'. Later examples of the name may come from Freemantle (Hants), *Freitmantell* 1181.

Freen: *v.* FRAIN
Freeney: *v.* FRANEY
Freer: *v.* FREAR
Freeth, Freke: *v.* FIRTH
French, ffrench: Simon *le Frensch* 1273 RH (W); John *le Frenche* 1278 Ronton (St). OE *frencisc*, ME *frennsce, frenche* 'French'.
Frenchum: *v.* FRANSHAM
Frend: *v.* FRIEND
Freney: *v.* FRANEY
Frensham: *v.* FRANSHAM
Frere: *v.* FREAR
Freshfield: *v.* FRECHEVILLE
Freshney: *v.* FRISKNEY
Frett: Metonymic for *Fretter*.
Fretter: Henry *le Fretter* 1332 SRWa. A derivative of ME *frette*, OFr *frete* 'interlaced-work', used of ornaments (especially for the hair) consisting of jewels or flowers in a network, hence a maker of these. cf. a frette of goold (c1385 NED), frette of perle (1390).

Frewen, Frewin, Frewing, Frowen, Frowing, Fruen, Fruin: *Freowinus, Freuuinus* 1066 DB (Sf, Ess); *Frewinus* c1150 Gilb (L), 1175 P (Ha); Richard, Henry *Frewine* 1221 ElyA (Sf), 1230 P (Ha); Walter *Frewyne* 1313 Glast (Do); John *Froweyn* 1394 LLB H; Edward *Frewinge* 1665 HTO. OE *Frēowine* 'noble-friend'. Occasionally we have forms with *Fra-*, William *Frawin* 1221 AssWa, from OE *Frēawine* 'ruler-friend', which may also appear as *Frewinus* (PNDB 253).
Freyne: *v.* FRAIN
Friar: *v.* FREAR
Frid, Fridd, Fryd: *v.* FIRTH
Friday, Fridaye: Chetel *Friedai* 1086 DB (Nf); Ralph *Fridai* c1167 AC (Lei); William *Fridey* 1214 Cur (Ess). OE *frīgedæg* 'Friday', perhaps for one born on that day. If the 17th-century phrases *Friday-face* 'a gloomy expression', *Friday-food*, *Friday-feast* 'a fast-day meal' are old, we might have a nickname for one as solemn and gloomy as a Friday fast-day.
Friend, Frend: Robert *Frend'* 1166 P (Nt); Gervase *Lefrend* 1221 Cur (Mx). OE *frēond* 'friend'.
Frier: *v.* FREAR

Frift, Fright: *v.* FIRTH
Friman: *v.* FREEMAN
Friskney, Freshney: Adam *de Freskenay* 1193 P (L). From Friskney (Lincs).
Frith: *v.* FIRTH
Frobisher: Geoffrey *le Furbisur* c1260 LeiBR; Henry *le Fourbissor* 1306 AD v (Sa); Richard *Forbour, Forbysschour* 1359–60 ColchCt; John *Frobyser* 1517 GildY; Christian *Fribysher* 1582 RothwellPR (Y); William *Frubbisher* 1714 FrY. OFr *forbisseor* 'furbisher'. cf. FURBER.
Fromant, Froment, Fromont: *Frumond* 1086 DB (Y); *Fromont* de Macels Hy 2 DC (L); Richard, Thomas *Fromund* 1203 P (Do), 1243 AssSt. OFr *Fromont*, OG *Frumund*.
Frome, Froom, Froome, Vroome: Æðelweard *æt Frome* c1038 OEByn (He); Peter *de Froma* 1170 P (So). From Frome (Dorset, Hereford, Som).
Frost, Forst: Aluuin, William *Forst* 1066 DB (Ha), 1199 AssSt; Lefstan, Gilbert *Frost* c1095 Bury (Sf), 1195 P (Wa). OE *forst, frost* 'frost', perhaps used in the sense of 'frosty', 'cold as frost', 'without ardour or warmth of feeling' (c1385 NED), or 'with the appearance of being covered with frost', 'with hoary, white hair' (*frosty berd* 14.. NED).
Froud, Froude, Frowd, Frowde, Frood, Frude: (i) Richard, Siward *Frode* 1184 P (D), 1187 P (Sx); William *Froud* c1203 StCh; William *le Frode* 1334 SRK; Robert, John *Frowde* 1525 SRSx, 1545 SRW. OE *frōd* 'wise, prudent'. (ii) *Frodo* liber homo 1066 DB (Sf); *Frodo* prepositus c1115 Bury (Sf); Hugh *filius Frodonis* 1121–48 Bury (Sf); *Frode* 1296 Wak (Y). ON *Fróði*, ODa *Frothi*. OE *Frōda* is found only once, and OG *Frodo* is rare. In Normandy *Frodo* may be ON (PNDB 256); *Frodo* 1086 DB was a brother of the abbot of Bury and was *genere Gallus*. Although there is no clear evidence, the possibility that the personal name gave rise to a surname cannot be excluded.
Frowen, Frowing, Fruen, Fruin: *v.* FREWEN
Fry, Frye: William *Frie* 1195 P (Sx); Robert *le Frye* c1248 Bec (W). OE *frīg* 'free'. cf. FREE.
Fryer: *v.* FREAR
Fryman: *v.* FREEMAN
Fuche, Fudge, Fuge, Fuidge: Robertus *filius Fuche* a1170 Gilb (L); *Fuche* Bassat c1200 Seals (Nth). A pet form of *Fulcher*, or *Fucher*. Gilebertus *filius Fulcheri* (c1130 Whitby) is also called Gilebertus *filius Fuche* (c1125 ib.). Robertus *filius Fuch'* is identical with Robertus *filius Fulcheri* 1210 Cur (Db), whilst Henry *Fulcher* is also called Henry *Fouch* 1297 Coram. *v.* FULCHER.
Fucher, Fudger: *v.* FULCHER
Fudge, Fuge: *v.* FUCHE
Fugeman: 'Servant of *Fuge* or *Fouche*.' *v.* FUCHE.
Fugere: *v.* FULCHER
Fuggle, Fuggles: *v.* FOWLE
Fugler: *v.* FOWLER
Fuidge: *v.* FUCHE
Fuke: *v.* FOLK
Fulcher, Fulger, Fulker, Fulscher, Fucher, Fudger, Fugere, Futcher, Folger, Folker, Foker, Foulcher,

Foulger, Foulser, Foucar, Volker, Fullagar, Fullager: *Fulcher* 1066 DB, c1095 Bury (Sf); Seuuale *filius Fulgeri* Hy 2 DC (L); *Fulcarius* 12th DC (Lei); Rogerus *fiius Foukere* 1201 Cur (O); Roger *Fulchier* 1167 P (Ha); Ralph *Fulcher* 1182 P (Sf); Peter *Fulker'* 1212 Cur (W); Eustace *Folchir* 1212 Fees (Ha); Nicholas *Fuker'* 1234 Fees (D); Warin *Fucher* 1235 Fees (Ess); John *Foucher'* 1242 Fees (W); Robert *Folgar* 1327 SRSf; William *Fouger* 1327 SRWo; Robert *Fowcher* 1524 SRSf. OFr *Foucher, Fouquier,* from OG *Fulchar, Fulcher* 'people-army'. OE *Folchere,* from which these surnames have sometimes been derived, is not recorded after 824. Occasionally we may have ODa *Folkar.*

Fulford: Robert *de Fulfort* 1219 AssY; Richard *de Fulford* c1280 SRWo; Thomas *Fuleford, Fulleford* 1327, 1332 SRSx. From Fulford (Devon, Som, Staffs, ERYorks).

Fulk, Fulkes, Fulks: *v.* FOLK

Fulker, Fullagar, Fullager: *v.* FULCHER

Fullalove, Fullelove, Fullerlove, Fulleylove, Fullilove: Henry *ffulofloue* 1327 SRC; William *ffuloflof* 1332 SRCu. A nickname, 'full of love', a translation of the French *pleyn d'amour.* cf. BLANDAMORE.

Fullen: *v.* FULLOON

Fuller, Voller, Vollers: Roger *Fulur* 1219 AssY; Reginald *fullere* 1221 ElyA (Sf); William *le Fulur* 1221 Ass (Wa); Simon *le Voller* 1316 Oseney (O); John *Follere (Vollere)* 1317 AssK. OE *fullere,* OFr *fouleor, foleur* 'a fuller of cloth'. The raw cloth had to be *fulled,* i.e. scoured and thickened by beating it in water, a process known as *walking* because originally done by men trampling upon it in a trough. Hence *Walker,* by the side of *Fuller* and *Tucker* from OE *tūcian,* originally 'to torment', later 'to tuck', 'to full'. These three surnames seem to be characteristic of different parts of England. In general, in ME, *Fuller* is southern and eastern; *Walker* belongs to the west and north; *Tucker* is south-western. The French form *fuller* occurs in the whole of England and is often a translation of *walker* or *tucker. v.* MESO 100–1.

Fullerlove, Fulleylove: *v.* FULLALOVE

Fullick, Fullicks, Follick: Adam *de Fullewyk* 1296 SRSx. From Fulwick's Copse in Lurgashall (Sussex), *Fullykland* 1586 PN Sx 113.

Fulljames: *v.* FOLJAMBE

Fulloon, Fullen: Ralph *le fullun* 1219 AssL; William *le Fulun* 1223 Pat (Y). OFr *fulun* 'fuller'.

Fullshawe: Henry *de ffulshaghe* 1332 SRLa. 'Dweller by the muddy wood', OE *fūl, sceaga.*

Fullstone: *v.* FOULSTON

Fullwood, Fulwood: Adam *de Foulewode* 1326 Wak (Y). From Fulwood (Lancs, WRYorks). Also becomes *Fullward* and *Fuller:* Avory *Fullward, Fuller alias Fullwood* 1703, 1719 SaltAS (OS) x.

Fulscher: *v.* FULCHER

Funk: William *Funke* 1314 NorwDeeds; John *le Funke* 1327 SRSo; Nicholas *Founk* 1396 FrY. ME *funke, founck* 'a spark of fire' (MED a1393), cf. 'Funke or lytylle fyyr, *igniculus, foculus*' c1440

PromptParv. As a nickname, perhaps 'fiery, hotheaded'.

Funnell: *v.* FURNELL

Furbank: *v.* FIRBANK

Furber, Forber: Elfwin *Furbor* 1180 Oseney (O); Roger *le Furbur* 1199 P (Lo); Adam *le Forbour* 1333 ColchCt. OFr *forbeor, fourbeor, furbeor* 'furbisher of armour, etc.' (c1415 NED). *v.* also FROBISHER.

Furlong, Furlonge, Forlong, Furlonger: Robert *Furlang* 1242 Fees (D); John *de Forhlangh* 1250 Fees (Sf); Richard *de Furlang* 1260 AssLa; John *Forlong* 1316 Oseney (O); John *atte Forlange* 1327 SRSx. This can hardly mean 'dweller by a furlong'. OE *furhlang,* lit. 'a furrow long', came to mean the length of a field and a division of an unenclosed field. In the 14th century it was used to translate Latin *stadium* in the sense of 'the course for footraces'. cf. 'þei that rennen in þe ferlong for þe pris' c1380 Wyclif; 'Yif a man renneþ in the stadie or in the forlong for the corone' c1374 Chaucer. Hence *furlonger* (and *atte furlong* as a surname) may have been used of a runner famous for his exploits in the 'forlong'.

Furmage, Furmedge, Firmage: Herbert *furmage* 1160 P (L); Luke *Formage* 1280 AssSo; Henry *Firmage* 1524 SRSf. OFr *fourmage,* modFr *fromage* 'cheese' (14.. NED), metonymic for FIRMINGER.

Furman: *v.* FIRMIN

Furmenger, Furminger: *v.* FIRMINGER

Furnace, Furnass, Furness, Furniss, Furnish, Fourniss, Varnish: Michael *de Furneis* 1171 P (La); Anselm *de Furnes* 1198 P (We); John *Fornace* 1505 FrY. From Furness (Lancs). *v* FURNEAUX.

Furneaux: Anketillus *de Furnels* 1086 ICC (C); Odo *de Fornelt* 1086 DB (So); Simon *de Furneaus, de Furnellis* 1220, 1235 Fees (Herts); John *de Furneals* 1238 Fees (D); Henry *de Furnaus, de Furnell', de Fornell', de Furnellis* 1210–12 Cur (Ess, So). From Fourneaux (Calvados, La Manche) 'furnaces'. Furneux Pelham (Herts), named from Richard *de Furneals* (12th century), occurs as Pelham *Furnelle* (1240), *Forneys* (1291), *Furneus* (1293), *Furnysshe* (1541) and *Funish* (1700 PN Herts 184). There has thus been confusion with *Furnace* and *Furnell.*

Furnell, Fournel, Funnell, Funnelle, Funel: Alan, Richard *de Furnell'* 1191 P (O), 1206 Cur (Y); John *Funnell* 1553 SxW. OFr *fournel* 'furnace' or from one of the French places named Fournal or Fournel. *v.* FURNEAUX.

Furner, Fournier: William *le Furner,* Simon *Furner* 1208, 1212 Cur (Y); Martin *le Forner* 1283 LLB A. OFr *fornier, furnier* 'baker' (1441 MED).

Furnival, Furnivall, Furnifall: Gerard *de Furniualla* 1171–84 DC (L). From Fournival (Oise, Orne).

Furr: Reginald, Robert *Furre* 1193, 1202 P (L, Ess). ME *furre* 'a coat or garment made of or trimmed with fur' (c1375 MED), for a wearer, maker or seller of this.

Fursdon: (i) William *de Fursdon* 1281 PN D 521;

George *Fursdon* 1642 PrD. 'Dweller by the furze-covered hill', OE *fyrs* and *dūn*. (ii) John *de la Fursen* 1318 Pat (D). 'Dweller in the furze' (weak pl.), cf. William *indefurse* 1189 Sol.

Furse, Furze, Furseman, Furzeman, Furzer: John *de la Fursa* 1168 P (D); John *atte Furse*, Sibel *atte Ferse* 1296 SRSx. 'Dweller by the furze-covered land' (OE *fyrs* 'furze').

Fursey, Fussey, Fuzzey, Forsey: John *Forshay* 1431 AD ii (Do); John, Roger *Fursey* 1583 Musters (Sr), 1642 PrD. 'Dweller by the furze-covered enclosure', OE *fyrs* and (*ge*)*hæg*.

Fuster: *v.* FEWSTER
Futcher: *v.* FULCHER
Fynes: *v.* FIENNES

G

Gabb: Walter, Thomas *Gabbe* 1275, 1327 SRWo. ME, OFr *gab* 'mockery, deceit', for *gabber* 'deceiver, liar': William, Stephen *le Gabber* 1230 P (D), 1279 RH (O).

Gabler: Goda *Gabblere* 1193–1212 Clerkenwell (Lo); Reginald *le Gabler* 1230 P (Ha). OFr *gabelier* 'tax-collector' or OFr *gableor* 'usurer'.

Gabriel: *Gabriel* filius Reginaldi 1212 Cur (Sx); *Gabriele* Spyg 1296 SRSx; Roger, Nicholas *Gabryel* 1296 SRSx, 1327 SRSf. Hebrew *Gabriel*, never a common name.

Gage, Gauge: Alice *Gage* 1310 ColchCt; Robert *Gauge* c1315 Calv (Y). ONFr *gauge* 'a fixed measure' (1432 MED), used by metonymy for a measurer or tester.

Gager, Gaiger: Andrebode *Gangeor* (sic) 1066 Winton (Ha); Henry *le Gaugeor* 1305 LoCt; Laurence *Gauger* 1327 *SR* (Ess). AFr *gaugeour*, OFr *gauger* 'gauger', 'exciseman' (1444 MED).

Gaillard: *v.* GALLIARD

Gain, Gaine, Gaines, Gains, Gayne, Dingain, Engeham, Ingham: William *Ingania, Inganie* 1086 DB (Hu, Nth); Vitalis *Engaine*, Richard *Ingaine* 1130 P (Nth); Ralph *Engaigne* 1158 P (Cu); William *de Engain* 1208 FFHu; Richard *Ingan* 1228 Cl (Gl); John *en Gayne* alias *den Gayne* 1271 Ipm (Sf); John *le Gayne* 1275 Wak (Y); William *Denganye, de Engann'* 1279 RH (C); Richard *Ingayn* 1310 LLB D. OFr *engaigne*, Lat *ingania* 'trickery, ingenuity'. The family has left its name in Colne Engaine and Gaynes Park (Essex), in D'Engaine's Fm (Cambs) and in Aston Ingham (Hereford). The family name is only rarely spelled *de Engaine*. For this, cf. the French surnames *Dejour, Denuit, Damour*, elliptic for (*homme*) *d'amour*, etc. (Dauzat). *Ingham* has other derivations.

Gaish: *v.* WACE

Gait, Gaite, Gaites, Gaitt: (i) Stephen, Thomas *Gayt(e)* 1297 SRY, 1331 FrY; John *Gaytt, Gate* 1390, 1416 FrY; Richard *Gaites* 1561 ib. These northern forms are probably from ON *geit* 'goat', but some may belong below. (ii) Reginald *Gayt* 1139 Templars (O); Robert *le Gayt* 1205 Cur (O); William *le Guaite* 1208 FFSt. OFr *gaite* 'watchman', a doublet of WAIT.

Gaiter, Gayter, Gaytor, Gayther, Geater, Geator: Michael *le Geytere* 1279 RH (Hu). A derivative of ON *geit*, ME *gayte* 'goat', hence 'goat-herd'. The frequency of the names may be due to the absorption of *gaythird* 'goat-herd': John *le Gaythirde* 1301 SRY, Robert *Gayterd* 1466 FrY.

Gaitskell, Gaitskill, Gaskell, Gaskill: Benjamin *de Gaytscale* 1332 SRLa; Edward *Gaskell* 1560 LaWills; Richard *Gatskell, Gaytscalle* 1595–6 ib.; Richard *Gaitskell* 1632 ib. From Gatesgill (Cumb), earlier *Geytescales*.

Galbraith, Galbreath: Gillescop *Galbrath, Galbraith* 1208–46 Black; William *Galbrath* 1269 AssNb. OGael *Gall-Bhreathnach* 'stranger-Briton', a name given to Britons settled among Gaels.

Gale, Gayle: (i) *Gualo* legatus 1219 AssY; *Galo* 1230 ClR (Nantes); Gilbert, Alicia *Gale* 1202 AssL, 1275 SRWo; William *le Gal* 1285 *Ass* (Ess); Juliana *le Gale* 1327 SRC. Chiefly, no doubt, from OE *gāl* 'light, pleasant, merry; wanton, licentious'. But also from the central French form of OG *Walo* (*v.* WALE). (ii) Robert *le Geil* 1186 P (Wo). Identical with modern French *Gail* 'gay, joyous', from the simplex of *gaill-ard*. *v.* GALLIARD. (iii) Philip *de la Jaille* 1208 P (Ha); William *ate Gaole* 1317 AssK; Thomas *del Gayle* 1365 FrY; Robert *de Gale* 1402 FrY. The modern surnames represent the Norman pronunciation of ONFr *gaiole, gaole*, ME *gay(h)ole, gayll(e), gaile*, surviving in the official spelling *gaol*, but replaced in pronunciation by the OFr *jaiole*, ME *jaiole, jayle*, which is also represented in the above forms. 'At the gaol', 'jailer'. cf. GALER.

Galer, Gayler, Gaylor, Jailler: Robert *le Gaoler* 1255 *Ass* (Ess); Richard *le Gaylor* 1275 SRWo; Richard *le Gayoler* of Newgate 1300 LoCt; William *le Gaoler* of Nottingham 1302 NottBR. ONFr *gayolierre, gaiolere*, OFr *jaioleur* 'gaoler, jailer'. *v.* GALE.

Gales: Mager' *Galeys* 1279 RH (C); Henry *le Galeys, le Waleis* 1299, 1305 LoCt. The central French form of *Wallis*, or of OG *Walo*. *v.* WALES.

Galey: *v.* GALLEY

Galilee, Gallally, Galley: William *de la Galilye* 1337 Cl; Ralph *Galile* 1539 FeuDu; John *Gallale* 1539 Bardsley (Du). OFr *galilee* 'porch or chapel at the entrance to a church', those at Durham and Ely being particularly famous. The reference may be to the keeper or to one who lived near. Bardsley cites John and Robert *Galley* (1551) whom the historian of Newcastle identifies as members of a family of *Galilee*.

Gall, Gaul, Gaw: Walter *Galle* c1170 Gilb (L);

138

Adam, Richard *Galle* 1221 AssWa, 1275 SRWo; John *Gal* 1334 Black; William *Gaw* 1397 ib. Celtic *gall* 'foreigner, stranger', found in Irish, Gaelic and Breton. It occurs in Perthshire and Aberdeen where the common pronunciation was *Gaw* and was used of Lowlanders. In England it is found in the Welsh border counties and also in Lincolnshire where it was of Breton origin. In Brittany where the name was common, it was applied to immigrants from France.

Gallacher, Gallagher, Gallaher: Ir *O Gallchobhair* 'descendant of *Gallchobhar*' (foreign help).

Gallant: *Waland* 1066 DB (Wo); *Galant* fitz Richard 1210 FFEss; Adam *Galland* 1274 RH (Ess); Thomas *Galaunt* 1275 RH (Sf); John *Galant* 1326 FFEss. OFr *Galand, Galant*, OG *Waland*. The surname is also from OFr, ME *galant* 'dashing, spirited, bold'.

Gallard: *v.* GALLIARD

Gallatly: *v.* GOLIGHTLY

Gallear, Galler: *v.* WALLER

Galletley, Galletly: *v.* GOLIGHTLY

Galley, Gallie, Gally, Galey: Henry *Galye* 1219 AssY; Adam *del Galay* 1304 FrY. Either 'man from the galley' or OFr *galie, galee*, ME *galai, galy(e)* 'a galley' used by metonymy for a galley-man, rower. *v.* also GALILEE.

Galliard, Gaillard, Gallard, Gaylard, Gaylord: *Gaylardus* 1206 PatR; Robert *Gaylard* 1225 ClR; John *Galard* 1232 FineR; Sabina *Geylard* 1295 ParlR (Ess); Alexander *Galyard* 1426 FrY. OFr *Gaillart*, OG **Gailhard* 'lofty-hard', or OFr *gaillard, gaillart*, ME *gaillard, galiard* 'lively, brisk; gay, full of high spirits' (c1390 MED).

Gallier(s): *v.* WALLER

Galliford: *v.* GULLIVER

Galling: Margaret *Gaddling* 1260 AssC; John *Gallyng* 1296 SRSx. OE *gædeling* 'companion', ME *gadeling* 'fellow, vagabond'.

Galliot, Galliott: Wydo *Galiot* 1230 P (D); William *Galyot* 1275 AssSo. OFr *galiot* 'sailor in a galley, galley-slave, pirate', ME *galyot* 'pirate' (c1425 (rare) MED). Noted also in the sea-board counties of Essex, Kent, Sussex and Suffolk (1296–1327).

Galliver: *v.* GULLIVER

Gallon: Walter *Galun* 1220 Cur (So); Thomas *Galon* 1275 SRWo. OFr *Galon*, cas-régime of OG *Walo*. *v.* GALE, WALE. *Galun* may be a diminutive of *Galo* (*Gal-un*). or has been influenced by ME *galun* 'gallon'.

Gally: *v.* GALLEY

Gallyer: *v.* WALLER

Galpin, Galpen: Robert, William *Galopin* 1195 P (Wa), 1201 AssSo; William *Galpyn* 1279 AssSt. OFr *galopin* from *galoper* 'to gallop', 'messenger, page; turnspit, scullion in a monastery' (1567 NED), especially the latter.

Galsworthy, Golsworthy, Galsery: Thomas *Gallysworthy* 1524 Hoskins; Thomas *Galsworthie* 1558 HartlandPR; Nectanus, Elizabeth *Galsworthe* 1560, 1571 ib.; William, Joan *Galsery* 1598, 1625 ib. From Galsworthy (Devon).

Galt, Gault, Gaught, Gaut, Gaute: Godfrey, William *Galt* 1198 FFNf, 1202 P (Y); William *Galt* 1367 Black (Perth). In England, a nickname from the boar or hog, ME *galte, gaute, gault*, ON *goltr, galte*. In Scotland, like *Gall*, it is found in Perth and Aberdeen (as *Gaut* in 1649) and is regarded by Scots as a variant of *Gaul* or *Gauld*.

Gamage, Gammage, Gammidge, Camidge, Cammidge: Godfrey *de Gamages* 1158 P (He); Philip *de Camiges* 1275 RH (W); Alicia *Gamage* 1279 RH (O); William *Camage* 1583 FrY. From Gamaches (Eure). *v.* ANF.

Gaman: *v.* GAME

Gambell, Gamble, Gambles, Gammell, Gammil: *Gamel* 1066 DB; *Gamel* Auceps 1158 P (Y); Simon, Adam *Gamel* 1202 AssL, 1260 AssY; Jordan *Gambel* 1297 MinAcctCo; John *Gamyll* 1597 FrY. ON *Gamall*, ODa, OSw *Gamal* 'old'.

Gamblin(g): *v.* GAMLIN

Gambray: *v.* CAMBRAY

Game, Games, Gaman, Gamon, Gamman, Gammans, Gammon, Gammond, Gammons: Richard *Gamen* 1251 FFEss, 1275 RH (Nf); Roger, John *Game* 1268 AssSo, 1377 LLB H; John, Hugh *le Gamene* 1275 RH (Ha), 1309 SRBeds; John *Goodgame* alias *Game* 1549 FFHu. OE *gamen*, ME *gamen, game* 'game', a nickname, no doubt, for one fond of or good at games, cf. GOODGAME, but also one given to the winner of 'the gamen', the prize in a foot-race. cf. 'Men usen ofte þis gamen, þat two men . . . rennen a space for a priis, and he þat comeþ first to his ende shall have þe gamen þat is sett, wheþer it be spere or gloves [v.l. gleyves] or oþir þing þat is putt' (c1380 NED). cf. GLEAVE, and *v.* GAMMON.

Gamlin, Gamlane, Gamlen, Gamblin, Gambling: Odo *filius Gamelin* 1086 DB (So); *Gamelyn* de Cottyngwith 1347 AD iv (C); James, Ralph *Gamelin* 1262 *For* (Ess), 1279 RH (O). *Gamel-in*, a diminutive of *Gamel*. *v.* GAMBELL. *Gamel* and *Gamelinus* are used of the same man (1218 AssL).

Gammage: *v.* GAMAGE

Gamman(s): *v.* GAME

Gammell, Gammil: *v.* GAMBELL

Gammidge: *v.* GAMAGE

Gammon, Gamon: Roger, Margery *Gambun* 1209 P (Wa), 1222 Cur (O); Richard, John *Gambon* 1260 AssC, 1327 SRC. A diminutive of *gamb*, the Norman form of *jambe* 'leg'; 'little leg'. cf. Fr *Gambet, Gambin, Gambon*. *mb* would be assimilated to *mm*, hence *Gammon*. *v.* also GAME.

Gander: Roger, William *Gandre* 1275 RH (Sf), 1327 LLB E; Reginald *le Gandre* 1327 SRSo. OE *gan(d)ra* 'gander'.

Gandey, Gandy: John *Gameday* 1327 SRSf. 'Servant of *Game*.' *v.* DAY. A Suffolk name.

Ganson: *v.* GAWENSON

Gant: *v.* GAUNT

Ganter: *v.* GAUNTER

Gape, Gapes: William *Gape* 1243 AssSo. OFr *gape* 'weak, enfeebled'.

Gapp: Richard *gappe* 1198–1212 Bart; Savatus *del Gap* de Torp 1275 RH (Nf); Nicholas *Gap* ib.;

Thomas *atte Gap* 1327 SRSf. ME *gappe*, ON *gap* 'chasm', 'breach in a wall or hedge', in Norfolk and Suffolk 'dweller by a gap in the cliffs'.

Garard: *v.* GERARD

Garbe, Garber: Henry *Garbe* 1275 RH (Nf). ONFr *garbe* 'wheatsheaf', first recorded in NED in 1502. The word must be much older. The Latin *garba* is found in 1103 (MLWL) and the term must have been in common use in reference to tithes. *Garber* may mean a binder of wheat into sheaves or a collector of tithes. *Garbe* is metonymic.

Garbett, Garbutt: (i) *Gerbodo* 1086 DB; *Gerbodo del Scalt* 1185 P (L); William *Gerbode* 1185 P (Hu); Thomas *Gerbot* 1302 AssSt; John *Garbot* 1397 FrY; James *Garbutt* 1602 FrY. OG *Gerbodo* 'spear-herald'. (ii) *Gerbertus, Gereberct, Girbertus* 1086 DB; *Gerbertus de Sancto Claro* 1199 Cur (Sf); Robert *Gerbert* 1100–13 Rams (Herts), 1174 P (Berks), 1187 P (W); William, Elyas *Girbertus* 1130 P (W). OFr, OG *Gerbert, Girbert* 'spear-bright'. (iii) *Gerboldus de Curcy*, Hugo *filius Gerbold* 1219 AssY; William *Gerebald* 1221 ElyA (C); Adam *Gerbaud* 1300 Rams (Hu). OG *Gerbald, Gerbold* 'spear-bold'. *Gerbodo* and *Gerbald* were early confused: cf. *Gerbod'* . . . *et Willelmus filius Gerboud* (both of Grindleton) 1219 AssY; William *Garbode, Garbolde* 1275 RH (Nf).

Gard, Guard: Richard, John *le Gard* 1275 SRWo, 1279 RH (C); William *la Garde* 1309 SRBeds. OFr *garde* 'guard, watchman'.

Garden, Gardyne: William *del Gardin* c1183 AC (O); William *Gardin* 1220 Cur (Hu); John *atte Gardyne* 1296 SRSx. ONFr *gardin* 'garden' (a1325 MED). Metonymic for *Gardener*. cf. JARDIN.

Gardener, Gardenner, Gardiner, Gardinor, Gardner, Gairdner: Anger *gardiner* a1166 Seals (L); William *le gardinier, le Gardenier* 1199, 1201 P (R); Andrew *Gairner* 1663 Black; Thomas and Rose *Gardiner, Gardner* 1730, 1733 HorringerPR (Sf). ONFr **gardinier* corresponding to OFr, modFr *jardinier* 'gardener' (a1325 MED). Walter *le gardiner* (1292 SRLo) was a fruiterer. *Gairdner* is Scottish. *v.* GARNER.

Garey, Geary: *Gheri* 1066 DB (Sa); *Geri* 1203 AssSt; *Geri filius Gunni* 1150–60 DC (L); Ralph *Gari* 1196 Cur (Nth); Richard, Aluredus *Geri* 1200 P (Sa), 1221 ElyA (Nf); Ralph *Gary* 1249 FFC; Roger *Gairy* 1301 SRY. ON *Geiri*, ODa *Geri* 'spear'. *Gari* is probably a Norman form. *Geri*, with hard *G* (as here) is difficult to distinguish from OFr *Geri* (with *j*-sound) in *Geary, Jeary*.

Garford, Garforth, Garfath, Garfirth, Garfit: William *de Gereford* 1219 AssY; Henry *de Garforde* 1260 Oseney; Richard *Garford* 1447 FFEss; Rycherd *Garforth* 1558 RothwellPR (Y). From Garford (Berks), or Garforth (WRYorks).

Gargate, Gargett: Reginald, Richard *Gargate* 1130, 1166 P (O, Co); John *Garget* 1210 Cur (So). OFr *gargate, garguett* 'throat'.

Garland, Garlant: (i) Robert *Gerland* 1221 AssWa; Adam *Garlaund* 1293 FFEss; William *Garland* 1293 Fees (D). Metonymic for *garlander* 'a maker of *garlands*', metal chaplets or circlets

for the head adorned with gold or silver: cf. William *Garlander* 1319 SRLo. (ii) John, Robert, William *de Garland(e)* 1190 P (Ha), 1225 Pat (Y), 1208 Cur (Ess). 'Dweller by the gore-land', OE *gāra* 'triangular piece of land'.

Garlic, Garlick, Garlicke: Robert *Garlec* 1273 RH (C); Gilbert *garlek* 1277 Ely (Sf); John *Garlyke* 1491 FrY. OE *gārlēac* 'garlick', used of a seller of garlick: cf. Luke *le Garlekmongere* 1309 LLB D; Thomas *Garleker* 1387 FrY.

Garman, Garmons, Garment: *Gormundus* 1208 Cur (So); Alanus *Garmundus* 1177 P (Nf); William *Gormund* 1255 RH (W). OE *Gārmund* 'spear-protector'. *v.* GORMAN.

Garmonsway, Garmondsway: Ralph *de Garmundeswaie* 12th FeuDu; Robert *de Garmundeseye* 1242 AssDu; William *Garmonsway* 1446 FrY. From Garmondsway (Durham).

Garnell: John *Gardinal* 1325 FFEss. For CARDINAL.

Garner, Garnar, Garnier, Gerner: (i) *Garnerius de Nugent* 1170–83 NthCh (R); Geoffrey *Gerner* 1272 FFEss. OFr *Garnier*. *v.* WARNER. (ii) William *del Gerner* 1332 SRLa. OFr *gerner, gernier* 'storehouse for corn', hence 'keeper of the granary'. (iii) *Garner* (1540 Black) is a late form of *Gardner*: Matthew *Gardner, Garner* 1706–9 Bardsley.

Garnet, Garnett, Warnett: *Garnet* 1409 Bardsley; Ricard *Gernet* 1086 DB (Ess); Roger, Benedict *Gernet* 1170, 1195 P (Nt, La); Robert *Warinot* 1275 RH (Hu); John *Garynot* (*Gerynot*) 1327 *SR* (Ess); William *Garnett* 1379 PTY. A diminutive of OFr *Guarin, Warin*: OFr *Guarinot, Warinot*. *Garnet* is also occupational: Joceus, William *le Gerneter* 1296 SRSx, 1327 MEOT (La), from OFr *garnetier, gernetier* 'superintendent of the granary' (1454 MED), or '·maker of garnets', T-shaped hinges, of which the short cross-bar was fastened to the frame of a door, perhaps from ONFr *carne* 'hinge' (*kernettes* 1275, *gornettes* 1325, *garnettes* 1532 Building 297–8; *garnettes* 1459 NED).

Garnon, Garnons, Gernon, Garnham, Grennan: Robert *Gernon, Gernun, Greno, Grenon, Grino, Grinon* 1086 DB; William *de Perci cognomento Asgernuns, ove les gernuns* Wm I Whitby (Y); Willelmus *cum grinonibus* 1104 ELPN 159; Adam *as Gernuns* 1166 P (Ess); William *Asgernuns* 1175 P (Y); William *de Perci Ohtlesgernuns* c1180 Whitby (Y); Alexander *Gernum* (bis) 12th Gilb (L); Richard *gernun* 1221 ElyA (Sf); Abel *Agernun* 1248 FFEss; William Bought called *Gernon* 1310 LLB D; John *Gernon* 1327 SRDb; Henry *Garnon* 1524 SRSf; John *Garnham* ib.; Thomas *Garnome* 1533 SIA xii; Nicholas *Garnom* 1568 SRSf; Thomas *Garnam, Garnham* ib. OFr *grenon, gernon* 'moustache'. Early examples are often prepositional, 'with the moustache(s)', a distinguishing characteristic which readily gave rise to the nickname. All the Normans on the Bayeux Tapestry are represented as clean-shaven. This nickname in the form *Algernon* was ultimately adopted as a christian name. Already in the 12th century *Gernun* is found occasionally as *Gernum*. This later became *Garnom* and *Garnam* and finally *Garnham* as if derived from a place-name. In the 1524 Subsidy Roll for Suffolk four men of this name were assessed in Bacton: Thomas *Gernon*, Nicholas *Gernown*, John and Edmund *Garnon*. In the same parish, in 1568, all four men of this family are called *Garnham*, the only form found in the 1674 Hearth Tax. This is the usual modern form, *Gernon* and *Garnon* being rare. *Grennan* is from the variant OFr *grenon*.

Garrad, Garred, Garratt, Garrett, Garretts, Garritt, Gerrad, Gerratt, Gerred, Gerrett, Jared, Jarrad, Jarred, Jarratt, Jarrett, Jarritt, Jerratt, Jerreatt, Jerred: *Geraddus* filius Simonis 1242 Fees (L); *Gerad* 1272 Ipm; *Jaret* Havelok 1539 FeuDu; John *Gerad* (*Gerard'*) 1230 P (So); Peter *Geraud* son of Robert *Gerold* 1250–1 Fees (Nth); Thomas *Gerad* 1332 SRCu; Robert *Garad* 1540 NorwW (Sf); Thomas *Jarred* 1540 SxWills; John *Garrat*, William *Garrett* 1553–5 RochW; Robert *Jarratt* 1597 SRSr. For GERALD or GERARD. Through loss of *l* or *r* respectively, both became *Gerad*, *Jerad* and developed alike.

Garrard: *v.* GERARD

Garraway, Garroway: (i) Ricardus *filius Garwi* 1188 P (Gl); William, Walter *Garwy* 1236 Ipm (Ess), 1327 SRWo; John *Gorewy* 1317 AssK. OE *Gārwīg* 'spear-war'. (ii) Walter *de Garewy* 1228 Cl. From Garway (Hereford).

Garrish: *v.* GERISH

Garrison: (i) Nicholas *de Gerdeston* 1204 AssY. From Garriston (NRYorks). (ii) James *Gerardson*, *Garardson* 1423–9 FrY; Thomas *Garratson*, John *Garretson* 1550 Pat. 'Son of Gerard.'

Garrod, Garrood, Garrould: *v.* GERALD

Garson: Reginald *Garcon* 1177 P (Y); Hugh *le Garchun* 1242 P (Ess). OFr *garcon*, *garchon* 'valet'.

Garston, Garstone, Gaston: (i) John *de la Garston'* 1210 Cur (Sr); John *at(t)e Gaston*, *Garston* 1327, 1332 SRSx. 'Dweller by the grass-enclosure' (OE *gærstūn*) or, possibly, 'warden of the *garston*', an enclosure near the village where cattle were kept. (ii) Adam *de Gerstan* 1264 Ipm (La). From Garston (Lancs).

Garth: John, Mariota *del Garth* 1297 MinAcctCo (Y), 1332 SRCu. 'One in charge of enclosed ground, a garden or paddock', ME *garth*, ON *garðr*.

Garton: Robert *de Gertuna* c1163 Gilb; Robert *de Garton* 1249 IpmY; William *Garton* 1346 FFEss. From Garton (ERYorks), or from minor places of this name.

Gasche: *v.* WACE

Gascoign, Gascoigne, Gascoin, Gascoine, Gascoinge, Gascoyne, Gasquoine, Gaskain, Gasken, Gaskin, Gaskins, Gasking: (i) Bernard *Gascon'* 1206 Cur (Nth); William *le Gascun* 1208 P (Y). AFr *Gascon*, ME *Gascoun*, *Gascon* 'a Gascon', 'a native of Gascony' (a1375 NED). This does not seem to have survived, unless it has been absorbed by *Gasken* and *Gaskin(s)*. (ii) Philip *le Gascoyn* 1266 FineR (Sa); Peter *Gascoying* 1274 RH (D); Geoffrey *Gascoyne* 1275 RH (Nf); Joan *Gas-choyn* 1469 GildY; William *Gasquyn* 1473 ib.; John *Gasqwyn* 1486 GildY, John *Gascoyng* 1505 ib., Dom. John *Gascon* 1509 ib., Mag. John *Caswin* 1528 ib.; John *Gascon*, Thomas *Gaskyn* 1524 SRSf. OFr *Gascuinz* adj., 'of Gascony', 'a Gascon'. In the 15th century and later, *Gascon* occurs as *Gaskin*, *Gascogne*, *Gascoigne*, which NED suggests may be due to the influence of *Gascogne* 'Gascony'. Some of the above forms are certainly from the adjective. (iii) Robert *de Gascoin* 1243 AssSo; Nicholas *de Gascoigne* 1340 LLB F; William *Gascoigne* 1389 FFHu. From Gascony (Fr *Gascogne*).

Gash, Gashion: *v.* WACE

Gaskell, Gaskill: *v.* GAITSKELL

Gason, Gass: *v.* WACE

Gassman, Gastman: Adam *Gasman*, Richard *Whasman* 1346 FA (Sf). 'Servant of *Gass* or *Wace*', with intrusive *t* in *Gastman*. *v.* WACE.

Gasson: *v.* WACE

Gast: *v.* GHOST

Gastall: *v.* WASTALL

Gastman: *v.* GASSMAN

Gaston: *v.* GARSTON

Gate, Gates: Ailricus *de la Gata* 1169 P (D); Ralph *de Gates* 1206 Cur (O); Gilbert *atte Gate* 1260 AssC; Cristina *Gate* 1275 SRWo; Richard *Overthegate* 1327 SRDb; Thomas *atte Gate*, Custancia *del Gates* 1379 PTY. 'Dweller by the gate(s)', OE *gatu*, plural of OE *geat*. *v.* YATE. In the Scandinavian counties we may also have ON *gata* 'road'. cf. STREET.

Gatecliff, Gatliff, Getliff: Thomas *Gaytclyff* 1457 FrY. From Gatley (Ches), earlier *Gateclyve*.

Gateley, Gately, Gatley, Gatlay: Ralph *de Gateleia* 1086 DB (Nf); Simon *de Gatle* 1203 FFK; Henry *Gateleye* 1327 SRWo. From Gateley (Norfolk), or Gatley (Ches, Hereford).

Gater: Walter *le Gater* 1279 RH (O); Robert *Gater* 1301 SRY; William *le Gatier* 1332 SRSx. (i) A derivative of OE *gāt* 'goat', hence 'goat-herd', with preservation today of the unrounded northern *ā*. cf. GOATER, GAITER. (ii) In the north, 'dweller by the road', from ON *gata*. (iii) 'dweller by the gate', *v.* GATE.

Gaterell: *v.* GATHERAL

Gatheral, Gatherall, Gaterell, Gatterel, Gatrall, Gatrell, Gatrill, Gattrell: Weekley takes *Gatherall* literally as a nickname, but all are probably voiced forms of CATTERALL, etc.

Gathercole: William, Richard *Gaderecold* 1327 SRSf; Thomas *Gadercold* 1524 SRSf; James *Gathercoal*, *Gathercole* 1597, 1611 Gardner (Sf). There can be no association with charcoal or cabbage as the second element is clearly *cold*. To the medieval physiologist, melancholy and choler were dry and cold. When old, a man's blood was said to wax dry and cold and cold was associated with weakness. Hence, probably, a nickname for an old man, one who 'gathered cold' and weakness.

Gatherer: Roger *le gaderer* 1275 RH (L). A derivative of OE *gaderian* 'to gather', a collector of money. ME *gather* was used of collecting dues from gild-brethren, rent, tithes, etc.

Gatland: William *Gatelond* 1327 SRSx; Ralph *atte Gatelond* 1332 ib. 'Dweller on the land with or by a gate' or at the goat-land.

Gatliff: v. GATECLIFF

Gatrell, Gatterel: v. GATHERAL

Gattiker: William *de Gatacra* 1161 P (Sa). From Gatacre (Salop) or Gateacre (Lancs).

Gatward: William, Richard *le Gateward* 1255 Ass (Ess), 1262 MEOT (Herts); Walter *Gatward* 1524 SRSf. OE *geat-weard* 'gate-keeper', or 'goat-ward, goat-herd' (OE *gāt*).

Gauche: John *Gauch* 1260 AssC. OFr *gauche* 'left-handed, awkward'.

Gaudin, Gauden: *Waldinus* 1066 DB (So), 1086 DB (Y, L); *Gaudinus* 1188 P (Nf); Peter, Roger *Gaudin* 1237 Fees (D), 1275 RH (Sf); Roger *Waudin* 1243 Fees (Sa). AFr *Waldin*, OFr *Gaudin*, a diminutive of OG names in *Wald-*. v. WALDING.

Gaught: v. GALT

Gaukrodger: v. GAWKRODGER

Gaul: v. GALL

Gauld: Jas *Gald* 1550 Black; John *Gauld* 1686 ib. Gael *gallda* 'pertaining to the Lowlands'. v. GALL, GALT.

Gault: v. GALT

Gaulter, Gaultier: v. WALTER

Gaunson: v. GAWENSON

Gaunt, Gant: (i) Richard *le Gaunt* 1219 Cur (K); Maurice *le Gant* 1225 AssSo. ME *gaunt, gant* 'slim, slender', or 'haggard-looking, tall, thin and angular' (1440 MED). (ii) metonymic for GAUNTER 'glove-maker'. (iii) Gilbert *de Gand, de Gant* 1086 DB; Gilbert *de Gaunt* 1219 Cur (L). From Ghent (Flanders).

Gaunter, Ganter: Lefwinus *le Wanter* 1172 Oseney (O); Adam *le Gaunter* 1220 Cur (Mx); Adam *le Ganter* 1279 RH (O). OFr *gantier, wantier* 'maker or seller of gloves' (1263 MED).

Gaut, Gaute: v. GALT

Gautier: v. WALTER

Gavin, Gaven, Gauvain, Gauvin, Gawen, Gawn, Gawne, Wawn, Wawne: *Wawanus filius Ricardi* 1208 Cur (Ess); Goseline *filius Gawyne* 1279 RH (C); *Gawynus de Suthorp'* 1332 FFK; *Gaven* Richardson 1631 Bardsley; *Gawne* Gilpin 1653 ib.; William *Walwein* 1169 P (Do); Robert *Wawayn* 1255 RH (W); Matilda *Wawwayne* 1315 Wak (Y); John *Walweyn*, Alice *Waweins* 1327 SRC; Adam *Wawayne* c1372 Black; Emma *Gawyn* 1379 PTY; William *Wawne* 1502 Black; Alexander *Gavin* 1647 ib. *Gavin*, still a common christian name in Scotland, is the Scottish form of the English *Gawayne* and the French *Gauvain*, the name of the son of King Arthur's sister. In the Welsh Arthurian romances it is found as *Gwalchmai*, perhaps 'the Hawk of the Plain' (Jackson), and is latinized by Geoffrey of Monmouth as *Walganus*, a form which has led to the suggestion that there was an alternative name *Gwalchgwyn* 'white falcon'. The name was also common in Brittany which may partly account for its frequency in the eastern counties.

In central French the Anglo-Norman *Walwain* became *Gawain* or *Gauvain*, with the common substitution of *G* for *W*. *Walwain* may still survive in *Walwin*. v. also GAWENSON.

Gaw: v. GALL

Gawenson, Gaunson, Ganson: Alexander *Gawensone* 1563 Black (Nairn). 'Son of *Gavin*.'

Gawkrodger, Gawkroger, Gaukrodger, Gaukroger: Rauffe, William *Gawkeroger* 1539 RothwellPR (Y); John *Gawkrycher* 1553 FrY; Danyell *Corkroger* 1685 FrY. 'Awkward or clumsy Roger', a Yorkshire name, from dial. *gawk*.

Gawler, Gowler: Ralph *Gauelere* 1206 P (Do); William *le Gavelere* 1305 FFEss. ME *gaveler, goveler, gouler* 'usurer', from OE *gafol* 'tribute, rent, interest'.

Gawn, Gawne: A Manx name from *Mac-an-Gabhain* 'the smith's son': *MacGawne* 1422, *Gawen* 1517 Moore. cf. Irish *McGowan* and Gaelic *McGavin*. v. also GAVIN.

Gay: (i) Osward *le Gay* 1176 P (Sr); Gilbert *Gay* 1191 P (L). ME *gai(e)*, OFr *gai* 'full of joy, lighthearted' (c1390 MED). (ii) Hilda *de Gay* 1192 P (O); William *de Gaia* 1203 AssSt. From some French place; perhaps Gaye (La Manche).

Gaylard: v. GALLIARD

Gayle: v. GALE

Gayler, Gaylor: v. GALER

Gaylord: v. GALLIARD

Gaymar, Gaymer: Rannulf *filius Gaimar'*, *Gaimer* 1193–5 P (L); Rannulf *Gaimer* 1197 ib.; Peter *Gaymer* 1219 FFEss. OFr *Gaimar*, OG *Weimar, Waimer, Guaimar*.

Gayter, Gaytor: v. GAITER

Gaze: v. WACE

Geake, Jeeks, Jecks, Jex: Walter *Geek* 1275 RH (L); Henry *le Geke, le Gekke* 1279 RH (O); Walter *Jekkes* 1524 SRSf. ME *geke, gecke* 'fool, simpleton' (1515 NED). v. also JACK.

Gear, Geare, Geear, Geer, Geere: Albert, Joscelin *Gere* 1133–60 Rams (Sf), 1221 AssWo. ME *gere* 'sudden fit of passion', 'wild or changeful mood', whence GERISH.

Gearing, Geering: William *Gering* 1202 AssL; Sewal *Geryng* 1296 SRSx; Hugh, Peter *le Geryng* 1327 *SR* (Ess). ME *gering*, recorded twice (c1300) apparently in the sense 'villain'.

Geary, Gerrey, Gerrie, Gerry, Jaray, Jearey, Jeary, Jary, Jarry: *Gericus de Gilling* 1208 Cur (Y); Willelmus *filius Gerici* 1214 Cur (L); John, Richard *Geri* 1195 P (O), 1221 AssWa; John *le Geri* 1276 RH (Berks); Richard *Jery* 1279 RH (Hu). OFr *Geri*, OG *Geric;* also a nickname from ME *ge(e)ry* 'changeable, giddy', applied by Chaucer to Venus. v. also GAREY.

Geater, Geator: v. GAITER

Geaves: v. JEEVES

Gebb: v. JEBB

Geddie: v. GIDDY

Gedge: Thomas *Geg* 1205 Cur (Nf); Walter *le Geg* 1221 ElyA (Hu); William *Gegge* 1263 AssLa; Alice *la Gegges* 1310 ColchCt; John *Gedge* 1568 SRSf. ME *gegge* a contemptuous term applied to both men and women. cf. 'Thus arraied gooþ þe gegges, And alle wiþ bare legges' (1387 NED).

Gedye: v. GIDDY
Geen: v. JEAN
Geer(e): v. GEAR
Geering: v. GEARING
Geeves: v. JEEVES
Geffen, Giffen, Giffin: Peter, Rose *Geffen* 1332 SRWo, SRWa; Nycolas *Gyffen* 1524 SRSf; Robert *Giffen* 1660 ArchC 30. The Subsidy Rolls for Worcestershire (1327) and Warwickshire (1332) contain at least 40 surnames in *-en* of a type hitherto unnoted. They are usually names of men, occasionally of women, and are found side by side with the more common type *Geffes, Hobbes, Tomes, Watts*. The suffix is added to pet-forms of French personal-names common among the peasants, usually masculine (*Jacken, Kytten, Nicken, Tommen, Watten*), occasionally feminine (*Maggen, Molden* (Maud), *Magoten*). In addition to *Geffen*, this suffix survives in the modern *Dawn, Edden, Hobben, Hudden, Judden* and *Tibbins* and has contributed to *Gibben, Hicken, Hitchen* and *Hullin*. It seems clear that we have a genitive singular, *Geffen, Dawn*, etc., parallel to *Jeffs, Dawes*, etc., but the form is difficult. Our knowledge of the 12th- and 13th-century written language of this area is scanty. Of the spoken language we know nothing. In early ME the genitive singular *-an* of the weak declension would have become *-en*. But at an early date the whole of the singular appears to have been re-formed on the analogy of the nominative singular, and the plural on that of the nominative plural, giving a singular in *-e* and a plural in *-en*, with a genitive plural *-ene*. The *-e* of the genitive singular was then supplanted by *-es* from the strong declension. In the West Midlands and the south the weak declension survived, but only in the plural. Presumably these pet-names of French origin were adopted at a time when the Old English system of declensions was breaking up and the inflexions were in a state of flux. They would be used most commonly in the nominative and when a possessive was required the common form of genitive in *-es* was normally used. It may be that in the West Midlands, when genitives of these pet-names were first required, the genitive singular in *-en* was still in use in the spoken language and persisted, side by side with that in *-es*, just as strong and weak plurals interchange in the Devonshire place-names *Hayes* and *Hayne*.

Geldard, Geldart: William *le Geldehyrde* 1284 Wak (Y); John *Gelderd* 1494 GildY; John *Geldert* 1511 FrY. ME *gelde* 'sterile, barren', and OE *hierde* 'tender of the "geld" cattle'.

Gelder: v. GILDER
Gelding, Gilding: Geoffrey *Geldyng* 1296 SRSx; Thomas *Gelding* 1327 ib. ON *geldingr* 'a gelded person, eunuch' (a1382 MED), an opprobrious nickname.

Gell, Gelle, Jell: *Gelle* Bakur 1275 Wak (Y); *Gelle* Winter 1279 RH (C); John *Jelle* 1296 SRSx; John *Gelle* 1301 SRY. *Gell*, a pet form of *Jelion* or *Juliana*. v. GILLIAN.

Gellatly: v. GOLIGHTLY
Gellibrand: v. GILLEBRAND
Gelling: *Mag Gelain* 1222, *Mac Gilleon, Gellen* 1511, *Gelling* 1626. Manx for *Giolla-Guillin* 'Guillin's servant' (Moore).
Gellion: v. GILLIAN.
Gellman, Gelman: v. GILLMAN
Gem: *Gemma* 1219 AssY; *Jemma* 1283 FFEss; Alan *Gemma* 1198 P (Nth); Semannus *Gemme* 1205 Cur (Nf); Simon *Gimme* 1232 Pat (L); Walter *Gemma* 1301 AD ii (Y); Agnes *Jemme* 1379 PTY. The above personal-names are those of women as is that of *Jimme* wife of Robert Feysant (1286 AssCh), but the name was also undoubtedly masculine: *Gemme* brother of Gilbert (1251 AssLa); *Gemme* Campion, whose wife Magge is mentioned, and *Gemme* the gardiner, presumably a man (1306 Wak). cf. *Jimme* Balder 1286 AssCh. This must be the vernacular pronunciation of *James*, used for men and women alike. The surname is indebted to both the masculine and the feminine name.

Gemmell, Gemmill: Gabriel *Gymmill*, William *Gemmill* 1599 Black. A late Scottish pronunciation of *Gamel*. v. GAMBELL.

Gemson, Gimson, Jimpson: Robert *Gimson, Gemson* 1332 SRCu, 1379 PTY. 'Son of *Jimme* or *Gem.*' v. GEM.

Genn: v. JEAN
Genner, Genower: v. JENNER
Gent, Jent: Robert *le Gent* 1195 P (Ha); John *Gent* 1200 P (Wo). OFr *gent*, ME *gente* 'well-born', 'noble', hence 'noble in conduct, courteous' (c1300 MED).

Gentle, Gentles, Gentile, Jentle: Osbert *le Gentil* 1202 P (Ha); John (*le*) *Gentil* 1242 Fees (W). OFr, ME *gentil* 'high-born, noble' (c1225 MED).

Gentleman: Nicholas, William *Gentilman* 1273 RH (Beds), 1301 SRY. 'A man of gentle birth' (a1275 NED).

Geoffrey, Geoffroy: v. JEFFRAY

George, Georgeson: *Georgius* Grim 12th DC (L); Hugo *filius Georgii* 1222 Cur (Nf); William *George* 1412 LLB I; William *Georgeson* 1471 Black (Coupar). Fr *Georges*, Lat *Georgius*, from Greek Γεωργός 'land-worker, farmer'. The name was introduced into England by the Crusaders but was never common before the Hanoverian succession in the 18th century.

Gepp, Jepp, Jeppe, Jepps: *Geppe* Werri 1228 FeuDu; *Geppe* filius Hugonis 1258 Kirkstall (Y); *Jep* le Wyte 1296 SRSx; William *Jep* 1225 Pat; William *Geppe* 1327 SRSf. A pet-form of *Geoffrey*.

Gepson: v. JEPPESON

Gerald, Gerold, Garrould, Garrod, Garrood, Jarraud, Jarrod, Jarrold, Jarrott, Jerrold, Fitzgerald: Robertus *filius Geraldi, Geroldi, Giroldi, Girold* 1086 DB (Do, W); Philippus *filius Geroldi* 1119 Bury (Sf); *Geroudus* filius Radulfi 1166–75 DC (L); William *Geroud* 1200 P (Y); Adam *Jeroldus* 1221 ElyA (Sf); Robert *Gerold* 1250 Fees (Nth); John *Jerald* 1275 RH (Sf); Richard *Gerald* 1277 Ely (Sf); Thomas *Garold* 1524 SRSf; Elizabeth *Jarrald* 1730 SfPR. OG *Gerald*, *Girald* 'spear-ruler', a name introduced by the Normans, fairly common, but less so than *Gerard* with which it was early confused: Adam *Gerold*, *Girardus*, *Gerard* 1219–46 Fees (La), Nicholas *Garolde* alias *Garard* 1535 NorwW (Nf). Garret *Fitzgarret* 1586 (SPD) is for *Fitzgerald*. *v.* GARRAD.

Gerant, Gerrans, Gerring, Jerrans, Jarrand: (i) Turstinus *de Giron*, *de Girunde* 1086 DB (K); Walter *de Gyrunde*, *Gerun*, *de Gerunde*, *Gerunde* 1279–92 FFEss. From Gironde (Gascony). (ii) *Gerinus*, *Girinus* 1086 DB (Wa, Ha); Serlo *filius Gerini* 1208 Cur (Ess); Henry *Girun* 1210 Cur (C); Richard *Gerrun* c1250 Rams (C); John *Geryn* 1300 LoCt; Robert *Jeryn* 1319 SRLo; Richard *Geroun*, *Geround* 1327 SRC. OFr *Gerin*, *Jerin*, OG *Gerin*, a diminutive of a name in *Ger-*, plus the suffix *-in*, and, occasionally, *-un*. One *Gerin* was a pet-name for *Gervasius* (Forssner). *v.* also JEROME.

Gerard, Gerrard, Garard, Garrard, Jarrard. Jerrard: *Gerardus*, *Girardus* 1086 DB; *Gerardus* 1134–40 Holme (Nf), 1149–62 DC (L); *Jerard* filius archidiaconi Hy 2 ib.; John, Hugo *Gerard* Hy 2 DC (L), 1199 P (Nth); William *Gerart* 1281 AssSt; Henry *Jerard* 1284 FFEss; John *Gerrard*, Thomas *Garard*, William *Garrarde* 1412, 1429, 1458 FrY. OFr *Gerart*, *Girart*, OG *Gerard*, *Girard* 'spear-brave'. Willelmus *filius Gerardi* de Kiluington is also called William *Gerard*' (1219 AssY). *v.* also GARRAD, GERALD.

Gerham: *v.* JEROME

Gerish, Gerrish, Garrish: Umfrey *le Gerische* 1275 RH (O); William *Girisshe* 1370 Eynsham (O). ME *gerysshe* 'changeful, wild, wayward' (c1430 NED). cf. 'Madnesse that doth infest a man ones in a mone the whiche doth cause one to be geryshe, and wavering witted, not constant, but fantasticall' (1547 NED).

German, Germann, Germain, Germaine, Germing, Jarman, Jarmain, Jarmains, Jerman, Jermine, Jermyn, Jermynn: (i) *Germanus* 1086 DB, c1150 DC (L); *Jerman* filius Willelmi 1248 FFEss; John *Jarman* 1227 Pat (Nf); Philippus *Germani* 1236 Fees (Do); William *Jermain* 1279 RH (O); Nicholas *Germeyn* 1292 LLB A; Richard *Germeyn*, *Jermin* 1317 AssK; Margery *Jerman* 1524 SRSf. OFr *Germain*, Lat *Germanus* 'a German'. *v.* JERMEY. (ii) Gilbert *le German* 1318 Pat (Sf). 'The German.'

Gernon: *v.* GARNON

Gerrad, Gerratt, Gerred, Gerrett: *v.* GARRAD

Gerrans: *v.* GERANT

Gerrard: *v.* GERARD

Gerrey, Gerrie, Gerry: *v.* GEARY

Gerring: *v.* GERANT

Gerrish: *v.* GERISH

Gervase, Gervis: *v.* JARVIS

Gervers: Probably a late form of GERVASE.

Gething, Gettens, Gettings, Gettins, Gitting, Gittings, Gittins: Eynon *Gethin* 1332 Chirk; Robert *Gettyns* 1500 FrY; Richard *Gittin* 1603 Bardsley (Ch). Welsh *Gethin*, perhaps from *cethin* 'dusky, swarthy'.

Getliff: *v.* GATECLIFF

Ghost, Gast: Aluiet *Gæst* 1066 ICC (C); John *le Gast* 1275 SRWo; Bartholomew (*le*) *Gost* 1327 SRSf. OE *gæst* (*gāst*) 'demon'.

Gibb, Gibbes, Gibbs: *Gibbe* de Huckenhale 1179 P (Nt); *Gibbe* 1183 DC (L); Winc' *Gibbe* 1290 AD iv (Nf); Thomas *Gibbes* 1327 SRSo. *Gibb*, a pet form of *Gilbert*. cf. *Gibertus* le Vag' 1332 SRSr. *v.* GIPP.

Gibben, Gibbens, Gibbin, Gibbins, Gibbings, Gibbon, Gibbons: (i) Ralph *Gibiun* (*Gibbewin*) 1176 P (O); Geoffrey *Gibewin*, *Gibwin*, *Gibeuin*, *Gubewin* 1196, 1208, 1213 Cur (So, Nth, Bk). OFr *Giboin*, OG *Gebawin* 'gift-friend', surviving in Marsh Gibbon (PN Bk 54). (ii) *Gebon*, *Gilbert* Peke 1466–7 Oseney (O); Vitalis, Richard *Gibun* c1176 Bart, 1202 P (Sx); Thomas *Gibon* 1317 AssK. *Gibb-un* a diminutive of *Gibb* (Gilbert). (iii) William *Gibben* 1332 SRWa. *v.* GIBB, GEFFEN.

Giblett, Giblin, Gibling: *Gibelinus* serviens 1199 P (Nth); Segerus *Gibelin* 1206 Cur (Co); Dera *Gibelot* 1279 RH (C); John *Gebelot* 1327 SRC; Simon *Gibeloun* 1327 SRSf. *Gib-el-in*, *Gib-el-un*, *Gib-el-ot*, double diminutives of *Gibb*.

Gibson, Gibbeson: Henry *Gibsone* 1311 NottBR; Richard *Gibbeson* 1327 SRWo. 'Son of *Gibb*.' May also be a contraction of (Robert) *Gibonson* 1484 FrY.

Giddy, Geddie, Gedye: Herbert *Gidi* 1115 Winton (Ha); Walter *le Gidye* 1219 AssY; Roger *Geddy* 1230 P (Y). OE *gydig*, *gidig* 'possessed of an evil spirit', 'mad, insane'. cf. William *Gidyheved* 1347 LLB F.

Giffard, Gifford, Jefferd, Jefford: *Gifardus* 1086 DB, Hy 2 DC (L); Johannes *filius Giffard*' 1200 P (C); Walter *Gifard*. *Gifhard*, *Giffart* 1084–6 GeldR, DB, InqEl; William *Giffard* 1158 P (Wa); Reginald *Gifford* 1260 AssC; Philip called *Giffard* 1311 LLB D. OG *Gifard*, or OFr *giffard* 'chubby-cheeked, bloated'.

Giffen, Giffin: *v.* GEFFEN

Gigg, Giggs: Hugo *Gigge* 1220 Cur (Sf). ME *gigge* 'a flighty, giddy girl' (a1225 NED).

Giggle: *v.* JEKYLL

Gilbert, Gilbard, Gilbart, Gilbeart, Gilburt, Gillbard, Guilbert, FitzGilbert: *Gislebertus* 1066 DB (W); *Gilbertus* presbiter c1150 Gilb (L); Willelmus *Gilberti* 1202 Cur (W); Robert *Gylebert* 1235 AD v (Nf); Robert *Gilberd* 1240 Rams (C); William *Gilbert* 1290 Crowland (C); John *Gilbard* 1304 FFSf; Margery *Gilberdes* 1330 AD vi (W); Henry *Gylbart* 1332 SRSt. OG *Gisilbert*, *Gislebert* 'pledge- or hostage-bright', OFr *Gislebert*, *Gil(l)ebert* (*Guilbert*). The frequency of *Gilberd* suggests that this, with *Gil(l)bard*, may at times belong to *Goldbard*, though *Gilbeard* certainly occurs for *Gilbert*.

Gilbertson: Nicholas *Gilberdson* 1379 PTY. 'Son of *Gilbert*.'

Gilbride: *Ghilebrid* 1066 DB (Y); *Gilbryde* Macgideride 1147–60 Black. Gael *Gille Brighde* 'St Bride's servant'.

Gilchrist, Gilcriest, Gilcrist, Gillchreest, Gill-

crist, Gilgryst: *Gillecrist* 1202 P (Cu); Kilschyn *Gilcrist* 1296 Black. Gael *Gillacrist* 'servant of Christ'. *Gillchreest* is Manx.

Gildea: Ir *Giolla Dé* 'servant of God'.

Gilder, Gilders, Gelder, Guilder: Stephen *le Gelder* 1281 LLB B; John *le Gilder* 1306 ib. C. A derivative of OE *gyldan* 'to gild', a gilder (1550 NED).

Gilders: Ralph *del Gildhus* 1176 P (Y), George *Gildus* 1638 Bardsley. Probably 'caretaker of the guildhall'.

Gildersleeve, Gildersleve: Roger *Gyldenesleve* 1275 RH (Nf); John *Gildensleve*, Jeffrey *Gildsleeve*, Robert *Geldyngsleffe*, Richard *Gyldersleve* 1524 SRSf. 'Man with the golden sleeve' (OE *gylden*).

Gilding: *v.* GELDING

Gildon: Wlgar *se Gildene* c945 OEByn; Henry *le Gulden*, *Gilden* 1325 ParlWrits (Do). Simon *le Geldene* 1327 *SR* (Ess). OE *gylden* 'golden', perhaps 'golden-haired'.

Gilduff: *v.* DUFF

Giles, Gyles, Jiles: *Gilo*, *Ghilo* 1086 DB; Wido *filius Gisel* Hy 2 DC (L); *Gisle, Egidius, Gilo, Gile* de Gousle Hy 2, 1183–7 DC (L); *Gile* de Costeshal' 1196 P (L); *Gilo* Hose 1210 Cur (W); Ailward, Godfrey *Gile* 1176, 1191 P (Bk, Nth); William *Gyles* 1296 SRSx; William *Gilis* 1317 AssK; Nicholas *Gisel* 1346 FA (Sf). The DB *Gilo* has been identified with OG *Gilo*, equivalent to *Gislebertus*, and this is supported by the forms *Gisel*, *Gisle*. The latinization of this by *Egidius* shows that the scribe associated the name with *Giles*, a difficult name, regularly translated *Egidius*, from Greek αἰγίδιον 'kid'. The name of the 7th-century Provençal hermit St *Ægidius* spread widely and survives as *Gidi*, *Gidy* in southern France, as *Gili*, *Gilli* in the Alpes-Maritimes, elsewhere as *Gile*, *Gille*. The popularity of this form in England is proved both by the number of churches dedicated to St Giles and by the frequent medieval *Egidius*. In the 12th century it was confused with and absorbed OG *Gilo* and *Gisel*, a short form of *Gilbert*. *v.* JELLIS.

Gilfillan: *Gillefalyn* c1214 Black; Ewin *Gilfillane* 1516 ib. Gael *Gille Fhaolàin* 'servant of (St) Fillan'.

Gilfoyle: Ir *Giolla Phóil* 'servant of (St) Paul'.

Gilgryst: *v.* GILCHRIST

Gilham: *v.* GILLAM

Gilkison: Robert, John *Gilc(h)ristson* 1332 SRCu, 1499 Black; William *Gilkersone* 1559 ib.; James *Gilkisone* 1672 ib. 'Son of Gilchrist.'

Gill: (i) *Ghille, Ghile, Ghil* 1066 DB (Y); Gamel *filius Gille* 1185 Templars (Y); Henricus *filius Gilli*, *Gille* 1200 DC, P (L); Johannes *filius Gille* 1297 SRY; Ralph, Robert *Gille* 1202 AssL, 1332 SRCu, 1379 PTY. OIr **Gilla*, ON *Gilli* 'servant'. (ii) Elias *de la Gyle* 1269 Ipm (Y); Thomas *del Gille* 1246 AssLa; Michael *del Gill* 1332 SRCu. 'Dweller in the deep glen or ravine', ME *gille*, ON *gil* (a1400 MED). Both these northern names are pronounced with a hard *g*. (iii) Samuel, Roger *Gille* 1206 Cur (Ess), 1279 RH (O); Thomas *Gylle* 1296 SRSx; John *Jylle* 1312 LLB D. The Irish-

Norwegian personal name *Gille* was not used in the south, but both in the north and the south *Gille* is found as a pet-form of *Gillian* and gave rise to surnames *Gill*, *Gell* and *Jell*. *v.* GELL.

Gill, Gell, MacGill, MacKill: Harald *Gille* (an Irishman) 1103, *MacGylle* 1430, *McGell* 1504, *McGill, Gell* 1511 Moore; Patrick *M'Kille* 1475, James *M'Gill* 1572 Black. Manx *Gill* and *Gell*, Irish *Gill* and Galloway *MacGill*, *MacKill* are all from Ir, Gael *gille* 'servant'.

Gillam, Gillham, Gilliam, Gillum, Gilham: *Giliaum* Spyser 1379 PTY; Peter *Gillame* 1276 LLB B; Arnold *Gilleme* 1283 ib. A; William *Giliam* 1379 PTY; Robert *Gylham*, Thomas *Guyllam* 1524 SRSf. English forms of French *Guillaume*. *v.* WILLIAMS.

Gillard, Jillard, Jellard: *Gillard*, with a hard *g*, is Fr *Guilard*, corresponding to Norman WILLARD. With a *j*-sound, it is a derivative of *Gille* (Giles), Fr *Gillard*. *v.* GILES.

Gillebrand, Gillibrand, Gellibrand: William *Gilebram'* 1219 AssL; John *Gilibrond* 1278 AssLa; Richard *Gelybrond* 1562 PrGR (La). OG *Giselbrand* 'hostage-sword'. In Suffolk, this became *Gillibrowne* (1576) and *Gillibourne* (1620 Lit-SaxhamPR).

Gillespie, Gillespey, Gillaspy, Gilhespy: Ewan *filius Gillaspeck* 1175–99 Black; *Gillescop* de Cletheveys 1220–40 ib. Gael *Gilleasbuig* 'the bishop's servant'.

Gillet, Gillett, Gillatt, Gillitt, Gilliat, Gilliatt, Gilyatt, Gilyott, Jillett, Jillitt, Jellett: (i) *Wiotus* (*Guillotus*) 1175 P (Berks); *Guillotus* le Hauberger 1319 SRLo. Fr *Guillot*, a hypocoristic of *Guillaume* (William), a doublet of WILLET. *Gilot* de Portesmue (1292 SRLo) and *Guylote* Belebouche (1319 SRLo) are both called also *William* (1290 LLB G, 1300 LoCt). Surnames would appear as *Gilot*, *Gillot* and cannot be safely assigned here. Pronounced with *G* hard. (ii) Robert *del Gilheved* 1332 SRCu. 'Dweller at the head of the glen' (ON *gil*). This would become *Gillett*, with hard *G*. (iii) *Gilot* de Lackenby 13th Guisb (Y); *Gilot* de Paris 1280 Oseney (O); John *Gilet* 1243 AssDu; Peter *Gyllot* 1260 AssY; William *Gilot* 1296 SRSx. Whilst these forms cannot be distinguished from (i) above, *Gilot* must also correspond to Fr *Gillet*, *Gillot*, diminutives of *Gille* (Giles) and would become *Gillett*, etc., with a *j*-sound. (iv) *Gillota* 1198 FF (Sf), 1221 AssWa; *Gelot* (m) Webester 1379 PTY; *Gillot* (f) 1379 PTY; John *Gillote* 1279 RH (C); Richard *Gilote* 1324 AD vi (K); Peter *Giliot* 1333 Kirkstall (Y); William *Geliot* 1379 PTY; Robert *Jelott* 1512 GildY. *Gillota* is a diminutive of *Gilia*, the femine of *Giles*: *Egidia* de Clere 1203 Cur (Sf). *Giliot* is a diminutive of *Gillian* or *Juliana* and has given *Gilliat* and *Gilyott* which belong only here and have also become *Gillett*, etc. *Gelot* (m) is a diminutive of *Giles* or of *Julian*. *Gillot* (f) may also be a dimi utive of *Gill* (Gillian). (v) *Gillatt*, in particular, and all except *Gilliat* and *Gilyott* may be late forms of *Gillard*.

Gillham, Gilliam: *v.* GILLAM

Gillian, Gillion, Gillions, Jillions, Gellion, Jellings, Jillings: *Giliana* 1198 FF (Sf); *Jilianus* filius Geroldi 1206 Cur (C); *Jeliana* Falcard 1274 1pm (Cu); *Gilianus* de Levekenore 1279 RH (Bk); Adam *filius Jelion'* 1279 RH (C); *Giliana* Damyñan 1315 AD i (Nth); Robert *Gilion* 1279 RH (C); John *Gilian* 1327 SRDb; Matilda *Jeliane* 1379 PTY; John *Jelyon* 1524 SRSf. Colloquial pronunciations of *Julian* or, more commonly *Juliana. v.* JULIAN. *Juliana* de Scaccario (1194 Cur) is also called *Giliana*, as is Juliana, wife of Henry Escrop (13th Whitby). The seal of *Juliana*, wife of Robert de Vendore, is inscribed SIGILL' GILIANE (12th DC) and a deed of Osbert Cirotecarius and *Juliana* his wife has a seal with the same form of the wife's name (1230 Oseney).

Gilliat(t): *v.* GILLET

Gillibrand: *v.* GILLEBRAND

Gillies, Gillis: *Gillise* c1128 Black; John *Gyllis* 1521 ib. Gael *Gille Iosa* 'servant of Jesus'.

Gilliver: William *Girofre, Gylofre, Gelofre* 1210 P (Sf), 1275, 1327 SRWo. OFr *girofle, gilofre*, ME *gylofre, gilliver* 'clove', used for sauces, hence, perhaps, a grower of gillyflower or a sauce-maker. It might also refer to one who held land by a rent of a clove of gilly-flower.

Gillman, Gilman, Guillerman, Gellman, Gelman, Wellemin, Wellerman, Wellman, Welman, Willmin, Willman, Wilman, Willament, Williman, Williment, Willimont, Willment: *Wileminus* 1220 Cur (O); Anketinus *filius Gilmyn* 1279 RH (C); *Gilmyn* de Perham 1327 SRSx; John *Wilemyn* 1275 RH (Lo); William *Ghylemyn* 1297 MinAcctCo (Co); John *Wylemyn* 1301 LLB B; William *Gillemyn* 1317 AssK; Ralph *Welemyn* 1327 SRC; Matilda *Gelemyn* ib.; Thomas *Wylman* 1524 FrY; Richard *Williman* 1544 RothwellPR (Y); William *Gylman* son of William *Gylmyn* 1549 FrY. OFr *Guillemin*, Norman *Willemin*, diminutives of *Guillaume, Willelm. v.* WILLIAMS.

Gillmore: *v.* GILMOUR

Gillson, Gilson: Thomas, John *Gilleson* 1324 Wak (Y), 1332 SRCu; John *Gylesson(e)* 1348 LLB F, 1372 LoPleas. 'Son of *Gill* or of *Giles.*'

Gillum: *v.* GILLAM

Gilman: *v.* GILLMAN

Gilmour, Gilmore, Gilmer, Gillmor, Gillmore: (i) *Gilmor* 1133–56 Black (Cu); Richard *Gilemor* 1228 FFHu; Gillechad *Gillamor* 1304 Black. Ir, Gael *Gille Moire* 'servant of (the Virgin) Mary'. (ii) William *de Gyllingmor* 13th Guisb (Y). From Gillamoor (NRYorks).

Gilroy, Gildroy: Ewen *Gilry* 1331 Black. Ir, Gael *Giolla rua* 'servant of the red-haired lad'.

Gilson: *v.* GILLSON

Gilyatt, Gilyott: *v.* GILLET

Gimson: *v.* GEMSON

Ginger: Roger *Gingiure* 1221 AssGl; William *Gyngeuer* 1262 FFEss; Roger *Ginger* c1280 St Thomas (St). ME *gingivere, gyngure, gingere* 'ginger', for a dealer in ginger, or, possibly, also for a hot-tempered or a reddish-haired man.

Ginn, Gynn: Henry, Roger *Gin* 1191 P (Nf), 1221 FFSt; Walter *Gynn* 1275 SRWo. ME *gin, ginne*, an aphetic form of OFr *engin* 'skill, ingenuity' (c1200 MED), 'snare, trap' (a1250). cf. JENNER.

Ginner: *v.* JENNER

Giot: *v.* WYATT

Gipp, Gipps, Gypp, Gypps: *Gippa* de Neuhus 1150 DC (L); *Gippe* filius Ailsi 1202 FFL; Walter, Edmund *Gippe* 1188 P (L), 1227 FFSf; Agnes *Gyppes* 1352 ColchCt. A pet-name of *Gilbert.* cf. *Gilebertus* filius *Gippe* de Cheyle, *Gilebertus* de Cheiles Hy 3, 1256 Gilb (L). cf. GIBB.

Gipson, Gypson: Robert *Gipson* 1524 SRSf. 'Son of *Gipp.*'

Girdler, Gurdler, Gurtler: Luke *le Gerdler* 1277 LLB A; William *Gurdeler* 1279 RH (O); Henry *le Girdlere* 1295 MESO (Nf). A derivative of OE *gyrdel* 'girdle', a girdle-maker (1356 MED).

Girle: Geoffrey *Gurle* 1275 RH (Sf); William (*le*) *Gurle* 1296, 1327 SRSx. ME *gurle* 'youth, maiden' (c1300 MED).

Girling: *v.* CODLIN

Girton, Girtin, Gurton, Gretton, Gritton, Gritten: Godmarus *de Grettona* 1086 InqEl (C); Engenulfus *de Grettona* 1172 P (Nth); Richard *de Grittone* 1279 RH (C). From Girton (Cambs, Notts), Gretton (Glos, Northants).

Gitting(s), Gittins: *v.* GETHING

Gladden, Gladding, Glading: *Gledingus* 1196 Cur; Robert *Glading*, Susan *Gladden*, Stephen *Gladin* 1674 HTSf. OE **Glæding*, from OE *glæd* 'glad'. cf. GLADE, GLADWIN.

Gladdish: *v.* GLADWISH

Glade: (i) Willelmus *filius Glade* 1202 AssL. OE **Glæd*, the simplex of **Glæding* and **Glædwine.* (ii) Richard *in the Glade* 1275 SRWo. 'Dweller in the glade', the more likely source.

Gladhill: *v.* GLEDHILL

Glading: *v.* GLADDEN

Gladman: *Glademanus* 1066 DB (Sf); William *Gladman* 1327 SRY. OE **Glædmann.*

Gladwin: *Gladuin(e)* 1066 DB (L, St); *Glad(e)-wine* c1113 Burton (St), c1180 ArchC vi, 1207 AssBeds; Henry, Peter *Gladewine* 1148 Winton (Ha), 1210 Cur (C); Robert *Gledewyne* 1317 AssK. OE **Glædwine*, unrecorded in OE, but fairly common in the 12th century.

Gladwish, Gladdish: Roger *de Gledewysse* 1296 SRSx. From Glydwish in Burwash (Sussex).

Glaisher, Glaysher, Glazyer, Glazier: Thomas *le glasyer* 1297 MinAcctCo; Robert *le Glasiere* 1327 SR (Ess). A derivative of OE *glæs* 'glass', glass-maker (1296–7 MED).

Glandfield, Glanfield, Glenfield: These names may derive from *Clanefeld:* cf. Clanfield, Clanville (Hants), Clanvill (Som), Clanville (Wilts), Glanvill Fm (PN D 629), Glenfield (Leics), all identical in origin; or from *Glanville.* Ann *Glanvill* (1706) is called *Glanfield* in 1712 in the ShotleyPR (Sf). cf. Glandfield's Fm in Felsted: *Glaunvylles* 1360, *Glandfield* 1593, from William *de Glaunvilla* 1200 (PN Ess 423). The surname Glanfield is still found at Witham, not far from Felsted.

Glanvill, Glanville, de Glanville: Robert *de Glamuilla, de Glanuill', de Glauilla* 1086 DB (Nf, Sf); William *de Glanvile* 1127–34 Holme (Nf). From Glanville (Calvados). *v.* OEByn, ANF.

Glascock, Glascott, Glasscock, Glasscote: Walter *de Glascote* 1332 SRSt; From Glascote (Warwicks), *Glascote* Hy 2, *Glascocke* 1667 PN Wa 26.

Glasgow, Glasscoe: John *de Glasgu* 1258 Black. From Glasgow.

Glassbrook, Glazebrook: Geoffrey *de Glasebroc* 1246 AssLa; William *de Glasebrok* 1350 FFY; Richard *Glasbroke* 1525 SRSx. From Glazebrook (Lancs), or from minor places of this name.

Glassman: Richard *le Glasmon* 1327 SRSt. OE *glæs* and *mann*, 'dealer in glass-ware'.

Glave(s): *v.* GLEAVE

Glaysher, Glayzer, Glazier: *v.* GLAISHER

Glazebrook: *v.* GLASSBROOK

Gleadell, Gleadle: *v.* GLEDHILL

Gleave, Gleaves, Glave, Glaves: William *Glaiue* 1202 FFNf; William *Gleiue* 1227 AssBeds; William *Gleue* 1283 SRSf. OFr *glaive, gleive*, ME *gleyve, gleve* 'lance', a name for a spearman or for a winner in a race in which the lance set up as a winning-post was given as a prize. *v.* GAME.

Gledhill, Gledall, Gleadell, Gleadle, Gladhill: Adam *de Gledehyll* 1277 Wak (Y); Robert *Gledall, Gledhell, Gleydell* 1571–1603 RothwellPR (Y); Launcelot *Gleadell, Gleadall* 1600–10 ib. From Gledhill (WRYorks).

Gleed: *v.* GLIDE

Glen, Glenn: (i) Gregory *Glen* 1230 Cur (Sf); Adam, William *de glen* 1327 SRLei; Thomas *Glenne* 1340–1450 GildC. From Glen (Leics). (ii) Colban *del Glen* 1328 Black; John *de Glene* c1377 ib.; William *Glen* 1452 ib. (Paisley). From the lands of Glen in Traquair (Peebles).

Glendening, Glendenning, Glendinning, Clendenin, Clendennen, Clendinning, Clindening: Adam *de Glendonwyn* a1286 Black; Robert *Glendonying* 1599 ib.; Isabel *Glindinine* 1667 ib. From Glendinning in Westerkirk (Dumfriesshire).

Glenfield: *v.* GLANDFIELD

Glew, Glue: Radulfus *filius Gleu* 1219 AssY; William *Gleu* 1168 P (Nf); Rannulf *Glowe* 1201 P (So); Peter *Glew* 1301 SRY. OE *glēaw* 'wise, prudent', occasionally used as a personal-name.

Glide, Glyde, Glede, Gleed: Walter *Glide* 1225 AssSo; Thomas *le Glede* 1277 ib.; Richard *le Glyde* 1296 SRSx. OE *glida*, ME *glede* 'kite' (a1398 MED).

Gloster: Durandus *Gloecestra, de Glouuecestre* 1086 DB; William *de Glocestria* 1242 Oseney (O). From Gloucester.

Glover: Gilbert, William *le Glouere* 1250 MESO (Nf), 1278 AD iv (Sr). A derivative of OE *glōf* 'glove', maker or seller of gloves (1355 MED).

Glozier: Roger *Glosere*, William *Glosur'* 1279 RH (C); Robert *Glosier* 1674 HTSf. A derivative of ME *glosen*, OFr *gloser* 'to make glosses upon, expound, interpret', a commentator (c1400 MED).

Glue: *v.* GLEW

Goacher, Goucher: Willelmus dictus *Godechere*

1343 Black. ME *chere*, OFr *chier* 'face', one of good aspect, cheerful appearance.

Goate: (i) William *le gat* 1139 DC (Nt); Suein *Got* 1166 P (Nf); Hugo *Gat* 1219 AssL; John *le Got* 1254 Pat. OE *gāt* 'goat'. *v.* also GAIT. (ii) Alexander *de Gote* 1288 PN Sx 356, Peter *atte Gote* 1327 SRSx, John *de la Gote* 1329 FrY. 'Dweller by the watercourse or sluice', ME *gote*. *v.* PN C 327, MELS 80. As *gott* is found later for both 'goat' and 'watercourse', these surnames may have contributed to *Gott*.

Goater: Thomas, John *le Goter(e)* 1327, 1333 MEOT (O, Ha). A derivative of OE *gāt* 'goat', goatherd. *v.* also GATER.

Goatman: Ralph *Gateman* 1183 P (Nth); Nicholas *Gooteman* 1455 GildY. OE *gāt* and *mann*, goatherd. cf. Osbert *Gotenecherl* 1183 P (Wa), Reiner *le Gotegrom* 1335 FFSf.

Gobat: *v.* GODBOLD

Gobert: *v.* GODBERT

Godbear, Godbeer, Godber, Godbehear, Godbeher, Godbehere, Goodbeer, Goodbehere: (i) Robert *Godebere* 1296 SRSx. A nickname 'good beer'. cf. GOODALL. (ii) John *Godbehere* 1456 Cl (Lo); Geoffrey *Godbeherinne* 1277 LLB B. Either *God be her(inne)* 'May God be in this house' or *Gōd be her(inne)* 'May it be well in this house'. Such names were common but are usually obsolete. cf. Gilbert *Godbiemidus* 1219 AssL. *v.* GODSAFE.

Godbert, Gobert: *Godebert* 1086 DB (Ess); Robertus *filius Goberti* ib.; Ricardus *filius Godebert* 13th Lewes (Nf); Roger *Godberd, Godbert* 1200–1 P (Y, Nt); William *Godebert* 1221 AssSa; William *Godebrich* 1262 For (Ess); Gilbert *Godebrith* 1327 SRSf; John *Gobard* 1335 AssSt. OG *Godebert* 'god-bright'. *Godebrich* (rare) suggests the possibility of an unrecorded OE *Godbeorht*.

Godbold, Godbolt, Godball, Gobat: *Godeboldus* 1086 DB; Adam *filius Goboldi* Hy 3 Colch (Ess); William *Godebald'* 1206 Cur (Beds); Henry *Gobaud, Gubaut* 1242 Fees (D); John *Gobaut* 1316 FA (Wa); John *Godebold* 1317 FFEss; John *Godball* 1485 RochW. OG *Godebald* 'god-bold'.

Goddard, Godard, Godart: *Godardus* de Clakesbi c1160–6 DC (L); Robert *God(d)ard* 1208 Cur (Ha); Wlfrich *Godard* 1221 *ElyA* (Nf); Symon *Godhard* 1299 LLB C. OFr *Godard*, OG *Gotahard, Godhard* 'god-hard'.

Godfrey, Godfray, Godfree, Godfery, Gotfrey: *Godefridus* 1086 DB; *Godefridus filius Baldewini* 1138 NthCh (L); Symon *Godefrei* 1221 *ElyA* (Sf); Alan *Godefre* 1252 Rams (Hu); Maud *Godefray* 1277 Ipm (Nt); OFr *Godefroi(s)*, OG *Godefrid* 'god-peace'.

Godin: *Godun* le Bere 1279 RH (C); Philip *Guodun, Guodin* 1280 AssSo; Henry *Godyn* 1386 LLB H. OFr *Godin, Godun*, diminutives of OG names in *God-*.

Godley, Godly, Goodley: Richard *de Goddeley* 1275 RH (D); Robert *de Godely* 1296 SR (Sx). From Goodley (Devon), Godley (Ch), Godley Bridge (Surrey) or Godley's Green (Sussex).

Godman, Goddman, Goodman, Goudman, Gut-

man: (i) *Godman(nus)*, *Godeman(us)* 1066 DB; *Godeman* de Waledena 1176 P (Herts); *Godman* de Offenchurche 1221 AssWa; Astcelinus *Godeman* 1115 Winton (Ha); Nicholas *Godman* 1188 BuryS (Sf). OE *Godmann* or OG *God(e)man*. (ii) Henry *le Godman* 1275 RH (C); Gerard *Gudman* 1352 FrY; John *Goodman* 1365 ColchCt. 'Good man' (cf. Anketin *Bonhomme* 1274 FFC), or 'master of a household'. *v.* BONHAM. (iii) *Guthmund, Gudmund, Godmund* 1066 DB; *Gudmund* del celer 1121–48 Bury (Sf); William *Gudmund* 1190 P (Wo); Hugh *Gothemund* alias *Gutmund* 1265 Ipm (Wo); John *Gotemund* 1274 RH (Ess); Richard *Guthmund, Godmund* 1275 RH (Sf); Adam *Guthmond* 1327 SRSf; Nicholas *Gooteman, Goteman, Godman* 1466, 1467, 1472 GildY. ON *Guðmundr*, ODa *Guthmund* or OE *Guðmund*.

Godrich, Godridge: *v.* GOODRICH

Godsafe, Godsave, Godsalve, Godseff, Godsiff: Nicholas *Agodeshalf* 1206 P (Sx); Alexander *Agodeshalve* 1260 AssC; Hugo *Ogodishalve, Ongodishalve* 1264, 1271 LeicBR; William *of e Godeshalve* 1311 NottBR; William *a Codeshalf* 1332 SRLo; Henry *Godsalve* 1337 FrY; John *Godeshalf* 1376 ib.; Eustace *Godsafe*, John *Godsaff* 1662 HTEss. ME *on* (*a*) *Godes half* 'in God's name, for God's sake', a nickname, due no doubt, to the frequent use of the phrase. The surname was common and widely distributed. The seal of Matthew son of Robert *a Godeshalf* (1202–16 ELPN) bore the legend 'Sigill. Mathei *ex parte Dei*', so that already at the beginning of the 13th century the surname had become hereditary in London. For similar oath-names, *v.* GODBEAR. cf. Geoffrey *Godesgrace* 1220 Cur (Sr), Robert *Godesblescinge* 1225 AssSo, Richard *Godesname* paternoster 1298 LoCt, William *Goddesbokes* 1308 FrY, Roger *Godesfast* 1392 LLB H, Henry *Godsake* 1514 NorwW, Olive *Goadebles* 1269 Pat, William *Godthanke* 1275 RH (Nf), William *Godwotte* 1352 PatR, William *Godhelp* 14th AD iv (Sr). For similar names of French origin, *v.* PARDEW.

Godsal, Godsall, Goodsell, Gotsell, Gutsell: Godwin *Gotsaule* 12th ELPN; William *God saule* 1197 FF (Nf); Ralph *Godsoule* 1219 AssY; Amicia *Godsol* 1279 RH (C); Ralph *Godsale* 1379 PTY; Thomas *Godsalle* 1518 FrY. 'Good soul', 'an honest fellow'.

Godsell, Godsil: Hugh *de Godeshill* 1225 AssSo, *de Godeshull'* 1230 P (Ha); Thomas *de Godeshelle* 1309 LLB D; Richard *Godeshulle* 1327 SRSx. From Gadshill (Kent), Godshill (Isle of Wight), *Godesill* 1393, Godshill (Hants) or Godsell Fm (Wilts), all originally *Godeshyll* 'god's hill'.

Godsman, Goodsman, Goodisman: *Godesman* 1066 Winton (Ha); *Godesman* de Spalding 1158 DC (L); Astin, Thomas *Godesman* 1214 Cur (L), 1248 FFEss. OG *Godesman* 'the man of the god', or a description, 'the man of God', a name for a clergyman or for one noted for his piety. cf. Willelmus *homo dei* 1195 P (L), Richard *Homedeu* 1216 Oseney (O).

Godsmark: Henry *Godesmerk* 1296 SRSx; William *Godesmark* 1327 ib. 'One bearing God's mark, the sign of the plague.' cf. 'He also was full of Godys markys' 1531; 'the markes of the plague, commonly called Goddes markes' 1558; 'Some with God's markes or Tokens doe espie, Those Marks or Tokens shew them they must die' 1630 NED.

Godson, Goodson: (i) *Godsune* 1086 DB (Ess), 1191 P (K); Alwinus *Gode sunu* 1066 DB (So); William *Godsune* 1200 P (Lo); Benedict *Godsone* 1298 FFC; Richard *Goddesone* 1332 SRSt. *Gode sunu* may be 'son of Goda' (masc. or fem.) or, possibly, OE *Godsunu* (either OE *god* 'God' or *gōd* 'good' and *sunu* 'son'), the probable source of the rest, though OE *godsunu* 'godson' is also possible. (ii) Thomas filius *Gode* 1302 SRY; Roger *Godessun'* 1205 Cur (Ess); Adam *Godesone, Godessone* 1294, 1303 LLB A; Richard *Godissone* 1402 FFSf. Either 'son of God', a short form of such names as *Godwine, Godrīc*, etc., or 'God's son', or 'son of *Gode* (f)'. cf. GODSMAN. Ekwall suggests (ELPN 41) that Adam *Godesone* (*Godessone*) 1294–1305 was a son or descendant of *Godeson le Megucyer* (1235). If so, he was called both 'Godson' and 'son of *Gode*', a pet form of *Godsunu*. (iii) William *Godesone* 1252 Rams (Hu); Ralph *le Godesone* 1296 SRSx; Sarra *Goudesone*, William *le Goudesone* 1332 SRSx; Robert *Goodsone* 1377 AD vi (He). OE *gōd* 'good' and *sunu* 'son'. *Godson* in NED is always *godson*, never *godeson*. In the York plays, *Gud sonne* 'good son' is a common term of address. cf. William *Goodefader* 1418 Pat (Ess).

Godward: Wlmarus filius *Godwardi* 12th DC (L); Alicia *Godword* 1252 Rams (Hu); John *Godward* 1568 SRSf. Late OE *Godweard*, 'God or good' and *weard* 'protector'.

Godwin, Godwyn, Goodwin, Goodwins, Goodwyn: Ailmar filius *Goduini* 1086 DB; Ricardus filius *Godwini* 1219 AssY; Walter *Godwin'* 1177 P (Nf); Nicholas *Godwyn* 1239 FFC; Richard *Godwynn* 1296 FrY; William *Goudwyne* 1327 SRSx; Robert *Gudwen* 1327 SRC; William *Godewynes* 1327 SRWo; John *Gudwyn* 1388 FrY. The common OE personal name *Godwine*, from *god* 'god' or *gōd* 'good' and *wine* 'friend, protector, lord', which survived the Conquest. *Gōdwine* became Godwin and *Gōdwine* Goodwin. If *Godwynn* and *Gudwen* are reliable, we have occasionally the feminine OE **Godwynn*.

Goff, Goffe: Bertram, Nicholas, Thomas *Goffe* 1208 FFL, 1327 SRWo, 1332 SRWa. Ir, Gael *gobha*, Welsh, Breton *gof*, Cornish *gov* 'smith'.

Golbourn: *v.* GOLDBOURN

Gold, Goold, Gould: (i) Hugo filius *Goldæ* 1086 DB (Sf); Ralph filius *Golde* 1193 P (Beds); *Golde* Bassat 1279 RH (C); Walter *Golde* 1165 P (D); Ralph *Golde* 1268 AssSo; John *Gulde* 1297 MinAcctCo. OE *Golda* (m), or *Golde* (f). (ii) Thomas *le Gold* 1327 SRSx; John *le Goulde* 1332 ib. A nickname, 'golden-haired'. (iii) Thomas *withe Gold* 1220 Pat (St). Presumably 'rich'.

Goldbard, Goldbart: (i) *Goldebrict'* de Dunewic' 1203 Cur (Sf); Richard *Goldberd* 1230 P (Wa);

Odin *Goldeberd, Guldebort* 1327, 1332 SRSx. OE *Goldbeorht* 'gold-bright'. (ii) William *Gulberde* 1220 FFEss; Richard, Philip *Geld(e)berd* 1296 SRSx. 'Golden beard', OE *gylden, beard*.

Goldbourn, Golborn, Golbourn, Goulborn, Goulborne: Richard *de Goldburn* 1332 SRLa. From Golborne (Lancs, Ches).

Goldburg, Goldburgh: Ricardus *filius Goldburg* c1179 Bart (Lo); Richard *Goldburc* 1210 Cur (Lei). OE *Goldburg* (f) 'gold-fortress'.

Golden, Goolden, Goulden: Walter *Guldene, le Gelden*' 1212 Cur (Ha); Hilde *Golden*' 1279 RH (C). OE *gylden* 'golden-(haired)'. cf. Richard *Guldenheved* 1222 DBStP.

Golder, Goulder: (i) Henricus *filius Goldere* 1197 P (Ess); John, Adam *Golder(e)* 1296 SRSx, 1327 SRSf. OE *Goldhere* 'gold-army', of which only one other example is known, in 1086, at Colchester. (ii) Matthew *de Goldore* 1275 RH (Herts); Richard *de la Goldore* 1295 MELS (Sr). 'Dweller at the bank where marigolds grow' (OE *golde, ōra*), as at Goldor (Oxon).

Goldfinch: William *Goldfing* 1260 AssC; Robert *Goldfynch* 1277 AssSo; Philip *le Goldfynch* 1307 AssSt. A nickname from the bird, OE *goldfinc*.

Goldfoot: Robert *Geldenefot, Gildenefot* 1188 P (Nf), 1213 Cur (Nf). OE *gylden* and *fōt* 'golden foot', a curious nickname.

Goldhawk: *Goldhac, Goldhauek* Hy 2, 1212 Bart (Lo); *Goldhevek de* Lond(on) 1212 Cur (Sr); Robert *Goldhauek* 1219 FFEss; Swein *Goldhauc* 1235 FFEss. Late OE *Goldh(e)afoc* 'gold hawk'.

Golding, Goolding, Goulding: *Goldinc* 1086 DB (Ess); *Golding* Aldred a1224 Clerkenwell (Mx); William, Richard *Golding* 1202 AssL, 1210 Cur (C); William *Gulding* 1327 SRSx. Late OE *Golding*.

Goldman: Adam *Goldeman* 1297 SRY; Maud *Goldman* 1393 LoPleas. OE *Goldmann*, first recorded on an Essex coin c1066 (Grueber).

Goldney: Richard *Goldeneghe* 1345 LLB F. 'Golden eye.'

Goldrich: *Goldrich* 1066 DB (Ess); *Golricus* de Skegeness 1218 AssL; William *Goldrych* 1344 ChertseyCt (Sr); Robert *Goldwright* 1500 ERO. OE *Goldrīc* 'gold-ruler'.

Goldsborough, Goldsbrough, Gooldsbury, Gouldesborough, Gouldsbury, Goulsbra: Walter *de Goldisburc* 1206 P (Y); John *Goldsborough*, Lawrence *Goldesberry* 1674 HTSf; John *Goldsbrow* 1784 SfPR. From Goldsborough (NR, WRYorks).

Goldsby: Ralph *de Golkesbi* 1202 AssL. From Goulceby (Lincs).

Goldsmith, Gouldsmith: Roger *Goldsmiz* 1250 MESO (Nf); Thomas *Goldsmith* 1255 *Ass* (Ess); John *le Goldesmethe* 1309 LLB D. OE *goldsmið* 'goldsmith'.

Goldspink: Robert *Goldspynk* 1524 SRSf. 'Goldfinch.'

Goldston, Goldstone, Gouldstone, Goulston, Goulstone, Golston, Goldson, Golson, Gulston, Gulson: (i) *Goldstan, Golstan* 1066 DB (K, Ess); Wulfric *filius Goldston* 1180 P (K); Richard *Golstan* 1185

Templars (Ess); Robert, Walter *Goldstan* 1202 AssBeds, 1214 Cur (Bk); Robert *Goldstone* 1312 LLB D; Thomas *Golston, Golson* 1524 SRSf; John and Mary *Goldson, Goldston* 1795, 1798 HorringerPR (Sf). OE *Goldstān* 'gold stone'. (ii) John *de Goldeston* 1312 FFEss; Ambrose *Golson* 1523 SRK. From Goldstone (Kent), earlier *Goldstaneston*, or Goldstone (Salop).

Goldway: Tocwy *filius Goldwy* 1182 RBWo; Thomas *Goldweg* 1297 MinAcctCo. OE *Goldwīg* 'gold-warrior', not otherwise known.

Goldwin, Goldwyn: *Golduinus* 1066 DB (Sx); *Goldewinus* 1221 *ElyA* (Sf); William *Goldwyn* 1256 AssNb; Richard *Goldwyne* 1317 AssK. OE *Goldwine* 'gold-friend'.

Golightly, Gallatly, Galletley, Galletly, Gellatly, Gelletly: Rannulf *Golicthli* 1196 P (C); Adam *Golictlik* 1201 Cur (Nt); Howe *Golichtly* 1221 AssWa; Henry *Gellatly, Galighly* a1291 Black, 1296 CalSc; Gilbert *Galetly* 1592 Black. 'Go lightly', a nickname for a messenger.

Golland: *v.* JOLIN
Golley: *v.* GULLY
Gollin(s): *v.* JOLIN
Golsworthy: *v.* GALSWORTHY
Gomer: *v.* GUMMER
Gomme, Goom, Gum, Gumb, Gumm: Simon *Gumme* 1247 AssBeds; Henry *le Gome* 1275 SRWo; John *Gom* 1279 RH (C); Walter *Gomme* 1297 MinAcctCo; Nicholas *Gumes* 1327 SRSf; John *(le) Goom* 1340 AssC. OE *guma* 'man'.

Gonville: Hugh *de Gundeuilla, de Gundeuille* 1155 NLC (Bk), 1225 AssSo; Adam *Goundevyle* 1332 SRDo. From Gondouville (Seine-et-Marne).

Gooch, Goodge, Goudge, Gouge, Gudge, Gutch: Robert, Felicia *Goch* 1203 Pl (Sa), 1306 IpmGl; John *Guch*, William *Gugge* 1327 *SR* (Ess); John *Gooch* 1374 ColchCt; William *Goch* or *Gouche* 1509 LP (Lo). Welsh *coch* 'red'. *v.* also GOUGH.

Good, Goode, Goude, Gudd, Gude, Le Good, Legood, Leegood: *God* 1066 DB (K, Sx, W); *Goda, Gode* (m), *Gode, Goda* (f) ib.; *Goda* de West Wicumbe 1194 Cur (Bk); Odo *se Gode* 960 OEByn; Æilgyuu *Gode* 1050–71 ib.; Edwardus *bonus* 1204 P (O); Gilbert *le Gode* 1212 Cur (Bk); Robert *Gode* 1221 AssGl; William *Goude* 1297 MinAcctCo; Thomas *le Goude* 1327 SRSx; Andrew *Gude* 1537 FrY. As *le Gode* is much the most common form, this is usually a nickname from OE *gōd* 'good', but a personal name cannot be ruled out, either OE *Goda* (m) or *Gode* (f).

Gooda: *v.* GOODER

Goodall, Goodale, Goodayle, Goodhall: Toka *Godala* 1181 P (Sf); Roger *Godhal*' 1221 AssSa; William *Godale* 1244 Rams (Beds); John *Godhale* 1297 MinAcctCo; John *Gudale* 1379 PTY; James *Goodall* 1581 RothwellPR (Y); William *Guidaill* 1657 Black (Kirkwall). 'Good ale', a brewer or seller of good ale.

Gooday, Goodey, Gooddy, Goody: For GOOD-DAY, or 'dweller at the good enclosure' (OE *gōd, (ge)hæg*): John *de Goday* 1327 SRSt; or for GOODIFF.

Goodbairn, Goodban, Goodband: William *Godbarn* 1203 Cur (L); Robert *Gudbarn* 1379 PTY. ME *gōd-barn* 'good child', confined to the Scandinavian counties. cf. GOODCHILD.

Goodbeer, Goodbehere: v. GODBEAR

Goodbody, Goodboddy: Richard *Godbodi* 1221 AssGl; John *Godbody* 1308 AssSt; John *Goodbody* alias *Goodman* 1468 Ewen (Nf). 'Good body' (OE *gōd, bodig*), used as an epithet of courteous address, also equivalent to French *Beaucorps* and to *Goodman*.

Goodcheap, Goodchap: Walter *Godchep* 1166 P (Nf); William *Gudchep* 1236 Bart (Lo); Hamo *Godchape* 1315 ib. OE *gōd* 'good' and *cēap* 'barter, price'. ME *good cheap* was used of a state of the market good for the purchaser, when prices were low (a1325 MED), hence 'one who gives a good bargain'. The nickname might also have been taken from the vendor's cry.

Goodchild: Henry *Goddechild'* 1211 Cur (Ess); Robert *Godchild* 1237 FFEss; Willelmus *Bonus Puer* c1250 Rams (C); Richard *Godechild* 1327 SRC; Gilbert *Goodchilde* 1366 LLB G. OE *gōd* 'good' and *cild* 'child'. cf. GOODBAIRN. The first form suggests that the source may occasionally be 'godchild'.

Goodday: Stephen *Godeday* 1301 SRY; Wylliam *Goodday* 1524 SRSf. For GOODENDAY or, possibly, 'good servant', v. DAY.

Goodenday: ME *godne dæie* c1205, *godun dai* c1250, *god dai* a1300 NED, 'Good day', a salutation on meeting or parting: 'Have a good day!' 'God give you good day!' cf. Walter *Godemorwe* (*Godemorwen*) 1327 *SR* (Ess).

Goodenough, Goodnow, Goodner, Goodanew: (i) Alan *Godinoch, Godinogh'* 1212 Cur (Y), 1297 MinAcctCo; William *Godinogh* 1225 AssSo; William *Godinowe* 1309 NottBR. A nickname, probably for one easily satisfied. cf. Robert *Welynogh* 1260 AssC, William *Welynough* (*Welynou*) 1327 *SR* (Ess). (ii) Roger *Godecnaue* 1220 Oseney (O); Hervicus *Godcnave* 1225 Pat (Nt); Hugo *Gudknave* 1269 AssNb; John *Goddeknawe* 13th Shef (Y). OE *gōd* and *cnafa.* 'boy, servant'. It is not surprising, in view of the apparent contradiction in terms and the unpleasant associations of the modern *knave*, that this name survives only in disguise. For *knave*, NED gives the forms *knaf* c1375, *knaffe* 1481 and *knawe*: *knave-line* became *knauling*. With the loss of *k*, *Godenaf* would easily be confused with Goodenough and *God(e)-nawe* with Goodnow and Goodanew, which preserve the now dialectal *enow* for *enough*. The synonymous OE *cnapa* 'boy, servant', also gave rise to a surname: Ernald *le Godeknape* 1308 AD vi (Sf), Martin *Godeknape* 1327 SRC.

Gooder, Goodere, Gooders, Gooda, Gouda: *Godere* 1066 DB (Ess, Sf); John *Godere* 1317 AssK; John *Gooder* 1564 ShefA. OE *Gōdhere* 'good army'.

Goodered: v. GOODREAD

Gooderham, Goodram, Goodrum, Guthrum: *Guðrum* 12th Whitelock; Gerard *filius Gudram,* *Guðram* 1201 P (L); Brictiua *filia Guderam* 1202 AssL; *Guderam* Gleve 1283 SRSf; Hugh *Godrum* 1260 AssL; Thomas *Guderam, Godram* 1283, 1327 SRSf; Thomas *Goodrum* 1577 Musters (Nf); Widow *Guderum, Goddram* 1674 HTSf; Godfrey *Gooderham* 1681 NorwDep; Geoffrey *Goodrum* 1765 FrYar. ON *Guðormr* 'battle-snake'. *Guðrum*, *Gudram*, the name of the first Danish king of East Anglia, is preserved in the York street-name Goodramgate (PN ERY 289). There has probably also been some confusion with ON *Guðrún* (f), OG *Godram* (m), and OE *Gōdrūn* (f), the last of which is the origin of Gutter Lane (London), v. ELPN 41. But for these as surnames the evidence is slight.

Gooderidge: v. GOODRICH

Goodes, Goodess: *Godise* 1066 DB (Y); *Godehese* 1198 P (K); Johannes *filius Goduse* 1190 P (Y); *Godusa* 1208, 1220 Cur (Y, L); Roger *Godhus* 1279 RH (C); Hugh *Godhos* ib. (Bk); William *Godhose* 1296 SRSx; John *Godhous* 1327 SRSf; William *Goudese* 1327 SRSx. *Godus* (f) must derive from the solitary OE *Godhyse* (966 BCS 1181), which suggests that *Edus* and *Aldus* may go back to OE **Eadhyse, *Ealdhyse. v.* EDIS, ALDIS.

Goodesmith, Goodsmith: John *Godesmaghe* 1351 FrY; Margaret *Goodsmyth* 1525 SRSx. 'Relative of *Gode*', cf. HUDSMITH.

Goodeve: *Godgeua, Godiua, Godeue* 1066 DB; *Godiua* 1221 AssWa; William *Godyeue* 1327 SRSf; Edward *Godyf* 1527 RochW; Edmond *Goodeve* 1662 HTEss. OE *Godgifu* (f) 'god or good gift'. v. also GOODIFF.

Goodfar, Goodfare: Gilbert *Goudefeyre* 1332 SRSx; Robert *Gudefeir* 1379 PTY. One of 'good appearance, demeanour', from ME *feyr*, an aphetic form of *effeir* from OFr *aferir* 'to be proper, meet'.

Goodfellow: Richard *Godfelage* 1192 P (Nth); Roger *Godfelawe* 1274 RH (Ess). ME *god felawe* 'good fellow', a good companion. cf. John *Trewfelagh* 1379 PTY.

Goodgame: Robert *Godgame* 1185 Templars (Herts); Walter *Godgamen* 1279 RH (Hu). 'Good sport.' v. GAME.

Goodger, Gudger: Robert *Gudger* 1616 RothwellPR (Y); Joseph *Goodger, Goodyer* 1738, 1760 WordwellPR (Sf). A late development of GOODYEAR.

Goodhall: v. GOODALL

Goodhand: Aluric *Godhand* c1095 Bury (Sf). 'Good hand.' v. HAND. Henry *Goudenhond* 1332 SRSx. This is probably 'golden hand'.

Goodhart, Goodheart: John *Godhierte* 1221 Cur (Herts); John *Goudhert* 1327 SRSo. 'Good heart.'

Goodhead: (i) William *Godheved* 1222 Pat (Herts). 'Good head', OE *hēafod*. (ii) William *Godhed* 1327 SRWo. ME *godhede* 'goodness'. cf. Richard *Godnesse* 1327 SRSf.

Goodhew, Goodhue, Goodhugh: *Got hugo* 1086 DB (Ess); *Godhuge* c1095 Bury (Sf); Robertus *filius Godhu*, Robert *Godhuge* 1181, 1222 DBStP; Roger *Godhou* c1240 *ERO* (Ess); Robert *Godhewe* 1311 ColchCt; Richard *Godhowe*, William *God-*

hewen 1327 *SR* (Ess); John *Godhiwe, Goudhywe* 1327, 1332 SRSx; John *Godhewyn* 1333 FFSf; William *Goodhewe* 1383 LLB G. ON *Guð(h)ugi*, no doubt the opposite of *Ill(h)ugi, Illhuge* 11th Saga Bk xii, 137, Radbode *filius Illhuge* 1166 P (Nf). The surname may also mean 'good servant', ME *god* and *hewe*, from OE *hīwan* (plural) 'members of a household'. cf. GOODHIND.

Goodhind: William, Geoffrey *Godhine* a1224 Clerkenwell (Mx), 1230 P (Nth). ME *god* 'good' and *hine* sg, from OE *hīwan* pl. 'member of a household', 'a lad, boy, stripling'; 'a good lad'. *v.* also GOODHEW.

Goodier: *v.* GOODYEAR

Goodiff, Goodey, Goody: (i) Nota *Godwyf* 1311 ColchCt; Margaret *Godewyf* 1374 FFHu. ME *good-wife* 'mistress of a house'. cf. GOODMAN. *Goodey* is a shortened form. cf. *hussey* from *hūs-wīf* and *Goody* or *Goodwyff* Wilkes (1559 NED). (ii) John *Godyf* 1279 RH (O); Thomas *Godif* 1297 SRY. These forms are too early to be regarded as a form of *good-wife*. They are probably from OE *Godgifu* (f). *v.* GOODEVE. This was confused with OE *Godgȳð* (f) and also with *good-wife*: William *Godith(e), Godyth, Gwodyf* 1317 AssK. *Godyf* widow of John Clare is also called *Goditha* Clare de Strode ib.

Gooding, Goodinge, Goodings, Godding, Goding: *Godinc* 1066 DB; *Goding* ib., c1113 Burton (St); Robert *Goding* 1185 Templars (Ess); Peter *Godding* 1274 RH (Sf). *Gooding* is from OE *Gōding, Godding* from OE *Gōding*. In 1208 P (Sf), *Goding* is an alternative for *Godmer*, and so a pet-form of names in *God-*.

Goodison: Nicholas *Godithson* 1332 SRCu; Robert *Guditson*, John *Godyeson* 1379 PTY. 'Son of *Godith*', OE *Godgȳð* 'god or good battle', a woman's name long in use: *Godith* 1206 Cur (Beds), *Godit* 1199 ChR, *Gudytha* Foloufast 1379 PTY.

Goodlad, Goodlatte, Goodlet, Goodlett: Robert *Godelad* 1301 SRY; William *Godlad* 1332 SRCu; William *Goodlad* 1464 GildY; Robert *Guidlett* 1574 Black (Ross); John *Guidlat* 1602 ib. 'Good lad', 'good servant'.

Goodlake, Goodluck, Gullick, Gulick, Cutlack: *Gotlac* 1066 DB (Ch); Robertus *filius Guthlach* 1187 P (La); Symon *Goddeloc, Godeloc* 1247 FFC; Hosebert *Gotloc, Guzloc*, John *Gudloc* 1279 RH (O); Isabella *Gullake* 1327 SRSo; Henry *Cutlake* 1538 NorwW. OE *Gūðlāc* 'battle-play', or, possibly, ON *Guðleikr*.

Goodlamb: *Godlamb* 1086 ICC (C); *Godlambus* 1114–30 Rams (C); *Godlamb* de Well', de Lenn' 1166 P, 1206 Cur (Nf); Herveus *filius Godlamp* 1221 ElyA (C); Roger *Godlamb* 1230 P (Nf); William *Godlomb* 1274 RH (Nf). OE *Gōdlamb*, an original nickname 'good lamb', recorded once before the Conquest. Probably also a nickname.

Goodland: (i) Gilebertus *filius Godland'* 1201 Cur (Nf); Hugo *Godlond* 1279 RH (O). OG *Godland*. (ii) Henry *de Godland* 1379 PTY. 'Dweller by the good land.'

Goodlet: *v.* GOODLAD
Goodley: *v.* GODLEY
Goodliff, Goodliffe: *Gothlif* 1086 ICC (C); *Godelief* 1197 P (K); Maud *Goodleef* 1272 Bart (Lo); John *Godelef* 1296 SRSx; William *Godeloues* 1327 SRWo. OE *Godlēof* (m) or OE *Godlēofu* (f) 'good or god dear', long used in Kent: *Godlefe* (f) 1508 ArchC xxx.

Goodlud: This may be a corruption of *Goodlad*, but is more probably for 'good lord'. cf. the legal 'M'lud': John *Godlord* 1332 AD v (Wa); Ralph *Goodlord* 1387 NorwW (Nf).

Goodman: *v.* GODMAN
Goodner: *v.* GOODENOUGH
Goodram: *v.* GOODERHAM
Goodread, Goodred, Goodreds, Goodered: *Gudret, Godred* 1066 DB (L, Y); *Gudred* de Cnappewelle 1102–7 Rams (C); *Godred* 1200 FFL; *Ragemerus filius Gutred* 1204 P (L); Henry *Guthred* c1214 StGreg (K); John *Godred, Ysabell Godrad, Godrid* 1279 RH (C); Alexander *Godered* 1325 FFK; William *Goodrede* 1460 FrY. ON *Guðrøðr*. The surname may also be ME *god rede* 'good counsel'. cf. the Scottish *Meiklereid*, Robert *Smalred* 1176 P (Y), Philip *Lytylred* 1372–6 Gaunt.

Goodrich, Goodridge, Gooderidge, Gooderick, Goodrick, Goodricke, Godrich, Godridge, Goodwright: *Godric* 1066 DB; Gaufridus *filius Godrici* 1207 Cur (Bk); Ambrosius *filius Godrige* 1279 RH (C); Ralph *Godric'* 1199 P (Wo); Hugo *Godriche* 1221 ElyA (Sf); John *Godrige* 1279 RH (C); John *Godryk* 1313 FFEss; James *Goodrich* 1341 ColchCt; William *Godright* 1363 LLB G; Albreda *Goderik* 1381 PTY; Simon *Goderich* 1388 LLB H; William *Guderyk* 1475 GildY; John *Guddrig* 1477 FrY; Elizabeth *Gutteridge, Goodritch* 1659, 1666 HorringerPR (Sf); John *Goodridg* 1662 HTEss. OE *Godrīc* 'good or god ruler'. *v.* also CUTTERIDGE. Occasionally the surname is local in origin: Thomas *de Goderigge* 1275 RH (W).

Goodrum: *v.* GOODERHAM
Goodsell: *v.* GODSAL
Goodsir: Thomas *Goudsyre, Goodsire* 1375 LoPleas, 1384 LLB H. ME *gudsire, goodsir* 'grandfather' (c1425 NED). Probably a term of address. cf. GODSON, SWEETSER.

Goodsman: *v.* GODSMAN
Goodson: *v.* GODSON
Goodspeed: Ralph *Godisped* 1275 RH (Herts); Walter *Godspede* 1275 SRWo. 'God speed (you)', a wish for success for one setting out on an enterprise (1526 NED).

Goodswen, Goodswin, Goudswen: Herbert *Godsuain* c1155 DC (L); William *Godswein* 1206 Cur (L); Roger *Gudswen* 14th Lewes (Nf). ME *god swain* (ON *sveinn*, ODa *sven*) 'good servant'. cf. Roger *Godyoman* 1297 SRY.

Goodway: *Goduui* 1066 DB (C); *Godwi* 1188 BuryS (Sf); Henry *Godwi* 1212 Cur (Berks); William *Gudeway* 1448 FrY. OE *Godwīg* 'good or god-strife'.

Goodwin: *v.* GODWIN
Goodwright: *v.* GOODRICH

Goodyear, Goodyer, Goodier, Goudier: Cest', Henry *Godyer* 1279 RH (Hu), 1295 ParlR (Ess); Henry, Annc' *Godyar* 1285 *Ass*, 1301 ParlR (Ess); John *Godhyer* 1296 SRSx; William *Godeyer*, Maud *Godeyiere* 1301 SRY; Henry *Goudhier*, William *Godier* 1327 SRSx; Agnes *Goudyer* 1327 SRSx; John *Goodyer* 1456 FrY; John *Godeyere* 1467 AD vi (Mx); Robert *Gudyere* 1513 GildY; William *Goodeare* 1566 FFHu; Jeremiah *Goodyear* 1682 FrY. ME *goodyeare, goodier, goodere, goodye(e)re* 'good year', an expletive used in questions, 'What the good year?'. Possibly elliptic for 'as I hope to have a good year' (c1555 NED).

Gook: Alan *Gok* 1219 AssL; Thomas *Gouk'*, Richard *Gouc* 1219 AssY; Thomas *Gauke* 1424 FrY; John *Gook* 1432 ib. ON *gaukr* 'cuckoo', ME *goke, gowke* (a1300 MED).

Gookey: Willelmus *filius Goci* 1121–38 Bury (Sf); *Goche* 1166 P (Nf), 1186–1210 Holme (Nf); Roger *Goki* 1191 P (Cu); Ralph *Goky* 1218 AssL. ON *Gauki*.

Goold: v. GOLD
Goolden: v. GOLDEN
Goolding: v. GOLDING
Gooldsbury: v. GOLDSBOROUGH
Goom: v. GOMME

Goose: Hugo, Richard *Gos* 1176, 1191 P (L, Y), 1210 Cur (C); Hugh *le Gos* 1227 AssBeds; Hamo *le Gous* 1231 FFC; Alice *Gous* 1297 MinAcctCo. OE *gōs* 'goose'. v. also GOSS.

Gooseman: Gilbert *Gosman* 1246 AssLa. OE *gōs* and *mann* 'tender of the geese'. cf. GOSSARD.

Goosey, Goozee: (i) Robert *Gosege* 1167 P (D); Peter *Goseie* 1199 P (Nth); Henry *Goseye* 1327 SRWo. 'Goose-eye.' cf. John *Gosebody* 1297 MinAcctCo, Roger *Gosefot* 1212 Fees (Berks), Gocelin *Gosethrote* 1200 Oseney (O). (ii) Walter *de Gosey* 1242 Fees (Berks). From Goosey (Berks).

Gorch, Gordge: Herveus, Osbert *Gorge* 1185 P, 1221 Cur (Sf). OFr *gorge* 'throat'. *Gorgerer*, from OFr *gorg(i)ere*, was a not uncommon occupational term for a maker of gorgers or gorgets or armour for the throat and possibly also for a maker of chin-cloths or wimples for covering the throat: Alexander *le Gorgerer* 1220 Cur (Mx), called also *le Gorgeur* (1221 ib.), Andrew *le Gorgerer* Hy 3 Colch (Ess). The surname is metonymic for *gorgerer*. cf. Simon *Gorget* 1327 SRC.

Gordon, Gurden: The home of the Scottish Gordons was in Berwickshire where there is a place Gordon from which the family probably took its name. The earliest member noted is Richer *de Gordun* lord of the barony of Gordon in the Merse (1150–60). His son was Thomas *de Gordun* (Black). The surname is found early in England: Adam *de Gurdun* 1204 P (Ha) who probably came from a French place named Gourdon (Saône-et-Loire, etc.). The names of Geoffrey *Gurdun* 1220 Cur (K), Adam *Gordon* 1279 RH (C), etc., are probably identical with Fr *Gourdon* which Dauzat takes as a diminutive of OFr *gourd* in the sense 'dull, stupid, boorish'.

Gore: Ralph *de la Gare* 1181 P (K); John *de*

Gore 1257 ArchC iii; Alan *ate Gore* 1274 RH (Ess). 'Dweller by the triangular piece of land' (OE *gāra*), as at Gore Court (Kent) and Gore (Wilts).

Gorer: Equivalent to *ate Gore*.

Goring, Goringe, Gorin: Geoffrey *de Garinges* 1192 P (Sx); Orvietus *de Goringes* 1255 Cur (Y); Robert *Goring* 1327 SRSx; William *Goringe* 1583 Musters (Sr). From Goring (Oxon, Sussex).

Gorman: William *Gorman* 1296 SRSx; Adam *Garman* 1327 ib. v. GORE, GORER and GARMAN. Also for Irish *MacGorman*, *O'Gorman* 'son or descendant of *Gorman*', a diminutive of *gorm* 'blue'.

Gorrell, Gorrill: (i) William, Henry *Gorel* 1176 P (K), 1319 SRLo, 1221 Cur (D). ME *gorrell* 'a fat-paunched person', from OFr *gorel* 'pig'. (ii) Margeria *Gorulf* 1296 SRSx; John *Goroulfe* 1327 SRWo. OE *Gārwulf* 'spear-wolf'. (iii) 'Dweller by the muddy spring', as at Gorwell (Essex) or Gorrel (Devon): Walter *de Gorewell* 1274 RH (Ess); or by the muddy hill: Cecily *de Gorhull* 1246 AssLa; or at a muddy nook as at Gorrel Fm (Bucks), earlier *Gorhale*.

Gorst: Roger *de la Gorste* 1275 SRWo; Agnes *del Gorstes*, Ralph *in le Gorstes* 1281 MELS (Wo). 'Dweller among the gorse' (OE *gorst*).

Gorstidge, Gorsuch, Gostage, Gostige, Gossage: John *de Gosefordsik* 1332 SRLa; Henry *Gorsage* 1579 Bardsley; Roger *Gorsuche* 1602 PrGR; Henry *Gorstich* 1669 Bardsley. From Gosfordsich (Lancs).

Gosling, Gossling, Gostling: Henry *Goseling* 1260 AssC; Robert *Goseling*, Maud *Gosselyng* 1327 SRC. ME *goslyng* 'gosling'. *Gosling* is, no doubt, often a late development of *Goslin* (v. JOCELYN), but these forms are much too early for such a development. They are earlier, too, than the earliest *o*-form in MED (*gosselyng* c1350).

Goss, Gosse, Joass, Joce, Jose, Joss, Jossc: *Gotso dapifer* 1130 P (St); *Gosce*, *Joce de Brunna* Hy 2, 1195 DC (L); Hugo, Geoffrey *Gosse* 1202 AssL, 1251 Rams (Hu); Richard *Goce* 1205 P (Sf); Thomas *Joce*, William *Josse* 1327 SRSx. OFr *Joce, Josce, Gosse*, OG *Gozzo, Gauz*. Also a pet-name of *Gocelin*: *Gosse* or *Gocelin de Mealtun* c1160 DC (L); *Jose* or *Jocelinus de Baillol* 1164–66 Bury (Sf). *Joss(e)* is also for Breton *Judoc*. v. JOYCE, and also GOTT.

Gossage: v. GORSTIDGE

Gossard, Gozzard, Gozzett: Walter *Goseherd* 1236 *Ass* (Ha); John *le Goshurde* 1327 SRSx. OE *gōs* and *hierde* 'goose-herd' (*gozzard* 1771 NED).

Gosselin: v. JOCELYN

Gosset, Gossett, Jossett: Robert, Isabella *Josset* 1279 RH (C). A diminutive of *Gosse, Josse*. v. GOSS.

Gossip, Gossop: Ulfketil *Godsib* 1229 Cl (Nf); William *Godsip* c1248 Bec (Nf); John *le Gossib*, *Gossyp* 1319 AssSt. OE *godsibb* 'godfather, godmother', later 'a familiar acquaintance or friend'.

Gosson: William *Gosson'* 1327 SRC. Perhaps an assimilated form of GODSON. cf. 'Godson or gosson, *Filiolus*' c1440 PromptParv. Or for (William) *Gotson* 1314 Wak (Y). 'Son of *Gotte*.' v. GOTT.

Gostage, Gostige: v. GORSTIDGE

Gostling: v. GOSLING, JOCELYN

Gothard: Geoffrey *Gothirde* 1229 Cl (O); Reginald *le Gateherde* 1275 SRWo; Geoffrey *le Gotherde* 1332 SRSx. OE *gāt, hyrde* 'goat-herd'.

Gotobed, Gotbed: John, Richard *Gotobedde* 1269 Barnwell (C), 1309 SRBeds; William *Gawetobedde* 1332 SRSx; Charles *Godbed* 1760 Bardsley. There can be little doubt that this nickname means what it says. cf. William *Gatorest* Hy 3 Gilb (L), John *Gobiside* 1379 PTY, Nicholas *Gabyfore* 1430 FeuDu, Serle *Gotokirke* 1279 RH (C).

Gotsell: v. GODSAL

Gott, Gotts: *Gotte filius Wulfrici* 1188 P (Y); Gilbertus *filius Gotte* 1195 P (L); Godui *Gott* c1095 Bury (Sf); Haldan' *Gotte* 1202 AssL; Geoffrey *Gottes* 1346 FA (Nf). *Gocelin*, pronounced *Gotselin*, had pet-forms *Gosse* (v. GOSS, JOYCE) and *Got*, both from *Gots*: cf. *Gocelin* Bouer; Thomas *Gotsone* Bouer 1319 Pat (Hu), i.e. Thomas son of *Got* Bouer, where *Got* is clearly short for *Gocelin*. In Yorkshire and Lincolnshire, this may be of Breton origin. But the 11th-century Godui *Gott* is too early for this development and is probably from OE *gutt*, ME *gutt, gotte* 'gut, guts', formerly in polite use, meaning also 'a corpulent or greedy person'.

Goubert: v. JOBERT

Goucher: v. GOACHER

Goud-: v. GOOD-

Goudge, Gouge: v. GOOCH

Goudie, Goudy: Scottish variants of *Goldie*, found in Edinburgh from 1598 as *Gowdie, Gaudie, Goddie* (Black).

Gough, Goff, Goffe: Griffin, Robert *Gogh* 1287 AssCh, 1327 SRSo; Thomas *Goughe* 1576 SRW. Welsh *coch* 'red'. v. also GOOCH.

Goul(d)-: v. GOLD-

Goundry: v. GUNDREY

Gourd: Henry *Gourdemaker* 1327 SRY. A maker of bottles or cups (OFr *gourde*).

Gover: (i) Gilbert *Gofar'* 1223 Cur (O); Gilbert, John *Gofaire* 1240 Oseney (O), 1260 Husting; Geoffrey *Gouayre* 1242 Ct (Ha); James *Gafaire* 1327 FrY. 'Go fairly', ME *faire* 'beautifully', 'gently, quietly'. Either one who walks beautifully or, more probably, one who goes gently, uses gentle means (ELPN). cf. Margerie *Gangefeyr* 1451 Rad (C). (ii) Walter *gouyere* 1296 SRSx; John *Gouere*, William *Gover*, Richard *le Gofiar* 1327 SRSo; Thomas *Gover* 1380 SRSt. This form, which will also account for *Govier*, is difficult. It cannot be the East Anglian dialectal *goave* 'to store grain', as suggested by Weekley and Harrison, for that word derives from ME *golfe* and retains its *l* until the 16th century. These surnames, too, are southern and western which dissociates them also from Harrison's alternative suggestion, ME *gofe* 'to stare stupidly', which is a Scottish word.

Gow: Richard *Gowe* 1230 P (So); George *Gow* 1580 Black. Gael *gobha* 'smith'.

Gowen, Gowing: v. MacGOWAN

Gower, Gowar, Gowers, Guwer: (i) Willelmus *filius Goer* c1160 Gilb (L); *Goerus* Pellipar' 1296 SRSx; William *Goer, Guer* c1150, 1187 Gilb (L); Alan *Goiher, Guher* 1176, 1179 P (Y); Jordan *Guuer* 1202 P (So); Thomas *Guwer, le Goher* 1221 Cur (O); Stephen *Gower (le Goher)* 1230 P (Y); Adam *Goier* 1327 SRSf. OFr *Go(h)ier*, OG *Godehar* 'good army'. *Gohier* also denoted an inhabitant of the *Goelle*, the country north of Paris, anciently *Gohiere*, hence *le Goher*. The term seems also to have been applied to a man from Gouy. William *de Goiz* is also called *le Goeir* 1212 Cur (Beds). (ii) Walter *de Guher* 1130 P (Carmarthen). From Gower (Glamorgan).

Gowler: v. GAWLER

Gozzard, Gozzett: v. GOSSARD

Grace, Gras, Grass: (i) William *le Gras* 1199 P (Gl), 1202 AssL, 1219 AssY; Roger *le Gras*, Rogerus *Crassus* (identical) 1200 Cur (St); Simon, William *Grace* 1310 ColchCt, 1332 SRSt. OFr *gras* 'fat'. v. CRASS, GROSS. Great Graces in Little Baddow owes its name to Nicholas *le Gras* (1275 PN Ess 235). Or from OFr *grace*, ME *grace, gras* 'a pleasing quality', i.e. 'attractive, charming' as opposed to John *Gracemauuais* 1247 AssBeds 'the ungracious'. (ii) William *atte Grase* 1327 SRSo; Robert *atte Gresse* 1381 SRSt. OE *græs* 'grass', also 'pasture', hence 'one who puts out cattle to grass', 'a grazier'.

Grace, Gracey, Gracie, Grece: Robertus *filius Grecie* 1188 BuryS (Sf); *Grecia* 1201 P (We), 1221 AssGl, AssWa; *Gracia* 1213 Cur (Sr), 1247 AssBeds; *Gratia* 1221 Cur (Berks); *Gracia* de Saleby 1232–35 Gilb (L); Henry *Grece* 1275 RH (Nth); Gilbert *Gracye* 1296 SRSx; William *Grece* 1297 SRY; Adam *Grace* 1302 SRSf. We are clearly concerned with a single woman's name, perhaps a derivative of OG *grisja* 'grey'. OFr *gris*, 'grey' is found in ME as *grece, greyce*. The name was latinized by the scribes as *Gratia* and popularly associated with OFr *grace*. v. also GRASSICK.

Graddige, Gradidge: From Graddage Fm in Clayhidon (Devon), earlier *Greatediche*, where lived William *atte Graddich* in 1330 (PN D 611).

Graeme: v. GRAHAM

Graft: Robert *Graf* 1279 RH (O); John *Graff* 1414 FrY. cf. Thomas *Graffard* 1200 P (Y). This latter was a Norman term for a public scribe or scrivener, from OFr *grafer* 'to write'. OFr *grafe* 'stylus', 'pencil' is here used for the wielder of the pen.

Grafton: William *de Graftona* 1130 P (Lei); John *de Grafton'* c1280 SRWo; John *Grafton* 1443 FFEss. From one or other of the many places of this name.

Graham, Grahame, Graeme, Grayham, Greim: The first of the Grahams in Scotland was William *de Graham* (1127 Black). A Norman, he took with him the Norman form of his surname which derives from Grantham (Lincs), found in DB as both *Grantham* and *Graham*. In Scotland it occurs as *Grame* in 1411 and *Graym* in 1467 (Black).

Grainge: v. GRANGE

Graley: v. GREALEY

Grammer: Robertus *Gramaticus* 1201 Cur (Y). In the margin: 'Robertus clericus et persona est'. Richard *le Gramarie, le Gŕamary, le Gramayre,* William *Gramayre* 1219 AssY; Andrew *le Gramare* 1284 FA (Y). OFr *gramaire* 'grammarian, scholar, astrologer'.

Grand: v. GRANT

Grandage, Grandorge, Grandidge: William *Grain de Or* (*Graindorge*) 1166 RBE (Sf); Thomas *Grandage* 1379 PTY; Roger *Grandorge* 1459 Balliol (O); Widow *Grandish* 1674 HTSf. OFr *grein de orge* 'barleycorn'.

Grandison: Otho *de Grandissono* 1280 Glast (So); Peter *de Grandisson* 1335 IpmW; Roger *Graundisson* 1397 FrY. From Granson on the lake of Neuchâtel, v. Wagner. cf. also Stretton Grandison (Hereford) from William de Grande Sono 1303.

Grange, Grainge: William *de la Graunge* 1275 RH (Ess); Laurence *atte Grange* 1296 SRSx. 'Dweller near, or worker at a grange', AFr *graunge,* OFr *grange* 'granary, barn' (a 1325 MED).

Granger, Grainger: William *le grangier* c1100 MedEA (Nf); Reginald *le Granger* 1219 FFSf; Walter *le Graunger* 1247 AssBeds; John *Grainger* Hy 6 AD vi (Wo). AFr *graunger,* OFr *grangier* 'one in charge of a grange, a farm-bailiff'.

Grant, Grand, Le Grand, Legrand: (i) Hugo *Grandis* 1084 GeldR (W); Gilbert *Grant, Grandus* 1183, 1192 Eynsham (O); William *le grant* 1189–1210 Holme (Nf); Thomas *le Graunt* 1219 AssY; Agnes *Grant* 1221 ElyA (Sf). AFr *graund, graunt,* OFr *grand, grant* 'great'. Ekwall notes (ELPN) that William *grandis* or *le grant* (c1150–60) was a son of Wlfwin *Graunt, Grand, grant* (1108–30) and inherited his byname, which was evidently given him for distinction from Wulwinus *juvenis* (c1130), so that *grand* here means 'elder, senior'. In most instances it probably means 'tall'. (ii) Petrus *filius Grente* 1166 P (Y); Robert *filius Grante* 1208 P (Gl); *Grante* le Chapman 1274 RH (D); William *Grent* 1204 P (O); Robert *Grente* 1327 SRSx. This must be a survival of the OE *Grante, Grente* found in several place-names. v. PN ERY 89, DEPN.

Grantham: Thomas *de Grantham* 1220 Cur (Herts). From Grantham (Lincs).

Grason: v. GRAVESON

Grassick, Grassie, Grass, Gracey: John *Grasse* alias Cordonar 1539 Black; Donald *Grasycht* 1548 ib.; John *Graissie* or *Grecie* 1632–3 ib. Gaelic *greusaich, griasaich,* originally 'decorator, embroiderer', later 'shoemaker'.

Grassman: Walter *Graysman* 1297 MinAcctCo; Mable *Gresman* 1319 *SR* (Ess). OFr *graisse, greisse, gresse* 'grease' and *man,* 'a seller of grease'.

Grater: John *the Gratere* 1223 MESO (Y); Stephen *le Gratier* 1305 Pinchbeck (Sf); Juliana *la Gratour* 1327 MESO (Ha). OFr *grateor, gratour,* *gratier* 'one who grates', probably a furbisher.

Gration: v. GRAVESON

Gratton, Grattan, Gratten: Robert, William *de* *Gratton* 1327 SRDb, 1337 IpmNt; John *de Grattone* 1348 DbAS xxxvi. From Gratton (Derby, Devon), probably also one of the sources of Irish *Grattan*.

Gravatt, Gravett, Grevatt: Ralph *de Grauette* 1208 P (Ha); Ascelina *de Lagravate* 1210 Cur (Ha); John *atte Grevette* 1288 PN Sx 17; William *de Greuett', Richard de la Greuett'* 1296 SRSx. OE **gräfet, *græfet,* a derivative of OE *gräf, gräfe* 'grove' and the diminutive suffix *-et,* from residence near a little grove. The term is found chiefly in Sussex and Surrey. v. MELS.

Grave, Graves: Lefsi *filius Greiue* 1161–77 Rams (Nf); Æthewold *filius Greui* ib.; Adam *filius Graiue* 1221 ElyA (C); *Greive* de Pincebec 1232 Pat (L); Robert, Walter *Greyue* 1255 NottBR, 1327 SRC; Hubert, Thomas *le Greyve* Hy 3 Colch (Sf), 1275 RH (Nf); William *le Grayue* 1334 FFLa; John *Graue* 1379 PTY; Hugo *Graves* 1540 FrY. This is usually from ME *greyve,* from ON *greifi* 'steward', 'a person in charge of property', in its later forms confused with GRIEVE. In South Yorks in the 16th century, *grave* (*grayves*) interchanges with *grieve* (*grevys*) in the same sense (NED). We have also to deal with a personal name ON *Greifi,* a byname from ON *greifi,* ODa, OSw *grefe* 'count, earl', which may survive in *Greavy.* This appears in DB in 1066 as *Greue* (L) and in 1130 P (L) in Turstin' *filius Greue,* where the *e* is due to the OEScand change of *ei* to *e* and is one source of *Grieve.* The forms *filius Graiue, Greiue* may mean 'son of the *greyve*' and survive as GRAVESON.

Graveney, Greveney: Alard *de Gravenni* 1207 Cur (Sf); Robert *de Graveney* 1230 Cur (K); John *Graveneye* 1376 AssLo. From Graveney (Kent).

Gravenor, Gravener: Robert *le Grant Venur* 1293 AssSt; John *Gravener* 1524 SRSf. OFr *grand* 'great' and *veneor* 'hunter'.

Graver: William *le Grevere* 1275 SRWo; Roger *le Graueur* 1279 MEOT (Sr); Peter *le Grauere* 1293 MESO (Y); John *Grafour,* carver 1414 FrY. OE *grafere, græfere,* OFr *graveur* 'engraver, sculptor'. cf. Robert *le Orgraver* 1308 Wak (Y) 'gold engraver' and Adam *le Selgraver* 1332 MESO (Lo) 'engraver of seals'. *Gravere* may also mean 'digger', from OE *grafan* 'to dig'. Piers *le Graver* was killed by the collapse of the (coal)pit in which he was working by himself at Silkstone (Db) in 1290 (MedInd.).

Graveson, Grayson, Grason, Grayshan, Grayshon, Gration, Graveston, Grayston, Graystone: Richard *Grayveson* 1327 Wak (Y); John *Graiveson* 1332 SRCu; John *Graveson* 1379 PTY; John *Grayfson* 1381 PTY; Thomas *Grayson* 1426 FrY; John *Grason* 1542 GildY. 'Son of the *greyve* or steward.' v. GRAVE and cf. GRIEVESON. A Lancs and Yorks name, all the modern variants being still found in the Leeds district. *Grayveson, Graysoun* and *Grayveston* are all found in the Preston Guild Rolls.

Gray, Grey, Le Grey: (i) Baldwin *Grai* 1173 P (Bk); William *Grei* 1198 FFHu; William *le Greie,* Sewyn *le Gray,* Philip *le Grey* 1296 SRSx. OE *gräg* 'grey', probably 'grey-haired'. (ii) Anschitill *Grai,* *de Grai* 1086 DB (O); Henry *de Gray* 1196 P (Nt). From Graye (Calvados).

Grayham: *v.* GRAHAM

Grayshan, Grayshon, Grayson: *v.* GRAVESON

Grayston, Graystone: William *Graistaine, de Graystanes* 1332 SRCu, 1380 FeuDu. 'Dweller by the grey stone(s)', as at Greystones (Sheffield). *v.* also GRAVESON.

Grazier: William *le Grasiere, le Grazur* 1279 RH (Bk), 13th Guisb (Y); Richard *le Grasiere* 1325 Oseney (O). 'One who grazes or feeds cattle for market', a derivative of OE *grasian* 'to graze'.

Grealey, Greally, Grealy, Greeley, Greely, Graley, Grayley, Gredley, Gridley, Gridly, Greasley, Gresley, le Gresley, Legresley, Grisley, Grealis, Grellis: Albert *Greslet* 1086 DB (Ch); Robertus *Greslatus* 1127 Seals (La); Robert *Greslet* 1130 P (Y); Robert *Greilli* 1133–60 Rams (Beds); Alexander *Grisle* 1148 Winton (Ha); Albert *Gresley, Gresle* 1153–68 Holme (Nf), 1182 P (L); Robert *Gresle, de Gredlei,* 1196–7 P (L), *Gredlei* 1200 Cur (L); Albert *Grelli* c1200 WhC (La); Henry *Gredle, Greslei* 1212 Cur (K); Robert *Gresle, Grelle, de Grellay, Gredlegh* 1212 Fees (La, Sf, L, O); Robert *Grelay* (*Gresle*) 1230 P (La); Thomas *Greley, Graley* (son of Robert) 1235 Fees (La); Thomas *Greyley, Grayly, Gresley* 1235, 1242 Fees (La, O, Sf); Thomas *Gredley* alias *Grelley* 1271 Ipm (R); Margaret *le Grele* 1295 Barnwell (C); Thomas *Gridly* 1674 HTSf. OFr *greslet* 'marked as by hail', i.e. pitted or pock-marked. *le Gresley* is still found in the Channel Islands and *Greslé, Grêlé* in France. *Greasley* and *Gresley* are also local in origin, from Greasley (Notts) and Gresley (Derby), pronounced *Greasley*, identical in meaning: William *de Greseleg'* 1198 P (Nt/Db), Nigel *de Greseleg'* 1204 P (Db). As both places also appear as *Griseleia,* William *de Griseleia* 1130 P (Nt/Db), this may sometimes have given modern *Grisley.* In early forms, the nickname has been confused with the place-name. *Grealley, Greeley, Greely,* are also for Ir *Mag Raoghallaigh* 'son of *Raoghallach*'.

Greasley, Gresley, Gresly: William, Nigel *de Greseleia* c1130 StCh, 1208 P (La); William *de Gresley* 1373 IpmNt; John *Gresley* 1445–6 FFWa. From Greasley (Notts), or Gresley (Derby). *v.* also GREALEY.

Greathead, Greathed, Greated: John *Gretheved* 1278 LLB B; Thomas *Gretehed* 1351 Whitby (Y). 'Big head' (OE *grēat, hēafod*).

Greatwood: Richard *Gretword* 1196 P (Nt); Gilbert *de Gretewurthe* 1214 Cur (Nth). From Greatworth (Northants).

Greaves, Greeves, Greve, Greves: Geoffrey *de la Greue* 1203 P (Lei); Walter *in the Greve* 1220 Pat (St); Richard *del Greues* 1246 AssLa; Richard *de Greves* 1259 AssCh; Alexander *del Greue* 13th WhC (La); Adam *del Grefes* 1314 Wak (Y); John *del Grayfe* 1363 FrY. From Greaves in Preston (Lancs) or from residence in or near a grove or groves (OE *grǣfe* 'brushwood, thicket, grove'). This appears as *greyve* c1475 and there has been

confusion with *Grave* and *Grieve* which occurs as *greeve* (1629) and *greave* (1844).

Greavison: *v.* GRIEVESON

Greavy: *v.* GRAVE

Grece: *v.* GRACE

Gredley: *v.* GREALEY

Greed: William, Robert *Grede* 1185 P (Y), 1242 Fees (D). According to NED, *greed* is a back-formation from *greedy* and does not occur before 1609. The back-formation appears to have taken place much earlier.

Greedy: Matildis *Gredi* 1209 P (L); Helyas *le Gredie* 1269 LeiBR. OE *grǣdig* 'ravenous, voracious, gluttonous'.

Greeley, Greely: *v.* GREALEY

Green, Greene, Grene: Geoffrey *de Grene* 1188 P (K); Richard *de la Grene* 1200 P (Nf); Geoffrey *Attegrene* 1206 AssL; Walter *ad Grenam* 1210 Cur (L); William *del grene* 1221 ElyA (Nf); Alexander, William *Grene* 1230 P (Y), c1248 Bec (O); John *en le grene,* Robert *Othegrene,* Henry *on the grene* 1274–99 MELS (Wo); John *super le Grene* 1327 SRDb. OE *grēne* 'green', usually from residence near the village green. Occasionally we may have *green* in the sense 'young, immature'. cf. the French *Vert, Levert* which Dauzat refers to 'la *verdeur* de l'homme, sa vigueur, sa jeunesse, sa vivacité'; or a personal name. cf. Godwin *Grenessone* 1115 Winton (Ha), Peter *filius Grenii* 1196 P (Y), Matthew *filius Grene* 1202 Cur (Sr).

Greenacre: Richard *de Grenacres* 1332 SRLa, *de Grenacr* 1335 WhC (La). 'Dweller by the green field(s)' (OE *æccr*).

Greenall: *v.* GREENHALGH

Greenberry, Greenburgh, Greenbury: William, Turstan *de Greneberge* 1205 P (Y), 1207 Cur (Lei); John *de Grenberwe* 1279 RH (O); Ed. *Grenebury* 1544 FrY. From Grandborough (Bucks), earlier *Greneberge,* or 'dweller by the green hill'.

Greener: (i) Robert *de la Grenehore* 1275 RH (Sf). 'Dweller by the green bank' (OE *ōra*). *v.* GREENHALGH. (ii) John *le Greener* 1332 SRWo. 'Dweller by the green.'

Greenfield: Peter *de Grenefeld* 1242 Fees (Sf); John *de Grenefeud* 1296 SRSx. 'Dweller by the green field.'

Greengrass: Richard, Alice *de Grenegres* 1275 RH (Sf), 1327 SRSf. 'Dweller at the green grassy-spot' (ON *gres*). All examples are from Suffolk, with *-gres.*

Greenhalgh, Greenhalf, Greenhall, Greenall: Richard *de Grenhal'* 1230 P (Sa); William *de Grenol* 1246 AssLa; Matill' *de Grenehalgh,* William *de Grenolf, de Grenholl'* 1332 SRLa. From Greenhalgh (Lancs), pronounced *Greener.* Probably also from Greenhaugh (Northumb).

Greenham, Grinham: Simon *de Gryndham* 1268 AssSo; Ralph *de Greneham* 1275 RH (Sf). From Greenham (Som, Berks).

Greenhead: (i) Robert *Grenhod* 1221 ElyA (Sf); William *Grenhoud* 1327 SRSx; John *Grenehed,* Alice *Greenhood* 1423, 1449 NorwW. OE *grēne,* *hōd* 'green hood', from a partiality for this head-dress. (ii) Robert *de la Greneheved* 1290 Black. From Greenhead (Peeblesshire, Northumberland) or from residence near a green hill.

Greenhill, Grinnell: William *de Grenehill'* 1200 P (Beds); Symon *de la Grenehell* 1270 ArchC v; Gilbert *ate Grenehelle* 1317 AssK. From one of the small places called Greenhill or from residence near a green hill.

Greenhough, Greenhow, Greenhowe, Greenough: Toka *in Grenehoga* 1066 DB (Nf); Geoffrey *de Grenhou* 1219 AssY; Robert *de Grenehowe* 1332 SRCu; John *Greenough* 1682 PrGR. From Green-hoe (Norfolk) or Greenhow (NR, WRYorks).

Greenhouse: William *de Grenhous* 1279 RH (C). 'Dweller at the house on the green.'

Greenist: Richard, Giles *de Gren(e)hurst* 1246 AssLa, 1251 AssY; Walter *de Greneherst* 1296 SRSx. 'Dweller by the green wooded-hill' (OE *hyrst*).

Greenley, Greenly, Grindlay, Grindley, Grinley: William *de Grenlay* 1275 RH (Nt); William *de Grinle* 1279 RH (C). From Little Gringley (Notts), Grindley (Staffs) or residence near a green clearing.

Greenman, Greenmon: John *Greneman* 1357 ColchCt. 'Dweller by the green.'

Greenough: *v.* GREENHOUGH

Greensmith: Thomas *Grenesmyth* 1523 RochW. 'Coppersmith.'

Greensted, Grinstead, Grinsted: William *de Grenested'*, *de Grinstede* 1230 P (Sx), 1327 SRSf. From Greenstead, Greensted (Essex) or Grinstead (Sussex). *v.* GRIMSTEAD.

Greenstreet: Bartholomew *de Grenestrete* 1257 ArchC iii; Peter *atte Grenestrete* 1327 SRSx. 'Dweller by a green road.'

Greenward: Adam *Grenewerde* 1276 RH (Y). Apparently 'keeper of the (village) green' (OE *weard*).

Greenway, Greenaway: William *de Greneweie* 1214 Cur (K); Robert *Grenewey* 1279 RH (O), 1327 *SR* (Ess); John *atte grenewey* 1327 SRSo. 'Dweller on the green way.'

Greenwell: Thomas *de Grenewille* 1279 RH (O). 'Dweller by the green (grassy) spring or stream.'

Greenwood: John *del Grenewode* 1275 Wak (Y). 'Dweller by the green wood.'

Greer: *v.* GRIERSON

Greeson: *v.* GRIEVESON

Greet: (i) Philippus *filius Grete* 1201 Cur (Nth); *Greta* 1219 AssY, 1260 AssC; Æðelwold *ðes Greta* c900 OEByn; Æðelmæres *Greatan* (gen.) 1017 ib.; Maud, William *Grete* 1243 AssDu, 1296 SRSx; Henry, Gilbert *le Grete* 1279 RH (Bk), 1287 AssCh. OE *grēat* 'big, stout' or, less commonly, from *Greta* (f), probably short for *Margareta*. (ii) Philip *de Grete* 1204 Cur (St); Rannulf *de Grete* 1207 Cur (Gl); Peter *de Grete* 1255 RH (Sa). From Greet (Glos, Salop, Worcs). Or local. cf. Alexander *de la Grete* 1240 Fees (K), from residence at some gravelly spot, or, perhaps more probably, from working in a gravel-pit.

Greethurst: Stephen *de Gruthurst* 1221 AssWo. From a lost place *Greethurst* in Yardley (Worcs).

Greeves: *v.* GREAVES

Greg, Gregg, Greggs: William *Gregge* 1234 Fees (Do); Henry *Gregge* 1306 FFEss; John *Greggez* 1504 FrY. A short form of *Gregory*.

Greggor, Gregor: Robert son of *Gregor* c1240 Black (Coldingham); John son of *Gregor* 1332 SRCu; Richard *Gregour* 1373 ColchCt. The vernacular form of *Gregory*.

Gregory, Gregori, Grigorey: Willelmus *filius Gregorii* 1143–7 DC (L); *Gregorius* c1150 Black; *Grigarius de Bristwic'* 1214 Cur (Y); *Grigori de Bertune* 13th AD iv (Wa); Peter *Gregory* 1279 RH (Beds); John *Grigory* 1280 AssSo; John *Gregory* 1296 SRSx. Fr *Grégoire*, Lat *Gregorius*, from Gk γρηγόριος a derivative of γρηγορέω 'to be watchful', at times confused with Lat *gregarius* from *grex, gregis* 'herd, flock'. Common in both England and Scotland.

Gregson, Grigson: William *Griggesson* 1327 SRC; Richard *Gregson* 1332 SRCu. 'Son of Greg or Grig', i.e. Gregory.

Greif: *v.* GRIEVE

Greim: *v.* GRAHAM

Grennan: *v.* GARNON

Grenville, Grenfell: Gerard *de Grenvill'* 1161 P (Bk); Eustace *de Greinuill'* 1197 P (Ess); William *de Grenefell* 1363 FrY. From Grainville-la-Teinturière (Seine-Inférieure). *v.* ANF.

Grerson: *v.* GRIERSON

Gresham: William *de Gresham* 1199 Pl (Nf); Thomas *Gresham* 1446 AssLa; Richard *Gressam* 1551 FrY. From Gresham (Norfolk).

Gresley: *v.* GREALEY, GREASLEY

Gretton: *v.* GIRTON

Grevatt: *v.* GRAVATT

Greveney: *v.* GRAVENEY

Greves: *v.* GREAVES

Greville: William *de Greiuill'* 1158 P (Nb). From Gréville (La Manche).

Grew, Grewe: Roger *le Grue* 1230 MemR (So); Gerard *la Grue* 1246 Ipm (Y). OFr *grue* 'crane'.

Grewal: Thomas *Gruel* 1327 SRC. OFr *gruel* 'fine flour, meal', a name for a miller or a baker.

Grewcock, Grocock, Grocott, Groocock, Groucock, Groucutt, Growcock, Growcott: Margeria *Groucok* 1275 SRWo; William *Grucock* 1312 AssSt. ME *grew* 'crane' plus *cock*, a formation similar to that of *Peacock*.

Grey: *v.* GRAY

Gribben, Gribbin, Gribbon: *v.* CRIBBIN

Gribble, Gribbell: Walter *atte Gribbele* 1330 *SR* (D). From residence near a crabtree or black-thorn (ME *gribbele*). *v.* also GRIMBLE.

Grice, Grise, Griss, Le Grice, Le Grys: Richard, Eustace *Gris* 1176, 1193 P (Nth, K); Robert, John *le Gris* 1198 FF (Nf), 1202 AssL; Leticia *Grise* 1317 AssK; Thomas *Grys* 1327 SRSx; Walter *Griss* 1337 ColchCt; Richard *Grice* 1413 FrY. ME *grise, grice* from ON *gríss* 'a pig' (c1230 MED) or ME *gris, grice* from OFr *gris* 'grey', grey-haired (c1395 MED).

Gricks: *v.* GRIGG
Gridley: *v.* GREALEY
Grief: *v.* GRIEVE
Grier: *v.* GRIERSON

Grierson, Grerson: Gilbert *Greresoun* 1411 Black; William *Grerson* 1451 ib.; Gilbert *Greir, Greirsone* 1676–7 ib.; *Grierson* alias *M'Gregor* 1704 ib. 'Son of *Gregor*.'

Grieve, Grieves, Greif, Grief, Grieff, Greeff: Farðain *Greva* c1050 YCh; Johan *Greve* 1199 P (W), 1296 Black; William *Greue* 1327 MEOT (L); John *le Greue* 1332 ib. (Nf); John *Grefe* 1470 Black; Laurence, Richard *Greif* 1493 ib., 1529 FrY; John *Grieff* 1605 Black; John *Grieve* 1782 ib. Scottish and Northern English *grieve* is the normal representative of ONorthumb *grǽfa*, corresponding to WS *gerēfa* 'reeve' (NED). Originally 'governor of a province', it came to mean 'overseer, manager, head workman on a farm, farm-bailiff'. This is the origin of the Scottish *Grieve* and probably of the first Yorkshire example, though this might be a byname from the personal name discussed under *Grave*. One would not expect an Old Northumbrian form in Wilts, Lincs or Norfolk. The Wilts example is also probably from the personal name. The Norfolk example is certainly and the Lincs one probably the occupational term. Thuresson explains these as due to the influence of *reve* 'reeve' on the ground that the Scandinavian change of *ei* to *e* occurs only in personal names. As the personal name is the occupational term used as a byname, there seems no reason why both should not undergo the same development and these forms from the eastern counties where Scandinavian influence was strong should be derived from ON *greifi* 'steward'. cf. GRAVE.

Grieveson, Greavison, Greeson, Greson: Emma *Grefeson* 1379 PTY; Robert *Greveson* 1498 FrY; John *Greason* 1637 Bardsley (La). 'Son of the bailiff.' *v.* GRIEVE.

Griffin, Griffen: *Grifin* 1066 DB (Co, Ch, St, Wa); *Griffin* filius Gurgan 1130 P (Pembroke); Osbertus *filius Griffini* 1153–68 Holme (Nf); *Gruffin* son of Oweyn 1285 Ch (Radnor); Robert *Grifin* 1148 Winton (Ha); Godfrey, Robert *Griffin* 1197 P (Wa), 1219 AssSo; John *Griffen* c1230 StThomas (St). *Gruffin, Griffin*, a pet-form of MW *Gruffudd*; in the Welsh border counties introduced direct from Wales, in the eastern counties by the Bretons who came over with the Conqueror and were numerous there. cf. *Griffinus* Bret Hy 2 DC (L).

Griffith, Griffiths: *Gruffyd* ap Madog Vnyon 1392 Chirk; Jone *Gryffyth* 1524 SRSf. OW *Griph-iud*, MW *Gruffudd*, noted in Wales in 1150. The second element is *iud* 'chief'. cf. *Griffinus* seu *Griffith* Kynaston 1428 FA (Sa).

Grigg, Griggs, Gricks, Grix: *Gricge, Grigge* 1275 RH (Sf); *Grigge* Suel 1327 SRC; William *Grig* 12th DC (L); Warin *Grygge* 1282 FFEss; John *Gregge* 1282 FFEss; Robert *Grigges* 1341 AD iii (Hu); John *Gregge, Grigge* 1343, 1345 LLB F; *Grig* is a short form of *Gregory*. cf. GREG.

John *Grygges* was the son and heir of *Gregory* le Bacer 1345 AD i (Herts). The frequency of *Grigg* as compared with *Greg* is due to the fact that *Grigg* was also a nickname: Stephen *le Grig* 1327 SRSx: ME *grigg(e)*, 'a diminutive person, a dwarf' (a1400–50 NED). There appears to be no connexion with 'a merry grig'.

Grigorey: *v.* GREGORY
Grigson: *v.* GREGSON

Grill, Grills, Grylls: John *Grylle* 1327 SRSf; John *Grille* 1346 FA (Sf). ME *grill(e)* 'fierce, cruel', from OE *gryllan* 'to gnash the teeth, rage'.

Grimble, Grumble, Grumell, Gribbell, Gribble: *Grimbald* 1066, 1086 DB; *Grimbaldus, Grumbaldus* Pancefot 1272 Forssner; *Grymbald* Fraunceys 1310 AssSt; Robert, William *Grimbald* 1153–63 Templars (O), 1207 Cur (Nth); Radulfus *Grumbaldus* 1185 Templars (O); Warin *Grimboll* 1275 RH (Sf); Martin *Grumbold* 1327 SRC; Richard *Grymbyll* 1524 SRSf. OG *Grimbald* 'helmet-bold'. *Grimbald* became *Gribald* through assimilation of *mb* to *bb*: cf. *Gribaut*, Guido *Gribaud* 1275 RH (Nf). *v.* also GRIBBLE.

Grimby: William *de Grenebi* 1178 P (L). From Granby (Notts).

Grime, Grimes, Grimm, Grimme: (i) *Grim, Grimus, Grimmus* 1066 DB; *Grim* de Leuertona 1175 P (Nt); Godwin, Bernard *Grim* 1170, 1183 P (Nf, C); Alan *Grime* 1279 RH (C); William, Thomas *Grym* 1309 FFSf, 1332 SRSt; Geoffrey, John *Gryme* 1327 SRY, 1379 PTY. ON *Grímr*, ODa, OSw *Grim*. This should give *Grime(s)*. *Grimmus* may belong below. The common early form *Grim* as a surname cannot be definitely assigned. It is certainly at times for *Grimm*. (ii) Edricus *Grim, Grimma, Salvage* 1066 DB (Sf); Peter *le Grim* 1327 SRSx; John *le Grymme* 1332 SRSt. *le Grim* is from OE *grim* 'fierce, grim', a nickname clearly borne by Edricus Grim.

Grimmet, Grimmett, Grumitt, Grummett, Grummit, Grummitt: (i) Roger, John *Grymet* 1251 AssY, 1297 SRY; Vyncent *Grumet* 1275 RH (W). A diminutive of *Grim*, a short form of *Grimbald*. *v.* GRIMBLE. (ii) Thomas *Grimuld*, William *Grimald* 1327 SRSf. OG *Grimbald*, becoming *Grimaud, Grimet*. (iii) John *Grymyld, Grymyd* 1379 PTY. ON *Grímhildr* (f) 'helmet-battle'.

Grimmond, Grimond: John *Griman* 1534 Black (Perth); Anna *Grimen* 1657 ib.; John *Grimmond* 1665 ib. A form of M'CRIMMON with excrescent *d*.

Grimsdell: Adam *de Grimisdale* 1332 SRCu. From Grinsdale (Cumb).

Grimsell: Robert *de Grimeshull'* 1221 AssWo. From Grimes Hill (Worcs).

Grimshaw: Richard *de Grymeschagh, de Grymeschawe* 13th WhC, 1284 AssLa; Henry *de Grimeshagh* 1400 IpmLa. From Grimshaw (Lancs).

Grimson: Arne *Grimsune* Wm 2 Whitby (Y). 'Son of *Grímr*.' *v.* GRIME.

Grimstead, Grimsted: Walter *de Grimestede* 1201 P (W). From Grimstead (Wilts). Also from Grinstead (Sussex): Thomas *de Grimstede* 1327 SRSx. *v.* GREENSTED.

Grimward, Grimwade, Grimwood: *Grimward* de Cuthmund 1199 FineR; *Grimwardus* 1222 ClR; Robert *Grimward* 1247 FineR (L); Thomas *Grymward* 1327 SRSf; William *Grymwade* 1524 SRSf; Edmund *Grimwood* 1674 HTSf. OG *Grimward* 'helmet-guard'.

Grindal, Grindall, Grindel, Grindell, Grindle: (i) Ædricus *Grendel* 1180 P (Wo); Robert *de Grenedala* 1166 P (Y); Walter *de Grendale* 1242 Fees (L); Stephen, Benedict *de Grindale* 1297 AssY, 1332 SRCu. From Greendale (Devon), Grindale (ERYorks) or residence in a green valley. (ii) Richard *de Grenehull'* 1221 AssSa. From Grindle (Salop) or residence near a green hill.

Grinder: William *le grindere* 1230 P (So); Stephen *le Grindar* 1274 RH (Sa). OE *grindere* 'grinder of corn, miller'. In medieval England the reference may also have been to a sharpener of iron tools (grindstones or grindelstones are mentioned 1228); or to a grinder of colours for painters (1352 Building 171).

Grindlay, Grindley, Grinley: *v.* GREENLEY
Grinham: *v.* GREENHAM
Grinnell: *v.* GREENHILL
Grinstead, Grinsted: *v.* GREENSTED
Gripp: (i) Hugo *filius Grip* 1086 DB (Do); Robert, John *Grip* 1195 P (Y), 1275 SRWo. ON *Gripr*, ODa *Grip*. (ii) Walter *del le Grip* 1279 AssNb; John *atte Grype* 1332 SRSx. 'Dweller in the deep valley', as at Crypt Fm (Sussex), OE *gripu* 'kettle, caldron', used topographically, *v.* MELS.

Grisdale, Grisedale: Simon *de Grisdale* 1332 SRLa; William *de Gresdale* 1359 FrY; William *Grisedayle* 1526 FrY. From Grisedale (Cumb).

Grise, Griss: *v.* GRICE
Grisley: *v.* GREALEY
Grissom, Grissin, Grisson: John *Grisun* 1221 AssWa. OFr *grison* 'grey'.
Gritton: *v.* GIRTON
Grix: *v.* GRIGG
Grocock, Grocott: *v.* GREWCOCK
Gronow: Kenwrig *ap Grono* 1391 Chirk. Welsh *Goronwy, Gronw, Gronow,* OW *Guorgonui*.
Groocock: *v.* GREWCOCK
Groom, Groome: Richard *Grom* c1100 MedEA (Nf); Ernald *le Grom* 1187 P (Gl); Robert *Groum* 1327 SRWo; Roger *le Groom* 1351 AssEss. ME *grom(e)* 'serving-man, manservant', often applied to shepherds. cf. Richard *le Gotegrom* 1335 FFSf, John *Lambegrom* 1279 RH (C), John *Schepgrom* 1327 *SR* (Ess), Richard *Plougrom* 1319 *SR* (Ess).
Groser: John *Grocer* 1350 ColchCt. OFr *grossier* 'wholesale-dealer'.
Gross, Grose, Groos, Gros, Le Gros: Willelmus *filius grosse* 1086 InqEl (Sf); Gerardus *filius Grossi* 1176 P (Y); Willelmus *Grossus* 1086 DB (Nf); Adam *le.Gros* 1186–1210 Holme (Nf); William *le Groos* 1314 FFEss. Lat *grossus* 'thick', OFr *gros* 'big, fat', used occasionally as a personal-name. *v.* CRASS, GRACE.
Grosset: Richard *Grosset* 1279 RH (O). A diminutive of GROSS.
Grosvenor: Robert *le gros Venour* c1200 WhC

(La); Warin *le Grovenur* 1259 AssCh. Fr *gros veneur* 'chief huntsman'.
Groucock, Groucutt: *v.* GREWCOCK
Grout, Grut, Grute: Edwin, Geoffrey *Grut* 1066 DB (Ess), 1199 P (L); Walter, Robert *Groute* 1297 MinAcctCo, 1447–8 FFSr. OE *grūt* 'groats, coarse meal', cf. ON *Grautr*, an original nickname from ON *grautr* 'porridge'. *v.* OEByn 376.
Grove, Groves: Ralph *de Graua* 1119–27 Colch (Ess); Osbert *de la Graua* 1197 FF (Bk); John *de la Grove* 1275 SRWo; Robert *ate Groue* 1317 AssK; William *Grove* 1327 SRDb. 'Dweller by the grove', OE *grāf*.
Grover: William *Grouar* 1332 SRSx. 'Dweller by the grove.'
Growcock, Growcott: *v.* GREWCOCK
Grubb, Grubbe: Richard, John *Grubbe* 1176 P (Bk), 1203 P (Sx). The name was fairly common and is probably ME *grubbe* 'grub', used in the 15th century of a short, dwarfish individual.
Grumble, Grumell: *v.* GRIMBLE
Grumitt, Grummett: *v.* GRIMMET
Grut(e): *v.* GROUT
Grylls: *v.* GRILL
Guard: *v.* GARD
Gubb: Robert, Richard *Gubbe* 1296 SRSx, 1319 Bart (Lo). A short form of *Gubiun*. *v.* GUBBIN.
Gubbin, Gubbins: Hugo *Gubiun* 1130 P (Nth), 1256 AssNb; Richard *Gubun, Gubiun, Gybun, Gubyun* 1219 Cur; Hugo *Gobyon* 1242 Fees (Beds); Thomas *Gubin* 1279 RH (O). OFr *Giboin*, with *u* for *i* through the influence of the neighbouring sounds. *v.* GIBBEN.
Gubell: *Gubaldus* c1130 ELPN; Willelmus *Guboldus* 1192 P (L); Alice, Robert *Gubald* 1201 P (L), 1219 AssY. OE **Gūðbeald* 'battle-bold'.
Gude: *v.* GOOD
Gudge: *v.* GOOCH
Gudgeon, Gudgin: Peter *Guggun* 1206 Cur (L); Robert *Guiun* 1221 Cur (W); Henry *Gojun* 1332 SRSt; Thomas *Goodgeon* 1613 FrY. ME *gojon, gogen,* OFr *goujon* 'gudgeon', perhaps 'greedy', or 'big-headed', or one who will take any bait, 'credulous, gullible'.
Gudger: *v.* GOODGER
Guest: Benwoldus *Gest* c1100 OEByn; Richard, Thomas *le Gest* c1248 Bec (Mx), 1275 SRWo. ON *gestr* 'guest, stranger'.
Guilder: *v.* GILDER
Guilding: *v.* GELDING
Guillerman: *v.* GILLMAN
Guiness, Guinness: For MAGUINESS.
Gull: Alured, Geoffrey *Gulle* 1200 FFEss, 1218 AssL; Richard *le Gul* 1279 RH (O). ME *gulle* 'gull' or ME *gull,* ON *gulr* 'pale, wan'.
Gullick, Gulick: *v.* GOODLAKE
Gulling: Roger *Gulling* 1203 P (Ha). ME **gulling* 'the pale one'. *v.* GULL.
Gulliver, Gulliford, Galliford, Galliver: William *Gulafra* 1086 DB (Sf); Philip *Golafre* 1166 RBE (Sf); William *Golefer* 1459 Cl (Mx); Henry *Gullifer, Gulliford* 1654, 1670 Bardsley. OFr *goulafre* 'glutton', a very common name.

Gully, Gullyes, Golley: John, Thomas *Gulias* 1202 AssL, 1229 Cl (So); Hugh *Golie* 1206 P (O); Jordan *Gulie* 1225 AssSo; Geoffrey *Golias* 1275 RH (Nf). ME *golias* 'a giant', from the Hebrew *Goliath*. Wyclif uses both *Goliath* and *Golie*; Chaucer and Shakespeare have *Golias*.

Gulson, Gulston: *v.* GOLDSTON

Gumb, Gumm: *v.* GOMME

Gumbel: Durandus *Gumboldus* 1148 Winton (Ha); William *Gumbald'* c1216 Seals (Sf). OFr *Gombaut*, OG *Gundbald* 'battle-bold'.

Gummer, Gomer: (i) *Gumer* 1091–1102 Rams (Hu); *Guthmarus* clericus c1170 Rams (Nf); Johannes *filius Gudemer'* 1219 AssL; Abraham *filius Gumari* 1219 Cur (C); Simon *Gumer* 1276 RH (Y). OE **Gūðmǣr* 'battle-famous'. (ii) *Godmarus* 1066 DB (Sf), 1255 Rams (Beds), 1279 RH (Hu); Willelmus *filius Gomer* 1191 P (C); Colin *Godmar* 1255 Rams (Hu); Robert *Gomar* 1279 RH (Hu); William *Godmer* 1332 SRWa. OE *Gōdmǣr* 'good-famous'.

Gun, Gunn, Gunns: *Gunne* 1142 NthCh (L); *Gun* Hy 2 DC (L); Warin, William *Gun* 1218 AssL, 1275 RH (Sf); Robert *Gunn* 1297 Wak (Y). ON *Gunnr* 'battle', or, perhaps, *Gunne*, a pet-form of *Gunnhildr*. *v.* GUNNETT.

Gundrey, Gundry, Goundry: *Gundricus* 1100–13 Rams (Herts); William *Gundrey* 1296 SRSx. OG *Gundric* 'battle-ruler', OFr *Gondri*.

Gundy: William *Gundi* 1279 RH (Hu); John *Gondy* 1327 SRC. OG *Gundi*.

Gunhouse: *v.* GUNNIS

Gunnell: *Gunnild* 1066 DB (Sx), c1172–80 DC (L); *Gunnilla* 1214, 1219 Cur (Sr, L); Robert *Gunnilt* Hy 2 DC (L); Stephen, John *Gunnild* 1240 Rams (Nf), 1327 SRC; Simon *Gunel* 1240 FFEss. ON *Gunnhildr* (f) 'battle-battle'. *v.* GUNNETT.

Gunner: (i) *Gunneuare, Gunnor* 1066 DB; *Gunware* Hy 2 DC (L), 1219 AssY; *Gunnora* 1207–8 Cur (So, Nb); William, Simon *Gunnore* 1275, 1279 RH (Sf, Bk); William *Gunwar* 1279 RH (C). ON *Gunvor*, ODa *Gunwǫr, Gunnor* (f), a common Norman name, usually latinized as *Gunnora*. (ii) Thomas *le gonner* 1285 PN Ess 21. ME *gonner* 'gunner' (1391 MED).

Gunnett: *Gunnota* 1279 RH (O); William *Gonnote* 1327 SRSf. *Gunnot*, a diminutive of *Gunne*, a pet-form of *Gunnhildr*. *Gunnilda*, daughter of Fulco, is also called *Gunnota* (1207 Cur).

Gunning: *v.* GUNWIN

Gunnis, Gunhouse: Herveus *de Gunnesse* 1202 AssL. From Gunness (Lincs).

Gunson: Eustace *Gunson* 1279 RH (C). 'Son of *Gunn*.' Henry *Gunneson* (1278 AssLa) is identified by the editor as Henry son of *Gunnild*.

Gunter, Gunther: *Gunterus* 1094–1100 NthCh (Nth), 1214 Cur (Sr); *Guntier filius Herberti* 1165 P (Ha); William *Gunter* 1205 Cur (Berks), 1221 *ElyA* (Sf). OFr *Gontier*, OG *Gunter* 'battle-army'.

Gunthorp, Gunthorpe, Guntrip: Yvo *de Gunethorp* 1207 Cur (Nth); William *Gunthropp* 1623 Bardsley. From Gunthorpe (Lincs, Norfolk, Northants, Notts, Rutland).

Gunton: Bartholomew *de Guneton* 1195 P (Nf, Sf); Matthew *de Gunetun'* 1226 Cur (Nf); Henry *Gonton* 1309 Wak. From Gunton (Norfolk, Suffolk).

Gunwin, Gunning: *Gundewinus* cortinarius 1130 P (Sr); Thomas *Gundewin* 1228 Cl; William *Gundewyne* 1296 SRSx; Jo. *Guninge* 1674 HTSf. OG *Gund(e)win* 'battle-friend'. In Corton (Suffolk) in the reign of John, *Gundewyn'* de Nethergate held land which was held in 1275 by Gerald *Gunwine* or *Gundwyne* by heredity (RH).

Guppy: Nicholas *Gopheye* 1327 SRSo; Robert *Guppey* 1392 LoPleas. From Guppy (Dorset).

Gurden: *v.* GORDON

Gurdler: *v.* GIRDLER

Gurling: *v.* CODLIN

Gurnett: Alexander, Robert *Gurnard* 1275 RH (D), 1327 SRSx. ME *gurnard, gurnade*, a fish with a large spiny head and mailed cheeks, with a throat almost as big as the rest of its body, so called because of the grunting noise it makes.

Gurney: Hugo *de Gurnai* 1086 DB (Ess, So); Adam *de Gurnay* 1196 P (Nth). From Gournai-en-Brai (Seine-Inférieure).

Gurtler: *v.* GIRDLER

Gurton: *v.* GIRTON

Gutch, Guthrum: *v.* GOOCH, GOODERHAM

Gutman: *v.* GODMAN

Gutridge, Gutteridge: *v.* CUTTERIDGE, GOOD-RICH

Gutsell: *v.* GODSAL

Guy, Guye, Guys, Gye, Why, Whye, Wye: (i) Willelmus *filius Widonis, Guidonis* 1086 DB; Turstanus *filius Witdo*. ib.; *Why* de la Haie c1200 MELS (Sx); *Guido* de Hathfeld' 1200 Cur (Mx); Richard *Wi* 1188 P (O); William *Wy* 1297 MinAcctCo; John *Gy* 1317 AssK, 1319 SRLo; Richard *Guy* 1384 LoPleas. OFr *Guy*, OG *Wido*, a common French name, usually latinized as *Wido*, occasionally as *Guido*. *Why*, much rarer than *Guy* today, is the Norman form. (ii) John *le Gy* 1327 SR (Ess). OFr *gui* 'guide'.

Guyat, Guyatt: *v.* WYATT

Guyer, Gyer: Henry *le Gyur* 1271 Ch (Do); Thomas *Gaiour* 1327 SR (Ess). OFr *guyour, guieor* 'guide'.

Guymer, Gymer: *Gyomarus* 1101–16 MedEA (Nf); Robertus *filius Guimer* 1204 P (Y); *Guiomarus* filius Warnerii 1210 P (Y); Robert *Guymer* 1277 *Ely* (Sf). OG *Wigmar* 'battle-famous'. *v.* also WYMER.

Guyon: *v.* WYON

Guyot, Gyatt: *v.* WYATT

Gwilliam, Gwillim: Hova, Jankyn *ap Gwillym* 1391 Chirk; Lewis *Gwillam* 1630 SaAS 2/iv. Welsh forms of *William*.

Gwinn, Gwyn, Gwynn, Gwynne, Wyn, Wynne: Thomas *filius Win* 1255 RH (Sa); *Wyn, Win* 1280 SaAS 2/xi (Ellesmere); *Gwyn* 1327 SRSa; *Gwynne* ap Griffud ap Tudur 1474 Chirk; William *ap Guyn*, David *ap Gwyn*, Philip *Wyn* 1327 SRSa; Thomas *Gwynne* 1481–2 FFSr. Welsh *gwyn* 'fair, white'. *v.* also WINN.

Gye: *v.* GUY
Gyer: *v.* GUYER
Gyles: *v.* GILES
Gymer: *v.* GUYMER

Gynn: *v.* GINN
Gypp(s): *v.* GIPP
Gypson: *v.* GIPSON
Gyves: *v.* JEEVES

H

Habberjam: *v.* HABERGHAM, HABERSHON

Habbeshaw, Habeshaw, Habishaw: William *le Haubergier* 1201 P (Nth); Reginald *le Hauberger, le Haubeger* 1275 RH (Lo), *le Haberger* 1281 LLB A. OFr *haubergier* 'maker of hauberks or coats of mail' (1481 NED). cf. HARBISHER.

Habbijam, *v.* HABERGHAM, HABERSHON

Haberer: *v.* HARBERER

Habergham, Habberjam, Habbijam: Matthew *de Habercham* 1269 InqLa; Lawrence *Haberjam* 1551 FFLa; John *Habergam* 1574 LWills. From Habergham Eaves (Lancs). The modern pronunciation is *Habbergam* (DEPN), but was once clearly *Habberjam*, which has been confused with the later pronunciation of *Habershon*.

Habershon, Habberjam, Habbijam: Edmund *Habirgent* 1416 NorwW (Nf); Edward *Haberjon* 1565 ShefA; John *Haberdejohn* 1592 ArchC 48; William *Haberjamb* 1735 FrY. Metonymic for a maker of habergeons, sleeveless coats or jackets of mail or scale armour, worn also as a rough garment for penance. ME, OFr *haubergeon*, a diminutive of *hauberc*. cf. HABBESHAW. *Habershon* and *Habbijam* are both still found in Sheffield, the latter being a direct descendant of the 1565 *Haberjon*. cf. HABERGHAM.

Habeshaw, Habishaw: *v.* HABBESHAW

Hack: *v.* HAKE

Hacker: Adam *le Hakkere* 1262 MEOT (Herts); John *Hakyere* 1296 SRSx. A derivative of ME *hacken* 'to hack', one who hacks, a cutter, probably a wood-cutter. Or, perhaps, 'a maker of *hacks*', used in ME of agricultural tools such as mattocks and hoes.

Hackett, Haggett, Haggitt, Acket, Acketts: *Haket* de Rideford c1160–66 DC (L); *Haket* filius Clac 1193 FF (L); Walter *Achet* 1086 DB (Bk); Ralph *Hacget* 1131 FeuDu; Rolland' *Haget, Haket* 1158 1179 P (Y, L); Geoffrey *Haget, Hachet* 1191 P (Y). An AN diminutive of ON *Haki*, OSw *Haki*, ODa *Hake*. Occasionally we may have a nickname from a fish: John *Hakede* 1327 SRSf, Roger *Hakat* 1327 SRC, from *hacaed* (*haket*) 'a kind of fish' mentioned in a 14th-century copy of the foundation charter of the Abbey of Ramsey.

Hacking: William *de Hakkyng* c1283 WhC (La). From Hacking (Lancs).

Hackling, Haclin, Ackling: *Hakelinus* 1192 P (Lo); *Hakelinus* filius Jurneth 1199 MemR (Sf). A

double diminutive of ON *Haki, Hak-el-in*. cf. HACKETT.

Hackman: William *Hakeman* 1197 P (C); William *Hacman* 1204 Cur (D). 'Servant of *Hake*.'

Hackney, Hakeney, Hakney: (i) Benedict *de Hakeneye* 1275 RH (Lo). From Hackney (Middlesex). (ii) Adam called *Hakenay* 1316 Black; John *Hakeney* 1327 *SR* (Ess), 1329 ColchCt; William Mopps *Hakeneyman* 1327 Pinchbeck (Sf). OFr *haquenée*, ME *hakenei* 'an ambling horse or mare, especially for ladies to ride on'. cf. PALFREY and PALFREYMAN.

Hackwood: John *Hackewude* 1230 P (Sx); Thomas *Hackewode* 1327 SRSx. 'Hack wood', a nickname for a wood-cutter.

Haclin: *v.* HACKLING

Hacon: *Hacun, Hacon* 1066 DB; *Hacon* de Crokestun c1160 DC (L); Robert *Hacun* 1221 AssSa; Semann' *Hacon* 1275 RH (Sf). ON *Hákun* 'high race'.

Hadaway: *v.* HATHAWAY

Hadcock: *v.* ADCOCK

Hadden, Haddin, Haddon: (i) Ailwin *de Haddun'* 1159 P; Philip *de Haddon* 1267 AssSo; John *de Hadden* 1323 IpmNt; Thomas *Haddun* 1379 PTY. From Haddon (Derby, Dorset, Northants, Hunts), or Haddon in Shute (Devon). (ii) Ulkill, Bernard *de Hauden* 1165–71, 1296 Black (Roxburgh); William *Haulden* 1328 ib.; Silvester *Hadden* 1514 ib. From the barony of Hadden or Halden (Roxburgh).

Haddock, Haddacks, Haddick: Richard, William *Haddoc* 1208 ChR (Sf), 1228 FeuDu; John *Haddock'* 1302 SRY. *Haddock* is the local pronunciation of *Haydock*, but this will not account for these early forms. We may have a nickname from the fish, first recorded in 1307 (MED), not inappropriate in Suffolk for a seller of haddocks. The Durham name is probably from a personal name, a diminutive of OE *Æddi* (Bede), with inorganic *H*. cf. *Addoch* de Eselinton 1187 P (Nb); *Addoc* c1220 FeuDu, William *Addoc* 1243 AssDu.

Hadenham: *v.* HADMAN

Hadfield: Wido *de Hadfeld'* 1190 P (Ess); Matthew *de Hadefeld* 1288 AssCh; Richard *Hadefeld* 1401 AssLa. From Hadfield (Derby).

Hadgkiss: *v.* HODGKIN

Hadkins: *v.* ADKIN

Hadley, Hadlee: Matilda *de Hadlega* 1194 P (Sf); Warin *de Hadlai* 1212 P (Y); Richard *de Hadlege*

1311–12 FrC; John *Hadley* 1390 FFEss. From Hadleigh (Essex, Herts, Salop, Suffolk), or Hadley (Worcs).

Hadman: John *Hadenham, Hadman,* William *Hadnam* 1524 SRSf. From Hadenham (Bucks): Geoffrey *de Hadenham* 1235 Fees (Bk).

Hafter: Hugh, Robert *le Haftere* Hy 3 AD ii (Mx), 13th Lewes (Nf). A derivative of OE *hæft* 'handle', a maker of handles for tools (1598 NED).

Hagan, Hagen, Hagon, Hain, Haine, Haines, Hains, Hayne, Haynes, Heyne, Heynes, Hanes: *Hagene, Hagana* 1066 DB (He, Nf); *Hagena* Jugement 1130 P (Sf); Rogerus *filius Hane* 1198 FFNf; *Hagan(us)* 1199 FFSt, 1240 Rams (Nf); Alicia *filia Hahen* 1202 FFNf; *Heyne* le Forester 1274 Wak (Y); Adam *filius Hayne* 1332 SRLa; Ulricus *Hagana* 1066 DB (Sf); Peter *Hain* 1200 P (Do); Amfridus *Hane* 1209 P (St); Walter *Hein* 1279 RH (C); John *Hagun* ib. (O); Richard *Hagyn* 1304 LoCt; Alice *Heynes* 1327 SRSo; Margery *Haynes* 1352 ERO; Robert *Haynesson* alias *Hayn* 1398 FrY. ODa *Haghni,* OSw *Hagne,* or OG *Hagano, Hageno. v.* also HAIN. *Hagan* may also be for *O'Hagan.*

Haggard, Haggart, Hagard: Alice *Haggard* 1275 SRWo. ME, OFr *hagard* 'wild, untamed'.

Haggas, Haggis, Haggish: Richard *del Haghous* 1327 SRY; Gilbert *of Haggehouse* 1394 Black; John *Hagas* 1401 FrY; William *Haggus* 1427 Black; Richard *Haggas* 1486 GildY; Christopher *Haghus* 1532 LWills; John, Richard *Haggis* 1547 Black, 1637 SfPR. NED has *hag-house* (1733) '? a place for storing firewood'. *Hag* is a northern and Scottish word from ON *hǫgg* 'a cutting blow, hewing of trees', common in northern place-names. A *hag-house* was probably a wood-cutter's hut and the surname one for a wood-cutter. *Haggis* is a common place-name in the Scottish Lowlands.

Haggett, Haggitt: *v.* HACKETT

Hagtharp: Robert *de Hakethorp* 1251 AssY. From Hackthorpe (Westmorland).

Haig: Peter *del Hage* 1162–6 Black, *de la Haga* 1162–90 ANF. The Haigs of Bemersyde derive from the district of La Hague (La Manche). *v.* ANF.

Haig, Haigh, Hague: Jollan *de Hagh'* 1229 Cl (Y); William *del Haghe* 1327 SRY. From Haigh (Lancs, WRYorks) or 'dweller by the enclosure' (OE *haga* or ON *hagi*).

Haile, Haill, Hails, Hayle, Hayles: (i) *Haile(s)* and *Hayle(s)* are Scottish and Northern English forms of HALE(s). cf. Haile (Cu): *Hale* c1180 and William *de Hales* 1349 FrY; William *Hayles* 1456 ib. The Scots *Hailes* derives from Hailes in Colinton (Midlothian, East Lothian): William *de Halis* 1189–98 Black; John *Hayles* 1408 ib. (ii) William, Richard *de Hayles* 1273, 1279 RH (Wa, O). From Hailes (Glos), distinct in origin from HALE. *v.* also HAYLOCK.

Hailey, Haily, Haley, Haly, Hayley: William *de Hayleg'* 1251–2 FFWa; Roger *de Hayleye* 1328 IpmGl; Thomas *Haley* 1420–1 IpmNt. From Hailey (Oxon), or 'dweller at the hay clearing'.

Haim, Haimes, Haymes, Hamon: *Hamo, Haimo, Hamon* 1086 DB; *Hamon* de Hauton c1135 DC (L); *Haim* de Branzton' 1202 FFL; *Heimes* de Henford' 1203 Cur (Nf); Richard, John *Haym* 1279 RH (O), 1327 SRSo; John *Hamon'* 1279 RH (C); Thomas *Hamun* 1296 SRSx. OFr *Haim, Haimon, Aymes,* OG *Haimo* 'home', a popular Norman name. *Hamo* is the OFr cas-sujet, *Hamon* the cas-régime. *v.* HAMMOND.

Hain, Haine, Hayne, Heyne: (i) William *de Heghen* 1289 PN D 544; William *atte Heyene* 1327 SRSo; Martin *de la Heghen* 1333 PN D 129. *Hayes* and *Hayne,* respectively strong and weak plurals of *hay,* are common place-names in Devon, particularly in the south-east, and are found elsewhere in the west country. *v.* PN D 129–30. 'Dweller on the farm or holding.' cf. HAY. (ii) William *le Heyne* 1327 SRSt. ME *heyne, haine, hayn* 'a mean wretch, niggard' (c1386 NED).

Hain(e)s: *v.* HAGAN

Hair, Haire, Hare, O'Haire, O'Hare, O'Hear: William *Hare* 1366 Black (Edinburgh); Patrick *Ahayr(e), Ahaire, Ahar, Hayre, Hair, Hare* 1415–38 ib. (Ayr). Ir *Ó hĺr* 'descendant of *Ír*' (sharp, angry). *v.* also AYER, HARE.

Hairon: *v.* HERON

Haizelden: *v.* HAZELDEN

Hake, Hakes, Hack: Turkil *Hako* 1066 DB (Nf); Leuiua *filia Hacke* 1218 AssL; Gilbert *Hake* 1257 FFSf; Robert *Hakke* 1375 Lewes (Nf). ON *Haki,* ODa *Hake* 'hook, crook', an original nickname.

Hakeney: *v.* HACKNEY

Hakluyt: Walter *Hakelutel* 1255 RH (Sa); John *Hackelut* 1323 AssSt. 'Hack little', a nickname for a lazy wood-cutter.

Haldane, Halden, Haldin, Hallding, Holdane: *Haldein, Haldanus, Halden* 1066 DB; *Haldeynus* 1109–31 Miller (C); *Halden* filius Eadulf a1124 Black (Glasgow); *Haldane* de Hemingburgh 1208 AssY; Goduinus *Haldein, Halden* 1066, 1086 DB (Nf); Robert *Haldein* 1170 P (Ess); Roger *Haldane* 1255 Black; William *Halden* 1286 AssCh; Simon *Holdeyn* 1358 FFSf. ON *Halfdanr,* ODa *Hal(f)dan,* Anglo-Scand *Healfdene* 'half Dane'.

Hale, Hales: William *de Hales* 1180 P (Sa); Robert *Attehal'* 1212 Cur (L); Morus *de la Hale* 1214 Cur (K); John *del Hale* 1220 Cur (Herts); Nicholas *en la Hale* 1275 SRWo; John *in the Hale* 1296 SRSx. From residence in a nook, recess or remote valley. OE *halh* (nom.) becomes *Haugh, Hauff, Hallowes.* The dative *(atte) hale* becomes *Hale. v.* also HAILE, HEAL.

Haler, Hayler, Haylor, Hayllar: William *le Haliere* 1279 RH (O); John *Haler* 1373 ColchCt; Thomas *Hayler,* Elizabeth *Haler* 1555, 1556 SxWills. Perhaps a derivative of ME *halien* 'to hale, haul, drag', from OFr *haler* 'to pull', a carrier, porter (1479 NED); also, probably equivalent to *atte Hale* 'one who dwelt in a retired spot', etc. *v.* HALE.

Haley: *v.* HAILEY

Halfacre, Halfacree: Henry *Halfacr'* 1297 MinAcctCo; Alexander *atte Helfakere* 1333 MELS

(So). From Halfacre in Northill (Cornwall), or one who lived on a homestead consisting of a half-acre.

Halfhead, Halfhide, Halfhyde: Robert *de Halve-hid'* 1212 Cur (Herts); Roger *atte Haluehyde* 1332 MELS (Sr); John *de Halfhyde* 1332 SRSt; William *Halfhed* 1536 Eynsham (O). From Half Hyde (Herts), Half Hides (Essex) or from residence on a homestead consisting of half a hide (OE *healf, hīd*).

Halfnight, Halfnights: William *Halfchniet, Halfchnigt* 1169–70 P (Gl); Asce *Halvecniht*, Ace *Dimichevaler* 1213 Cur (Ha); Thomas *le Halveknight* 1327 AD ii (Ha). OE *healf* and *cniht* 'a half-knight', probably one who held half a knight's fee, one who held his land by service of paying half the cost of providing a knight or armed horseman in the army for forty days. The surname may also be a derogatory nickname for one who was only 'half a knight'. Such compounds were not uncommon: Godfrey *le Halveloverd, -laverd* 1207 Cur (Ess), 'half-lord', a lord to whom only half a man's service was due. cf. also Simon *Halvedievel* 1212 Cur (Mx), William *Halfhund* 1203 P (Ha) 'half-hound', Michael and Roger *Halfplow* 1327 SRSf who probably each owned a half-share in the plough.

Halford: Thomas *de Haleford* 1200 P (K); Robert *de Halford* 1327 SRLei; Robert *Halford* 1500–1 FFWa. From Halford (Devon, Salop, Warwicks), or the lost Haleford in Kent (PN K 187).

Halfpenny, Halpenny: Adam *Halpeni* 1275 SRWo; Richard *Halfpany* 1296 SRSx. Halfpenny Field in Elm (Cambs) was so called because the tenants had to contribute a half-penny for each acre to the repair of the neighbouring Needham Dyke (PN C 268). Some such custom or a similar rent may have given rise to the name.

Halfyard: Stephen *atte Halvezerd* 1327 SRSo. OE *healf* 'half' and *gierd* 'yard', one who lived on a homestead consisting of half a yard-land. In Great Waltham (Essex) the virgate or yard-land of 30 acres was called a *yerd* and divided into halves and quarters. cf. *Camyshalfeyerde* (1497 PN Ess 580).

Haliday, Halladay, Halladey, Halleday, Halliday, Hallidie, Holiday, Holyday, Holladay, Holliday: Reginald *Halidei* 1179–94 Seals (Beds); Suein *Halidai* 1188 P (Nt); Thomas *Holidaie* 1524 SRSf; John *Halladay* 1666 FrY; John *Holliday*, Robert *Holladay* 1674 HTSf. OE *hāligdæg* 'holy-day, a religious festival', a name frequently given to one born on such a day. cf. CHRISTMAS.

Halksworth: *v.* HAWKESWORTH

Hall, Halle, Halls: Warin *de Halla* 1178 P (Ess); Robert *de la Hall'* 1199 MemR (Ha); Alan *atte Halle* 1296 SRSx; Roger *de Hall* 1327 SRDb; Richard *in the Halle* 1332 SRWa. 'Worker at the hall' (OE *heall*). *v.* HALLMAN.

Halladay, Halladey: *v.* HALIDAY

Hallam, Hallum, Hallums: (i) Adam *de Hallum* 1297 SRY; John *de Hallum* 1328 WhC (La). From Hallam in Sheffield (WRYorks), *Hallun* DB. (ii) Richard *de Halom* 1327 SRDb; Henry *de Halom*

1392 FrY. From Kirk or West Hallam (Derby), *Halun* DB. As both these are from dative plurals, respectively 'at the rocks or slopes' and 'at the nooks', *Hallums* must have a different origin, from Hallams Fm in Wonersh (Surrey), *Hullehammes* 1418, where in 1327 lived John *atte Hulhamme*, by the enclosure(s) near the hill (PN Sr 254).

Hallard: *v.* ADLARD, HALLWARD

Hallas: *v.* HALLOWES

Hallaway: *v.* ALAWAY

Hallawell: *v.* HALLIWELL

Hallding: *v.* HALDANE

Halleday: *v.* HALIDAY

Haller: Robert *Haller* 1332 SRSr. For *atte Hall. v.* HALL.

Hallett: *v.* ADLARD

Halleybone, Hallybone: Stephen *de Haliburn'* 1222 Cur (Ha). From Holybourne (Hants).

Hallfield: Robert *Hallefeud* 1296 SRSx. 'Dweller by the field near the hall.'

Halliday: *v.* HALIDAY

Halline: William *le Hallehyne* 1332 SRSt. 'Servant at the hall.' *v.* HINE.

Hallis: *v.* ALIS

Hallison: *v.* ALISON

Halliwell, Hallawell, Hallewell, Hallowell, Holliwell, Hollowell: Osbert *de Haliwell'* 1200 P (Sf); Robert *Halwewoll*, Martin *de Halgewelle* 1275 RH (Do, D); Editha *atte Holywelle* 1327 SRSo. From Halliwell (Lancs), Holwell (Dorset, Oxon), Holywell (Hunts, Northumb), or 'dweller by a holy spring'.

Hallman, Halman: (i) Æluric *Halleman* c1095 Bury (Sf); Gilbert *le Halleman* 1301 NottBR. 'Servant at the hall.' (ii) William, John *Haleman* 1327 SR (Ess), 1379 AssEss. 'Dweller in the *hale.' v.* HALL, HALE.

Hallmark: *v.* ALLMARK

Halloway: *v.* ALAWAY

Hallowbread, Hollowbread: William, John *Halibred* 1309 SRBeds, 1317 AssK; — *Hollibred*, Widdow *Hollowbred* 1674 HTSf. 'Holy bread.' cf. Richard *le Halywaterclerc* 1285 Ass (Ess).

Hallowell: *v.* HALLIWELL

Hallowes, Hallows, Hallas: William *in le Halowe* 1276 RH (C); Simon *del Halghe* 1337 FrY; Thomas *Hallowes* 1446 ib. 'Dweller in the *halh* or deep valley.' *v.* HALE.

Hallsworth, Hallworth: *v.* HOLDSWORTH

Hallum(s): *v.* HALLAM

Hallward, Hallard: Ricardus *Halwardus* 1185 Templars (Wa); Gervase *le Halleward* 1250 FFEss. 'Keeper of the hall', OE *heall* and *weard.*

Hallway: *v.* ALAWAY

Hallybone: *v.* HALLEYBONE

Halman: *v.* HALLMAN

Halpenny: *v.* HALFPENNY

Halse: (i) Alfric *Hals* c1100 OEByn; Robert *Hals* 1182 P (D), 1185 Templars (L). OE *heals* 'neck', a nickname. cf. SHORTHOSE. (ii) Sampson *Attehalse, Athalse* 1251 AssSo. 'Dweller at the neck of land' (OE *heals*), as at Halse (Devon, Som).

Halstead, Halsted, Alstead: (i) Ralph *de Hal-*

steda 1181 P (Sf); Henry *de Alsted* 1274 RH (Ess). From Halstead (Essex, Kent, Leics) or Hawstead (Suffolk). (ii) Willyam *del Hallested, del Hallstudes* 1340 WhC (La). 'Worker at the hall-buildings', horseman, cowman, etc.

Halter: Robert *le Haltrere* 1296 LLB B. A derivative of OE *hælftre* 'halter', maker or seller of halters. In 1301 Henry *le Haltrehere* was owed 62*s.* by the Commonalty of London for halters for horses (LLB C).

Halton: Algar *de Haltona* 1084 GeldR; Walter, Richard *de Halton* 1270 FFL, 1332 SRCu; Henry *Halton* 1407 AssLo. From Halton (Bucks, Ches, Lancs, Lincs, Northumb, Salop, WRYorks).

Haly: *v.* HAILEY

Ham, Hamm, Hamme, Hams: Robert *de la Hamme* 1275 RH (Sx); Robert *atte Hamme* 1296 SRSx; Henry *Ham*, William *Hamme* 1279 RH (C, O); Hugh *in the Hamme* 1327 SRSo. 'Dweller on the flat, low-lying land by a stream' (OE *hamm*).

Hamblin(g): *v.* HAMLIN

Hambro, Hamburgh: Richard *de Hambir'*, Robert *de Haneberg'* 1279, 1281 Eynsham (O). From Handborough (Oxon).

Hambury: *v.* HANBURY

Hames: Thomas *del Hames* 1332 SRCu. From Hames Hall in Papcastle (Cumb).

Hamill: *v.* HAMMEL

Hamlin, Hamlen, Hamlyn, Hamblen, Hamblin, Hambling: Robertus *filius Hamelin* 1130 P (D); *Hamelin* 1166 RBE (Y), 1206 Cur (L); Thomas, Walter *Hamelin* c1230 Barnwell (C), 1243 AssSo; Thomas *Hamblyn*, Bartholomew *Hamling* 1568 SRSf. *Haimelin, Hamelin*, a diminutive of OG *Haimo*.

Hamm(e): *v.* HAM

Hammel, Hamill: Aldan *Hamal* c1055 OEByn; Gregory *Hamel* c1170 Riev (Y). OE *hamel* 'scarred, mutilated'.

Hammer: John *le Hammer'* 1332 SRSx. 'Dweller in the *hamme.*' *v.* HAM, HAMMING. Or metonymic for a maker or user of hammers, perhaps a hammer-smith. cf. Geoffrey *wythe Hameres* 1303 Pat.

Hammett: William *Hamet* 1297 MinAcctCo. *Ham-et*, a diminutive of OG *Hamo.*

Hamming: Richard *Hammyg* 1275 SRWo; James *Hammyng* 1327 SRSx; Robert *Hommyng* 1327 SRSo. OE **hamming* 'dweller in the *hamme'*. *v.* HAM. The surname appears side-by-side with *atte hamme.*

Hammond, Hammand, Hammant, Hamman, Hammon: (i) *Hamandus* Cocus 1140–5 Holme (Nf); *Hamo, Hamandus* elemosinarius c1140 DC (L); Walter, Adam *Hamund* 1242 Fees (He), 1280 AssSo; Richard *Hamond, Hamon* 1327, 1332 SRSx. OFr *Hamond*, OG *Hamon* with excrescent *d.* *v.* HAIM. (ii) *Haimund'* Peccatum 1121–48 Bury (Sf); *Hamo* Pecce 1156–60 ib.; Willelmus *filius Haymundi* 1221 Cur (Sr); Roger *Haymund* 1275 RH (Ha); John *Hemund* ib. (K); William *Heymond, Heymund* 1327 SRSf, 1346 FA (Sf). *Haimund*, from OG *Haimon*. This probably survives also as *Hayman.*

Hamon: *v.* HAIM

Hampden: Alexander *de Hamden, de Hampeden* 1274 FFO, 1275 RH (Bk); Simon *de Hamden* 1334–5 SRK; Edmund *Hampden* 1413 Goring. From Hampden (Bucks).

Hamper: John *le Hanaper* 1236–41 StP (Lo); John *Hanapier* c1260 *ERO;* Geoffrey *le Hanaper* 1279 RH (C). OFr *hanapier* 'maker or seller of goblets'.

Hampshire, Hamshere, Hamshar, Hamsher, Hamshaw, Hampshaw: (i) Thomas *de Hallumschire* 1296 Wak (Y); Richard *de Halumpschyre* 1348 DbAS 36; John *Hamshaw, Hampshawe* 1506, 1555 FrY; John *Hamschyer* 1507 GildY. From Hallamshire (WRYorks). (ii) Robert *Hamptessire* 1296 SRSx; Thomas *Hamshere* 1523 SRK. From Hampshire.

Hampson, Hamson: John *Hammonson* 1332 SRCu; Robert *Hamsone, Hameson* 1354 FrY, 1379 PTY; Henry *Hampson* 1540 FrY. 'Son of Hamo or Hamon(d).'

Hampton: Philip *de Hamtona* 1166 Oseney; Edith *de Hampton'* 1221 AssWo; Richard *Hampton* 1327 SRSx. From one or other of the many places of this name.

Hanbury, Handbury, Hambury: William *de Haneberge* 1196 FFSt; Euller' *de Hambir'* 1221 AssWo; Philip *de Hannbir'* 1230 P (Wo); John *de Hambury* 1327 AssSt. From Hanbury (Staffs, Worcs).

Hance: *v.* HAND, HANN

Hancell: *v.* ANSELL

Hancock, Hancox, Handcock: *Hanecok* Birun 1276 RH (Y); Thomas *Hancoc* 1274 RH (Sa); John *Hancokes* 1316 Wak (Y); Thomas *Handcocke* 1632 RothwellPR (Y). A diminutive of HANN. *Hannecok* le Nunne (1297 Wak) is also called *Henricus* (1297 SRY).

Hand, Hands: *Honde* Cotrell 1288 AssCh; Johannes *cum manu* c1200 Dublin; Richard *Hand* 1279 RH (Beds); Robert *Hond* 1296 SRSx; Walter *Handes* 1332 SRWa. For Handsacre (Staffs) and Handsworth (WRYorks) Ekwall postulates an OE **Hand*, originally a nickname from *hand.* cf. FOOT. *Honde* may well be a survival of this. The surname may also refer to some peculiarity of the hand or to skill in its use. cf. GOODHAND.

Handasyde, Handisyde, Handysyde, Hendyside: Richard *de Hanggandsid*, Adam *Hangalsyde* 1398, William *Hangitsyde* 1494, John *Handisyde* 1665. From Handyside near Berwick (Black).

Handbury: *v.* HANBURY

Handcock: *v.* HANCOCK

Handford, Handforth, Hanford, Hanfirth: Simon *de Hanford'* 1230 P (So); John *de Hondford* 1325 AssSt; Richard *Hanford* 1468–9 FFWa; John *Handford* 1642 PrD. From Hanford (Dorset, Staffs), Handforth (Ches), or Hannaford (Devon).

Handley, Handlay, Hanley, Hanly: Gilbert *de Hanlega* 1185 P (Wo); Laurence *de Hanlaye* 1219 AssY; Robert *de Handlegh* 1314 IpmGl; John *Hanley* 1426 IpmNt; Robert *Handley* 1611 Bardsley. From Handley (Ches, Derby, Dorset,

Northants), Hanley (Staffs, Worcs), or Handley Farm in Clayhanger (Devon).

Handscombe: v. HANSCOMB
Handsley: v. HANSLEY
Handslip: v. HANSLIP
Handson: v. HANSON
Handysyde: v. HANDASYDE
Hanes: v. HAGAN
Hanfirth, Hanford: v. HANDFORD

Hanke, Hanks: *Anke* Hy 2 DC (L); *Hanke* 12th ib.; *Anke* de Ankinton' 1194 P (L); *Hank'* carpentarius 1280 Oseney (O); Roger *Hanke* 1275 RH (Nf); Ralph *Hancks* 1642 PrGR. *Hank* is usually regarded as a Flemish pet-form of *John*. The early examples above are undoubtedly of Scandinavian origin, from ON *Anki*, a diminutive of some name in *Arn*-.

Hankin, Hankins, Hanking: (i) *Hankynus* 1285 Oseney (O); *Hanekyn* de London 1300 LLB C; Hugh *Hankyn* 1327 SRC; Alice *Hankynes* 1337 ColchCt. A diminutive of *Hann*. cf. HENKIN. (ii) *Hondekin* the Barbur 1286 AssCh; *Handekyn* Starky 1287 ib. A diminutive of *Hand* (*Hond*). v. HAND. (iii) Willelmus *filius Hamekin* 1232 Pat (L); Thomas *Hamekyng* 1327 SRSx. A diminutive of *Hame* (Hamo). v. HAIM.

Hanley, Hanly: v. HANDLEY

Hann: *Hann, Hancock* and *Hankin* are usually regarded as Flemish forms of *John*, but they are probably English formations, sometimes from *Johan* 'John'. *Henecoc* Cotun is probably identical with *John* de Coton (1319 SRLo). *Hanne* was a very common christian name in 13th-century Yorkshire (1274–97 Wak). Camden takes *Hann* as a pet-name of *Randolph*, rhymed on *Rann* which is possible, though *Randolph* was by no means a popular name. *Hann* is certainly in some instances a pet-name for the common *Henry* (cf. *Harry*): cf. *Hanne* or *Henry* de Leverpol 1323 InqLa. Richard *Hannesone* (1379 NottBR) is identical with Ricardus *filius Henrici* (1365 ib.).

Hannibal: v. HUNNABLE

Hansard: Gilbert, Roger *Hansard* c1170 Riev (Y), 1243 AssDu; William *Haunsard* 1230 P (Sr). OFr *hansard* 'cutlass, poniard', for a maker or seller of these. The surname is much too early to denote a Hanseatic merchant.

Hanscomb, Hanscombe, Handscomb, Handscombe: Alan de *Hanscombe* 1255 Rams (Beds). From Hanscombe End in Shillington (Beds).

Hansell, Hansill: v. ANSELL

Hansley, Handsley: John de *Hannesley* 1275 RH (Nt). From Annesley (Notts).

Hanslip, Handslip: Winemarus de *Hanslepe* 1086 DB (Nth); John de *Hannslap* 1227 AssBk. From Hanslope (Bucks).

Hansom: John *Hansom* bricklayer 1659 FrY; Thomas *Hanson* son of John *Hansome* bricklayer 1664 ib. For HANSON.

Hanson: (i) John *Handson* 1327 SRY; William *Hondesone* 1332 SRSt. 'Son of *Hand*.' (ii) John *Hanson* 1332 SRCu; Ralph *Hanneson* 1350 Putnam (La). 'Son of *Hann*.'

Hanton: Gervase de *Hanton'* 1200 P (Ha). From Southampton (Hants).

Happe: Aldwin' *Happe* 1194 P (Sx); John *le Hap* 1296 SRSx. OE *gehæp* 'fit'.

Happs: v. APPS

Harbach: v. HERBAGE

Harber, Harbor, Harbour, Arber: Geoffrey, John *Herbour* 1279 RH (Bk). OE *herebeorg* 'shelter, lodging', metonymic for HARBERER.

Harberd, Harbert, Harbird: v. HERBERT

Harberer, Haberer: Geoffrey *le Arbrer* 1205 Cur (Mx); Richard *le Erbrer* 1315 Bart (Lo); Augustine *le Herberer* 1319 Husting. A derivative of ME *hereber(e)ʒen* 'to provide lodgings', a lodging-house keeper.

Harbidge: v. HERBAGE

Harbinson, v. HERBERTSON

Harbisher: Edric (*le*) *Herberg(e)or* 1184–5 P (Wo); Thomas *le Harbergur* 1198 P (Sx); William *le Herbejour, le Herbyiour* 1298 Ipm (Db), 1343 DbCh. OFr *herbergeor*, also a derivative of OFr *herbege*, 'host, lodging-house keeper'. cf. HABBE-SHAW.

Harbison: v. HERBERTSON

Harbolt, Herbolt: Gilbert, Ralph *Harebald* 1279 RH (O), 1297 MinAcctCo. OG *Haribald* 'army-bold', OFr *Herbaud*.

Harbor: v. HARBER

Harbord: Wulfwine *Hareberd* c1100 OEByn (So). OE *hār* and *beard*, 'grey-beard'. v. also HERBERT.

Harbott: v. HERBERT

Harbottle: Richard de *Herbotell* 1323 FrY; Thomas *Hardebotyll* 1513 RochW; John *Harbottle* 1543 Bacon (Sf). From Harbottle (Northumb).

Harbour: v. HARBER

Harbud: v. HERBERT

Harcourt: William de *Harewcurt* 1055 OEByn; Philip de *Harecourt* 1139 Templars (Sx). From Harcourt (Eure).

Harcus, Harkess, Harkus, Arkus, Arkush: Adam *of Harcarres* 1216 Black; John *de Harkers* 1329 ib.; William *Harkes* 1444 ib.; Alexander *Harkass* 1547 ib.; Janet *Arcus* 1668 ib. From Harcarse (Berwickshire).

Hard, Hardes, Hards: (i) *Hardo* de Acolt 1212 Cur (Sf); Roger *Hard* 1275 RH (L). OE **Heard* 'hard', or a nickname 'harsh, severe'. Sometimes for HARDY: Robert *Hard*, *Hardi* Hy 3 Gilb (L). (ii) Gilbert *del Hard* 1232 Pat (L). 'Dweller on the hard, firm ground' (1576 NED).

Harder: John, William *Harder(e)* 1220 Cur (Do), 1332 SRLa. A derivative of OE *heardian* 'to make hard', used of metals by Chaucer and in ME of hardening dough with heat. A hardener of metals or a baker.

Hardey, Hardie: v. HARDY

Hardiman, Hardeman: Walter *Hardiman* 1327 SRSx. 'Bold man.' v. HARDY.

Harding, Arding: *Hardingus* c1095 Bury (Sf); *Ardingus* 1200 Oseney (O); Roger, Richard *Harding* 1199 P (Nth), 1204 AssY; Hugh *Arding* 1244 Oseney (O). OE *Hearding* 'hard'.

Hardisty, Hardesty: John *de Hardolfsty* 1379 FrY; William *Hardosty* 1450 ib.; John *Hardesty* 1659 ib. From Hardistys in Nesfield or Hardisty Hill in Fewston (WRYorks).

Hardman: *Hardman(nus)* c1095 Bury (Sf), 1168–75 Holme (Nf); Robert *Hardman* 1188 BuryS (Sf). OE **Heardmann* 'hard man', a late formation with *-mann*, a type common in the eastern counties.

Hardware: Robert, Samuel *Hardware* 1551 ArchC 42, 1682 PrGR. Metonymic for *hardware-man*: Lambert *Hardwareman* 1473 GildY.

Hardwick, Hardwicke, Hardwich, Hardwidge: Anketill' *de Herdewic'* 1221 AssWa; Richard *de la Herdewyk* 1243 MELS (So). From one of the numerous Hardwicks (OE *heordewīc* 'sheep-farm'), or 'shepherd'. cf. WICH.

Hardy, Hardee, Hardey, Hardie, Le Hardy: William *Hardi* 1194 P (Y); William *le Hardy* 1206 P (L), 1220 Ass (Berks). ME *hardi* 'bold, courageous'.

Hare, Hares: (i) Walter (*le*) *Hare* 1166, 1171 P (Sr); John *le Hare* 1197 P (Nf). OE *hara* 'hare', a nickname for speed or timidity, cf. 'liouns in halle, and hares in the feld' (c1330 MED). *v.* also HAIR. (ii) A nickname from the hair (OE *hær*): Godefridus *cum capillo* c1200 Dublin; Henry *Mytehare, Myttehere* 1253–4 ELPN. *mid the here* 'with the hair'. cf. BEARD, HEAD. (iii) Ralph *del Hare* 1309 SRBeds. 'Dweller on the stony-ground', OE *hær*. *v.* DEPN, s.v. *hār*.

Harenc: *v.* HERRING

Harewood: *v.* HARWOOD

Harfoot: Harold *Haranfot* 1038 OEByn; Robert, Samson *Harefot* 1170 P (L), 1221 AssWo. The byname of Harold, son of Cnut, is, no doubt, an anglicizing of ON *harfótr* 'hare's foot', a nickname for a swift runner. cf. 'Harald, Godwyne sone; He was cleped Harefot, For he was urnare god' (c1330 MED). The surname may also be English in origin.

Harford: *v.* HEREFORD

Hargent: *v.* ARGENT

Harger: *Hardgarus* 1112 Bury (Sf); Willelmus *filius Hargari* 1121–48 ib.; Thomas *Hardgare* 1260 AssC; Baldewynus *Haregar*, Rogert *Hargar'* 1279 RH (C). OG *Hariger, Harger* 'army-spear'.

Hargreave, Hargreaves, Hargrave, Hargraves, Hargreves, Hargrove, Hargroves: Geoffrey *de Haregraue* 1188 P (Db); Henry *de Hargreue* 1332 SRLa; William *Hargreave*, Richard *Hargreaves* 1672 HTY. From Hargrave (Ches, Northants, Suffolk), or Hargreave Hall (Ches).

Harker: Robert *le Herkere* 1280 AssSo; Ralph *Harka* 1479 GildY. A derivative of ME *herkien* 'to listen', an eavesdropper.

Harkin, Harkins, Harkiss: Edwinus, Rogerus *filius Hardekin* 1175 P (Nf); John *Hardekyn, Herkyn* 1327 *SR* (Ess). A diminutive of HARD.

Harkus: *v.* HARCUS

Harland: Peter *de Herland'* 1221 AssWa; Adam *Herlond* 1332 SRWa; Thomas *Harland* 1525 SRSx. From Harland Edge (Derby), Harlands Wood (Sussex), or 'dweller by the boundary wood'.

Harle: *v.* EARL

Harley, Harly: Juhel *de Harelea* 1166 P (Y); Henry *de Hareleye* c1280 SRWo; William *Harley* 1379 IpmGl. From Harley (Salop, WRYorks), or 'dweller at the hares' wood'.

Harlin, Harling: *v.* HURLIN

Harliss: *v.* ARLISS

Harlock, Horlock, Horlick: Borewoldus *Horloc* 1066 Winton (Ha); Edwardus *Horloch, Harloch* 1187–8 P (Lo); Richard *Horloc* 1206 P (Co). 'Grey lock', OE *hār, locc. v.* OEByn, ELPN.

Harlow, Harlowe, Arlow: Osbern, Thomas *de Herlaue* 1121–48 Bury, 1205 Pl (Herts); Walter *de Harlow* 1327 SRY; Thomas *Harlowe* 1442 AssLo. From Harlow (Essex), or Harlow Hill (Northumb, WRYorks).

Harman, Harmand, Harmon, Harmond, Hearmon, Herman, Hermon: *Hermannus dapifer* 1101–25 Holme (Nf); Alexander *filius Hermanni* 1191 P (Sr); Willelmus *Hermannus* 1141–9 Holme (Nf); Robert *Hereman* 1196 P (Nf); William *Heremond* 1296 SRSx; John *Harman* 1327 SRSf. OFr *Herman(t)*, from OG *Hariman, Her(e)man* 'warrior'.

Harmer, Harmar, Hermer: (i) *Heremerus de la Bolde* 1176 P (St); Willelmus *filius Hermeri* 1208 Cur (L); Walter *Hermer* 1327 SRSf; Richard *Harmer* 1524 SRSf. OG *Her(e)mar* 'army-famous'. (ii) William *de Hermer'* 1207 Cur (Sx); Simon *de Haremere* 1296 SRSx; William *Harmere* 1428 FA (Sx). *Harmer*, still found in Burwash, Battle, Hastings, and Winchelsea, and over the border in Kent, at Tunbridge Wells, is here local in origin, from Haremere Hall in Etchingham (PN Sx 456).

Harmond: *v.* HARMAN

Harmsworth: Robert *de Hermodesworthe* 1340 CorLo. From Harmondsworth (Middlesex), *Hermodesworth* 1233.

Harn: *v.* HERN

Harness: *v.* ERNEST

Harnett, Harnott: *v.* ARNALD

Harniman: *v.* HERNAMAN

Harold, Haroll, Harald, Harrald, Harrold, Harral, Harrall, Harrel, Harrell, Harrad, Harrod: (i) *Haraldus, Harold, Herald, Herold, Horoldus, Haral, Heral* 1066 DB; *Haraldus* Hy 2 DC, 1212 Cur (L); Ralph *Harold* 1171 P (Y); Radulfus *Haroud'* . . . predictus Radulfus *Harold'* 1196 FF (Y); Philip *Harald* 1327 SRSx; Lawrence *Horold* 1333 FFSf. (ii) *Hereuuoldus* 1066 DB (Sf); Gacobus *Herewald* 1275 RH (Sf); David *Harwald* ib.; Thomas *Harwold* 1331 LLB E; Thomas and Dorathy *Harwold, Harrold* 1664, 1666 Great WelnethamPR (Sf); George and Elizabeth *Hurrell, Harrold* 1780, 1782 ib. The chief source of these names is ON *Haraldr*, ODa, OSw *Harald*, a name very common in DB, but usually referring to King Harold. *Harrod* is from *Haroud*, whilst *Herald* and *Herouldus* would give *Herald* and *Herod*. The latter might also derive from OG *Hairold, Herold*. There has also been confusion with OE *Hereweald* 'army-power', particularly in Suffolk where there was also a late confusion with *Hurrell*.

Harp: Roger *atte Harp* 1327 SRSo; John *atte Harpe* 1361 LLB G. OE *hearpe* 'harp', in the compound *sealthearpe*, was used of a harp-shaped contrivance for sifting and cleansing salt and survives in South Harp in South Petherton (Som). cf. also Harp House in Eastwood (Essex), near the marshes where there were salt pans. *v.* MELS 92. The second reference, from London, is probably due to residence at the sign of the harp. Ralf *Harpe* (1241 FFBk) is probably metonymic for 'harper'.

Harper, Harpour, Harpur: Robert *le Harpur* 1186 P (Ha); Reginald *le Harper* 1275 SRWo. The surname is common and widely distributed. *Harper*, now the usual form, is from OE *hearpere* 'harper', *Harpour* and *Harpur* from AFr *harpour*, OFr *harpeor*, the common form in early sources.

Harpin: Geoffrey *Harpin* e Hy 2 DC (L); William *Harepin* 1185 Templars (Wa), *Harpin* 1231 Guisb (Y), 1243 AssDu. OFr *harpin* 'harper'.

Harraden, Harradine, Harradence, Harridine: William *de Harewedon* 1327 SRSx. From Harrowden (Beds, Northants).

Harrall, Harrell: *v.* HAROLD

Harrhy, Harrie, Harries: *v.* HARRY

Harriman, Harryman: Henry *Henriman* 1332 SRCu. 'Servant of *Henry*.'

Harrington, Harington: William *de Harinton'* 1202 AssL; Richard *de Harington* 1274 RH (L); John *Harington'* 1327 SRLei. From Harrington (Cumb, Lincs, Northants).

Harrismith: *v.* ARROWSMITH

Harrison, Harrisson, Harison: Henry *Hennerissone* 1354 Putnam (Ch); Robert *Harriesone* 1355 LoPleas; John *Herryson* 1372 FFHu; William *Henryson* 1376 FrY; John *Herryson, Harryson* 1445 Shef (Y). 'Son of *Henry*.'

Harrod, Harrold: *v.* HAROLD

Harrop, Harrup, Harrap: Richard, Hugh *de Harop* 1185 P (Nb); William *de Harrope* 1242 AssDu; William *Harrop* 1367 FFY; John *Harop, Herrop* 1476, 1478 Cl (Lo). From Harehope (Northumb), or Harrop, Harrop Dale, Harrop Hall (WRYorks).

Harrower, Harrowar, Harwar: Geoffrey *Haruer* 1255 MEOT (Ess); Geoffrey *le Harewere* 1275 RH (Nf); Ralph *le Harwere* 1327 SRSf; John *Harower* 1379 PTY. A derivative of ME *harwen* 'to harrow', a harrower (c1475 MED).

Harrowsmith: *v.* ARROWSMITH

Harry, Harrie, Harrhy, Harries, Harris, Harriss: *Herre* de Camera 1176 P (Nf); *Harry* Haket 1270 ArchC 5; *Hanry* Wade, *Hary* de Kent, *Herri* de Merowe 1292 SRLo; Nicholas *Herri* 1327 SRWo; William *Herry* 1337 ColchCt; Richard *Harry* 14th Shef (Y); William *Harrys* 1406 Eynsham (O); Lawrence *Harryes* 1468 Fine (Herts). *Harry* was the regular pronunciation of *Henry* in the Middle Ages but is rarely found in documents where the name is usually in the Latin form *Henricus*. *v.* HENRY.

Harryman: *v.* HARRIMAN

Harsant, Harsent Hersant, Hassent, Arson, Assan: *Hersent* 1166 RBE (Nf), 1208 Cur (Gl); Roger *Harsent* 1276 RH (C); William *Herseynt* 1297 MinAcctCo; John *Hersent* 1327 SRSf; John,

William *Arsent* 1327 SRC; John *Harsand*, Henry *Harshand* 1440, 1493 ShefA (Y); William *Areson* 1520 FrY. OFr *Hersent, Hersant* (f), OG *Herisint* (f) 'army-truth'.

Harsnett: Robert *de Hassnade, de Halstnade* 1215–27 StGreg (K); Benedict *de Halssnod* 1334 SRK; Richard *Halsnoth* 1474 CantW; Roger *Harslett* 1513 ib.; Thomas *Halsnoth* alias *Awstnet* 1523 LP (Lo); William *Alsnoth* 1524 WBCinque; Walter *Hawsnode* 1565 ib.; Marten *Halsnode, Halsnothe* 1566, 1570 ib.; William *Hassnod* 1647 ib.; Robert *Halsenorth* 1664 HTSo. From Ayleswade in Frittenden (Kent), *Halsnod'* 1224. Samuel *Harsnett*, later archbishop of York, b. 1561, son of William *Halsnoth*, baker, of Colchester, when appointed Master of Colchester Grammar School in 1586, signed as *Harsnet*, although his name is entered six times as Mr. *Halsnothe* (ER li, 10).

Hart, Harte, Heart, Hort, Hurt: Ælfric *Hort* c1060 OEByn (Ha); Roger *Hert* 1166 P (Nf); Reginald *Hurt* 1185 Templars (Beds); Simon *le Hert* 1197 FF (K); Godrich' *le Hurt* 1220 Fees (Berks); Richard *Hort* 1221 AssWa. OE *heorot*, ME *hert* 'hart'. In ME *heorot* became *hurt*, roughly west of a line from Dorking to Birmingham, and this has occasionally survived, though often replaced by the standard *hart* from *hert*.

Hartell, Hartill, Hartle, Hartles: Robert *de Herthil* 1176 P (Db). From Harthill (Ches, Derby, WRYorks).

Hartford: *v.* HEREFORD

Hartley: Robert *de Hertlay* 1191 P (Y); Nicholas *de Hertlegh* 1327 SRSo; Richard *Hertlay* 1379 PTY; William *Hartley* 1621 SRY. From Hartley (Berks, Devon, Dorset, Hants, Kent, Northumb, Westmorland), or Hartleigh in Buckland Filleigh (Devon).

Hartrick, Hartwright: *v.* ARKWRIGHT

Harvey, Harvie, Hervey: *Herveus* 1086 DB; *Herueu de berruarius* 1086 DB (Sf); *Heruei de Castre* 1157–63 DC (L); *Herui* de Burc Hy 2 Gilb (L); Willelmus *filius Hervici* 1242 Fees (Sf); William *Hervi, Herevi* 1190 BuryS, 1196 Cur (Sf); William *Hervy* 1232 FFEss; Richard *Herfu* 1327 SRSx. OFr *Hervé*, OBret *Aeruiu, Hærviu* 'battle worthy', a name introduced by Bretons at the Conquest. Occasionally OG *Herewig, Herewicus* 'army-war'.

Harwar: *v.* HARROWER

Harward: *v.* HEREWARD

Harwarth: *v.* HAWORTH

Harwin: *Harduuinus, Haruinus* 1066 DB (Nf, Sf); *Hardewinus* 1208 Cur (Herts); Walter *Hardwin* 1207 Cur (Gl); Henry *Harwyn* 1456 NorwW. OFr *Harduin*, OG *Hardwin* 'firm friend'.

Harwood, Harewood: Hubert *de Harewda* 1176 YCh; Bernard *de Harewode* 1242 Fees; Alice *Harewode* 1327 SRSo. From Harwood (Devon, Lancs, Northumb, NRYorks), Harewood (Ches, Hereford, WRYorks), or Horwood (Devon), *Harewde* 1219.

Haselar, Haseler: *v.* HASLER

Haseldene, Haseldine, Haseltine: *v.* HAZELDEN

Hasel: *v.* HAZEL

Haselgrove: v. HAZELGROVE
Haselhurst: v. HAZELHURST
Haselwood: v. HAZELWOOD
Haskell: v. ASKELL
Haskey: v. ASKEW
Hasking, Haskin(s): v. ASKIN
Haskow: v. ASKEW

Haslam, Haslem, Haslum, Hasleham, Haslen, Heslam, Aslam, Aslen: Hugh *de Haslum, de Hesellum* 1246 AssLa; Benjamin *Aslin* 1674 HTSf. From Haslam (Lancs) or 'dweller by the hazels', OE *hæsel*, ON *hesli*.

Haslegrave: v. HAZELGROVE
Hasleham: v. HASLAM
Haslehurst: v. HAZELHURST
Haslen: v. HASLAM

Hasler, Haselar, Haseler, Heasler: Robert *de Heselhour', de Haselore* 1221 AssWa, 1287 AssSt. From Haselour (Staffs) or Haselor (Warwicks, Worcs).

Haslett, Haslitt: v. HAZLETT
Haslewood: v. HAZELWOOD

Haslin, Hasling: Geoffrey *Alselin* 1086 DB (Ess); William *Haslin* 1148–56 Seals (L); Radulfus *Halselinus* 1176 P (Db); Roger *Haucelin* 1196 P (Y); William *Hauselin, Hanselin, Halselin* 1211–12 Cur (L); John *Halselyn* 1327 SRSx. *Alselin* is OG *Anselin*, with assimilatory change of *n* to *l*. v. ANSELL, ANSLYN.

Haslin, Hasling, Hesling, Heslin, Hessling: Robert *Hasling* 1275 SRWo; Walter *atte Haselyng* 1327 SRSx; Peter *atte Heselyng* 1332 ib. 'Dweller by the hazel-copse', OE **hæsling*.

Haslock, Hasloch, Hasluck: *Aslac, Aseloc, Haslec* 1066 DB (L, Nf, Sf); *Haselac molendinarius* 1177 P (L); Ricardus *filius Aslac* 1197 P (L); Radulfus *filius Oselach* 1189 P (Sf); William *Aselach', Aslac* 1189 P (Y, Nf); Petronill *Oslok* 1327 SRSf; Richard *Hasloke* 1536 NorwW (Nf). ON *Áslákr*, ODa, OSw *Aslak*.

Haslop, Haslip, Haslup, Haselup, Hazelip, Heaslip, Heslep, Heslop, Hislop, Hyslop: John *Heslop* 1414 FrY. 'Dweller in the hazel-valley', OE *hæsel*, ON *hesli* and OE *hop*.

Haspineall: v. ASPINALL
Hassard: v. HAZARD
Hasselby: From Asselby (ERYorks). cf. AXLEBY.

Hastain: v. HASTING

Hasted: William *Halstead*, Thomas *Hawstead*, Thomas *Hastead* 1674 HTSf. A late development of *Halstead*.

Hastie, Hasty: (i) Robert *Hastif* 1202 Cur (W); Richard *Hasty* 1221 AssWa; Richard *le Hastie* 1326 LaCt. OFr *hastif, hasti*, ME *hasty* (c1340 NED) 'speedy, quick'. (ii) Picot *filius Asti* 1203 P (L); William *Asti* 1212 Cur (Nf); Francis *Asty* 1674 HTSf. *Asti* is a pet-form of Norman *Asketin* from ON *Ásketill*. v. ASKELL. *Hasti*, like *Hastin* and *Hasluck*, has an inorganic *H. Hasti de Bolebi* (12th DC) is identical with *Asketinus de Bolebi*.

Hastin: v. ASKIN

Hasting, Hastain: Walter *Hastinc* 1190 P (Cu); Aitrop *Hasteng* 1194 StCh; Hamo *Hasting'* 1235

Fees (Bk). *Hastang (Hastenc, Hasten)* is a Norman personal name, doubtless of Scandinavian origin, from ON *Hásteinn*.

Hastings may be a patronymic of *Hasting*, 'son of *Hastang*', but is, no doubt, usually local in origin, from Hastings (Sussex): Robert *de Hastinges* 1086 DB, Hugh *de Hasting* 1130 P (Lei).

Hastler: Henry *le hasteler* 1190 P (Ha). AFr **hasteler*, from **hastele*, a diminutive of *haste*, Fr *hâte* 'a spit'. 'One who roasts meat', 'a turn-spit', also 'the officer of the kitchen who superintended the roasting of meat'.

Hatch: Gilbert *ad Hacce* 1185 Templars (Ess); Adam *del Hach* 1221 ElyA (Nf); Henry *Hache* 1230 P (Sf); Walter *ate Hacche* 1297 MinAcctCo. From Hatch (Beds, Hants, Som, Wilts), or from residence near a hatch or gate (OE *hæcce*), generally one leading to a forest, sometimes a sluice.

Hatchard: v. ACHARD

Hatcher: John *Hetchere* 1296 SRSx; Andrew *Hatcher* 1560 SxWills. 'Dweller by the gate.' v. HATCH.

Hatfield, Hatfeild, Hatful, Hatfull: Tata *æt Hæðfelda* c1050 OEByn; William *de Hatfeld* 1119–27 Colch (Ess); Robert *de Hattefeld* 1343 FFY; Thomas *Hatfeld* 1412 AssLo. From Hatfield (Essex, Hereford, Herts, Notts, Worcs, ER, NRYorks), or Heathfield (Som, Sussex).

Hathaway, Hathway, Hadaway: (i) *Hadeuui* 1066 DB (He); *Hathewi* 1175 P (Wo); William *Hatewi, Hadewi, Hathewy* 1178, 1181 P (He), 1221 AssWa; Nigel *Haðewi* 1208 P (Gl); Thomas *Hatheweye* 1380 SRSt. OE *Heaðuwīg* 'war-warrior' (rare), or OG *Hathuwic, Hadewic*. (ii) William *de Hathewy* 1294 FFEss. 'Dweller by the heath-way', OE *hæð, weg*.

Hathersich, Heaversedge: Matthew *de Hauersegge* 1190 P (Y), *de Hathersich'* 1219 AssL, *de Hathersage* 1254 AssSt. From Hathersage (Derby).

Hathorn: v. HAYTHORNE

Hatry: v. DAWTREY

Hatt, Hatts: (i) Roger, Randulf *Hat* 1148–67 ELPN, 1168 P (Do). OE *hætt* 'hat', metonymic for *Hatter*. (ii) Thomas *del Hat* 1279 RH (O); Richard *atte Hatte* 1327 SRWo. 'Dweller by the hill' (OE *hætt*), as at Hathitch Fm or Hathouse Fm (Worcs).

Hatter: Reginald, William *le Hattere* 1212 Cur (Berks), 1262 *For* (Ess). A maker or seller of hats (1389 NED).

Hattrell: Vilein, John *Haterel* 1210, 1221 Cur (Nth, Nt). *Haterel* is used in the York Plays (c1440) of 'dress, attire'. It is probably a derivative of OE *hæteru* 'clothes' and here probably denotes a tailor. cf. Elias *le Hatermongere* 1251 Oseney (O), a dealer in clothing.

Hattrick: Richard *Hatheriche* 13th Cust; Claricia *Hatheric*, Alice *Haterich* c1280, 1332 SRWo. OE *Heaðurīc* 'war-ruler'.

Hauman: Alan *Hagheman* 1275 RH (Ha). 'Dweller by the enclosure', OE *haga*.

Havekin: v. HAWKIN

Havelock: *Haveloc* c1210 Fees (Co); William,

Robert *Havelok* 1327 *SR* (Ess), 1369 LoPleas. ON *Hafleikr* 'sea-port'.

Haven: Nigel *de Hauen*' 1200 P (Ha); Philip *atte Hauene* 1269 AssSo. 'Dweller by the harbour', OE *hæfen* 'haven'.

Haverfield: Matilda *de Hauerfeld* 1327 SRSf. 'Dweller by the oat-field', ON *hafri* 'oats'.

Havers: Hugh, Simon *Hauer* 1199 P (Nf), 1230 P (Ess). OE *hæfer* 'he-goat'.

Haverson, Haversum: Hugo *de Hauersham* 1190 P (Beds); Nicholas *de Haversam* 1279 RH (Bucks). From Haversham (Bucks).

Havill, Havell, Hovell, Hovil: Ralph *de Halsuilla* 1084 GeldR (W), *de Haluile* 1086 DB (W); Ralph *de Hauvill*' Hy 2 Fees (Nf), *de Alta Villa, de Havill*' 1198 ib.; Henry *de Hautvill*' 1242 Fees (Bk); Lucas *de Houyle* 1327 SRSf; Alice *Havell* 1464 NorwW. The DB tenant-in-chief *de Hal(s)-uilla* came from Hauville (Eure), *Alsvilla* 1050, *Hasvilla* 11th, others from Hauteville la Guichard (La Manche), earlier *Hautteville*. Both became *Hauvill* and *Havill*, the former also developing into *Hovell*.

Haw, Hawes: (i) Richard *Haga (de Haga)* 1175 P (L); Roger *de la Hagh* 1255 RH (W); Peter *in le Hawe* 1279 RH (C); Margery *del Hawe*, Caterina *Hawe*, John *atte Hawe* 1327 SRSf. 'Dweller by the enclosure', OE *haga* or ON *hagi*. (ii) *Hawe* 1260 AssY, 1277 Wak (Y); *Hawe* de Bolinton 1286 AssCh; William, Thomas *Hawe* 1275 SRWo, 1307 Wak (Y). *Hawe* is clearly a pet-form of some common name, but of what it is difficult to decide. It may be for OE *Hafoc*, from the diminutives *Havekin, Havecot. v.* HAWKIN, HAWKETT.

Haward: *Hauuart* 1066 DB (Y); *Haward* de Wihton 1166 P (Nf); William, Stephen *Haward* 1327 SRC, 1332 SRCu. ON *Hávarðr*, ODa *Hawarth*, OSw *Havardh* 'high or chief warden or guardian,' cognate with OG *Howard*.

Hawarth: *v.* HAWORTH

Hawes, Hawyes: *Hawis* 1208 Cur (Sf); *Hawisia* 1214, 1215 Cur (Sf, Beds); Robert *Hawyse*, William *Hawys* 1279 RH (O); John *Hawys*, Margery *Hawis* 1327 SRSf. OFr *Haueis*, OG *Hadewidis* 'battle-wide' (f).

Hawk, Hawke, Hawkes, Hawks, Hauke: (i) *Hauok* 1066 Winton (Ha); *Willelmus filius Hawoc* 1240-5 Black; Roger *Hauech*' 1176 P (Do); Robert *Hauk* 1269 AssNb; Walter *le Hauek* 1296 SRSx; Thomas *Haukes* 1460 FrY. Osbertus *filius Hauoc* c1115 OEByn (O) is probably to be identified with Osbern *Hauoc* (ib.). His father bore the OE name of *Hafoc* 'hawk'. In *le Hauek* we have clearly a nickname 'hawk', indicative of a savage or cruel disposition. Sometimes the simple *Hauoc* is used by metonymy for 'hawker' or with reference to the holding of land by providing hawks for the lord. In 1130 (P), Ralph *Hauoc* owed the exchequer two 'Girfals', gerfalcons or hawks. *Hawkes* may also be from *Hawkins*: William *Hawkys* or *Hawkyns* 1539 Oxon. (ii) William *del Halk* 1188 BuryS (Sf); Adam *de Halk* 1260 AssC; William *atte Halk*, Alan *Hauke* 1327 SRSf. 'Dweller in the nook or corner' (ME *halke*).

Hawken: *v.* HAWKIN

Hawker: Robert *le Hauekere* 1214 Cur (Gl); Mabill' *Haueker* 1221 ElyA (Sf); Robert *le Hauker* 1283 SRSf. OE *hafocere* 'falconer, hawker'.

Hawkesworth, Hawksworth, Halksworth: Laurence *de Houkeswurda* 1194 P (Nt); Robert *de Hauekeswrth* 1226 FFY; John *Hawkesworth*' 1395 AssL. From Hawksworth (Notts, WRYorks).

Hawkett, Hawkitts: Henry *Havekot* 1275 RH (Nf). A diminutive of OE *Hafoc*: *Havek-ot*. cf. HAWKIN.

Hawkey: *v.* HAWKSEY

Hawkin, Hawken, Hawking, Hawkings, Hawkins, Havekin: *Haukynus* le cotoler 1313 FrY; *Haukyn* Skinner 1332 SRCu; Robert *Hauekin* 1248 PN Ess 333; John *Havekyn* 1275 RH (K); Richard, Alexander *Haukyn* 1297 MinAcctCo, 1311 LLB D; Margery *Haukyns* 1327 SRWo; John *Haw-kynge* 1570 FrY. *Hawkin* has been regarded as a pet-name for *Henry*, from *Halkin*, but no such form has been adduced. Such a formation from such a common name seems likely, but there must be another source. Harrison cites:

Wo was *Hawkyn*, wo was Herry!
Wo was Tomkyn, wo was Terry!

But as *Tomkyn* is certainly not a pet-name for *Terry*, it is a fair assumption that *Hawkyn* is not for *Herry*. Our earliest forms are *Havekyn* which persists until at least 1365 (AD ii). This must be for *Havek-in*, a diminutive of OE *Hafoc*, which was still in use in the middle of the 13th century (*v.* HAWK) and had at least one other diminutive, *Havekot* (*v.* HAWKETT).

Hawkley: Philip *de Hauecleia* 1221 AssWo; Hugh *de Hauckelegh* 1346 SRWo. From Hawkley (Hants), Hawkley Farm in Pensax (Worcs), or 'dweller by the hawk-wood'.

Hawksey, Hawkey: William *Hauekesega* 1191 P (Nth); William *Hauekeseye* Hy 3 Colch (Ess). 'Hawk's eye', a nickname. The Manchester Hawk-seys may preserve an old form of HAWKSHAW.

Hawkshaw: Adam *de Haukesheye* 1285 AssLa; Thomas *Haukshawe* 1375 AD iv (Wa). From Hawkshaw (Lancs).

Haworth, Harwarth: Robert *de Hawrth* 1200 P (Y). From Haworth (WRYorks).

Hawson: Simon, Richard *Haweson* 1331 AssSt, 1424 DbCh. 'Son of *Haw*.'

Hawtayne: *v.* HAWTIN

Hawthorn, Hawthorne: William *de Hagethorn* 1155 FeuDu; Henry *atte Hauthorn* 1327 SRWo. From Hawthorn (Durham) or from residence near a hawthorn (OE *hagþorn*).

Hawtin, Hawtayne: (i) Walter *Halteyn* 1134-40 Holme (Nf); Eborard *Halthein* 1146-75 MedEA (Sf); Theobald *Hauthein*, *Halþein* 1153-68 Holme (Nf), *Hautein* 1198 FF (L). OE *heall-þegn* 'hall-thane'. one who resides in or is occupied in a hall. (ii) Robert *Hauteyn, Auteyn* 1242 Fees (L); Walter *Haweteyn* 1277 LLB A. OFr *hautain* 'proud, haughty'.

Hawtrey: *v.* DAWTREY

Hawyes: *v.* HAWES

Hay, Haye, Hayes, Hays, Hey, Heyes, Heighes:
(i) Richard *de Hay* 1170 P (L); Robert *de la Haie* 1185 Templars (Herts); Roger *del Heys* 1275 RH (Nf); William *de Hayes* ib. (Nth); Henry *del Haye*, Stephen *in the Haye* 1275 SRWo; Thomas *atte Heye* 1327 SRSo. 'Dweller by the enclosure' (OE *(ge)hæg*), as at Hay (Hereford) or Hayes (Devon, Dorset). In ME *hay* also meant 'forest fenced off for hunting'. *v.* HIGHE, O'HEA. (ii) Willelmus *filius Hai* 1168 P (Bk); Ricardus *filius Haye* 1205 Cur (Nf); Robert, Roger *Hai* 1150 Eynsham (O), 1163–6 Seals (Sx). There is recorded in a dubious charter of 704 an OE *Hæha* or *Heaha* which Redin derives from OE *hēah* 'high'. Compounds with *Hēah-*, such as *Hēahbeorht*, *Hēahstān*, etc., were common in OE and two otherwise unrecorded compounds, *Hēahsige* and *Hēahhild* (f), suggest that the first theme long remained popular: *Hiechsi* 1066 Winton (Ha), Walter *filius Hehilde* 1201 Cur (L). A short form of these names, *Hēah(a)*, may well have existed in OE and may survive in the post-Conquest *Hai*. *v.* HAYCOCK. (iii) Robert *le Hay*, *le Heye* 1275 RH (Nf, Bk); Roger *le Hay* ib. (Sx). OE *hēah* 'high, tall'. cf. 'He was strong man and hey' (c1300 NED). *v.* HIGHE.

Haycock, Haycocks, Haycox, Heycock: Robert *Heykok* 1296 SRSx; Ralph *Haycok* 1311 FFEss. *Hai-coc*, a diminutive of *Hai*. *v.* HAY, HICKOX.

Haycraft, Haycroft: Hugo *de la Heycroft* 1279 RH (O); Richard *atte Haycroft* 1332 SRSx. 'Dweller by the hay-croft', OE *hēg*.

Hayday: Geoffrey *Hechdai*, *Hegday*, *Heagday* 1180–5 P (Nth); Alicia *Hedei* 1327 SRWo. OE *hēah-dæg* 'a day of high celebration, a solemn or festal day'. cf. HALIDAY.

Hayden, Haydon, Heyden, Heydon, Heiden: Thomas *de Haiden'* 1200 Pl (Ess); William *de Heydon* 1303 IpmGl; Walter *Haydon* 1327 SRSo. From Haydon (Dorset, Som, Wilts), Haydon Bridge (Northumb), or Heydon (Cambs, Norfolk).

Haydock, Haddock: Hugo *de Haidoc* 1212 Fees (La); Robert *Haddocke*, *Haydock* 1669, 1671 LaWills. From Haydock (Lancs), pronounced *Haddock*.

Hayer: Richard *le Heyer* 1274 RH (Gl). 'Dweller by the enclosure.' *v.* HAY and also AYER.

Hayes, Hease, Heyes: Hugh *de la Heise* 1197 Eynsham (O); Robert *de Hese* 1209 P (Nf); Henry *Heyse* 1240 Rams (C); Michael *atte hese* 1296 SRSx. 'Dweller by the brushwood' (OE *hæs*), as at Hayes (Kent, Middlesex), Hays (Sussex), Heaseland and Heasewood Fm (Sussex). *Heise* is from OFr *heis* 'brushwood'.

Hayesman: *v.* HEASEMAN

Hayhoe, Hayhow, Heigho, Heyo, Higho: John *Heyhowe*, *Hihoo* 1524 SRSf. 'Dweller by the high ridge', OE *hēah*, *hōh*.

Hayhurst: Thomas *de Hayhurst*, *de Heyhurst* 1246 AssLa, 1327 SRSx; John *Hairst* 1662 PrGR. 'Dweller by the high wood.'

Hayland, Heyland, Highland, Hyland: Nicholas *de Haylaund* 1255 AssSo; Wulford *atte Heghelonde* 1275 RH (K); Thomas *de Heyeland* ib. (Sx).

'Dweller by the hay-land or the high-land', OE *hēg* or *hēah* and *land*.

Hayler, Haylor: *v.* HALER

Hayles: *v.* HAILE

Haylet, Haylett: *Hegelot* 1134–40 Holme (Nf); *Heylot* 1279 RH (C); Robert, Emma *Heylot* ib. (Beds, Hu). *Hai-el-ot*, a double diminutive of *Hai*. *v.* HAY.

Hayley: *v.* HAILEY

Haylock: *Heiloc* 1188 BuryS (Sf); Nicholas *Heilok* ib.; William *Heylok* 1327 SRSf. Probably OE *Hægluc*, a diminutive of *Hægel*, unrecorded, but found in Hailsham, Hayling and Hazeleigh. In 1327 SRSf, *Hayl* is found seven times as a surname: John *Hayl*, Robert *Heyle*. This might well be OE *Hægel*, surviving as *Haile*.

Hayman, Heaman, Heyman, Highman, Hyman: William *Hayman* 1312 AD iv (D); Walter *Heyman* 1332 SRWa. The first element is doubtful. It may be OE *(ge)hæg*, 'dweller by the enclosure', for *atte Hay* (cf. HAY); or keeper of the enclosure (cf. HAYWARD); or OE *hēg*, *hīg* 'hay', seller of hay. cf. Henry *Heimongere* 1230 P (L); or even 'tall man', OE *hēah*. *v.* also HAMMOND.

Haymes: *v.* HAIM

Hayne: *v.* HAIN, HAGAN

Hayselden: *v.* HAZELDEN

Haysom, Haysum: John *Heysone* 1300 LLB C. 'Son of *Hay*.'

Hayter, Haytor: William *Haytere* 1260 AssC; Reginald *le Heytur* 1296 SRSx. For *atte Heyte*. *v.* HEIGHT.

Haythorne, Hathorn, Heathorn, Hethron: Philip *Haythorn* 1332 SRSr. From OE *hægþorn*. *v.* HAWTHORN.

Hayton: William *de Haitun* c1147–54 YCh; Adam *de Hayton'* 1202 P (Nt); Henry *de Heyton'* 1327 SRLei; Robert *Hayton* 1415 IpmY. From Hayton (Cumb, Notts, Salop, ERYorks).

Hayward, Heyward: Godric *Heiuuard*, Brihtmer *Haiuuard* c1095 Bury (Sf); Richard *Haiward* 1166 P (Nf); William *le Heiward* c1179 Bart (Lo). The original duties of the hayward seem to have been to protect the fences round the Lammas lands when enclosed for hay (Coulton), hence his name, OE *hege-weard* 'guardian of the fence or hedge'. This *heȝe* was a dead hedge easily erected and removed, forming an enclosure (OE *(ge)hæg* from which, to judge from the early and regular variation between *heiward* and *haiward*, and from his more general duties of preventing cattle from breaking through into the enclosed fields and growing crops, the hayward seems also to have been called *(ge)hægweard* 'enclosure-protector'. cf. also (from *Piers Plowman*): 'Canstow . . . haue an horne and be haywarde, and liggen oute a nyghtes, And kepe my corn in my croft fro pykers and þeeues?'. In the Parish Register of Horringer (Suffolk) c1670–80 *Hayward* is regularly written *Howard*, and in the Walthamstow Toni court-rolls from 1678 to 1882 the marshbaley is often called the *hayward* or *howard*, so that some of our Howards were probably Haywards. *v.* HOWARD.

Haywood, Heywood, Heawood, Highwood: Anselm *de Haiwod* c1199 StThomas (St); Adam *de Heyuuode* 1246 AssLa; Arnold de *Hewode* 1275 RH (W). From Haywood (Hereford, Notts, Salop, Staffs) or Heywood (Lancs, Wilts), or from numerous minor places.

Hayzeldene: *v.* HAZELDEN

Hazard, Hazzard, Hasard, Hassard, Haszard, Assard: (i) Hugo *Hasard* 1170, 1190 P (Ha), *Halsard* (*Hasard'*) 1178 P (Ha); William *Halsart'* (*Hausard'*) 1177 P (Sr); Gilbert *Hausard* 1196 P (Y). Probably OE *hals* 'neck' plus the pejorative suffix *-ard*, a nickname for one with some peculiarity of the neck. cf. TESTAR. (ii) Geoffrey *Hasard* 1185 Templars (L); Walter *Hassard* 1197 FFK; Sybil *Hasard'* 1201 AssSo. *Hasard* is common and cannot always be from *Halsard*. It may be OE *hasu* 'grey' plus *-ard*, 'grey-haired', or Fr *hase* 'a female hare' plus *-ard*, parallel with *Hare*, or, perhaps more frequently, OFr *hasard*, ME *has(s)ard*, *haz(z)ard* 'a game at dice' (MED c1300), used of a gambler or one prepared to run risks. cf. John *Hasardour* 1366 ColchCt, ME, AFr *hasardour* 'a dicer, gamester' (1368 MED). This metonymy existed already in French. cf. 'vous n'etes que un *hasart*. Et ledit Robin dist: Je ne suis point *hazart*. Cellui est *hazart* qui joue sa femme aux dez' (Du Cange, *s.v.* 'hazardour').

Hazel, Hazell, Hasel, Hasell, Haisell, Heazel, Heazell, Hessel, Hessels: Alured *del Hesel* c1182 MELS (Wo); Gamel *Hesel* 1203 P (L); Hugh *de Hesill* 1204 AssY; William *atte Hasele* 1275 SRWo; John *Hasyl* 1327 *SR* (Ess); Henry *de Hessell* 1341 FrY. 'Dweller by the hazel', OE *hæsel*, ON *hesli*, as at Hessle (ER, WRYorks), Heazille Barton, Heazle Fm (Devon), etc.

Hazelden, Hazeldene, Hazeldeane, Hazeldine, Hazeldon, Hazeltine, Hazledine, Hazzledine, Haiselden, Hasleden, Haseldene, Haseldine, Haseltine, Haszeldine, Hayselden, Haizelden, Hayzelden, Hayzeldene, Heselden, Heseldin, Heseltine, Heselton, Hesleden, Hesselden, Hesseltine, Hestleton: Robert *de Heseldene* 1243 AssDu; Alexander *de Haselindene* 1258 Kirkstall (Y); Reginald *de Haselden'* 1275 RH (W); William *de Heseldenn* 1296 SRSx; Richard *Hessletine* 1632 YWills. From Heselden (Durham), Haselden (Sussex), Haslingden (Lancs), Hazledon Fm (Wilts), *Heseldene* c1130, or from residence in a hazel-valley. There has been some confusion with *Hazelton*.

Hazelgrove, Hazelgreaves, Haselgrove, Haslegrave, Heaselgrave, Heselgrave, Hesselgrave, Hesselgreaves: Richard *de Hasilgref* 1297 SRY. From Hesselgreave (WRYorks), Hazel Grove (NR Yorks), or residence in a hazel-valley (OE *hæsel*, ON *hesli* 'hazel' and ON *gryfja* 'hole, pit').

Hazelhurst, Hazlehurst, Haselhurst, Haslehurst: Henry, John *de Haselhurst* 1332 SRLa, SRSr. From Hazelhurst (Lancs, Surrey, Sussex) or 'dweller by a hazel-wood'.

Hazelman, Hazleman: For *atte Hasele. v.* HAZEL.

Hazelip: *v.* HASLOP

Hazelrigg, Hazlerigg: Alan *de Hesilrig* 1279 AssNb. From Hazelrigg (Cumb, Lancs, Northumb).

Hazeltine: *v.* HAZELDEN

Hazelton, Haselton, Hastleton, Heselton, Hestleton: Robert *de Haselton* 1274 RH (Gl); Geoffrey *de Heseleton* 1275 RH (Nf). From Hazelton Bottom (Herts), Hazelton Wood (Essex), both originally *Haselden*, Hazelton (Glos), or Hesselton (NRYorks). *v.* HAZELDEN.

Hazelwood, Hazlewood, Hazzlewood, Haselwood, Haslewood, Heaslewood, Heselwood, Heslewood, Hesselwood, Aizlewood: Ernald *de Heselwude* 1191 P (Y); John *Haselwod* 1332 SRSx. From Hazelwood (Devon, Derby, Suffolk, Surrey, WRYorks), Hesslewood (ERYorks), or residence near a hazel-wood.

Hazlett, Hazlitt, Haslett, Haslitt, Heaslett, Hezlet, Hezlett: (i) John *Haselette* 1332 SRSr; William *atte Hasellette* 1333 MELS (Sr). 'Dweller by a hazel-copse', as at Haslett Copse (Sussex), OE **hæslett*, a common term in Essex, Kent and Surrey. (ii) William *Hesilheued* 1421 FrY. From Hazelhead (Lancs, WRYorks), or 'dweller by the hazel-hill', OE *hēafod*.

Hazzard: *v.* HAZARD

Hazzledine: *v.* HAZELDEN

Hazzlewood: *v.* HAZELWOOD

Heacock: *v.* HICKOX

Head, Heads, Heed: (i) Hubertus *cum testa* 1130 P (D); Ralph *Heued'* 1166 P (Nf); Thomas *Hede* c1246 Calv (Y). A nickname from OE *hēafod* 'head'. (ii) Thomas *del Heved* 1275 RH (Nt); Roger *Byheved* 1285 AssCh; Walter *Othehede* 1331 DbCh. 'Dweller by the promontory or hill, or near the source of a stream or the head of a valley', OE *hēafod*.

Headland: John *de* (*del*) *Hevedlond* 1275 RH (Sf). 'Dweller by the headland', here on the Suffolk coast.

Heafield: *v.* HIGHFIELD

Heal, Heale, Heales, Hele: William *de Lahela* 1130 P (Ha); William *in Thehele* 1234 MELS (So); Roger *de Hele* 1242 Fees (D); Hugh *Attehele* 1306 FFSo. Hele and Heale are very common place-names in Devon, less frequent in Somerset, and occasionally noted in Hants, Wilts, Worcs and Surrey. The surname is from residence in a nook or secluded place, from ME *hēle* from OE *heale*, dative singular of *healh*, corresponding to the Anglian dative *hale*, frequent as HALE.

Heald, Held, Hield, Hields: Adam *de Helde* 1207 P (K); Richard *del Helde* 1246 AssLa; Hamon *Attehelde* c1260 ArchC 34; Eustace *ater Hylde*, Matthew *atte Hulde* 1296 SRSx; Robert *Heild* 1605 FrY; William *Hield* 1706 ib. From residence near a slope, OE *helde*, *hi(e)lde*, *hylde*.

Heaman: *v.* HAYMAN

Heams: *v.* EAMES

Heard: *v.* HERD

Hearder: *v.* HERDER

Heardman: *v.* HERDMAN

Hearle: *v.* EARL

Hearne: *v.* HERN
Heart: *v.* HART
Hease: *v.* HAYES
Heaselgrave: *v.* HAZELGROVE
Heaseman, Heasman, Hayesman, Easman: Simon *le Heysman* 1275 RH (Nf). 'Dweller in the brushwood'. *v.* HAYES. *Hayesman and Easeman* are found side by side in Kent.
Heasler: *v.* HASLER
Heaslett: *v.* HAZLETT
Heaslewood: *v.* HAZELWOOD
Heaslip: *v.* HASLOP
Heath: John *de la Heth* 1248 FFEss; Laurence *atte Hethe* 1296 SRSx; Peter *del Heth* 1297 SRY; Alan *Othehethe* 1332 SRSt. 'Dweller on the heath', OE *hǣð*.
Heathcock: Walter *Hathecok* 1274 RH (Ess). A nickname from the heathcock, the black grouse (1590 NED).
Heathcote, Heathcoat, Heathcott: Godfrey *de Hetcota* 1166 P (Db); Ralph *de Hethcote* 1227 AssSt. From Heathcote (Derby, Warwicks). In Yorkshire, pronounced *Hethkett*.
Heather: John, Henry *le Hether* 1327 SRWo, 1332 SRSr. For *atte hethe*. *v.* HEATH.
Heatherington: *v.* HETHERINGTON
Heathfield: Livesa *de Hethfeld* 1276 RH (O); Adam, Isabel *atte Hethfeld* 1327 SRSo, 1332 SRSx. From Heathfield (Sussex) or dweller on the heath-land (OE *hǣð, feld*).
Heathman: *v.* HEATHER
Heathorn, Heathron: *v.* HAYTHORNE
Heaven(s): *v.* EVANS
Heaver: Geoffrey *Heuere* 1297 MinAcctCo. A derivative of ME *heve* 'to lift, raise', a porter, carrier. (1586 NED). *v.* HEVER.
Heaversedge: *v.* HATHERSICH
Heaward, Heaword: Robert *Heaward* 1585 Shef; George *Heaword* 1681 ib. *v.* HOWARD.
Heawood: *v.* HAYWOOD
Heazell: *v.* HAZEL
Hebb: *Hebbe* Capell 1284 Wak (Y); Herberdus, Juliana *Hebbe* 1279 RH (Hu), 1296 SRSx. *Hebb*, a short form of *Hebert*, i.e *Herbert*. *v.* HEBBARD.
Hebbard, Hebard, Hebbert: Henry, Reginald *Hebert* 1279 RH (O); Adam *Hebert* ib. (Beds). *Hebert*, for *Herbert*, with loss of the first *r*.
Hebblethwaite, Hebblewaite, Hebblewhite, Hepplewhite, Ebblewhite: Agnes *de Hebletwayt* 1379 PTY; John *Ebyllthwayte* 1455 GildY; John *Epulweyte* 1481 SIA xii; Johanna *Hebbylewhayt* 1526 GildY; Alexander *Hebylthwat* 1528 FrY; Christabel *Hebeltwhitt* 1624 LaWills. From Heblethwaite near Sedbergh (WRYorks).
Hebborn, Hebburn: *v.* HEPBURN
Heberden: *v.* HIBBERDINE
Hebson: Thomas *Hebson* 1326 Wak (Y). 'Son of *Hebb*.'
Heck: John *del Hek* 1219 AssY, *de Hecke* 1242 Fees (Y). From Heck (WRYorks) or 'dweller by the gate', from *heck*, a northern form of *Hatch*.
Heckingbottom: *v.* HIGGINBOTHAM
Heckler: William *le Hekeler* 1297 Wak (Y). A

derivative of ME *hekel* 'to heckle', a heckler or dresser of hemp or flax (1440 MED).
Hedge, Hedges: Ailmar *Hegge* 1227 AssBeds; Robert *atte Hegge* 1256 AssSo; Richard *de Hegges* 1296 SRSx; Robert *del Hegges* 1301 SRY; Roger *in the Hegg* 1327 SR (Ess). 'Dweller by the hedge(s) or enclosure(s)', OE *hecg*.
Hedgecock, Hedgcock, Hedgecoe: John *Hechecok* 1327 SRC. Probably for HITCHCOCK. cf. ALCOE.
Hedger: Henry *le Hegger* 1327 SRSx; John *Heggere* 1332 SRSr. A parallel to HEDGMAN and HEDGE.
Hedgman: Richard *le Hegman* c1240 *ERO;* John *Heg(ge)man* 1305 HPD, 1327 *SR* (Ess); Ralph *Hedg(e)man* 1524 SRSf. 'Dweller by the enclosure.'
Heed: *v.* HEAD
Heginbotham, Heginbottom: *v.* HIGGINBOTHAM
Heiden: *v.* HAYDEN
Heighes: *v.* HAY
Heigho: *v.* HAYHOE
Height, Hight, Hite: Henry *de la Heyt* 1275 RH (Db); Robert *atte Heyte* 1279 RH (O). 'Dweller at the height' or top of the hill, OE *hīehþu*, ME *heyt* 'height, top, summit'.
Heighton: *v.* HIGHTON
Held: *v.* HEALD
Helder: Hugh, Cristiana *le Heldere* 1212 Cur (Herts), 1279 RH (C). Either (i) a derivative of OE *healdan* 'to hold', a tenant, occupier. cf. HOLDER; or (ii) a toponymic from OE *hylde* 'slope', equivalent to *atte held*, 'dweller on the slope'. cf. HEALD; or, possibly, for 'the elder' with inorganic *H*.
Hele: *v.* HEAL
Heley: *v.* ELY
Helin: *v.* ELION
Helis: *v.* ELLIS
Hell: Johannes, Fulco *filius Hel'* 1279 RH (Hu); Wulfwin, Roger *Helle* 1188 P (Ess), 1221 *ElyA* (Nf). This may occasionally be for HILL, preserving the south-eastern form: William *atte Helle* 1296 SRSx, but in surnames, as in place-names, this usually takes the standard form. The surname is clearly chiefly from a personal name *Helle*, a pet-form of *Ellis* (*v.* ELCOCK) or of some name in *Hil(d)*-, or perhaps of *Helen*. *v.* HELLCAT.
Hellass: *v.* HILLHOUSE
Hellcat, Hillcoat: Ralph, Walter *Hellecoc* 1202 AssL, 1219 AssY; Roger, John *Hellecok(e)* 1276 RH (Gl), 1327 Pinchbeck (Sf). *v.* ELCOCK, HELL.
Hellen(s): *v.* ELION, ELLEN
Heller: Alexander *Huller, Heller* 1327, 1332 SRSx. A derivative of ME *hell, hull*, OE *hyll* 'dweller on the hill'.
Helliar, Hellier, Hellyer, Helyer, Hilliar, Hillier, Hillyar, Hillyer, Hilyer: Robert *le Heliere* 1275 RH (K); Gilbert *le Helyere* 1280 MESO (Ha); Robert *le Hillier* 1347 Cl (Beds). A derivative of OE *helian* 'to cover, roof', a slater or tiler. cf. Walter *Helier vel Tiler* c1450 NED.
Hellin(s): *v.* ELION, ELLEN
Helling, Hellings: Ralph *de Helling'* 1191 P (L). From Healing (Lincs). *v.* also ELION.

Hellis: *v.* ELLIS: Probably also for HELLASS.

Hellman, Helman: William *Helman* 1274 RH (Ess). 'Dweller on the hill.' cf. HELLER.

Hellon: *v.* ELION

Hellyer: *v.* HELLIAR

Helm, Helme, Helms: Nicholas *de Helm* 1180 P (Sr); William *Helmis* 1279 RH (Bk); Hugh *del Helm* 1296 Wak (Y); Richard *ate Helme* 1327 SRWo; William *del Helmes* 1366 SRLa. OE *helm* 'a covering', later, in dialects, 'roofed shelter for cattle', used, presumably for a herdsman.

Helmsley: *v.* HEMSLEY

Hely: *v.* ELY

Helyer: *v.* HELLIAR

Hembrey, Hembry, Hemery: *v.* AMERY

Hembrow, Hembury: *v.* EMBERY

Hemes: *v.* EAMES

Hemmett: *v.* EMMATT

Hemming, Hemmings: *Hemmingus* 1066 ICC; *Hemming* de Welega 1166 P (Ess); Walter, William *Hemming* 1170 P (So), 1221 AssWo. ON *Hem(m)-ingr*, ODa *Hem(m)ing*.

Hemmingway, Hemingway: John *de Hemyngway*, William *Hemyngway* 1379 PTY; Richard *de Hemmyngway* 1309 Wak; Robert *Hemmyngwaye* 1561 Pat (Y). 'Dweller by Hemming's path', from an unidentified minor place, probably in Yorks.

Hempenstall: *v.* HEPTONSTALL

Hemphrey, Henfrey: *Heinfrid'* de Colecestr' 1197 P (Ess); *Hemfridus* 1214 Cur (Nth); Margareta *Henfrey* 1327 SRSf; Wylliam *Hemffrey* 1524 SRSf. OG *Haimfrid*, *Heinfrid*, OFr *Hainfroi*.

Hempson, Hemson: Roger *Hemson, Hempson* 1524 SRSf. For EMSON, or *Hemingson*: Suein *Hemmingessune* 1166 P (Nt).

Hems: Walter *de Hemma* 1182 P (Sa); Richard *de la Hemme* 1275 RH (W); John *en le Hemme* 1300 AssSt. From The Hem (Salop), Hem (Montgomery), or 'dweller by the border', OE *hemm* 'hem'.

Hemsley, Hemesley, Helmsley: William *de Helmeslac* c1160–83 YCh; Walter *de Helmeslay* 1260 IpmY; William *de Helmesley* 1373 FFY; William *Hemsley* 1477 IpmNt. From Helmsley (NRYorks), *Elmeslac* DB, *Helmesley* 12th, *Hemesley* 1548.

Hemson: *v.* HEMPSON

Henchcliffe: *v.* HINCHCLIFFE

Hencher: *v.* HENSHALL

Henday, Hendey: *v.* HENDY

Henderson: William *Henrison* 1374 Black; David *Hennerson* 1504 ib.; James *Hendirsoune* 1553 ib. 'Son of *Henry*.' cf. HENDRIE.

Hendisson: William *Hendissone* 1327 SRSf. 'Son of *Hendy*.'

Hendra: John *del Hendre* 1370 MinAcctCo. From one of the Cornish places named Hendra, *hen dref* 'old homestead'.

Hendrie, Hendrey, Hendry: *Hendrie* Ralstoun 1519 Black; *Hendrye* Stanford 1593 EA (OS) ii (Sf); John *Hendre* 1359 Putnam (Co); Hendyre *Hendry* 1562 Black. OFr *Henri*, with intrusive *d*. *v.* HENRY.

Hendy, Henday, Hendey: Henricus *filius Hendy* 1279 RH (O); William *Hendi* 1198 FF (Sr); Robert *le Hendy* 1275 RH (Nf). ME *hendy* 'courteous, kind, gentle', used also as a personal-name. *Hendyman* was also a common surname and a personal-name: *Hendeman* del Ho 1259 AD iii (K); *Hendeman* Oldlegh 1260 AssC.

Hendyside: *v.* HANDASYDE

Henfrey: *v.* HEMPHREY

Henkin, Hinkins: (i) *Hanekin, Henekin* le Rede 1299 LoCt; William *Henekyn* 1327 *SR* (Ess); John *Hinkins* 1787 Bardsley. A diminutive of *Hen* (Henry). cf. HANN, HANKIN. (ii) Thomas *Hendekyn* 1337 LLB F. A diminutive of *Hendy*.

Henley, Henly: Gilbert *de Henlega* 1181 P (Wo); Robert *de Henlay* 1270 IpmY; William *Heneley* 1392 IpmNt. From Henley (Oxon, Salop, Som, Suffolk, Surrey, Warwicks).

Henman: William *Henman* 1327 SRSo; Richard *Heneman* 1327 SRSf. Probably 'man in charge of the hens'.

Henn: (i) *Henna* Curi 1192 P (Lo); Johannes *filius Hen* 1275 RH (Nt); Euerard *Henne* 1202 P (L). *Henn*, like *Hann*, was a pet-name for *Henry*. cf. HENKIN. *Henna* is the corresponding feminine. Forssner cites *Henrica* (without date). (ii) Colemannus, Thomas *le Hen* 1275 RH (Sf). A nickname from the hen.

Hennessey, Hennessy, Hennesy, Henesy: Irish *Ó hAonghusa* 'descendant of *Aonghus*' (one-choice).

Hennion: *v.* ENNION

Henry, Henrey, Henery, Heneries, Fitzhenry: *Henricus* 1066, 1086 DB; Thomas *Henery* 1275 RH (K); Richard *Henry* 1293 Fees (D); Adam *Henris* 1323 AssSt; John *Fitz Henrie* 1346 Ipm. OFr *Henri*, OG *Haimric*, *Henric* 'home-rule', after the Conquest one of the most popular Norman names. The English form was *Herry* or *Harry*, with pet-forms *Henn*, *Hann*, and diminutives *Henkin*, *Hankin*, *Henriot*, and a pet-form *Hal* which may survive in *Hawkins*. *v.* also HARRY, HERIOT, HENDRIE.

Henshall, Henshaw, Hensher, Hencher: (i) Peter *de Henschal* 1332 SRCu. From Henshaw (Northumb). (ii) Richard *de Henneshagh* 1365 Bardsley (Ch); Sysley *Henshall* (*Henshawe*) 1570 ib. From Henshaw in Prestbury (Ches).

Hensman, Hinckesman: William *Henxman* 1413 Cl; Thomas *Hengysman* 1460 RochW; John *Hengestman* 1473 SIA xii; Thomas *Hinchman* son of Thomas *Henchman* 1674 Bardsley. OE *hengest* 'stallion' and *mann*, a groom, later a squire or page of honour, and also 'sumpter-man, carrier'.

Henson (i) Hugh Balle *Heyneson* 1304 Cl. 'Son of *Hayne*'. *v.* HAGAN. (ii) William *Hendisson* 1327 SRSf; William *Henson* 1381 PTY. 'Son of *Hendy*.'

Henty: Robert, John *de Hentye* 1327, 1332 SRSx. From Antye Fm in Wivelsfield (Sussex).

Hepburn, Hebburn, Hebborn: Adam *de Hepburne* 1271 Black; Thomas *de Heburn'* 1279 AssNb; John *Hebburn* 1407 FrY. From Hepburn (Northumb), or Hebburn (Durham).

Heppenstall: *v.* HEPTONSTALL

Hepplewhite: *v.* HEBBLETHWAITE

Heptonstall, Heptinstall, Heppenstall, Heppinstall, Hempenstall: John *de Heptonstall* 1296 Wak (Y); William *Heptinstall* 1558 RothwellPR (Y); Matthew *Hepinstall* 1668 ib. From Heptonstall (WRYorks).

Hepworth, Hipworth: Eadward *de Heppeworde* 1121–48 Bury; Stephen *de Heppeworth'* 1330 FFEss; Richard *Hyppeworthe* 1387 *Petre*; John *Hepworth* 1414 IpmY. From Hepworth (Suffolk, WRYorks).

Herald, Heraud, Herold, Herod, Herrald, Herrold, Herrod: *Herouldus, Hairaudus* 1066 DB; William *Herode* 1279 AssNb; John *Heraud* 1296 SRSx; Peter *Herodes* 1297 SRY; Seman *Erode, Harrold, Herodes* 1297 SIA x. These surnames may derive from ON *Haraldr,* OG *Hairold, Herold* or from OE *Hereweald. v.* HAROLD. They may also be from ME *heraud, herault, herode, haraude* 'herald' (c1385 MED), from OFr *heraut, herault.* Weekley explains *Herod* as a stage braggart. Dauzat similarly derives the rare French *Herode* from the Biblical name which Michaëlsson considers a suitable nickname from the name of the King of the Jews who slaughtered the Innocents and is often mentioned in the *chansons de geste.* There seems to be no clear evidence for this in England. In Wace's *Roman de Rou,* Harold occurs as *Heraut.*

Herbage, Harbach, Harbage, Harbidge: Probably for *atte herberge* from OFr *herberge* 'hostel, shelter'. Equivalent to HARBISHER.

Herbert, Herbit, Harbard, Harberd, Harbert, Harbird, Harbord, Harbot, Harbott, Harbud, Harbut, Harbutt, Fitzherbert: *Herbertus, Hereberd* 1086 DB; *Herebertus* capellanus 1148–56 Bury (Sf); William *Herebert* 1206 P (Do); Richard *Herbert, Herebert, Herberd* 1221 AssWo; Johannes *Herberti* 1230 Cl (Nf); Reginald *le Fitz Herbert* 1347 Ipm; Christopher *Harbart* 1550 FrY; Philip *Herbert* son of John *Harbart* 1609 FrY; William *Harbatt* son of Richard *Harbart* 1626 FrY; William *Harbort* 1626 Bardsley. OFr *Herbert* from OG *Hariberct, Her(e)bert* 'army-bright'. Introduced by the Normans, but much less common than *Hugh.* Diminutives were formed but have not survived: *Herbelott* Someter 1296 SRSx, Richard *Herbelot* 1327 ib., Alexander *Herbelyn* 1376 ColchCt, Robert *Herbekyn* 1296 SRSx.

Herbertson, Harbertson, Harburtson, Herbinson, Herbison, Harbinson, Harbison: Archibald *Herbertson* 1525 Black (Glasgow); William *Herbesone* 1555 ib. (Berwick); Richard *Harbertson* 1605 ib. (Glasgow). *Herbisone* is found in Glasgow in 1551 and the development is shown in *Harberson, Harbeson, Harbisone* 1706 (Black). An intrusive *n* in this last gave *Harbinson.*

Hercock, Hircock: John, Henry *Hercok* 1327 SRSf. *Her,* a short form of *Herbert* or *Herman* and *cock.* cf. *Here (Herbertus* CR) de Oxhei 1230 P (Herts).

Herd, Heard, Hird, Hord, Hurd: William *Lehird* Ric 1 Cur (L); Thomas *Hord'* 1221 AssSa; Reginald *le Herd* 1243 AssSo; Richard *le Hurde* 1296 SRSx. OE· *hierde* 'herd', 'hersdman'. For the dialectal forms, *v.* MEOT 254–7.

Herder, Hearder, Horder: Nicholas *le Herder* 1327 SRSo; John *Hurder* 1333 MEOT (So). A rare name. A derivative of ME *herden, hurden* 'to take care of, to tend', from OE *hierde* 'herd'. 'A herdsman.'

Herdman, Heardman, Hurdman: Osbert *Hirdman* 1166 P (Nf); Simon *le Hyrdeman* 1181 P (K); Henry *Erdman* 1260 AssC; John *le Herdman,* Walter *Herdman* 1296 SRSx. OE *hierdeman* 'herdman', one who tends sheep, cattle, etc.

Herdsman: Robert *Herdesman* 1367 ColchCt (Ess). 'Servant of the herd', or more probably 'of one named Herd'.

Herdson: Thomas *Hirdson* 1332 SRCu; Gilbert *Herdson* 1415 PrGR. 'Son of the herd.'

Here: Simon *le Here* 1275 RH (Nf); Alan *Here* 1276 RH (Y). OE *hēore, hýre,* ME *here* 'gentle, mild, pleasant'.

Hereford, Herford, Harford, Hartford: Ilbert *de Hertford* 1086 DB, *de Hereforda* 1086 ICC (Herts); Walter *de Hereford* 1158 P (Wa); Richard *de Herfordia* 1185 Templars (Herts). From Hertford (in which the *t* was early lost as in the modern pronunciation *Harford*), Hereford, or Harford (Devon, Glos).

Hereward, Harward: *Hereuuard, Heruart* 1066 DB; *Herewardus* de Barneby 1219 AssY; Walter, Alexander *Hereward* 1156–80 Bury (Sf), 1221 AssGl; Reynold *Harward* 1523 SRK. OE **Hereweard* 'army-guard'.

Hering: *v.* HERRING

Heriot, Herriot, Herriott, Heryet, Herratt, Herrett, Herrits, Herritts: German *de Heriet (de Herierð)* 1176 P (Ha); Richard *de Heriett, de Herierd* 1197–8 FF (Bk, Beds). From Herriard (Hants). The Scots *Heriot* is from the lands of Heriot (Midlothian): Laurence *de Herryhot* 1221–38 (Black).

Heritage, Herrtage: John *Heritag'* 1279 RH (O); John *Erytage* 1279 RH (Hu); William *Heritage* c1280 Whitby (Y). ME *heritage* from OFr *eritage, heritage* 'property, especially land, which devolves by right of inheritance'; used in 1390 of heirs collectively. Here, perhaps, an heir.

Herman, Hermon: *v.* HARMAN

Hermer: *v.* HARMER

Hermitage, Armatage, Armatys, Armitage, Armytage: Richard *de Ermitage* 1259 AssCh; Hugh *del Hermytage* 1296 PN Wa; John *de Armitage* 1423 Shef (Y). ME *(h)ermitage,* OFr *hermitage* 'hermitage' (c1300 MED). From Armitage (Staffs), Hermitage Fm in Little Packington (Warwicks), where there were early hermitages, or 'dweller by or in a hermitage'.

Hermitte, Armett, Armit, Armitt: William *lermite* 1196 P (Y); William *le Heremit* 1208 Cur (Y); Andrew *Ermite* 1255 RamsCt (Hu); Thomas *Harmyt* 1526 RochW; John *Harmet* 1549 GildY. ME *hermite, ermite,* OFr *(h)ermite* 'hermit' (a1225 MED).

Hern, Herne, Hearn, Hearne, Hurn, Hurne, Harn: Gunnora *de la Hurn'* 1212 Cur (Ha);Walter *Atehurne* 1267 AssSo; Henry *en le Hurne* 1279 RH (Bk); Ralph *in þe Hurne* 1279 RH (O); William *del Herne* 1327 SRSf; John *ate Hirne* 1327 SRSx; Robert *Herne*, John *Harne* 1524 SRSf. From residence in a nook or corner of land or in a bend (OE *hyrne*) as at Herne (Kent) or Hirn (Hants). For the variation in the vowel, cf. HERST. *Hern* is also a ME form of HERON.

Hernaman, Herniman, Harniman, Horniman: Hugo *Herneman* 1428 FA (W); John *Hernaman*, William *Hurnaman*, Richard *Hornaman*, 1547, 1668 DWills. Identical in meaning with *atte Herne*.

Herod, Herold: *v.* HERALD

Heron, Herron, Herroun, Hairon: (i) Ralph *Hairun* 12th DC (L); William *Herun* 1212 Fees (Do); Roger *Heirun* 1221 AssWa; John *Heroun* 1298 LLB B. OFr *hairon*, AFr *heron*, ME *heiroun*, *heyron* (a1302 NED), *herne* (13..), *heron* (c1386) 'heron', a nickname for a thin man with long legs. *v.* HERN. (ii) Drogo *de Hairum, de Harum* 1131, 12th Riev (Y), Drogo *Hairun* 1196 P (Y); William *de Harum, de Herun* c1150, 1175 ib. (Y). From Harome (NRYorks), DB *Harun, Harem, Harum*. There has clearly been confusion with the more common nickname. Jordan *Herum, Hayrun* 1232, 1234 Riev and William *Herun, Heyrun* 1256 AssNb were probably of the same family.

Herratt, Herrett: *v.* HERIOT

Herrick: *Eiric, Eric, Erich* 1066 DB; Siwate *filius Airic* Hy 2 DC (L); John *Eirich* 1211 FrLeic; Nicholas *Heyryke* 1524 ib.; John *Eryke* 1568 ib.; Edward *Hericke* 1620 ib. ON *Eiríkr*, ODa, OSw *Erik*.

Herring, Hering, Harenc: Ralph *Hareng* 1166 Eynsham (O); Peter *Harang* 1210 Cur (Y); Nigel *Haring* 1275 RH (C); Roger *Hering* 1279 RH (O). Early examples are from OFr *hareng* 'herring'; later we have ME *hering* from OE *hǣring, hēring*. Metonymic for a dealer in herrings. cf. Theobald *le Heryngmongere* 1212 Cur (Berks), Symon *Haryngbredere* 1274 RH (Lo), Walter *le Heringman* 1327 SRSf. *Hering* is common in Suffolk in 1327 SR.

Herriott: Walter *Henriot* 1327 SRSo; Henry *Henryot* 1327 SRSt. A diminutive of *Henry*. *v.* also HERIOT.

Herritts: *v.* HERIOT

Herrod: *v.* HERALD

Herroun: *v.* HERON

Herrtage: *v.* HERITAGE

Hersant: *v.* HARSANT

Herst, Hirst, Hurst, Horst: Thomas *de Herst* 1066 DB (Sx); Helias *de Hirst* 1177 Templars (Y); Walter *del Hurst* 1196 P (Bk); Robert *de la Hurste* 1214 Cur (Sr); Nicholas *Horst* 1220 AssSt; William *del Hirst* 1275 Wak (Y); Henry *Attehurst* 1277 AssSo; William *ater*, Robert *ate*, Peter *de la Herst* 1296 SRSx; Joan *upe*, Geoffrey *uppe the Hurst* 1332 SRSx. OE *hyrst* 'wood, wooded hill'. The surname may derive from Hirst (Northumb), Hirst Courtney (Yorks), Temple Hirst (Yorks),

Hurst (Berks, Kent, Warwicks) or Hurstpierpoint (Sussex), earlier *Herst*, or, more frequently, from residence near a wood or wooded hill. The variant forms are due to different developments in ME of OE *y* which, in general, became *e* in the south-east, especially Essex and Kent, *i* in the north and the east midlands and *u* in the west and central midlands and the southern counties.

Herve: A Jersey name. *v.* HARVEY.

Hervey: *v.* HARVEY

Heryet: *v.* HERIOT

Heselden, Heseldin, Heseltine: *v.* HAZELDEN

Heselgrave: *v.* HAZELGROVE

Heselton: *v.* HAZELTON

Heselwood, Heslewood: *v.* HAZELWOOD

Hesketh, Heskett, Heskitt: Robert *de Heskeythe* 1332 SRLa; John *de Hesketh* 1338 WhC; Thomas *Hesketh* 1390 AssLa. From Hesketh (Lancs, NRYorks), or Hesket (Cumb).

Heslam: *v.* HASLAM

Heslin, Hesling: *v.* HASLIN

Heslop: *v.* HASLOP

Hespe: *v.* APPS

Hessel: *v.* HAZEL

Hesselden: *v.* HAZELDEN

Hesselgrave, Hesselgreaves: *v.* HAZELGROVE

Hesselwood: *v.* HAZELWOOD

Hestleton: *v.* HAZELTON

Hetherington, Heatherington: Richard *de Hetherington* 1298 AssL; Edmund *de Hetherynton* 1316 AssNth; Mr. *Etherington* 1672 HTY. From Hetherington (Northumb), or 'dweller at the enclosure on the heath'.

Heugh: *v.* HOW

Hever: Walter *de Hevre* 1203 Cur (K). From Hever (Kent). *v.* HEAVER.

Hew: Dyonisia *le Hewe* 1279 RH (Bk); Thomas *le Heue* 1283 SRSf. ME *hewe* 'a domestic, a servant', a singular formed from ME *hewen*, OE *hīwan* 'members of a household, domestics'. *v.* also HUGH.

Hewar: *v.* HEWER

Heward, Hewart: *v.* HOWARD

Hewartson, Hewertson, Huartson, Huertson: 'Son of *Huard*.' *v.* HOWARD.

Hewat: *v.* HEWET

Hewell: Thomas *Huhel* 1260 AssC; Sampson *Hugheles* 1296 SRSx. A diminutive of *Hugh*. cf. HEWLETT, HEWLINS.

Hewer, Hewar: Alwinus *Heuere* 1066 Winton (Ha); Hugh *le Hewer* 1255 Ass (Ess); Benedict *le Huwere* 1279 RH (C). ME *hewere (huwere)*, a derivative of OE *hēawan* 'to hew', 'a hewer' (a1382 MED), a cutter of wood or stone, probably the latter.

Hewertson: *v.* HEWARTSON

Hewes: *v.* HUGH

Hewet, Hewett, Hewat, Hewit, Hewitt, Howat, Howatt, Howett, Howitt, Huet, Huett, Huitt, Huot: (i) Roger *Huet, Huiet* 1182, 1185 P (D); William *Heuet* 1221 AssSa; Roger *Hughet* 1280 AssSo; John *Howet* 1316 ERO; Roger *Howat* 1327 SR (Ess); Ricot *Huot*, Thomas *Huwet* 1327 SRSx;

William *Howit* 1444 FrY; Alisoune *Hewat* 1662 Black. Diminutives of *Hugh.* cf. HUGGETT. (ii) Occasionally local in origin, from residence in a clearing. At Hewitts in Chelsfield and at Hewitts in Willesborough (Kent) lived families named *de la Hewatte* (1270), *de la hewett* (1301), *atte Hewete* (1338 PN K 16, 421). OE *hīewett* 'cutting', here used of a place where trees had been cut down.

Hewetson, Hewitson, Hewison, Huetson, Huison, Huitson: Henry *Hwetsone* 1363 FrY; Richard *Huetson* 1379 PTY; Thomas *Hewetson* 1489 LLB L; John *Hewyttson* 1544 FrY. 'Son of *Hewet.*'

Hewgill: *v.* HUGILL
Hewin(s): *v.* EWAN
Hewish: *v.* HUISH
Hewison, Hewitson: *v.* HEWETSON
Hewit, Hewitt: *v.* HEWET
Hewkin: *v.* HUKIN

Hewlett, Hewlitt, Howlett, Hulatt, Huleatt, Hulett, Hullett, Hullot: Agnes *Hughelot* c1248 Bec (Nf); Thomas *Huwelot* c1250 Rams (Hu); Richard *Hulot* 1275 RH (Sf); Walter *Howlot, Hughlot* 1310, 1311 LLB D; John *Huelot* 1327 SRWo; John *Hoghlot* 1357 Calv (Y); Robert *Hulat* 1381 SRSf. A double diminutive of *Hugh, Hugh-el-ot.*

Hewlins, Hewlings, Howlin, Howling, Howlings, Huelin, Huglin, Hulance, Hulin, Hullin, Hullins: *Hugelyn* Bourþeyn, *Hugelinus* cubicularius 1052–65 Rams (Hu); *Hvchelinus* parcherius 1066 Winton (Ha); Galfridus *filius Hugelini* 1169 P (Do); *Huelinus* de Fednes 1221 Cur (Bk); Robert *Huelin* 1202 P (Wa); Hugo *hugelini* 1222 DBStP; William *Hugelin* 1230 P (Ha); William *Huhelyn* 1267 AssSo; Richard *Hulin* 1275 RH (Sf); John *Huwelyn* 1327 SRWo; Thomas *Howelyn* 1327 SRSf; John *Hullyng* 1428 FA (W); Robert *Howlinge* 1549 NorwW (Ess). OFr *Hugelin, Huelin, Hulin,* from OG *Huglin,* a diminutive of *Hugo.* There was also a feminine form: Tomas *filius Hugolinae* 1185 P (C), *Hugolina* 1219 AssY, 1309 FFEss.

Hews: *v.* HUGH
Hewson: *v.* HUGHSON
Hext: Walter *Hexte*, Nicholas *Exte* 1327 SRSo. ME *hext*, from OE *hēhst* 'highest', 'tallest'.

Hey-: *v.* HAY-
Heyden, Heydon: *v.* HAYDEN
Heyer: *v.* AYER
Heyne(s): *v.* HAGAN, HAIN
Heyo: *v.* HAYHOE
Hezlett: *v.* HAZLETT
Hibbard, Hibberd, Hibbert: *v.* ILBERT
Hibberdine, Heberden: Ralph *de Iburgedenn* 1279 *Ass* (Sx); William *de Hyburdenn, de Hyburgdenn, de Hybourghedene* 1296, 1327 SRSx; Matthew, Henry *Hiberden* 1507 SxAS xl; Richard, John *Hyberden, Hyberdyn* 1525 SRSx; Roger *Heberden* 1525 FFEss; Nicholas *Hibberdine* 1622 Greenwich-PR. From a lost Heberden in Madehurst (Sussex), last recorded in 1795.
Hibberson: *v.* IBBERSON
Hibbin, Hibbins: James *Hybbyns* 1555 Pat;

Thomas *Hebins* 1560 Bardsley. *Hibb-in*, a diminutive of *Hibb,* from *Hebb.*

Hibbitt, Hibbott: *v.* IBBOTT
Hibble, Hible: *v.* IBELL
Hibbs: *v.* IBBS
Hichens: *v.* HITCHEN
Hichisson: John *Hichsone* 1332 SRLa; John *Hichenson* 1535 KentW. 'Son of *Hitch* or *Hitchen.*'

Hick, Hickes, Hicks, Hix: *Hikke* de Sauteby 1276 RH (Y); *Hyk* serviens 1286 Wak (Y); Richard *Hick'* 1302 SRY; William *Hickys* 1332 SRWa; Henry *Hix* 1484 FrY. *Hick*, a pet-form of *Ricard. v.* RICHARD, HITCH.

Hicken: Isabella *Hicken* 1332 SRWa. *v.* HICK, GEFFEN.

Hickin, Hicking: *Hekyn* de Wath 1379 PTY; David *Hicun* 1275 RH (Sf); Alicia *Hykyn* 1379 PTY. *Hicun, Hicin,* diminutives of *Hick.*

Hickinbotham: *v.* HIGGINBOTHAM
Hicklin, Hickling: (i) Iuo *de Hickelinge* 1163–6 Holme (Nf); William *de Hikelyng* 1327 SRSt. From Hickling (Norfolk, Notts). (ii) Robert *Hikeling* 1212 Fees (La); John *Hykelyng* 1327 SRSx; William *Hykelyn* 1332 SRSt. *Hik-el-in*, a double diminutive of *Hick.* The *Hikeling*-forms may be early examples of loss of *de. v.* above.

Hickman, Higman: *Hykeman* 1279 RH (O); *Hykemon* Smert 14th AD iii (Wo); Richard *Hykemon,* Juliana *Hykemones* 1275 SRWo; Walter *Hikeman* 1279 RH (O). 'Servant of *Hick*', used also as a personal-name.

Hickmott: Thomas *Hikemot* 1460 RochW. 'Hick's brother-in-law.' *v.* HITCHMOUGH.

Hickox, Heacock: *Hikoc* 1279 RH (Hu); *Hekoc* de Par 1366 SRLa; William *Hekoc* 1219 AssY; William *Hycoxe* 1555 Pat. *Hekoc* is probably from *Hēa-coc,* a diminutive of OE **Hēah.* This would become *Heacock,* and, with shortening of the vowel, *Hickock.* cf. HAY, HAYCOCK.

Hickson, Hickeson, Hixson: Stephen *Hykson* 1381 PTY; John *Hixon* 1450 Rad (C). 'Son of *Hick.*

Hiddleston: *v.* HUDDLESTON
Hide, Hides, Hyde, Hydes: (i) Robert *de la Hyda* 1188 P (Do); Avice *atte Hyde* 1296 SRSx; John *of then hyde* 1299 MELS (Wo). OE *hīd* 'a hide of land', probably 'holder of a hide'. (ii) Gilbert *filius Hide* 1185 Templars (Ess); *Hida* de Knapwell 1255 RamsCt (Hu). The personal-name appears to be feminine, possibly *Ida. v.* IDA. cf. Gilbert *Hidecock* 1286 FFSf.

Hider, Hyder: Robert *le Hider* 1309 MESO (Sx); Hugh *Hyder* 1389 AD vi (Do). 'Holder of a hide.' cf. Roger *Hydeman* 1252 Rams (Hu). *v.* HIDE.

Hie: *v.* HIGHE
Hield, Hields: *v.* HEALD
Higdon: Richard son of *Hykedon* 1313 ChambAcctCh; John *Hikedun* 1221 AssWo, 1273 RH (Wo); Thomas *Hykedon, Hekedon* 1327 SRC. *v.* RIGDEN.

Higgett, Higgitt: *Hyket* 1279 RH (O); John *Hykot, Hicoth* 1317 AssK. A diminutive of *Hick,* with late voicing of *k.*

Higginbotham, Higginbottam, Higginbottom, Higenbotham, Higenbottam, Higinbothom, Higgenbottom, Heckingbottom, Heginbotham, Heginbottom, Hickinbotham: Alexander *de Akinbothun* 1246 AssLa; Nicholas *Hichinbothome* 1579 Bardsley (Ch); Mary *Higginbotham* alias *Hickabotham* 1695 DKR 41. From Oakenbottom in Bolton-le-Moors (Lancs), probably originally **æcen-botme* 'oaken-valley', becoming *Eakenbottom, Ickenbottom*. This was then associated with *hickin* or *higgin*, a Lancashire and Cheshire dialect-word for 'mountain-ash'.

Higgins, Higgens, Higgon, Higgons: *Hygyn* de Bowland 1379 PTY; John *Hygyn* 1377 AssEss, *Hygyns* 1452 AD i (Wo). A diminutive of *Higg*, a voiced form of *Hick*. v. HICKIN, HIGGS.

Higginson: Alan *Hygginson* or *Hickynsone* 1552 Oxon. 'Son of *Hickin* or *Higgin*.'

Higgs: *Hegge* Hog 1286 AssCh; Richard *Higge* 1275 RH (Nf). A voiced form of *Hick*.

Higham, Hioms, Hyam, Hyams: Osward *de Hecham* 1176 P (Ess); Hugo *de Hegham* 1198 P (K). From one of the Highams.

Highe, Hie: (i) Gilbert *le High* 1327 SRSx. OE *hēah* 'high, tall'. (ii) Robert *atte Heghe* 1327 SRSx; Richard *atte High* 1332 ib.; both assessed in Heighton (Sussex). 'Dweller on the height or hill', OE *hēah* 'high' used substantively. v. MELS and cf. HEIGHT.

Highfield, Heafield: Robert *de Heghefeld* 1275 RH (Ha); John *de Hefeld*', William *de Hyefeld* 1332 SRSr. 'Dweller by the high field or open-country.'

Highland: v. HAYLAND
Highman: v. HAYMAN
Higho: v. HAYHOE

Highstead, Highsted, Histead, Hysted: Helewis' *de Heghested* 1296 SRSx; Thomas *Highstede*, Lawrance *Histed* 1473, 1494 ArchC 41. From Highstead in Sittingbourne (Kent).

Hight: v. HEIGHT

Highton, Heighton: John *atte Heghetun* 1296 SRSx. From Heighton (Sussex).

Highwood: v. HAYWOOD
Higman: v. HICKMAN

Higson: Roger *Higson* 1487 LLB L. 'Son of *Higg*.'

Hilary: v. HILLARY
Hilbert: v. ILBERT

Hild: *Hilda* de Tidintun Hy 2 DC (L); *Hilda* de Gay 1192 P (O); Hereward, Arnald *Hilde* 1168, 1200 P (Do, Ha). *Hilda* (f), a short form of a name in *Hild*-, e.g. OG *Hildigard* (f), or OE *Hildgȳð* (f).

Hildebrand, Hilderbrand: *Hildebrand* lorimarius 1086 DB (Nf); Brand *filius Hildebrand* 12th DC (Nt); Adam *filius Heudebrand* 1210 Cur (Nf); Geoffrey *Hildebrant* 1195 P (Nf); Gregory *Hildebrand* 1275 RH (L); John *Heldebrond* 1296 SRSx. OG *Hildebrand, Eldebrand* 'battle-sword', occasionally, in the Danelaw, also ON *Hildibrandr*.

Hilder: William *le Hilder*' 1332 SRSx. 'Dweller on the slope', from OE *hylde*. cf. HEALD.

Hildyard, Hilliard, Hillyard: *Hildiard*' de Trule 1206 Cur (Sr); *Hyldeiard* (f) 1228 FFEss; Robert *Hildyard, Hiliard* 1276 RH (Y); Peter *Hildeyerd*' 1297 SRY. OG *Hildigard, Hildiardis* (f) 'war-stronghold', not a common name.

Hilger: (i) *Ilgerus* 1086 DB, 1221 AssWa; *Ilger*' de Wilberfoss' 1219 AssY; Walter *Ylger* 1191 P (Sf); John *Ilger* 1239 FFSf; Emma *Hilger* 1279 RH (O). OG *Hildeger, Hilger* 'battle-spear', not uncommon, invariably as *Ilger*. (ii) Willelmus *filius Hildegari* c1250 Rams (Hu); William, Julian *Hildegar* 1267–85 Rams (Nf), 1279 RH (Hu); Geoffrey *Hildegor* 1221 ElyA (Sf). ODa *Hildiger*. The name is limited to East Anglia.

Hill, Hille, Hills: Gilbert *del Hil* 1191 P (Nf); William *attehil* 1260 AssC; Simon *Hille* 1273 RH (Wo); William *o the hil* 1313 AddCh (C); Matilda *Hilles* 1327 SRSo. 'Dweller on the hill', OE *hyll*. The surname is partly from a personal-name *Hille*, a pet-form of some such name as *Hilger* or *Hillary*: Rogerus *filius Hille* 1221 Cur (D).

Hillary, Hillery, Hilary, Elleray, Ellery, Elray: (i) *Hilarius Brunus* 1177 P (Wo); Richard *Ilarie* 1227 AssSt; Willelmus *Hillar*' (*Ylarius*) 1230 P (Wo); Roger, William *Hillari* 1275 RH (L), 1283 AssSt; William *Hillary, Illore* 1308–9 ib. Fr *Hilaire, Hilari*, Lat *hilaris* 'cheerful', the name of several saints, in particular St Hilarius of Poitiers (d. 368). The name was popular in France and not uncommon in England. (ii) *Eularia, Eilaria, Yllaria* Trussebut 1200, 1204 Cur; *Eularia* de Hulle 1200 Cur (Beds); *Eularia, Elaria* 1212 Cur (So, L); *Illaria, Ilaria, Hillaria* 1219 AssY. This woman's name is not, as has been suggested, a feminine of *Hilarius*, but *Eulalia*, a latinizing of Greek εὔλαλος 'sweetly-speaking'. It was the name of the patron saint of Barcelona, not uncommon in Spain and France (*Eulalie*), and survives as a French surname in the popular form *Aulaire*. There was a masculine form, probably absorbed by *Hillary*: *Eularie* (nom.) de Hegge 1212 Cur (Y); *Eularius* de Syre 1214 Cur (Sr); *Illarius, Hillarius* de Bechamton' 1208 Cur (So); *Eylarius* de Bachamton 1214 ib. (Ha).

Hillas: v. HILLHOUSE
Hillcoat: v. HELLCAT
Hillen: v. ELION

Hiller: Peter *Hiller* 1432 FrY. 'Dweller on the hill.' cf. HELLER.

Hillers: v. HILLHOUSE
Hillery: v. HILLARY

Hillhouse, Hilhouse, Hillas, Hillers, Hillis, Hellass: Nicholas *del Hellus* 1235 RH (Bk); Grace *Hellhouse* 1598 Bardsley (Essex). 'Dweller at the house on the hill.' cf. BULLAS.

Hilliar: v. HELLIAR
Hilliard: v. HILDYARD

Hilling, Hillings: Robert, Richard *Hilling* 1206, 1212 Cur (Nth, Lei). Probably OE **hylling* 'hill-dweller'. v. also ELION.

Hillis: v. HILLHOUSE

Hillman: John *Hildman* 1327 SRY. 'Dweller by the slope' (v. HEALD) or 'servant of *Hild*'. Also 'hill man'. cf. HELLMAN.

Hillson: (i) Alexander *Hildson* 1332 SRCu. 'Son of *Hild*': (ii) Walter *Hillessone* 1381 SRSf. 'Son of *Hill*.'

Hillyar: *v.* HELLIAR

Hillyard: *v.* HILDYARD

Hilton: Roger *de Hiltun* 1132 Riev; Robert *de Hilton* 1343 FFY; John *Hilton* 1393–4 FFSr. The usual sources of the name are, no doubt, Hilton (Derby, Hunts, Staffs, NRYorks), or Hilltown (Devon), but occasionally a personal name may be involved, cf. Ralph *filius Hilton* 1219 AssY.

Hinchcliffe, Hinchliff, Hinchliffe, Henchcliff, Henchcliffe, Hinchsliff: John *de Hengeclif* 1324 Wak (Y); Agnes *de Hingeclif* 1327 ib.; John *Hyncheclyffe* 1441 ShefA; William *Hynseclif* 1485 FrY; Henry *Henseclyf* 1552 ib.; John *Hinchliffe* 1633 ShefA. From Hinchcliff (WRYorks).

Hinckesman: *v.* HENSMAN

Hinckley, Hinkley: Anfred *de Hinkelai* 1176 P (Lei); Roger *de Hinckelee* 1208 Cur (W); John *de Hynkeley* 1332 SRSt. From Hinckley (Leics).

Hind, Hinde, Hindes, Hinds, Hynd, Hynds: Cristiana, Henry *Hynde* 1285 *Ass* (Ess), 1332 SRSt. OE *hind* 'female of the deer', perhaps 'timid as a hind'. Late examples may be from *Hine*, with excrescent *d* (1520 NED).

Hindley, Hindeley, Hyndley: Simon *de Hindelay* 1219 AssY; Robert *de Hindeley* 1243 AssDu; John *Hyndeley* 1340–1450 GildC. From Hindley (Lancs), or Hiendley (WRYorks).

Hindson: John *Hyndson* 1493 LLB L. 'Son of the hind.'

Hine, Hines, Hyne, Hynes: William, Robert *le Hyne* 1240 Eynsham (O), 1254 AssSo, 1256 AssNb. ME *hine* 'hind, servant'. *v.* MED.

Hingle: *v.* INGALL, INGELL

Hinkins: *v.* HENKIN

Hinsull: *v.* INSALL

Hinton: Robert *de Hintona* 1086 ICC; Thomas *de Hyneton*' 1230 Cur (Do); Thomas *Hynton* 1385 FFEss. From one or other of the many places of this name.

Hipkin, Hipkins, Hipkiss: cf. *Hyppe* 1275 RH (Nf); Lefsius *Hippe* 1275 RH (Sf); John *Hipecok*' 1243 AssSo. *Hyppe* is an unvoiced form of *Hibb*, from *Heb, Hipkin*, like *Hipecok*, a diminutive.

Hipperson: *v.* IBBERSON

Hipworth: *v.* HEPWORTH

Hircock: *v.* HERCOCK

Hird: *v.* HERD

Hirst: *v.* HERST

Hiscocks: *v.* HITCHCOCK

Hislop: *v.* HASLOP

Histead: *v.* HIGHSTEAD

Hitch, Hitches, Hytch: *Hiche* de Sadinton 1198 FrLeic; *Hicche uenator* 1202 P (Hu); Walter *Hicch* 1279 RH (Hu); Stephen *Hiche* 13th Lewes (Nf); John *Hyches* 1319 AD iv (Hu). *Hich*, a pet-form of *Richard*, was common in the 13th century, particularly in Cheshire.

Hitchcock, Hitchcox, Hitchcott, Hiscock, Hiscocks, Hiscox, Hiscott, Hiscutt, Hiskett: *Hichecoc* 1260 AssCh; *Hichecok* 1275 RH (Y); *Higecok*

Trente 1310 LLB D; Richard *Hichecokes* 1327 SRWo; John *Higecok* 1327 SRC; William *Hygecok*, *Hichecok* 1329, 1360 AD i, vi (Do); Nicholas *Hekkox* son of Abraham *Heskcok* 1636 Bardsley. A diminutive of *Hich*. *v.* HITCH.

Hitchcoe: For HITCHCOCK. *v.* ALCOE.

Hitchen, Hitchens, Hitcheon, Hitchin, Hitchins, Hitching, Hitchings, Hichens: (i) *Hichoun* 1286 AssCh; John *Hichun* 1279 RH (O). *Hich-un*, a diminutive of *Hich*. cf. Robert *Hichel* 1327 SRWo. *v.* HITCH. (ii) John *Hychen* 1332 SRWa. *v.* HITCH, GEFFEN. (iii) Geoffrey *de Hicchen* 1321 LLB E. From Hitchin (Herts).

Hitchman: Richard, William *Hicheman* 1238 AssSo, 1279 RH (O). 'Servant of *Hich*.'

Hitchmough: Robert *Hichmughe* or *Hytch-moughe* 1584 Oxon (La). 'Brother-in-law of *Hich*.' cf. HICKMOTT, WATMOUGH.

Hite: *v.* HEIGHT

Hix: *v.* HICKS

Hixson: *v.* HICKSON

Hoad, Hoath: John *del Hoth* 1275 RH (Nf); Simon *atte Hothe* 1296 SRSx, 1317 AssK. From Hoath (Kent), or 'dweller on the heath', from OE *hāþ*, ME *hōth*, a by-form of *hæþ* 'heath', a Kent and Sussex form.

Hoadley: William *de Hodlegh* 1296 SRSx. From Hoathly (Sussex).

Hoar, Hoare, Hore: (i) William *Hore* 1188 BuryS (Sf); Robert, William *le Hore* 1203 AssSt, 1221 AssWo. OE *hār* 'hoar, grey-haired'. (ii) Gilbert *de Hore* 1200 P (Sx); Richard *de la Hore* 1230 P (D). From Ore (Sussex) or 'dweller by the bank', OE *ōra*. *v.* NOAR.

Hoather, Hother: 'Dweller on the *hoath* or heath.' *v.* HOAD and cf. HEATHER.

Hob, Hobb, Hobbes, Hobbis, Hobbiss, Hobbs: *Hobbe* Litel 1176 P (Sa); *Hobb(e)* 1198 Cur (Nth), P (Y), 1205 Cur (Wo); Osbert, Ralph *Hobbe* 1204 P (R), 1230 P (Wa). Agnes *Hobbis* 1279 RH (Hu); Isabella *Hobbes* 1327 SRWo. *Hobb*, a pet-form of *Robert*, rhymed on *Rob*.

Hobart: *v.* HUBERT

Hobbins: (i) Henry, Alice *Hobben* 1327 SRWo, 1332 SRWa. *v.* HOB, GEFFEN. (ii) Richard *Hobbyn* 1408 PN Ess 53. A diminutive of *Hobb*. *Hobbins* may have become *Hobbiss*.

Hobday, Hobdey: William *Hobday* 1469 KentW. 'Servant of *Hobb*', '*Hobb* the servant', *v.* DAY.

Hobgen: John *Hobjohn* 1526 SxWills. A combination of *Hobb* and *John*, perhaps 'rustic, boorish John'. cf. *Hobhouchin*, a name for the owl (1682 NED).

Hobkinson: *v.* HOPKINSON

Hobkirk: *v.* HOPKIRK

Hoblin, Hobling, Hoblyn: *Hobelyn* Flemyng 1373 ColchCt; William *Hobelyn* 1374 ib. *Hob-el-in*, a double diminutive of *Hob*.

Hobson, Hopson: John *Hobbessone* 1327 *SR* (Ess); John *Hobsone* 1327 Wak (Y). 'Son of *Hob*.'

Hochkins: *v.* HODGKIN

Hockaday, Hockerday: John *Hockedeȝ* Hy 2 Suckling (Sf); Simon *Hochede* 1206 P (Bk);

Henry *Hokedey* 1296 SRSx. ME *Hocedei, Hokedey*, the second Tuesday after Easter Sunday, in former times an important term-day, on which rents were paid, etc., Hock-day and Michaelmas dividing the rural year into its summer and winter halves. From the 14th century it was also a popular festival. A name for one born at this time. cf. PENTECOST, CHRISTMAS, MIDWINTER.

Hockeridge: *v.* HOCKRIDGE

Hockold: Adam *de Hockewald* 1275 RH (Nf). From Hockwold (Norfolk).

Hockridge, Hockeridge: Stephen *de Hokeregge* 1275 RH (K); Maurice *de Haukerigge* 1333 PN D 365. From Hawkridge (Kent), from OE *hōc*, or from Hawkeridge (Devon, Wilts) or Hawkridge (Devon), from 'hawk'. Hawkridge in Morebath is *Hockerige* in 1596.

Hodd, Hoddes, Hodds, Hodes, Hood, Hoods: Osbernus *Hod* c1100–30 OEByn (D); Walter *Hod* c1200 ArchC 6; Gilbert *Hodde* 1225 AssSo; Robert *Hood (Hod)* 1230 P (Y); Philip *Hodde, Hudde* 1305 LoCt; Willeame *Hood* 1320 Merton (O); John *Hoddes* 1524 SRSf. OE *hōd*, ME *hod, hud, hood, hodde* 'hood'. A maker of hoods. Hamo *Hode* is also called *Hodere* (1317 AssK). Occasionally *Hood* is local, from Hood in Rattery (Devon): Jurdan *de Hode* 1242 Fees (D).

Hodder: John *le Hoder* 1220 Cur (Ess); William *Hudere* 1279 RH (C). A derivative of OE *hōd* 'hood', a maker of hoods. cf. HODD, HOTTER. John *Hoder* (1361 ColchCt) is also called *Hodmaker* and *Hodman*.

Hodge, Hodges: *Hogge* 1208 FFL, 1212 Cur (Cu); William *Hogge* 1297 MinAcctCo; Alicia *Hogges* 1327 SRSo; William *Hodges* 1524 SRSf. A pet-form of *Roger*. Chaucer's cook 'highte *Hogge* of Ware' is invoked 'Now tell on, *Roger* . . .'

Hodgeon, Hodgens, Hodgins: *v.* HODGSON

Hodgett, Hodgetts: William *Hogettes* 1408 AssCh (St). A diminutive of *Hodge*.

Hodgkin, Hodgkins, Hodgkiess, Hodgkiss, Hadgkiss, Hodgskin, Hodgskins, Hochkins, Hotchkin, Hotchkis, Hotchkiss: Robert *Hochekyn* 1327 SRSt; John *Hogekyn* 1453 AD ii (Pembroke); Richard *Hoggekynes* 1445 AD vi (Nf); William *Hochekys* 1470 AD iv (Sa); Robert *Hodgekin* 1524 SRSf; Charles *Hodgskines* t. Eliz Bardsley; John *Hotchkis* 1690 DKR 41 (Sa). *Hogge-kin*, a diminutive of *Hodge*.

Hodgkinson, Hodgkison: John *Hogkynson* 1459 PrGR; Ewan *Hodg(e)kynson* 1582 ib. 'Son of *Hodgkin*.'

Hodgson, Hodgshon, Hodgens, Hodgin, Hodgins, Hodgeon, Hodson: Henry, William *Hoggeson(e)* 1325 LaCt, 1381 PTY; John *Hodgeson* 1525 FrY; Thomas *Hodshon* 1528 GildY; Richard *Hodson* 1582 PrGR; James *Hodgshon* 1591 LaWills; William *Hodgson* 1602 PrGR; Elizeus *Hodgeon* 1682 ib. 'Son of *Hodge*.' In PrGR, *Hogeson* is common before 1582 and *Hodson* and *Hodgeon* are clearly the same name.

Hodkin: *Huddekyn* 1324 LaCt. 'Little Hugh.' *v.* HUDD.

Hodkinson, Hodkison, Hodskinson: Ellen *Hodkinson*, Richard *Hodskinson* 1626, 1661 LaWills. 'Son of *Hodkin* or of *Hodgkin*.'

Hodson: William *Hodson*, Robert *Odeson* 1379 PTY; John *Hodessone* 1385 LLB H. 'Son of *Odo*.' *v.* also HODGSON.

Hoe(s): *v.* HOW

Hogarth: *v.* HOGGARD

Hogben, Hogbin: Thomas *Huckebone* 1479 ArchC 39; Robert *Hucbone* 1500 ib.; Peter *Hugbone* 1549 ib.; John *Hogben* 1588 ib. 35. From *huck-bone* 'the hip-bone or haunch-bone', hucklebone, found in Craven dialect (Yorks) as *hug-baan*. The origin of *huck* is obscure, but it may be from a Teutonic root **huk-* 'to be bent'. cf. ON *huka* 'to crouch, sit bent, sit on the haunches' and *huck-backed* 'hump-backed, crump-shouldered' (1631 NED). This Kentish surname is, no doubt, synonymous with the Scottish *Cruickshank*.

Hogg, Hogge: Ailmer, William *Hog* 1079 Rams (Hu), 1174–80 StP (Lo); Alice, William *le Hog* 1279 RH (O), 1296 SRSx; Adam *le Hogge* 1332 SRLa. OE *hogg* 'pig'.

Hoggar, Hogger: John *le Hoggere* 1327 SR (Ess); William *Hogir* 1327 SRSx. A derivative of OE *hogg*; 'hog-herd'.

Hoggard, Hoggart, Hoggarth, Hogarth, Hoggett: William *Hoggehird* 1279 AssNb; Richard *le Hoghird* 1327 SRY; John *Hoggard* 1461 FrY; John *Hoggerd* 1509 ib.; Henry *Hogget, Hogged* 1627 Bardsley. OE *hogg* and *hierde*, 'swine-herd'. *v.* HOGG.

Hoghton: *v.* HOUGHTON

Hoile, Hoiles: *v.* HOYLE

Holbem, Holben: William, Walter *de Hol(e)bem(e)* 1242 Fees (D), 1296 SRSx. From Holbeam (Devon), Holbeanwood in Ticehurst, or Holban's Fm in Heathfield (Sussex).

Holbert, Holbird, Hulbert, Hulburd: *Holbertus venator* 1168 ArchC 5; William, John *Holdebert* 1205 P (Wa), 1219 AssY; John *Hulberd* 1524 SRSf. These surnames, rare in early sources, probably derive from an unrecorded OE **Holdbeorht* 'gracious-bright'. Old English names in *Hold-* are rare and late, only *Holdburh* (f), *Holdfrið* (f), and *Holdwine* being recorded in independent use.

Holbrook, Holbrooke, Houlbrook, Houlbrooke: Richard *de Holebroc* 1189 Sol; William *atte Holebrok* 1296 SRSx; John *Holebrok* 1327 SR (Ess). From Holbrook (Derby, Dorset, Suffolk), or 'dweller by the brook in the hollow'.

Holcombe, Holcomb, Holcom: Brihtmer *æt Holacumbe* c1100–30 OEByn; Adam *de Holecumb* 1256 AssSo; John, Thomas *Holcombe* 1525 SRSx. From Holcombe (Devon, Dorset, Glos, Lancs, Oxon, Som).

Holcroft, Holdcroft, Houlcroft, Houldcroft: Robert *de Holecroft* 1246 AssLa; John *Holecroft* 1327 SR (Ess); Richard *Holdcroft* 1569 Bardsley. From Holcroft (Lancs).

Hold, Hould: *Ysopa Hold* 905 ASC A; Aluredus *Holde* 1198 P (K); Elyas *Lehold* 1205 ChR (W);

Caterina *le Holde* 1327 SRSf. ON *hǫldr* 'a nobleman in rank beneath a *jarl*'.

Holdam: *v.* HOLDHAM

Holdane: *v.* HALDANE

Holden, Holdin, Houlden, Houldin, Howlden: Robert *de Holden* 1285 AssLa; William *Holeden* 1327 SRSx; Richard *atte Holdene* 1331 FFK. From Holden (Lancs, WRYorks) or from residence in a hollow valley (OE *holh, denu*).

Holder, Houlder: Geoffrey *le Holder* 1262 MEOT (Herts); Robert *le Holdere* 1274 RH (Gl). A derivative of OE *haldan* 'to hold', an occupier, possessor, probably a tenant or occupier of land (a1400 MED). *v.* also HELDER.

Holderer: Very rare. Probably for HOLDER.

Holdford, Holdforth: *v.* HOLFORD

Holdham, Holdam, Holdom, Holdum: Robert *Holdom* 1477 FrY. Probably for OLDHAM.

Holdman: Thomas *Holdeman* 1312 ColchCt. Either 'servant of the noble' (*v.* HOLD) or for OLDMAN. *Aldman* and *Holdman* interchange in 1240 *Ass* (Sf).

Holdroyd: *v.* OLDROYD, HOLROYD

Holdship: William *Holshep* 1327 SRWo. OE *holdscipe* 'loyalty'.

Holdsworth, Holesworth, Holsworth, Houldsworth, Houdsworth, Hallworth, Hallsworth: John *de Haldeworth* 1273 RH (Y); John *de Halworth*, Richard *de Haldeworthe* 1379 PTY; Joshua *Houldsworth* 1593 Oxon (Y); Robert *Haulsworth* or *Holdsworth* 1595 ib.; Thomas *Haldsworth*, Jenetta *Halsworth* 1616, 1621 RothwellPR (Y); Thomas *Holdsworth* 1639 ib. This appears to be a specifically West Riding surname from either Holdsworth in Eckington or Holdsworth in Ovenden (WRYorks), both originally *Haldeworth* with a late intrusive *s*.

Hole, Holes, Houle: William *de la Hole* 1200 P (D); Alice *Attehole* 1279 AssNb; Hugh *del Hole* 1296 Wak (Y); John *Houll* 1433 FrY. 'Dweller in the hollow', OE *hol, holh*, dat. *hole*.

Holeman: 'Dweller in the hollow.' cf. Robert *le Holare* 1275 SRWo.

Holeyman: *v.* HOLYMAN

Holford, Holdford, Holdforth, Houlford: Jordan *de Holeford* 1179 P (So); John *de Holeford* 1296 SRSx. From Holford (Som) or Holford Fm in Chailey (Sussex).

Holgate: John *de Holegate* 1200 P (Y); Gommer *de Holgate* 1343 FFY; John *Holgate* 1525 SRSx. From Holgate (WRYorks), or 'dweller by the hollow road'.

Holgreaves, Houlgrave: Roger *de Holingref* 1297 SRY. From Hollingreave (WRYorks).

Holiday, Holladay: *v.* HALIDAY

Holland, Hollands: Begmundus *de Holande* c975 LibEl (Ess); William *de Holaund* 1246 AssLa. From Holland (Essex, Lancs, Lincs).

Hollaway: *v.* HOLLOWAY

Holleman: *v.* HOLYMAN

Hollen(s), Holles, Hollis: *v.* HOLLIES

Hollest: *v.* HOLLIST

Holley, Holly: (i) Leouuine, Alfwinus *Holege*

c1095 Bury (Sf), 1166 P (Nf); John *Holeghe* 12th ELPN; John *Holey, Holley* 1332 SRCu. OE *hol, ēage* 'hollow-eye'. (ii) Adam William *de Holleye* 1327 SRSf. 'Dweller by the clearing in the hollow', OE *hol* and *lēah*. *v.* also HOLLIES.

Holleyman: *v.* HOLYMAN

Holliday: *v.* HALIDAY

Hollier, Hollyer, Hullyer: Robert *le Holyere* 1309 SRBeds; Adam *Holiere* 1327 *SR* (Ess). OFr *holier, huler*, a variant of *horier, hurier*, ME *holer, holyer, hullor* 'whoremonger, debauchee'.

Hollies, Holles, Hollis, Holliss, Hollen, Hollens, Holling, Hollings, Hollins, Hollay, Holley, Holly: Adam *atte Holies, atte Holye* 1275, 1327 SRWo; Robert *del Holins* 1297 Wak (Y); Nicholas *del Holyn* 1301 SRY; John *in the Holis* 1327 SRSf; Richard *del Holyes* 1332 SRSt; John *Holyn* 1428 FA (Wo); John *Holyns* 1431 FA (Wo); William *Holling* 1649 FrY. Dweller by the 'holly, holm-oak', OE *holegn, holen*, ME *holi(e), holin. v.* also HOLLEY.

Holliman: *v.* HOLYMAN

Hollingrake, Hollindrake, Hollinrake, Hollenrake: Adam *del Holirakes* 1275 Wak (Y); John *of Holynrakes* 1315 ib.; Anna *Hollenrecke* 1644 RothwellPR (Y). From some small spot in the West Riding.

Holling(s): *v.* HOLLIES

Hollingshead, Hollingshed, Hollinshead: Richard *de Holineside* c1220 FeuDu; John *del Holynshede* 1408 Bardsley (Ch). From Hollingside or Holmside (Durham).

Hollins: *v.* HOLLIES

Hollinshead: *v.* HOLLINGSHEAD

Holliss: *v.* HOLLIES

Hollist, Hollest: Alice *de Holhurst* 1296 SRSx. From Hollist House in Easebourne (Sussex).

Holliwell: *v.* HALLIWELL

Hollman: *v.* HOLMAN

Hollock, Hollocks, Hollox, Holock: Walter *de Holoc* 1208 ChR (Sf); Walter *Hollock* 1327 SRSo; John *ate Holock'* 1332 SRSr; John *del Hollokes* 1549 SxWills. 'Dweller by a little hollow', OE *holoc*, a diminutive of *hol*.

Holloman: *v.* HOLYMAN

Hollow, Hollows: Peter *in le Holwe* 1279 RH (C); Thomas *de Hollowe* 1327 SRWo. 'Dweller in the hollow', OE *holh*.

Holloway, Hollaway, Hollway, Hollwey, Holoway: Richard *de Holeweia* 1130 P (D); John *de la Holeweye* 1275 AssSo; John *Holewey* 1279 RH (O); John *del Hollewaye* 1308 Wak (Y); Hugh *atte Holewey* 1310 LLB D; Edward *Hollaway* 1674 HTSf. 'Dweller by a sunken-road', OE *holh, weg*.

Hollowbread: *v.* HALLOWBREAD

Hollowell: *v.* HALLIWELL

Hollox: *v.* HOLLOCK

Hollway, Hollwey: *v.* HOLLOWAY

Hollyer: *v.* HOLLIER

Hollyhock: *v.* HOLYOAK

Hollyman: *v.* HOLYMAN

Hollyoak: *v.* HOLYOAK

Holm, Holme, Holmes, Holms: Roger *de Holm*

a1186 Seals (Lei); Urkell' *de Holmes* 1219 AssY; John *atte Holme* 1296 SRSx; William *del Holmes* 1327 SRDb, 1332 SRCu'. From residence near a piece of flat land in a fen or by a piece of land partly surrounded by streams (ON *holmr*). ME *holm* also derives from OE *hole(g)n*, ME *holin*, *holm* 'holly, holm-oak' which survives in Holne (Devon) and Holme (Dorset, WRYorks). *v.* also HULM, HOME, HUME.

Holman, Hollman: John *Holman, Holeman* 1327 *SR* (Ess). OE *holh* and *mann* 'dweller by a hollow'.

Holmer, Homer: (i) Andrew, Robert *de Hol(e)-mere* 1227 AssBk, 1279 RH (O), 1327 SRSf. From Holmer (Bucks, Hereford) or 'dweller by a pool in the hollow' (OE *holh, mere*) as at Homer (Devon). (ii) John *Holmar'* 1296 SRSx; Richard *le Holmare* 1332 SRSr; William *le Holmere* 1340 MESO (Ha); Thomas *Holmer*, Edward *Homer* 1603 SRWo. 'Dweller by a holly-bush' (OE *holen*, ME *holm*), or on flat land near water (ME *holm*, ON *holmr*). *v.* HOLLIES, HOLM, HOMER.

Holmwood: *v.* HOMEWOOD

Holock: *v.* HOLLOCK

Holoway: *v.* HOLLOWAY

Holroyd, Holroyde, Holdroyd, Howroyd: Thomas, Andrew *Holerode* 1296 SRSx; Gilbert *de Holrode* 1327 SRSf; George *Holroyd* 1709 FrY. 'Dweller at the clearing in the hollow.'

Holt, Hoult: Hugo *de Holte* 1185 Templars (K); Simon *del Holt* 1230 P (Wa); Walter *in the Holte* 1260 MELS (So); Hugh *atte Holte* 1268 PN Sr 175. From Holt (Dorset, Hants, Leics, Norfolk, Staffs, Warwicks) or from residence in or near a wood (OE *holt*).

Holtby, Houltby: William *de Holtebi* 1208 Pl (Y); William, John *de Holteby* 1303 FFY, 1396 AssL. From Holtby (NRYorks).

Holter: Richard *le Holtar'* 1327 SRSx. 'Dweller by the wood.'

Holtham, Holtom, Holttum, Holtum: Matilda, Alan *de Holtham* 1200 P (L), 1256 AssNb. 'Dweller at the enclosure in the wood', OE *holt, hamm*. Richard *de Holtham* 1327 *SR* (Ha) came from Holtham in East Tisted (Hants). *v.* also HOTHAM

Holtie: William *de Holetye* 1296 SRSx. From Holtye Fm (Sussex).

Holway: *v.* HOLLOWAY

Holyday: *v.* HALIDAY

Holyman, Holeyman, Holleman, Holleyman, Holliman, Holloman, Hollyman: Roger *Haliman* 1212 Fees (Berks); William *Holyman* 1276 RH (L); Richard *Hollyman* Eliz Bardsley. OE *halig, mann* 'holy man', a nickname, probably pejorative. cf. Richard *Holifader* 1327 SRSo, Roger *Holymoder* Hy 3 Colch (Herts).

Holyoak, Holyoake, Hollyoak, Hollyoake, Hollyhock: Godric *de Haliac* Hy 2 Seals (Sf); Gerard *de Haliach* 1188 P (Lei); Peter *de la Holyok* 1300 MELS (Wo). From Holy Oakes (Leics) or from residence near a holy-oak or gospel-oak, an oak marking a parish-boundary where a stoppage was made for the reading of the Gospel for the day

when beating the bounds during the Rogation Days.

Home, Homes: Robert *del Houme* 1222 Cur (Nf); Alan *de Home* 1275 SRWo; Henry, William *Home* 1279 RH (O); Walter *of the home*, John *atte Home* 1327 SRWo; Andrue *Holmes*, John *Home*, Richard *Homes* 1524 SRSf. 'Dweller by a *holm* or by a holm-oak.' *v.* HOLM, HUME. The Scottish *Home* and *Hume* derive from the barony of Home in Berwickshire: William *of Home* 1268, Alexander *de Hume* 1408 (Black).

Homer, Homere: (i) Identical with HOLMER. (ii) John *le Heaumer* 1220 Cur (Lo); Richard *le Heumer* 1284 LLB A; Mannekin *le Haumer* 1298 ib. B. OFr *heaumier, heumier* 'maker of helmets'.

Homeward: Peter *de Homewerth* 1296 SRSx; John *atte Homewerthe*, Robert *Homworth* 1332 ib. From residence at a homestead by the river-meadows (OE *hamm, weorð*).

Homewood: William *atte Homewode* 1279 PN Sr 331; Simon *atte Homwode* 1296 SRSx. From residence by a 'wood near the manor-house', OE **hām-wudu*, surviving as Home Wood, Holmwood, and probably also as HOMEWARD.

Homfray: *v.* HUMPHREY

Hond: *v.* HAND

Hone, Hones: Walkelin *de Hone* 1200 P (Ha); John, Thomas *Hone* 1276, 1279 RH (Berks, O); Godfrey *de la hone* 1296 SRSx; James *atte Hone* 1342 MELS (So). 'Dweller by some prominent stone or rock', OE *hān*, often a boundary-stone.

Honebone: *v.* HONEYBOURNE

Honer: Robert *le honer* 1230 P (Lo). A derivative of OE *hān* 'stone' in the sense 'whetstone' (c1325 NED), a sharpener of tools, a grinder or honer (1826 NED).

Honex: *v.* HUNWICK

Honey: Geoffrey *Hony* 1275 SRWo; Richard *Honey* 1279 RH (C); Robert *le Hony* 1296 SRSx. OE *hunig* 'honey', used as a term of endearment, 'sweetheart, darling' (a1375 MED).

Honeybourne, Honeyburne, Honeyban, Honeybun, Honebone, Hunnybun: Robert *de Hunuburn'* 1221 AssGl; William *de Honybourn'* 1327 SRWo; Thomas *Honeybunn* 1802 PN Mx 55. From Cow Honeybourne (Glos) or Church Honeybourne (Worcs), pronounced *Hunnybun*.

Honeycomb, Honeycombe, Unicum, Unicume: Robert *de Honicomb'* 1327 SRSo. 'Dweller in the "honey", pleasant, fertile valley.'

Honeyman, Honneyman: (i) Robert, Everard *Huniman* 1199 FrLeic, 1235 Fees (Nth); Osbert *Honiman* 1279 RH (O); John *Honyman* 1296 SRSx. OE *hunig* and *mann*, 'seller of honey'. cf. Richard *Honymanger* 1382 AD i (W). (ii) *Hunman* 1066 DB (Bk); *Hunemannus* 12th Rams (C); Gillebertus *filius Honemann'* 1199 FF (W); John *Huneman* 1260 AssC; Thomas *Honeman* 1275 RH (Sf). OE *Hūnmann*.

Honiatt, Honiett, Onyett: William *Honiet*, Reginald *Honyet* c1280 SRWo; Peter *Onyett*, *Honyot* 1279 RH (O), 1327 SRWo; John *Oniet*,

Roger *Onyott* 1327 SRSo. OE **Hungēat* 'young bear-Geat'.

Honick: *v.* HUNWICK

Honneyball, Honneybell: *v.* HUNNABLE

Hood: *v.* HODD

Hoodlass, Hoodless, Huddless, Hudlass, Hudless: William *Hodeles* 1292 FrY; Robert *Hudelesse* 1545 ib.; Thomas *Hoodles* 1568 SRSf; William *Hudlass* 1713 FrY. 'Hoodless', one who did not wear a hood. cf. HODD.

Hoof, Hooff: *v.* HOW

Hook, Hooke, Hookes, Huk, Huke, Huck, Hucke, Hucks: (i) Halwun *Hoce* 1050-71 OEByn (D); Hervicus, Richard *Hoc* 1218 AssL, 1230 P (Berks); John *Hook* 1327 *SR* (Ess); Adam *Huke* 1524 SRSf. OE **Hōca,* or OE *Hōc,* from *hōc* 'hook', probably denoting a man with a hooked or bent figure. Or metonymic for *Hooker.* (ii) Robert *de Hoke* 1192 P (K); Gilbert *de Huc* 1219 AssY; Geoffrey *de la Hoke* 1242 Fees (D); Gervase *ad Hokys* 1244 Rams (Beds); Richard *del Hokes* 1277 Wak (Y); John *atte Houke* 1332 SRSr. From Hook (Hants, Surrey, Lancs, Wilts, WRYorks), Hooke (Dorset), or from residence near a bend or hill-spur (OE *hōc*). This is the common source.

Hooker: Osmundus cognomento *Hocere* c975 LibEl; William, Osbert *Hoker(e)* 1199 P (Nf), 1219 AssL; John *le Hoker, le Houker* 1327, 1332 SRSx; Richard *Hooker* 1558 SxWills. OE, ME *hōcere,* a maker of hooks or an agricultural labourer who uses hooks. Also equivalent to *atte hoke* 'dweller by a hill-spur or bend'.

Hookins, Hookings: *v.* HUKIN

Hooman: *v.* HUMAN

Hooper: Adam, Philip *le Hoper(e)* 1228 Cl (W), 1297 MinAcctCo; William *le Houper* 1327 SRSo; Richard *Hoper,* couper 1367 FrY; Ralph *Hooper* 1444 AD vi (D). A derivative of OE *hōp* 'hoop', a maker or fitter of hoops, cooper.

Hoose: *v.* HOUSE

Hooson, Hoosun: *v.* HUGHSON

Hope, Hopes: Robert *de Hope* 1255 RH (Sa); John *atte hop* 1296 SRSx; Robert *del Hope* 1302 SRY. From Hope (Derby, Salop, NRYorks, etc.), or from residence in or near raised land in a fen, or a small enclosed valley (OE *hop*).

Hopkin, Hopkins, Hopkyns: *Hobekinus* 1224 Cur (St), 1231 Oseney (O); *Hopkyn* 1324 LaCt; William *Hobkyn,* Richard *Hobkyns* 1327 SRWo; William *Hopkyn,* John *Hopkynes* 1327 SRSt. *Hobbe-kin,* a diminutive of *Hobb* (Robert). *v.* HOB.

Hopkinson, Hobkinson: Richard *Hobbekynessone* 1354 Putnam (Ch), John *Hopkynson* 1469 FrY. 'Son of *Hobkin.' v.* HOPKIN.

Hopkirk, Hobkirk: James *Hopkirk, Hobkirk* 1574, 1679 Black. From Hopekirk (Roxburghshire), pronounced *Hobkirk.*

Hopper: Waldr', Edric *le Hoppere* 1203 P (W), 1204 Cur (Wo). A derivative of OE *hoppian* 'to hop, leap, dance', a dancer.

Hopping: William *Hopping* 1327 SRSo. Probably OE **hoping* 'dweller in a *hop'. v.* HOPE.

Hopson: *v.* HOBSON

Hopton: Thomas *de Hopeton'* 1196 P (Sf); Robert *de Hopton* 1250 IpmY; William *Hopton* 1478 FFEss. From Hopton (Derby, Hereford, Salop, Suffolk, WRYorks).

Hopwood: William *de Hopwod, de Hopwode* 13th WhC, 1298 AssLa; William *Hopwod'* 1379 PTY; John *Hopwood* 1642 PrD. From Hopwood (Lancs).

Horberry, Horbury: Jordan *de Hordbir'* 1204 AssY. From Horbury (WRYorks). This form confirms Ekwall's alternative etymology, *hordburg* 'treasure-burg'.

Hord: *v.* HERD

Horder: Ælfwine *ðe Hordere* 1001 OEByn (W); Ordric *hordere, þe hordor* 11th (1333) ASCh 220 (Sf); Simon *le Horder* 1225 AssSo. OE *hordere* 'keeper of the hoard or treasure', 'treasurer', 'keeper of provisions'. Ordric was the cellarer of the abbey of Bury St Edmund's. *v.* also HERDER.

Hore: *v.* HOAR

Horlick, Horlock: *v.* HARLOCK

Horn, Horne: (i) Lifwine *Horn* 1066-86 OEByn; Aluuinus *Horne* 1066 DB (Mx); Wulmer, Herui, Robert *Horn* 1166 P (Nf), 1185 Templars (So), 1197 P (Sf). Metonymic for HORNBLOWER or HORNER. (ii) Roger *de Horne* 1208 Cur (Sr); William *de la Horn* 1261 PN Sx 379; Thomas *atte Horne* 1327 SRSo. From Horne (Rutland, Som, Surrey) or from residence near a spur or tongue of land or a bend, OE *horn(a).*

Hornagold, Hornigold: John *Hornyngold* 1524 SRSf; Widow *Hornigold, Hornegold* 1674 HTSf. From Horninghold (Leic).

Hornblow, Hornblower, Horniblow, Orneblow: John, Geofffrey *le Hornblauere, -blawere* 1255, 1285 *Ass* (Ess); Adam *Horneblawer* 1301 SRY. OE *hornblāwere* 'horn-blower'. In the Middle Ages workmen were called to work by the ringing of bells or by a horn. In 1320, at Caernarvon, Walter de la Grene was paid 1*d.* per week 'for blowing the horn' (Building 62). cf. Thomas *Blauhorn* 1303 Pat, Alice *Blawhorn* 1379 PTY.

Hornbuckle: *v.* ARBUCKLE

Hornby: William *de Horneby* 1205 Pl (Y), 1296 SRNb; John *Hornby* 1376 IpmGl. From Hornby (Lancs, Westmorland, NRYorks).

Horner, Hornor: William *le Hornare* 1275 SRWo; Matilda, Clement *le Hornere* 1279 RH (O), 1302 LLB C. A derivative of OE *horn,* a maker of horn spoons, combs, etc. Later, also a maker of musical horns, and also one who blows a horn. Adam *le Horner* 1297 SRY is also called *le Harpour.*

Horniman: *v.* HERNAMAN

Horrabin, Horabin, Horobin: Henrie *Horerobyn* 1596 DWills; William *Horabin* 1783 ib. 'Grey Rabin or Robin', OE *hār* and a pet-name of *Robert.* cf. *Jolyrobin* 1332 SRCu; Agnes *Greyadam* 1297 MinAcctCo.

Horrey: *v.* HURRY

Horridge: (i) Richard *de Hawerugge* 1297 MinAcctCo. From Hawridge (Bucks). (ii) Thomas *de Horewich* 1327 SRDb. From Horwich (Lancs).

(iii) Richard *de Horugg* 1275 RH (D). From one of the five places in Devon named Horridge.

Horrod: Richard *Horhod* 1293 AssSt. 'Grey hood', OE *hār, hōd*.

Horsbrugh, Horsburgh: Symon *de Horsbroc* 1214–49 Black; William *de Horsbrok* 1329 ib. (Peebles); Alexander *Horsbruik* 1550 ib.; *Horsborrough* 1686 ib. From Horsburgh in Innerleithen (Peebles).

Horscraft, Horscroft, Horsecroft: John *de Horscrofte* 1274 RH (Ess); John *atte Horscrofte* 1333 MELS (So). 'Dweller by, or worker at an enclosure for horses.'

Horsegood: *v.* OSGOOD

Horsler: *v.* OSTLER

Horsnail, Horsnaill, Horsnall, Horsnell, Horsenail, Horsenell, Arsnell: Henry, Richard *Horsnail* 1221 AssSa, c1248 Bec (Berks). *Horse-nail*, a horseshoe-nail (1432 MED), frequently mentioned in medieval accounts. Either a maker of these or a nickname for a shoer of horses.

Horst: *v.* HERST

Hort: *v.* HART

Horton: Leofwine Godwines sunu *æt Hortune* c1018 OEByn; Alan *de Hortun* c1160–80 YCh; Richard *de Horton'* 1255 ForNth; William *Hortone* 1334–5 SRK. From one or other of the many places of this name.

Horwich: Robert *de Horwich* 1332 SRLa. From Horwich (Lancs).

Horwick: Walter *de Horewyk* 1327 SRSx. 'Dweller at a muddy dairy-farm', OE *horh, wīc*.

Horwood: Osbert *de Horwude* 1214 Cur (Ha); William *del Horewode* 1332 SRSt. 'Dweller near a muddy wood', as at Horwood (Bucks, Devon).

Hosbons: *v.* HUSBAND, OSBORN

Hosburn: *v.* OSBORN

Hos(e)good: *v.* OSGOOD

Hosey: *v.* HUSSEY

Hosier: William *Husier* 1180 Oseney (O); John *le Huser* 1182–7 Clerkenwell (Lo); Nicholas, Yuo *le hosier* 1197 P (Lo, Y); Alexander *le Hoser* 1200 Cur (Sx). A derivative of OE *hosa* 'hose', dealer or maker of stockings and socks (1381 MED). Early *husier* points to an OFr **hosier*. cf. OFr *heuse* (*huese, house, hose*) 'boot', hence 'shoe-maker'.

Hosken, Hoskin, Hosking, Hoskings, Hoskins, Hoskyns, Hoskison, Hoskisson: *Osekin* 1274 RH (Lo); Robert *Osekin* ib.; Peter *Osekyn* 1306 FFEss; Thomas *Hoskyns* 1463 AD vi (Berks); William *Hoskyn* 1472 KentW. A diminutive of *Os-*, a short form of such names as *Ōsgōd, Ōsbeorn, Ōsmǣr*, etc.

Hosker: *Osgarus* de Bedeford 1066 DB (Beds); Robert *Hoseger* 1199 FF (R); William *Hosker* 1375 ColchCt. OE *Ōsgār* 'god-spear'.

Hosler: *v.* OSLAR

Hosmer: *v.* OSMER

Hossell: William *del Hostel, del Ostel* 1222 Cur (Do); John *del Hostell* 1332 SRCu. OFr *ostel, hostel* 'lodging, inn', hence inn-keeper. cf. OSTLER. William was a brother of the Abbot of Ford and may have been responsible for the abbey's entertainment of guests.

Host, Hoste, Ost: Elias, John *le host* 1254 AssSo, 1279 RH (C); Richard *le Ost, Lost* 13th Guisb (Y). OFr *oste, hoste* 'host, guest'; an inn-keeper (c1290 NED).

Hoster: Stephen *Hodestre* 1379 AssEss. A feminine form of HODDER. A rare surname. cf. BAXTER.

Hostler, Hosteller: *v.* OSTLER

Hotchen, Hotchin: *v.* HUTCHIN

Hotchkin, Hotchkiss: *v.* HODGKIN

Hotham, Holtham: Robert *de Hotham* 1202 AssL; Walter *de Hothum* 1327 SRY; John *Hotham* 1381 LoPleas. Usually from Hotham (ERYorks), but occasionally perhaps from Holtham or Hougham (Lincs). *v.* also HOLTHAM.

Hother: *v.* HOATHER

Hotson: *v.* HUDSON

Hott: Robert, Geoffrey *Hot* 1195 P (Y), 1275 SRWo; William *Hotte* 1327 SRSf. OFr *hotte* 'basket' (a1400 MED). 'Basket-maker.' *v.* HOTTER and cf. BANNISTER.

Hotter: William, John *le Hottere* 1275 SRWo, 1331 LLB E. A derivative of OFr *hotte* 'basket', a basket-maker. cf. HOTT. Hotters (*hottarii* 1284, *hottatores* 1295) were also carriers of wicker panniers (*hotti* 1208, *hottes de wekere* 1441) full of sand for making mortar. *v.* Building 353–4.

Hottot: Hugo *de Hotot* 1086 DB (C); William *hotot, de hotot* 1148 Winton (Ha). From Hottot-les-Bagues or Hottot-en-Auge (Calvados). *v.* OEByn.

Houchen, Houchin: *v.* HUTCHIN

Houdsworth: *v.* HOLDSWORTH

Houf, Hough: *v.* HOW

Hougham, Huffam: William *de Huham* 1207 P (K). From Hougham (Kent), formerly spelled *Huffam* (Lower).

Houghton, Hoghton, de Hoghton, Howton: William *de Hoctona, de Hohton'* 1115 Winton (Ha), 1208 Cur (Sx); Symon *de Howtone* 1279 RH (C). From one of the Houghtons.

Houlbrook(e): *v.* HOLBROOK

Hould: *v.* HOLD

Houl(d)croft: *v.* HOLCROFT

Houlden, Houldin: *v.* HOLDEN

Houlder: *v.* HOLDER

Houldershaw: *v.* OLDERSHAW

Houldsworth: *v.* HOLDSWORTH

Houle: *v.* HOLE

Houlford: *v.* HOLFORD

Houlgrave: *v.* HOLGREAVES

Hoult: *v.* HOLT

Houltby: *v.* HOLTBY

Hound: Bonde *Hund* 1166 P (Nf); Alice *le Hound* 1327 SRSf. OE *hund* 'hound, dog'.

House, Hows, Howse, Hoose: Simon *Hus* 1226 Eynsham (O); Geoffrey *de la House*, Richard *Hous* 1279 RH (Hu, O); Walter *del Hus* 1289 AssCh; William *atte House* 1331 FFK; Nicholas *Howse*, Robert *Howes* 1524 SRSf. One employed at 'the house' (OE *hūs*), probably a religious house, convent (a1160 MED). *House* and *Howse* may sometimes be for *Howes*.

Household: William, Richard *Housold* 1279 RH (Hu), 1327 SRC. Metonymic for *Householder* 'one who occupies a house as his own dwelling' (c1387–95 MED).

Houseman, Housman: John *Houseman* 1365 ColchCt. *v.* HOUSE.

Houser: *v.* HOUSE, HOUSEMAN

Houston, Houstoun: Finlay *of Huwitston*, alias Finlawe *de Hustone* 1296 Black; John *de Howistone* 1406 ib. (Paisley); Patrick *de Huyston* 1415 ib. (Glasgow); Alexander *Howstoun* 1460 ib. From the barony of Houston (Lanark).

Hovell, Hovil: *v.* HAVILL

How, Howe, Howes, Hows, Hoe, Hoes, Hoo, Heugh, Hough, Hoof, Hooff, Houf, Houfe, Huff, Hughf, Hughff: William *de Ho* 1121–48 Bury (Ess); Eustace *de Hou* 1190 P (Ess); Alured *de la Ho* 1199 P (Wo); Benedict *de Ho, de Hoes', de Howe*, Marjoria *de Howes* (his wife) 1211–12 Cur (Lei); Walter *de Howes, de Hou, de Hoes* 1212 Cur (Nt); Herebertus *Alahoge* 1240 Rams (Nf); Gilbert *ate How* 1296 SRSx; William *ate Howes* 1327 SRC; Thomas *de Hoo* 1332 SRSx; Henry *del Hoe* 1332 SRSt; William *de Huff* 1379 PTY; William *Hough* 1564 Bardsley; Thomas *Hoofe* 1626 FrY; Arthur *Houfe* 1743 ib. OE *hōh* 'heel', 'projecting ridge of land', was common in place-names in the sense of 'a spur of a hill', 'steep ridge', or 'a slight rise'. It is especially common in Bedfordshire and Northants, fairly so in Suffolk, Essex, Herts and Bucks, and very common in Northumberland and Durham. The nominative singular gives *Hough*, in Scotland and Northern England *Heugh*. The dative singular *hō* becomes *hoo* or *hoe*, a later form *hōge* giving *howe*. From the nominative plural *hōs* we have *hose* and from the later *hōgas*, *howes*. The surname may derive from Hoe (Norfolk), Hoo (Kent), Hooe (Devon, Sussex), Hose (Leics), Heugh (Durham, Northumb), Hough (Ches, Derby), often pronounced *Hoof*, *Huff*, or from residence near a *hōh*. *Howe* may also be from ON *haugr* 'mound, hill' and without other evidence cannot be distinguished from *howe* 'ridge'. It is certainly the origin of Howe (Norfolk) and of Howe Hill in Kirkburn (ERYorks), near which there is a tumulus beside which lived Robert *atte Hou* in 1333 (PN ERY 166). *Howes* often refers to groups of tumuli. *How* is also a form of *Hugh*, and *Howes* of *Hughes* and *House*.

Howard, Howerd, Heward, Hewart, Huard, Huart: (i) *Huardus, Houart* 1086 DB (He, Lei, Sf, W); Willelmus *filius Huward* 1170 P (Nb); *Huwardus, Huardus de Bikeleg'* 1214–19 Cur (D); *Huart de Noerel* 1216 PatR (Ess); *Heward de Horewell* 1279 RH (C); Geoffrey *Hohard* 1194 P (Nf); Geoffrey *Huard* 1209 P (Nf); John *Huward* 1279 RH (O); Robert, John *Heward* 1313 Wak (Y), 1337 ColchCt. OFr *Huard* from OG *Hugihard* 'heart-brave'. As *Hugh* appears in ME as both *How* and *Hew*, this is the origin of *Heward* and a source of *Howard* but there has been confusion with OG *Howard* below, the cognate *Haward* of Norse origin, and also with *Hayward*. (ii) *Houar-*

dus 1066 DB (Ess); *Howard* 1101–7 Holme (Nf); Willelmus *filius Howard* 1188 BuryS (Sf); *Owardus, Houwardus, Howardus* (identical) 1221–2 Cur (Sf); Geoffrey *Houward* 1210 Cur (C); Robert, William *Howard* 1221 ElyA (Nf), 1312 ColchCt. OG *Howard, Howart* 'high or chief warden'. Confused with *Haward*, which is sometimes found for the Norfolk *Howard*. cf. 'my Lord *Haward*' (1503), 'Henry *Hawarde*, Esq., son of Sir Thomas *Hawarde*, Viscount Bindon' who succeeded as Viscount *Howard* of Bindon (1565–6 Bardsley). (iii) John *Howeherde* 1348 DbAS 36. 'Ewe-herd' from OE *ēowu* and *hierde*, a rare but contributory source. *v.* EWART.

Howarth, Howorth, Howourth: Randal *Howarth* 1532 Bardsley. The surname is common in Manchester and Leeds. In the former it is from Howarth in Rochdale (Lancs), in Leeds it is, no doubt, often a corruption of *Haworth*.

Howat, Howatt: *v.* HEWET

Howatson: Jok *Howatson* 1569 Black. 'Son of Howett.' *v.* HEWET.

Howchin: *v.* HUTCHIN

Howel, Howell, Howels, Howells: (i) *Huwal* West Wala cyning (King of the West Welsh) 926 ASC D; Morganus *filius Hoel* 1166 P (Sa); *Hoelus* de Charlion 1184 P (Glam); *Howell' filius Ade* (Walensis) 1221 AssSa; Geffrei *Hoel* c1100–30 OEByn (D); Bald', William *Hoel* 1183 P (W), 1221 ElyA (Nf); Robert *Howeles* 1210 Cur (Nth); John *Houeles* 1280 AssSo; John *Howel* 1313 FFC; William *Huwel* 1331 AssSt. OW *Houel*, OBret *Houuel, Huwel, Huwal, Howael;* in the Welsh border counties from Wales, in the eastern counties, where Bretons were numerous, direct from Brittany. *v.* also POWELL. (ii) Walter *de Huwella* 1165 P (L); Alfredus *de Howella* 1177 P (L). From Howell (Lincs).

Howers: Walter, Henry *le Howere* 1275 RH (K), 1327 SRDb. 'Dweller near a ridge or hill.' OE *hōh* or ON *haugr* plus *-er*. Equivalent to *atte Howe. v.* HOW.

Howetson: William *Howetson* 1379 PTY. 'Son of *Howett.*'

Howett: *v.* HEWET

Howieson, Howison: John *Howison* 1450 Black; Alan *Howesson* 1474 NorwW (Sf). 'Son of *Howe*' (Hugh), or, perhaps, an assimilated form of *Howetson.*

Howitt: *v.* HEWET
Howkins: *v.* HUKIN
Howlett: *v.* HEWLETT
Howlin(g): *v.* HEWLINS
Howman: *v.* HUMAN
Howroyd: *v.* HOLROYD
Howse: *v.* HOUSE, HOW
Howson: *v.* HUGHSON
Howton: *v.* HOUGHTON
Hoyer: *v.* AYER
Hoyle, Hoyles, Hoile, Hoiles: Henry *att Hoyle* 1379 PTY. A south Yorkshire dialectal pronunciation of HOLE.

Huard: *v.* HOWARD

Huban, Huband: John *Huebarne* 1301 SRY. 'Hugh's bairn.' cf. GOODBAIRN.

Hubbard, Hubbert: *v.* HUBERT

Hubberstey: John *Hubersty* 1452 FrY. From Hubbersty, a lost place in Cockerham (Lancs).

Hubbold, Hubball, Hubble: *Hubald de Bereford'* 1205 P (He); Hugo *Hubald, Hubolt* 1086 DB, ICC (Beds); Bernard *Hubold* 1148 Winton (Ha); Henry *Hubaut, Hubald, Hubalt* 1199, 1205 P (Wa); William *Hubball* 1640 SaltAS (OS) xv. OG *Hugibald, Hubald* 'mind-bold', OFr *Hubaut*.

Hubert, Hubbard, Hubbart, Hubbert, Hobart: Eudo *filius Huberti* 1086 DB (Ha); *Hubert de Bissoppesgate* 1292 SRLo; Roger *Hubert* 1199 FF (Nth); Thomas *Huberd (Hubert)* 1230 P (Do); William *Hoberd* 1291 FFSf; Roger *Hubard* 1327 SRSo; John *Hobart* 1346 FA (Sf). OG *Hugibert, Hubert* 'mind-bright'.

Hubling: William, Thomas *Hubelin(e)* 1327 SRSf, 1348 DbAS 36. *Hub-el-in*, a double diminutive of *Hubb*, a short form of *Hubald* or *Hubert*. cf. Amyas *Hubbe* 1327 SRSf.

Hucheson: *v.* HUTCHINSON

Huck, Hucks: *Hucche* purs c1150 DC (L); Gamel *filius Hucca* 1185 Templars (Y); *Hucke* 1221 *ElyA* (Nf); William *Hukke* 1279 RH (Hu); William *Huckes* 1568 SRSf. OE **Ucca*, a petform of OE *Ūhtrǣd*. cf. Huctredus *filius Ucke* 1212 Fees (La). cf. HUG, HUGMAN and *v.* HOOK.

Huckel, Huckell, Huckle: Reginald, Jocelin *Huckel* 1209 P (C), 1225 AssSo. A diminutive of *Huck*.

Hucker: John *le Hukker'* 1307 MESO (So); John *le Hucker'* 1333 ib. A derivative of ME *hucke* 'to bargain', a petty dealer.

Huckin: *v.* HUKIN

Huckle: *v.* HUCKEL

Hudd: *Hude de Rafningeham* 1177 P (Sf); *Hudde de Bosco* 1210 P (Nf); *Hudde de Pesefurlang* 1246 AssLa; William, Reginald *Hudde* 1230 P (Sa, Y). *Hudde* was very common and is a petform of *Hugh*: Hugo *filius Johannis ... Johannes pater ipsius Hudde* 1212 Cur (Y); *Hugo Sturdy* 1219 AssY, *Hudde Sturdi* 1230 P (Y). It appears to have been used also for *Richard*: Bardsley's *Ricardus* de Knapton and Cristiana *Hud-wyf* (1379 PTY) is not absolutely conclusive, but his '*Ricardus dictus Hudde* de Walkden' (1346 Cl) leaves no doubt. Also found as *Hutte* (1246 AssLa).

Huddart: *v.* WOODARD

Hudden: William *Hodden* 1332 SRWa. From *Hudde*, or *Hodde* (1211 FFL). *v.* HUDD, GEFFEN.

Huddle: *Hudd-el*, a diminutive of *Hudd*. cf. the double diminutive in: William, Richard *Hudelin* 1208 P (L), 1247 AssBeds.

Huddleston, Huddlestone, Huddelston, Hudleston, Hudlestone, Hiddleston: Richard *de Hudelesdun* 1200 Cur (Y). From Huddleston (WRYorks).

Hudgell: *v.* HUDSWELL

Hudman: Roger *Hudman* c1248 Bec (Do). 'Servant of *Hudd*.'

Hudsmith: Thomas *Huddemogh* 1332 SRLa;

William *Hudmagh* 1379 PTY; Thomas *Huddesmawth* 1464 FeuDu; Cuthbert *Hodgemaght, Hodgemaughthe* 1545–6 NorwW (Nf); Ralph *Hudsmyth* 1582 PrGR. 'Hudd's brother-in-law.' cf. Richard *Gepmouthe* and *v.* WATMOUGH.

Hudson, Hutson: John *Hudsone, Hutson* 1323 Wak (Y), 1568 SRSf. 'Son of *Hudd*.'

Hudswell, Hudgell: Geoffrey *de Huddeswell'* 1206 P (Y). From Hudswell (NRYorks).

Hue: *v.* HUGH

Huelin: *v.* HEWLINS

Huett: *v.* HEWET

Huff: *v.* HOW

Huffam: *v.* HOUGHAM

Huffington: Alan *de Huffintone* c1270 ArchC 34; Margery *Uffington* 1553 ib. 37. From Ufton Court in Tunstall or Uffington Fm in Goodneston (Kent).

Hug: Galfridus *filius Hugge* 1301 SRY; Robert, William *Hugge* 1180 P_(Y), 1279 RH (O). OE **Ugga*, a pet-form of *Ūhtrǣd*. cf. *Uctredus pater Henrici et Ugge avus suus* 1212 Cur (Y). cf. HUCK, OUGHTRED.

Huggard: Richard *Huggard* 1535 LWills. From *Hug-ard*, a variant of *Huard*.

Huggens: *v.* HUGGIN, HUGGON

Huggett, Huget: (i) A variant of *Hewet*, from *Hug-et*, a diminutive of *Hugh*. Huggett's Lane in Willingdon (Sussex) owes its name to Helwis' *Hugot* 1296 SRSx, *Huwet* 1327 ib., and Huggett's Fm in Heathfield (Sussex) to William *Hughet* 1296 SRSx. It is *Huggetts* in 1614 (PN Sx 425, 467). (ii) Robert *de Hugat'* 1219 AssY; Isabel *Hugate, Hugitte* 1440 ShefA. From Huggate (ERYorks).

Huggill: *v.* HUGILL

Huggin, Huggins: Reginaldus *filius Hugin* Hy 1 Fees (So); *Hugyn* 1246 AssLa; Robert, John *Hugyn* 1327 SRSx, 1337 FFSt; William *Hugyns, Amisia Hugines* 1327 SRWo. *Hug-in*, a diminutive of *Hugh*. Also for *Huggen*: Robert *Huggen* 1332 SRWa. *v.* GEFFEN.

Huggon, Huggons, Hugon: *Hugun filius Ricardi* c1250 Rams (Hu); Richard *Hugons* 1327 SRSo; Hugh *Hugune* 1379 PTY; William *Hugon* 1432 FrY. There seems to be no evidence for the use in England of OFr *Hugon*, cas-régime of *Hugues*. *Hugun* is a diminutive of *Hug*, i.e. *Hugh*. For the series *Hugun, Hugin, Huget*, cf. that of *Burdun, Burdin, Burdet*, s.n. BURDEN.

Huggonson: 'Son of *Hugun*.'

Hugh, Hughes, Hugo, Ugo, Hue, Huws, Hew, Hewes, Hews, How, Howe, Howes, Hows, Fitz-Hugh, Fitzhugues: *Hugo* 1066 DB (Hu, Sf); Willelmus *filius Hugonis* 1084 GeldR (W); Reginaldus *le fiz Hugonis* 1195 P (Lei); *Howe Golichtly, Howe caretarius* 1221 AssWa; Edde *filius Hugh* 1279 RH (C); *Hwe purte* 1292 SRLo; *Hue de Clopham* ib.; Rogerus *Hugo* 1185 Templars (Db); Ralph, Robert, William *Howe* 1221 AssWa; Richard *Hue* 1275 SRWo; Richard *Huwe* 1279 RH (C); Constance *Huwes* 1279 RH (O); William *Hewe* 1291 LLB A; John *Hugh* 1296 SRSx; John *Hugh (Huwe)* 1327 *SR* (Ess); Thomas *Hughes* 1327 SRSo;

John *Fitz Huwe* 1344 Ipm; Thomas *Howe. Huwe* 1353–4 ColchCt; Richard *Houwes* 1359 Putnam (So); Elysabeth *Hewes* 1524 SRSf. OFr *Hue*, from OG *Hugo* 'heart, mind', a very popular name after the Conquest. It is usually found in the Latin form *Hugo*, the vernacular forms being *Hewe* and *Howe*, all of which survive as surnames. The popularity of Hugh is clearly shown by its 14 variants in modern surnames and by numerous derivatives in *-in*, *-on*, *-et*, *-ot*, *-kin*, *-son*, *-man*, and by double diminutives in *-el-in*, *-el-et* and the French double diminutive *Huchon*. Of these derivatives there are some 90 different modern forms and the list is probably not complete. In Scotland and Ireland *Hugh* is frequent for an original Gaelic *Aodh*, in Argyllshire for *Eòghann* and in north and north-west Scotland for *Uisdeann*. In Ireland, Hughes and MacHugh are regarded as equivalent to MacKay. In Wales it has become *Pugh. Hew, How* and *Hawes* have alternative origins. *v.* FITHIE.

Hughf, Hughff: *v.* HOW
Hughill: *v.* HUGILL
Hughman: *v.* HUMAN

Hughson, Huson, Hewson, Hooson, Hoosun, Howson: Wlfuric *Hugo sune* 1066 InqEl; Richard *Hughson* 1310 LLB D; William *Huggesone* 1327 SRWo; Henry *Howsone* 1332 SRCu; Michael *Hwesone* 1378 ColchCt; Thomas *Hughesson* 1389 FrY; William *Hewson* 1437 FrY; Henry *Hooson* 1635 RothwellPR (Y); Thomas *Hueson* 1653 ib. 'Son of *Hugh*.'

Hugill, Huggill, Hughill, Hewgill, Howgill: Matilda *de Hogyll* 1379 PTY (Sedbergh). From Howgill in Sedbergh (WRYorks) or Hugill (Westmorland).

Huglin: *v.* HEWLINS
Hugman: William *Uggeman, Huggeman* 1301 SRY. 'Servant of *Ugge.*' *v.* HUG.
Hugo. *v.* HUGH
Hugon: *v.* HUGGON

Huish, Huyshe, Hewish: Robert *de Hiwis* 1194 P (D); William *de Hewis* 1207 Cur (Do); John *de Hewish* 1278 AssSo. From one of the places named Huish in Devon, Dorset, Somerset or Wilts.

Huison, Huitson: *v.* HEWETSON
Huitt: *v.* HEWET
Huk, Huke: *v.* HOOK

Hukin, Hukins, Hewkin, Hookins, Howkins, Huckin: John *Hukyns* 1332 SRWa; John *Hukyn* 1337 BarkingAS ii (Ess); Thomas *Howkyn* 1378 Balliol (O). A diminutive of *How* or *Hew*, i.e., *Hugh* plus *-kin*.

Hulance: *v.* HEWLINS
Hulatt, Huleatt, Hulett: *v.* HEWLETT
Hulbert, Hulburd: *v.* HOLBERT
Hulin: *v.* HEWLINS

Hull, Hulles, Hulls: (i) Peter *de Hull* 1199 AssSt; John *ate Hulle* 1297 MinAcctCo (Mx); Robert *in le hull* 1327 SRDb. From Hull (Ches). *atte hulle* is a southern and west-midland form of *hill*, 'dweller on a hill', but this has, no doubt, usually assumed the standard form. *v.* HILL. (ii) Henry, Simon *Hulle* 1309 Wak (Y), 1312 CochCt; John

Hull 1332 SRCu. The surname is most commonly from a personal name *Hulle: Hulle* le Bule 1201 P (St), *Hulle* son of Stephen 1227 AssBeds, *Hulle* de Alperam 1259 AssCh. A pet-form of *Hugh* or of its common diminutives *Hulin, Hulot*. In 1380 John *Hulle*sone Rudde held a tenement formerly *Hugh* Rudde's (AD v). John was the son of *Hulle* or *Hugh* Rudde.

Hullah, Huller: Ralph *le Hullere* 1327 SRSx; Richard *le Huller* 1332 SRSr. 'Dweller by a hill' from OE *hyll*, equivalent to *atte hulle*. This would survive as there was no common standard word. The south-eastern *Heller* also survives. cf. BRIDGER.

Hullett: *v.* HEWLETT
Hullin, Hullins: *v.* HEWLINS. Also for *Hullen*: Richard, Thomas *Hullen* 1332 SRWa. *v.* HULL, GEFFEN.
Hullot: *v.* HEWLETT
Hullyer: *v.* HOLLIER

Hulm, Hulme: Turstinus *de Hulmo* 1169 P (Hu); Geoffrey *de Hulm* 1202 P (La); John *de Hulm* 1260 AssCh. ODa *hulm*, corresponding to ON *holmr. v.* HOLM. From Hulme (Staffs) or one of the places of the same name in Cheshire or Lancashire. *v.* HUME.

Hulman: Roger *Hul(le)man* 1327 SRSo, 1359 Putnam (So). 'Servant of *Hull*' or 'dweller by a hill', equivalent to HULLAH.

Hulson: Thomas *Hull(e)son* 1308, 1333 FrY. 'Son of *Hull*.'

Hulton: Jelvorth *de Hulton'* 1206 Cur (La); Adam *de Hulton* 1246 AssLa; William *Hulton* 1418–19 FFWa. From Hulton (Lancs, Staffs).

Hum, Humm: Gilbert *Om* 1177 P (Ha); Ernald *Hum* 1208 Cur (L); John *Humme* 1229 Cl (Sf); Geoffrey *le Home* 1296 SRSx. OFr *homme* 'man'. cf. MAN.

Human, Hughman, Howman, Uman: Matill' *filia Hiweman* c1248 Bec (W); *Hugeman* de Assinton 13th *Stoke* (Sf); Nicholaus *filius Howemanni, filius Huemanni* 1252 Rams (Hu); Willelmus *filius Howman* 1276 RH (Hu); William *Hiweman* c1248 Bec (W); Humfrey *Huueman* 1277 *Ely* (Sf); John *Human* 1279 RH (C); William *Huweman* (*Howeman*) 1327 SR (Ess). The forms would suggest 'servant of *Hugh*' and the surname may sometimes have this meaning, but such a combination as a personal name is rare or unique. In late OE times names in *-mann* were popular and new combinations were formed. This is a similar late formation, **Hygemann*, the first element *hyge* 'mind', cognate with the OG *hugi* of *Hugh*, found in OE *Hygebeald* and *Hygebeorht*. Compounds of *Hyge-* were in use after the Conquest: *Hygemund*: Gamel filius *Higmund* 1185 Templars (Y), and *Hygerǣd*: Willelmus filius *Hugered* 1198 P (Sx). *Howman* as a surname might also mean 'dweller by a hill-spur or hill', equivalent to HOWERS. *v.* HOW.

Humberston, Humberstone, Humblestone, Humerstone, Hummerston, Hummerstone: Ralph *de Humberstein* 1180 P (L). From Humberstone (Leics, Lincs).

Hume: Walter *de Hulmo* (*Humo*) 1221 Cur (Sf); Ralph *de la Hume* 1275 RH (Nf); Walter *Hume* 1275 RH (Sf). ODa *hulm* with loss of *l* before the labial. *v.* HOLM, HOME.

Humfress, Humfrey: *v.* HUMPHREY

Humm: *v.* HUM

Hum(m)erstone: *v.* HUMBERSTON

Humpherson, Humpherston: John *Humphreson* 1663 Bardsley (Ch). 'Son of *Humphrey*.'

Humphery: *v.* HUMPHREY

Humphrey, Humphreys, Humphries, Humphris, Humphriss, Humphry, Humphryes, Humphrys, Humphery, Homfray, Humfress, Humfrey: *Hunfridus, Humfridus* 1086 DB; *Humfridus* 1186-88 BuryS (Sf); William *Humfrey* c1240 Fees (Beds); William *Humfray, Umfrey* 1293 AssSt; Roger *Houmfrey* 1311 LLB B. OG *Hunfrid, Humfrid*.

Hunger: *Hungar* Cofrich 1166 P (Nf); *Hunger* 1167 ib.; *Ricardus filius Hundger* 1185 Templars (L); Turstinus *Hunger* 1176 P (Nth); William *Hungere* 1198 P (K). OE *Hungār*, unrecorded, but both themes are common in OE.

Hunn: (i) *Robertus filius Hunne* c1155 DC (L); Brictmerus *filius Hunne* 1193 P (Nf); Robert, Elwin *Hunne* 1166 P (C), 12th FeuDu. OE *Hun(n)a*. (ii) Seman', Martin, Robert *le Hunne* 1277 Ely (Sf), 1279 RH (C), 1288 RamsCt (Hu). As the nickname is East Anglian, it may be ON *húnn* 'young bear'.

Hunnable, Hunneyball, Hunneybell, Hunnibal, Hunnibell, Hannibal, Honeyball, Honneybell, Honniball: *Anabul* 1379 PTY; Roger, George *Anabull(e)* 1499, 1539 DbCh; Thomas *Hannyball* 1513 Oxon; John *Anyable* 1568 SRSf; Simon *Honeyball* 1792 SfPR; Elizabeth *Hunnibal(d)* 1821, 1824 ShotleyPR (Sf). *Anabul* is clearly for *Anabel*, from *Amabel*. *v.* ANNABLE. These surnames are late corruptions of this. There is no evidence for the use of *Hannibal* as a christian name in England before 1619 in Cornwall: *Hannibal* Gammon (ODCN). As a surname, we find Matthew *Hanibal* (1255 Cl), Peter *Haniballus* (Bardsley), both described as 'civis Romanus' and obviously Italians. A Roman surname from the Carthaginian Hannibal is somewhat surprising.

Hunnex: *v.* HUNWICK

Hunnings: *Huning* 1086 DB; *Hunningus de Cliva* 1176 P (Sa); Alexander, William *Hunning* 1269 AD iv, 1275 RH (Sf). OE *Hun(n)ing*, 'son of *Hun(n)a*'.

Hunnybun: *v.* HONEYBOURNE

Hunt: Humphrey *le Hunte* 1203 FFSx; Ralph *Hunte* 1219 AssY. OE *hunta* 'hunter, huntsman'.

Hunter: Simon *Huntere* 1220 Cur (Beds); Juliana *la Hunter* 1312 ColchCt. A derivative of OE *huntian* 'to hunt', 'huntsman' (c1250 MED).

Hunting: *Hunting* c1095 Bury (Sf); *Hunting* filius Hanuse 1193 P (Y); Geoffrey *Hunthing* 1209 P (Lei); Roger *Hunting* 1275 RH (K). OE *Hunting* a derivative of OE *Hunta* 'hunter', recorded only once before the Conquest (c1060).

Huntingdon, Huntington, Huntinton: Eustace *de Huntedune, de Huntendone* 1086 OEByn; Humphrey *de Huntendun'* 1202 SP1 (Beds); William *de*

Huntinton' c1280 SRWo; Robert *Huntyngdon* 1375 AssLa. From Huntingdon (Hunts), or Huntington (Ches, Hereford, Salop, Staffs, NRYorks).

Huntley, Huntly: Thomas *de Huntelega* 1176 P (Gl); Thomas *de Hunteley* 1280 AssSo; John *Hunteleye* 1374-5 FFSr. From Huntley (Glos), or 'dweller by the hunter's wood'.

Huntman, Huntsman: John *Hunteman* 1219 Fees (Sf); John *Hunteman, Huntesman* 1347, 1348 FA (Sf). A compound of OE *hunta* 'huntsman' or ME *hunte* 'the act of hunting' and *mann*, either in the sense 'hunter' or 'servant of the hunter'. Occasionally we may have an unrecorded OE personal name *Huntmann*, a compound of *Hunta* and *-mann*, an addition to these late compounds in *-mann*. It is found in Suffolk in 1199 (SIA iv).

Hunwick, Hunwicke, Hunwicks, Hunnex, Honex, Honick: Walter *de Honewyke* 1296 SRSx; Richard *de Hunewyke* 1307 FFEss. 'Dweller at the honey-farm', or, bee-keeper. OE *hunig, wīc*.

Hunwin: *v.* UNWIN

Huot: *v.* HEWET

Hupple: Juliana *Huppehulle* 1279 RH (O); Adam *Uppehull* 1327 SRSo. Dweller 'up the hill'.

Hurd: *v.* HERD

Hurdman: *v.* HERDMAN

Hurl, Hurle, Hurles, Hurll: *v.* EARL

Hurlbatt, Hurlbut, Hurlbutt: John, Robert *Hurlebat* 1327 *SR* (Ess), 1333 *SR* (Ha). A nickname from a game. 'Pleying at þe two hande swerd, at swerd & bokelere, & at two pyked staf, at þe hurlebatte' (c1450 MED). It took its name from 'short battes of a cubit long and a halfe, with pykes of yron, and were tied to a line, that when they were throwne, one might plucke them again' (1565-73).

Hurley, Hurly: John *de Hurleia* 1210-11 P (W); Richard *de Hurleye* 1327 SRWo; John *Hurleye* 1340-1450 GildC. From Hurley (Berks, Som, Warwicks).

Hurlin, Hurling, Hurlen, Harlin, Harling, Arling, Urlin, Urling, Urlwin, Harwin, Herwin: Balduinus *filius Herluini* 1066 DB; *Herluinus, Urleuuine* 1086 DB; *Herlewine* de Sumerfeld' 1191 P (K); *Harlewyn* 1279 RH (C); John *Erlewin* 1225 Pat (K); Roger *Herlewyn* 1230 P (Do); Simon *Arlewine* 1242 Fees (Beds); Peter *Harlewyne* 1279 RH (C); Richard *Urlewyn'* ib. (O); William *Harlyn* 1327 SRSx; Alice *Hurlewyne* 1332 SRSr; Agnes *Herlyng* 1379 PTY; Thomas *Harlewyn*, Robert *Harlyng*, John *Harwyn* 1524 SRSf; Roger *Urlen* 1581 Oxon; Marmadux *Urlin* (siue, ut Atavi scripsere, *Earlewyn*) 1654 CAPr 34; Mr. *Urling* 1698 ib. OFr *Herluïn, Arluïn*, OG *Erlewin, Herlewin* 'earl-friend'. *Url-* is an Anglo-Norman spelling.

Hurlston, Hurlestone: (i) Henry *Hurleston* 1474 Bardsley; Philip *Hurlestone* 1642 PrD. From Hurleston (Ches). (ii) John *Huddilston, Hudelston, Hodelston, Hudleston* or *Hurleston* 1509 LP. *Hurleston* is here an unusual development of HUDDLESTON, found side by side with *Hurlston* in Bradford (WRYorks).

Hurman: Walter *Hurneman* 1297 MinAcctCo. 'Dweller in the nook.' *v.* HERN.

Hurne: *v.* HERN

Hurran, Hurren: William *Hurant* 1086 DB (Sf); William *Hurand* 1245 *Ass* (Ess); Edmund *Hurryng* 1524 SRSf. OFr *hurand, hurant* from OFr *hure* 'hair' and the suffix *-and, -ant*, hence 'the shaggy-haired one'.

Hurrell: Roger *Hurel* 1154 Riev (Y), 1170 P (Nb). An *-el* diminutive of OFr *hure* 'hair' in the same sense as *Hurran*.

Hurry, Hurrey, Hurrie, Horrey, Horry, Orrey, Orry, Ourry, Oury, Urry, Urie, Ury: *Vlfric, Vlfricus, Vlricus* 1066 DB; *Urrius* de la haie c1148 EngFeud (He); Reginaldus *filius vrri* 1182-98 Bart (Lo); *Urric'* Arbelestier 1194 CurR (Ess); *Wlricus* Balistarius 1233 Fees (Ess); *Hurri* c1250 Rams (Hu); Walter, Herueus *Urri* 1208 Cur (Sr), 1209 P (Nf); Gilbert *Uri* 1214 Cur (L); Alan *Hurry* 1219 FFEss; Geoffrey *Orry* 1235 Fees (Sa); Walter *Horry* 1290 Fees (Wt); John *Ourry* 1297 MinAcctCo; John *Ulricus* 14th AD vi (C). A Norman pronunciation of OE *Wulfrīc*. *v.* WOOLRICH.

Hurst: *v.* HERST

Hurt: *v.* HART

Husband, Husbands, Hosbons: Ernald, Robert *Husebond'* 1176 P (Y), 1231 Pat (Nb); Robert *le Hosebonde* 1279 RH (C). Late OE *hūsbonda* 'householder'; farmer, husbandman.

Husey: *v.* HUSSEY

Husher: *v.* USHER

Huskinson, Huskison, Huskisson: 'Son of *Oskin*.' *v.* HOSKEN.

Huson: *v.* HUGHSON

Hussey, Hussy, Husey, Hosey: (i) Walter *Hosed, Hosatus* 1086 DB, *Hosethe* c1100 OEByn (D); Henry *Hoese, Huse* 1153, 1185 Templars (O); Geoffrey *Hoset* (*Hose*) 1168 P (W); William *Hose, Huse* 1221 AssGl; Richard *le Hose* 1243 AssSo; Geoffrey *Husey* 1275 RH (W); John *Hussee* ib. (Nt); Richard *Hussi* 1275 SRWo; Henry *Hosey* 1296 SRSx. OFr *hosed* (*housé*), Lat *hosatus* 'booted'. (ii) Richard, Rose *Husewif* 1192 P (Sx), 1279 RH (C); Margeria *Hosewyf* 1327 SRC; Roger *Huswyffe* 1435 AD i (Herts). ME *hus(e)wyf* 'mistress of a family; wife of a householder; a domestic economist', applied to a woman, a compliment; to men, derogatory. This became *hussie* in the 16th century. The surname is not to be associated with the modern meaning of *hussy*. The word was also used as a woman's name: *Husewyua* (*Husewyf*), widow of Adam Brist (1317 AssK).

Hustler: *v.* OSTLER

Hustwayte, Hustwitt: William *de Husthayt* 1219 AssY. From Husthwaite (NRYorks).

Hutchin, Hutchins, Hutchings, Hutchence, Hutchens, Hutcheon, Hutchons, Hotchen, Hotchin, Houchen, Houchin, Howchin: *Huchun* Aleyn 1277 Wak (Y); *Hucohun* le Cu 1292 SRLo; Gilbert *Huchun* 1296 SRSx; John *Huchon* 1321 FFSf; John *Howechoun* 1327 SRSf; John *Huchin*, Richard *Huchins* 1327 SRWo; Edith *Huchenes* 1332 SRSt; John *Huchouns* 1337 ColchCt; Cecily *Howchyngs* 1523 NorwW (Nf); John *Howchyn* 1524 SRSf. OFr *Huchon*, a double diminutive of *Hue* (Hugh), common in Picardy, corresponding to OFr *Hueçon, Huesson*, modFr *Husson*. It was used as a christian name in Scotland (*Hucheon* Fraser 1422) where it also became a surname (John *Hutching* 1525, Helen *Huchown* 1547) and was adopted in Gaelic as *Huisdean* or *Uisdean* (Black). *v.* MC-CUTCHEON

Hutchinson, Hutcherson, Hucheson, Hutchingson, Hutchison: Isota *Huchonson* 1379 PTY; John *Hucheson* 1440 ShefA (Y); John *Huchynson* 1475 GildY; Tomasine *Hutcherson* 1674 EA (OS) i (Sf); Abell *Hutchison* 1679 RothwellPR (Y). 'Son of *Huchun*.' *v.* HUTCHIN.

Huthwaite: Adam *de Hothwayt* 1260 AssLa; Thomas *de Hothuait* 1332 SRCu. From Howthwaite (Cumb), Huthwaite (NRYorks), or Hucknall under Huthwaite (Notts).

Hutler: Wlward *Hutlawe* 1279 RH (C). *v.* OUTLAW.

Hutson: *v.* HUDSON

Hutton: Ernewi *de Hottona* 1175 P (Y); Nicholas *de Hutune* 1246 AssLa; John *Hutton, Huttun* 1403 IpmY, 1502 FFEss. From one or other of the many places of this name.

Huxley: Robert *de Huxeleg'* 1260 AssCh; Thomas *de Huxeley* 1332-3 SRSt; William *Huxley* 1530 FFEss. From Huxley (Ches).

Huxster, Huxter: Lecia *la hucstere* 1277 *Ely* (Sf); Amable *la Hukkester* 1310 ColchCt; William *le Hukester* 1327 SRSf; Richard *Huxster* 1662 HTEss. ME *huckestere*, feminine of *huckere* (*v.* HUCKER), 'pedlar, hawker', used chiefly of women.

Hyam(s): *v.* HIGHAM

Hyde(s): *v.* HIDE

Hyder: *v.* HIDER

Hyland: *v.* HAYLAND

Hyman: *v.* HAYMAN

Hyndley: *v.* HINDLEY

Hynes: *v.* HINE

Hyslop: *v.* HASLOP

Hysted: *v.* HIGHSTEAD

I

Iago: v. JAGO

I'Anson: John *Janson, I'anson* 1569, 1673 FrY; Nehemiah *Janson, I'anson* 1615, 1673 ib. For JANSON.

Ibberson, Ibbeson, Ibbison, Ibbotson, Ibbetson, Ibbitson, Ibotson, Ibeson, Ibison, Hibberson, Hipperson: Henry *Ibbotson* 1379 PTY; John *Ibotessone* 1392 NottBR; Anthony *Ibbison* 1596 FrY; Roger *Ipperson, Ibbatson* 1611–14 Bardsley; George *Ibberson* 1695 Shef. 'Son of *Ibbot.*'

Ibbott, Ibbett, Ibbitt, Hibbit, Hibbitt, Hibbott: *Ybot, Ibbota* 1286, 1314 Wak (Y); *Hibbot* 1379 PTY; Roger *Ybott* 1415 LLB I; John *Hybbot* 1550 Pat. *Ibb-ot*, a diminutive of *Ibb. Hibbot* is a diminutive of both *Ibb* (Isabel) and of a man's name: *Hibot'* de Buskeby 1379 PTY, probably from *Hilbert* or *Ilbert*. v. ILBERT.

Ibbs, Hibbs: *Ibbe* 1324 LaCt; Adam *Ibbe* 1334 ColchCt; John *Hibson* 1442 Bardsley. *Ibb*, a petform of *Isabel* or of *Ilbert*.

Ibell, Hibble, Hible: cf. John *Ibelsone* 1381 SRSt. *Ib-el*, a diminutive of *Ibb*.

Ibson: William, John *Ibbeson* 1324 LaCt, 1332 SRCu. 'Son of *Ibb.*'

Icemonger, Isemonger: Ailred *Ismangere* 1165–72 P (K); Hervey *le Ismongere* 1248 FFEss. OE *īsern, īsen, īren* 'iron' and *mangere*, 'ironmonger'. v. IREMONGER.

Ickeringill, Ikringill: *Icornegill'* 1379 PTY; Benjamin *Ickeringill* 1670 FrY; William *Ickeringale, Hickeringill* 1679, 1700 FrY. From a lost place in Skipton (WRYorks), *Ecorngill* 1329, *Ickering-Gill* 1822 (PN WRY v, 71).

Ida, Ide: *Ida* 1175 AD i (Mx), 1207 Cur (L); William *Ide, Yde* 1279 RH (C), 1296 SRSx. *Ida*, an OG name from *id-* 'labour', popular among the Normans.

Iddenden, Iddenten, Iddenton, Idenden: Godleue *Ydendene* 1442 ArchC xi. From Iddenden Fm in Hawkhurst (Kent).

Iddins: v. IDDON

Iddison: Thomas *Idonson*, Richard *Ideson* 1379 PTY. 'Son of *Idon.*' v. IDDON.

Iddon, Iddins: *Idonea* Hy 2 DC (L), 1205 Cur (Lei); Willelmus *filius Ydeneye* 1297 SRY; Nicholaus *filius Ydon'* 1297 MinAcctCo; *Idone* 1327 SRSo; William *Idony* 1274 RH (Lo); Robert *Ydany* 1300 Ipm (K); Robert *Ydeyn* 1327 SRC. Probably ON *Idunn, Iðuna* (f), from *iðja* 'to do,

perform' and *unna* 'to love'. It was latinized as *Idonea* 'suitable'. The vernacular form was *Idony*.

Idel: v. IDLE

Idelson: 'Son of *Idell.*' v. IDLE.

Iden: Osbert *de Idenn* 1296 SRSx. From Iden Green in Benenden or Iden Manor in Staplehurst (Kent).

Idle, Idel, Idell: (i) Wrennus *filius Ydel* 1193 P (He); *Idellus* 1202–7 Black (Glasgow); William, John *Idel(e)* 1199 FF (Nth), 1332 SRSr; William *Ydil* 1343 Black. Welsh *Ithell*, MW *Ithael* 'lord-bountiful'. In England, the surname may also be OE *īdel* 'lazy'. cf. ITHELL. (ii) Ailsi *de Idla* c1190 Calv (Y); John *del Idle* 1317 AssK; John *dil Idle* 1327 SR (Ess). Fom Idle (WRYorks) or from residence in an island (AFr *idle*, OFr *isle*).

Ifould: Benedict *de Ifold* 1296 SRSx. From Ifold Ho (Sussex).

Iggleden, Iggledon, Igglesden, Iggulden: Richard *Igolynden*, John *Igulden* 1475, 1536 ArchC 31. From Ingleden (Kent).

Ikin: Richard *Idekyne* 1324 FA (W). A diminutive of *Ida*.

Ikringill: v. ICKERINGILL

Ilbert, Hilbert, Hibbard, Hibberd, Hibbert: *Ylebertus* c1150 Gilb (L); *Hildebertus* 1150–60 DC (L); Willelmus *filius Hiberti* 1163 ib.; Estmundus *filius Hilbert* 1205 Cur (Nf); *Ilbert* de Betelintun' 1212 Cur (Berks); Walter *Ilberd (Hilbert)* 1230 P (Y); Martin *Yllebert* 1243 AssSo; Margaret *Hilbert* 1283 SRSf; Roger *Hileberd* 1327 SRSo; John *Heebarde* 1568 SRSf; James *Hibbert* 1591 Bardsley. OG *Hildeberht* 'battle-glorious', OFr *Ilbert*.

Iles, Isles: John *del Ile* 1275 RH (Sf); Ralph *Iles* 1560 FrY. 'Dweller in the isle' (OFr *isle*, Fr *île*). v. ILLES.

Iliff, Iliffe, Ilieve, Ilive: *Æillovus*, identical with *Illivus* 1212 Cur (Cu, Nb); *Ilyf* de Wyn 13th FeuDu; Francis *Ilive* 1622 Bardsley; John *Iliff* 1640 ib. A form of ON *Eilifr*. v. AYLIFF.

Illes: (i) Ralph *Ille* 1202 P (Nf), 1275 RH (Sf). ME *ille* 'bad, evil'. (ii) Baldwin, Andrew *del Ille* 1255 RH (O), 1332 SRCu. 'Dweller in the island.' v. ILES.

Illingworth, Illingsworth: Alice *de Illingworth* 1314 Wak (Y); John *de Illyngworth'* 1379 PTY; Richard *Illyngworth* 1454 IpmNt. From Illingworth (WRYorks).

Image: Richard *Image* 1563 Bardsley. Metony-

mic for *Imager*: Alexander *le Ymagour* 1305 LLB
B. OFr *ymageour*, *ymagier* 'maker of images,
carver, sculptor'.

Imbrey, Imbrie: *v.* AMERY

Imm, Imms, Ims: Thomas *Imme* 1243 AssSo;
Geoffrey *Ymme* 1332 SRSr. OG *Emma, Imma*.

Immink: *v.* EMENEY

Impey, Impy: John *atte Imphage* 1327 SRSx;
John *de Impey* 1327 SRSf. 'Dweller near a hedge
or enclosure made of saplings, or an enclosure for
young trees' (OE **imphaga, *imphæg*), as at Emply
(Surrey), Empty (Northants) or Imphy Hall
(Essex).

Imray, Imrie: *v.* AMERY

Ince: *v.* INNES

Inchbald: *Hengebaldus* (Sa), *Ingelbald* (D) 1086
DB; *Ingeboldus (Engebald', Ingelbold')* filius Kar-
lonis 1221 AssGl; William *Ingebald* 1379 PTY;
Emma *Inchebald* ib. OG *Engelbald, Ingilbald*
'Angle-bold'.

Ind: Nicholas *Attehende* 1332 SRSt; Robert *de
Ynde* 1369 LLB G. 'Dweller at the end (of the
village).'

Inderwick, Enderwick: Roland *de Inuerwic'*
c1190 Black; Robert *Inderwick* or *Innerwick* 1652
ib. From Innerwick (East Lothian).

Ineson: Thomas *Idonson*, John *Ineson* 1379
PTY. 'Son of *Iddon*.'

Ingall, Inggall, Ingold, Ingle, Ingles, Hingle:
Ingold 1066 DB (Y), c1095 Bury (Sf); *Ingoldus*
1114–30 Rams (Hu); *Ingald'* Ledbater' 1221
AssWa; *Ingol* Textor c1250 Rams (Hu); Edmund,
Peter *Ingold* 1274 RH (Sf), 1312 LLB D; Geoffrey
Ingal 1279 RH (Hu); Roger *Hyngoll* 1524 SRSf.
Anglo-Scand *Ingald, Ingold*, OSw *Ingæld*, ON
Ingialdr 'Ing's tribute'.

Ingate: Matilda *de Endegate* 1327 SRSf; Robert
Ingate 1568 SRSf. From Ingate (Suffolk).

Ingell, Ingels, Ingle, Ingles, Hingle: (i) Emma,
William *Ingel* 1279 RH (Hu), 1327 SRC; William
Ingelle 1381 SRSt. ODa *Ingeld*, ON *Ingialdr*. cf.
INGALL. (ii) *Ingulf, Ingolf* 1066 DB; Adam
Ingulf 1229 Cl (Sf); Richard, Thomas *Ingolf* 1327
SRSx, 1391 FrY. ON *Ingólfr*, ODa, OSw *Ingulf*
'Ing's wolf'. The surname may also be from OG
Engenulf, Ingenulf: Engenulfus, Ingenulf 1086 DB,
Ingenolf 1212 Cur (Nth), *Engenolfus* 1219 Cur
(Beds).

Inger, Inker, Ingerson: *Ingeuuar, Imgarus* 1066
DB; Roger *Inger* 1255 RH (W); Peter *Ingarson*
1546 FrY. ODa, OSw *Ingvar*, ON *Yngvarr*.

Ingersoll, Inkersole: Roger *de Hynkersul* 1321
Shef. From Inkersall (Derby).

Ingham: Alwinus *de Ingham* 1049–52 OEByn
(O); Roger *de Ingham* 1162–8 Holme (Nf). From
Ingham (Lincs, Norfolk, Suffolk). *v.* also GAIN.

Ingillson: *v.* INGLESON

Ingle, Ingles: *v.* INGALL, INGELL

Inglebright, Engelbert: *Engelbricus* 1066 DB
(Mx); *Engelbricht* de Stanlega 1176 P (So); *Ingelberd* c1190 DC (L); Robert *Ingelberd'* 1230 P (Y);
Robert *Ingelbert* 1275 RH (L); Arnald *Ingelbright*
1373 LLB G. OFr *Engilbert, Englebert*, OG *Engelbert, Ingelbert* 'Angle-glorious'.

Ingleby, Ingilby: Goslanus *de Engelby* 1157
Gilb(L); Thomas *de Ingelby* 1280 FFY; John
Ingelby 1370 IpmGl. From Ingleby (Derby, Lincs,
NRYorks).

Inglefield: William *de Englefeld* 1185 P (St);
Philip *de Ingelfeld* 1355 LLB G; Stephen *Ingylfeld*
1407 LLB I. From Englefield (Berks), or Englefield
(Surrey), *Ingelfeld* 1282.

Inglesent: Willelmus *filius Ingelsent'* 1219 AssY;
William *Inglesant* 1379 PTY; William *Inglissent*
1447 FrY. OG *Ingilsind(is)* (f).

Ingleson, Ingillson: Thomas *Ingleson* 1458 FrY.
'Son of *Ingle*.' *v.* INGALL, INGELL.

Inglett: (i) *Engelardus* de Strattone 1166 RBE
(Sa); Robertus *filius Ingelard'* 1221 AssGl; Isa-
bella, John *Ingelard* 1279 RH (Beds). OG *Engel-
(h)ard, Ingilard* 'Angle-hard'. (ii) Willelmus *filius
Ingelot* 1200 P (L); William, Reginald *Ingelot* 1279
RH (O), 1327 SRC. *Ingel-ot* a diminutive of
Ingel-, a short form of such names as *Ingelbald,
Ingelbert*, etc.

Ingley: Laurencius *filius Ingelieth* 1221 ElyA
(Nf); Peter *Inglyth* 1395 EA (OS) i (C). For
INGREY, through an interchange of liquids in the
combination *n—r*; *Ingrith* becoming *Inglith*.

Inglis, Inglish: *v.* ENGLISH. Occasionally we may
have OFr *Engelais* (f), OG *Engilheid: Engelise* 1190
P (W), *Engeleisia* 1200 P (W); *Ingeleis* 1202 AssL,
1205 Cur (Herts).

Ingold: *v.* INGALL

Ingoldby, Ingoldsby: Nigel *de Ingoldebi* 1208–9
Pl (L); Ralph *de Ingaldesby* 1275 RH (L); William
de Ingoldesby 1371 AssL; Ralph *Ingoldesby* 1439–40
FFWa. From Ingoldsby (Lincs).

Ingpen: *v.* INKPEN

Ingram, Ingrams, Ingrem: *Ingelram* de Sayı
c1140 Holme (Nf); *Ingelrannus* tanurus 1148–66
NthCh (Nth); *Engelrannus* clericus c1150–60 DC
(Nt); *Radulphus filius Engelram* 1158 P (Y);
Ingeram de Helesham Hy 2 DC (L); *Ingerannus*
capellanus 12th DC (Nt); John *Engelram* 1132
Riev (Y); John *Ingelram (Ingeram)* c1138 Whitby
(Y); John *Ingeram* c1150 Whitby (Y); Robert
Engram c1220 Guisb (Y); Richard *Ingram* c1250
Calv (Y). OG *Engel-, Ingelramnus, -rammus*
'Angle-raven', OFr *Enguerran, Engerran*.

Ingrey: *Ingrede* 1066 DB (Y); *Ingreda* 1101–16
Holme (Nf); *Ingerithe, Ingeride* Hy 2, 1163 DC
(L); *Ingerid, Ingrith'* 1221 AssWa; Alexander
Ingerith' 1221 ElyA (Sf); Thomas *Ingrid* 1279 RH
(Hu); Thomas *Ingre* c1320 Layer; Edward *Ingreth,
Ingry* 1558, 1563 ib. ODa *Ingrith*, OSw *Ingridh*
and ON *Ingiriðr* have all contributed to this
name, the former being perhaps a little more
common.

Inions: *v.* ENNION

Inker: *v.* INGER

Inkersole: *v.* INGERSOLL

Inkpen, Inkpin, Ingpen: Richard *de Ingepenne*
1255 RH (Bk). From Inkpen (Berks).

Inman: William *Inman* 1379 PTY. OE *inn*
'abode, lodging' and *mann*. 'Lodging-house
keeper.'

Innes, Ince: (i) John *de Ines, de Ince* 1401 AssLa;

Henry *de Ines* 1415 IpmLa; Edmund *Ins, Ince* 1474 Cl (Sf). From Ince (Ches, Lancs), or Innes (Cornwall). (ii) Walter *de Ineys* 1226 Black; William *de Inays* 1296 ib.; Robert *de Innes* 1389 ib. From the barony of Innes in Urquhart (Moray).

Insall, Inseal, Insole, Insoll, Insull, Hinsull: Richard *de Inneshal'* 1327 SRWo; John *de Insale* 1341 NI (Wo); Philip *Insoll* 1603 SRWo. From a place *Insoll* in Elmley Lovett (Worcs), no longer on the map, first recorded as *Inerdeshell* in 1275 and last as *Insoll* in 1642 (PN Wo 241).

Inskip, Inskipp, Inskeep: Margery *de Inskip* 1246 AssLa; John *Inskip* 1401 AssLa. From Inskip (Lancs).

Inston, Instone: Sibilla *de Inardeston'* 1275 SRWo. From Innerstone (Worcs).

Inward, Inwards: Roger *de Ynewrðe* 1202 P (Nth). From Inworth (Essex), *Inward* 1467. *Inward* and *Inwood* have been confused. Sarah *Inward*, daughter of Richard *Inwood*, died in 1685 (Weekley).

Inwood, Innwood: Thomas *de Inwode* 1327 SRSo. 'Dweller by the 'in-wood', the home-wood, as opposed to the 'out-wood'.

Ipsen: William *de Ipstone* 1220 AssSt. From Ipstones (Staffs) or Ipsden (Oxon).

Irby, Ireby: Hugh, Ailsi *de Yrebi* 1193 P (L), 1195 P (Cu); William *de Irby* 1280 IpmY; Richard *Yrby* 1341 IpmGl. From Irby (Ches, Lincs, NRYorks), or Ireby (Cumb, Lancs).

Ireland: Ralph *de Ibernia, de Irlande* 1200, 1210 Oseney; Robert *de Irlonde* 1327 SRSx; John *Ireland* 1458 FFEss. 'The man from Ireland.'

Iremonger, Ironmonger: Richard *Yernmonger* Hy 3 Gilb (L); John *le Irmongere* 1255 RH (O); John *Irinmongere* 1279 RH (Bk); Elyas *le Ironmongere* 1294 AssSt; Roger *le Ernmongere* 1327 SRSt; John *le yremongere* 1327 SRC; John *le Yernemanger* 1332 MESO (Y). OE *īren* 'iron' and *mangere*, 'ironmonger'. Identical with ICEMONGER. *Ern-, Yern-* in Yorks, Lincs and Staffs is from the ON *earn, jarn* 'iron'.

Ireton, Irton: Richard, Henry *de Irton'* 1218 AssL, 1272 AssSt; William *de Yrton'* 1351 AssL. From Ireton (Derby), or Irton (Cumb, NRYorks).

Irish: Richard *Ireis* 1169 P (Sa); William *le hyreis* 1227 FFSf; Robert *le Irish* 1356 AssSt. OFr *Ireis* 'Irish', later replaced by the English form.

Ironmonger: *v.* IREMONGER

Ironside: Hugh *Irninside*, Thomas *Irenside* 1297 Coram (L); John *Irenside* 1333 FrY. OE *īren* and *sīd* 'iron-side, warrior'. *Irnenside* preserves the adjectival inflexion. cf. *mid irenen neilen* c1175 NED. The first and most famous bearer of this nickname was Edmund Ironside, so called for his doughtiness: '*Iren-sid* wæs geclypod for his snellscipe' 1057 ASC D. cf. 'Edmundes sones *wiþ þe Irenside*' c1350 Brut.

Irvin, Irvine, Irving, Ervin, Erving, Urvine: Robert *de Hirewyn* 1226 Black; Simon *de Irwyn* 1296 AssCh; Adam *Irvine* 1455 Black. From Irvine (Ayrshire) or Irving (Dumfries). There has

been confusion with ERWIN.

Irwin: *v.* ERWIN

Isaac, Isaacs, Isacke, Isaacson: *Isac* 1086 DB; Willelmus *filius Ysac* 1206 Cur (Ess); Henry *Isaac* 1275 SRWo; Walter *Isak* 1327 SRSo; John *Isakson* 1379 PTY. Hebrew *Isaac*, from a root meaning 'laugh'. The name was not confined to Jews and the medieval surname was certainly not Jewish.

Isabel, Isbell, Isbill: *Isabel* 1141–9 Holme (Nf), c1160 DC (Lei); William *Isabelle* 1202–16 StP (Lo); William *Isabel* 1275 SRWo; John *Isbel* 1379 PTY. *Isabel*, a form of *Elizabeth*, which seems to have developed in Provence. A very popular name, with pet-forms *Ibb, Libbe, Nibb, Tibb, Bibby, Ellice*, and various diminutives.

Isard, Iseard, Isitt: *v.* ISSARD

Isdale, Isdell: *v.* ESDAILE

Isham, Isom, Issom: Henry *de Isham* 1206 Cur (Nth); John *Isom* 1713 FrLeic. From Isham (Northants).

Isherwood, Esherwood, Usherwood: William *de Yserwude* 1246 AssLa; Adam *de Esherwode* 1332 SRLa; Robert *Issherewood*, John *Ussherwood* 1524 SRSf. From an unidentified place, probably in Lancs.

Isles: *v.* ILES

Ismay: *Ysemay* de Mult' 1275 RH (L); Ralph *Isemay, Hyssmaye* 13th Shef (Y); William *Ysmay* 1327 SRDb. This somewhat rare woman's name might possibly be an unrecorded OE **Ismæg*, but *Is-* is unknown in OE names and *-mæg* is found as a second theme in only three late names. cf. also *Idemay* la Frye 1327 SRSo. The equation of the earliest example, *Isemay* (1227 AssBk), with *Isemeine* (cf. EMENEY) suggests a continental origin. *Is-* occurs in a number of OG names. Förstemann derives *Macharias* from a root **mag*, related to OHG *magan* 'might'. Forssner suggests that the OFr *Maissent* may contain the same first element, from OG **Magisind*, **Megisind*. Hence, *Ismay* may, perhaps, be from an OG **Ismagi*, **Ismegi*.

Isom: *v.* ISHAM

Ison: William *Ideson* 1583 RothwellPR (Y). 'Son of Ida.'

Issard, Issett, Issit, Issitt, Issott, Issolt, Isard, Iseard, Isitt, Iszard, Iszatt, Izard, Izat, Izatt, Izant, Izod, Izzard, Izzett, Ezard: *Iseldis* 1086 DB (Do); *Ysoude* 1186–1210 Holme (Nf); *Hysode* 12th DC (L); *Ysout* 1200 Oseney (O); *Isolda* 1200 Cur (Lei), 1219 Cur (Sf), AssY; *Ysolt* 1201 Cur (Y); *Isouda, Iseuda* 1214 Cur (Sx, Lei); *Isota* Holebrook 1327 SRSo; *Isata* 1459 FrY; *Izota* 1603 SRWo; Thomas *Isolde* 1275 RH (Sf); Robert *Isaud* 1316 Wak (Y); Thomas *Isoude* 1326 FFEss; Margaret *Isod*, John *Isot* 1379 PTY; John *Esod* 1496 FrNorw; Joane *Isard*, Rachel *Izatt*, Henry *Izod* 1626, 1666, 1668 Bardsley; Robert *Issitt* 1763 FrLeic. OFr *Iseut, Isalt, Isaut, Ysole*, OG **Ishild* 'ice-battle'.

Ithell: *Itel* Karlo 1160 P (Sa); *Ithel* de Landinab 1215 Cur (He); Ralph *Ithel* 1336 AssSt. Welsh *Ithell*, MW *Ithael*. cf. IDLE, BITHELL.

Ivatt, Ivatts: *Iuetta* 1166 P (C), 1175 DC (L),

1221 AssWa; Richard *filius Iuotte* 1270 RamsCt (C); John *Ivette* 1262 FFSf; William *Ivet* 1271 ForSt; John *Iuot* 1327 SRC. A diminutive of OFr *Iva*, feminine of *Ivo*. cf. IVE.

Ive, Ives: Herbertus *filius Iuonis* 1086 DB; *Iue* de Verdun 1101–7 Holme (Nf); *Iuo, Hiue* de Gausla 1155–60 DC (L); Roger *Yuo* 1175 P (L); Thomas, Henry *Ive* 1274 RH (So), 1280 FFEss; John *Ives* 1327 SRSx. OFr *Ive, Yve(s), Ivon*, particularly common among the Normans and Bretons.

Ivers: *v.* IVOR

Iveson, Ivison: Adam *Iveson* 1383 Shef (Y). 'Son of *Ive*.'

Ivey, Ivy: Geoffrey *de Iuoi, de Iuei* 1161–2 P (O). From Ivoy (Cher).

Ivor, Ivers, Iverson: *Juuar* 1066 DB (Sa); *Iware* diaconus 1140–53 Holme (Nf); *Iuor* paruus 1161 P (Wo); Robert *Yuor* 1296 SRSx. ON *Ívarr*, ODa *Iwar*, OSw *Ivar* 'yew-army'.

Ivory, Ivery: (i) Roger *de Iuri, de Iueri* 1086 DB (Bk); G. *de Iverio*, Matillis comitissa *de Ibreio* 1215 Cur (O). From Ivry-la-Bataille (Eure), earlier *Ibreium*. (ii) *Ivory* Malet 1270 Bardsley; Thomas son of *Ivorie* 1332 SRCu; Alice *Yuory* 1296 SRSx; William *Ivory* 1364 LLB G. A diminutive of *Ivor*.

Izard, Izatt, Izant, Izod, Izzard, Izzett: *v.* ISSARD

J

Jack, Jacka, Jacke, Jackes, Jacks, Jagg, Jaggs, Jakes, Jeeks, Jecks, Jex: Petrus, Andreas *filius Jake* 1195–7 P (Co); Normannus *filius Jacce* 1218 AssL; *Jake* Heriel 1275 RH (Gl); Robertus, Johannes *filius Jake* 1279 RH (C), c1315 Calv (Y); *Jakes* Flinthard 1292 SRLo; *Jak* del Thorp 1332 SRCu; *Jagge* the jogelour 1377 Piers Plowman; William *Jagge* 1251 Rams (Hu); William *Jake* 1260 AssC; Geoffrey, Richard *Jakes* 1269 AssSo, 1296 SRSx; Agnes, William *Jakkes* 1279 RH (Hu), 1366 Eynsham (O); William, Robert *Jacke* 1302 AssSt, 1332 SRWa; John *Jak* 1327 SRC; Adam *Jeke* 1332 SRWa; John *Jekes* 1346 ColchCt; Walter *Jekkes* 1524 SRSf; Thomas *Jagges* 1568 ib. The ODCN, following E. W. B. Nicholson (1892), derives *Jack*, the commonest pet-name of *John*, from *Jankin*, a diminutive of *Jan*, *Jehan* (John). According to this theory, *Jankin* became *Jackin* and was then shortened to *Jack*, a process completed by the beginning of the 14th century. Both *Jack* and *Jake* are certainly found for *John* towards the end of the 13th century: *John* or *Jacke* le Warner 1275 RH (C); *John* or *Jakke* de Bondec 1279 RH (Bk); *Jake* or *John* de Couentre 1292 SRLo, 1300 LoCt. *Jankin* was a 14th-century diminutive of *John*. v. JENKIN. But it is difficult to believe that the 1195 *Jake* and the 1218 *Jacce* can derive from *Jankin*. In France, *Jacques* (James) was so common a name that it became the normal term for a *peasant*, just as, in England, *Jack* became a synonym for *man* or *boy*. It would be strange if so popular a French name did not appear in England. Though rare, undoubted examples of *Jacques* are found: *Jacobus* or *Jakes* Amadur 1275 RH (L); *Jakes* or *James* Flinthard 1292 SRLo, 1300 LoCt. The diminutives *Jackett*, *Jacklin*, *Jakins*, correspond to the French *Jaquet*, *Jacquelin*, *Jacquin*, from *Jacques*. v. also JAMES. *Jakes*, *Jeeks*, *Jex*, show the same vowel development as *James*, *Jeames*, *Jem*.

Jackalin: v. JACKLIN

Jackaman: *Jakemyn* le Hatter 1314 LLB D; *Jakemina* 1321 FFEss. A diminutive of *Jacqueme*, a Picard form of *James*, from **Jacomus*. Also feminine, and has probably become JACKMAN. *Jakemin* de Sessolu 1302 LoCt is also called *James*.

Jackett, Jacketts, Jacot: William *Jaket* 1296 SRSx. A diminutive of *Jack*. The feminine *Jaketta* (1300 LoCt) was a pet-name for *Jakemina*.

Jacklin, Jackling, Jackalin: *Jakelinus* 1219 Fees (Y); *Jakelinus* de Bouele 1327 SRSx; Elias *Jakelyn* 1296 SRSx; Edmund *Jakelin* 1327 SRSf. A double diminutive of *Jack*. *Jacolin* hugelin (1292 SRLo) is also called both *James* and *Jack* (1291 LLB A).

Jackman, Jakeman: Robert, William *Jakeman* 1296 SRSx, 1327 SRSf; Robert *Jacman* 1379 PTY. 'Servant of *Jack*.' v. also JACKAMAN.

Jackson, Jacson, Jagson, Jaxon: Adam *Jackessone* 1327 SRSf; Adam *Jakson* 1353 AssSt; John *Jakeson* 1438 AD i (L). 'Son of *Jack*.'

Jacob, Jacobs, Jacubs: *Jacob* c1250 Rams (Hu); Agnes *Jacobes* 1244 Rams (Beds); Walter, Alan *Jacob* c1250 Rams (Hu), 1324 FFK; Emma *Iacop* 1332 SRSr. The medieval surname was not Jewish. *Jacob* is found before the Conquest as the name of an ecclesiastic. After the Conquest, it is impossible to decide how common the name was as the Latin *Jacobus* was used for both *Jacob* and *James*.

Jacobson: William *Jacobson* 1332 SRCu; Peter *Jacobbesson* 1375 ColchCt. 'Son of *Jacob*.'

Jacoby, Jacobi: Robertus *filius Jacoby* 1297 SRY; Thomas, Pieres *Jacoby* 1275 RH (Nf), 1338 LoPleas. A preservation of the Latin genitive *Jacobi* '(Son) of *Jacobus*', Jacob or James.

Jacot: v. JACKETT

Jacox: v. JEACOCK

Jacques, Jacquet, Jacquot, Jaques, Jaquest, Jaquet, Jaquin, Jaquiss: Either late introductions from France or a refashioning of *Jakes*, *Jackett*, etc., after the French. Camden notes such a tendency in the 16th century 'which some Frenchified English, to their disgrace, have too much affected'. *Jaquest* and *Jaquiss* are certainly English forms.

Jaffray, Jaffrey: v. JEFFRAY

Jagg, Jaggs: v. JACK

Jaggar, Jaggars, Jagger, Jaggers: Thomas *Jager*, John *Jagher* 1379 PTY; Katerina *Jeggar* 1480 GildY. A West Riding name, from *jagger* 'carrier, carter; pedlar, hawker' (1514 NED). It may also be from *Jaggard*, with loss of d.

Jaggard: Aldred, William *Jagard* 1194 Cur (W), 1279 RH (C); John *Jakard* 1296 SRSx. *Jack-ard*, a hypocoristic of *Jack*.

Jago, Jagoe, Jeggo, Iago: *Jago filius Ytel* 1185 P (He); William *Jeago* 1221 AssSa; Thomas *Jagoo* 1524 SRSf. Welsh *Iago*, Cornish *Jago* 'James'.

Jagson: v. JACKSON

Jailler: v. GALER

Jaine: v. JAN

Jakeman: v. JACKMAN

Jakes: v. JACK

Jakins, Jakens, Jeakins, Jeakings: *Jakin* de Lagefare 1202 FFEss; Robert *Jacun* Hy 3 HPD (Ess); Claritia *Jagun* 1275 RH (Nf); John, William *Jakyn* 1296 SRSx, 1314 FFK; Robert *Jeakins* 1806 Bardsley. *Jak-un, Jak-in*, diminutives of *Jak* (James). v. JACK.

James: *Jacobus* 1160 DC (L); *Jam'* de Sancto Hylario 1173–6 NthCh (Nth); *Jamos* (*Jacobus*) de Vabadun 1221 Cur (Sf); *James* or *Jacobus* de Audithleg' 1255 RH (Sa); Walter, Emma *James* 1187 P (Gl); Cristiana, Thomas *Jemes* 1279 RH (C), 1332 SRWa. *Jacob* was latinized as *Jacŏbus*, but in late Latin became *Jacŏbus* and *Jacŏmus*. From the former came French *Jacques*, English *Jacob* and Welsh *Iago*, from the latter, Spanish *Jayme*, OFr *James, Gemmes*, AFr *Jam* and English *James*. In early documents the name is usually *Jacobus*, but *James* is occasionally found in the 12th and 13th centuries, sometimes alternating with *Jack* or its diminutives *Jackamin, Jackett* and *Jacklin*. The vernacular form was *Gemme* or *Jemme* (both masculine and feminine), and occasionally *Jimme*. v. GEM.

Jameson, Jamieson, Jamison: William *Jamesson* 1379 PTY; John *Jameson* 1440 FrY; Richard *Jamieson* 1642 PrGR. 'Son of *James*.'

Jan, Jans, Janse, Jannis, Jane, Janes, Jaine, Jayne, Jaynes, Jeynes: Simon *Ianes* 1297 MinAcctCo; William *Jan* 1327 SRSo; John *Janne* 1327 SRC; Thomas *Jannes*, John *Janys* 1327 SRWo; Robert *Jans, Jance* 1539–40 Bardsley; John *Jane* 1548 Oxon. *Jan*, from *Johan*. v. JOHN.

Janet, Jennett: Willelmus *filius Jonet* 1297 SRY; *Jonot* 1308 Wak (Y); John *Ionet* 1297 MinAcctCo; Robert, Simon *Janot* ib., 1327 SRSx. *Janot, Jonet, Jonot*, diminutives of *Jan, Jon*, from *Johan*. *Jennett* is from *Jehan*. v. JOHN.

Janin, Jannings: v. JENNINGS

Janks: v. JENKIN

Janman, Jenman: Richard *Janeman* 1327 SRSx; Wyote *Janemon* 1327 SRWo. 'Servant of *Jan*.' v. JOHN.

Jannis: v. JAN

Janson: Henry *Jannesonne* 1327 SRSt. 'Son of *Jan*.'

Jaques, Jaquest, Jaquet, Jaquiss: v. JACQUES

Jaram: v. JEROME

Jaray: v. GEARY

Jardin, Jardine: Winfredus *de Jardine* a1153 Black (Kelso); Humphrey *del Gardin* 1194–1211 ib.; Matilda *atte Jardin*, Mabilia *Jardyn* 1296 SRSx. 'Dweller near, or worker at a garden', central OFr *jardin*.

Jared: v. GARRAD

Jarmain, Jarman: v. GERMAN

Jarmay, Jarmey: v. JERMEY

Jarrad, Jarred, Jarratt, Jarrett, Jarritt: v. GARRAD

Jarrand: v. GERANT

Jarrard: v. GERARD

Jarraud, Jarrod, Jarrold, Jarrott: v. GERALD

Jarry: v. GEARY

Jarville: William *de Iarpunuill'* 1173 KRec xviii; John, Laurence (*de*) *Jarpe*(*n*)*ville, Charpeneuill* 1258, 1285, 1296 PN Ess 128; Alice *Jarpenvil* 1301 SRY; William *Jerpeville* 1327 *SR* (Ess); John *Gardeuill'* 1376 AssEss; Gerald *de Charpeuile* 14th *Petre* (Ess); John *Gerdevyle, Jardevelde* 1423 ib., 1473 *ERO* (Ess); Richard *Jard*(*e*)*feld* 1507, 1527 FFEss. From Gerponville (Seine-Inférieure), cf. Gerpins in Rainham (PN Ess 128).

Jarvis, Jervis, Jervois, Jervoise, Gervase, Gervis: (i) *Geruasius* Painel 1158–66 DC (Lei); *Garvasius* Godihalt 1275 SRWo; John *Geruas'* 1202 P (Sa); Thomas *Geruais* 1230 P (Nf); William *Gerveys* 1270 AssSo; Richard *Jerfeys* 1327 SRSx; Thomas *Jerveys* 1360 ColchCt. OG *Gervas*, OFr *Gervais*(*e*). (ii) Robert *de Gerewall'* 1275 SRWo; John *Gerveux* 1360 FrY; William *de Gervaux* 1370 ib.; William *Gerveys* 1395 ib.; John, Richard *Gervas* 1435 ib.; Thomas *Jarvis* 1713 ib. Though usually from the personal name, these names, in Yorkshire in particular, are at times from Jervaulx (Yorks), of which the pronunciation (now obsolescent) is *Jarvis*, earlier *Gervaus* 1200, *Jervax* 1400, *Gerveis* 1530, *Gervis* 1577 (PN NRY 250).

Jary: v. GEARY

Jaxon: v. JACKSON

Jay, Jaye, Jayes, Jays, Jaze, Jeayes, Jeays, Jeyes: Peter *le iai* 1195 P (C); Gilbert *Jai* (*Gai*) 1202 P (L); Walter *le Jay* 1225 AssSo. OFr *jay, gai*, Fr *geai* 'jay', chatterer.

Jaycock(s): v. JEACOCK

Jayne(s): v. JAN

Jeacock, Jeacocke, Jacox, Jaycock, Jaycocks: William *Jacok* 1327 SRSf; John *Jecok* 1375 ColchCt; John *Jecokes* 1381 AssWa; Elizabeth *Jeacock* 1712 Bardsley. *Jak-coc*, a pet-form of *Jack*.

Jeafferson, Jeaffreson: v. JEFFERSON

Jeakins, Jeakings: v. JAKINS

Jealous: Ralph *Jelus* 1230 Pat (K); John *Jelous* 1327 *SR* (Ess). ME, OFr *gelos* 'wrathful, furious' (c1385 MED).

Jean, Jeanes, Jeans, Jeens, Jenn, Jenne, Jenness, Jennis, Jenns, Geen, Genn: (i) William *Gene* 1275 RH (Sf); Thomas *Gennes* 1297 MinAcctCo; Alice *Genne* 1327 SRSf; Thomas *Geene* 1378 FrY; Mary *Jeenes* 1663 Bardsley. *Jen*, from *Jehan*. v. JOHN. (ii) Henry, Francis *de Gene* 1255 RH (St), 1309 LLB D. From Genoa.

Jearey, Jeary: v. GEARY

Jearum: v. JEROME

Jeavons: v. JEVON

Jeay(e)s: v. JAY

Jebb, Gebb: William *Gebbe* 1327 SRSf; Lucas *Jebbe* 1508 FrY. A voiced form of *Gepp* (Geoffrey).

Jebson, Jibson: Robert *Gebbesson, Gebisson* 1442, 1453 Shef. 'Son of *Gebb*.'

Jeckell(s): v. JEKYLL

Jecks, Jeeks: v. GEAKE, JACK

Jeeves, Jeves, Geaves, Geeves: *Geua* 1120–3 EngFeud, Hy 2 Gilb (L), 1221 AssWa; Willelmus *filius Geue* 1208 Cur (Nb); *Geva* Mullyng 1313 AD iv (Lo); Richard *Geves* 1279 RH (O); Thomas

Geue, Adam *Geues* 1327 SRWo; Thomas *Jeve* 1327 SRSo. Bardsley takes *Jeeves* as identical with *Geff*, a pet-name of Geoffrey, but this accounts neither for the long vowel nor for the *v*. It is a pet-name for *Genevieve*, a favourite name in France, where St Geneviève is the patron saint of Paris. Its use in England in the 12th–14th centuries seems to have escaped notice. A 12th-century Lincolnshire deed of a woman named *Geua* has attached to it her seal, with the legend: SIGILL' GENEVEVE F' ARNALD (DC). *Geva*, wife of Segar, is also called *Eva* (1199 CurR).

Jeff, Jeffe, Jeffes, Jeffs: *Geffe* 1260 AssCh; Ralph *Jeffe* 1275 RH (D); Richard *Geffes*, William *Geffe* 1332 SRWa. *Geff*, a pet-form of *Geoffrey*. cf. Alicia *Gefraywif*, Alicia *Gefdoghter* 1379 PTY. *v.* also GEFFEN.

Jeffcock, Jeffcoat, Jeffcoate, Jeffcote, Jeffcott, Jefcoat, Jefcoate, Jefcott, Jephcott: (i) Geoffrey *Geffecoke* 1327 SRWo; William *Gefcok* 1332 SRSt; Emota *Jeffecockes* 1380 SRSt; Agnes *Jeffcott* 1616 Bardsley. A diminutive of *Jeff*. cf. Thomas *Gepcok* 1360 Cl (K). (ii) Thomas *Geuecok* 1332 SRWa; John *Jevecok* 1454 RochW. A diminutive of *Geva* (Geneviève). *v.* JEEVES. *Jevecok* became *Jevcok*, and was then assimilated to *Jeffcock*. As often, the suffix *-cock* has become *-cott* or *-coat*.

Jefferd: *v.* GIFFARD

Jeffers: *v.* JEFFRAY

Jefferson, Jeafferson, Jeaffreson: Robert *Geffreysone* 1344 AssSt; Alice *Geffrason* 1488 GildY; John *Jeffrason* 1528 FrY. 'Son of Geoffrey.'

Jefford: *v.* GIFFARD

Jeffray, Jeffrey, Jeffreys, Jeffree, Jeffress, Jeffries, Jeffry, Jeffryes, Jeffares, Jefferey, Jefferies, Jefferis, Jefferiss, Jeffery, Jefferys, Jefferys, Jeffers, Jeoffroy, Jaffray, Jaffrey, Geffers, Geoffrey, Geoffroy: *Goisfridus, Gaufridus, Gosfridus* 1086 DB; *Galfridus* c1150 DC (L); Simon *filius Gosfrei* 1210 Cur (Nf); Walter *Geffrei* 1203 Cur (Nf), *Gefray* 1243 AssSo; Agnes *Geffreys* 1283 SRSf; Robert *Geoffray* 1293 AssSt; William *Geffrey* 1296 SRSx; John *Gaffry* 1327 SRSo; Hugo *Jafres* 1327 SRSt; Joan *Jeffray* 1327 SRC; Henry *Geffreys* 1332 SRSt; John *Geffre* 1333 AD iv (Nth); Symon *Geffris* 1340 SRWo; Roger *Jeffray* 1379 PTY; William *Jaffrey* 1450 SIA xii; John *Jafery* 1499 NorwW; Philip *Jeffereyes* 1566 ChwWo; Robert *Jeffers* 1689 FrY; Robert *Jefferys* 1723 ib. ME *Geffrey*, from OFr *Geuffroi, Jeuffroi* or OFr *Jefroi*, representing two or, possibly, three OG names usually latinized in early documents as *Galfridus* or *Gaufridus* (most commonly) and *Goisfridus* or *Gosfridus*. *v.* Forssner 101–2, 125–6.

Jeggo: *v.* JAGO

Jeggons: *v.* JUGGINS

Jekyll, Jeckell, Jeckells, Jickells, Jickles, Jiggle, Jockel, Giggle, Jockelson: *Judichel uenator* 1066 DB (C); *Judicaelis* 1066 ICC (C); *Iuichel', Iuchel presbiter* 1086 DB (Sf); *Gykell, Jukel* de *Jertheburc* c1170, 1182 Gilb (L); *Johannes filius Jokell', Jukell'* 1218 AssL; *Jukel Brito* 1207 Cur (Nf); *Gigelle Belle* 1276 RH (Y); John *Iekel* (*Iukel*) 1174

P (Ha); John *Gikel* 1201 P (L); Thomas *Jokel* 1296 SRSx; Robert *Jekel* 1312 FFEss. OBret, OC *Iudicael*, which became *Iedecael*, modern *Gicquel*, *Iezequel* (Loth) and survives in French as *Jézéquel*. The name is found at Bodmin (c1000) as *Gyðiccæl* (PNDB). In England the personal name was particularly common in Yorkshire and Lincolnshire and in districts where the Breton contingent settled after the Conquest. *v.* also JOEL, GOSS.

Jell: *v.* GELL
Jellard: *v.* GILLARD
Jellett: *v.* GILLET
Jellings: *v.* GILLIAN
Jellis, Jelliss: Robert *Geliss*, John *Gelis* 1527 Black; Andrew *Jeeles* 1681 ib. For GILES.
Jempson, Jemson: *v.* GEMSON
Jencken: *v.* JENKIN
Jenckes: *v.* JENKS
Jeneson: William *Geneson* 1346 AssSt. 'Son of John.' *v.* JEAN.
Jenkin, Jenkins, Jenking, Jenkings, Jenkyn, Jenkyns, Jencken, Junkin: *Janekyn* de sancto Iohanne 1260 Oseney (O); *Jonkin* the Turnur 1288 AssCh; *Jenkin* le persones 1327 SRSt; Richard *Janekyn* 1296 SRSx; William *Jonkyn* 1297 Ipm (Do); William *Jankins* 1327 SRWo; Richard *Jenkins* 1327 SRSo; William *Junkin*, George *Jonkyng* 1469, 1530 FrY. A diminutive of *Jan, Jon, Jen* (John). *v.* JEAN, JOHN. cf. *John* nicknamed *Janekin* de Bocking Ed 3 PN Ess 461; Henry *Janekynesmon* Hastang (1319 SaltAS x), 'servant of John Hastang junior'. His father was alive and his servants were Henry *Jonespaneter* Hastang and Richard *Jonesprest* Hastang, so that *Janekyn* clearly means 'Young John'.

Jenkinson, Jenkerson, Jenkison, Junkinson, Junkison: Robert *Jonkinson* 1379 PTY; William *Jenkynson* 1484 FrY. 'Son of *Jenkin*.'

Jenks, Jenckes, Janks: Walter *Jenks* 1542 Oseney (O). A contraction of *Jenkin, Jankin*.

Jenman: *v.* JANMAN

Jenn, Jenne, Jenns: *v.* JEAN. The Cornish *Genn, Gynn* may be for *Jennifer*.

Jennens: *v.* JENNINGS

Jenner, Jenoure, Genner, Genower, Ginner: Richard *lengignur, lenginnur* 1191–7 P (Y); William *Enginur* 1202 Cur (Sf); Robert *le enguigniur* 1221 AssWo; Robert *le Ginnur* 1229–30 Clerkenwell (Lo); Ralph *Gynnour* 1301 SRY; William *le Genour* 1324 RamsCt; Robert *Jenour* 1327 SRSf. OFr *engigneor, enginior* 'engineer, maker of military machines' (c1380 MED). In the 12th century *ingeniator* was used of men who combined the duties of master-mason and architect. Ailnoth *ingeniator*, a military architect, was surveyor of the king's buildings at Westminster and the Tower in 1157 and was in charge of building operations at Windsor 1166–73. He repaired Westminster Abbey after a fire and superintended the destruction of the castles of Framlingham and Walton (MedInd 108).

Jenness: *v.* JEAN
Jennett: *v.* JANET

Jennifer, Junifer, Juniper: Mabilia *Jeneuer* 1296 SRSx; Henry *Juneuyr* 1332 ib.; Joshua *Junefer* 1623 SfPR; Captain *Jenifer* 1667 Pepys; John *Juniper* 1753 Bardsley. Welsh *Gwenhwyvar* (f), from *gwen* 'fair, white' and (*g*)*wyf* 'smooth, yielding', found in Shropshire as *Gwenhevare* in 1431 and in Cornwall as *Jenefer* (1554) and *Junipher* (1691).

Jennings, Jennens, Jennins, Jenings, Jenyns, Janin, Jannings, Jouning: *Janyn* le Breton 1332 SRLa; *Jenyn* de Fraunce 1379 PTY; Roger *Jonyng* 1296 SRSx; John *Ianin* 1297 MinAcctCo; Walter *Jannen*, Richard *Janyns* 1327 SRWo; John *Janyng* 1327 SRSx; Thomas *Jenyn* 1428 FA (Sx); Cristofer *Jenyng* 1532 FrY. Diminutives in *-in* of *Jan*, *Jon*, *Jen*. *v.* JOHN. cf. *John* or *Janyn* Nichol(e) 1413–17 LLB I.

Jennis: *v.* JEAN

Jennison: Robert *Genyson* 1491 GildY; William *Jenyson* 1518 FrY. 'Son of *Jenin*.' *v.* JENNINGS.

Jenns: *v.* JEAN

Jent: *v.* GENT

Jentle: *v.* GENTLE

Jeoffroy: *v.* JEFFRAY

Jephcott: *v.* JEFFCOCK

Jephson: Hugh *Geffesone* 1327 SRWo. 'Son of *Geff*', i.e. Geoffrey.

Jepp, Jeppe, Jepps: *v.* GEPP

Jeppeson, Jepson, Gepson: John *Gepsone* 1326 Wak (Y); John *Jepson* 1379 PTY. 'Son of *Gepp*.'

Jerams: *v.* JEROME

Jeray: *v.* GEARY

Jerdan, Jerden, Jerdein, Jerdon: Jon *Jerdein* 1563 Black; Andrew *Jerdon* 1659 ib. Scottish forms of JARDIN.

Jeremy, Jermyn: *Iheremias* de Tornhill' 1189 P (Y); *Geremias, Jeremias* Banastre c1200 Rad (C); *Gereminus* de Eclefeld', *Jeremias* de Ecclesfeld' 1219 AssY; Johannes *Jheremie* 1193 P (Y); Thomas *Jeremye* 1225 Pat; William *Germin* 1253 HPD (Ess). *Jeremias* is a latinization of the Greek form of the Hebrew *Jeremiah* 'May Jehovah exalt', in the vernacular *Jeremy*. cf. 'þe propheci þat said was þoru *Jeremi*' (Cursor Mundi). *v.* JERMEY. *Gereminus* is a hypocoristic.

Jermain, Jerman, Jermin, Jermine, Jermyn, Jermynn: *v.* GERMAN

Jermey, Jermy, Jarmay, Jarmey, Jarmy: Johanna *Germye, Jermye* 1303, 1346 FA (Sf); Thomas *Jarmy* 1652 Bardsley (Nf). One would naturally assume that *Jermey* was identical with *Jeremy* and Bardsley cites a late example: *Jeremye* or *Jermy* Gooch from Norfolk (1617, 1652). He also notes that Blomefield, the Norfolk historian, states definitely that the true origin of *Jermy*, a Norfolk surname, is *Jermin* and cites Sir John *Germyn* or *Jermy* (1300). The truth is that *Germin* was used for both *Jeremy* and *Germain* and here the vernacular *Jermy* prevailed. *v.* GERMAN, JEREMY.

Jernegan, Jerningham: *Gernagus* filius Hugonis 1166 P (Y); *Gernagan* de Tanefeld, Hugo *filius Jernagan* 1204 AssY; Hubert *Gernagan* 1166 RBE (Sf); Aluredus *Gernegan* 1170 P (Y); Hubert *Jernegan, Jarnegan* 1218, 1222 FFSf; John *Gernyngham, Jerningham* 1472, 1503 Copinger (Sf); Edward *Jermingham* 1510 ib.; Henry *Jernegam* 1572 Bardsley (Nf). The surname, now rare, is found particularly in Suffolk where Little Stonham, also known as *Stanham Gernagan* (1244 FFSf), was long held by the family of Hubert *Jarnegan* (1222 FFSf). In 1086 (DB) land was held in Stonham by Earl Alan and Iuichel the priest (*v.* JEKYLL) and there can be little doubt that *Gernagan* is a Celtic name brought over by the Bretons at the Conquest, probably identical with OBret *Iarnuuocon* (*Iarnogon* 1062 Loth) 'iron-famous'.

Jerome, Jerrom, Jerrome, Jerromes, Jerams, Jerram, Jerrams, Jerrim, Jearum, Jaram, Gerham: *Geram* Hy 2 DC (L); *Geram* de Curzun 1206 FineR (Bk); *Jeronimus, Geronimus, Gerarmus* de Curzun 1206–11 Cur (Berks, St); *Jerom'* de Ponte Burgi 1219 AssY; *Jeronimus* de Normaneby 1230 P (L); William *Geran'* 1194 CurR (Sa); Roger *Geram* 1333 AD ii (Lei); Peter *Jerrome* 1604 FrY; Joseph *Jerram* 1729 Bardsley. It is clear that two distinct personal names were early confused. OG *Ger(r)am, Gerrannus* 'spear-raven' would certainly be taken as the name of *Geram* de Curzun were it not for the forms *Jeronimus, Geronimus* which point clearly to *Jerome*, Greek Ἱερώνυμος 'sacred name', Italian *Geronimo*, French *Jérôme*. The name of the translator of the Bible does not seem to have been very popular in England. *Gerrannus* may also have become GERRANS or JERRANS. *v.* GERANT.

Jerrans: *v.* GERANT

Jerrard: *v.* GERARD

Jerratt, Jerreatt, Jerred: *v.* GARRAD

Jerrold: *v.* GERALD

Jerrom(e), Jerrim: *v.* JEROME

Jervis, Jervois, Jervoise: *v.* JARVIS

Jesson: *v.* JUDSON

Jessop, Jessopp, Jessope, Jessup, Jessep: William *Josep* 1296 SRSx; William *Josop*, John *Jesop* 1379 PTY; Joan *Josopp, Jesopp* 1524 SRSf. A pronunciation of *Joseph*.

Jester: John *Gestour* 1377 ColchCt. A derivative of OFr *geste, jeste* 'exploits'; ME *gester* 'a mimic, buffoon, merry-andrew' (c1362); 'a professional reciter of romances' (c1380).

Jestice: *v.* JUSTICE

Jetson: *v.* JUDSON

Jeudwin, Jeudwine: *Jeldewin* 1157 P (Sx); *Joldewinus* filius Sauarici 1158 P (Sx); *Jodewinus* 1214 Cur (Sx); Martin *Gaudewyne* 1296 SRSx; Gilbert *Goldewyne, Geldewine* 1317 AssK; John *Jeldewyne, Jewdewyne*, Agnes *Joidewyne* 1327 SRSx; John *Joldewyne, Judewyne* 1332 ib.; John *Judwyn* 1534 SxWills. AFr *Jeudewin*, a Norman form of OE *Goldwine*. *v.* GOLDWIN.

Jeune, June, Lejeune: Richard *le Jeune* 12th Lichfield (St); Matilda *Jun* 1279 RH (C); John *le June* 1301 SRY. Fr *jeune* 'young'. cf. JEVON.

Jeves: *v.* JEEVES

Jevon, Jevons, Jeavons: (i) Alexander *le iouene* Hy 2 DC (L); John *le Jofne* 1200 Cur (Herts);

Bartholomew *le Joevene, le Juvene* 1254–69 Rams (Beds); Robert *le Jeofne, le Jevene* 1242–55 Fees (Nth); Thomas *le Geven*' 1279 RH (O). OFr *jovene*, Lat *juvenis* 'young'. cf. JEUNE. (ii) *Jeuan* Vachann 1391 Chirk; Ririt *ap Jeuan* ap Eigon 1393 ib.; *Jevan* or *Evan* Thomas 1600 Bardsley (Glam); Thomas *Ieuane* 1436 Oseney (O); John *Jevanne* 1459 ib. Welsh *Ieuan*, later *Evan*, 'John'.

Jew: *Gewe* de Sumerkotes 1275 RH (L); Richard *Jue* 1314 FFEss. From *Jull* (Julian or Juliana). Also a nickname: Thomas *le Jeu* 1275 RH (Nt), 'the Jew'.

Jewell, Jewels: *v.* JOEL. The surname may also be metonymic for jeweller, goldsmith: Robert *le*, Alicia *la Jueler* 1319 SRLo.

Jew(e)sbury: *v.* DEWSBURY

Jewett, Jewitt: *v.* JOWETT

Jewhurst: *v.* DEWHIRST

Jewison, Jewisson: Henry *Jewetson* 1533 GildY. 'Son of *Jewet*.' *v.* JOWETT.

Jewkes: *v.* JUKES

Jewry, Jury: Richard *ate Jewerye*, atte *Giwerye* 1327, 1332 SRSx; William *Jury* 1495 ArchC 42. 'Dweller in the Jewry, the Jews' quarter, the Ghetto.' AFr *juerie*, OFr *juierie, jurie*.

Jewson, Juson: Richard *Juwesone, Jullesome, Jullesone* 1333, 1340, 1341 ColchCt. 'Son of *Jull*.'

Jewster: *v.* JUSTER

Jex: *v.* GEAKE, JACK

Jeyes: *v.* JAY

Jeynes: *v.* JAN

Jibson: *v.* JEBSON

Jickells, Jickles: *v.* JEKYLL

Jickling: *Jukelinus, Jukellus* de Smetheton' 1200 Cur (Y); Edward *Jeglin* 1662 *HTEss*. A diminutive of *Jukel*. *v.* JEKYLL.

Jiggen(s), Jiggins: *v.* JUGGINS

Jiggle: *v.* JEKYLL

Jiles: *v.* GILES

Jillard: *v.* GILLARD

Jillett, Jillitt: *v.* GILLET

Jillings, Jillions: *v.* GILLIAN

Jimpson: *v.* GEMSON

Jinkin, Jinkins, Jinkinson, Jinks: Johanna *Jinckson* 1578 Bardsley: Mary *Jynckes* 1615 Moulton (Sf). Late developments from JENKIN.

Joan, Joanes: *v.* JOHN

Joass: *v.* GOSS

Job, Jobe, Jobes, Jope, Jopp, Jubb, Jupe, Jupp: *Jop* serviens Osulf 1185 P (Co); *Joppe* filius Harde-kin 1199 P (L); *Jubbe* de Donewiz 1275 RH (Sf); *Job* Molendinar' 1296 SRSx; William *Job* 1202 FFNf; Elyas *Jubbe* 1230 P (Nf); Henry *Joppe* 1255 RH (W); Walter *Jobbe* 1275 SRWo; Eudo *le Jope* 1290 SRSr; William *Jopes* 1296 SRSx; Richard *Joup, Joup* 1327, 1332 SRSx. Often, no doubt, as suggested by Bardsley and Weekley, from the Hebrew *Job* 'hated, persecuted', a frequent character in medieval plays. The genitive of *Job* in Orm is *Jopess*. For the variation between *Jop* and *Job*, cf. *Gipp* and *Gibb*, *Gepp* and *Jebb*. There is no evidence for OG *Joppo* in England as suggested in ODCN. We have also clearly a nick-

name. Jupeshill Fm in Dedham (Essex) derives from Matthew *le Jop* (Ed 3 PN Ess 387), OFr *jobe* 'a fool'. cf. *joppe* 'fool', *joppery* 'folly', from Lat *joppus* (PromptParv). We may also be concerned with ME *jubbe, jobb(e)* (c1386 NED), a large vessel for liquor, holding 4 gallons. Hence a nickname for one who could carry that quantity or a trade-name for a maker of *jubbes*. OFr, ME *jube, jupe* 'a long woollen garment for men' (c1290 NED) may also, as an occupation-name, have contributed to the frequency of these surnames.

Jobar, Jobber, Jubber: Alan *Iober* 1317 AssK; Robert *Jobour, Jober* 1356, 1369 LLB G; Thomas *Jobber* 1524 SRSf. Probably occupational, 'maker of woollen garments' (ME *jube*) or of large vessels (ME *jobbe*). *v.* JOB. Perhaps also to be associated with East Anglian dialect *to job* 'to peck with the beak, or with the mattock'. *Nut-jobber* was formerly a name for the nuthatch, which has become a surname.

Jobbins, Jobin: *Jobin* Don 1271 ForSt; Ern' *Jobin* 1173 P (He). A diminutive of *Job*.

Jobborn, Jobern, Joberns: Probably a substitution of *-bern* for *-bert* in *Jobert*. *Ketelbern* and *Ketelbert* frequently interchange.

Jobert, Joubert, Jubert, Goubert: John, Robert *Joyberd* 1256 Ass (Ha), 1327 SR (Ess). *Goisbert* de Inge (1141) gave his name to *Ginges Joberti* (1230), now Buttsbury (Essex). OG *Gautbert* be-came OFr *Jaubert, Joubert, Jobert*, and also *Gois-bert, Joibert*, through association with OFr *joie*.

Jobin: *v.* JOBBINS

Joblin, Jobling, Joplin, Jopling: Abraham *Joblin* 1652 FrY; Henry *Jobling* 1738 Bardsley; Hannah *Joplin* 1742 ib.; Elizabeth *Jopling* 1763 ib. A double diminutive of *Job, Job-el-in*, used in OFr of a beg-gar and in English of 'a sot, a fool'.

Jobson, Jopson: Joppe son of *Joppeson* 1332 SRCu; Ralph *Jopson* 1382 Whitby (Y); Richard *Jobson* 1491 FrY. 'Son of *Job*.'

Joce: *v.* GOSS

Jocelyn, Joscelyn, Joscelyne, Josselyn, Joselin, Joslen, Joslin, Josling, Josolyne, Joseland, Josland, Goslin, Gosselin, Goseling, Gosling, Gossling, Gostling, Gosland: *Gozelinus, Gos(c)elinus* 1086 DB; *Joscelinus, Gotcelinus, Goscelinus* de Stalham 1149–66 Holme (Nf); *Goslanus, Goslein, Goslinus, Jos-lanus* de Engelby 1154–84 Gilb, DC (L); *Joslinus* Hy 2 DC (L); *Joslenus* But 1175 P (L); Willelmus *filius Jocealini, Jocelini, Gosceami, Josealmi* 1208–12 Cur (L); Robert *Goselin* 1185 Templars (L); Walter *Joslein, Joslani, Goslein* 1195-8 P (Y); Ralph *Jocelin*' 1198 Cur (Nf); Edrich *Gocelin*' (*Goscelin*') 1204 P (L); Ralph *Joscelin* 1208 Cur (Nth); William *Joclenne* 1243 AssSo; Thomas *Gosselyn* 1327 SRC; John *Gostelen, Gosteleyn* 1462 NorwW (Nf); John *Gostlyng* 1526 ib. (Sf). OFr *Goscelin, Gosselin, Joscelin*, OG *Gautselin, Goz(e)lin*, diminutives of compounds with *Gos-* or *Goz-*, or of OFr *Josse* (OBret *Judoc*). *v.* also GOSS, GOTT, GOSLING.

Jockel, Jockelson: *v.* JEKYLL

Joel, Joels, Joell, Jewell, Jewels, Joule, Joules,

Jowle, Juell, Joelson, Jolson: *Joel, Jool, Jol (Johol)* de Lincolnia c1051 (1334) Rams; *Judhel* de Totenais 1086 DB (D); *Johel* de Helsam c1160 DC (L); *Juhel* de Harelea 1166 P (Y); *Joel* de Creton 1195 FF (C); *Juel(us)* de Vautort 1214 Cur (Co); Richard *Juel* 1247 AssBeds; Alan *Joel* 1256 AssNb; William *Jool* 1332 SRSx; William *Juwel* 1358 AD vi (Beds); Roger *Juylle* 1383 Cl (Co); John *Jewell* 1462 FrY; John *Joulle* 1579 Bardsley; Augustine *Jowles* 1650 ib.; Joane *Jule* 1704 ib. OBret *Iudhael*, from *Iud-* 'lord, chief' and *haël* 'generous'. cf. JEKYLL. The personal name was common in Devon and Cornwall and the Breton districts of Yorks and the Eastern counties. *Jewell* is now common in North Devon.

Joesbury: *v.* DEWSBURY

Joester: *v.* JUSTER

John, Johnes, Johns, Johnys, Joan, Joanes, Jone, Jones, Joynes, Fitzjohn: *Johannes* c1140 DC (L); Alanus *filius Jene* 1275 RH (L); Willelmus *filius Gene* 1276 RH (Y); Walterus *filius Jone* 1279 RH (Hu); *Jon* 1292 SRLo; Richard *le Fitz Joan* 1327 SRSo; *Johan* 1379 PTY; Petrus *Johannis* 1230 Cl (Sf); Thomas *John* 1279 RH (Bk); Matilda *Jones* ib. (Hu); Arnold *Johan* 1280 LLB A; Robert *Jhoun* 1295 Barnwell (C); Thomas *fiz Jon* 1296 SRSx; Richard *Jon*, Robert *Jone* 1327 SRSx; Roger *Jonis* 1327 SRSf; Robert *Johns* 1327 SRSo; Robert *Joyne*, June 1524 SRSf. Hebrew *Johanan* 'Jehovah has favoured', usually latinized as *Johannes* in early documents, OFr *Johan, Jehan, Jean*. By the beginning of the 14th century *John* rivalled *William* in popularity and has always been a favourite name. The feminine *Joan*, latinized as *Johanna*, was also common and had the same forms and pronunciation as *John*. The surname may derive from either. *Johan* became *Jan* and *Jon*, and *Jehan* became *Jen*, with diminutives *Janin, Jonin, Jenin; Janet, Jonet, Jenet; Jankin, Jonkin, Jenkin*. A pet-form was *Han*, with diminutives *Hancock, Hankin. Jack* is sometimes for *John*. The Welsh form was *Ieuan, Evan* (*v.* JEVON, EVANS). The form *Ioan* was adopted for the Welsh Authorized Version of the Bible, hence the frequency of the Welsh patronymic *Jones*. For *Joynes*, *v.* JOHNSON. *v.* also JACK, JAN, JEAN, JENKIN, JENNINGS, JINKIN, HANN, HANCOCK, HANKIN, HENKIN.

Johncock, Johncocks, Johncook: John *Johncock* 1525 ArchC 30. A diminutive of *John*.

Johnson, Jonson, Joinson, Joynson: John *Jonessone* 1287 AD i (Sr); Wautier *Jonessone* 1296 CalSc (Berwick); John *Jonesone* 1321 AD i (Sr); William *Johnson*, Robert *Johanson, Jonson* 1379 PTY; Robert *Joynson* 1582 Bardsley (Ch); Jone *Geynson* 1595 ib.; Thomas *Jeynson* 1667 ib. 'Son of *John*.' *Joynson* is a Cheshire form, from *Jeynson*, from *Jeyn. v.* JAN.

Johnston, Johnstone: (i) Caterina *Jonstons* 1327 SRSf. For *Johnson*, with intrusive *t*. (ii) Alan *de Johannestun* 1227 AssSt; Peter *de Jonestone* 1299 ib. From Johnson Hall (Staffs). (iii) Gilbert *de Jonistoune* 1195–1215 Black. From Johnstone in

Annandale (Dumfries), named from *John*, father of Gilbert.

Joice: *v.* JOYCE

Joiner, Joyner: John *Joinur* 1195–1215 S⁴P (Lo); William *le juinnur, Joinier, Joyner* 1204, 1218–33 ELPN; John *le Jeynuur* 1296 FFEss. AFr *joignour*, OFr *joigneor* 'joiner' (1322 MED).

Joinson: *v.* JOHNSON

Jolin, Jolland, Jollands, Jowling, Gollan, Golland, Gollin, Gollins: *Jollanus, Joelinus* Hy 2 DC (L); *Goillanus, Gollanus* de Aute(r)barg(e) ib.; *Jollein* 12th ib.; *Iolanus, Joelinus* de Nouilla ib.; *Gollinus (Joelinus)* de Pomereia 1214 Cur (D); Adam *filius Jollein, Joulen* 1219 AssL; *Juelinus (Joelus)* de Wic 1220 Cur (O); *Joelus, Joelinus, Jollinus, Jollanus, Joylin* de Sowe 1221 AssWa, 13th AD ii (Wa); Alexander *Jolleen* 1196 Cur (L); William *Goelin* 1212 Cur (O); Richard *Joelan'* 1214 Cur (Beds); Roger *Jollein* 1219 AssL; Geoffrey *Joelin, Jolin* 1221 AssWa; William *Joylin* 1279 RH (C); William *Gollayn* 1408 FrY; Thomas *Gollan, Golland* 1412, 1481 ib. *Joel-in*, a diminutive of *Joel*. For the suffix and development, cf. JOCELYN.

Jolivet: Adam *Joliuet* 1279 AssSo. A diminutive of JOLLIFF.

Jolland(s): *v.* JOLIN

Joll(es): *v.* JULL

Jolliff, Jolliffe, Jolley, Jollie, Jolly, Jollye, Joly: John *le Goly* 1275 RH (W); John *Jolif* 1279 RH (Hu); Walter *Jolyf* 1281 LLB B; John *Joly* 1415 FrY. ME, OFr, *jolif, joli* 'gay, lively'.

Jolson: *v.* JOEL

Jone(s): *v.* JOHN

Jonson: *v.* JOHNSON

Jope, Jopp: *v.* JOB

Joplin, Jopling: *v.* JOBLIN

Jopson: *v.* JOBSON

Jordan, Jordain, Jorden, Jordens, Jordin, Jordon, Jourdain, Jourdan, Jourdon: *Jordanus* presbiter 1121–48 Bury (Sf); *Jurdanus* de Brakenberge 12th DC (L); Robert *Jurdan* a1182 Seals (Y); John *Jorden* 1202 FFC; Walter *Jourdan* 1327 SRSx; William *Jurdain* 1332 SRSt. The name of the River Jordan, used as a christian name by returning crusaders who brought back with them Jordan water for the baptism of their children. The name became very common. *v.* JURD, JUDD.

Joscelyn, Jos(e)land, Joselin: *v.* JOCELYN

Jose: *v.* GOSS

Joseph, Josephs: *Josephus* 1086 DB; *Joseph* 1141–9 Holme (Nf), 1187 DC (L); Umfridus *filius Josep* 1205 Cur (Herts); Henry, William *Joseph* 1191 P (Ha), 1205 Cur (Sf). Hebrew *Joseph* 'May Jehovah add'. *v.* JESSOP.

Josephson: John *Josepsone* 1332 SRCu. 'Son of *Joseph*.'

Josland, Joslen, Joslin, Josling, Josolyne: *v.* JOCELYN

Joss(e): *v.* GOSS, JOYCE

Josselyn: *v.* JOCELYN

Jossett: *v.* GOSSET

Jotcham: *v.* JUDSON

Joubert: v. JOBERT
Joule(s): v. JOEL
Jóuning: v. JENNINGS
Jourdain, Jourdan, Jourdon: v. JORDAN
Jowett, Jowitt, Jewett, Jewitt, Juett: *Juetta* Ric 1, 1201, 1214 Cur (L, Lei, Nf); *Juheta* Vidua 1200 Cur (L); *Joetta* 1219 AssY; *Juwete* 1227 AssSt; *Juhota* 1329 AD iv (Wa); William *Juet* 1279 RH (Hu); Robert *Iuwet* 1297 MinAcctCo; William *Jouet* 1299 AssSt; Ludowycus *Gouet* 13th WhC (La); Richard *Jouot* 1300 AssSt; Roger *Guet* 1317 AssK; Robert *Jowet* 1379 PTY; Lawrence *Jewet* 1458 FFHu; Thomas *Jewitt* 1488 GildY. *Jou-et, Jou-ot,* diminutives of *Juwe, Jowe,* from *Jull.* *Juetta,* which was common, was a pet-name of *Juliana,* of which *Jull* was a short form, as *Jell* and *Jill* were of the common pronunciations *Jelian* and *Jillian. Juetta* de Locton' 1212 Cur (L), is twice called *Juliana. Jull* was also a short form of *Julian.* v. JULL, GILLIAN.

Jowle: v. JOEL
Jowling: v. JOLIN
Jowsey: v. JOYCE
Joy, Joye, Joyes: Manser *filius Joie* 1186 P (L); *Joia* 1195 FFEss, 1221 AssWa; Robert *Ioie* c1155 'DC (L); Lefwin *Joie* 1166 P (Nf); Ricardo *Gaudio* (abl.) c1176 Bart (K). Either from *Joia,* a fairly frequent woman's name, or from the common noun *joy. Joie* was also masculine. cf. *Joie,* husband (*vir*) of Joan de Lalleford 1219 Cur (O).

Joyce, Joice, Joisce, Joss, Josse, Joicey, Joysey, Jowsey: (i) *Josce, Iocius* c1140–50 DC (L); *Gocius* de Huptuna Hy 2 NthCh (Nth); Isaac *filius Joscei* 1208 Cur (Mx); Johannes *filius Jocey* 1275 RH (Sf); *Josce* or *Joice* 1313, 1320 LLB D, E; Robert *Joysy* 1533 RochW; Swithin *Joyce* 1568 FFHu; William *Joyse* 1574 ib. Breton *Iodoc,* the name of a saint, son of Judicael, who had a hermitage at the modern St Josse-sur-Mer (ODCN). Earlier examples of the surname (*Joce*) cannot be distinguished from those of GOSS. Two farms in Essex, Joyce's Fm, derive respectively from Robert and John *Joce* (1353, 1398 PN Ess 303, 309). (ii) *Jocea* 1199 CurR; *Juicia* 1211, 1212 Cur (Do, Nt); *Jocosa* de Huntynfeld 1346 FA (Sf). A feminine form of *Joceus, Jodoc.* (iii) Occasionally the surname may derive from Jort (Calvados). cf. Burton Joyce (Notts), from Geoffrey *de Jorz* 1234 (*Jorce* 1327, *Joce* 1433, *Joys* 1535 PN Nt 157).

Joyner: v. JOINER
Joynes: v. JOHN
Joynson: v. JOHNSON
Joysey: v. JOYCE
Jubb: v. JOB
Jubber: v. JOBAR
Jubert: v. JOBERT
Juckes: v. JUKES
Judd, Jutte: *Judde* Rampe 1246 AssLa; *Judde* Clubbe 1260 AssCh; *Judde* de Halifax 1309 Wak (Y); Hugo, Henry, John *Judde* 1204 P (He), 1279 RH (C, O); Alan, John *Jutte* 1260 AssC, 1279 RH (C); Thomas *Joudde* 1297 MinAcctCo; Richard *Joddes* 1327 SRWo. *Judd, Jutt,* pet-names

for *Jordan,* from *Jurd,* with the common interchange of voiced and voiceless final consonants.
Jude: Hugo *filius Jude* 1193 P (L); Herueus, John *Judas* 1191 P (C), 1327 SRWo; William, Reyne *Jude* 1211 Cur (D), 1279 RH (O); Simon *Jude, Judde* 1327, 1332 SRSx. *Judas* is the hellenized form of Hebrew *Judah,* the name of a son of Jacob, of which *Jude* is an abbreviation. There is little evidence for its use in medieval England, but it was occasionally used, either from the name of the Apostle Jude, sometimes called Judas, or through the popularity of the story of Judas Maccabaeus. *Jude* appears to be also a variant of *Judd.* cf. Alicia *Judedoghter* 1379 PTY.

Juden: Adam *Judden* 1327 SRWo; Nicholas *Jurdan,* Walter, William *Judden* 1332 SRWa. Either an assimilated form of *Jurdan* (Jordan), or *Judd-en.* v. GEFFEN.
Judge, Judges: Adam *le Jugge* 1309 MEOT (Wo); Thomas *Judges* 1524 SRSf. OFr *juge* 'judge'.

Judkins: v. JUGGINS
Judson, Jutson, Jutsum, Jutsums, Justum, Justham, Jotcham, Jetson, Jesson: John *Judson* 1324 Wak (Y); Henry *Juddessone* 1370 AD vi (Ch); John *Jutsam* 1581 DWills; Prudence *Jutsham* 1611 ib.; Agnes *Jutson* 1635 ib.; John *Jutsum* 1725 ib.; Barbara *Jetsome* 1735 ib.; John *Jesson* ib. 'Son of *Judd* or *Jutt.*'

Juell: v. JOEL
Juett: v. JOWETT
Juggins, Jeggons, Jiggen, Jiggens, Jiggins: *Jecun* de Sutton 1190 P (Sa); *Jukin* le Walshe 1323 AssSt; William *Jokin* 1275 RH (Sf); John *Jokyn* 1296 SRSx, 1327 SRSf; John *Joukyn* 1303 AD v (W); Thomas *Jukyn* 1327 SRSx; Robert *Gygoun* 1377 AssEss; John *Jowkyn* 1379 PTY; John *Jeggon* 1590 Bardsley (Ess); Thomas *Juggins* 1650 ib.; William *Jigins* 1662 HTEss. Bardsley derives *Juggins* from *Judkin,* a diminutive of *Jordan,* his earliest example being Thomas *Judkins* (1648). This is a formation one would have expected to be common and early, but in the light of the above forms *Judkin* is probably from *Jukin,* with intrusive d. *Jek-un, Juk-in, Jok-in* are diminutives of *Jok* or *Juk,* a short form of Breton *Judicael,* with its variants *Juk-, Jok-, Jek-, Gik-.* v. JEKYLL, JUKES. cf. Thomas *Juket,* John *Joket* 1296, 1332 SRSx. *Jowkyn* suggests also a derivation direct from *Jull.* cf. Robert *Julkynesone* 1332 SRSx. cf. JOWETT.
Juggler: William *le Gugelour* 1250 AssSt; Lucy *Jugeler* 1260 AssC. OFr *jo(u)glere, jougelour* 'juggler'. cf. TREDGETT.
Jukes, Juckes, Jewkes, Jugg: Adam *Jock* 1279 RH (O); Robert *Jokke* 1327 SRSo; John *Iucke, Iukkes* 1360 Eynsham (O); John *Jokes* 1381 SRSt. A short form of *Jukel, Jokel,* from Breton *Judicael.* v. JEKYLL.
Julian, Julians, Julien, Jullens, Jullion, Jullings: *Julian* de Horbelinghe Hy 2 Gilb (L); *Juliana* de Haketoren 1185–7 DC (L); Hugo *filius Juliani* 1212 Cur (Y); Gunnilda *filia Juliane* 1211 Cur (K); Walter *Julien* 1200 P (L); John *Juliane* 1275 SRWo;

Henry *Julian* 1327 SRSf; John *Julion* 1327 SRC; John *Julyoun* 1346 FA (Sf). In ME, *Julian* was both masculine and feminine and both are represented in the surnames. Lat *Julianus*, from *Julius*, the name of a Roman *gens*, and *Juliana*, its feminine, were both names of saints and both names were popular, the latter particularly as *Gillian*.

Jull, Joll, Jolles: Tomas *filius Golle* 1196 P (Y); *Golle* 1203 P (Ess), 1219 AssY (f); *Jowe* 1227 AssBk, 1327 SRDb, SRSt; Richard *Juwe* 1288 Rams (C); John *Jowe* 1297 MinAcctCo; Robert *Julle* 1317 AssK, 1327 SRSx; William *Jolle* 1327 SRSx; William *Goll* 1421 FrY. A short form of *Julian* or *Juliana*. cf. GILL from GILLIAN.

Jullings: *v.* JULIAN

June: *v.* JEUNE

Junifer, Juniper: *v.* JENNIFER

Junkin: *v.* JENKIN

Junkinson, Junkison: *v.* JENKINSON

Jupe, Jupp: *v.* JOB

Jurd: *Jurdy* 1275 RH (Sf); Adam *Jorde* 1210 P (Nf); John, Robert *Jurd(e)* 1209 P (Hu), 1275 SRWo. A pet-form of *Jordan*.

Jury: *v.* JEWRY

Juson: *v.* JEWSON

Just: Gilebertus filius *Juste* 1203 P (L); *Justus* de Thurlestun(e), Martin *Justuse* of Thurleston Hy 3 AD ii, iii (Sf); Martin, Roger *Justus* of Thurlestone (brothers) 1292 AD ii (Sf). A rare name. The only evidence noted for a meaning 'the just' is Thomas *le Guste* 1327 SRSo. *Justus*, Lat *justus* 'just', the name of a 4th-century bishop of Lyons, has given rise to the French surnames *Just, Juste* and *Jux* and the derivatives *Juteau, Jutot* (Dauzat). It was rare in England but certainly gave rise to a hereditary surname near Ipswich in the 13th century.

Juster, Jewster, Joester: John *le justur* 1230 P (Sx); Robert *le Gustur* 1255 Ipm (So); John *Justere* 1279 RH (O); Walter *Justour* 1327 SRSx. AFr *justour*, OFr *justeor, justeur* 'jouster' (c1400 MED). To give young knights practice in deeds of arms and their elders excitement, tournaments or jousts were held. They sprang up in France in the 12th century and were popular with the Anglo-Norman knights. 'These early tournaments were very rough affairs, in every sense, quite unlike the chivalrous contests of later days; the rival parties fought in groups, and it was considered not only fair but commendable to hold off until you saw some of your adversaries getting tired and then

to join in the attack on them; the object was not to break a lance in the most approved style, but frankly to disable as many opponents as possible for the sake of obtaining their horses, arms, and ransoms.' William the Marshal, later Earl of Pembroke and regent of England during the minority of Henry III, the most brilliant jouster of his day, 'made a very good income out of his tournaments' (EngLife 202).

Justham: *v.* JUDSON

Justice, Jestice: William *la Justis* 12th AD iii (Sf); Thomas *Justic'* 1202 AssL; Robert *la justice* 1220 Bart (Lo); Peter, Roger *le Justice* 1255 RH (Sa). OFr *justise, justice* had various senses, 'uprightness, equity, vindication of right, court of justice, judge', etc., of which the first to be adopted in England was 'the exercise of authority in vindication of right by assigning reward or punishment'. As early as c1172 it was used of judicial officers or judges (*Justices et baruns* NED) and that is often its sense as a surname. cf. William *Justyse* then constable 1253 Lewes (Nf). Sometimes it may be a shortening of OFr *justiceor* (c1330 NED): John, Tiphina *le Justiser* 1322 AD vi (D). The variation between *le* and *la*, though not to be taken too seriously, may point to the use of the abstract *justice*. Weekley (*Surnames* 221n.) points out that in one of the Chester plays the speakers included 'Veritas, Misericordia, Justitia, and Pax' and that here we have a plausible origin of the names *Verity*, *Mercy* or *Marcy*, *Justice* and *Peace*.

Justin, Justins: *Justinus* Clericus 1175–80 Holme (Nf); *Justina* 1221 AssWo; *Justinus* filius Wakerild 1229 Pat (Sx); Ralph *Justyn* 1327 SRSf; John *Justyn* 1327 SRSx. *Justinus*, a derivative of Lat *justus* 'just', the name of two Byzantine emperors and of Justin Martyr (d. 163 A.D.), has given rise to the French surnames *Justin* and *Jutin* (Dauzat). The association of the name with *clericus* and the existence of *Justina*, which must be associated with the 4th-century martyr St *Justina*, patron saint of Padua, previously not noted in England before the 18th century (ODCN), suggest that *Justinus* was used occasionally in this country. But *Justinus* is also certainly a latinization of ON *Iósteinn*, which is found in DB in 1066 as *Justen*, *Justan* and *Justinus* (PNDB) and this would certainly be at home among the Scandinavian names of Norfolk and Suffolk.

Justum, Jutson, Jutsum: *v.* JUDSON

Jutte: *v.* JUDD

K

Kadwell, Kadwill: *v.* CADWALL

Kaighan, Kaighin: A Manx name, contracted from *Mac Eachain* 'son of *Eachan*' 'horse-lord': *MacCaighen* 1422, *Kaighin* 1611 Moore. cf. MᴀᴄEACHAN, MᴄGACHAN, common in Galloway.

Kain, Kaine: *v.* CAIN

Kaley: *v.* CALEY

Kalker: *v.* CHALKER

Kane: *v.* CAIN, CANE

Kaneen: A purely Manx name, contracted from *Mac Cianain* 'son of *Cianan*': *Kynyne* 1422, *Keneen* 1666, *Kaneen* 1740 Moore.

Kanter: *v.* CANTER

Kaplan, Kaplin: *v.* CHAPLAIN

Kapper: *v.* CAPPER

Karck, Kark: *v.* CARKER

Karl(e): *v.* CARL

Karslake: *v.* CARSLAKE

Kater: *v.* CATER

Kates: *v.* CATES

Katin: Richard, Walter *Catin* 1177, 1200 P (Wa). A diminutive of *Cat*, a short form of *Catharine*, *Cat-in*.

Katte: *v.* CATT

Kave: *v.* CAVE

Kay, Kaye, Kayes, Keay, Keays, Keeys, Key, Keye, Keyes, Keys, Keyse: (i) Britius *filius Kay* 1199 P (Nth). OW *Cai*, MW *Kei*, from Lat *Caius*. Not a common name but probably used by the Bretons as well as in Wales and the Welsh border counties. It is the origin of the Cornish *Key*. (ii) Cecilia *de Kay* 1199 P (Gl); John *del Cay* 1207 P (Lo); William *atte Keye* 1372 LoPleas. OFr *kay*, *cay*, ME *kay(e)*, *key(e)*, *keay* 'quay' (1306 MED), from residence near or employment at a wharf or quay. (iii) Richard *Ka*, Adam *Kay* 1219 AssY; Adecok *Kay* 1246 AssLa; Alicia *Ka*, *Kay* 1297 MinAcctCo (Y); Donald *Ka* 1399 Black; Thomas *Kay* 1552 ib.; Thomas *Keay* 1758 FrY. ME *ka*, *kae*, *kay*, from ON *ká* 'jackdaw'. In the north and Scotland, OE, Scand *ā* remained in ME, often spelled *ai*, *ay*. NED has *Cais* 'jackdaws' c1450. In FrY between 1355 and 1461 the surname occurs as *Caa* (1461), *Kaa* (1433), *Cay* and *Kay* (thrice each). It is difficult to believe, however, that *kā* had become *kay* by 1219. Whilst most of the Yorkshire, Lancashire and Lowland *Kay(e)s* are nicknames from the bird, there is probably some other source. In Lancashire and Cheshire we find a ME *kei*, Da dialect *kei* 'left'

(hand or foot) about 1300 and this survived in these dialects until the 19th century. As Cotgrave uses the word in 1611 (*Gauchier* left-handed, key-fisted) it was probably more widely distributed and we have a nickname 'left-handed, clumsy'. The surname may also be metonymic for *key-er* 'a maker of keys' (cf. KEAR) or from office, a key-bearer, key-keeper. (iv) Geoffrey *Cai* 1197 P (Nf); William, Roger *Keys* 1275 SRWo, 1444 AD i (Berks); William *le Kay* 1296 SRSx; Benedict *Cay* 1297 FFSf; Stephen, Edmund *Kay* 1327 SRSf; Hugh *Kegh*, William *le Keye* ib.; Geoffrey *Kay* 1331 AssSt. In these counties *kā* became ME *co(o)*, now COE. A Scandinavian nickname from *kei* 'left-handed' would be at home in Norfolk, Suffolk, Derbyshire and Staffordshire. In Sussex *le Kay* is probably for *de Kay* 'at the quay'. 'Key-bearer' is possible in all, and *Cai* in Worcestershire and possibly in Norfolk and Suffolk. The Manx *Kay* is for *Mackay*.

Kayley: *v.* CALEY

Kayne: *v.* CAIN

Kayser: *v.* CAYZER

Keable: *v.* KEEBLE

Keach, Keattch: *v.* KEECH

Kear, Keer, Care: Adam *filius Cheigher* 1178 P (Nb); Robert *le Keyere* 1275 RH (K); William *le Keer* 1303 MESO (Lei); Richard *le Kayer* 1287 LLB A; Richard *Kere* 1322 FFEss. OE **cægere*, from OE *cæg* 'key', a maker of keys. The first example probably means 'Son of the key-smith'.

Kearsey: *v.* KERSEY

Kearsley, Keasley, Kersley, Carslaw, Carsley, Caselaw, Caseley, Casley, de Casley, Cassley: Simon *de Caresle* 1206 Cur (Wo). From Keresley (Warwicks), pronounced *Carsley*, or Kearsley (Lancs, Northumb).

Keat, Keate, Keates, Keats, Keet, Keit, Keyte, Kett, Ketts, Kite, Kyte: (i) Ailnoð, Richard *Kete* 1166 P (Nf), 1221 ElyA (Sf); Robert *Chet* 1183 Boldon (Du); Richard *Kyte* 1243 AssSo; William *Ket* 1275 RH (Nf); Peter *le Kyte* 1327 SRSx; John *Kette* 1327 SRC. OE *cȳta*, ME *kete*, *kyte* 'kite', a rapacious person. (ii) Ralph *atte Kete* 1292 PN K 493. This survives in Kite Fm which Löfvenberg has shown (StudNP 17) derives from OE *cȳte* (f), **cyte* (m) 'hut', some kind of shed or outhouse for cattle or sheep. The surname probably denotes a herdsman.

Keatley: *v.* KEIGHLEY

Keattch: v. KEECH
Keay(s): v. KAY
Kebbell, Kebell, Keble: v. KEEBLE
Kedge, Ketch: Alured *Keg'* 1177 P (Nf); Alexander *Kech* 1221 *ElyA* (Nf); William *Kigge* Hy 3 Gilb (L); Richard *le Keg'* 1332 SRSx. East Anglian dialectal *kedge* 'brisk, lively'. cf. '*Kygge*, or ioly' c1440 PromptParv. Perhaps a palatalized form of Da, Norw *kiæk*, Sw *käck* 'bold, brisk'.

Keeble, Keable, Kebbell, Kebell, Keble, Kibbel, Kibble, Kibel: Æluric *Chebbel* c1095 Bury (Sf); William, Salomon *Kebbel* 1214 Cur (K), 1263 FFEss; Thomas *Kibel* 1275 RH (L); Henry *Kybbel* 1327 SRC; John *Kebyll*, Richard *Kebull* 1524 SRSf. OE **cybbel*, perhaps the source of *kibble* 'cudgell' (1397 MED). A maker or seller of cudgels, or, perhaps, originally, one stout and heavy as a cudgel.

Keech, Keetch, Keach, Keattch, Keitch: Reginald, Hugo *Keche* 1206, 1219 Cur (C, Sr). ME *keech* 'a lump of congealed fat; the fat of a slaughtered animal rolled up into a lump', used in the 16th century for a butcher: 'Did not goodwife Keech the Butchers wife come in then?' (Henry IV); 'I wonder, That such a Keech can with his very bulke Take vp the Rayes o' th' beneficiall Sun, And keepe it from the Earth' (Henry VIII), where the reference is to Cardinal Wolsey, a butcher's son.

Keed: Henry, Simon *Kede* 1275 RH (Sf), 1327 SRC; William *Keed* 1524 SRSf. ME *kide, kede* 'kid'.

Keemish: v. CAMMIS

Keen, Keene, Keenes, Keens: Ricardus *filius Kene* 1188 P (D); Alexander *filius Kene* 1202 AssL; Adam, Hugo *Kene* 1207 Cur (Sf), 1221 AssWo; Richard *le Kene* 1297 MinAcctCo (O). *Kene* is a short form of OE names in *Cēn-* or *Cyne-*, such as survive in *Kenward, Kenway, Kerrich*, etc. *le Kene* is OE *cēne*, ME *kene* 'wise, brave, proud'.

Keep: Thomas *ate Kepe* 1327 SRSx; Robert *de Kepe* 1332 SRCu. One employed at a keep or castle (a1586 NED). Perhaps 'jailer'.

Keeper: William *le Kepere* 1279 RH (Hu); Simon *Kepere* 1327 SRSx. Identical in meaning with KEEP.

Keer: v. KEAR
Keet: v. KEAT
Keetch: v. KEECH
Keetley: v. KEIGHLEY
Keeys: v. KAY
Kegan, Keggin, Keggins: A Manx contraction of *Mac Taidhgin* 'son of little *Tadhg*', the poet (Moore).

Kehoe: v. KEYHO
Keig, Kegg: Muircheartach *Mac Taidhg* 1159, *Mac Keg* 1511, *Kegg* 1630, *Keige* 1653 Moore. 'Son of *Tadg*', the poet, philosopher. Irish *Teague*, *MacTague*.

Keighley, Keighly, Keightley, Keitley, Keatley, Keetley, Kightly, Kitlee, Kitley: Henry *de Kythelay* 14th Calv (Y). From Keighley (WRYorks).

Keit: v. KEAT
Keitch: v. KEECH

Keitley: v. KEIGHLEY
Kelham, Kellam: Peter *de Kellum* 1204 Pl (Nt); William *Kelom* 1327 SRLei; John *Kellom* 1447 IpmNt. From Kelham (Notts).

Kell, Kells: Reginaldus *filius Chelle* 1219 AssL; *Chel* filius Mabillæ c1250 Rams (C); Ansfredus, Isabella *Kelle* 1176 P (Ha), 1311 RamsCt (Hu). ON **Kel*, OSw *Kæl*, shortened from *Ketill*. v. KETTLE.

Kellaway: v. CALLAWAY
Kellett, Kellet, Kellitt: Adam, William *de Kellet* 1194 P (Cu), 1279 FFY; Mariota *Kelitt* 1327 SRC. From Kellet (Lancs), or Kelleth (Westmorland).

Kellog, Kellogg: Geoffrey *Kyllehog* 1277 FFEss; Walter *Kelehoog* 1369 PN Ess 456; John Ryche alias *Kelhoge* 1541 FFEss. 'Kill hog', a name for a butcher. cf. Gilbert *Killebole* 1327 SRLei; Richard *Kilfole* 1442 AssLa.

Kelly, Kelley, Kellie: In Ireland for *O'Kelly*, Ir *Ó Ceallaigh* 'descendant of *Ceallach*' (war). In Galloway and the Isle of Man, where it is as common as in Ireland, it is for *MacKelly*: *McKelly* 1429, *Kellye* 1601 Moore. It may also be local in origin, in Scotland from Kelly near Arbroath or Kellie in Fife: John *de Kelly* 1373 Black; in England, from Kelly (Devon), from Cornish *celli* 'wood, grove': Warin *de Kelly* 1194 P (D).

Kelman: William *kelman* 1257 MEOT (Y); John *Keleman* 1328 MESO (L). Probably 'a maker of kells or calls', from ME *kelle*. cf. Symon *le keller* 1322 FrY, and CALLER. It might also be from ME *kele* 'ship', a worker on keels, flat-bottomed vessels, a bargeman.

Kelner: v. KILNER
Kelsall, Kelshaw, Kilshall, Kilshaw: Richard *de Kelsale* 1260 AssCh; John *de Kelshulle* 1340 AssLo; John *Kelesall* 1379 PTY. From Kelsall (Ches), Kelshall (Herts), or Kelsale (Suffolk).

Kelway: v. CALLAWAY
Kemball: v. KEMBLE
Kember: Roger *le Kembar'* 1327 SRSx; Peter *le Kembere* 1333 MESO (Ha). A derivative of OE *cemban* 'to comb', a comber of wool or flax. cf. KEMPSTER.

Kembery, Kembry: v. CAMBRAY
Kemble, Kemball, Kimball, Kimbell, Kimble, Kimmel, Kemple: (i) Turbet *filius Chembel* 1130 P (W); Richard *Cembel* 1185 P (Hu); Roger *Cumbel*, *Chimbel, Kymbel, Kimbel* 1191-3 P (Wa); John, Richard *Kenebelle* 1327 SRSf; Simon, William *Kymbel* ib. OW *Cynbel*, from *cyn* 'chief' and *bel* 'war'. cf. *Cymbeline (Cunobelinus)*. (ii) Robert *Kinebald* 1215-21 AD iv (So); Ralph *Kenebold* 13th AD ii (Wt); William *Kembald* 1302 SRSf; William *Kenebold*, Nicholas *Kembold* 1327 SRSf; Samuel *Kembull* 1621 Buxhall (Sf); Susan *Kemball* 1638 ib. OE *Cynebeald* 'family-, kin-bold', a name which does not seem to be recorded after the 9th century but which must have continued in use. (iii) Hugo *de Kenebell'* 1196 Cur (Bk); Roger *de Kinebelle* 1255 RH (Bk); Thomas *de Kymble* 1327 SRC. From Kimble (Bucks).

Kemmery: v. CAMBRAY

Kemp, Kempe: Eadulf *Cempa* 902 OEByn (W); Edmund *Kempe* c1100 MedEA (Nf); Ralph *le Kemp* 1296 SRSx. OE *cempa* 'warrior', ME *kempe*, also 'athlete, wrestler'. *v.* CAMP.

Kempster: Agnes *Kembestere* 1252 Rams (Hu); Dionisia *le Kemstere* 1317 Oseney (O); Agnes *Kempster* 1327 SRC. The feminine form of *Kembere* (a1400 NED). *v.* KEMBER.

Ken, Kenn: (i) Robert *le Chien* (*Chen*) 1183 P (Co); Willelmus *Chen, Canis* 1212, 1219 Fees (Ess); Henry *le Kenne* 1337 SRSx. AFr *ken, chen,* OFr *chien* (Lat *canis*) 'dog'. (ii) Sewulf, John *de Ken* 1170, 1176 P (D, So). From Kenn (Devon, Som).

Kendal, Kendall, Kendell, Kendle, Kindell: John *de Kendale* 1332 SRLa. From Kendal (Westmorland).

Kendrick: *v.* KENRICK, KERRICH

Kenion, Kennion: *v.* KENYON

Kenmare, Kenmore, Kenmir: Richard *Kenemer* 1277 Ely (Sf); John *Kenemer,* Thomas *Kenemere* 1296 SRSx. OE *Cynemǣr,* a personal name found in several early place-names, but recorded only in the reign of Edward the Confessor as the name of a moneyer. It occurs also as the name of a 12th-century cowman: terram que fuit *Chinemeri* bouarii, a1183 EngFeud.

Kennard: *v.* KENWARD

Kennaway: *v.* KENWAY

Kennedy: *Gilbert mac Kenedi* c1180 Black; Huwe *Kenedi* 1296 CalSc. Ir *Ó Cinnéide* 'ugly head'.

Kennerley, Kinnerley: Hugh *de Kenardel'* 1243 AssSo. From Kennerleigh (Devon).

Kennish: *v.* KINNISH

Kenrick, Kendrick, Kenwrick, Kenwright: Hugo *filius Chenwrec* 1160 P (Sa); Ennian *filius Kenewrec* 1161 ib.; *Kenwrec* Walensis 1195 P (Sa); *Kenrig* de Gretewurth' 1219 Cur (Nth); *Kenwrig* ap Madog Duy 1391 Chirk; *Kendrick* Eyton 1602 Bardsley (Ch); *Kenrick* Evans 1613 ib.; Nicholas *Kenewrec* 1327 SRSo; Richard *Kendrick* 1593 Bardsley (Ch). Welsh *Cynwrig,* from *cyn* 'chief' and (*g*)*wr* 'man, hero' plus the suffix of quality. *v.* also KERRICH.

Kent: Nicholas *de Kent* 1185 Templars (Wa); William *Kent* 1296 SRSx; John *a Kent* 1524 SRSf, 1525 SRSx. 'The man from Kent.'

Kentish, Kintish, Cantes: William *Centeis* c1165 Bury (Sf); Richard (*le*) *Kenteis* 1176 P (Lei); Ralph *Canteis, le Kenteis* 1208 Cur (Sf); Richard *Kentissh* 1332 SRSx. OFr *Kanteis, Kenteis* 'Kentish (man)', influenced by OE *Centisc.*

Kenward, Kennard: *Keneward* lingedraper 1198–1212 Bart (Lo); Walterus *filius Kenewardi* 1214 Cur (Wa); *Kynnard* Delabere 1590 AD v (Gl); Agnes, Walter *Kyneward* c1250 Rams (Beds); Nicholas *Kenward* 1274 Wak (Y); Simon *cuneward* 1297 MinAcctCo (Mx). OE *Cēnweard* 'bold guardian' or *Cyneweard* 'royal guardian'.

Kenway, Kennaway: *Kenewi* 12th MedEA (Nf), 1279 RH (C); Robertus *filius Kenewi* 1198 Cur (K); William *Chienewe* 1130 P (Ha); Ralph *Kenewi* 1221 *ElyA* (Sf). OE *Cēnwīg* 'bold war' or *Cynewīg* 'royal war'.

Kenwrick, Kenwright: *v.* KENRICK, KERRICH

Kenyon, Kenion, Kennion: Robert *de Kenien* 1212 Fees (La); Jordan *Kenyan* 1260 AssLa; Nicholas *Kynion* 1288 AssCh. From Kenyon (Lancs).

Keown: *v.* MacOWEN

Ker, Kerr: *v.* CARR

Kerb(e)y: *v.* KIRKBY

Kerk: *v.* KIRK

Kerkham: *v.* KIRKHAM

Kerl(e)y: *v.* KIRKLEY

Kerman: *v.* KIRKMAN

Kermode, Cormode: *Mac Kermott* 1430, *Mac Cormot* 1511, *Kermod* 1586 Moore. A Manx contraction of *MacDermot.*

Kerrell, Kirrell, Kirriell, Kriel, Croyle: Robert *de Cruel* 1086 DB (Sx); Simon *de Crieil* 1170 StGreg (K); Bertram *de Criel, de Crioille* 1221 StGreg, 1252 *ERO*; William *de Kiriel* 1287 FFHu; John *Kyriel* 1332 SRSr; John *Kyrrell,* Edward *Kerrell* 1583 Musters (Sr). From Criel-sur-Mer (Seine-Inférieure).

Kerrich, Kerridge, Kerrage, Carriage, Kerrick, Kirrage, Kenrick, Kendrick: *Kenricus* (2), *Chenricus, Chericus* (identical) 1066 DB (Sf); *Chenric* ib. (Nth); *Cenric, Chenrich* 1095 Bury (Sf); John *Kendrich* 1279 RH (C); John *Kerrych, Kenrich* 1297, 1299 Ipm (Sf); Thomas *Kenrick* 1299 Gardner (Sf); John *Kenrich, Kerrich* 1327 SRSf, *Kerrick* 1330 Gardner (Sf); Robert *Kerysche* 1524 SRSf; Susannah *Carriage* daughter of Thomas *Kerridge* 1632 Bardsley; Samuel *Kerridge* 1671 SfPR. OE *Cynerīc* 'family-ruler', which in Suffolk would become *Kenrich.* There is little evidence for OE *Cēnrīc.* The surname might also have become *Kenwright* and have been refashioned as *Courage.* *Kerridge* might also be local, from Kerridge (Cheshire, Devon).

Kersaw: *v.* KERSHAW

Kersey, Keresey, Kearsey, Kiersey, Carsey: Ralph *de Karesey* 1279 RH (C); Adam *de Kersey* 1325 FFEss. From Kersey (Suffolk).

Kershaw, Kersaw: Adam *de Kyrkeschawe* 1307 Wak (Y); Geoffrey *del Kyrkeshagh* 1390 Bardsley (La). From Kirkshaw in Rochdale (Lancs) or from residence near the 'church-wood'.

Kerslake: *v.* CARSLAKE

Kersley: *v.* KEARSLEY

Kerswell, Kerswill: *v.* CARSWELL

Kertess: *v.* CURTIS

Kerton: *v.* KIRTON

Kesby: *v.* KISBY

Keslake: *v.* CARSLAKE

Kessell: *v.* KESTEL

Kestel, Kestell, Kessel, Kessell: John *de Kestel* 1297 MinAcctCo. From Kestell (Cornwall).

Ketchell, Kitchell: William, John *Kechel* 1221 AssWo, 1279 RH (Hu). ME *kechel, kichel* (*v.* NED) 'a cake given as almes in the name, or for the sake, of God'. cf. Chaucer's 'A Goddes *kechel*' where some MSS read *kichel,* so called because godfathers and godmothers used commonly to give them to their godchildren when they asked a blessing. The surname probably denotes a maker or seller of these small cakes.

Ketchen: *v.* KITCHEN
Ketcher: *v.* CATCHER
Kett, Ketts: *v.* KEAT
Kettell: *v.* KETTLE
Ketteridge, Kettridge, Kitteridge, Kittredge: Adam, Roger *Keterych(e)* 1317 FFEss, 1379 ColchCt; Thomas *Kederych* 1524 SRSf. Probably an Anglo-Scandinavian hybrid *Cytelrīc, a compound of ON *Ketill* and the common OE second theme *-rīc.* cf. KETTLEBURN.
Kettle, Kettles, Kettless, Kettel, Kettell, Kittel, Kittle: Grym *Kytel* 972 BCS 1130 (Nth); *Chetel* (Ha), *Chitel* (Co), *Ketel* (Gl, La, Nf, Sf, Y), *Kitel* (Nf, So) 1066 DB; *Ketel* filius Eutret 1212 Cur (Cu); Roger *Chetel* 1180 P (Nth); Edricus *Keteles* c1188 BuryS (Sf); Hulf *Ketel* 12th Seals (Nf); William *Kitel* 1243 AssSo. ON *Ketill* '(sacrificial) cauldron', anglicized as *Cytel*, from which comes *Kittel*.
Kettleburn: *Ketelbern* (Wo), *Chetelbern* (L, Nt, Nf) 1066 DB; *Ketelbern* Hy 2 DC (L), 1211 Cur (Y); Roger, Walter *Ketelbern* 1192 P (Sx), 1221 AssWa; William *Ketelbern'*, *Cutelbern* c1248 Bec (Bk); Robert *Ketelbarn* 1324 FrY. ON *Ketilbiǫrn* '(sacrificial) cauldron-bear', late OE *Cytelbearn*, *Ketelbern*.
Kettless: *v.* KETTLE
Kettridge: *v.* KETTERIDGE
Kew, Le Keux, Lequeux: Roger *le Cu* 1196 FFNf; William *Kue* 1203 P (Lei); William *le Keu* 1231 FFC; Hugh *le Kew* 1246 AssLa. OFr *queu, keu, kieu, cu* 'cook', probably one who sold cooked meat, keeper of an eating-house. *v.* also KEYHO.
Kewen, Kewin: A Manx contraction of *Mac Eoin* 'John's son': *McJon* 1417, *M'Kewne* 1504, *Kewyne* 1540 Moore.
Kewish: A similar Manx contraction of *Mac Uais* 'the noble's son': *Kewish* 1618 Moore.
Kewley, Cully: Hunfridus *de Cuelai* 1086 DB (Nf); Hugh *de Cuilly, de Cully* 1313–14 Bardsley. From Cully-le-Patry (Calvados). The Manx *Kewley* is for COWLEY.
Key, Keye, Keyes, Keys, Keyse: *v.* KAY
Keyho, Keyhoe, Kehoe, Kew: Robert *de Cahou, de Cayho, de Kaiho* 1195–6 P (Bk); William *de Kehou, de Caihou* 1205 Cur (C), P (K); William *de Kayu* 1230 P (Ess), Wilkin *de Keu* ib. (C). All these men came from Caieu, a lost town in the vicinity of Boulogne-sur-Mer (Pas-de-Calais), recorded as *Cahu, Kaeu, Kaio, Kayhou, Keu* (Fees). Kew (Surrey), recorded only from the 14th century, has not been noted as a surname.
Keynes: *v.* CAINES
Keyser, Keysor, Keyzor: *v.* CAYZER
Keyte: *v.* KEAT
Kibbel, Kibble: *v.* KEEBLE
Kichin: *v.* KITCHEN
Kid, Kidd, Kidde, Kidds, Kyd, Kydd: Unfrei *cide* Hy 2 DC (L); William, Ralph *Kide* 1181, 1198 P

(Sf, Nth). ME *kid(e)* 'kid'. Also, occasionally, a voiced form of *Kitt*, a pet-name for Christopher: Robert *Kyd* de Dunde 1357 Black. Or metonymic for KIDDER.
Kiddell, Kiddle: Simon *Kidel* 1219 Fees (K); William *Kyddall* 1554 FrY. AFr *kidel, kydel*, OFr *quidel, cuidel* 'kiddle', 'a Wicker engine whereby fish is caught' (Cotgrave); a dam, weir or barrier in a river with an opening fitted with nets, etc., for catching fish. One in charge of a fishing-weir. cf. Katharine *Kydelman* 1327 *SR* (Ess).
Kidder: Ailric *(le) Chidere* 1190–1 P (Wa); Roger *Kidere* 1233 FFLa; Thomas *le Kidere* 1301 SRY; Richard *le Kedere* 1310 LLB D. Fransson explains this as 'kiddier, hawker, badger', of obscure origin, and compares MDu *keder* 'one who announces or proclaims', first recorded in NED in 1552. The first example is early for a Dutch loan-word and we may have a derivative of ME *kidde* (of unknown origin) 'a faggot or bundle of twigs, brushwood, etc.' (c1350 MED), a woodman, a cutter or seller of faggots. cf. *Kidberers* 1477 MED.
Kidgell, Kiggel, Kigelman: Godwin *Kiggel*, Siger *Kigel* 1221 ElyA (Sf, Nf); William *Kegghel* 1327 SRSf; Margery *Kedgell*, John *Kegel* 1524 SRSf. OE *cycgel* 'cudgel'; a maker or seller of cudgels.
Kidman: Richard *Kideman* 1221 ElyA (Nf); Alan *Kydeman* 1275 RH (Nf). Man in charge of the kids.
Kidson: John, Richard *Kydson* 1522 FrY, 1531 GildY. 'Son of *Kid*' (Christopher). *v.* KID, KITSON.
Kiersey: *v.* KERSEY
Kigelman, Kiggel: *v.* KIDGELL
Kightl(e)y: *v.* KEIGHLEY
Kilbride: John *de Kilbrid* 1202–7 Black. From Kilbride (Lanarks). *v.* also BRIDSON, McBRIDE.
Kilby, Kilbey, Killby, Kilbuy: William *de Kilebi* 1202 AssNth; Thomas *de Kylby* 1327 SRLei; Richard *Kylby* 1396 AssWa. From Kilby (Leics).
Kilduff: *v.* DUFF
Kilham, Killham: Stephen, Everard *de Killum* c1160–9 YCh, 1219 AssY; William *de Kilham* 1337 FFEss. From Kilham (Northumb, ERYorks), or Kilham in Kirk Neuton (Cumb).
Kill, Kille: *Cille* 1066 DB (Y); Godwine *filius Chille* 1187 P (St); Robert *Kille* 1185 Templars (L); Robert *Kyl* 1327 SRSf. Probably ODa *Killi* or *Kille.*
Killigrew: John *de Kelligreu* 1176 P (Co). From Killigrew (Cornwall).
Killip: *M'Killip* 1430, *Killop* 1540 Moore. A Manx contraction of *MacPhilip* 'son of *Philip*'.
Kilmartin: Ir *Mac Giolla Mhártain* 'son of (St) Martin's servant'.
Kilner, Kelner: William *le Kylnere* 1292 MESO (La); Robert *Kilner* 1305 ib. (L). A derivative of OE *cylene* 'kiln', one in charge of a kiln, limeburner.
Kilpatrick, Killpatrick: (i) Stevene *de Kilpatric* 1296 Black; Nigel *Kilpatrick* 1302 ib.; Thomas *de Kylpatrik* 1468 ib. From one or other of the Scottish

places of this name, e.g. Kilpatrick in Closeburn (Dumfries), East, West Kilpatrick (Dumbarton). (ii) In Ireland for *Mac Giolla Phádraig*, an older form of *Fitzpatrick* (MacLysaght).

Kilroy: Ir *Mac Giolla Rua* 'son of *Gilroy*'.

Kilshall, Kilshaw: *v.* KELSALL

Kilvert: *Kilvert* filius Ligulfi c1015 PNDB (Y); *Chiluert* 1066 DB (Y, L); Geoffrey *Culverd*' 1207 Cur (L); Robert *Culuert* 1211 AssWo; John *Culuert, Kiluerd* 1283–4 Balliol (O). Probably an ON **Ketilfrøðr*, ODa **Ketilfrith*, anglicized as **Cytelferð* which became **Cylferð*. *v.* PNDB 215.

Kimball, Kimbell, Kimble, Kimmel: *v.* KEMBLE

Kimberley, Kimberely, Kimberlee: William *de Chineburlai* 1161 P; Robert *de Kynmerley* 1300 ForNt; Thomas *de Kymberle* 1338 LLB F. From Kimberley (Norfolk, Notts, Warwicks).

Kincaid, Kincade, Kinkead: Robert, David *de Kyncade* 1450, 1467 Black; Thomas *Kyncayd* 1545 ib. From the lands of Kincaid in Campsie (Stirling).

Kincey: *v.* KINSEY

Kindell: *v.* KENDAL

Kindersley: *v.* KINNERSLEY

King, Kinge, Kings: (i) *King*' 1201 Cur (C), 1219 ib. (Sr); Mariota filia *King* . . . William *King* 1259 RamsCt (Hu). OE *Cyng*, an original nickname from OE *cyning, cyng* 'king'. (ii) Ælwine *se Cyng* 1050–71 OEByn (D); Wlfric *Ching* c1130 ELPN; Geoffrey *King* 1177 P (C); Wuluricus, Gaufridus *le King* 1182–1200 BuryS (Sf); Juliana *la Kinges* 1275 SRWo, 1285 *Ass* (Ess). OE *cyning, cyng* 'king', a nickname from the possession of kingly qualities or appearance. Also a pageant name, one who had acted as king in a play or pageant, or had been King of Misrule, or 'king' of a tournament.

Kingett, Kinggett: Robert, John *Kynget* 1296 SRSx, 1317 FFEss; John *Kyngot* 1327 SRWo. *King-et, King-ot*, diminutives of *King*, the personal name. cf. the double diminutive: William *Kyngelot* 1328 ArchC 33.

Kinghorn, Kinghorne, Kinghan, Kingan: Adam *de Kyngorn, de Kynghorn* 1204–11, 1357 Black; James *Kinghorne* 1597 ib. (Dunfermline); Alexander *Kingarn* 1679 ib. (Kirkcudbright); John *Kinging* 1684 ib.; Andrew *Kingan* 1689 ib. (Kirkcudbright). From the barony of Kinghorn (Fife).

Kingsford: Edwin *de Kingesford* 1185 Templars (Ess); John *de Kyngesford*', *de Kyngesford* 1221 AssWa, 1327 SRWo. From Kingsford (Devon, Essex, Warwicks, Worcs).

Kingsley: William *de Kingesle* 1246 AssLa; Richard *de Kyngesleye* 1327 SRSt; John *Kyngesley* 1421–2 FFWa. From Kingsley (Ches, Hants, Staffs).

Kingsman: Godwin *Kingesman* 1166 P (Nf); William *Kingesman* 1184–1215 AD iv (Lo). 'The king's man', a surname common in Norfolk and Suffolk where it probably meant one who had commended his services to the king and not to some baron. cf. Walter *Kingesbonde* 1205 P (Nb), Godwin *Kingesreive* 1208 FFL.

Kingson: Godricus *Chingessone* 1066 Winton (Ha); Ælfmær *Cynges sune* 1100–30 OEByn (D);

Henry *Kingessone* 1224–46 Bart (Lo). 'Son of *Cyng*', from OE *Cyng*, or of *King*. *v.* KING.

Kingston, Kingstone: Alan *de Kingistona* 1175 P (Y); Nicholas *de Kyngeston* 1247 FFO; Thomas *Kyngeston* 1398 FFEss. From one or other of the many places of this name.

Kinkead: *v.* KINCAID

Kinlay, Kinley: A Manx contraction of *MacCinfaolaidh* 'son of *Cinfaoladh*' 'wolf-head': *Kinley* 1604 Moore. The name may also be English: Thorold *de Kynely* 1220 FFEss. Probably from Kenley (Surrey).

Kinman, Kynman: *Keneman* c1250 Rams (Nf); Richard *Kineman* 13th *Binham* (Nf); Robert *Kynemon*, Richard *Kenemon* 1327 SRWo. OE *Cynemann* 'royal-man', recorded only once, c770 in Worcester. More commonly, OE *cȳna* and *mann* 'cows' man', herdsman. cf. Ralph *Kenegrom* 1235 Bart.

Kinnaird: Richard *de Kinnard* 1204–14 Black; Rauf *de Kynnard* 1296 ib. (Fife); Thomas *de Kynnarde* 1431 ib.; Erche *Kinʒerd* 1567 ib. (Kelso). From the barony of Kinnaird (Perth).

Kinnerley: *v.* KENNERLEY

Kinnersley, Kinnersly, Kindersley, Kynnersley: Hugh *de Kinardesle(g)* 1208 Cur (He), 1221 AssWo. From Kinnersley (Hereford, Salop, Surrey, Worcs).

Kinnish, Kennish: A Manx contraction of *Mac Aenghuis* 'son of *Aenghus*': *McInesh* 1511, *Kynnish* 1626, *Kenish* 1649 Moore. cf. MAGUINESS.

Kinsey, Kincey, Kynsey: William *Kynsei* 1306 IpmGl; George *Kynsey, Kyngsey* 1525 SRSx; Robert *Kensaye* 1558 Pat (Sx); Margery *Kynsee* 1584 StratfordPR; Joseph *Kinsey* 1648 FrYar. OE *Cynesige* 'royal-victory'.

Kinsley, Kynsley, Kinslea: Ralph *de Kineslea* 1191 Pl (Ess); John *de Kyneslay* 1244–5 IpmY; Robert *Kynslay* 1542 RothwellPR (Y). From Kinsley (WRYorks).

Kinsman: William *Kinesman* 1198 FFNf; John *Cunesmon* 1275 SRWo. ME *cunnes, kinnes*, genitive of *kin* and *man*, 'kinsman', a relative by blood (or, loosely, by marriage).

Kintish: *v.* KENTISH

Kipping, Kippen, Kippin: Alwinus *filius Cheping* 1086 DB (Berks); Mafrei *filius Kipping* 1170 P (Nth); *Kipping de Burehamton*' 1243 AssSo; John, Richard *Kipping* 1195 P (Wa), 1206 Cur (Ess). OE *Cypping*, an original nickname from the Germanic root **kupp-* 'to swell, be swollen', used of a man of fat, rotund appearance (Tengvik).

Kipps: Ulwardus *Cheppe* 1066 Winton (Ha); Wolberne, Robert *Kippe* 1202 AssL, 1279 RH (C); Richard *Keppe* 1327 SRSx. OE **Cyppe*, the simplex of *Cypping*, with the same meaning. *v.* KIPPING.

Kirk, Kirke, Kerk, Kyrke: Reginald *Attekireke* 1209 FFL; Richard *Attekirck* 1301 SRY; Adam *Ofthekirke* 1308 Pat (Sf); John *be ye kyrk* 1438 DbCh. 'Dweller by the church', ON *kirkja*.

Kirkbride, Kirkbright: Richard *de Kirkebryd* 1274 Ipm (Cu). From Kirkbride (Cumb).

Kirkby, Kirkebye, Kirby, Kerbey, Kerby: Godebold *de Kirkebi* 1121–48 Bury (Sf); Ketellus *de Kerkebi* 1191 P (Y); Richard *Kyrby* 1524 SRSf. From one of the numerous places named Kirby or Kirkby.

Kirkham, Kirkam, Kerkham: Simon *de Kirkeham* 1219 AssY. From Kirkham (ER, WRYorks).

Kirkhouse, Kirkus: John *Kirkhous, Kirkeasse* 1446 FrY, 1618 YWills. 'One employed at the church-house.' *v*. KIRK.

Kirkland, Kirtland, Kirtlan: Michael *de Kerkeland*' 1196 P (Cu); John *de Kyrkeland* c1280 Black (Berwick); Samuel *Kirtland* 1802 Oseney (O). From Kirkland (Cumb, Lancs; Ayr, Dumfries, Lanarks).

Kirkley, Kirkly, Kirtley, Kerley, Kerly: William *de Kirkelee* 1200 Cur (Sf). From Kirkley (Northumb, Suffolk).

Kirkman, Kirman, Kerman: Robert *Kirkeman* 1230 P (Y); Roger *le Kirkeman* 1259 Calv (Y). ON *kirkja* and ME *man*, 'custodian of a church'. cf. CHURCHMAN.

Kirkus: *v*. KIRKHOUSE
Kirrage: *v*. KERRICH
Kirrell, Kirriell: *v*. KERRELL
Kirtland: *v*. KIRKLAND
Kirtler: *v*. CURTLER
Kirtley: *v*. KIRKLEY

Kirton, Kerton, Kurton: Lambert *de Kirketon*' 1219 AssL; William *Kirton* 1508 FrY. From Kirton (Lincs, Notts, Suffolk).

Kisby, Kesby: Ralph *de Kisebi* 1205 Cur (L). From Keisby (Lincs).

Kiss, Cuss, Cusse, Cush: Amice, John *Kisse* 1327 SRLei; William, Thomas *Kysse* 1329 FFSf, 1430 FrYar; John, Edmond *Cusse* 1545, 1576 SRW; Laurence *Kyshe*, Sarah *Kish* 1573, 1765 Bardsley. Metonymic for KISSER.

Kissack, Kissock: Gilbert *McIssak* 1418, *Kissak* 1599 Moore. A Manx contraction of *MacIsaac* 'Isaac's son'.

Kisser, Kissa: William *Kisere* 1224–46 Bart; Richard *le Kissere* 1288 LLB A; Hugh *le Kysser*, *le Cussere, le Kisehere* 1292 SRLo, 1294 LLB A, 1307 Husting; Margaret *Cusser* 1298 IpmY; Benjamin, Edward *Kishere* 1738, 1750 Bardsley. 'A maker of (leather) armour for the thighs', from OFr *cuisse* 'thigh', cf. 'cuisses, armour for the thighs' (Cotgrave). The kissers were cordwainers.

Kitchell: *v*. KETCHELL
Kitcheman: *v*. KITCHINGMAN

Kitchen, Kichin, Kitchin, Kitching, Ketchen, Ketchin: Henry *atte Kychene* 1311 ParlWrits (Sx); Nicholas *atte Kechene* 1327 SRSo; Robert *del Kychin* 1359 FrY; Thomas *Kytchyng* 1513 GildY. 'Worker in a kitchen' (OE *cycene*).

Kitchener, Kitchiner: (i) William *le Cuchener* 1332 MEOT (Sr); Thomas *Kytchener, Kitchynner* 1472 FrY, 1494 GildY. A derivative of OE *cycene* 'kitchen', one employed in a kitchen, especially in a monastery (c1440 MED). (ii) Robert *de Kechenor*' 1207 Cur (Sx). From Kitchenour (Sussex).

Kitching: *v*. KITCHEN

Kitchingman, Kitcheman, Kitchman: John *Kychynman* 1379 PTY; Thomas *Kechynman* 1475 GildY; Jenet *Kycheman* 1553 RothwellPR (Y); William *Kitchingman* 1583 FrY. *v*. KITCHEN, KITCHENER.

Kite: *v*. KEAT

Kitson: William *Kittesson* 1340 Crowland (C); Thomas *Kytson* 1357 ib. 'Son of *Kit*.'

Kitt, Kitts: *Kytte* the Soper 1286 AssCh; Roger son of *Kytt* 1297 Wak (Y); Wigar, Amfridus *Kitte* 1173–9 Clerkenwell (Mx), 1190 Oseney (O). *Kytte* is a pet-form of *Christopher* and of *Katharine*. The surname was common and may also be metonymic for KITTER.

Kittel: *v*. KETTLE

Kitter: Walter *le Kittere* 1177 P (Y); Holbe *Kittere* 1221 AssWo. A derivative of ME *kitte* (1362 MED) 'a wooden vessel made of hooped staves', a maker of kits (tubs, milking-pails, etc.). cf. Richard *le Kittewritt*' 1275 MESO (Y), 'kit-wright'.

Kitteridge: *v*. KETTERIDGE

Kittermaster: Ida *de Kidministre* 1230 P (Wo); Symond *Kytermyster* 1524 SRSf; Thomas *Kiddermaster* 1637 EA (NS) ii (Sf); William *Kittermaster* 1663 Bardsley. From Kidderminster (Worcs).

Kittle: *v*. KETTLE
Kittredge: *v*. KETTERIDGE

Knape: John *le Knape* 1332 MEOT (Nf). OE *cnapa* 'youth, servant'.

Knapman: *v*. KNAPP, KNAPPER

Knapp: William *atte Kneppe* 1294 PN Sr 89; Henry *de Cnappe* 1301 PN D 81; John *Knappe* 1279 RH (Bk). 'Dweller at the top of the hill or on a hillock' (OE *cnæpp*) as at Knapp (Devon) or Knapp Fm (Sussex).

Knappen: Henry *Knappyng* 1327 SRSf. OE **cnæpping* 'dweller on the hill'. *v*. KNAPP.

Knapper: William *Knapper* 1360 FFSx; Andrew *Knapere* 14th Rad (Sf). Identical in meaning with KNAPP, KNAPMAN, KNAPPEN.

Knappett: Thomas *Knapet* 1378 LLB H; John *Nappett* 1473 FrY. Perhaps a diminutive of KNAPE.

Knatchbull: John *Knechchebole, Knetchebole* 1375 ColchCt; Thomas *Knechboll*, John *Knachbull* 1481, 1504 KentW. ME *knetch, knatch* 'to knock on the head, fell' and *bull*, 'Fell bull', a nickname for a butcher.

Kneal, Kneale: *McNelle* 1408, *MacNeyll* 1430, *Kneal* 1598 Moore. A Manx contraction of *MacNiall* 'Niall's son'. *v*. NEAL.

Kneen: A purely Manx name, probably identical with KANEEN. It seems to have been confused with NIVEN: Jenkin *M'Nyne* or *Mac Nevyne* 1429, 1430 Moore.

Knell, Knill: Alvredus *de Knelle* 1220 Cur (Sx); Gilbert *de Knille* 1279 RH (C); William *atte Knelle* 1296 SRSx. 'Dweller by the knoll', OE **cnyll(e)*, as at Kneela (Devon), Knell House (Sussex), Knill (Hereford), Nill Well (Cambs).

Kneller: William *Kneller* 1327 SRSx. Identical in meaning with KNELL.

Knevet, Knevit: v. KNIVETT

Knife: Alwyne *Knyf* 1139 Templars (O); John *Knif'* 1277 AssSo. OE *cnif* 'knife', metonymic for *knife-smith*, cutler: v. NAYSMITH.

Knifton: v. KNIVETON

Knight, Knights: (i) *Chenicte* 1066 DB (Y); Johannes *filius Cnith* 1182–1211 BuryS (Sf); Gamell' *filius Cniht* 1219 AssL. OE *Cniht*. (ii) Godefridus *Niht*, Oschetel *Cniht* 1166 P (Nf); Walter *le Knit* 1200 Oseney (O); William *Knicht'* 1221 AssWo; John *Knyght* 1275 RH (Sf); Beatrix *Knictes* 1279 RH (Hu); Alicia *Knyghtes* 1327 SRSo; Henry *le Nyte* 1327 SRSx. OE *Cniht* or *cniht* 'servant', 'knight, feudal tenant bound to serve as a mounted soldier', 'a common soldier'.

Knightley, Knightly: Jordan *de Knitteleg'* 1207 Pl (St); Robert *de Knyghteleye* 1351 Ronton; Richard *Knyghtley* 1411 FFEss. From Knightley (Staffs).

Knighton: Alexander *de Cnichteton'* 1181 P (Wo); Ralph *de Knichton* 1222 AssSt; Hugh *de Knyghton'* 1327 SRLei; Thomas *Knyghton* 1503 FFEss. From one or the other of the many places of this name.

Knill: v. KNELL

Kniveton, Knifton: Matthew *de Knyveton* 1275 AssSt. From Kniveton (Derby), pronounced *Nifton*.

Knivett, Knyvett, Knevet, Knevit, de Knevett, Nevet, Nevett, Nevitt: Leuricus, Nicholas *Cnivet* 1087–97 Crispin (Mx), 1185 Templars (Herts); William, Osbert *Knivet* Hy 2 DC (L), 1199 AssSt; Ernald *Knikt* 1275 RH (Nf); Thomas *Knifet* ib. (L); Walter *le Knift* 1279 ib. (O); John *Knyft*, *Knyvet* 1311, 1337 ColchCt. A Norman pronunciation of *Knight*, owing to the French difficulty with the *h* of *cniht*. Mathew *de Knyvet* 1273 RH (Nt) must be identical with Matthew *de Knyveton* above and William *de Knyvet* 1327 SRDb must similarly be for *Knyvet'*, i.e. *Kniveton*. Alexander *de Knyft* 1279 RH (O) is an error for *le Knyft* (cf. Walter *le Knift* above). There is no evidence for a place *Knevet* and the modern *de Knevett* is either a perpetuation of one of these errors or due to a late prefixing of an unetymological *de*.

Knock, Knocker: Thomas *atte Knocke* 1296 SRSx; Nicholas *Knok* 1279 RH (Beds). 'Dweller by the hill (OE *cnocc*) as at Knock Hatch (Sussex), Knock Fm (Kent). v. MELS.

Knoll, Knollys, Knowles, Nowles: Robert *de la Cnolle* 1185 P (D); Theobald *de Chnolle* 1242 Fees (K); Thomas *Knolle* 1279 RH (C); William *atte Knolle* 1296 SRSx; Adam *del Knol* 1318 AssSt; Christopher *Knolles* 1407 FrY. 'Dweller at the top of a hill' (OE *cnoll*), as at Knole (Kent, Sussex),

Knowle (Devon, Dorset, Som, Warwicks).

Knoop, Knope, Knopp: Osgod *Cnoppe* 1066 OEByn (Ess); William, Walter *Knop* 1327 SRC, SRSf. OE *cnoppa*, ME *knop(p)*, *knope* 'a small rounded protuberance, knob', used also of the knope of the knee and the elbow-joint.

Knorr: Richard *de Knarre*, *de Knorre* 1279 RH (C). From Knarr Fm or Lake (Cambs).

Knott: (i) *Cnut*, *Cnud*, *Canut* 1066 DB; Randulfus *filius Cnut* 1191 P (D); *Knot* pater Alani, Alanus filius *Knod* 1202 AssL; Radulfus *filius Knut* 1203 P (Y); Walter, Robert *Cnot* 1165 P (Sf), 1185 Templars (Herts); William *Cnotte* 1206 Cur (Beds); William, John *Knotte* 1221 AssWo, 1260 ELPN; Stephen *le Knotte* 1296 SRSx; Hugo *Knout'* 1301 SRY. The personal name is ON *Knútr*, ODa, OSw *Knut*, an original nickname from ON *knútr* 'knot', occasionally, perhaps, the rare OE *Cnotta*. *Knut* (Canute) was still in use in the 13th century. The surname is usually a nickname from OE *cnotta* 'knot', used of a thickset person. (ii) Emma *del Knot* 1332 SRCu. 'Dweller on the hill' (ME *knot*) as at Knott End (Lancs).

Knotter: John *Knotter* 1524 SRSf. Equivalent to KNOTT (ii).

Knottson: 'Son of *Knut*.' v. KNOTT (i).

Knowler, Knowlder, Knowlman: John, Walter *le Knollere* 1296 SRSx; Wilmore *Knowleman* 1616 Bardsley. Found side by side with *atte Knolle*, v. KNOLL.

Knowles: v. KNOLL

Knowling: William *Knollyng* 1327 SRSx. OE *cnolling* 'dweller at the top of the hill'. v. KNOLL, KNOWLER.

Knox: John *de Cnoc* 1260 Black; Hugo *Cnox* c1272 ib., Alan *de Knockis* 1328 ib. From Knock (Renfrew).

Kortwright: v. CARTWRIGHT

Krabbe: v. CRABB

Kriel: v. KERRELL

Krips: v. CRISP

Kristall: v. CHRYSTAL

Kroll: v. CROWL

Krook: v. CROOK

Kurton: v. KIRTON

Kyd(d): v. KID

Kynaston: Walter *de Kynwardeston'* c1295 Glast (So); Ralph *de Kinastan* t Ed 3 Rydware; William *Kynastone* 1418 LLB I. From Kynaston (Hereford, Salop).

Kynman: v. KINMAN

Kynnersley: v. KINNERSLEY

Kynsey, Kynsley: v. KINSEY, KINSLEY

Kyrke: v. KIRK

Kyte: v. KEAT

L

Labbet: *v.* ABBATT

Labern: *v.* LAYBORN

Labey: *v.* ABBA

Lace: OFr *laz, las,* ME *lace* 'cord'; metonymic for *Lacer,* a maker of cords or strings: Richard *le Lacir* 1278 LLB B; William *le Lacer* 1292 SRLo, 1298 Wak (Y).

Lacey, Lacy, Lassey, de Lacey, de Lacy: Ilbert *de Laci,* Roger *Laci* 1086 DB; Henry *de Lasci* 1185 Templars (L). From Lassy (Calvados).

Lachlan, Laughlan, Laughland: *Lohlan* 1158–64 Black; Eugene *filius Loghlan* 1296 ib.; Reginald son of *Lauchlan* 1327 ib.; Adam *Lachlane* 1417 ib.; Robert *Laughland* 1642 ib. Gael *Lachlann,* earlier *Lochlann* 'lake or fjord-land', i.e. Scandinavia, Norway, the personal name denoting 'one from Lachlann'.

Lacklison: William *Lauchlanesone* 1497 Black. For MacLACHLAN.

Ladd, Ladds: Godric *Ladda* c1100 OEByn (So); Richard *Ladde* c1175 EngFeud (Nth); Walter *le Ladd'* 1242 Fees (K). The common English *lad,* of obscure origin, originally 'servant or man of low birth'. cf. 'to make lordes of laddes' (*Piers Plowman*); 'A ladde . . . Borne he was of pouere lynage' (Robert of Brunne).

Lade: Richard, Petronilla *de la Lade* 1214 Cur (C), 1275 SRWo. 'Dweller by the road, path or watercourse', OE (*ge*)*lād.*

Ladler, Laidler: Walter *le Ladelere* 1278 Misc (Wa); John *le Ladeler* 1327 SRY; Nicholas *Ladelere* 1377 AD iii (Hu). 'A maker of ladles', OE *hlædel* and *-er,* cf. Nicholas *Ladel* 1187–9 Ek, William *Ladyl* 1337 CorLo.

Ladye: William *le Lady* 1340 AssC. A nickname.

Ladyman: Rannulf (*le*) *Lauediman* 1202 FFL, 1214 Cur (Nth); Geoffrey *le Leuediman* 13th Guisb (Y); Roger *Ladyman* 1296 MEOT (Herts). 'The lady's servant', OE *hlæfdige* and *mann.*

Laffeaty, Laffitte, Lafitte: *v.* FATES

Lafflin, Laffling: An English pronunciation and spelling of *Laughlan.*

Lainer, Leiner: Hugo *le Layner* 1279 MESO (Y); Goceus (Joyce) *le Leyner, le Laner, le Wollemongere* 1292 SRLo, 1312 LLB D, 1301 Husting. OFr *lainier, lanier* 'woolmonger'.

Laing, Layng: Thomas *Laing* 1357 Black (Dumfries). A Scottish variant of LANG.

Laird: Roger *Lawird, lauird* 1257 Black (Ber-

wick); Thomas *Lairde* 1552 ib. (Glasgow). A Scottish form of LORD, 'landlord, land-owner'.

Laister: *v.* LEICESTER

Lake, Lakes: Richard *de la Lake* 1200 P (Sa); Robert *Attelake* 1242 P (Sr). 'Dweller by the stream', OE *lacu.*

Lakeman: John *Lakeman* 1320 HPD (Ess). 'Dweller by the stream.'

Laker: (i) William *le Lakere* 1325 MESO (Ha); Adam *Lakyare* 1391 ib. (Sx); Robert *Laker* 1545 SxWills. From OE *lacu* 'stream'. *v.* LAKE, LAKEMAN. (ii) Osbert *Laycar* 1274 RH (Ess); John *le Leykere* 1309 SRBeds, 1327 FFK. ME *leyker,* ON *leikari* 'player, actor'. cf. Richard *Leyk* 1292 SRLo, from ME *leyk* 'play, sport'. cf. GAME.

Lamb, Lambe, Lamm: *Lamb* dispensator 1161 Dugd v. 421; *Lambe* de Harewude 1290 ShefA; Ædward, Wulmar *Lamb* 1195 P (K), 1230 P (Nf); William, Roger *le Lamb* 1279 RH (C), 1296 SRSx. A nickname from the animal or a shortened form of *Lambert.* Occasionally from a sign: William *atte Lamme* 1320 LLB E.

Lambard, Lambart, Lambarth, Lambert, Lambirth, Lamburd, Lampard, Lampart, Lamperd, Lampert, Lammert, Limbert: (i) Gozelinus *filius Lamberti* 1086 DB (L, Y); *Lambertus* 1142 NthCh (L), 1219 AssY, 1221 AssWo; Ricardus *filius Lambricht* 1148 Winton (Ha); *Lambricthus, Lambrihtus* 1196–7 P (Bk); Constantinus *filius Lambrichti* 1220 Cur (Sf); *Lambard* 1296 Black; Richard *lambert* 1148 Winton (Ha); Simon *Lamberti* 1212 Cur (Berks); Peter *Lamb'rt, Lamberd'* 1220 Cur (Nf); John *Lambard* 1250 Fees (Sx); William *Lambryt* 1279 RH (Hu); Thomas *Lambrygt, Lambrith* 1280 AssSo; Thomas *Lamparde* 1544 RochW; Mr *Limbert* 1587 EA (NS) ii (Nf). OFr *Lambert,* OG *Lambert, Lanbert* 'land-bright', a popular name from the 12th century, probably introduced from Flanders where St Lambert of Maestricht was highly venerated. Late OE *Landbeorht* was rare but was used after the Conquest and has contributed to the surname. *v.* LAMBRICK. (ii) William *Lambhyrde* 1255 Ass (Ess); Robert *le Lambhurde* 1288 Ct (Ha); Hugh (*le*) *Lambehird* 1309 Wak (Y); William *Lambeherde* 1332 SRSx. OE *lamb* and *hierde* 'lamb-herd'.

Lamberton, Lamerton: William *de Lamberton* c1136 Black; John *de Lambertoune* c1200 ib.; William *de Lambirtoun* 1300 ib.; Robert *Lamberton* 1672 HTY. From the barony of Lamberton

(Berwick). Occasionally perhaps from Lamerton (Devon), *Lambertone* 1232, and cf. John *de Lamerton*' 1206 P (D).

Lambie, Lamby, L'Ami, Lammie, Lampey: Robert, Henry *Lambi* 1203 P (Nth), 1281 Black (Dundee); Mariora *Lammeis dothyr* 1527 ib. (Strathdee); George *Lammie* 1628 ib. ON *Lambi*.

Lambirth: *v.* LAMBARD

Lambkin: *Lambekyn* Flandrensis 1178 P (Nb); *Lamekin filius Beatricis* 1188 P (Bk); Nicholas *Lambekyn* 1301 SRY; John *Lamkyn* 1379 ColchCt. *Lamb-kin*, a diminutive of *Lamb* (Lambert).

Lamborn, Lamborne, Lambourn, Lambourne, Lamburn, Lamburne: Ralph *de Lamburne* 1198 FFEss; Alice *de Lamborne* 1278 CtW; John *Lambourn* 1451 AssLa. From Lambourn (Berks), or Lambourne (Essex).

Lambrick: Richard *Lambrich* 1327 SRSf. OE *Landbeorht. v.* LAMBARD.

Lambshead: Suetman, Agnes *Lambesheved* c1130 ELPN, 1279 RH (Hu). A nickname. cf. John *Lomesfot* 1327 SRSo.

Lambson: *v.* LAMPSON
Lamburd: *v.* LAMBARD
Lamburn(e): *v.* LAMBORN
Lamerton: *v.* LAMBERTON
Lamey, L'Ami, L'Amie: *v.* AMEY, LAMBIE
Lamm: *v.* LAMB

Lammas, Lammers: Brictius (*de*) *Lammasse* 1190–1 P (Nf); William *de Lammers* 1248 FFEss. From Lammas (Norfolk) or Lamarsh (Essex), both DB *Lamers*.

Lammert: *v.* LAMBARD
Lammey, Lammie: *v.* LAMBIE

Lammiman, Lamyman: Alexander *Lamaman* 1463 FrY; Richard *Lambeyman* 1521 GildY; John *Lamyman* 1525 FrY. 'Servant of *Lambie*' or of *Lambin. v.* LAMPEN.

Lammin(g): *v.* LAMPEN

Lammond, Lamond, Lamont: *Laumannus filius* Malcolmi 1230–46 Black; Molmure *filius Lagman* 1290 ib.; *Lawemund* McGreghere 1292 ib.; John *Lawmond* 1466 ib.; John *Lamond* 1674 HTSf. MIr *Lagmand*, from ON *Lǫgmaðr* 'lawman'. *v.* MACLAMON, LAWMAN.

Lampard, Lampart, Lamperd, Lampert: *v.* LAMBARD

Lampen, Lampin, Lammin, Lamming: *Lambinus* Frese 1181 P (K); *Lambinus* 1197 P (K), 1221 Cur (C); Robert *Lambin* 1292 SRLo; John *Lambryn* 1302 FFSf, 1305 LLB B; Roger *Laming* 1683 Bardsley. *Lamb-in*, a diminutive of *Lamb* (Lambert). *Lambert* de Langham (1283 SRSf) is also called *Lambinus*.

Lampet, Lampitt, Lamputt: John *de Lampet*, Agnes *Lampit* 1327 SRSf; William *atte Lamputte* 1332 SRSr. 'Dweller near, or worker at the clay-pit', OE *lām* 'loam', *pytt* 'hollow'.

Lampey: *v.* LAMBIE

Lampson, Lambson, Lamson: Adam *Lambeson* 1332 SRCu; Thomas *Lamson* 1464 Cl; William *Lampson* Eliz Bardsley. 'Son of *Lamb* (Lambert).'

Lamyman: *v.* LAMMIMAN

Lancashire, Lankshear, Lankshire: Richard *de Lancastreschire* 1387 AssL; Robert *Lancashire* 1604 ChW; Robert *Lankshire*, John *Lankshear* 1693, 1805 Bardsley. 'The man from Lancashire.'

Lancaster, Langcaster, Lankester, Loncaster, Longcaster: William *de Lonecastre* 1175 StCh; John *de Lancastre* 1327 SRC; Thomas *de Langcastre* 1327 *SR* (Ess); Alice *Longcaster* 1494 GildY; Ales *Lankester* 1565 SfPR. From Lancaster.

Lance: *Lance* Bliaut 1185 NthCh (Nth); *Lance* prepositus 1219 AssL; Alice, John *Lance* 1196 FFNf, 1237 Oseney (O). OG *Lanzo*, a hypocoristic of names in *Land-*.

Land, Lawn: Thomas *de la Lande* 1205 P (Nth); James *de la Launde* 1262 AssSt; Widdow *Lawne* 1674 HTSf. 'Dweller by the glade', as at Launde (Leics), ME *launde*, OFr *land*.

Lander(s): *v.* LAVENDER

Landray, Landrey, Landry, Laundrey: (i) *Landri, Landric(us)* 1086 DB; Willelmus *filius Landrei* 1219 Cur (L); Gerard *Landri* 1198 P (D). OFr *Landri*, OG *Landric(us)* 'land-ruler'. (ii) Ricardus *de la Lavendaria* 1219 Cur (So); Robert *de la Lauendrie* 1278 AssSo. 'Worker in a wash-house', ME *lavendrie*.

Landseer: Gilbert *de la Landsare* 1243 AssSo; Thomas *de la Landschare* 1274 RH (So). 'Dweller by the boundary or landmark', OE *landscearu*.

Lane, Lanes, Loan, Lone, Lones: Ralph *de Lane* 1176 P (K); Osbertus *in Lane* 1212 Cur (Sr); Adam *Ithelane* 1227 AssBeds; Walter *atte Lane* 1260 AssC; Nicholas *atte Lone* 1275 SRWo; Roger *de la Lone* 1279 AssSt; Bartholomew *Lane* 1292 FFSf; Thomas *in le lone* 1327 SRDb. 'Dweller in the lane', OE *lanu. Lone* shows the characteristic *o* of the West Midland dialects.

Lang, Lange, Long, Lung: Ætheric *ðes Langa* 972 OEByn (Nth); Leofwine *Lange* 1070 ASC E; Berard *Long* 1121–48 Bury (Sf); Godfrey *Lunge* 1179 P (Gl); Nicholas *le Long, le Lung* 1290–2 LLB C; William *Lange* 1296 Black; Adam *ye Langge* 1297 SRY. OE *lang, long* 'long, tall'. *Lang* is Scottish and Northern English.

Langbain: *Langebeyn* 1101–7 Holme (Nf); John *Langebayne* 1306 Riev (Y). ON *Langabein* (by-name), 'long bone', perhaps 'long leg'.

Langbant: William *Langbarne* 1327 SRY. 'Tall child', OE *lang, bearn.* cf. GOODBAIRN.

Langbridge: William *de la Langebrigge* 1199 Cur (Sr). 'Dweller by the long bridge', OE *lang, brycg.*

Langdale: Henry *de Langdale* 1332 SRCu; Patrick *de Langedale* 1362 AssY; John *Langdale* 1402 IpmY. From Langdale (Westmorland).

Langdo(w)n: *v.* LONGDEN
Langford: *v.* LONGFORD

Langham: Walter, William *de Langham* 1201 Pl (Do), 1327 SRLei; Thomas *Langham* 1392 CtH. From Langham (Dorset, Norfolk, Rutland, Suffolk), Langham ⌐ow (Lincs), or Longham (Norfolk), *Langham* 1254.

Langhurst, Longhurst: Richard *de Langherst*' 1221 Cur (Sr); Robert *de Longehurst* 1332 SRSx.

'Dweller by the long wooded hill' (OE *hyrst*), as at Longhirst (Northumb).

Langland(s): *v.* LONGLAND

Langley, Longley, Longly: Richard *de Langelega* 1191 P (Sa); Simon *de Longelay* 1297 SRY. From one of the many Langleys or 'dweller by the long wood or clearing' (OE *lang, lēah*).

Langman: *v.* LONGMAN

Langridge, Langrick, Longridge, Longrigg: Thomas *de Langgerugge* 1175 P (So); Dionisia *de Langerig* 1253 AssSt; Robert *de Longrigge* 1276 ib.; Thomas *de Langerigg* 1332 SRCu. 'Dweller by the long ridge' (OE *lang, hrycg*, ON *hryggr*), or from Langridge (Som), Langrigg (Cumb), or Longridge (Lancs).

Langrish, Langrishe: Robert *de Langerisce* 1199 Pl (Ha); Ralph *de Langris* 1222 Acc; Hugh *Langrisch*' 1332 SRDo. Usually no doubt from Langrish (Hants), but occasionally perhaps it may be a nickname, cf. Robert *le Langerus* 1200 Cur, a derivative of OFr *langeuer* 'lassitude, inertia'.

Langshaw: *v.* LONGSHAW

Langstaff: *v.* LONGSTAFF

Langthorp, Langthorpe, Longthorp: Stephen *de Langetorp* 1212 Cur (Y). From Langthorpe (NRYorks).

Langton, Longton: Osbert *de Langeton*' 1191 P (L); William *de Longetone* 1332 SRLa. From Longton (Lancs, Staffs) or one of the Langtons.

Langtree, Langtry: Siward *de Langetre* 1206 Cur (La). From Langtree (Devon, Lancs).

Lank: Avice *Lanke* 1275 RH (Nf). OE *hlanc* 'long, narrow', i.e. tall and thin.

Lankester: *v.* LANCASTER

Lankshear, Lankshire: *v.* LANCASHIRE

Lapage, Lappage: John *Lawpage* 1379 PTY; Robert *Lappadge*, Thomas *Lappage* 1568 SRSf. 'Page, servant of *Law* (Laurence).' ME, OFr *page*.

Lappin, Lapping: Robert, Beatrix *Lapyn* 1320 FFK, 1481 FrY. OFr *lapin* 'rabbit'.

Larcher, L'Archer: *v.* ARCHER

Larder: Bernard *Larderer* 1130 P (W); Peter *de Larder*' 1173 P (Ha); Thomas *del Larder* 1304 Cl. David *Larderer* is identical with David *le Lardener* (c1170 Riev). *v.* LARDNER. *Larderer* is a derivative of OFr *lardier*, originally 'a tub to keep bacon in', later, 'a room in which to keep bacon and meat'; hence, 'officer in charge of the larder'.

Lardner: Dauid *Lardener, le Lardener, Lardiner* 1161–81 P (Y); Thomas *le Lardiner* 1193 P (Sr). AFr *lardiner* 'officer in charge of a larder', also 'the officer who superintended the pannage of hogs in the forest'.

Large, Lardge: Geoffrey *(le) Large* 1204–5 P (Nth). OFr *large* 'generous'.

Lark, Larke, Laverack, Laveric, Laverick: Juliana *laueroc* 1243 AssDu; Ralph *Larke* 1275 RH (Nf); William *le Lauerk* 1332 SRSx. A nickname from the lark (ME *larke, lavero(c)k*, OE *lāwerce*).

Larkin, Larking: *v.* LORKIN

Larmer, Larmo(u)r: *v.* ARMER

Larner, Lerner: Larner's Wood in Little Saxham (Suffolk) owes its name to the family of Edmund *de Lauueney* (1327 SRSf). Other members were John *Lawney* (1381 SRSf) and James *Larner* (1562 Saxham PR). The wood is *Lawners* Wood in 1638 (ib.).

Larrett: Richard *Laryot* 1524 SRSf; Thomas *Larret* 1674 HTSf. A diminutive of *Larry*, a pet-form of *Laurence*.

Larwood: Geoffrey *de Larwode* 1299 NorwDeeds; William *Larwoode* 1524 SRSf; Thomas *Larwood* 1577 Musters (Nf). From some minor place, as yet unidentified but probably in Norfolk.

Lascelles: Peter *de Laceles* c1150 Riev (Y); Pigot *de Lasceles* 1185 Templars (Y). From Lacelle (Orne).

Lasenby: *v.* LAZENBY

Lashford: *v.* LATCHFORD

Lashmar, Lashmore: *v.* LATCHMORE

Lass, Less: William, Thomas *Lesse* 1276 RH (Lei), 1327 *SR* (Ess); Ralph *le Lasse* 1332 SRSx; Herry *Lasse* 1524 SRSf. OE *lǣssa* 'less', ME *lesse*, *lasse* 'smaller', perhaps 'the younger'.

Lasseter: *v.* LEICESTER

Lassey: *v.* LACEY

Last: Thomas, Richard *Last* 1385 FFSf. ME *last, lest* 'a wooden mould of the foot for a shoemaker', used of a maker of such. cf. Thomas *le Lastur* 1275 AssSo, Hugo *Lastemaker* 1395 NottBR.

Latch, Latches, Letch, Leche, Leach, Leech: Richard *del Lech* 1177 P (Y); Cristiana *de Lech* 1210 Cur (Gl); Ralph *de la Leche* 1214 Cur (Sr); Peter *de la Lache*, Henry *del Lache* 1297, 1308 Wak (Y). From Lach Dennis or Lache (Ches), Eastleach or Northleach (Glos), or from residence near a stream or some wet place (OE **læcc, *lecc* 'stream'). *v.* also LEACH.

Latchford, Lashford, Letchford: Philip *de Lecheford* 1279 RH (O). From Latchford (Ches, Oxon).

Latchmore, Lashmar, Lashmore, Lechmere: William *Lechemere*, John *Lachemer* 1296, 1327 SRSx. From Lashmars Hall (Sussex).

Latham, Lathem, Lathom, Laytham: Robert, Henry *de Latham* 1204 AssY, 1327 SRSo; Robert *Lathom, Laytham* 1494 FFEss, 1563 Pat (L). From Latham (WRYorks), Lathom (Lancs), Laytham (ERYorks), or 'dweller at the barns'.

Lathe, Leath, Leathes: Gilbert, Richard *del Lathes* 1296 FrY, 1332 SRLa; Adam *del Laythes* 1332 SRCu; John *del Leth* 1379 PTY. 'Worker at the barn(s)', ON *hlaða*. cf. Henry *Latheman* 1278 AssLa. *Leath* is a Lancashire and Cumberland dialect form.

Latimer, Lattimer, Lattimore, Latner: Hugo *Latinarius, Interpres, Hugolinus Interpres* 1086 DB (Ha); Robertus *Latinus, Latinarius* 1086 DB (K), *Latimir* 1087 DM (K); Ralph *Latimarus* 1086 DB (Ess); Gocelinus *le Latimer* 1102–7 Rams (C); William *(le) Latimier, le Latimer* 1163–85 P (Y); Richard *le Latener* 1332 MEOT (Ess); Richard *Latoner, Latomer* notary 1485 GildY. Lat *latimarus, latinarius, latinus, interpres*, OFr *latinier, latim-(m)ier* 'interpreter', lit. a speaker of Latin (a1225 MED). 'Latonere, or he that usythe Latyn speche'

(PromptParv). cf. Hugo *Latyn* 1327 SRSf. *v.* also LATNER.

Latner: Alan, Richard *le Làtoner* 1306 MESO (Nf), 1311 LLB D; William *le Latouner* 1327 SRSf. ME *latoun* 'brass' from OFr *laton*, 'worker in or maker of latten' (1339 MED). *v.* also LATIMER.

Latta, Lattey, Latto: James *Lattay, Lata* 1677, 1709 Black. Scottish forms of LAWTEY.

Latter: Thomas *le Latier* 1199 ChR (Do); Robert *le Latthere* 1318 LLB E; Robert *Latter* 1327 Wak (Y). A derivative of OE *lætt* 'lath', a lath-maker.

Laughlan(d): *v.* LACHLAN

Laughton: William *de Lactone* 1185 Templars (L); Walter *de Laughton'* 1327 SRLei; Thomas *Laughton* 1541 CorNt. From Laughton (Leics, Lincs, Sussex, WRYorks).

Launder: *v.* LAVENDER
Laundrey: *v.* LANDRAY

Laurence, Laurance, Laurens, Lawrance, Lawrence, Lorence, Lorenz, Lowrance: *Laurentius* cellerarius 1141–9 Holme (Nf); *Laurencius* molendinarius 1219 AssY; John *Lorence* 1268 FFSf; Benedict *Laurenz* 1292 FFHu; John *Laurens*, William *Lorens* 1296 SRSx; William *Lourance*, Lucus *Lowrance* 1374, 1481 FrY. Latin *Laurentius*, a common name from the 12th century, with pet-names and diminutives, *Lawrie, Laurie, Lowrie, Larry, Lorry, Law, Low, Larkin, Lorkin*. There was also a feminine form: *Laurencia* 1201 FFEss, 1296 SRSx.

Lavender, Launder, Lander, Landers: Ysabelle *la Lauendere* 1253 Oseney (O); Ralf *la Lavendere* 1268 AssSo; Thomas *Launder* 1331 FrY; Elyzabeth *Lander* 1524 SRSf. OFr *lavandier* (masc.), *lavandiere* (fem.) 'one who washes', 'washerman, washerwoman' (c1325 MED).

Laverack, Laverick: *v.* LARK

Law, Lawes, Laws: John *de la Law'* 1208 Cur (Wo); William *de Lawe* 1229 Cl (Ess); Hugh *del Lawe* 1309 Wak (Y); William *Law* 1279 RH (C); Nicholas *Lawes* 1539 FeuDu. OE *hlāw* 'hill, burial mound', which became *low* in the south but *law* in the north. The surname may also be a pet-name of Laurence: *Lawe* del Park 1275 SRWo, *Lawe* Robynson 1379 PTY. cf. LOW.

Lawday: *v.* LAWTEY

Lawless: Thomas *Lagheles* 1360 FrY; Richard *Lawles* 1533 KentW. ME *laweles, laghles* 'uncontrolled by the law, unbridled, licentious'; for *lawless-man* 'an outlaw'.

Lawman: *Lagman* 1066 DB (Y); *Laghemannus* ib. (Ess); *Lageman* 1219 AssY; Alwold, Brictric *Lageman* 1066 DB (L); Hugo *Lageman* c1210 Fees (Ha); Geoffrey *Lauman* 1214 Cur (Herts); William *Laweman* 1279 AD i (Nf). ODa, OSw *Lag(h)man*, ON *Logmaðr*. Adam son of *Lagheman* took his father's name as his surname, Adam *Laweman* (1246 AssLa). Alwold and Brictric *Lageman* were 'lawmen' of Lincoln (Anglo-Scand *lagman* 'one whose duty it was to declare the law').

Lawn: *v.* LAND

Lawrance, Lawrence: *v.* LAURENCE

Lawrenson: Walter *Laurenceson* 1480 Black. 'Son of *Laurence*.'

Lawrey, Lawrie, Lawry, Lorie, Lorrie, Lory: Simon *filius Lari* 1197 FFL; William *Larie* 1279 RH (Bk); Hugh *Laurie* 1784 Bardsley. A diminutive of *Laur* (Laurence). *v.* also LOWREY.

Lawson: Richard *Lawisson* 1327 SRC; Henry *Laweson* 1379 PTY. 'Son of *Law*' (Laurence). *v.* LAW.

Lawtey, Lawty, Leuty, Lewtey, Lewty, Loalday, Luty, Lawday: Huctredus *Leute* 1212 Fees (La); Alan *Leaute* 1256 Rams (C); Thomas *Lawtye* 1613 YWills. OFr *leaute* 'loyalty'.

Lawton: Adam *de Lauton'* 1205 P (La); Philip *de Lauton* 1281 AssCh; Robert *Lawton* 1642 PrD. From Lawton (Ches, Hereford).

Lax: *Lax* de Ludham 1141–9 Holme (Nf); Thomas *Lax* 1351 FrY. ON *Lax*, a nickname from the salmon, otherwise unrecorded in England.

Lay(e): *v.* LEA

Layborn, Laybourn, Labern, Leeburn, Leyborne, Leyburn, Lyburn: Robert *de Leburn'* 1192 P (K); Richard *de Laibrunn* 1204 AssY; Roger *de Leiburn'* 1214 Cur (K); Henry *Laburn* 1488 FrY. From Leybourne (Kent) or Leyburn (NRYorks).

Laycock, Leacock: Ralph *de Laycok*, Roger *de Lacok* 1247, 1250 AssSt. From Lacock (Wilts) or Laycock (WRYorks).

Layen: *v.* LAYNE

Layer, Leir: (i) Hugh *de Leir* 1275 RH (L); William *de Leyre* 1291 LLB A. From Leire (Leics) or one of the three Layers in Essex. (ii) Alice *la Eyr* (*Leyr*) 1327 *SR* (Ess); Gilbert *Leyr* ib.; William *le Eyr* 1327 SRSf. 'The heir.' *v.* AYER. *Leyer* was also a name for the layers or setters who placed in position the stones worked by the (free)-masons: *cubitores* 1252, *positores* 1365, *leggeres* 1282, *leyers* 1412 (Building 31).

Layfield, Leighfield, Leyfield, Lyfield: Hugo *Layfeld* 1442 FrY; William *Leyfeld* 1484 LLB L. 'Dweller by the lea-field', the pasture, grass-land, as at Leyfield (Notts).

Layland: *v.* LEYLAND

Layman, Leyman: William *Leyman* 1327 SRSx; John *Layman* 1524 SRSf. 'Dweller by the wood or clearing.' *v.* LEA.

Layne, Layen: William *de la Leyne* 1275 MELS (Sx); Henry *atte Layne* 1327 SRSx. 'Dweller by the open tract of arable land at the foot of the Downs.' *v.* MELS.

Laytham: *v.* LATHAM

Layton, Leighton, Leyton, Lighten, Lighton: Richard *de Lecton'* 1201 P (Sa); Roger *de Leyton'* 1276 RH (Hu); William *de Leghton* 1287 AssCh. From Layton (Lancs, NRYorks), Leighton (Beds, Ches, Hunts, Lancs, Salop) or Leyton (Essex), of varied origins. John *atte Layhton* 1390 MELS (Wo) may have lived at a homestead where leeks were grown or may have been a worker in the kitchen-garden (OE *lēac-tūn*).

Lazar: Thomas *le Lazur* 1280 AssSo; William *le Lazer* 1297 Wak (Y). 'The leper' (ME *lazare* 1340 NED).

Lazenby, Lasenby: Robert *de Leisingeby* 1204 Pl (Y); John *de Laysingby* 1361 AssY; William *Laysyngby* 1421IpmNt. From Lazenby (NRYorks), or Lazonby (Cumb).

Lea, Lee, Legh, Leigh, Ley, Leys, Lay, Laye, Lye, Lyes: Ailric *de la Leie* 1148–66 NthCh (Nth); Liffild *de Lega* 1176 P (Ess); Turgod *de la Lea* 1193 P (Wa); Philip *de Lye* 1198 Fees (W); Henry *del Lea* 1203 P (La); William *de la Le* 1207 Cur (Berks); Pagan *a la Legh* 1208 Cur (Y); John *de Leye* 1275 SRWo; Simon *atte Lee*, Richard *atte Legh* 1296 SRSx; John *del Lee* 1384 FrY; Hugh *atte Leygh* 1392 MELS (Sr). From one of the many places named Lea, Lee, Leigh, Leighs, or Lye, or 'dweller by the wood or clearing'. OE *lēah* (nominative) became ME *legh, leigh;* the dative *lēa* became *lee*, and the later dative *lēage* gave ME *leye, lye*.

Leach, Leech, Leetch, Leche: Robert *Leche* c1250 Rams (Hu); John *Lache* Hy 3 Colch (C); Edmund *le Leche* 1279 RH (O). OE *lǣce* 'leech', 'physician'.

Leachman, Leechman: Adam *Lacheman* 1210 Cur (Y), 1212 Cur (Ha); William *Lachman* 1327 SRSf. OE *lǣce* 'leech' and *mann*, 'servant of the physician'.

Leacock: *v.* LAYCOCK

Leadbeater, Leadbeatter, Leadbetter, Leadbitter, Ledbetter, Lidbetter: Ingald' *Ledbater'* 1221 AssWa; Walter *Ledbeter*, *le Ledbetere* 1256 AssNb; Henry *Leadbetter* 1645 YWills; Mr *Leadbutter* 1674 HTSf. OE *lēad* and *bēatere* 'a worker in lead'.

Leader, Leeder, Lader, Ledder: Ralph *ledere* 1243 AssDu; Henry *le leeder* 1328 Pinchbeck (Sf); Jo. *Leader* 1674 HTSf. OE *lǣdere* 'leader', in the sense 'driver of a vehicle, carter' (1423 MED). In the north, 'leading coal, manure, etc.' is still used even though the driver of the loaded vehicle may not be leading a horse. In the Middle Ages, the particular commodity carried was often named: Richard *Bredleder* 14th Whitby, Robert *Cornlader* 1372 ColchCt, Laurence *le Maltlader* 1294 MEOT (Herts), William *Waterladar'* 1177 P (Wa). The reference may also be to pleasure: Richard *Pleyledere* 1327 SRSo. cf. PLAYER, and *dawnceleder* s.n. DANCE. Fransson derives the surname from OE *lēad* 'lead' in the sense 'plumber'. This certainly survives in *Ledder* which is rare. cf. 'wages of a *ledder* soldering the gutters over the great gate' (1344 Building 266).

Leadsom: *v.* LEDSAM

Leaf, Leafe, Leefe, Leif, Lief, Life: Godwin *Lief* 1198 P (Nf); Alice *le Lef*, Loue *þe Lef* 1279 RH (C, Hu); John *(le) Leef* 1318 Crowland (C); Henry *Lyf* 1327 SRSf; Henry *Lief* (*Leef*) 1327 *SR* (Ess); Lucia *le Lyf* 1327 SRSo; William *Leof* 1332 SRWa. This is usually from OE *lēof* 'dear, beloved' but occasionally it may derive from *Lēof, a short form of *Lēofrīc*, *Lēofwine*, etc. This is not evidenced with certainty in OE but its existence is suggested by *Lif* sacerdos 12th DC (L).

Leak, Leake, Leek, Leeke, Leeks, Leck: (i)

Walter, Ralph *de Lek* 1202 AssL, 1219 AssY; Henry *de Leek* 1290 AssCh. From Leak (NRYorks), Leake (Lincs, Notts), Leek (Staffs) or Leck (Lancs). (ii) John *Leke* Hy 3 Gilb (L); Ralph *Leecke* 1279 RH (Beds). Metonymic for LEAKER.

Leaker: Adam *lekere* 1279 MESO (Y); William *le Leker* 1293 ib. A derivative of OE *lēac* 'leek', a seller of leeks. cf. Hugh *le Lekman* 1319 MESO (Nf).

Leal, Leale, Lealman: Andrew *Leal* 1479 Black; William *Leleman* 1297 SRY, 1363 FrY. ME *lele*, OFr *leial* 'loyal, faithful'.

Leaman, Leamon: *v.* LOVEMAN

Lean, Leane: Hugo *Macer* 1208 Cur (O); Walter *Lene* 1276 RH (Y); John *Leane* 1317 AssK. OE *hlǣne* 'lean, thin' (Lat *macer*). Also for MacLEAN.

Leaper, Leeper: Robert *le Lepere* 1185 Templars (Wa); Henry *Leper* c1200 DC (Nt); William *le Leapere* 1295 AD vi (K). Either OE *hlēapere* 'leaper, dancer, runner, courier' or a derivative of OE *lēap* 'basket', 'basket maker'. cf. John *le Lepmaker* 1338 MESO (Nf). *v.* also LEPPER.

Leaphard: *v.* LEOPARD

Leapingwell: *v.* LEFFINGWELL

Leapman: 'Basket-maker'. cf. LEAPER.

Learmond, Learmont, Learmonth, Learmount, Leirmonth: William *de Leirmontht* 1408 Black. From Learmonth (Berwicks).

Learmouth: William *Lermouth* 1438 FrY. From Learmouth (Northumb).

Leary: *v.* O'LEARY

Leason: *v.* LEESON

Leat, Leate, Leates, Leatt, Leet, Leete: William *Bytherlete* 1279 AssSo; John *atte Lete* 1330 PN D 172. 'Dweller by the conduit or watercourse' (OE *gelǣt*), as at Leat (Devon) or The Leete (Essex).

Leath(es): *v.* LATHE

Leather, Leathers, Leatherman: Robert *Lether* 1524 SRSf. Probably a dealer in leather or one who used leather in his work. cf. John *Lethercarver* 1404 AD iv (Nth). 'Leather-dyer' was an occupation-term in London in 1373 (MEOT).

Leaver: *v.* LEVER

Leaves, Leeves: Leue *Leue* 1066 DB (Hu); *Leva* vidua c1188 BuryS (Sf); Thomas *Leve* 1229 Pat (Do). OE *Lēofa* (m) or *Lēofe* (f). Sometimes, apparently, topographical: Robert *Intheleves* 1322 LLB E.

Leavett, Leavitt: *v.* LEVET

Leavey, Levey, Levi, Levy, Lewey, Lewy, Lovie: *Leuui* 1066 DB; Ricardus *filius Lefwi* 1171–2 MedEA (Sf); Agnes *filia Lewi* 1221 AssSa; Thomas *Leui* 1228 Eynsham (O); Robert *Levi* 1275 SRWo; Geoffrey *Leuwy* 1301 ParlR (Ess). OE *Lēofwīg* 'beloved warrior'. Modern *Levi* is usually the Hebrew *Levi* 'pledged' or 'attached'.

Leavold, Levell, Lovold: *Leuot* 1066 DB (Ess); *Lewold'*, *Liwwoldus*, *Luwold'* 1066 Winton (Ha); Simon *filius Lefwaldi*, *Lefwoldi*, *Leualdi* c1165–80 Bury (Sf); William *Leuald* c1250 Rams (Nf); John *Levold* 1275 RH (K); John *Levell* 1568 SRSf; James *Leavold* 1674 HTSf. Late OE *Lēofweald* 'beloved power or ruler'.

Lebbell: Robert *Lebel*, *le Bel* 1235 Fees (So). 'The beautiful.' *v.* BELL.

Lebby: *v.* LIBBY

Lechmere: *v.* LATCHMORE

Leck: *v.* LEAK

Lecomber: *v.* CAMBER

Lecount: *v.* COUNT

Ledder: *v.* LEADER

Ledger, Leger: *Leodegar*' 1192 P (Ha), 1209 FFEss; *Leodegarus* de Dive 1212 Cur (Nth); Adam, William *Leger* 1279 RH (C), 1305 FFEss; Richard *Leggere* 1377 LLB H. OFr *Legier*, OG *Leodegar* 'people-spear', common throughout France and Normandy through the memory of St Leger, a 7th-century bishop.

Ledingham: Hugh *de Ledenham* Hy 2 Gilb (L). From Leadenham (Lincs).

Ledsam, Ledsham, Ledsome, Ledson, Leadsom: Nigel *de Ledesham* 1219 AssY; Cuthbert *Ledsome* 1606 Bardsley; Sarah *Ledson* 1809 ib. From Ledsham (Ches, WRYorks).

Ledster: *v.* LISTER

Ledwich, Ledwidge: Roger *de Ledewich* 1221 AssSa. From Ledwyche (Salop).

Lee: *v.* LEA

Leeburn: *v.* LAYBORN

Leece, Leese: *Lecia* 1172–80 DC (L); Willelmus *filius Lecie* 1219 AssY; Godfrey, William *Lece* 1296 SRSx, 1394 AD iv (Sf). OFr *Lece* (f). *v.* LETTICE.

Leech: *v.* LEACH

Leechman: *v.* LEACHMAN

Leeder: *v.* LEADER

Leefe: *v.* LEAF

Leegood: *v.* GOOD

Leek(s): *v.* LEAK

Leeman: *v.* LOVEMAN

Leeper: *v.* LEAPER

Lees: Roger *de Leges*, *de Lees* 1212 Cur (K). The plural of LEA.

Leese: Alan *de la Laese* 1276 ArchC vi; Robert *de la Lese* 1290 FFHu; Robert *atte Leese* 1315 MELS (Sr). 'Dweller by the pasture' (OE *lǣs*). *v.* also LEECE.

Leeson, Leason: John, Roger *Leceson* 1332 SRCu, SRSx. 'Son of *Lece*'. *v.* LEECE.

Leest: Peter, Thomas *de la Leste* 1275 RH (K), SRWo. 'Dweller by the path or track' (OE *lǣst* '(foot)step, track'.

Leet(e): *v.* LEAT

Leetch: *v.* LEACH

Leeves: *v.* LEAVES

Lefeaver, Lefever, Lefevre: *v.* FEAVER

Leffek: *v.* LEVICK

Leffingwell, Lepingwell, Leppingwell, Leapingwell: Avina *de Leffeleswell* 1258 FFEss; William *de Lefheldewelle* 1291 EAS xxi; Richard *Leffendewelle* 1357 FFEss; William *Leffingwell* 1465 EAS xxi; John *lepyngwell* 1539 ib.; William *Leapingwell* 1709 DKR 41 (Ess). *Lepingwell* derives from Leppingwells in Little Maplestead, Essex, which is called *Leffingwelles* in 1561 and owed its name to the possessions here of the family of Robert *de Leffeldewelle* (1302) who is called *Leffingwell* in an Elizabethan transcript of the Court Rolls. The family, *Leffingwell* in the 15th century and *Leppingwell* in the 16th, took its name from a lost place *Liffildeuuella* (DB) which may survive in a corrupt form in Levit's Corner in Pebmarsh into which their possessions extended. *v.* PN Ess 446–7.

Le Fleming: *v.* FLEMING

Lefort: *v.* FORT

Lefridge: *v.* LEVERAGE

Legard: Godefridus *filius Leggard* 1204 P (Sx); Osbertus *filius Leggardi* 1205 Cur (Nf); *Leggard* Joseph 1327 SRC; John, Adam *Legard* 1275 SRWo, 1296 SRSx; Hugh, Thomas *Leggard* 1275 Wak (Y), RH (Nf); William *Lyggard* 1379 PTY. OFr *Legard*, OG *Leudgard*, *Liudgard* 'people-protection'. There was also a feminine: *Ligarda* 12th DC (L), *Legarda* 1230 P (He), from OG *Leutgarda*.

Legat, Legate, Legatt, Leggat, Leggate, Leggatt, Leggett, Leggitt, Leggott: Hugolinus *Legatus* 1084 GeldR (So); Peter *Legat* 1199 P (Co); Ralph *le Legat* 1279 AssNb; Richard *Leget* 1379 PTY. ME, OFr *legat* 'ambassador, deputy'. Often a pageant-name. In 1377, in the procession for the entertainment of Richard, the young son of the Black Prince, was 'one stately attired like a pope, whom followed twenty-four cardinals, and after them eight or ten with black visors, not amiable, as if they had been legates from some foreign prince' (Stow). *v.* LEGWOOD.

Leger: *v.* LEDGER

Legg, Legge: Alueredus, Ædwardus *Leg* 1176, 1185 P (Gl, Nb); John, Robert *Legg(e)* 1327 SRC, SRSx. ME *legg*, ON *leggr* 'leg'. ON *Leggr* was used as a personal-name but no examples have been noted in England. The nickname is confirmed by Rannulf *Jambe* 1221 AssWa.

Legh: *v.* LEA

Legood: *v.* GOOD

Legrand: *v.* GRANT

Legresley: *v.* GREALEY

Le Grice, Le Grys: *v.* GRICE

Legwood: Thomas *Legwood*, Benjamin *Leggett*, Edmund *Legitt*, Henry *Legate* 1674 HTSf. A corruption of LEGAT.

Lehern: *v.* HERON

Leicester, Leycester, Lester, Lestor, Lessiter, Lisseter, Laister, Lasseter: Hugo *de Legrecestra* 1130 P (Lei); Nicholas *de Leycester* 1287 AssCh; Richard *de Laycestre* 1305 FrY; Henry *Lycester* 1381 PTY; William *Leycetter* 1480 GildY; Henry *Lasisture* 1503 ib.; Richard *Lasseter* 1550 SxWills; Nicholas *Lessetur* 1603 SfPR. From Leicester.

Leif: *v.* LEAF

Leigh: *v.* LEA

Leighfield: *v.* LAYFIELD

Leighton: *v.* LAYTON

Leiner: *v.* LAINER

Leiper: A Scottish form of LEAPER (1608 Black).

Leir: *v.* LAYER

Leirmonth: *v.* LEARMOND

Leishman, Lishman: William *Leischman* or *Leschman* 1466 Black; John *Lecheman* or *Lesche-*

man 1560 ib.; Roger *Lisheman* 1605 FrY. Scottish forms of LEACHMAN.

Leitch: Patrick *Leich(e)*, *Lech(e)* 1440–82 Black. Scots for LEACH.

Lejeune: *v.* JEUNE

Le Keux: *v.* KEW

Leleu: *v.* LOW

Lely: *v.* LILEY

Leman, Lemon: *v.* LOVEMAN

Lemarchand, Le Marchant: *v.* MARCHANT

Le May: *v.* MAY

Lemm: Eustac' *filius Lemme* 1275 RH (Nf); Geoffrey, Thomas *Lem* 1218 AssL, 1296 SRSx. *Lemme*, a hypocoristic of OE *Lēofmǣr* or *Lēodmǣr*. cf. LEMMER.

Lemmer: *Lefmer, Leodmar, Ledmær, Leomar, Lemer* 1066 DB; Robertus *filius Lemmer, Lefmer* 1203–4 P (Y); Robert, William *Lemmer* 1221 ElyA (C), 1332 SRSx; John *Ledmer* 1316 FFK. OE *Lēodmǣr* 'people-famous' or *Lēofmǣr* 'dear-famous'.

Lemmon: *v.* LOVEMAN

Lempriere: John *Lemprere* 1420 DKR 41 (Jersey). 'The emperor', a nickname or pageant-name. In England, of Huguenot origin.

Lenard: *v.* LEONARD

Lenfestey: *v.* VAISEY

Leng: Symon *Lenge* 1275 RH (Nf). The comparative of OE *lang* 'tall'.

Lenn: *v.* LYNN

Lennard: *v.* LEONARD

Lennox, Lenox: John *of Levenax* 1400 Black; John *de Lenox* 1428 ib. (Glasgow); George *Lennox* 1542 ib. (Glenluce). From the district of Lennox (Dunbarton).

Lenthal, Lenthall, Lentell, Lentle: William *Lentale* 1369 LLB G. From Leinthall (Hereford).

Leo, Leon: *Leo camerarius* 1121–48 Bury (Nf); *Leo, Leon de Romeslega* 1271 AssSt; Hugo *Leo* 1180 P (Lo); William, John *Leon* 12th Seals (So), 1279 RH (O). OFr *Leon*, Greek λέων, Latin *leo* 'lion', the name of several popes who were canonized. *v.* LYON.

Leonard, Lenard, Lennard: *Leonardus de Berhedon'* 1219 Cur (R); Radulphus *filius Lennardi* 13th Rams (Hu); Stephanus *Leonardus* 1221 AssWo; William, Agnes *Leonard* 1279 RH (Hu), 1296 SRSx. OG *Leonhard* 'lion-bold', a name not so common in England as one would have expected in view of the number of churches dedicated to St Leonard, the patron saint of captives.

Leopard, Leaphard, Leppard, Leppert, Lippard: William *Lepard* 1296 SRSx; John *Lyppard* 1327 SR (Ess). A nickname from the leopard.

Le Patourel: Ralph *Pasturel* 1166 RBE (L). A Norman diminutive of *pastour* 'shepherd', surviving in the Channel Islands. *v.* PASTOR.

Le Pelley: *v.* PELLY

Lepick: *v.* PIKE

Lepingwell: *v.* LEFFINGWELL

le Poideven, Le Poidevin: *v.* POIDEVIN

Leppard, Leppert: *v.* LEOPARD

Lepper: Geoffrey *Lepere* 1221 Cur (Ess);

Richard *le Lepor* 1298 Wak; William *Lepper* 1674 HTSf. ME *lepre* 'a leper'. Hospitals for lepers were not uncommon in medieval England and the use of *leper* as a byname is attested by the survival of LAZAR. That this surname is now very rare is not surprising. It may well often be concealed in *Leopard*. The frequent early form *leper(e)* is often for *Leaper*.

Leppingwell: *v.* LEFFINGWELL

Lequeux: *v.* KEW

Lerner: *v.* LARNER

Lesley, Leslie, Lesslie: (i) Robert *de Leslie* 1272 Black; Symon *de Lescelye* or *Lesellyn* 1278 ib. From Leslie (Fife). (ii) *Lecelina de Clinton'* 1207 Cur (O); *Lecelina* 1220 Cur (Herts); Ralph *Letselina* 1101–16 MedEA (Nf); Adam *Lestelin* 1327 SRSf; Thomas *Lestelin* (*Lessely*) 1346 FA (Sf); John *Leslyn* 1524 SRSf; Robert *Lesle* 1674 HTSf. *Lec-el-in*, a double diminutive of *Lece*. *v.* LEECE.

Less: *v.* LASS

Lessells: Alan *de Lascels* a1173 Black; David *Lessellis* 1560 ib. A Scottish form of LASCELLES.

Lessiter: *v.* LEICESTER

Lester: (i) William *de Lestra* 1084 GeldR (So). From Lestre (La Manche). (ii) Andrew *le lestere* 1327 Pinchbeck (Sf). *v.* LISTER. *v.* also LEICESTER.

Lestrange, L'Estrange: *v.* STRANGE

Lesuard: For *le su-hierde* 'the sow herd'. *v.* SEWARD.

Le Sueur: a Jersey name. 'Shoemaker.' *v.* SEWER.

Letch: *v.* LATCH

Letcher: (i) Henry *Lacher* 1224 Cur (Y); Walter *le Lecher* 1272 MESO (Ha). Fransson explains *Lecher* as a derivative of ME *leche* 'to cure', physician, a possible explanation of the form but unlikely in view of the frequency of *Leche* 'physician', apart from the fact that it would become modern *Leacher* which does not seem to exist. The surname is a derivative of *læcc* 'stream', with the same meaning as LATCH, LETCH. (ii) James *Lecchur* 1269 AssNb; Nicholas, Thomas *Lechour* 1327 SRC, SRSf. ME *lech(o)ur*, OFr *leceor* 'lecher'. The surname is rare, probably usually disguised as *Leger*.

Letchford: *v.* LATCHFORD

Letson, Lettsome: John *Letesson'* 1327 SRC; Elizabeth *Letsome* 1775 Bardsley. 'Son of *Lett*.'

Lett, Letts: Gerardus *filius Lete* 1208 FF (C); Ralph *Lette* 1296 SRSx. *Lett*, a pet-form of *Lettice*.

Lettice: *Leticia* Hy 2 DC (L), 1206 Cur (Ess), 1221 AssSa; John *Letice* 1247 AssBeds; Warin *Letiz*, Margaret *Letice* 1275 RH (Sf). Latin *laetitia* 'joy'.

Lettsome: *v.* LETSON

Leuty: *v.* LAWTEY

Levell: *v.* LEAVOLD

Levene: *v.* LEWIN

Levenger: *v.* LOVEGUARD

Lever, Levers, Leaver: (i) Ralph *le Levere* 1276

RH (Lei); William *le Levere* 1294 AssSt. OFr *levre* 'hare', a nickname either from speed or timidity. Sometimes, no doubt, a shortening of *leverer* 'a hunter of the hare', 'harrier': Roger *Leuerier* c1230 Barnwell (C), Hugo *Leverer* 1242 Fees (Nb). cf. MAULEVERER. (ii) Dande *de Leuer* 1246 AssLa; Ralph *atte Levere* 1387 AD vi (Sx). From Great or Little Lever (Lancs) or from residence near reedy ground (OE *lǣfer* 'rush, reed, iris').

Leverage, Leverich, Leverick, Leveridge, Lefridge, Livery, Liverock, Loveredge, Loveridge, Loverock, Luffery: *Lefric, Leuric* 1066 DB; *Leofricus* 1066 InqEl; *Lowric* presbiter 1066 Winton (Ha); Willemus *filius Lefrich'* 1196 Cur (Lei); Thomas *filius Leueric'* 1219 AssY; William *Leuric* 1086 DB (O); Walter *Lufrich* 1206 P (W); Robert *Leffrich* 1240 DBStP (Ess); Robert *Leverik'* 1276 RH (L); John *Leveriche* 1279 RH (C); Henry *Leverige* ib.; William *Loverich* 1279 RH (O); Richard *Liuerich* 1309 SRBeds; Richard *Loverik* 1350 LLB F. OE *Lēofrīc* 'beloved ruler'.

Leverett, Leveritt: (i) *Leuret* 1066 Winton (Ha), DB (K); Danielis *filius Lefredi* 1202 FFK; Thomas *filius Lofridi* 1229 Pat (K); Emma, Robert *Luuered* 1221 *ElyA* (Sf), 1227 AssBeds; William *Leverad* 1255 RH (W); William *Lefred* 1274 RH (Ess); William *Loverede* 1279 RH (C); John *Leverede* 1327 *SR* (Ess). OE *Lēofrǣd* 'dear-counsel'. (ii) Peter *Leverot* 1224 FFEss; Agnes, William *Leverit* 1279 RH (O). AFr *leveret* 'young hare'.

Levermore: *v.* LIVERMERE

Leversage, Leversuch: *v.* LIVERSAGE

Leveson, Lowson: *Leofsuna, Lefsune, Leuesuna* 1066 DB; *Leuesune* 12th Gilb (L); Hugo *Lovesone* 1230 Pat (Nb); Richard *Levesone* 1255 RH (O); Adam *Leveson'* 1275 SRWo; Walter *Lufesone* 1279 RH (O); Richard *Livesone* 1279 RH (C). OE *Lēofsunu* 'beloved son'.

Levet, Levett, Levitt, Leavett, Leavitt, Livett, Livitt: (i) *Leuiet, Leueget* 1066 DB; *Lefget* c1095 Bury (Sf); *Levetus* 1146-53 Rams (Hu); *Leuiet* 1166 P (Nf); *Liviet* 1205 Cur (C); Manewine *Leuiet* 1188 BuryS (Sf); Gilbert *Liuet* 1200 P (Gl); William *Liuet* (*Luuet*) 1205 P (L); Adam *Leuet* 1221 AssWa; John *Lefet* 1285 *Ass* (Ess). OE *Lēofgēat* 'beloved Geat'. The personal name may sometimes be the woman's name OE *Lēofgȳð* 'beloved battle': *Leued* 1066 DB, *Liuitha, Liuete,* 1221 AssWa, *Leuith'* 1221 AssSa, *Leffeda* Rugfot 1230 Pat (Sf), *Livith, Livid* 14th Rams (Hu). *Levet(t)* may also be a nickname from OFr *leuet* 'wolf-cub', a diminutive of OFr *leu* 'wolf'. cf. LOVETT. (ii) William *de Lieuet* 1196 P (Y). From one of the places named Livet in Normandy.

Levey: *v.* LEAVEY

Levick, Leffek: (i) Hardekin *filius Leueke* 1175 P (Nf); *Leweke* de Rouington 1246 AssLa; *Lefeke* Daffe 1279 RH (Beds); William *Leuke* 1204 P (O); Amicia *leueke* 1277 Ely (Sf). OE *Lēofeca*, a diminutive of *Lēofa*. This may also have become *Luke*. *v.* also LIVICK. (ii) Osbert *le Eveske* 1189 Dugd vi; Henry *Leveske* 1200 P (Hu); John *Levick* 1674 HTSf. OFr *eveske*, ModFr *évêque*

'bishop'. In *Levick* the article has coalesced with the noun. This was then re-divided as *le Vick* and survives as VECK, VICK.

Levin, Levine: *v.* LEWIN

Levinge, Levings, Lewing, Liveing, Living, Livings, Loving, Lowing, Lowings: *Leuing, Liuing, Louincus* 1066 DB; *Leouing', Leowing', Leuing', Lewing', Luuing'* 1066 Winton (Ha); *Levingus* 1198 P (L); Richard *Livinge* 1259 FFEss; Henry *Lywing* 1272–80 Bart (Lo); Robert *Levinge* 1275 SRWo; William *Leuing'* 1297 AssY; William *Lovinge* 1674 HTSf. OE *Lēofing, Lȳfing.*

Levingston(e): *v.* LIVINGSTON

Levitt: *v.* LEVET

Levy: *v.* LEAVEY

Lew: (i) Adam *de Lewe* 1191 P (Gl); Alice *ate Lewe* 1279 RH (Hu). 'Dweller by the hill', OE *hlǣw*. (ii) Robert *le Leu* 1207 ChR (Do). AFr *leu* 'wolf'. *v.* LOW.

Lewcock: *v.* LOWCOCK

Lewer(s): *v.* EWER

Lewes: John *de Leuwes* 1296 SRSx. From Lewes (Sussex).

Lew(e)y: *v.* LEAVEY

Lewin, Lewins, Lewens, Leven, Levene, Levien, Levin, Levine, Livens, Lowen, Lowin: Wlfricus *filius Leofwini* 1010 OEByn; *Leuuin, Leuinus, Lifwinus, Liuuinus* 1066 DB; *Lowinus* Rex 1185 Templars (Sa); *Leowinus* pater Normanni 1206 Cur (Sr); Iwanus *filius Lofwini* 1212 Fees (La); Hugo *filius Lewyn* 1230 P (Y); Hugo *filius Levine* 1232 Pat (L); John *Lewyn* 1230 P (Nth); Henry *Lowyn* 1275 SRWo; William *Lowen* 1275 RH (Sf); Robert *Lefwyne*, Roger *Livene* 1279 RH (O, C); Robert, Andrew *Leuene* 1327 *SR* (Ess); John *Liuene* ib. OE *Lēofwine* 'beloved friend'. In the Isle of Man, *Lewin* has the same origin as *Gelling*, but the *Giolla* has transferred only *l* to *eoin* instead of *Gill*: *McGilleon, MacGillewne* 1511, *Lewin* 1627, *Lewne* 1628, *Lewen* 1698 Moore.

Lewing: *v.* LEVINGE

Lewis, Louis, Lowis: *Lowis* le Briton 1166 RBE (Ess); *Lodowicus* clericus 1205 Cur (R); Walterus *filius Lowis* 1209 P (Wa); Robert, Geoffrey *Lowis* 1202 P (La, L); William *Lewys* 1267 FFSf, 1309 LLB D. *Lewis* is an Anglo-French form of Old Frankish *Hlúdwig* 'loud battle', latinized as *Ludovicus* and *Chlodovisus*, gallicized as *Clovis* or *Clouis*, Fr *Louis*. In Wales it was used for *Llewelyn*: *Llewelyn* ap Madoc alias *Lewis* Rede 1413 Bardsley.

Lewsey, Lewzey: Azor *filius Lefsi* 1066 DB (Nt); *Lefsius* Hippe 1275 RH (Sf); William *Lefsi* 1221 *ElyA* (C); Helena *Lewsay* 1486 GildY. OE *Lēofsige* 'dear victory'.

Lewt(e)y: *v.* LAWTEY

Ley: *v.* LEA

Leyborne, Leyburn: *v.* LAYBORN

Leycester: *v.* LEICESTER

Leyfield: *v.* LAYFIELD

Leyland, Layland: Aldulf *de Leilande* 1203 FFK; Robert *de Layland'* 1219 AssY; William *de Leylond* 1339 LoPleas; Richard *Leyland* 1418–19 FFWa. From Leyland (Lancs), or 'dweller by the untilled land'. Occasionally perhaps from Ealand (Lincs), cf. Walter *de Leilande* 1205 P (L), *de Eiland* 1205 Cur (L).

Leyman: *v.* LAYMAN

Leyton: *v.* LAYTON

Libby, Lebby: John son of *Libbe* 1298 Wak (Y); William *Lybbe* 1506 Oxon. Pet-names for *Isabel*. *v.* IBBS and cf. the diminutive: John *Libet* 1319 AD v (Sr).

Licence: *v.* LYSONS

Liddall, Liddel, Liddell, Lidell, Liddle, Lydall: Richard *de Lidel* 1202-34 Black (Largs); Geoffrey *Liddel* 1266 ib. (Roxburgh); Christiana *de Lydell* 1370 FrY. From Liddel (Cumb, Roxburgh).

Lidgate, Liggat, Liggatt, Liddiatt, Lidgett, Lyddiatt, Lydiate: Ralph *de Lidgate* 1230 P (Sx); William *de Lydyathe* 1242 Fees (La); Philip *atte Lidgate* 1274 Wak (Y); Richard *de la Lydeyate* 1280 AssSt; John *atte Lygate* 1332 SRSx. 'Dweller by the swing-gate' (OE *hlidgeat*), as at Lidgate (Suffolk) or Lydiate (Lancs).

Lidster: *v.* LISTER

Lief, Life: *v.* LEAF

Liell: *v.* LYAL

Light, Lyte: (i) Thomas *de Leht* 1275 RH (K); Richard *atte Lighte* 1317 MELS (Sx). OE *lēoht* 'light', probably 'light place', hence 'dweller in a clearing or glade'. (ii) John *le Lyt* 1266 AssSo. OE *lȳt* 'little'. (iii) Thomas *le Leht* 1275 RH (K); Thomas *Lyght* 1377 ColchCt. OE *lēoht* 'light'; active, bright, gay.

Lightband, Lightbound, Lightbown: William *Litebonda* 1195 P (Cu); James *Lightbowne* 1682 PrGR. The first element may be OE *lēoht* 'light', but *Lite-* in compounds is often for *Little*, OE *lȳt*. Hence 'gay, active' or 'little husbandman, peasant'. *v.* BOND.

Lightbody: (i) Katerina *litlebod'* 1327 SRC. 'Little body', 'little person' (OE *lȳtel*). cf. BODDY. (ii) William *Leichtbody* 1552 Black, John *Lychtbodie*, *Lightbody* 1574, 1678 ib. 'Active, gay individual' (OE *lēoht*).

Lightburn: (i) Geoffrey *Lithbarn* (*Lytbarn*) 1327 SR (Ess). 'Active or little child' (cf. LIGHTBAND, GOODBAIRN), or from OE *līðe* 'gentle, mild'. (ii) Rober *Lightborn* 1593 Bardsley (La). From Lightburne in Ulverston (Lancs).

Lighten, Lighton: *v.* LAYTON

Lightfoot: William *Lihfot* eHy 2 Seals (O); Hugh *Lihtfott* 1206 Cur (L); John *Lyghtfot* 1296 AssCh. OE *lēoht* 'light' and *fōt* 'foot', one with a light, springy step, a speedy runner, messenger. cf. *Lyghtefote Nuncius* in the Towneley Play of *Cæsar Augustus* and John *Litefot*, cacher' 1274 RH (Nf).

Lightlad: Elias *Lithelad* 1327 SRDb. Perhaps 'mild, gentle lad' (OE *līðe*), or, 'active or little lad'. cf. LIGHTBAND, LADD.

Lightoller, Lightollers, Lightouler, Lightowler, Lightowlers: Michael *de Lightholres* 13th WhC (La). From Lightollers (Lancs).

Lightwood: John *de Lightwood* 13th Shef. From Lightwood in Norton (Derbyshire).

Lilbourn, Lilbourne, Lilburn, Lilburne: Alexander *de Lilleburna* 1170 P (Nb); John *de Lilleburn* 1327 SRY; Stephen *Lylborn* 1434-5 FFSr. From Lilbourne (Northants), or Lilburn (Northumb).

Lile: *v.* LISLE

Liley, Lilley, Lillie, Lilly, Lely: Thomas son of *Lylie* 1296 Wak (Y); Alan *Lilie* 1247 AssBeds; Hugh *Lily* 1275 RH (L); William *Lely* 1275 RH (Nf). *Lylie* is probably a pet-form of *Elizabeth*. The diminutive *Lilian* occurs in Geoffrey *Lilion* 1279 RH (Beds) and the modern surnames *Lelliott*, *Lilliard* point to other early derivatives. Occasionally the surname derives from Lilley (Herts) or Lilly (Berks): Nicholas *de Lilleye* 1342 LoPleas.

Lilleker, Lillico: *v.* LITHGOE

Lilleyman, Lilliman, Lillyman, Lithman, Litman, Littman, Lyteman, Lutman, Luttman, Lulman: *Lutemannus* 1066 Winton (Ha); *Liteman de Clunton'* 1176 P (D); Rogerus *filius Liteman* 1204 Cur (Sf); *Lillemannus* Pastor 1212 Cur (Y); Reginaldus *filius Luteman* 1221 AssGl; Robert, Geoffrey *Litleman* 1202 AssL, 1221 *ElyA* (Sf); Roger *Lelman* 1212 Cur (Y); Robert *Lulleman* 1235 Fees (C); Adam *Lilleman* 1260 AssY; Richard *Liteman* 1275, 1279 RH (Nth, Beds); Malina *Lyleman* 1297 Wak (Y); Gilbert, William *Lyteman* 1305 SIA iii, 1327 SRSx. OE **Lȳtelmann* 'little man', an original nickname. For the development, cf. Lilly Wood and Plantation (PN Ess 396, 420), both *Littlehei*.

Lillywhite, Lilywhite: John *Lyliewhyt* 1376 ColchCt; Stephen *Lylywythe* 1398 Balliol (O). 'White as a lily', originally used of a woman. For a man, a nickname for one with a complexion fair as a woman's.

Liman, Limon: *v.* LOVEMAN

Limbert, *v.* LAMBARD, LOMBARD

Limer, Lymer: Thomas *Limer, Lymer* 1219 AssY; John *le Limer* 1279 RH (Hu). A derivative of OE *līm* 'lime', a whitewasher.

Limmer, Lumner: Ralph *le Liminur*, Robert *le Luminur* 1230 Oseney (O); Reginald *le Eluminur* 1257 ib.; Reginald *le Ylluminur* 1265 FF (O); John *le Leominur*, Richard *Lemner* 1275 SRWo; John *le Lumynour, le Alumynour* 1282, 1291 AD iv (Sr); Edmund *le lumner* 1327 SRSt; Thomas *Lymnour* 1493 LLB L. OFr *enlumineor, illumineor* 'an illuminator of manuscripts'.

Linacre, Linaker, Lineker, Liniker, Linnecar, Linnecor, Linnekar, Linegar, Linnegar: Godwin *de Linacra* 1086 DB (C); Alan *de Linacre* 1227 AssSt. From Linacre (Lancs), Linacre Court *alias* Lenniker (Kent), or 'dweller by the flax-field'.

Lincey: *v.* LINDSAY

Linch, Lince, Linck, Link, Lynch: Geoffrey *Linch* 1228 FFSf; Gilbert *de la Lynche* 1275 SRWo; Robert *de Bynithelinche* 1278 AssSo; Robert *Lincke* 1279 RH (C); Simon *atte Lynke* 1296 SRSx; Robert *atte Linch* 1327 ib. 'Dweller by the hill' (OE *hlinc*). *Lynch* may be Ir *Ó Loingseacháin* 'descendant of *Loingseach*' (sailor).

Lincoln, Linkin: Aluredus *(de) Lincolia* 1086 DB. From Lincoln.

Lind, Lynde, Lynds: Robert *de la Linde* 1185 P

(Sr); Richard *atte Lynde* 1275 SRWo. 'Dweller by the lime-tree' (OE *lind*).

Linder: Richard *le Lyndere* 1327 SRSx. *v.* LIND and p. xv.

Lindhurst, Lyndhurst: Herbert *de Lindherst* 1169 P (Ha); Robert *de Lyndhurst* 1268 AssSo; William *Lyndherst* 1392 CtH. From Lyndhurst (Hants), or 'dweller by the lime-wood'.

Lindley, Lingley, Linley: Siward *de Lindele* 1204 AssY; Thomas *de Linleia* 1204 P (Do); Matthew *de Linlee, de Lindleg'* 1205–6 Cur (Herts); Martin *de Lingleg'* 1219 Fees (Do); Richard *de Linlegh'* 1221 AssSa, *de Lingl'* 1251 Fees (Sa); Jordan *de Lynley* 1275 Wak (Y). From Lindley (Leics, WRYorks), Linley (Salop, Wilts), or from residence near a lime-wood (OE *lind, lēah*) or a clearing where flax was grown (*līn-lēah*).

Lindsay, Lindsey, Lincey: Thomas *de Lindesie* 1207 FFL. From Lindsey (Lincs).

Line, Lines, Lyne, Lynes: *Lina* 1181 P (O), 1195 Cur (So), 1202 FFL; William, Thomas *Lyne* 1296 SRSx, 1332 SRWa; Reginald *Lynes* 1340 AssC. *Lina*, a pet-form of such women's names as *Adelina, Emelina, Lecelina*, etc.

Linegar: *v.* LINACRE

Lineham, Lynam, Lynham: Walter *de Linham* 1205 P (D). From Lyneham (Devon, Oxon, Wilts). Also Ir *Ó Laigheanáin* 'descendant of *Laidhghnean*' (snow-birth).

Linford, Linforth, Linfoot: Geoffrey *de Lineford'* 1202 FFNf. From Linford (Bucks) or Lynford (Norfolk).

Lingley: *v.* LINDLEY

Link: *v.* LINCH

Linkin: *v.* LINCOLN

Linklater: Criste *Ælingeklæt* 1424 Black; Andro *Lynclater, Lincletter, Linclet* 1504 ib.; Thomas *Linkletter* 1634 ib. A distinctively Orkney name from Linklater (South Ronaldsay, North Sandwick), or Linklet (North Ronaldsay).

Linley: *v.* LINDLEY

Linn: *v.* LYNN

Linnecar, Linneker, Linnegar: *v.* LINACRE

Linnett, Linnit, Linnitt: *Linota* 1279 RH (O); Robert, Thomas *Linet* 1275 RH (Sx), 1317 AssK; Walter *Lynot* 1389 LLB H. *Lin-et, Lin-ot*, diminutives of *Lina* (*v.* LINE), or nicknames from the linnet (ME *linet*, OFr *linot*).

Linney, Linny: *Linniue* 1185 Templars (Herts); Eustace *Linyeve*, Geoffrey *Lyneue*, William *Linyiue* 1279 RH (C); Richard *Lyneue* 1327 SRSf. OE *Lindgifu, *Lindgeofu (f) 'shield-gift'.

Lint: Metonymic for *Linter*.

Linter: Robert *le lynetier* 1263 MESO (Sx); Walter *le Lintere* 1275 SRWo. A derivative of ME *lynet, lynt* 'flax', a dresser of flax.

Lipp: Ælfsinus *Lippe* 958 OEByn; Edwardus *Lipe* 1066 DB (Do); Roger *Lippe* 1148 Winton (Ha), 1210 Cur (Nth). The OE example is certainly a nickname from OE *lippa* 'lip'. Post-Conquest examples are common, though the modern name is rare, and we may also have a pet-name *Leppe* or *Lippe*, from an OE name in *Lēof-*. cf. *Leppe*

c1190 DC (L), 1198 P (Y); *Lepsy* 1275 RH (Nf), Robert *Lipsi* 1196 P (Co), for *Lēofsige*; *Lepstan(us)* 1066 Winton (Ha), for *Lēofstān*. *v.* PNDB § 90, pp. 91, 315.

Lippard: *v.* LEOPARD

Lippett, Lippitt: William *Lypet* 1296 SRSx; Roger *Lypat* 1327 ib. A diminutive of *Lipp*.

Lippiatt, Lippiett, Lipyeat: Roger *de la Lypiat* 1242 P (So); Thomas *atte Lippȝete* 1333 MELS (So). From Lypiate (Som) or Lypiatt (Glos); or 'dweller by a *leap-gate*, a low gate in a fence which can be leaped by deer, while keeping sheep from straying' (OE *hlīepgeat*).

Lipson: *Lepstan'*, *Lippestanus* bittecat 1066 Winton (Ha); Juliana *Lepsone* 1283 SRSf. 'Son of *Lēofstān*.' *v.* LIPP. Also from Lipson (Devon).

Lishman: *v.* LEISHMAN

Lisle, Lile, Lyle, de Lisle, De L'Isle, de Lyle: Hunfridus *de Insula* 1086 DB (W); Peter *de Isla* 1166 RBE (Y); Ralph *de Lile* 12th DC (L); Robert *del Ile* 1311 FrY; Henry *Lyle* 1319 Crowland (C). AFr *del isle* '(dweller) in the isle'. *Isle* is a common French place-name and the surname may sometimes derive from Lille (Nord), but it may also be of English origin. Robert de Insula, Bishop of Durham in 1274, was the son of poor crofters at Lindisfarne and took his name from Holy Isle.

Lison: *v.* LYSONS

Lisseter: *v.* LEICESTER

Lister, Lyster, Litster, Lidster, Ledster, Lester: Ralph *Litster* 1286 Wak (Y); John *le Letstere* 1305 FFSf; Richard *le Lyster* 1327 SRDb; John *le Listere*, Peter *le lestere* 1327 SRSf. A derivative of ME *lit(t)e* 'to dye', a dyer. An Anglian surname.

Litcook, Litson, Litt: *Litecock* de Salford 1246 AssLa; Simon *Lytecok* Ed 3 Battle (Sx); Roger *Lutesone* 1321 AssSt; John *Litecok* 1327 SR (Ess). *Litecok* is a pet-form of *Litt*, a short form of such names as *Litman, Litwin*.

Lithgoe, Lithgow, Lythgoe, Lillico, Lilleker: Symon *de Lynlithcu* 1225 Black; John *de Lithcu* 1312 CalSc; James *Lithgo* 1552 Black; Robert *Lynlytgow* 1599 ib. From Linlithgow.

Lithman, Litman: *v.* LILLEYMAN

Litson: *v.* LITCOOK

Litster: *v.* LISTER

Litt: *v.* LITCOOK

Little, Littell, Lytle, Lyttle: Eadric *Litle* 972 OEByn (Nth); Lefstan *Litle* c1095 Bury (Sf); Thomas *le Lytle* 1296 SRSx. OE *lȳtel* 'little'.

Littleboy: Robert *litelboie* 1206 FrLeic; John *Lytelboye* 1384 Add 27671 (Ha). 'Little boy.'

Littlechild: Ralph *Litechild* 1209 P (Lei); Richard *Litilchilde* 1524 SRSf. 'Little child.'

Littlefair: Agnes *Lutfair* 1381 SRSt. 'Little companion' (ME *fere, feir*).

Littlejohn, Littlejohns, Litteljohn: *Litel Jon* 1350 ColchCt; John *Lytelion* 1372 ib. 'Little John', often, no doubt, for a giant.

Littlepage: Ralph *Litelpage* 1314 LLB D. *v.* LITTLE, PAGE.

Littleproud: Goderun *Litteprot* 1066 Winton (Ha); Matilda *Lytillprowd* 1379 PTY. A hybrid,

OE *lȳtel* 'little' and OFr *prut, prud* 'worth, value'. The wife of Henry *Lytilprud* (1301 NottBR) was Hawisia '*Crist a pes*' whose constant cry 'Christ have peace!' suggests her husband deserved his nickname.

Littleton, Lyttleton: Driu *de Litletun*' 1210 P(W); Thomas *de Luttelton* 1358 SRWo; John *Lytelton* 1416 IpmNt. From one or other of the many places of this name.

Littlewood: Geoffrey *de Litelwode* 1275 Wak (Y); Robert *atte Lytlewode* 1327 SRWo. 'Dweller by the little wood.'

Littleworth: Hugo *de Litlewurd* 1180 P (Wa). From Littleworth (Warwicks).

Littley: (i) Walter *litel eie* 1162 DC (L). A nickname, 'little eye'. (ii) Juliana *Littlehey* 1327 *SR* (Ess). 'Dweller at the little enclosure' (OE *lȳtel*, *(ge)hæg*), as at Littley Green or Littley Wood (Essex).

Littman: *v.* LILLEYMAN

Litton, Litten, Lytton: Gamel *de Litton* 1175 YCh; Henry *de Lideton*' 1212 Fees (Do); Thomas *de Lytton* 1327 SRDb; Robert *Lytton* 1403 FFEss. From Litton (Derby, Dorset, Som, WRYorks).

Litwin: *Lihtuuinus* 1066 DB (Sf); Walterus nepos *Lituini, Lictwine* 1172, c1175 DC (L); *Licthwinus* 1235 CartAntiq (Ess); Guthmarus filius *Lithwini* c1250 Rams (Nf); John *Lutewin* 1194 Cur (Beds); Herveus *Lightwyne* 1285 *Ass* (Ess); Hugh *Lithwyne, Lightwyne* 1312, 1346 ColchCt; John *Lytzwyne* (*Lytwyne*) 1327 *SR* (Ess); William *Litwyn* 1441 FrY. An unrecorded OE personal name *Lēohtwine* 'bright friend'.

Livard, Luard, Lyward: *Leuuard, Liuuard* 1066 DB (K, Nt); Madducus *filius Luardi* 1170 P (L); *Lefwardus* filius Gode 1197 P (K); *Lewardus* filius Ainilde 1207 Cur (Sr); Willelmus *filius Leuardi* 1214 Cur (K); Nicholas *Lefward* 1212 Fees (Wo); Peter *Loward* 1332 SRSr. OE *Lēofweard* 'beloved guardian'. We should have expected *Leward* as the normal development. Perhaps the final *d* was lost (cf. *Lefwarus* c1250 Rams) and the surname absorbed by *Lewer*. After the revocation of the Edict of Nantes in 1678, *Luard* was re-introduced by a Huguenot from Caen, Robert Abraham Luard, who became the ancestor of the Luards of Essex and Lincs (Lower). This is a Germanic name from the roots *Hlod-* and *-ward* 'glory-protector', French *Louard*.

Liveing, Living, Livings: *v.* LEVINGE

Livemore: To the question 'Why do you call yourself *Livemore*? Your name ought to be *Livermore*', a schoolboy of about 12 in the 1930's replied: 'Yes, sir. My father's name is *Livermore*, but when my mother registered my birth, the registrar left out the *r*, and my name's *Livemore*.'

Livens: *v.* LEWIN

Livermere, Livermore, Levermore: Raulf *de Lieuremere* 1087–98 Bury (Sf). From Livermere (Cambs, Suffolk).

Liverock: *v.* LEVERAGE

Liversage, Liversedge, Liversidge, Leversage,

Leversuch: Robert *de Luvereseg*', *de Liverseg*' 1212 Cur (Y). From Liversedge (WRYorks).

Livesay, Livesey, Livsey: Henry, Adam *de Liuesay* 13th WhC, 1332 SRLa; Christopher *Levesey* 1455 IpmNt. Usually no doubt from Livesey (Lancs), but occasionally perhaps from OE *Lēofsige* 'dear-victory'.

Livett, Livitt: *v.* LEVET

Livick, Livock : Walter *Lyvoke* 1369 LLB G. A variant of *Levick* or *Leffek*. As names in *Lēof-* became *Lief-, Live-, Lēofeca* would become ME *Liveke*.

Livingston, Livingstone, Levingston, Levingstone: Archibald *de Levingestoune* 1296 Black. From Livingston (West Lothian).

Llewellin, Llewellyn, Llewelyn, Llewhellin: *Lewelinus* Bochan 1198 P (Sa); *Thlewelin* ap Euer 1287 AssCh; Tudor ap *Llywelyn* 1391 Chirk; Roger *Lewelin* 1255 AssSa; Peter *Lewlyn* 1275 SRWo; Peter *Lewelyne* 1301 SRY. Welsh *Llywelin*, often explained as 'lion-like', but probably from *llyw* 'leader'.

Lloyd, Lloyds, Loyd: Richard *Loyt* 1327 SRWo; Ithell *Lloit* 1391 Chirk; Richard *Lloyd* 1524 SRSf. Welsh *llwyd* 'grey'.

Loader, Loder: Emma *la Lodere* 1279 RH (O); Simon *le Loder* 1332 SRWa. Either a derivative of ME *lode* 'to load', a carrier, or equivalent to *atte Lode*. *v.* LOADES, LODDER.

Loades, Loads: Wulfward *de la Lada* 1194 P (So); John *ate Lode* 1327 SRSx. 'Dweller by the path, road, or watercourse' (OE *(ge)lād*), as at Long Load (Som) or Load Fm in Kingsley (Hants).

Loadman, Loadsman: John *Lademan* 1301 SRY; Petronilla *Lodman* 1341 ColchCt. OE *lād* 'way, course; load, burden' and *mann*. Either 'carrier' or 'dweller by the road or stream'. cf. LOADER.

Loalday: *v.* LAWTEY

Loan: *v.* LANE

Loaring: *v.* LORING

Lob, Lobb: Godric *Lobbe* Hy 1 ELPN; 1236 FFBk. OE *lobbe* 'spider', a nickname. Also from Lobb (Devon, Oxon): Philip *de Lobbe* 1242 Fees (D).

Lock, Locke, Locks: (i) Leuric *Loc*, Leovric *Locc* 1130 P (Wa), 1130 Cur (Ha); Eustace *Loc* 1235 CartAntiq (Ess). OE *loc(c)* 'lock (of hair)', probably a nickname for one with fine curls. (ii) William *de Lok* 1230 P (Berks); Robert *Atteloke* 1300 LoCt. OE *loc(a)* 'enclosure'. ME *loke* was also used of a barrier in a river which could be opened or closed at pleasure (c1300 NED). Along the Lea it was used of a bridge, *unum pontem alias Lok* (1277). *v.* PN Ess 585. The surname may thus have reference to residence near an enclosure or bridge or may be used of the keeper of the lock or bridge.

Locker: (i) Henry *le Lokkere* 1292 MESO (La); William *Locker* 1301 SRY; Richard *le Lokker* 1327 SRDb. A derivative of OE *loc(a)*, equivalent to *atte Lock* (*v.* LOCK) and *Lockman*: Scanard *Loceman* 1279 RH (C), Geoffrey *Lockeman* 1334

LLB E. 'Dweller by the enclosure' or 'keeper of the bridge'. cf. Sewal, William (*le*) *Locward* 1327 *SR* (Ess), from ME *loc* and OE *weard* 'ward, guardian'. (ii) Peter *le Loker* 1221 AssWo; John *Lokar*' 1279 RH (O); Adam *Lokere* 1296 SRSx. Some of these forms, which are common, may belong above. *Lokere* may also be a derivative of OE *loc* 'lock', equivalent to *Locksmith* or *Lockyer*; or of OE *lōcian* 'to look, see', equivalent to *Looker* 'shepherd'.

Lockett, Lockitt: *v.* LUCKETT

Lockeyear: *v.* LOCKYER

Lockhart: (i) Symon *Locard* 1153–65 Black; Warin *Lockard* 1190 BuryS (Sf); Jordan *Lokard* 1203 P (Nf). Probably an OG *Lochard* 'stronghold-hard'. (ii) Uruay *le Lockhert* 1203 AssNth (C). OE *loc* 'enclosure, fold' and *hierde*; herdsman in charge of the sheep or cattlefold. cf. Roger *le Medherd* 1317 MEOT (O), herd in charge of grazing cattle.

Lockier: *v.* LOCKYER

Lockless: John *Locles* 1327 *SR* (Ess); Austen *Lockeles* 1568 SRSf. OE *loc* 'lock of hair' and *lēas* 'free from', a nickname for one with straight hair, as opposed to *Bald* and *Curl*.

Locksmith: Walter, Roger *le Loksmyth*' 1255 *Ass* (Ess), 1293 Pinchbeck (Sf); John *Loc Smyth* 1279 AssNb; Robert *Locsmyth* 1279 RH (Hu). OE *loc* 'lock' and *smið*, 'locksmith'. cf. William *Locwricht* 13th AD iv (Lo).

Lockwood: Henry *de Locwode* 1294 AssSt; Adam *de Lokwode* 1352 FFY; Richard *Lokwode* 1455 LLB K. From Lockwood (WRYorks), or 'dweller by the enclosed wood'.

Lockyer, Lockyers, Lockyear, Lockier, Lokier: John, Henry *le Lokier* 1221 AssWa, 1275 RH (Lo); Simon *le Lokyere* 1296 SRSx, 1316 FFK. A derivative of OE *loc* 'lock', 'locksmith'. *v.* also LOCKER.

Locock: *v.* LOWCOCK

Lodder: Richard (*le*) *Lodere* 1234, 1247 Oseney (O). OE *loddere* 'beggar'. *Lodere* cannot be distinguished from forms for LOADER.

Loder: *v.* LOADER

Lodge: Adam *atte Logge* 1327 SRSf; John *del Loge* 1379 PTY. ME *logge* 'small cottage, place to rest in'. cf. 'Logge, or lytylle howse' PromptParv. 'Dweller at the cottage', but probably often in a more technical sense, with reference to the masons' *logge* (1332, 1351) 'the building on which the life of the temporary community of masons centred.' *v.* Building 39–40. *atte Logge* may often denote the warden of the masons' lodge.

Loft, Lofts: Matthew *ad le Loft* 1279 RH (Hu); Hugh *ate Lofte* 1317 AssK. ME *lofte* 'upper-chamber, attic'. Hardly 'dweller on the upper-floor', possibly 'servant of the upper-chamber'. *Lofte* may have been used in the same sense as *Lofthouse*.

Lofthouse, Loftus: Peter *de Lofthusum* 1166 P (Y); Ralph *de Lofthus* 1219 AssY; John *del Lofthouse* 1365 FrY; John *Loftus* 1505 GildY. This common Yorkshire name may mean 'dweller at the house with an upper floor' (ON *lopthús*) but

is probably usually from Lofthouse (WRYorks (3)), Loftsome (ERYorks) or Loftus (NRYorks).

Logan: Robert *Logan* 1204 Black; Walter, Thurbrand *de Logan* 1230, 1272 ib. From Logan (Ayr), or from minor places of this name.

Loker: *v.* LOOKER

Loller: Elfred *le Lollere* 1133–60 Rams (Hu), Alfward, Robert *Lollere* 13th ib., 1279 RH (C). A very rare and interesting name. Perhaps from ME *lolle* 'to droop, dangle; to lean idly, to recline in a relaxed attitude', hence 'an indolent fellow'. It is, however, possible that *Lollere* is an early ME *lollere* 'mumbler', applied to pious persons and substituted in the 14th century for *Lollard* as a description of the Lollards. As Alfred's wife Edgiva became a nun at Ramsey, she was a pious woman and it is reasonable to suppose that her husband was also pious (ELPN).

Lomas, Lomax, Loomas, Lummis, Lummus: Richard *Lumas*, *Lumax*, Geoffrey *Lomax* 1602, 1622, 1642 PrGR; John *Lummis* 1674 HTSf. From a lost place Lomax, earlier *Lumhalghs*, the name of a district south of the Roch in Bury (Lancs).

Lomb, Loombe, Loom, Loomes, Lumb, Lum: (i) Houward, Simon *Lomb* 1198 FFNf, 1252 Rams (Hu); Ralph, Sibilla *le Lomb* 1327 SRSx, SRSf. *v.* LAMB and cf. Robert *lumbekin* 1277 Ely (Sf), either 'little lamb' or *Lambkin*, the origin of the surname of Tony *Lumpkin*. (ii) John *del Lumme* 1327 Wak (Y). 'Dweller by the pool', as at Lumb (Lancs), OE **lum(m)*.

Lombard, Lumbard, Lumbert, Limbert: (i) *Lumbardus* 1203 Cur (Y); William *Lumbart* 12th DC (L); Martin *Lumbard*' 1208 Cur (Nt). OFr *Lambert* (*v.* LAMBARD), with the same vowel-development as in *Lomb*. (ii) Peter *le Lumbard*' 1193 P (Hu); Brankeleon *le Limbard* 1293 AssSt; Pelle *le Lombard* 1319 SRLo. 'A Lombard', a native of Lombardy, originally *Langobardus* 'long beard'. In the Middle Ages these Italian immigrants were moneylenders and bankers and the surname may sometimes mean 'banker'.

Loncaster: *v.* LANCASTER

Londesborough, Lownsbrough: Osward *de Launeburc*' 1219 AssY; Thomas *de Lownesburgh* 1354 FrY. From Londesborough (ERYorks).

London, Lundon, Lonnon, Lunnon: Ælfstan *on Lundene* a988 OEByn (K); Leofsi *de Lundonia* 1066 DB; Bernardus *Lundonie* 1086 ib. From London. cf. William *Londoneman* 1309 SRBeds.

Londsdale: *v.* LONSDALE

Lone: *v.* LANE

Loney: *v.* LOONEY

Long: *v.* LANG

Longbone, Longbones: An anglicizing of LANGBAIN. cf. Walter *le Longebak* 1332 SRLa.

Longbotham, Longbottom: Richard *Longbotehom* 1379 PTY; Agnes *Longbothom* 1539 RothwellPR (Y); Thomas *Longbottom* 1557 Bardsley. 'Dweller in the long bottom or valley.'

Longcaster: *v.* LANCASTER

Longden, Longdin, Longdon, Langdon, Langdown: Ælfward *æt Langadune* c1050 OEByn (Wo);

Chetelbern *de Longedun* Hy 2 Seals (Wa); Maurice *de Langedun* 1201 FFK; Reginald *de Langedon'* 1221 AssSa (St); Alan *de Longedon'* ib. (Sa). From Langdon (Devon, Dorset, Essex, Kent), Longden (Salop) or Longdon (Salop, Staffs, Worcs).

Longfellow: Jacobus *Langfelley* 1475 FrY; Maria *Langfellow* 1639 RothwellPR (Y). 'Tall fellow.'

Longfield: John, Roger *de Longefeld* 1317 AssK, 1332 SRLa. 'Dweller by the long field.'

Longford, Langford: Osm' *de Langeford'* 1130 P (W); Henry *de Longeford'* 1242 Fees (La). From Langford (Norfolk) or Longford (Derby, Glos, Hereford, Middlesex, Salop, Wilts).

Longhurst: *v.* LANGHURST

Longland, Langland, Langlands: Thomas *de Longelond* 1296 SRSx; Ralph *atte Longelonde* 1332 SRSr; John *Langlandes* 1458 FrY. 'Dweller by the long piece of land.'

Longley: *v.* LANGLEY

Longman, Langman: Alice *Longemon* 1275 SRWo; Agnes *Langeman* 1279 RH (Bk); William *Longeman* 1292 SRLo. 'Tall man.'

Longridge, Longrigg: *v.* LANGRIDGE

Longshaw, Langshaw: John *de Langchawe* 1297 SRY. From Longshaw (Derby).

Longstaff, Longstaffe, Langstaff: Richard *Langstaf* 1210 P (We); Hugo *Longstaf* 1210 FrLei. 'Long staff', probably, as suggested by Bardsley, a nickname for a bailiff, catchpoll, or other officer of the law.

Longthorp: *v.* LANGTHORP

Longton: *v.* LANGTON

Longueville, Longville, Longfield, Longwell, Longwill: Henry *de Longauilla* 1185 Templars (L); Henry *de Longavill'* 1229 Cur (Ess); Thomas *de Longevill* 1336 FFEss; John *Longuevyle, Longwyle, Longvyle* or *Longefyld* 1509 LP (Bk). From Longueville-la-Gifart, now Longueville-sur-Scie (Seine-Inférieure).

Lonnon: *v.* LONDON

Lonsdale, Londsdale: Ralph *de Lounisdale* 1260 AssY; John *de Lonesdale* 1301 FFY; Thomas *Lounsdale* 1419 IpmY. From Lonsdale (Lancs, Westmorland).

Look: *v.* LUKE

Looker, Loker, Luker: (i) John *le Lokar,* Robert *Louker* 1327 SRSo; William *Lookar* 1582 Oxon (Ha). A derivative of OE *lōcian* 'to look'; one who looks after something, a shepherd or farm-bailiff (NED). *v.* also LOCKER. (ii) Simon *de Lucre* 1256 AssNb. From Lucker (Northumb).

Loomas: *v.* LOMAS

Loombe, Loom(es): *v.* LOMB

Looney, Loney: Gillacrist *O'Luinigh* 1090, *M'Lawney* 1504, *Lownye* 1540, *Looney* 1644, *Loney* 1681 Moore. A Manx contraction of *O'Luinigh* 'descendant of *Luinigh',* from *luinneach* 'armed'. Survives in Ireland as *O'Looney, Looney.*

Loos, Loose: Stephen, William *de Lose* 1200 P (Sf), 1204 FFK. From Loose (Kent) or Lose (Suffolk).

Loraine: *v.* LORRAIN

Lord: William *le Lauerd* 1198 P (Sf); Gilbert *Louerd* c1202 NthCh (Nth); John *le Lord* 1252 Rams (Hu). OE *hlāford* 'lord, master', often, no doubt, a nickname for one who aped the lord, or for a lord's servant.

Lording: Geoffrey *Lauerding* 1198 P (Sf); Richard *Louerding* 13th Binham (Nf); Thomas *Lording* 1327 SRSf. OE **hlāfording* 'son of the lord', or, perhaps 'follower, servant of the lord'.

Lorence, Lorenz: *v.* LAURENCE

Lorie: *v.* LAWREY

Lorimer, Lorrimar, Loriner: Goldwin' *lorimar* c1130 AC (Lo); Hernisus *le lorinner* 1166 P (Y); Aimar *lorimer* a1174 Clerkenwell (Lo); Reginald *le Lorimier* 1185 P (Gl); David *le Loriner* 1301 MESO (Wo). OFr *loremier, lorenier* 'lorimer, spurrier'.

Loring, Loaring: Geoffrey *(le) Lohareng'* 1158–59 P (St); Dauit *le Loreng* 1197 FFNf; Thomas *Loring* 1280 AssSo. OFr *le Lohereng* 'the man from Lorraine'.

Lorkin, Lorking, Larkin, Larkins, Larking: Adam *Lartkyn* 1296 SRSx; Thomas *Lorekyn* ib.; Thomas *Lorkyn* 1327 SRC; Robert *Larkyn* 1524 SRSf. A diminutive of *Lar-, Lor-,* pet-forms of *Laurence.*

Lorrain, Lorraine, Lorain, Loraine: Eustache *de Lorreyne* 1333 Black. From Lorraine.

Lorrie: *v.* LAWREY

Lorriman: William *Loryman* 1540 FrY; William *Lurryman* 1662 PrGR. 'Servant of *Lorrie'* (Laurence).

Lorrison: Robert *Lowryson* 1471 Black; Thomas *Lorisoun* 1551 ib. 'Son of *Lowrie* or *Lorrie'* (Laurence).

Lory: *v.* LAWREY

Lothian, Louthean, Lowthian: Ranulph *de Louthyan* 1256 AssNb; John *de Loudonia* 1327 Black (Berwick); Alice *Louthian* 1364 AssY. From Lothian (Scotland).

Lott, Lotte, Lots: (i) Alwin *Loth* 1162 P (K); William *Lot* 1275 RH (Sf); John *Lotte* 1275 RH (Nf); Andrew, John *Lote* 1279 RH (C), 1317 FFEss. There is no evidence for the early use of the Biblical *Lot* in England, but the first form may be this in its French form *Loth* which was common in Brittany. There was a woman's name *Lota* 1279 RH (C), probably a pet form for such names as *Allot* (Alis), *Amelot* or *Emelot* (Amelina), *Ellot* (Ellen), *Gillota* (Gilia), etc., which is probably the usual source. (ii) Richard, William *at(t)e Lote* 1296 SRSx, 1332 SRSr. OE *hlot* 'lot, portion', here used of 'a share of land'. 'Holder of an allotted share of land.'

Loud, Lowde: (i) *Lude* 1185 Templars (Y); Richard *Lud* 1221 Cur (D); Reginald *Lude* 1215 Cur (Sr); William *Loud* 1242 Fees (D). *Lude* must be the OE **Hlūda* postulated by Ekwall to explain Loudham (Suffolk) and Lowdham (Notts). It is from OE *hlūd* 'loud'. The surname might also be a nickname for a noisy individual. (ii) Robert *de la Lude* 1225 AssSo; Henry *atte Lude* 1275 SRWo;

John *ate Lude* 1327 SRC. 'Dweller by the roaring stream', from OE **hlȳde*, as at Lyde (Hereford, Som), or from OE **hlūde*. *v.* MELS. (iii) Richard *de Luda, de Louthe* 1319 SRLo, 1325 *Cor.* From Louth (Lincs), named from the River Lud.

Louden, Loudon, Loudoun, Lowden, Lowdon: James *de Loudun* c1189 Black; Adam *Loudin* c1280 Balliol; John *de Louden* 1332 SRCu. From Loudoun in the district of Cunningham (Ayr), or for LOTHIAN.

Louis: *v.* LEWIS

Loukes: *v.* LUKE

Lound, Lount: *v.* LUND

Loury: *v.* LOWREY

Louth, Lowth: *v.* LOUD (iii)

Love: (i) *Lufe* c1095 Bury (Sf); Radulfus *filius Luue* 1176 P (Nt); Galfridus *filius Love* 1208 Cur (Nf); *Love Meel* (f) 1315 Bart (Lo); Gilbert *Luue* 1177 P (C); Peter *Love* 1255 FFEss. OE *Lufu* (f), from OE *lufu* 'love', a popular and widely distributed woman's name, or OE *Lufa* (m). (ii) Alan, Robert *le Love* 1279 RH (C). AFr *louve*, feminine of *loup* 'wolf', occasionally alternating with the diminutive: Martin *Lovel, Love* 1346, 1348 FA (Sf). *cf.* LOW.

Loveday, Lowday: *Leuedai* (*Liuedai*) 1066 DB (So); *Leuedæi* c1095 Bury (Sf); *Luveday* Vidua 1205 Cur (Nth); *Lovedaia* 1302 FFC; Æluric *Leuedey* c1095 Bury (Sf); Robert *Luvedey* 12th AD iii (K); Walter *Loveday* 1256 FFEss; Adam *Lowday* 1524 SRSf. OE *Lēofdæg* (f) 'dear day', a common medieval christian name in use from before the Conquest to the 20th century. It still survives in Cornwall and Devon, sometimes as *Lowdy*. *cf. Lowdye* Trelogan 1601 Bardsley. As a surname, it may also be from ME *love-day*, a day appointed for a meeting between enemies, litigants, etc., with a view to the amicable settlement of disputes, being given to children born on such a day. *cf. Loveday* wife of Robert Christemasse 1381 SRSf.

Lovegood: Richard *Livegod'* 1204 Cur (Wa); Alexander *Louegod* 1327 SRSf; William *Levegood* 1398 LLB H. The variation in the vowel points to a first element *Lēof-*, hence from OE *Lēofgod* 'beloved god or good', a rare OE personal name recorded only once as the name of a moneyer in the reign of Ethelred II. Its occurrence as a surname proves it must have remained in use after the Conquest.

Loveguard, Lugard, Lugger, Levenger: *Lefgar, Leueger* c1095 Bury (Sf); *Leuegarus* mercator 1199 P (Ess); Edward *Leuegar* 1199 P (D); Richard *Leugar* 1272 AD i (Lo); John *Leugor*, William *Leuegor* 1327 SRSf; Richard *Loueger* 1327 SRSo. OE *Lēofgār* 'beloved-spear'. In *Loveguard* and *Lugard* the *d* is excrescent, in *Levenger* the *n* is intrusive as in *Messenger*.

Lovekin, Lufkin, Lucken, Luckens, Luckin, Luckins, Lukin, Lukins, Lukyn: *Luuekin* 1221 AssSa; *Lovekinus* 1255 RH (O); *Lovekyn* 1279 RH (C); Osbert *Lovekin* 1275 SRWo; John *Loukin*, Robert *Lukyn* 1297 MinAcctCo; Robert

Lufkyn 1524 SRSf; Maistres *Lovekyn, Luffkyn* 1542-3 Bardsley. *Love* plus the diminutive suffix *-kin*, 'little Love', either a pet-name or an affectionate attribute. Occasionally, perhaps also 'little she-wolf'. *v.* LOVE, LOW.

Lovel, Lovell, Lowell: Ricardus *lupellus* c1118 AC (Sx); William *Luuel* 1130 P (O); Willelmus *Luvel, Lupellus* 1206 Cur (O); William *Luvel, Luel* 1212 Fees (Sf); Philip *Lowel* 1255 RH (O); Richard *Luvel* alias *Lowel, Lovel* 1263 Ipm (So). AFr *lovel* 'wolf-cub', a diminutive of AFr *love* 'wolf'. Like the alternative diminutive *lovet*, it was common and widely distributed. Richard Luvel above was 'of Kari Lowel barony', and was descended from William, Earl of Yvery, who was called *Lupellus* to distinguish him from his father Robert who had acquired the nickname *Lupus* because of his violent temper. Here the diminutive is clearly used in the sense 'the younger'. Used also as a personal name: *Luuellus* 1145-7 Colch (Ess); *Lovel* le Clark 1274 RH (Ess). *cf.* LOVE, LOW, LOVETT.

Lovelace, Loveless, Lowles, Lowless: Edith *Luvelece* 1243 AssSo; William *Luuelaz* c1250 StGreg (K); John, Albricus *Loveles* 1251 FrLei, 1275 RH (Sf); Richard *Lovelas*, John *Lovelace* 1344, 1367 PN K 407; Robert *Lufelesse* 1444 Calv (Y). OE *lufu* 'love' and *-lēas* 'free from, without', 'loveless'. The common form is *Loveles*. Occasionally we may have 'love lass' from ME *las(se)*. *cf.* Alan *Luveswain* 1166 P (Y). 'Love lace', a dandy, is less likely. OFr *laz*, ME *las* meant 'cord'. The sense *lace* is not recorded in England before 1550 (NED).

Lovelady: Adam *Luvelavedy* 1297 Wak (Y); Adam *Loveladi* 1314 ib. An obvious nickname for a philanderer.

Loveless: *v.* LOVELACE

Lovelock, Loveluck: I. *Luveloc* 1283 SRSf; William *Louelok* 1327 *SR* (Ess). A nickname for a dandy, a wearer of pendant locks of hair falling over the ears and cut in a variety of fashions. They were common in the 16th century and apparently much earlier. Walter (*le*) *Loveloker'* (1279 RH (O)) must have been a maker of these.

Lovely: John *Lovely* 1319 AssSt; Henry *Loveliche* 1406 LLB I; William *Loveliche*, Matthew *Louledge*, John *Lowledge* 1524 SRSf. ME *luuelich* 'lovely'.

Loveman, Lowman, Luffman, Leaman, Leamon, Leeman, Lemmon, Leman, Lemon, Liman, Limon: *Leman* 1066 DB (Ha); *Lufmancat* 1066 Winton (Ha); *Lemannus* de Fordham 1175-86 Holme (Nf); Reiner *Leman* 1185 Templars (Ess); William *Luveman* 1211 FrLeic; Aumfridus *Leofman* 1221 AssWo; Wfricus *Lefman* c1250 Rams (Hu); William *Lemmon* 1275 SRWo; Elyas *Loveman* 1276 RH (Y); Henry *Lemman* 1327 SRSx; Thomas *Leaman* 1568 SRSf. OE *Lēofmann* 'beloved man', a rare personal name of which only three pre-Conquest examples are known. The surname has been reinforced by the common ME *leofman, leman, lemman* 'lover, sweetheart': Robert *le*

Leman 1285 Pinchbeck (Sf). *Luve-, Loveman* may mean 'servant of *Love*'.

Loven: (i) *Luuunus* 1066 DB; *Leuunus* 1086 DB; Robertus *filius Louun* 1160 P (Sa); Ralph *Lovyn* 1345 ColchCt. OE **Lēofhun* 'beloved young bear', a rare name, unrecorded in OE. (ii) Jocelin *de Luvan* 1187 Gilb (L); Godfrey *de Luvein* 1195 P (K). From Louvain. The more common source.

Lover: William *le Lovere* 1275 RH (Nf); Alice *Louer* 1327 SRSf. ME *lovere* 'lover, sweetheart'.

Loveridge: *v.* LEVERAGE

Lovering: William *Luuering* 1203 P (Sr), Thomas, Martin *Lovering* 1275 RH (D), 1327 SRSo. OE **Lēofhering, *Lēofring* 'son of *Lēofhere*' 'beloved-army'.

Loverock: *v.* LEVERAGE

Lovett, Loveitt, Lovitt: William *Louet, Loueth, Luueth* 1086 DB (Berks, Nth); Geoffrey *Luvet* c1125 StCh; Robert *Lovit* 1279 RH (Bk). OFr *louet* 'wolf-cub', a diminutive of *lou* 'wolf', occasionally alternating with a diminutive in -*el*: Robert *Luvet, Luvell*' 1206 Cur (R). cf. LOVEL.

Lovick: This may be (i) from *Loveke* from OE *Lēofeca*. *v.* LEVICK. (ii) from *Lufwic* becoming *Lowik*. *v.* LOWICK.

Lovie: *v.* LEAVEY

Loving: *v.* LEVINGE

Lovney: Mabilia *de Luveny, de Loveny* 1242 Fees (L). From Louvigny (Calvados).

Lovold: *v.* LEAVOLD

Low, Lowe, Lowes: (i) John *le Lu* 1207 P (Gl); Robertus *Lupus*, Robert *le Lu* 1221 AssWa; Walter *le Lou* 1242 Fees (D). OFr *lou* 'wolf', occasionally interchanging with the diminutive: Gregory *le Lu, Lupus, Lupet* 1221 Cur (D), Martin *Lovel* or *Love* 1346, 1348 FA (Sf). (ii) Turgot *Lag* 1066 DB (Y, L); William *le Low* 1284 AssLa; Martin *le Low* 1275 RH (Lo). ON *lágr* 'low, short'. (iii) Robert *de la Lowe* 1275 SRWo; Roger *del Lowe* 1288 AssCh; Stephen *Atteloue* 1301 SRY. OE *hlāw* 'hill', 'burial mound'. cf. LAW. (iv) From a pet-name of *Laurence*. cf. Simon *Loustepsone* 1297 SRY.

Lowcock, Locock, Luckcock, Luckcuck, Luckock, Lucock, Lewcock: *Luuecok, Leucok* Schayf(e) 1246 AssLa; *Lovekoc de Wlvedale* 1275 Wak (Y); *Lokoc de Heppewrth* 1286 ib.; Peter *Luuecok*' 1221 AssWa; Geoffrey *Luvecoc, Lucoc* 1259, c1308 Calv (Y); Henry *Lovecok* 1274 RH (Ess); William *Loukok* 1327 SRDb; Robert *Lukok* 1338 FrY; William *Locoke* 1531 FrY; John *Lewcocke* 1674 HTSf. A diminutive of OE *Lufa*. cf. LOVE.

Lowday: *v.* LOVEDAY

Lowde: *v.* LOUD

Lowell: *v.* LOVEL

Lowen, Lowin: *v.* LEWIN

Lower: *v.* EWER

Lowery: *v.* LOWREY

Lowick: Balde *de Lufwic* 1200 Cur (Nth). From Lowick (Lancs, Northants, Northumb).

Lowing: *v.* LEVINGE

Lowis: *v.* LEWIS

Lowless: *v.* LOVELACE

Lowman: Richard *de Lumene* 1242 Fees (D). From Uplowman (Devon). *v.* also LOVEMAN.

Lownsbrough: *v.* LONDESBOROUGH

Lowrance: *v.* LAURENCE

Lowrey, Lowrie, Lowries, Lowry, Lowery, Loury: *Lowry* Smith 1467 Black; Robert *Lowri* 1332 SRCu; Gilbert *Lowrie* 1497 Black. A pet-form of *Laurence*. A Border form. cf. LAWREY. *Lowry* may also be from Lowery (Devon), whence the surname *de Loveworþe* (1256 PN D 245).

Lowrieson, Lowrison: Robert *Lowryson* 1471 Black. 'Son of *Lowrey*.'

Lowson: (i) Geoffrey *le Leuesone* 1309 SRBeds. 'Beloved son', OE *lēof* and *sunu*. cf. LEAF. (ii) Richard *Lowson* 1381 PTY; William *Loweson* 1456 FrY. 'Son of *Low*', a pet-name of *Laurence*. *v.* also LEVESON.

Lowth: *v.* LOUD

Lowther: William *de Laudre* 1184 P (We); Henry *de Louthere* 1230 Cur (Y); Hugh *de Louthre* 1342 FFY; William *Lowther* 1672 HTY. From Lowther (Westmorland), *Lauder* c1180.

Lowthian: *v.* LOTHIAN

Lowthorpe, Lowthrop: Walter *de Luitorp* 1161 P (Y). From Lowthorpe (ERYorks).

Loyd: *v.* LLOYD

Luard: *v.* LIVARD

Lubbock: Robert *de Lubyck* 1276 RH (L). From Lubeck.

Lucas: *Lucas* c1150 DC (Nt); Euerard *Lucas* 1153–85 Templars (Herts). The learned form of *Luke*.

Luce, Lucia: *Lucia* c1150 DC (L), 1205 Cur (Sf); Richard, Asselyna *Luce* c1230 Barnwell (C), 1332 SRSx. *Lucia*, feminine of Lat *Lucius*, from *lux* 'light'. St Lucia, martyred at Syracuse under Diocletian, was a popular medieval saint whose name was common in England as *Luce*.

Luck(es): *v.* LUKE

Luckett, Locket, Lockett, Lockitt: Eudo, Walter *Loket* 1275 RH (Nf), 1389 FrY; Matilda *Luket* 1418 Bardsley (Y). A diminutive of *Luke*.

Luckhurst, Lukehurst: This Kentish surname must derive from Luckhurst in Mayfield (Sussex), itself a corruption of the first part of *Lukkars Croche* 1553, *Luckers Crouch* 1823, where probably lived Henry *Luggere* in 1296 (PN Sx 382).

Luckin: *v.* LOVEKIN

Lucking: William *Luueking* 1188 P (Lei); Nicholas *Loveking* 1275 SRWo. OE **Lēofecing* 'son of *Lēofeca*'. cf. LEVICK. *Lucking* may also be a late development of *Lovekin*.

Luckman: *v.* LUKEMAN

Luckock, Lucock: *v.* LOWCOCK

Lucy, Lucey: (i) William, Cecilia *Lucy* 1297 MinAcctCo, 1327 SRSo *v.* LUCE. (ii) Richard *de Luci* 1135–54 Bury (Sf). From Lucé (Orne).

Ludkin, Ludkins: Adam *Lotekyn, Ludekyn* 1311 LLB D; Hugh *Lutkyn* 1332 SRSt. A diminutive of the *Lote* discussed under LOTT or of *Lutt*.

Ludlow: William *de Ludelawa* 1182 P (Sa); John *de Lodelawe* 1327 SRWo; George *Ludlow* 1545 SRW. From Ludlow (Salop).

Luff: William, Simon *Lof* 1177, 1185 P (C, Nth); William, Geoffrey *Luffe* 1188 P (Co), 1309 SRBeds. OE *lēof* 'beloved' or **Lēof*, with change of stress to *leōf, lōf*. cf. LEAF. Or OE **Luffa*, a geminated form of *Lufa*. cf. LOVE.

Luffingham: William *de Lufham* 1199 FF (R). From Luffenham (Rutland).

Luffman: *v.* LOVEMAN

Lufkin: *v.* LOVEKIN

Lugard, Lugger: *v.* LOVEGUARD

Luke, Luck, Luckes, Look, Looks, Loukes: (i) *Luke* 1277 Ipm (Nt); William, Thomas *Lucke* 1279 RH (C), 1332 SRSt; Simon *Luk* 1286 Ipm (Sf); Godfrey, John *Lukke* 1327 SRSf, 1381 ArchC iii; John *Louk* 1327 SRSf; Robert *Lukes* 1376 LoPleas; John *Look* 1379 ColchCt. *Luke* or *Luck* was the popular form of *Lucas*, Greek *Λουκᾶς*, a man from Lucania. *v.* also LEVICK. (ii) Lucas *de Luk', de Lukes* 1274 RH (Lo); Richard *Luike* 1279 RH (C). From Luick (Liège).

Lukehurst: *v.* LUCKHURST

Lukeman, Luckman: 'Servant of *Luke*.'

Luker: *v.* LOOKER

Lukin(s): *v.* LOVEKIN

Lulman: *v.* LILLEYMAN

Lum, Lumb: *v.* LOMB

Lumbard: *v.* LOMBARD

Lumley, Lumbley: William *de Lumeley* 1235–6 AssDu; Marmaduke *de Lomley* 1348 FFY; William *Lumley* 1672 HTY. From Lumley (Durham).

Lummis, Lummus: *v.* LOMAS

Lumner: *v.* LIMMER

Lumsden, Lumsdaine, Lumsdon: William *de Lumisden* 1166–82 Black; Adam *de Lumesdene* 1212 P (Du); John *de Lummysden* c1335 Black. From Lumsden in Coldingham (Berwick).

Lund, Lunt, Lound, Lount: Ralph *de la Lunde* 1183 P (Y); Geoffrey *de Lund* 1200–30 Seals (Nf); John *del Lound* 1327 SRSf; John *Lunt* 1524 SRSf. From Lund (Lancs, Yorks), Lunt (Lancs), Lound (Lincs, Notts, Suffolk), or 'dweller by the grove' (ON *lundr*).

Lundon: *v.* LONDON

Lung: *v.* LANG

Lunniss: Richard *Londoneys* 1279 RH (C); Robert *Lundenissh* 1327 SR (Ess). 'The Londoner.'

Lunnon: *v.* LONDON

Lupino: A theatrical family of Italian origin, established in England since 1642. The Victoria and Albert Museum possesses a handbill of that date, beginning: 'Signor Luppino will present Bel and the Dragon newly arrived from Italy ...' The surname is an Italian diminutive, corresponding to the French *Lovell* and *Lovett*, ultimately from Latin *lupus*, 'wolf-cub'.

Lupton: Robert *de Lupton'* 1297 SRY; Roger *Lupton* 1506 FFEss; Andrew, Peter *Lupton* 1642 PrD. From Lupton House (Devon), and probably also from an unidentified Lupton in Yorks.

Lurey, Lurie, Delhuary: John *del Ewry* 1379 PTY. ME *ewerye*, a room where ewers of water, table-linen, etc., were kept. 'Sergeant or groom of the Ewery.' cf. EWER.

Lusher: *v.* USHER

Luter, Lutter: (i) Alvredus *le Lutur* 1221 Cur (K); John *le Leuter, le Leutour, Luter* 1304–10 LLB B, C, D; Idonea *Lutier* 1358 AD ii (Mx). OFr *leuteor*, or a derivative of ME *lute* 'to play on the lute', a lute-player. (ii) William *Lelutre* 1130 P (Ess); Geoffrey, Ralph *Lutre* 1204 StP (Lo), c1208 FrLeic; Ralph, William *le Lutre* 1207 Cur (Sx), 1235 AD i (Mx). OFr *loutre* 'otter', metonymic for *Lutterer* 'otter-hunter'.

Luther: Ralph *Luther* 1529 GildY; John *Luthur* 1674 HTSf. 'Lute-player', Fr *luthier*. There is no evidence for the personal-name *Luther* in medieval England.

Lutman: *v.* LILLEYMAN

Lutt: Simon, Seman *Lutte* 1279 RH (Hu), 1327 SRSf. OE **Lutt(a)*, from the root *lut-* in OE *lӯtel*. cf. *Lutting* c1095 Bury (Sf) 'son of **Lutt(a)*', Ralph, John *Lutting* 1185 P (Nf), 1357 FrY.

Lutterer: Ralph *le Lutrer, le Luterer* 1220 Cur, 1232 Fees (Bk). A derivative of OFr *loutre* 'otter', an otterhunter. cf. LUTER.

Luttrell: Geoffrey *Lutrel* 1194 P (Nt); Alexander *Lutterel* 1268 AssSo. A diminutive of OFr *loutre* 'otter'. Ralph *Lutrel* is also called *le Lutrer* 1219 Cur (Bk). cf. LUTTERER.

Luty: *v.* LAWTEY

Lyal, Lyall, Lyel, Lyell, Liell: Johannes *filius Lyelli* 1329 Black; *Lyell* Robson 1541 Bardsley; John *Lyell* 1408 FrY; John *Liel* 1411–34 Black. A hypocoristic of *Lyon* (*v.* LYON and cf. John *Lyot* 1327 SRDb), or of its diminutive *Lionel*.

Lyburn: *v.* LAYBORN

Lydall: *v.* LIDDALL

Lyde: *v.* LYTH

Lye(s): *v.* LEA

Lyfield: *v.* LAYFIELD

Lyle: *v.* LISLE

Lymburner: Geoffrey *Limbarner* John FFEss; Alexander *le Lymbrennere* 1240 FFEss; Robert *Lymbrinner* 1327 SRY. OE *līm* plus a derivative of OE *beornan* or ON *brenna* 'to burn', a limeburner, a maker of lime by burning lime-stone.

Lymer: *v.* LIMER

Lynam: *v.* LINEHAM

Lynch: *v.* LINCH

Lynde: *v.* LIND

Lyndhurst: *v.* LINDHURST

Lyne: *v.* LINE

Lyner: Gilbert *le Lyner* 1279 RH (Hu); John *Lynar* 1327 SRSx. OFr *linier* 'maker or seller of linen cloth'.

Lynham: *v.* LINEHAM

Lynn, Lynne, Linn, Lenn: Ædricus *de Lenna* 1177 P (Nf). From King's Lynn (Norfolk).

Lyon, Lyons: (i) *Lyon* son of *Lyon* 1293 AssSt; Ricardus *Leo* 1176 P (O); Thomas *Lioun* 1287 AssCh; William *le Leoun* 1290 Fees (Wt); William *Lyon* 1327 SRSf; Johanna *le Lyon* 1332 SRSx. Either from *Lyon*, the popular pronunciation of *Leo* or *Leon*, or a nickname from the lion. (ii) Azor *de Lions* 1159 P (Nf); Geoffrey *de Liuns* 1170 P (Nf); Henry *de Lyons* 1296 SRSx. As early forms of the surname, which is not uncommon, invariably end in -*s*, this must be from Lyons-la-Forêt (Eure) and not from the better-known Lyons, earlier *Lugudunum*, Fr *Lyon*.

Lysons, Licence, Lison: Godfrey *de Lisun* 1195 P (So); William *Lycens* 1524 SRSf. From Lison (Calvados).

Lyster: *v.* LISTER
Lyte: *v.* LIGHT
Lyteman: *v.* LILLEYMAN
Lyth, Lythe, Lyde: (i) Richard *de la Lid'* 1212 Cur (Bk); Robert *de Litha* 1214 Cur (Y); Adam *atte Lythe* 1275 SRWo; Abraham *atte Lyde* 1296 SRSx. 'Dweller by the slope' (OE *hliþ, hlid*, ON *hlið*), as at Lythe (NRYorks), Lyth (Westmorland) or Lydd (Kent). (ii) Gonnilda *le Lyth* 1279 RH (Bk). OE *liðe* 'mild, gentle'.

Lythgoe: *v.* LITHGOE
Lytle, Lyttle: *v.* LITTLE
Lyttleton: *v.* LITTLETON
Lytton: *v.* LITTON
Lyward: *v.* LIVARD

M

Mabb, Mabbs: *Mabbe* 1293 AssCh, 13th WhC (La); Ralph, John *Mabbe* 1278 LLB B, 1300 Oseney (O); John *Mabbys* 1309 SRBeds. A pet-name for *Mabel.*

Mabbett, Mabbitt, Mabbot, Mabbott, Mabbutt: *Mabota* Ryder 1379 PTY; Richard *Mabot* 1509 Oxon; William *Mabbett* 1646 Bardsley. *Mabb-ot,* a diminutive of *Mabb.*

Mable, Mabley, Mably: Rogerus *filius Mabilie* 1130 P (Nth); *Mabilia* c1150 DC (L), 1221 AssGl; Arnaldus *Mabilie* 1185 Templars (Ess); John *Mabile* 1274 RH (Ess); John *Mably* 1279 RH (C). *Mabel* or *Mabley* was the popular form of *Amabel.* *v.* ANNABLE.

Mabson: William *Mabbeson* 1332 SRLa; William *Mabbesson* 1381 SRSf. 'Son of *Mabb.*' *Mabbesson* may be for *Mabbetson.* cf. William *Mabotson, Mabetson* 1379 PTY. 'Son of *Mabbett.*'

McAdam: Dolfinus *mach Adam* 1160–2 Black; John *M'Cadame* 1609 ib. 'Son of *Adam.*'

Macaddie, Macadie: John *McChaddy* 1596 Black. Anglicized forms of Gaelic *MacAda* or *MacÁdaidh*, the Gaelic dialectal form of Lowland *Adie. v.* ADEY.

Macalaster, Macallaster, Macalister, McAllister, Maccalister: Ranald *Makalestyr* 1455 Black. Gaelic *MacAlasdair* 'Son of *Alexander.*' *v.* CALLISTER.

McAlery: *v.* McCHLERY

Macall: *v.* McCALL

Macallan: Dungall *M'Alayne* 1376 Black. 'Son of *Allain.*'

Macally, McAlley: *v.* MACAULAY

Macalpin, McAlpine: John *MacAlpyne* c1260 Black. 'Son of *Alpin.*'

McAndrew: Donald *Makandro* 1502 Black. 'Son of *Andrew.*'

Macara, Maccarra: John *M'Ara* 1614 Black. 'Son of the charioteer' (OGael *ara*).

MacArthur, Maccairter, Maccartair, McCarter: Gyllemechall *M'Carthair* 1569 Black; Dougall *M'Arthour* 1580 ib.; Patrick *McKairtour* 1630 ib. Gaelic *MacArtair* 'Son of *Arthur.*'

Macartney, Macartnay, Maccartney: Gilbert *McCartnay* 1529 Black (Galloway); Thomas *McCartnay, Makartnay* 1562 ib.; Helen *Macartney* 1588 ib. (Dumfries). Ir *Mac Cartaine*, a variant of *Mac Artáin* 'son of *Art*'.

Macasgill, Macaskill, Maccaskell, Maccaskill,

Mackaskill: Gilbert *Mac Askil* 1311 Pat (Du). Gaelic *MacAsgaill* 'Son of *Askell.*'

Macaskie, McCaskie: Gilbert *Makasky, Makaskel* 1316, 1318–9 Cl (IOM). Gaelic *MacAscaidh* 'Son of *Ascaidh*', a pet-form of *Askell.*

McAteer: *v.* MACINTYRE

Macaulay, Macauley, McAuliffe, Macalley, Maccally: Iwar *McAulay* 1326 Black; John *Makalley* 1602 ib. In Dumbartonshire, from Gaelic, Ir *MacAmhalghaidh* 'Son of *Amalghaidh*', an old Irish personal-name; in the Hebrides, from Gael *MacAmhlaibh* or *MacAmhlaidh*, OIr *Amlaib*, ON *Oláfr* 'relic of the gods'.

Macauslan, Macausland, Macauslane, McCausland: Malcolm *Macabsolon* 1308 Black; Alexander *Macausland* 1421 ib. 'Son of *Absalom.*'

McBeath, Macbeth: An old Gaelic personal-name, 'son of life'.

MacBrayne: Eugenius *Makbrehin* 1525 Black. 'Son of the judge', Ir *brehon*, Gael *breithean*.

McBride, McBryde: Cristinus *McBryd* 1329 Black. 'Son of (the servant of St) Bride.'

MacByrne: *v.* BYRNE

Maccabe, M'Cabe: Hugh *MacCabe* 1368 Black (Ireland). Irish *Mac Cába* 'Son of *Cába*' (cape, hood).

Maccaffie: *v.* McFEE

MacCaffray, MacCaffery, Caffray, MacGaffrey: Duncan *Macgoffri* 1319 Cl. Irish *Mac Gafraidh* 'Son of *Godfrey.*'

McCall, Maccaull, Macall, Mackail, Mackall: Robert *M'Kawele* 1370–80 Black; Finlay *Makcaill* 1506 JMac; John *M'Call* 1583 Black. Gaelic *MacCathail* 'Son of *Cathal*', Ir, Gael *Cathal*, OW *Catgual* 'war-wielder'.

MacCallum: Gilbert *MacCalme* 1631 Black (Ayr); Iain *M'Callum* 1647 ib.; Archibald *M'Callome* 1661 ib. Gaelic *MacCaluim* 'son of the servant of *Calum*'.

M'Calman, Maccalmon, Maccalmont: Gill. *M'Colemane* c1180 JMac; Gilbert *M'Calmont* 1581 Black; Alexander *McAlman* 1682 ib. Irish *Mac Calmáin, Mac Colmáin.* 'Son of *Colmán.*' *v* COLEMAN.

Maccartair, McCarter: *v.* MACARTHUR

MacCarthy, MacCartie: Douenald Roth' *Mackarthi* 1285 Pat. Irish *MacCárthaigh* 'Son of *Cárthach*', earlier *Caratācos.* cf. CRADDOCK.

Maccartney: *v.* MACARTNEY

MacCashin: *v.* CASHEN

McCaskie: v. MACASKIE

McCausland: v. MACAUSLAN

McChlery, McCleary, McCleery, McAlery: Malcom *M'Cleriche, M'Clery* 1461, 1475 Black; Duncan *McInclerycht* 1537 ib.; Finlay *M'Aclerich* 1638 ib. Gaelic *Mac an chlerich, M'a'chleirich* 'Son of the clerk or cleric'.

McClarron: v. McLAREN

McClean: v. MACLEAN

McClement(s): v. MACLAMON

McCloud: v. MACLEOD

McCloy: Donald *Clowie* or *Makcloye* 1537–40 Black. Gaelic *MacLughaidh* 'Son of Lewie', a petform of *Lewis*.

McClure, Maclure, MacCloor, Macleur: (i) John *McLur* 1526 Black; Thomas *Maklure* 1532 ib. (Carrick); Gilleane *MacIloure* 1618 ib.; John *M'Clour* 1664 ib. (Appin). Gaelic *M'Ill'uidhir* 'son of the servant of *Odhar*'. (ii) In Ireland sometimes an anglicization of *Mac Giolla Uidhir*, from *odhar* 'dun-coloured'.

McClymont: v. MACLAMON

Maccolman: v. M'CALMAN

McComb, McCombe: Gilchrist *Makcome* 1526 Black. Gaelic *MacThóm* 'Son of Tom'.

M'Combie, Maccomie: Ferquhair *McCombquhy* 1556, John *M'Comy* 1571, John *Makthomy* Makgilleweye 1586 Black. Gaelic *MacComaidh*, from *MacThomaidh* 'Son of Tommy'.

McConachie, McConaghey, Macconkey: Gilbert *Maccoignache* 1296 CalSc; Angus *M'Conchie* 1493 Black. Gaelic *MacDhonnchaidh* 'Son of Duncan'.

MacCone: v. MACOWEN

Macconnal, McConnell: The Irish name is sometimes from *MacConnaill* 'Son of Conall', but is usually, as in Scotland, a variant of *Macdonald*.

MacCoole: v. MACDOUGALL

McCorkell, Maccorkill, Maccorkle: *M'Thurkill, M'Kurkull* 1661, 1663 Black. v. CORKHILL.

McCormac, Maccormack, McCormick: Gillecrist *mac Cormaic* 1132 Black. Irish *Mac Cormaic* 'Son of Cormac'. v. CORMACK.

McCorquodale, Maccorkindale: Ewen *Mactorquedil* or Ewgyne *M'Corqueheddell* 1430 Black. Gael *MacCorcadail* 'Son of Thorketill'. v. CORKHILL.

Maccoubrie, McCoubrey: John *Makcopery* 1513, Henry *McCowthry* 1539 Black. Gael *Mac Cuithbreith* 'Son of Cuthbert'.

McCrae, Maccraith: v. MACRAE

M'Crimmon: Johne *Mcchrummen* 1533 (Inverness), Hector *M'Crimmon* 1595 Black (Skye). Gael *Mac Cruimein* 'Son of Rumun', ON *Hrómundr* 'famed protector'.

Maccrindell, Maccrindle, MacRanald: John *M'Rynald* or *Makrynnild* 1483, Donald *McRanald* Vaan 1506, Malcome *McRyndill*, James *Mc Crynnell* 1526 Black. Gael *Macraonuill* 'Son of Raonull', i.e. *Ranald*.

McCrossan: Irish *Mac an Chrosáin* 'Son of the rhymer'.

McCubbin, McCubbine, McCubbing: Martin

M'Cubyn 1376, John *Makcubyng* 1567 Black. 'Son of *Cubbin*', i.e. *Gibbon*.

MacCure: v. MACIVER

MacCurtin: v. CURTIN

McCutcheon, Maccutchen, MacHutchin: John Roy *Makhuchone* 1495, James *McCutchone* 1686 Black. 'Son of Hutcheon.' v. HUTCHIN.

MacDermot, McDermott: Nemeas *Mactarmayt* 1427 Black; Alexander *M'Dermite* 1687 JMac. 'Son of Diarmaid', OIr *Diarmait* 'freeman'.

Macdonald, MacDonnell, McConnell: Robert *Dovenald* 1257 Dublin; Dovenilt *Macdencuilt*, Conoye *Mac Deuenilt* 1264 ib. Gael *Mac Dhómhnuill*, pronounced *Mak oonil*, 'Son of Donald'.

McDonaugh, McDonogh: 'Son of Duncan'. v. McCONACHIE, DUNCAN.

Macdougal, McDougall, MacDool, Macdouall, McDowall, McDowell, MacCoole: Duncan *Makdougal* c1230 JMac; Omertach *Macdowyyll*, Molawelyne *Macduulle* 1264 Dublin; Fergus *MacDowilt* 1296 CalSc; Robert *M'Kowele* 1370–80 Black; Nigel *MakCowl* 1497 ib. Gael *MacDhùghaill* 'Son of Dhubgall'. v. DOUGAL.

Macduff: Roger *Macedugh* 1264 Dublin; Malisius *mc Duf* 1284 Black. Gaelic *Mac Dhuibh* 'Son of Dubh' (black).

MacDuffie: v. McFEE

MacEachan: v. KAIGHAN

Macellar, Maceller: v. MCKELLAR

McElroy, MacIlroy: Michael *M'Gilrey, M'Ylroye* 1376, 1500 Black. Irish *Mac Giolla Rua* 'Son of the red-haired lad'. cf. GILROY, MILROY.

MacEwan, McEwen, Macewing: Gilpatrick *mac Ewen* 1219 Black. Gael *MacEoghainn* 'Son of Ewen'.

Macey: v. MASSEY

McFadden, McFadyean, MacFadyen, McFadzean: *Padyne* Regane 1264 Dublin; Malcolm *Macpadene* 1304, John *McFadyeane* 1457, Donald *M'Fadzeane* 1473 Black. Gael *MacPhaidin* or *MacPhaidein* 'Son of Paidean' or Little Pat.

Macfail, Macfall, Mackfall, MacPhail, MacVail: Gillemore *M'Phale* 1414, Donald *M'Pawle* 1490, Gylleis *Makfaill* 1492 Black. Gael *Mac Phàil* 'Son of Paul'. cf. QUAYLE.

Macfait, M'Fate, M'Feate: Finlay *M'Fead* 1485, Gilcrist *McPaid* 1539, Robert *M'Faitt* 1596 Black. Gael *Mac Pháid* 'Son of Pate'.

MacFarlan, Macfarlane, Macfarland, Macparlan, Macpartland: Malcolm *Mcpharlane* c1385 Black. Gael *MacPharlain* 'Son of Parlan', OIr *Partholon* (Bartholomew).

M'Farquhar: Malmur *Mac Hercar* c1200 JMac. 'Son of Farquhar.'

McFee, Macfie, MacPhee, Macphie, Maccaffie, Machaffie, McDuffie: Thomas *Macdoffy* 1296 CalSc; Archibald *McKofee* 1506, Morphe *mcphe* 1531, Ewin *McAphie* 1681 Black. Gael *MacDhubhshith* 'Son of Dubhshithe' (black man of peace).

McGachan: v. KAIGHAN

MacGaffrey: v. MACCAFFRAY

McGee, McGhee, McGhie, Magee, Maggee:

Gilmighel *Mac Ethe* 1296 CalSc; *McGethe* 1297 Pat; *Macge* or *Mageth* 1339, Robert *Macgye*, *M'Gy* 1444–9 Black. Irish *Mag Aoidh* 'Son of *Aodh*'. cf. MCKAY.

MacGeorge: *v*. MACINDEOR

McGibbon, Mackibbon, McKibbin: Thomas *Makgibbon* 1507 JMac. 'Son of *Gibbon*.'

McGill: Maurice *Macgeil* 1231, James *M'Gill* 1550 Black. Gael *Mac an ghoill* 'Son of the Lowlander or stranger'. cf. GALL.

MacGillivray, MacGilvray: Archibald *McIluray* 1542, Farquhar *MacGillivray* 1622 Black. Gael *Mac Gillebhrath* 'Son of the servant of judgement'.

MacGilp: *v*. MCKILLOP

McGinley: *v*. KINLAY

MacGorman: *v*. GORMAN

MacGowan, McGowing, McGown, MacGoun, MacGown: Gilcallum *McGoun* 1503, Gilbert *Makgowin* 1526 Black. Gael, Ir *Mac a' ghobhainn* 'Son of the smith'.

McGrath, McGraw: *v*. MACRAE

MacGregor, McGreigor, McGrigor: Duncan *M'Greg(h)ere* 1292 JMac. 'Son of *Gregor*.'

McGuinness: *v*. MAGUINESS

McHaffie: *v*. McFEE

Machen: *v*. MASON

MacHendrie, MacHenry, Mackendrick: John *M'Henri* 1370–80, *McHenrik* 1590 Black. Gael *MacEanruig* 'Son of *Henry*'.

Machent, Machon: *v*. MASON

MacHutchin: *v*. McCUTCHEON

MacIlduff: *v*. DUFF

MacIlroy: *v*. McELROY

Macilvride, Macilvreed: Colanus *McGilbride* 1363, Nigel *M'Ylwyrd*, *Makkilbreid* 1476–8 Black. Gael *Mac Giolla Brighde* 'Son of the servant of St Bride'.

Macindeor, Mackindewar, Mackinder, M'Jarrow, M'Jerrow, MacGeorge: Colin *Macindoyr* 13th, Gillaspy *McIndewir* 1541, *McInder* 1613, John *Macjore* 1691, John *M'George* 1726 Black. Gael *Macindeoir* 'Son of the stranger', pronounced *Makinjor*, hence *M'Jarrow*, *MacGeorge*.

MacInnes, Mackinnes, Mackiness: Donald *McKynes* 1514, Allester *M'Callen M'Aneiss* 1574 Black. Gael *MacAonghuis* 'Son of *Angus*'.

McIntosh, Mackintosh: Farchard *Mctoschy* 1382, Alexander *Mackintoche* 1390 Black. Gael *Mac an toisich* 'Son of the chieftain'.

Macintyre, McEntire, McAteer, McTear: Nicholas *Mac in tsair* 1268, Paul *M'tyr* 1372, Gildow *Makintare* 1506 JMac. Gael *Mac an tsaoir* 'Son of the carpenter'.

MacIver, Macivor, Maccure, Mackeever: Malcolm *McIuyr* 1292 Black. Gael *MacIomhair* 'Son of *Ivar*' (ON *Ivarr* 'bow-army').

M'Jarrow: *v*. MACINDEOR

Mack: *Maccus* de Leum 1176 P (Nb); Hugo *Mac* 1188 P (Wo); John *Mack* 1327 SRSo. OC *Maccos*, OIr *Maccus*, an Irish adoption of ON *Magnus*.

Mackail, Mackall: *v*. McCALL

Mackay, McKay, McKee, McKey, Mackey,

Mackie, McKie: Cucail *Mac Aedha* 1098 Moore; Gilchrist *M'Ay* 1326, Odo *Macidh* 1433, Gilnew *McCay* 1506 Black. Gael *Mac Aoidh* 'Son of *Aodh*'.

McKellar, MacKeller, Macellar, Maceller: Patrick *McKellar* 1436 Black; Archibald *Makelar* 1488 ib. (Argyll); Duncan *McCallar*, *Makcallar* 1500 ib. (Dumbarton). Gaelic *Mac Ealair* 'son of *Ealair*', the Gaelic form of Lat *Hilarius*.

McKelly: *v*. KELLY

McKenna, Mackinney: William *M'Kinnay* 1544 Black. Gael *MacCionaodha* 'Son of *Cionaodh*'.

Mackenzie: Makbeth *Makkyneth* 1264 Black; Nevin *M'Kenze* 1473 JMac. 'Son of *Coinneach*' (comely).

McKibben: *v*. MCGIBBON

McKillop, McGilp: Finlaius *Macpilibh* 1433, William *Makillop* 1526, Donald *M'Gillip* 1532 Black. Gael *Mac Fhilib* 'Son of Philip'.

McKisack, MacKissack: *v*. KISSACK

Mackown: *v*. MacOWEN

MacLachlan, McLauchlane, Maclaughlan, MacLoughlin: *v*. LACHLAN

Maclaine: *v*. MACLEAN

Maclamon, Maclamont, Macclemment, McClements, Macclymond, McClymont: Gael *MacLaomuinn* 'Son of *Lamont*'. *v*. LAMMOND.

McLaren, Maclauren, Maclaurin, McClarron: Donald *Maklaurene* 1586, Laran *McLaran* 1592 Black. Gael *Mac Labhruinn* 'Son of *Labhran*'. *v*. LAURENCE.

MacLean, Macclean, Maclaine, Maclane: Lachlan *M'Gilleon* 1436, Alexander *McKlane* 1684 Black. Gael *Mac Gille Eoin* 'Son of the servant of St John'.

MacLeod, McCloud: Gillandres *MacLeod* 1227 Black. Gael *MacLeòid* 'Son of *Leòd*' (ON *Liótr* 'ugly').

Macleur, Maclure: *v*. MCCLURE

McManus: *v*. MAGNUS

McMichael: *v*. MICHAEL

Macmillan, MacMullan: John *Macmullan*, *Makmylan* 1454–87 Black. Gael *MacMhaolain* 'Son of the tonsured one'.

MacNab: Mathew *M'Nab* 1376 Black. Gael *Mac an Aba* 'Son of the abbot'.

MacNachtan, MacNaghten: *v*. MACNAUGHTON

McNamara, MacNamara: *Mac Conmera* 1311 Moore; *Mac Namara* 1511 ib.; *McNameer*, *McNamear* 1610, 1793 ib. An anglicized form of Gaelic *Mac con-mara* 'son of the hound of the sea'.

MacNaughton, MacNaghten, MacNachtan: Gillecrist *Mac Nachtan* 1247 Black; Donald *Macnachtane* 1431 ib. (Dunkeld); Maureis *McNauchtane* 1510 ib. Gaelic *Mac Neachdainn* 'son of *Neachdain*', the Pictish *Nechtan* 'pure'.

McNeal, McNeil: *v*. NEAL

MacNevin, MacNiven: . NIVEN

McNichol: *v*. NICHOLAS

McOmish, Maccomish: Donald *McHomas* 1688, Archibald *M'Comash* 1696 Black. Gael *Mac Thomais* 'Son of Thomas'.

MacOwen, MacCown, MacCone, Mackeown,

Cowan, Keown: 'Son of *Ewen*'. *v.* MACEWAN, OWEN.

McParlan(d), McPartland: *v.* MACFARLAN

McPhail: *v.* MACFAIL

McPhee: *v.* MCFEE

McPheeters: Thomas Moir *McGillifedder* 1607, Duncan *M'Fater* 1694 Black. Gael *Mac Gille Pheadair* 'Son of (St) Peter's servant'.

Macpherson: Alexander *Makfersan* c1447, Bean *Makimpersone* 1490 Black. Gael *Mac an Phearsain* 'Son of the parson'.

McQueen, MacQueen, Macqueen: Hector *Mac-Souhyn* 1271 Black; Luke *Macquyn* 1403 JMac; Finlay *M'Quene*, Gillereoch *M'Queane* 1541 ib. Gaelic *Mac Shuibhne* 'son of *Suibhne*', from *suibhne* 'pleasant'.

M'Quisten, McQuistin: Kenneth *M'Hustan* 1542, John *Macquiestoun* 1662, Donald *M'Houstone* 1664 JMac. 'Son of *Húisdean*.' *v.* MCCUTCHEON.

Macrae, McRaith, Macraw, Macray, McRea, McCrae, McCraith, McCraw, McCrea, McCreath, McCreith, Mackereth: *Maccret* mac Iodene a1200 Dublin; *Macrath* ap Molegan 1296 CalSc; Alexander *Macrad* c1225, Patric *M'Re*, *M'Rey* 1376, Adam *M'Creich* 1438 Black; Richard *Makereth* 1526 FrY; John *Makcra* 1621 Black. Gael *Macrath* 'son of grace', an old personal-name.

MacRanald: *v.* MACCRINDELL

M'Sorley: *v.* SUMMERLAD

McTaggart, MacTaggert: Ferchar *Machentagar*, *Mackinsagart* 1215 Black; Otes *Mactagart* 1511 Moore. Gael, Irish *Mac an tsagairt* 'Son of the priest'.

MacTague, MacTeague, MacTigue: 'Son of the poet'. *v.* KEIG.

Mactavish: Doncan *M'Thamais* 1355, Duncan *McTawisch* 1480, Thomas *McTaevis* 1515 Black. Gael *Mac Támhais* 'Son of *Tammas*', Lowland Scots for *Thomas*.

McTear: *v.* MACINTYRE

McTurk: John *Makturk* 1538 Black. Gael *Mac Tuirc* 'Son of *Torc*' (boar).

Macwilliam: Edward *Makwillyam* 1461 Fine (Ess). 'Son of *William*'.

Macy: *v.* MASSEY

Maddams: John *Madame* 1327 SRY. A nickname.

Madder, Madders, Mader: Thomas *Mader* 1221 Cur (Nf); Jacobus *le Madur* 1275 RH (L). OE *mædere* 'madder', used for *madderer* 'dyer with or seller of madder'. cf. Walter *le Maderere* 1317 FFEss, Thomas (*le*) *Maderman* 1293 LLB A, 1300 LoCt, Robert *madermanger* 1230 P (Nth).

Maddison, Madison: Thomas *Madyson* 1425 FrY; William *Maddison* 1430 FeuDu; Edmund, Lancelot *Madyson* 1532 LP (Nth), 1537 FFEss. Usually a by-form of MATHIESON 'son of Matthew', but occasionally perhaps from *Maddy*, a pet-form of MAUD.

Maddock, Maddocks, Maddox, Maddick, Madicks, Madocks, Mattack, Mattacks, Mattock, Mattocks, Mattick, Mattuck: *Madoch* 1066 DB (Gl); Oenus *filius Madoc* 1160 P (Sa); *Maddock*

le Waleys 1283 AssSt; William *Madoc* 1274 RH (Sa); Robert *Mattok* 1290 AssCh; Robert *Madduk*', Stephen *Madek*' 1297 MinAcctCo (W, Co). OW *Matōc*, Welsh *Madawc*, *Madog* 'goodly'.

Madel(l): *v.* MALE

Mader: *v.* MADDER

Madge, Maggs: *Magge* 1246 AssLa, c1248 Bec (Wa); Ailmundus, John *Magge* 1200 P (L), 1279 RH (Hu); John *Magges* 1327 SRSf. *Magge* may be *Magg*, a short form of the common *Magot*, *Magota* 1208 Cur (Nf), a hypocoristic of *Margaret*, or for *Madge* (*Margery*).

Madgett: William *Maggard* 1327 SRSf; Samuel *Maggett* 1647 RothwellPR (Y). *Magge* (Margery), plus the suffix -(h)ard.

Madle: *v.* MALE

Maffey: *v.* MORFEY

Maffre: *Matfridus*, *Mafrei* filius Kipping 1185–6 P (Nth); Henry *Matefrei* 1208 Cur (Sf); Francis *Maffry* 1674 HTSf. OFr *Mafreiz*, OG *Mathefrid* 'power-peace'.

Magee: *v.* MCGEE

Mager: *v.* MAUGER

Maggs: *v.* MADGE

Magill: *v.* MCGILL

Magnus, Magnusson, Manus, McManus: *Magnus* de Weitecroft Hy 2 DC (L); Hugo *Magnus* c1114 Burton (St); John *M'Manis* 1506 Black. ON *Magnus*, Lat *magnus* 'great'. The first of this name was Magnus I, King of Norway and Denmark (d. 1047), named after Charlemagne (Carolus *Magnus*), under the impression that *Magnus* was a personal-name. It became the name of many Scandinavian kings and was very popular in Shetland where *Magnusson* also survives as *Manson*. In Scotland it has given *McManus*.

Magowan: *v.* MACGOWAN

Magrath, Magraw: *v.* MACRAE

Magson: William *Maggessone* 1327 SRSf; Hugh *Maggesone* 1332 SRSt. 'Son of *Magg* (Margaret).'

Maguiness, Maguinness, Magennies, Maginniss: Irish *Mag Aonghuis* 'Son of *Angus*'. cf. Scottish MACINNES.

Mahood: *v.* MAUD

Maiden, Maydon: Robert *Maiden*, *Maide* 1197–8 P (Nf); Adam *le Maiden* 1279 RH (C). 'The maiden', a derogatory nickname.

Maidens: Geoffrey *Maidens* 1225 AssSo; Thomas *del Maydenes* 1345 AssSt. cf. PARSONS.

Maides: Abram *Maide* 1185 P (Co); John *Mayde* 1327 SRWo. 'The maid.' cf. MAIDEN.

Maidman, Maidment, Maitment: Richard *Maydenemon* 1275 SRWo; Robert *Maideneman* 1327 SRSx; William *Maideman* 1332 SRSr. 'Servant of the maidens.'

Mailer, Mailler, Maylor, Meyler: (i) *Meilerus* frater Laissioc 1160 P (Sa); Robertus *filius Meilir* 1255 RH (Sa); William *le Maillier* 1203 P (Wa), *le Mailur* 1262 HPD (Ess); Ralph *Meillur* 1227 AssBeds; Walter *Meyler* 1255 RH (Sa); Philip *le Mayllur* 1268 AssSo. The surname is usually occupative, from ME *amel*, with loss of *a* in *ameillur*

(OFr *esmailleur*), 'enameller'. cf. AMBLER. We have also a Welsh personal-name, *Meilyr*, OW **Maglorīx* (Jackson 625). There was a Breton saint *Maglorius*. (ii) In Scotland, from Mailer in Forteviot (Perthshire): Johan *de Malere* 1296 Black (Perth).

Main(e), Mains: *v.* MAYNE

Mainer: *v.* MAYNER

Mainerd: *v.* MAYNARD

Mainwaring, Manwaring, Mannering: Ralph *de Maisnilwarin* 1185 P (L); Thomas *de Meinwaring* 1260 AssCh; Randoll *Manwaryng* Hy 8 StarChSt; Arthur *Mainering* 1714 Shef. From a place named Mesnilwarin 'the manor of Warin'.

Mair: Symon *le Mare* 1296 Black (Perth); John *Mair* 1453 ib. Gael *maor* 'officer'. In Scotland 'Mair was the designation of an officer who executed summonses and other legal writs' and was used not only of the king's herald or sergeant but also of such officers as a head forester. *v.* also MAYER.

Maisey, Maizey, Maysey, Meysey, Meazey: Geoffrey *de Maisi* 1130 P (Sr). From Maizy (Aisne) or Maisy (Calvados).

Maitland: Richard *Maltalant* 1170 P (Nb); William *Mautalent* 1208 Cur (Nb), 1221 Black; Gilbert *de Maltalent* c1215 Black; Richard *de Mauteland* a1315 ib.; Robert *Matilland*, *Maitland*, 1417, 1424 ib. In England, where the surname was not uncommon, this appears to be a nickname for one with discourteous, unpleasant manners (OFr *maltalent*), but in Scotland there are sufficient examples with *de* to show that it derives from a place-name. Dauzat derives the French surname from Mautalant (Pontorson) 'peu gracieux'.

Major: *v.* MAUGER

Majoribanks: *v.* MARJORIBANKS

Makepeace, Makepiece: Gregory *Makepais* 1219 FrLeic; Thomas *Makepays* 1340 FFSt. 'Make peace', peace-maker.

Makin, Makins, Making, Makings, Meaken, Meakin, Meakins, Meakings, Meekings, Meekins, Mekking: (i) *Maikin* de Eylesburi 1212–23 Bart; *Maikin* Sutor 1311 HPD (Ess); Peter *Maykyn* 1319 FFEss; John *Maykyn*, *Makyn* 1362, 1368 LLB G; John *Mekyn* 1486 KentW; Thomas *Meekin* 1622 PrGR; William *Makin*, Widow *Makinge* 1674 HTSf. *May-kin*, a diminutive of *May*, a hypocoristic of *Mayhew* (Matthew). (ii) Robert *Maidekyn* 1327 PN K 554; Jeva *Maydekyng* 1327 SRC. *Maide-kin*, 'little maid', a nickname.

Malcolm: Norman *filius Malcolumbe* 1066 DB (L, Y); *Malculum* 1192 P (Sa); *Maukolum* 1207 Cur (Ha); Aleyn *fitz Maucolum* 1296 Black. Gaelic *Mael Coluimb* 'devotee of (St) *Columba*'. As a surname its use is comparatively modern.

Malcolmson, Malcomson: Symon *Malcomesson* 1296 Black. 'Son of *Malcolm*.'

Mald: *v.* MAUD

Male, Males, Madle: Robert *le Masle* 1187 P (Berks); Osbert *le Madle* 1202 FFEss; Stephen *Male* 1230 P (Ess). OFr *masle* 'male, masculine'.

William *le Masle* (1280), *le Madle* (1303), or *le Male* (1305) has left his name in Marles Fm in Epping Upland (PN Ess 24). For forms, cf. GREALEY.

Malet: *v.* MALLET

Malin, Malins, Mallin: *Malina* 1212 Cur (Nt); *Malyn* del Wllehous 1277 Wak (Y); John, Richard *Malin* 1297 SRY, 1327 SRDb; John *Malynes* 1358 Putnam (Wa). *Mal-in*, a diminutive of *Malle* (1297 Wak), a pet-name for *Mary*.

Malindine: *v.* MALLANDAIN

Maliphant: Geoffrey *Malenfant* 1205 P (Sf); William *Malefant* 1448 Pat. OFr *mal enfant* 'naughty child'.

Malise, Meliss, Melles, Mellis, Melliss, Mellish: *Malis* c1190 Black; Gillemycell *Malys* 1481 ib.; John *Mellish* 1771 ib.; David *Meliss* 1773 ib. Gael *Maol Iosa*, EIr *Mælisu* 'tonsured servant of Jesus'.

Malkin, Maulkin: Ricardus *filius Malkyn* 1297 SRY; John *Malekin* 1284 RamsCt (Hu); William *Malkyn* 1297 MinAcctCo. A diminutive of *Mall* (Mary).

Malkinson: Walter *Malkinesone* 1327 SRSx. 'Son of *Malkin*.'

Mallandain, Mallandaine, Mallandin, Mallendine, Mallindine, Malidine: Gerard de *Manegeden* 1208 FFEss. From Manewden (Essex), formerly pronounced *Mallendine*.

Mallard: For *Maylard*, or, perhaps, OFr *malard* 'wild drake'.

Malleson: William *Malleson* 1332 SRCu. 'Son of *Mall* (Mary).'

Mallet, Mallett, Mallette, Malet: Robert *Malet* 1086 DB (Sf); William, Gilbert *Malet* 1166 DC (L), 1185 Templars (So); William *Malait* 1230 P (K); Irveyus *Maleit* ib. (Berks). *Maleit* is OFr *maleit*, past participle of *maleīr*, 'cursed'. This is certainly the origin of some Norman surnames, but the three DB tenants-in-chief, frequently mentioned and invariably as *Malet*, may have brought with them a Norman patronymic, a diminutive of *Malo*, the popular form of the name of St *Maclovius*, a 6th-century Welsh monk who worked in Brittany, which survives in Saint-Malo and in the church of Saint-Maclou in Rouen. *Malo*, *Malet* and *Maclou* survive in France, the latter, particularly in Seine-Inférieure, Eure and Calvados. Tradition claims that the surname of William Malet, founder of Eye Priory, arose 'ob bellicam fortitudinem eo quod in præliis hostes ut malleo contunderet'. This is supported by the form *Gulielmo agnomine Mal(l)eto* in Orderic and William of Poitiers. When William Malet was banished in 1109, his son Hugh took the name of *Fichet* which was retained by his son Hugh, although his eldest son reverted to *Malet* (A. Malet, *An English Branch of the Malet Family* (1885), 7, 23–4, 102–3). This undoubtedly implies that Hugh regarded both surnames as nicknames with very similar meanings, both suited to a knight expert in the use of lance (cf. FITCH) and mace, the *mailz de fer* of the *Chanson de Roland*. OFr *maillet*, *mallet*, a diminutive of *mail*, *mal* (Lat *malleus*) 'hammer'. cf.

OFr *mailleor* 'hammerer, smith', and v. MARTEL. In England the chief source of the surname is *Mal-et*, a diminutive of *Mall* (Mary): *Maleta* 1219 AssY. *Mallet* may also be a late development of *Mallard*.

Mallin: v. MALIN

Mallinson, Mallison: John *Malynessone* 1317 Pat (Y); Thomas *Malisone* 1445 Black (Aberdeen). 'Son of *Malin*.' *Mallison* may also derive from *Mallet* (Mary): William *Malitesoun* 1469 Black (Aberdeen).

Mallory: Geoffrey *Maloret* 1086 DB (Do); Richard *Mallorei* c1155 DC (Nt); William *Maleuerei* 1170 P (Y); Henry *Mallore* 1195 P (Db); Robert *Mallory* 1255 Fees (Nth). OFr *maloret* (*maleuré*, *maloré*) 'the unfortunate', 'the unlucky'.

Mallot: *Malota* 1221 AssWa; Isabella *Malot* 1327 SRSf; Mariota *Mallot* 1332 SRCu. *Mal-ot*, a diminutive of *Mall* (Mary).

Malone: Ir *Ó Maoileoin* 'descendant of *Maoleoin*' (servant of St John).

Malpas, Malpass, Melpuss, Morpuss: Henry *Malpas*, *Maupas* 1203 Cur (Y), 1219 AssY; Walter *de Malpas* 1275 SRWo. From Malpas (Ches, Cornwall) or some French Malpas or Maupas.

Malster: Robert *le Maltester* 1279 MESO (Y); John *le Malstere* 1327 SRSf. A feminine form of *Malter*, as a surname, used only of men.

Malt: v. MAUD

Maltas: v. MALTHOUSE

Maltby, Maultby: Robert *de Maltebi* 1169 P (Nf); Andrew *de Malteby* 1219 AssY; Robert *Maltby*, *Mawteby* 1378 AssLo, 1439–40 Past. From Maltby (Lincs, NR, WRYorks), or Mautby (Norfolk).

Malter: (i) Roger, John *le Malter* 1319 *SR* (Ess); 1336 ColchCt. A derivative of OE *mealt* 'malt', a maltster. cf. Hugh *le Maltmakere* 1255 RH (Bk), Peter *le Maltmetere* 1271 AD i (Mx), William *Maltmelnere* 1214 FFK, John *le Maltemeller* 1327 Pinchbeck (Sf). (ii) John *Maletere* 1198 FFK; Ralph *de Maleterr'* 1211 Cur (Nb). From some French place *Maleterre* 'poor ground'.

Malthouse, Malthus, Maltus, Maltas: Fulk *atte Malthuse* 1297 MELS (Sx); William *Malthouse* 1497 FrY. 'Worker at the malt-house.'

Maltman: Richard *Maltmon* 1332 SRWa; John *Malteman* 1471 Eynsham (O). cf. MALTER.

Maltravers: v. MATRAVERS

Malyan, Malyon: John *Marion*, *Malyon* 1351–4 PN Ess 483. *Marion*, a diminutive of *Mary*, with change of *r—n* to *l—n*.

Man, Mann: *Man* 1066 DB (Y, Sf); Ricardus, Hugo *filius Man* 1188 P (L), Hy 3 Colch (Ess); Algar, William *Man* 1141 ELPN, 1185 Templars (Y); Alan *le Man* 1288 FFSf; Walter *le Mon* 1327 SRDb. The OE personal name *Mann* 'man' was still in use, though not common, in the 12th century and was sometimes, no doubt, adopted as a surname. The usual source is OE *mann* 'man' though the exact sense is not always clear. A common meaning is, no doubt, 'servant' as in the

compounds *Harriman*, *Ladyman*, *Monkman*, etc. Sometimes it may correspond to such a phrase as *homo Bainardi* 'the man of Bainard', one who owed him feudal service. At times it may have reference to a lower rank in the social scale, *nativus* 'bondman'. In 1279 Ralph de Ginges granted to Simon de Duntona (both of Essex) Peter *Man* son of Robert *Man* his *nativus* with all his family and all his chattels for 40s. sterling (Bart i. 503).

Manby: Antonius *de Manebi* 1181 P (L); Hugh *de Mageneby* 1226 FFY; Thomas *de Mauneby* 1336 FFY; Thomas *Manneby* 1403 IpmY. From Manby (Lincs), *Magnebi* 1212, or Maunby (NRYorks), *Magnebi* 1166.

Mancell: v. MANSEL

Mancer: v. MANSER

Manchip: v. MANSHIP

Manclark, Moakler, Mockler, Mokler: Roger *Malclerc* 1194 Cur (W); Walter *Mauclerc* 1207 Cur (L); Walter dictus *Manclerc* 1279 RH (O); John *Maucler* 1317 AD iv (Wa); William *Manclark* 1524 SRSf. OFr *mal*, *mau* and *clerc* 'bad cleric'. Walter *Mauclerc* 1275 RH (L) was Bishop of Carlisle. Pierre de Bretagne, similarly nicknamed, was unfrocked (Dauzat). *Manclark* is from *malclerc* with dissimilation of *l—l—r* to *n—l—r*; *Moakler*, *Mockler* are from *Maucler(c)*.

Mandeville, Manvell, Manville, Manwell: Goisfridus *de Magna uilla*, *de Manneuille* 1086 DB (Ess, K); Ernulf *de Mandeuill'* 1158 P (W); William *de Manevell'* 1210 Cur (Bk); William *de Manewell* 1296 SRSx. The Mandevilles, earls of Essex, came from Manneville (Seine-Inférieure); the Mandevilles of Earl's Stoke and Devon, from Magneville (La Manche); the undertenants of Montfort and the counts of Meulan, from Manneville-sur-Risle (Eure). v. ANF. Others may have come from Manneville (Calvados).

Manger, Monger: William *Manger'* 1255 RH (W); Richard *le Manger* 1275 SRWo; Robert *Monger'* 1316 Wak (Y). OE *mangere* 'monger, dealer, trader'.

Mangnall, Mangold, Manknell: Geoffrey *Mangwinel* 1204 Cur (Pembroke); Stephen *Manguinel* 1212 Cur (Wa); Thomas *Mangenel* 1327 SRSx; John *Mangel*, *Mangulle* 1363, 1390 LLB G, H. 'A worker of the mangonel', OFr *mangonelle* 'a war engine for throwing stones'.

Manistre, Manisty: (i) William *Mannol(f)stygh* 1315–16 Wak (Y); Richard *Manaste* 1422 FrY. Manesty in Borrowdale (Cumberland) is *Manistie*, *Maynister* in 1564 (PN Cu 353). Whether the Yorkshire surnames derive thence is not certain but *Manesty* is a normal development of *Mannolfstygh* and Cumberland surnames are not uncommon in Yorkshire. (ii) William *Manitre* 1674 HTSf; John *Manister*, *Manester* ib.; Edmund *Manistre* ib.; Robert *Mannestey* ib. From Manningtree, on the Essex side of the Stour. Usually *Manitre*, it occurs as *Manystre* in 1291 and 1343 (PN Ess 343) and this appears to have been the local pronunciation which became *Manister*, *Manisty*.

Mankin: *Manekyn le Heumer* 1318 Pat (Lo);

Stephen, William *Manekyn* 1242 Fees (K), 1327 *SR* (Ess). *Man-kin*, a diminutive of *Man*, and, possibly, also of the noun, whence a nickname 'the little man'.

Manknell: *v.* MANGNALL

Manley, Manly, Manleigh: William *de Manelegh'* 1202 Fees (D); Alexander, James *Manly* 1363 AssY, 1642 PrD. From Manley (Ches, Devon), or 'dweller by the common wood'.

Mannell: *v.* MEYNELL

Mannering: *v.* MAINWARING

Manners: Reginald *de Meiniers* c1180 ANF (Sx); Walter *de Maners* c1230 Barnwell (C). From Mesnières (Seine-Inférieure). *v.* ANF.

Manning: *Mannicus* 1066 DB (Ess); Algarus *Manningestepsune* c1130 ELPN; Seman *filius Manning* 1181 P (Ess); Ainulf, Richard *Manning* 1190 P (K), 1221 *ElyA* (Sf). OE *Manning*.

Mansel, Mansell, Mancell, Maunsell: *Mansell de Patleshull* 1203 AssSt; Thomas *filius Manselli* 1256 AssNb; Turstinus *Mansel* 1148 Winton (Ha); Robert *le Mansel* 1171 P (Ha); Andrew *Maunsel* c1180 Black. From a personal-name or from OFr *Mancel*, an inhabitant of Maine or its capital Le Mans. In France *Mansel* was also a feudal tenant, occupier of a *manse*, land sufficient to support a family.

Manser, Mancer: (i) *Manasserus* de Danmartin 1166 RBE (Sf); *Manserus* filius Joia 1186 P (L); *Maneserus Judeus* 1191 P (L); *Manaserus* de Hasting', de Hamwold' 1207-8 Cur (Sx, K); *Manasserus, Manser* Aguliun 1211-12 Cur (Ha); Ranulfus *filius Manser* 1221 *ElyA* (Sf); *Mancerus* le Parmenter 1296 SRSx; Walter *Manser* 1250 Fees (Sf); Alan *Mauncer* 1296 SRSx; John *Maunser* 1327 *SR* (Ess). There can be little doubt that this must be the Hebrew *Manasseh* 'one who causes to forget', used undoubtedly of Jews (*Manaser* Judeus 1219 AssY), but also of others. The DB tenant-in-chief *Manasses* was presumably a Norman, whilst frater *Manasserus* of the Hospital of St John of Jerusalem (1219 Cur, Beds) cannot have been a Jew. Mansers Shaw in Battle owes its name to the family of *Manasseh* de Herst, William Fitz *Manser* of Herst and *Manserus* de Scotegny (PN Sx 500). (ii) Nicholas *le Mauncer* 1297 LLB B; Richard *le mancher* 1292 SRLo. A derivative of OFr *manche* 'handle, haft', a maker of hafts for knives. Richard is also called *le Haftere* (1301 Husting).

Manship, Manchip: Ailsi *de Menscipe* (*Maneschipe*) 1167 P (Y); Philip *Mansipe* 1189 P (Nf); John *Manshipe* 1247 AssBeds; Robert *Mansipe* 1279 RH (O); Alexander *de Manshipe* 1319 SRLo; John *Manschupe* 1327 SRSo. From Minskip (WRYorks), Manships Shaw (Surrey) or Manchips Field in Bishop's Stortford (Herts), all from OE *gemænscipe* 'community, fellowship', used of land held in common, and also in its abstract sense.

Manson: (i) John *Mannisson* 1305 FFSf. 'Son of *Mann*.' (ii) Angus *Mangson* 1446 Black (Kirkwall); David *Manson* 1504 ib. For *Magnusson*. Common in Shetland.

Mantel, Mantell, Mantle: Turstinus *Mantel* 1086 DB (Bk); Robert *Mantell'* 1176 P (Berks). OFr *mantel* 'cloak, mantle', a nickname or trade-name.

Manton: Odinell *de Maneton'* 1202 AssNth; Thomas *de Maneton* 1227-8 FFEss; William *Mantoun* 1327 SRC. From Manton (Lincs, Notts, Rutland, Suffolk, Wilts).

Manus: *v.* MAGNUS

Manvell, Manville: *v.* MANDEVILLE

Manwaring: *v.* MAINWARING

Manwell: *v.* MANDEVILLE

Manwood: Alice *de la Manewod* 1332 SRSx. 'Dweller by the common wood', OE *(ge)mæne* and *wudu*.

Manyweathers: cf. FAIRWEATHER.

Maples: Robert *atte Mapele* 1285 Ass (Ess); John *Mapel* 1327 SRC; John *del Mapples* 1348 Shef. 'Dweller by the maple(s)', OE *mapul*.

Maplethorpe, Mapplethorp: Gilbert *de Maupertorp'* 1219 AssY. From Mablethorpe (Lincs).

Marber, Marbrow, Marbler: Reginald *le Marbrer* 1230 P (Ess); Godfrey *le Marbeler* alias *le Marberer* 1265 Ipm (Sr); Walter *le Marbeler, le Marbrer, le Marberer* 1281, 1288 LLB B, 1292 SRLo. OFr *marbrier* 'quarrier, hewer of marble', carver or worker in marble. At Westminster in 1385 Thomas Canon of Corfe, marbrer, was paid £30 6*s.* 8*d.* for making stone images in the likeness of kings, to stand in the Great Hall. Marble was also used for paving in churches, etc. In 1312 Adam le Marbrer undertook to pave part of St Paul's with squares of marble (Building 32, 147).

Marble: Robert *Marbull*, Hugh *Marble* 1479, 1531 AD i (Mx). Metonymic for *Marbler*.

March: Henry, William *de la Marche* 1295 Barnwell (C), 1307 Oseney (O); Hugo *atte Marche* 1349 LLB G. 'Dweller by the boundary', ME, OFr *marche*.

Marchant, Marchent, Marchand, Marquand, Merchant, Le Marchand, Le Marquand, Le Marchant, Lemarchand: Roger *Marcand* (*Marchand'*) 1202 P (Berks); Roger *Marchaunt*, Herueus *Merchant* 1219 AssY; Ranulph *le Marchand* 1240 FFEss; Reginald *le Marchant* 1247 FFC; Thomas *le Markaund* 1274 RH (So). OFr *marchand, marchëant* 'merchant, trader'.

Marchbank(s): *v.* MARJORIBANKS

Marcy: Ralph *(de) Marci* 1086 DB (Ess). From Marcy (La Manche). *v.* also MASSEY.

Mares: *v.* MARRIS

Margary, Margery: *Margeria* 1219 AssY; Galfridus *filius Margerye* 1221 *ElyA* (Sf); Robert, John *Margerie* 1195 P (Gl), 1275 RH (K); Agnes *Mariory* 1327 SRSf. *Margerie* was a French popular form of *Marguérite* (Margaret).

Margerison, Margereson, Margerrison: Robert *Mariorison* 1379 PTY. 'Son of *Margery*.'

Margerson, Margesson, Margison: Richard *Margison* 1683 EA (OS) iv (Sf). 'Son of *Margery*.' Also for *Margetson*.

Margetson, Margitson: Richard *Margretson* 1381 PTY; Thomas *Margetson* 1425 DbCh. 'Son of *Margaret*.'

Margetts: John *Margaret'* 1275 RH (Sf); John *Marget* 1524 SRSf. From *Margaret* 'pearl', a common medieval woman's name, found as *Merget* in 1460 and *Margat* in 1534 (ODCN).

Mariner, Marriner, Marner: Hugo *le marinier* 1197 P (O); Ace *Meriner* 1211-23 Clerkenwell (Lo); Ivo *le Mariner* 1228 Cl (Bk); Peter *le Marner* 1327 SRSx. AFr *mariner*, OFr *marinier*, *marnier*, *merinier* 'sailor, seaman'.

Marion, Marians, Maryan, Maryon, Marrian, Marrion: *Marion* Lambert 1379 PTY; John *Mariun* 1279 RH (C); Richard *Marioun* 1350 LLB F. A diminutive of *Mary*.

Maris: *v.* MARRIS

Marjoribanks, Majoribanks, Marchbank, Marchbanks: John *Marjoribankis* 1550 Black; James *Marchbank* 1664 ib. The barony of Ratho was granted to Robert Bruce as a marriage portion to his daughter Marjorie on her marriage in 1316 to Walter, High Steward of Scotland, ancestor of the royal house of Stewart (Burke). The lands, known as Ratho-Marjoribankis, came into the possession of a family named Johnson who assumed the surname of Marjoribanks (Black).

Mark, Marke, Marks: (i) Rogerus *filius Markes* 1207 Cur (Ha); *Marc* le draper 1292 SRLo; Robertus *Marcus* 1148 Winton (Ha); Philip *Marc* 1209 P (Nt); Robertus *Markes* 1288 RamsCt (C). *Mark*, Lat *Marcus*. Never a very common name. (ii) Adelolfus *de Merc* 1086 DB (Ess); Geoffrey *de Merc* 1130 P (Ess). From Marck (Pas-de-Calais). (iii) Simon *del Merc* 1208 Cur (Ess); Matilda *de la Merke* 1227 FFEss; Aylward *atte Merke* 1296 SRSx. 'Dweller by the boundary', OE *mearc*.

Marker: (i) Symon *filius Markere* 1168 P (D); *Markerus* de Torneberga 1176 P (Bk); Walter, Eborard *Marker* 1297 SRY, 1309 SRBeds. Probably an OG *Marchari* 'boundary-army'. *Mearc-* seems not to occur as an OE theme. (ii) William, Agnes *le Marker(e)* 1185 P (Ess), 1260 Oseney (O); Reginald *le Merkere* 1275 RH (Nf). Thuresson's suggestion that this is a derivative of OE *mearcian* 'to mark', a marker of game or a stamper or brander, is not satisfying. The name may at times mean 'dweller by the boundary' (cf. MARK) but examples are more numerous than usual for such a toponymic. It may be a survival of OE *mearcere* 'notary, writer'.

Markham: Jordan, Roger *de Marcham* 1204 Pl (Nt); Richard, Emma *de Markham* 1259 FFEss, 1371 AssL; John *Markham* 1408 IpmNt. From Markham (Notts).

Markson: William *Markeson* 1445 FrY. 'Son of *Mark*.'

Marler, Marlor: Hugo *le Merlere* 1275 SRWo; Thomas *le Marlere* 1277 *Ely* (Sf); William *marlur* 1297 MinAcctCo (Y). A derivative of ME, OFr *marle* 'marl', a hewer or quarrier of marl. cf. William *le Marlehewere* 1327 SRSt.

Marley, Marlee: William *de Merlai* c1145-65 Seals; Thomas *de Mardele* 1208 Pl (Y); John *de Marley* 1285 Riev; William *de Marleye* 1306 FFEss. From Marley (Devon, Kent, WRYorks), Marley Farm in Brede (Sussex), or Mearley (Lancs), *Merlay* 1241.

Marlow, Marlowe: Edric *Merlaue* 1066 DB (Bk); Wido *de Merlaue* 1225 Cur (Bk); Richard *de Merlawe* 1325-6 CorLo; Joan *Marlowe* 1534 CantW. From Marlow (Bucks), but there was evidently also some confusion with MARLEY, cf. Richard *Merleye*, and Alice *Marlowe* his wife, 1488, 1494 ArchC xxxix.

Marner: *v.* MARINER

Marney, Marnie, de Marney: Robert *de Mareigni* 1168 P (Ess); William *de Marenni* 1207 Cur (Ess), *de Marny* 1284 FFEss. From Marigni (La Manche).

Marquand: *v.* MARCHANT

Marr, Marre, Marrs: Roger, James *de Mar* 1182 P (Y), 1296 Black (Aberdeen); Ralph *atte Mar* 1297 SRY; William *del Marre* 1302 SRY. From Marr (WRYorks), High or Low Marr in Wheldrake or The Marrs in Swine (ERYorks), Mar (Aberdeenshire), or from residence near a pool or marsh (ON *marr*).

Marrable: Roger *Mirabell'* 1230 P (D); Richard *Marabile* 1244 Rams (Beds); Robert *Merable* 1327 PN Wt 253. *Mirabel*, a woman's name latinized as *Mirabilis* 1210 Cur (Wo) 'marvellous, wonderful'.

Marriage: Alice *Marriage* 1616 Bardsley (Wa); Samuel *Marredge* 1626 ib. (Mx); Stephen *Marridge* 1709 ib. (Lo). In Essex and Suffolk, probably from a lost place in Finchingfield or Aythorpe Roding, OE *(ge)mære* and *hæcc* 'boundary-gate', found as a surname: William *Marhach'*, *Mar(r)ach* 1377, 1379 AssEss. Marriage Fm 'boundary-ridge' (PN K 386) and Marridge 'meadow-ridge' (PN D 285) both gave rise to surnames in the 13th century.

Marrian, Marrion: *v.* MARION

Marrin: *Marinus* clericus 1192 P (Lo); *Marina* 1230 P (Nt), 1302 FA (Bk); Walter *Maryne* 1327 SRSo. There were several saints named *Marinus* and one *Marina* (Lat *marinus* 'of the sea'). Neither name was common in England.

Marriott, Marritt, Marryatt: *Mariota* Hoppesort 1195 FFSf; *Mariota* 1200 P (Lei), 1219 AssY; William, Hervicus *Mariot* 1185 Templars (Wa), 1210 Cur (C). *Mari-ot*, a very common diminutive of *Mary*. *Marryatt* is probably from OE *Mærgeat*: Richard *Meryet* 1297 MinAcctCo; William *Mariet* 1327 SRDb. cf. MERRETT.

Marris, Maris, Mares: Clarenbodo *de Maresc*, Richard *de Maris* 1086 DB (Bk, K); William *de Mares* 1191 P (K); Aldwin *des Mareis* 1199 P (Gl); Henry *Mareys* 1252 Rams (Hu); Walter *del Mareys*, Richard *de Marise* 1275 SRWo. From (Le) Marais (Calvados) or from residence near some marsh (OFr *marais*, Norm-Picard *marese*).

Marrow, Marrows: John *Marwe* c1208 FrLeic; Geoffrey *le Marewe* 1276 RH (C). ME *marwe* 'companion, mate, lover'.

Marryatt: *v.* MARRIOTT

Marsden: Alan *de Marchesden* 1246 AssLa; Johanna *de Merssden* 1379 PTY; Peter *Marsden* 1459 Kirk. From Marsden (Lancs, WRYorks).

Marsh, Mersh: Godard *le la Merse* 1194 P (So); Henry *del Merse* 1212 Cur (Y); William *atte Mersche* 1296 SRSx. 'Dweller near a marsh' (OE *mersc*).

Marshall, Marschall, Marskell, Mascall, Maskall, Maskell, Maskill: Goisfridus *Marescal* 1084 GeldR (W); Hugo *Maskercal* 1087–97 Crispin (Mx); William *Marescald* 1100–30 OEByn; Roger *Mascherell* 1130 P (L); Rainald *le mareschall* c1140 DC (L); Robert *Maskerel* 1166 RBE (Sf); Henry *le Marscal* 1238 AssSo; John *Marschal* 1296 SRSx. OFr *mareschal, marescal, marescald, marechault*, 'one who tends horses, especially one who treats their diseases; a shoeing smith, a farrier' (1258 NED). Early examples may refer to a high officer of state (cf. the Earl Marshal). Later, the surname is equated with *Smith* and *Faber*. Mascallsbury in White Roding (from Robert *le Marescal* 1235) is *Maskerelesburi, Maskelesbury* 1351, *Mascallesbury* 1476 (PN Ess 495).

Marshman, Mashman: Edmund *le Mersman* 1233 HPD (Ess); John *Mershman* 1301 ArchC 9. 'Dweller in the marsh.' John *Mersman* and Richard *ate Mersshe* lived in the same parish (1317 AssK). cf. William *le Mersher* 1327 SRSx.

Marskell: *v.* MARSHALL

Marsom, Marson: Robert *Marson* 1596 Musters (Sr). From Marston, a common place-name, often spelled and pronounced *Marson*. Later, the surname acquired an intrusive *t*, restoring it to its earlier form. *Marson* is now less common than *Marston*, while *Marsom* is rare after about 1720. At Olney (Bk), Thomas and Elizabeth *Marson* (1796–8) appear as *Marston* in 1801 and 1804, whilst their daughter Sophia (d.1806) is called *Marson*. At Church Leigh (Staffs), William, son of James *Marston* (b.1685), was baptized as *Marston* in 1721, but is called *Marson* on his tombstone (1787), whilst his son was baptized and married as *Marston* but buried as *Marson* which has since been the family name. *v.* MARSTON.

Marsters: *v.* MASTER

Marsterson: *v.* MASTERSON

Marston: Hugh *de Merstona* 1170 Eynsham; William *de Merstun*' 1231 Cur (Herts); Sylvester *de Marston* 1349–51 FrC; John *Marsten* alias Mason 1565 NorwDep. From one or other of the many places of this name, or from Merston (Kent, Sussex, Wight). *v.* MARSOM.

Martel, Martell: *Martellus* 1163–6, c1187 DC (L); *Martel* Saladin 1222 Cur (Nf); Goisfridus *Martel* 1086 DB (Ess); William *Martel* 1148 Eynsham (O). The personal name is a hypocoristic of *Martin*. The surname may derive from this (cf. Martin *Martel* Hy 2 DC (L)) or be a nickname from OFr *martel* 'hammer' (1474 NED), here, no doubt, the *martel de fer*, the iron hammer or mace of medieval warfare. The first bearer of the name was Charles son of Pépin d'Héristal 'qui martela les Sarrasins' at the battle of Poitiers in 732 and received the name of Charles *Martel* (Moisy). Later, the name was probably occupational, 'smith'.

Marter, Martyr: Robert *Lamartre* 1130 P (O); Walter *martre* 1148 Winton (Ha); William *le Marter* 1275 SRWo. A nickname from the weasel, OFr *martre*, ME *martre, marter*.

Martin, Martins, Marten, Martens, Martyn, Martyns: *Martinus* 1066 Winton (Ha), c1166 NthCh (Nth); Walter, Helewis *Martin* 1166 RBE (C), Ric 1 Cur. MedLat *Martinus*, a diminutive of *Martius*, from *Mars* the god of war. A very popular christian name and an early surname. The Manx *Martin* is a contraction of KILMARTIN.

Martinson: John *Martynson* 1463 Black. 'Son of *Martin*.'

Marton, Martin, Merton: Adam *de Mertuna* 1189 Sol; Thomas *de Marton* 1212 P (Y); Ellis *de Martin*, William *de Mertton*' 1249 AssW; John *Merten* alias Noble, William *Martene* alias Perham 1545, 1576 SRW. From one or other of the many places called Marton, Merton, or Martin.

Martyr: *v.* MARTER

Marval, Marvel, Marvell: (i) Richard *Merveyle* 1275 RH (C); Roger *Marvell* 1524 SRSf. OFr *merveille* 'the marvel'. cf. William *le Merveillus* 1186 P (L) 'the wonderful'. (ii) Ranulph *de Mereville* 1306 FFEss. From Merville (Nord, Somme). (iii) Marvell (Isle of Wight) derives from a family of Merryfield: *de Meriefeld* 1255, *Marfeides* 1558, *Marvell* 1608 (PN Wt 102).

Marwood: (i) William *Marwod, de Marrewod* 1312, 1365 FrY; William *Marwood* 1559 Pat (D). From Marwood (Devon, Durham). (ii) The name may sometimes represent OFr *Malregard* 'evil look, evil eye', *v.* OEByn 322, and cf. Richard *Malregard* c1170 Riev; Walter *Malreward* 1200 Cur; Thomas *Maureward* 1208 Cur (Do); Robert *Mareward* 1242 Fees (W). Goadby Marwood (Leics) owes the second part of its name to William *Maureward* who held part of the manor in 1316.

Maryan, Maryon: *v.* MARION

Maryson: Willelmus *filius Marie* 1292 ELPN is identical with William *Marysone* 1298 LoCt. 'Son of *Mary*.'

Mascall: *v.* MARSHALL

Maser: Adam, William, Walter *le Mazerer* 1275 RH (Nth), 1307 LLB C. *Maser* is metonymic for *maserer*, a maker of masers (ME *maser*, OFr *masere* 'a maple-wood bowl'). *v.* MASLEN.

Mash: Robert *Masshe* 1524 SRSf. Probably for MARSH.

Masheder, Masheter, Mashiter, Massheder, Mesheder, Messiter: Richard *Maschrother* 1498 FrY; Robert *Masherudder* 1517 GildY; Peter *Mashrether* 1584 Bardsley (Ess); Janet *Masheder*, Agnes *Masheter* 1637 LaWills; Ellen *Masheder* or *Mashred* 1663 ib. Although the evidence is not quite conclusive, this seems to be a nickname for one who steeped malt. cf. 'Maschel, or rothyr, or mascherel. *Remulus, palmula, mixtorium*' (Prompt-Parv). 'A rudder (so called from its resemblance in shape), or instrument to stir the meash-fatte with' was one of the instruments of the brewhouse. Peter Mashrether came from Chigwell, not far from Mashiter's Hill in Romford, so called from a family of Mashiter.

Mashman: *v.* MARSHMAN

Maskall, Maskell, Maskill: *v.* MARSHAL

Maskery, Maskrey: Henry *le Macegre* 1260 AssY; Syremon *le Macekre* 1275 SRWo; Henry *Maskery* 1327 SRDb. OFr *macegref*, an altered form of *macecrier* 'butcher'. cf. MASSACRIER.

Maslen, Maslin: (i) Ricardus *filius Mascelin* 1187 P (Sa); Alexander *filius Macelini, Mazelini* 1203 Cur (Bk); Richer *Mazelin* 1168–75 Holme (Nf); William *Masselyn* 1327 SRC. OFr *Masselin*, OG *Mazelin*, a diminutive of *Mazo*. It might also be a double diminutive of *Maci* or *Masse* 'Matthew'. There was also a feminine *Mazelina* (1212 Cur (Nf), 1221 AssWa), probably a diminutive of *Matilda*. (ii) William *le Mazelin* 1282 AD ii (Mx). OFr, ME *maselin*, 'mazer, bowl of maple-wood', used by metonymy for a maker of these. William *le Mazeliner* 1283 LLB A (perhaps the same man as the above) is also called *le Mazerer* (1281), *le Mazener* (1282), *le Maceliner* (1292 ib.). cf. MASER.

Mason, Massen, Masson, Machen, Machent, Machin, Machon: John *Macun* c1130 AC (Lo); Ace *le mazun* 1193 P (He); Richard *machun* 12th DC (L); Roger *le Mason'* 1200 Oseney (O); Godfrey *le Mascun* 1203 FFEss; Osbert *le Masson* 1279 RH (O); Adam *le Machon* 1279 AssNb; Richard *Machen* 1284 AssSt; Thomas *Machyn* 1439 AD iv (Wa). ONFr *machun*, OCentrFr *maçon, masson* 'mason'. *v.* also MAYSON.

Massacrier: William *the Massacrer* 1235 FFY; Roger *le Macecrer* 1243 AssSo. OFr *macecrier* 'butcher'. A very rare surname. cf. MASKERY.

Masse: Osbertus *filius Masse* 1177 P (Sf); *Masse faber* 1219 AssY; Osbert *Masse* 1194 P (Nf). A pet-form of *Matthew*.

Massen: *v.* MASON

Masset: *Masota* de Middeton 1327 SRSx; *Mazota* Vyncent 1332 ib.; Richard *Masothe* 1279 RH (Bk); Richard *Masote* 1332 SRSx. A feminine diminutive of *Masse*, i.e. *Matthew*.

Massey, Massie, Massy, Macey, Macy: (i) *Mathiu, Maci* de Mauritania 1086 DB (Berks, Gl); *Masci* filius Mathei 1198 P (Nf); Alan *Macy* 1275 RH (Sf); William *Massy* 1330 NottBR. A pet-form of *Matthew*. (ii) Hamo *de Masci* 1086 DB (Ch), 1179 P (Db); Hugo *Maci* 1086 DB (Ha), *Mascy* 1221 Cur (Hu); John *de Maci* 1221 Cur (Mx). Hamo de Masci came from Macey (La Manche). Others may have come from Massy (Seine-Inférieure), Macé-sur-Orne (Orne) or La Ferté Macé (Orne). (iii) Ralph *Marci, de Marcei* 1086 DB (Ess); William *de Marsei* 1180 P (Nt). From Marcy (La Manche). Ralph's name survives in Stondon Massey, developing thus: *de Marcy* (1238), *Masse* (1542), *Massie* (1642 PN Ess 81).

Massinger: *v.* MESSENGER

Masson: *v.* MASON

Master, Masters, Marsters: (i) Robert *le Meistre*

1202 Cur (Berks); John *Maister* 1225 Lewes (C); Hubert *Mastres* 1279 RH (Hu); John *Mastere* 1379 PTY. ME *maister*, OFr *maistre* 'master'. The exact signification is not clear. It may refer to a schoolmaster (cf. 'Maystyr, *Magister, didascolus, petagogus*' PromptParv), to the master of a farm or house, or to the master of an apprentice. (ii) William *atte Maystres* 1327 SRSt. 'One who lived at the master's (house)', his servant, or, possibly, his apprentice. In Scotland the eldest sons of barons and the uncles of lords were called 'Masters'.

Masterman: John *Maystreman* 1327 SRC. 'Servant of the Master.'

Masterson, Marsterson: Robert called *Maistersone* 1300 Black (Galloway); Hugh *le fiz Mestre* c1320 Calv (Y); John *Maisterson* 1323 FrY. 'Son of the Master.'

Masterton: William *de Mastertone* 1296 Black (Fife); Symon *de Maysterton* 1357 ib.; Thomas *Masterton* 1476 ib. From the lands of Masterton (Dunfermline).

Mather, Mathur, Mathers, Matthers: Alan *le Mathere* 1249 AssW; Beatrix *Matther* 1396 NottBR; Margaret *Mather* 1524 SRSf; Thomas *Mathar* 1621 SRY. OE *mæðere* 'mower', reaper', not, as Guppy thought, confined to Lancs, Northumb, and Derby.

Mathes, Mathez, Mathie, Mathis, Mathys, Matthes, Matthey, Matthys: *Mathe* 1195 P (Nt); William son of *Mathie* 1332 SRCu; Hugh *Mathi* 1221 Cur (Herts); William *Mathy* 1275 RH (W); Henry *Matthe* 1279 RH (C); John *Mathis* 1674 HTSf. *Math* or *Mathi*, pet-forms of *Matthew*.

Matheson: *v.* MATHIESON

Mathew: *v.* MATTHEW

Mathieson, Mathison, Matheson, Matthison: John *Mathyson* 1392 Black (Angus). 'Son of *Mathi*.' *v.* MATHES.

Mathis: *v.* MATHES

Matland: *v.* MAITLAND

Maton, Matten, Mattin, Matton: William *Matun* 1275 RH (Nf); Matheon *Mateon* 1327 SRC; Robert *Maton*, William *Mathon*, Adam *Mathin* 1379 PTY. Diminutives of *Matthew*, from *Math* or *Mat*.

Matravers, Matraves, Mattravers, Maltravers: Hugo *Maltrauers, Malus Transitus* 1084 GeldR (So); Walter *Maltrauers* 1130 P (Do); Walter *de Matrauers* 1194 Cur (W). OF *mal travers* 'bad (difficult) passage'. One would assume that this was a place-name, like *Malpas* but no such French place has been noted, although the 1194 form suggests there was one. If a nickname, it probably denotes a man difficult to pass, one who can look after himself, a stout soldier.

Matt, Mattes, Matts: Adam *Matte* 1275 RH (W); Simon *Mat* 1309 FFEss. In view of the existence of *Matkin* and *Maton*, there must have been a diminutive *Mat* from *Matthew*. The surname may also be metonymic, for MATTER.

Mattack: *v.* MADDOCK

Mattar: *v.* MATTER

Matten: v. MATON
Matter, Mattar: Arnald *Matere* 1214 Cur (L); Richard *le Mattere* 1310 LLB B. A derivative of OE *matte* 'mat'. cf. John *Mattemaker* 1381 AssWa.
Matters: Alexander *Matras* 1379 PTY; John *Matres* 1438 FrY. *Matters* is, no doubt, for *Matres* 'mattrass', metonymic for 'mattrass-maker'. cf. Alice *Matresmaker* 1381 PTY.
Matthers: v. MATHER
Matthes: v. MATHES
Matthew, Matthews, Mathew, Mathewes, Mathews: *Mathiu, Matheus* 1086 DB; *Matheus* Baret c1150–5 DC (L); Alan *Mathew* 1260 AssC; John *Mathows* 1395 Whitby (Y). Hebrew *Mattathiah* 'gift of Jehovah', latinized as *Matthaeus* and *Mathaeus*, which in France became respectively *Mathieu* and *Mahieu* (v. MAYHEW). The name was introduced into England by the Normans and became very popular, with a variety of pet-forms and diminutives. v. also MACEY, MASSE, MASSET, MASSEY, MATHES, MATON.
Matthewman: Hugh *Mathewman* 1379 PTY; John *Mathyman* 1564 ShefA. 'Servant of *Matthew*.'
Matthewson, Mathewson: John *Matheuson* 1416 FrY; George *Mathowsone* 1539 FeuDu. 'Son of *Matthew*.'
Matthey, Mathie: v. MATHES
Mattick: v. MADDOCK
Mattimoe: William *Matheumogh* 1327 SRDb; Ann *Mathemore* 1619 GreenwichPR. 'Relative of *Matthew*.' cf. WATMOUGH.
Mattin: v. MATON
Mattingley, Mattingly: Stephen *de Madingel'*, *de Matingel'* 1206 Cur (Sr, Ha); Peter *de Mattingeley* 1249 IpmHa. From Mattingley in Heckfield (Hants).
Mattingson, Mattinson, Mattison, Matterson: Robert *Mattison* 1635 FrY; Thomas *Matterson* 1672 FrY. Probably from *Matonson* or *Mattinson* with the same development as *Pattinson*. v. MATON
Mattleson: v. MAUD
Mattock: v. MADDOCK
Matton: v. MATON
Mattravers: v. MATRAVERS
Mauchan: v. MAUGHAM
Maud, Maude, Mahood, Mawhood, Mald, Malt, Mault, Mold, Mould, Moulds, Moult, Mowat: *Mathild, Mathildis* 1086 DB; *Mahald regina* 1119 Colch (Ess); *Matilda* c1140 Holme (Nf); *Matildis* c1150 Gilb (L); *Mactilda* 1154–69 NthCh (Nth); *Matillis* temp. Stephen DC (L); *Mactildis* Hy 2 DC (L); *Mahald* 1172–80 DC (Lei); *Mahalt* Hy 2 Gilb (L), 1197 P (Wo); *Mahaut vidua* 1190 BuryS (Sf); Comitissa *Malt* 1275 RH (Sf); *Moude de Seint edmund* 1292 SRLo; *Mauld* 1303 ODCN; *Maud* 1314 Cl; Robert '*Maldes*man of the Ker' 1327 Pat (Y); *Molde, Moolde* 1450 ODCN; *Mawte* 1502 BuryW (Sf); Gilbert, William, Robert *Mald'* 1190 P (Ess, R, W); Smale *Mautild* 1199 P (Nf); Hugh *Mold* 1275 RH (Wo); Geoffrey *Maude* 1279 RH (Hu); John *Malt* 1279 RH (C); Gilbert *Maughtild* 1327 SR (Ess); William *Matild'* 1327

SRC; Geoffrey, Agnes *Molt* 1327 SR (C, Sf); Edmund *Mohaut* 1332 SRLo. OG *Mahthildis*, introduced into England at the Conquest. William I's queen, Matilda, is called *Mold* by Robert of Gloucester. *Matilda* is a learned form, rarely found in medieval surnames and now completely lost unless it is the source of the very rare *Mattleson*. A pet-form *Till*, however, survives in *Till(e)*, *Tilley, Tillie, Tilly*, in the diminutives *Tillet(t)*, *Tillott*, and in *Tillotson, Til(l)son*. The common vernacular forms *Mahald, Mahalt*, have given *Mald, Malt, Mault, Maud, Mold, Mould(s)* and *Moult*. In *Mahald* and *Mahalt* the *l* was vocalized, giving *Mahaud, Mahaut*, now *Mahood, Mawhood, Mowatt*. cf. also MAUDSON, MAWSOM, MOLSON.
Maudling: Simon *Maudeleyn'* 1279 RH (O); John *Maudeleyne* 1368 FrY. Hebrew *Magdalen* 'woman of Magdala', a somewhat uncommon christian name in the 13th century.
Maudsley, Maudslay, Mawdsley, Mawdesley: Adam *de Moudesley* 1257 Bardsley (La); William *de Maudesley* 1401 AssLa; Robert *Mawdesley* 1476 FrY. From Mawdesley (Lancs).
Maudson, Maulson: Ralph *Maldesone* 1327 SRSx; John *Mauldsone* 1376 Black (Fife); John *Maltson* 1438 FrY. 'Son of *Mald*' or *Matilda*. v. MAUD. cf. MAWSOM.
Mauduit, Mawditt, Mudditt: Gunfridus *Maledoctus* 1084 GeldR (W); William *Maldoit, Malduith, Malduit* 1086 DB (Ha); Otuell *Malduit* 1169 P (Ess); Richard *Maudut* (*Maudit*) 1229 Cur (Bk). OFr *mal-duit*, Lat *male doctus* 'badly educated'.
Maufe: v. MAW
Mauger, Mager, Mayger, Major: Hugo *filius Malgeri* 1086 DB (Ess); Drogo *filius Matelgerii* ib. (D); *Malger filius Gilleberti* 1150–60 DC (Nt); *Maugerus episcopus* 1212 Fees (Wo); John *Mauger, Malger* 1250 Fees (So); 1272 AssSo; Thomas *Mauger'* 1260 Oseney (O). OFr *Maugier*, OG *Madalgar, Malger* 'council-spear'. Tolleshunt Major (Essex) owes its attribute to the DB *Malger* (Tolshunt *Major* 1480 Pat).
Maugham, Maughan, Mauchan: John *de Machen* 1263 Black (Lanark); Adam *Mauchan* 1300 ib.; Richard *Maghan*, John *Mawgham* 1476, 1537 FrY. From earlier Machan, now Dalserf (Lanark).
Maul, Maule, Maull: Robertus *filius Malle* 1297 SRY; Gerard *Malle* 1297 MinAcctCo (Bk). A pet-name for *Mary*.
Mauleverer: William *Malleu(e)rier* 1159, 1166 P (Y); Ralph *Mauleverer* 1204 AssY. OFr *mal leverier*, Lat *malus leporarius* 'poor harrier'.
Maulkin: v. MALKIN
Maulson: v. MAUDSON
Mault: v. MAUD
Maultby: v. MALTBY
Maurice, Morrice, Morris, Morriss, Fitzmaurice: *Mauricius de Edligtona, de Creona* c1176, c1190 DC (L); Fulco *filius Mauricii, Moriz* 1185 Templars (L); Ricardus *filius Morys* 1297 SRY; Josce *Mauricii* 1191 P (Lo); Richard *Maurice* 1252 Rams (Hu); John *Morice* 1275 RH (Bk); Simon *Morys* 1296 SRSx; Robert *Morisse* 1308 StThomas (St);

Nicholas *le fiz Mouriz* 1314 Cl. Lat *Mauritius* 'Moorish, dark, swarthy', from *Maurus* 'a Moor'. *Maurice* is the learned form, *Morice* the common popular one. *Morris* may also be a nickname: Robert *le Moreys* 1274 RH (So), 'the swarthy'.

Maw, Mawe, Mowe, Maufe, Muff: (i) William *Mawe* 1275 RH (Nf), 1322 FrY; William *Mogge, Mugh* Ed 1 NottBR; Robert *Mouth, le Mogh* 1336–7 ib.; William *Magh'* 1381 PTY. OE *māge* 'female relative', ME *maugh*, used vaguely of a relative by marriage; in the north of a brother-in-law. cf. 'Mow, husbondys syster, or wyfys systyr, or syster in lawe' (PromptParv). This will give *Maufe* and *Muff*. (ii) *Mauua* 1066 DB (Sf); Godefridus, Galfridus *filius Mawe* 1199 P (L), 1297 MinAcctCo (Y); Johannes *filius Mawe* 1256 AssNb. Ekwall takes the DB name as OE **Mawa* and compares OG *Mawo*. cf. Agnes *Mawedoughter* 1381 SRSt and the diminutive *Moco(c)k* 1297, 1307 Wak (Y). We may also have a nickname from the sea-mew, OE *mǣw*: Henry *le Mou* 1327 SRWo. cf. ME *mawe, semawe* (c. 1450 NED), 'Mowe, byrd, or semewe' (PromptParv), and *v.* MEW. (iii) Sibilla *de la Mawe* 1275 RH (Sf); William *de Mawe* ib.; William *atte Mowe*, John *Mowe* 1327 SRSf. 'Dweller by the meadow', OE **māwe*.

Mawd(e)sley: *v.* MAUDSLEY

Mawditt: *v.* MAUDUIT

Mawer, Mower: John *le Mawere, le Mowere* 1225 AssSo; Robert *le Mouer* 1263 ArchC iv (K); John *le Mawer* 1297 SRY; Roger *le Mower* 1305 Pinchbeck (Sf); Alan *Mawer* 1332 SRCu. A derivative of OE *māwan* 'to mow', 'a mower' (c1440 NED). OE *aw* became ME *au* north of the Humber and remained; to the south it became *ou*. *Mower* may also be occasionally a dialectal form of MOORE: Laurance *a Mower* 'at the moor', Ezabell *Mower* 1562 RothwellPR (Y).

Mawhood: *v.* MAUD

Mawsom, Mawson: John *Malteson* 1332 SRSr; William *Mawson* 1382 Calv (Y). 'Son of *Maud*' or 'son of *Maw*'.

Maxwell: Herbert *de Makeswell'* 1190 P (Y); John *de Maccuswell* 1221 Pat (Scotland); Eymer *de Mackisuuell* 1262 Black (Peebles). From Maxwell, a salmon pool on the Tweed near Kelso Bridge.

May, Le May, Maye, Mayes, Mays, Mayze, Mey, Meye, Meys, Lemay: Johannes *filius Maie* 1274 RH (L); Elena *filia May* 1301 SRY; *May* de Hindley 1379 PTY; William *Mai* 1167 P (Nf); William *le Mai* 1177 P (Nf); Thomas *le Mey*, Goscelin *Mey* 1221 ElyA (Sf); John *Meys* 1276 RH (Gl); Stephen *Mayes* 1332 SRWa. ME *may* 'young lad or girl' or *May*, a hypocoristic of *Matthew*, from *Maheu, Mayhew*.

Maycock, Meacock, Mycock: *Maicoc le Crou*-der 1284 AssLa; William *Maycock, Moycock* 1323 AssSt; Thomas *Macok*, John *Moycok* 1327 SRDb; John *Mecocke* 1585 Oxon. *Mai-coc*, a diminutive of *May*, from *Mayhew* (Matthew).

Maydon: *v.* MAIDEN

Mayer, Mayers, Mayor, Meier, Meyer, Meyers: William *le Maier* 1243 AssSo; Henry *Meyer,*

Bartholomew *le Meyre* 1275 RH (Nf); David *le Meir* 1276 RH (L); Alan *Mair* 1279 AssNb. Occasionally we may have OFr *maire* 'mayor', but the term was limited in England to mayors of boroughs, much less numerous than the corresponding, but less dignified, 'mayors' of France and Scotland (*v.* MAIR). It may have been sometimes a nickname for one who aped the mayor. Usually the surname is synonymous with MYER, OFr *mire*, ME *mire, meir, meyre* 'physician'. The modern surname is often Jewish and German, from Ger *meier* 'steward, bailiff; farmer'.

Mayger: *v.* MAUGER

Mayhew, Mayo, Mehew: *Maheo* de Charun 12th DC (Lei); Geoffrey *Maheu* c1240 Fees (Bk); John *Mahyw*, William *Mahu* 1296 SRSx; William *Mayhew* 1351 ColchCt; John *Mayho* 1428 LLB K; John *Mayhow*, Wylliam *Mayo* 1524 SRSf. OFr *Mahieu*, a common Norman form of *Matthew*.

Maylard, Maylett, Mallard: *Meillardus, Maillard* 1221, 1226 Fees (Gl); *Mallard(us)* 1148 Winton (Ha), 1229 Cl (Gl); Gilbert *Maillard* 1185 Templars (Lo); William *Maillard'* 1209 Cur (Nt); John, Andrew *Mallard* 1219 Cur (Nt), 1296 SRSx. OFr *Maillart*, OG *Madalhard* 'council-strong'.

Maylor: *v.* MAILER

Maynard, Mainerd: *Meinardus uigil* 1086 DB (Nf); Thomas *filius Meinard* 1202 AssL; Richard, Robert *Mainard* 1195, 1198 P (Sf, Ha). OFr *Mainard, Meinard*, OG *Maganhard, Meginard* 'strength-strong'.

Mayne, Maynes, Main, Maine, Mains: (i) *Main* 1135 Oseney (O), 1168 P (W); *Mein* 1198 P (O); Robert *Main* 1204 AssY; John *Mayn* 1255 RH (Bk). OG *Maino, Meino* 'strength'. (ii) Robert *le meyne* 1285 Kirkstall (Y); Richard *le Mayne* 1327 SRSx. OFr *magne, maine* 'great'. (iii) Walter *Asmeins* 1223 Pat (Gl); William *Asmayns* 1230 P (L). A nickname from OFr *mayns*, the man 'with the hands'. (iv) Adam *de Meine* 1205 P (So); Robert *de Maine* 1213 Cur (So). From the French province of Maine. (v) Johel *de Meduana, de Mayne* 1212, 1237 Fees (D). From Mayenne. (vi) In Scotland, ON *Magnus* became (*Mac*)*Manus* and *Main* (*M'Manis* 1506, *M'Maines* 1673 Black). *Main* is common at Nairn and in Aberdeenshire.

Maynell: *v.* MEYNELL

Mayner, Maynor, Mainer: *Mainerus filius* Roberti 1207 Cur (L); Walkevinus *filius Mainer* 1210 Cur (C); Hugo *Mainer* 1279 RH (C); William *Mayner* 1328 FrY. OG *Maginhari* 'army-might'.

Mayo: *v.* MAYHEW

Mayor: *v.* MAYER

Maysey: *v.* MAISEY

Mayson: (i) William *Mayson, Mayeson* 1327 SRY, 1332 SRWa; John *Mayesson* 1369 AD iv (Nf). 'Son of *May*.' (ii) Adam de Morton, *mayson* 1371 PTY; John *Mayson* 1379 PTY; Alexander *Mason, Mayson* blaksmyth 1520, 1542 FrY. A northern spelling of MASON.

Mayze: *v.* MAY

Meacham, Meachem, Meachim, Meachin, Mee-cham: Anne *Machin, Macham* 1615, 1620 Lit-

SaxhamPR (Sf); Robert *Meacham* 1676 ib. Late developments of MACHIN. *v.* MASON.

Meacock: *v.* MAYCOCK

Mead, Meade, Meads: (i) John *Atemede* 1248 FFEss; Richard *inthemede* 1332 MELS (Sr); John *del Mede* 1379 PTY; John *a Mede* 1454 KentW. 'Dweller in or by the mead', OE *mæd.* (ii) Richard *Mede* 1190 P (Wa). Either an early example of loss of the preposition, or metonymic for MEADER. cf. Matillis *Medewif* 1327 SRY.

Meaden: Hugo *ate Medende* 1332 SRSr. 'Dweller by the meadow-end.'

Meader, Medur: Alexander *le Meder, le Medier, Medarius* 1180, 1200 Oseney (O), 1188 P (Bk); Thomas *Meder* 1332 SRSr. A derivative of OE *meodu* 'mead', Lat *medarius* 'a maker or seller of mead'. cf. John *Medemaker'* 1332 MESO (Nf). Or 'dweller by the mead'. cf. MEAD. Such toponymics are common in 1332 SRSr.

Meadow, Meadows, Medewe: Henry *I'the, de la Medewe* 1280 MELS (Wo); Henry *del Medue* 1283 Ipm (Db); Richard *atte Medeue* 1327 SRSx. 'Dweller by the meadow', OE *mæd, mædwe.*

Meadowcroft: Peter *de Medwecroft* 1246 AssLa. From Meadowcroft in Middleton (Lancs).

Meadway, Medway: Alexander *at þe Medewaye* 1302 MELS 129 (Sx); John *atte Medeweie* 1327 ib. 'Dweller by the river Medway.'

Meager, Meagers, Meagher, Megar: Geoffrey *le Megre* 1179 P (Ess); Robertus *Macer,* Robert *le Megre* 1210 Cur (Wa), 1221 AssWa. ME, OFr *megre,* Lat *macer* 'thin, lean'.

Meaken, Meakin(g)s: *v.* MAKIN

Meale, Meals: Geoffrey, Simon *Mele* 1279 RH (C), 1300 LLB B. OE *melo* 'meal', metonymic for a maker or seller of meal. *Melemakers* in York were millers. cf. Adam *le Melemakere* 1274 Wak (Y), Roger *le Meleman* 1275 SRWo, Gilbert *le Melemongere* 1296 SRSx.

Mear, Meares, Mears, Meers: Robert *atte Mere* 1269 AssSo; Adam *del Mere* 1307 Wak (Y). 'Dweller by the pool (OE *mere*) or the boundary (OE *(ge)mære).*'

Measham, Measom, Messam, Messum: William *de Meysham* 1248 AssSt. From Measham (Leicester). The surname occurs as *de Meysam* 1305, *Measham* 1421, *Measam* 1633, *Messam* 1661 DbAS 36, Thomas *Mesham,* Maute *Messume* 1524 SRSf.

Meazey: *v.* MAISEY

Meazon: *v.* MESSENT

Medcalf(e): *v.* METCALF

Medcraft: William *de Medecroft* 1313 Eynsham (O). 'Dweller at the meadow-croft.'

Medewe: *v.* MEADOW

Medley, Medlay: Thomas *Medlay* 1419 IpmY; Benedict *Medley* 1496–7 FFWa; Christopher *Medelay* 1504 CorNt; Robert *Medley* 1672 HTY. From Medley (Oxon), or perhaps Madely (Glos), *Methlegh* 1234, but the examples are late and a nickname may also be involved.

Medlicott, Medlycott: Lewelin *de Modlincot* 1255 RH (Sa). From Medlicott (Salop).

Medur: *v.* MEADER

Medway: *v.* MEADWAY

Meecham: *v.* MEACHAM

Meek, Meeke, Meeks: Richard *Mek* 1229 Pat (So); Robert *le Meke* 1300 FrY. ON *mjúkr,* ME *meke* 'humble, meek'.

Meekin(g)s: *v.* MAKIN

Meers: *v.* MEAR

Meese: Richard *del Mes* 1276 AssSt. From Meece (Staffs).

Meetham, Metham, Mettham, Mettam: Thomas *de Metham* 1276 RH (Y). From Metham (ERYorks).

Meffan, Meffen: *v.* METHUEN

Meffatt, Meffet: *v.* MOFFAT

Megar: *v.* MEAGER

Meggat, Meggett, Meggitt: (i) George *Meggott* 1677 Bardsley. *Megot,* a variant of *Maggot,* a diminutive of *Magg, Megg* (Margaret): *Megota* de Rypon 1309 Wak (Y). (ii) Randulf *de Meggate* c1190 Black. From Megget in Yarrow (Selkirk).

Megginson: For MEGGISON with intrusive *n.*

Meggison: Robert *Meggotson* 1379 PTY. 'Son of *Meggot* (Margaret).'

Megson: Johannes *filius Megge* 1279 RH (O); Adam *Meggesone* 1332 SRCu. 'Son of *Megg* (Margaret).'

Mehew: *v.* MAYHEW

Meier: *v.* MAYER

Meikle, Mickle: William *Mykyl* 1382 Black; Bessie *Mekill* 1609 ib.; William *Meikill* 1616 ib. MScots *mekill, meikill* 'big'.

Meiklejohn, Micklejohn, Mucklejohn: *Mekle John* Burne 1495 Black; William *Meiklejohne* 1638 ib. 'Big John.'

Melady: *v.* MELODY

Melhuish, Mellhuish, Mellish: John *de Melewis* 1242 Fees (D); Elinora *de Melhywys* 1274 RH (D); John *Mellishe* 1583 Musters (Sr); George *Melhuish* 1642 PrD. From Melhuish Barton (Devon).

Meliss: *v.* MALISE

Mellanby: Alan *de Melmerby* 1316 FrY; Walter *Mellerby* 1412 ib. From Melmerby (Cumb, NRYorks).

Mellard: *v.* MILLWARD

Meller, Mellers: Roger *le Meller* 1319 Crowland (C), 1327 SRSf. 'Miller.'

Mellichap: *v.* MILLICHAMP

Mellin: *v.* MELVILL

Melling, Mellings: Henry *de Mellinges* 1194 P (La). From Melling (Lancs). *v.* also MELVILL.

Mellis, Melliss: Joan *de Melles* 1327 SRSf; John *Melys,* Thomas *Mellice* 1524 SRSf. From Mellis (Suffolk). *v.* also MALISE.

Mellish: *v.* MELHUISH

Mellor, Mellors: Richard *de Meluer* 1246 AssLa. From Mellor (Lancs).

Mellowship: *v.* MILLICHAMP

Mellsop: *v.* MILSOPP

Melody, Melady: *Melodia* 1212 Cur (Berks); Richard *Melodie* 1279 RH (O). From a woman's name, *Melodia.*

Melpuss: *v.* MALPAS

Melsom(e), Melson: *v.* MILLSOM

Melvill, Melville, Melvin: Geoffrey *de Maleuin*, 1161–3, 1165–71; Hugh *de Malleville* c1202 Black. The surname appears as *Meiluill* 1520, *Melwin* 1550 and is commonly pronounced *Melvin*, besides *Mellin, Mellon, Melling*. James Melville the reformer spelled his name indifferently *Melville* and *Melvin* (Black). The surname usually derives from Melville (Midlothian), itself named from Geoffrey de Mallaville who came from Emalleville (Seine-Inférieure).

Membery, Membry, Membury: Richard *de Membri, de Membyr'* 1201 AssSo, 1242 Fees (D); John *de Membury* 1327 SRSo. These Somerset surnames derive from Membury (Devon). *v.* also MOWBRAY.

Memory: *v.* MOWBRAY

Menel, Mennell: *v.* MEYNELL

Menzies: A Scottish form of MANNERS, spelled *de Meyneris* or *Meinzeis* 1306–29, *Meygnes* 1425, *Menyhes* 1428, *Mengues* 1487, *Mengzes* 1572. Pronounced *Meeng-us* or *Mingies* (Black). For the *z*, cf. DALYELL.

Mercer, Mercier, Merchiers: Gamel *mercer* 1168 P (L); John *le mercier* 1196 P (Gl); Hamo *le Merchier* 1204 Cur (O); Richer *le Mercher, le Mercer* 1298 LLB B. OFr *mercier, merchier* 'merchant', one who deals in textile fabrics, especially silks, velvets and other costly materials (NED).

Merchant: *v.* MARCHANT

Meredith: *Mereduht* ap Grifin 1248 Ipm (Mon); William *Meredich* 1191 P (St). OW *Morgetiud*, MW *Maredudd*, Welsh *Meredydd*.

Merewether: *v.* MERRYWEATHER

Merioth, Meriott, Meritt, Meryett: *v.* MERRETT

Merivale: Geoffrey *de Miriuall'* 1206 Pl (Y); William *de Muryvale* 1332 SRSt; Richard *Meryvale* 1418 LLB I. From Merevale (Warwicks), *Mirival* c1190, or 'dweller in the pleasant valley'.

Merrall, Merrell, Merrill: *v.* MURIEL

Merrett, Merrett, Merritt, Merrit, Merritt, Merioth, Meriott, Meritt, Meryett: (i) Alric *filius Meriet*, Ælric *Meriete sune* 1066 DB; Ægelricus *filius Mergeati* c1086 Crispin; *Meriet* c1113 Burton (St), 1200 Oseney (O); Ralph, Symon *Meriet* 1202 AssL, 1255 RH (Bk); John *Meryet* 1316 FA (W); John *Meryatt* 1375 ColchCt. OE *Mǣrgēat* 'famous Geat'. *v.* MARRIOTT. (ii) Hardinus *de Meriet* 1084 GeldR (So); Henry *de Merieth* 1185 Templars (So). From Merriott (Som).

Merriday, Merredy, Merridew: John *Meridewe* 1379 PTY. An English and Irish form of MEREDITH. Bardsley gives two examples of men called both Meredith and Meriday in 1596–8 and 1680–2.

Merrikin: William *Marekyn*, John *Marykyn* 1390, 1458 FrY. A diminutive of *Mary*.

Merriman, Merriment: Adam *Murymon* 1332 SRSt; John *Meryman* 1359 LLB G; Adam *Myryman* 1379 PTY. 'The merry man.' *v.* MERRY.

Merritt, Merriott: *v.* MERRETT

Merryweather: *v.* MERRYWEATHER

Merry: Gilbert *le mirie* 12th DC (Lei); John *Myrie* 1219 AssY; Robert *Merye* Edw 1 Battle (Sx). OE *myrige*, ME *mirie, merie, murie* 'merry'.

Merryweather, Merrywether, Merriweather, Merewether: Henry *Meriweder* 1214 Cur (Beds); Robert *Muriweder* 1223 Pat (O); Roger *Mirywoder* 1260 AssC; John *Mereweder* 1345 ColchCt. OE *myrige* 'merry' and *weder* 'weather', a common term for fair weather, used as a nickname for a gay or blithe fellow. cf. FAIRWEATHER.

Merton: *v.* MARTON

Meryett: *v.* MERRETT

Mesheder: *v.* MASHEDER

Message: Metonymic for MESSENGER.

Messam: *v.* MEASHAM

Messenger, Massinger: Lucas *le mesagier* 1193 P (Nth); Richard, Hugh *le Messager* 1211 Cur (Mx), 1221 AssSa; William *le Messinger* 1293 Guisb (Y); Robert *le Massager* 1317 AssK; Richard *Messenger* 1377 LoPleas; Walter *Massynger* 1428 FA (W). OFr *messagier, messager*. 'A messenger' (a1225 NED).

Messent, Meazon, Mezen, *Meisent, Moysent* Hy 2 DC (L); *Maysant* 1197 FF (Y); Helie *Moysant* 12th DC (L); William *Maysaunt* 1297 SRY. OFr *Maissent* (f), OG *Mathasuent(a)* or **Magisind, Megisend* (Forssner). Measant's Charity alias Messants Fm in Debden (Essex) owes its name to John *Meysaunt* or *Mesande* (15th PN Ess 524).

Messer: Roger *Messer* 1172–80 DC (L); Erkenbald *le Messer* 1180 P (L); William *le Messier* 1187 P (Nt). OFr *messier, messer* 'harvester', or more probably 'hayward'.

Messiter: *v.* MASHEDER

Messum: *v.* MEASHAM

Metcalf, Metcalfe, Medcalf, Medcalfe, Mitcalfe: Adam *Medecalf'* 1301 SRY; John *Metcalf, Medcalfe* 1423, 1463 FrY; William *Meatecalf* 1560 FrLeic; Mark *Meadcalfe* 1568 Oxon; John *Madcalfe* 1674 HTSf. It is quite clear that Bardsley's derivation of this much discussed Yorkshire name, from *Medcroft*, is untenable. The first form supports Weekley's 'mead-calf'. Harrison's 'mad calf' need not be seriously considered. Forms are late and the unfortunate gap between 1301 and 1423 makes any explanation speculative. OE had *metecorn* 'corn for food' and *mete-cū* 'a cow that is to furnish food'. A similar formation **mete-cealf* 'a calf to be fattened up for eating' might have existed and given rise to a nickname 'fat as a prize-calf' (cf. *Duncalf* as a nickname). Such a calf would be turned out in the lush grass of the meadow, the meaning of *mete-cealf* (never a common term) forgotten, and the first element associated with *mead*, hence the variation between *Metcalf* and *Medcalf*.

Metham: *v.* MEETHAM

Methuen, Methven, Meffan, Meffen: Robert *de Methven* 1233–55 Black; Roger *de Methfenn* 1296 CalSc; Roger *Meffen* a1320 Black. From Methven (Perthshire).

Mettam, Mettham: *v.* MEETHAM

Meux, Mewes, Mewies, Mewis, Mews, Mewse: John *de Mehus* 1196 FF (Y); Hugo *de Mues* 1201 P (Lei); Thomas *de Meuse* 1282 FFEss; Andrew

Mewes 1371 FFHu; Roger *Meux* 1403 FrY; Lodewycus *Mewys* 1428 FA (W). From Meaux (ERYorks), pronounced *mews*, to rhyme with *sluice. v.* PN ERY 43–4, where the different forms are illustrated.

Mew: (i) Algarus *filius Meawes* 1016 OEByn; Robert *Meu* 1275 SRWo; William *Mew* 1284 RamsCt (Hu); William *le Mew* 1296 SRSx; John *Meau, Meaw* 1312 LLB B. OE *mǣw, mēaw* 'a gull', also 'a sea-mew'. *Mēaw* was used as a personal name in OE (Redin). *v.* also MAW. (ii) Geoffrey *Muwe* 1275 RH (Nf). OFr *mue*, a cage for hawks, especially when mewing or moulting (13.. NED), used by metonymy for *Mewer*. This was probably more common than appears. When OE *ǣw* and OFr *u* had fallen together, this would be indistinguishable from *Mew* above. (iii) William *de la Muie, de la Mue* 1199 P (D). 'One in charge of the mew.' *v.* MEWER.

Mewer, Meur, Meurs, Muer, Muers, Mure: Robert, Alan *le Muer* 1195 P (Ess), 12th DC (L); Adam *Muier* 1199 P (L). A derivative of OFr *mue* 'a cage for hawks', used of one in charge of the mews where hawks were kept whilst moulting. cf. William *Meweman* 1279 RH (O). The surname may have been confused with *Muir*.

Mewes, Mewies, Mewis, Mews, Mewse: *v.* MEUX

Mewett, Mewitt: Richard *Mewot* 1279 RH (Hu). A diminutive of *Mew*.

Mewha: Richard *de Mewy* 1242 Fees (D). From Meavy (Devon).

Mey: *v.* MAY

Meyer, Meyers: *v.* MAYER

Meyler: *v.* MAILER

Meynell, Maynall, Mennell, Menel: (i) Robert *de Meinil, de Maisnil, del Maisnil*, 1166–77 P (Y), *del Meisnil* 1195 P (Ha), *del Menill* 1199 P (Y), *de Mesnill'* 1219 AssY; Hugh *de Meynyl* 1260 AssLa; Nicholas *(de) Menil* 1276 RH (Y); Henry *Meynel* 1321 FFEss. Meynell Langley (Derbyshire) was held by Robert *de Maisnell* temp. Henry I. The family came from one of the French places named Mesnil, from OFr *mesnil*, Lat **mansionile*, diminutive of *mansio* 'abode, habitation', used of the country domain where a noble lived with his family and retainers. As a surname it may also be used of a member of the household, retainer. (ii) *Mehenilda* vidua c1250 Rams (Nf); *Maghenyld* 1275 RH (Nf); Alan *Mahenyld* 1275 RH (Nf); Ralph *Manel* 1279 RH (Hu); Henry *Manild*, Hugh *Maneld* 1327 SRSf; John *Maynild* 1327 SR (Ess); Thomas *Maynell* 1426 PCC; William *Menneld* 1546 FrY. OG *Maginhild* (f) 'strength (in) battle'. This has also become MANNELL.

Meysey: *v.* MAISEY

Mezen: *v.* MESSENT

Miall, Miell, Myall, Myhill: *Mihil* Cristen 1549 Bardsley; John *Mihell* 1524 SRSf; Priscilla *Miell* 1779 Bardsley. *v.* MICHAEL.

Miatt, Miot, Myott: Probably diminutives of *My*, from *Myhel*, i.e. Michael.

Mich: *Miche* de Sancto Albano 1275 RH (Lo);

Robert, Adam *Miche* 1279 RH (Hu), 1327 SR (Ess). A pet form of *Michel*, i.e. Michael. cf. Johannes *filius Michecok* 1322 SRLa. Also synonymous with MUTCH.

Michael, Michaels, McMichael: *Michaelis* de Areci c1160 DC (L); *Michael* 12th DC (L); John *Makmychell* 1507 Black. Hebrew 'Who is like the Lord?' *Michael* is the learned form. The popular pronunciation was from the French *Michel* which survives as MITCHEL. The OFr popular form was also used in England. *v.* MIALL. Butler, in *Hudibras*, rhymes St *Michael's* with *trials*. In ME *Michaelmas* is found both as *Mielmasse* and *Mighelmasse*, and the *Cursor Mundi* has a form seynt *Myghell*, surviving as MIGGLES. In Orkney St *Michael's* is pronounced St *Mitchell's*. St Michael's, Cornhill, was *Saint Mihills* in 1626 (Bardsley). Miles's Lane (London) was *Seint Micheleslane* 1303, *Saynte Mighelles Lane* 1548 (Ekwall). *Miles* Coverdale, the translator of the Bible, when in Germany, called himself *Michael* Anglus. Thus *Miles* may derive from *Michael* through the form *Miel*.

Michaelson: John *Michaelson* 1646 Black. 'Son of *Michael*.'

Michell: *v.* MITCHEL

Michelson: *v.* MITCHELSON

Michie: *Michy* Nycholson 1446 Black; John *Mychy* 1473 ib. A Scottish diminutive of *Mich*, from *Michael*.

Michieson: Tawis *Michison* 1415 Black. An anglicizing of *MacMichie*.

Mickle: *v.* MEIKLE

Micklejohn: *v.* MEIKLEJOHN

Micklem, Miklem: John *de Mychelham, Mykelham* 1296, 1327 SRSx; Fraunces *Mycklem* 1561 BishamPR (Berks). From Mickleham (Surrey).

Middle: (i) Richard *le Midel* 1279 RH (O). A nickname, for one who was neither *Bigg* nor *Small*. (ii) Simon *atte Middele* 1327 SRSo. OE *middel* 'middle' used topographically. Probably 'dweller in the middle of the village'.

Middlemas, Middlemass, Middlemiss, Middlemist, Midlemas: The Middlemasses were vassals and tenants in and around Kelso and took their name from 'lie Middlemestlands' in Kelso. The surname occurs as *de Meldimast* 1406, *Myddilmast* 1439, *Midlemes* 1612, *Midlemist* 1670 and *Midlemiss*, 1685 Black.

Middleton, Myddleton: Robert *de Mideltone* 1166 Eynsham; William *de Midelton* 1327 SRSx; John *Middilton* 1409–10 FFWa. From one or other of the many places of this name, or occasionally from one of the Milton's, many of which represent an OE *middel-tūn* 'middle farm'.

Midnight: Wlfrich *Midnith* 1199–1208 Clerkenwell (Lo); William *Midnicht*, Osbert *Midnihte* 1221 AssWa; John *Midnyght* 1327 SR (Ess). The contrasting *Midday* is found from the 14th to the 16th century: Adam *Midday* 1335 FFNf, Robert *Myddaie* 1568 SRSf. Birth at noon or midnight might well have been considered sufficiently noteworthy to warrant commemoration by name.

Midwinter: *Midwinter* 1188 P (Berks); John

Midwinter c1248 Bec (W); Geoffrey *Midewynter* 1275 SRWo. OE *midwinter* 'midwinter, Christmas'. A name for one born at Christmas. cf. CHRISTMAS, NOEL, YOULE, and John *Midsumer* 1224 Cur (Sf). The surname may also be local: John *de Midwinter* (1238), from Midwinter (PN D 435).

Miell: *v.* MIALL
Mier(s) *v.* MYER
Miggles, Mighell, Mighill: *Mighell* Axendall 1598 Bardsley; Adam, John *Miggel* 1327 SRSf; Richard *Mighell* 1327 *SR* (Ess). *v.* MICHAEL.

Mignot, Mignott, Minet, Minett, Minette, Minnett, Minnitt, Mynett, Mynott: Peter *Mignot*, *Minnot* 1191, 1201 P (K); Robert *Mignot, Minot* 1232, 1237 Oriel (O); Nicholas *Mynyot* 1379 PTY; William *Minet* 1524 SRSf. OFr *mignot* 'dainty, pleasing'. Also a diminutive of *Minn: Minnota* (f) 1274 FFEss. *v.* MINN. *Minet* is a Huguenot name but was in use in England centuries earlier.

Miklem: *v.* MICKLEM
Milborrow, Millborough: Walter *Milburegh, Milburew* 1275, 1279 RH (O). OE *Mildburh* (f) 'mild-fortress', daughter of a Mercian king, an abbess and saint much venerated in the Middle Ages. The christian name *Milborough* was still in use in Shropshire in the 18th century.

Milbourn, Milbourne, Milburn, Millbourn, Millbourne, Millburn: Hugh *de Meleburn* 1201 Pl (Do); Walter *de Milleburne* 1251 IpmY; William *Milbourne* 1465 FFEss. From Milborne (Dorset, Som), Milbourne (Northumb, Wilts), Milburn (Westmorland), or Melbourne (Derby), *Mileburne* DB.

Mildenhall, Mindenhall: Andrew *de Mildenhale* 1170–83 Bury (Sf). From Mildenhall (Suffolk, Wilts).

Mildmay: Walter *Myldemay* 1483 AD i (Gl). 'Gentle maiden.' cf. John *Mildeman* 1381 SRSf and the opposite, John *Wyldmy* 1287 LLB A 'wild lad'.

Miles, Myles: *Milo* 1086 DB; Johannes filius *Mile* 1150–60 DC (L); *Milo* Noyrenuyt 1230 P (Berks); Nicholaus filius *Miles* 1297 SRY; Nicholaus *Miles* 1177 P (Sx); Henry, Richard *Mile* c1225 Fees (Beds), 1230 P (Berks); Agnes *Milys* 1297 MinAcctCo; Walter *Miles* 1327 SRSx. OFr *Milon, Miles*, OG *Milo*. The christian name is usually latinized as *Milo*. The early vernacular form in English appears to have been *Mile*, as in modern French *Mile, Mille. Miles* has been noted only twice. As a surname, *Miles* is ambiguous, being sometimes Lat *miles* 'soldier'. cf. Ralph *Miles* 1324 Cor, identical with Radulpho *Milite* 1319 SRLo. Another Ralph *Miles*, a fishmonger, of Bridge Ward (1292 SRLo), founded a chantry for his late lord *Milo*, no doubt *Miles* de Oystergate, fishmonger (1291 Husting). Ralph had adopted his master's christian name as his surname. *Miles* may also be from *Miel, v.* MICHAEL.

Mileson: Elisota *Milesson* 1379 PTY. 'Son of *Miles*.'

Milford, Millford: Hugh *de Mileford'* 1208 FFY; William *de Melleford* 1347 AssLo; John *de Milford'* 1379 PTY. From Milford (Derby, Hants, Wilts, WRYorks), or Long Melford (Suffolk).

Milk: Ailmar *Melc* 1066 DB (Ess); Henry, Geoffrey *Melc* 1279 RH (C); William *Mylk* 1367 FrY. OE *meolc* 'milk', perhaps a nickname for one whose drink was milk, effeminate, spiritless. cf. MILSOPP. Or for one with milk-white hair. cf. Hugh *Milkeheued* 12th DC (L). But more probably metonymic for a seller of milk. cf. Robert *le Milker* 1221 AssWa, William *le Milkster* 1246 AssLa, Geoffrey *le melkmakiere*, John *le melkberere* ('carrier') 1285 *Ass* (Ess).

Mill: (i) Richard *de la Melle* 1200 Cur (Sx); Walter *Attemille* 1242 P (Sx); John *atte Mulle* 1327 SRSo. An assimilated form of OE *mylen* 'mill'. *v.* MILN. (ii) *Mylla* 1246 AssLa; *Milla* c1250 Rams (C); *Mille* Cruche 1275 RH (Nf); Richard *Mille* 1279 RH (C), 1316 Wak (Y), *Mylle* 1296 SRSx. This is usually regarded as a variant of *Miles*, but the evidence points rather to a short form of a woman's name, perhaps *Millicent*.

Millachip: *v.* MILLICHAMP
Millage, Milledge: *v.* MILLIDGE
Millard: *v.* MILLWARD
Millbourn(e), Millburn: *v.* MILBOURN

Miller, Millar: Ralph *Muller* 1296 SRSx; Reginald *Miller* 1327 SRSx; John *Millare* 1467 Black. An assimilated form of MILNER. *Millar* is Scottish.

Millerchip, Millership: *v.* MILLICHAMP

Millett, Milot: *Milot* c1248 Bec (W); Hugo *Milot* 1206 Cur (Nf); Roger *Millot* 1275 RH (Nt); Richard *Mileth* 1279 RH (O); Richard *Myles* or *Mylot* 1453 RochW. A diminutive of *Mile. v.* MILES.

Millford: *v.* MILFORD

Millhouse: Henry *del Melnehous* 1327 SRDb; Joan *del Milnhous* 1331 Wak (Y). 'At the mill-house', a miller.

Millican, Milliken, Millikin, Milligan, Mulligan, Mullikin: Molior *Omolegane* 1264 Dublin; Thomas *Ameligane, Amuligane* 1477, 1485 Black; Cuthbert *Amullekyne* 1578 ib.; John *Myllikin* 1593 ib; John *Mulligane* 1630 ib; Thomas *Mulliken* 1672 ib. Gael *Maolagan*, OIr *Maelecán*, a double diminutive of *mael* 'bald', 'the little bald or shaven one', monk, disciple. Irish *Ó Maoileacháin, Ó Maoileegáin*, 'descendant of *Maolagán*'.

Millicent: *Milisendis* lotrix 1179 P (O); *Milesent, Melisentia* 1208 Cur (St); William *Melisent* 1221 AssSa; Robert *Milisant* 13th Guisb (Y); John *Milicent* 1279 RH (Hu); William *Mylecent, Milsent* 1296, 1332 SRSx. OG *Amalasuintha* 'work-strong' became *Melisenda*, the name of a daughter of Charlemagne, and, as OFr *Milesindis, Milesenda, Miles(s)ent*, was brought to England in the 12th century.

Millichamp, Millichap, Millicheap, Millachip, Millichip, Millinchip, Millerchip, Millership, Mellichap, Mellowship: Roger *de Millinghope* 1199 P (Sa); Roger *de Miligehop'* 1255 RH (Sa). From Millichope (Salop).

Millidge, Milledge, Millage: Roger *de Melewich* 1198 P (St), *de Mulewic* 1219 AssSt. From Milwich (Staffs).

Millington: Peter *de Milington'* 1206 FFY; James

de Milyngton 1371 FFY; Roger, Thomas *Myllyngton* 1525 SRSx. From Millington (Ches, ERYorks), or 'dweller at the farm with a mill'.

Millmaker: Adam *le Melemakere* 1274 Wak (Y); William *Melmaker* 1453 Black. 'Maker of meal', miller. *v.* MEALE.

Millman, Milman: Robert *Melneman* 1373 ColchCt; William *Melman* 1447 CarshCt (Sr); John *Myllman* 1642 PrD. 'Worker at the mill', cf. John *milne knave* 1348 DbAS xxxvi, and *v.* MILLWARD.

Millner: *v.* MILNER

Mills, Milles, Millis: John *Myls* 1336 LLB F. *Mills* is much more common than *Mill* and may be from the plural, 'dweller by the mills' or a patronymic, from *Miles* or *Mill*.

Millsom, Millson, Millsum, Milsom, Melsom, Melsome, Melson: (i) Richard *Milleson* 1309 AssSt; Thomas *Milsson* 1379 PTY; Robert *Melsam* 1524 SRSf; Thomas *Melson* 1674 HTSf. 'Son of *Miles*' or of *Milla* (f). (ii) Simon *Mildesone* 1327 SRSo. 'Son of *Milde*', OE *Milde* (f): *Milda* 1066 DB (Sf); Osbertus *filius Milde* Hy 2 DC (L).

Millward, Millwood, Milward, Millard, Mellard, Mullard: John *le Milleward* 1279 RH (Hu); Cecilia *le Mulvard* 1286 ELPN; Richard *Meleward* 1296 SRSx; Walter *le Milneward* 1300 LoCt; Robert *le Moleward* 1327 SRDb; Richard *Millard* 1696 Bardsley. OE *myle(n)weard* 'keeper of a mill, miller'. Fransson notes that this is very common in the southern and western counties, elsewhere the common form is *Milner*. Equivalent to *atte Mille*: John *atte Mylle* otherwise called *Mylleward* 1426 AD v (Sx). cf. also the approbrious nickname: William *Offelle* alias *Milleward* 1429 AD i (Do).

Miln, Milne, Milnes, Milns, Milln, Millns, Mylne: Richard *atte Mulne* 1275 SRWo; Nicholas *atte Melne* 1296 SRSx; Robert *del Miln* 1332 SRCu. 'Dweller or worker at the mill' (OE *mylen*). *v.* MILLWARD.

Milner, Millner: John *le Mulnare* 1275 SRWo; Robert *le Milner* 1297 SRY. This may be an OE *mylnere* or a derivative of ME *mylne* 'mill', hence 'miller'. Examples of ME *melnere, mulnere* are much less frequent than one would expect. The surname is most common in the north and eastern counties, where Scandinavian influence was strong and may thus often derive from ON *mylnari* 'miller'. *v.* MILLWARD.

Milot: *v.* MILLETT

Milroy: For Manx *Mac Gilroy* or Scots *M'Ilroy*. *v.* MCELROY.

Milsom, Milson: *v.* MILLSOM

Milsopp, Melsopp: Ranul *milcsoppe* 1221 ElyA (Sf); Symon *Melksop* 1237–45 Colch (Lo); Roger *Milcscoppe* Hy 3 Stone (St); John *Milesop* 1279 RH (O). ME *milksop* 'a piece of bread soaked in milk' (c1386 NED), used of 'an effeminate, spiritless man or youth'.

Milton: Boia *on Mylatune* 972 OEByn; Alan *de Milton* 1235 FFO; Robert *Milton* 1360 IpmGl. From one or other of the many places of this name,

sometimes from Middleton, and occasionally from Melton (Leics, Lincs, Norfolk, ER, WRYorks).

Milward: *v.* MILLWARD

Minchin: Aluredus, Peter *Minchun* 1190, 1205 P (Wo, D); Robert *Mincin* 1381 SRSf. OE *mynecen* 'nun', a nickname.

Mindenhall: *v.* MILDENHALL

Miner, Miners, Minor, Minors: Jordan *le mineur* 1195 P (Co); Adam *le Miner* 1212 Cur (L); Henry *le Minur* 1224 Pat (Db). OFr *mineor, mineur* 'miner'.

Minet(t): *v.* MIGNOT

Mingay, Mingey: Johannes *filius Menghi* c1154–5 DC (L); Robertus *filius Mingghi* 1178–81 Clerkenwell (Ess); Andrew *Mengy* 1262 For (Ess); Richard *Mingy* 1276 FFEss. *Menguy*, a Breton name, 'stone dog', from Breton *men* 'stone' and *ki* 'dog'.

Minn, Minns, Mynn: *Minna* 1202 AssBeds; Gostelynus *Mynne* 1327 SRSf; John *Mynnys* 1524 SRSf. *Minna*, a pet-form of some woman's name, perhaps from *Ameline, Emeline*, or from *Ismenia (Imyne)*. For a diminutive *Minnota*, *v.* MIGNOT.

Minnett, Minnitt: *v.* MIGNOT

Minor(s): *v.* MINER

Minstrell: Hugo Harper *de Wolpet*, tregettour, alias dictus Hugo *Mynstrall* de Bildeston, jogelour 1483 EwenG 90. cf. TREDGETT.

Minter, Mintor: William *le Myntere* 1221 AssWa; John *Muneter* 1296 SRSx; Hamo *le Meneter* 1296 FFEss. OE *myntere* 'moneyer'.

Miot: *v.* MIATT

Miskin: William *le Meschin* 1161 P (Wa); Alan *de Perci le Meschin* c1180 Whitby (Y). OFr *meschin* 'young man', used to distinguish son from father.

Mitcalfe: *v.* METCALF

Mitcham, Mitchem, Mitchum: Wulfward *de Michham* 1190 P (Sr). From Mitcham (Surrey).

Mitchel, Mitchell, Michell: (i) *Michel* de Whepstede 1327 Pinchbeck (Sf); *Michele* Michel 1327 SRSo; *Mitchell* M'Brair 1490 Black (Galloway); Gilbert, Robert *Michel* 1205, 1219 Cur (Nb, So). Examples of *Michel* as a christian name are rare; the clerks regularly used *Michael*. In 1198 *Michael* de Middelton held a quarter of a carucate in Middleton (Wilts) by service of keeping the king's wolf-hounds (Fees). About 1219 William *Michel* received 3½*d.* per day for keeping two wolf-hounds and in 1236 Richard *Michel* held a cotset in Middleton for a similar service. The relationship between the three men is not stated but it appears a reasonable assumption that they were of the same family and that *Michael* de Middleton had two sons who derived their surname *Michel* from their father's christian name. The clerk gave the christian name its usual learned form, the surname in the form in use. *v.* MICHAEL. (ii) Roger *Michil* 1202 Cur (W); Ralph *le Muchele*, Geoffrey *Michel* 1230 Pat; Gilbert, Robert *Michel*, Adam *le Mechele (Muchele)* 1280 AssSo; John *Mochel* 1327 SRSo; Thomas *Mechel* Ric 2 PN Ess 320. OE *mycel*, ME *michel, mechel, muchel* 'big'. This survives as *much* and, as a surname, MUTCH. The survival of *Mitchell* alone as a surname is due to the influence of the personal name *Michel*, a form which cannot be distinguished from the adjective when there is no article.

Mitchelson, Mitchellson, Michelson: Roger *Michelson* 1383 DbCh. 'Son of *Michel*' (Michael).

Mitchenall, Mitchener, Mitchiner, Mitchner, Mitchimer: Henry *de Michenhale* 1347 PN Sr 349; Richard *Mychenall* 1524 SRSx; Thomas *Mychinall*, John *Mychinor* 1583 Musters (Sr); Pawle *Mychenor*, Robert *Michenour* 1596 ib. Probably from Michen Hall in Godalming (Surrey).

Mitcheson, Mitchison: Adam *Michesone* 1348 DbAS 36; William *Mitchesonne* 1568 SRSf. 'Son of *Mich* or *Michie*.'

Mitchinson: Ann *Mitchinson* 1749 Bardsley. 'Son of *Michel*', with change of *l—n* to *n—n*.

Mitford: John *de Midford'* 1196 P (Du); Robert *de Mitford* 1256 AssNb; Hugh *Mitford* 1412 IpmY. From Mitford (Northumb).

Mitton, Mitten: (i) Alan, Jordan *de Mitton'* 1219 AssY, 1246 AssLa. From Mitton (Lancs, Worcs, WRYorks). v. MUTTON. (ii) Simon *a Myddethune* 1296 SRSx; William *a Middeton* 1327 ib.; Richard *Middeton* 1332 ib. 'Dweller in the middle of the village.'

Moakler: v. MANCLARK

Moat, Moatt, Mote: William *de la Mote* 1305 FFEss; Stephen *ate Mote* 1317 AssK. 'Dweller at the castle', ME, OFr *mote*.

Mobbs: Wylliam *Mobbys* 1524 SRSf. A variant of MABBS.

Moberley, Moberly, Mobberley: Patrick *de Moberleia* 1190–1200 EChCh; Ralph *de Modberleg* 1260 AssCh; John *Moburlee* 1369 LLB G. From Mobberley (Ches).

Mockler: v. MANCLARK

Mockridge: v. MOGGRIDGE

Moffat, Moffatt, Moffett, Moffitt, Muffatt, Muffett, Meffatt, Meffet: Nicholas *de Mufet* a1232 Black; Thomas *Moffet* 1296 ib. From Moffat (Dumfries).

Mogg: William, Henry *Mogg(e)* 1195 P (Lei, Gl). *Mogg*, a pet-name for *Margaret*. cf. *Mogota* de Ripon; *Mogota* Maure 1313, 1325 Wak (Y); for the more common *Magot*.

Moggridge. Mogridge, Mockridge, Muggeridge, Muggridge, Mugridge: John *Moggrydge* 1544 AD v (W), John *Moggeridge* 1671 DWills. From Mogridge (Devon).

Moir: Robert *More* 1317 Black (Aberdeen). Gael *mòr* 'big'.

Moise: v. MOYSE

Mokler: v. MANCLARK

Mold: v. MAUD

Molin, Molins: Jon *de*, Adam *del Molyn* 1274 RH (Ess), 1289 AssSt; William *de Molyns* 1297 MinAcctCo (Co). From a French place *Moline(s)*, or 'dweller by the mill(s)'. v. also MULLIN.

Molineux, Molyneux: Richard *de Mulinas*, *de Molinaus* 1212 Fees (La); Adam *de Mulyneux*, *de Mulinas* 1235 Fees (Y); Roger *de Molineus* 1259 AssLa. According to Dauzat, the Fr *Molyneux* is an alteration of *molineur* 'miller', v. MULLINER. This

may be the case with Adam *le Molineus* 1242 Fees (La), Richard *Mollineux* 1374 IpmLa, but clearly a French place-name Moulineaux is also involved.

Moll: Walterus *filius Molle* 1203 P (Db); *Molle* litel 1277 Ely (Sf); Alan, Adam *Molle* Hy 3 Gilb (L), c1250 Rams (Nf). A pet-name for *Mary*.

Mollet, Mollett: *Molot* 1290 AssCh; Roger *Molot* 1275 RH (Nf); Ralph *Molet* 1327 SRSf. *Mol-ot*, *Mol-et*, diminutives of *Moll* (Mary).

Mollinson: From an unrecorded *Mollin*, a diminutive of *Moll*. cf. MALLINSON.

Mollison, Mollyson: Thomas *Mollysone* 1589 Black (Aberdeen). 'Son of *Molly*.'

Molson, Moulson: (i) Robert *Mollesone* 1323 AssSt, 1324 Wak (Y). 'Son of *Moll* (Mary).' (ii) John *Moldesone* 1327 SRWo. 'Son of *Mold*.' v. MAUD.

Molton: v. MOULTON

Momerie: v. MOWBRAY

Mompesson, Mumberson, Mumbeson: Philip *de Munpincun* Hy 2 DC (L); Edward *Mounpesoun* 1327 SRC; Edward *Momperson* 1694 Bardsley. From Montpinçon (Calvados, La Manche).

Moncaster: v. MULCASTER

Monday, Mondy: Symon *Moneday* 1279 RH (Hu); William *Monday* 1317 AssK; John *Monenday* 1332 SRSx. OE *mōnandæg* 'Monday'. Perhaps a name given to one born on that day, or to a holder of *Mondayland*, land held on condition of working for the lord on Mondays.

Moneypenny, Monypenny: Richard *Monipenie* 1200–11 Black; William, Richard *Manypeny* 1229 Pat (So), 1256 RamsCt (Hu). 'Many pennies', a nickname for a rich man, or ironically, for a poor one.

Monger: v. MANGER

Monk, Monck, Monnick, Munck, Munk: Aylric *Munec* c1045 ASWills; Regenolde *ðam Munece* a1103 OEByn; William *Munc* 1222 FFEss; Walter *le Monec* 1243 AssSo; Richard *le Monk* 1327 SRWo. OE *munuc*, *munec* 'monk', originally occupational, later a nickname.

Monkhouse: Roger *del Munkhous* 1379 PTY; Alice *Munckus* 1602 Bardsley; Thomas *Munkas* 1660 ib. 'Worker at the monks' house.'

Monkman, Munkman: Robert *Monekisman* 1179 P (L); Edward *le Munekesman* 1199 Cur (Ha); John *Monkeman* 1276 RH (Y); John *Munkman* 1332 SRCu. 'Servant of the monks.'

Monks, Munks: (i) Agnes, Mariota *le Monekes* 1274 RH (Ess), 1279 AssSo. 'The monk's servant.' (ii) Henry *de Monkes* 1332 SRLa; William *del Munkes* 1332 SRCu. 'Servant at the monks', one employed at a monastery.'

Monkton, Munkton: Edward *de Munketon'* 1202 FFY; Robert *de Moneketon* 1346 IpmW; Thomas *de Munkton'* 1395 AssL. From Monkton (Devon, Dorset, Durham, Kent, Som, Wilts, WRYorks).

Monroe: v. MUNRO

Monsey: v. MOUNCEY

Montacute, Montagu, Montague: Drogo *de Montagud*, *de Monte Acuto* 1084 GeldR (So); William *de Montacute* 1255 AssSo; William *de Montagu* 1312 LLB B. The DB family came from Montaigu-le-bois or from Montaigu (La Manche) and have left their name in its Latin form in Montacute (Som) and in its French form in Shepton Montague and, disguised, in Sutton Montis in the same county. Later, Montacute itself, no doubt, gave rise to a surname.

Montford, Montfort, Mountford, Mountfort, Mumford, Mundford, Munford: Hugo *de Montford, de Montfort* 1086 DB, *de Munford* 1086 InqEl, *de Mundfort* 1087 InqAug; Ralph *de Munford* 1159 P (K), *de Muntford* 1200 P (Gl); Simon *de Mumford, de Munford* 1242 Fees (K). The DB undertenant came from Montfort-sur-Risle (Eure). Others later may have come from some other French Montfort. Many of the early forms are indistinguishable from those of Mundford (Norfolk) from which *Mumford* and *Mun(d)ford* may also derive: Richard *de Mundeford* 1247 FFC.

Montgomerie, Montgomery, Montgomrey: Hugo *de Montgomeri, de Montgumeri* 1086 DB (St); William *de Mungumeri* c1159 StCh. From Sainte-Foy-de-Montgomery and Saint-Germain-de-Montgomery (Calvados).

Moodey, Moody, Mudie: Alwine *Modi* c1100–30 OEByn (D); Godric *Modi* c1150 DC (Nt); William *Mudy* 1365 Black. OE *mōdig* 'bold, impetuous, brave'.

Moon, Moone, Munn: (i) William *de Moion, de Moiun, de Moine, de Mouin* 1086 DB (Do); Reginald *de Moyn, de Moyun, de Moun, de Mohun* 1239–53 AssSo. From Moyon (La Manche). (ii) Robert *Mone* 1260 AssY; Thomas *le Mun* 1275 RH (Nf); Geoffrey *le Moun'* 1279 RH (Beds). AFr *moun, mun* 'monk'. cf. MOYNE.

Moor, Moore, Moores, Moors, More, Mores: (i) Johannes filius *More* 1185 Templars (L); *Morus* de la Hale 1214 Cur (K); *More* Kalendrer 1332 SRLo; Hugo *Maurus* 1186 P (C); William, Osbert *Mor* 1198 FFEss, 1227 FFSf; Thomas, Hugh *le Mor* 1201, 1205 Cur (K, Beds). The personal-name *More* is from OFr *Maur* (Latin *Maurus*), in the vernacular *More*, either 'a Moor' or 'swarthy as a Moor'. There was a 6th-century saint of this name. *le Mor* is a nickname (OFr *more* 'Moor', swarthy). (ii) William *de More* 1086 DB (Sf); Lefric *de la Mora* 1169 P (Nth); Matthew *del More* 1275 Wak; Thomas *atte More*, Simon *atte Moure* 1296 SRSx; John *Bythemore* 1327 SRSo; John *in le Mor* 1332 SRSt. From Moore (Ches), More (Salop) or from residence in or near a moor (OE *mōr* 'moor, marsh, fen').

Moorcock: *Morecok* Chepman 1327 SRSo; Walter *Morcoc* c1160 Colch (Sf), 1202 AssL; John *Morekoc, Morecok* 1283 Battle (Sx), 1327 *SR* (Ess). Either a diminutive of *More* (*Morcoc*), v. MOOR; or a nickname from the moorcock.

Moorcroft, Morecraft: Richard *de Morcroft* 1366 SRLa. 'Dweller at the croft on the moor.'

Moorey: (i) Robert *de la Morhage* 1207 P (Db). 'Dweller at the enclosure on the moor', as at Moorhay (Devon). (ii) William *de Morewraa* 1332

SRCu. 'Dweller at the nook on the moor' (ON *vrá*).

Moorhouse, Morehouse, Morres: William *de Morhuse* 1180 P (Y); Matilda *del Morhouse* 1301 SRY; Geoffrey *atte Morhouse* 1327 SRSo; William *Morhous* 1440 ShefA; George *Morras* or *Morehouse* 1680 LaWills. From Moorhouse (WRYorks) or from residence at a house on the moor or marsh. OE *mōr* and *hūs*. This may have become MORRIS.

Mooring, Moreing: Richard *Moring* 1275 SRWo, 1327 SRSx; Henry *Morynge* 1327 SRWo. Perhaps OE **mōring* 'dweller on the moor'.

Moorman, Moreman, Morman: Ralph *le Morman* 1287 SRSf; William *le Moreman* 1327 SRSf. OE **mōrmann* 'marsh-dweller'.

Moorshead: John *Murside* 1260 AssLa. 'Dweller at the edge of the marsh.'

Moorwood, Morwood: Ralph *de Morewode* 1275 RH (L). 'Dweller by the moor-wood.'

Moppett: Probably a diminutive of *Mopp*, a variant of *Mobb, Mabb*, pet-names for *Mabel*. cf. Ivetta, William *Mopp(e)* 1243 AssDu, 1279 RH (O), the diminutive *Moppel*, Fulco *Moppel* 1251 Rams (Hu), and the double diminutive *Moppelin*, Ralph *Moppelin* 1195 P (L).

Morand, Morant, Murrant: *Morandus* de Kerkebi 1176 P (Y); *Morant* filius Ernis 1198 FF (Nf); *Moraunt* Lambard 1317 AssK; Hugo *le Demurant* 1182 P (K); William *Morand'* 12th DC (L); Richard *Morant* 1200 P (D); William *Morand, Morant* 1210–11 Cur (Sx); John, Thomas *le Moraunt* 1297 Coram (Sf), 1320 FFSf; Margery *Demoraunt* 1379 PTY. OFr *Moran, Morant*, probably OG **Modrannus*, or a nickname, aphetic for OFr *demorant* (*demeurant*), present participle of *demeurer* 'to reside', residing, staying, probably 'a sojourner', a stranger who stays.

Morce, Morss: John *Morice, Morce* 1382 AssC. For MORRIS.

Mordaunt: William *mordaunt* 1148 Winton (Ha); Eustace *le Mordant* 1176 P (Bk). OFr *mordant*, present participle of *mordre* 'to bite', 'biting, sarcastic'.

Morel, Morell, Morill, Morrell, Morrill: *Morel* 1086 InqEl (Nf); *Moræl* of Bæbbaburh 1093 ASC E; *Morellus* 1191 P (Sf); Peter, Milo *Morel* 1164, 1196 P (O, Bk). A diminutive of either *More* or OFr *more* 'brown, swarthy as a Moor'. v. MOOR.

Moreland, Morland: Edith *de la Morland* 1257 MELS (So); Henry *atte Morlonde* 1296 SRSx; William *de Moreland* 1327 SRY. 'Dweller on the moor-land.'

Moreman: v. MOORMAN

Moreton: v. MORTON

Morfey, Morffew, Morphey, Morphy, Morphew, Maffey: Wido *Malfeth* 1130 P (Nth); William *Malfet* 1163–6 Seals (Sx); Simon *(le) Malfe* 1176, 1184 P (Nth, C); Lucas *Maufe, Malve* 1196, 1205 Cur (Nth); Simon *Malfei* 1198 FF (Nf); John *Malefay* 1307 Wak (Y); Thomas *Mauphe, Maufe, Maufie* 1221 AssWa; Laurence *Maufei*, Andrew *Maufee* 1327, 1332 SRSx; Elias *Maifai*, William

Mayfai 1327 SRSx; Richard *Maffay* 1498 SxWills; John *Morfewe* 1564 SfPR; Jedion *Morphewe* 1629 ib.; John *Morfee* 1679 ib. OFr *malfé, malfeü*, 'representing a barbarous Latin *male-fatus* and *male-fatutus*' (Weekley), 'ill-omened', a term of abuse applied to the Saracens and the devil. cf. *Hobgoblyng*, goblin mauffé (Palsgrave); *malfé, maufé, maufeit, maffé, malfait, malfee* 'devil, demon' (Godefroy). The normal development would be *Mauffey*. With the loss of *r* in pronunciation, *Mau-* (*Maw-*) and *Mor-* were indistinguishable. For the *ph*, cf. FARRAR and PHARAOH.

Morgan, Morgans: *Morganus* 1159, 1166 P (Gl, Sa); *Morgund* 1204–11 Black; Isabella, John *Morgan* 1214 Cur (Berks), 1279 AssNb; John *Morgane* 1419 Black. OBret, OW, Cornish *Morcant*, Welsh *Morgan*, Pictish *Morgunn*, a very old Celtic name.

Morhall, Morrhall, Morral, Morrall: Gilbert *de Morhalle* 1332 SRLa. 'Dweller at the hall on the moor.'

Morin, Morren, Morrin: Rogerus *filius Maurini, Morini* 1086 ICC (C); *Morin'* del Pin 1130 P (Lei); Robert, Ralph *Morin* c1140 DC (L), 1183–4 EngFeud (Nth). OFr *Morin*, a diminutive of *More*. *v.* MOOR.

Morison: *v.* MORRISON
Morland: *v.* MORELAND

Morley, Morely, Moorley: Milo *de Morleia* 1196 P (Bk); Ralph *de Morleg* 1230 P (Db); Thomas *Morleigh* 1377 IpmW. From Morley (Derby, Durham, Norfolk, WRYorks), or Moreleigh (Devon).

Morman: *v.* MOORMAN
Morphew, Morphey: *v.* MORFEY
Morpuss: *v.* MALPAS
Morrall: *v.* MORHALL
Morrell, Morrill: *v.* MOREL
Morren, Morrin: *v.* MORIN
Morres: *v.* MOORHOUSE
Morrice: *v.* MAURICE

Morrick: Nicholas, Hugo *de Morewic* 1190 P (He), 1219 AssY. 'Dweller at the dairy-farm in the fen or on the moor', OE *mōr* and *wīc*.

Morris(s): *v.* MAURICE

Morrish: John *Morysch* 1416 LLB I; Humfrey *Mores, Morrishe* 1569, 1602 Oriel (O). For MORRIS. cf. NORRISH, PARISH.

Morrison, Morison, Moryson: Robert *Morisson* 1379 PTY; Andrew *Morison* 1463 Black. 'Son of *Maurice*.'

Mortimer, Mortimore, Mutimer: Ralph (*de*) *Mortemer, de Mortuo Mari* 1086 DB; Peter *Mortemer* 1296 SRSx; Elizabeth *Mottimer* 1712 SfPR. From Mortemer (Seine-Inférieure).

Morton, Moreton: Robert *de Mortone* 1130 P (W); William *de Moreton, de Morton* 1218 FFO, 1307 IpmGl; Thomas *Morton* 1432–3 FFSr. From one or other of the many places of this name.

Morwood: *v.* MOORWOOD

Moseley, Mosely, Mosley, Mosleigh, Mossley, Mozley, Mozeley: Suen *de Moseleia* 1195 P (Wo); William *de Moseleg* 1271 AssSt; Alan *de Moselegh* 1332 SRLa; John *Mosley* 1414 FFEss. From Moseley (Staffs, Worcs), Moseley in West Dean (Glos), or Mowsley (Leics).

Moss, Mosse: David *del Mos* 1286 AssCh; Stephen *atte Mos* 1327 SRSt; Robert *del Mosse* 1327 SRDb. 'Dweller by the moss or morass', Oe *mos. Mosse* was also a common form of Jewish *Moses*: *Mossus* cum naso 1183 P (Nf), Master *Mosse* the Jew of London 1260 AssY and this has probably contributed to the surname. Ailmerus *filius Mosse* or Almer *Mosse* 1153–68, 1186–1210 Holme (Nf) was probably English. cf. Richard, Henry *Mosse* 1250 *Ass* (C), 1275 RH (L).

Mote: *v.* MOAT

Mothers: *Moder* c1095 Bury (Sf); Vlfgiet *Moder* 1162 P (Nth); Alicia *le Moder'* 1279 RH (C). ON *Móðir*, ODa, OSw *Modher*. Also a nickname.

Mothersole, Mothersill: John *Mothersole* 1674 HTSf. These surnames may be a dialectal pronunciation of Moddershall (Staffs): William *de Modreshalle* 1305 StThomas (St). But we are probably also concerned with a nickname: Richard *Modisoule;* Hugh *Modysowel* 1275, 1308 Wak (Y), 'brave, proud soul', OE *mōdig, sāwol*. In Ralph *Modersoule* 1313 Cl (La), we have an oath-name, 'by my mother's soul'.

Motton: *v.* MUTTON

Mottram, Motteram: John *de Mottrum* 1287 AssCh; Richard *Motteram* 1541 CorNt; John *Motrum* 1678 NorwDep. From Mottram (Ches).

Mouat, Mouatt, Mowat, Mowatt: Robert *de Montealto* 1124–53 Black; Robert (*de*) *Muhaut* 13th Riev (Y); Alexander *de Mohaut, Mouhat* 1198–1218 Black; Simon *de Munhalt* 1197 P (Y); Richard *de Mohaud* 1208 Cur (Y); Thomas *de Moaud* 1219 AssY; John *Mowet* 1410 Black. From a French place Montaut (several). The surname may also have become *Mahood, Mawhood* (*v.* MAUD), and, occasionally may mean 'meadowward', or hayward (cf. MAW): Roger *le Mowerd* 1280 AssSo.

Moubray: *v.* MOWBRAY
Mould(s): *v.* MAUD
Moule(s): *v.* MULE
Moulson: *v.* MOLSON
Moult: *v.* MAUD

Moulton, Molton, Multon: Ælfgar *de Muletune* c975 LibEl (Sf); Thomas *de Moleton, de Multon* 1166 P (L), 1327 SRLei; John *Multon* 1482 FFEss. From Moulton (Ches, Lincs, Norfolk, Northants, Staffs, Suffolk, NRYorks), or Molton (Devon).

Mouncey, Mounsey, Mounsie, Monsey, Muncey, Munsey, Munsie, Munchay, Mungay: William *de Moncels, Moncellis, Muntcellis, Muncellis* 1086 DB; Milisant *de Muncehaus*, Edonea *de Munchaus* 1185 Templars (L); William *Munci* 1198 FF (Gl); Walter *de Mouncy, de Munsy* 1300 LoCt. William de Moncels of DB came from Monceaux (Calvados). Edonea *de Munchaus* is also called *de Herste* and had a son, Waleran, called both *de Herste* and *de Muncaus*. They came from Monchaux (Seine-Inférieure) and their name survives in

Herstmonceux (Sussex), pronounced *Hurstmoun-sies*. *Mungay* may also be for *Mountjoy*.

Mount, Mounter: Richard *del Mount* 1301 SRY; John *le Mountere* 1305 MESO (Ha); Richard *le Monter* 1327 SRSo. 'Dweller by the mount, hill' (OE *munt*).

Mountford, Mountfort: *v.* MONTFORD

Mountjoy, Mungay: Gilbert *de Montgoye* 1219 AssY; Elias *Munjoye* 1243 AssSo; Robert *de Mount-gay, de Mungay* 13th WhC (La); John *Mount-joye* 1307 AssSt. From Montjoie (La Manche).

Mountney, Mounteney: Robert *de Munteigni* 1177 P (Ess); Michael *de Munteny* 1208 Cur (Nf). From Montigni (Calvados, La Manche, etc.).

Mouth: (i) Robert *Muth* 1183 P (Ess). OE *mūð* 'mouth'. cf. BOUCH. (ii) William *atte Muthe* 1315 PN Sr 294. 'Dweller at the junction of the streams' (OE *(ge)mȳðe*), as at Meath Green (Surrey).

Mowat(t): *v.* MAUD, MOUAT

Mowbray, Mowbury, Moubray, Momerie, Mul-berry, Mulbery, Mulbry, Mumbray, Mummery, Memory, Membry: Rodbeard *a Mundbræg* 1087 ASC E; Roger *de Mulbrai, de Mubrai* c1130 Whitby (Y), *de Molbrai* c1150 ib.; Paganus *de Moubrai* 1150 Eynsham (O); Roger *de Munbrai, de Moubrai* 1185 Templars (L, Y); William *de Mumbray* 1242 Fees (K); Richard *Mulberye* 1381 SRSf; John *Mowbray, Memory, Membry* 1714, 1725, 1748 FrLeic; Samuel *Mowbery* 1745 ib. From Montbrai (La Manche).

Mowe: *v.* MAW

Mower: *v.* MAWER

Mowling: *v.* MULLINGS

Mowll, Mowle, Mowles: John *Moule* or *Moulde* 1584 Bardsley. For MULE or MAUD.

Mowse: Æluric *Mus* 1066 ICC (C); Geoffey *le Mus, le Mous* 1296, 1332 SRSx. OE *mūs* 'mouse'.

Mowson: Margarita *Mowson* 1549 Rothwell PR (Y). Probably for *Mollson* 'Son of Mary'.

Moxon, Moxom, Moxson, Moxsom: Siuuard *Mocesun* 1087–98 Bury; John *Mokesson* 1379 PTY; John *Moxson* 1499 Calv; Thomas *Moxon* 1588 Rothwell PR (Y). The first example is from OE *Mocca*, found twice in early documents, but later examples are more probably for 'son of *Mog*', i.e. Margaret, with *-gs-* assimilated to *-ks-*.

Moyce, Moyes: *v.* MOYSE

Moyle: William, Richard *Moil* 1275 SRWo, 1359 Putnam (Co); William *le Moil* 1327 *SR* (Co); David, Richard *Moill* 1393 Chirk, 1504 Black. Cornish *moel*, Ir, Gael *maol* 'bald'.

Moyne: Robert *le Muine* 1141–51 Colch (Ess); Ralph *Moin* 1168 P (Sx); Henry *le Moygne* 1255 Ass (Ess). OFr *moine, muigne, moigne* 'monk', originally of office, later a nickname. Geoffrey *le Moine* was constable of the castle of Newcastle in 1219 (AssY).

Moyse, Moyses, Moyce, Moyes, Moise: Gauf-ridus *filius Moyses* 1210 Cur (Nf); *Moys' de* Bil-ham 1230 P (Y); Elyas *Moyses* 1196 P (Y); William *Moyse* 1274 RH (Ess). Fr *Moise*, Hebrew *Moses*.

Moz(e)ley: *v.* MOSELEY

Much: *v.* MUTCH

Muckle, Mutchell: Richard *Mukel* 1255 RH (Sa); Agnes *la Muchele* 1279 RH (O). OE *mycel* 'big'. cf. MITCHEL.

Mucklejohn: *v.* MEIKLEJOHN

Mudd: *Modde* 1307, 1315 Wak (Y), 14th Shef (Y); Hugo *Mud* 1205 P (Sf); Cristofor *Mod* 1327 SRSf; Widow *Mud* alias *Mutt* 1625 EA (NS) ii (Sf). Perhaps OE **Modd*, a short form of names in *Mōd-*, though these were rare. cf. *Modingus, Modinc* 1066 DB (Beds, Ess); Hugh *Moding'* 1275 SRWo; William *Modbert* 1274 RH (Sa).

Muddeman, Muddiman: Richard *Modimon* 1275 SRWo. 'Brave, courageous man.' cf. MOODEY.

Mudditt: *v.* MAUDUIT

Mudie: *v.* MOODEY

Muers: *v.* MEWER

Muffatt, Muffett: *v.* MOFFAT

Muggeridge, Muggridge: *v.* MOGGRIDGE

Muir, Mure: Thomas *de la More* 1291 Black; Elizabeth *Mure* 1347 ib.; Aleusa *en le muyre* 1348 DbAS 36; John *Muyr* 1470 Black. 'Dweller by the moor.' Chiefly Scottish. Perhaps also for MEWER.

Muirhead: William *de Murehede* 1401 Black; David *Muirheyd* 1527 ib. 'Dweller at the head of the moor.' Common in Scotland.

Mulberry, Mulbry: *v.* MOWBRAY

Mulcaster, Muncaster, Moncaster: Walter *de Mulecastr'* 1219 AssY; John *Muncaster* 1675 HTSf. From Muncaster (Cumb).

Mule, Moule, Moules: David *le Mul* 1199 P (Wo); Yuo *Mul* 1206 P (L); Baldewin *Mule* 1225 Pat; William *le Moul* 1327 SRSt. OE *mūl*, ME *moul* 'mule'. This would have become *mowl* but was ousted by OFr *mule* in the 13th century.

Mullard: *v.* MILLWARD

Mullet, Mullett: John *Mulet* 1275 RH (Sf), 1311 ColchCt. Perhaps a diminutive of OFr *mule* 'mule'. Or, possibly, a nickname for a seller of mussels (OFr *mulet*). Michaëlsson notes that on the Nor-mandy coast he is called 'Moulettes' from his cry. His real name is unknown to most of his customers.

Mulligan: *v.* MILLICAN

Mullin, Mullen, Mullins, Mullens, Mullings, Molins: Ralph *de Molins* 1159 P; Adam *del Molyn* 1289 AssSt; John *de Molyns* 1341 LoPleas; Edward *Mullens* 1545 SRW; William *Mullyns* 1642 PrD. 'Dweller at the mills', Fr *moulins*, or from one or other of the numerous French places of the name. *v.* also MOLIN.

Mulliner, Mullinar, Mullinder, Mullinger: San-cheus *Moliner* 1275 RH (L); Walter *le Moliner* 1283 SRSf; William *Molindiner* 1327 SRSo; Wil-liam *Mullinder* 1612 Shef (Y); Francis *Mullender, Mullenger*, Sam *Mulliner* 1674 HTSf. OFr *molinier* 'miller'.

Mullings, Mowling: William *Molling'* 1292 SRLo; Geva *Mullyng* 1313 AD iv (Lo). OE **mulling* 'darling' (c1450 NED).

Multon: *v.* MOULTON

Mumberson, Mumbeson: *v.* MOMPESSON

Mumbray: *v.* MOWBRAY

Mumford: *v.* MONTFORD

Mummery: *v.* MOWBRAY

Muncaster: v. MULCASTER

Muncey, Munchay: v. MOUNCEY

Munday, Mundie, Mundy: Richard, Thomas *Mundi* 1239 Rams (Nf), 1291 AssCh; John. Walter *Mundy* 1327 SRSf, SRY. ON *Mundi*.

Mundford, Munford: v. MONTFORD

Mungay: v. MOUNCEY, MOUNTJOY

Munkton: v. MONKTON

Munn: v. MOON

Munnings: *Mundingus* 1066 DB, c1095 Bury (Sf); Maurice *Munning* 1221 AssWa; Gilbert *Monding*, William *Munding*, Robert *Munnyng* 1327 SRSf. OE *Munding 'son of *Munda*'. OE *Munda 'protector' is unrecorded but is the first element of Mundford (Norfolk) and Mundham (Norfolk, Sussex).

Munro, Munroe, Munrow, Monro: Gael *Rothach* 'man from Ro'. 'According to a tradition which may be substantially correct the ancestors of the Munros came from Ireland, from the foot of the river Roe in Derry, whence the name *Bunrotha*, giving *Mun-rotha* by eclipsis of *b* after the preposition *in*' (Watson).

Munsey, Munsie: v. MOUNCEY

Murch: Geoffrey *Morch* 1327 SRSf; Hugh *Murch* 1651 DWills. 'Dwarf.' cf. '*Murche*, lytyll man. *Nanus*' PromptParv.

Murchie, Murchison, MacMurchie: Kathel *Mac murchy* 1259 Black; John *Murchosone* 1473 ib. Gael *MacMhurchaidh* 'son of *Murchadh*' 'sea-warrior'.

Murdoch, Murdock: *Murdac, Murdoc, Meurdoch* 1066 DB (Y); *Mariedoc* Bohhan 1160 P (Sa); Geoffrey, Roger *Murdac* 1130 P (Y), 1182 StCh; Ralph, Sibilla *Murðac* 1197, 1199 P (Db, Gl); Nicholas *Murdoc* Hy 3 AD i (Bk). An anglicizing of OIr *Muireadhach*, OW *Mordoc*, MGael *Muireadhaigh*, Gael *Murdoch* 'mariner'. Introduced into Yorkshire before the Conquest by Norwegians from Ireland.

Murgatroyd: John *Mergetrode* 1379 PTY; Bryan *Murgetroyde* 1647 RothwellPR (Y). From a lost Yorkshire place, 'Margaret's clearing'.

Muriel, Murrell, Murrells, Murrill, Merrall, Merralls, Merrell, Merrells, Merril, Merrill, Merrills, Mirralls: (i) Ougrim *filius Miriel*' 1188 P (L); *Mirielis, Muriella* de Stokes 1203 Cur (Bk); Johannes *filius Miriald*' 1208 Cur (Y); Godric *Miriild, Mirild*', *Mirield* 1184–8 P (L); Robert, Richard *Muriel* 1195 P (L), 1221 *ElyA* (Sf); Simon *Mirield* 1323 AD v (Nf); John *Myrel* 1327 SRSf; Richard *Meryel*, Walter *Merel* 1381 SRSf; William *Meryellys*, Thomas *Merelles* 1524 SRSf. *Muriel*, much the least common form as a surname, is of Celtic origin, found in Welsh as *Meriel, Meryl*, and in Irish as *Muirgheal*, earlier *Muirgel* 'sea-bright'. It was brought from Brittany by the Normans, hence its popularity in Lincolnshire, East Anglia and Essex, and also in Yorkshire where it may also have been introduced earlier by Scandinavians from Ireland. The name occurs in ON as *Mýrgjol*, daughter of a King of Dublin. In Staffordshire and the Welsh border counties, it came, no doubt, direct from Wales. (ii) Adam *de Merihel*

1275 RH (Sf); Nicholas *de Meriel* 1276 RH (Y); Walter *de Merihil* 1283 SRSf; Ralph *Muryhull* 1332 SRSt. From residence near some pleasant hill.

Murphy: Ir *ÓMurchadha* 'descendant of *Murchadh*' 'sea-warrior'.

Murrant: v. MORAND

Murray, Murrey, Murrie, Murry: William *de Moravia* 1203 Black; Alan *de Morref* 1317 ib.; Andrew *Moray* 1327 ib. From the province of Moray (Scotland). Some of the modern names may be from ME *murie*. v. MERRY.

Murrell, Murrill: v. MURIEL

Murton: William *de Murton*' 1221 AssWa (Lei); William *Murtone* 1375 ColchCt. From Murton (Durham, Northumb, Westmorland, NRYorks).

Musgrave, Musgrove: Alan *de Musegrave* 1228 Cur (Nb); Thomas *de Musgraue* 1362 AssY; Robert *Musgrave* 1413 IpmY; Philip *Musgrave, Musgrove* 1642 PrD. Usually no doubt from Musgrave (Westmorland), but occasionally perhaps from Mussegros (Normandy), cf. Charlton Musgrove (Som) from Richard *de Mucegros* t John.

Mushet, Muskett: Robert, Osketell' *Muschet* Hy 2 DC (Nt), 1177 P (Sf); William *Musket* c1210 Fees (Nf); William *Mouchet* 1327 SRC. OFr *mouchet, mouschet, mousquet* 'a musket; the tassell of a sparhawke' (Cotgrave), 'a lytell hauke' (Palsgrave).

Mussard, Mussared: Hascoit *Musard, Musart* 1086 DB (Berks, Bk); Alfricus *Musard* 1134–40 Holme (Nf). OFr *musard* 'absent-minded, stupid' (c1300 NED).

Mustard, Mustart: Adam, William *Mustard*' 1191 P (Y), 1206 P (He). OFr *mostarde* 'mustard', perhaps one with a sharp, biting tongue, but usually, no doubt, a dealer in mustard, by metonymy for *mustarder*. cf. John *le Mustarder* 1327 SRC, Adam *le Mustardman* 1327 SRSf.

Mustell, Mustill, Mustol, Muzzel, Muzzle: Robert *Mustail* 1175–90 Seals (Y); Roger *Musteile* 1177 P (L); Hugh *Mustell*' 1208 Cur (Gl); William *Mustol*' 1208 Cur (Nf). OFr *musteile, mustoile* 'weasel'.

Musters, Mustre: Robert *de Mosteriis, de Mosters* 1086 DB (L, Nt); Robert *de Mustres* 1185 Templars (Y); Lisiard *des Mustiers* 1197 P (L). From Moutiers-Hubert (Calvados).

Musto, Mustoe, Mustoo, Mustow: Ralph *atte Mustowe* 1327 SRSx. 'Dweller by the moot-stow', OE (*ge*)*mōt-stōw*, a common name for the meeting-place of a hundred.

Mutch, Much: William *Moch* 1275 RH (Nf); Richard *Muche* 1374 Ipm (Ess). ME *moche, muche* 'big'.

Mutchell: v. MUCKLE

Muter, Mutter, Mutters: Grinchetell' *Mutere*, Hugo *le Motere* 1130, 1175 P (L); William *le Mouter* 1327 SRWo. OE *mōtere* 'public speaker'.

Mutimer: v. MORTIMER

Mutton, Motton: Stephen *Muton*' 1195 Oseney (O); Robert *Mouton*', *Mutun* 1219 Cur, 1242 Fees (Lei); William *Moton* 1327 SRSx. OFr *mouton* 'sheep', a nickname, or metonymic for OFr *mou-*

tonier, a keeper of sheep, shepherd: Hugh *Motoner* 1275 RH (Lo).

Mutton, Mitton, Mytton: William *de Mitton*, *de Mutton* 1286–7 AssSt. From Mitton (Lancs, Worcs, WRYorks) or Myton (Warwicks, Salop, NRYorks).

Muttycombe: A Somerset name, from Mothecombe (Devon), pronounced *Muddicombe*, where the surname was *de Modecumbe* 1238, *de Muthecumbe* 1244 (PN D 277).

Myall: *v.* MIALL

Mycock: *v.* MAYCOCK

Myddleton: *v.* MIDDLETON

Myer, Myers, Mier, Miers: (i) Herewardus *le Mire, Medicus* 1212 Cur (Berks); Thomas *le*

Myre 1256 AssNb. OFr *mire* 'physician'. (ii) Hugo, Adam *del Mire* 1274 Wak (Y), 1332 AssLa. 'Dweller by the marsh', ON *mýrr*.

Myhill: *v.* MIALL

Mylechreest, Mylchreest, Mylecrist: *MacGilchreest* 1511, *McYilchrist* 1713, *Mylechreest* 1717. Manx *Mac Giolla Chreest* 'son of Christ's servant' (Moore).

Myles: *v.* MILES

Mylles: *v.* MILLS

Mynett, Mynott: *v.* MIGNOT

Mynn: *v.* MINN

Myott: *v.* MIATT

Mytton: *v.* MUTTON

N

Nabb, Nabbs, Napp: *Nabbe* Brodeye 1298 Wak (Y); *Nabbe* son of Broun 1308 ib.; John *Nap* 1279 RH (C); Gregory *Nabbys* 1524 SRSf. *Nabb* and *Napp* are probably parallels to *Nobb* and *Nopp*, pet-names for *Robert*, rhymed on *Rab* and *Rob*. cf. Robert *Nabelot* 1524 SRSf and *v.* NOBBS, ROBLETT.

Nadler: *v.* NEEDLER

Naesmith: *v.* NAYSMITH

Nail: William, Geoffrey *Nayl* 1255 RH (Bk), 1327 *SR* (Ess). Metonymic for NAYLAR.

Nailer: *v.* NAYLAR

Naisbet, Naisbitt: *v.* NESBIT

Naish: *v.* ASH

Naismith: *v.* NAYSMITH

Nalder: *v.* ALDER

Naldrett: *v.* ALDRITT

Nangle: *v.* ANGLE

Napier, Naper, Napper: Peter *Napier* 1148 Winton (Ha); Ralph (*le*) *Naper, le Napier* 1167–71 P (Ess); Reginald *le Nappere* 1225 AssSo. OFr *napier, nappier* from *nappe* 'table-cloth'. 'Naperer, one who has charge of the napery or table-linen' (1880 NED).

Napleton: *v.* APPLETON

Napp: *v.* NABB

Nares: Simon *le Neir* 1221 AssGl; William *le Nayr* 1297 SRY. AFr *neir* 'black'.

Narracott: William *de Northecote* 1330 PN D 31. From Narracott (Devon).

Narramore, Narrowmore: Reginald *Bynorthemore* 1318 PN D 481. 'Dweller north of the moor', as at Narramore (Devon).

Narraway, Narroway: Nicholas *Bynortheweye* 1333 PN D 453. 'Dweller north of the road', as at Narraway (Devon).

Nash: *v.* ASH

Nasmyth: *v.* NAYSMITH

Nass: *v.* NESS

Nave: John *le Cnaue* 1221 AssWa; Simon *Knave* 1296 SRSx. OE *cnafa* 'child, youth, servant', often used of servants: William *Margeriknave* 1307 Wak (Y). *Nave* may also be metonymic for *Naver*: Eadric *Nauere* 13th AD iv (Lo), Richard *le Navere* 1275 RH (Nf), a maker of naves of wheels, from OE *nafa, nafu*. cf. Adam *Nawrith* 1301 SRY 'nave-wright'.

Nay: *v.* NYE

Naybour: *v.* NEIGHBOUR

Naylar, Nayler, Naylor, Nailer: Stephen *le*

Nailere 1231 Pat (Lo); James *le nayler* 1273 FrY. A derivative of OE *nægel* 'nail', a maker of nails (c1440 NED).

Nayshe: *v.* ASH

Naysmith, Naismith, Naesmith, Nasmyth: Roger *Knifsmith* 1246–89 Bart (Lo); Adam *Knyfsmith* 1285 AssLa; Saman *le Knyfsmyth* 1310 LLB D; William *Knysmyt* 1326 AssSt; Robert *Knysmithe* 1594 Bardsley; John *Naysmith* n.d. ib. OE *cnīf* 'knife' and *smið* 'smith', a cutler.

Neachell: *v.* ETCHELLS

Neal, Neale, Neall, Neel, Neele, Neeld, Neels, Neil, Neild, Neill, Niall, Niel, Nield, Niell, Niles, Nigel, Nihell, Nihill, McNeal, McNeil, McNiel, O'Neal, O'Neill: Willelmus *filius Nigelli* 1086 DB (Bk); *Neel* 1170–82 YCh (Y); *Niel* de Wellebek 1260 AssY; Achyne *mac Nele* 1289 Black; Willelmus *filius Nele* 1304 SRY; *Neil* Carrick c1314 Black (Galloway); *Nile* Hog 1557 Black (Stirling); Willelmus *Nigelli* 1195 FF (W); Robert *Nel, Neel* 1208–10 Cur (Berks); Nicholaus *Nigelle* 1252 Rams (Hu); Henry *Nel* 1260 AssC; Robert *Neel* 1294 AssSt; Roger *Niel* 1319 FFSf; John *Nihell* 1565 Bardsley; Matthew *Nihill* 1796 ib. OIr *Niáll*, Gael *Niáll* 'champion', latinized by Adamnan as *Nellis*. The name was carried to Iceland by the Scandinavians as *Njáll*, taken to Norway, then to France and brought to England by the Normans. It was also introduced direct into north-west England and Yorkshire by Norwegians from Ireland. It was usually latinized as *Nigellus* through an incorrect association with *niger* 'black'. *Neil* and *Nigel* are now mainly Scottish. In Yorkshire it is found as *Nell*. Robertus *filius Nigelli* and Robertus *Nel* (1221 AssWa) are identical.

Neam, Neame: Richard *le Naim* 1170–8 P (L); John *Nepos, le Neim* 1214 Cur (Sr); John *le Neim* c1280 SRWo; Henry *Neem*, John *le Naym* 1327 SRDb, SRWo; John *Naym* 1431 FA (Wo). OE *ēam* 'uncle' with the initial *N-* due to misdivision of syllable. *v.* also EAMES. But Fr *nain* 'dwarf' is probably also a source of the name.

Neap, Neep: Peter, John (*le*) *Nep* 1279 RH (Bk, Hu); Richard *Nepe* 1524 SRSf. OE *nǣp* 'turnip'.

Neat, Neate: Probably OE *nēat* 'ox, cow', metonymic for 'cowherd'. cf. William *Nethirde* 1301 SRY, Hubert *le Netdriver* 1295 SIA xiii (Sf). Or a nickname: cf. Ascer *Neteheved* 1200 Cur (L), 'ox-head'.

Neatby: John *de Nateby* 1350 FFC. From Nateby (Lancs, Westmorland).

Neave, Neaves, Neeve, Neeves, Neve: Robert *le Neve* 1242 Fees (K); Andrew *Neve* c1250 Rams (Beds). OE *nefa*, ME *neve* 'nephew'. Also a nickname for a prodigal or parasite: 'neuerthryfte, or wastour' PromptParv.

Neck: Henry *Nekke* 1279 RH (C); Richard *Necke* 1327 SRC. A nickname for one with some peculiarity of the neck. cf. Symon *Nekeles*, probably identical with Symon *Chortneke* 'short neck' 1275 RH (Nf), Geoffrey *Neckebon* 1316 FFC.

Needham, Nedham: John, Robert *de Nedham* 1275 RH (Db), 1305 LoCt; John *Needhom* 1371 FFEss. From Needham (Derby, Norfolk, Suffolk).

Needle: Metonymic for NEEDLER.

Needler, Neelder, Nelder, Nadler: Peter *le Nedler'* 1221 AssSa; Richard *Nedlere, Neldere* 1235 Oseney (O); Robert *le Nadlere* 1309 LLB D, 1327 *SR* (Ess). OE **nædlere* 'needler' from *nædl* 'needle'. A maker of needles (1362 NED). *Neelder* and *Nelder* are due to metathesis of *dl*. In ME *Nadler* was the regular form in Essex and common in London.

Neel(e), Neeld, Neels: v. NEAL

Neep: v. NEAP

Neeve(s): v. NEAVE

Neighbour, Naybour: Ralph *Nechebur* 1222 DBStP (Herts); William *le Neybere* 1309 SRBeds; Bartholomew *Neighebour* 1327 *SR* (Ess). OE *nēahgebūr* 'neighbour'.

Neil(d), Neill: v. NEAL

Neilson, Nielson, Nilson: John *Neylsone* 1510 Black; John *Nilsoune* 1654 ib. 'Son of Neil.'

Nelder: v. NEEDLER

Neldrett: v. ALDRITT

Nell: *Nelle* de Wynter, de Soureby 1274 Wak (Y); Henry *Nelle* 1297 MinAcctCo (R). OIr *Nel, Niáll. v.* NEAL.

Nelm(e)s: v. ELM

Nelson: John, Robert *Nelleson* 1324 Wak (Y), 1332 SRCu. 'Son of Nell.' v. NELL.

Nephew: Thomas *le Neveu* 1268 AssSo; John *Neveu* 1274 RH (Nf). OFr *neveu* 'nephew'.

Nesbit, Nesbitt, Naisbet, Naisbit, Naisbitt, Nisbet, Nisbit: Robert *de Nesbit* 1160–1200 Black; William *de Nesebite* c1250 FeuDu. From Nesbit (Berwicks, Northumb) or Nesbitt (Durham, Northumb).

Nesfield, Nessfield: William *de Nesfeld* 1345 FFY; Richard *de Nessfeld* 1381 PTY; Aliua *Nesfeld* 1395 Whitby. From Nesfield (WRYorks).

Ness, Nass, Noss: Robert *de Nesse* 1177 P (Y); William *de Nes* 1275 RH (Sf); Agnes *ate Nass* 1279 RH (O). 'Dweller on the headland', OE *næss*, as at Nass (Glos) or Ness (Ches, NRYorks). John *atte Nasse* lived at Noss Point in Brixham in 1330 (PN D 508). Occasionally these modern forms may be for ASH, NAYSHE: Walter *ate Nesse* or *ate Neysshe* 1317 AssK. Nicholas *de la Nesse* in 1279 lived at Ashes Fm, Icklesham (PN Sx 512).

Nessling, Neslen: Nicholas *Nestlyng* 1524 SRSf; Peter *Nestlyn* ib.; Widow *Neslin* 1674 HTSf. 'Nestling'.

Netherton: Petronilla *de la Netherton'* 1275 SRWo; Walter *atte Nuthereton* 1330 MELS (Sr). 'Dweller at the lower farm', as at Netherton (Northumb, Worcs).

Netherwood: Thomas *de Netherwode* 1274 RH (Ess). 'Dweller by the lower wood.'

Nettelfield: Roger *de Netelfed'* 1221 AssWo. 'Dweller by the land overgrown with nettles.'

Netter: John *le Nettere* 1298 LLB B; Christina *Netter* 1367 ColchCt. A derivative of OE *net(t)* 'net', a net-maker. cf. John *le Netmaker* 1336 ColchCt.

Nettleton: John *de Neteltone* c1220–30 RegAntiquiss; Covecok *de Nettelton* 1309 Wak; George *Nettleton* 1621 SRY. From Nettleton (Lincs, Wilts), or 'dweller by the enclosure where nettles grow'.

Neve: v. NEAVE

Nevett, Nevitt: v. KNIVETT

Nevill, Neville, Nevile, Newill: Ralph *de Neuilla*, Richard *de Nouuilla* 1086 DB; Gilbert *Neuille, de Nouila* 1142–60 DC (L); John *de Newill'* 1235 Fees (W). The Nevilles of Raby came from Néville (Seine-Inférieure). v. ANF. Others may have come from Neuville (Calvados) or other French places of the same name.

Nevin: v. NIVEN

New: (i) William *le Neuwe* 1221 AssWa; Walter *le New* 1234 FFC; John *le Nywe* 1333 AD v (L). OE *nīwe*, ME *newe* 'new', 'the newcomer', the more usual source. (ii) John *atte Newe* 1327 SRSo; Petronilla *ate Nywe* 1332 SRSr. From residence near a yew tree, OE *ēow, īw*. v. p. xiv.

Newall: v. NEWHALL

Newbald, Newbold, Newbolt, Newbould, Newboult, Newball: Robert *de Newebolt* 1175 P (Wa); John *de Neubald'* 1219 AssY; William *de Newbold'* 1299–1300 FFWa; Roger *Neubolt* 1350 LLB F; Thomas *Newball* 1653 FrY. From Newbald (ERYorks), or Newbold (Ches, Derby, Lancs, Leics, Northants, Notts, Warwicks, Worcs). Variants *Newbatt, Newbart, Newbert* are said to be peculiar to Notts (Bardsley).

Newbon, Newbond, Newbound: Hugo *le Neubonde* 1271 Rams (C); William *Newebonde* 1275 SRWo. 'The new *bond*', v. BOND.

Newcomb, Newcombe, Newcombes, Newcome: Alan *le Neucument* 1175 P (L); William *Neucum* 1183 Boldon (Du); Walter *le Neucumen* 1185 Templars (L); Richard *Newecume* 1195 P (L). OE *nīwe* and *cumen, cuma* 'newly-arrived stranger'.

Newell: Thomas *de Newell* 1201 FFEss. For NEVILL. Ralph *Nuuel* 1209 P (Y). For NOEL.

Newey, Neway: Thomas *de Newehawe* 1327 SRSf. 'Dweller at the new enclosure.'

Newhall, Newall: Robert *de Niwehal'* 1195 P (Y). 'Dweller at the new hall.'

Newhouse, Newis, Newiss: Ralph *de Niwehus* 1176 P (Y); William *ate Neuhous* 1327 SRC; John *Newis* 1672 FrY. 'Dweller at the new house.'

Newill: v. NEVILL

Newland, Newlands: Samson *de la Niwelande* 1188 P (K); William *atte Niwelond* 1327 SRSo.

From a place called Newland(s) or 'dweller at the newly cleared or newly acquired land'.

Newman, Nieman, Niman, Nyman: Stangrim *Noueman* 1166 P (Nf); Godwin *Nieweman* 1169 P (O); Ailwin *le Newman* 1195 P (Ess); William *þe Niweman* 1227 Eynsham (O); Robert *le Nyman* 1296 SRSx. 'The new man, newcomer', OE *nēowe*, *nīwe*, *nīge* and *mann*.

Newmarch: Adam *de Neumarche* 1242 Fees (Nt). From Neufmarché (Seine-Inférieure). *v.* ANF.

Newsam, Newsham, Newsholme, Newsom, Newsome, Newsum: Robert *de Neusum* 1195 P (Y); Robert *de Neusom* 1275 Wak (Y); Ralph *Newsame* 1598 RothwellPR (Y). From Newsham, Newsam or Newsholme, common north-country names, all 'at the new houses'.

Newton: Alward *de Niwetuna* 1066 DB (Nf); Robert *de Neweton'* 1190 P (Y); Stephen *de Neuton'* c1280 SRWo; William *Neuton* 1370 IpmNt. From one or other of the many places of this name.

Ney: *v.* NYE

Niall: *v.* NEAL

Nicholas, Nicholass, Nicolas, Nicklas, Nicklass, Nickcols, Niccols, Nichol, Nicholds, Nicholes, Nicholl, Nicholls, Nichols, Nickal, Nickalls, Nickel, Nickell, Nickells, Nickels, Nickle, Nickol, Nickolds, Nickolls, Nickols, Nicol, Nicole, Nicoll, Nicolle, Nicolls, Nickolay, Nicolai, Nicolay, McNichol, McNicol, McNickle: *Nicolaus* 1086 DB; *Nicholaus* presbiter 1147–66 Gilb (L); *Nicolus* Hy 2 DC (L); Maucolum *fiz Nicol* 1296 Black; Waleram *Nicholai* 1198 Cur (Sf); John *Nichole* c1270 ERO; Dovenald *Macanecol* 1294 JMac; William *Nicholas* 1311 AD i (Beds); Robert *Nicholes* 1322 AssSt; Andrew *Nicoles* 1327 SRSo; Gylbryd *Nycholay* 1446 Black; James *Nickle* 1650 Black; William *Nickless* 1783 SfPR. Lat *Nicolaus*, Greek Νικόλαος 'victory-people' was a very popular medieval name as is proved by its numerous forms as a surname, its diminutives and pet-forms. The vernacular form was *Nicol*. Fairly common, too, was the feminine *Nic(h)olaa* 1207–8 Cur (Hu, Gl), corresponding to the French *Nicole*, which may account for surnames with a final *-e*. *Nickolay* is a survival of the Latin genitive: Patrick *Nicholai* (1436 Black) is the same man as Patrik *Nicholsone* (1446 ib.). *v.* COLLIN.

Nicholetts: John *Nicholetes* 1327 SRWo; Henry *Nicolet* 1347 AD vi (K). A diminutive of *Nic(h)ol*, i.e. *Nicholas*.

Nicholl(s): *v.* NICHOLAS

Nicholson, Nickelson, Nicolson: Michael *Nycholson* 1443 Black; Peter *Nicholasson* 1459 Oseney (O); Thomas *Nicolson* 1496 LLB L; Mallie *Niclasson* 1663 Black. 'Son of *Nichol(as)*.'

Nickall(s), Nickell(s): *v.* NICHOLAS

Nickerson, Nickinson, Nickisson: For NICHOLSON. cf. HERBERTSON.

Nickes, Nicks, Nix: John son of *Nyk* 1316 Wak (Y); Henry *Nix* 1279 RH (O); Nicholas *Nike*, *Nicks* 1355, 1385 DbAS 36. A pet form of *Nicholas*. cf. John *Nicholls* alias *Nicks* 1697 DKR 41 (O).

Nickle: *v.* NICHOLAS

Nicklen, Nicklin: Nicholas, Robert *Nykelin* 1387 AssSt. A double diminutive of *Nick* (Nicholas).

Nickman: John *Nikeman* 1327 SRSf. 'Servant of *Nick*', a short form of *Nicholas*.

Nickol, Nickolay, Nickolds: *v.* NICHOLAS

Nickson, Nixon, Nixson: Robert *Nikkesune* 1309 NottBR; John *Nickeson* 1332 SRWa; John *Nyxon* 1450 Rad (C). 'Son of *Nick*.'

Nicoll(s), Nicolay: *v.* NICHOLAS

Nie: *v.* NYE

Nield, Niell: *v.* NEAL

Nielson: *v.* NEILSON

Nieman: *v.* NEWMAN

Nifton: The local pronunciation of Kniveton (Derby).

Nigel: *v.* NEAL

Nightingale, Nightingall, Nightingirl: Walter *Nichtegale* 1176 P (Gl); Richard *Nihtingale* 1227 AssBeds; Alan *Nightegale* 1260 AssC; Henry *Nitingale* 1281 LLB B. OE *nihtegale* 'night-singer','nightingale', a common nickname for a sweet singer.

Nighton: *v.* KNIGHTON

Nihell, Nihill: *v.* NEAL

Niker: William *le Niker* c1240 Colch (Ess); Cecilia *Niker* 1327 SRC. OE *nicor* 'water-monster, water-sprite'.

Niles: *v.* NEAL

Nilson: *v.* NEILSON

Niman: *v.* NEWMAN

Nind: Adam *Attenende* 1260 MELS (So); Thomas *atte Nende*, *atte Ynde* 1327, 1332 SRWo. 'Dweller at the end' (of the village). OE *ende*. *v.* p. xiv.

Nineham, Ninham, Ninnim: Rare surnames, from *atten innome*, *atte ninnome*, one who dwelt by a piece of enclosed ground (OE **innām*, ME *innom*). The term is common in field-names, survives in Inholms (PN Sx 29), Ninehams (PN Sr 312), and occurs as *Nynnom*, *Inums*, *Innims* and (PN Ess 583) as *Nynnams*. *v.* p. xiv.

Nisbet, Nisbitt: *v.* NESBIT

Niven, Neven, Nevin, Nevins, MacNevin, MacNiven: *Nevinus* c1230 Black; *Neuyn* filius Ade 1332 SRCu; Thomas *filius Neuini* 1295 JMac; Thomas *Maknevin* 1528 ib.; Thomas *Nevin* 1538 Black; John *M'Nivaine* 1638 ib.; John *Nivine* 1675 ib. Ir, Gael *Naomhin* 'little saint'.

Nix: *v.* NICKES

Nixon, Nixson: *v.* NICKSON

Noad, Noades, Nodes: Adam *Node* 1297 MinAcctCo; Thomas *Noades* 1692 ERO. Richard *ate Node* lived at the Node in Codicote (Herts) c1282–5 and Adam *atten Ode* at the Nodes in Totland (Isle of Wight) in 1311 (PN Herts 110). *Ode* is from OE *ād* 'pile, heap, funeral pile'; its exact sense in these place-names is doubtful. *v.* p. xiv.

Noah: Probably for NOAR.

Noake, Noakes, Noaks: *v.* OAK

Noar: Walter *Nore* 1275 RH (L); John *at(t)e Nore* 1314 LLB E, 1332 SRSt. From residence near a shore, bank, or, very commonly, a steep slope, OE *ōra*. cf. Nore Fm (PN Sr 227), the home of John *Attenore* in 1263. In Sussex, Surrey, Devon and Middlesex it has become *Nower*. cf. ORE. Nore Hill (PN Sx 70), the home of Richard *atte Noure* in 1353, is from OE *ōfer* in the same sense. cf. OWER. *v.* p. xiv.

Nobbs, Nobes, Nopps, Nops: *Nobbe* Caipe 1202 AssL; Wido *Nobbe* c1248 Bec (O); Philip *Noppe* 1279 RH (Hu); William *Nobys* 1327 SRSf. *Nobb* is a rhymed pet-form of *Robert*, from *Rob*. *Noppe* is a variant with the common interchange of voiced and unvoiced consonants.

Noble, Nobles: Peter *Noble* 1185 Templars (Wa); Robert *le Noble* 1206 Cur (Hu). Fr *noble* 'well-known, noble'.

Noblet, Noblett: (i) Ordric, Walter *Noblet* 1187 P (Berks), 1206 P (Hu). A diminutive of *Noble*. (ii) Hugh, John *Nobelot* 1327 SRC, SRSf. *Nob-el-ot*, a double diminutive of *Nobb*. *v.* NOBBS.

Nock: *v.* OAK

Nodder, Nother, Nothers: William *Nadder* 1219 AssY; William *Nedder* 1260 AssY; Hugh, John *le Nodder* 1314, 1316 Wak (Y); George, Thomas *Nother* 1601 FrY. The well-known Yorkshire *Nodder* is diffidently explained by Bardsley as 'a nickname for one of sleepy or apathetic habits: one who nodded'. It is probably a nickname, with a typical Yorkshire sting, from OE *nædre*, ME *nadder*, *nedder* 'adder'. The initial *n* was lost in ME through misdivision of *a naddre* as *an adder*, a combination which would not occur in the surname. *Nedder* is still a northern dialect form. *Nodder*, from *Nadder*, is an inverted spelling and pronunciation, due to the unrounding of *o* to *a*, found in Yorkshire, certainly in the 15th century, and possibly earlier: cf. John *Stapper*, *Stopper* 1464, 1483 FrY (*v.* STOFFER). The 1314 *Nodder* is too common to be an error for *Nedder*. There are early examples of variation between *Mall* and *Moll*, *Nabb* and *Nobb*, and in the Wakefield Court Rolls of *Magota* and *Mogota*. *Nother*, also a Yorkshire name, is due to the common dialectal interchange of *d* and *th* in *fadder* and *father*, etc.

Nodes: *v.* NOAD

Noe: *v.* NOY

Noel, Nowell, Nowill: *Noel* 1130 P (Lo), 1200 Cur (Nth); Geoffrey *Noel* Hy 2 DC (R); William *Nowel* 1248 FFHu. OFr *noël* 'Christmas', a name given, like the English *Christmas* and *Midwinter*, to one born at that festival.

Noice, Noise: *v.* NOY

Noke, Nokes: *v.* OAK

Nolda, Nolder: *v.* ALDER

Nopps, Nops: *v.* NOBBS

Norbrook: *v.* NORTHBROOK

Norburn, Norbron: Thomas *de Nortburne* 1275 RH (K). 'Dweller by the north brook.'

Norchard: *v.* ORCHARD

Norcliffe, Norclyffe: *v.* NORTHCLIFFE

Norcombe: *v.* NORTHCOMBE

Norcott: *v.* NORTHCOTE

Nordaby: Walter *Northinbi*, Robert *Northiby* 1297, 1301 SRY; John *Northobe* 1535 GildY; Nicholas *Northaby* 1617 FrY. 'Dweller to the north

of the village', ON *norðr í bý*. cf. WESTOBY.

Norem: *v.* NORTHAM

Norfolk: William *de Norfolc* 1154–76 YCh; Robert *de Norfolk'* 1228 Cur (C); John *Northfolk*, *Norfolk* 1377 AssEss, 1380 AssLo. 'The man from Norfolk.'

Norgate, Norgett: Siward *de Nordgat'* 1198 P (K); Gilbert *de Northgate* 1239 Rams (Nf); Trikke *del Nortgate* 1277 Wak (Y); Elvina *de Norgate* 13th Rams (Nf). From residence near the north gate of a town or castle.

Norgrove: Thomas *de Norgrave* 1311 Rams (Hu). One who lived near the north grove.

Noridge: *v.* NORRIDGE

Norkett, Norkutt: *v.* NORTHCOTE

Norman, Normand: (i) *Norman, Normannus* 1066 DB; *Norðman* 1066–70 Bury (Sf); *Norman* c1113 Burton (Staffs); *Normannus* 1230 P (Ha); Reginaldus *filius Normandi* 1220 Cur (Ess); Hugo, William *Norman* 1171 P (W), 1185 Templars (Herts); Robert *Norþman* 1279 RH (O); William *Northeman* 1301 SRY. OE *Norðmann* 'dweller in the North, Scandinavian, especially a Norwegian', recorded as a personal name from the second half of the 10th century and fairly common in 1066. (ii) John *Normand* c1216 Calv (Y); John *le Norman*, Nicholas *le Normand* 1221 AssWa; Alexander *le Normaunt* 1273 RH (L). OFr *Normand, Normant* 'a Norman'.

Normanville: Emma *de Normanuill'* 1195 P (Sx); Isabel *Normafeld* 1535 RochW; John *Normavell* 1571 YWills. From Normanville (Seine-Inférieure).

Norridge, Noridge: This may be identical with NORTHRIDGE. cf. Norridge in Upton Scudamore (Wilts), *Northrigge, Norrigge* 1203 (PN W 156). Or it may be a phonetic rendering of NORWICH.

Norrie, Norry: *v.* NORTHEY

Norrington: John *Noryngton* 1523 SRK. From Norringtonend Fm in Redbourn, the home of Alice *de Northington* in 1296 (PN Herts 79), or Northingtown Fm in Grimley (PN Wo 128), where lived Robert *de Norinton'* in 1275 (SRWo), or from Norrington in Alvediston (Wilts), *Northintone* 1227 PN W 199, all originally *norð in tūne* 'to the north of the village'. cf. NORTHINGTON and *v.* SINTON. This may also be a dialectal pronunciation of *Northampton*: cf. Henry *de Norhantona* 1165–71 Colch (Ess); Peter *Norampton* 1352 ColchCt and Northington (Hants), *Northametone* 903, *Norhameton* 1167.

Norris, Norriss, Norreys: (i) Robert *norreis* 1148 Winton (Ha); William *le Norreis* 1163–1200 Seals (Gl); Robert *le Norais* c1170 Riev (Y). AFr *noreis, norreis* 'northerner'. A very common name, particularly in the midlands and the south. Used also as a personal name: *Norreis* 1180 P (Y), *Noreis de Blida* c1200 DC (Nt). (ii) Robert *le Noris* 1297 SRY; Alice *la Norisse*, Agnes *le Norice* 1310, 1337 ColchCt; John *Norice* 1317 AssK. OFr *norrice* 'nurse'. Less common than (i). (iii) Adam *de Northus*, *de Norhuse* 1206 Cur (Ess). 'Dweller at the north house.'

Norrish: Rosa *Noryssh* 1459 GildY; Robert

Nores, Norish, Norysche 1509 Oriel (O); Raff *Norysche*, John *Noresse* 1555, 1558 RothwellPR (Y). A late development of NORRIS. cf. PARISH.

Norrison: Philip *le Noriscun*, John *le Norisoun* 13th AD ii (Wa); John *Norrison* 1672 FrY. OFr *norriscun* 'nursling'.

North: Aylmar *del North* 1230 P (Sf); John *de North* 1257 FFC; William *North* 1296 SRSx; Agnes *Bynorth* 1301 ParlR (Ess). 'Man from the north', or 'dweller to the north'.

Northall: William *de la Northalle* 1280 MELS (So). 'Dweller at the north hall.'

Northam, Norem: William *de Northam* 1214 Cur (Wa). From Northam (Hants, Devon).

Northard: Probably 'dweller to the northward'. cf. John *Anorthward* 1275 RH (Berks), which may also have become *Northwood*.

Northbrook, Norbrook: Hugo *de Nordebroc* 1190 P (K); Gilbert *de Norbroc* 1205 P (Wa); Philip *de Northebrok* 1327 SRSx. From a place called Northbrook or 'dweller north of the brook'.

Northcliffe, Nortcliffe, Norcliffe, Norclyffe: Henry *de Northclyf, del Northeclif* 1307, 1309 Wak (Y); John *de Norclif* 1327 SRC. 'Dweller by the north cliff.'

Northcombe, Norcombe: Stephen *de Northcumb'* 1230 P (D). From Northcombe in Bovey Tracey or in Bratton Clovelly (Devon).

Northcote, Northcott, Norcott, Norkett, Norkutt, Notcutt: Nicholas *de Northicote* 1199 AssSt; William *de Nordcote* 1205 P (Gl); John *atte* Northcote 1296 SRSx. From one of the places named Northcote or Northcott in Devon, from Norcott in Northchurch (Herts), or from residence at the cottage to the north. cf. NARRACOTT.

Northend: Peter *de Northende* 1279 RH (Beds); Thomas *del Northend* 1307 Wak (Y). 'The man from the north end (of the village).'

Northern, Northen: William *le Northerne* 1252 Rams (Hu); Richard *le Northryn, le Northren* 1317 Wak (Y); William *Northene* 1327 SRSf. OE *norþern* 'the man from the north'.

Northey, Norey, Norrie, Norry: Thomas *de Northie* 1200 P (K); John *de Norhie* 1205 Cur (Sx). From various minor places, compounds of *north* and varied suffixes: (*ge*)*hæg* 'enclosure': Northey Wood in Ugley, *Norhey* (1345 PN Ess 554), Northay in Hawkchurch, John *de Northeheye* (1280 PN D 656), Northey Wood in Anstey (PN Herts 171); *ēa* 'river': Northey in Whittlesey, near the Cat's Water, (*Northee* 1280 PN C 261); *ēg* 'island': Northey in Bexhill (PN Sx 493), Northey in Bury (Hunts), *Northeya* (c1350 PN BedsHu 208); *hōh* 'ridge': Northey Wood in Shudy Camps (Cambs), *Norro* 13th, *Northou* 1260 (PN C 105), Northey in Turvey (Beds), *Northho* 1242 (PN BedsHu 49).

Northington: William *de Northentone* 1327 SRSf. v. NORRINGTON and SINTON.

Northop: John, Thomas *Northupp(e)* 1296 SRSx. Probably 'Dweller north up (in the village).'

Northridge: William *de Northerugg'* 1332 SRSx. 'Dweller on the north ridge.'

Northrop, Northrope, Northrupp: Reginald *de Northorp'* 1219 AssY. From Northorpe (ERYorks).

Northway, Norway: Richard *de Northweye* 1275 SRWo; Geoffrey *Bynorthweye* 1280 MELS (So). 'Dweller to the north of the road.' William *Bynorthewey* lived at Northway in Widdecombe in the Moor in 1330. At Whitestone (Devon) in 1344, Roger *Bynortheweye* lived at Norway and Ralph *Bysouthweye* at Southway. They owed their names to the fact that they lived respectively to the north and south of the main road which separates the farms (PN D 529, 457). cf. NARRAWAY.

Northwood, Norwood: Painot *de Norwude* 1176 P (D); Alexander *de Nordwuda* 1190 P (K); Geoffrey *Northwud'* 1205 Cur (Nf). From one of the places named Northwood or Norwood 'north wood', or from residence to the north of a wood. William and David *Bynorthewode* (1330, 1333) lived north of woods now represented by Northwood Fm in Okehampton and Morchard Bishop respectively (PN D 205, 409).

Norton: Osuuardus *de Nordtone* 1066 DB (K); Leofwin *de Norton'* 1177 P (L). From one of the numerous Nortons. It may also derive from some place called *norð in tūne* (place) 'to the north of the village': Walter *de Northinton'* 1275 SRWo came from Norton Fm in Suckley (Worcs) where the corresponding place to the south of the village is Sindon's Mill. v. SINTON. This type was very common in Sussex: William *Anortheton*, Margery *atte Northetone* and John *atte Northon* (both in Combes), Walter *de Northeton* 1296 SRSx. v. also NORRINGTON and NORTHINGTON.

Norwell: Henry *de Northewelle* 1296 SRSx. 'Dweller by the north spring or stream.'

Norwich: Goscelinus *de Norwic* 1086 DB (Nf); Richard *de Northwyco* 1296 SRSx. From Norwich (Norfolk) or 'dweller at the north dairy-farm'.

Norwood: v. NORTHARD, NORTHWOOD

Noss: v. NESS

Notcutt: v. NORTHCOTE

Nothard, Nutter: Nicholas *le noutehird* 1296 FrY; Henry *le Nauthird* 1308 Wak (Y); Margaret *Nutter* 1562 RothwellPR (Y). ON *naut* 'beast, ox' and OE *hierde* 'herd', cowherd.

Nother(s): v. NODDER

Notman: v. NUTMAN

Nott: Roger *Not* 1100–30 OEByn; Algar *le Notte* 1183 P (So); Henry *le Not* 1210 Cur (St). OE *hnott* 'bald-headed, close-cropped'.

Nottage, Nottidge: Thomas *Nuthech* 1220 Fees (Berks); Alan *Nuthach* 1224 Cur (Ess). A nickname from the nuthatch.

Notting: Siward *Noting* 1219 AssL; Adam *Nottyng* 1327 SRSf. OE **hnotting* 'the bald-headed one'.

Nourse: v NURSE

Nowell, Nowill: v. NEWELL, NOEL

Nowers: Roger *de Nuiers* 1199 Fees (Nf); Alexander *de Nowers* 1230 P (Wa). From Noyers (Eure). v. ANF, NOAR, OVER, OWER.

Nowles: v. KNOLL

Noy, Noyce, Noyes, Noe, Noice, Noise: *Noe*

c1125 StCh; Thomas *filius Noe* 1185 Templars (Wa); William, Simon *Noysse* 1327 SRSf. Hebrew *Noah* 'long lived'. Not a common medieval name. No doubt also from the medieval drama.

Nugent: Philip *de Nugent* 1203 Pl (Sa); Philip *Nogent* 13th Ronton; Richard *de Nugent* 1293 AssSt; John *Nogent* 1340 CorLo. From one or other of the many French places called Nogent.

Nunhouse, Nunniss: William *Nunhouse* 1379 PTY. 'Worker at the nuns' house', servant of the nuns. cf. MONKHOUSE.

Nunn, Nunns: (i) Eluiua *nonna* 1155–66 Holme (Nf); Alice *Nunne* 1243 AssDu, *la Nonne* 1275 RH (Nth); Robert, Hannecok *le Nunne* 1252 Rams (Hu), 1297 Wak (Y). Where the christian name is that of a woman, this is a surname of office. Applied to a man (as most commonly), it is a nickname for one meek and demure as a nun. (ii) Robert *del Nunnes, othe Nonnes* 1297 SRY, 1309 LLB D; John *atte Nunnes* 1325 Cl. 'Servant at the nuns' ', identical in meaning with NUNHOUSE and *Nunman:* Walter *Noneman* 1217 Pat (Y). Roulf, predecessor of Simon de Kime, gave 60 acres in Lincs to the nunnery of Elstow (Beds) which Nicholas *le Nunneman* held by service of 15*s.* per annum (1212 Fees).

Nunney, Nunny: Robert, Beatrice *de Nonhey* 1327 SRSf. From residence near an enclosure belonging to the nuns.

Nunniss: *v.* NUNHOUSE

Nunweek, Nunwick: Geoffrey *de Nunnewich* 1193 P (Y). From Nunwick (Northumb).

Nurrish: *v.* NURSE

Nursaw, Nurser, Nursey: *v.* NUSSEY

Nurse, Nurrish, Nourse: Joan *Nurys*, Magota *le Nuris* 1379 PTY. OFr *nurice* 'nurse'. *v.* NORRIS, NORRISH.

Nurser, Nussey: *v.* NURSAW

Nussey, Nussie, Nursey, Nursaw, Nurser: Robert *de Nussey*, John *de Nussay* 1379 PTY; Richard *Nussey* 1605 FrY; William *Nursay*, Thomas *Nursaw* 1707, 1747 ib. From Nussey Green in Burnsall (WRYorks).

Nutbeam, Nutbeem, Nutbeen: John *ate Notebem* 1279 RH (O); William *atte Nhutbyme* 1332 SRSx. 'Dweller near a prominent nut-tree or hazel' (OE *hnutbēam*). John *atte Notebeme* 1327 SR (Ha) came from Nutbane in Weyhill (Hants).

Nutbrown: William *Nuttebrun* 1185 Templars (Y); Willelmus *filius Nutebrun* 1203 P (L); Richard *Nutebrune* 1296 SRSx. 'Nut-brown', a nickname from the complexion, used also as a personal name.

Nutman, Nuttman, Notman: John *Noteman*, William *Nuteman* 1275 RH (Nf, L). 'Servant of *Nott*' or 'dealer in nuts'.

Nutt: William *Nutte* 1181 P (Nth); Richard *le Nute* 1274 RH (K); John *Nutte, Nutt* 1379 PTY, 1523 CorNt. OE *hnutu* 'nut', a man with a round head or a brown complexion.

Nuttall, Nuthall: Richard *de Nutehal'* 1201 Pl (Nt); Stephen *de Notehale* 1269 RegAntiquiss; John *Notehal* 1354 ColchCt; Peter *Nutill* 1375 FFY. From Nuthall (Notts), or Nuttall (Lancs).

Nutter: Robert *le Notere* 1221 AssWa; Adam *le Notyere* 1293 AssSt; Dyonisia *Notur* 1302 Oseney (O). OE *nōtere* 'scribe, writer' or a derivative of OFr *note* 'note', 'secretary'. *v.* also NOTHARD.

Nye, Nie, Nay, Ney: Robert *Nay* 1207 FFEss; Robert *Atteneye* 1269 AssSo; William *Atteneye* 1276 AssSo; Gilbert *de la Nye* 1315 FFEss. From residence near some low-lying land. ME *atten ye, eye* became *atte nye, neye*. cf. Nye in Winscombe (Som). Neigh Bridge in Somerford Keynes (Wilts) is from OE *ēa* 'by the stream'. *v.* REA, RAY, RYE.

Nyman: *v.* NEWMAN

O

Oade, Oades, Oaten, Oates, Oats, Ott, Otten, Otton: *Ode, Odo, Otho* 1066 DB; Radulfus *filius Ode* c1160 DC (L); Willelmus *filius Ote (Otte)* 1177 P (Ess); William *Ode* 1213 Cur (Sf); Cristiana *Odes* 1275 RH (Nth); Andrew *Otes* 1275 RH (Nf). OG *Odo, Otto* 'riches', OFr *Odes, Otes* (cas-sujet), *Odon, Otton* (cas-régime). Both survive, though the latter is seldom recorded. Belchamp Otton (Essex) owes its attribute (*Otes* 1254, *Oton* 1255) to *Otto* (temp. Hy 2), descendant of *Otto* or *Odo* (DB). *Oade* may also be local in origin. *v.* NOAD.

Oak, Oake, Oaks, Oke, Noak, Noake, Noakes, Noaks, Nock, Noke, Nokes: Henry *atte Noke* Hy 3 PN Ess 140; Adam *at þe Ock* 1273 RH (Sa); Thomas *del Oke* 1275 RH (Bk); Thomas *atten Oke* 1296 SRSx; Henry *atte Nok* 1326 PN Ess 145; John *atte Noke* 1327 SRSx; Robert *atte Nokes* 1332 SRWo; Richard *en le Okes* 1383 StThomas (St). From residence by an oak or a group of oaks (OE *āc*), with variation between *atten oke(s)* and *atte noke(s). v.* also ROKE.

Oakden, Ogden: Elias *de Akeden, de Aggeden* 1246 AssLa; Richard *de Okeden* 1332 SRLa; William *Ogdin* 1612 FrLeic. From Ogden (Lancs).

Oaker: Henry *Oker* 1275 RH (Sf); Walter *Oaker* 1279 RH (C). 'Dweller by the oak.' cf. OAK.

Oakey: *v.* OKEY

Oakley, Oakeley, Okeley, Okely: Hervey, Philip *de Ocle* 1199 AssSt, 1246 IpmGl; Richard *de Okeley* 1327 SRLei; John *Okelee* 1377 AssEss; Robert *Okeleye* 1545 SRW. From one or other of the many places of this name, or from Oakle Street (Glos), Oakleigh (Kent), or Ockley (Surrey).

Oakman: Alexander *filius Okeman* 1219 AssY; Robert *Okman* 1296 SRSx. OE *Ācmann* 'oak-man'.

Oastler: *v.* OSTLER

Oaten, Oat(e)s: *v.* OADE

Oatway: *v.* OTTOWAY

Obin: *v.* ALBIN

Obray: *v.* AUBRAY

O'Brian, O'Brien, O'Bryan, O'Bryen: Irish *Ó Briain* 'descendant of *Brian*'.

O'Byrne: *v.* BYRNE

O'Clery: Ir *Ó Cléirigh* 'descendant of the clerk'. cf. MCCHLERY.

O'Connell: Ir *Ó Conaill* 'descendant of *Conall*', Celtic *Kunovalos* 'high-powerful'.

O'Connor: Ir *Ó Conchobhair* 'descendant of *Conchobhar*' 'high-will'.

Odam, Odams, Odom, Odhams: Walter, Robert *Odam* 1313 Wak (Y), 1327 SRSf; John *Odames* 1327 SRSt. OE *āðum*, ME *odam* 'son-in-law'.

Odart: *Odard* 1086 DB; Eilsi *filius Odardi* 1188 P (Y); Peter, Walter *Odard* 1206 ClR, 1332 SRCu. OG *Authard, Othard, Odard* 'riches-hard'.

Odd, Odde: Asketinus *filius Od* 1163 DC (L); Odd *atte Flete* 1327 SRSx; Gilbert, Richard *Odde* 1225 AssSo, 1284 Wak (Y). OE *Odda* or ON *Oddr*.

Oddie, Oddey, Oddy: John *Ody* c1280 SRWo, 1390 CorW; Robert *Odye* 1576 SRW; William *Oddy* 1657 FrY. A diminutive of ODD.

Odell, O'Dell: Simon *de Wahella* 1195 P (Beds); Simon *de Wahull* 1212 Pl (K); Robert *de Wodhull* 1314–16 AssNth; John *Odyll, Odell* 1545, 1576 SRW. From Odel (Beds), *Wahelle* 1162, *Woodhull* 1276, *Odyll* 1494.

Odgear, Odger, Odgers, Oger, Ogier: *Ogerus Brito* 1086 DB (Lei); *Ogerus filius Ogeri* 1196 Cur (D); *Odgarus de Lind'* 1214 Cur (Sr); Nicholas *Oger* 1296 SRSx; Peter *Ogger* 1306 LoCt. OFr *Ogier*, OG *Odger, Og(g)er* 'wealth-spear'.

Odhams: *v.* ODAM

Odlin, Odling: *Odolina* 1086 DB; *Odelina* 1198 FFSf, 1207 Cur (Do); *Hodlyn* 1315 Wak (Y); Robert *Odelyn* 1250 Fees (Nf); Henry *Odelin* 1276 RH (Y). OG *Odelin* (m) or *Odelina* (f), double diminutives of *Odo. v.* OADE.

Odom: *v.* ODAM

O'Donnell: Ir *Ó Domhnaill* 'descendant of *Dhomnall*'. *v.* DONALD, MACDONALD.

O'Donoghue, O'Donohue, Donohue, Donaghy, Donahue: Ir *Ó Donnchadha* 'descendant of *Donnchadh*'. *v.* DUNCAN.

O'Donovan: Ir *Ó Donnabháin* 'descendant of *Donndubhán*' (dark brown).

O'Dowd: Ir *Ó Dubhda* 'descendant of *Dubhda*' (black).

O'Duffy, Duffy: Ir *Ó Dubhthaigh* 'descendant of *Dubhthach*'.

Offer, Orfeur: (i) William *le Orfere* 1265 Pat; William *atte more, orfrer* 1292 SRLo; John *Ourefre, Ourefyre* 1327 SRSf. *Orfrer* is found as an occupational name in London and probably meant 'a maker of orphrey or gold-embroidery', OFr *orfreis*, MedLat *aufrisium*, a modification of Lat *auriphrygium*, cf. OFFICER. (ii) William *le Orfeuere* 1235 FFHu; Thomas *le Orfevre* a1284 NottsBR; Robert *Lorfeure* 1319 SRLo. OFr *orfevre* 'goldsmith'.

254

Officer: Alicia *aurifrigeria* 13th SRLo; Adam *le Orfreyser* 1302 FrC. Probably a corruption of OFr *orfroisier* 'a maker of orphrey or gold-embroidery'. *v.* OFFER.

Offield, Ofield: *v.* OLDFIELD

Offord: Robert *de Offewurth*' 1221 AssWa; Robert *de Offorde* 1327 SRSf; Thomas *de Offord* 1374 FFEss. From Offord (Hunts, Warwicks).

O'Flaherty: Ir *Ó Flaithbheartaigh* 'descendant of *Flaithbheartach*' (bright ruler).

O'Flinn, O'Flynn: Ir *O Floinn* 'descendant of *Flánn*' (red).

Ogden: *v.* OAKDEN

Oger: *v.* ODGEAR

Ogilvie, Ogilvy, Ogilwy: Alexander *de Oggoluin* a1232 Black; Patrick *de Oggiluill* c1267 ib.; Walter *de Ogilby* 1425 ib.; Thomas *of Oglevy* 1466 ib. From the barony of Ogilvie in Glamis (Angus).

Ogle, Ogles: Robert *de Ogle* 1181 P (Nb); Agnes, Gilbert *Dogel* 1221 Cur (Nb); Robert *Ogill*' 1379 PTY; Richard *Ogle* 1519 FFEss. From Ogle in Whalton (Northumb).

Oglethorpe: Hemer *de Oclestorp*' 1219 AssY; William *Ogylsthorpe* 1407 IpmY; Maria *Oglethorpe* 1621 SRY. From Oglethorpe (WRYorks).

O'Gorman: *v.* GORMAN

O'Grady: Ir *Ó Grádaigh* 'descendant of *Gráda*' (noble).

O'Hagan: James *Ohagan* 1280 Pat. Ir *Ó hÁgáin* 'descendant of *Ógán*' (young).

O'Haire, O'Hare, O'Hear: *v.* HAIR

O'Hea, Hay, Hayes: Ir *Ó hAodha* 'descendant of *Aodh*' (fire).

O'Kane: *v.* CAIN

Oke: *v.* OAK

Okeley, Okely: *v.* OAKLEY

O'Kelly: *v.* KELLY

Okey, Oakey: (i) *Aki* (Sf), *Achi* (L, Sf, Wa) 1066 DB; *Oky, Hoky* Ed 3 Rydware (St); Henry *Aky, Oky* 1221 AssGl; William, Elyas *Oky* c1250 Rams (Hu), 1327 SRSf. ODa *Aki*, OSw *Ake*. (ii) Cecilia *de Okeye* 1275 SRWo; Robert *de Okhei* 1327 SRWo. 'Dweller near an oak-copse' (OE *āc* and *(ge)hǣg*).

Olarenshaw: *v.* OLLEREARNSHAW

Old, Olds, Ould, Oulds: Boia *þe Ealde* c980 OEByn; Willelmus *Vetus* 1183 P̄ (Lo); Gerardus *Senex* 1193 P (Berks); Henry *le Olde*, Roger *Old* 1327 SRSf. OE *eald* 'old' (Lat *vetus, senex*), not necessarily implying old age. Wulfstan *Ealda* was so called to distinguish him from Wulfstan *Geonga* 'the young' c1060 OEByn (K).

Oldacre, Oldaker: Helyas *de Aldeacris* 1231 Guisb (Y). One who lived by the old ploughed field (OE *æcer*). cf. OLDFIELD.

Olden: *v.* ALDEN

Older: *v.* ALDER

Oldershaw, Houldershaw: Hugh *de Alreschawe* 1307 AssSt. 'Dweller by the alder-wood', ME *aldershawe*, OE *alor, sceaga*.

Oldfield, Offield, Ofield, Allfield: Agnes *de Aldefeld* 1221 ElyA (Sf); Robert *de le Aldefeld* 1279 RH (C); Adam *del Oldefeld*' 1297 SRY; Salkyn *Eldefeld* 1327 *SR* (Ess). 'Dweller by the old field', OE *eald, feld*, as at Allfield (Salop), Alfell Fm in Elmstead (Essex), Ofields (Warwicks) and Oldfield Grove in Langley (Essex). In Cambridgeshire, this has become The Offal (Comberton), Offal End (Haslingfield) and Offals Wood (Steeple Morden).

Oldham, Oldam: Achard *de Aldeham* 1218–19 FFK; Richard *de Oldham* 1384 IpmLa; Robert *Oldum* 1470 Cl (Lo); Ralph *Oldham, Oldam* 1508, 1514 CorNt; John *Owldam* 1599 SRDb. From Oldham (Lancs), or 'dweller by the long-cultivated river flat'.

Oldis: *v.* ALDIS

Oldknow: William *Aldinoch* 1203 P (L). OE *eald, genōh* 'old enough'. cf. GOODENOUGH.

Oldland, Olland: Wluard *Oldelond* 1221 ElyA (Nf); Hugh *de la Aldelond*', *del Heldelonde* 1260–70 MELS (So); William *de Oldlond* 1276 RH (Gl); Henry *de Aldelonde* 1296 SRSx; John *atte Oldelond* 1327 SRSo. 'Dweller at the old estate', as at Oldland (Glos) or Oldland(s) (Sussex).

Oldman, Olman: William *Aldeman* 1196–1237 Colch (Ess); Robert *Oldman* 1275 RH (Nf); Marjery, Joan *Oldmanes* 1310 ColchCt. OE *eald* 'old' and *mann*. This has, no doubt, also become ALLMAN.

Oldridge: *v.* ALDRICH

Oldroyd: Adam *de Olderode* 1316 Wak (Y); Robert *Ouldroyde* 1666 RothwellPR. 'Dweller at the old clearing', OE *eald, rod*, Yorks dialectal *royd*.

Oldwright: *v.* ALLRIGHT

O'Leary, Leary: Ir *Ó Laoghaire* 'descendant of *Laoghaire*' (calf-keeper).

Olerenshaw: *v.* OLLEREARNSHAW

Oliff(e): *v.* OLLIFF

Oliphant, Olivant: David *Olifard* 1141 Black; Robert *Oliphard* c1148 EngFeud (He); John, Hugh *Olifard* 1179 P (C), 1208 (Wo); William *Olyfat* 1296 Black; William *Holifarth* 1300 ib.; William *Olivant* 1572 LaWills. A difficult name. Derivation from ME *olifant* 'elephant' is impossible. The persistent medial *f* (except for the solitary *terram Olivard* 1186–8 BuryS) dissociates the name from *Oliver*. A compound of ON *Óleifr* and the French suffix *-ard* might be suggested were it not for the fact that the persistent medial *i* of *Oliphant* does not appear in *Olliff* before the 14th century. From OFr *olif* 'olive-branch' (Godefroy) a pejorative *Olifard* may have been formed, a derisive nickname for one who preferred an olive-branch to more martial weapons. The development was *Olyphard* 1249, *Olifaunt* 1317, *Oliphand, Olyfant* 1326 (Black), due to interchange of *r* and *n* in the combination *l—r*. *Oliphant* became the common form by association with *olifant* 'elephant'. Sometimes we may have a late surname from a sign: Isabell *del Olyfaunt* 1318 LeicBR.

Olive, Ollive: *Olyve* 1202 AD ii (Nth); *Oliva* 1207–8 Cur (O, Wo); Richard *Olive* 1279 RH (O); John *Olyve* 1310 FFEss. Latin *oliva* 'olive'. There were two saints named *Oliva*, one the patroness of olive trees.

Oliver, Olivier, Olliver: *Oliverus* 1086 DB; *Oliuerus* de Vendouer 1149–62 DC (L); Jordan *Oliver, Oliuier* 1201 AssSo, 1204 P (Co); Willelmus, Jordanus *Oliueri* 1206 P (Co), 1223 Pat (D); Robert *Olyveyr* 1260 AssC; Ralph *Olifer* 1327 SRWo. The French *Olivier*, recorded in 1011, was at first southern and later became common through the influence of the *Chanson de Roland*. Dauzat takes it as symbolic, from *olivier* 'an olive branch', the emblem of peace. This can hardly be the origin of the name of the peer of Charlemagne which is probably Teutonic. The suggested derivations from ON *Óláfr* and OG *Alfihar* are both difficult phonetically.

Olland: *v.* OLDLAND

Ollerearnshaw, Ollerenshaw, Olarenshaw, Olerenshaw, Olorenshaw: Adam *del Helerinshagh*, John *del Olrynshagh* 1327 SRDb. 'Dweller by the alder-wood.'

Olley, Ollie: *v.* DOYLEY

Ollier: *v.* OYLER

Olliff, Oliff: *Olefus* (*Olafus*) 1221 Cur (Sa); Robert *Olef* 1275 SRWo; John *Olof* 1296 SRSx; Adam *Olif* 1379 PTY. ON *Óleifr*, ODa *Óláfr* 'ancestral-relic', the name of a Norwegian king and saint.

Olman: *v.* OLDMAN

O'Looney: *v.* LOONEY

Oman, Omond: Leuric *Omundi filius* c1095 Bury (Sf); John *Omond* 1327 SRSf; Edduard *Homondsone* 1546 Black (Orkney); Edward *Omand* or *Omandson* 1576 ib. ON *Hámundr* 'high protector' or *Ámundi* 'great-grandfather-protector'. An Orkney and Shetland name.

O'Neal, O'Neill: *v.* NEAL

Onians, Onion, Onions, O'Nions, Onyon: Thomas *Onoiun* 1279 RH (C); Robert *Oygnoun* 1295 Husting; Robert *Onnyon* 1568 SRSf; Thomas *Oynion, Onion* 1686–9 ShotleyPR (Sf). OFr *oignon* 'onion', for an onion-seller. More commonly for ENNION.

Onraet: Walter *Unred* a1200 Dublin; Alredus *Vnred*' 1230 P (Nf); John *Onrett* 1275 RH (K). OE *unrǣd* 'evil counsel, folly'. cf. Adam *Huncouthe* 1379 PTY.

Onyett: *v.* HONIATT

Oram: *v.* ORME

Orange, Orringe: *Orengia, Horenga* 1201, 1204 Cur (O); *Orenga, Orenge* 1226 FFEss, 1247 AssBeds, 1296 SRSx; Sibel, John *Orenge* 1296 SRSx; Alexander *Orrynge* 1327 SRWo. From a woman's name *Orenge*, of doubtful etymology. It is found too early to be associated with the orange. William *de Orenge* (1086 DB) probably came from Orange (Mayenne), but as no later examples have been noted, this topographical source is probably not to be considered.

Orbell: *Orabilis* (f) 1221 Cur (K); *Orabla, Orable, Arable* de Meyhamme 1243 Fees (K); *Orabilia* 1273 FFEss; *Orabella* 1275 AssSt; John *Orable* 1279 RH (C); Adam *Orbel* 1327 SRSf. This woman's name can hardly be the Scottish *Arabella*, found in the 17th century as *Arbell*. Lyford (1655)

derives *Orabilis* from Lat *orabilis* 'easy to be entreated', a derivation clearly implied by the 13th-century scribes, and probably correct, being a formation parallel to *Amabilis*. *v.* MABLE.

Orchard, Norchard: Alexander *de Orchyard* 1225 AssSo; Emeric *del Orchyard* 1244 AssSo; William *Orchard* 1279 RH (O); Richard *ate Orchard, Atten Orchard* 1316 Ipm (Wo), *atte Norchard* 1332 SRWo. From residence near or employment at an orchard, OE *ortgeard, orceard*.

Ord, Orde: Henry *de Orde* 1209 P (Nb); Adam *of Horde* 1296 Black; Andrew *de Ord* t Robt I ib.; Alexander *Ord* 1596 ib. The first of these is from East Ord (Northumb), the others are from Ord, later Kirkurd (Peebles), or from the lands of Ord (Banff). But a personal name may also be involved, cf. Henry *filius Ord*' 1206 Pl (K).

Ordway: *Orduui* 1066 DB (Hu); Ricardus *filius Ordwi* 1185 P (Gl); Radulfus *filius Ordewi* c1250 Rams (Hu); Thomas *Ordwy*, Ralph *Ordwey* 1276 RH (Beds). Late OE *Ordwīg* 'spear-warrior'.

Ore: William, Simon *de Ore* 1207, 1208 Cur (Sx, K); Walter *Ore* 1210 Cur (C). From Oare (Berks, Kent, Wilts) or Ore (Sussex). No doubt also from residence near a shore or slope (OE *ōra*), though the local names seem usually to have become NOAR or NOWERS.

O'Regan, Regan: Padyne *Regane* 1264 Dublin. Ir *Ó Riagáin* 'descendant of *Riagán*' (little king).

O'Reilly: William *Orailly* 1451 Pat. Ir *Ó Raghailligh* 'descendant of *Raghallach*' (valiant).

Orfeur: *v.* OFFER

Organ, Organe: Robert, Thomas *Organ* 1210 Cur (K); 1332 SRSt. This is sometimes metonymic for ORGANER. John *Organ* of Treworian (Co) was the son of *Organa*, wife of Ives de Treworian (1325 AD v). cf. *Organus* Pipard 1236 Fees (O).

Organer: Walter *le Organer* 1332 SRSr; John *Organer*, apothecary 1374 ColchCt. A derivative of ME *organ*, in early use, of a variety of musical (especially wind) instruments. 'A musician, a player or maker of the organ.' cf. John *le Orgeniste* 1241 FFY, Adam *le Organystre* 1327 Pinchbeck (Sf). OFr *organiste, organiste* 'organist'.

Orgar, Orger: *Orgar, Orger* c1095 Bury (Sf); Water *filius Ordgeri* c1150 DC (L); Roger *Orgar*' 1198 FFNf; Geoffrey *Ordgar* 1226 ClR (C). OE *Ordgār* 'point-spear'.

Orgel, Orgill: Edmund *Liorgil*' 1198–1211 StP; Walter *Orgouyl* 1297 MinAcctCo; Gerard *Orgul* 1305 LoCt. OFr *orgueil* 'pride'. cf. PRIDE.

Oriel: *Oriholt, Oriolda* de Endrebi 1206–7 Cur (Y); *Oreute* Cur (Nt); Robertus *filius Oriold* 1230 P (He); Roger *Oriel* 1276 LLB A. OG *Aurildis, Orieldis* (f) 'fire-strife'.

O'Riordan: *v.* REARDON

Orlebar: Alur' *de Orlinberga* 1130 P (Nth); Thomas *Orlibar* 1732 SfPR. From Orlingbury (Northants).

Orledge, Orlich: John *Orlog* 1356 ColchCt. OFr *orloge* 'clock', metonymic for *orlogier* 'clockmaker'. cf. John, Adam *Orloger* 1295 Barnwell (C), 1311 ColchCt.

Orme, Ormes, Oram, Orum, Orrom: *Orm* 1066 DB (Y); *Orm* de Hedoc 1169 P (La); *Orum* 1175 P (Db); John *Orm* 1275 SRWo; Augustin *Orumme* 1327 SRSf. ON *Ormr*, ODa, OSw *Orm* 'serpent'. *Oram* and *Orum* are due to the strongly trilled *r*.

Orneblow: *v.* HORNBLOW

Orpen, Orpin: Elyas *Orpyn* 1298 Seals (Nth); Elizabeth *Orpen* 1665 HTO. cf. *Auripigmentum* . . . a couleur lyke golde, in englysshe *Orpine* (1548 NED). Fr *orpin* is given by Littré as a generic term for *Sedum* (yellow stonecrop), the name of a succulent herbaceous plant, *Sedum Telephinum*, a native of Britain, found in cottage gardens and esteemed as a vulnerary. From its tenacity of life it was called *Live-long* (a1387 NED). 'Orpyn, herbe, *Crassula major, et media dicitur* Howsleek, *et minima dicitur* stoncrop', c1440 PromptParv. One of the medicinal plants that gave rise to surnames.

Orpet, Orpett: William *Orpede* 1230 P (Wa); Walter *le Orpede* 1255 RH (Bk). OE *orped* 'stout, strenuous, valiant, bold'. cf. William *Orpedeman* a1223 Clerkenwell (Lo).

Orr: (i) Roger, William *Orre* 1202 AssL, 1277 Wak (Y); Robert *Orre* 1334–5 SRK. ON *Orri*, originally a byname 'black-cock'. (ii) Agnes, Peter *de Ore* 1210–11 PWi, 1264–5 IpmW; William *de Ore* 1334–5 SRK. From Oare (Berks, Kent, Som, Wilts), Ore (Sussex), or 'dweller by the bank or ridge'. (iii) Donald *Oure* 1512 Black; John *Or* 1578 ib. Gaelic *odhar* 'dun, of sallow complexion'.

Orred, Orrett: *Huredus* c1250 Rams (Hu); William *Orede* 1275 RH (Sf); Nicholas *Ored* 1279 RH (O). OE *Wulfrǣd* 'wolf-counsel'. cf. HURRY.

Orrey: *v.* HURRY

Orrick, Orridge: Reinaldus *filius Ordrici* 1114–30 Rams (Hu); Walter, William *Ordrich* 1193, 1196 P (Wa, Bk); Thomas *Orridge* 1778 HorringerPR (Sf). OE *Ordrīc* 'spear-powerful', a late OE name, common in Domesday Book.

Orringe: *v.* ORANGE

Orriss, Orys: *Oratius presbiter* 1193 P (Ess); Richard *Oras* 1312 FFEss; William *Orice* 1668 SfPR; Henry *Orris* 1674 HTSf. Latin *Horatius*, the name of a Roman *gens*, best known from Horatius Cocles, the defender of the bridge, and the poet Quintus Horatius Flaccus. The name has not previously been noted in England before the Renaissance when it apparently was introduced from Italy as *Horatio*.

Orrom: *v.* ORME

Orry: *v.* HURRY

Orsborn: *v.* OSBORN

Orton, Overton: (i) Æðelweard *of Ortun* c1051 OEByn; Henry *de Orton* 1229 FFO; Hugh *Orton* 1357 IpmNt. From Orton (Cumb), or from Nether, Over Worton (Oxon), *Orton* 1191. (ii) Hugh *de Overtuna* c1150 StCh; Bartholomew *de Ouerton'* 1203 AssNth; Adam *atte Overton* 1275 MELS (Wo); Geoffrey *de Overton* 1324 Oriel (O). From one or other of the many places called Overton, or from Orton (Hunts, Leics, Northants, Warwicks, Westmorland), all with OE *ōfer, ofer, ufera* as the

first element. In the absence of medieval forms the two names cannot be distinguished.

Orum: *v.* ORME

Orwin: *v.* ERWIN

Osbaldeston, Osbaldiston, Osbaldstone, Osboldstone, Osbiston: Adam *de Osbaldeston* 1292 WhC (La); Elizabeth *Osbosstone* 1552 RothwellPR (Y). From Osbaldeston (Lancs).

Osband: *v.* OSBORN

Osbiton: Roger *de Osberton'* 1242 Fees (Nt). From Osberton (Notts).

Osborn, Osborne, Osbourn, Osbourne, Osburn, Osbon, Osband, Orsborn, Usborne, Hosburn, Hosbons: *Osbern* 1066 DB; *Osbernus filius Willelmi* 1221 Cur (Bk); Henry *Osbern* 1260 AssC; Henry *Oseburn* 1297 MinAcctCo; John *Osebarn* 1296 SRSx; Walter *Osborn* 1310 FFC; Andrew *Housborn*, Walter *Hosebarn* 1327 SRSo; Elena *Usburne* 1381 PTY; John *Usbarne* 1467 KentW; William *Osbon* 1792 Bardsley. Late OE *Ōsbern*, from ON *Ásbiǫrn*, ODa *Asbiorn* 'god-bear'. The name is found in England before the Conquest and may be of direct Scandinavian origin. It was also common in Normandy whence it was often brought over by Normans after the Conquest.

Oscroft: Thomas *de Oxcroft* 1327 SRDb. 'Dweller by the ox-croft.'

Osgood, Hosegood, Hosgood, Horsegood, Angood: *Asgot, Ansgot, Angot, Osgot* 1066 DB; *Osgot* c1095 Bury (Sf); *Angothus clericus* c1166 DC (Lei); Henricus *filius Osegod* 1199 FF (Nth); Galfridus *filius Angod'*, *Angot* 1208 Fees, 1212 Cur (Bk), identical with Galfridus *Angod* 1235 Fees (Bk); Matilda *Angot* 1198 FF (Nf); William *Osgot'*, *Osegod* 1202 FF (Nf), 1213 Cur (Sf); Petrus *Angoti* 1209 P (Nf); Robert, John *Hosegod* 1275 RH (W), 13th AD iii (Beds). Late OE *Ōsgod, Ōsgot*, from ON *Ásgautr*, ODa, OSw *Asgut, Asgot*. This was common in Normandy in the forms *Ansgot, Angot*, hence *Angood*, ANGOLD. *Hosegood* is the Anglo-Scandinavian *Osgod* with retention of the inorganic *H* so frequently prefixed by Norman scribes.

O'Shea, O'Shee, Shea, Shee: Ir *Ó Séaghdha* 'descendant of *Séaghdha*' (stately, majestic).

Oslar, Osler, Hosler: William *Osselur, Oiselur* 1170, 1171 P (Y); Alberic *le Oselur* 1208 FFC; Thorald *le Osiller* 1250 Fees (L); Robert *le Oyseler* 1255 AssSo; Godfrey *le Hoselur* 1279 RH (C); William *le Vsseler* 1332 SRSr. OFr *oiseleor, oiseleur* 'bird-catcher, fowler'. Forms in *-er* may be from OFr *oiselier* 'seller of game, poulterer'.

Osman, Osmant, Osment, Osmint: *v.* OSMOND

Osmer, Hosmer, Usmar: *Osmar, Osmer* 1066 DB (Lei, D); *Osmer ater Dune* 1296 SRSx; William *Osmere* 1230 P (D); Chaneys *Usmer* 1589 ArchC 48. OE *Ōsmǣr* 'god-fame'.

Osmond, Osmon, Osmund, Osman, Osmant, Osment, Osmint: *Osmund* 1066 DB; *Osemundus clericus* 1222 Cur (Gl); Roger *Hosemund* 1199 FF (Nth); Robert *Osemund* 1221 ElyA (Nf); Richard *Osemond* 1297 MinAcctCo (O); William *Osman* 1367 ColchCt; Edward *Osmand* 1660 Bardsley.

OE *Ōsmund* 'god-protector', or Norman *Osmund* from ON *Ásmundr*, ODa, OSw *Asmund*.

Ost: *v.* HOST

Ostle: For *atte ostle*, metonymic for *Ostler*.

Ostler, Oastler, Hosteller, Hostler, Horsler, Hustler: William *Hostiler* 1190 Eynsham (O); Robert, Edid *le Osteler* 1204 AssSt, 1260 Oseney (O); Robert *le Hostler* 1275 RH (Nf); Henry *Husteler* 1301 SRY; Thomas *Ostler* 1562 FrY; Mr *Husler* 1674 HTSf; William *Oastler* 1738 FrY. OFr *ostelier, hostelier*, ME *(h)ostiler, (h)osteler* 'one who receives, lodges or entertains guests, especially in a monastery' (c1290 NED), 'keeper of a hostelry or inn' (c1365 ib.). This also came to mean 'a stableman', modern *ostler* (c1386 NED), a meaning less probable here.

Ostridge: John *Ossreche*, Matilda *Ostrich* 1327 SRSf; Thomas *Ostriche* 1421 LLB I. OFr *ostrice, hostrige* 'a hawk', used by metonymy for *ostricer* 'a keeper of goshawks, hawker, falconer'. cf. William *(le) ostricer* c1160 DC (L).

O'Sullivan, Sullivan: Ir *Ó Súileabháin* 'descendant of *Súileabhán*' (black-eyed).

Oswald, Osswald, Oswell: *Osuuald, Osuuoldus* 1066 DB (So, Sr); Robertus *filius Oswaldi* 1240 Rams (Nf); Simon *Aswald* 1279 RH (O); John *Oswald* 1327 SRSx. OE *Ōsweald* 'god-ruler', or, possibly, also ON *Ásvaldr*. The christian name occurs as *Oswell* (1540) and *Oswall* (1620 Bardsley).

Oswick: John *de Oxewic* 1206 Cur (Nf). From Oxwick (Norfolk).

Oswin: *Oswinus* c1250 Rams (C, Nf); Roger *Oswin* 1221 Cur (Ess). OE *Ōswine* 'god-friend'.

Othen: *Oinus dacus* 1066 DB (Ess); Henry *Othyn* 1296 SRSx. Anglo-Scand *Ōðin*.

Ott, Otten: *v.* OADE

Ottaway: *v.* OTTOWAY

Otter: *Otre* 1066 DB (D, Y); Walterus *filius Otheri, Other* 1086 DB; *Other* Pilemus 1187 P (Nf); Roger *Oter* 1185 P (C); John *Otir* 1230 P (Ha); Symon *Other* 1279 RH (C); Mariota *Otre* 1297 SRY. ON *Óttar* 'terrible army', anglicized in OE as *Ohthere;* or, more commonly, ME *oter* 'otter', metonymic for 'otter-hunter': Adam *Loterhunt, le Oterhunter* 1246 AssLa.

Otterway: *v.* OTTOWAY

Ottewell, Ottewill, Ottiwell, Otterwell: Willelmus *filius Otuelis* c1150 DC (L); *Otuell* Malduit 1169 P (Ess); William *Ottiwell* 1564 Bardsley. OFr *Otuel*, interchanging with *Otoïs*. *v.* OTTOWAY. cf. *Otuelis, Otewicus de Clipeston* 1207 Cur (Nf). The christian name was still in use in the 17th century.

Otton: *v.* OADE

Ottoway, Ottaway, Otterway, Ottway, Otway: *Otewi* 1202 AssL; *Otewicus le Poher* 1221 Cur (Sx); *Otewi de Esthall* 1228 Eynsham (O); Roger *Otway* 1260 AssLa; Hugh *Otewy* 1319 SRLo. OFr *Otoïs*, OG *Otwich*.

Oughtred, Outred, Ughtred: *Vctred* 1066 DB (D); *Uthret* ib. (Sf); Ysabella *filia Uhtredi* 1207 Cur (Ess); *Utred de Norflet* 1214 Cur (K); Roger *Uctred, Hutred* 1260 AssY; Roger *Outred* 1297 MinAcctCo (O). OE *Ūhtrǣd* from *ūht(e)*

'twilight, dusk, dawn' and *rǣd* 'advice, counsel, wisdom'.

Oughtright: *v.* OUTRIDGE

Ould: *v.* OLD

Ourry: *v.* HURRY

Outlaw: Alan *le Vtlage* 1230 FFSf; John *le Utlawe* 1316 FFC; Robert *Outlawe* 1327 SRC, SRSf. ME *outlawe* from ON *útlagi* 'outlaw'. Occasionally used as a personal name: *Hutlage* de Wrmedale Ed 2 AD i (Gl).

Outred: *v.* OUGHTRED

Outridge, Outteridge, Oughtright, Utteridge, Uttridge, Utridge: John *Outrich* 1333 ERO (Ess); William *Utteredge, Utteridge* 1663 Buxhall (Sf), 1674 HTSf. OE **Ūhtrīc* 'dawn-powerful', unrecorded in OE.

Ovens: John *Attenouene* 1276 AssSo; John *atte Oven* 1299 MELS (Wo); William *ate Ouene* 1317 AssK. 'One who lived near, or worked at an oven or furnace' (OE *ofen*), probably an old iron-furnace or a charcoal-furnace.

Over: Thomas *atte Overe*, William *del Overe* 1275 SRWo; Walter *atte Novere* 1327 ib. From Over (Cambs, Ches, Glos), or from residence near a bank or steep slope (OE *ōfer*). cf. OWER, NOAR, NOWERS.

Overal, Overall, Overell, Overill: William *Oueral* 1217 Pat; William *del Overhall* 1316 Wak (Y); Thomas *Overell* 1632 ERO; Thomas *Overill* 1674 HTSf. 'Dweller at the upper hall.' *Overell* and *Overill* might mean 'over the hill', but may be due to late weakenings of *Overhall*.

Overbeck: Thomas *Overthebek* c1270 Whitby (Y); Hugh *Overbecke* 1301 SRY. 'Dweller beyond the stream', ME *beck*, ON *bekkr* 'brook, beck'.

Overend: William *de Overende* 1279 RH (Bk). 'Dweller at the upper end (of the village).'

Overton: *v.* ORTON

Overy: (i) Robert *Overhe* 1279 RH (C); Richard *Oueree* 1314 Oseney (O). 'Dweller beyond the stream', OE *ēa.* (ii) Alexander *Overye, Overey* 1328 ArchC 33. 'Dweller beyond the low-lying land' (OE *ēg*). *v.* NYE, REA.

Owen, Owens: *Uwen* Wenta cyning 926 ASC D; *Ouen* 1066 DB (He); *Oenus filius* Madoc 1160 P (Sa); Robertus *filius Owen* 1221 Oseney (O); Ralph *Oein, Owein* 1221 AssWa; John *Owain* 1242 Fees (Sa); Henry *Oweyn, Ewayn* 1286-9 Balliol (O); Robert *Owyng* 1430 Oseney (O). OW *Oue(i)n*. *v.* EWAN.

Ower, Owers: Alexander *del Owre* 1240 PN K 72; Richard *de Owre* 1310 Balliol (O); John *Owers* 1524 SRSf. From Ower (Hants) or Owermoigne (Dorset), The Nower (Kent), or from residence near a bank or steep slope (or banks or slopes). OE *ōfer*. cf. OVER, NOWERS. Occasionally this is from OE *ōra* in the same sense. cf. Ores Fm (PN K 508), The Owers (PN Sx 83) and *v.* NOAR.

Owles: Gilbert *Vle* 1176 P (Nt); Stevyn *Owle*, Thomas *Owles* 1524 SRSf. OE *ūle* 'owl'.

Owlett: William *Owlete* 1524 SRSf. 'Little owl.'

Oxborough, Oxborrow, Oxbrow, Oxburgh, Ox-

bury: William *de Oxeburg'* 1275 RH (Nf). From Oxborough (Norfolk).

Oxenford: *v.* OXFORD

Oxer: Adam *Oxehird* 1327 Wak (Y); William *le Oxherd* 1332 SRLa. 'Ox-herd.' cf. OXNARD.

Oxford, Oxenford: Ulric *de Oxenford* 1086 DB (K); Walter *de Oxenforde, de Oxford* 1319 SRLo, 1341 LoPleas. From Oxford.

Oxlade: Michael *de Ocslade* 1279 RH (O). 'Dweller in the oak-valley', OE *āc, slæd.*

Oxley, Oxlee: Robert *de Oxeleia* 1227 FFSt; John *de Oxleye* 1310 LLB D; Thomas *Oxley* 1505, 1541 CorNt. From Oxley (Staffs) or Ox Lee in Hepworth (WRYorks).

Oxman: John *Oxeman* 1201 Cur (K); Richard *le Oxeman* 1289 AssCh. OE *oxa* 'ox' and *mann* (NED c1830), 'oxherd'.

Oxnard: William *Oxenhird'* 1301 SRY; John *le Oxenhurde* 1327 MEOT (Ha); Josias *Oxenerd, Oxnerd, Oxnard* 1645, 1646, 1671 FrY. OE *oxnahyrde* 'oxherd'.

Oyler, Ollier: Richard *Oylere, le Oyller'* 1248 Ass (Ha), 1281 MESO (L); Reginald *le Oyler* 1286 ib. (Lei). OFr *olier, huilier* 'maker or seller of oil'.

Ozanne: *Osanna* 1160 P (He), 1208 Cur (Do); Reginaldus *filius Osanna* 1180 P (Y); Walter *Ossenna* 13th AD i (Herts); John *Osan* 1279 RH (Bk); Richard *Osan, Ossan* 1296–7 Wak (Y). *Osanna*, a woman's name, from a Hebrew liturgical word used among the Jews, meaning 'save now', or 'save pray'. Latinized as *Hosanna*. Dauzat derives the name from the medieval feast of Palm Sunday, called *Osanne* or *Ozanne* from the hosanna sung on that day.

P

Pace, Paice, Pays, Payze, Peace: John *Pais* 1219 FrLeic; Roger, Ralph *Pays* 1275 RH (Nf); William, John *Pace* 1242 Fees (D), 1269 Ipm (D); John *Pax* 1275 RH (D); Peter *Pece* 1302 SRY. ME *pais, pes(e)*, OFr *pais*, Lat *pax* 'peace, concord, amity'. As ME *pasches* appears also as *paisch, peice, peace*, and Easter eggs are still called *Pace* eggs, later examples may be a variant of PASH.

Pacey, Pacy: Robert *de Peissi* 1158 P (Nt), *de Pacy* 1214 Cur (Wa). From Pacy-sur-Eure (Eure).

Pack, Packe, Paik, Pakes: *Payke* 1260 AssC; Johannes *filius Pake* 1279 RH (C); John *Pac* 1190 BuryS (Sf); Roger *Pake* 1195 P (Lei); Richard *Packe* 1221 *ElyA* (Sf); Richard *Pake, Packe* 1311, 1340 ColchCt; Joan *Pakes* 1312 ib. OFr *Pasques, Paque* 'Easter', *v.* PASH. cf. the diminutives in *Pakerel* 1251 Rams (Hu), Robert *Pakerel* 1201 AssSo, *Paket* 1190 P (Wa), Walter *Paket* 1176 P (O).

Packard: William *Pachart* 1208 P (L); Geoffrey, Henry *Pac(k)ard* 1327 SRSf. *Pack*, plus the suffix *-hard*.

Packer: Henry, Robert *Packer(e)* 1209 FrLeic, 1221 *ElyA* (Sf); John *le Pakkere* 1254 ArchC xii. A derivative of ME *packe* 'to pack', probably a wool-packer.

Packington, Pakington: Robert *de Pakinton'* 1195 P (Db) ; David *de Pakington* 1244 AssSt; Richard, Robert *de Pakynton* 1332 SRWa. From Packington (Leics, Staffs, Warwicks).

Packman: *v.* PAKEMAN

Pacock: *v.* PEACOCK

Paddock: Thomas, Walter *Paddoc* 1279 RH (C), 13th AD ii (Berks). OE **padduc* 'frog'.

Padgett: *v.* PAGET

Padgham: Hugh, Roger *de Pageham* 1206 Cur (Ha), 1255–6 FFSx; Edwarde *Pagham* 1576 HTY. From Pagham (Sussex).

Padley: Nicholas *de Paddeleye* 1275 RH (Db); Henry *de Padelay* 1379 PTY; William *Paddeley, Padley* 1504, 1508 CorNt. From Padley (Derby), or Padley Common (Devon).

Paenson: *v.* PENSON

Paerson: *v.* PEARSON

Pagan: *v.* PAIN

Page, Paige: Ralph *Page* 1230 P (D); William *le Page* 1240 FFEss. OFr *page* 'page'.

Paget, Pagett, Padgett: William, John *Paget* 1327 SRSx, 1359 ColchCt. A diminutive of PAGE.

Paice: *v.* PACE

Paige: *v.* PAGE

Paik: *v.* PACK

Paikin: Richard *Paykin* 1327 SRSf; Grigge *Pakyn* 1327 SRC. A diminutive of *Pay* or *Pa. v.* PAY, PAW.

Pain, Paine, Paines, Pane, Panes, Payan, Payen, Payn, Payne, Paynes, Pagan, Pagon, FitzPayn: Edmund *filius Pagen* 1086 DB (So); Reginaldus *filius Pain* 1185 Templars (L); *Payn* de Weston 1268 AssSo; Radulfus *Paganus* identical with Radulf *Pagenel* 1086 DB (So); John *Pane* 1190 P (Wo); Rotrotus *Pagani* 1195 P (Lei); Robert *Pain* 1200 P (Ha); William *Paen* 1220 Cur (So); Ralph *Payn* 1221 *ElyA* (C); Stephen *Paynes* 1230 Pat; John *Pagan* 1275 SRWo; Thomas *Payen* 1296 SRSx; Roberd *le filz Payeng', filz Payn* 1305 SRLa. OFr *Paien*, from Lat *paganus*, originally 'villager, rustic', later 'heathen'. Lebel explains this as a name given to children whose baptism had been postponed. Dauzat prefers to regard it as a derogatory term applied to adults whose religious zeal was not what it should be. Radulfus *filius Pagani* is also called Radulfus *Paganus* and *Pagenel* already in 1086, that is, as son of Paganus he had adopted his father's christian name as his surname, *Pagenel* 'little Payn' distinguishing him from his father. In the 12th and 13th centuries *Payn* was a very common christian name and was, no doubt, given without any thought of its meaning. The surname is probably always patronymic.

Painter, Paynter: Richard *the Paintur* 1240 FFY; John *Peynter* 1317 AssK; Thomas *Peyntour* alias *Steynor* 1430 Oseney (O). AFr *peintour*, OFr *peintour, peintor* 'painter'.

Pairpoint: *v.* PIERPOINT

Paish: *v.* PASH

Paiton: *v.* PAYTON

Pakeman, Packman: Henry *Pacheman* c1160 ELPN; Simon *Pakeman* (*Pacchem'*) 1202 P (Nt), 1221 Cur (Lei); William *Pakeman* 1278 AssSo; John *Packeman, Pakeman* 1352, 1360 ColchCt. Perhaps 'servant of *Pake*' (*v.* PACK), but usually ME *pake, packe* 'pack, bundle', plus *man*, 'hawker, pedlar'.

Pakes: *v.* PACK

Pakington: *v.* PACKINGTON

Palairet: A Huguenot name, Fr *Pailleret*, a diminutive of *Pailler*, denoting the owner of a *grenier a paille* 'a straw-rick, farm-yard'.

Paler, Payler: Ralph *le Paeler, le Payller* 1193

P (We), c1297 MESO (Wo). A derivative of ME *payle* or OFr *paelle* 'pail, pan'. A maker or seller of pails.

Pales: Metonymic for PALER.

Palfrey, Palfery, Parffrey, Parfrey: Hunfridus *Palefrei* 1148 Winton (Ha); Ralph *Palefray* 1183 Boldon (Du); Philip *Pawfry* 1605 LitSaxham PR (Sf); Ro. *Parfry*, An. *Paufry*, Ro. *Pawfery*, Jea. *Payfrey* 1674 HTSf; Francis *Parfree* bapt. 1742, Frances *Palfrey* widow bur. 1797 Rushbrook PR (Sf). OFr *palefrei* 'saddle-horse, palfrey', by metonymy for PALFREYMAN. cf. Adam *le Palefreur* 1255 *Ass* (Ess).

Palfreyman, Palfreeman, Palfreman, Palframan, Palphreyman, Parfrement: John *le Palfreyman* 1279 RH (C); John *Palfreman* 1333 MEOT (So); John *Palframan* 1379 PTY. 'Man in charge of the palfreys.' For *Parfrement*, cf. PALFREY.

Pallant: John *ate Palente* 1285 *Ass* (Sx); John *de Palenta* 1296 SRSx. From The Pallant (OE *palant* 'palace, enclosure'), the south-eastern quarter of the city of Chichester, a peculiar of the Archbishop of Canterbury, with special 'palatine rights'.

Pallis: (i) Henry *Paillehus* 1166 P (Y). A hybrid, Fr *paille* 'straw' and OE *hūs* 'house', a worker at the straw-rick. (ii) Augustin *de la Paleysse* 1327 SRSf. Rather OFr *palis, paleis* 'palisade' than AFr *paleis* 'palace'. Hence, 'dweller by the fence or palisade'.

Palliser, Pallister, Palser, Roger *Paleser* 1315 Wak (Y); Richard *Palicer* 1381 SRSt; William *Pallester* 1598 FrY. A derivative of OFr *palis, paleis* 'palisade', a maker of palings or fences. cf. William *Palycemaker* 1379 PTY.

Palmar, Palmer, Paumier: Sagar *Palmer* 1176 P (D); Wiger *le Palmer* 1191 P (L); Richard *le Paumere* 1198 FF (Mx). OFr *palmer, paumer* 'palmer, pilgrim to the Holy Land', so called from the palm-branch he carried.

Palphreyman: *v.* PALFREYMAN

Palser: *v.* PALLISER

Pammenter: *v.* PARMENTER

Pan, Pans: Lefwin, Aldwin *Panne* 1176 P (Nth), c1250 Rams (Nf). Probably metonymic for PANNER.

Panckridge, Pankridge: (i) *Pancrace* Grout 1532 Bardsley; Richard *Pancras* 1296 SRSx; Robert *Panckridge* 1698 Bardsley (La). From *Pancras*, a saint to whom eight churches are dedicated in the south-eastern counties, three of them in Sussex. The London church of St. Pancras was *Pancradge* church in 1630. (ii) William, John *de Panegregg'* (1296 SRSx) were connected with Pannelridge Wood in Ashburnham (Sussex), *Panegregg'* 1296, *Panyngrigge* 1366, while Penkridge (Staffs), *Pancriz* DB, *Pencrich* 1156, may be another source of the name.

Pane(s): *v.* PAIN

Pankhurst: *v.* PENTECOST

Pannaman: Thomas *le Paynerman* 1301 SRY; Adam *Panyarman* 1354 Putnam (L). 'A hawker who carries fish or other provisions in a pannier.' *v.*

PANNER (ii), and cf. Ranulf *Panermaker* 1305 *ERO*, Ralph *le Paniermakier* 1310 MESO (Ess), 'a maker of panniers'. The surname may also be a south-eastern form of PENNYMAN.

Pannaman: *v.* PENNYMAN

Pannell: *v.* PAYNELL. Also metonymic for *Panneler:* Simon *Paneller'* 1240 Eynsham (O); Martin *le Panneler* Hy 3 AD ii (Mx). ME *panel* 'a pannel of wainscot, of a saddle, etc.', hence a maker of panels.

Panner, Panniers: (i) Peter, John *le Panner* 1262 *For* (Ess), 1268 AssSo. A derivative of OE *panne* 'a pan', 'one who casts pans', synonymous with (Cristin *le) Pannegetter* 1250 MESO. (ii) Æluric *Paner* c1095 Bury (Sf); John *Panier* 1209 P (W); Nicholas *Paner* 1216 ChR; Edith *Panier* 1279 RH (C). OFr *paniere*, AFr *paner*, ME *panier* 'a basket' (c1300 NED). This might be metonymic for 'a basket-maker', or a hawker. *v.* PANNAMAN.

Pannett: *Painotus* de Norwude 1176 P (D); *Painot* 1200 P (Y); Richard *Painot* 1200 P (Y); Thomas *Paynet* 1332 SRSx. OFr *Payen* plus the diminutive suffixes -ot, -et. *v.* PAIN, PAYNELL.

Pannifer: *v.* PENNYFATHER

Panson: 'Son of *Pain*'. *v.* PAIN, PANNETT, PENSON.

Panter, Panther: Reginald *le Paneter* 1200 Cur (K), *le Panetier* 1206 P (K); Warin *le Paneter* 1230 Cl (Ha). AFr *paneter*, OFr *panetier*. 'A household officer who supplied the bread and had charge of the pantry' (1297 NED). The panter of a monastery also distributed loaves to the poor.

Pantrey, Pantry: John *de la Paneterie* 1274 RH (Lo); Robert *atte Panetrye* 1332 SRSx. 'The officer of the pantry.' *v.* PANTER.

Pape: Stubhard, Blachemannus *Pape* c1095 Bury (Sf), 1178 P (Sr); William, Adam *la Pape* 1207 Cur (Bk), 1268 AssSo. Some of the earlier forms, particularly those with an English christian name may be from OE *pāpa* 'pope' which became ME *pope* and survives as POPE. Those with the article and French christian names are from OFr *pape* 'pope'. A nickname for one of an austere, ascetic appearance, or a pageant-name.

Papigay, Pebjoy, Pobgee, Pobjoy, Popejoy, Popjoy: Robert *Papejay* 1321 AssSt; Robert *Papyngeye* 1371 Cl (Nf); Robert *Popungey* 1397 NorwW (Nf); Roger *Popyngeay* 1410 AD i (Mx); William *Popjoy* 1759 Bardsley; John *Pobjoy* 1784 ib. ME *papejai, popingay*, OFr *papegai* 'parrot', either a nickname from the bird or a title for the winner in the sports. cf. 'Papegay, a parrot or popingay; also a wooden parrot (set up on the top of a steeple, high tree, or pole) whereat there is, in many parts of France, a generall shooting once euerie yeare; and an exemption, for all that yeare, from *La Taille*, obtained by him that strikes downe the right wing thereof (who is therefore tearmed *Le Chevalier*); and by him that strikes downe the left wing (who is tearmed, *Le Baron*); and by him that strikes downe the whole popingay (who for that dexteritie or good hap hath also the title of *Roy du Papegay*, all the yeare following)' (Cotgrave). Stow notes a similar prize of a peacock for running at the quintain.

Papillon: Turoldus *Papilio* c1095 Bury (Sf); Ridellus *Papillun* 1162 P (Nth); Thorald *le Papillon* 1250 Fees (Do). OFr *papillon*, Lat *papilio* 'butterfly', 'un surnom d'homme inconstant, imprudent' (Dauzat).

Paragreen: *v.* PILGRIM

Paramor, Paramore, Parramore: John *Paramour* 1296 SRSx, 1372 ColchCt. ME, OFr *par amour* 'with love', 'lover, sweetheart'.

Parchment: Walter *Perchamunt* 1200 P (L). Metonymic for OFr *parcheminier* 'maker or seller of parchment': Gille *Parcheminer* 1180 P (Sa), Richard *parchment maker, Parchemener* 1413, 1420 Oseney (O).

Parden: *v.* PARDON

Pardew, Pardey, Pardy, Pardoe, Perdue: Richard *Parde* 1228 FFSf; Robert *Pardey* 1296 SRSx; Henry *Pardeu* 1332 SRWa; Walter *Perdu* Ed 3 Rydware (St). An oath-name, *par Dieu*, perhaps shortened from *de par Dieu* (Lat *de parte Dei*) 'in God's name'. Common in ME as *pardee:* 'I have a wyf, pardee, as wel as thow' (Chaucer). Such names were common. cf. PURDAY, PUREFOY, GODSAFE, and Adam *Parmafey* 1327 SRSf, Rychard *Parmafoye* 1568 SRSf, Richard *Parmoncorps* 1332 SRSx, Alan *Par la Roy* 1302 SRY.

Pardner, Partner, Partener: Walter *le Pardoner* 1322 ParlWrits (C). 'The pardoner', a licensed seller of indulgences.

Pardon, Parden: Alfred, Thomas *Pardon* 1327 SRWo, 1347 Cl (L). Metonymic for PARDNER.

Parent, Parrent, Parrant: Gerald *parent* Hy 2 DC (L); Geoffrey *Parent* 1185 P (Nth); William *(le) Parent* 1316 AssSt, 1327 SRSt. Weekley and Dauzat take this to be a surname of relationship. This is vague. We may well have OFr *parant, parent*, adj. used figuratively of a fine appearance, 'powerful' (Godefroy).

Parfait, Parfett, Parfit, Parfitt, Perfitt, Parfect, Perfect: Vnfridus *parfait* 1115 Winton (Ha); Richard *Parfeit, Parfet* 1196 Cur (So); William *Perfyt* 1383 LLB H; Richard *Parfytte* 1568 SRSf. ME *perfit, parfit* from OFr *parfeit, parfit* from Lat *perfectus* 'perfect'. *Parfit(t)* and *Parfett* are the most common forms today. *Perfect* is fairly frequent but is late and due to the influence of the reconstructed, learned spelling of the adjective.

Parffrey, Parfrey: *v.* PALFREY

Parfrement: *v.* PALFREYMAN

Pargeter, Pargetter, Pargiter: Willelmus *Dealbator* 1207 Cur (Nf); James *Pergetor* 1533 Bardsley (Nf); Edmund *Pargitur* 1617 ib. Pargetting at Marlborough is mentioned in 1237. It was allied to daubing, plaster being used instead of clay or loam. The surface of the parget might be finished smooth, with a coat of whitewash, or as roughcast with sand or small stones. cf. 'Stephen the Dauber who pargetted the long chamber' at Corfe in 1285 (Building 191).

Parham, Perham, Parram, Perram: Turmod *de Perham* 1066 DB (Sf); William *de Perreham* 1187

P (Sx); William *de Parham* 1264 RegAntiquiss; John *Parham* 1366 IpmW. From Parham (Suffolk, Sussex), or 'dweller by the homestead where pear-trees grow'.

Paris, Parris, Parriss: (i) Geruase *de Paris* 1158 P (Lo); Willelmus *Parisiensis* 1185 Templars (L); William *de Paris* 1238 AssSo. From Paris, the usual derivation. William *de Paris* Hy 2 DC is identical with Willelmo *Paride* c1150 ib. Here *Paris* (abl. *Paride*) appears to be identical with *Parisiensis* 'the Parisian'. (ii) Magister *Parisius* 1157–63 DC (L); Reinger *filius Paridis* 1203 Cur (Sx); *Parisius Miles* 1311 Battle (Sx); Ralph *Paris* c1220 NthCh (Nth); Richard *Parys* 1293 Fees (D); Adam *Parisson* 1332 SRCu. This is from a personal name which, to judge from the number of early examples without a preposition, was not uncommon. It is the French popular form of (St) *Patrick*, Lat *Patricius* 'patrician', the origin of French *Paris, Patrice, Patris*. The variant *Paris, Paridis* must be due to the influence of the Trojan *Paris*, unknown as a personal-name in either England or France.

Parish, Parrish: John *Parisshe, Pareys* 1462–4 LLB L. Identical with PARIS. Paris Hall in North Weald Bassett (Essex), named from Richard *de Paris* (1276), is *Parrishe* in 1593 (PN Ess 87). This development of final *sh* from *s* is found already in 1319 in *Wrabenash* for Wrabness (PN Ess 358). Consequently, in William de *Parysch* 1379 PTY we probably have the same development. Derivation from *parish* is very unlikely. cf. MORRISH, NORRISH.

Park, Parke, Parkes, Parks, Duparc, du Parcq, Duparcq: Henry *del Parck* 1272 AssSt; Iselota *atte Park* 1285 AD vi (K); Agnes *del Parkes*, Henry *del Parks* 1304 MELS (Wo). ME *parc, parke* (13th NED), from OFr *parc* 'lists', 'enclosed space', 'park', 'enclosure'. The surname may denote residence in or near a park or enclosure but is, no doubt, often synonymous with PARKER. cf. PANTREY. Modern *Park(e)* is sometimes a contraction of PARRACK. *Duparcq* is a Guernsey name.

Parker, Parkers: Anschetil *Parcher* 1086 DB (So); Geoffrey *parchier* c1145–65 Seals (Nb); Claricia *le Parkeres* 1327 SRSo. AFr *parker*, OFr *parquier, parchier, parker* 'parker', 'one in charge of a park', 'park-keeper' (1321 NED).

Parkhouse: John *del Parkhouse* 1379 PTY. 'Dweller at the house in the park.'

Parkhurst: William *de Parkhurst* (1327 SRSx) lived at Parkhurst Fm in Tillington (Sussex). There are two other Parkhursts in Sussex and others elsewhere.

Parkin, Parkins, Parkyn, Perken, Perkin, Perkins, Purkins: Edmund *Perkyn* 1327 SRSf; Robert *Parkyn* 1327 SRSt; Walter *Perkyns* 1327 SRWo; Maud *Parkynes* 1332 SRWa. 'Little Peter', from *Per* (*Peres*) and *-kin*. *v.* PIERCE.

Parkinson, Parkerson: John *Parkynson* 1379 PTY; William *Perkynsone* 1382 AssWa; Emmot *Parkyngson* 1540 Whitby (Y). 'Son of *Perkin*.'

Parkman: Richard *Parcman* 1307 MEOT

(Herts); Richard *Parkeman* 1429 LLB K. ME *park* and *man*, identical with PARKER.

Parlabean, Parlby: Richard *Parlebien* 1200 P (L); Roger *Parleben* 1231 FFC. Fr *parle bien* 'speak well'. cf. John *Parlefrens* 1283 Battle (Sx).

Parlane: *v.* MACFARLAN

Parlett: Herlewin *Perlet* 1180 P (Nf); Walter *Parlet* 1218 FFSf. A double diminutive of *Per*, contracted from *Per-el-et*. cf. PARKIN.

Parlour: (i) Robert *Parler* 1086 DB (W); Richard *le Parlour* 1219 Rams (Hu). OFr *parlier*, AFr **parlour* 'avocat, discoureur' (Godefroy), 'lawyer', perhaps 'chatterbox'. Also probably 'the servant who attended the parlour', originally the conversation and interview room in a monastery. cf. Richard *atte Parlur* 1296 SRSx. (ii) Henry, Simon *le Perler* 1291 LLB A, 1297 FFEss. A derivative of ME, OFr *perle* 'pearl', a seller of pearls, or perhaps 'maker of glass pearls', 'paternostrer' (Ekwall). *v.* PEARL.

Parmenter, Parminter, Pammenter, Parmeter, Parmiter: Robert *Parmenter* 1177 P (Lei); Vmfridus *parmentier* 1198 P (K); William *le Parmenter* 1204 Cur (O); Robert *le Parminter* 1221 AssWo; Thomas *le permeter* c1250 Rams (C); William *Parmater* 1381 SRSf; Thomas *Parmiter* 1674 HTSf. OFr *parmentier, parmetier* 'tailor'.

Parnall, Parnell, Parnwell, Purnell: Petronilla Ric 1 DC (L); *Purnelle, Petronille, Peronelle* Kepeherme, -harm 1249, 1250, 1253 Oseney (O); *Pernel, Parnell* la Brune 1268, 1280 AssSo; Johanna *Peronele* 1250 Fees (C); Agnes *Peronell* 1274 Wak (Y); Roger *Pernel* 1295 Barnwell (C); Edith *Purnele* 1297 MinAcctCo (W); Robert *Parnel* 1332 SRSt. *Petronilla*, a feminine diminutive of the Latin *Petronius*, was the name of a saint much invoked against fevers and regarded as a daughter of St Peter. The name was accordingly considered to be a derivative of *Peter* and became one of the most popular of girls' names, the vernacular *Parnell* being still used as a christian name as late as the 18th century in Cornwall. *Parnwell*, in spite of its local appearance, is a corruption, in use in 1670 as a christian name, *Parnwell* Graystocke (LaWills) and in 1801 as a surname, William *Parnewell* (Bardsley).

Parr, Par: (i) Robert, Margeria *Perre* 1275 RH (Y), 1327 SRSf. OFr *Perre, Pierre* 'Peter'. (ii) Henry *de Par* 1284 AssLa; Richard *del Par* 1356 LLB G; Thomas *Par* 1402 FA (We). From Parr (Lancs), or 'dweller at the enclosure'.

Parrack, Parrick, Parrock: Artur *de Parrok* 1212 Fees (Ha); John *atte Parrok* 1296 SRSx; Walter *Parrok* 1299 LoCt. OE *pearroc* 'paddock, enclosure', 'Parrocke, a lytell parke, *parquet*' (Palsgrave). Sometimes this has given a modern PARK. Park Fm in Great Horkesley, *Parrokyslond* Ric 2, owes its name to the family of Elias *del Parrok* (1276 PN Ess 393).

Parram: *v.* PARHAM

Parramore: *v.* PARAMOR

Parrant: *v.* PARENT

Parratt, Parrett: *v.* PARROT

Parrell, Parren: *v.* PERRIN

Parrick, Parrock: *v.* PARRACK

Parris, Parrish: *v.* PARIS, PARISH

Parrot, Parrott, Parratt, Parrett, Parritt, Perot, Perott, Perratt, Perret, Perrett, Perrot, Perrott, Porrett, Porritt: *Perot* 1246 AssLa; William *Peret* 1066 DB (Sf); Ralph *Perot* 1235 Fees (Ess), 1279 RH (Beds); William *Poret* 1301 SRY; John *Parrat* 1344 LoPleas; William *Parotte* 1470 LLB L; John *Porrett, Perott, Parott, Parrett* 1520 Oxon. Diminutives of *Perre* (Peter) plus the suffixes *-et, -ot*. *Parratt* and *Perratt* are also from *Pirard* or an undocumented *Perard*. *v.* PIRRET. Also a nickname from the parrot, itself nicknamed from *Perot*: William *le Perot* 1277 ParlWrits (Wo).

Parry: John *ap Harry* 1407 AD iii (He); Morres *Parry*, John *Apharry* 1527, 1528 LP; Richard *Upharry* 1545 SRW; Margery *A parry*, Harrye *Aperry* 1556, 1557 LedburyPR (He); Thomas *Parrye* 1557 Pat (Gl). Welsh *ap Harry* 'son of *Harry*'.

Parsey: *v.* PEARCEY, PERCY

Parsloe, Parslow, Parsley, Paslow, Pasley, Pashley, Pashler: Radulfus *Passaqua* 1086 DB (Bk); Ralph *Passelewa* 1104–6 Bury (Sf); Hamo *passelowe* 1194 Cur (Bk); Edmund *Passeleye* 1314 AssK; Simon *Passelegh* (*Passelewe*) 1327 *SR* (Ess); Nycholas *Passhloo* 1524 SRSf; Edward *Parsley* 1637 EA (NS) ii (Sf). OFr *Passelewe* 'cross the water'. *v.* PASSMORE. cf. Alan *Pasewater* 1439 NorwW (Nf), John *Paswater* 1568 SRSf. The Domesday tenant's name survives in Drayton Parslow (Bucks). cf. also Parsloes in Dagenham (Ess): *Passelewesmede* 1390, *Pashlewes* 1456, *Parslo(w)es* 1609, 1634 (PN Ess 92).

Parson: William *Persun* 1197 P (Nf); Richard *la Persone* 1221 AssWo; Robert *Parson* 1296 SRSx. OFr *persone*, ME *persone, persoun* 'priest, parson'.

Parsons: (i) Roger *le Persones* 1323 AssSt; Alicia *le Parsones* 1327 SRWo; Isabella *Parsones* 1327 SRSo. This is an elliptic genitive, 'the parson's servant'. cf. Eudo *homo persone* 1210 Cur (C), Henry *le Personesman* 1327 SRDb. (ii) Gilbert, Stephen *ad Parsons* 1297 MinAcctCo; Ralph *del Persones* 1323 AssSt; William *atte Personnes* 1327 SRSf; Gilbert *atte Parsones* 1332 SRSx. This again is elliptic, one who lived (or worked) 'at the parson's (house)', at the parsonage.

Parsonson, Parsison, Parsizon: Stephanus *filius persone* 12th DC (L); Thomas *le Fiz la Persone* 1250 FFL; John *le Personesone* 1312 AssSt. 'Son of the parson.'

Partener: *v.* PARDNER

Partington: Henry *de Partinton* 1260 AssCh; Hugh *de Partyngton* 1401 AssLa. From Partington (Ches).

Partlan: *v.* MACFARLAN

Partleton: Stephen *de Pertlington* 1327 SRSx. From Pattleton's Fm in Westfield (Sussex), *v.* PN Sx 506.

Partner: *v.* PARDNER

Partrick, Partridge, Patriche: Ailward *Pertriz* 1176 P (D); Geoffrey *Perdriz* 1197 FF (Ess); John

Perdrich 1244 FFSt; Philip *Partrich* 1260 AssCh; Henry *Pertrik* 1274 RH (Nf); Thomas *le Partrich* 1327 SRSo; Sibil *Partryge* 1332 SRSt; John *Pattriche* 1579 Gt Welnetham PR (Sf); John *Pattridge* 1622 ib. ME *pertriche*, OFr *perdrix* 'partridge'. The surname is very common and whilst often a nickname from the bird, it probably also means 'a hunter or catcher of partridges'. cf. Thomas *Pertricour* 1279 RH (Hu), Nicholas *le Pertricour* 1324 Wak (Y), from AFr **perdrichour, *pertricour*. In the 1524 Suffolk Subsidy Roll the name appears as *Partriche* (frequent), *Parterych, Patrick, Pattrik* and *Patryk*, and in the Hearth Tax for 1674 as *Partridge, Pattridge, Pattrige, Pateridge, Pattarage, Pattrage* and *Putteridge*. *Patriche*, which is rare, is due to the loss of the first *r*, and a similar loss in *Partrick* gave rise to *Patrick*, so that some of our *Patricks* owe their name to the bird and not to the saint.

Pascall, Paskell, Pasquill: *Paskell* Langdon 1606 Bardsley (Co); John *Pascal* 1221 AssWa; William *Pascale* 1275 SRWo; William *Paschale* 1327 SRSf. Fr *Pascal*, the name of a 9th-century pope and saint, from Latin *paschalis* 'pertaining to Easter'. cf. OBret *Paschael* (Loth).

Pascoe: *Pascow* Meneux 1424 LLB I; Simon *Pascoe* 1372 ColchCt; John *Pascowe* 1443 AD iv (Co). A form of *Pascall*, long surviving in Cornwall. *Paskell* Langdon (1606) is called *Pascowe* in 1571 (Bardsley).

Pasfield: *v.* PASSFIELD

Pash, Pashe, Paish, Pask, Paske, Pasque: Hugo *filius Pasch'* 1279 RH (C); Thomas *Paske* 1253 Oseney (O); Felic' *Pasch'* 1279 RH (C); William *Pasques, Paskes* 1311 LLB D, 1319 SRLo; Walter *Passh'* 1327 SRWo. ME *pasche(s), paske(s)*, OFr *pasche, pasque(s)* 'Easter', from Hebrew *pesakh* 'a passing over', used as a personal name for one born at Easter. cf. OBret *Pasc* (Loth). cf. William *Paskessone* 1293 FFC 'son of *Paske*'.

Pashler: *v.* PARSLOE

Pashley: Robert *de Passelegh* 1303 FA (Sx). From Pashley in Ticehurst (Sussex). *v.* also PARSLOE.

Paske: *v.* PASH

Paskell: *v.* PASCALL

Paskerful: *v.* BASKERVILLE

Paskin, Paskins: *Pasken* de Stafford, Ralph *Pasken, Paschen* 13th StThomas, Ronton (St). OW *Paskent*, MW *Pascen*, from Lat *Pascentius* (Förster).

Pasley, Paslow, *v.* PARSLOE

Pasmore: *v.* PASSMORE

Pasque: *v.* PASH

Pasquill: *v.* PASCALL

Pass, Passe: *Passe* de Albeneye 1230 P (Nt); John *Passe* 1275 RH (Nf), SRWo. Probably a pet-form of *Pascall*. cf. *Passe* 'Easter' (1533 NED).

Passage: Ralph *de Passagio*, Agnes *del Passage* 1275 RH (Sf). From residence in a passage or narrow lane.

Passant, Passavant: *Passeuant* 1155 FeuDu; William *Passavant* 1198 Cur (L); Andrew *Passe-*

avant 1212 Cur (Ha); Robert *Passaunt* 1314 Pat (Y). OFr *passe avant* 'go on in front', perhaps a herald or messenger.

Passenger: Robert *le Passager* Hy 3 AD iii (Sr); Rebecca *Passenger* 1771 Bardsley. OFr *passager* 'wayfarer'.

Passfield, Pasfield: Andrew, William *de Passefeld'* 1214 Cur (Ess), 1345 LLB F. From *Passefelda* (1062), now Paslow Hall in High Ongar (Essex). *v.* PN Ess 73.

Passifull: *v.* PERCEVAL

Passmore, Pasmore: William, Richard *Passemer* 1199 P (Nth), 1242 Fees (D); Walter *Passemore* 1266 AssSt. OFr *passe mer* 'cross the sea', seafarer, sailor. In England the second element was associated with *mere*, interchanging, as often, with *more*. A type of surname common both in France and England. *v.* PASSANT, PARSLOE, and cf. Richard *Passeboys* 'wood', Adam *Passebusck* 'bush' 1297 SRY, Alfwin *Passeculuert* 1166 P (Sx) and the French *Passedouet* (canal), *Passefons* (fountain), *Passepont* (bridge), *Passerieu* (stream). These Dauzat plausibly suggests mean 'one who has to cross the bridge, stream or water, or pass the spring or fountain to reach his home'. cf. PERCEVAL.

Paster: This is, no doubt, often for PASTOR, but must also be a derivative of OFr *paste* 'paste or dough', a baker, synonymous with (John) *Pastemakere* 1340 AssC. cf. Tewaldus *Paste* 1159–85 Templars (Lo); Gilbert *Paste* 1210 Cur (C).

Pasterfield, Pasterful: *v.* BASKERVILLE

Paston: Geoffrey *de Paston'* 1202 AssNth; John *de Pastone* 1321 CorLo; William *Paston* 1414 FFEss. From Paston (Norfolk, Northants, Northumb).

Pastor: Gerardus *pastor* 1140–53 Holme (Nf); Godrich *le Pastur* 1227 Pat (Nf); Dionisius *Pastour* 1317 AssK. AFr *pastour*, OFr *pastor, pastur* 'herdsman, shepherd'. In early sources *Pastor* is often Lat *pastor* 'shepherd'. cf. Willelmo *pastore* 12th DC (L).

Patch: Seman *Pac, Pach* 1177–8 P (Sx); Nicholas *Pacche* 1248 Oseney (O); Henry *Patche* c1248 Bec (Do); William *Payche* 1327 SRSf. *Pache* is a ME form of *pasches* 'Easter'. *v.* PACK, PASH.

Patchett: *Pachet* 1221 AssWa; Gerard, William *Pachet* 1183, 1195 P (Berks, Lei); Richard *Pascet* c1198 Bart (Lo). A diminutive of *Patch*.

Patchin: John *Pachun, Pachon* 1279 RH (O); Robert *Pachyns* 1296 SRSx. Diminutives of *Patch*.

Patching: Elena, William *de Pacching*(*g*) 1327 SRSx, *SR* (Ess). From Patching (Sussex) or Patching Hall (Essex).

Pate, Pates: Aluric, Osbert *Pate* c1100–30 OEByn (D), 1196 P (Bk). ME *pate* 'head, skull', a nickname (cf. HEAD), or a pet-name for *Patrick. v.* PATEMAN.

Pateman, Patman, Pattman: *Patein* or *Pateman* Broin 1407 CalSc; Jordan *Pateman* 1219 AssY; Peter *Patemon* 1275 SRWo; John *Patman* 1524 SRSf. A pet-form of *Patrick*.

Patent: Thomas *Paton, Paten*, John *Patten*, Edward *Patent* 1524 SRSf. Late forms, with excrescent *t*, of PATON, PATTEN, PATTON.

Paternoster: *Paternoster* de Mumbi Hy 2 DC (L); Roger *Pater noster* 1185 Templars (L); Robert *Paternoster* 1197 FF (Bk), 1221 AssWa. The first words of the Latin Lord's prayer are recorded as a noun, ME *paternoster* (c1250 NED) in the sense '(bead in a) rosary'. Here we have the word used both as a personal-name and, by metonymy, for 'a maker of paternosters, rosaries, chaplets, beads strung together for pattering aves' (Bardsley), a natural shortening of the fuller *paternosterer*: William *le Paternostrer* 1280–95 LLB A, B, Jordan *paternosterer* 1303 LoCt. There is a Paternoster Row near St Paul's Cathedral and another near Carlisle Cathedral and there was formerly one near Chertsey Abbey, all centres of this once important industry. In the 14th century the term used was *paternostermaker*: Nicholas *Paternostermaker* 1388 LoCt. Sometimes the name is due to the service by which land was held. In the reign of Edward I John *Paternoster* held a virgate of land in East Hendred (Berks) now called Paternoster Bank by service of saying a paternoster every day for the King's soul (PN Sr 380). In the same reign Alice *Paternoster* held land in Pusey in the same county by service of saying five paternosters a day for the souls of the king's ancestors and Richard *Paternoster* on succeeding to an estate in the same parish, instead of paying a sum of money as a relief, said the Lord's Prayer thrice before the Barons of the Exchequer, as John his brother had previously done (Lower).

Paterson: *v.* PATTERSON

Pateshall, Patsall: Simon *de Pateshylla, de Pateshull* 1190 P (Nth); John *de Pateshull* 1298 AssL; Richard *Patsale* 1506 FFEss. From Pattishall (Northants).

Patey: Walter *Pati* 1275 SRWo; John *Patey* 1381 PTY. A diminutive of *Pate* (Patrick).

Patman: *v.* PATEMAN

Patmore, Pattemore: Walter *de Patemere* 1208 Cur (Herts); Richard *de Patmere* 1332–3 FFSr. From Patmore (Herts).

Paton, Patton: *Paton* 1332 SRCu; *Patone* de Hangaldsyde, *Patrick* Hangangside 1467, 1469 Black; *Pattoun* Millar 1492 ib.; Hugo *Patun* 1230 Pat (Nb); James *Patoun* 1279 RH (Beds); John *Paton* 1413 FFC; Thomas *Pattoun* 1538 Black; Thomas *Patton* 1547 ib. *Pat-un*, a diminutive of *Pat(e)*, i.e. *Patrick*.

Patriche: *v.* PARTRICK

Patrick, Pattrick: *Patricius* 1175–96 YCh (Y); *Patricius clericus* 1214 Cur (Sf); William *Patric* 1130 P (K); William *Patrik* c1180 WhC (La); John *Pateric* 1229 Cl (Ireland). OIr *Patraicc*, Lat *Patricius* 'patrician'. In England the name was chiefly northern. In Scotland *Patrick* was common in the west and became confused with *Peter*. The surname was common in Ayrshire. In Ireland it only became a popular christian name after 1600, due probably to the Scots settlers in Ulster.

Patry: *v.* PETRIE

Patsall: *v.* PATESHALL

Patt: (i) Gerard *de la Patte* 1219 MELS. Probably 'dweller by the marsh', OE **pat(t)e. v.* MELS. (ii) Hugo *Pat* 1206 P (He); William *Patte* 1297 MinAcctCo. Either identical with the above, with early loss of the preposition, or a pet-name of *Patrick*.

Patten, Pattin, Pattern: Anger, Robert *Patin* 1182 P (So), 1214 Cur (Ha); Rannulf *Aspatins* 1225 Pat. ME *paten* 'patten, clog' (1390 NED), often metonymic for *patoner* or *patynmáker*: Laurence *Patener* 1381 PTY, John *Patynmaker* 1379 ColchCt, 'a patten-maker'. *Aspatins* means 'the man with the pattens'. cf. 'Pateyne, fote vp berynge (pateyne of tymbyre, or yron, to walke with)' PromptParv. Way notes that pattens were used anciently by ecclesiastics, probably to protect the feet from the chill of the bare pavement of the church. *v.* also PATON.

Patterson, Paterson: William *Patrison* 1446 Black (Aberdeen); Donald *Patryson* 1490 ib.; Adam *Patersoun* 1499 ib. 'Son of *Patrick*.' This has probably also become *Pattison*.

Pattin: *v.* PATTEN

Pattinson, Patteson, Pattison, Pattisson, Pattyson, Patison: Nichole *Patonesone* 1305 Black; John *Patonson* 1332 SRCu; Alexander *Patynson* 1475 Black; Henry *Patyson* 1524 SRSf. 'Son of *Paton* (Patrick).'

Pattman: *v.* PATEMAN

Patton: John *de Patinton', de Patton'* 1221 AssSa, 1297 SRY. From Patton (Salop, Westmorland). *v.* also PATON.

Patvine: *v.* POIDEVIN

Paul, Paule, Paull, Pawle, Pole, Poles, Poll, Polle, Pool, Poole, Powell, Powle, Powles: *Powel* c1260 ODCN; Thomas *filius Pole* 1275 RH (Db); Stephen *le fiz Pauwel* 1276 AssLa; *Paulus Godchep* 1292 SRLo; Adam *filius Pole* 1323 AD v (St); Haldanus *Paulus* 1182 P (Sf); William *Pol* 1188 BuryS (Sf); William *Polle* 1193 P (L); Richard *Poul* 1224–46 Bart (Lo); John *Pol* 1275 SRWo; Nicholas *Pole* 1276 RH (Db); William *Poll* 1279 RH (O); John *Powel, Paul* 1292 SRLo, 1307 LLB C; John *Poul* (*Pouel*) 1293 Rams (Hu); John *Pool* 1324 FFEss; William *Powl* 1327 SRC; Adam *Poull* 1346 FA (Sf). Lat *Paulus* 'small'. As a christian name, examples are not common but it can hardly be regarded as 'a very rare name in the Middle Ages' (ODCN) in view of its numerous forms and derivatives. It was already a surname in the 12th century. Weekley regards the vogue of the diminutive *Paulinus* as largely due to Corneille but it is found in Domesday Book in 1066, in 1200–5 Cur (where it is indexed as *Paul*), and as a surname in the 13th century. The everyday form was *Pole* or *Poul* (Piers Plowman, Wyclif). The attribute of Belchamp and Wickham St Paul's (Essex) appears as *Pol(l)* 1285; *Poel* 1327, *Poulis* 1343, *Powel* 1358, *Poles, Poole* 1607. Pole Hill in Chingford is a relic of the manor of Chingford *Pauls* and Paul's Fm in Little Bardfield is *Pooles* in 1593.

v. PN Ess *s.nn.* cf. also *Pollekin* 1206 Cur (Sr), John *Polekin, Polekyn* 1279 RH (O), 1297 MinAcctCo, Jordan *Polekoc* 1250 Rams (Bk), Isabella *Polecok* 1274 RH (Berks). *v.* POWELL.

Pauley, Paulley, Pauly, Pawley: Geoffrey *Pauly* 1275 RH (C); Marjorie *Pawley* 1515 KentW. A pet form of *Paul.* cf. Wykkam *Pawley* (Wickham St Paul's) 1545 PN Ess 467.

Paulin, Pauling, Paulling, Pawlyn, Pawling, Pollins: *Paulinus* 1066 DB (So); *Paulinus* de Kirtlingtun Hy 2 DC (Nt); Johannes *filius Paulini* 1301 SRY; Basilia *Paulin* 1220 Cur (Mx); John *Paulyn* 1291 FFSf; William *Pawelyn* 1397 PrGR; William *Paulinge* 1607 Oxon (Wo). A diminutive of *Paul.* The feminine *Paulina* is occasionally found: *Paulina* 1169 P (K).

Paulley, Pauly: *v.* PAULEY

Pauncefoot, Pauncefote, Pauncefort, Ponsford: Bernard *Paunceuolt* 1086 DB (Ha); Hunfridus *pancheuot* 1148 Winton (Ha); Richard *Pancefot* c1180 DC (L), 1197 FF (Wo), *Panceuot* 1195 P (Gl); Richard *Pancefot* (*Paceford'*) 1220 Cur (He); Walter *Pauncefot* 1280 AssSo; Tracy *Pauncefoot, Pauncefort* 1702 DKR 41. Tengvik explains this name as 'paunch-face' from ME *panche* 'stomach' from OFr *pance*, ONFr *panche* (1375 NED) and OFr *volt* 'face', not an attractive etymology. His description 'The nickname may indicate corpulence and fleshiness' is, however, to the point, for the second element is, as Harrison has noted, OFr *volt* 'vaulted, arched', hence 'the man with the arched and rounded belly'. By the common Anglo-Norman interchange of liquids *Paunceuolt* would become *Paunceuort*, hence *Pauncefort* and there is some evidence of this in the 1220 *Paceford* and the form *Poncefortt* given by Lower which would give *Ponsford.* The surname may also derive from Ponsford (Devon), *Pantesfort* DB, *Pontesford* 1249 (PN D 561), the first form becoming *Pauncefort*, the second *Ponsford.*

Paveley, Pavly, Paveley, Pawley: Reginald *de Paueilli* 1190 P (W), Walter *de Pavily, de Pawely* 1235, 1250 Fees (W). From Pavilly (Seine-Inférieure).

Paver, Pavier, Pavior, Paviour, Pavyer: Walter *Pavier* 1212 Cur (Y); John *Pauur* 1252-3 Clerkenwell (Lo); William *le Pavour* 1281 LLB A, 1299 LoCt; Henry *le Paveor* 1327 SRWo. OFr *paveur* 'paviour', 'one who lays pavements' (1477 NED). The status and skill of the paviours varied from the masters of a craft to mere labourers who could only dig and ram. The more skilled were men of standing; in 1398 two paviours supped with the Fellows of New College, Oxford. The London Paviours were ultimately organized under the Wardens of the craft and their ordinances of 1479 are remarkably modern. They inveighed bitterly against 'fforeyns and laborers not havyng the verry kounyng of pavyng' . . . who 'take upon theyme the saide works of pavyng'. Each paviour was restricted to two labourers and apprentices were to be few. But, the bad worker was to 'take

up his werks agayn and make hit new and pay vjs viijd'. *v.* further, G. T. Salusbury, *Street Life in Medieval England* 13–39. Ornamental tiles and marble were used for paving the floors of cathedrals, palaces, etc. In 1308 Hugh le Peyntour and Peter the Pavier were employed 'making and painting the pavement' at St Stephen's Chapel, Westminster. *v.* Building 146–7, MARBER, PAVEY.

Pavett, Pavitt: John *Pavet* 1591 Bardsley. *Pav-et*, a diminutive of *Pavey.*

Pavey, Pavie, Pavis, Pavy: Ricardus *filius Pauee* 1156–85 Seals (Wa); Gillebertus *filius Pauie* 1172 P (So); *Pavia* 1206 Cur (Ess); *Paveya* 1219 AssY; Robert *Paui* 1219 AssY; Richard *Paveye* 1251 Fees (Wa). *Pavia*, a woman's name, may be OFr *pavie* 'peach' or *Pavie* 'a woman from Pavia' (Italy). The surname became confused with PAVER: Thomas *Pavey* alias *Paviour* 1719 DKR 41.

Pavley: *v.* PAVELEY

Paw, Pawe, Pea, Pee, Poe, Powe: Tedricus *Paue filius* c1095 Bury (Sf); *Pavo Cocus* 1203 AssSt; Robert son of *Pawe* 1277 Wak (Y); Walter, Robert *Pa Ric* 1 Gilb (L), 1260 AssY ; Robert *Paue* 1202 AssL; William, Morice *Powe* 1207 P (Y), 1327 SRSf; John, Richard *Paw*(e) 1312 AD ii (C), 1327 SRSx; John, William *le Poo* 1324 FFEss, 1332 SRSt; William, Thomas *Poo* 1327 SRSf, *SR* (Ess). *Paw* and *Powe* are from OE *pāwa*, *Pea* and *Pee* from OE *pēa*, *Poe* from ON *pá*, ME *pō* 'peacock', used both as a personal-name and as a nickname.

Pawle: *v.* PAUL

Pawley: *v.* PAULEY, PAVELEY

Pawling: *v.* PAULIN

Pawson: Simon, Hugh *Paweson* 1379 PTY, 1471 GildY. 'Son of *Pawe* (Peacock).'

Paxman: William *Paxman, Pakysman* 1439, 1443 LLB K. 'Servant of *Pack* or *Pake.*'

Paxton: Azelin *de Paxtun'* 1180 P (Lei); Richard *de Paxton* 1251 FFY; John *Paxton* 1489–90 FFWa. From Paxton (Hunts).

Pay, Pey: *Paie filius Wlstani, Paie Blancheard* 1142 NthCh (L); Elias, Richard *Pay*(e) 1275 RH (D), 1296 SRSx; Roger *Peye* 1293 AssSt. ME *pē* developed to *pai* which may explain some late forms of the surname as in *Paycock, Paybody*, but the above personal-name is much too early for this development. Peakirk (Northants) takes its name from St *Pega*, sister of St Guthlac, who is reputed to have established a cell there. One, at least of the above personal-names, is that of a man, and is probably a survival of OE *Pæga*, recorded only as the name of a monk and of an abbot.

Payler: *v.* PALER

Payman, Peyman, Peaman: John *Peman* 1327 SRC; William *Peyeman* 1351 AssEss. 'Servant of *Pea* or *Pay.*' *v.* PAW, PAY, PEACOCK.

Payn, Payne, Paynes: *v.* PAIN

Paynell, Panal, Panell, Pannell, Pennell: Radulfus *Pagenel, Paganellus* 1086 DB; Jordanus *Pænellus* 1130 P (Y); William *Painel* 1160 P (Y); Adam *Painell, Panell'* 1172 Gilb (L); William

Paynel 1268 AssSo. Lat *Paganellus*, OFr *Payenel*, diminutives of *Paganus* and *Payen*. v. PAIN.

Paynter: v. PAINTER

Pays, Payze: v. PACE

Payton, Peyton, Paiton: Matthew *de Peytun* 1240 FFEss; John *de Payton* 1292 FFEss; Edmund *Peyton* 1389 LoPleas; Ann *Payten* 1603 Ickworth-PR (Sf). From Peyton (Essex, Suffolk).

Pea: v. PAW

Peace: v. PACE.

Peach: v. PETCH

Peacher: v. PETCHER

Peachey: v. PETCH

Peacock, Peacocke, Peecock, Pacock, Pocock: *Pecoc* 1086 DB (Ess); *Pecoc* de Briminton 1285 AssCh; Roger *Paucoc* 1194 P (Co); Roger *Paucoc*, *Pecoc* 1194–5 P (Co); Richard *Pocok* 1225 AssSo; Simon *Pacock* 1297 SRY; Robert *Pecok* (*Paycok*) 1327 *SR* (Ess). OE **pēacocc* 'peacock', ME *pecok*, *pacok, pocok*, a nickname used also as a personal-name. v. PAW, PAY, PAPIGAY.

Peacop: v. PICKUP

Peagram, Peagrim: v. PILGRIM

Peak, Peake, Peek: (i) Richard *del Pec* 1192 Eynsham (O); William *de Peke* 1296 SRSx; William *atte Peke* 1321 LLB D. 'Dweller by the peak or hill', OE **pēac.* (ii) Uluric *Pec* c1095 Bury (Sf); Richard, Henry *le Pek* 1297 MinAcctCo, 1327 SRSx; William *Peke* 1327 SRC. Probably OE **pēac* used as a nickname for a stout, thick-set man. The surname is usually topographical in origin and *le* may be an error for *de*.

Peaker, Peakman: Walter *le peker* 1212–23 Bart (Lo). 'Dweller by the peak or hill.'

Peaman: v. PAYMAN

Pear, Peear, Peer, Pere: Osbert *Pere* 1230 P (Berks); Richard *le Pere* 1279 RH (Hu). ME *pere*, OFr *per, peer* 'a peer, paragon', also 'a match, companion'.

Pearce: v. PIERCE

Pearcey, Pearcy, Piercey, Piercy: Ralph *Perce-haie* 1086 DB (Berks); Walter *Percehaie*, *Percehaye* 1168 P (Y), 1280 Guisb (Y); Ralph *Parcehaye* 1247 AssBeds; Roger *Perseye* 1331 AD vi (Beds); Thomas *Pearcye* 1652 RothwellPR (Y). OFr *perce-haie* 'pierce hedge', from OFr *percer* 'to pierce' and *haie* 'hedge', which may have been used either of a hedge protecting a forest or enclosure, or of a military work. Hence either 'a poacher' or 'a warrior renowned for forcing his way through fortifications'. This may also have become PERCY, PARSEY.

Pearch: Geoffrey *del Perche* 1199 MemR (W); Adam *de Perche* 1221 Cur (Mx). ME *perche*, a measure of land, perhaps for one who cultivated this area. Or it may be used in its original sense 'rod', a measurer of land.

Peareth: Gamel *de Penred* 1190 P (Y). From Penrith (Cumb), still locally pronounced *Peereth*.

Pearl: Henry, Reginald *Perle* 1259 Oseney (O), 1316 WhC (La). ME, OFr *perle* 'pearl', metonymic for a seller of pearls. cf. PARLOUR.

Pearlman, Perlman: cf. PEARL, PARLOUR.

Pearman: Robert *Pyrman* 1296 SRSx; Gilbert *Perman* 1376 LLB H. A grower or seller of pears, OE *peru, pyrige*.

Pears(e): v. PIERCE

Pearson, Pearsons, Paerson, Peirson, Pierson: John *Pierisson* 1332 SRWa; Robert *Peresson* 1395 Whitby (Y); William *Pierson* 1412 WhC (La); John *Pereson* 1440 ShefA (Y). 'Son of *Piers* (Peter).' v. PIERCE.

Peartree: Richard de *Peretre* 1230 P (Nth); Emma *atte Peretre* 1279 RH (Hu); Robert *del Pertre* 1327 SRSf. 'Dweller by the pear-tree.'

Peascod, Pescod, Pescodd, Pescud, Peasegood, Peasgood, Pescott, Peskett, Bisgood: Richard *Pisecod* 1221 AssWa; John, Walter *Pesecod* 1279 AssNb, 1332 SRCu; William *Piscod*, *Puscod* 1327, 1332 SRSx; John *Pesegod* (*Pesecod*) 1317 AssK; John *Pasegude* 1441 GildY. OE *peose, pise* 'pea' and *codd* 'bag', a peascod, peapod; probably for a seller of peas. cf. Richard *pesemongere* c1198 Bart.

Pease: Thomas *Pese* 1194 Cur (Bk); Roger *Pise* 1206 Cur (Nf); Margeria *Pyse* 1327 SRSf. OE *peose, pise*, ME *pese* 'pea', metonymic for a seller of peas.

Peasey: v. PIZEY

Peatrie: v. PETRIE

Peberdy: v. PEPPERDAY

Pebjoy: v. PAPIGAY

Pechin: William *Peccin'* (*Peccat'*), Robert *Peccin* (*Peche*) 1176–7 P (Ha). A diminutive of PETCH.

Peck: (i) Richard *Pecke* 1187 P (Ha); Hervicus *Pecke* 1283 FFSf. This, like the topographical term below, might be for PEAK. Or it may be ME *pekke* 'a peck', metonymic for a maker of pecks or vessels used as a peck measure. cf. PECKAR. (ii) John *de Peck* 1275 RH (Lo); Henry *del Peck* ib. (L). 'Dweller by the peak', with vowel shortened.

Peckar, Pecker: Henry *Peckere* 1221 ElyA (C); Simon *le Peckere* 1279 RH (Hu). Either 'dweller by the hill' or 'maker of peck measures'. v. PECK. Or we may have a derivative of ME *pekken* 'to peck, snap up', used of one of acquisitive habits.

Peckett, Peckitt: William *Pecche*, *Pekat* 1088, c1100 Rams (C); William *Pechet* 1194 P (Ha); Robert *Pecket* 1198 FF (Nth). A diminutive of PETCH. William *Pekat* was of a Cambridgeshire family usually called *Pecche*.

Peddar, Pedder: William *le Pedder* 1165 P (Y); William *Peddere* 1243 AssDu. A derivative of ME *pedde* 'a pannier', hence 'one who carries goods for sale', 'a pedlar' (a1225 NED).

Pedlar, Pedler, Pidler: (i) William *Le Pedelare* 1307 MESO (Wo); Ralph *le Pedeler* 1332 SRWa; Martin *Pedeler* 1376 LoPleas. 'Pedlar, hawker' (1377 NED). (ii) Walter *Pedeleure* 12th HPD (Ess); William *Pe de levre* 1242 Fees (So); Cristina *Pede-leuere* 1327 *SR* (Ess). Fr *pied de lievre* 'hare-foot', speedy, nimble. cf. Alan *Pedeken* 1187 Gilb (L) 'dog-foot', Robert *Piedurs* 1199 P (O) 'bear-foot', John *Pedebef* 1381 SRSf. 'ox-foot'.

Pedlow, Pillow: Simon *Piedeleu*, William *Piedleu* 1367 LLB G. AFr *pie de leu*, Fr *Piédeloup* 'wolf-foot'. This may also have become PELLEW, PELLOW.

Pedrick: v. PETHERICK
Pee: v. PAW
Peech: v. PETCH
Peecock: v. PEACOCK
Peek: v. PEAK

Peel, Peele, Peile, Piele: (i) Walter, Henry *Pele* 1202 AssL, 1238 FFY; Robert *Peel* 1382 IpmNt. OFr *pel* 'stake', a nickname for a tall, thin person. (ii) Robert *de Pele* 1199 MemR (So); John *de Pele*, William *de la Pele* 1301, 1332 Kris. From Piel or Peel Island (Lancs), or 'dweller by the palisade', OFr *pel, piel,* cf. John *le Peler* c1280 SRWo.

Peers: v. PIERCE

Peever, Peevers, Peffer: Roger *Peiure* 1198 FFEss; William *Paiuer* 1219 AssY; William *Peyforer, le Peyfrer, Peyfore* 1293, 1301, 1324 FFEss; Vincent *le Peuerer, le Peuerier* Hy 3 AD ii (Mx); Roger *Peuere* 1297 MinAcctCo. OFr *peyvre* 'pepper', *peyvrier, pevrier* 'pepperer', both used at times of the same man.

Pegg, Peggs: Æluric *Pegga* 1165 P (Wa); Turbert, Stephen *Peg* 1192, 1195 P (Ha, Y); Ralph, Simon *Pegge* 1243 AssSo, 1301 SRY. ME *pegge* 'peg', metonymic for a maker or seller of pegs. We may also have a pet-name for *Margaret*. cf. Martin *Peggi* 1279 RH (O); John *Peggy* 1338 Oseney (O).

Pegram, Pegrum: v. PILGRIM
Peirce, Peirs(e): v. PIERCE
Peirson: v. PEARSON
Peiser: v. POYSER
Pelerin: v. PILGRIM

Pelham: Ralph, Peter *de Pelham* 1170 P (Herts), 1260 AssC; William *Pelham* 1350 IpmGl. From Pelham (Herts).

Pell, Pells, Pelly: *Pelle* 1274, 1316 Wak (Y); Walterus *filius Pelle* 1279 RH (Hu); *Pelle* chaundeler 1332 SRLo; Reginald *Pel* 1222 Cur (K); John, William *Pell(e)* 1260 AssC, 1279 RH (O); Robert, William *Pelleson* 1331 DbCh, 1412 GildY. *Pell* is a pet-form of *Peter*, with a diminutive *Pelly*. *Pelle* de Honeden (1296 Ipm (Sf)) is indexed as *Peter*, and *Pelly* Wyth (1278 Oseney (O)) is identical with *Peter* son of John (Ed.). cf. *Pell* Heigham (J. Kirby, *Suffolk Traveller*, 1764). *Pell* may also be OFr *pel* 'skin', for a dealer in skins. cf. FELL, PELLY, PILL.

Pellatt, Pellett: William *Pelet* 1297 Wak (Y), 1327 SRSx. Perhaps a diminutive of *Pell* (Peter), or, like Fr *Pelette*, of *pel* 'skin'.

Peller: William *le Peller'* 1263 MESO (Sx); John *le Pallere* 1327 SRSt. A derivative of OE *pæll, pell* 'costly cloak, purple cloth', for a maker or seller of these. cf. Rober Dun, *péller* 1332 SRLo. In Sussex, this might also mean 'dweller by the stream'. v. PILL.

Pellew, Pellow: Anketil *Pel de lu, Pealdelu, Piaudelu* 1195-7 P (L), 1202 AssL. OFr. *pel* (Mod Fr *peau*) *de lou* 'wolf-skin'.

Pelly, Le Pelley: Arnald *Pele* 1210 Cur (C); Gerard *le Pele* 1221 AssGl; Guillerm *le Peley* 1419 DKR 41. OFr *pele,* ModFr *pelé* 'bald'. v. also PELL.

Pelter, Pilter: William *le Peleter* 1219 AssY; Adam *le Peletur* 1296 SRSx; Henry *le Pelter* 1301 SRY; William *Pilter* 1332 SRSx. OFr *peletier* 'fellmonger, furrier' (1389 NED); also 'a dresser of fells'. Now a rare name.

Pemberton: Alan, Hugh *de Pemberton* 1212 Fees (La), 1387 IpmLa; John *Pemberton* 1443 FFEss. From Pemberton (Lancs).

Pender: v. PINDAR

Penderel, Penderell, Pendrell, Pendrill: Richard *Pendorayl* 1253-63 Seals (Lei). A derivative of Fr *pendre* 'to hang' and *oreille* 'ear', 'hang-ear'.

Pendergast: v. PRENDERGAST
Pendry: v. PENRY
Penfare: v. PENNYFATHER
Penfold: v. PINFOLD

Pengelley, Pengelly, Pengilly: John (*de*) *Pengelly* 1297 MinAcctCo. From Pengelly (Cornwall).

Penhale: Ralph *de Pennal* c1210 Fees (Co). From Penheale in Egloskerry (Cornwall).

Penkethman, Penkeyman: T. *Penkethmonne* 1525 GildY; Thomas *Pingithmoan* 1533 YWills. On the analogy of the numerous 14th-century Yorkshire surnames like *Matthewman*, this is rather 'servant of a man named *Penketh*' than 'the man from Penketh'.

Penn: (i) Warin *de Penne* 1176 P (St); Walter *de la Penne* 1196 P (Bk); John *ate Penne* 1297 MinAcctCo. From Penn (Bucks, Staffs) or from residence near a fold or hill, OE *penn* 'pen, fold' or OE *penn* 'hill'. The more usual source. (ii) Adam son of *Penne* 1277 Wak (Y); *Penne Ronge* 1327 SRC; John *Penn(e)* 1327 SRSx, *SR* (Ess); Katherine *Pennes* 1345 ColchCt. *Penne* is probably a pet-form of *Pernel.* v. PARNALL, PENNALL.

Pennall, Pennell, Pennells: (i) William *Pennel* 1377 ColchCt; Pethericke *Pernell, Pennell* 1580, 1583 Bardsley. An assimilated form of PARNALL. (ii) Aluredus *de Penhull'* 1221 AssWo. From Penn Hall in Pensax (Worcs), earlier *Penehull,* or from Penhill (Devon, NRYorks).

Pennefather: v. PENNYFATHER

Penner: John *le Penner* 1327 SRSo. A derivative of ME *pennen* 'to impound', pinder. Or, 'worker at the fold', or 'dweller on the hill'. v. PENN.

Penney, Pennie, Penny, Penning, Pennings: Gilebertus *filius Pening* 1206 P (L), probably identical with Gilebertus *Penning* 1204 P (L); Ralph *Penig* 1191 P (Hu); Ailnoth *Peni* 1204 Cur (Sr); William, Ralph *Pening* 1206 AssL, 1219 AssY; Alan *Pani* 1219 AssL; William *Peny* 1221 AssSa; Geoffrey *Pennyng'* 1305 Clerkenwell (Lo). This is usually a nickname from the coin, OE *pening, penig*, ME *peni. Pening* is clearly used as a personal name in Lincs in 1206 and may be a survival of a similar, unrecorded use in OE, thus lending support to the derivation of Penistone (WRYorks), earlier *Peningeston,* from this personal name. The surnames may also, at times, be patronymics.

Penniman: v. PENNYMAN
Penning, Penny: v. PENNEY

Pennycock, Pennycook, Pennycuick: David *de Penikok* 1250 Black, *de Penycuke* 1373 ib. From

Penicuik (Midlothian). The first two surnames are found early in the southern half of England and must be independent formations: God ... *Penigcoc* 1202 FFL; Thomas *Penycok*' 1379 PTY; John *Penycok(e)* 1452 AD v (W), 1483 AD i (Sr), 1485 AD iv (Ess). '*Cock* (son) or *cook* of Penny.'

Pennyfather, Pennefather, Pennyfeather, Penfare, Pannifer: Godwin *penifeder* 1066 Winton (Ha); Robert *Panyfader* 1296 SRSx; Geoffrey *Penifader* 14th AD iii (Wa); Thomas *Pennyfather* 1563 FFHu; Mary *Panifee*, Salmon *Panivie* 1749, 1781 SfPR. OE *penig* and *fæder* 'penny-father', a miser (1549 NED). cf. 'Pinse-maille, a pinch-pennie, scrape-good, niggard, penie-father' (Cotgrave). Pennyfeathers in High Roding was named from Richard *Panyfader* (1285 PN Ess 493). *Pannifer* preserves the south-eastern ME *pani*. For *Pannifer* and *Penfare*, cf. *granfer* for grandfather.

Pennyman, Penniman, Pannaman: Simon *Penyman* 1268 AssSo; William *Peniman* 1279 RH (C); Ralph *Panyman* 1296 SRSx. 'Servant of Penny.' *v.* also PANNER.

Penrose: Philip *de Penros* 1195 P (Co). From Penrose (Cornwall, Devon).

Penry, Pendry: Cadogann *Ab-Henry* 1294 Bardsley; Howel *ap Henri* 1316 ParlWrits; Joane *Pendrie* 1605 Bardsley (He); Joseph *Penry* 1748 ib. Welsh *ab, ap* 'son' and *Henry*, 'son of *Henry*'.

Penson, Pensom: (i) Richard *Paynesone* 1305 SIA iii. 'Son of *Pain*.' (ii) Thomas *Pennesone* 1337 ColchCt. 'Son of *Penn*.' (iii) Edmund *de Penson* 1297 MinAcctCo. From Penson (Devon).

Pentecost, Pentercost, Pentycross, Perrycost, Pankhurst: *Pentecoste de Wendleswurda* 1187 P (Sr); Gaufridus *filius Pentecostes* 1201 Cur (Mx); William, John *Pentecost* 1200, 1212 Cur (Sr, Sx); John *Pantecost* 1371 Cl (Mx); Rychard *Pencost* 1560 SxWills. OFr *Pentecost*, a name given to one born on that festival. The seal of Cristina *filia Pentecuste* (1250 Oseney) bore the legend: S. CRISTINE PEDTECOST. She had adopted as her surname the christian name of her father who was probably *Pentecost de Oxonia* (1230 ib). Pankhurst (Surrey), named from John *Pentecost* (1332 PN Sr 116), is *Pentecost* alias *Panchurst* in 1605.

Pepall, Peaple, Peopall, Peoples: Wyun son of *Pepel* 1246 AssLa; Hawis' *Pepell* 1301 SRY; John *Pepil* 1324 Wak (Y). Apparently a hypocoristic of *Pepin*.

Pepdie: *v.* PEPPERDAY

Pepin, Peppin, Pepys, Pippin, Pipon: Ralph, Henry *Pipin* 1086 DB (Lei), 1195 P (Y); John *Pepin* c1160 DC (L), 1202 FF (Nf); William, Walter *Pipun* 1176 P, 1212 Cur (Bk); Reginald *Peppin* 1205 Cur (Lei); William *Pippin* 1279 RH (Beds); John *Pepes*, Richard *Pepis* 1279 RH (C); William *Peps* 1377 AssEss; Widow *Peaps* 1671 HTSf. OFr *Pepin*, OG *Pipin, Pepin*, from the root *bib-* 'to tremble', popular in France in memory of the founders of the Carolingian monarchy, Pépin d'Héristal and Pépin le Bref, with the occasional variant *Pipun*. *Pepis* is a nominative form. Later examples of the surname may be from OFr *pepin*,

pipin 'seed of a fleshy fruit', used for a gardener.

Peppar, Pepper: Robert, Alice *Peper* 1197 P (Nf), 1241 FFEss. OE *pipor* 'pepper', metonymic for a dealer in pepper, a pepperer or spicer. John *Pepper* alias *Peyure* (1298 LoCt) alternated between the English and the French form of the name. *v.* PEEVER.

Pepperall: *v.* PEVERALL

Peppercorn, Peppercorne: Adam *Pepercorn* 1198–1212 Bart (Lo); Roger *Pipercorn* 1202 AssL; Richard *Pepercorne*, spysar 1379 PTY. OE *piporcorn* 'peppercorn', most probably a name given to a seller of peppercorns, a pepperer or spicer. But, in view of such phrases as 'peppercorn-sized' and 'peppercorn-hair', we may also have a nickname for a little man or one with darkish complexion or hair. Sometimes we may have reference to the holding of land at a peppercorn rent.

Pepperday, Pepdie, Peberdy, Pipperday: Stephen *Papedi* 1166 Black; Henry *Papedi* 1180 P (Y); Thomas *Popedy* 1260 AssY; John *Pabdy* 1381 PTY; Nichola *Pepdie* 1403 Black; John *Papeday* 1504 ib. An oath-name, OFr *pape-Dieu* '(by the) Pope-God'.

Pepperell, Pepperwell: *v.* PEVERALL

Peppin: *v.* PEPIN

Pepprell: *v.* PEVERALL

Pepys: *v.* PEPIN

Perceval, Percival, Percifull, Purcifer, Passifull: *Perceval* 1224 Pat; *Percival* Soudan 1414 AD vi (W); *Persefall* 1666 ODCN; William *Percevall*' 1229 Cl (Sa); Roger *Perceval* 1286 Ipm (So); John *Perseval* 1297 MinAcctCo; John *Percival* 1372 LoPleas; OFr *perce-val*, from OFr *percer* 'to pierce' and *val* 'valley', 'pierce the valley'. Such names were not uncommon in France. cf. *percebois* 'wood-borer', *perce-roche* 'rock-piercer', *perce-forêt* 'forest-piercer' which Harrison interprets as 'keen hunter'. It might also mean 'a poacher'. cf. PEARCEY, and William *Percevent* 1221 Cur (Mx), 'pierce-wind', from OFr *vent* 'wind', no doubt renowned for his speed. The 1224 Perceval was one of the servants of Faukes de Breauté, notorious for breaking into places where he should not. For *Purcifer*, a Yorkshire name, cf. the Yorks *Brammer* from *Bramhall*. cf. also PASSMORE. Occasionally, the surname may be topographical in origin. Richard *de Percevill* (1203 AssSt) may have come from one of the two places in Calvados named Perceval.

Percy, Persey, Parsey, Pursey: William *de Perci* 1086 DB (Y), c1133 Whitby; Walter *Perci*, Margaret *de Perci* 1185 Templars (L); Henry *Percy* 1332 SRSx; Rebecca *Parsy* 1702 SfPR. William de Perci, the Domesday tenant-in-chief and under-tenant of Hugh, earl of Chester, and ancestor of the second line of Percy, came from Percy-en-Auge (Calvados). *v.* ANF. Percy (La Manche), his traditional place of origin, and two other Percys in Calvados may also have contributed to the surname. cf. PEARCEY.

Perdue: *v.* PARDEW

Pere: *v.* PEAR

Perebourne: Walter *Perbrun* 1229 FFSf; Roger *Perebrun* 1275 RH (Sf). OE *pere* 'pear' and *brūn* 'brown', 'pear-brown', no doubt, a nickname for one of swarthy complexion. cf. NUTBROWN.

Peregrine: *v.* PILGRIM

Peres: *v.* PIERCE

Perfect, Perfitt: *v.* PARFAIT

Perham, Perram: *v.* PARHAM

Perken, Perkin(s): *v.* PARKIN

Perott: *v.* PARROT

Perowne: *v.* PERRIN

Perraton: *v.* PERRITON

Perratt, Perrett, Perrott: *v.* PARROT

Perrell, Perren: *v.* PERRIN

Perrie: *v.* PERRY

Perrier, Perryer, Peryer, Purrier, Puryer: (i) Robert *Perier* 1194 P (Lo); Henry *le Perer* 1217 Bart; Richard *Le Perur* 1288 MESO (Sx). OFr *perrier, perrieur* 'quarrier'. (ii) Ralph *Puriere* 1327 SRSx; William *le Piryere* ib.; John *Peryere* 1327 SR (Ess). 'Dweller by the pear-tree.' cf. PERRY.

Perriman, Perriment, Perryman, Periman, Peryman: Richard *Piriman* 1274 RH (Ess); William *Peryman* 1279 RH (C); Adam *Puryman* 1327 SRSo. 'Dweller by a pear-tree', OE *pyrige*. *v.* PERRY.

Perrin, Perring, Perrins, Parrell, Perrell, Parren, Perren, Perron, Perowne: *Perrinus* uadletus 1207 P (Nth); *Peryna* (f) 1280 FFEss; John *Pirun* 1166 P (Gl); Geoffrey *Perrun* 1185 Templars (L); Henry *Piron* 1194 Cur (O); William, John *Perel* 1222-3 Cur (Nf, Sr); John *Pirun* 1255 RH (W); Alexander *Peryn* 1268 AssSo; John *Perin* 1279 RH (C); Thomas *Paron* 1297 MinAcctCo; William *Peroun* 1327 SRSf; William *Peryng* 1332 SRSx. Diminutives of *Perre* (Peter) plus the suffixes -*in*, -*el*, -*un*. *Pirun* is an east French form from *Pier(r)un*. *v.* PIRRET. *Perowne* is a Huguenot name.

Perriton, Perraton, Purton: Eduuardus *de Periton* 1086 DB (Herts); Gervase *de Piriton'* 1200 P (So); Ascelin *de Periton, de Perton* 1207-8 P (O); Robert *de Puryton* 1269 AssSo; Walter *Piriton'* 1376 AssEss. From Pirton (Herts, Worcs), Pyrton (Oxon), Purton (Som, Wilts), or Purton End in Saffron Walden (Essex), all 'pear-tree farm'.

Perron: *v.* PERRIN

Perrott: *v.* PARROT

Perry, Perrie, Pirie, Pirrie, Purry, Pury, de Pury: Henry *de Peri, de Piri* 1176 P (St), 1199 AssSt; Richard *Pirie* 1198 P (K); William *de la Purie* 1243 AssSo; Gilbert *atte Pyrie* 1263 FFSr; Richard *del Piry* 1381 AssSt; Richard *atte Perye* 1392 MELS (Sx). 'Dweller by the pear-tree', OE *pirige, pyrige*. James *atte Pyrie* and John *Peryere* (1327 *SR*) both lived in Dedham (Essex). *v.* PERRIER, PERRIMAN.

Perrycoste: *v.* PENTECOST

Perryer: *v.* PERRIER

Perryman: *v.* PERRIMAN

Perse, Persse: *v.* PIERCE

Persey: *v.* PERCY

Peryer: *v.* PERRIER

Peryman: *v.* PERRIMAN

Pescod, Pescott, Peskett: *v.* PEASCOD

Pestell, Pistol: Robert, Nicholas *Pestel* 1221 AssSa, 1246 AssLa; Symon *Pystel* 1296 SRSx. ME *pestel* from OFr *pestel* 'an instrument for pounding things in a mortar', 'pestle'. cf. *Pestel*, of stampynge, Pila, pistillus, pistellus' PromptParv. Probably for a user of this instrument, a compounder of drugs, a spicer. For *Pystel*, cf. *pistil*, so called from its resemblance in shape to a pestle.

Pester, Pistor: Robertus *pistor* 1115 Winton (Ha); William, Symon *le Pestur* 1239 MESO (L), 1259 FFC; Richard *le Pester*, *le Pestour* 1279 RH (Beds); John *Pistor*, peleter 1281 LLB B; John *le Pistour* 1307 AssSt. AFr *pestour, pistour*, OFr *pestor, pesteur* 'baker'. In early sources, *Pistor* is common but is often the Latin *pistor* 'baker', clearly so when inflected as: Toli *Pistore* (abl.) c1140 StCh, Roberto *Pistori* (dat.) 1196 FF (D). Certain examples of AN *pistour* are rare. The legend on the seal of Turbernus *Pistor* (1200 Oseney) was SIGIL'L' TVRBERTI LE PESTVR. The modern *Pester* is not common; *Pistor* is rare. The feminine has also been noted: Alicia *le Pesteresse* 1270 RamsCt (C), as well as Robert *de la Pesterye* 1280 AssSo, 'of the bakery', cf. PANTER and PANTREY.

Pesterfield: *v.* BASKERVILLE

Petch, Petche, Petchey, Pechey, Peach, Peache, Peachey, Peech: Willelmus *Peccat'* 1086 DB (Ess, Nf); Haimund *Peccatum*, Hamo *Pecce* 1121-60 Bury (Sf); Rotbert *Pecceð* 1123 ASC E; God' *Pecce* 1165 P (Wa); Ralph *Pecche* 1168-75 Holme (Nf); William *Pesche* 1178 P (Y); William, Gilbert *Pechie* 1190, 1200 P (Ha, C); Geoffrey *Pech* 1191 P (L); Richard *Pechee* 1275 RH (Nf); Herbert *Pechy* 1275 RH (Berks). OFr *peche, pechie*, Lat *peccatum* 'sin', a curious nickname for Robert *Pecceð* (more commonly *Peche*), Bishop of Coventry in 1123. *v.* also PECHIN, PECKETT.

Petcher, Peacher: Adam *le Pechur* 1210 Cur (Do); Nicholas *le Peschur* 1221 AssWo; John *le Pechere* 1242 Oseney (O). OFr *pescheor, pecheour, pecher* 'fisherman'.

Petchey: *v.* PETCH

Peter, Peters, Petre: *Petrus* 1086 DB, Hy 2 Gilb (L); Ralph *Peter* 1195 P (Herts); Luke *Petre* 1282 LLB A; Elias *Petri* 1318 LLB E; William *Petres* 1327 SRSo. Lat *Petrus*, from Greek πέτρος 'rock'. *Peter* is the learned form, usually latinized in early documents. The popular form *Peres* (Fr *Piers*) was very common both as a christian name and a surname. *v.* PIERCE. The frequency of *Peters* as a surname is due to its late adoption by the Welsh.

Peterson: John *Peterson* 1375 LoPleas. 'Son of *Peter*.'

Pethard: William, Reginald *Petard* 1296 SRSx, 1436 CtH. A derogatory nickname from OFr *peter* 'to break wind' and the pejorative suffix -*hard*. *v.* PETTER (i).

Pether, Pethers, Pither, Pithers: Thomas *Pither* 1287 QW (Gl); John *Peter* or *Pether* 1526 Oxon. A west-country and Cornish form of *Peter*.

Petherick, Pethrick, Pedrick, Petterick: *Peth-*

roke 1547 Bardsley (Co); *Pethericke* 1579 ib. *Petrock*, a personal name common in Cornwall, commemorating the Cornish St Petrock.

Petifer: *v.* PETTIFER

Peto, Peyto: Robert *de Peytowe* 1222 Cur (W); Johannes *Pictavensis*, John *de Peyto* 1238, 1247 Fees (Bk). 'The man from Poitou', AFr *Peitow*. cf. POIDEVIN.

Petre: *v.* PETER

Petrie, Petry, Peatrie, Patry: Charles *Patre* 1513 Black; Andrew *Petre* 1530 ib.; Hendrie *Petrie*, Henry *Patrie* 1612–19 ib.; George *Paitrie* 1620 ib. Scottish diminutives of *Peter* or *Patrick*. In Arran and Kintyre *Patrick* became Gaelic *Pàdair* and *Pàtair* and was confused with *Peter*. *Patrick* Young, Dean of Dunkeld, is *Patry* Yhong (1452) whilst *Patrick* Roy Macgregor (1667) is usually called *Petrie* (Black).

Pett, Petts: *v.* PITT

Pettegree, Petegree, Petticrew, Petticrow, Pettigree, Pettigrew: Walter *Peticruw* 1227 *Ass* (Ess); Richard, Roger *Peticru* 1283, 1298 *Ass* (Ess, Sf); Thomas *Petykreu*, *Peticru* 1296 CalSc, 1297 MinAcctCo; John *Petegrew* 1346 FA (Sf); Robert *Pedgrewe* 1568 SRSf. The common belief that this name derives from a place in Cornwall is clearly untenable. There is no place of the name in that county, early forms have no preposition, and come from the eastern counties. Nor can the name be identical with *pedigree*, Fr *pied de grue* 'crane-foot', as early forms regularly have *t*, whilst the *g* does not appear before the 14th century. It is apparently *petit cru* 'little growth' (OFr *cru* 'growth, increase'), a nickname for a small man of stunted growth.

Pettengell, Pettingale, Pettingill: *v.* PORTUGAL

Petter: (i) John *le Petour* 1299 LLB B; John *Pethour* 1519 NorwDep. ME *-our* distinguishes this from the more common *Petter* 'dweller in a hollow'. Rolland *le Pettour* held land in Hemmingstone (Suffolk) by serjeantry of appearing before the king every year at Christmas to do a jump, a whistle, and a fart (*unum saltum, unum siffletum et unum bumbulum*) c1250 Fees. In 1330 the holder of the serjeantry is referred to as Roland *le Fartere* Ipm, and cf. John *le Fartere* 1327 SRLei. *Pettour* is from OFr *peter* 'to break wind', from which come the French names *Pétard, Peton, Petot*, and probably *Pétain*. Dauzat notes that at the end of the 19th century one family of *Pétard* had licence to change its name to *Pérard*. *v.* also PETHARD. (ii) For *atte pette*, *v.* PITT, PUTTER.

Pettifer, Pettifor, Pettyfar, Pettyfer, Petifer, Pettafor, Pettefar, Pettefer, Pettipher, Pettiver, Pettiford, Pottiphar, Puddepha, Puddifer: Herbertus *Pedesferri* 11th OEByn; John *Pedefer* 1190 P (Beds); John *Piedefer* 1198 P (Beds); William *Pedifer* 1221 AssWa; William *Petifer* 1327 SRSx; Richard *Pitifer* ib.; William *Pidefyr* 1332 SRSx; William *Putifer* 1382 RamsCt (Hu); William *Petefer* 1392 AD ii (Hu); Thomas *Petyver* 1524 SRSf. *Pedesferri* is Lat *pedes ferri* 'feet of iron', the rest are from OFr *pedefer*, i.e. *pied de fer* 'iron

foot', explained by Larchey as 'surnom de bon marcheur'. The name was common and sometimes used as a nickname alone: *Piedefer* 1186 P (Wo), *Pie de Fer* 1185 P (Nf), and may also have referred to an old soldier who had lost a foot. cf. the English translation, Roger and Geoffrey *Yrenfot* 1251 Rams (Hu) and the parallel John *Stelfot* 1301 LLB C. Bardsley notes the development to *Pottiphar* (1777), a natural development of *Putifer* (1382).

Pettinger: *v.* POTTINGER

Pettipher, Pettiver: *v.* PETTIFER

Pettit, Pettitt, Pettet, Petit, Petyt, Pittet: Aluric *Petit* 1086 DB (Ha); John *le Petit* 1228 FFEss. OFr *petit* 'little'.

Pettman: *v.* PITMAN

Petty, Pettie: William *Petie* 1198 FFNt; Walter *le Petiit* 1249 AssW; Thomas *Petyt* 1327 SRLei; Richard *Pettye* 1553 FFSt. Fr *petit* 'small', a not infrequent element in medieval names, cf. Walter *Petitclark* 1304 IpmGl; John *Petijohan* 1327 SRSx; William *Petitpas* 1199 Pl (K); Richard *Petitprudum'* 1230 Cur (L); John *le Petit Smyth* 1351 AssEss.

Peutherer: Lambert *le Peutrer* 1311 AD i (Mx); Geoffrey *le Peautrer* 1319 SRLo; Thomas *Powterer* 1472 GildY. AFr *peautrer*, OFr *peautrier* 'pewterer', a maker of pewter vessels (1348 NED). *Pewter, Pewtress* and *Powter* are metonymic.

Peverall, Peverell, Peverill, Peperel, Pepperall, Pepperell, Pepperwell, Pepprell: Geruasius *filius Peurelli* 1130 P (Lo); *Peverel* 1161–77 Rams (Hu), 1205 Cur (Ess); Rannulfus *Peurellus*, *Piperellus* 1086 DB (K, Ess); Richard *Peuerel* 1186–1210 Holme (Nf); William *Peuerell'* 1221 AssWa; William *Peperel* 1224 Clerkenwell (Mx). OFr *Peurel*, Lat *Piperellus*, a diminutive of OFr *pevre*, Lat *piper* 'pepper', used as a personal name. Tengvik suggests the reference may have been to one of small, rounded shape, 'peppercorn-sized', or to a man with a darkish complexion or hair. But it may well have been applied to a small man with a fiery, peppery temper.

Pewter, Pewtress: *v.* PEUTHERER

Pey: *v.* PAY

Peyman: *v.* PAYMAN

Peyser: *v.* POYSER

Peyto: *v.* PETO

Peyton: *v.* PAYTON

Pezey: *v.* PIZEY

Phair: *v.* FAIR

Phaisey: *v.* VAISEY

Phalp: *v.* PHILIP

Pharaoh, Pharo, Pharro: *v.* FARRAR

Phare: *v.* FARE

Phasey: *v.* VAISEY

Phayre: *v.* FAIR

Phear: *v.* FEAR

Pheasant: John *Faisant* 1166 P (Sx); Thomas *Fesaunt* 1221 AssWa; Richard *le Feisant*, *le Faisant* 1229 Cl (Jersey); Roger *Fesant* 1241 Oseney (O). A nickname from the pheasant, ME *fesaunt*.

Pheasey, Pheazey: *v.* VAISEY

Phelips, Phelops, Phelps: *v.* PHILIP
Phethean: *v.* VIVIAN
Pheysey: *v.* VAISEY
Phibbs: *v.* PHIPPS
Philb(e)y: *v.* FILBY
Philcott: A corruption of *Philcock. v.* PHILCOX.
Philcox, Phillcox: Betrice *Philekoc* 1283 SRSf; German *Philecok, Filcokes* 1307, 1314 Wak (Y). 'Son of *Phil*', a pet form of *Philip*, plus *cock. v.* FILL.
Philip, Philips, Philipse, Philipp, Philipps, Phil-liphs, Phillipps, Phillips, Phillipse, Philp, Philps, Phillp, Phillps, Phelips, Phelops, Phelp, Phelps, Phalp: *Filippus* de Crochesbi 1142–53 DC (L); *Philipus* Rabode c1150 Gilb (L); *Philippa* de Faia 1195 P (Sx); *Phelippus* 1290 Oseney (O); *Phelip* de Kocfeld 1292 SRLo; *Philp* Gledstanes 1541 Bardsley; Henry *Philip, Phelipe* 1275 RH (Nf); Maud *Philippes* 1279 RH (Hu); John *Felipe*, Gilbert *Phelip* 1296 SRSx; William *Phelipes* 1327 SRSt; Cecilia *Philipp* 1379 PTY; John *Phelpes* 1570 Bardsley; Peter *Philpe* 1698 DKR 41. Greek *Φίλιππος* 'horse-lover', usually latinized as *Philippus*. The vernacular form seems to have been *Phelip* which is not confined to the south-west as has been suggested. cf. Fr *Phélip, Félip*. It was also used as a woman's name, latinized *Philippa*. *Philp, Phelp* are contracted forms. For *Phalp*, cf. Fr *Phalip*. The popularity of the name is revealed by its pet-forms and derivatives. *v.* FILL, FILKIN, PHIPPS, PHILCOX, PHILLINS, PHILLOTT, PHILPOT, with its hypocoristics POTT, POTTELL, and POTKIN and their varied forms. Other derivatives surviving, but not well-evidenced are: *Philben, Philbin, Philpin, Phippard, Phippen*.
Philippot: *v.* PHILPOT
Philipson, Philippson, Phillipson: Gilbert *Phelipson* 1396 AssSt; John *Philipson* 1524 SRSf. 'Son of *Philip*.'
Phillins: A diminutive of *Phill* (Philip), plus *-in*.
Phillips: *v.* PHILIP
Phillipson: *v.* PHILIPSON
Phillott: *Philota* de Kender 1273 RH (Db). A diminutive in *-ot* of *Phil* (Philip), here feminine.
Phillpot: *v.* PHILPOT
Philp(s): *v.* PHILIP
Philpot, Philpots, Philpott, Philpotts, Phillpot, Phillpots, Phillpott, Phillpotts, Philippot: *Phelipot* Herneys 1377 AD ii (Beds); *Philipot* (f) 1379 PTY; John *Philipot* 1327 SRSx; Stephen *Philippot* 1336 AD v (K); John *Philippot, Phelipot, Philpot* 1367 LoPleas, 1378 LLB F, H. *Philip-ot*, a diminutive of *Philip*. From this were formed POTT, POTTELL and POTKIN.
Philson: *v.* FILL
Phimester, Phimister: *v.* FEMISTER
Phin, Phinn: *v.* FINN
Phipps: William *Fippe, Fyppe* 1227 FFBk, 1250 Fees (Sf); Henry, Geoffrey *Phippe* 1332 SRWa, 1337 *ERO;* John *Phippes* 1364 LoPleas. *Phip*, a pet-form of *Philip*.
Phizackerley, Phizaclea, Phizakarley: *v.* FAZACKERLEY

Physick, Visick: Richard *Physik* Ed 1 Malmesbury. Metonymic for *Physician*: John *le Fisicien* 1269 AssSt.
Phythian: *v.* VIVIAN
Pick: *v.* PIKE
Pickard: (i) Hugh *le Pycard* 1276 AssSt; John *Pikart* 1279 RH (Hu); Michael *le Pykard* 1289 LLB A; John *Picard* 1292 FFSf. 'The Picard', a man from Picardy. (ii) Paganus *filius Pichardi* 1160 P (Ha); *Picardus* filius Pagani 1208 Cur (Ha); Paganus, William *Pichard* 1169 P (Ha), 1198 FF (Sa); John *Pikhard* (*Pikard*) 1230 P (Ha). A French personal-name, compounded of *Pic* (cf. PICKETT) and *-hard*. On the analogy of *Richard*, this would become both *Pickard* and *Pitchard*, the latter, apparently, no longer surviving, but one origin of PITCHER.
Picker, Pickers: Richard *le Pickere* 1188 P (Y); Stephen *Pikere* 1199 P (K); Richard *le Pikere* Hy 3 AD iii (Ess). 'Maker or seller of pikes, pick-axes or picks', or 'fishmonger, seller of pike', or 'dweller on the hill'. *v.* PIKE.
Pickerell, Pickerill, Pickrell, Pickrill: Yuo *Pikerell* 1199 P (Nf); Richard *Pikerel* 1240 FFEss. ME *pykerel* 'a young pike'.
Pickering, Pickerin: Reginald *de Pichering'* 1165 P; Henry *de Pikeringes* 1246 FFO; John, William *Pykeryng* 1327 SRSo, IpmW. From Pickering (NRYorks).
Pickernell: *v.* SPICKERNALL
Pickersgill: Robert *Pickersgill* 1672 HTY; Elizabeth *Picersgill* 1679 Bardsley; Robert *Pickersgale* 1690 FrY. From Pickersgill Lane in Killinghall (WRYorks). ME *pyker* 'thief, robber' and *gil* (PN WRY v, 101).
Pickett, Picot, Pikett, Pykett, Piggot, Piggott, Pigot, Pigott: *Picot* de Grantebrige 1086 DB (C); *Pichot* de Lacele c1155 DC (L); *Pigotus* de Hutun Hy 2 DC (L); Robertus *filius Picot* 1166 RBE (Y); Roger *Picot* 1086 DB (Ch); Robert *Picot* 1140–5 Holme (Nf); William *Piket* 1177 P (Bk); Waubert *Pyket* 1277 LLB A; Peter *Picot, Pycot, Pygot* 1285 Ipm (C). We may occasionally have a nickname from OFr *picot* 'point, pointed object', but the surnames are probably usually from a personal name OFr *Pic*, plus *-ot* and, occasionally, *-et*. cf. PICKARD, of which *Pickett* may also be a late development.
Pickford: Alcock *de Pykeford* 1288 AssCh; Thomas *Pikeford* 1332 SRSx; Thomas *Pickford* alias Pickfatt 1649 DKR. From Pickforde in Ticehurst (Sussex).
Pickin, Picking: William *Pykyng* 1311 ColchCt; Thomas *Pykyn* 1353 ib. Probably OE **picing* 'dweller on the hill'. *v.* PIKE.
Pickis: Edmund *Pycoyse* 1524 SRSf. ME *pikois, pikeis* 'mattock'.
Pickles, Pickless, Pickle, Pighills: Richard *de Pighkeleys* 1379 PTY; Henry, Arthur *Pickles* 1571 LWills, 1672 HTY. 'Dweller at the small enclosure', ME *pightel, pighel*.
Pickman: Ralph *Pykeman* 1259 AD ii (Mx); Robert *Pyckeman* 1300 LLB C. *v.* PICKER, PIKE.

Picknett: Robert *Pikenot* 1175 P (Ha); Richard *Pikenet*, *Pikenot* 1206–8 Cur (Sf). *Pik-en-et*, *Pik-en-ot*, double diminutives of *Pic. v.* PICKETT.

Pickrell, Pickrill: *v.* PICKERELL

Pickstone, Pixton: Richard *Pixton'* 1209 P (Nf); Walter *Picxston* 1275 RH (K); Richard *Pikstan* 1296 SRSx. The surname has been noted in some six counties, always without qualification, and a topographical origin appears impossible. We probably have an unrecorded OE **Pīcstān*. *Piichel* is found in LVD and in Picklescott (Sa) and **Pīca* in Picton (Ch, NRY) and Pickworth (L, R).

Pickton, Picton: Geoffrey *de Piketon* 1191–4 YCh; William, John *de Piketon* 1251 AssY, 1327 SRDb. From Picton in Kirkleavington (NRYorks).

Pickup, Peacop: Edmund *Pickeupp* 1632 RothwellPR (Y). From Pickup or Pickup Bank (Lancs).

Picot: *v.* PICKETT

Pidgen, Pidgeon, Pidgon, Pigeon: William, Alan *Pigun* 1200 Cur (Nf), 1202 AssL; Ralf *Pyjun* 1268 AssSo. Fr *pigeon*, OFr *pipjon* 'pigeon', perhaps 'one easy to pluck'. Although definite identifications are impossible in Subsidy Rolls, those for Sussex suggest that *Pigeon* may also be *Petit Johan* 'Little John': Relicta *Pygon* 1296, Relicta *Pijohan*, John *Petijohan*, John *Pyion*, John *Petiion*, Thomas *Pyion* 1327.

Pidler: *v.* PEDLAR

Pie, Pye: (i) Ralph, Eustace *Pie* 1177 P (Y); 1210 Cur (C); William *le Pye* 1296 SRSx. This is certainly at times a nickname from the magpie, ME, OFr *pye*, *pie*. The surname is common, usually without the article, and may also be metonymic for a maker or seller of pies (ME *pie*). cf. Peter *Piebakere* 1320 LLB E, Adam *le Piemakere* 1332 SRLo, John *Pyman* 1524 SRSf. (ii) Stephen *atte Pye* 1347 LLB F. 'Dweller at the sign of the Pie.' cf. *'atte Pye* on the hope' 1340 LoPleas.

Piegrome: *v.* PILGRIM

Piele: *v.* PEEL

Pierce, Pieris, Piers, Pierse, Pearce, Pears, Pearse, Peers, Peirce, Peirs, Peirse, Peres, Perris, Perriss, Perse, Persse: *Peris* le ceynturer, *Peres* le cordener 1292 SRLo; Gilbert *Perse* 1198 P (Lo); Geoffrey *Peres*, *Pieres* 1237 HPD (Ess); Richard *Peris* 1275 SRWo; Adam *Pieris* 1332 SRWa; William *Peers* 1444 AD i (Gl). OFr *Piers*, nom. of *Pierre*, 'Peter', a common name, usually latinized as *Petrus*, with diminutives PARKIN, PARROT, PERRIN, PIRRET.

Piercey, Piercy: *v.* PEARCEY

Pierpoint, Pierrepoint, Pierpont, Pearpoint, Pairpoint: Reinaldus *de Perapund* 1086 DB (Nf); Richard *de Pierrepunt* 1178 P (Do); Roger *Perpunt* 1240 NottBR (Nt); Symon *de Perpoynt* 1316 FA (Nb). Godfrey and Robert *de Petroponte*, undertenants of William de Warenne in Suffolk and Sussex in 1086, came from Pierrepont (Seine-Inférieure). *v.* ANF. Others may have come from Pierrepont (Calvados), Saint-Nicholas-de-Pierrepont (La Manche), or Saint-Sauveur-de-Pierrepont (ib.). *v.* OEByn.

Piers, Pierse: *v.* PIERCE

Pierson: *v.* PEARSON

Pigache: Richard *Pigace* 1176 P (Gl); Ralph *Pigaz* 1219 AssY. Identical with French *Pigasse*, Norman-Picard *Pigache*, a variant of *Picasse*: a nickname from OFr *pic* 'pick-axe, hatchet', probably used of a workman.

Pigeon: *v.* PIDGEN

Pigg: Aluricus *Piga* 1066 DB (D); John *Pig* 1186 P (W); Robert *Pigge* 1277 Wak (Y). OE **picga*, **picg*, ME *pigge* (a1225) 'pig'. cf. HOGG.

Pig(g)ott: *v.* PICKETT

Piggrem, Pigram, Pigrome: *v.* PILGRIM

Pighills: *v.* PICKLES

Pike, Pyke, Pick, Lepick: (i) Aluric, Alwinus *Pic* 1066 DB (D, So); Fulco *picus* 12th DC (L); Hugo *Pik* 1177 P (O); Robert *le Pic* 1191 P (W); Henry *Picke* 1221 AssWo; William *le Pyc* 1296 SRSx; Nicholas *Pyke* 1344 FFC. These surnames have various origins. The DB examples are from OE *pīc* 'point, pick-axe', and may have the same sense as the corresponding Scandinavian nickname *Pik*, 'a tall, thin person'. Or it may denote a man armed with a *pīc*, a pikeman. Later examples may have the same meaning or may be nicknames from OFr *pic*, Lat *picus* 'wood-pecker' or from ME *pike* 'pike, fish'. Alexander *le pik* (1292 SRLo) was a fishmonger and owner of a ship. William, Robert and Stephen *Pikeman* (ib.) were also fishmongers. Here, *Pike* and *Pikeman* are both from *pike*, the fish, and mean 'sellers of pike'. (ii) Thomas *del Pic* 1220 FFEss; Ralph *del Pik'* 1292 QW (Herts). OE *pīc* 'point' in the sense of 'hill'. From residence near a hill as at Pick Hill (Ess, K), the former the home of Reginald *de Pike* (t Hy 3 PN Ess 29).

Pikesley: Hugo *de Pikesle* 1242 Fees (He). From Pixley (Herefords).

Pikett: *v.* PICKETT

Pilbeam, Pilbean, Pilbin: Adam *de Peltebhem* 1296 SRSx; Thomas *Peltebem* 1327 ib. This Sussex and West Kent name must derive from a lost place in Sussex. Pilbeams in Chiddingstone (Kent) is named from Her' *Peltebem* (1347 PN K 80).

Pilch: Ralph *Pilche* 1251 Rams (Hu); Richard *Pilche* 1275 SRWo. OE *pylece*, ME *pilche* 'a fur garment'. Metonymic for *Pilcher*.

Pilcher: Mabilia *Pullchare* 1214 FFSx; Hugh *Pilchere* 1271 FFC; Henry, Nicholas *le Pilchere* 1275 SRWo, 1317 AssK. A derivative of OE *pylece* 'a pilch', a maker or seller of pilches (an outer garment made of skin dressed with hair).

Pile, Pyle: Henry *de la Pil* 1221 Pat (So); Robert *Pile* 1243 AssSo; Robert *Attepile* 1274 RH (So). 'Dweller by the stake or post', OE *pīl*.

Pilfold: William *Pilefold* 1327 SRSx. From Pilfolds in Horsham (Sussex).

Pilgrim, Pilgram, Pagram, Peagram, Peagrim, Peggram, Pegram, Pegrum, Piggrem, Pigram, Piegrome, Pigrome, Pelerin, Peregrine, Paragreen: Hugo *peregrinus*, Hago (sic) *le pelerin* 1189–98, 12th MedEA (Nf); Hugo *Pilegrim* 1185 Templars (Wa); William *Pegerim*, *Pegrum* 1200 Cur (Do);

Eustace *Pelrim* 1221 *ElyA* (C); Robert *Peregrine* 1243 AssSo; William *Pylegrim* 1251 Rams (Hu); Robert *Pelrin, Pelgrim* 1260 AssC; William *Pegrin* 1275 RH (C); Symon *Pegrym* 1327 SRSf. ME *pelegrim, pilegrim*, OFr *pelegrin*, Lat *peregrīn-um* 'one that comes from foreign parts', used of one who had made the pilgrimage to Rome or the Holy Land (*pilegrim* c1200 NED). Occasionally used as a personal name: *Pelerin* 1206 P (Sx), sometimes given to or adopted by a pilgrim; William *Pelerin* de Albana is also called *Pelerine* de Albana, clerk (1272 Lewes (Nf)).

Pilkington: Alexander *de Pilkington, de Pilkinton* 1205 WhC, 1285 AssCh; John *Pylkyngton* 1470 Past. From Pilkington (Lancs).

Pill: Walter, John *Pille* 1197 P (O), 1275 SRWo. Probably OFr *pile* 'little ball, pill'. cf. BALL.

Pill, Pell: Robert *de la Pulle* 1221 AssWo; Hugh *de la Pille* 1225 AssSo; John *atte Pelle* 1332 SRSx. 'Dweller by the creek or stream', OE *pyll*.

Pillar, Piller, Pillers: (i) Roger, Dike *le Pilur* 1246 AssLa. OFr *pilleur* 'plunderer'. cf. '*Pylowre*, or he that pelyth other men, as cachpolls or odyre lyk, *pilator, depredator*' PromptParv. (ii) John *le Piler* 1327 SRSo; Thomas *Piler'* 1332 SRSr. 'Dweller by the stake or stream.' *v*. PILE, PILL. (iii) Thomas *Attepiler* 1231 Cl (O); Walter *de Piler'* 1279 RH (O). 'Dweller by the pillar', OFr *piler*.

Pilling, Pillings: Adam *Pilling* 1283 SRSf; Emma *Pylyng* 1296 SRSx; Thomas *Pillyng* 1344 AD i (Wa). OE **piling* 'dweller by the stake' or OE **pylling* 'dweller by the stream'.

Pillman: William *Pyleman* 1286 Wak (Y). 'Dweller by the stake or the stream.' *v*. PILE, PILL.

Pillow: *v*. PEDLOW.

Pilpot: For PHILPOT. Pilpot Wood in Calne (Wilts) is *Filpott* Coppice in 1650 (PN W 260).

Pim, Pimm, Pym, Pymm: *Pimme* filius Sirith 1204 Cur (St); *Pimme* forester 1246 AssLa; William, Henry *Pimme* 1250 Fees (Nt), 1279 RH (C); Agnes, Edmund *Pymm(e)* 1307 Wak (Y), 1316 AD ii (Nf). Bardsley explains this as a pet-form of *Euphemia*. In the two instances where certainty is possible it is clearly a man's name and is presumably the OE *Pymma* recorded once in LVD. cf. Gilbert *Pimming'* 1221 AssWa; William *Pymyng* 1295 FFEss. OE **Pymming* 'son of *Pymma*'.

Pimblett, Pimblott, Pimlett, Pimlott: Mergret *Pymlot* 1561 Bardsley. *Pim-el-et, Pim-el-ot*, double diminutives of *Pim*.

Pinch, Pinck: *v*. PINK

Pinchbeck, Pinchback: Walter *de Pincebec* 1202 AssL; John *de Pinchebeke* 1327 SRLei; William *Pynchebek* 1447 AssLo. From Pinchbeck (Lincs).

Pinchen, Pinchin, Pinching, Pinchon, Pinshon, Pinson, Pinsent: Hugo *filius Pinchonis, filius Pincun* 1121–33 Seals (O), Hy 2 DC (L); *Pincun* de Blacheshola 1166 P (Berks); Ralph *Pincun* 1166 RBE (L); Richard *Pincon* Hy 2 DC (Lei); William *Pynson* 1296 SRSx; Robert *Pynchoun* 1310 ColchCt; John *Pynsent* 1524 SRSf. OFr *pinçon, pinson*, Norman-Picard *pinchon* 'finch', used as a symbol of

gaiety, 'gai comme un pinson' (Dauzat), both as a nickname and a personal-name. Ekwall suggests a nickname from OFr *pinçon, pinchon* 'pincers, forceps'.

Pinckney: *v*. PINKNEY

Pinckstone: *v*. PINKSTONE

Pindar, Pinder, Pindor, Pender: Richard *le pynder* 1219 AssY; William *le Pendere* 1231 Pat (Ess); Richard *le Pundere* 1296 SRSx. A derivative of OE *(ge)pyndan* 'to impound, shut up'; pinder, an officer of a manor who impounded stray beasts. cf. Thomas *le Pendere* tunc prepositus de Atleford 1275 RH (K). *v*. also PONDER, POUNDER, POYNDER.

Pine, Pyne: (i) Bonde, Robert *Pine* 1101–7 Holme (Nf), 1181 P (Sa); Robert, William *Pin* 1208 Cur (Nth), 1221 AssSa; Henry *le Pyn* 1332 SRSx. OE *pīn* or OFr *pin* 'pine', a nickname for a tall, upright man. cf. PINNELL. (ii) Morin *del Pin* 1130 P (Lei); Alexander *de Pinu* 1169 P (D); Thomas *de Pyne* 1277 AssSo; John *atte Pyne* 1327 SRC. Combepyne and Upton Pyne (Devon) were held in the 13th century by a family of *de Pyn* who may have come from Le Pin (Calvados) or some other French place named from a prominent pine. The surname may also have arisen independently in England, 'dweller by the pine'.

Pinel: *v*. PINNELL

Pinfold, Penfold: Thomas *ate Pundfolde* 1296 SRSx; John *Pennefold* 1332 SRSx. 'One in charge of the pinfold or pound.' cf. PINDAR. The surname has probably also absorbed (Richard, Henry) *Pynfoul* 1322 LLB E, 1327 SRSf, 'pin, pen fowl'. cf. CATCHPOLE.

Pingstone: *v*. PINKSTONE

Pinion: *v*. BEYNON

Pink, Pinck, Pinks, Pinch: Sewine *Pinca* 1100–30 OEByn (D); Adam *Pinc* 1176 P (Y); Hugo *Pinch* 1190 P (L); Robert, Henry *Pinke* 1200 P (Ha), c1248 Bec (W); Lucia *le Pynch*, Dionisia *le Pinch* 1317 AssK. OE *pinca* 'chaffinch', with a variant *pinc*. cf. FINCH.

Pinkney, Pinckney: Ansculfus *de Pinchengi* 1086 DB (Bk); Robert *Pinkenie* 1184 P (Lo). From Picquigny (Somme).

Pinkstone, Pinckstone, Pingstone: Hugo *de Penkeston'* 1207 Cur (Nt). From Pinxton (Derby).

Pinn: (i) John *Pinne, Pynne* 1211 Cur (O), 1327 SRSf. OE *pinn* 'pin', for a pinmaker. *v*. PINNER. (ii) Geoffrey *de Pinne* 1230 P (Do); Richard *atte Pynne* 1327 SRSo. 'Dweller on the hill' (OE *penn*), as at Pinn or Pin Hill Fm (Devon). *v*. PENN.

Pinnell, Pinel: Ralph *Pinel* 1086 DB (Ess); Robert *Pinel* 1185 Templars (Wa). OFr *pinel* 'little pine-tree', a diminutive of OFr *pin* 'pine-tree'. A nickname (not uncommon), applied either affectionately to a tall, thin man, or derisively to a small weedy man.

Pinner: (i) Andrew, Richard *de Pinner* 1275 RH (Lo). From Pinner (Middlesex). (ii) Adam *le Pinare* 1244 MESO (Wo); Walter *le Pinnere* 1281 LLB B; Andrew *le Pynner* 1332 SRWa. A derivative of OE *pinn* 'a peg, pin', a pinmaker. Besides pins, the pinner also made wire articles, especially the small needles inserted in cards used in cloth dressing. (iii) Eborard *Penier* 1275 RH (L); Thomas *le Peniur* ib. (Nf); Maud *Penir* 1279 RH (C); John *le Peynur* ib. (Bk); Robert *le Penyr* 1327 *SR* (Ess). OFr *peigneor, peignier, pignour* 'a maker of combs'. William *le Pinour* (1292 SRLo) was also called William *le Horner* (1295 LLB A) and was, no doubt, a maker of horn combs. cf. also Juliana *le Pineresse, le Peÿneresse* 1281 MESO (Wo), a comber of wool or flax (OFr *peigneresse*).

Pinnick: *v.* PINNOCK

Pinnington, Pinington: Richard *de Pynyngton* 1332 SRLa. From Pennington in Leigh (Lancs).

Pinnion: *v.* BEYNON

Pinnix: *v.* PINNOCK

Pinnock, Pinnick, Pinnix: Nicholas *Pinnoch* 1199 P (W); Walter *Pinnok* 1255 RH (W). ME *pinnock* 'hedge-sparrow'.

Pinsent, Pinshon, Pinson: *v.* PINCHEN

Pinwill: Simon *Pynewelle* 1327 SRSx. From Pingwell Haw in Wilmington (Sussex).

Pinyon, Pinyoun: *v.* BEYNON

Pipe, Pipes: (i) Swan, William *Pipe* 1221 AssSa, 1227 FFBk; William *le Pype* 1274 AssSo. OE *pipe* 'pipe', metonymic for a piper, or, occasionally, the man's name *Pipe* recorded in Domesday Book, perhaps from the root of Fr *Pepin*, OG *Pipin*. There was also a woman's name *Pypa* (of Wytlesford 1260 AssC). (ii) Henry *de Pipa* 1152 StCh; John *del Pipe* 1267 Cl. OE *pīpe* was also used of a water-pipe, conduit or aqueduct, and of the channel of a small stream. The name may thus arise from residence near such a *pipe* or from Pipe (Hereford) where there is a brook, or from Pipehill (Staffs), earlier *Pipa*, where there are springs from which water has for centuries been piped to Lichfield.

Piper, Pyper: Jordan *Piper* 1185 Templars (So); William *le pipere* 1202 AssL. OE *pīpere* 'a player on the pipe, a piper'.

Pipon, Pippin: *v.* PEPIN

Pipperday: *v.* PEPPERDAY

Pirard: *v.* PIRRET

Pirie: *v.* PERRY

Pirkiss: *v.* PURCHAS

Pirret, Pirrett, Pirard: *Pirotus* 1154–61 Colch (Sf); *Pirot* 1204 Cur (Beds); Ralph *Pirot* 1176 P (Beds); Henry *Pirard* 1208 Cur (O); Richard *Pyrot* 1296 SRSx. From east French *Pier(r)ot, Pier(r)ard*, hypocoristics of *Pierre* (Peter). Now rare names, mostly absorbed by PARROT, etc.

Pirrie: *v.* PERRY

Piser: *v.* POYSER

Pistol: *v.* PESTELL

Pistor: *v.* PESTER

Pitcher, Pitchers: William *le Picher* 1243 AssSo; William *Pycher* 1289 FFSf. A derivative of OE *(ge)pīcian* 'to pitch', 'one who covers or caulks with pitch' (1611 NED). *Pitcher* is also a late form of PICKARD. Col. D. G. Pitcher notes an ancestor John *Pychard*, named in 1551 both *Pichard* and *Pichar*. In his will he calls his wife *Pytchard* and his

uncle William both *Pitchard* and *Pytcher*. cf. also William *Picard* or *Pitcher* (1648 Harrison).

Pither(s): *v.* PETHER

Pitman, Pittman, Pettman, Putman: Unban *Piteman* 1203 AssNth (Nf); Henry *Putman* 1296 SRSx; Walter *Petman* 1317 AssK. OE *pytt* and *mann*, 'dweller by the pit or in the hollow'.

Pitt, Pitts, Pett, Petts, Putt: Geruase *de la Puette* 1182 P (Sx); Maurice *de Pette* 1198 Cur (K); Thomas *de la Pitte, de la Pute* 1225 AssSo; Roger *de Pettes* 1276 ArchC vi; William *Bitheputte* 1277 AssSo; Thomas *ithe Putte* 1278 MELS (Wo); Gilbert *atte Pitte* 1294 PN Sr 151; John *ater Puttes* 1296 SRSx; Juliana *atte Pette* 1327 *SR* (Ess); Richard *Pyts* 1395 Whitby. From Pett (Kent), Pitt (Hants), or 'dweller by the pit(s) or hollow(s)', OE *pytt*.

Pitter: For *atte pitte*. cf. PITT, PUTTER.

Pittet: *v.* PETTIT

Pixton: *v.* PICKSTONE

Pizer: *v.* POYSER

Pizey, Pizzey, Pizzie, Peasey, Pezey, Pusey: Adam *de Pesy* 1220 Fees (Berks); Joan *de Pusye, de Pysy* 1277–8 AssSo; John *de Puseye, de Peseie* 1284, 1300 Oseney (O). From Pusey (Berks), *Pesei* DB, *Pusie* Wm 1 DEPN.

Place, Plaice: (i) William *de la Place* 1276 RH (L); John *atte Place* 1313 FFSf; Emma *del Place* 1332 SRCu. 'Dweller in the market-place', ME *place*. (ii) William *de Plaiz* 1190 P (Y); Roger *de Plaice* 1200 Cur (La); Richard *de la Pleyse, de la Plesse* 1277 AssSo. OFr *pleix, plais*, Lat *plexum*, 'an enclosure or coppice surrounded by a fence of living wood with interlacing branches'. The surname may be from some French place so named or may denote a forester. Also survives as PLEACE. (iii) Beatrice, Adam *Playce* 1297 SRY, 1332 SRCu; William *Plaice* 1346 Whitby (Y). These might be for *Plaiz*, with loss of the preposition. But they may also be OFr *plaise* 'plaice', so called from its flatness; either a nickname or a seller of plaice or fish in general.

Plaisted, Playsted, Plaster, Plested: Osbert *de la Plested'* 1221 AssWo; Alexander *atte Pleystude* 1327 SRSo. From residence near a place for play, OE **plegstede*. Chapel Plaster in Box (Wilts) was the home of John *atte Pleistede* in 1333 (PN W 83).

Plaistow, Plaistowe, Plaister, Plastow, Plaster, Plester: Robert *de Plegestoue* 1168 P (D); William *de la Pleystowe* 1275 RH (W); Cristian' *atte Pleystouwe* 1296 SRSx; William *Pleystowe* 1382 PN Herts 98. From residence at Plaistow (Devon, Essex, Surrey, Sussex), Playstow (Herts), Plaistows Fm, *Plasters* 1669, *The Plaisters* 1679 (PN Herts 98), Pleystowe Fm, *Plestore* 1596 (PN Sr 266), Plestowes Fm, *Plestowe* Ric 1, *Plesters* 1821 (PN Wa 249), Plaster Down (Devon), Plastow Green, Plasterhill Fm, or Plestor (Hants), or from residence near the village sports ground. OE *plegstōw* is more common than **plegstede*, and several of these modern places are in or near a large open space in the middle of the village. Plaistow in West Ham is pronounced *Plarstow*.

Plampin: v. BLAMPHIN

Plank: Maud *de la Plank* 1288 Ipm (W). 'Dweller by the plank' or narrow foot-bridge, ME *planke*.

Plant, Plante: William *Plante* 1262 *For* (Ess), 1279 RH (C); William *Plauntes* 1275 RH (Nf). Metonymic for a gardener or planter of various plants. cf. Henry *le Plaunter* 1281 Rams (Hu), Ralph *Plantebene* 1199 P (Nf) 'beans' and PLANTEROSE.

Planterose: Robert, Alice *Planterose* 1221 AssWa, 1272 RamsCt (C). 'Rose-grower.'

Plass: from *plais*. v. PLACE (ii).

Plaster, Plaister: Symon *le Emplastrer*, Robert *le Plastrer* 1276 LLB B; Hugo *le Playstrer* 1293 MESO (Y); Emma *le Plastrer* 1323 Bart (Lo); William *Plaister* 1646 FrY. OFr *plastrier* 'plasterer'. Richard *le Plasterer* of York and his mates (*sociis*) made the partition walls of the Queen's chamber of *plastre de Parys* at Scarborough in 1284 (Building 156). These names also represent a common pronunciation of PLAISTED and PLAISTOW.

Plastow: v. PLAISTOW

Plater, Platter: (i) William *le plater, le Platier*, armurer 1292 SRLo, 1311 LLB B; John *le Plater* 1300 LLB C; John *le Plattour* 1319 SRLo. A derivative of ME *plate*, a maker of plate-armour or of plates for armour. cf. John *Platesmyth* 1379 PTY. (ii) Herueus *Plaitere* Hy 3 Colch (Ess); Walter *Playtur* 1279 RH (Hu); Philip *le Pleytour* 1327 SRSf. A derivative of OFr *plait* 'plea' or OFr *plaitier* 'to plead', a pleader, advocate.

Platfoot: Matilda *Platfot* 1260 AssC. 'Flat-foot'. OFr *plat*.

Platner: John *le Platener* 1290 LLB A. A derivative of OFr *platon* 'metal plate', plate-maker.

Platt, Platts: John *de la Platte* 1242 P (Wo); Geoffrey *de Platte* 1285 AssLa; Henry *Atteplatte* 1327 SRSt; Robert *Plattes* 1590 FrY. 'Dweller by the small patch of land' (OE *plætt) or by a foot-bridge, dialectal *plat* 'foot-bridge' (1652 NED), from OFr *plat* 'flat surface', as at Platt Bridge (Lancs).

Platten: William, Walter *Platon* 1198 FFSf, 1327 SRWo. Metonymic for PLATNER.

Platter: William *Platter* 1332 SRSx. Probably 'dweller by the footbridge'. v. PLATT, PLATER.

Player: John, William *le Pleyer* 1296 MEOT (Herts), 1332 SRSr. OE *plegere* 'player', probably an athlete who distinguished himself on the *Plaisted* or *Plaistow*.

Playfair, Playfer: William *Playfayre* 1290 Black, 1570 FFHu. Probably 'play fairly'. cf. GOVER.

Playfoot: Richard *Pleyfote, Playfote* 1310–12 ColchCt. Probably 'splay-foot'. Loss or prefixing of initial *s* was common in the Essex dialect. The examples are early to be regarded as forms of *Playford*.

Playford: Fulcher' *de Pleiforda* 1130 P (Sf). From Playford (Suffolk).

Playsted: v. PLAISTED

Pleace, Please, Pleass: For PLACE (ii).

Pleaden: v. BLETHYN

Pleasance, Pleasaunce, Pleasants, Pleasant: (i) Reginald *de Pleisauns, de Plesence* 1275 RH (L); John *de Plesaunce, de Plesancia* of Lumbardy 1319 SRLo, 1339 LoPleas. From Piacenza (Italy), earlier *Placentia*. (ii) *Plesantia* West 1275 RH (Nf); Alicia *filia Plesance* 1279 RH (O); *Pleasant* Tarlton (f) 1681 Bardsley. *Plaisance* (OFr *plaisance* 'pleasure'), *Plaisant* (OFr *plaisant* 'pleasing'), women's names long in use.

Pleavin: v. BLETHYN

Plenty: Simon *Plente* 1230 P (Y); William *Plentee* 1243 AssSo. OFr *plente* 'abundance'.

Plested: v. PLAISTED

Plester: v. PLAISTOW

Pleven, Plevin: v. BLETHYN

Plewman: v. PLOWMAN

Plomer: v. PLUMER

Plott: John *atte Plotte* c1280 Bart (Herts); Henry *ate Plotte* 1317 AssK. 'Dweller on the small plot of ground', OE *plot*.

Plowden: William *de Ploden'* 1203 Pl (Sa); Roger *de Ploeden'* 1254 RH (Sa); Thomas *de Plowedene* 1327 SRSa. From Plowden (Salop).

Plowman, Plewman: Robert *Pleueman, Plouman* 1223 Cur (We); Philip *Ploman* 1255 *Ass* (Ess); John *(le) Plouman* 1275 RH (L); John *le Ploghman* 1275 RH (R); John *Plowman* 1345 AD i (L); John *Plewman* 1560 FrY. OE *plōh* 'plough' and *mann*, 'ploughman' (1271 NED).

Plowright: William *le Plowritte* 1279 RH (C); Robert *le Plogwryth* 1285 Wak (Y); Baldwyn *le Ploghwright* 1297 FFSf. OE *plōh* 'plough' and *wyrhta* 'wright', 'a maker of ploughs' (1285 NED).

Plucknett, Plumkett, Plunket, Plunkett: Hugh *de Plugeneio* 1163 Oseney; Hugh *de Plucheneit, de Plugenet* 1200 Oseney; Alan *Plugenet, de Pluckenet* 1270 AssSo; Robert *Plukenet* 1280 IpmW. From Plouquenet (Ille-et-Vilaine).

Pluckrose: William, Robert *Pluckerose* 1275 RH (Sf), 1296 SRSx. 'Pluck rose.' cf. John, William *Pullerose* 1296 SRSx, 1301 SRY. Lower mentions a friend of his who held land in Ashdown Forest (Sussex) of the Duchy of Lancaster by one red rose. 'On the front of a farm belonging to him is a large rose tree, to which the reeve of the manor periodically comes, and either *pluck*ing or *pull*ing a flower, sticks it into his button-hole, and walks off.'

Plum, Plumb, Plumbe: Geoffrey, Simon *Plumbe* 1208 ChR (Sf), 1251 Rams (Hu); John *Ploumbe* 1327 SRSf; Ralph *Plomme* 1327 SRDb; Nicholas *Plumme* 1469 LLB L. Common in early sources, without any sign of either article or preposition, almost invariably in the form *Plumbe*, this must be OFr *plomb*, Lat *plumbum* 'lead', used by metonymy for *plumber*. v. PLUMMER.

Plume: Alan *Plome* c1000 MedEA (Nf); Hugh *Plume* 1221 Cur (Do); Walter *Ploume* 1275 SRWo. OFr *plume*, Lat *pluma* 'feather', used of a dealer in feathers. v. PLUMER.

Plumer, Plomer: Walterus, Rogerus *plumarius* 1176 P (We), 1230 P (Nt); Roger *Plumer* 1185

Templars (Y); Turbertus *plumator* 1230 P (Sf); Simon *le Plumer* 1246 AssLa; Ralph *le Plomer* 1280 Oseney (O). AFr, OFr *plumier*, Lat *plumarius* 'a dealer in plumes or feathers' (1282 NED). MLWL records *plumator* 'flock-puller' in 1281 and *plumarium* 'feather-bed' in 1384, but does not include *plumarius*. John de Cestrehunte, *fethermongere* 1280 LLB A, is called *plumer* in 1281 ib. *Plumer* in early forms may sometimes mean 'plumber'. *v.* PLUMMER.

Plumkett: *v.* PLUCKNETT

Plummer, Plimmer: (i) Godric *Plumberre* 1102–7 Rams (Hu); Gillebertus *Plumbarius* 1183 P (C); Osbertus *Plumbarius, le Plumer* 1221–2 Cur (Mx); Ernald, Osbert *le plummer* 1225 FrLeic, 1227 Bart (Mx); Robertus *plumberius* 1230 P (Wa); Richard *le plumber* 1230 P (D); Peter *Plumber* 1256 AssNb; Robert *le Plummer* 1260 AssC; Simon *le Plommer* 1280 AssSo. The earliest examples seem to be a direct formation from OFr *plomb* 'lead', later assimilated to OFr *plummier, plommier* 'plumber' (1385–6 NED). *Plumbarius* is first recorded in MLWL in 1290 and *plummarius* in 1380. It has no example of *plumberius*. Early forms *plumer*, often undoubtedly for PLUMER, may sometimes belong here. (ii) This may sometimes be local in origin. Plummers in Kimpton (Herts) was the home of Thomas *de Plummere* in 1272, 'the pool by the plum-tree' (PN Herts 16). Plummer Wood in Thaxted (Essex) is *Plumetonemore* in 1348 (PN Ess 499).

Plunket(t): *v.* PLUCKNETT
Pluthero: *v.* PROTHERO
Poad, Poat, Podd, Pods: Richard *Pode* 1230 P (D); John *le Pod* 1275 RH (K). ME *pode* 'toad'.
Pobgee, Pobjoy: *v.* PAPIGAY
Pocket, Pockett, Pocketts: Adam, Geoffrey *Poket* 1210 Cur (C), 1258 FFEss. ME *poket*, a diminutive of AFr *poque*, 'a small pouch'. cf. POKE, POUCH.

Pocock: *v.* PEACOCK
Podd, Pods: *v.* POAD
Poe: *v.* PAW
Poel: *v.* PAUL, POWELL
Poggs: (i) William, Andrew *Pogge* 1286, 1309 Wak (Y). *Pogg* is a pet-name for Margaret, rhymed on *Mogg*. (ii) Imbertus *Pugeis* 1235 Fees (Ha); Robert *le Pugeys* 1286 Ipm (Sf); Alicia *Pogeys* 1327 SRC; Gregory *Pogeis* 1300 LLB B. Imbert *le Pugeys*, called also *de Salvadya* 'of Savoy' and *de Bampton* (Oxon), came to England with Queen Eleanor of Provence, who married Henry III on 20 January 1236 (Fees). He came from Le Puy-en-Velay (Haute-Loire) and has left his name in Stoke Poges (Bucks), *Stoke Pogys* (1514), *Stokbogies* (1526), and in Broughton Poggs (Oxon). The surname means 'man from Puy' or 'dweller by the hillock'. Le Puy is a common place-name in Anjou, Poitou, etc., and the surname may also have been introduced into England from one of these.

Pogson, Poxon: Richard *Pogson* 1440 ShefA (Y). 'Son of *Pog* (Margaret).'

Poidevin, Le Poidevin, le Poideven, Podevin, Patvine, Potvin, Potwin, Portwin, Portwine, Putwain, Puddifin, Puddifant, Puttifent: *Peiteuin de Eya* 1186 P (Sf); *Peyteuinus* le Esquier 1247 AssBeds; Rogerus *Peteuinus, Pictauensis* 1086 DB (Ess); Rogger *Peiteuin* 1094 ASC E; Ralph *Patefine* Hy 1 Whitby (Y); Odo *Petefin* ib.; Adam *Petevin* 1198 FFK; David *le Poitevin* 1199 AssSt; Rainer *le Payteuin* 1219 AssY; Richard *Patevin* 1242 Fees (Nb); William *Peytefin* 1247 AssBeds; Osemund *Petewin* 1279 RH (C); Preciosa *Potewyne* ib.; Reginald *Peytewin* 1296 SRSx. OFr *Poitevin*, AFr *Peitevyn*, a man from Poitou.

Pointel: Tedric *Pointel, Puintel* 1086 DB (Ess); Stephen *Puintel* 1166 P (Nf). OFr *pointel* 'point', 'a sharp pointed instrument', a diminutive of OFr *point* 'point', a nickname that might have been applied to a tall, thin man. The complete absence of any sign of the preposition *de* prevents any association with Pointel (Orne).

Pointer, Poynter: Benedict, Richard *le Puintur* 1206 P (Berks), 1212 Cur (K); Richard *le Pointur* 1213 FFC; Bartholomew *le Pointer* 1314 Oriel (O). A derivative of ME *poynte* 'a tagged lace or cord, of twisted yarn, silk, or leather' (1390 NED), from OFr *pointe* 'a sharp or pointed extremity'. 'A pointer', a maker of points for fastening hose and doublet together. We may also have a building-term. In roofing, the layers of tiles overlapped and the lowest layers, and sometimes all the layers, were pointed or rendered with mortar. This is called 'pointing' in 1265 and the slaters doing this work may well have been called *pointers* (Building 233–4).

Pointon, Poynton: Alexander *de Pochintun* c1155 Gilb; Jordan *de Poyngtun* c1200–10 RegAntiquiss; Alice *de Poynton* 1344 LoPleas; Robert *Pointon* 1419 FFEss. Usually from Pointon (Lincs), *Pochinton* DB, but occasionally perhaps from Poynton (Ches, Salop).

Points, Poyntz: Walterus *filius Ponz* 1086 DB (Berks); Ricardus *filius Puinz* 1185 Templars (So); *Puntius, Pontius* Arnaldi 1196 P (D); Reginald *Puinz, Poinz* 1176–7 P (Sr); Rannulf *Poinces* 1207 Cur (Sx). OFr *Ponz*, Latin *Pontius*, 'man from Pontus in Asia Minor', the name of a saint (*Pontius*) of Asia Minor whose cult was widely spread in the middle ages, surviving also in Fr *Pons*, *Ponce* and the Burgundian *Point*. The surname is also a nickname for a fop, the man with the points (*v.* POINTER): Geoffrey *Aspoinz* 1193 P (L), and may be local in origin: Hugh *de Poinz* 1221 Cur (So), Reginald *de Ponz, de Pontibus* c1222 InqLa, from Ponts (La Manche, Seine-Inférieure), Lat *pontes* 'bridges'.

Poke: Hugh, Robert *Poke* 1200 P (K); 1279 RH (Hu). ME *poke* 'bag', metonymic for *Poker*, 'maker of bags or small sacks': Ithel (*le*) *Poker* 1314, 1323 AssSt.

Pole(s): *v.* PAUL, POOL
Polglase: John *de Polglas* 1297 MinAcctCo. From Polglaze (Cornwall).
Poll: *v.* PAUL, POOL

Pollard: *Pollardus* Ostiarius 1201 Cur (Sf); *Pollardus* Forestarius 1207 Cur (Gl); Stephanus *filius Pollard* 1275 RH (K); William, Peter, Richard *Pollard* 1181, 1192, 1195 P (Sr, Herts, L). The personal-name *Pollhard* is a derivative of *Paul* which seems to have been pronounced *Poll* by the end of the 12th century. cf. *Pol* 1188 and *Polle* 1193 *s.n.* PAUL. The surname is also from a nickname *pollard* from ME *poll* 'to clip', *poll* 'the head', one with a close-cropped head or a big head. cf. BALLARD, TESTAR.

Pollins: *v.* PAULIN

Pollit, Pollitt: Henricus *filius Ypoliti* 1171 P (Y); *Yppolitus* de Pridias 1207 P (Ess); Walter, Geoffrey *Polite* 1222 Cur (Nth), 1285 *Ass* (Ess); Christina *Polytes* 1311 ColchCt. *Hippolytus*, Gk ʽΙππόλυτος 'letting horses loose', the name of a Roman saint martyred in 235, to whom the church of Ippollitts (Herts) is dedicated (*Polytes* 1412).

Pollock, Pollack, Pollok: Peter, John *de Pollok* c1172–8, 1304 Black; John *Pullok* 1453 ib. From Upper Pollock (Renfrew).

Polman: *v.* POOLMAN

Polson, Poulson, Poulsom, Poulsum: Adam *Poles(s)on* 1323–5 AssSt. 'Son of *Paul*.'

Pomeroy, Pomery, Pomroy, Pummery: Ralph *de Pomerai* 1086 DB (D, So); Ralph *Pomeria* ib. (So); Samson *de la Pumeray* 1200 Cur (O); Henry *de la Pomereie* 1225 AssSo; Robert *Pomeroy* 1327 SRSo. The DB tenant-in-chief, whose name survives in Berry Pomeroy and Stockleigh Pomeroy (Devon), came from La Pommeraye (Calvados). *v.* ANF. Others may have come from La Pommeraie (Seine-Inférieure) or Saint-Sauveur-la-Pommeraie (La Manche). The surname may also denote residence near an apple-orchard (OFr *pommeraie*). cf. APPLETON.

Pomfret, Pomfrett, Pomphrett, Pumfrett, Pontefract: Willelmus *de Pontefracto* 1191 P (Y); William *Puntfreit* 1200 Cur (Ess), *de Puntfreit* 1203 Cur (K); Matthew *de Pomfrait* 1275 RH (Lo); Robert *Pumfret* 1275 RH (Nf). From Pontefract (WR Yorks), Lat (*de*) *ponte fracto* '(at the) broken bridge'. *Punt-freit* is the Norman-French form, found also in Pomfret Mead (PN Ess 642). *v.* PUMFREY.

Pomfrey, Pomphrey: *v.* PUMFREY

Pond: William *del Pond* 1190 BuryS (Sf); John *de la Ponde* 1203 FFEss; Henry *Attepond* 1260 AssC; John *Ponde* 1262 *For* (Ess). 'Dweller by the pond', ME *pond*.

Ponder: William *le Pondere* 1279 RH (C); John *le Ponder'* 1306 RamsCt (Hu); Rychard *Ponder*, Thomas *Punder* 1524 SRSf. 'Dweller by the pond', cf. Richard *Pondeman* 1327 *SR* (Ess), or 'keeper of the pound'. *v.* POUNDER.

Ponsford: *v.* PAUNCEFOOT

Ponsonby: Alexander *de Ponsonby* 1332 SRCu; Dionisia *Pounsounby* 1401 LLB I; William *Ponsonbye* 1600 AssLo. From Ponsonby (Cumb).

Pont, Ponte, Punt: Amice *de Ponte* 1268 AssSo; Peter *del Pount* 1279 FFEss; William *Punt* 1316 FFEss; Walter *Pont* 1327 SRSf. 'Dweller by the

bridge', ME *pont*, *punt*, OFr *pont*, Lat *pons* 'bridge'.

Pontefract: *v.* POMFRET

Ponter, Punter: Walter *Punter* 1214 Cur (Nth); Stephen *le Punter* 1243 AssSo; John, Richard *Ponter* 1255 RH (Sa). 'Dweller by, or keeper of the bridge.' *v.* PONT, BRIDGER.

Pontis, Puntis: Robert *de Punteise* 1190 P (L); Adam *Pontis* 1275 RH (Nf); Henry *Ponteys* 1279 RH (Hu); James *Punteys* 1296 SRSx; John *de Pounteysse, de Pountoyse* 1300 LLB B, 1302 LoCt. From Pontoise (Seine-et-Oise).

Pook, Pouck: William *Puch* 1166 P (Nf); Richard *le Pouke* 1296 SRSx; John *le Puk* 1332 SRSx. OE *pūca* 'elf, sprite, goblin'.

Pool, Poole, Pole, Poles, Poll, Polle: Mauritius *de la Pole* 1176 P (D); Roger *de Pole* 1191 P (W); Thomas *del Pol* 1260 AssC; John *Pool* 1324 FFEss; Ralph *atte Polle* 1327 SRSx; William *atte Poule* 1327 SRSo; Thomas *del Polle* 1332 SRCu. From residence near a pool or tidal stream (OE *pōl*). All the modern surnames may also derive from PAUL.

Pooler: Equivalent to *atte Pole* (*v.* POOL) or POOLMAN.

Pooley: Walter *de Polhey* 1248 FFEss; William *de Poleye* 1273 RH (Bk); Elias *de Polye, de Polee* 1275 RH (Nf); William *de Polleye* 1275 SRWo; William *Polleye* 1346 ColchCt; John *Poley* 1379 AssEss. From residence near low-lying land or an enclosure by a pool (OE *ēg; (ge)hæg*). This sometimes becomes *Polley*. Hunt's Hall in Pebmarsh (Essex) is *Polheia* (1086), *Polleheye* (1238), *Pollyhall* (1446), *Pooley* t Eliz (PN Ess 450). Polly Shaw (PN K 40) has the same origin.

Poolman, Polman: Hugh *Poleman* 1260 ArchC iii; John *Polman* 1327 *SR* (Ess). 'Dweller by the pool.'

Poor, Poore, Power, Powers: (i) Drogo *poher* 1127 AC (Gl); Walter *le Poher* 1162 DC (L); Hugo *le Puhier* 1166 P (Sa); Hugo *Puher* 1170 P (Wo); John *le Poer* 1199 FF (Nth); Roger *le Puiher* 1204 Cur (Db); Philip *le Poyer, le Power* 1257 StThomas (St), 1292 AssSt; Richard *le Poier, le Pouer*, William *Pouwer* 1297 MinAcctCo (O); Stephen *le Poer, le Power, Power* 1296, 1327, 1332 SRSx. OFr *Pohier* 'a Picard'. Fairly common and almost invariably preceded by *le*. Without the article (Gilbert *Poer* 1274 FFSf), the source might, theoretically, be OFr *poer* 'power', but examples are so rare that all probably stand for *Pohier*. (ii) Walter *le Poure* 1163 Eynsham (O); Hugo *Pauper, le Pouere* 1191, 1206 Oseney (O); Roger *Pauper, le Poer, le Povr'* 1211–12 Cur (Nf); Roger *Pauper* (*le poure*) 1230 P (O). OFr *povre, poure* 'poor'. This, too, is common, but forms such as *poure, power* cannot safely be assigned to *Poher* or *povre* without other evidence. Geoffrey and William *Pouere*, customary tenants of the Bishop of Ely at Wetheringsett (Suffolk) in 1221 (*ElyA*) were not likely to be Picards. In London, Henry *Puer* or *Poer* (1300 LoCt) was probably of this nationality, but whether Geoffrey *le Power* (1299 ib.) and

John *le Poer* (1300 ib.) came from Picardy or were nicknamed 'the poor' cannot be determined.

Pope: Agnes, Hugo *le Pope* c1230 Barnwell (C), 1247 AssBeds; Henry *Pope* 1296 SRSx. ME *pope* from OE *păpa. v. PAPE.

Popejoy: *v.* PAPIGAY

Poppy: Jach', Geoffrey *Popy* 1275 RH (Nf), 1327 SRSf. A nickname from the flower.

Porcas: *v.* PURCHAS

Porcher: Edric *Porcher* 1185 Templars (Sa); Reginald *le Porker* 1221 AssWa; Thomas *le Porcher* 1275 SRWo. OFr *porcher, porkier* 'swineherd'.

Porkiss: *v.* PURCHAS

Porrett, Porritt: *v.* PARROT

Port, Porte: (i) Hugo *de Portu, de Port* 1084 GeldR (D), 1086 DB (K); Henry, Hawis *de Port* 1115 Winton (Ha), 1185 Templars (Berks). From Port-en-Bessin (Calvados). (ii) Walterus (*de*) *Extra Portam, de Horslaporte* 1199, 1200 Cur (L); Adam *de la Port* 1243 AssSo; Thomas *in the porte* 1275 SRWo; Alan *ad Portam* 1275 RH (L); Simon *Atteporte* ib. (Sx); Henry *Porte, de Porta* 1297 MinAcctCo. 'Dweller near or outside the town or castle-gate' (OE *port* 'door, gate', OFr *porte* 'entrance, door'); occupational, 'door-keeper, gate-keeper', equivalent to PORTER; 'dweller in the market-town or port' (OE *port* 'harbour, town').

Portal: A Huguenot name, southern French *Portal* 'dweller by the town-gate'.

Porter, Porters: (i) Willelmus *Portarius (Janitor)* 1183 P (Berks); William *le portier* 1190 P (Berks); Adam *le porter* 1202 AssL; Alice *le Porters* 1330 ColchCt. AFr *porter*, OFr *portier* 'door-keeper, gate-keeper'. Milo *Portarius* (1086 DB, Ha) performed porter-service at the jail or castle of Winchester. (ii) Nicholas, David *le portur* 1263 MEOT (Sr), 1279 AssSo; Andrew *Portour* 1356 ColchCt. OFr *porteour* 'porter', carrier of burdens. *Porter* 'door-keeper' also appears as *portour* in the 13th century (NED).

Portman, Portmann: John, Henry *Portman* 1225 AssSo, 1297 Ipm (Sf); Thomas *le Portman* 1275 SRWo. OE *portmann* 'townsman', 'portman', one of the body of citizens chosen to administer the affairs of a borough.

Portrait, Portrey: cf. John *le portreor* 1292 SRLo; Nicholas *le Portreour* 1312 LLB D. OFr *portraiour* 'painter (of pictures or portraits)'. The modern surnames appear to be metonymic, from OFr *pourtraict* 'portrait'.

Portugal, Pettengell, Pettengill, Pettingale, Pettingall, Pettingell, Pettingill, Puttergill: Walterus *filius Portingalliae* 1201 Cur (Sf); William *Potagal* 1214 Cur (Lei); Symon *Petingal* 1278 Oseney (O); William *Pettingall* 1568 SRSf; John *Portingale* 1569 SPD; Helena *Pettingall* 1607 RothwellPR (Y). ME *Portingale* 'Portugal' (c1386 NED), 'a Portuguese' (1497).

Portwin(e): *v.* POIDEVIN

Poser: *v.* POYSER

Posford: John *Posford, Potsforde* 1568 SR Sf. From Potsford Barn in Letheringham (Suffolk).

Poskitt: *v.* POSTGATE

Posnett: *v.* POSTLETHWAITE

Possell: *v.* POSTLE

Posselwhite: *v.* POSTLETHWAITE

Postan, Postans, Postance, Poston, Postons, Postin, Postings: Mabill', John *de la Posterne* 1203 P (Ess), 1242 Fees (W); John *Postans* alias Little John 1575 *ERO;* William *Poston* 1613 FrY. 'Dweller by, or keeper of the postern-gate', OFr *posterle, posterne.*

Postgate, Posgate, Postkitt, Poskett, Poskitt: Thomas *Postgate* 1349 Whitby (Y); Richard *Poskett* 1514 GildY; William *Posgate* 1648 YWills; Thomas *Poskitt* 1661 ib. From Postgate (NRYorks).

Postle, Postles, Posthill, Postill, Possell: *Postellus* 1176 P (Sr); *Apostollus* 1203 Cur (Mx); William, Richard *Postel* 1170 P (Nb), 1202 AssL; William *La Postle* 1300 LoCt; Ralph *Postle* 1300 LLB B; John *le Pusel* 1332 SRSx; Alice *Postill* 1500 NorwW (Nf). OE *apostol, postol*, OFr *apostle* 'apostle', both as a nickname or pageant-name and as a personal-name. cf. Fr *Apostol, Lapostolle*, which Dauzat explains as 'pape', an ironical nickname for a serious man. In OFr *apostole* was the original word for Pope.

Postlethwaite, Posselwhite, Posnett, Posnette: Thomas *Postilltwayte* 1467 GildY; Margaret *Postlewhaite* 1588 RothwellPR (Y); John *Postelwhat* 1584 LaWills; Gerard *Postlet* 1586 ib. From Postlethwaite in Millom (Cumb), now the name of a field in Mirehouse, first mentioned as a manor in 1278 (PN Cu). Bardsley notes that in Furness the name was colloquially pronounced *Poslett*, whence *Posnett.*

Poston: *v.* POSTAN

Pothecary, Potticary: William *Apotecarius, Ypotecarius* 1283–5 Oseney (O); Richard *Ipotecar'* 1297 SRY; Christopher *Potticary* 1591 Oxon (W). ME *apotecarie*, OFr *apotecaire*, MedLat *apothēcārius* 'storekeeper' (c1386 NED). Originally one who kept a store for spices, drugs and preserves, later one who prepared and sold drugs for medical purposes.

Potisman: *v.* POTMAN

Potkin, Potkins: William *Potechin* 1166 P (Nf); Roger, Reyner *Potekin* 1191 P (Nf), 1221 *ElyA* (Sf). 'Little Philip', from *Pot*, an aphetic form of *Philipot*, plus *-kin. v.* POTT.

Potman, Potisman: Nigellus *filius Poteman* 1185 Templars (K); *Poteman de Rokesakere* 1258 ArchC iii; Stephen, William *Poteman* 1296 SRSx, 1327 *SR* (Ess). Either 'servant of *Pott*' (*v.* POTKIN, POTT), or synonymous with POTTER and *potmaker*. cf. Richard *le Potmaker* 1297 Wak. The earliest example may mean 'son of the potman or potter'. The second example of the personal name is probably an original nickname. A personal name compounded of a French pet-form and English *-man* is unusual. cf. Richard *Potemay* 1332 SRSx, 'maid or servant of *Pot*'. *v.* MAY.

Pott, Pot, Potts: (i) Godwin, Richard *Pot* 1115 Winton (Ha), c1180 ArchC vi; Petronilla *Potes*

1311 ColchCt; Roger *Potte* 1352 ib.; William *Pottes* 1540 Whitby (Y). An aphetic form of *Philipot* 'little Philip' or metonymic for POTTER, 'a maker of pots'. (ii) Richard *de la Potte, Attepotte* 1221 Cur, 1228 Pat (Sx); Gilbert *atte Potte* 1332 SRSr. Margaret *atte Potte* (1296 SRSx) lived at either Pothill Fm or Potcommon in West Grinstead (Sussex). This is OE *pott* 'pot' used topographically of 'a hole or pit'. cf. Pott Hall (NRYorks) and *v.* MELS 156.

Pottage: John *Potage* 1296 SRSx. Metonymic for POTTINGER.

Pottell, Pottle: Durant, Richard *Potel* 1243 AssSo; 1279 RH (Bk). *Pot-el,* a diminutive of *Pot. v.* POTT. cf. the double diminutive *Potelinus* 1192 P (Lo), Mosse *Potelin* 1198 P (He).

Potter: Seuard *le potter* 1172 Gilb (L); Geoffrey *Poter* 1196 Cur (Lei); John *le Potier* 1197 P (Ess); Lambert *le Pottur* 1214 Cur (Ess). Usually late OE *pottere* 'potter', occasionally OFr *potier,* AFr **poteor.* A maker of earthenware vessels or of metal pots. The potter was sometimes also a bell-founder.

Potterell, Potterill: *v.* PUTTERILL
Potticary: *v.* POTHECARY
Pottinger: Walter *le Potagier* 1300 LoCt; Walter *le Potager* 1321 ParlWrits (O); John *Potyngar, Petynger* 1356, 1373 ColchCt. OFr *potagier* 'a maker or seller of pottage', a thick soup or broth (1572 NED). For the intrusive *n,* cf. MESSENGER, PASSENGER. *v.* POTTAGE.

Pottiphar: *v.* PETTIFER
Pottle: *v.* POTTELL
Pottock: *v.* PUTTOCK
Potvin, Potwin: *v.* POIDEVIN
Pouch: Simon, Thomas *Poche* 1327 SRWo. ME *pouche* 'pouch', by metonymy for POUCHER. Occasionally this may denote a member of the Society of *Pulci* or *Pouche* of Florence, frequent traders with London: Bernard *de la Pouche* 1319 SRLo, *de Pouches* of Florence 1330 Cl, *Pouche* of Lumbardia 1343 Cl.

Poucher: Philip, Robert *Poucher* 1275 RH (Sf), 1317 MESO (Lei). A derivative of ME, ONFr *pouche* 'pouch', a pouchmaker (1401 NED). cf. Richard *Pouchemaker* 1349 FrY.

Pouck: *v.* POOK
Pougher: A derivative of OE *pohha* 'a bag', synonymous with *poghwebbe.* cf. John *le Pogh-webbesone* 1306 AssSt, 'son of Poughwebbe', the weaver of bags.

Poulson, Poulsom, Poulsum: *v.* POLSON
Poulter: Aunger *le Poltur* 1222 Cur (Sr); Osbert *le puleter* 1230 P (Sa); Gilbert *Poleter* 1234 Oseney (O); Richard *Poulter* 1666 FrY. OFr *pouletier, poletier* 'poultry-dealer' (a1400 NED).

Poultney: *v.* PULTENEY
Pound, Pounds, Pund: (i) Ralph *de Punda* 1242 Fees (Ha); Nicholas *Attepounde* 1270 Eynsham (O). OE *pund* 'enclosure'. 'Dweller by the pound' or 'man in charge of the pound'. cf. PINDAR. (ii) Henry, William *Pund* 1206 P (K), 1221 Cur (Nth); Stephen *Pound* 1279 RH (C). Forms are

too early and too frequent for this to be for *atte pounde.* On the analogy of other names it should be metonymic for POUNDER which would then mean 'maker or seller of *pounds*'. This *pound* must be OE *pund* 'a weight' and *pounder* 'a maker of weights'.

Pounder: Gregory *le pundere* 1176 P (We); Hugo, William *Punder(e)* 1183 Boldon, 1212 Cur (Y). In the west midlands and the south ME *pundere* is for PINDAR and this form is used in the Boldon Book. With the exception of one from Sussex, all the examples of *punder* in Thuresson are from counties where *pinder* would appear as ME *pinder* or *pender* and are from ME *pounde* 'to impound', 'impounder', hence 'pinder'. All may be toponymics, 'dweller by the pound'. *Pounder* may also be 'maker of weights' (*v.* POUND) or occasionally, metonymic for *pundermaker:* Peter, William *le Pundermaker(e)* 1286, 1303 MESO (Nf), a maker of punders or auncels (a kind of balance).

Pountney, Poutney: *v.* PULTENEY
Powdrill: *v.* PUTTERILL
Powe: *v.* PAW
Powell, Poel: (i) Philip *ap Howel* 1285 Ch (Radnor); Hugh *Apowell* 1524 KentW; Richard *ap Hoell* 1544 AD v (Flint). An aphetic form of Welsh *ap Howell* 'son of Howel'. *v.* HOWEL. (ii) The seal of John *Paul* 1296 AD v (Sr) bears the legend S. JOH'IS POWEL. *v.* PAUL. (iii) Ralph *ate Powel* 1288 RamsCt (Hu). 'Dweller by the pool.' *v.* POOL. cf. Jordan *de Powella* 1184 P (Wa), John *de Pawel* 1339 Oseney (O). These unidentified place-names probably have a different etymology.

Power: *v.* POOR
Powick, Powicke: William *de Powic* 1202 FFY; Goda *de Powic'* 1221 AssWo. From Powick (Worcs).

Powis, Powys: Ernald *de Powis* c1148 EngFeud (He). From Powis, an ancient district in North Wales.

Powle, Powles: *v.* PAUL
Powter: *v.* PEUTHERER
Poxon: *v.* POGSON
Poynder: Isabella *le Puynder* 1279 RH (Bk). Identical with PINDAR. *uy* denotes the long front rounded *u*-sound from OE *y.* The surname may also be for POYNER, with intrusive *d.*

Poyner, Poynor, Punyer: Geoffrey *le Poinnur* (*Poignur*) 1220 Cur (Ess); William *le Poinur, le Pungneur* (*Puinur*) 1230 P (He, Y); R. *Poyner* 1283 SRSf; Richard *Punyer* 1327 Pinchbeck (Sf). OFr *poigneor* 'fighter'. cf. CHAMPION.

Poynton: *v.* POINTON
Poyntz: *v.* POINTS
Poyser, Poyzer, Peiser, Peizer, Piser, Pyser, Pyzer, Poser: Simon *le Peser* 1198 P (K); Elyas *Poyser* 1219 AssY; Josceus *le Pesur* 1224 Cur (K); William, John *Poser* 1275 RH (K), 1296 SRSx. AFr *peiser, poiser,* OFr *peseor* 'weigher', official in charge of the weighing machine. cf. I. *de la Payserie* 1317 Oseney (O).

Prater: *v.* PREATER
Pratt, Prett, Pritt: Wlfric *Prat,* Withmer' *Pret*

1179 Seals (Sf); Ædmund *Pret* 1192 P (Berks); Dereman *le Prat* 1198 Cur (K); Richard *Pritte* 1295 ParlR (Ess); William *le Pritte* 1332 SRSr. Harrison, Tengvik and PN Bk 46 derive this from OE *prætt* 'a trick'. The earliest example is Lefwinus *Prat* c1080 OEByn which the document explains '(id est) *Astutus*, quod ab inimicis saepe captus caute evaserit'. This is explained in NED as from an unrecorded adjective OE *prætt 'cunning, astute', the existence of which is supported by the forms *le Prat*, *le Pritte*.

Pray: Willelmus *de Prato* 1176 P (Do); Nicholas *de Pre* 1269 AssSo; Henry *de la Preye* 1279 RH (O). From residence near a meadow, OFr *pray*, Fr *pré*, from Lat *prātum* 'meadow'.

Prayer: Robert *de Praiers* 1161 P (Sx); John *de Prayers* 1306 FFEss; Thomas *Praeres* 1316 FA (Sx). From Presles (Calvados), *Praelliae* 1198, *Praeriae* 1269 (ANF).

Preacher: William *le precher* c1208 FrLeic; Hugo *le Prechur* 1247 AssBeds; Hugh *Precheour* 1297 SRY. OFr *precheor* 'preacher', probably a derogatory nickname.

Preater, Pretor, Prater: Willelmus *pretor* c1150 DC (L). Latin *praetor* used in the sense of 'reeve': Robertus *Pretor, Praepositus* 1208 Cur (Gl).

Precious, Pretious: *Preciosa* 1203 Cur (Herts); *Preciosa Potewyne* 1279 RH (C); Willelmus *Precios*' 1301 SRY; John *Precious* 1327 SRSf. Lat *Preciosa* 'of great value', used as a woman's name.

Preece, Prees: (i) Philip *de Pres* 1251 AssSt; Richard *de Prees* 1289 AssCh. From Prees (Salop) or Preese (Lancs). (ii) Griffin *ap Res, Apres* 1309, 1323 ParlWrits; John *Aprees* 1414 LLB I. Welsh *ap Rhys* 'son of *Rhys*'. (iii) Richard, Leticia *Pres* 1243 AssSo, 1303 FA (Sf). These forms are too early to be regarded as short for *ap Res* and unlikely to be associated with the Shropshire and Lancashire place-names. They may be ME 'Prees, or thronge. *Pressura*'. PromptParv.

Preist: *v.* PRIEST

Prendergast, Prendergrass, Prendergrast, Prenderguest, Pendergast: (i) Robert *de Prendergat*' 1225 Cur (L); Adam *de Prendrogest* 1354 FFY. From Prendergast near Haverfordwest (Pembroke), but these examples are perhaps rather to be connected with the following. (ii) Waldoev *de Prendergest* c1170 Black (Kelso); Adam *de Prendergest* c1240 ib.; Henry *de Prendregast, de Prendergest* 1296, 1325 ib. From Prenderguest Farm near Ayton (Berwick), which takes its name from the Welsh Prendergast.

Prentice, Prentis, Prentiss: John *Prentiz* 1295 Barnwell (c); Adam *Prentys* 1297 MinAcctCo. An aphetic form of ME, OFr *aprentis* 'apprentice', a learner of a craft. Roger and John *Prentiz* were assessed in the subsidy of 1319 (SRLo) and were presumably no longer apprentices. Either the surname had already become hereditary or it was a nickname as Ekwall suggests. cf. John Kyng called *Prentiz*, mercer 1350 LLB F, where *Kyng* appears to be the real surname, *mercer* the occupation, and *Prentiz* a nickname.

Prescot, Prescott, Preskett, Priscott: Gilbert *de Prestecota* 1175 P (D); Richard *de Prestecot* 1192 WhC (La). From residence or employment at the priests' house (OE *cot(e)* 'cottage', in place-names sometimes 'manor'), as at Prescot (Lancs, Oxon) or Prescott (Glos). In Devonshire there are three Prescotts, four Priestacotts, two Prestacotts, and one Pristacott.

Preskett: *v.* PRESCOT
Presland: *v.* PRIESTLAND
Presley: *v.* PRIESTLEY
Presman: *v.* PRIESTMAN
Press: *v.* PRIEST
Presser: *v.* PRESTER

Pressey: William *Presthey* 1377 AssEss. 'Dweller by the priests' enclosure' (OE *(ge)hæg*), as at Priesthaywood Fm in Wappenham (Northants).

Pressick, Prissick: Robert *de Prestewyke* 1296 SRSx; William *Presike* 1538 Riev (Y). From Prestwick (Bucks, Northumb, Surrey) or from employment at the priests' dairy-farm (OE *wīc*). Prissick Fm in Marton (NRYorks) is 'prieststream'. In Scotland, from Prestwick (Ayrshire): Bartram *de Prestwyc* c1272 Black (Paisley).

Pressland: *v.* PRIESTLAND
Pressley: *v.* PRIESTLEY
Pressman: *v.* PRIESTMAN
Pressney: *v.* PRESTNEY
Presswood: *v.* PRIESTWOOD
Prest: *v.* PRIEST
Prestage, Prestedge: *v.* PRESTWICH

Prester, Presser: Henry *le Prestre, le Prester* 1228, 1248 AssSt; Edmund *le Prestre* c1235 HPD (Ess). OFr *prestre* 'priest'. *v.* PRIEST.

Prestidge, Prestige: *v.* PRESTWICH

Prestney: Richard *de Prestonheye, Prestney* (1291 For, 1346 FA) came from Prestney's Fm in Great Horkesley (Essex).

Prestoe, Pristo: Eva *de Presthall* 1278 AssLa. From a lost place *Prestall* in Deane (Lancs), the name of which survives in Presto Lane.

Preston: Peter *de Prestun* 1185 Templars (Y); Laurence *Preston* 1327 SRSx. From one of the numerous places named Preston. *v.* PRIEST.

Prestwich, Prestage, Prestedge, Prestidge, Prestige: Thomas *de Prestwyc* 1230 P (La). From Prestwich (Lancs). *Prestage*, etc. show the local pronunciation. cf. Swanage, *Suuanwic* DB.

Prestwood, Preswood: *v.* PRIESTWOOD
Pretheroe: *v.* PROTHERO
Pretious: *v.* PRECIOUS
Pretlove: *v.* PRITLOVE
Pretor: *v.* PREATER
Prett: *v.* PRATT

Prettjohn, Prettejohn, Prettejohns, Prettyjohn, Prettyjohns: *Prestreiohan* 1219 AssL; *Prestre Johan* 1301 SRY; John *Prestrejohan* 1346 Pat (So). That England was fully abreast of the news of the world is shown by the occurrence of the name Prestreiohan borne by a Lincolnshire attorney. Tales of a great priest-king who ruled in central Asia were current in the twelfth century in Europe. He is first mentioned by a western chronicler in the middle of the century when Otto of Friesing tells how Johannes Presbyter won a great victory over the Persians and Medes. Between 1165 and 1177 a forged letter purporting to come from him was circulated in Europe. Some rumour of this must have reached Lincolnshire and caused at least one English child to be christened by the name of this suppositious eastern king (Sir Denison Ross in *Travel and Travellers of the Middle Ages*, ed. A. P. Newton, 174–94). No early example of *Prettyjohn* has been noted. The occurrence of *Prestrejohan* as a surname in 1346 suggests that this is the real origin. The name can never have been common. The meaning of *Prestre* would be known and the name assimilated to the later French form, becoming *Pretrejohn, Pretterjohn,* a form no longer suggesting *Prestrejohn* whose story was probably by then unfamiliar to the possessors of the name and they made it intelligible as *Prettyjohn*.

Pretty, Pritty: Robert *Prytty* 1327 SRSf; William *Pritty* 1428 FA (Sx); Thomas, Agnes *Praty* 1479 LLB L, 1524 SRSf. OE *prættig* 'crafty, cunning'.

Prettyman, Pretyman: Thomas *Pratyman, Pretyman* 1524, 1568 SRSf. Perhaps 'cunning man' or 'servant of a man named *Pretty*'. But cf. PRETTJOHN.

Prevost, Le Prevost: John *le Prevost* 1418 DKR 41. *Prevost* is a Huguenot name, *Le Prevost* a Guernsey one. Owing to its frequency, Dauzat regards the French *Prévost* as a nickname rather than from the office of provost.

Prew, Prow, Prue: Robert *Prue* 1270 AssSo; Robert *Prowe* 1276 RH (C); Ellis *Prew* 1280 AssSo; John *le Proo* 1332 SRSx. ME *prew, prue*, OFr *prou, preu* 'valiant, doughty'.

Prewett, Prewitt, Pruett: Matthew *Pruet* 1202 P (So); Richard *Prouet, Pruet, Prowet* 1278, 1280 LLB A. A diminutive of PREW.

Prewse: *v.* PROWSE

Price, Prise, Pryce, Pryse: (i) Jorwerth *ap Reys* 1393 LoPleas; John *Aprice* 1492 AD iii (Pembroke). Welsh *ap Rhys* 'son of *Rhys*'. (ii) Robert *Price* 1297 MinAcctCo; Richard *Prys* 1320 FFEss. ME, OFr *pris* 'price', metonymic for a fixer of prices. cf. *Prysare*, or settar at price, ynn a merket, or oþer placys; *Prysin'*, or settyn' a pryce (PromptParv).

Prichard(s): *v.* PRITCHARD

Pricher, Prickman: *v.* PRYKE

Prickett: William, Laurence *Priket* 1296 SRSx, 1325 AssSt. A nickname from the prickett, a buck in his second year (ME *priket*).

Pride, Pryde: John *le Pride* 1208 P (D); Richard, Robert *Pride* 1221 AssSa, AssWo. No doubt often a nickname or pageant-name from ME *pride* 'pride', but also clearly an adjective. The surname appears particularly in the Welsh border counties and may be from Welsh *prid* 'precious, dear'.

Prideaux: Nicholas *de Pridias* 1182 P (Co). From Prideaux (Cornwall).

Pridham, Prodham, Prudhomme: Gilbert *Prodhome, Prudume* 1176, 1197 P (Sr, W); Roger *Prodomme, Prodhomme* 1284, 1326 FFEss. OFr *prudhomme* 'upright, honest man; expert', used in the 13th century to distinguish the 'wiser' or 'lesser folk' (*prudhommes*) from the 'greater folk' or general mass. Pridhamsleigh (Devon) owes its name to John *Prodhomme* (1281 PN D 520).

Prier: *v.* PRIOR

Priest, Preist, Prest, Prestt, Press, Prust: Ælfsige *Preost* 963 OEByn (Herts); Asci *Preost* 1066 DB (Nf); Baldwin, Rodbert *Prest* 1176 P (L), 1188 BuryS (Sf); Robert *le Prest* 1243 AssSo; William *Prost* 1279 RH (O); Henry *Prust* 1279 RH (O), 1327 MEOT (Ha); Robert *le Preest* 1296 SRSx; Hugh *le Prist* 1327 ib.; John *le Preost* 1327 SRSo; Walter *Preyst* 1332 SRSx; Simon *le Prust* 1353 AssSt. OE *prēost* 'priest', in early examples denoting office but later usually a nickname for a man of 'priestly' appearance or behaviour or, no doubt, often for one of a most unpriestly character. *v.* PRESTER. As with *Parsons* and *Vickers*, we also find forms with an elliptic genitive and with *-son*: (i) Thomas *le Prestis* 1326 AD iv (Wa); Peter *Prestes* 1332 AD ii (Do); Cristina *Prestes* 1327 SRSo; 'servant of the priest'. (ii) Sarra *atte Prestes* 1327 SRSx; Richard *del Prestes* 1332 SRCu; 'servant at the priest's'. (iii) Thomas *fiz al prestre* 1230 Pat (Lo); William *le Prestesson* 1293 FFEss; Walter *Preesteson* 1316 Wak (Y); Adam *Prystesonne* 1327 SRSf; Thomas *Prestson* 1332 SRCu; 'son of the priest'. These do not seem to have survived, though both Bardsley and Harrison give *Presson*. The difficult combination of final consonants in *Prestes, Prests* has probably been assimilated to *Press*. In *Prestson*, a similar change would give *Presson*; an intrusive *t* would give *Preston* (cf. HOUSTON) and this common name (and the less common *Priston*) probably often means 'priest's son'. *Prestson* may have been simplified direct to *Preston*. *Prust*, which is rare and has been noted only in Somerset and London (where all varieties arrive), preserves the South-Western and West Midland ME rounded vowel, written *u, o, eo*.

Priestland, Presland, Pressland: Roger *de Preslond* 1305 FFEss. From residence near the priests' land as at Priestland Copse in Bampton (Devon), Priestlands in Horley (Surrey), which belonged to Reigate Priory, or Pressland in Hatherleigh (Devon).

Priestley, Priestly, Presley, Presslee, Presslie, Pressley, Pressly, Prisley: Samson *de Presteleia* 1198 P (Beds); Richard *de Presteley* 1297 Wak (Y); John *de Presle* 1311 LLB D; Richard *de Prestele* 1327 SRSx. 'Dweller by the priests' wood or clearing.' cf. Priestley (Beds, Herts, WRYorks), Prestley Wood (Wilts), Presley's Plantation in Norton (Notts), *Prisley* c1840.

Priestman, Presman, Pressman: Robert *Prestman* 1275 RH (Y); William *Prestesman* 1283 SRSf; Henry *le Prestesmon, le Prestemon* 1332 SRSt, 1333 AssSt; William *Priestman* 1393

NottBR. 'Servant of the priest' (OE *prēostesmann)
or 'of the priests' (*prēostamann).

Priestwood, Preswood, Presswood: William *de
Prestewude* 1176 P (St). From Prestwood (Bucks,
Sussex) or 'dweller by the priests' wood'.

Prigg: Henry *Prig* 1186 P (Wo); Simon, Adam
Prigge 1210 Cur (C), 1274 Wak (Y). Probably a
voiced form of ME *prikke. v.* PRYKE.

Prime: William, Ralph *Prime* 1275 RH (L),
1296 SRSx; Adam *Prymme* 1286 ForSt. OFr
prim(e) 'fine, delicate'.

Prin, Prinn, Prynne: William *Prin* 1275 RH
(Berks); Matilda *Pryn* 1275 SRWo; Nicholas
Prinne 1327 SRSx. OFr *prin* (Lat *primus*) 'first,
superior; small, slender'.

Prince, Prins: Robert *Prince* 1177 P (Cu);
Robert *le Prins* 1327 SRSx. Fr *prince* 'prince', a
nickname.

Prior, Prier, Pryer, Pryor: Roger *Priur* 1205 Cur
(Sf); Roger *le Priur* 1237 FFC; Nicholas *le Prior*
1268 AssSo; Robert *Pryer* 1274 RH (Ess). OE
prior or OFr *priur, priour* 'prior', originally a
surname of office, later a nickname. For Editha
le Priores 1327 SRSo, William *atte Priours* 1327
SR (Ess), and Thomas *Priorman* 1332 SRCu, cf.
PRIEST.

Priscott: *v.* PRESCOT
Prisley: *v.* PRIESTLEY
Prissick: *v.* PRESSICK
Pristo: *v.* PRESTOE

Pritchard, Prichard, Prichards: William *Prichard*
or *Ap-Richard* 1521 Oxon. Welsh *ap Richard* 'son
of *Richard*'.

Pritchet, Pritchett, Pritchatt: John *Prichet* 1309
FFSf, 1319 SRLo. Probably for PRICKETT, with
palatal *ch* for *k*.

Pritlove, Pretlove: Richard *Prykkeloue* 1296
SRSx; Alexander *Prikeloue* 1297 MinAcctCo. ME
prikke and OFr *love* 'wolf', 'prick wolf', a nickname, no doubt, for a hunter and killer of wolves.
cf. John *Prikehors* 1379 PTY 'prick horse', for a
hard rider, John *Prikehert* 1230 P (Sf), a hunter of
harts.

Pritt: *v.* PRATT
Pritty: *v.* PRETTY

Probert, Probets, Propert: Philip *ab Robert* Hy
3 AD iii (He); John *ap Ed ap Dafydd ap Robert*
1538 Chirk; Thomas *Uprobarte* 1540 Bardsley;
Joseph *Probert* 1792 ib. Welsh *ap Robert* 'son of
Robert'.

Probin, Probyn, Brobyn: John *Probyn* 1550
SxWills; Edward *Up Robyn* 1565 ShefA. Welsh *ab,
ap Robin* 'Son of *Robin*'.

Prockter, Procter, Proctor: Johanna *la Proketour*
1301 SRY; John *Proketour* 1326 FeuDu. ME
prok(e)tour, a contraction of Lat *procurator*
'manager, agent', commonly used of an attorney
in a spiritual court (c1380 NED). cf. Johannes *le
Procurator* 1279 AssNb.

Prodgers, Proger: John *ap Roger* 1538 Chirk;
Charles *Proger* 1607 Bardsley. Welsh *ap Roger*
'Son of *Roger*'.

Prodham: *v.* PRIDHAM

Profitt, PROFIT: *v.* PROPHET
Propert: *v.* PROBERT

Prophet, Proffitt, Profit: William *le Profete*
1220 Cur (Bk); Gunnora *Prophete* 1327 *SR* (Ess).
OFr *prophete* 'prophet', a nickname.

**Prothero, Protheroe, Protherough, Pretheroe,
Pluthero, Prydderch, Prytherch, Prytherick:** Wil-
liam *Prythergh* or *Protherugh* or *Protherough* 1581
Oxon; Rowland *Prythero* alias *Prothero* alias
Prytherch 1725 DKR 41 (Brecon). Welsh *ap
Riderch* 'son of *Riderch*' 'the reddish brown'.

Proud, Proude: Toui *Pruda, Prude* 1033 OEByn;
Orgar *le Prude* 1125 (c1425) LLB C; Richard
Prude 1185 Templars (Sa); William *le Proude* 1275
SRWo. Late OE *prūt, prūd* 'proud, arrogant'.

Proudfoot, Proudfoot: Gilbert *Proudfoot, Prudfot, Prutfoot* 1114–30 Rams, c1130 ELPN; Geoffrey *Prudfot* 12th MedEA (Nf); John *Prutfot*
1203 P (Ha). OE *prūd (prūt)* 'proud' and *fōt* 'foot',
'one who walks with a haughty step'. Gilbert
Proudfoot was sheriff of London c1140 and 'It is
interesting to find that the first known bearer of
the surname was a sheriff, thus a person who might
be justified in walking with a proud step' (ELPN).

Proudlove, Proudler: Thomas *Prudelove* 1289
AssCh. A nickname. cf. TRUELOVE, TRUSLOVE.

Proudman: William *Proudman* 1327 SRSf.
'Proud man' or 'servant of *Proud*'. cf. Thomas
Prudswain 1223 Cur (Sr), Olive *Prodemay* 1327
SRSf.

Prouse: *v.* PROWSE

Proust: Alan *Prouste* 1275 RH (L); Robert,
Simon *le Preust* 1297 MinAcctCo, 1314 AD iv
(Nth). Contractions of ME *prevost, provost* 'pro-
vost'. cf. Fr *Proust, Leproust*.

Prout: William *Prute* 1207 P (D); Thomas *le
Prute* 1274 RH (Gl); Robert *Proute* 1280 AssSo.
ME *proute* 'proud'.

Provan, Provand, Proven: Richard *de Prebenda*
c1190 Black; Stephen *Provand* 1489 ib.; Robert
Provane 1549 ib. From the lands of Provan, formerly a possession of the prebendary of Barlanark,
one of the canons of Glasgow Cathedral (Black).

Province, Provins: William *de Provinc* 12th DC
(L); Ralph *de Prouinz* 1202 P (Sx). 'Man from
Provence.'

Provost, Provest, Provis: Eanstan *Prafost* a925
OEByn (D); Uui *Provast* 11th ib. (D); Goscelin
Provost 1200 Cur (O); Geoffrey *le Provost* 1206
Cur (L); William *le Pruvost* 1219 Cur (Ha);
Richard *Provest* 1445 FrY; John *Provess*, William
Provise 1535, 1545 RochW. OE *prafost*, AFr *pro-
vost* 'provost'.

Prow: *v.* PREW

Prowse, Prouse, Prewse, Pruce: Richard *le Pruz*
1207 Cur (Herts); Adam *Pruce* 1225 AssSo; William *le Prouz* 1275 RH (D); Roger *le Prus* 1275
SRWo; William *Prous* 1279 RH (O). ME, OFr
prous, prouz 'valiant, doughty'.

Prudence: Robertus *filius Prudence* 1206 P (Sr);
Prudencia de Pavely 1210 Cur (Nf); Hugh, Adam
Prudence 1203 FFC, 1206 P (Sr). *Prudence*, Lat
prudentia 'prudence', a woman's name.

Prudhomme: v. PRIDHAM
Prue: v. PREW
Prust: v. PRIEST
Pryce, Pryse: v. PRICE
Prydderch: v. PROTHERO
Pryde: v. PRIDE
Pryer, Pryor: v. PRIOR
Pryke: William *Prike, Prikke* 1205–6 P (Wa); Geoffrey, Robert *Pricke* 1221 *Ely* (Nf), 1341 ColchCt; Alice, John *Prich*(*e*) 1295 Barnwell (C), 1327 SRC; Simon *Prike* 1340 FFSf. ME *prike, prikke* 'a point, prick', with occasional palatalized forms *priche*, also the name of a pointed weapon. The surname is probably metonymic for a maker or user of these. cf. Hamo *Pricchere* 1175 P (Do); William *Priker* 1256 AssNb; Hugh *le Prichere* 1327 *SR* (Ess); surviving as *Pricher*, and *Prickman* with the same meaning.
Prynne: v. PRIN
Prytherch, Prytherick: v. PROTHERO
Puckle, Puckell: (i) Richard *Puchel* 1200 P (Beds); Nicholas *Pokel* 1275 RH (K); John *le Pochel* 1297 MinAcctCo. OE *pūcel* 'little goblin, elf, sprite'. (ii) Robert *de Pukehole* 1296 SRSx. 'Dweller by the elf-hollow', OE *pūca, holh*.
Puddifant, Puddifin: v. POIDEVIN
Puddifer: v. PETTIFER
Puddifoot, Pudifoot, Puddefoot, Puddephat, Puddephatt, Puttifoot: Roger, Ralph *Pudifat* 1188 P (C), 1223 Cur (Herts); Herbert *Pudifot* 1212 Cur (Y); Richard *Pudifed*' 1213 Seals (O); Geoffrey *Putifat* 1221 ElyA (Sf); Robert *Podifat* 1288 LLB A, 1332 LoPleas. It is clear that the second element is not *foot* but *fat*, probably OE *fæt* 'vessel, vat'. The first is probably the dialectal *puddy, poddy* 'round and stout in the belly' from the Germanic root **pud*(*d*) 'to swell, bulge' found in *pudding*, OE *puduc* 'a wen' and the dialectal *pod* 'a large protuberant belly'. cf. LG *puddig* 'thick, stumpy'. An early English example may be (Rotberd) *Puddig* c1100–30 OEByn (D), though this may be merely a bad form for *Pudding*. The meaning of the compound is 'round and stout-vessel, cask, barrel', a nickname for a man with a prominent paunch, a parallel to PAUNCEFOOT and reminiscent of the 'barrel-bellied' monks mentioned under BARRELL.
Pudding: Ailword *Pudding* c1100–30 OEByn (D); Alured, Hugo *Pudding* 1176 P (Nth), 1219 AssY; John *Poddyng* 1297 MinAcctCo. Probably an *-ing* derivative of the root **pud*(*d*) discussed under PUDDIFOOT, a nickname for a round, stout man. The surname was common and may also be a nickname for a butcher, either from the sausages or puddings he sold (cf. the Yorkshire 'black-pudding') or from the puddings or offal from his slaughter-house, a perpetual nuisance to his neighbours, which gave name to Pudding Lane in London.
Pude: John *Pudde* 1186 P (W); Gilbert *Pud* 1213 Cur (Co). A nickname 'round and stout'. cf. PUDDIFOOT.
Pugh, Pughe, Pew: Richard *ap Hughe* 1563 AD

v (Montgomery); John *Apew, Pew* 1642 Bardsley. Welsh *ap Hugh* 'Son of *Hugh*'.
Pullan, Pullen, Pullein, Pulleine, Pulleyn, Pullin: Richard *Pulein* 1166 P (Nf), 1195 FF (Beds); Geoffrey *Poleyn* 1266 AssSo; Thomas *Pullan* 1509 GildY; John *Pullen* 1601 FrY. OFr *poulain* 'colt'.
Pullar, Puller: (i) Ralph *pullehare* 1189 Sol; William *Pullehare*, John *Pullehar* 1327 SRLei; Thomas *Pullehare* 1367 IpmW. A nickname, 'pull hare', cf. Alexander *Pullegandre* 1249 AssW; Roger *Pullegos* c1170 ELPN. (ii) John *de Pulhore* 1339 Black (Du); Henry *Pulour* 1379 ib. (Perth); Robert *Pullour* 1474 ib. 'Dweller by the bank of the pool or creek', OE *pull* and *ōra*.
Pullinger, Pillinger: v. BULLINGER
Pulman, Pullman: John *Pulman* 1525 SRSx; John *Pullman*, Roger *Pulman* 1642 PrD. 'Dweller by the pool', OE *pull* and *mann*.
Pulteney, Poultney, Pountney, Poutney: John *de Pulteneye* 1334 LLB E. From Poultney (Leics), DB *Pontenei*.
Pumfrett: v. POMFRET
Pumfrey, Pumphery, Pumphrey, Pumphreys, Pomfrey, Pomphrey: Edward *ap Humfrey* 1575 AD v (Sa); Anable *Pumfrey* 1633 Bardsley. Welsh *ap Humphrey* 'Son of *Humphrey*'. The surname may also be a doublet of POMFRET: John *Pounfrey* 1297 MinAcctCo (Co). Here, *Pounfrey* is for *Pountfreyt*. v. also BOUMPHREY.
Pummery: v. POMEROY
Punch: Godfrey, Philip *Punch*(*e*) 1181 P, 1275 RH (Sf); Seman *Ponche* 1327 SRSf. ONFr *Ponche*, OFr *Ponce*. v. POINTS.
Punchard, Puncher: Robert *Puncard* 1230 P (O); Oliver, Ralph *Punchard*(*e*) 1243 AssSo, 1255 Rams (Hu); Geoffrey *Puncard* alias *Punzard* 1265 Ipm (Berks); Fray *Punsard* 1279 RH (O). ONFr *Ponchard*, OFr *Ponsard*, a diminutive of *Ponce*. v. POINTS.
Pund: v. POUND
Punnett: Anna *filia Puinant* 1199 FFEss; *Puinant de Chelese* 1212 Cur (Herts); Richard *Poingiant, Pugnant, Puignant, Puinant, Puniant, Punat* 1086 DB; Roger *Puinnant, Poinant* 1194 Cur, 1196 P (Bk); John *Poygnaunt* 1278 AssSo; Thomas *Poynaunt* 1296 SRSx. Tengvik and Bardsley explain this as from OFr *puignant, poignant*, 'stinging, biting' (c1386 NED). Such a nickname and personal-name are possible. cf. MORDAUNT. The DB forms in particular, however, suggest a derivation from the present participle of OFr *poignier* 'to strike with the fist', *poignant* 'the striker, the fighter'. cf. *poniard*, a derivative of *poing* 'fist'. The surname survives in Poynatts Fm (Bucks), *Pinets* 1766 (PN Bk 179), and in Poynetts (Essex), *Poynes* 1412, *Poynattes* 1554 (PN Ess 143).
Punshon: Johannes *filius Puncon, Punzun* 1177, 1180 P (Cu); William *Puncun, Punzun* 1210 Cur (Nth). A diminutive of OFr *Ponce*. v. POINTS.
Punt: v. PONT
Punter: v. PONTER
Puntis: v. PONTIS

Punyer: v. POYNER

Purcell: Gaufridus *porcellus* 1130 P (Sr); Ralph, William *Purcel* 1159 P (St), 1230 P (Lei). OFr *pourcel* 'little pig'.

Purchas, Purchase, Purches, Purchese, Purkess, Purkis, Purkiss, Pirkis, Pirkiss, Porkiss, Porcas: William *Purchaz* 1190 P (Ess); Geoffrey *Purcaz* 1206 Cur (Ess); Roger *Purchas* 1239 Eynsham (O); William *Purkas* 1327 SRSf. OFr *purchas* 'pursuit, pillage', used as a name for messengers and couriers. Bardsley notes 'Purchase the Pursuivant' temp. Henry VI.

Purcifer: v. PERCEVAL

Purday, Purdey, Purdie, Purdy, Purdye, Purdu, Purdue: Gilbert *Purdeu* 1227 AssBeds; John *Purde* 1279 RH (C); John *Purdew, Purde* 1296, 1332 SRSx; John *Purdy* 1436 NorwW (Nf); Robert *Purdu* 1479 ib. An oath name, Fr *pour Dieu.* cf. Fr *Pourdieu* and v. PARDEW.

Purefoy: William, Henry *Parfei* 1195 FF, 1203 AssSt; Robert *Parfoy* 1296 SRSx; William *Purfey* 13th AD ii (Wa); Ralph *Perfai, Parfay* 1327, 1332 SRSx; William *Purefay* 1412 AD ii (Lei). AFr *par fei* 'by (my) faith'. *Parfoy* is central French *par foi.* The present spelling is a popular etymology, 'pure faith', which arose when *per, par* and *pur* fell together in pronunciation. cf. PURNELL and PARNALL. v. PARDEW.

Purkins: v. PARKIN

Purkiss: v. PURCHAS

Purnell: v. PARNALL

Purrier: v. PERRIER

Purry: v. PERRY

Purse: Hucche *purs* c1150 DC (L); Derewin *Purs* 1176 P (Bk). OE *purs* 'purse', by metonymy for PURSER.

Purser: Alexander *Purcir* 1279 RH (Bk); Roger *le Porser* 1299 LLB C; Adam *le Purser* 1332 SRLa. A derivative of OE *purs* 'purse', purse-maker. Robert *le Pursere* (1319 SRLo) was identical with Robert Neel, *burser* (1338 LoPleas) and was an associate of William de Borham, *pouchmaker* (1344 ib).

Pursey: v. PERCY

Purton: v. PERRITON

Purvis, Purves, Purvess: William *Purveys, Porveys, Purvys, Purvais* 1214–49, 1296 Black; Gilbert, Eva *Purveys* 1400 LLB I, 1450 NorwW (Nf); Thomas *Purvas* 1427 Black, *Purvis* 1524 SRSf; John *Parvysse* 1445 RochW. Neither Harrison nor Weekley give any evidence for their derivation from ME *parvis* 'porch' and Black's forms prove this etymology untenable. The original vowel was clearly *u* and the name goes back to AFr *purveier* 'to provide'. In 1451 John Graunger of the butlery of the Prioress of St Radegund, Cambridge, was

paid 3*s.* 'in regardo *pro officio Purvis domine*' (Rad 174), the editor explaining *Purvis* as 'a servant who acted as purveyor, *provisor*'. cf. OFr *porveor* 'provider' of supplies, especially in a hospital.

Purvey: John, Cons' *Purvey* 1279 RH (C). Either for *purveys*, with silent *s*, or metonymic for *purveyor.* cf. Alexander *Purveyance* 1623 Black.

Pury: v. PERRY

Puryer: v. PERRIER

Puscat: Robert *Pusekat* 1256 AssNb. 'Pussycat', a nickname. One example of the surname occurs in the London Telephone Directory for 1949.

Pusey: v. PIZEY

Putman: v. PITMAN

Putnam, Puttnam, Puttnum: Ralph *de Puteham* 1205 Cur (Bk). From Puttenham (Herts, Surrey).

Putt: v. PITT

Putter: John *le Putter* 1327 SRSx. 'Dweller by the pit or hollow.' cf. PITT.

Puttergill: v. PORTUGAL

Putterill, Puttrell, Potterell, Potterill, Pottrill, Powdrell, Powdrill: Roger *Putrel* 1166 RBE (Ess); Henry *Pultrel* 1180 P (Lei); Robert *Puterel, Putrell* 1199, 1200 Cur (Lei); Richard *Poterell*' 1235 Fees (Lei); William *Poutrel* 1316 AD vi (St); William *Powdrell* 1379 PTY; George *Powderhill* 1586 Oxon (Berks); Martin *Powdrill* 1592 ib. OFr *poutrel, potrel, pultrel, putrel, peutrel, poudrel,* MedLat *pultrellus,* 'a colt', probably denoting one of a lively, frisky disposition.

Puttifent: v. POIDEVIN

Puttifoot: v. PUDDIFOOT

Puttock, Puttack, Puttick, Puttuck, Pottock: Ælfricus *Puttuc* 1034 OEByn; Aluied *Pottoch* 1066 DB (So); Edricus *puttuc* 1148 Winton (Ha); John *Puttok* 1176 P (Herts); Thomas *Puttek*' 1297 MinAcctCo (Co); John *Pottock* 1332 SRSx. OE **puttoc* 'kite' (c1400 NED), 'metaphorically applied to a greedy, ravenous fellow' (Halliwell).

Putwain: v. POIDEVIN

Pyatt, Pyett, Pyott: Simon *Pyot* 1297 MinAcctCo; John *Pyet* 1308 LLB C; William *Pyatt* 1327 SRSo. A diminutive of OFr *pye* 'magpie'. v. PIE. *Pyatt* may also be a late development of *Pyard,* a pejorative from OFr *pye* and *-(h)ard*: John *Pyarde,* Nicholas *Piarde* 1327, 1332 *SR* (Ha), surviving in Pyott's Hill in Basing (Hants).

Pye: v. PIE

Pyke: v. PIKE

Pyle: v. PILE

Pymm: v. PIM

Pyne: v. PINE

Pyper: v. PIPER

Pyser, Pyzer: v. POYSER

Q

Quadling: v. CODLIN

Quaif, Quaife: William *Coyfe, Coif* 1260 AssC, 13th Gilb (L). OFr *coif* 'coif, a close-fitting cap', metonymic for *coifier* 'maker of coifs': William *Coifar* 1180 P (Bk); Bidan *le Coyfier* 1228 Cl (Ess); Geoffrey *Quayfere* 1301 SRY.

Quaile: v. QUAYLE

Qualter, Qualters, Qualtrough: Manx names for *MacWalter*: Thomas *MacWalter* 1308, *Mac-Qualtrough* 1429, *Qualtrough* 1430, *MacWhaltragh* 1511 Moore.

Quant: William *le Qwointe, le Coynte* 1254–67 Rams (Beds); Richard *le Queynte* 1256 Seals (Ha). OFr *cointe* (*quoint, cuinte*), ME *cointe, queynte, quante* 'wise, skilled, clever', also 'cunning, crafty' (a1225 NED).

Quantrell, Quantrill, Quarntrill, Quintrell: Ailric *Cointerell*, *Cuinterel* 1176, 1180 P (Co, K); William *Cuinterell* (*Cuonterel*) 1214 Cur (So); William *Queinterell* 1219 AssY; Adam *le Coynterel* 1281 QW (L); Robert *Quyntrel* 1332 SRSx. OFr *cointerel* 'a beau, a fop'.

Quarrell, Quarrelle: Osbert, Yvo *Quarel* 1175–6 P (So, Hu). OFr *quarel, quarrel* 'a short, heavy, square-headed arrow or bolt for cross-bow or arbalest' (a1225 NED). Metonymic for an arbalester.

Quarrie, Quarry: (i) Henry *de la Quarrere* 1279 RH (O); William *atte Quarere* 1332 SRSx. OFr *quarrere*, ME *quarer(e)* 'quarry' (13.. NED). (ii) Thomas *atte Querre* 1428 FA (Sr). ME *quarey, querry*, variants of *quarrer* (c1420 NED). Metonymic for QUARRIER. (iii) Alice Relicta *le Quarye* 1296 SRSx; Thomas *Quarry* 1524 SRSf. OFr *quarré*, ME *quarre* 'square; squarely built, stout' (1297 NED). 'Quarry, thykk mann, or womann, *Corpulentus, grossus*' PromptParv. (iv) The very common Manx *Quarry* is for *MacGuaire* 'son of *Guaire*': *MacQuarres* 1504 *MacWharres* 1511, *Quarry* 1684 Moore.

Quarrier: Henry *le Quarreur* 1275 SRWo; Henry *le Quarreour* 1324 Wak (Y); Walter *Quarer* 1333 MESO (Ha). OFr *quarreour, quarrier* 'quarry-man' (c1375 NED).

Quartermain, Quartermaine, Quarterman, Quatermain, Quatermaine: Herbert *Quatremains*, Robertus *Quatuormanus* 1187 Merton (O); Herbert *Quatermayns* 1230 P (O). AFr *quatremayns, quatremans* 'four hands', i.e. mail-fisted.

Quayle, Quail, Quaile: (i) *MacFayle* 1511, *Mac-*

Quayle, Quayle 1540 Moore. A Manx form of MACFAIL. (ii) Simon *Quayle* 1327 SRC. OFr *quaiłle* 'quail', noted for its supposed amorous disposition and timidity.

Quenell, Quennell, Quinnell: *Cvenild* monialis 1086 DB (Gl); *Quenilda* uxor Gimpi eHy 2 DC (L); *Quenill* 1221 AssWa; *Quenilla* (*Quenild*) 1221 Cur (Nf); William *Quenell* 1201 AssSo; Thomas *Quenild* 1275 RH (Nf); Richard *Quynel* 1286 Wak (Y). OE *Cwēnhild* (f) 'woman-war', first recorded in the 11th century.

Quick, Quicke: (i) Robert *Quic* 1279 RH (C); William *Quik* 1282 FFEss. OE *cwic* 'nimble, lively'. (ii) Gedmær *on Cuike*, Ricard *a Cuik* 1100–30 OEByn (D). From Cowick Barton (Devon) or Quickbury (Essex), DB *Cuica*. (iii) Afwardus *de Quike* 1179 P (Y); John *de Quyke* 1278 AssLa; Gilbert *de la Quyk* 1297 SRY; Adam *del Quyk* 1313 Wak (Y). From Quick Mere in Saddleworth (WRYorks), a lost Quick in Prescott (Lancs), or from residence near a poplar or aspen. cf. OE *cwicbēam* 'quickbeam, poplar', *cwictrēow* 'aspen'.

Quickly: William *Quiklich* 1260 AssC. 'Nimbly, in lively fashion.'

Quilliam, a Manx name from Irish *MacWilliam* 'William's son'.

Quilter: Richard *le cuilter* c1179 Bart (Lo); Ralph *le Cuiltier* 1186 P (Wa); William *le Quilter* 12th DC (L). A derivative of OFr *cuilte, coilte* 'a quilt', 'a maker of quilts or mattresses' (1563 NED).

Quincey, Quinsee, Quinsey, De Quincey: Saer *de Quincy* 1153–63 Templars (O); Henry *Quenci* Hy 2 DC (L). Saer de *Quincy*, ancestor of the earls of Winchester, came from Cuinchy (Pas-de-Calais). v. ANF. The name may have been reinforced by immigrants from Quincy-sous-Sénart (Seine-et-Oise) or Quincy-Voisins (Seine-et-Marne).

Quine, Quinn: *Mac Cuinn* 1027, Luke *Mac Quyn* 1403, *Quine* 1504. From *Mac Coinn* or *Mac Cuinn* 'son of *Conn*', from Ir *conn* 'counsel' (Moore). A Manx name.

Quinnell: v. QUENELL

Quinney: *Quinnye* 1429 Moore. Manx for *Mac-Connaidh* 'son of Connaidh' 'the crafty'.

Quinton: (i) Gladewin, Walter *de Quenton* 1176 P (Bk), 1221 AssWo. From Quinton (Glos, Northants, Worcs). (ii) Hugo *de Sancto Quintino* 1086 DB (Ha); Robert *de Quentyn* 1268 AssSo. From Saint-Quentin (La Manche) or, possibly,

286

Saint-Quentin-en-Tourmont (Somme). (iii) *Quintinus* 1086 DB; *Quintinus* Taleboth 1200 Cur (Bk); Geoffrey, William *Quintin* 1205 P (O), 1222 Cur (W); William *Quentyn* 1262 FFEss. OFr *Quentin*, Lat *Quintinus* 'fifth', popular in France from the cult of St Quentin of Amiens, and brought to England by the Normans. This was the common source of the medieval surname but seems to have been completely absorbed by *Quinton*. Occasionally the surname may have reference to tilting at the quintaine: John *Quynteyn* 1378 LoPleas.

Quirk, Quirke: Ceinnedigh *O'Cuirc* 1043, *McQuyrke*, *Quyrke* 1511 Moore. Manx for *Mac Cuirc* 'son of *Corc*' (heart). In Ireland, for *O'Cuirc*.

Quodling: *v.* CODLIN

R

Rabb: *Rab*' atte Wyk' 1332 SRSr; Walter *Rab* 1199 AssSt; Richard *Rabbe* 1296 SRSx. For *Robb* (*Robert*).

Rabbatts, Rabbets, Rabbetts, Rabbits, Rabbitt, Rabbitts, Rabett: (i) *Radboda*, *Rabbode* 1086 DB (Nf, Sf); *Radbode* filius Ilhuwe 1166 P (Nf); Philippus *filius Rabat* 1203 Cur (Y); *Rabot* de Bovington 1300 Guisb (Y); Philip *Rabot* Hy 2 Gilb (L); Sygwat *Radbode* 1275 RH (Nf). OG *Radbodo*, *Rabbodo* 'counsel-messenger'. (ii) Andrew *Robat* 1279 RH (Hu); Alexander *Robet* 1317 AssK; Thomas *Robot* 1327 SRC; Reginald *Rabett* 1524 SRSf. *Rob-et*, *Rob-ot*, hypocoristics of *Robert*. Rabbit's Fm in Dallington (Sussex) owes its name to John *Robet* (1288) and Richard *Rabett* (1482 PN Sx 474).

Rabjohn(s): *v.* ROBJANT
Rablan, Rablen, Rablin: *v.* ROBLIN
Rackliff(e): *v.* RADCLIFF

Radbourne, Radburn, Radbone, Redbourn, Redburn: William *de Redburn*' 1202 FFL; Bartholomew *de Redburn*' 1204 P (Herts); William *de Radburn*', *de Redburn*' 1219 AssY. From Radbourn (Warwicks), Radbourne (Derby), Redbourn (Herts) or Redbourne (Lincs).

Radcliff, Radcliffe, Radclyffe, Ratcliff, Ratcliffe, Ratliff, Ratliffe, Rattcliff, Rackcliff, Rackliff, Rackliffe, Redcliffe, Redclift, Reddecliff, Reddicliffe: Walter *de Radecliua* 1182 P (D); Robert *de Radeclyf* 1313 Wak (Y); Robert *Racclyff* 1496 Ipm (Sf); Henry *Rattcliffe* 1636 RothwellPR (Y); Elizabeth *Ratliff* 1792 SfPR. From Radclive (Bucks), Radcliffe (Lancs, Notts), Ratcliffe (Leics, Notts), Ratclyffe, Ratcliffes (Devon), or Redliff Hill (Warwicks), all meaning 'red cliff'.

Raddie: *v.* READY
Raddish: *v.* REDDISH
Raddle: *v.* RADWELL

Radford, Radforth, Radfirth, Ratford, Redford, Reddiford, Retford: John *de Radeford* 1209 P (Nt); Walter *de Redford*' 1230 P (Berks); Hugo *de Retford* 1275 RH (Nt); Geoffrey *de Ratforde* 1296 SRSx; Nicholas *atte Rydeforde* 1296 SRSx, *atte Redeford* 1305 MELS (Sx). From Radford (Devon, Notts, Oxon, Warwicks, Worcs), Ratford Fm (Sussex), Redford (Sussex) or Retford (Notts), all either 'red ford' or 'reed ford'. OE *rēad* 'red' would give both Radford and Redford, OE *hrēod* 'reed' would give Redford. Also 'dweller near a reedy ford'.

Radish: *v.* REDDISH
Radleigh, Radley: Osbert *de Radelega* 1177 P (Sr); Philip *de Radleg*' 1260 FFK; Adam *de Radelee* 1342–3 FFSr; Richard *Raddeley* 1471 Past. From Radley (Berks, Devon), or 'dweller at the red clearing'.

Radway, Reddaway, Rodaway, Rodway: Henry *de Radeweie* 1205 P (So); Stephen *Rodweye* or *Radwaye* 1581 Oxon; Richard *Reddaway* 1648 DWills. From Rodway (Som) 'road way', or Radway (Warwicks), Radway, Reddaway, Roadway (Devon), all 'red way' (OE *rēad*). Thomas *de Radeweye* (1242 Fees) came from Roadway, Geoffrey *de Radeweye* (ib.), from Reddaway.

Radwell, Raddle, Reddall, Reddell: Robert *de Radewelle* 1185 Templars (Beds); Robert de *Redewelle* 1274 RH (So). Usually from Radwell (Beds, Herts), occasionally from Redwell Wood (Herts), or 'dweller by the reed-stream'. Also 'dweller on the red hill': Richard *atte Redehulle* 1327 SRSo, or 'by the cleared woodland': Brun *de la Redeweld* 1296 SRSx. Certain forms suggest the possibility of a survival of OE *Rǣdweald* or *Rǣdwulf*, but the evidence is inconclusive: Ralph *Redwald*, William *Redolf* 1276 RH (O); Richard *Redwal* 1297 MinAcctCo.

Rae: Robert *Raa* c1231 Black. A Scottish form of ROE.

Rafe, Raff: *v.* RALF
Ragg: For WRAGG. A correspondent informs me that his pedigree proves that the surname was *Wragg*, but at the end of the 18th century, one son, by mistake of the clerk (presumably at his baptism), had his name entered as *Ragg*, which thereafter became his surname and that of his children.

Raikes: *v.* RAKE
Raiman: *v.* RAYMAN
Raimes, Reames: Roger *de Rames*, *de Ramis*, *de Raimis* 1086 DB (Mx, Ess, Sf); William *de Reimes*, *de Remes* 1199 MemR (Nf). From Rames (Seine-Inférieure). *v.* ANF.

Rain, Raine, Rayne: (i) *Regina* 1203 Cur (K); *Regin*' Prat 1275 RH (C); *Reina*, *Reyna* vidua 1214 Cur (Nth), 1244 Rams (Beds); Alan *Reyne* 1260 AssC; Hugo *Ragen*' 1275 RH (He); Alice *Reine* 1279 RH (C); William *le Reine* 1332 SRSx; John *Rayn*, Richard *Rayneson* 1379 PTY. Fr *Reine*, Lat *Regina* 'queen', a personal-name found in France; also a nickname, here derogatory. We may

288

also have a short form of names in *Regen*-, such as *Reyner*, *Reynold*, etc. *le Reine* is probably Fr *raine* 'frog'. (ii) Robert *de Ran*' c1180 Black. From Rayne (Aberdeenshire).

Rainbird, Raynbird, Rambart, Rambert, Ramart: *Rainbertus Flandrensis* 1086 DB (Gl); Willelmus *filius Reinbert* 1206 Cur (Mx); William *Reinberd*, *Reinbert*, *Renberd* 1208, 1212 Cur (Herts); Simon *Ramberd*, Stephen *Rambard* 1327 SRSx. OFr *Rainbert*, *Reinbert*, *Raimbert*, from OG *Raginbert*, *Reginbert* 'mighty guardian'.

Rainbow, Raybould, Rambaut, Ramble, Rammell, Rimbault, Renbold: *Raimbaldus* 1066 Winton (Ha); *Rainbaldus aurifaber* 1086 DB (Nf); Elward *filius Reinbaldi* ib. (Gl); *Reimbaldus* 1148–66 NthCh (Nth); *Rembaldus* 1168–75 Holme (Nf); Reginaldus *filius Renbald*, *Rainbaud* 1212 Cur (Wa); Johannes *filius Rambaldi* 1275 RH (Berks); William *Reimbaud* 1214 Cur (Mx); John *Rambald* 1332 SRSx; John *Reynbald* 1505 NorwW. OFr *Rainbaut*, *Raimbaut*, *Raimbault*, *Rambaut*, from OG *Raginbald*, *Rainbald*, *Reinbald* 'might-bold'.

Raincock: Robert, William son of *Raincok* 1332 SRCu; William, John *Rayncok* ib. *Rain-cok*, a diminutive of a short form of names in *Rain*-, e.g. *Rainball*, *Rainbert*, etc.

Rainer: *v.* RAYNER

Rainey, Rainie, Rainnie, Rainy, Raney, Rannie, Rennie, Renny: *Rayny* Voket 1409 Black; *Rany* Ra 1446 ib.; Henry *Raney* 1275 RH (Db); Thomas *Renie* 1279 RH (Beds); Symon *Renny* 1362 Black; Margaret *Rany* 1379 PTY; John *Rayny* 1436 Black; Walter *Rannie* 1453 ib.; John *Rany* 1510 ib.; Agnes *Reanie* 1636 ib. *Rayny*, with shortened vowel, *Rannie*, *Rennie*, pet-forms of *Reynold*. These names are Scottish. Similar forms seem to have arisen in northern England. In Ireland the name became *Mac Raighne*, *Ó Raighne*, with modern forms *Rainey*, *Raney*, *Reaney*, *Reanney*, *Reanny*, *Reany*, *Reinny*, *Rennie*, *Reyney*, *Ryney*. Theoretically, all these names could derive from Regny (Loire): Roger, William *de Reigni* 1157, 1195 P (D, Cu); William *de Reingny* alias *de Reyney* alias *de Reny* 1276 Ipm (Cu). The name was common in the 12th and 13th centuries and survives in Ashreigny (Devon) and Newton Reigny (Cumb), but there seems to be no connexion between this and the modern names.

Rainger: *v.* RINGER

Raistrick: *v.* RASTRICK

Rake, Raikes: John *de Rak*' 1242 Fees (D); Henry *de la Rake* 1275 MELS (Sx); Walter *Rake* 1279 RH (Hu); Beatrice *ate Rake* 1332 SRSr; Thomas *del Rakes* 1332 SRCu; Nicholas *Raikes* son of Thomas *Rakes* 1585 FrY. From residence near a pass or narrow valley (OE *hraca* 'throat') as at The Rake (Sussex), Raikes Fm (Surrey) or Raikes (WRYorks). *v.* MELS 160–1.

Raleigh, Raley, Ralley, Rally, Rawley, Rayleigh: Hugh *de Ralega*, *de Raalega* 1164, 1169 P (D); John *de Rallye* 1296 SRSx; Thomas *Ralegh* 1386–7 FFWa; Edmund *Rawley*, *Rayley*, *Raweleygh*, *Raleygh*, *Ralegh* or *Rawleigh* of Exeter 1509 LP.

From Raleigh (Devon), Rayleigh House in Morthoe (Devon), or Rayleigh (Essex).

Ralf, Ralfe, Ralfs, Ralph, Ralphs, Rales, Ralls, Rafe, Raff, Rau, Raves, Raw, Rawe, Rawes, Rawle, Rawles, Rawll: *Radulf*, *Radolf* 1066 DB; *Raulf*, *Raulfus clericus* c1095 Bury (Sf); *Radulfus* de Henlinton c1140 DC (L); Robertus *le fiz Raol* Hy 2 DC (L); *Raul* Cordel 12th NthCh (Nth); *Radufus* de Braibof c1200 DC (L); Edricus *filius Raw* Hy 3 Colch (Ess); *Rauf* c1350 Brut; *Raaph* 1387 Trevisa; Johannes *Radulphus* 1186–8 BuryS (Sf); Richard *Rau* 1212 Cur (Nf); Adam *Rauf* 1275 RH (Nf); Amic' *Raffe* 1279 RH (C); Simon *Raulf* 1296 SRSx; Denis *Rauf*, *Rolf* 1308 EAS xviii; John *Ralf* 1327 SRSx; Thomas *Raules*, John *Raweles* 1327 SRSo; Henry *Rawe* 1332 SRLa; Richard *Raaf*, Edward *Raphe* 1524 SRSf; Miles *Rawes* 1639 RothwellPR (Y). This may occasionally be ON *Ráðúlfr* but is usually from OG *Radulf*, the source both of Fr *Raoul* and the Norman *Radulf*, *Raulf*. The name had reached England before the Conquest and may have come direct from Scandinavia but was usually introduced from Normandy. It is very common indeed in the 12th century and almost invariably latinized as *Radulfus*. In spite of, or perhaps because of this popularity, it is rare as a surname before the 13th century when it is very common in a variety of forms. There has been some confusion with *Rolf*.

Ralling(s), Rallis: *v.* RAWLIN

Rallison: *v.* RAWLINGSON

Ralls, Ralph(s), Ralphson: *v.* RALF

Ram, Ramm: (i) Hendricus *Ram* 1188 Bury (Sf); Geoffrey *Ram* 1212 Cur (Nth), 1274 RH (Ess). A nickname from the ram, OE *ram(m)*. (ii) William, Giles *atte Ramme* 1307 LLB C, 1339 LoPleas. From the sign of the ram.

Ramage, Ramadge: Robert, Peter *Ramage* c1240 Fees (L), 1321 LLB E, 1304 Black (Perth). ME, OFr *ramage* 'wild', used of a hawk 'living in the branches', MedLat *ramaticus*, from *ramus* 'branch'.

Ramart, Rambart, Rambert: *v.* RAINBIRD

Rambaut, Rammell: *v.* RAINBOW

Ramsay, Ramsey, Ramshay: Æðelstanus *de Rameseia* c1036 OEByn (Ess). From Ramsey (Essex, Hunts). The Scottish Ramsays derive from Simund *de Ramesie* (a1175 Black) who went to Scotland from Ramsey (Hunts).

Ramsbotham, Ramsbottom: Roger *de Romesbothum* 1324 LaCt. From Ramsbottom (Lancs).

Ramsden: Roger *de Rammesden* 1195 FFL; John *de Rammesdenne* 1334–5 SRK; Peter *Ramsden* 1672 HTY. From Ramsden (Essex, Oxon).

Ramsey: *v.* RAMSAY

Ramshaw: *v.* RAVENSHAW

Ramshay: *v.* RAMSAY

Ramshead: William *Romesheued* 1327 SRDb. 'Ram's head', a nickname.

Ramshire: *v.* RAVENSHAW

Ranacre: *v.* RUNACRES

Ranald: *v.* RONALD

Rand, Rands, Rance: (i) *Rande* de Borham 1299

LoCt; Adam *Rand* 1275 SRWo; Thomas *Rande* 1327 SRSf; Richard *Randes* 1379 PTY; Rebecca *Rants*, *Rance* 1735–6 Bardsley. *Rand*, a pet-form of *Randolph*. (ii) Herlewinus *de Rande* 1176 P (Nth); Robert *de Randes* 1317 AssK. From Rand (Lincs), Rand Grange (NRYorks) or Raunds (Northants).

Randall, Randell, Randle, Randles, Randoll: *Randal* 1204 AssY; *Randle* de Stok 1260 AssCh; Thomas *Randel* 1250 FFSf; Richard *Randall* 1547 FFHu; *Rand-el*, a diminutive of *Rand* (Randolph).

Randerson, Randlesome: Thomas *Randalson* 1471 Black; William *Randerson* 1734 FrY. 'Son of *Randall*.'

Randolph, FitzRandolph: *Randulfus* c1095 Bury (Sf); Nicolaus *filius Randulphi* 1175–86 Holme (Nf); William, Robert *Randolf* 1260 AssC, 1275 RH (L); Ralph *Fetzrandolff* 1498 GildY. *Randolph* is ON *Rannulfr* 'shield-wolf', brought to England by the Normans as *Randulf*. It was confused with the equally common OG *Rannulf* 'raven-wolf', introduced at the same time: *Randolphus* de Brachenberch c 1155 Gilb (L), *Ranulfus* de Brachinberge 1160–6 ib.

Randy: Malie *Randie* 1573 Black (Perth). A pet-form of *Rand* (Randolph).

Raney: *v.* RAINEY

Ranigar: *v.* RUNACRES

Rank: John *Ronk* 1327 SRSf; William *Ronkes* 1332 SRCu. OE *ranc*, ME *rank* 'strong, proud'.

Rankill: Rogerus *filius Ranchil* 1130 P (Y); Rogerus *filius Rauenkil* 1170 P (La); Tomas *filius Ramkell'* 1191 P (Y); Robert *Ravenkil* c1138 Whitby (Y); William *Ramkil, Ranckil* 1204 AssY. ON *Hrafnkell*, OSw *Ramkel* 'raven-cauldron'.

Rankin, Rankine, Ranking, Ranken: *Rankin* de Fowlartoun 1429 Black; Reginald *Ranekyn* 1296 SRSx; Ralph *Rankin* 1301 SRY; Robert, John *Randekyn* 1327 SRSx, 1381 SRSf. *Rand-kin*, a diminutive of names in *Rand-*, e.g. *Randulf*, or *Ran-kin*, for *Rannulf*.

Rannard: *v.* REYNARD

Ranner: *v.* RAYNER

Rannie: An assimilated form of RANDY, or for RAINEY.

Ranscomb, Ranscombe, Ranscome: Thomas *de Rennescumbe, de Ramescumbe, de Ravenescumbe* 1203–6 Cur (K). From Ranscombe in Cuxton (Kent). Also from Ranscombe (Hants), Ranscombe Fm in South Malling (Sussex), one of the five Ranscombes in Devon, or Rainscombe House in Wilcot (Wilts), *Ranscombe* 1581, all 'raven's or ram's valley'.

Ransford: John *de Rammesford* 1327 SRSx probably lived at Ramsfold Fm in Lurgashall (Sussex).

Ranshaw: *v.* RAVENSHAW

Ransley: *v.* RAWNSLEY

Ranson, Ransom, Ransome: William *Randesson'* 1347 SR (C); John *Randson* 1395 Whitby (Y); Elizabeth *Ransom* 1518 NorwW (Sf); Adam *Ranson* 1524 SRSf. 'Son of *Rand*' (Randolph).

Rant: For RAND. A back-formation from *Rants*.

Ranwell: William *de Ranuill'* 1200 P (W); Adam *de Raineville* c1216 Calv (Y). From Ranville (Vosges).

Raper: *v.* ROPER

Rasch, Rash: *v.* ASH

Rashleigh: John *Atterashlegh* 1292 Ipm (D). From Rashleigh Barton (Devon).

Rasor: Baldewinus *rasor* 1130 P (O); Alan, Thomas *Rasur* 1159, 1196 P (O). OFr *rasor, rasur* 'razor', metonymic for a maker of razors. cf. Walter *le Rasorer* 1285 Wak (Y).

Raspberry: Marioth' *de Radespree* 1242 Fees (D). From Ratsbury (Devon).

Rastall: Roger, Walter *Rastel(l)* 1185 P (So), 1206 Cur (Ha). OFr *rastel* 'rake, mattock', either a maker or seller of rakes, or an agricultural labourer.

Rastrick, Raistrick, Rustrick: Roger *de Rastric* 1212 P (Y); John *de Rastrik* 1274 Wak; Katerina *Rastrik'* 1379 PTY. From Rastrick (WRYorks).

Ratchford: *v.* ROCHFORD

Ratcliff(e): *v.* RADCLIFF

Ratford: *v.* RADFORD

Rathbone, Radbone, Rathborne, Rathbourn: Richard, John *Rathebon* 1275 SRWo, 1347 AD vi (Ch); Robert, Richard *Rathebun(e)* 1297, 1327 SRY; Robert *Radbone* 1547 Bardsley. For this difficult name Harrison suggests an Irish or, preferably, a Welsh origin, Ir *Rathbane* 'white fort' or Welsh *Rhathbon* 'stumpy clearing or plain'. Bardsley, whose earliest example is 1547, doubtfully suggests a derivation from Ruabon. Early examples are rare and without any preposition. No satisfactory suggestion can be offered.

Ratliff(e): *v.* RADCLIFF

Ratnage: Richer *de Radenache* 1197 FF (Bk). From Radnage (Bucks) or Radnidge (Devon), *Rothenesse* 1292.

Ratter: Margeria *le Ratonner* 1327 SRSf. 'Rat-catcher', from OFr *raton* 'rat'.

Rattray: Thomas *de Rettre* 1253 Black; Adam *de Retref* 1294 ib.; William *Rettre* 1436 ib.; Silvester *Rettray* 1526 ib. From the barony of Rattray (Perth).

Rau: *v.* RALF

Raulin: *v.* RAWLIN

Raven, Ravens, Revan, Revans, Revens: Leduuinus *filius Reuene* 1086 DB (L); *Rauen* de Engelbi 1185 P (Y); Godric, William *Raven* 1133–60 Rams (Beds), 1188 P (Nb); Adam *Reven* 1279 RH (O); Elena *Ravenes* 1312 ColchCt; Walter, Alice *le Reven* 1327 SRWo, 1332 SRWa; William *Revance* 1520 NorwW (Nf); Alan *Rivance* 1534 ib. ON *Hrafn* or OE **Hræfn* 'raven', or a nickname from the bird, ON *hrafn*, OE *hræfn*. Occasionally from a sign-name: William *atte Raven* 1344 LLB F.

Ravenhall, Ravenhill, Revnell: (i) Willelmus *filius Rauenilde* 1297 SRY; William *Ravenild* 1276 RH (Y); Matilda *Rafenild* 1279 RH (C); John *Ravenell* 1700 Bardsley. ON *Hrafnhildr* (f). (ii) Nicholas *de Rauenhull'* 1230 P (He). From Ravenhill (NRYorks) or some other 'raven-hill'.

Ravening: *Rauening* de Raddon' 1194 P (Beds);

Ravening 1212 Cur (Bk); Simon *Ravening* 1248 FFEss; William *Rauenyng* 1297 MinAcctCo. OE **Hræfning*, an *-ing* derivative of OE **Hræfn*.

Ravenshaw, Ravensbear, Ramshaw, Ramshire, Ranshaw, Renshaw, Renshall, Renshell: Stephen *de Ravenshagh* 1332 SRLa; Ralph *Raynshae*, *Renshae* 1548, 1561 Bardsley (Ch); Robert *Ravenshaw, Ramshaw* 1606, 1617 ib.; Randle *Renshaw* 1613 ib.; John *Renshall* 1679 ib. 'Dweller by the raven-wood', as at Ravenshaw (Warwicks) or Renishaw (Derby).

Raw, Rawe: Edward *Bitherawe* 1279 AssSo; John *de Rawe* 1297 SRY, William *ate Rawe* 1332 SRSr; William *del Rawe* 1429 DbCh. 'Dweller by the hedgerow or in the row of houses or street', OE *rāw* 'row'. *v.* REW, ROW and also RALF.

Rawbone, Rabone, Rawbins, Raybon: William *Rabayn* 1301 SRY, 1332 SRLa; Thomas *Rawboon* 1492 FrLeic; Widow *Rawbones* 1674 HTSf. *Rabayn* is ON *rá-bein* 'roe-bone', a nickname for one with legs as speedy as those of a roe. cf. Henry *Coltebeyn* ('colt'), William *Gaytebayn* ('goat'), Alan *Kabayn* ('jackdaw') 1301 SRY. *Raybon* is from OE **rā-bān* 'roe-bone', showing the northern spelling of *rā*; *Rawbone* is a corruption of the midland and southern *Roebone*.

Rawcliff, Rawcliffe, Rawlcliffe, Rockcliffe, Rockliff, Rockliffe, Rowcliffe: Elsi *de Routecliua* 1170 P (Y); John *de Rouclef* 1332 SRCu. From Rawcliffe (NRYorks), Roccliffe (WRYorks), Rockcliff (Cumb), or Rowcliffe (Devon).

Rawdon: Walthef *de Raudon'* 1202 FFY; John *de Rawdon* 1379 PTY; John *Rawdon* 1459 Kirk. From Rawdon (WRYorks).

Rawes, *v.* RALF

Rawkins: Joane *Rawkyns* t Eliz Bardsley. *Rawkin* 'little Ralph'. *v.* RALF.

Rawland: *v.* ROWLAND

Rawlcliffe: *v.* RAWCLIFF

Rawle(s): *v.* RALF

Rawley: *v.* RALEIGH

Rawlin, Rawlins, Rawling, Rawlings, Rawlence, Rawlyns, Raulin, Raulins, Ralling, Rallings, Rallis: *Raulyn* le Forester 1277 Wak (Y); William *Raulyn* 1290 Eynsham (O); John *Rawlynes* 1343 AD iv (Wa); Walter *Rawling* 1520 NorwW (Nf); Catherine *Ralling* 1642 Black (Dumfries). OFr *Raul-in*, a diminutive of *Ralf*, both sometimes used of the same man: *Ralph de Knyghton . . . the above-mentioned Raulyn* 1377 LoPleas. *v.* RAWLINGSON.

Rawlingson, Rawlinson, Rawlison, Rallison: Richard *Rawlinson* 1538 Riev (Y); Robert *Rallinson* 1617 ShefA. 'Son of *Raulin*.' *v.* RAWLIN. Bardsley notes that in Furness and Cumberland, where Rawlinsons are numerous, *Rowland* is pronounced *Rawland* and *Rolland* and these Rawlinsons derive from *Rawlandson*, which became *Rawlinson*. *v.* ROLLINGSON.

Rawll: *v.* RALF

Rawnsley, Ransley: Margaret *de Rauenslawe* 1379 PTY; Nicholas *Raunsley, Rawnsley* 1564, 1565 ShefA; Joseph *Ransley* 1663 FrY. From an unidentified place, apparently in the West Riding.

Raworth: *v.* ROWARTH

Rawson, Rawsen: William *Raufson*, John *Rauson*, Richard *Raweson* 1379 PTY. 'Son of *Rauf* or *Rau*.' *v.* RALF.

Rawsthorn, Rawsthorne, Rawstorn, Rawstorne, Rawstron, Rosten, Rostern, Rosterne, Rosthorn, Rosson, Roston, Rostron: Richard *de Routhesthorn* 1246 AssLa; James *Rawstorne* 1599 FrY; Jane *Rosthern* 1613 Bardsley. From Rostherne (Ches).

Ray, Raye, Rey: Willaim *Lerei* 1195 FFNf; Robert *Raie* 1206 P (C); Henry *le Ray* 1296 SRSx. The most common source of these names is OFr *rei* 'king', occasionally used as a personal name: Thomas *filius Rey* 1279 RH (C). It may be a nickname denoting pride, one with the bearing of a king, or refer to the victor in some competition or sport such as shooting at the popinjay (cf. PAPIGAY). It might also be OE *rǣge* 'female of the roe' or, in the north, the dialectal pronunciation *ray* found in the 16th century for OE, ON *rā* 'roe'. *v.* also REA, RYE, ROY.

Raybon: *v.* RAWBONE

Raybould: *v.* RAINBOW

Rayer: *Raher'* 1137 Bart; Ricardus *filius Raher* 1206 Cur (Ess); Ralph *Raher* 1275 RH (Berks). OG *Radheri, Rathar, Rather* 'counsel-army', the name of the founder of St Bartholomew's Hospital.

Rayleigh: *v.* RALEIGH

Rayman, Raiman, Reaman, Reeman, Ryman: Robert *Ryman* 1327 SRSx; Simon *Reman* 1359 ColchCt; John *Rayman, Reyman* 1377 AssEss. 'Dweller by the low-lying land or the stream.' *v.* RAY, REA, RYE.

Raymond, Raymont, Rayment, Raiment: *Raimundus* 1086 DB (Ess); *Reimundus* 1121–48 Bury (Sf), 1214 Cur (Wa); Giraldus *Reimundus* 1086 DB (Ess); William *Reimunt* 1207 P (Ha); Ernald *Reimund'* 1208 P (K). OFr *Raimund, Raimond* from OG *Raginmund* 'counsel or might-protection'.

Raynbird: *v.* RAINBIRD

Rayner, Raynor, Rainer, Ranner, Reiner, Reiners, Reyna, Reyner, Renner: *Rainerus* 1086 DB; *Reynerus* cancellarius 1101–25 Holme (Nf); Ricardus *filius Rainer* 1148 Winton (Ha); *Renerus* c1250 Rams (Nf); Alexander *Reygner* 1229 Cl; William *Rayner* Hy 3 Gilb (L); William *Reyner* 1286 AssSt; Robert *Ranare* 1651 RothwellPR (Y). OFr *Rainer, Reiner, Renier*, from OG *Raginhari* 'counsel, might-army'.

Rea, Ree, Ray, Raye, Rey, Rye: Ralph *de la Reye* 1279 RH (O); William *atte Ree* 1285 Ass (C); William *bithe Ree* 1293 MELS (Wo); John *atte Reye* 1327 SR (Ess); William *atte Rea* 1327 SRSx. All these are local surnames from residence near a stream or low-lying land near a stream. OE *ēa* 'water', 'stream' had two datives, *īe and ēa*. OE *æt þære ēa* 'by the stream' became ME *at ther ee, atte ree*, hence *Rea* and *Ree*. OE *æt þære īe* became ME *at ther ie, ye, eye, atte rie, rye, rey*, hence *Ray(e), Rey, Rye*. OE *æt þære ēge, īge*, from OE *īeg, īg, ēg* 'island, piece of firm land in a fen', became ME *at ther eye, ye, atte reye, rye* which cannot be distinguished from the similar forms from OE *ēa* without further evidence. Michael *atte Ree* (1327 SRSx) is called *atte Rye* in 1332 (ib). Thomas *atte Ree* in 1332 probably lived at the same place as William *ate Rye* in 1359 (PN Sr 233), whilst both Walter *at Reghe* in 1287 and John *ate Ree* in 1332 lived at Ray Lodge (PN Sr 330). All these lived near a stream (*ēa*), as did Stephen *atte Ree* (1323 *For*) at Rye Mill in Feering (Essex). *v.* also RYE, NYE, YEA.

Reace: *v.* RHYS

Reacher: *v.* RICHER

Read, Reade, Reed, Red, Redd, Reid: (i) Leofwine *se Reade* 1016–20 OEByn (K); Aluric *pane Reda* c1100-30 ib. (D); William *Red* 1176 P (Gl), *le Red* 1332 SRSx; Hugo *le Rede* 1220 Cur (La); Hamo *le Reed* 1296 SRSx; Thomas *Read* 1327 SRSx. OE *rēad* 'red', of complexion or hair. *Reid* is Scottish. (ii) William *de Reved* 13th WhC; Ralph *de Rede* 1203 Cur (Herts); John *de Rede* 1327 SRSf. From Read (Lancs), earlier *Reved*, Rede (Suffolk) or Reed (Herts). (iii) Alwin *de Larede* c1160 MELS (Sx); Roger *de la Rede* 1208 P (D); Julian *atte Rede* 1296 SRSx; John *ater Rede* ib., identical with John *Rede* 1327 ib.; Thomas *atte Red* 1332 SRSx. From residence in a clearing, OE **rīed, *rȳd v.* RIDE.

Readdie, Readdy, Readey: *v.* READY

Reader, Readers, Reder, Reeder, Reeders: Adam, Symon *le Redere* 1279 RH (C), 1283 SRSf. A derivative of ME *redyn* 'to thatch with reed', 'a thatcher' (c1440 NED). Particularly common in Norfok (MESO 179). cf. THAXTER.

Readett, Readitt, Redit, Reditt, Riddett: Reymbro *ater Redette* 1296 SRSx. 'Dweller by the reedbed', OE **hrēodet.*

Readhead: *v.* REDHEAD

Reading, Readings, Redding, Reding, Reddin, Ridding, Riding, Rydings, Ruddin: Grifin *del Ruding* 1246 AssLa; Richard *del Ryding* 1277 Wak (Y); Sara *de Redyngg* 1311 ColchCt; William *atte Rydyng* 1339 AssSt. 'Dweller in the clearing', OE **rydding.*

Readman, Reedman, Redman: Robert *Redeman* 1274 RH (Ess); John *Redman* 1275 RH (Ha); Norchinus *le Redman* 1332 SRLa; Richard *le Redemon* 1332 SRSt; Alexander *Reademan* 1474 GildY. 'Reed-man', either a cutter of reeds or a thatcher. cf. READER. Possibly also a nickname, 'red man'. cf. READ.

Readwin, Redwin: *Redewinus* del Broc 1185 Templars (Sa); Robert, Richard, John *Redwyne* 1254 ArchC 12, 1327 *SR* (Ess), SRSx; Simon *Redwin* 1275 RH (K). OE *Rǣdwine* 'counsel-friend', a rare OE name.

Ready, Readey, Readdie, Readdy, Reddie, Reddy, Raddie: Robert *le Redye* 1260 AssY; John *Rady* 1327 *SR* (Ess). ME *rǣdi(ʒ), readi, redi* 'in a state of preparation, prompt, quick'.

Readyhough: *v.* RIDEALGH

Reaman: *v.* RAYMAN

Reames: *v.* RAIMES

Reaney: Henry *de Ravenhowe* 13th PN WRY i, 340; Thomas *de Ranaw* 1379 PTY; John *Ranoe*

1433 Wheat; Robert *Reanye* 1577 Edmunds; George *Rayney* or *Rayner* 1725 ib. This surname, though able not common, is a Sheffield name, always with this spelling. The correct pronunciation is *Rainey*, now being replaced by the spelling pronunciation *Reeney*. The above forms are all from around Penistone and Sheffield. The name derives from Ranah Stones in the township of Thurlstone in Penistone parish (WRYorks), called by T. W. Hall 'Raynah or Ranah, a farm-house in Thurlstone': *Reynoe* 1645 Bosville, *Renold stones* 1741 Edmunds. ON *hrafnhaugr* 'raven-hill'. *Rayner* above is a dialectal pronunciation.

Reaney, Reanney, Reanny, Reany, Raney, Rainey, Reney, Reinny, Reyney, Rennie, Ryney: Irish spellings of *Mac Raighne. v.* RAINEY.

Reap, Reape, Reep, Reepe: Roger, William *Repe* 1297 MinAcctCo (D), 1545 SRW; John *Reepe* 1642 PrD. Since the first named was paid *pro equis et aueriis non scriptis*, he was evidently concerned with horses, and was probably a carrier, *v.* RIPPER. A metonymic name from REAPER 'harvester' is much less likely.

Reaper: John, Mariota *Reper* 1327 SRSf. A derivative of OE *repan* 'to reap', reaper.

Reardon, Riordan, O'Riordan: Ir *Ó Rioghbhardáin* 'descendant of *Ríoghbhardán*' (royal-bard).

Reaves: *v.* REEVES

Record(s): *v.* RICKWARD

Red(d): *v.* READ

Redb(o)urn: *v.* RADBOURNE

Redcliffe, Redclift: *v.* RADCLIFF

Reddall, Reddell: *v.* RADWELL

Reddaway: *v.* RADWAY

Reddecliff, Reddicliffe: *v.* RADCLIFF

Reddie: *v.* READY

Reddiford: *v.* RADFORD

Reddihough, Reddyhoff: *v.* RIDEALGH

Redding: *v.* READING

Reddish, Redish, Raddish, Radish: John *de Reddich* 1202 FFL. From Redditch (Lancs, Worcs).

Redford: *v.* RADFORD

Redgewell: *v.* RIDGEWELL

Redhead, Readhead: Adam *Redhed* 1256 AssNb; John *Redheved* 1279 RH (C). 'Red head' (OE *rēad, hēafod*).

Redihalgh: *v.* RIDEALGH

Redit(t): *v.* READETT

Redman: *v.* READMAN, REDMAYNE

Redmayne: Norman *de Redeman* 1188 P (La); William *Redmaine* 1674 FrY. From Redmain (Cumb).

Redmond: Ir *Réamonn* or *Mac Réamoinn* '(Son of) *Remund*' (Raymond).

Redway: Walterus *filius Radewi, Redwi* 1165, 1169 P (L); Willelmus *filius Redwi* 1185 P (Wo); Gilbert, Andrew *Redwy* 1221 AssWo, 1279 RH (O). Late OE *Rǣdwīg* 'counsel-warrior'.

Redwin: *v.* READWIN

Ree: *v.* REA

Reece: *v.* RHYS

Reed: *v.* READ

Reeder(s): *v.* READER

Reedman: *v.* READMAN
Reeman: *v.* RAYMAN
Reep(e): *v.* REAP
Rees(e): *v.* RHYS
Reeson: Roger *Reuesone* 1296 Crowland (C); Adam *le Reuessone* 1327 SRSf. 'The reeve's son.'
Reeve: Walter, James *le Reve* 1220 FrLeic, 1281 LLB A. OE *(ge)rēfa* 'reeve'.
Reeves, Reaves: (i) Richard *del Reves* 1332 SRLa. 'Servant at the reeve's (house).' (ii) John *atte Reuese* 1327 SRWo. 'Dweller at the border' of a wood or hill (OE *efes* 'edge'; ME *atter evese*). *v.* EAVES.
Regan: *v.* O'REGAN
Reid: *v.* READ
Reiner: *v.* RAYNER
Reinny: *v.* RAINEY
Relf, Relfe, Relph, Realff: *Richolf* de Gameltun' 1210 Cur (Y); *Riculfus* 1212 ib.; *Ricolfus* filius Ailwini 1219 Cur (Sx); Robert *Reolf* 1296 SRSx; John *Relf* 1327 ib. Probably OFr *Riulf*, from OG *Ricwulf*.
Remfrey, Remfry, Renfree: *Rainfridus* 1086 DB (L); *Reinfridus* 12th DC (L); Gilebertus *filius Reimfridi, filius Reynfrey* 1213 Cur (Cu), 1230 P (La); Roger *Reymfrey* 1221 Cur (So). OG *Raganfrid, Rainfrid* 'might-peace'.
Renaud, Renaut: *v.* REYNOLD
Renbold: *v.* RAINBOW
Reney: *v.* RAINEY
Renfree: *v.* REMFREY
Rengger: *v.* RINGER
Renhard, Rennard: *v.* REYNARD
Rennell: *v.* REYNOLD
Renner: Aluuinus *Rennere* c1134 Black (Govan); Richard *Renner* 1319 *SR* (Ess); John *le Renner* 1340 MEOT (La). A derivative of OE *rennan* 'to run', 'runner', probably a messenger or courier. *v.* also RAYNER.
Rennie, Renney, Renny: *v.* RAINEY
Rennison, Renison, Rennilson, Renilson, Renson: John *Renisson* 1327 SRC; John *Rendelson* 1694 Black. 'Son of *Reynold*.'
Renshall, Renshell, Renshaw: *v.* RAVENSHAW
Renyard: *v.* REYNARD
Ressler: *v.* RESTLER
Rest: *Reste* c1135 DC (L); Walterus *filius Reste* 1176 P (L); John *Rest* 1447 LLB K. A short form of OG *Restold. v.* RESTALL.
Restall, Restell: *Restaldus, Restolt* 1086 DB; *Restold'* 1130 P (O); Gillebertus *filius Restaldi* 1206 Cur (L); Hugh, Peter *Restwald* 1279 RH (O). OG *Restold, Restald*, a Frankish name, perhaps of Celtic origin.
Restler, Ressler: Robert, William *le Wrastler* 1317 MEOT (O), 1332 SRWa; Henry *Wrasteler* 1440 ShefA. OE *wræstlere* 'wrestler'.
Retchford: *v.* ROCHFORD
Retford: *v.* RADFORD
Retter: Alice *le Retour* 1279 RH (O); William *Retour* 1332 SRSx. OFr *retier* 'net-maker'.
Revan, Revans, Revens: *v.* RAVEN
Revel, Revell, Revill, Reville, Reavell: *Reuel* de

Teteneia Hy 2 DC (L); Paganus *revellus* 1130 P (Herts); Robert, Hugh *Reuel* 1177, 1196 P (Ess, Nth); Richard *Revel(l), Rivel(l)* 1210 Cur (So). OFr *revel* 'pride, rebellion, sport', from *reveler* 'to rebel'. The font-name *Revel* was common in OFr and ME and may actually be from Lat *rebellus*. The surname is also metonymic for *Reveler* which survives.
Revere: (i) Paul *Reyvere* 1255 RH (Bk); William *le Reuere* 1316 FFK; John *Reuere* 1375 ColchCt. ME *revere* 'reiver, robber'. (ii) John *ater Reure* 1296 SRSx; Robert *atte Revere* 1327 SRSx; Matilda *atte Riuer* ib.; Adam *atte Eure* ib. 'Dweller on the slope or brow of the hill' (OE **yfer* 'edge').
Revis, Rivis: Adam *de Rievalle, de Ryvaus* 1333 Riev (Y); Richard *Ryvax* 1414 GildY; Thomas *Revis, Rivice* 1588, 1618 FrY. From Rievaulx (Yorks), pronounced *Rivers*.
Revnell: *v.* RAVENHALL
Rew, Rue: Robert *ate Rewe* 1297 MinAcctCo; William *in therew* 1327 SRSo. 'Dweller in the row of houses or in the street' (ME *rew*, OE *ræw*), as at Rewe (Devon). cf. RAW.
Rey: *v.* RAY, REA
Reyna: For RAYNER or RAINEY.
Reynard, Renhard, Rennard, Renyard: Rogerus *filius Rainardi, Rainart* 1086 DB (Nf); Elias *Reynardi* 1205 Holme (Nf); Henry *Renard* 1325 Orig (Ha). OFr *Reinart, Renart*, OG *Raginhard, Rainard* 'counsel-brave'.
Reyner: *v.* RAYNER
Reynold, Reynolds, Reynalds, Reynell, Renaud, Renaut, Renals, Rennell, Rennels, Rennoll: Willelmus *filius Rainaldi* 1086 DB; *Reinaldus* camerarius 1121–48 Bury (Sf); *Rennaldus* filius Berwaldi Hy 2 DC (L); *Renalt* de Saint Leger ib.; William *Reynaud* 1272 HPD (Ess); John *Reynald* 1275 SRWo; Henry *Reynel* ib.; Adam *Renaud* 1297 MinAcctCo; William *Reynold* 1299 FFEss; John *Rennold* 1327 SRC; John *Rennels* 1788 Bardsley. OFr *Reinald, Reynaud*, OG *Raginald* 'counsel-might', latinized as *Reginaldus*. Some of the numerous instances of *Rainald* in England may be from ON *Ragnaldr*, but most were introduced from France and Normandy where both the OG and ON forms contributed to its popularity.
Reynoldson: Richard *Raynoldson* 1379 PTY. 'Son of *Reynold*.'
Rhodes, Rhoades, Road, Roads: Hugh *de Rodes* 1219 AssY; Alexander *de la rode* 1277 Ely (Nf); John *atte Rode* 1294 RamsCt (Beds); Robert *del Rodes* 1332 SRLa; Robert *Roades, Rhoades* 1660, 1676 FrY; Thomas *Rhodes* 1678 ib. 'Dweller by the clearing(s)', OE *rod(u)*, as at Roade (Northants), Rhode (Devon), etc.
Rhys, Reace, Reece, Rees, Reese, Rice: *Hris* 1052 ASC C; *Rees* 1066 DB (Ch); *Resus* filius Griffini 1178 P (D); Griffinus *filius Res, Ris* 1198–9 P (Sa, Gl); *Rice* or *Rise* Powell 1570 Oxon; William *Res* 1203 Cur (L); John *Rees* 1288 FFSf; Walter *Rys* 1327 SRWo; John *Ryce* 1524 SRSf. OW *Rīs*, Welsh *Rhys* 'ardour'.

Ricard, Riccard: v. RICHARD

Rich, Riche, Riches, Ritch: (i) Godwinus *Diues*, *le Riche* 1177, 1185 P (L); Mosse *le Riche* 1195 P (Gl); William *Riche* 1296 SRSx. OFr, ME *riche* 'rich'. (ii) Ricardus *de la Riche* 1200 P (Ha); Alexander *atte Riche* 1296 SRSx. 'Dweller by the stream' (OE *ric), as at Glynde Reach (Sussex). v. MELS 166. (iii) *Riche* Algar 1296 SRSx; Richard *Ryches* 1296 SRSx. A diminutive *Rich* from *Richard* to which some examples without the article belong, e.g. Adam *Rych* 1281 FFSf. cf. RICK.

Richard, Richardes, Richards, Ritchard, Ricard, Ricarde, Ricards, Riccard, Rickard, Rickardes, Rickards, Rickeard, Rickerd, Rickert, Ricket, Rickets, Rickett, Ricketts: *Ricard* 1066 DB; *Richardus* Basset 1127-34 Holme (Nf); *Ricard* de Linlee c1166 NthCh (Sa); Juliana, Thomas *Richard* 1276 RH (O), 1296 SRSx; Adam *Ricard* 1327 SRSo; Thomas *Richardes* 1327 SRWo; William *Ricardes* 1327 SRSo; Hester *Rickett* 1606 Bardsley; David *Rickart* 1651 Black. AN *Ricard*, CentralFr *Richard*, OG *Ric(h)ard* 'powerful-brave', one of the most popular names introduced by the Normans. Usually latinized as *Ricardus*, the common form was *Ricard* whence the pet-form *Rick*, etc. *Richard* has given *Richie, Ritch*, etc. For other pet-forms, v. HICK, HITCH, DICK, with their derivatives. cf. also the double diminutive *Richelot* 1188 P (L), 1219 AssY, Robert *Richelot, Rikelot* 1191-2 P (L); Richard *Rykelot* 1315 FFEss. *Ricket*, often a late development of *Rickard*, may also be from the diminutive *Ric-ot*: *Ricot* Huot 1327 SRSx. *Richard* occasionally interchanges with *Richer*: *Ricardus, Richerus* filius Bondi, filius Stannardi 1134-45 Holme (Nf). v. also HUDD, RICKWARD.

Richardson, Richarson: Murdac *Richardesson* 1359 Black; William *Richardson* 1381 PTY; Agnes *Richarson* 1470 GildY; George *Richison* 1683 RothwellPR (Y). 'Son of *Richard*.'

Richell, Rickel, Rickell, Rickells: *Rikilda* 1197 FF (Sf); Willelmus *filius Richild, Rikilde* 1212 Cur (Herts); Thomas *Richil* 1275 RH (Nb); Geoffrey, Hugh *Rikild* 1279 RH (Hu, O); Robert *Rykeld* 1279 RH (O); Walter *Rychyld* 1297 MinAcctCo; Thomas *Rikel* 1327 SRSx. OG *Richild, Richeldis* (f), Fr *Richeut*. cf. RICHOLD.

Richer, Reacher, Ricker, Rickers: *Richerius* clericus, *Ricerus* 1086 DB (Sf); *Richer* de Brunho 1219 AssY; William, Geoffrey *Richer* 1236 Oseney (O), 1260 AssC; Isabell' *Ryker* 1332 SRSx. OG *Richer(e), Riker*, OFr *Rich(i)er, Ricier*.

Richey, Richie(s): v. RITCHIE

Richmond, Richmont: Roger *de Richemund* 1199 CartAntiq; Adam *de Richemond* 1296 SRNb; William *Richemound* 1326 CorLo. From Richmond (Surrey, NRYorks), but early examples may be from one of the many French places of this name.

Richold: *Ricolda* mater Baldeuini 1151-4 Bury (Sf); Johannes nepos *Richold* 1177 P (L); Osbertus *filius Rikoldi* 1208 P (Y); *Richolda* uxor Pagani 1213 Cur (Sr); Walterus *Ricaldes* c1100 MedEA

(Nf); Ralph *Richold* 1297 MinAcctCo. *Richolda* is from OG *Richoldis* (f), a form of *Richild*, which survives as *Richell* and *Rickell(s)*. Some of the forms above are from OG *Ricoald, Ricold, Richold* (m), which has certainly contributed to *Richold*, and probably also to *Rickell(s)*.

Rick, Ricks, Rix: (i) *Rike* 1260 AssCh; Ralph *Rixe* 1279 RH (C); Ema *Ricke*, David *Rickes* 1327 SRSf; Richard *Rycke*, Milcentia *Ryckes* 1330, 1351 ColchCt. *Rick*, a pet-form of *Ricard*. v. RICHARD. (ii) Osbert, John *de la Rixe* 1274 RH (So); Roger *ate Rixe* 1302 PN D 545; William *atte Ryxe* 1333 MELS (So). 'Dweller by the rushes', from West Saxon *rixe, rexe*, a metathesized form of OE *risc, rysc* 'rush', which survives as *rix, rex* in the dialects of Dorset, Somerset and Devon. cf. Rix, Rixdale (Devon). The plural has become RIXON.

Rickard(s), Rickeard: v. RICHARD

Rickcord: v. RICKWARD

Rickel, Rickell(s): v. RICHELL, RICHOLD

Ricker(s): v. RICHER

Rickerd, Rickert, Rickett(s): v. RICHARD

Rickson: v. RIXON

Rickward, Rickword, Rickwood, Rickcord, Record, Records: *Richewardus* de Westberi 1190 P (Bk); *Rikeward* Kupere 1296 SRSx; Robert *Rikeward* 12th DC (L); Walter *Rykeward* 1275 RH (Nf); Roger *Recard* 1393 NorwW (Sf); John *Recorde* 1409 RochW; William *Rekerd* 1455 NorwW (Nf); John *Record, Rikecord, Rikeworth* 1595, 1599, 1601 Bardsley. OFr *Ricoart*, OG *Ricward* 'powerful-guardian'. *Recard* might also be from *Ricard* (Richard): *Rec'* pentecoste, *Rec'* bene 1292 SRLo. *Rickwood* may also, occasionally, be from OG *Ricoald* 'powerful-might': *Rikewaud'* 1215 Cur (Sx). cf. RICHOLD.

Ridal, Rideal, Riddall, Riddell: Alan *de Ridale* c1160-75 YCh; Nicholas *de Ridal* 1222 FFY; William *Rydale, Riddall* 1338 FFEss, 1672 HTY. From Rydal (Westmorland), or Ryedale (WRYorks). v. also RIDDELL.

Riddell, Riddel, Riddall, Riddle, Riddles: *Ridel* Papillun 1163 P; *Ridel* de Kisebi e Hy 2 DC (L); Goisfridus, Geva *Ridel* 1086 DB, 1138-47 P (Ch); William *Ridell'* 1205 Pl (Nth); Reginald *Ridel* 1327 SRLei. A nickname from OFr *ridel* 'a small hill', though its exact significance as a personal name is obscure. v. OEByn 380.

Riddett: v. READETT

Ridding: v. READING

Riddiough: v. RIDEALGH

Ride, Ryde, Rude: Roger *de la Rude* 1176 P (Sr); Robert *de la Ryde* 1294 LLB C; Richard *ate Rude* 1297 MinAcctCo. 'Dweller in the clearing', OE *ried, *ryd. Survives also as READ.

Ridealgh, Ridehalgh, Redihalgh, Reddihough, Reddyhoff, Readyhough, Riddiough: William *de Redihalgh* 1324 LaCt; Robert *del Riddyough* 1397 PrGR; Edward *Riddihough, Riddihalgh* 1682 ib. From Higher Ridihalgh (Lancs).

Rideout, Ridout, Ridoutt: Elyas *Rydhut* 1274 RH (So); Ellis, John *Ridut* 1276, 1278 AssSo; William

Rydhowt 1379 PTY. Probably 'ride out', a nickname for a rider. cf. Adam *Rideway* 1219 AssY.

Rider, Ryder: John, Thomas *le Rider* 1204 AssY; Richard *Ridere* 1212 Fees (Cu). Late OE *rīdere* 'rider', probably 'knight, mounted warrior' (c1085 NED). Also 'dweller by the clearing' (v. RIDE). Henry *at Ryde* is identical with Henry *Ryder* (1599 PN Sr 149).

Ridge: Geoffrey *de la Rigge* 1166 P (Ha); Edith *atte Rigge* 1327 SRSo. 'Dweller on the ridge', OE *hrycg. v.* also RUDGE.

Ridgeway, Ridgway: Gilbert *de Ruggeweie* a1183 EngFeud (Gl); Walter *de Regewey* 1262 ArchC iii; William *de Rygeway* 1310 DbCh. 'Dweller by the ridgeway' (OE *hrycgweg*) or from a place named Ridgeway.

Ridgewell, Ridgwell, Redgewell, Redgwell: Thomas *de Redeswell* 1281 FFEss. From Ridgewell (Essex).

Riding: v. READING

Ridler: Geoffrey *le ridelere* 1230 P (So); Andrew *le Rydelere* 1294 RamsCt (Beds). A derivative of ME *rid(e)len* 'to sift', from OE *hriddel* 'a sieve', a sifter of corn or a sifter of sand and lime in making mortar.

Ridley: Elyas *de Redleg'* 1227 FFK; Alexander *de Rydeleye* 1279 AssNb; Henry *Rydleye* 1300 IpmGl. From Ridley (Ches, Essex, Kent, Northumb).

Ridout: v. RIDEOUT

Rigby, Rigbey: Gilbert *de Rigebi* 1208 P (L); Henry *de Ryggeby* 1285 AssLa; Thomas *Rygby* 1453 FFEss. 'Dweller at the farm on the ridge', ON *hryggr* and *bý*.

Rigden: Richard *Rikedoun* 1317 AssK; Reginald *Rykedoun* 1327 SRSx; William *Rigden*, 1557 ArchC 34. This name must be taken with HIGDON, earlier *Hikedun*. Both names look like place-names but neither is ever found with a preposition and no place-names of similar form are known. *Ricardun* is a diminutive of *Ricard* (Richard). The *-ar-*, being unaccented, was weakened to *-e-* and then lost, giving *Ricdun*. This, with partial assimilation, would become *Rigden*. *Hikedun* is a variant based on the rhymed *Hick*.

Rigg, Rigge, Riggs: William (*de*) *Rigge* 1197-8 P (Sa); John *del Rigg* 1332 SRCu. 'Dweller by the ridge', ON *hryggr*.

Rigglesford, Riggulsford: v. WRIGGLESWORTH

Rigley: v. WRIGLEY

Rigmaiden: John *de Ryggemayden* 1285 AssLa. From Rigmaiden (Cumb).

Riley, Ryley: John *de Ryeley* 1284 Wak; Henry *de Ryley* 1327 SRDb; John *Ryley* 1488 CorNt. From Riley (Devon), High Riley (Lancs), or 'dweller at the rye clearing'.

Rimell: Elias *filius Rimilde* 1201 Cur (So); *Rimilda Vidua* 1201 ib. (Ha); Rogerus *filius Rimilde* 1203 ib. (Nf); Robert *Rimel* 1327 SRWo; Agnes *Rymyld* 1332 SRWa. OE *Rimhild* 'border-war', a rare and late woman's name.

Rimer, Rimmer, Rymer: Warin *Rymer* 1229 Pat (Y); Richard *le Rimour* 1277 WhC (La). A derivative of ME *rimen* 'to rime' or AFr *rimour, rymour* 'a rimer, poet'.

Ring, Ringe, Rings: Eilwinus, Robert *Ring* 1207 ChR (Nf), 1279 RH (C). Probably metonymic for *Ringer* (ii) 'bell-ringer', or, perhaps, for a maker of rings, jeweller.

Ringer: (i) Two examples of OE *Hringhere* have been noted: *Ringer* 12th Searle 562; *Ringer'* filius Alani 1219 AssL. There is no evidence for the formation of a surname from this, but it might have contributed to *Ringer* which has other origins. (ii) Hugo (*le*) *Ringere* 1207 Cur (Sf); William *le Ringere* 1327 SRSf. A derivative of OE *hringan* 'to ring', 'a bell-ringer' (c1425 NED). cf. Henry *Ringebell* 1275 RH (Sf). (iii) Richard *le Wringar* 1327 SRSx. A derivative of OE *wringan* 'to wring, squeeze', perhaps a wringer or presser of cheese. cf. Richard *le Chesewryngere* 1281 MESO (L).

Ringer, Rengger, Rainger: Radulfus *filius Raingeri* 1147-53 DC (Nt); John *Rynger* 1319 SR (Ess). OFr *Rainger*, from OG *Reginger*. Richard *Renger*, alderman, sheriff and mayor of London, was the son of *Rainger* (Ricardus *filius Reinger* 1221 StP) and is usually called Richard *Reinger* or *Renger* (1225 Pat), having adopted or acquired his father's name as his surname. This at once became hereditary, for his sons, Richard and John, are both called *Renger* in 1235 (FFEss). The family bought an estate in Essex which is called *Renggers* in 1318, the 'inheritance of John *Renger'* in 1277, and is now represented by Ringer's Farm in Terling (PN Ess 297).

Ringrose: John *Ringerose* 1259 NorwDeeds; John *Ringros* 1332 SRCu; Thomas *Ryngotherose* 1332 SRLa; William *Ringrose* 1535 LWills. A nickname 'ring rose', the exact significance of which is obscure, cf. PLUCKROSE. The forms lend no support to Harrison's derivation of the second element from OE *rǣw* 'row'.

Riordan: v. REARDON

Ripley: Bernard, Roger *de Rippeley* c1175-83 YCh, 1242 Fees (Nb); Richard *Rypplay* 1381 PTY. From Ripley (Derby, Hants, Surrey, WRYorks).

Ripper: Adam *le Ripier(e)* 1279 RH (O); Gilbert *le Riper* ib. (Beds). A derivative of ME (*h*)*rip* 'basket', maker or seller of baskets. *Rypier* was used in 14th century London of those who brought fish from the sea for sale in the city.

Risbridger, Rusbridger: John *Rysebrigger* 1497 SRSr. 'Dweller by the brushwood-bridge or causeway' (OE **hrīs-brycg*), as at Rice Bridge (Sussex), Risebridge (Essex), Rising Bridge (Northants), Ridgebridge (Surrey), etc.

Rise: William *de Ris* 1210 Cur (Nt); Robert *del Rys* 1332 SRLa. From Rise (ERYorks) or 'dweller in the brushwood', OE *hrīs*.

Risher: v. RUSHER

Ritch: v. RICH

Ritchard: v. RICHARD

Ritchie, Richey, Richie, Richies: Duncan *Richie* 1505 Black. A Scottish diminutive of *Rich* (Richard).

Rivers: Gozelinus *de Lariuera* 1084 GeldR (W),

de Riuere, de Riuaria 1086 DB (So); Gozelinus *Riuere, Riuere* ib.; Walter *de la Rivere* c1150 Riev (Y); John *de Rypariis* 1286 FFEss. From La Rivière (Calvados, Pas-de-Calais) or other places of the same name. Tengvik suggests also a possible derivation from OFr *rivere*, 'dweller by the river'. How far later examples are from this or from a French place-name can only be decided by detailed investigation in each case. It is noteworthy that the preposition is always *de la*. For Matill' *atte Riuer*, John *Riuer* 1327 SRSx, a different etymology is essential. *v.* REVERE.

Rivett: John *Ryuet* 1327 SRSf. ME *ryvet, revette* 'a rivet', metonymic for *riveter*: Richard *le reveter* 1313 FrY, John *Reveter* 1381 PTY.

Rivis: *v.* REVIS

Rix: *v.* RICK

Rixon, Rixom, Rixson, Rickson: (i) Richard *Rikson* 1457 LLB K; William *Rixon* 1621 Oriel (O). 'Son of *Rick*.' (ii) Cristiana *atte Ryxen* 1395 FFSo. 'Dweller among the rushes.' *v.* RICK.

Roach, Roch, Roche: (i) John *de Roches* 1086 DB (Beds); Lucas *des Roches* 1249 Fees (Ha). From Les Roches (Seine-Inférieure). An occasional source. (ii) John *Roche* 1195 P (So); Ralph *de la Roche* 1195 P (Co), 1220 Cur (Sx); Roger *atte Roche* 1351 ColchCt. 'Dweller by the rock', ME, OFr *roche*. Robert *atte Roche* lived at Roach Fm in 1330 (PN D 578).

Road, Roads: *v.* RHODES

Roadnight, Road-Night, Rodnight: Robert *Rodcnicht*, John *le Rodknicht* 1221 AssWa; John *Rodknyth* 1332 SRWa. OE *rādcniht* 'mounted servant or retainer'.

Roaf, Roalfe: *v.* ROLF

Roake: *v.* ROKE

Roan, Rone: Willelmus *de Rotomago* 1148 Winton (Ha). From Rouen. cf. þe cite of *Roen, Roan, Rone* 1418–20 LondEng.

Roback: *v.* ROEBUCK

Robart(s): *v.* ROBERT

Robathan: *v.* ROWBOTHAM

Robb, Robbs, Robe: *Robe coccus* 1196 P (W); *Robbe* Cuth 1199 P (L); Richard *Robbe, Robe* 1177–8 P (Sx); Richard *Robbe* 1212 Fees (So); Simon *Robes* 1319 ELPN; Adam *Robbes* 1327 SRSf. A pet-form of *Robert*.

Robberds: *v.* ROBERT

Robbie, Robey: Beatrix *Robbie*, Issobell *Robie* or *Robye* 1597 Black (Aberdeen). A Scottish diminutive of ROBB.

Robbings, Robbins: *v.* ROBINS

Robe: *v.* ROBB

Robearts, Robers: *v.* ROBERT

Robens: *v.* ROBINS

Roberson: *v.* ROBERTSON

Robert, Roberts, Robart, Robarts, Robberds, Robearts, Robers: *Rodbertus, Rotbert, Robert* 1066 DB; Willelmus *filius Roberti* 1086 DB (K); *Rotbertus* 1134–40 Holme (Nf); *Rodbert* prest 1188 BuryS (Sf); John *Roberd* 1279 RH (Bk); William *Robert* 1292 FFEss; William *Robbard* 1296 SRSx; Richard *Roberdes* 1327 SRWo; Thomas *Robart*

1332 SRSt; Roger *Robardes* 1341 AD iv (Sa). OFr *Rodbert, Robert*, OG *Rod(b)ert* 'fame-bright'. It was introduced by Normans during the reign of Edward the Confessor and became very popular. Pet-forms and diminutives were formed early, *Robin* being particularly common. *v.* also DOBB, HOB, NOBBS, HOPKIN, ROPKINS, ROBJANT. The vowel has sometimes been unrounded to *a. v.* DABBS, RABB, RABBATTS.

Robertson, Roberson: William *Robertsone* 1327 SRDb; John *Roberdeson* 1354 AssSt; Andrew *Robersoun* 1450 Black (Arbroath); John *Robertsoune* 1464 ib. (Leith). 'Son of *Robert*.'

Robeson: George *Robesoun* 1633 Black. Perhaps 'Son of *Robe*' (Robert), but also a reduced form of *Robertson* or *Robinson*.

Robey, Roby: *v.* ROBBIE. May also be local from Robey (Derby) or Roby (Lancs).

Robins, Robyns, Robbins, Robbings, Robbens, Robens: *Robinus probator* 1198 P (Mx); *Robinus* 1206 Cur (C); Richard *Robin* c1248 Bec (Mx); Walter *Robyn* 1279 RH (O); Margaret *Robines* 1279 RH (C). A diminutive of *Rob* (Robert); *Robin* and *Robert* are used interchangeably: *Robin* or *Robertus* 1206 Cur (L); *Robinus, Robertus de Leic'* 1212 Cur (Nth); *Robert* called de Tylemount . . . the above *Robins* (sic) 1300 LoCt.

Robinson, Robison: John, Richard *Robynson* 1324 Wak (Y), 1332 SRLa; Thomas *Robyson* 1379 PTY; John *Robynson* 1426 Black; Donald *Robison, Robertson* 1446 ib.; James *Robison* (signs *Robinson*) 1808 SfPR. Usually 'Son of *Robin*', but also for *Robertson*, through *Roberson*.

Robjant, Robjohn, Robjohns, Rabjohn, Rabjohns: *Robezun de Weleford* 1166 P (R); William *Robegance* 1279 RH (C). *Rob-eç-un*, a double diminutive of *Rob* (Robert). For the formation, cf. HUTCHIN, and the French *Robeçon, Robichon, Robuchon*. The *ch* is the Picard form. Robjohns in Finchingfield (Essex) is named from Robert and Simon *Robechun, Robichun, Robchon* (1285, 1299, 1306) and is *Robjents* in 1777 (PN Ess 427).

Roblett: Richard *Robeloth* 1221 ElyA (Sf); Nicholas *Robylot* 1327 SRWo; Thomas *Roblet* 1524 SRSf. A double diminutive of *Rob* (Robert), *Rob-el-ot*.

Roblin, Rablan, Rablen, Rablin: Simon *Robelyn* 1276 RH (Beds). *Rob-el-in*, a similar diminutive of *Rob* or *Rab* (Robert).

Robotham, Robottom: *v.* ROWBOTHAM

Robson: Willelmus *filius Rob* 1327 SRDb; Richard *Robson* 1379 PTY. 'Son of *Rob*' (Robert).

Roby: *v.* ROBEY

Roch(e): *v.* ROACH

Rochelle, Rockall, Rockell, Rotchell: William *de Rokella* (*Rochella*) 1175 P (Beds); Philip *de la Rokele, Rochelle* 1203, 1207 FFEss; John *Rockel* 1275 RH (W). From La Rochelle or some French place by a rock (*roche*, Norman *roque*).

Rochester, Rogister: Turoldus (*de*) *Rouecestra* 1086 DB (Ess); Robert *Rouchestre* 1377 AssEss. From Rochester (Kent).

Rochford, Ratchford, Retchford: Waleram *de*

Rocheforde 1198 FF (Nt). From Rochford (Essex, Worcs).

Rock(s): *v.* ROKE

Rockall, Rockell: *v.* ROCHELLE

Rockcliffe: *v.* RAWCLIFF

Rocker, Rokker, Rooker, Rucker: William *le Rockere* 1228 Cl (Ireland); Richard *le Roker, le Rockare* 1279 RH (O); John, Lucas *Rockere* 1296 SRSx. Bardsley cites Juliana *Rokster* 1388, a derivative of ME *rok, rocke* 'distaff', a spinner. *Rocker* may be a masculine derivative of this, 'a maker of distaffs'. Or 'dweller by the rock'. *v.* ROKE.

Rockliffe: *v.* RAWCLIFF

Rodaway: *v.* RADWAY

Roddis: *v.* ROODHOUSE

Rodger(s): *v.* ROGER

Rodgie: John *Roger, Rogy, Rogie* c1525 Black; Helen *Rogie* or *Rodgie* 1597 ib. A Central Scottish pronunciation of *Roger*.

Rodgman, Roggeman: Richard *Rogerman* 1332 SRCu. 'Servant of *Roger*.' cf. William *Robertman* 1332 SRCu, William *Thomasman* 1379 PTY.

Rodhouse: *v.* ROODHOUSE

Rodney: Richard, William *de Rodeneye* 1304 Glast, 1331 IpmW; Walter *Rodney* 1520 FFEss. From an unidentified place on the borders of Somerset and Wilts, cf. *Radaneheye* 1282 Glast.

Rodnight: *v.* ROADNIGHT

Rodway: *v.* RADWAY

Roe, Roo: Ului *Ra* 1095 Bury (Sf); William *le Roe* 1170 P (Wa); Reginald *le Ro* 1188 BuryS (Sf); Benedict *le Roo* 1270 FFEss; Isolda *Ro, Roo* 1314–16 Wak (Y). OE *rā*, ME *rō* 'roe'. These names are midland and southern forms. In the north, *rā* remained unrounded and survives as RAE and RAY.

Roebotham: *v.* ROWBOTHAM

Roebuck, Roback: Adam *Rabuck* 1246 AssLa; Matilda *Robuc* 1297 SRY. OE *rā* and *bucc* 'roebuck'.

Rofe, Roff: *v.* ROLF

Roffey: Flavyen *de Rughehege* 1239 FFSf; Amfr' *de la Rogheye* 1275 RH (K). 'Dweller by some rough enclosure' as at Rolphy Green or Roffy (PN Ess 271, 477).

Roger, Rogers, Rogger, Rodger, Rodgers: *Rogerus* marescalcus 1066 DB (Ess); *Rogerius, Rogerus* 1086 DB; Richard *Roger* 1263 ArchC iv; William *Rogger* 1296 SRSx; Henry *Rogeres* 1327 SRWo. OFr *Roger, Rogier,* OG *Ro(d)ger* 'fame-spear'. The name was introduced from Normandy where OG *Rodger* was reinforced by the cognate ON *Hróðgeirr*. In England it was very popular, with pet-forms *Hodge* and *Dodge* and their derivatives, but it was not so productive of direct diminutives as Richard and Robert, only *Roget* and *Rogerun* having been noted: Robert *Rogeroun* 1327 SRSf. *Rogers* is the common form, with *Rodgers* in Scotland.

Rogerson: Donald *Rogerson* 1364 Black; William Rogerson 1379 PTY. 'Son of *Roger*.'

Roget, Rogett: Robert, Walter *Roget* 1279 RH (O), 1296 SRSx. *Rog-et*, a hypocoristic of *Roger*.

Roggeman: *v.* RODGMAN

Roginson: John *Rogesoune* 1570 Black. 'Son of *Roger*'. The modern form is eccentric, based on the variation between *Robinson* and *Robison*, etc.

Rogister: *v.* ROCHESTER

Rohan: Alan *de Roham* 1190 P (Sf). From Rohan (Morbihan).

Rohard: *v.* ROWARTH

Roke, Roake, Rock, Rocke, Rocks, Rook: Robert *Dellroc* c1182 MELS (Wo); Peter *de la Roke* 1243 AssSo; Richard *del Ak, atte Rok'* 1275, 1327 SRWo; Ralph *ater Oke, atte Oke* 1296, 1327 SRSx; Geoffrey *atte Ock, atter Ok* 1296, 1332 ib; William *atte Rock, atter Ok* 1296, 1327 ib.; Nicholas *de Aka* called *othe Roke* 1313 LLB E; Robert *of ye Rook* 1318 ib.; William *Attroc* 1327 SRWo; Henry *del Rook* 1332 SRSt; Richard *Bytherok'* 1333 MELS (So). ME *atter oke, atte roke* 'at the oak.' In ME the vowel sometimes became short, *v.* OAK, hence *Rock*, but where there is no confirmatory evidence, this may be from ME *rok* 'rock'. William *de Rok* 1242 Fees (Nb) came from Rock (Northumb) 'rock', but Rock (Devon, Worcs), Roke (Oxon) and Rook (Devon) all derive from *āc* 'oak'. *v.* OAK.

Rokker: *v.* ROCKER

Rolance, Roland: *v.* ROWLAND

Roleston: *v.* ROLLESTON

Rolf, Rolfe, Rolph, Roalfe, Roles, Rollo, Roll, Rolle, Rolles, Rolls, Roff, Roffe, Roaf, Rofe, Roof, Roofe, Rouf, Rouff, Rove, Row, Rowe, Rowes, Rowles, Ruff, Rulf, Rule: *Rolf* 1066 DB (Nt, Nf); *Roulf* ib. (Lei); Turstinus *filius Rolf, Rou, Roffi* 1086 DB; Robertus *filius Rolui, Roulf* ib.; *Roolf* 1142 NthCh (L) (a peasant); *Rolf* de Ormesby 1147–66 Gilb (L); *Rothof* filius Ketelli c1155–60 DC (L); *Rodulfus* filius Ketelli c1160–66 ib.; Martin *Rof* 1242 Fees (D); Robert *Rolf* Ed 1 Battle (Sx); William *Roulf* 13th Gilb (L); William *Rowe* 1275 RH (Sf); Robert *Rolle* 1279 ib. (Beds); Matilda *Rolles* ib. (Hu); Roger *Rolves* ib. (O); John *Roolf* 1296 SRSx; Robert *Roulfes* 1327 SRWo; Juliana *Roules* 1327 SRSo; John *Rowes* 1333 ColchCt; Thomas *Rowf* 1524 SRSf; William *Rowle* 1662 FrY; Richard *Rowles* 1675 FrY. ON *Hrólfr,* ODa, OSw *Rolf.* Found as the name of a peasant in Danish Lincs, it must sometimes be Anglo-Scandinavian, but the name was also common in Normandy where it became OFr *Roul, Rou,* often latinized as *Rollo* and it is to this that the frequency and variety of the surnames are due. *Roulf* may be a contracted form of ON **Hróðwulf,* the ultimate source of *Hrólfr.* There has been confusion with RALF. Some of these names have alternative origins.

Rolin, Roling: *v.* ROLLIN

Rolinson, Rolison: *v.* ROLLINGSON

Roll, Roll(es): *v.* ROLF

Rolland: *v.* ROWLAND

Rollason, Rollerson: *v.* ROLLINGSON

Roller: John *le Rollere* 1274 Wak (Y); Philip *le Roulour* 1327 SRSo, *le Rouller* 1337 FFSo. A derivative of ME *rolle,* OFr *rolle, roolle, roulle* 'a roll, piece of parchment'. Probably a maker or seller of rolls of parchment.

Rolleston, Rollston, Roleston, Rolston, Rolstone, Roulston, Roulstone, Rowleston, Rowlstone, Rowstone: Simon *de Roluestona* 1170 P (Lei); Robert *de Rolleston'* 1181 P (Nt). From Rolleston (Notts), *Roldeston* DB 'Hróald's farm', Rolleston (Leics, Staffs, Wilts) or Rowlston (ERYorks), all earlier *Rolvestun* 'Rolf's farm'.

Rollet, Rollett, Rollit, Rollitt: *Roelet* 1208 Cur (Ha); William *Raulot* 1279 RH (C); John *Raulot* 1296 SRSx. *Roelet* is a hypocoristic of *Rowland*. cf. ROWLATT, ROWLING. *Raulot* is a diminutive of *Raul* (Ralph). cf. RAWLIN. The normal development would be to *Rawlett*, the spelling *Rollet* being due to the influence of the common *Rolland*. *Rawlett* survived until 1670 (Bardsley).

Rollin, Rolling, Rollings, Rollins, Rolin, Roling: (i) John *Rolins* 1327 SRSf; John *Rolyns* 1327 SRSo. A diminutive of *Roll* (Rolf) or *Roland* (Rowland). *v.* ROLF, ROWLAND. cf. Richard *Rollevilain* 12th Riev (Y), 'Roll's villein'. The paucity of early examples suggests that *Rollin(g)* is often a late spelling for *Rawlin(g)*. cf. ROLLET. It may also be identical with ROWLING. (ii) Roger *de Rolling* 1275 RH (K). From Rowling Court in Goodnestone or Rowling Street in Bilsington (Kent). *v.* PN K 532.

Rollingson, Rollinson, Rollason, Rollerson, Rollison, Rollisson, Rolinson, Rolison: William *Rollandson* 1590 LaWills; John *Rollingson* 1596 ib. 'Son of *Roland*.' Common in Furness, side by side with ROWLINSON, where it has also become RAWLINGSON.

Rollitt: *v.* ROLLET
Rollo: *v.* ROLF
Rollons: *v.* ROWLAND
Rollston: *v.* ROLLESTON
Rolt, Roult: *Rold* 1066 DB. From ON *Hróaldr*. *v.* ROWAT.

Romain, Romaine, Roman, Romans, Romayn, Romayne: *Romanus* le corduaner 1221 Cur (Y); Adam *Romanus, Romayn* 1207–8 Cur (Sr); Reginald *le Romayn* 1275 RH (L); John *Roman* 1367 ColchCt; George *Romans* 1636 FrY. OFr *Romeyn* or *romeyn* 'a Roman'. *Romanus* was the name of two martyrs and a 7th-century bishop of Rouen. Only one English example of this personal-name has been noted, but it may sometimes be the source of the surname.

Romanes, Romanis, Romans: Philip *de Roumanoch* c1250 Black; Alexander *Romannois* 1508–20 ib; John *Romanoss* 1567 ib.; James *Rolmainhous, Romanis* 1642 ib. From Romanno in Newlands (Peebles-shire).

Rombulow: *v.* RUMBELLOW

Rome, Room, Roome: William *Rome* 1296 SRSx; John *de Rome* 1379 PTY; John *Roome* 1654 FrY. Either an immigrant from Rome or, perhaps, a pilgrim back from Rome. cf. ROMER. *Room* is the old pronunciation of *Rome* which Shakespeare rhymes with *doom* and *groom*, a pronunciation still used by Donne and Pope.

Romer, Roomer, Rummer: (i) Cristiana *la Romere* 1274 RH (Sf); John *Romere* 1296 SRSx. ME *romere* 'one who had made the pilgrimage to Rome'. For *Roomer, v.* ROME. *Rummer* shows a shortening of the vowel. (ii) William *de Romara* 1190 P (L). William de Roumare, earl of Lincoln, made a yearly payment to Rouen Cathedral from his rent of Roumare (Seine-Inférieure) near Rouen.

Romilly: Alexander *de Romeilli*, Alexander *Rumeilli* 1190, 1193 P (O); Alice *de Romeilli, de Rumelly* 1197, 1230 P (Cu, Y). From Remilly (La Manche). *v.* ANF. Richard *de Romilly* (1198) came from Romilly (Eure), ib. Alan *de Romely* 1262 AssSt may have come from Romiley (Ches).

Romney, Rumney: Robert *de Romenel, de Rumenae* 1086 DB (K); Ralph *de Romeney* 1279 RH (O). From Romney (Kent).

Ronald, Ronalds, Ranald: John *Rannald* 1463 Black; John *Ronald* 1655 ib. A Scottish equivalent of *Reynold*, but derived from ON *Rǫgnvaldr* which became OIr *Ragnall*, Gael *Raonull*.

Ronaldson: Doul *Ranaldsone*, Dowill *M'Renyll* (son of *Ronald* Alanson) 1511 Black. 'Son of *Ronald*.'

Ronson: *v.* ROWNSON
Roo: *v.* ROE
Roobottom: *v.* ROWBOTHAM
Roodhouse, Rodhouse, Roydhouse, Roddis: Henry *del Rodehouse* 1379 PTY; John *Roidosse, Roiddus* 1539–40 RothwellPR (Y); Joan *Roydhouse* 1549 ib.; John *Rodhouse* 1552 ib. 'Dweller at the house in the clearing.' *v.* RHODES, ROYDS.

Roof(e): *v.* ROLF
Rook, Rooke, Rookes, Rooks, Ruck: William *Roc* 1185 Templars (O); William *le Roke* 1243 AssSo; William *Ruk* 1296 SRSx; Richard *le Rouke* 1327 SRSo; Adam *Rucke* 1327 SRSf. OE *hrōc* 'rook', a nickname. *v.* also ROKE.

Rooker: *v.* ROCKER
Rookledge: *v.* ROUTLEDGE
Room(e), Room(e)s: *v.* ROME
Roomer: *v.* ROMER
Roope: *v.* ROPE
Roos(e): *v.* ROSS
Root, Roote, Rootes, Roots: Æðelstan *Rota* 955 OEByn (W); Walter, Ralph *Rote* 1185 Templars (L), 1216–36 Miller (C); John *Rotes* 1643 ArchC 48; William *Root* 1644 FrY. OE *rōt* 'glad, cheerful'. Occasionally also ME *rōte* 'psaltery', metonymic for RUTTER.

Rope, Ropes, Roope, Rupp: Richard *Rop* 1327 SRC. Metonymic for *Roper*.

Roper, Rooper, Raper, Rapier: Roger *Raper* 1219 AssY; Richard *le Ropere* 1220 Cur (Herts); Agnes *Raper* 1430 FeuDu; Alice *Rooper* 1450 Rad (C). A derivative of OE *rāp* 'rope', 'a roper, rope-maker'. *Roper* is the normal southern development. *Raper* persisted in the north.

Ropkins: Adam, Joan *Robekyn* 1279 RH (O), 1332 SRSx; Richard *Ropkin* 1524 SRSf. *Rob-kin*, a diminutive of *Rob* (Robert).

Rosamond: *v.* ROSEMAN

Rose, Royce, Royse: (i) *Rothais* 1086 DB (Herts); *Rohesia* 1219 AssY; *Roes'* de Killum ib.; Thomas *filius Rose* 1279 RH (C); *Rosa* Weuere 1327 SRSx; Robert, Peter *Rose* 1302 LoCt, 1327 SRWo; Richard *Roys* 1327 SRSf; Richard *Royse, Rose* 1604, 1609 Shef. OG *Hrodohaidis, Rothaid* 'fame-kind' (f), common among the Normans as *Rohese, Roese,* later *Royse,* becoming ME *Rose,* as if derived from *rosa* 'rose'. (ii) Robert *de la Rose* 1242 Fees (O); Adam *atte Rose* 1305 LoCt. From the sign of the rose.

Roseman, Rosamond, Rosoman: *Rosamunda* 1206 Cur (Sf); John *Rosemound* 1356 LLB F; Nicholas *Rosamon* 1359 Putnam (Co). OG *Rosemunda* (f).

Roskin: *v.* RUSKIN

Rosling, Rosslyn, Rusling: Robertus *filius Rozelin, Rotselini* 1086 DB; *Rocelin* de Riggesbi c1150 Gilb (L); Thomas *Roscelin* 1221 AssGl; John *Russelyn* 1316 Wak (Y); Amycia *Roslyn* 1327 SRC. OFr *Roscelin, Rocelin,* OG *Ruozelin, Roscelinus,* a double diminutive of OG *Rozzo.*

Rosoman: *v.* ROSEMAN

Ross: (i) *Rozo* 1086 DB (W); *Rosce* de Pileham 1196 P (L); Johannes *filius Rosce* 1197 P (K); Robert *Roce, Rosce* 1195, 1199 P (Nth); Richard *Rosse* 1327 SRC. OG *Rozzo,* a hypocoristic of compounds in *Hrod-.* Willelmus *filius Roce* 1207 Cur (Ess) is also called Willelmus *filius Rocelini* and William *Roce.* (ii) Anschetillus, Serlo *de Ros* 1086 DB (K, Beds); Bernard *de Rosse* 1177 P (Y); Philip *de Roos* 1246 AssLa. The families of Ros of Bedfordshire and of Kent came from Rots (Calvados), that of Roos of Helmsley from Roos (ERYorks), others from Roose (Lancs) or Ross (Hereford, Northumb).

Rossall: Robert *de Roshal* 1221 AssSa. From Ross Hall (Salop) or Rossall (Lancs).

Rossel, Rossell: Robertus *filius Rocel* 1214 Cur (L); Reginald, William *Rosel* 1182, 1195 P (Y, Do); Patriz *Rozel* 1185 Templars (Db). OFr *Roc-el,* a diminitive of *Rosce. v.* ROSS.

Rosslyn: *v.* ROSLING

Rosson, Rosten, Rostern, Rosthorn, Roston, Rostron: *v.* RAWSTHORN

Rotchell: *v.* ROCHELLE

Roth: Adam, Henry *atte Rothe* 1346 ColchCt, 1353 LLB G. 'Dweller in the clearing', OE **roþ,* as at Roe (Herts) or Rothend (Essex).

Rotheram, Rotherham, Rudderham, Rudrum: Richard *de Roderham* 1256 AssNb; Henry *de Rotherham* 1356 AssSt. From Rotherham (WRYorks).

Rotherforth: *v.* RUTHERFORD

Rothman: John *Rotheman* 1327 *SR* (Ess); Richard *Rothemon* 1342 AssSt. 'Dweller in the clearing.' *v.* ROTH.

Rothwell, Rowell: William *de Rowell'* 1200 P (Nth); William *(de) Rowell'* 1212 Fees (L); Robert *de Rothewelle* 1297 MinAcctCo. From Rothwell (Lincs, Northants, WRYorks).

Roubottom: *v.* ROWBOTHAM

Rouf(f): *v.* ROLF

Rough, Ruff: (i) John *le Rug* 1279 RH (O);

Geoffrey *Rugh* 1297 SRY. OE *rūh* 'rough'. (ii) John *ate Rogh* 1332 SRSx. 'Dweller by the rough, uncultivated ground', OE *rūh* used topographically.

Roughhead, Rowed, Ruffhead: Robert *Ruhaued* 1170–87 ELPN; Alexander *Ruhheued* 1218 FFSf; Robert *Roheued* c1230 P (Hu); John *Roughheved* 1304 AssSt; John *Rouhed* 1384 LoPleas; William *Roughed* 1524 SRSf. OE *rūh* 'rough' and *hēafod* 'head', 'one with rough, shaggy hair'.

Roughley: John *atte Roughle* 1351 Putnam (Sr). 'Dweller by the rough clearing', OE *rūh, lēah.*

Roukin: Agnes *Roulekin* 1275 RH (L). *Roul-kin,* a diminutive of *Roul* (Rolf).

Roulson, Rouson, Rowson: Thomas *Roulfisson'* 1327 SRC. 'Son of Rolf.'

Roulston(e): *v.* ROLLESTON

Roult: *v.* ROLT

Rounce: *v.* ROUND

Rouncewell: *v.* ROUNSEFELL

Round, Rounds, Rounce: Ralph *Rund'* 1202 FFEss; Alecok *Ronde* 1246 AssLa; Alan *Lerond* 1377 AssEss. OFr *roond* 'rotund, plump'.

Roundell: William *Rundel, Roundel* 1150 Oseney (O), 1301 SRY. A diminutive of ROUND.

Roundtree: *v.* ROWNTREE

Rounsefell, Rounsevall, Rounsivelle, Rouncewell, Rounswell: Geoffrey *de Runceual* 1254 *Ass* (Ess); Richard *Runcyual, Runsifal* 1296, 1327 SRSx. From Roncesvalles in the Pyrenees where there was a Priory of St Mary of which the Hospital of Our Lady of Rouncevale at Charing Cross was a cell.

Rountree: *v.* ROWNTREE

Rous, Rouse, Rowse, Ruse, Russ: Wilekin *Rous* 1225 AssLa; John *Russe* 1218 Fees (W); Symon *le Rus* 1253 FFHu; Margareta *le Ruse* 1285 FA (St). ME, AFr *rous(e)* 'red'.

Rouson: *v.* ROULSON

Roussell: *v.* RUSSEL

Rout: Clarice *atte Route* 1296 SRSx; Henry *Route* 1317 AssK. Probably 'dweller by the rough ground', OE **rūt. v.* MELS 171.

Routledge, Rutledge, Rudledge, Rookledge, Rucklidge: Symon *Routlage* 1494 Black; David *Routlesche* 1512 ib.; William *of Retleche,* William *Routleth* Hy 8 PN Cu 25; Jorge *Rutliche* 1524 SRSf; Martin *de Rotheluche* 1537 Black; John *Rutledge, Routledge* 1606, 1639 FrY; Abraham *Roottlidg, Rookledge, Rockleidg* 1657, 1670, 1679 RothwellPR (Y). Harrison's derivation from Routledge (Cumb) is unlikely as the only place of the name in that county is Routledge Burn which is not recorded before the 16th century and probably derives from the surname. This is a border name, English rather than Scottish, from some place which still remains unidentified.

Rove: *v.* ROLF

Rover, Ruffer: John *le Rofere* 1279 MEOT (Sr); John *Rouer(e)* 1297 MinAcctCo, 1375 ColchCt. A derivative of OE *hrōf* 'roof', a constructor or repairer of roofs.

Row, Rowe: (i) Geoffrey *le Ruwe* 1195 P (Lei); Richard, John *le Rowe* 1260 AssCh, 1327 SRC; Walter *le Rowe, le Rouwe* 1262 *For* (Ess), 1320

FFEss; William *Rowe* 1275 RH (Sf). OE *rūh* 'rough'. cf. ROUGH and *v.* also ROLF. (ii) Richard *atte Rowe* 1306 AssSt; John *de Rowe* 1317 AssK; Robert *del Rowe* 1327 SRSf. 'Dweller in the row of houses or in the street', OE *rāw. v.* RAW, REW.

Rowarth, Roworth, Raworth, Rohard: *Rohard-(us)* 1086 DB (So); Hugo *filius Rohard* 1193 P (He); Benedictus *filius Ruardi* 1219 AssY; Peter *Ruard'* 1220 ClR (L); Alice, Joan *Roward* 1279 RH (O), 1327 *SR* (Ess). OFr *Rohart, Roart*, OG *Hrodhard, Rodhard* 'glory-brave'. This has probably also become ROWAT. *Rohard* is rare.

Rowat, Rowatt, Rowett: *Rold* 1066 DB (L); Alanus *filius Ruhald'* 1175 P (Y); *Roaldus* filius Alani 1213 Cur (Nth); Robert *Rohald'*, *Roald, Ruald* 1214 Cur (Wa); John *Makrowat* 1513 Black (Wigtown); John *Rowett* or *Rowatt* 1585 ib. (Glasgow). ON *Hróaldr*, ODa, OSw *Roald. v.* ROLT. From *Roald* we probably also have RO-WELL, and from *Roaud*, the vocalized form undocumented, *Rowat*. The name may also derive from *Rohart. v.* ROWARTH.

Rowberry, Rowbrey, Rowbury, Rubery, Ruberry, Rubra: Roger *de Rubury* 1327 SRWo. From Roborough (Devon), Rowberrow, Ruborough Hill (Som) or Rowborough (Isle of Wight), all 'rough hill'.

Rowbotham, Rowbottam, Rowbottom, Roubottom, Robathan, Robotham, Robottom, Roebotham, Roobottom: Dorythye *Robotom* 1546 Bardsley; Oliver *Robotham* 1592 ib.; Thomas *Rowbotham* 1613 ib. 'Dweller in the rough valley', probably in Lancashire.

Rowcliffe: *v.* RAWCLIFF

Rowed: *v.* ROUGHEAD

Rowell: For ROTHWELL, or 'dweller by the rough hill' (OE *rūh* and *hyll*), as at Rowell (Devon) where the surname is *Rowehill* in 1333 (PN D 491).

Rower, Royer: Roger *le Roier* 1176 P (Herts); Gilbert *le Roer* 1185 Templars (Sa); John *le Rohier* 1195 P (Nf); Ralph *le Rowere* 1240 Oseney (O); John *Royer* 1279 RH (Hu); John *le Rouier* 1327 SRSx. OFr *roier, rouwier, roer, rouer* 'wheelwright'. Dyonisia *la Rowere* was owed money for *wheels* by the Commonalty of London in 1301 (LLB C).

Rowet, Rowett: (i) William *Roet* 1219 Cur (Nf). *Ro-et*, a diminutive of *Ro(w)*, i.e. *Rolf*. (ii) Richard *atte Rouette* 1296 SRSx. 'Dweller by the rough ground', OE **rūwet*.

Rowland, Rowlands, Rawland, Rolland, Rollons, Roland, Rolance: (i) *Rolland* 1086 DB; *Rolandus, Ruelandus* Decanus 1133-60, 1188 Rams (Hu); *Rollandus* de Dinan c1155 DC (L); *Roudlandus* de la Genouerai Hy 2 DC (Lei); *Roulandus* de Withcala 12th DC (L); *Roelandus* 1212 Cur (Berks); *Rotelandus* Dauvers 1214 Cur (Bk); *Rodlandus* 1240 Rams (Nf); Nicholas *Ruel'* (*Rueland'*, *Roelent*) 1219 Cur (Nf, D); Simon *Rolland'* 1218 AssL; William *Roulland'* 1221 AssGl; Geoffrey *Rodland* 1244 Rams (Beds); Nicholas *Roland* 1303

FFEss. OFr *Rollant, Rolant, Rolent, Roulent*, OG *Hrodland, Rodland* 'famous land'. A popular name, largely due to *Roland*, the most famous of the peers of Charlemagne. In the *Chanson de Roland* it appears as *Rollanz* and *Rollant*, and in the *Cursor Mundi* as *Rauland*. It was introduced by the Normans and has numerous derivatives, some of which have been confused with those of *Ralf*. (ii) Ralph *de Rowlond* 1296 SRSx; Alan *de Roland* 1327 SRDb. From Rowland (Derby) or Rowland Wood in Slinfold (Sussex).

Rowlandson: 'Son of *Rowland*.' cf. William *Roulandman* 1332 SRCu. *v.* ROLLINGSON, ROW-LINGSON, ROWNSON.

Rowlatt, Rowlett: William *Roulot* 1327 SRSf. A hypocoristic of *Rowland*. cf. ROLLET.

Rowlerson: *v.* ROWLINGSON

Rowles: *v.* ROLF

Rowleston: *v.* ROLLESTON

Rowley: William, Adam *de Ruelay* 1219 AssY; Geoffrey *de Roweleye* c1280 SRWo; John *Rowley* 1348-9 IpmNt. From Rowley (Devon, Durham, Staffs, ER, WRYorks), or Rowley Hill (Essex).

Rowling, Rowlins: *Roelin, Rohelin* 1195 P (Cu); Adam, Geoffrey *Roulin* 1327 SRSf. *Roel-in, Roul-in*, hypocoristics of *Rowland. v.* ROLLIN.

Rowlingson, Rowlinson, Rowlison, Rowlerson: John *Rowlinson* 1608 LaWills. 'Son of *Rowland*.' *v.* ROLLINGSON, ROWNSON.

Rowlstone: *v.* ROLLESTON

Rowney: Agnes *de Rowenheye* 1275 SRWo; Walter *ate Roueneye* 1279 RH (O); Walter *de Rounhey* 1309 SRBeds; Beatrice *Roweney* 1327 *SR* (Ess). From Rowney Green (Worcs), Rowney Wood (Essex), or from residence near a rough enclosure (OE *rūh, (ge)hæg*).

Rownson, Ronson: Richard *Rowlandson* or *Rownessonn* 1607 LaWills; John *Rowanson* or *Rownson* 1639 ib.; John *Rowlandson* or *Rownson* 1715 ib. A north Lancashire form of ROWLAND-SON.

Rowntree, Rountree, Roundtree: Robert *Rountre* 1301 SRY; John *Roundtree* 1659 Bardsley. 'Dweller by the rowan-tree.'

Rowse: *v.* ROUS

Rowson: *v.* ROULSON

Rowstone: *v.* ROLLESTON

Rowstron: *v.* RAWSTHORN

Rowton: Ivo *de Roweton'* 1255 RH (Sa); William *atte Ruetune* 1275 RH (K); Robert *atte Rowetoune, atte Rugheton* 1327, 1332 SRSx. From Rowton (Salop, ERYorks) or 'dweller by the rough enclosure', OE *rūh, tūn*.

Roy: Adam *le Roy* 1268 FFSf; Simon *Roy* 1279 RH (C). OFr *roi* 'king', used also as a personal-name: *Roi* de Scallebi 1188 P (L). *v.* RAY.

Royce: *v.* ROSE

Roycraft, Roycroft: *v.* RYCROFT

Roydhouse: *v.* ROODHOUSE

Royds: Adam *de Roides* 1379 PTY. A Yorkshire dialect pronunciation of RHODES.

Royer: *v.* ROWER

Royle: Bernard *de Royl* 1230 Cl; William *de*

Roille 1290 AssCh; Nicholas *Royle* 1551 FFSt. From Royle (Lancs).

Ruber(r)y, Rubra: *v.* ROWBERRY

Rubottom: *v.* ROWBOTHAM

Ruck: *v.* ROOK

Rucker: *v.* ROCKER

Rucklidge: *v.* ROUTLEDGE

Rudd: Gerard, William *Rudde* 1189 P (Y), 1199 AssSt. OE **rud-*, the root of OE *rudig* 'ruddy', *rudduc* 'red-breast'.

Rudderham: *v.* ROTHERAM

Ruddick, Ruddock, Rudduck: Azor *Ruddoch* 1176 P (Beds); Matilda *Ruddoc* 1275 SRWo. OE *ruddoc* 'robin-redbreast'.

Ruddiforth: *v.* RUTHERFORD

Ruddin: *v.* READING

Rude: *v.* RIDE

Rudeforth: *v.* RUTHERFORD

Rudge: (i) William *de Rugge* 1196 P (St). From Rudge (Glos, Salop). (ii) Walter *de la Rugge* 1243 AssSo; Alan *atte Rugg* 1296 SRSx; Geoffrey *ate regge* ib.; Roger *othe Rugge* 1327 SRWo. From residence near a ridge (OE *hrycg*). In ME this became *rugge, regge, rigge* in different dialects. *Regge* does not seem to have survived. For *rigge* *v.* RIDGE. *Rudge* is still used for *ridge* in Worcs where it is found in Rodge Hill. (iii) Roger *Rugge* 1195 P (D); Osbert *le Rugg'* 1275 RH (K); Gilbert *Rougge* 1377 AssEss. AFr *rug(g)e*, Fr *rouge* 'red', i.e. 'red-haired'. cf. ROUS.

Rudgeley: *v.* RUGELEY

Rudledge: *v.* ROUTLEDGE

Rue: *v.* REW

Ruff: *v.* ROLF, ROUGH, ROW

Ruffer: *v.* ROVER

Ruffet, Ruffett: Roger *Rucfot* 1205 P (Y); John *Rofot* 1277 AssSo; Henry *Rugfot* 1297 MinAcctCo; Adam, Arnold *Roufot* 1327 *SR* (Ess), 1360 ColchCt. OE *rūh* 'rough, hairy' and *fōt* 'foot', the exact meaning being obscure.

Ruffhead: *v.* ROUGHEAD

Rugeley, Rudgeley, Rudgley: Giles *de Rugeleye* 1301 AssSt. From Rugeley (Staffs).

Rulf: *v.* ROLF

Rumball, Rumbell, Rumbold, Rumbolt, Rumbol, Rumboll, Rumble, Rumbles: *Rumbaldus* 1086 DB (Gl); Robert, Roger *Rumbald* 1191 P (Ess), 1195 P (Cu); William *Rumbol'* 1222 Cur (Ha); William *Rumbolt* 1327 SRC. OG *Rumbald*.

Rumbellow, Rumbelow, Rombulow: Robert *Romylow, Rombilow* 1524 SRSf; William *Rumbilow, Rumbelow* ib. Bardsley, Harrison and Weekley agree in taking this name as a nickname for a sailor from the meaningless combination of syllables sung as a refrain whilst rowing, an explanation unlikely in itself, as there is no evidence for the use of *rumbelow* as a generic name for a sailor, whilst the nickname seems quite unsuited to the first known bearer of the name, Stephen *Romylowe*, constable of Nottingham Castle in 1347. Of ten examples of his surname only one contains a *b* (*Rombylou* 1351 Pat) whilst two, *de Romylo* (1346 Pat) and *de Romylou* (1363 NottBR), point clearly to a place-name ending in *-low*. This must be identical in origin with The Rumbelow in Aston (Warwicks), *Rumbelowe* 1461, the home of Richard *de Thrimelowe* in 1334. A second example of the same name is Tremelau Hundred (Warwicks) and a third is Rumbelow in Wednesfield (Staffs), *le Thromelowe* 1339, *Romylowe* 1420 (PN Wa 31). All three are from OE *æt þrēom hlāwum* (dweller) 'by the three mounds or barrows'. The Suffolk surname probably originated in Suffolk.

Rumford, Rumfitt: Warin *de Rumford* c1233 HPD (Ess). From Romford (Essex).

Rummer: *v.* ROMER

Rumney: *v.* ROMNEY

Rump: Thurstan, Robert *Rumpe* c1095 Bury (Sf), c1170 Rams (C). ME *rumpe* 'buttocks'. cf. dial. *rump* 'an ugly rawboned animal', used contemptuously of a person (EDD).

Runacres, Runacus, Runagle, Runeckles, Runecles, Runicles, Runnackles, Runnacles, Runnagall, Runneckles, Runnicles, Ranacre, Ranigar: Alan *de Ruynacres* 1246 AssLa; Richard *de Reinacre* 1261 ib.; Richard *de Rynacres* 1332 SRLa; William *Renacles* 1500 FrLeic; Alice *Renakers* 1568 SRSf; Alice *Runnaker* 1575 SfPR; Widow *Runnicre* 1674 HTSf; Elizabeth *Runicles* 1798 SfPR; Mark *Runnacles* 1815 ib. 'Dweller by the rye acre(s)' (OE *rygen, æcer*), as at Renacres (Lancs).

Runcie: Roger, Laurence *Rouncy* 1230 Eynsham (O), 1276 RH (O). ME *runcy, rouncy* 'rouncy, nag', for RUNCIEMAN.

Runcieman, Runciman, Runchman: Adam *Runciman* 1697 Bardsley. 'Man in charge of the rouncies.'

Rundall, Rundell, Rundle: (i) Richard, Herbert *Rundel* Hy 2 DC (Lei), 1197 P (Nf). OFr *rondel*, a diminutive of *rond*. *v.* ROUND. (ii) Thomas *de Rundal* 1275 RH (K). From Rundale in Shoreham (Kent).

Runnackles, Runnagall: *v.* RUNACRES

Rupp: *v.* ROPE

Rusbridger: *v.* RISBRIDGER

Ruse: *v.* ROUS

Rush: John *ate Russh'* 1332 SRSr. 'Dweller among the rushes', OE *rysc* 'rush', used collectively.

Rusher, Risher: John *le Russere*, Geruase *le Rischere* 1296 SRSx. A derivative of OE *rysc* 'rush', a cutter or seller of rushes. cf. Alan *le Rusmangor* 1210 Oseney (O). Also 'dweller among the rushes'. cf. RUSH.

Rushton: Robert *de Riston'* 1203 AssNth; John *de Russheton'* 1340 Crowland; John *Russheton* 1433–4 FFWa. From Rushton (Ches, Northants, Staffs), the last two are *Risetone* DB.

Ruskin, Roskin: *Rosekin* 1220 FFEss; John *Rosekyn* 1389 FFC; John *Ruskyn* 1498 RochW. A diminutive of *Rosce*. *v.* ROSS.

Rusling: *v.* ROSLING

Russ(e): *v.* ROUS

Russel, Russell, Russill, Rousel, Rousell, Roussel, Roussell: *Russel* c1095 Bury (Sf); *Russellus de Suberton'* 1212 Cur (So); Ralph, Robert *Russel*

1115 Winton (Ha), 1169 P (Do); John *Roussel* 1297 MinAcctCo. OFr *rous-el*, a diminutive of *rous* 'red', used also as a personal-name.

Russon: Peter *Russessone* 1308 AD i (Hu); Hugh *Rosesone* 1342 AD vi (St); John *Rossissone* 1365 AD ii (Sf). 'Son of *Ross* or of *Rose*.'

Rust: Cenwold *Rust* 1016–20 OEByn (K); Robert, Richard *Rust* 1148 Winton (Ha), 1275 RH (Nf). OE *rūst* 'rust', used of reddish hair or complexion.

Ruston, Rustom: Richard *de Ruston'* 1194 P (L); Randle *de Ruston* 1260 AssCh; John *Ruston* 1379 PTY. From Ruston (Devon, Norfolk, NRYorks), or Ruston Parva (ERYorks).

Rustrick: *v.* RASTRICK

Ruth: William *Ruth* 1180 P (L), 1275 RH (Nf). ME *reuthe* 'pity'.

Rutherford, Rutherfoord, Rutterford, Rotherforth, Ruddiforth, Rudeforth: William *de Rwthirford* a1200 Black; Nicholas *de Rothirford* 1296 ib.; Nicholas *Rotherforth* 1645 FrY; John *Rudderforth* 1758 ib. From Rutherford (Roxburghshire, NRYorks).

Rutledge: *v.* ROUTLEDGE

Rutt: Godric *Rute* 1166 P (Nf); William *le Rutte* 1278 RH (O); James *Rutt* 1524 SRSf. Metonymic for RUTTER 'player on the rote'.

Rutter: Simon *le rotur* Hy 2 DC (Lei); Reginald *Ruter* 1210 Cur (Cu); Thomas *le Roter* 1251 Fees (Wa); Thomas *le rotour*, Richard *le routour* 1297 MinAcctCo; John *Rutter* 1524 SRSf. OFr *roteor*, *roteeur*, *routeeur* 'a player on the rote', a musical instrument, a kind of fiddle (a1300 NED). The forms in *-er* may be from OFr *rotier*, *routier* 'robber, highwayman, ruffian' (1297 NED).

Rutterford: *v.* RUTHERFORD

Rycroft, Rycraft, Roycraft, Roycroft: Richard *de Riecroft* c1230 Barnwell (C); Richard *de Ruycroft* 1325 AssSt. 'Dweller by the ryecroft', OE *ryge, croft*.

Ryde: *v.* RIDE

Ryder: *v.* RIDER

Rydings: *v.* READING

Rye: (i) Hubert *de Ria* 1169 P (Nf). From Ryes (Calvados). If this has survived, it is rare. (ii) Matillis *de la Rye* 1237 CartAntiq (Ha); William *de Rye* 1240 FFEss; Geoffrey *ate Rye* 1297 MinAcctCo. Usually from ME *at ther ye*, becoming *at the rye* 'at the island or low-lying land', as in Rye (Sussex), The Rye (Bucks), Rye House (Herts), etc. *v.* also REA.

Ryecart: Fulco *de Ruycote* 1259 Oseney (O). From Rycote (Oxon).

Ryland, Rylands, Rylance: Stephen *de Riland* 1232–45 RegAntiquiss; John *de Rylaundes* 1281 AssLa; Thomas *de Rilond* c1296 AssCh. 'Dweller by the land where rye is grown.'

Ryley: *v.* RILEY

Ryman: *v.* RAYMAN

S

Saayman: *v.* SEAMAN

Saban, Sabben, Saben, Sabin, Sabine: *Sabina* 1186–1210 Holme (Nf), 1220 Cur (K, Sr); Rogerus *filius Sabini* 1252 Rams (Hu); Richard *Sabin* 1221 AssWa; John *Sabine* 1279 RH (C). There were three saints named *Sabinus* and one *Sabina*. Lat *Sabinus* 'a Sabine'. In England, the woman's name was much the more common.

Saber: *v.* SEABER

Sablin, Sabline: Willelmus *filius Sabeline* 1182–3 StP (Lo); *Sabelina* 1197 P (Lo), 1211 Cur (Mx); Roger *Sabelyn* 1297 MinAcctCo (O). *Sab-el-in(a)*, a double diminutive of *Sabin(a)*.

Sach, Sacher, Satch: Henry *le Sachiere* 1280 MESO (Ha); John *le Sachere* 1294 RamsCt (Hu). OFr *sachier* 'maker of sacks'. cf. SACKER. *Sach, Satch* are metonymic.

Sack: Symon *Sac'* c1250 Rams (C); William *Sak* 1327 *SR* (Ess). OE *sacc* 'sack'. Metonymic for SACKER.

Sacker, Sackur, Secker, Saker: Geoffrey *Sakker* t John ELPN; Hugh *le Saker* 1225 AssSo; Eva *le Seckere* 1277 Wak (Y). A derivative of OE *sacc* or ON *sekkr* 'sack'. 'A maker of sacks or coarse cloth, sackcloth.' cf. Ralph *Sakeman* 1209 P (Hu), Henry *le Sacwebbe* 1279 AssSo.

Sackville, Sackwild: Richard *de Sachanuilla, de Sacheuilla* 1086 DB (Herts, Ess); Simon *Sakeuilla* 1154–89 Colch (Ess); Alexander *de Saccauill', de Saccheuilla, de Sakeuill'* 1162–98 StP (Lo); William *de Sauchevilla* 1176 P (Bk). Round's derivation of the Sackvilles, later dukes of Dorset, from Sauqueville (Seine-Inférieure) is accepted by Loyd. Their identification of the Essex DB under-tenant, of a different family, as coming from Secqueville-en-Bessin (Calvados) depends solely on the fact that the place is 11 kilometres from Ryes, the place of origin of Eudo Dapifer under whom he held. The early forms of Secqueville are *Sicca Villa* (1077), *Secheville* (1155), *Secqueville* (1217), which do not fit in with those of Sackville and probably survive as SETCHFIELD. Richard probably came, as suggested by Dupont, from Sacquenville (Eure), recorded as *Sachenville* (1195), *Sakenvilla* (c1210), *Sackevilla* (1220). *v.* OEByn, ANF.

Sadd: Roger *Sad* 1086 DB (Nf); Henry *Sadde* 1229–41 StP (Ess). ME *sad(de)* 'serious, discreet, firm'.

Saddler, Sadleir, Sadler, Sadlier: Simon *le* *Sadelere* 1288 MESO (Sx); Peter *le Sadelare* 1296 Wak (Y). A derivative of OE *sadol* 'saddle', a maker or seller of saddles (1389 NED).

Saer: *v.* SAYER

Saffell, Saffill, Saffle, Safhill: *Safugel* 1066 Winton (Ha); Willelmus *filius Safoul* 1182–1200 BuryS (L); Rannulfus *filius Safugel, Safuwel, Sefugel* 1196–7 P, 1200 Cur (Sf); *Sefull* the chaplain 1268 AD ii (Sf); Halwær *Sæfugulasuna* c1150 YCh; John *Seful* 1275 SRWo; Robert *Sefoul* 1279 RH (O); John *Safowel* 1327 *SR* (Ess); John *Sefughel* 1332 SRSx; John *Safoul* 1376 AssEss; John *Saffull* 1434 FFEss. AScand *Sæfugul*, from ON *sæfogl* 'sea-bird', especially the cormorant, not recorded as a personal name in Scandinavia but common in England after the Conquest.

Saffer, Saffir: Robert *le Saffere*, John *Saffare* 1275 SRWo. Probably OFr *saffre* 'glutton'. *v.* also SAVARY.

Saffery, Saffrey: *Safrei* 1198 FF (Sf); *Sefridus* 1214 Cur (Sx); *Saffredus* 1214 Cur (Bk); Robert *Safrey* c1230 Barnwell (C); William, Roger *Sefrey* 1275 RH (Nf); Bryan *Saffrey* 1327 SRC. OE *Sæfrið* 'sea-peace', a personal name recorded in the 9th and 10th centuries, and then not until the 12th. *v.* also SAVARY.

Saffill, Saffle, Safhill: *v.* SAFFELL

Safford: John *de Safford* 1296 SRSx. From Seaford (Sussex).

Sagar, Sager, Saiger, Saggers, Seagars, Seager, Seagers, Seegar, Seeger, Segar, Seger, Segger: *Sagar* 1066 DB (D); *Segarus* ib. (Ess); Galfridus *filius Seger* 1222 Pat (D); Walter *Sagar* 1195 P (Do); Ralph *Segar* 1207 Cur (Beds); John *Seger* 1275 RH (Nf). OE *Sægār* 'sea-spear', unrecorded in OE, but fairly common from 1066 onwards. *Seager* would naturally become *Sigger* and be confused with SIGGERS.

Sage: Robert *le Sage* 1185 P (Sa); Ralph *Sage* 1190 BuryS (Sf); Petronilla *la Sage* 1206 FFSt. OFr *sage* 'wise'.

Saggers, Saiger: *v.* SAGAR

Sailer, Saylor, Seiler, Seiller, Seyler: Herbert *le Sayllur* 1191–1210 YCh; Hugh *le Saylliur* 1275 RH (Sf); Robert *le Salyour* 1327 SRSf; John *Sayller* 1327 *SR* (Ess). OFr *sailleor, salleor, sailleur, saillur* 'dancer'.

Sailes, Sails: Hugh *de Sailes* 1219 AssY; Agnes *del Sayles*, William *Saylles* 1379 PTY. From Sales

(Lancs), *Saylys* c1535, or from residence near a pool or pools (ON *seyla*). v. PN La 217.

Sainer: v. SENIOR

Saines, Sains: *Sæuuine, Seuuinus, Sauuin, Sauinus* 1066 DB; *Sewinus* 1207 Cur (Ess); Petrus *Sewinus* 1242 Fees (W); William *Sewine* c1250 Rams (C); Thomas *Sewyne* 1327 *SR* (Ess). OE *Sæwine* 'sea-friend'. One would expect this to become *Sewin* or *Sawin* but such forms would inevitably be contracted in everyday speech. cf. Saintbury (Gl), *Seinesberia* 1186, probably from *Sæwines-burg* (DEPN).

Sainsberry, Sainsbury: Reginald *de Seinesberia* 1190 P (Gl). From Saintbury (Glos).

Saint, Sant, Sants, Saunt: Roger *le Sent* c1250 Riev (Y); Hugh *Sant* 1270 RamsCt (C). ME *seint*, *saint*, AFr *seint*, OFr *sant* 'saint', a nickname.

Sainter: v. SENTER

Sait: *Saiet* 1066 DB (Beds, O), 1115 Winton (Ha); *Saegeat* 1077 PNDB (Wo); Thomas *Seiete* 1115 Winton (Ha); Robert *Seyet* c1240 Fees (Bk). OE *Sægēat* 'sea-Geat'.

Saker: v. SACKER

Salaman, Salamon, Salamons, Salomon, Salomons, Salman, Salmen, Salmon, Salmond, Salmons, Samman, Sammon, Sammonds, Sammons: *Salomon* 1066 DB (Y); *Salamon clericus* 1121–48 Bury (Sf); *Salomon* (a chaplain) 1159 Black (Roxburgh); Hugo *filius Salman* 1219 AssY; *Salman* Salman 1382 LoPleas; *Salamon* Salmon 1394 ib.; Roger *Salmon* 1210 Cur (Beds); Robert *Salemon*' 1212 Fees (L); Lambert *Saumon* 1242 Fees (Ha); Geoffrey *Saleman* c1248 Bec (Sf); Adam *Sauman* 1275 RH (L); William *Sammoun* 1279 RH (Hu); Willelmus dictus *Salomon* 1287 Husting; William *Saleman* 1296 SRSx; Richard *Salman, Salamon* 1301 LoCt; John *Sawmond* 1494 Black; Thomas *Samond* 1524 SRSf; James *Salmond* 1546 Black. OFr *Salomon, Salemon*, a Hebrew name, from *shalom* 'peace'. *Salomon* was the common medieval form, used in the Vulgate, by Tyndale and Cranmer and in the Rheims version (1582). *Solomon* is the form used in the Geneva Bible and the Authorized Version. The *dictus Salamon* of 1287 shows that it was occasionally a nickname, probably 'the wise', but the name was not uncommon from the 12th to the 14th centuries and was not confined to Jews. It is found as the name of a cleric, a chaplain and a canon. Occasionally the modern *Salamon(s)*, *Salomon(s)* may be Jewish. *Solomon(s)* certainly is. Tengvik and Wallenberg consider the surname may also be OE, ME **saleman* 'salesman', evidenced in NED from 1642. This appears unlikely. There is no example of *le saleman*. The form shows a natural weakening of the vowel on the way from *Salaman* to *Salman*, which is certainly found as the personal name. There seems no reason to doubt that Thomas *Salamon, Salomon* (1317), who probably gave name to Salmans in Penshurst (Kent), was a descendant of a *Salamon* (PN K 93). John *Saleman* (1319 SRLo) was a son of *Solomon* Burghard. The *d* of *Salmond* is late and excrescent.

Sale, Sales: Robert *de la Sale* 1243 AssSo; Nicholas *ate Sale* 1296 SRSx; Edmund *del Sale* 1327 SRSf; John *Sales* 1524 SRSf. Dweller *atte sale*, from OE *sealh, salh* 'sallow', used of certain species of *Salix* of a low-growing or shrubby habit, as distinct from osiers or willows. The surnames may also derive from OE *sæl* 'hall', servant at the hall. Hugh *de la Sale* (1277 So) and Philip *de la Sale* (Wo) are also called *de Aula* (MELS).

Salesbury: v. SALISBURY

Salingar, Salinger, Sallagar, Seliger, Selinger, Sellinger: Reginaldus *de Sancto Leodegario* 1176 P (Wo); John *de Sentliger* 1327 SRSx; Thomas *Sillinger* 1327 SRWo; Richard *de Seyntliger* 1332 SRSx; John *Selyngier* 1423–66 Bart (Lo). From Saint Léger-aux-Bois (Seine-Inférieure) or Saint-Léger (La Manche). v. ANF.

Salisbury, Salisberry, Salesbury, Salusbury, Salsbury: William *de Salesberie* 1115 Winton (Ha). From Salisbury (Wilts). In Lancashire, from Salesbury (Lancs): Bernard *de Salesbiry* 1246 AssLa.

Salkin, Salkind, Sawkins: *Salkyn* Eldefeld 1327 *SR* (Ess); Robert, William *Salekyn* 1255 RamsCt (Hu), 1307 AD iv (K); John *Saukyn* 1359 Putnam (Co). This might be from *Saul* but is probably from the more common *Salaman*: *Sale-kin* 'little Salaman'.

Sall, Salles: (i) Warin *de Salle* 1202 FFNf. From Sall (Norfolk). (ii) Robert *del Sal(l)* 1297 MinAcctCo; John *atte Salle* 1327 SRWo; John *del Sal* 1332 SRCu. 'Servant at the hall' (OE *sæl*, or in Cumb, ON *salr*). (iii) Johannes *filius Salle* 1308 RamsCt (Nf). A pet-name, perhaps from *Salaman*.

Sallagar: v. SALINGAR

Sallaway: v. SALWAY

Sallis(s): v. SALLOWS

Sallitt: *Salide* 1066 DB (Ha); Ailwardus *filius Salide* 1195 P (Berks); *Selide le Cupere* 1195 P (Nf); John, Matill' *Selide* 1206 P (Gl), 1221 ElyA (Sf); Robert *Seled*' 1252 Rams (Hu); William *Saled* 1297 MinAcctCo (Mx). OE **Sælida*, an original nickname, not recorded before the Conquest, from OE *sælida* 'seafarer, pirate'.

Salloway: v. SALWAY

Sallows, Sallis, Salliss: Nicholas *de Sallowe* 1254 RH (Sa); Robert *ate Salwe* 1297 MinAcctCo; William *Salowes* 1524 SRSf. 'Dweller by the willows' (OE *sealh*), though the examples are chiefly singular.

Salman, Salmen, Salmon, Salmond, Salmons: v. SALAMAN

Salsbury: v. SALISBURY

Salt, Sault: Nicholas *de Salt* 1199 AssSt; William *de Saut* 1203 Pl (St); Hugh *de Salt* 1332–3 SRSt. From Salt (Staffs), *Saute* 1236.

Salter, Saulter, Sauter, Sautter, Sawter: (i) Robert, Philip *le Salter* 1243 AssSo, 1262 *For* (Ess); Thomas *le Selter* 1296 SRSx. OE *sealtere* 'maker or seller of salt'. cf. John *Saltman* 1327 SRSf, Laurence *le Saltmetere* 1300 LoCt. William *le Saltere* 1279 AssNb is also called *le Salterer*, i.e. *Psalterer*, 'player on the psaltery', a stringed instrument like a harp. Thus *Salter* is at times identical with *sautreor*, a derivative of OFr *saltere* 'psaltery'. (ii) John *le Sautreor* 1276 LLB B; William *le Sautreour*, minstrel to the Lady Margaret, Queen of England 1304 LLB C. A derivative of OFr *sautere* 'psaltery'.

Saltern, Salterne: Henry *de Salterne* 1333 *SR* (D); John, Stevyn *Saltern* 1524 SRSf. 'Worker at the salt-house', OE *sealt-ærn*, as at Saltren's Cottages in Monkleigh (Devon).

Salthouse, Salters: Adam *de Salthus* 1274 RH (Nf); John *Saltos* 1525 SRSx; Janet *Saltehowse* 1562 LaWills; William *Saltus* 1662 ib. From Salthouse (Norfolk), from minor places where there were saltworks, as at Salthouse in Lytham and Salthouse in Furness (Lancs), or 'worker at the salt-house'. For *Salters*, cf. DUCKHOUSE and DUCKERS.

Saltman: Henry, John *Saltman* 1315 Norw-Deeds, 1327 SRSf. 'Maker of salt.'

Saltmarsh, Saltmarshe: Robert *de Saltemers* 1130 P (Gl); Geoffrey *de Saltmarais* 1219 AssY; Robert *de Saltemerhs* 1332 SRLei; Thomas *Saltmarsch* 1419 IpmY. From Saltmarsh (Glos, Hereford), Saltmarshe (ERYorks), or 'dweller by the brackish marsh'.

Salton, Saltoun: Matilda *de Saleton* 1219 AssY; William *de Saulton* 1357 Black (Linlithgow); John *Saulton* 1536 ib. From Salton (NRYorks, East Lothian).

Saltonstall, Sattenstall, Sattersall: William *de Saltonstal* 1275 Wak (Y); Richard *de Saltonstall'* 1379 PTY; Richard *Saltonstall* 1610 Oxon (Ess); Anne *Salthingston* 1642 Bardsley (Herts). From Saltonstall in Warley (WRYorks).

Salusbury: *v.* SALISBURY

Salvidge: *v.* SAVAGE

Salvin: *v.* SAUVAIN

Salway, Salwey, Sallaway, Salloway, Selway: *Salewi* de Blipesdune 1185 Templars (So); Walter, Adam *Salewy* 1275 SRWo; Robert *Saleway* 1327 SRSo. This is clearly from a personal-name, apparently an unrecorded OE **Sælwīg* 'prosperity-war'.

Sam, Samme, Sammes, Samms, Sams: *Samme Parvus* 1275 RH (L); Richard *Sammys* 1458 NorwW (Nf). A pet-form of SAMPSON. *Samson Fullon'* 1265 Calv (Y) is also called *Samme* (c1260 ib.). There was also a pet-form *Sampe*: Huelin *Sampe* 1276 RH (L).

Sambell: *v.* SEMPLE

Samber: *v.* SEMPER

Sambridge: Richard *de Samebrugg'* 1279 RH (O); Matilda *atte Samesbrugg* 1296 SRSx. The Sussex place is now Salmons Bridge in Tillington. Probably 'dweller by a bridge used in common' (OE **sam-brycg*). *v.* MELS 177.

Sambrook, Sambrooke: Thomas *de Sambrok* 1258 FFSt. From Sambrook (Salop).

Samman, Sammon, Sammonds, Sammons: *v.* SALAMAN, SEAMAN

Samper: *v.* SEMPER

Sampford: *v.* SANDFORD

Sample: *v.* SEMPLE

Sampson, Samson, Samsin, Sansam, Sansom, Sansome, Sanson, Sansum: (i) *Sanson* 1086 DB; *Samson, Sansone, Sampson* Takel(l) Hy 2 DC (L); *Samson* Cornuwala c1170 Riev (Y); Hugo *Samson* 1130 P (Nt); Philip *Sampson* 1192 WhC (La); Hemericus *Samsun* 1221 Cur (So); William *Sansum* 1260 AssCh; Marget *Sansom* 1524 SRSf. OFr *Sanson, Samson*, the name of a Welsh bishop (fl. 550) who crossed over to Brittany and founded the abbey of Dol where he was buried and venerated as a saint. Whether his name is the Biblical *Samson* or one of Celtic origin is uncertain. The name was popular in Yorkshire and the eastern counties where it was introduced by the Bretons after the Conquest, and also in the Welsh border counties where it no doubt came from Wales. (ii) Occasionally the surname may be local in origin: Ralph *de Sancto Samsone* 1087 InqAug (K), Albert *de Samsona* 1086 InqEl (C). Probably from Saint-Samson (Seine-Inférieure), or from Saint-Samson (Calvados), Saint-Samson-de-Bonfosse (La Manche) or Saint-Samson-de-la-Roque (Eure).

Samter: *v.* SANTER

Samuel, Samuels, Samwell: *Samuel* 1198 Cur (K); *Samuelis* Gille 1206 Cur (Ess); Adolfus *Samuel* c1160 DC (L); William *Samwel* 1279 RH (O). This Hebrew name, 'name of God', is not common in the Middle Ages, but the surnames are not necessarily of Jewish origin.

Samways: Robert *Samwis* 14th AD i (Nth). OE *sāmwīs* 'dull, foolish'.

Sanctuary, Santry, Sentry: John *Seyntwary(e)* 1517 Landwade (C), 1524 SRSf. ME *seintuarie*, OFr *saintuarie* 'a shrine'. As suggested by Lower, this is probably for one who has taken sanctuary in a church or monastery. For *Sentry*, cf. 'He hath no way now to slyppe out of my hands, but to take sentrie in the hospital of Warwick' (1590 Nashe).

Sand, Sandes, Sands, Sandys: William *de Sandes* 1205 Cur (Sr); Walter *de la Sonde* 1248 FFSr; Andrew *atte Sonde* 1296 SRSx; Reginald *del Sond* 1298 Ipm (Sf); Thomas *Attensandes* 1301 SRY; Gilbert *del Sandes* 1332 SRCu. 'Dweller on sandy soil or by the sands', OE *sand* 'sand'.

Sandal, Sandall: (i) Peter *de Sandal* 1188 WhC (La). From Sandal Magna, Kirk or Long Sandall (WRYorks). (ii) Rogerus *filius Sandolf'* 1208 P (Gl); *Saundulfus* 1221 AssWa; Thomas *Sandolf* 1327 SRSf. ON **Sandúlfr*.

Sandars, Sander, Sanders, Saunder, Saunders: *Sandre* c1248 Bec (O); *Sander* 1255 RH (Sa); Henry *Sandres* 1275 SRWo; William *Sandre, Saundre* 1316-17 AssK; Richard *Saunder* 1332 SRSt. *Sander*, a pet-form of *Alexander*.

Sanday: *v.* SANDEY

Sandcraft: Robert *de Sandecroft* 1200 FFSf. From residence near a sandy croft.

Sandeford: *v.* SANDIFER

Sandell, Sandells, Sandels, Sandhill: (i) William *de Sandhull* 1276 AssSo; Walter *de Sandhell* 1327 SRSx; William *atte Sandhille* 1332 SRSx. Dweller by a sand-hill.' OE *sand, hyll*. (ii) Alexander *de la Sandhelde* 1275 AD i (Sx); William *ater Sandhyld* 1296 SRSx. 'Dweller by a sandy slope.' OE *sand, hylde*.

Sandelson: For SANDERSON.

Sandeman: John *Saundirman* 1379 PTY; David *Sandeman* 1628 Black (Perth); Richard *Sandeman, Sandiman* 1645, 1674 FrY. 'Servant of *Saunder*' (Alexander). cf. Robert *Alexsanderman* 1379 PTY.

Sandercok: John, William *Sandircok* 1425 AD i (K). A diminutive of *Sander*.

Sanders: *v.* SANDARS

Sanderson, Saunderson: Adam *Saunderson* 1349 LoPleas; Robert *Saundreson* 1464 FeuDu. 'Son of *Sander*' (Alexander).

Sandes: *v.* SAND

Sandever: *v.* SANDIFER

Sandey, Sandy, Sanday: (i) Hugo *de Sandeia* 1202 AssBeds. From Sandy (Beds). (iii) Adam *Sandi* 1332 SRCu. ON *Sandi*. cf. SANK.

Sandford, Sanford, Sampford: Jordan *de Sandforda, de Samford*' 1175, 1190 P (W); Bartholomew *de Sandford* c1280 SRWo; John *Sandford* 1473 IpmNt; James *Sanford* 1642 PrD. From Sandford (Berks, Devon, Dorset, Oxon, Salop, Westmorland), or Sampford (Devon, Essex, Som).

Sandhill: *v.* SANDELL

Sandifer, Sandiford, Sandeford, Sandever, Sandyfirth: Richard *de Sandiforth* 1286 Wak (Y); John *de Sandeforthe* 1379 PTY. From an unidentified Sandiford, apparently in Yorkshire.

Sandle: For SANDAL or SANDELL.

Sandler: *v.* SANTLER

Sandro: Adam *de Sandewra* 1332 SRCu. From Sandraw (Cumb).

Sandy: *v.* SANDEY

Sandyfirth: *v.* SANDIFER

Sandys: *v.* SAND

Sangar, Sanger, Songer: John *le Songere* 1296 MEOT (Herts); Richard *le Sangere, le Songer* 1327 SR (Ess). OE *sangere, songere* 'a church-singer, chorister'.

Sangster: Sibilla *Sangistere* 1327 MEOT (Ha); Adam *le Songster* 1327 ib. (La); James *Sankstar* 1452 Black (Aberdeen). OE *sangestre*, feminine of *sangere*, though not always used of a woman. In Scotland 'a chorister'.

Sanguine, Sangwin, Sangwine: John *Sanguin* 1194 P (Gl); William *Sangwyn* 1270 AssSo. ME, OFr *sanguin* 'of a sanguine complexion'.

Sank: William *samke* 1221 ElyA (Sf). A rare surname. *Samke* is an interesting example, hitherto unnoted, of the vitality of the Anglo-Scandinavian name-system in the eastern counties. It is of a type noted by Stenton in the Danelaw: ON *Steinki*, a short form of a name compounded with *Stein-, Anke* (ON *Anki*), from ON *Arnkell*, etc. *Samke* may be from ON **Sandúlfr* (cf. SANDAL), or, possibly, from *Sanni*, a pet-form of ON *Sandi*, both recorded in 12th-century Lincolnshire charters (IPN 185). *Sandi* is the first element of Saundby (Notts).

Sankey, Sanky: Gerard *de Sanki* t Hy I Fees;

Roger *de Sonkey* 1246 AssLa; William *Sanky* 1292 AssCh. From Sankey (Lancs).

Sankin: John *Sampkin* 1351 ERO (Ess); William *Samkyn* 1358 LLB G. 'Little *Samme*', a diminutive of *Samson*, plus *-kin*.

Sanne, Sans: A diminutive of *Sanson*: Eynon son of *Sanne* 1260 AssCh. cf. William *Sampson* ib.

Sansam, Sansom(e), Sanson, Sansum: *v.* SAMPSON

Sant: *v.* SAINT

Santer, Saunter, Samter: John *Sancterre* 1260 AssC; John *Sanzterre, Santerre, Sauntere* 1275 RH (L). OFr *sanz terre* 'without land'. cf. *Lackland*, the nickname of King John. *v.* also SENTER.

Santler, Sandler, Sendler: (i) Robert *de Sancto Elerio* 1219 AssL; Roger *de Seinteler* 1235 Fees (Nth); Peter *de Saint Elena*, Hilary, Leyre 1268–9 AssSo. From Saint-Hilaire-du-Harcouët (La Manche). *v.* ANF. (ii) Geoffrey *de Sancto Laudo* 1148 Winton (Ha); Hubert *de Sancto Lot* c1158 EngFeud; Gilbert *de Sanlo* c1150 DC (L); Adam *de Sainlow* 1275 RH (L); Agnes *Senclowe, Seyntlowe* 1422, 1444 Rad (C). From Saint-Lô (La Manche, Somme) or Saint-Laud (Maine-et-Loire).

Santry: *v.* SANCTUARY

Saper, Sapier: *v.* SOPER

Sapsed, Sapsford, Sapstead, Sapsworth: Richard *de Sabricheword*' 1230 P (Lo). *Sapsworth* or *Sapseth* was the old pronunciation of Sawbridgeworth (Herts) which is *Sapsforde* in 1568. *Sapseth* became *Sapsed*, and, with an intrusive *t*, *Sapstead*.

Sara, Sare, Sarra, Sarre: *Sarra* c1160 DC (L), 1219 AssY; Benedictus *filius Sarre* 1169 P (Nf); Alan *Sare* 1296 SRSx; Adam *Sarre* 1317 FFEss. Hebrew *Sara(h)* 'princess'. *Sare* may also be for SAYER.

Sarch: *v.* SEARCH

Sare: *v.* SARA, SAYER

Sarel(l): *v.* SARL

Sargaison: *v.* SARGEANTSON

Sargant, Sargeant, Sargeaunt, Sargent, Sargint, Sarjant, Sarjeant, Sarjent, Seargeant, Searjeant, Sergant, Sergean, Sergeant, Sergeaunt, Sergent, Serjeant, Serjent: Edric *le sergant* Hy 2 DC (L); Thomas *Seriant* 1185 Templars (O); Robert *le Serjaunt* 1221 Cur (Lei); Thomas *le Sergeant* 1266 AssSt; John *Sargeant* 1396 FFSf; Thomas *Sarjeant* 1689 FrY. OFr *sergent, serjant*, probably in general 'servant' (c1200 NED). Often latinized as *serviens*. Other possible meanings are: 'an officer charged with enforcing the judgements of a tribunal, arresting offenders, or summoning persons to appear before a court' (a1300 NED) or 'a tenant by military service under the rank of a knight' (c1290 NED).

Sarge: *v.* SEARCH

Sargeantson, Sargentson, Sargeson, Sarginson, Sargison, Sargisson, Sargaison, Sarjantson, Sergenson, Serginson, Sergison, Surgison, Serjeantson: William *Sergantson* 1379 PTY; Thomas *Sargenson, Sardganson* 1477, 1488 GildY; Thomas *Sarganson* 1538 SfPR; Margareta *Sergison* 1593 RothwellPR (Y); James *Sargeson* 1740 FrY. 'Son of the serjeant.'

Sark, Sarkes: v. SEARCH

Sarl, Sarll, Sarel, Sarell: *Sarlo* Iuuenis 1091–3 LVH; *Sarle* Tinctor 1274 RH (Hu); Matilda, Thomas *Sarle* 1275 RH (C), 1327 SRSf, SRSx; Robert *Saryll*, clericus 1412 FrY; Thomas *Serle*, capellanus, filius Roberti *Sarle*, clerici 1438 ib.; Edward *Sarel* 1788 Bardsley. Anglo-Scandinavian or Norman *Sarli*, *Sarle*, from ON *Sǫrli*. This is the ON cognate of OG *Sarilo* which survives as SEARL, and is more common. In later examples, *Sarle* may be a development of *Serle*.

Sarre: v. SARA

Sarson, Sarsons: (i) Adam *Sareson* 1285 LLB A; John, Peter *Sarson* 1332 SRCu. 'Son of *Sara*' (cf. Gilebertus *filius Sarre* 1327 SRC), or 'son of *Saer*' (cf. Richard *Saressone* 1327 SRSf). v. SAYER. (ii) Oliver *Sarazin* 12th DC (Lei); Philip *le Saracin* 1201 AssSo; Stephen called *Saracen* 1281 AssCh. OFr *Sarrazin* 'a Saracen', used as a nickname for one of swarthy complexion.

Sartin, Sartain, Sarton, Sattin, Sertin: William *Certayn* 1394 LLB H; Richard *Sartin* 1693 DKR 41 (W). OFr *certeyn* 'self-assured, determined'.

Sarvent: v. SERVANT

Sarver: Turstan *le seruier* 1197 P (Nf); Thomas *Server* 1516 LLB F. OFr *serveur* 'servant'.

Sarvis: v. SERVICE

Satch: v. SACH

Satchel, Satchell: Nicholas, Thomas *Sachel* 1243 AssSo, 1327 SRSo. OFr *sachel* 'a little bag', for a maker of these. cf. SACH.

Satchwell: v. SETCHFIELD

Sattenstall, Sattersall: v. SALTONSTALL

Satterthwaite, Satterfitt, Setterfield: William *Setterthwaite* 1614 FrY; Charles *Satterthwait* 1625 ib.; Thomas *Satturwaite* 1653 ib. From Satterthwaite in Hawkstead (Lancs).

Sattin: v. SARTIN

Saul, Saull, Sawle: Ricardus *filius Sawl* 1198 AC (Lo); Ralph *Saule* 1255 Rams (Hu); John *Sawle* 1296 SRSx. Hebrew *Saul* 'asked for'. Not a common medieval name.

Sault: v. SALT

Saulter: v. SALTER

Saunder(s): v. SANDARS

Saunderson: v. SANDERSON

Saunt: v. SAINT

Saunter: v. SANTER

Sausby: Probably a phonetic spelling of *Saursbye* for SORBIE.

Saut(t)er: v. SALTER

Sauvage: v. SAVAGE

Sauvain, Sauvan, Sauven, Savin, Salvin, Selwin, Selwyn, Selwyne, Sylvaine: (i) *Siluein* de Torp 1170 P (Wa); Ricardus *filius Seluein* 1195 FF (Nth); Robertus *Siluein*, *Seluenus* 1127–34, c1140 Holme (Nf); Henry *Siluain* Hy 2 Gilb (L); Osbert *Seluein* 1162 P (Y); Robert *Seluan* 1185 Templars (L). *Silvanus*, a Latin cognomen, from *silva* 'wood', the name of the god of the forests and also of a saint. (ii) William *Salvayn*, *Salven* c1170 Riev (Y); Geoffrey *Selvayn*, *Salvan'* 1242 Fees (L); Hugo *Salveyn*, *Selveyn* ib.; Robert *Selveyn*, *Selweyn* 1244, 1271

AssSt. This may, at times, be from *Silvanus* but is more often from OFr *salvagin* 'wild, savage'. cf. Thorpe Salvin (WRYorks) from Henry *Selvein* (temp. Ric. 1). (iii) *Seleuuinus* 1066 DB (W); Paganus *filius Selewin'* 1203 P (Beds); Roger *Selewyne* Hy 3 AD ii (Mx); Juliana *Selewyne* 1332 SRSx. **Selewine* 'hall-friend', unrecorded in OE, is found once in DB and again in the 13th century. Always rare, it is one origin of *Selwin*.

Savagar, Savager, Saveker, Savigar, Savigear: Humfridus *de Sancto Vigore* 1168 P (W); Thomas *de Saint Vigor* 1268 AssSo. From Saint-Vigor (La Manche, etc.).

Savage, Savaage, Savege, Savidge, Sauvage, Salvage, Salvidge: Edric *Saluage* 1066 DB (He); Edricus cognomento *Silvaticus* 1067 OEByn; John *Saluage* 1166 P (Nf); William *le Saluage* 1194 Cur (Sa); Robert *le Sauuage* 1198 FF (Sr); Ralph *le Savage* 1268 FFSf. OFr *salvage, sauvage*, Lat *silvāticus*, in popular Latin *salvāticus;* 'savage, wild' (a1300 NED).

Savary, Savery, Savory, Savoury, Severy: Joldewinus *filius Sauarici* 1158 P (Sx); Jocelinus *filius Sephari, Sefar, Safar* 1195 Oseney (O), filius *Saphar, Safari* 1200 ib., filius *Seauary* 1210 ib.; Willelmus *filius Saveric, filz Saviere* 1206–7 Cur (Do); Philip, William *Savery* 1276 RH (Lei), 1327 SRC; Robert *Sauerai, Seffray* 1327, 1332 SRSx. OFr *Savari*, OG *Sabaricus, Savaricus*. This may also have become SAFFER; its forms are confused with those of SAFFERY.

Saveall, Savell: v. SAVIL

Savege, Savidge: v. SAVAGE

Savigny: Ralph *de Sauenie, de Sauigneo, de Sauigni* 1086 DB; Jordan *de Saueigni* 1196 P (Nt). The DB under-tenant came from Savenay (Calvados). v. ANF. Others may have come from Savigni (La Manche) or Savigni-le-Vieux (La Manche).

Savil, Savill, Savile, Saville, Saveall, Savell, Saywell, Seville: John *de Sayvill* 1246 FFY; Stephen *de Savile* 1277 FFY; Robert *Sayuill* 1379 PTY; John *Sayvell* 1431 Calv; Rosemunda *Savell* 1549 RothwellPR (Y); Thomas *Savil* 1672 HTY. Perhaps from Sauville (Ardennes, Vosges), or Sainville (Eure-et-Loir). Sometimes maybe for SAFFELL.

Savory, Savoury: v. SAVARY

Saward, Soward: v. SEWARD

Sawbridge: Ysaac *de Salebrigg'* 1221 AssWa. From Sawbridge (Warwicks). v. also SEABERT.

Sawdon, Sawden: Ralph *de Saldene* 1257 AssY; Robert *Sawdan* 1502 GildY; John *Sawdon* 1525 SRSx. From Sawdon (NRYorks), *Saldene* 1289.

Sawell: v. SEWALL

Sawers: Jordan *le Sawer* 1257 MEOT (Y); Baldwin *le Sawere* 1270 AD iii (K); Cetil *Sower* 1332 MEOT (L); William *Sawer*, Robert *Sawyer* 1524 SRSf. This surname is much less frequent, both in early documents and today, than *Sawyer* which is therefore unlikely to be, as suggested by NED, an altered form of *sawer* 'one who saws'. The earliest example of *sawer* in NED is from a 1379 Yorkshire surname which is late and throws no light on the meaning. The early examples above are probably from OE *sāwere* 'a sower (of seeds)'. In the 16th century *sawer* may well be a slurred pronunciation of *sawyer*.

Sawkins: *v.* SALKIN

Sawle: *v.* SAUL

Sawter: *v.* SALTER

Sawyer, Sawyers: Nicholas *le Sagyere* c1248 Bec (Berks); Humfrey *le Sayhare, le Sawyere*, Robert *le Sawyere, le Saweare* 1270 AssSo; Richard *le Sawier'* 1278 LLB B; Philip *le Sagher* 1324 Wak (Y); John *le Saghiere* 1327 SRSx. A derivative of ME *saghe, sawe* 'to saw', 'a sawer of timber, especially in a saw-pit' (1350 NED). ME *saghier* also became *sayier* and survives as SAYER, a form which might also derive from OFr *seieor* 'sawyer'. *v.* also SAWERS, SEWER.

Saxby: (i) Nicholas, Simon *de Saxebi* 1200 P (Lei), 1202 AssL. From Saxby (Leics, Lincs). (ii) Jordan *Sacheespee* 1183 P (Y); Robert *Sakespe* 1206 Cur (L); Thomas *Sakespey* 1296 SRSx; John *Saxepe* 1327 ib. 'Draw sword', a name for a trainer in swordsmanship. cf. Fr *Sacquépée* and John *Draweswerd* 1327 SRSf.

Saxon, Saxton, Sexton: Jordan *de Saxton*, Simon *de Sexton* 1208 Cur (Y, C). From Saxton (WRYorks) or Saxton Hall and Saxon Street (Cambs). *v.* also SEXTEN.

Say, Saye: Jordan *de Sai* 1161 Eynsham (O). From Sai (Orne).

Sayburn: *v.* SEABORN

Sayce, Seys: Em' *Seis* 1255 RH (Sa); Jeven *Sais* 1392 Chirk. Welsh *sais* 'Saxon, Englishman'.

Saycell: *v.* CECIL

Sayer, Sayers, Sayre, Saer, Sare, Seyers, Sear, Seares, Sears, Seear, Seers: (i) *Saher* de Arcelis 1147–53 DC (L); Stephanus *filius Seir* 1148–52 Bury, *filius Saheri (Saieri)* c1160 DC (L); *Seherus, Seiherus* de Quenci c1155 RegAntiquiss (L); *Seyr'* de Quinci 1205 ib.; Robertus *filius Seer* 12th DC (Nt); *Saerus* Thomasseruaunt Clench 1318 Pat (Ess); Richard *Sayer* 1230 P (D); Nicholas *Sare* 1275 SRWo; Godwin *Seer* 1279 RH (C); Stephen *Saer* 1281 LLB A; Thomas *Sare*, John *Sayer* 1292 FFEss; Robert *Saier*, Roger *Sayher* 1322, 1324 ib.; Roger *Seyer* 1302 LLB B. *Saer, Sayer* is a personal-name common in early records in a variety of forms. It is obviously Norman, though of Old German origin, perhaps OHG *Sigiheri* (Ekwall). *Sear(s), Seers*, etc. seem to derive only from the personal name. *v.* SARA, SEARSON. (ii) Richard *le Saer* 1204 AssY; Humfrey *le Sayhare, le Sawyere* 1270 AssSo; Robert *le Sayer* 1284 LLB A; Geppe *le Sahar* 1285 Wak (Y); Alice *Sayeres* 1310 EAS xx; Robert *Saer, Sawer, Sare, Saare* 1465–87 Combermere (Ch); John *Sare* or *Sayer* 1605 ChwWo. This common occupational name, with its varied early and modern forms, has five different origins. It is clearly a form of SAWYER (*le Sayhare* or *le Sawyere* 1270), or of SEWER (iii), *le Syur* or *le Sayur* 'sawyer' (1286), and may occasionally be a derivative of OE *secgan* 'to say', 'a

professional reciter' (c1330 NED, with forms *seg-ger, seiere, saier*). It may also be an aphetic form of ME *assayer* from AFr *assaior, assaiour* 'one who assays or tests', 'an assayer of metals', or 'a fore-taster of food, etc.' (1370 NED). Or, especially in later examples, it may be from OFr *saier*, from *saie* 'silk, serge', 'a maker or seller of say'.

Sayles: *v.* SAILES

Saylor: *v.* SAILER

Sayner, Saynor: *v.* SENIOR

Sayre: *v.* SAYER

Saysell: *v.* CECIL

Sayward: *v.* SEWARD

Saywell: John *Seywell* 1600 FrLeic, Henry *Seewell* 1754 ib. For SEWALL or SEWELL. *v.* also SAVIL.

Scafe, Scaife, Skaife: Geoffrey *Skaif'* 1219 AssY, 1240 AssLa; Robert *Scafe* 1418 FrY. ON *skeifr*, NEng dial *scafe* 'crooked, awry; awkward, wild'.

Scale, Scales, Schoales, Scholes, Scoles: Richard *del Scoles* 1275 Wak (Y); Adam *de Scoles* 1285 AssLa; Thomas *del Scales* 1332 SRCu; William *del Scale* ib.; John *del Scholes* 1379 PTY. 'Dweller by the hut(s) or shed(s)' (ON *skáli*, ME *scale, scole*), as at Scales (Cumb, Lancs), Scholes (WRYorks) or Scole (Norfolk).

Scarf, Scarfe, Scarff, Scarffe: John *Scarf* 1260 AssY; Henry *Scharf* 1275 RH (L). ON *skarfr* 'cormorant'.

Scargill: Warin *de Scakergill'* 1177 P (Y); William *de Skaregile* 1285 IpmY; John *Scargill* 1459 Kirk. From Scargill (NRYorks).

Scarlet, Scarlett: William *Scarlet* 1185 Templars (O); Geoffrey *Escarlata* 1195 P (W); Ralph *le Escarlet* 1220 Cur (So). OFr *escarlate* 'scarlet'. Probably a dealer in 'scarlet', the name of a cloth already in 1182 (P): 'x ulnis de escarleto'.

Scatchard: John *Skacher* 1327 SRSf; Thomas *Scochard* 1336 AD v (K); John *Scacharde*, William *Skachade* 1381 SRSt. Probably a derivative of ONFr *escache*, OFr *eschace*, modFr *échasse* 'a stilt'. *Skacher* may be 'maker of stilts'; *scachard* is a pejorative, perhaps, as suggested by Harrison, a nickname for a long-legged bird such as the heron, later applied to a man. Dauzat explains the French *Eschasseriaux* as 'man with a wooden leg'.

Scattergood: Henry *Skatergot* 1219 AssY; Walter *Skatergod* 1247 AssBeds; Robert *Scatergod* 1327 SRY. 'Scatter goods', a nickname for a spendthrift or, possibly, for a philanthropist.

Schoales: *v.* SCALE

Schoemaker: *v.* SHOEMAKE

Schofield, Schoefield, Scholefield, Scholfield, Scolfield, Scoffield, Scofield: John *de Scholefeld* 1343 WhC (La); Richard *de Skolefeld* 1363 FrY; Anne *Scofeld* 1561 RothwellPR (Y); John *Schofeld* 1592 ib. 'Dweller by a field with a hut' (ON *skáli*, OE *feld*), a common Lancashire and Yorkshire name.

Scholar, Scholard, Scholer, Schollar, Scholler, Scollard, Scoular, Scouler, Scouller: Adam *del*

Scoler 1332 SRLa; Henry *Scoular* 1525 Black. Probably 'dweller by the shieling with a hut', ON *skáli, erg.*

Schol(e)field: *v.* SCHOFIELD

Scholes: *v.* SCALE

Scholey, Schooley, Scollay: John *de Scolay* 1379 PTY. Probably 'dweller by the low-lying land with a hut', ON *skáli*, OE *ēg.*

Schoolcraft, Scowcroft: Richard *de Schalecroft* 1246 AssLa; Richard *Scowcroft* 1689 Bardsley. 'Dweller by the croft with a hut', ON *skáli*, OE *croft.*

Schorah: *v.* SCORAH

Schrieve: *v.* SHERIFF

Science: *Sciencia* filia Gerardi 1260 AssC; *Sciencia* ate Watere 1332 SRSr; Roger *Science* 1642 PrD. Spanish and Provençal *Sancha, Sanchia* (f). Introduced into England in 1243 by the marriage of Richard of Cornwall to *Sanchia*, daughter of the Count of Provence. It appears in ME as *Cynthia, Scientia, Science,* and later as *Sens, Sence, Sense, Saints, Sanche,* cf. *Sanche* widow of John Strelley 1502 AD iii (Nf), James Bynde and *Sanctia* or *Sence* his wife 1620 ODCN.

Scoffield, Scofield: *v.* SCHOFIELD

Scoles: *v.* SCALE

Scollan: *v.* SCOTLAND

Scollard: *v.* SCHOLAR

Scollay: *v.* SCHOLEY

Scorah, Scorer, Scorrer, Schorah: William *le Scorur* 1297 SRY; Alice *la Scoriere* 1327 *SR* (Ess). A derivative of OFr *escorre, escourre* 'to run out', a scout, spy, or of OFr *escurer* 'to scour', a scourer, cleanser.

Scothern, Scothorne, Scothron, Scottorn: Hugh *de Scotþorn* 1279 RH (O). From Scothern (Lincs).

Scotland, Scollan: (i) *Scotlandus* 1081 Bury (K); *Scollandus* 1086 DB (Sx); *Scotlande* 1101–7 Holme (Nf); Gaufridus *filius Scollandi* 1130 P (Ha); William *Escoland* 1155 FeuDu; Jordan *Escotland* 1196 P (L); Thomas *Escollant* 1198 FFK; William *Scotland* 1332 SRSx. *Scotland, Scolland* is a personal name found in Normandy but not in Germany. It is formed from the name of the *Scots,* plus *-land.* (ii) Galfridus *de Scotland'* 1193 P (Ess); Geoffrey *de Scolaund* 1268 AssSo. From Scotland. Much rarer than the personal name. In Scotland, from Scotland Well in Portmoak (Kinross): Richard *de Scocia* 1178–80 (Black).

Scotney: Hugo *de Scotini* 1143–7 DC (L); Walter *Escoteni, Escoteigni* 1195–6 P (L); William *de Scoteny* 1219 AssY. From Etocquigny (Seine-Inférieure). Scotney Castle (Sussex) was built c. 1180 by Walter *de Scotiniis. v.* ANF.

Scotson: Gilbert *Scotessun'* 1131 FeuDu; Alexander *Scotteson* 1379 PTY; John *Scotchson* 1689 FrY. 'Son of Scot.' *v.* SCOTT.

Scott, Scotts, Scutt, Scutts: (i) Uchtred *filius Scot* c1124 Black (Selkirk); Roger, William *Scot* c1150–60 DC (L), 1183 Boldon (Du); Gillebertus *Scottus* 1177 P (C); Hunfridus, Robertus *le Scot* 1194 P (W), 1197 P (Wa); Aluredus *Scotticus* 1198 P (K); Adam *le Scot* c1221 Black (Dryburgh);

John *le Escot* 1260 AssC. (ii) Godwin, Lefstan *Scut* 1185 P (Nf), 1190–1200 Seals (Sf); John *le Scut* 1248 *Ass* (Ha); William *le Skut* 1327 SRSx. *Scott* is one of the twelve commonest surnames in Scotland, a border name, from OE *Scott,* originally 'an Irishman', later 'a Gael from Scotland'. In the English border counties where the surname is also common the name means 'a man from Scotland', not necessarily a Gael. The surname may also derive from a personal-name, OE *Scott.* According to Guppy, *Scott* is well-established in the eastern counties whilst the Scutts of Dorset are as numerous as the Scotts of Devonshire or Yorkshire. The 12th-century Scots of eastern England may well have been retainers of David I, King of Scotland, who succeeded to the extensive lands of Waltheof, Earl of Huntingdon, on his marriage to Waltheof's daughter. Many of these must have remained in England and their surnames became hereditary for in the 1327 Subsidy Roll for Suffolk there are 35 men called *Skot.* Some may have been retainers of Scottish nobles who accepted Edward I's overlordship and fought against Bruce. The surname, too, may in part have absorbed *Scutt,* also found in the east. This is probably OFr *escoute* 'a spy' which would become ME *scut* and be confused with *scot.*

Scotter: Roger *de Scotre* 1202 FFL. From Scotter (Lincs). Also for SCOTTOW.

Scotter, Scutter: Alan, John *Scutard* 1279 RH (C, O); Hugh, Walter *Scotard* 1327 SRC, *SR* (Ess). A pejorative of OFr *escoute* 'spy' or of ME *Scot* 'Scott'.

Scotton, Scotten: Andrew *de Scotton'* c1200–10 RegAntiquiss; Ralph, John *de Scotton* 1250 IpmY, 1347 FFY. From Scotton (Lincs, NR, WRYorks).

Scottorn: *v.* SCOTHERN

Scottow, Scotto: Hervei *de Scothoue* 1177 P (Nf). From Scottow (Norfolk). *v.* also SCOTTER.

Scoular, Scouler, Scouller: *v.* SCHOLAR

Scovell, Scovil: Ralph *de Scouilla* 1194 P (Bk). From Escoville (Calvados).

Scowcroft: *v.* SCHOOLCRAFT

Scowle: *Scule, Escule* 1066 DB; *Scul* c1155 DC (L); Robert *Scule* c1165 Bury (Sf); William *Scowle* 1273 RH (L); Richard *Scoule* 1297 SRY. ON *Skúli,* ODa *Skule,* probably from *skýla* 'to protect'.

Scrimgeour, Scrimgeoure, Scrimger, Scrimiger, Scriminger, Scrimygeour, Scrymgeour, Scrimshaw, Skrimshaw, Skrimshire: Richer *le schirmisur* 1154–89 DC (L); William *Lescermissur* 1180 P (Sf); Symon *Leskirmisur* 1221 Colch (Ess); Gilbert *le Skermisur* 1222 AssWa; Alexander *Skrymchur* 1387 Black; Thomas *Skrymshire* 1465 ib.; Thomas *Skrymsher, Skrymshawe* 1520, 1533 FFSt; James *Skrympshire* 1723 DKR 41 (St). OFr *escremisseor, -our, eskermisor, scremisseur* 'fencing-master'. *Scrimshaw* and *Skrimshire* are more common in England, *Scrimgeour* in Scotland, where Black also gives the forms *Skrimagour* (1411), *Scrymgeoure* (1456), *Scrimigeor* (1503) and *Scrymger* (1541). In spite of the re-enactment in 1285 of the Assize of Arms of 1181, fencing was regarded as unlawful. The keeping of fencing-schools was forbidden in the City of London 'as fools who delight in mischief do learn to fence with buckler, and thereby are encouraged in their follies'. Fencing-masters were legally denominated as rogues and vagabonds and classed with stage-players, bearwards, gipsies and other undesirable characters. *v.* NQ 198, 231–4. cf. SKIRMER and CHAMPION.

Scripps: *v.* CRISP

Scripture: Ricardus *scriptor* 1158 P (So); John *Scripture* 1686 Bardsley. A refashioning of Lat *scriptor* 'writer, clerk'.

Scriven, Scrivens, Scrivins, Scrivings: Richard *le Scrivein* 1208–13 Fees (O); Gervase *le Escriuein* 1278 AssSo; Richard *Scrivin* son of Norman *Scrivin* 1294 AD vi (K). OFr *escrivain, escrivein* 'writer', one who writes and copies books, manuscripts, etc.; also a clerk (a1300 NED).

Scrivener, Scrivenor: Simon *Scriuiner* 1218–22 StP (Lo); Kemma *Scriuener* 1311 ColchCt. A derivative of *scrivain* with the same meaning as SCRIVEN.

Scrutton, Scruton: Thomas *de Scruton* 1364 FFY; Daniell *Scrutton* 1568 SRSf; Edward *Scruton* 1672 HTY. From Scruton (NRYorks).

Scrymgeour: *v.* SCRIMGEOUR

Scudamore: *v.* SKIDMORE

Scurrell: *v.* SQUIRREL

Scutt, Scutts: Godwin, Lefstan *Scut* 1183 P (Nf), 1190–1200 Seals (Sf); William *le Scutt, le Skut* 1222 Acc, 1327 SRSx; William *Skutt* 1545 SRW. A nickname from *scut*, originally used of the tail of the hare, particularly noticeable when the animal was fleeing, and later of the hare itself, cf. 'Scut, hare', c1440 PromptParv.

Scutter: *v.* SCOTTER

Seaber, Seaberg, Seaburgh, Seabury, Sebry, Saber, Sibary, Siberg, Siberry, Sibery, Sibree: (i) *Seburga* filia Oseberti 1222 Cur (O); William *Sibry* c1227 Fees (Y); Alan *Sibri* 1276 RH (Y); John *Seber* 1279 RH (C); John *Seburuh* 1279 RH (Hu); John *Sabourgh* 1327 *SR* (Ess); William *Seburgh*, Margaret *Seborw* 1327 SRSf. OE *Sǣburh* (f) 'sea-fortress', of which only one earlier example has been noted, in LVD (11th cent.). The early *Sibry* forms may have been influenced by OE *Sigeburh* 'victory-fortress', an early OE woman's name, found in place-names, but not known to have survived the Conquest. (ii) Warin *de Seberg'* 1230 P (Do). From Seaborough (Dorset). Also, perhaps, from Seaborough Hall (Essex), which is found as *Seueberghe* 1293, *Sebergh* 1334, *Sebarhall* 1544, *Sibbery Hall* 1805 (PN Ess 164).

Seabert, Seabridge, Seabright, Sebert, Sebright, Seebright, Sibert, Sawbridge: *Sebertus* 1199 MemR (Gl); Ricardus *filius Sebriht* 1200 P (Lei); Gaufridus *filius Sabricti* 1210 Cur (C); William *Sebright* Hy 2 PN Ess 235; Richard *Sebriht* 1279 RH (O); Peter *Sabright* 1290 Cl (Ess); Robert *Sebriche*, Michael *Sebryth* 1327 SRSf. OE *Sǣberht* 'sea-bright', the name of a 7th-century king of Essex, found occasionally until the 10th century, and then not until 1199. The surname has probably been reinforced by OE *Sigebeorht* 'victory-bright', the name of an early king of Essex and much more common in OE than *Sǣbeorht*. This, too, certainly survived the Conquest but is rare: Wlfwardus *filius Sibrith* 1189–1200 BuryS (Sf), *Sibryth* 1275 RH (Sf), John *Sybrith* 1327 SRSf. William *Sebright* has left his name in Great Seabrights in Great Baddow (Essex), *Sowbridge* 1777 (PN Ess 234). *Sǣbeorht* is the first element in Sawbridgeworth (Herts).

Seaborn, Seaborne, Seabourn, Seabourne, Sebborn, Sibborn, Sibbons, Siborne, Siburn, Sayburn: *Sabernus* Monachus, Philippus *filius Seberni* 1114–30 Rams (Hu); Margareta *filia Seberni* 1207 Cur (Mx); Nel, John *Sebern* 1190 BuryS (Sf), 1275 SRWo; Sayer *Sabarn* 1327 *SR* (Ess); John *Sabern* 1377 AssEss. OE *Sǣbeorn* 'sea-warrior', of which the earliest known examples are those above.

Seach: *v.* SYKES

Seader: Peter, Ralph *le sedere* 1221 ElyA (C), 1263 MEOT (Sr). OE *sǣdere* 'sower'.

Seaford, Seaforth, Seafourth: Hugh *de Seford'* 1208 Pl (Herts); William *Seford* 1327 SRSx; Humphrey *Seaford* 1642 PrD. From Seaford (Sussex).

Seagars, Seager(s): *v.* SAGAR

Seagood, Segot: Adam *Segud* 1317 AssK; Alan *Segode* 1327 SRY; Katerine *Seegode* 1450 RochW; John *Saygude* 1473 GildY. An unrecorded OE *Sǣgōd* 'sea-good'.

Seagram: Ernald *Segrom* 1307 MEOT (Wo); John *le Segrom*, Richard *Segrom* 1327 SRSx. OE *sǣ* 'sea' and ME *grom* 'servant', probably 'seaman, sailor'. cf. SEAGRIM.

Seagrave, Seagrief, Seagrove, Segrave: Thomas *de Segraua* 1180 P (Lei). From Seagrave (Leics).

Seagrim, Seagrin: *Sagrim* 1066 DB (Nth, St); *Segrim* de Haltun c1155 DC (L); *Sagrim* carnifex 1190 P (Hu); Seeman *Seegrim* c1248 Bec (Sf); John *Sagrim* 1327 *SR* (Ess); John *Sigrym* 1327 SRSo. ON *Sægrímr*, ODa *Segrim* 'sea-protector'. cf. SEAGRAM.

Seagrove: *v.* SEAGRAVE

Seal, Seale, Seales, Seals, Seel, Seels, Zeal, Zeale: (i) Ralph *de la Sele* 1168 P (D); Robert *ate sele* 1332 SRSr. From employment at the hall (OE *sele*) or, perhaps, 'dweller by the sallow copse' (OE **siele, *sele*). Seal (Kent), Seale (Surrey) and Sele (Sussex) are probably from *sele*. (ii) Ralph *de Sseill* 1185 Templars (Wa). From Seal (Leics). (iii) Hugh *le Sele* c1113 Burton (St); Roger *Sele* 1198 P (Nf). Probably metonymic for SEALER. cf. Everard *de Sigillo* (*del Sael*) 1219 Cur (Sf). But *le Sele* suggests a nickname from the seal (OE *seolh*, ME *sele*).

Sealeaf: *Saloua* 1066 ICC (C); Robertus *filius Seluue* 1190 BuryS (Sf); *Salove* 1203 Cur (Mx); Agnes, John *Seloue* 1308 EAS xviii, 1327 SRSf; John *Salove* 1327 *SR* (Ess). von Feilitzen derives the 1066 personal name from an unrecorded OE woman's name **Sǣlufu* 'sea-love'. This would account for all the above forms but would give a modern *Sealove*. In DB *Lēof-* usually appears as

Leue-, but also as *Liue-* and occasionally as *Luue-*. An OE **Sǣlēofu* (f) 'sea-love' would give modern *Sealeaf* and this could be the source of all the above. cf. LEAF, GOODLIFF.

Sealer: Robert, William *Seeler* 1221 AssGl, 1230 Cl (Db); Walter *le Seler* 1327 SRSf; Richard *le Sealer* 1328 LoPleas. A derivative of ME *sel, seel, seal* from OFr *seel* 'a seal'; 'a maker of seals'. Hugh *le Seler* of York in 1333 made a new seal for the bishopric of Durham (MedInd 132). Numerous examples of *Seler* are found but it is usually impossible to decide whether they belong to *Sealer* or to *Sellar. v.* also SEAL. As Cotgrave has *sele* for *saddle* and Palsgrave '*Seale*, horse harnesse', *Sealer* must sometimes mean 'saddler'.

Sealey, Seally, Sealy, Seeley, Seelly, Seely, Selley, Selly, Silley, Silly, Ceeley, Ceely, Ceiley, Cely, Zealey, Zealley, Zelley: Richard *Seli* c1200 Gilb (L); Roger (*le*) *Seli* 1205 P (He); Roger *Cely* 1255 RH (Sa); Richard *Sely*, John *Celi* 1275 SRWo; Thomas *Sali* 1279 RH (Hu); Thomas *Sali, Sely* 1281, 1286 LLB B; Thomas *Zely* 1327 SRWo. OE *sælig* 'happy, blessed', whence modern *silly*, often misunderstood in the phrase 'Silly Suffolk'. This was also used as a woman's name: *Sela* 1219 AssL, *Sely* filia Nicholai 1221 AssWo, *Sely* Percy 1327 SRSo.

Seaman, Seammen, Seamons, Seeman, Seman, Semens, Semmens, Seyman, Saayman: *Seman* 1066 DB (Sr), c1155 DC (L), 1211 Cur (So); *Seman le* Erl 1327 SRSx; Rufus, Richard *Seman* 1182–1211 BuryS (C), 1235 FFEss; Geoffrey *Semman* 1292 SRLo; Robert *Sayman* 1379 PTY. OE *Sǣmann* 'sea-man'.

Seamer, Seamour: (i) *Sæmar, Samar, Semær, Semar, Semer* 1066 DB; *Semarus* Cham 1179 P (D); *Semer de* Risenberg' 1212 Cur (Bk); Geoffrey *Semare* 1251 Rams (Hu); Henry *Semer* 1275 RH (Do); John *Samar* 1279 RH (C); George *Seama* 1558 RattlesdenPR (Sf). OE *Sǣmǣr* 'sea-famous'. Not quite so common as *Sǣmann*. (ii) Ioscelinus, Petronilla *de Semere* 1176 P (Y), 1329 ColchCt. From Seamer (NRYorks) or Semer (Norfolk, Suffolk). (iii) John (*le*) *Semere* 1327 SRSo, 1340 MESO (Ha). OE *sēamere* 'tailor'. cf. SIMESTER.

Seanor: *v.* SENIOR

Search, Sarch, Sarge, Searight, Seawright, Serrick, Serck, Sark, Sarkes, Surrage, Surridge: (i) *Saric, Seric* 1066 DB; William *Serych* 1296 SRSx; Reginald *Serich, Serche* 1297 Coram; John *Sarich, Serich* 1296, 1299 FFEss; Richard *Sarich* 1327 *SR* (Ess); Emma, John *Serch*(*e*) 1332 SRSx, SRSt; Alan *Serech* 1359 FFSt. OE *Sǣrīc* 'sea-ruler', frequent in post-Conquest sources (PNDB). This would regularly give ME *Saric, Seric*, which would normally appear as *Sarridge, Serridge*. These do not seem to survive but have probably been absorbed by *Surridge* which, with *Serrick*, is still found in Sussex, and is, no doubt, the direct descendant of the 1296 *Serych*. All the southern Surridges cannot have brought back to their native south a name acquired by migration north. For *Serrick* and *Sea(w)right*, cf. ALDRICH and ALL-

RIGHT. With loss of the unstressed vowel, *Saric, Seric* would become ME *Sarc, Serc*, giving modern *Sarch, Sarge, Search, Serck* and *Sark*. (ii) *Siric, Syric, Seric* 1066 DB; *Siricus* de Lenna 1210 Cur (Nf); R. *Siricus* 1114–77 Rams (Hu); Hugo *Serich* 1206 P (Ha); Hugo *Sirich*(*e*) 1230 P (Berks), 1327 SRSf; Aubert, Roger *Syrik* 1275 RH (L). OE *Sigerīc* 'victory-powerful'. Occasionally also ON *Sigrikr*, ODa *Sigrik*. The vowel of *Sirich* was early lowered to *e* in *Serich* which would then develop like *Serich* from *Sǣrīc*.

Seares: *v.* SAYER

Seargeant, Searjeant: *v.* SARGANT

Searl, Searle, Searles, Searls, Serle, Serrell: *Serlo* 1066 DB (Ess); *Serlo* le Flemyng c1150 Gilb (L); *Serle* Gotokirke 1279 RH (C); *Serill'* Pynder 1379 PTY; Adam, Hugo *Serle* 1226 FFBk, 1250 Fees (Do); Hugh *Sereleson* 1320 ParlWrits (Y); William *Serell'* 1379 PTY. OG *Sarilo, Serilo*, (Romance) *Serlo*, probably related to OE *searu* 'armour', cognate with ON *Sǫrli. v.* SARL. The name was frequent in Normandy and common in England after the Conquest.

Searson: Ralph 'Johnesservaunt *Searessone* de Sutton' 1317 Pat (L). Ralph was the servant of John, son of *Seare* (i.e. *Saer*) de Sutton. *v.* SAYER.

Seath: William *Ateseth'* 1275 SRWo. 'Dweller by the pit or pool', OE *sēaþ*.

Seaton, Seton: (i) Adam *de Seton* c1194–1214 Black; Alexander, Serlo *de Seton* 1225, c1250 ib. From Seaton (Haddington). (ii) Ralph *de Seton'* 1207 P (Nb); Robert *de la Setene* 1296 MELS (Sx); John *Seeton* 1557 CorNt. From Seaton (Cumb, Devon, Durham, Northumb, Rutland, ER, NRYorks), or 'dweller by the plantation or the cultivated land', OE *seten, v.* MELS 183. Occasionally a personal name may also be involved, cf. Madoch *filius Setun'* de Sutton 1187 P (Sa).

Seavers, Sever, Severs: *Seuare* 1185 Templars (So); *Sephare* 1188 BuryS (Sf); Radulfus *filius Sefare* 1221 ElyA (Sf); *Seuar'* Boykin 1277 Ely (Sf); William, Hugh *Seuare* 1185 P (Co), 1285 FFEss; Walter *Sefare* 1230 P (Beds); Thomas *Safare* (*Savare*) 1327 *SR* (Ess); William *Sefare*, Ralph *Seffare* 1327 SRSf. An unrecorded OE woman's name, **Sǣfaru* 'sea-passage', of which the above are the earliest known examples.

Seaward: *v.* SEWARD

Seawright: *v.* SEARCH

Sebbage: Adam *de Seuebech*, William *Seuebeche* 1327 SRSx. From Seabeach in Boxgrove (Sussex), *Sebeche* in 1521, now pronounced *Sibbidge*.

Sebborn: *v.* SEABORN

Sebert: *v.* SEABERT

Sebley: *v.* SIBLEY

Sebright: *v.* SEABERT

Sebry: *v.* SEABER

Secker: *v.* SACKER

Seckerson, Secretan: *v.* SEXTEN

Secular, Seckler: Nicholas *le Seculer* 1197 P (He), *le Secler, le Seccoler* 1250 Fees (He); Walter *le Seculer* 1255 RH (Sa); Robert *Seclermunck'* 1301 SRY. OFr *seculier* 'secular, lay, temporal'. Med-

Lat *secularis*, by which the name is translated (1206 ChR), meant 'secular, of this world', and, as a noun, 'layman, member of the secular clergy'; cf. *secularitas* 'worldliness, worldly life'. *Seclermunck* was probably a nickname for a monk of worldly life and the surname in general 'worldly'.

Sedge: Richard *de la Seg'* 1230 P (D); Thomas *atte Segh* 1308 Ipm (Wo). 'Dweller by the sedgy or reedy spot' (OE *secg* 'sedge, reed').

Sedgefield, Sedgfield: Peter *de Seggesfeld* 12th FeuDu; William *de Segefeld* 1243 AssDu; John *de Seggefeld'* 1361 AssY. From Sedgefield (Durham).

Sedger: Osbert, Gilbert *Seggere* 1200 Cur (Sf), 1275 RH (O); Richard *le Segger'* 1292 MESO (La). A derivative of OE *secg* 'sedge'. cf. Richard *le Seggemaker* 1306 AssSt and *v.* SEDGMAN.

Sedgman: cf., at King's Hall, Cambridge 'For wages of Brown, *seggeman*, for thatching walls, 7*d.* Also in reward to 6 boys carrying *segge*, 6*d.*' (1428) and in 1439 'for the dinners of 2 *seggethakkers* for 4 days, 16*d.*' (Building 226).

Sedgwick, Sedgewick, Sedgewicke, Sidgewick, Sidgwick: John *de Segheswyk*, Thomas *de Sigeswik* 1379 PTY. From Sedgwick (Westmorland) or Sedgewick Castle in Nuthurst (Sussex).

Sedman: *v.* SEEDMAN
Sedwick: For SEDGWICK.

See: Richard *Attesee* 1297 SRY; Berthram *del See* 1312 ColchCt. This surname is not uncommon, both near the coast and well inland. Hence 'dweller by the sea' or 'by a pool' (OE *sæ* 'sea, lake, pool'). Löfvenberg has also noted a third type in Somerset, in the neighbourhood of Bridgwater and at Sea near Ilminster: Bricius *de la Seo* 1262; William *Bythesee* 1336, John *Bitheseo* 1364. This he derives from OE **sēoh*, dat. **sēo* 'watercourse, drain'. *v.* MELS 179–80.

Seear: *v.* SAYER
Seebright: *v.* SEABERT
Seed, Seeds: Johannes *filius Sede* 1210 Cur (Nf); Gilbert, William *Sede* 1275 RH (L), 1327 SRWo. Metonymic for SEEDMAN, but also from an OE **Sida*, a short form of late names recorded after the Conquest, from OE *sidu* 'custom, manner; morality, purity': OE *Siduwine: Seduuinus* 1066 DB (D), Ricardus *filius Sidewini* 1188 P (K); **Sidumæg: Sedemæi* 1185 Templars (K), Robert *Sedemai* 1180 P (Sf); **Sidumægden* (f): *Sedemaiden* c1095 Bury (Sf); **Sidumōd* (f): Ælfget *Sedemode filius* c1095 ib.; and **Sidulufu* (f), **Siduwulf*, found in place-names (NoB 33). *Sede-* may be from **Seodu-*. *v.* PNDB § 13, 359.

Seedman, Sedman: Robert *Sedeman* 1219 Cur (Nf), c1248 Bec (Wa). 'Dealer in seeds.' This might also be from OE *Sidumann: Sydeman* 931 BCS 674; *Sideman* presbiter 974 (1334) Rams. cf. SEED.

Seegar, Seeger: *v.* SAGAR
Seel: *v.* SEAL
Seel(e)y: *v.* SEALEY
Seeman: *v.* SEAMAN
Seener: *v.* SENIOR

Seers: *v.* SAYER
Seeviour: *v.* SEVIER
Segar, Seger: *v.* SAGAR
Segger: *v.* SAGAR, SEDGER
Seggins: *v.* SEGUIN
Segot: *v.* SEAGOOD
Segrave: *v.* SEAGRAVE
Seguin: *Segwinus* 1208 Cur (Y); *Segwin'* forestarius 1209 P (Sf); William *Seguin* 1177 P (O); Richard, Alan *Segin* 1276 RH (L), 1279 RH (C). Identical with French *Seguin* which Dauzat derives from OG (Visigothic) *Sigwin* 'victory-friend'. *Segwinus* 1210 Cur (L) was a citizen of Cologne.

Seignior: *v.* SENIOR
Seiler, Seiller: *v.* SAILER
Seivwright: *v.* SIEVWRIGHT
Selborne, Selbourne, Selburn, Selburne: Robert *de Seleburn* 1272 FFEss; William *Selebourne* 1327 SRSx; John *Selbourne* 1362–4 FrC. From Selborne (Hants).

Selby, Selbey, Selbie: William *de Selebia* 1175 P (Y); Hugh *de Seleby* 1219 AssY; Robert *Selby* 1395 IpmGl. From Selby (WRYorks).

Selden, Seldon, Seldom: Roger *de Seldon'* 1199 Pl (Wa); William *de Selkedon* 1296 SRSx; Robert *Selden, Selkeden* 1525 SRSx; Richard *Seldon*, William *Selden* 1642 PrD. From Seldon in Hatherleigh (Devon), or Selden Farm in Patching (Sussex). The latter is the source of the surname of the famous lawyer, John Selden (1584–1654), whose memory is associated with West Tarring (Sussex).

Self, Selfe: *Saiulfus, Sahulfus, Saulf, Saolf, Saul, Seulf* 1066 DB; Robert *filius Seulfi* 1185 Templars (Berks); William *Sewolf* 1296 SRSx; John, William *Self* 1327 SRSf. OE *Sæwulf* 'seawolf'.

Seliger, Selinger: *v.* SALINGAR
Sell, Selle, Sells, Zell, Zelle: Humfrey *ater Selle* 1296 SRSx. OE (*ge*)*sell* 'shelter for animals' or 'herdsman's hut'. *v.* MELS 181. Probably for a herdsman.

Sellar, Sellars, Seller, Sellers, Sellors, Sellier, Cellier, Zeller: (i) Alriz *Sellere* 1086 InqEl (C); Alwinus *leseller* 1115 Winton (Ha). Either OFr *selier, seller* 'sadler' (1311 NED) or ME *seller* from OE *sellan* 'to give, hand over', 'a seller, dealer' (c1200 NED). Tengvik and Fransson regard the latter as an improbable meaning for the surname. But VENDER still survives. cf. Henricus *Venditor* 1274 RH (L). Sanson *Sellarius* of Yorkshire in 1175 (P) paid 5 marks into the exchequer for selling shields to the king's enemies and Walter *Sellarius* of Warwickshire was fined half-a-mark in 1183 (P) for false description of his wares (*pro falso clamore*). Bodo or Bondo *Sellator* (1175–7 P, Sf) was a sadler (*sellator* 'sadler' 1224 MLWL), but this may be a translation of either the French *seller* or the English *sadler*. Philip *le Celler* (1319 SRLo) is also called *le Sadeler* (1320 LLB E). The frequent form *Seler*, sometimes for *Sealer* and sometimes for *cellar*, may also mean 'sadler'. Sellars in Barnston (Essex) owes its name to Thomas *Seler* (1396 PN Ess 470). cf. *Sele*, horsys harneys (Cotgrave). (ii) Ordingus *cellerarius* 1121–48 Bury (Sf); William *Sellerarius* 1185 Templars (Wa); Robert *le Celerer* 1297 SRY; William *Sellerer* 1419 LLB I. A form of *cellarer*, identical in meaning with *atte celer* (*seler*). (iii) Gudmund *del celer* 1121–48 Bury (Sf); Richard *ate Celer*, taverner 1308 LLB B; William *atte Seler*, *Selere* 1365 LLB G, F. AFr *celer*, OFr *celier* 'a cellar' (a1225 NED), 'a store-house or store-room for provisions; a granary, buttery or pantry'. ME, AFr *celerer* (a1300 NED) was the officer of a monastery, etc., who had charge of the cellar and provisions. Later, it was used of a taverner.

Sellerman: John *Celereman*, Patric *Celererman* 1332 SRCu. Respectively 'worker in the "cellar" ' and 'servant of the cellarer'.

Selley, Selly: Richard *de Selleia* 1203 AssSt. From Selly Oak (Worcs). *v.* also SEALEY.

Sellier: *v.* SELLAR

Sellinger: *v.* SALINGAR

Sellman, Selman, Sillman, Silman: Ailricius *Seliman* 1169 P (Nth); Thomas *Selman* 1275 RH (W); John *Seliman* 1279 RH (C); Robert *Salyman* 1327 *SR* (Ess); Claricia *Selimon*, Henry *Selmon* 1327 SRWo. OE *sǣlig* and *mann* 'happy man'. Occasionally used as a personal name: *Selmon'* de Copmanford 1279 RH (Hu). Sometimes 'Servant of *Sely*'. John *Sely* and Walter *Selyman* lived in the same parish (1327 SRSo). cf. Joan *Saliwymman* 1276 LLB B and SEALEY.

Selvester: *v.* SILVESTER

Selway: *v.* SALWAY

Selwin: *v.* SAUVAIN

Seman: *v.* SEAMAN

Sember: *v.* SEMPER

Semens: *v.* SEAMAN

Semkin: *v.* SIMKIN

Semmence, Semmens: Usually for SIMMONDS, occasionally for *Seamons*. *v.* SEAMAN.

Semper, Sember, Samber, Samper, Simper, Symper: Richard *de Sancto Petro*, *de Sempere*, 1256 AssNb; Richard *Saunper* 1256 FFNb; Simon *Saumper* 1345 AssSt; John *de Seyntper* 1353 AssSt; Ralph *de Seynpere* 1371 DbCh; Urian *Seintpier* 1419 IpmY; John *Semper* 1466 DbCh; John *Simper* 1674 HTSf. Geoffrey de Clinton, chamberlain of Henry I, came from Saint-Pierre-de-Semilly (La Manche). The Count of Meulan and his undertenants, the Mandevilles, were associated with the abbey of Saint-Pierre-des-Preaux.

Sempkins: *v.* SIMKIN

Semple, Sempill, Sambell, Sample, Simble, Simpole: Robertus *de Sancto Paulo* 1159 P (Beds); Symon *Sempol* 1271 RamsCt (C); Simon *Senpol* 1274 ib.; Agnes *Seynpol* 1289 ib.; John *Sampol* 1351 FrY; Thomas *Seintpoule*, *Seinpoull* 1403, 1418 IpmY; Cicily *Sampule* 1413 GildY; Nicholas *Sempool* 1421 NorwW (Sf); Anna *Sampall*, *Sampoll* 1515, 1524 GildY. From one of the French places named Saint-Paul or from Saint-Pol (Pas-de-Calais, Nord). The Scottish *Semple* has a different origin. Black's forms show clearly that it is identical with SIMPLE. From 1315 to 1574 the vowel is invariably *i* or *y*: *Sympil*, *Simpil*, *Simple*. The *e* first appears in 1691 (*Sempell*).

Senchel(l): *v.* SENESCHAL

Sendall, Sendell: John *Sendal* 1303 FA (Sf); John *Sendale* 1374 LoPleas. Among the materials bought for Edward I in 1300 were sindon, or *sendal*, a silk cloth, at 16*s.* the yard, samite, also silk at £4 10*s.*, silken cloth of gold at 26*s.* 8*d.*, cloth of gold of Tartary at 36*s.*, and of Turkey at no less than £7 the yard (METrade 423). The surname probably denotes a merchant who sold sendal or one who made garments of sendal.

Sendler: *v.* SANTLER

Seneschal, Seneschall, Senchell, Senescall, Senecal, Sensicall, Sensicle, Senskell: Alan *le Seneschall* 1194 AssSt; Ralph *le Seneschall'* 1222 Cur (Sx); William *le Seneschel* 1243 AssSo; Thomas *Senycle* 1395 Cl (Lo); Sarah *Senskell* 1693 Bardsley. OFr *seneschal* 'seneschal', an official in the household of a sovereign or great noble, to whom the administration of justice and the entire control of domestic arrangements were entrusted. In a wider use, a steward, 'major-domo' (1393 NED). *Senescal* and *Senecal* were Norman forms (Moisy). cf. MARSHALL and MASKALL.

Senett: *v.* SINNATT

Sengel: *v.* SINGLE

Senhouse: Robert *de Sevenhowes*, John *de Senehowes* 1346 FrY. From Hallsenna in Gosforth (Cumb), earlier *Sevenhoues* 'seven hills', *Hall Senhouse* 1668 (PN Cu 395).

Senior, Seniour, Senier, Seanor, Seener, Seignior, Senyard, Sainer, Sayner, Saynor, Seyner, Sinyard, Synyer: Walter *Seignure* 1164 P (Nf); Hugh *Seinure* 1212 Fees (Nf); Thomas *le Senyur* 1271 AssSt; Robert *le Seynur* 1275 RH (Sf); Henry *Senior* 1279 RH (O); Hugelyn *le Seygnur* 1280 AssSo; Thomas *Senyer* 1332 SRCu; William *Synyer* 1379 PTY. OFr *seignour* 'lord', Lat *senior* 'older'. Perhaps a name of rank, 'lord of the manor', or a nickname for one who aped the lord, or 'the senior, the elder'.

Senneck, Sinnocks: John *Seuenok* 1521 RochW; George *Sennok* 1532 ib. *Sennocke* is the old pronunciation of Sevenoaks (Kent), still used as the name of an hotel and an engineering firm.

Sennett, Sennitt: *v.* SINNATT

Sensicall, Sensicle, Senskell: *v.* SENESCHAL

Senter, Center, Sainter, Santer: Edmund *Sein(e)-tier* 1160–8 ELPN; Benedict *le Seintier* 1197 P (Lo), *le Sentier* 1206 P (Y), *campanarius* c1216–22 Clerkenwell (Lo), *le Seincter* c1230–40 ib.; Simon *le Sainter* 1219 AssY; Roger *Santer*, *le Sainter* 1333 Riev (Y). OFr *saintier* 'bell-founder', the French equivalent of the English BILLITER. *v.* also CENTURY.

Sentry: *v.* SANCTUARY

Seppings, Sippings: Nycolas *Sevenpennys*, Wylliam *Sevynpenys* 1524 SRSf; Hamond *Sepens* ib.; Francis *Sipins*, George *Sepings* 1674 HTSf. A nickname, 'seven-pence'. cf. HALFPENNY.

Serck: *v.* SEARCH

Sergant, Sergean, Sergeant, Sergeaunt, Sergent, Serjeant, Serjent: *v.* SARGANT

Sergenson, Serginson, Sergison, Serjeantson: *v.* SARGEANTSON

Serkitt: *v.* CIRCUITT

Serle: *v.* SEARL

Sermin, Sermon, Surman: Richard *le Sermoner*, Ralph *Sermoner* 1212 Cur (Herts, O); Hugh *le Sarmener* 1269 AssSo; Herbert *le Sarmuner* (*Sermunur*) 1220 Cur (Sf). ME *sermoner*, *sarmoner*, OFr *sermounier* 'preacher, speaker'. The modern surnames are metonymic.

Serrell: *v.* SEARL

Serrick: *v.* SEARCH

Sersmith: *v.* SHEARSMITH

Sertin: *v.* SARTIN

Servant, Servante, Servent, Sarvent: Adam *le Serviant* 1242 P (So). OFr *servant*, *serviant* 'serviteur' (Godefroy). Probably equivalent to *serviens* 'sergeant'. cf. William *Seruantman* 1379 PTY 'the sergeant's man'.

Service, Servis, Servais, Servaes, Sarvis: Walter *Cerveise* 1177 P (O), 1206 Cur (O); William *Ceruaise* 1230 P (Berks); Robert *Cereveyse*, *Sereveyse* 1279 RH (O). OFr *cervoise* 'ale', for a seller of ale, a taverner.

Sessions: Esueillardus *de Seissuns*, *de Soissuns* 1181, 1190 P (C); Riulfus *de Sessuns* Hy 2 (1212) Fees (Berks). From Soissons (Aisne).

Setch: Probably for SACH.

Setchell: For SATCHEL.

Setchfield, Satchwell: Ralph *de Secchevill'* 1176 P (D); Geoffrey *de Saccheuill'* 1198 P (Nt). From one of the two Secquevilles in Normandy. *v.* SACKVILLE. Heanton Satchville (Devon) was held by John *de Sicca Villa* in 1242 (Fees) and Thorpe Satchville (Leics) by Ralph *de Secheville* in 1212 (RBE).

Seton: *v.* SEATON

Setter, Setters: (i) Stephen *le Setere* 1262 MESO (Ha); Symon, Philip, Henry *le Setere* 1280 ib. (ii) Roger *le Settere* 1278 LLB A; Robert *Setter* 1292 SRLo; Isabel *Settere* 1354 ColchCt. *Setter* was common in London as a surname and as an occupational term. Riley took it to mean 'an arrow-smith'. Weekley noted that in 1314 John Heyroun, *settere*, and William *le Settere* were called in as experts to value an embroidered cope and explained the term as 'a maker of *sayete*, a kind of silk'. Fransson adopts this etymology, 'silk-weaver', from OFr *saietier*. Ekwall points out that whilst this meaning may suit the Hampshire forms *setere*, it hardly fits the London examples, *setter(e)*, invariably with a double *t*. He further notes that Alexander *le Settere* in 1307 received £10 in part payment of £40 for an embroidered choir cope bought of him and undertook well and fittingly to complete it. He was an embroiderer who made copes. *Setter* is from ME *setten* 'to set', used of placing ornaments, etc., on a surface of metal or on garments. *v.* SRLo 357. *Setter* was also an occupational term in York. This Thuresson similarly derives from OE *settan* 'to set', one who

sets or lays stone or brick in building, and compares *rogh setter* 'a rough-stone mason' (1435 NED). This was a common term in building: 'the layers, *setters*, or wallers, who placed in position the stones worked by the (free) masons'. They are called *cubitores* at Westminster in 1252, at Corfe in 1280 and at Caernarvon in 1282; *positores* at Windsor in 1365 and Westminster in 1385; *leggeres* and *setteres* at Newgate in 1282; *leggers* at St Paul's in 1382 and *leyers* at Cambridge in 1412. The contemporary term at York was *setters* (Building 31).

Setterfield: *v.* SATTERTHWAITE

Setterington: John *de Setrinton'*, *de Seteryngton* 1200 FFY, 1272 FrY; Adam *de Setryngton* 1367 FFY. From Settrington (ERYorks).

Sevenoaks: Michael *de Sevenoke* 1258 AssSo; Peter *Seuenok* 1332 SRSx. 'Dweller by the seven oaks', as at Sevenoaks (Kent).

Sever(s): *v.* SEAVERS

Severwright: *v.* SIEVWRIGHT

Severy: *v.* SAVARY

Sevier, Sevior, Seviour, Sevyer, Seeviour, Siveyer, Sivier, Sivyer: Edith *Siuiere* 1274 RH (Ess); Ralph *le Siviere* 1279 RH (C); Walter *le Seuyare* 1327 MESO (Ha). A derivative of OE *sife* 'sieve', a sieve-maker (c1440 NED).

Seville: *v.* SAVIL

Sewall, Sawell: *Sauualdus*, *Sauuold*, *Seualdus*, *Seuuold* 1066 DB; *Seuuale* filius Fulgeri Hy 2 DC (Lei); *Sewaldus de Cornhull'* 1214 Cur (Ess); William *Sewald* 1220 Fees (Berks); Roger *Sewale* 1275 SRWo; Nicholas *Sewal* 1279 Calv (Y); Thomas *Sewold* 1317 AssK; John *Sawalle*, Cristina *Sewalle* 1327 SR (Ess); John *Sawold* 1377 AssEss. OE *Sæweald* 'sea-power'. Now rare, largely absorbed by SEWELL. cf. SAYWELL.

Seward, Sewards, Sewart, Seaward, Saward, Saword, Sayward, Suart: (i) *Sauuard*, *Seuuard*, *Seuuart* 1066 DB; *Sewardus de Hohton'* 1199 Cur (Hu); *Sewarde* 1275 RH (Nf); Richard *Seward* 1275 RH (Sa); John *Sewar* 1275 RH (W); William *Saywart* 1385 Combermere (Ch). OE *Sæweard* 'sea-lord'. (ii) *Siuuard* 1066 DB, *Seuuardus* Exon; *Siuuart* 1066 DB (Nt); *Siuuard* c1095 Bury (Sf), c1150 DC (L); *Sigwardus* peregrinus c1155 DC (L); Richard *Siward*, *Suard* 1235 Fees (O); Richard *Siward* 1241 FFEss, *Syward* 1260 AssC. OE *Sigeweard* 'victory-lord' and ODa *Sigwarth* are frequent in DB but the forms cannot be distinguished with certainty. In the Danelaw, the latter is more likely. *Siward*, at times, alternates with *Seward*, which may also be from *Sæweard*, from which all the modern surnames may derive. *Seward*, *Sewart* and *Suart* may also be from *Sigeweard* or *Sigwarth*. (iii) Cecilia *Sueherd* 1379 PTY. OE *sū* 'sow' and *hierde* 'herd', 'sow-herd'. cf. SWINERD. This may occasionally be the source of *Seward*, *Sewart* or *Suart*.

Sewell, Sewill: (i) *Siuuoldus* 1066 DB (So); *Siwaldus* c1250 Rams (Hu); Henricus filius *Sewal'* 1221 AssWa; Richard *Suuel* 1212 Cur (L); John *Sewale* 1277 FFC; Richard *Suel* 1297 MinAcctCo.

OE *Sigeweald* 'victory-ruler' or ON *Sigvaldr*, both
in ME appearing as *Sewal*, a form indistinguish-
able from those of *Sǣweald*. (ii) Ebrardus *de
Seuewell*' 1193 P (Bk); Walter *de Siwell*' 1196 Cur
(Nth); Simon *de Siwelle* 1200 Eynsham (O); Wal-
ter *de Seuewell*' 1222 Cur (D). From Sewell (Beds),
Seawell (Northants), Sywell (Northants), Showell
(Oxon), or Sowell (Devon), all 'seven springs'.
Seawell occurs as *Seywell* in 1681 and 1930. Thus
both Sewall and Sewell may become SAYWELL.

Sewer: (i) William *Suuer* 1185 Templars (Ess);
Roger *le Suhur* 1220 Cur (Lo); Geoffrey *le Suur*
1240 FFEss; Peter *le Suour* 1283 SRSf. This rare
name has no less than four origins, with a variety
of similar forms frequently very difficult to assign
definitely. The most common is OFr *suor, suour,
suur, seur* 'shoemaker'. *v.* also SOUTAR. (ii) Nicholas
le Seur 1284 LLB A; Robert *le Seure* 1301 SRY;
John *le Seuwour, le Seour* 1311 LLB D. An aphetic
form of AFr *asseour*, OFr *asseoir* 'to cause to sit,
to seat', 'an attendant at a meal who superintended
the arrangement of the table, the seating of the
guests, and the tasting and serving of the dishes'
(a13.. NED, with forms *sewere, sawere, sewre*).
(iii) Gilbert *le Suir* 1222 DBStP; Roger *le Syur* 1225
AssSo; Humfrey *le Syur, le Sawyere, le Sayhare*
1270 AssSo; John *le Syur, le Sayur* 1286 MESO
(Nf); Philip *le Ciour, le Syour* 1316 Wak (Y). OFr
seieor, syeeur, scieur, saieur 'sawyer'. Humfrey le
Syur's name appears in both French and English
forms which have given modern *Sewer, Sawyer*,
and *Sayer*. (iv) Richard *le Sewer* 1279 MESO (Y);
Margery *Sewer* 1327 SRC. A derivative of OE
sēowian 'to sew', 'a sewer, tailor' (1399 NED, with
forms *sewer, sawer, sower*). The feminine form
survives as SOUSTER.

Sewter: *v.* SOUTAR
Sexon: *v.* SEXTEN
**Sexten, Sexton, Sexstone, Sexon, Seckerson,
Secretan:** Tomas *Sekerstein* 1203 P (Y); Gilbert *le
Segerstein* 1285 Ass (Ess); William *le Sekersteyn*
1296 SRSx; Thomas *Segrestan* 1299 LLB B;
Henry *le Secrestein* 1327 SRSf; John *Sekesteyn*
1310 EAS xx; William *Sexstain* 1327 SRSx; Peter
Sexten 1327 SRWo; Thomas *Sexton, Sexten* 1524
SRSf. AFr *segerstaine*, OFr *segrestein, secrestein*,
MedLat *sacristānus*, a doublet of *sacristan* (1303
NED), 'sexton', originally 'the officer in a church
in charge of the sacred vessels and vestments', not,
as now, the grave-digger.

Seyler: *v.* SAILER
Seyman: *v.* SEAMAN
Seymour, Seymoure, Seymore, Seymer: Gauf-
ridus *de Sancto Mauro* 1159 P (Hu); Henry *de
Seimor* 1203 AssSt; Henry *de Seintmor* 1251
FFHu; Henry *de Seynmor, de Seymmor, de Sem-
mor* 1272 AssSt; Robert *Seymor* 1344 LoPleas.
From Saint-Maur-des-Fossés (Seine). Also from
Seamer (Yorks): John *Saymor* 1416 FrY.

Seyner: *v.* SENIOR
Seys: *v.* SAYCE
Shackcloth: Probably a corruption of SHACK-
LOCK.

Shackel, Shackell, Shackle, Shackles, Skakle:
Robertus *filius Scakel* Hy 2 DC (L), Robert
Scakel ib.; Herbert *Scakel* ib.; William *Shakelle*
1379 PTY. *Schakel* is an anglicizing of Anglo-
Scand *Skakel*, from ON *Skǫkull* (byname), OSw
Skakli, the latter occurring in Scagglethorpe (ER,
WRYorks).
Shacklady: *v.* SHAKELADY
Shackleton: Hugh *Schacheliton* 1246 AssLa;
Hugh *de Shakeldene* 1302 SRY. From Scackleton
(NRYorks), a Scandinavianized form of OE
Scacoldenu. The surname preserves the original
English *Sh-*.
Shackley: *v.* SHAKERLEY
Shacklock, Shatlock, Shadlock: Roger, Richard
Schakeloc 1187 P (Gl), 1246 AssLa; Robert
Shakeloc 1227 AssSt; Adam *Schakelokes* 1316
Wak (Y); John *Shadlock* 1524 FrY. 'Shake lock',
a nickname for one with a habit (not unknown
today) of shaking back his long hair (note the
1316 plural *locks*), or metonymic for a gaoler,
either as a shaker of locks or from ME *schaklock*
'fetters'.
Shackman: Henry *Shakeman* 1221 FFEss. cf.
SHAKELADY.
Shackshaft: *v.* SHAKESHAFT
Shad: Durand *Scad*, John *Shad* c1140
ELPN, 1326 FFEss; Nicholas, Ida *Schad* 1255
RH (W), 1275 SRWo. A nickname from the fish,
OE *sceadd* 'a shad', the importance of which is
shown from the existence of a 'shad season' in OE
times.
Shaddick, Shaddock, Shadwick: *v.* CHADWICK
Shade, Schade: Lucas *Shadue* 1203 Cur (C);
Hugo *Scade (Schade)* 1221 Cur (Lei); Andrew
Shadewe 1314 LLB D; Ralph *Shade* 1296 SRSx.
OE *sceadu*, ME *shade, shadwe* 'shadow', perhaps a
nickname for a very thin man. Also 'dweller by
the boundary' (OE *scēad*): Richard *de la Schade*
1230 P (D).
Shadlock: *v.* SHACKLOCK
Shadwell: William, Roald *de Schadewelle* c1176–
90 YCh, 1261 FFO; Thomas *de Shadewelle* 1349
IpmW; John *Shadwell* 1576 SRW. From Shadwell
(Middlesex, Norfolk, WRYorks).
Shafe: *v.* SHAW
Shairp: *v.* SHARP
Shakelady, Shacklady: Richard *Shakelauedy*
1332 SRLa; Richard *Shaklady* 1384 FFLa;
Rowland *Shakelady* 1529 ib. 'Known in Lanca-
shire as a corruption of the ancient local surname
of Shackerley (Lower). Clearly an unwarranted
local derivation. 'Shake lady.' Forssner suggests
'house-tyrant'.
Shakelance: Henry *Shakelaunce* 1275 RH (Nth);
Robert *Schakelaunce* 1327 SRSf. 'Shake lance', a
spearman. cf. SHAKESPEAR.
Shakerley, Shackley: Henry *de Shakresleghe,
de Shakerleghe* 1332 SRLa. From Shackerley or
Shakerley (both Lancs).
Shakesby: Richard, John *Shakespey* 1292 EwenG
(Y), 1296 SRSx; Walter *Shakespye* 1342 Ewen
(Sr). For SAXBY, *Sakespe* 'draw sword', with early

substitution of the English *Shake-* for the French *Sac-*.

Shakeshaft, Shakesheff, Shackshaft: William *Shakeshaft* 1332 SRLa, 1542 PrGR; Henry *Shakshaft* 1674 HTŚf. 'Shake shaft', OE *sceaft* 'shaft, spear'.

Shakespear, Shakespeare, Shakspeare: W. *Sakespere* 1248 Ewen (Gl); W *Shakesper'* 1318 ib. (St); Simon *Shakespere, Schakespere* 1324 AssSt, 1327 SRSt; Robert *Schaksper* 1379 PTY. 'Shake spear', a spearman, a common type of surname. cf. SHAKELANCE, SHAKESHAFT, etc. above, and John *Shakstaf* 1423 LLB K, Geoffrey *Schakeheved* 13th Rams (Hu), John *Shakeleg* 1333 ColchCt, William *Schaktre* 1301 SRY, Richard *Schakerake* 1379 *Coram* (Ha). 'Never a name in English nomenclature so simple or so certain in its origin. It is exactly what it looks—Shakespear' (Bardsley). To which Weekley adds that 'no European philologist of any reputation would dissent from this opinion' (*Words Ancient and Modern* 204). And there the name could be left but for Ewen's elaborate and pretentious ten-page disquisition in support of his preconceived theory that such names cannot be nicknames (*History of British Surnames* 312–322). An ignorance of phonetics and OE nomenclature is bolstered up by a confused collection of examples, some irrelevant, some proving conclusively the very etymology he wishes to disprove, the whole aptly summarized by Weekley as 'etymological moonshine'. Unrepentant, Ewen returned to the fray with an elaborate pedigree of the name, *partly conjectural* (his own italics) in his *Guide to the Origin of British Surnames* (91–97), beginning with OE *Sceaftloc* and ending with *Shakeberry*. Apart from the fact that *Sceaft* is unknown as an element in OE personal-names, it would become *Shaft* and not *Shake* or *Skathe*. Eliminating from the pedigree all compounds of these, we are left with *Shaftspere* (1501) and *Scapespere* (1523), obviously 16th century corruptions or errors of transcription, and *Shafsbury* (1688), clearly originating from the Dorset Shaftesbury. This leaves high and dry, in solitary seclusion, the conjectural OE *Sceaftloc*, presumed ancestor of an illegitimate progeny.

Shallcrass, Shallcross: *v.* SHAWCROSS

Shank, Shanks: Lefuine *Scanches* c1095 Bury (Sf); Rotbern *Sceanca* 1100–30 OEByn (D); Walter, Robert *Schanke* 1177, 1190 P (D, Herts); Stephen *Schankes* 1275 RH (Nf); John *Shonke* 1349 LoPleas. OE *sceanca* 'shank, leg', a nickname.

Shaper: Julia *Schaper* 1332 SRSx. A derivative of ME *schapen* 'to shape', a tailor. *v.* SHAPSTER.

Shapler: Gervase, Ralph *le Chapeler* 1214 Cur (Sr), 1230 MemR (K). OFr. *chapelier* 'maker or seller of hats' (1601 NED). The name is also found in the AFr form *capelier*: Baldwin, Benedict *le capel(l)er* 1216–20 Clerkenwell (Lo), 1291 Cur (Mx).

Shapster: Matilda *Shapistre* 1275 RH (Sf); Sarra *le Shapester* 1327 SRWo. The feminine form

of SHAPER. ME *schapen* is a new formation from the substantive *schap*. The OE verb was *scieppan*, whence SHIPSTER.

Shard, Sheard, Sheards: William *atte Sharde* 1275 SRWo; Adam *atte Sherd* 1332 SRWa; Hugo *del Sherd* 1354 Putnam (Ch). 'Dweller by the cleft or gap', OE *sceard.*

Sharman, Shearman, Sheerman, Sherman, Shurman: Roger *sereman* 1207 FrLeic; William *le Shereman* 1281 LLB B; John *Sherman* 1327 SRSf; Philip *Shareman* (*Sharman*) 1327 *SR* (Ess). OE *scēarra* 'shears' and '*mann*', a shearer of woollen cloth.

Sharp, Sharpe, Sharps, Shairp: Healðegn *Scearpa* 1026 OEByn (K); Ailmer *Scharp* 1184 P (Herts); Richard *Serp* 1210 Cur (C); Aylmer *Sarp* 1228 FFEss; Alan *Sharp* 1296 SRSx. OE *scearp* 'sharp, quick, smart'. *Shairp* is Scottish.

Sharples, Sharpless: John *de Scharples* 1246 AssLa; John, Adam *de Sharples* 1332 SRLa; Robert *Scharpiles* 1418 IpmY; Richard *Sharplys* 1543 CorNt. From Sharples (Lancs).

Sharrock(s): *v.* SHORROCK

Shatlock: *v.* SHACKLOCK

Shave(s): *v.* SHAW

Shaw, Shawe, Shafe, Shave, Shaves, Shay, Shayes, Shea: Simon *de Schage* 1191 P (Berks); Richard *de la Schawe* 1275 SRWo; John *ate Shaw* 1295 ParlR (Ess); Henry *del Schawe* 1307 Wak (Y); William *Bithe Shaghe* 1333 MELS (So); Richard *Shay*, Hugh *Shey* 1564 ShefA (Y). 'Dweller by the wood', OE *sceaga*, as at Shaw (Berks, Lancs, Wilts). *Shay* is a Yorkshire dialect form, found also in Devon where *shave* and *shafe* are also found. Shaugh (Devon), pronounced *Shay*, is *Shaue* 1281, *Sheagh* 1535, *Shea* 1584, *Shaff* 1584, *Shaye* t Hy 8 (PN D 258). Shave Cross (Dorset) and Shave Fm (Som) both derive from *sceaga*. *Shea* is also for O'SHEA.

Shawcross, Shalcross, Shallcrass, Shallcross, Shellcross: Benedict *de Shakelcros* 1327 SRDb; Matilda *de Shalcros* 1348 DbAS 36. From Shackelcross (Derby).

Shear: *v.* SHEER

Sheard: *v.* SHARD

Shearer, Sheara, Sherar, Sherer, Sharer, Shirer: Robert *le Sherer* 1231 FFC; William *Le Scherer'*, *Le Schirere* 1305 MESO (Ha). A derivative of OE *sceran* 'to cut', 'one who removes the nap of cloth by shearing', identical in meaning with SHEARMAN, SHARMAN.

Shearman: *v.* SHARMAN

Shearsmith, Sersmith: Walter *Scheresmythe* 1325 ParlWrits (Gl); Geoffrey *Sheresmyth* 1391 FrY. 'A maker of shears, scissors', OE *scēarra* and *smið.*

Shearwood: *v.* SHERWOOD

Sheather: Henry, Richard *le Schether(e)* 1302 FrY, 1304 LoCt; Robert, Alexander *le Shether* 1334 LLB E, FrLeic. 'Maker of sheaths' (OE *scǣþ, scēaþ*).

Sheep: Simon *Shep* 1221 AssWa; Thomas *Sheep* 1321 FFSf. OE *scēap* 'sheep'. A nickname, but also, probably, for a shepherd or a dealer in sheep: John *Shepgrom* 1327 *SR* (Ess), Alexander *Shepmongere* 1227 AssBeds.

Sheepshanks: William *Shepescanke* 1224 Cur (Nf), 1379 PTY. 'With legs like a sheep' (OE *sceanca* 'leg'). Yorkshiremen were partial to this type of name: Symon *Doggeschanke* c1246 Calv (Y), William *Pyshank* 1373 FrY 'magpie-legs', John *Philipschank* 1379 PTY 'sparrow-legs'.

Sheepwash, Shipwash: Robert *Sepwas, de Sepwass*' 1279 RH (O); Philip *atte Shepewassh* 1332 SRSx. 'Dweller near a place for washing sheep' (OE *scēapwæsce*) as at Sheepwash (Devon, Northumb) or Sheepwash Fm in Nuthurst (Sussex).

Sheer, Sheere, Sheeres, Sheers, Sher, Sherr, Shere, Shear, Shears: Walter *Leschir* 1193 P (Berks); Reginald *le Scher* 1327 SRSt. OE *scīr*, **scǣre* 'fair, bright'. *Shear(s)*, if the spelling is to be relied on, may be metonymic for SHEARSMITH.

Sheldon: Roger *de Scheldona* 1189–90 P (St); Cecily *de Sheldon* 1248 FFK; John *Sheldone* 1367 IpmGl. From Sheldon (Devon, Derby, Warwicks).

Sheldrake, Sheldrick, Shildrake, Shildrick: Roger *Scheldrac* 1195 P (Ess); Adam *le Sceldrake* 1275 RH (Sf). 'Sheldrake', a bird of the duck tribe, remarkable for its bright and variegated colouring (c1325 NED).

Shellabear: v. SHILLABEER

Shellcross: v. SHAWCROSS

Shelley, Shelly: Matildá *de Selleg*, Richard *de Selueleg*' 1201 Pl (Sf); Henry *de Schellay* 1297 SRY; Roger *de Shelley* 1379 PTY; John *Shelley* 1473–4 FFSr. From Shelley (Essex, Suffolk, WRYorks).

Shelton: Robert, John *de Schelton*' 1191 P (St), 1260 AssY; John *Shelton*' 1385 AssWa. From Shelton (Beds, Norfolk, Notts, Salop, Staffs).

Shemmans, Shemming: v. SHIMMINGS

Shepard, Shepeard, Sheperd, Shephard, Shepheard, Shepherd, Sheppard, Shepperd, Sheppherd, Shippard: William *Sepherd* 1279 RH (O); Henry *Sephurde* 1296 SRSx; Emma *le Schepherde* 1297 MinAcctCo; Walter *le Shepperde* 1307 FFSf; Alice *the Schiphird* 1307 Wak (Y); Avice *la Schepherdes* 1311 ColchCt; John *Shipherde* 1317 AssK; Walter *le Sheparde* 1327 SRWo; Adam *le Shepherd* 1328 Crowland (C); Robert *le Shephard* 1330 FFSr. OE *scēaphyrde* 'shepherd'. This may also occasionally have absorbed *shipward*; William *le Shipward* 1357 Putnam (He), Hugo *Shipward* 1471 FrY. Probably OE **scēap-weard* 'sheep-ward'. Thomas *Shypward* (1432) and John *Shipward* (1467), both domiciled in Bristol, were probably ship-masters (OE *scipweard*). v. MEOT.

Shepherdson, Sheperdson, Sheppardson, Shepperdson, Shepperson, Shipperdson: John *Schephirdson* 1332 SRCu; Ralph *Schiperdson* 1509 GildY. 'Son of the shepherd.'

Sheppick: Henry *de Schepewic* 1275 RH (Nt). 'Dweller or worker at a sheep-farm' (OE *scēapwīc*). cf. Shapwick (Dorset, Som).

Sher: v. SHEER

Sherar: v. SHEARER

Sherard: v. SHERRARD

Shercliff, Sheircliffe, Shirtcliffe, Shirtliff, Shetliff, Shortliffe: John *de Shirclyf* 1379 PTY; Thomas *Shirtliffe* 1510 ShefA; Richard *Shirtcliffe* 1564 ib.; Robert *Sheirclyff* 1593 ib. From Shirecliff in Sheffield (Yorks).

Shere: v. SHEER

Sherer: v. SHEARER

Sheriff, Sheriffs, Sherriff, Sherriffs, Shireff, Shirreff, Shirreffs, Shirrefs, Shiriff, Shreeve, Shreeves, Shreve, Shrieve, Shrieves, Shrive, Shrives, Schrieve: Æthelwine *Sciregerefa* 1016–20 OEByn (K); Hugo *le Sirreve* 1212 Cur (Lei); Alan *Sciriue* 1219 AssL; Walter *Sherrev*' 1220 Cur (K); Thomas *Shyrreue* 1230 P (Ha); John *Schiref* 1273 RH (Nb); Thomas *Shreeve* 1457 Bacon (Sf); Robert *Shryve* 1568 SRSf. OE *scīrgerēfa* 'sheriff'. v. SHIRRA.

Sherlock, Shurlock: Ælfwerd *Scirloc* c1002–19 OEByn; Ralph *Shirloc* 1159 P (Lo). OE *scīr* 'bright, shining' and *loc(c)* 'lock (of hair)'. 'Fair-haired.'

Sherman: v. SHARMAN

Sherr: v. SHEER

Sherrard, Sherreard, Sherrad, Sherratt, Sherred, Sherrett, Sherrott, Sherard: William *Shirard* 1298 AssSt; Richard *Schirard* 1323 AD v (St); William *Sherard* 1337 AssSt; William *Sherratt* 1578 AD vi (Ch). OE *scīr* 'bright' plus the French intensive suffix *-(h)ard*.

Sherriff: v. SHERIFF

Sherwen, Sherwin: Gilbert *scerewind*', *scorewint* Hy 2 DC (L); William *Scherewind* 1187 P (Cu); John *Shirwyn* 1479 NorwW (Nf); John *Sherwyn* 1524 SRSf. 'Cut wind', from OE *sceran* 'to cut' and *wind*, used of a swift runner.

Sherwood, Shearwood: William *de Shirewude* 1219 AssY; Alan *de Shirewod* 1327 SRSx; John *Shirwod* 1405 IpmY; Elizabeth *Sherwood* 1539 CorNt. From Sherwood (Notts), or 'dweller by the bright wood'.

Shetliff: v. SHERCLIFF

Shettle: v. SHUTTLE

Shield, Shields: (i) Robert *Scild* 1206 P (Y); William *Sheld* 1267 AssSt. OE *scild, sceld* 'shield', probably for a maker of shields. cf. *scyldwyrhta* c1114 MLWL, Geoffrey *le Seldmakere* 1285 MESO (Ess), Adam *Scheldman* 1327 SRSf. (ii) Roger *ate Schelde* 1332 SRSr. 'Dweller by the shelter' (OE *scild, sceld* 'protection') or 'by the shallow place' (OE **scieldu*).

Shildrake: v. SHELDRAKE

Shillabeer, Shillibeer, Shellabear: From a lost Shillibeer in Meavy (Devon), last recorded c1587, with a surname *Shullebere* in 1333 (PN D 230).

Shilling: John *Eschelling* 1176 P (So); Geoffrey *Scelling* 1188 P (So); John *Eskeling* 1221 AssGl; William, John *Schilling* 1275 RH (Nf), 1309 AD iv (Wa). Apparently a nickname from OE *scilling* 'shilling'. There is no evidence for a personal-name as suggested by Bardsley and Harrison.

Shimmin: Dermot *MacSimon* 1366, *MacShemine* 1430, *Shimin* 1614 Moore. Manx *McSimeen* 'little Simon's son'.

Shimmings, Shimmin, Shimmins, Shemming, Shemmans: Roger *Scymming*, John *Schemmeng* 1279 RH (C); Richard, John *Shymmyng* 1297 MinAcctCo, 1332 SRWa; Robert *Shimmon*, Amy *Shimming*, Ann *Shimman* 1775, 1787, 1793 SfPR. Perhaps OE **sciming* 'the fair one', from OE *scīma* 'bright'.

Shingler: Roger *le Shinglere* 1335 MEOT (Ess); William *Shyngelere* 1381 SRSt. A derivative of ME *schinglen* 'to cover with shingles', a roofer.

Shingles: John, Henry *S(c)hingel* 1327 SRSx, SRSf. ME *shingle* 'a wooden tile', metonymic for SHINGLER.

Shinn, Shynn: Herveus *Schin* 1165 P (Sf); Hugo *Scin* 1190 P (He). Probably OE *scinn*, ME *shin* 'skin', the native equivalent of ON *skinn*. *v.* MESO 119–21. Metonymic for a skinner. *v.* SHINNER.

Shinner: John *le Scinner* 1279 RH (C); Geoffrey *le Schinnere* 1296 SRSx; John *Schynnere*, Adam *Le Schinner* 1305 MESO (Ha, So). A derivative of OE *scinn* 'skin', a skinner. *v.* SHINN, SKINNER.

Shipley, Shiplee: Hugh *de Sciplay* 1219 AssY; Robert *de Sheplay* 1375 FFY; Robert *Shipleye* 1402–3 FFWa. From Shipley (Derby, Durham, Northumb, Salop, Sussex, WRYorks), or 'dweller by the sheep pasture'.

Shipman: (i) *Schipemannus* 1130 P (R); *Scipmanus* c1250 Rams (Nf); Hubert *Scipman* 1221 ElyA (Hu); Simon *le Sipman*, *Schipman* 1267, 1290 HPD (Ess). OE *scipmann* 'seaman, sailor'. William *Scipman* (1243 AssSo) was drowned from a boat in the water of the Parret. (ii) Richard *le Schepman* 1296 MEOT (Herts); Adam *le Schepman* 1316 ib. (Ess). OE *scēap* 'sheep' and *mann*, 'shepherd'. In certain dialects, OE *scēap* became ME *ship* and *shipman* may sometimes mean 'shepherd'. *v.* MEOT 63, 257.

Shipp: Roger *de*, *del Schipp* 1288 AssCh; Walter *del Schippe* 1297 SRY. Richard Stonham *atte Shippe* withouten Crepulgate (1423 LondEng 149) lived at the sign of the ship but early examples of such sign-names are rare and the above examples are probably identical in meaning with SHIPMAN 'sailor'.

Shippard: *v.* SHEPARD

Shippen: William *Shepene* 1317 AssK; Adam *atte Shupene* 1327 SRWo; Henry *ate Shypene* 1341 ib. OE *scypen* 'cattle-shed', either from residence at a place named from such, as Shapens (PN Ess 521), Shippen (PN D 495), Shippen (WRYorks) or Shippon (Berks), or from employment there, 'cattle-man, cowman'.

Shipperbottom: *v.* SHUFFLEBOTHAM

Shipperdson: *v.* SHEPHERDSON

Shipster: Alice *La Seppestre* 1296 SRSx; Matilda *le Scipstere* 1320 Oseney (O); John *Shepster* 1379 ColchCt. A derivative of OE *scieppan, sceppan* 'to create', ME *shippen* 'to shape', 'a female cutter-out of material, a dressmaker' (1377 NED). Now a rare surname.

Shipwash: *v.* SHEEPWASH

Shipwright: Warin *Sipwriet* t John HPD (Ess); Alice *le Schipwrith* 1279 AssNb; John *le Shipwrighte* 1309 FFEss. OE *scipwyrhta* 'a man employed in the construction of ships'.

Shirer: *v.* SHEARER

Shirley: William *de Schirle* 1219 AssY; Ralph *de Shirleye* 1318–19 FFWa; William *Shirley* 1442–3 FFSr. From Shirley (Derby, Hants, Surrey, Warwicks, WRYorks).

Shirman: Ufegeat *Scireman* 1000–14 OEByn (K); William *Schiremon* 1275 SRWo. OE *scīrmann, scīremann* 'sheriff', also 'bailiff, steward'.

Shirra: The Scottish pronunciation of SHERIFF: Elspeth *Shirra* 1676 Black (Edinburgh).

Shirt: Godwin *de la Sirte* 1179 P (Sr); John *atte Shurte* 1296 SRSx. 'Dweller by the detached piece of land', OE *scyrte* 'skirt, piece cut off'.

Shirtcliffe, Shirtliff: *v.* SHERCLIFF

Shitler: *v.* SHUTLAR

Shocker: John *le Schokere* 1296 SRSx. An occupational-name from ME *schokken* 'to heap up, arrange sheaves in a shock'.

Shoebotham, Shoebottom: *v.* SHUFFLEBOTHAM

Shoemake, Shoemaker, Schoemaker: Hugh *S(c)homaker* 1365 ColchCt. 'Shoemaker', from OE *scōh*.

Shoesmith, Shoosmith: William *Le Shosmith, Sosmyth* 1288 MESO, 1296 SRSx. OE *scōh, smið* 'shoeing-smith', maker of horseshoes.

Shooter, Shotter, Shuter: Robert *scotere* 1148 Winton (Ha); Stephen *le Shotiere* 1255 Ass (Ess); Henry *Schuetere* 1275 SRWo; William *Schoter* 1316 NottBR; Henry *le Shotter* 1320 AssSt; John *le Schotiere* 1327 SR (Ess); John *Schewter* 1379 PTY; Richard *Shoiter, Shooter* 1554 Shef, 1579 ShefA; John *Shuter* 1784 Bardsley. A derivative of OE *scotian* 'to shoot', 'shooter, archer'. *S(c)hoter* may also derive from ME *schōten*, from OE *scēotan*, through a shifting of the vowel-stress from *scēotan* 'to shoot'. This also gave *sheter*, now *Sheeter*: Ralph *Scheter* 1297 SRY, Robert *Schetere* 1327 SRSf.

Shopper: Thomas *atte Shoppe* 1341 LLB F; John *Shopper* 1353 Putnam (W). 'Shop-keeper.'

Shore, Shores: William *del Shore* 1332 SRLa. 'Dweller by the shore', ME *schore*.

Shorrock, Shorrocks, Sharrock, Sharrocks, Shurrock: Richard *de Shorrok* 1332 SRLa; George *Sharrocke* 1682 PrGR. From Shorrock Green (Lancs).

Short, Shortt: Ordric *Scort* 1176 P (Do); Richard *le Sorte* 1269 AssSo; William *Short* 1327 SRSx. OE *sceort* 'short'.

Shorthose, Shorthouse, Shortose, Shorters, Shortis, Shortus: (i) William *Shorthose* 1260 AssLa; Henry *Schorthose* 1275 Wak (Y); Robert *Shortus* 1585 Oxon; Martha *Shorthouse* 1731 SfPR. A translation of *Curthose* 'short boot'. Trevisa (1387) translates Higden's 'filio Roberti *courtehose*' by 'Robert *Schorthoses* sone' (Groups 62). cf. Adam *Sortkyrtell* 1256 AssNb 'short-gown', Robert *langhose* 1277 Ely (Sf) 'long boot'. (ii) Robert, John *Schorthals* 1198 P (K), 1219 AssL. 'Short neck',

OE *h(e)als*. cf. Rogerus *longhals* c1200 Dublin. *v.* WHITEHOUSE.

Shortliffe: *v.* SHERCLIFF

Shortreed: Martin, Simon *Shortrad(e)* 1274 RH (Ess), 1327 SRY. 'Short counsel', OE *sceort, ræd*, 'short' in the sense 'limited'. cf. 'My wit is short' (Chaucer) and Robert *Smalred* 1176 P (Y).

Shotter: *v.* SHOOTER

Shotton: Robert *de Schottun* c1180 Black (Kelso); Huwe *de Shottone* 1296 ib. (Roxburgh); Ralph *del Schoton* 1327 SRDb. From Shotton (Durham, Northumb), or 'dweller by the enclosure on the slope'.

Shoulders: Rau *Sculdur* 1100–30 OEByn (D); Robert *Schuldre* 1275 RH (Nf); Simon *Shulder* 1327 SRSx. OE *sculdor* 'shoulder', a nickname for one with broad shoulders or some peculiarity of the shoulders.

Shouler: *v.* SHOVELLER

Shove: Aluricus *Scoua* 1066 DB (Herts); Leuuinus *Scufe* c1067 OEByn; *Scoua* 1086 DB (Herts); Wulnod *Scoue* 1185 Templars (K). Probably OE **scufa*, a derivative of *scūfan* 'to thrust, push'. cf. SHOWERS.

Shovel, Showl: Turoldus *scuuel* 1148 Winton (Ha). Metonymic for SHOVELLER.

Shovelbottom: *v.* SHUFFLEBOTHAM

Shoveller, Shouler, Showler: William *le Schovelere* 1301 MEOT (O); Walter *le Shouelere* 1314 ib. (Herts); Nicholas *Schoueler, Schoveler* 1366 ColchCt. A derivative of ME *schovelyn* 'to shovel'. One who works with or makes shovels.

Showers: Richard *le Shouere* 1297 MinAcctCo (W). A derivative of OE *scūfan* 'to thrust, push', a nickname, no doubt, for one of violent habits. cf. SHOVE, and SHOWLER for SHOVELLER.

Showl: *v.* SHOVEL

Showler: *v.* SHOVELLER

Shrapnel: Richard *Sharpanel* 1218–22 Cockersand (La); Richard *Shrapnell* 1706 DKR 41 (W). A metathesized form of *Charbonnel*. *v.* CARBONELL.

Shreeve(s): *v.* SHERIFF

Shrewsbury, Shrosbree: John *Shrouesbury* 1280 SRSt; William *de Schrouesbir'* 1332 SRLo. From Shrewsbury.

Shrieve(s), Shrive(s): *v.* SHERIFF

Shrubb: Robert *Shrub* 1288 FFSf; John *in the Scrobbes* 1327 *SR* (Ess). 'Dweller by the shrub(s)', OE *scrybb*.

Shubotham: *v.* SHUFFLEBOTHAM

Shufflebotham, Shufflebotam, Shovelbottom, Shipperbottom, Shoebotham, Shoebottom, Shubotham: Richard *de Schyppewallebothem* 1285 AssLa; James *Shepobotham* 1579 Bardsley; John *Shippobotham* 1582 ib.; George *Shupplebotham* 1621 ib.; Charles *Shifabothom* 1626 ib.; James *Shipplebotham* 1642 ib.; Richard *Shufflebotham* 1674 ib. From Shipperbottom (Lancs).

Shurlock: *v.* SHERLOCK

Shurrock: *v.* SHORROCK

Shuter: *v.* SHOOTER

Shutlar, Shutler, Shuttler, Shitler, Shittler: William *le Scuteler* 1177 P (Nf); John *Scutelere* 1296 SRSx; Hugo *le Scotiler* 1327 SRSt. Thuresson explains this as a derivative of OE *scutel* 'dish, platter', 'a scullion' or a dealer in crockery. This would account for the above forms and *Shutler*, but the existence of *Shitler* and the possibility that *Shettle* may be metonymic for *Shutler*, implies an OE *y*. *Shitler*, often *Shutler*, and the implied *Shetler* are derivatives of OE *scytel*, ME *shittle, schetylle, schutylle*, an instrument used in weaving, a shuttle, and the surnames denote a maker of shuttles or, more probably, 'a weaver'. cf.

> 'My godsire's name, I tell you,
> Was *In-and-In Shittle*, and a weaver he was,
> And it did fit his craft; for so his shittle
> Went in and in still, this way and then that way.'
> (Ben Jonson, *Tale of a Tub*, iv. 2.)

Shutt, Shut, Shutte, Shutts: Wulfsige *Scytta* c1050 OEByn (Herts); Liuricus *Shitte* 1165 P (Sf); Michael *Shut* 1296 SRSx; John *Schut, Shit* 1327 SRSf. OE *scytta* 'shooter, archer'.

Shutter: Simon *le Shutter* 1332 SRWa. OE *scytere* 'archer'.

Shuttle, Shettle: William *le Schutel* 1296 SRSx; Simon *Shitel* 1313, 1314 Pat (Y). ME *shytell, shuttle* 'inconstant, variable, fickle, flighty' (c1440 NED). Also metonymic for SHITLER, SHUTLAR.

Shuttleworth, Shuttlewood: Henry *de Schutlesworth* 1246 AssLa; John *de Shutelisworth* 1338 WhC; James *Shittleworth*, John *Shettleworth*, Grace *Shettlewood* 1662 HTEss. From Shuttleworth (Lancs), Shuttlewood in Bolsover (Derby), or Shuttleworth, now Littleworth, in Rossington (WRYorks).

Sibary, Siberg, Siberry: *v.* SEABER

Sibbett, Sibbit, Sibbitt: *Sebode* c1095 Bury (Sf); William *Sibode* 1206 P (So); Walter *Sybod* 1221 AssWa; William *Sibbitt* 1581 FrY; Roger *Sybbett* 1594 ib. OG *Sigibodo* 'victory-messenger'.

Sibble, Sibbles: Walter *filius Sibile* 1189 Sol; *Sibilla* 1219 AssY, Cur (Nth); Walter *Sibilla* 1170 P (Berks). Fr *Sibille* (f). *v.* SIBLEY.

Sibbons, Sibborn: *v.* SEABORN

Sibert: *v.* SEABER

Sibley, Sibly, Sebley: Geoffrey *Sibilie* 1275 RH (Sf); William *Sibeli, Sibli* 1279 RH (Hu); Richard *Sebely* 1327 SRSf. *Sibyl*, Greek Σίβυλλα, Lat *Sibilla*, the name of the priestess who uttered the ancient oracles, a common woman's name after the Conquest, in the vernacular *Sibley*.

Siborne: *v.* SEABORN

Sibree: *v.* SEABER

Sibson: John *Sibson, Sibbeson* 1314, 1316 Wak (Y); William *Sibbison* 1327 SRC. 'Son of Sibb', a pet-form of *Sibyl*. cf. John son of *Sibbe, Sibbe Hamond* 1297, 1306 Wak.

Siburn: *v.* SEABORN

Sicely: *v.* SISLEY

Sich: *v.* SYKES

Sid(d)enham: *v.* SYDENHAM

Side, Sydes: Herbert *de Side* 1221 AssGl; Henry *Beside* 1290 *ERO;* Michael *Aside* 1327

SRSx; Adam *del Syde* 1332 SRSt. 'Dweller by the slope', OE *sīde*, as at Syde (Glos).

Sidebotham, Sidebottom: Hugh *de Sidbothume* 1289 AssCh. 'Dweller in the wide valley', OE *sīd*. Sometimes pronounced *Siddybottarm*.

Sideman: *v.* SEEDMAN

Sidey: Laurence *de Sydhaghe*, Alan *de Sidhey* 1327 SRSf; John *Sidey* 1524 SRSf. 'Dweller by the wide enclosure.'

Sidg(e)wick: *v.* SEDGWICK

Sidney, Sydney: John *ate Sydenye* 1332 SRSr; William *Sydny* 1428 FA (Sx). 'Dweller by the wide well-watered land' (OE *sīd, īeg*), as at Sidney Fm in Alfold (Surrey). The name is usually derived from St Denis (Normandy) but proof is lacking. The only evidence noted is: Roger *de Sancto Dionisio* 1212 Fees (Nf), John *Seyndenys* 14th ArchC 29 and this is certainly not conclusive. Harrison's William *Sidney* (1325) cannot be from St Denis. His name belongs above.

Sier: *v.* SIRE

Sievwright, Sivewright, Seivwright, Severwright: Simon *le siuewricht'* 1219 AssY; John *le Syvewryct'* 1301 SRY. OE *sife* and *wyrhta* 'maker of sieves'.

Siffleet, Sifleet, Siflet: John *Sifled, Syflede* 14th AD iv (Wa); William *Syflete, Syfflett* 1490–1508, c1566 ArchC 49. OE *Sigeflǣd* (f) 'victory-beauty', which must have remained in use after the Conquest.

Siggers, Siger: *Sigar* 1066 DB (W); *Sigarus* ib. (C); *Sigar* c1095 Bury (Sf); *Sigherus* 1180–1207 Rams (Nf); *Sigerus* c1250 ib. (Beds); Edricus *Sigarus* 1066 DB (Sf); Eluiua *Sigar* 1221 ElyA (Nf); William *Siger* 1275 RH (Nf). This may be OE *Sigegār* 'victory-spear' or ON *Sigarr*, ODa, OSw *Sighar*, or OG *Sigger*. The form *Sigar* goes better with OE *Sigegār* than with ODa *Sighar*, which should have become *Sigher, Sier* in English (ELPN).

Siggs: *Sigga* 1162 DC (L); *Sigge de Anemere* 1275 RH (Nf); Aunketillus *Sigge* 1214 Cur (Do); John *Sygges* 1524 SRSf. *Sigga* (f), a short form of ON *Sigríðr*, ODa *Sigrith*: *Sigreda* 1066 DB (Y).

Sikes: *v.* SYKES

Silabon, Silburn: *v.* SILLIBOURNE

Silcock, Silcocks, Silcox: *Silcokkus de Altricheham* 1283 Cl (Ch); *Silkoc of Middlewich* 14th AD iv (Ch); William *Selecok* 1327 SRSo; John *Silcok* 1379 PTY. *Sil-coc*, a diminutive of *Sil*, a short form of *Silvein* (*v.* SAUVAIN) or *Silvester*.

Silk: Ædwardus, John *Selk(e)* 1170 P (So); William, John *Silke* 1350 LLB F, 1353 Putnam (W). OE *seolc* 'silk', metonymic for a worker or dealer in silk. cf. Alice *la Selkwimman* 1334 ColchCt.

Silkin: John *Selekyn* 1327 *SR* (Ess). *Sil-kin*, a diminutive of *Sil*. cf. Silcock.

Sill, Sills: Robert *Sille* 1397 PrGR. A short form of *Silvein* or *Silvester*. *v.* SILCOCK.

Silley: *v.* SEALEY

Sillibourne, Silabon, Silburn: Adelina *Salibern* 1279 RH (Hu); John *Selybarn'* 1297 SRY; Robert

Seliberne 1332 SRSt; Richard *Selbarn* 1407 FrY; John *Sillibarn* 1528 ib.; James *Silburne* 1689 ib. OE *sǣlig, bearn* 'happy child'. cf. SELLMAN.

Sillman: *v.* SELLMAN

Silly: *v.* SEALEY

Silver: (i) Lucas, John *Siluer* 1205–13 Seals (L), 1301 SRY. OE *silfor* 'silver', metonymic for a silversmith. cf. Robert *Silverhewer* 1212 Cur (Y), William *Sylvereour* 1417 FrY. (ii) Thomas *atte Selure* 1327 SRWo; Thomas *of the silvere* 1332 ib. 'Dweller by the silvery stream', OE **seolfre, *sylfre*, as at Silver Beck (Cumb) or Silver (Devon). *v.* MELS.

Silverlock: Adam *Seluerloc* 1221 AssWo; John *Silverloc* 1268 AssSo. 'Silver lock', silvery-haired.

Silvester, Selvester, Sylvester, Siveter, Siviter: *Siluester capellanus* Hy 2 DC (Lei); *Seluester filius Walteri* 1204 Cur (Y); Thomas *Silvestr'* 1212 Fees (Ha); William *Silvester* 1250 Fees (La); William *Sevester* 1455 LLB K. Lat *Silvester* 'dweller in the forest', the name of three popes, which seems to have been first used in England by clerics. *Sevester* gives the clue to the origin of *Siveter* and *Siviter*. In modern French we have the popular forms *Sevestre* and *Sivestre* by the side of *Silvestre*. The loss of the second *s* would give *Seveter, Siveter*.

Sim, Simm, Simms, Sims, Symms, Syms, Sime, Simes, Syme, Symes: *Sym* Clerk 1446 Black; Ralph *Simme* 1317 AssK; John *Symme* 1345 ColchCt; Robert *Symmes* 1379 PTY. *Sim(m)*, a pet-form of *Simmond*, or *Sime* of *Simon*.

Simble: *v.* SEMPLE

Simco, Simcoe: Probably for SIMCOCK. cf. ALCOE.

Simcock, Simcocks, Simcox, Symcox, Sincock: Robert *Symcot* (sic) 1275 RH (C); Simon *Simecok* 1327 SRSo; Thomas *Symcokes* 1395 AssSt. 'Little *Sim*' (Simon), *Sim* plus *cock*.

Sime(s): *v.* SIM

Simeon, Simeons, Simion: Ricardus *filius Simeonis* 1219 Cur (Bk); *Simeon* 1220 Cur (Berks); Robert *Simeon* 1254 FFHu; William *Symeon* 1278 FFSf. The Hebrew *Shimeon* 'hearkening' appears in the English versions of the Old Testament as *Simeon*, occasionally *Shimeon*, but in the New Testament as *Simon* (except in one instance). The forms were kept distinct, as separate names, in the Middle Ages, *Simon* being much more common.

Simer: Walter *le Simer* 1243 AssSo. A derivative of either OE *sīma* 'cord, rope', a roper, or of OE *sīman* 'to load', a loader. Very rare.

Simester, Simister: Peter *le Semester* 1275 RH (L); Alicia *Semester* 1376 MESO (Y); Julia *Semster* 1380 SRSt; Margaret *Sembster* 1381 PTY. OE *sēamestre*, feminine of *sēamere* 'sewer, tailor', sempstress; used also of a man. cf. SEAMER.

Simey: Robert *Sygemay* 1275 Wak (Y). OE **Sigemǣg* 'victory-kinsman', of which this is the only known example. An addition to the late compounds of *-mǣg*, noted by von Feilitzen: *Sǣmǣg* (1185), *Sidmǣg* (1185), *Wulfmǣg* (1063). *v.* NoB 33, 87. A very rare surname.

Simison: *v.* SIMONSON

Simkin, Simkins, Simkiss, Simpkin, Simpkins, Simpkiss, Semken, Sempkins, Sinkin, Sinkins, Sinkings: *Symekyn* Sadeler 1378 LoPleas; Anand *Simekin* 1199 SIA iv; William *Symkyn* 1524 SRSf. *Sim-kin* 'Little Sim' or Simon. Used as a diminutive: *Symond* or *Symkyn* Skynner 1466 AD v (Wa).

Simmance, Simmans, Simmens, Simmins: *v.* SIMMONDS

Simmer, Simmers, Symmers, Symers: George *Symmer* 1529, John *Symer* 1641. Scottish forms of SUMMER. Black notes *Sumer* and *Somyr* from c1200–1478, after which the vowel varies between *u* and *i*. OFr *som(m)ier*, used both of a pack-horse and a sumpter.

Simmie: Alexander *Simmey* 1613 Black (Aberdeen). A diminutive of *Sim*.

Simmonds, Simmons, Simmance, Simmans, Simmen, Simmens, Simmins, Semens, Semmence, Semmens, Simond, Simonds, Symmons, Symonds, Fitzsimmons: *Simund* danus 1066 DB (Wa); *Simundus* 1134–40 Holme (Nf); *Symundus* de Ludham 1150–60 Holme (Nf), *Simon* de Ludham 1155–89 ib.; *Simund, Simon* clericus de Abi Hy 2 DC (L); *Simond* Moysaunt 1426 LondEng; Robert *Simund* 1222 Cur (W); John *Symont* 1260 AssC; William *Simon, Simond* 1291 LLB A; Margery *Simondes* 1308 EAS xviii; Hugo *le Fiz Simond, filius Simonis* 1325 ParlWrits (Herts). *Simon* 1066 DB (Wo), also *Simundus* (ib.), is elsewhere called '*Simund* quidam, genere Danus' (PNDB). His name was thus ON *Sigmundr*, ODa *Sigmund* 'victory-protector' which was already confused with *Simon*. Some, at least, of the Norfolk and Lincolnshire personal names were Scandinavian and contributed to the surname. Others may have been introduced from Normandy. Here, in addition, we have to reckon with the Hebrew *Simon* and OG *Sigmund*, cognate with ON *Sigmundr*. After the Conquest, in England, *Simund* was a common AFr form of *Simon*. Wycliffe uses *Symound* for Simon Peter; Simon de Montfort is called *Simond* by Robert of Gloucester. Adam *Cimond* (1292 SRLo) is identical with Adam *Simon* (1292 LLB A) and Adam *son of Simon* (1290 Pat). It is thus impossible to distinguish between the various origins. *v.* SIMON.

Simmonite, Simonett, Simonite, Simnett: William *Symonet* 1327 SRSt; Asselin *Simonett'* 1346 LLB F. *Simon-et*, a diminutive of *Simon*. Simon Corder is also called *Simonet* 1377 LoPleas. Another diminutive, *Simon-el*, has not survived: Philip *Simenel* 1200 P (Ha), Henry *Symnell* 1373 Bart (Lo). cf. also Lambert *Simnel*.

Simner, Simnor: For SUMNER.

Simon, Simons, Simans, Symon, Symons, Fitzsimon, Fitzsimons: *Simon* 1134–40 Holme (Nf); *Symon* de Cheurolcurt c1150 DC (Nt); William *le fiz Simon* Hy 2 DC (L); William, John *Simon* 1291 LLB A, 1296 SRSx. The Hebrew *Shimeon* may have been influenced by Greek Σίμων, from σιμός 'snub-nosed'. *Simon* and *Simond* were very popular and had a variety of diminutives. *v.* SIMEON, SIMMONDS.

Simond(s): *v.* SIMMONDS

Simonson, Simison, Simyson, Symondson: Philip *Simondson* 1430 FrY; Marques *Symondesson* 1473 ParlR. 'Son of *Simond* or *Simon*.'

Simper: *v.* SEMPER

Simpkiss, Simpkiss: *v.* SIMKIN

Simpkinson, Sinkinson: William *Symkynson* 1381 PTY. 'Son of *Simkin*.'

Simple: Reginaldus *Simplex* c1160 Gilb (L); Robert *le Sinple* 1202 AssL; Hugh *le Simple* 1243 AssSo. OFr *simple* 'free from duplicity, dissimulation or guile; honest, open, straightforward'.

Simpole: *v.* SEMPLE

Simpson, Sympson, Simson: Richard *Symmeson* 1353 AssSt; Adam *Symson* 1395 Whitby (Y); John *Simpson* 1397 Calv (Y); Henry *Symmesson* 1450 Rad (C); John *Symson* or *Sympson* 1487 LLB L. 'Son of *Simm*' (Simon). Three places named Simpson in Devon, earlier *Siwineston*, gave rise to surnames in the 13th century.

Sinclair, Sinclaire, Sinclar, St Clair: Hubertus *de Sancto Claro* 1086 DB (So); Richard *de Sencler* ib. (Nf); Richard *de Seincler* 1194 Cur (Nf); Ralph *de Seintcler* 1197 P (So); Emma *de Sancler* 1198 FF (K); John *de Sentcler* 1327 SRSx. The tenants of Eudo Dapifer in Essex came from Saint-Clair-sur-Elle (La Manche). *v.* ANF. The Sinclairs of Caithness appeared in Scotland c1124–53, coming, according to Black, from Saint-Clair-l'Evêque (Calvados). The frequency of the surname in Caithness and the Orkneys is due to the adoption by tenants of the name of their overlord. The name appears as *Sincklair* in 1634.

Sincock: *v.* SIMCOCK

Singer, Singers: Lucas *le Syngere* 1296 SRSx; William *le Syngur* 1297 SRY. A derivative of OE *singan* 'to sing', a singer.

Single, Sengel: Alan *de la Sengle* 1296 SRSx; John *ate Sengle* 1327 ib.; Widow *Singull* 1674 HTSf. 'Dweller by the burnt clearing', OE **sengel*.

Singler: Arnald *Singlere* 1195–1215 StP; Richard *le Sengler* 1317 FFEss. ME *sengler, syngler*, OFr *sengler, seingler* 'singular', perhaps 'living alone, solitary'.

Singleton: Adam *de Singelton'* 1220 Cur (La); Geoffrey *de Sengelton* 1296 SRSx; Adam *de Syngleton* 1379 PTY. From Singleton (Lancs, Sussex).

Sinkin(s): *v.* SIMKIN

Sinkinson: *v.* SIMPKINSON

Sinnatt, Sinnett, Sinnott, Senett, Sennett, Sennitt, Synnot, Synnott, Synott: *Synodus* c1095 Bury (Sf); Robertus *filius Sinothi* 1200 P (St); Dionisia *filia Sinod* 1207 Cur (Herts); Stephen *Sinot, Sinut* 1275 RH (Sf); Warin *Sinat* 1276 RH (C). OE *Sigenōð* 'victory-bold', DB *Sinod*.

Sinnocks: *v.* SENNECK

Sinton: Aldich *de Suthinton'* 1275 SRWo; Henry *de Sothinton'* ib.; Adam *a Suthetun*, Robert *atte Suthethun*, William *de Suthetun* 1296 SRSx; John *de Sothynton, de Sutingthun* 1296 SRSx; Thomas *Southetoun* 1327 SRSx; John *de Sotinton* 1327 SRSx; William *de Sotiton* 1332 SRSx; Agnes *de Suthyngton*, Richard *de Sotyng-*

ton ib. Like WESTINGTON, this surname was common in Sussex where it has been noted in some 35 parishes between 1296 and 1332. In Worcestershire it derives from Sodington, Leigh Sinton or from Sindon's Mill in Suckley, (the place) 'south in the *tūn*' (*Suthiton, Sothyntone* 1275) as opposed to that 'north in the *tūn*', now Norton Fm. cf. also Siddington (Glos) and Southington in Selborne (Hants). Similar place-names were formed also from *east, north* and *west* and survive in Eastington (Devon, Dorset, Glos, Worcs) and Norrington (Herts, Wilts, Worcs). As surnames, *Astington, Norrington, Uppington* and *Westington* survive. *Southeton* and *Sotiton* would become indistinguishable from SUTTON. For a similar northern formation of Scandinavian origin, *v.* SOTHEBY and WESTOBY. In Scotland the surname derives from the barony of Synton (now included in Ashkirk, Selkirkshire); Andrew *de Synton* (1165–1214 Black).

Sinyard: *v.* SENIOR

Sippings: *v.* SEPPINGS

Sirdifield, Sirdyfield, Cedervall, Surrell: Richard *de Surdeual* 1086 DB (Y); Robert *de Surdeuall'* 1197 P (We); John *Sowrdewall* 1488 GildY; Richard *Surwald* 1516 ib. From Sourdeval (Calvados, La Manche).

Sire, Sier, Sirr, Surr, Syer, Syers: Geoffrey *Sire* 1177 P (Nf); Matheus *le Sire* 1201 Cur (Nt); Ralph *le Seyr* 1296 SRSx; Walter *Surr* 1327 SRC. OFr *sire*, ME *sire, sier* 'master', a nickname; also used of an elderly man. *Surr* may be from OFr *sor, sieur*, oblique case of *sire*.

Sired, Sirett, Sirette, Sirrett, Syrad, Syratt, Syred, Syrett: *Sired, Siret* 1066 DB; *Sigreda* 1066 DB (Y); *Sired(us)* 1095 Bury, 1213 Cur (Sf); Willelmus *filius Sigerith* 1197 P (Y); *Sireda* de Kirkby 1332 SRCu; Wulfwine *Sired* 1077 OEByn (So); Robert *Sired* 1198 FFK; Roger *Syred* 1306 FFSf. OE *Sigerǣd* 'victory-counsel' (m), or, at times, ON *Sigriðr* (f).

Sirkett: *v.* CIRCUITT

Sisley, Sicely: *Cecilia* celleraria Hy 2 DC (Lei); Henricus *filius Cecilie* 1210 Cur (Db); Willelmus *Cecilie* 13th Kirkstall (Y); Henry *Cecili* 1279 RH (C); Richard *Cecely* 1296 SRSx; Roger *Cysely* 1332 SRWa. OFr *Cecile*, Lat *Caecilia*, feminine of *Caecilius*, from *caecus* 'blind'. The martyred St Cecilia was the patron saint of musicians and her name, introduced into England by the Normans, soon became very popular as *Cecely* or *Sisley*, with pet-forms *Siss, Sissel, Sisselot* and *Sissot*.

Sismore, Sissmore, Sizmore, Sizmur: Thomas *Sysmore* 1432 *Petre* (Ess); John *Sysemore* 1591 ChWo. OFr *sis mars* 'six marks', cf. DISMORE.

Sisson, Sissons, Sissens: Thomas *filius Sisse* 1297 SRY; Robert *Cisson,* John *Sisson* 1379 PTY; Edward *Sissons* 1641 FrY. 'Son of *Ciss*' (Cecily).

Sisterson: *Cissota* 1298, 1309 Wak (Y); Agnes *Sissotson* 1470 GildY. 'Son of *Cissot*', a diminutive of *Ciss* (Cecily).

Sitch: *v.* SYKES

Siveter, Siviter: *v.* SILVESTER

Sivewright: *v.* SIEVWRIGHT

Siveyer, Sivier: *v.* SEVIER

Sizer: William *Sisar* 1379 PTY; Robert *Syser* 1524 SRSf. ME *sysour* 'assizer', a member of the assize, sworn recognitor.

Sizmore, Sizmur: *v.* SISMORE

Skaife: *v.* SCAFE

Skakle: *v.* SHACKEL

Skeat, Skeats, Skett, Skeet: *Scet, Schett* 1066 DB (Nf); Ricardus *filius Schet* 1166 P (Nf); Nicholas, Walter *Sket* 1201 P (Sa), 1275 RH (Nf); Robert *Skeet* 1327 SRSf. ON *skjótr* 'swift, fleet', used also as a personal-name.

Skeffington, Skiffington, Skevington, Skivington: Simon *de Scheftinton* 1193 P (Lei); Henry *de Skefyngton* 1327 SRLei; John *Skevyngton* 1520 FFSt. From Skevington (Leics).

Skegg: Thomas *Skegge* 1379 PTY. ON *skegg* 'beard'.

Skelton: Hamo, John *de Skelton'* c1160–93 YCh, 1286 FFY; John *Skelton* 1410 FFEss. From Skelton (Cumb, ER, NR, WRYorks).

Skepper: Simon *Sceppere* 1221 *ElyA* (C); Walter *le Skeppere* 1281 MESO (L). A derivative of ON *skeppa* 'basket', a maker of baskets. *v.* SKIPP.

Skermer: *v.* SKIRMER

Skerratt, Skerrett, Skerritt, Skirrett: (i) Eudo *de Skirwiht* 1285 IpmCu. From Skirwith (Cumb), formerly pronounced *Skerritt*. (ii) Alice *Skyrewhit* 1327 *SR* (Ess); Thomas, Roger *Skyrewyt* 1332 SRSr; John *Skyrwhyt* 1377 ColchCt. ME *skirwhit(e)*, apparently an alteration by popular etymology of OFr *eschervis*, a variant of OFr *carvi* 'carraway', a species of water parsnip formerly much cultivated in Europe for its esculent tubers which were used for sauce or physic, cf. *Skyrwyt*, herbe or rote, c1440 PromptParv. Metonymic for a grower of white parsnips.

Skett: *v.* SKEAT

Skevens: Walter *Skyuein, Schyuein* 1277 *Ely* (Sf); Richard *Skeuyn* 1301 SRY. ME *skeuayne, skeuyn,* ONFr *eskevein,* OFr *eschevin* 'steward of a guild' (1389 NED).

Skidmore, Skitmore, Scudamore: Hugh *de Scudimore* 1167 P (He); Peter *de Skidemor* c1170 Glast (So); Geoffrey *Escudemor', Eskidemor'* 1242 Fees (W); Peter *de Skydemore* 1282 FFC; Richard *Skidmore* 1576 SRW. From an unidentified place, probably somewhere in the west or south-west.

Skiffington: *v.* SKEFFINGTON

Skill: William *Skille* 1279 RH (O); William *Skyl* 1302 AssSt. ON *skil*, ME *skill* 'reason, discernment'. cf. Geoffrey *Scilful* 1279 RH (C), William *Skylful* 1327 SRC and *v.* SKILLMAN.

Skilleter, Skilliter: John *Skellattour* 1327 *SR* (Ess); John *Skelete* 1332 SRCu. A derivative of ME *skelet* 'skillet' (a1403 NED), a maker of skillets.

Skillman: John *Skyleman* 1275 RH (Nf); Matthew *Skylman* 1327 SRC. An anglicization of ON *skilamaðr* 'trustworthy man'.

Skin: Roger, Simon *Skin* 1221 AssWo, 1279

AssNb; Cecilia *Skynn* 1301 SRY. ON *skinn* 'skin'. Metonymic for SKINNER.

Skinner, Skynner, Skyner: Robert *le Skynnere* 1263 MESO (Sx); Ralph *le Skinnere* 1269 AD i (Herts). A derivative of ON *skinn* 'skin', a skinner. cf. SHINNER.

Skipp: Osbert *Sceppe* 1210 Cur (C); John *Skip* 1282 LLB A; William, Walter *Skyp* 1296 SRSx, 1310 ColchCt; John *Skep*, William *Skypp* 1327 SRC. ON *skeppa*, ME *scepp(e)* 'basket', metonymic for SKEPPER and, probably, for SKIPPER.

Skipper: Geoffrey *le Skippere* 1285 *Ass* (Ess); Robert *le Skypper* 1286 AssSt. A derivative of ME *skip* 'to jump', a leaper, jumper, or one who moves lightly and rapidly. Later examples may be for SKEPPER (cf. SKIPP) or for ME *skypper* 'master of a ship' (1390 NED).

Skirmer, Skermer, Skurmer: Richard *le Skiremar'*, Thomas *le Scuremer*, Hugh *Skermere* 1279 RH (O); William *le Skurmere* 1296 SRSx; Robert *le Skirmer* 1332 SRLa. A derivative of ME *skurmen, skirmen*, from OFr *eskirmir, eskermir* 'to fence', 'a fencing-master'. cf. SCRIMGEOUR.

Skirrett, Skivington: *v.* SKERRATT, SKEFFINGTON
Skitmore: *v.* SKIDMORE
Skreven: Henry *Screuyn* 1297 MinAcctCo (Y); William *de Skrevyn* 1309 FrY. From Scriven (WRYorks).
Skrimshaw, Skrimshire: *v.* SCRIMGEOUR
Skurmer: *v.* SKIRMER
Skynner: *v.* SKINNER
Slack, Slacke: (i) Gerebod *le Slac* 1195 P (L); Thomas *Slak* 1359 LLB G. OE *slēac, slæc* 'lazy, careless, slow'. (ii) Thomas, Nicholas *del Slac, slakk* 1275 Wak (Y), 1331 WhC (La). 'Dweller in the shallow valley', ON *slakki*.
Slade: Sabern *de la Slade* 1255 FFEss; Reginald *atte Slade* 1306 AD v (Mx); Walter *in the Slade* 1327 SRSf. 'Dweller in the valley', OE *slæd*.
Slape: Adam *de la Slape* 1276 AssSo; Elena *atte Sclape* 1327 SRSo. 'Dweller near a miry place or marsh' (OE *slæp).
Slate: Roger *Slat* 1221 AssGl. Metonymic for *Slater*.
Slater, Slator, Sclater, Slatter: Thomas *le Sclatere* 1255 MESO (Wo); Saundr' *le Sclattur* 1278 Oseney (O); Roger *Sclatiere* 1279 RH (O); Walter *Sclatter* 1279 RH (Bk); Thomas *Slater* 1297 SRY. A derivative of ME *sclate, slate*, OFr *esclate* 'slate' or ME *sclat, slatt*, OFr *esclat* 'slat', slater.
Slaughter, Slagter: (i) Robert *de Scloctres* 1191 P (Gl); Robert *de Sloutre* 1251 Eynsham (O); Mariota *de la Sloghtere* 1296 SRSx; John *Sloutere* 1327 SRWo. OE *slōhtre* 'slough, muddy place', the source of Upper and Lower Slaughter (Glos) and minor places in Sussex, as Slaughterford Fm, Slaughterbridge Fm and Slaughterwicks Barn. *v.* MELS 190. (ii) Thomas *le Slaghterere* 1296 FFEss; Henry *le Sclaufterer*, Stephen *le Slawterer* 1327 SRSf; Roger *Slaghtere* 1360 FFSf; Walter *Slautere* 1381 SRSf. A derivative of ME *slahter* 'slaughter' (a1300 NED), 'a killer of animals, a butcher' (1648 NED).

Slaven, Slavin: Roger *Sclauin* 1177 P (Sf); Goditha *Sclauine* 1221 AssSa. ME *sclaueyn, slaveyn, slavyne*, OFr *esclavine* 'a pilgrim's mantle'.

Slay, Slee, Sleigh, Sleith, Sleath, Sligh, Sly: Walter *Sleh* 1219 FFEss; Thomas *Sleh, Slei, Slegh* 1219 AssL; Robert *Sley* 1221 AssWa; John *le Slege* 1273 RH (O); Ralph *Sly* 1273 RH (Hu); John *Slygh* 1327 SRSx; John *le Slegh* 1333 FrY; John *Slee* 1446 FrY. ME *sleȝ* from ON *slœgr* 'clever, cunning' became *slee* in the north and *sligh, sly* in the south and midlands. 'Skilful, clever, expert' (c1200 NED). For *Sleath, Sleith*, cf. the pronunciation of Keighley. In 1247 AssBeds we have both William *le Slaer* and John *Slay* and in 1311 ColchCt William *Slayare*. The latter is a derivative of ME *slaye* 'an instrument used in weaving', 'a maker of slays', synonymous with SLAYMAKER, and *Slay* must here be used in the same sense. The common forms today are *Slee* and *Sly*.

Slaymaker: John *Slaymaker* 1379 PTY; Henry *Slaymaker* or *Slymaker* 1594 Oxon. 'A maker of slays', ME *sleȝe, sleye, slay(e)* 'an instrument used in weaving to beat up the weft', 'a weaver's reed or shuttle'. Always a rare name. Formerly more common, but now apparently extinct, was *Slaywright*: Robert *le Sleywrihte* 1334 ColchCt. *v.* MESO 167 and cf. SLEEMAN.

Slayter, Slaytor, Sleator: Roger *Sleghtere* 1304 FFEss; William *le Sleghtere* (*Sleyter*) 1327 *SR* (Ess); William *le Sleter* 1327 SRSx. A derivative of OE *slyht* 'slaughter', slaughterer, butcher.

Sleath: *v.* SLAY
Sleator: *v.* SLAYTER
Slee, Slay: Stephen *del Sle* 1274 RH (Ess). 'Dweller by the grass-grown slope', OE *slēa, as at Slay Down (Wilts). *v.* also SLAY.
Sleeman, Slemmonds, Slemming, Slemmings, Slimming, Slimmon, Sliman, Slyman: Thomas *Sleman* 1277 Wak (Y); Auicia *Scleyman* 1327 SRC. May be 'cunning, sagacious man', 'dweller by the grassy slope', or 'maker of slays'. *v.* SLEE, SLAY, SLAYMAKER.
Sleeper: Hugh, John *le Slepere* 1212 Cur (K), 1232 FFEss. ME *sleper* 'sleeper', used of an indolent or inactive person (a1225 NED).
Sleigh, Sleith: *v.* SLAY
Slemmonds, Slemming(s), Sliman, Slimming, Slimmon: *v.* SLEEMAN
Sling: Reyner, Robert *Sleng(e)* 1221 ElyA (Nf), 1298 Wak (Y); William *Slinge* 1279 RH (Hu); Robert *Slyngg* 1327 *SR* (Ess). ON *Slengr*; cf. Norw *sleng* 'idler'. This would become *Sling*, early examples of which may, however, be metonymic for SLINGER.
Slinger: William *Slinger, Slinge* c1248 Bec (Wa); John *Slingere* 1297 MinAcctCo; Adam *le Sclynggere* 1327 *SR* (Ess). A derivative of ME *slingen* 'to sling', slinger, a soldier armed with a sling (1382 NED). As *le slengg', slyngges* is found in 1323 and 1348 for the stout ropes hitched round large blocks of stone and over a hook as a means of lifting them during building operations (Building

322), *slinger* probably also denoted workers of these slings.

Slingsby: Roger *de Slingesby* 1219 Cur (Y); Higdon *de Slyngesby* 1379 PTY; Henry *Slingsby* 1672 HTY. From Slingsby (NRYorks).

Slipper: William *Slipere* c1248 Bec (Mx); Laurence *Slyper* 1332 SRSx. A derivative of ME *slipe* 'to polish, sharpen', probably a sword-sharpener. cf. William *Suerdsliper* 1313 Wak (Y).

Sloley: *v.* SLOWLY

Sloman, Slowman, Sluman: William *Sloman* 1327 SRSx; Henry *Sloghman* 1392 AD i (Ess). 'Dweller by the slough.' *v.* SLOUGH.

Sloper: Agatha, Geoffrey *le Slopere* 1279 RH (Hu), 1286 MESO (Nf). A derivative of ME *slop(e)* 'slop, outer garment, tunic, etc.', a maker or seller of these. cf. Emma *le Sclopmongere* 1317 Oseney (O).

Slot, Slott: Walter *de la Slot* 1275 RH (Nf). An early example of ME *sclott* (c1475 NED), glossed *limus*. 'Dweller by the muddy place'.

Slough, Slow, Slowe: Ulric *a teslo* c1095 Bury (Sf); Hemming *de Slo* 1196 P (Bk); Unfridus *de la Slowe* 1225 Pat (Bk); Hugh *Aterslo* 1228 FFEss; Richard *atte Slouh* 1275 SRWo; John *dil Slow* 1327 SRSf; Walter *atte Slogh* 1337 LLB E. 'Dweller by the slough or miry place' (OE *slōh*). Occasionally, *Slow* may be a nickname from OE *slāw* 'slow, sluggish, dull': Richard *Slou* 1296 SRSx.

Slowly, Sloley: Juliana *de Sloleg* 1221 AssWa; Peter *de Sloleye* 1275 RH (Nf). From Slowley (Warwicks) or Sloley (Norfolk).

Slowman, Sluman: *v.* SLOMAN

Sly: *v.* SLAY

Slyman: *v.* SLEEMAN

Smail, Smailes, Smails: Richard *de Smegle* 1296 SRSx. These surnames, with, probably, *Smiles*, still found in Sussex and West Kent, derive from Broxmead, Brooksmarle (Sussex) or a lost vill of *Smeghel* in the east part of the county. From OE **smēagel* 'burrow', the compound meaning 'badger-hole'. *v.* PN Sx 262. *Smail* is also a later northern and Scottish form of *Small*: Henry *Smailes* 1640 FrY (Christopher *Smales* 1627 ib.), Henry *Smaill* 1657 Black.

Smale, Smales, Small, Smalles, Smalls, Smeal, Smeall: William *Smale* 1221 ElyA (C), 1275 SRWo; Alexander *le Smele* 1221 AssSa; William *le Smale* 1294 RamsCt (Hu); Thomas *Small* 1360 Black. OE *smæl* 'small, slender, thin'. *Smeal* is from ME *smel* (c1275 NED). *v.* SMAIL.

Smallbone, Smallbones: Wilk *Smalbon* 1198 FrLeic; John *Smalbayne* 1301 SRY. OE *smæl* and *bān* (in Yorks, ON *bein*) 'small bone', a nickname, probably 'short legs'.

Smalley, Smally: William *de Smalleghes* 1325 Wak; Richard *de Smalley* 1388–9 FFWa; Alexander *Smalley, Smalley* 1532, 1537 CorNt. From Smalley (Derby).

Smallfield, Smawfield: Thomas *de Smalfeld* 1290 ShefA; John *de Smalefeld* 1296 SRSx. 'Dweller by a small field' (OE *smæl, feld*).

Smallman, Smallsman, Smalman: Hubert *Smale-*

man 1209 FFSf; Richard *Smaleman* 1275 RH (Sf). In Durham the *smaleman* (OE **smælmann*) is coupled with thanes and drengs in an order which suggests he is inferior to both (*de Tainis et Dreinis et Smalemannis* 1130 P). Two Essex examples *Smallemanneslond* 1367, *two Smallmannes lond* (1405 PN Ess 584) seem to confirm that we have here the name of a particular type of tenant.

Smallpage: Elizabeth *Smalpage* 1579 RothwellPR (Y). cf. LITTLEPAGE.

Smallpeace, Smallpeice, Smallpiece: Geoffrey *Smalpece* 1414 PN Ess 545. Probably 'Dweller by or holder of a small enclosure'. ME *pece*, dial. *piece* 'piece of land, enclosure, field'.

Smallridge, Smaridge: Henry *de Smalrug* 1221 AssWo; William *de Smalerugge* 1330 PN D 96. From Smallridge in Langtree and in Axminster (Devon), *Smarige* 1086, *Smalrigge* 1200 PN D 634, or from residence near a narrow ridge (OE *smæl, hrycg*).

Smallshaw: (i) Dobbe *de Smaleschawe*, Roger *Smalchaghe* 1298, 1316 Wak (Y). 'Dweller by a small wood' (OE *sceaga*). (ii) William *Smalsho* 1378 PN Ess 481, 1420 LLB I. Perhaps a nickname 'Small shoe' (OE *scēo*). Or from a lost place *Smelesho* 1297 Coram (Beds).

Smallthwaite: *v.* SMITHWHITE

Smallwood: William *Smalwud* 1220 Cur (Ess); John *de Smalwode* 1332 LLB E; Richard *Smalwode* 1401 AssLa. From Smallwood (Ches), or 'dweller by the small wood'.

Smaridge: *v.* SMALLRIDGE

Smart: Lifwinus *Smart* c1180 ArchC viii; William *Smert* 1275 SRWo. OE *smeart* 'quick, active, prompt'.

Smawfield: *v.* SMALLFIELD

Smead, Smeath: *v.* SMEED

Smeal(l): *v.* SMALE

Smeathers: 'Dweller on the level ground.' *v.* SMEED.

Smeathman: Robert *Smytheman* 1379 PTY; Christopher *Smethman, Smoothman* 1600, 1628 FrY. 'Smooth, suave man.' *v.* SMEED.

Smeaton, Smeeton, Smeton, Smieton, Smitton, Smiton: (i) Henry *de Smithetone, de Smeithtone* 1296, 1359 Black; Alexander *Smethytone* 1506 ib.; Erasmus *Smittoune* 1613. From the lands of Smytheton, now Smeaton (Midlothian). (ii) Johel *de Smetheton*, Jukel *de Smitheton* 1201, 1204 Pl (Y); Robert *de Smytheton* 1340 FFY; John *Smeton* 1379 PTY. From Smeaton (NR, WRYorks), Smeeton Westerby (Leics), or Smeetham Hall (Essex), all OE *smiþatūn* 'the smiths' enclosure'.

Smeed, Smeeth, Smead, Smeed, Smee: (i) Richard *Smethe* 1202 P (Co); William *le Smeth*, Philip *le Smeþe* 1279 RH (O, Hu). OE *smēþe* 'smooth, polished, suave'. (ii) Laurence *de Smethe* 1275 RH (K); William *del Smethe* 1327 SRSf. From Smeeth (Kent), or 'dweller on the smooth, level place', OE *smēþe*.

Smelt: Alwine *smelt* 1040–2 OEByn; Richard *Smelte* 1230 Cur; John *le Smelt* 1334 SRK; Robert *Smelt* 1415 IpmY. OE *smelt* 'sardine, smelt', clearly a nickname, probably also 'a seller of smelts', and possibly a patronymic, though the personal name is not recorded after DB, cf. *Smelt* 1035 Redin (Do), *Esmellt*, *Esmeld* 1066 PNDB (K, Sx). If the spellings are reliable, John *Smolt* 1318 FFEss, 1405 IpmY, would lend support to a possible nickname from OE *smelt*, *smolt*, *smylte* 'mild, peaceful' (PNDB 367).

Smeton, Smieton: *v.* SMEATON

Smewing: *Smeuuin* 1066 DB (So); *Smeuuinus* 1086 ib. (O); *Smewinus* c1130 Ewen (Do); Martin, John *Smewyne* 1256 *Ass* (Ha), 1327 *SR* (Ess); Matilda *Smywyne* 1332 SRSx. OE **Smēawine* 'sagacious friend'.

Smidman: Henry *Smythman* 1379 PTY. 'The smith's assistant.'

Smisson: *v.* SMITHSON

Smith, Smithe, Smyth, Smythe, Smye: (i) Ecceard *Smið* c975 OEByn (Du); Ælfword *þe Smith* c1100 ib. (So); William *le Smyth* 1275 AssSo; Julian' *le Smithes* 1279 RH (O); John *Smye* 1524 SRSf. OE *smið* 'smith, blacksmith, farrier'. Early examples are common in the Latin form FABER. (ii) William *atte Smithe*, Thomas *de la Smythe* 1313 AD i (Sx); Robert *atte Smyth* 1332 SRSx. 'Worker at the smithy', OE *smiþþe*.

Smither, Smithers: John *Smythiere* 1379 AssWa. 'Smith, hammerman.' cf. 'The Jorneymen . . . of all oþer Craftes . . . except hakmen and smythers wurche in hur own houses and nott in hur masters housz' (1435 NED).

Smitherman, Smythyman: Robert *Smythyman* 1309 Cl (Y). 'Smithy man', worker at the smithy.

Smithies, Smithyes, Smythyes: John *del Smythy* 1332 SRLa, 1385 ShefA; John *Smythes, Smythies* 1568 1586 FrY; Thomas *Smiddies* 1629 ib. 'Worker at the smithy', ME *smythy*.

Smithson, Smythson, Smisson: Reginald *le Smythessone* 1296 SRSx; Henry *le Smithson* 1324 Wak (Y); Peter *Smitson* 1327 SRY. 'Son of the smith.'

Smithwhite, Smorthwaite, Smorfit, Smurthwaite, Smurfit, Smallthwaite: Henry *de Smetwayt* 1285 AssLa; Thomas *de Smythuait* 1327 SRY; Matilda *Smarthwate* 1489 GildY; Robert *Smerwhaitt* 1518 ib.; Thomas *Smirthwaite* 1577 FrY; Thomas *Smorthwait* 1627 ib.; Matthew *Smurwhaite* 1657 ib.; Edward *Smurfett* son of Matthew *Smurfett* 1713 ib. In Cumberland there is a Smaithwaite in Keswick and another in Lamplugh, *Smathwaitis* c1280, *Smerthwayte* 1530, *Smethwayte* 1552 (PN Cu 314, 407), whilst in Guiseley (Y) we have *Smerthwayt* 1323 Calv, 'small clearing' (ON *smár*). In Cumberland, too, we find two Smallthwaites, neither recorded before 1611, which may be identical in origin, with late substitution of English *small* for Scandinavian *smár*. The first two examples above may contain OE *smēðe* 'smooth'.

Smithwick: Adam *de Smithewyk* 1327 SRSx; Roger *de Smythewyk* 1332 SRSx. From Smethwick (Ches), or from a lost Smithwick in Southover (Sussex), last recorded c1608 (PN Sx 323).

Smithyman: *v.* SMITHERMAN

Smiton, Smitton: *v.* SMEATON

Smollett: John *Smalheued* 1332 SRWa; William *Smalhed, Smallyd* 1524 SRSf, 1547 EA (NS) ii (Sf). 'Small head.'

Smorfit, Smorthwaite, Smurfit, Smurthwaite: *v.* SMITHWHITE

Smye, Smythe: *v.* SMITH

Snail: Hamelin *Sneyl* 1221 *ElyA* (Sf); Geoffrey *Snayl* 1277 *Ely* (C). OE *snegel, snægel* 'snail', of persons, 'slow, indolent'.

Snake: William *Snak* 1327 SRSx. OE *snaca* 'snake'. A nickname.

Snape, Snepp: Agnes *del Snappe* 1242 Rams (Hu); John *atte Sneppe* 1327 SRSx; Robert *de Snape* 1355 FFY; Roger *Snape* 1525 SRSx. From Snape (Suffolk, NRYorks), or 'dweller by the pasture', OE *snæp*, ON *snap*.

Snarey, Snary: *Snarri* de Wurðintona 1169 P (Wa); Richard *Snarri* 1200 P (Ha); Andrew *Snary* 1224 FFEss. ON *Snari*, from ON *snarr* 'swift'.

Snawdon: *v.* SNOWDEN

Snead, Sneed, Snoad, Snode, Snee: Ailnoth *de Snode* 1214 Cur (K); Robert *del Sned*, Agnes *Sned* 1275 SRWo; Robert *atte Snede* 1327 SRWo; John *Snode* 1327 SRSf. 'Dweller by a clearing or piece of woodland', OE *snæd*, hence *Snead*, OE *snād*, hence *Snoad*, as at Snead Fm in Rock (Worcs), Snoad's Hole in Linton, Snoad Farm in Otterden and Snoadhill in Betterden (Kent).

Sneezam, Sneezum: Richard *de Snetesham* 1161 P (Nf). A local pronunciation of Snettisham (Norfolk).

Snel, Snell, Snelle: Johannes *filius Snel* 1196 P (Y); Alexander *filius Snell'* 1219 AssY; William *Snel* 1185 Templars (K); Edwinus *Snell'* 1195 FF (Nf); Thurstan *le Snel* 1223 Cur (Sr). OE *Snell*, from OE *snel(l)* 'smart, active, bold' or the adjective as a nickname. In Yorks and Norfolk we may have ON *Snjallr*.

Snelgar: *Snelgarus* 1191, 1196 P (Sx, Do); *Snelgarus* de Broke 1205 Cur (K); Thomas *Snelgar* 1243 AssSo; Richard *Snelgorr* 1450 ArchC vii. An unrecorded OE **Snelgār* 'bold-spear'. cf. SNEL.

Sneller: William, Richard *Snellard* 1205 P, 1275 RH (D). A hybrid compound of *Snel* and Fr *-ard*.

Snelling: *Snellinc* 1066 DB (C); *Snelling* 1204 P (Ess); Andrew, Brithmarus *Snelling* 1222 Pat (Herts), c1250 Rams (Nf). OE *Snelling*, a derivative of *Snell*.

Snellman, Snelman: John *Snelman* 14th AD iv (Ess). 'Bold, active man', or 'servant of *Snel*'. *v.* SNEL.

Snepp: *v.* SNAPE

Snider, Sniders, Snyder, Snyders, Sniderman: John *Snyther* 1332 SRSx; John *Sniders* 1674 HTSf. A derivative of OE *snīðan* 'to cut', cutter, tailor.

Snoad, Snode: *v.* SNEAD

Snook, Snooks: Eduuardus *Snoch* 1066 DB (K); *Stenesnoc* ib. (Ha); John, Thomas *Snok* 1222 DBStP, 1356 ColchCt; Robert *Snouk* 1327 SRSo. Lower, followed by Bardsley and Weekley, derives this surname from the old pronunciation of Sevenoaks and states that Sussex deeds relating to a family of Snooks give all the modes of spelling from *Sevenoakes* down to *S'nokes*. The pronunciation was *Sennocke*, with stress on the first syllable, which is still used occasionally. We should not expect this to become *Snook* and it certainly cannot account for the early forms above. These must go back to an OE **snōc* 'a projecting point of land', used as a nickname for a long-nosed individual, or from an OE **snōc* 'snake' which appears to have been used as a personal-name in Snorscomb (Northants), *Snoces cumb* 944 DEPN.

Snow: Richard *Snow* 1221 AssWo; Robert *Snou* 1239 FFSf; Gilbert *Snawe* 1327 *SR* (Ess); William *le Snow* 1327 SRSx. OE *snāw* 'snow', a nickname for one with snow-white hair. Haylwardus *Snew* (c950 OEByn) is said to have been so called *propter albedinem*.

Snowball: Robert *Snawbal* 1301 SRY; Roger *Snowbald* 1327 SRSt; Robert *Snaubal* 1332 SRLa. OE *snāw*, ME *snow* and ME *ball*, 'a white streak, a bald place', a nickname for one with a snow-white patch of hair, or, possibly, with a whitish bald spot amid jet-black hair. *Snowbald* may be evidence of the latter meaning, from ME *ballede*, or the *d* may be excrescent. cf. BALD, BALL.

Snowden, Snowdon, Snawdon: Henry *de Snewedon* 1277 FFEss; Matthew *de Snoudon'* 1278 AssSo. From Snow End (Herts), *Snowdon* 1362, Snowdon (Devon), or Snowden (WRYorks).

Soal(l): *v.* SOLE

Soame, Soames, Somes: Warin *de Saham* 1086 InqEl (C); Henry *Somes*, William *Soumes*, Widow *Soames* 1674 HTSf. From Soham (Cambs, Suffolk).

Soane(s): *v.* SON

Soar, Soares, Soars: John, Roger *le Sor* 1176 P (Do), 1229 Cl (Co); John *le Soor* 1327 SRSf. OFr *sor* 'reddish-brown'. cf. SORREL.

Soards: *v.* SWORD

Soden, Soldan: *v.* SOWDEN

Sole, Soles, Soal, Soall: (i) William *de la Sole* 1207 Cur (Sx); Thomas *atte Sole* 1294 PN Sr 101; Hamo *de Soles* 1242 Fees (K). 'Dweller by the miry place', OE *sol* 'mud, wallowing place for animals', as at Soles (Kent). (ii) Osbert, Walter *Sole* 1203 Cur (Nf), 1207 Rams (C); Godfrey, Osbert *le Sol* 1274 RH (Ess), 1275 SRWo. OFr *sol* 'sole, lonely'.

Sollas, Sollis: Walter, Robert *Solace* 1269 AssNb, 1372 LLB H. ME *solas*, OFr *solaz* 'comfort'.

Soltan: *v.* SOWDEN

Somer(s): *v.* SUMMER

Somerscales: *v.* SUMMERSCALE

Somerset, Somersett, Sommersett, Summersett: Walter *de Sumerset* 1206 Pl (L); John *de Somersete* 1331 IpmW; Edmund *Somerset* 1545 SRW. 'The man from Somerset.' But John, Robert *de Somersete* 1319 SRLo, 1352 AssLo, may owe their names to the London parish of St. Mary Somerset.

Somervell, Somerville, Somervaille, Sommerville, Summerville: Adam *de Somervila* 1153 Templars

(O); William *de Summeruill'* 1158 P (Y). Probably from Graveron-Sémerville (Nord).

Somes: *v.* SOAME

Sommer(s): *v.* SUMMER

Sommerlat: *v.* SUMMERLAD

Somner: *v.* SUMNER

Son, Sonn, Sone, Sones, Soan, Soane, Soanes, Soans: John *Sune* 1203 P (Wa); James *le Sone* 1275 AD iii (Mx); Roger *le Son* 1327 SRSf; William *Sones* 1327 SRWo; Thomas *Sonne* 1327 SRDb; Robert *Soones, Soane*, John *Soanes* 1674 HTSf. OE *sunu*, ME *sone* 'son', perhaps 'the younger', junior.

Songer: *v.* SANGAR

Songhurst, Songest: William *de Sunghurst* 1332 SRSr. From Song Hurst in Ewhurst (Surrey) and from Songhurst Fm in Wisborough Green (PN Sx 135).

Soord: *v.* SWORD

Soothill, Soutell, Suttill, Suttle: Michael *de Sothil, de Suthill'* 1207 P, 1208 Cur (Y); John *Sootell* 1472 GildY; Katerina *Sottell* 1497 ib.; Robert *Suttell* 1526 ib.; William *Suttle* 1679 FrY. From Soothill (WRYorks). *v.* also SUTTLE.

Soper, Soaper, Sopper, Saper, Sapier: Edgar *le soppier* 1138–60 ELPN; William *(le) Sopere* 1195–6 P (Gl); Roger *Sapere* 1243 AssDu; Alexander *le Soppere* c1260 *ERO* (Ess); Emma *la Sapere* 1301 SRY. A derivative of OE *sāpe* 'soap', a maker or seller of soap.

Sorbie, Sorby, Sorsbie, Sorsby, Sowerby, Sowersby, Surbey: Odierna *de Sourebi* 1195 P (Cu); Richard *Surby* 1381 LoPleas; William *Sourby* 1381 PTY; Isabel *Soreby* 1485 GildY; Thomas *Sowerbye* 1597 Oxon (C); Christopher *Saursbye* 1615 Shef; Robert *Sorsbie* 1626 ib. Sowerby 'farm or village in marshy ground' is a common place-name in Cumberland, Westmorland, Lancashire and Yorkshire. Sowerby near Inskip (Lancs) is *Sorbi* in DB. The unetymological medial *s* in *Sorsby* is found in 1202 in *Kirkesoresbi* for Castle Sowerby (Cumb). The most common form today is *Sowerby*. In Sheffield, *Sorby* is usual.

Sorley: *v.* SUMMERLAD

Sorrel, Sorrell, Sorrill: William *Sorell'* 1130 P (Sf); Thomas, William *Sorel* 1175 P (Nf), 1185 Templars (Herts). OFr *sorel*, a diminutive of *sor* 'reddish-brown'.

Sorrie: Ralph, Fulco *Sori* 1275, 1276 RH (Nf, L); Robert *le Sorei* 1279 RH (O). OE *sārig* 'sorry, sad'.

Sorsbie, Sorsby: *v.* SORBIE

Sotham, Sothcott: *v.* SOUTHAM, SOUTHCOTT

Sotheby, Suddaby, Sutherby: Stephen *de Sottebi* 1194 P (Y); John *Suthiby*, Robert *Suthinby* 1297 SRY; William *Sothybe* 1479 GildY; John *Suddebe* 1516 ib.; John *Sotheby* 1674 HTSf. ON *suðr í bý* (the man who lived) 'south in the village'. *v.* WESTOBY.

Sotheran, Sothern, Sotheron, Southan, Southon, Southerin, Southern, Southorn, Sudran, Sudron, Sutherin, Suthern, Sutherns, Suthren: Geoffrey *le Sutherne* 1243 AssSt; Robert *le Sotherun, le*

Sotheren 1297 SRY, MinAcctCo (Y); John *le Southeren* 1307 Wak (Y); Henry *le Suthreen* 1325 AssSt; Hugh, Henry *le Sotheron* 1327 SRDb; Agnes *le Southeron* 1327 SRWo; Richard *Sotheran* 1352 FrY; Thomas *Sothryn* 1387 AD iv (Y); Robert *Sudurrom* 1496 GildY; William *Sothoryng* 1524 SRSf; Andrew *Suddren* 1755 FrY. *Southern* and *Sothern* are from OE *sūðerne* 'southern', the man from the south. For this NED has one metathesized form *southren* c1386 and *southron*, originally Scottish and northern, from c1470. This it regards as an alteration of *southren* with the ending probably modified on the analogy of *Briton, Saxon*. The above forms, much earlier, and mostly from Scandinavian counties, suggest that some may derive from ON *suðrænn* 'southern'. The intrusive *e* of *Sotheran*, etc., found in most forms is probably due to the strongly trilled northern *r*. The sole example of this form in NED is from the northern *Cursor Mundi* (a1300), *sotherin englis*.

Souch: *v.* SUCH

Souster: Cristiana *Seustere* 1279 RH (Hu); Alice *Sewstere* 1301 SRY; Emma *le Sowester* 1307 Cl; Juliana *le Suster* 1309 SRBeds; Margery *le Sewester* 1326 Wak (Y). ME *sewester, sowester* from OE *sēowian* 'to sew', 'a woman who sews, a sempstress', the feminine of SEWER.

Soutar, Souter, Souttar, Soutter, Sowter, Sueter, Suter, Sutor, Sewter, Sutters: Lewinus *sutor* 1066 Winton (Ha); Nicholas *le Soutere* 1263 MESO (Sx); John *le Sutere* 1273 RH (C); William *le Soutare*, Richard *Suter*, Roger *Soutere* 1327 SRSx; Nota *la Souteres* 1312 ColchCt; John *Sowter* 1379 PTY. *Sutor*, which is now rare but was very common in the 12th century, is Lat *sutor* 'shoemaker', often a translation of OE *sūtere*, the source of the remaining forms.

South: William *de la Sothe* 1273 RH (D); Isabella *South* 1297 MinAcctCo; William *del South* 1379 PTY. 'Man from the south', a synonym for *Southern* and *Sotheran*. cf. BYSOUTH.

Southall: Nicholas *de Suthalle* 1273 RH (Nf). 'Dweller at the south hall.'

Southam, Sotham: Thomas *de Suham* 1199 Pl (Nth); Ralph *de Sutham* 1237 WhC; William *de Southham* 1305 IpmGl; John *Southam* 1371 FFEss. From Southam (Glos, Warwicks), or 'dweller to the south of the village'.

Southan, Southerin, Southern: *v.* SOTHERAN

Southcott, Sothcott: Geoffrey *de Suthcot* 1229 Cur (K); Stephen *de Southcote* 1305 IpmW; John *Suthcote* 1398 FFEss. From Southcot (Berks), or 'dweller in the southern cottage'.

Southerland: *v.* SUTHERLAND

Southey: Peter *de Suthag'* 1219 AssY; John *Ofthesuthhey* 1315 FFEss; Sara *Bysoutheya* 1330 PN D 613; Christopher *Southey* 1642 PrD. From Southey in Culmstock (Devon), Southey Green (Essex), Southey Wood in Ufford (Northants), or Southey in Ecclesfield (WRYorks).

Southgate, Suggate, Suggett, Suggitt: Osbert *de Sudgate* 1197 P (Ess); Alice *de Southgate* 1327 SRSf; Richard *Suggett* 1516 GildY. 'Dweller

near the south gate', especially of some ancient town.

Southland: Christiana *ate Southlande* 1317 AssK. 'Dweller by the southland.'

Southon, Southorn: *v.* SOTHERAN

Southouse: Gilbert *atte Suthhuse* 1296 SRSx; William *atte Southouse* 1327 ib. 'Dweller at the south-house.'

Southward is a corruption of SOUTHWOOD or SOUTHWORTH. Southward Downs in Aldbourne (Wilts) were probably by *Southwode* (1509 PN W 293).

Southwick: Ogga *æt Suthwycan* 972 OEByn (Nth); William *de Sudwic* 1202 AssNth; Thomas *de Suthewyk* 1332 SRSx; William *Southwyke* 1363 IpmGl. From Southwick (Durham, Glos, Hants, Northants, Sussex, Wilts).

Southwood, Sowood: Elfere *de Sudwude* 1202 P (Nf); William *de Suthwud* 1225 FFEss; Margaret *Suwode* 1296 SRSx. 'Dweller near the south wood.' Or 'to the south of the wood': Roger *Bisothewode* 1283 Battle (Sx).

Southworth: Gilbert *Southworthe, de Sotheworth* 1281 AssLa. From Southworth (Lancs). Confused with SOUTHWOOD. Southwood Fm in Walton-on-Thames is *Suthwode* 1235, *Sutheworthe* 1337 (PN Sr 98).

Souttar, Soutter: *v.* SOUTAR

Sowden, Soden, Soltan, Soldan, Sultan: Alan *Soldenc, Soldench'* 1166, 1175 P (Y); *Soutan, Soldangus* Ric 1 Cur (K); Henry *Soldan* 12th FeuDu; Roger *le Soudan* 1208 Cur (Y); Robert *le Sowden'* 1279 RH (Bk). OFr *soudan* 'sultan', occasionally, perhaps, a nickname, but often a pageant-name from the Soldan of the Saracens. cf. 'He that playeth the sowdayn is percase a sower. Yet if one should . . . calle him by his owne name . . . one of his tormentors might hap to breake his (one's) head' (Sir Thomas More).

Sowerby, Sowersby: *v.* SORBIE

Sowman: John *Southman* 1332 SRSx. 'Man from the south' or 'dweller to the south'.

Sowood: *v.* SOUTHWOOD

Sowter: *v.* SOUTAR

Spackman: *v.* SPEAKMAN

Spaight: *v.* SPEIGHT

Spain: Richard *de Espaigne* 1177 P (Ess); Thomas *Spane* 1302 SRY; Thomas *de Spaigne* 1318 LLB E; John *Spayne* 1327 SRC. Alueredus *de Hispania* (1086 DB) came from Épaignes (Eure). Herueus *de Ispania* (ib.) was probably a Breton and may have come from Espinay (Ille-et-Vilaine). *v.* ANF. Later, the name probably derives from Spain, especially in the case of London merchants.

Spalding, Spaulding: Gilbert *de Spaldingis* 1175 P (L). From Spalding (Lincs).

Spalton, Spolton: Henry *Spalding*, carpenter 1633 FrY; Mathew *Spaldinge*, carpenter, son of Henry *Spaldinge* 1662 ib.; Henry *Spawlden*, son of Henry *Spalden*, carpenter 1672 ib.; Marcus *Spaldinge*, carpenter, son of Mathew *Spalton*, carpenter 1689 ib.; Mathew *Spalding*, son of Mathew

Spalding, carpenter 1702 ib.; Henry *Spaldon*, son of Henry *Spaldon*, taylor 1713 ib. Most, if not all of the above freemen of York were members of the same family of *Spalding*, of which *Spalton* is one of several dialectal pronunciations.

Spare: Walter, John *Spare* 1186 P (So), 1268 AssSo. 'Frugal', from OE *spær* 'sparing'.

Sparhawk: *v.* SPARROWHAWK

Spark, Sparke, Sparkes, Sparks: William *Sperc* 1202 AssL; Ralph *Sparke* 1221 ElyA (Sf); John *Sparkes* 1301 SRY. ON *sparkr*, *spræk* 'lively, sprightly'.

Sparling, Sperling, Spurling: Jordan son of *Sparling* 1148–67 ELPN; Alexander *filius Esperling'*, *Sperleng* 1173, 1193 P (Lo); Alexander, Simon *Sperling* a1187 ELPN, 1219 AssY; John *Spurlang* 1221 AssWa; Ralph *Esperlang'* 1221 Cur (Herts); Ælstanus *Sperling* c1250 Rams (Nf). Probably, as suggested by Ekwall, OE *Spyrling*, from *Spyrtling*, a metathesis of *Sprytling*, a diminutive of *Spryt(t)el*, the first element of Spridlington (Lincs), *Spredelintone*, *Sperlinctone* DB. *v.* ELPN.

Sparr, Sparre: William *de la Sparre* 1263 MELS (Sx); John *atte Sparre* 1296 SRSx. 'Dweller by the enclosure', OE *spearr*.

Sparrow, Sparrowe: Richard, *Sperewe* 1160–5 ELPN; Ralph *Sparewe* 1182 P (Nf); Ibbota *Sparow* 1325 Wak (Y). OE *spearwa* 'sparrow', lit. 'flutterer'.

Sparrowhawk, Sparhawk: *Sparhauoc*, *Sperhauoc*, *Sperafoc* 1066 DB (Nt, Sf); *Sparhauec* vtlagus 1172 P (Nth); *Sparhauk* Outlaw 1327 SRSf; Geoffrey *Sparheuec*, Robert *Sperhauec* 1221 AssWa; Thomas *Sparhauk*, William *Sparhawk* 1327 SRSf. OE *Spearh(e)afoc* 'sparrow-hawk', found as a personal name before the Conquest. As a byname, the surname must be both patronymic and a nickname.

Sparshatt, Sparshott: Peter *de Sparshete* 1327 SRSx. From Sparshot (Sussex).

Spashett, Spatchett: Hugo *Pachat*, Robert, Leticia *Spachet* 1327 SRSf. For PATCHETT, with inorganic initial *S*. cf. STURGE.

Spaulding: *v.* SPALDING

Spawforth: *v.* SPOFFORD

Speak, Speake, Speaks, Speck, Speek, Speeks, Speke: William *Spec*, *Spech* 1086 DB (Beds); Walter *Espec* 1130 P (Y); Ailfwin *Speke* 1180 P (Bk); William *le Spec* 1195 P (Do). OFr *espech(e)*, *espek* 'woodpecker'.

Speakman, Spackman: Nigel *Spakeman* 1195 P (Ess); William *Spakeman*, *Spekeman* 1297 MinAcctCo (O). ME *spekeman* 'advocate, spokesman' (1340 NED).

Spear, Speare, Speares, Spears, Speer, Speers: Walter *Speare* 1185 P (So); Henry *Spere* 1246 AssLa. OE *spere* 'spear', for *Spearman*.

Spearman: John *Spereman*, *Spermon* 1327 SR (Ess), SRSt. 'Spearman.'

Speck: *v.* SPEAK

Speed: Godfrey *Sped* 1185 P (Sf); John *Spede* 1277 Ely (Sf), 1296 SRSx. OE *spēd* 'speed, success, wealth'.

Speers: *v.* SPEAR

Speight, Speaight, Spaight, Spieght: William *Speyt*, *Speght* 1297 MinAcctCo (Y), 1332 SRCu; John *Speht*, *Speght* 1313, 1315 Wak (Y). OE *speoht*, *speht*, ME *speight* 'wood-pecker' (c1450 NED).

Speirs: *v.* SPIER

Spellar, Speller: Robert *Speller'* 1202 AssL; Gerard *le Speller* 1301 ParlR (Ess). Probably a derivative of OE *spellian* 'to speak, discourse', a speaker, preacher or a professional story-teller.

Spellen, Spelling: Edmund *Spelyng* 1327 SR (Ess). Perhaps a derivative of OE *spellian* with the formative suffix -*ing*, in the same sense as SPELLAR.

Spellman, Spelman: John *Speleman* 1273 RH (Nt), 1327 SR (Ess). OE *spell* 'discourse, homily, story' and *mann*, equivalent to SPELLAR. *v.* also SPILLMAN.

Spence, Spens: Simon *del Spens*, *de la Despense* 1300 Guisb (Y); Amice *atte Spense* 1327 SR (Ess); William *atte Spence* 1327 SRWo. ME *spense*, *spence*, from OFr *despense* 'larder', one who worked at or was in charge of the buttery. cf. SPENCER. Alan *de la Spense* sometarius Domini Roberti de Shirlaunde (1317 AssK) is also called Alanus *sometarius*, Alanus *seruiens* and Alanus *homo Domini Roberti*. He was the servant or pack-horse driver who carried the provisions to the buttery.

Spencer, Spenser: Robert *le Despenser'* 1204 Cur (Sa); William *le Spencer* 1275 RH (Ha); Ralph *le Spenser* 1275 RH (Sf); Richard *le Espenser* 1279 RH (Beds). AFr *espenser*, OFr *despensier* 'dispenser (of provisions)', a butler or steward (a1300 NED).

Spender: Henry *le Despendur* 1214 Cur (Wa); Peter *de Spendure* 1227 AssSt; Agnes *Spendure* 1301 SRY; Adam *le Spendur* 1327 SRSt. An aphetic form of ME, OFr *despendour* 'a steward' (1340 NED).

Spendlove, Spendlow, Spenlow, Spindelow: Ralph *Spendeluue* 1219 AssL; Robert *Spendelove* 1256 AssNb; Henry *Spendelowe* 1309 SRBeds; Walter *Spenlowe* 1433 GildY; Amy *Spenderlow* 1794 SfPR. 'Spend love', one generous with his love, from OE *spendan* 'to spend, employ lavishly, squander' and *lufu* 'love'.

Spens: *v.* SPENCE

Spenser: *v.* SPENCER

Sperling: *v.* SPARLING

Sperrin, Sperring: *v.* SPURREN

Spice: William, Clement *Spice* 1326 FFSf, 1399 FFC. ME *spice*, OFr *espice* 'spice', metonymic for SPICER.

Spicer: William *le Espicier* 1184 P (K); Bertram *le Specier* 1200 P (Ha); Robert *le Spicer* 1201 AssSo; Hugo *le Especer* 1214 Cur (C); John *Spicer* ElyA (C). OFr *espicier*, *especier* 'a dealer in spices; an apothecary or druggist' (1297 NED).

Spickernall, Spickernell, Spicknell, Pickernell: Richard, Walter *Spigurnel(l)* 1192 P (Lo), 1205 Cur (Y); John *Spigernel* 1259 Crowland (C);

Nicholas *Spikernel* 1275 RH (Nf); Edmund *le Espycurnel'*, Geoffrey *Espigurnel* 1285 *Ass* (Ess); Adam *Sprigunnel* 1297 Wak (Y). ME *spigurnel* 'a sealer of writs'.

Spieght: *v.* SPEIGHT

Spier, Spiers, Speir, Speirs, Spyer, Spyers: William *le Spiour* 1302 ChambAcctCh; Robert *Spyer* 1379 PTY. A derivative of ME *espyen*, OFr *espier* 'to spy', a spy, watchman. cf. 'The wayte (var. *spiere*) that stood upon the toure of Jezrael' (Wyclif).

Spillman, Spilman: Goduine *filius Spilemanni* c1095 Bury (Sf); *Spileman* c1095 Bury (Sf), c1160–65 NthCh (Nth), 1166 P (Nf); Berdic *Joculator*, Adelina *Joculatrix* 1086 DB (Gl, Ha); Edwine *Spileman* 1103–15 OEByn (D); William *Spileman* 1167 P (Ha); Swayn *Spileman* 1204 AssY. The Latin *Joculator* is probably a translation of OE **spilemann* 'jester, juggler'. We are also clearly concerned with a personal name, one of the nicknames used as personal names which were not uncommon in the 12th century. There has been some confusion with SPELLMAN. cf. William *Spileman, Speleman* 1221 Cur (Ha).

Spilsbury: William *de Spellesbury* 1180 Eynsham; Philip *de Spillesbury* 1327 SRWo; Thomas *Spellsbury* 1599 ChwWo. From Spelsbury (Oxon), *Spillesbury* 1343.

Spindelow: *v.* SPENDLOVE

Spindler: William *le Spinlere* 1236 FFSx; William *le spindlere* 1297 MinAcctCo. A derivative of OE *spinel* 'spindle', a maker of spindles.

Spink, Spinke, Spinks: Roger *Spinc* 1133–60 Rams (Beds); Thomas *Spink* 1256 AssNb. ME *spink* 'a finch', especially a chaffinch.

Spinner: John *le Spinner* 1270 MESO (Wo); Thomas *Spinnere* 1356 AD i (D). A derivative of OE *spinnan* 'to spin', 'a spinner of wool, yarn, etc.' (1393 NED).

Spir, Spire: Thomas, William *Spir* 1229 Pat (Ess), 1279 RH (C); Thomas *le Spyr* 1296 SRSx. OE *spīr* 'spike, stalk, tapering stem', probably a nickname for a tall, thin man.

Spirett, Spirit: Osbert, Robert, Geoffrey *Spirhard* 1206 Cur (Nf), 1219 AssY, 1221 *ElyA* (Sf). OE *spīr* plus the French suffix *-hard*, perhaps in an intensive sense, 'the tall one'. cf. POLLARD.

Spiring: William, Lyme *Spiring* 1229 Pat (So), 1250 Fees (Gl); Henry *Spiryng* 1275 SRWo. OE **spīring*, a derivative of *spīr*, 'the tall one'.

Spitteler, Spittler: Synonymous with *atte Spitele* and (Adam) *Spitelman* 1176 P (Y). *v.* SPITTLE.

Spittle, Spittall, Spittel, Spital, Spittles: Geoffrey *del Hospital* 1210 Cur (So); Adam *del Spitell* 1307 Wak (Y); Walter *atte Spitele* 1332 SRSx. 'Dweller at or attendant in a hospital', ME *spitel*, OFr *(h)ospital*.

Spittlehouse: Robert *de Spytelhous* 1440 ShefA. 'Dweller or worker at the hospital-house.'

Spofford, Spofforth, Spawforth: Hynge *de Spoufford'* 1212 Cur (Y). From Spofforth (WRYorks).

Spolton: *v.* SPALTON

Spooner: Roger *Lesponere* 1179 P (Y); Thomas,

Robert *le Sponere* 1221 AssL, 1254 FFEss. OE *spōn* 'chip, splinter' is recorded in 1316 in the sense 'roofing-shingle' and c1340 as 'spoon'. The surname may therefore mean 'maker of spoons', but, as it is mainly a northern name and *spone* 'shingle' is a northern term (Building 229), the meaning is probably in general 'maker of shingles'.

Spoor, Spore: *v.* SPURR

Sprackling, Spratling, Sprankling: *Sprachelingus* 1130 P (Lo); *Sprakelingus* 1200 P (K); Robertus *filius Sprakeling* 1204 P (W); Vnspac *Spracheling* 1166 P (Nf); John, Gervase *Sprakeling* 1170–87 ELPN, 1204 P (W). OE *Spracaling*, an anglicizing of ON *Sprakaleggr* 'man with the creaking legs'.

Spragg, Spragge, Sprague, Sprake: Richard *Sprak* 1327 SRSf; Reginald *Sprag* 1303 FA (Sf); Alice *Sprakes* 1359 Putnam (So). *Sprag* is a voiced form of *sprak*, a metathesis of *spark*. cf. Wilts dial. *sprack* 'lively' and *v.* SPARK.

Sprankling, Spratling: *v.* SPRACKLING

Spray, Sprey: (i) Geoffrey *Espray, Lesprai* 1205 Cur (L); John *Spraye* 1319 SRLo. ME *spray* 'slender shoot or twig'. (ii) William *de Spray, Espray* 1180–1 P (D). From Sprytown (Devon), DB *Sprei*.

Sprigg, Spriggs: William *Sprig* 1199 P (Nf); Osbert *Sprigge* 1206 P (D). ME *sprigge* 'twig'. cf. Lonsdale dialect *sprig* 'a small, slender person'.

Spring: William *Esprinc* Hy 2 DC (L); Henry *le Springe* 13th FeuDu; William *Spring* 1280 Riev (Y). Probably a nickname for an active, nimble individual, from ME *spring* 'spring', the season when young shoots spring or rise from the ground. There appears to be no evidence for a topographical origin.

Springall, Springell, Springhall, Springle, Springate: *Springald* 1195 P (Gl); *Springaldus, Springoud* 1197 P, 1220 Cur (Ess); Robert *Springout* 1245–6 Seals (Nth); Emma *Springhalt* 1272 AssSt; Adam *Springald* 1275 Wak (Y); Walter *Springaud* 1279 RH (O); John *Springot* 1297 MinAcctCo; William *Springold* 1310 ColchCt; Deynes *Springat* 1327 SRC; William *Springate* 1814 SfPR. OFr *espringalle*, AFr *springalde* 'an engine of the nature of a bow or catapult used in medieval warfare for throwing heavy missiles' (a13.. NED). Early examples are probably metonymic for a soldier in charge of such engines but we are also concerned with ME *springal(d)*, of doubtful origin, perhaps a derivative of *spring*, 'a young man, youth, stripling' (c1440 NED). There has, no doubt, been confusion with SPRINGETT.

Springer: William, Simon *Springer* 1185 Templars (K), 1296 SRSx. A derivative of OE *springan* 'to jump', a jumper, perhaps a nickname, 'nimble, lively'.

Springett: William *Pringet* 1193 P (Wa); William *Springet* 1262 For (Ess), 1296 SRSx. A diminutive of SPRING, 'a lively young man'. cf. SPRINGALL.

Sprot, Sprott: *Sprot* 1066 DB (Ess), c1130 ELPN; *Sprot de Spaldintona* 1176 P (Y); Willelmus *filius Sprot* ib.; Alduinus, Ralph, William

Sprot c1140 ELPN, 1176 P (Ess), 1199 P (Beds). OE **Sprot(t)* 'sprout, shoot', considered by von Feilitzen to be possibly Scandinavian, but more probably native, from the same root as SPARLING.

Spurling: *v.* SPARLING

Spurr, Spoor, Spore: Peter *Spore* (*Spure*) 1230 P (Sx); Osmund, Alice *Spore* 1274 RH (Ess), 1303 FA (Sf). OE *spura, spora* 'spur', metonymic for (John) *Spureman* 1222 Cur (Nf), 'spurrier'.

Spurren, Spurring, Spearon, Sperrin, Sperring, Sperryn: Hugo *Esporun, Spurun* 1141–2 StP, 1185 Templars (Ess); William *Sporun* 1212 Cur (Y); William *Esperun* 1227 AssBeds; Thomas *Sperun* 1274 RH (Ess). OFr *esporon, esperun* 'spur', metonymic for SPURRIER. Richard *le sporiere* (1281 LLB B) is also called *Sporon*. cf. Henry *Speroner, le Esporoner* 1296, 1301 LLB C, B.

Spurrier: Walter *Spurier* t. John HPD (Ess); Benedict *le Sporier* 1298 LoCt; Roger *Spurreour* 1360 FrLeic. A derivative of OE *spura* 'spur', 'spur-maker'.

Spyer: *v.* SPIER

Squiller: Robert *Lescuieler, le Esquieler, le Squieler* 1219–21 Cur (Nth); John *le Squiller* 1334 LLB E. AFr *sculier*, OFr *esculier, escuillier, esquelier* 'maker or seller of dishes' (often of gold or silver); also 'servant in charge of the scullery' (NED).

Squire, Squires, Squier, Squiers: Alword *se Scuir* 1100–30 OEByn (D); William *Scuer* c1180 Bury (Sf); Richard *Lesquier* 1197 P (Gl); Simon *Esquier* 1206 Cur (R); Roger *le Esquier* 1228 FFEss; Roger *Squier* 1293 Fees (D). OFr *escuyer, escuier*, ME *squyer* 'shield-bearer, esquire'. In the early examples, used of a young man of good birth attendant on a knight (c1290 NED). The sense of personal attendant or servant is not recorded before 1380.

Squirrel, Squirrell, Scurrell, Squirl: Ralph *Squrel* 1221 AssWa; William *Scurell* 1230 P (Nf); Geoffrey *le Esqurel* 1274 RH (Sf); Peter *Squirel* 1301 SRY. AFr *esquirel*, OFr *esquireul, escureul* 'squirrel' (a1366 NED). Used contemptuously of men in the 16th century, but as a surname, probably a nickname denoting agility or thrift. For *Squirl*, cf. the northern dialect form *swirl*.

Stable, Stables: (i) Walter *de la Stable* 1275 SRWo; Robert *del Estable* 1270 AssSo; Robert *atte Stable* 1327 SRSx. OFr *estable* 'a stable', equivalent to STABLER, but occasionally, perhaps, denoting one who lives near a stable. (ii) Roger *Estable, Stable* 1199 ChR, 1200 P (So); William *Stable* 1250 Fees (So). OFr *stable, estable* 'steadfast in purpose or resolution; sound in counsel or judgement, trustworthy' (a1275 NED).

Stableford, Stableforth: *v.* STAPLEFORD

Stabler, Stabeler: Laurence *le Stabler* 1196 FFEss; Alan *le Establer* 1257 MEOT (Y). OFr *establier* 'stable-keeper' (14.. NED), also 'stable-man, ostler'.

Stace: *Stacius* 1147–65 Colch (Ess); *Stacius* de Hant' 1187 P (Ha); John, Roger *Stace* 1275, 1279 RH (Lo, Hu). *Stacius* is a latinization of *Stace*, the vernacular form of *Eustace*.

Stacey, Stacy: *Stacy* Hernowe 1327 SRSo; Robert *Staci* 1270 Eynsham (O); William *Stacy* 1275 RH (D); Lucia *Eustasy* 1327 SRSo. A diminutive of *Stace*. *Staci* de Gynes (1292 SRLo) is called *Eustace* (1299 LLB C).

Stack: Robert *Stac* 1199 P (Bk); Simon *Stakke* 1244 Fees (Ha). ON *stakkr* 'hay-stack', either metonymic for *Stacker*, a builder of stacks, or a nickname for one hefty as a hay-stack.

Stackard: Robert *le Stacker* 1264 AD i (Herts); William *le Stackere* 1327 SRSf. A maker of hay-stacks. The modern form is probably very late, with excrescent *d*.

Stackpoole: Walter *de Stakepol* a1200 Dublin. From Stackpoole (Pembrokeshire).

Staff: William *Staf* 1177 P (Sf); Thomas *le Staf* 1297 FFEss. OE *stæf*, used by Chaucer as a type of thinness or leanness:

Ful longe were his legges and ful lene,
Ylyk a staf, ther was no calf ysene.

Stafford, Staffurth: Robert *de Stadford* 1086 DB; Robert *de Stafford'* 1177 P (St); Adam *de Stafford* c1280 SRWo; John *Stafford* 1423 AssLo. From Stafford (Staffs), East, West Stafford (Dorset), Stowford (Devon), *Staveford* 1086, or 'dweller by the ford marked with staves'.

Stagg: Robert *Stagge* 1198 P (Sx); Richard *Stagge* 1243 AssDu. OE *stagga* 'stag'.

Stain: *v.* STEIN

Stainer, Steiner, Steynor: Henry *Stainer* 1319 SR (Ess); John *le Stainer* 1327 SR (Ess); William *le steignour* 1353 FrY; Thomas *Peyntour* alias *Steynor* 1430 Oseney (O). A derivative of ME *steyne* 'to stain' (1388 NED). 'Paid to Thomas *Staynour* of Windsor for painting the fenestral like a glass window, 4*d*.' (1427 Building 174).

Staines: Richard *de Stanes* 1275 RH (K). From Staines (Middlesex).

Stainthorp, Stainthorpe: Gilbert *de Steyndrope* 1346 LLB F. From Staindrop (Durham).

Stair, Stairs: William *de Stegre* 1195 P (K); Robert *atte Steghere* 1296 SRSx. OE *stǣger* 'stair', used in Kent and Sussex of an ascent, rising ground. cf. Stairbridge Fm in Bolney, Steer's Common in Kirdford (Sussex), the Stair (Kent).

Staker: Stephen *Staker* 1242 Fees (Lei). 'One who drives in stakes', or 'dweller by the stake'.

Stakes: (i) William *de Lestake* 1214 Cur (Bk); Alice *ate Stake* 1332 SRSr. 'Dweller by the stake' (OE *staca*), probably a boundary-post. (ii) Geoffrey, Hugh *Stake* 1199 P (Nf), 1203 Cur (C). OE *staca* 'a stake'. cf. STAFF.

Stalker: Walter *le Stalkere* 1202 P (Nt); Nicholas *Stalkere* 1252 Rams (Hu). A derivative of ME *stalke*, OE **stealcian* 'to walk stealthily, to pursue game by stealthy approach'.

Stallan, Stallen, Stallon, Stallion: Alfwin *Stalun* 1202 FF (Nf); Alexander *Stalon* 1275 SRWo; John *Staloun* 1327 SRSf. OFr *estalon* 'a stallion' (a1388 NED); applied to a person, 'a begetter' (c1305); 'a man of lascivious life'. cf. 'þe monke þat wol be stalun gode . . . He schal hab wiþute danger. xii. wiues euche ȝere' (c1305 NED).

Stallard, Stollard: Sybyll *Stalward, Stallard* 1572, 1573 LedburyPR; Thomas *Stollard* 1645 Bardsley. A variant of STALLWOOD.

Stallman, Stalman: Adam *de Stalmyn* 1292 QW (La). From Stalmine (Lancs).

Stallwood: Reiner *Stalewurd* 1227 Pat (Nf); John *le Stalwrthe* 1279 RH (O); William *Staleworthe* 1327 SR (Ess). OE *stælwierðe* 'sturdy, robust; brave, courageous'.

Stallworthy, Stolworthy: Thomas *Stalworthi* 1285 Pinchbeck (Sf); John *Stalworthy* 1327 SRSf. An altered form of *stalworth*, after *worthy* (c1250 NED).

Stamer: Æðelwearde *Stameran* 1015 OEByn; John *Stamer* 1296 SRSx; Robert *le Stamere* 1327 SRSx. OE **stamera* 'stammerer', from OE *stamerian* 'to stammer'.

Stammer, Stammers, Stanmore: *Stanmar* 1066 DB (Sf); *Stanmarus* c1250 Rams (Nf); *Stanmer* 1095 Bury (Sf); Widwinus *Stammere* 13th Bart (Lo); Robert *Stammers* 1674 HTSf. A late OE *Stānmær* 'stone-fame', chiefly East Anglian. Also local, from Stanmore (Middlesex) or Stanmer (Sussex): Robert *de Stanmere* 1206 Cur (Mx); Reginald *de Stanmere* 1296 SRSx.

Stamp, Stamps: Salamon, John *de Stampes* 1191 P (Lo); Thomas *Stampe* 1424 FFEss. From Étampes (Seine-et-Oise), earlier *Estampes*.

Stanberry, Stanborough, Stanbury, Stanbra: Alan *Stanborw* 1279 RH (C). This form represents an unrecorded OE woman's name **Stānburh* 'stone-fortress': *Stamburc* 1086 DB (Ess), *Stanburch* 12th LVD. *Stanbury* is common in Devon where it is probably from Stanborough. The Lancashire *Stanbury* is from Stanbury (WR Yorks).

Standage: *v.* STANDISH

Standalone, Standerline: Richard *Standalan* 1332 SRCu. 'Stand alone', a nickname for a resolute, self-reliant man.

Standfast: Thomas *Stanfast, Stampfast* 1279 RH (O); Robert *Stantfast* 1296 SRSx. A nickname for one of steadfast, resolute character. cf. Gudytha *ffoloufast* 1379 PTY.

Standidge: *v.* STANDISH

Standing: Robert *Standing* 1553 WhC (La). Probably from Standen in Lancashire where *Standen* and *Standing* are both found as surnames.

Standish, Standage, Standidge: Ralph *de Stanedis* 1206 Cur (La); 'Herriesservant *Standich* de Clyfford' 1377 Pat (Wa). From Standish (Lancs, Glos).

Standwell: Richard *Standwele* 1309 Wak (Y). cf. 'Beo stalewurðe & stond well' a1225 NED, and STANDFAST.

Stanger: Whilst not common, the name seems to be more frequent in Kent and Sussex than in Yorks and Lancs. The northern surname is from Stanger in Embleton or Stangrah in Whitbeck (Cumb): Robert *de Stangre* 1332 SRCu, or, possibly, from Stanghow (NRYorks), all from ON

stŏng 'pole'. In the south, from residence near a stony gore: Jordan *de Stangar* 1327 SRSo; Henry *Stangor* 1327 SR (Ess). There was a place (*to*) *stangare* in the bounds of Upminster in 1062 (PN Ess 131), OE *stān* 'stone', *gāra* 'triangular piece of land'.

Stanham, Stannum: Robert *de Stanham* 1177 P (Sf). From Stonham (Suffolk).

Stanhill, Stonhill, Stonnill: (i) Robertus *filius Stanilde* 1095 Bury (Sf); *Stonilda* 1185 Templars (K); Adam *filius Stanilde* 1198 FFSf; Robert, Thomas *Stonild* 1305 FFSf. An unrecorded OE woman's name **Stānhild* 'stone-war'. (ii) Henry *atte Stonhill* 1305 PN Sr 154. 'Dweller by a stony hill', OE *stān, hyll*.

Stanhope: Swayn *de Stanhop* 1242 AssDu; William *Stannop* 1327 SRSf; Richard *Stanhope* 1427 IpmNt. From Stanhope (Durham), or 'dweller at the stony valley'.

Stanhurst: Hugo *de Stanhurst* 1230 P (K). From residence near a stony, wooded hill (OE *stān, hyrst*).

Stanier: *v.* STONEHEWER

Staniford, Staniforth, Stanyforth: Matild' *de Staniforþe* 1297 SRY. 'Dweller by a stony ford', probably near Sheffield (Yorks) where the surname is common.

Staniland: William *atte Stanylond* 1272 AssSt. 'Dweller by the stony land.'

Stanistrete: *v.* STONESTREET

Stanlake: Thomas *de Stanlac'* 1221 Cur (Sf). 'Dweller by the stony stream.' OE *stān, lacu.*

Stanley, Stanly, Stanleigh: Robert *de Stanleya* 1130 P (St); Alan *de Stanlai* 1208 P (Y); Hugh *de Stanleye* 1323 IpmNt; Richard *Stanley* 1398 IpmGl. From Stanley (Derby, Durham, Glos, Staffs, Wilts, WRYorks).

Stanmore: *v.* STAMMER

Stannah: *v.* STANNER

Stannard, Stonard, Stonhard, Stonner, Stannett: *Stanhard, Stanhart, Stanardus, Stanart* 1066 DB; *Stannard* 1095 Bury (Sf); *Stanardus* le Couhirde 1327 SRC; Ralph *Stanhard* 1221 ElyA (Sf); Richard *Stanhert* ib.; Henry, Walter *Stonhard* 1222 DBStP (Herts), c1250 Colch (Herts); Laurence *Stannard* 1327 SRC. OE *Stānheard* 'stone-hard', a late name, common after the Conquest, especially in the east.

Stannas, Stanners, Stannis, Stannus: Robert *de Stanehouse* 1275 RH (Nb). 'Dweller at the stonehouse.'

Stanner, Stannah: Nicholas *de Stanhoe* 1146–8 MedEA (Nf). From Stanhoe (Norfolk).

Stannett: *v.* STANNARD

Stannum: *v.* STANHAM

Stansfield, Stansfeld: Richard *Stanesfeld* 1275 RH (Y); William *de Stanesfeld* 1330 FFEss; Edward *Stanesfeld* 1523 CorNt. From Stansfield (Suffolk, WRYorks).

Stanton, Staunton: Godwine *æt Stantune* c1055 OEByn; Walter *de Stanton'* 1199 Pl (Nt); John *de Staunton* 1290 FFO; John *Stanton* 1395–6 FFSr; Robert *Staunton* 1445–6 IpmNt. From one or other of the many places called Stanton or Staunton, all 'enclosure on stony ground'.

Stanyer: *v.* STONEHEWER

Stanyforth: *v.* STANIFORD

Stap: William *a la Stappe* 1275 SRWo; Robert *atte Stappe*, Robert *Stappe* 1332 SRSx; OE *stæpe*, a side-form of *stepe* 'step'. Probably 'Dweller by the stepping-stones or footbridge.' *v.* MELS 198.

Staple, Staples: Walter *de Stapel*' 1275 SRWo; Osmund *atte Staple* 1279 PN Sr 253; Richard *de Staples* 1321 FFEss; John *Stapel* 1325 ib. 'Dweller by a post or posts', OE *stapol* 'post, pillar', as at Staple (Kent) or Staple Fitzpaine (Som).

Stapleford, Stableford, Stableforth: Alfgar, Richard *de Stapleford* 1177 P (Ess), 1277 IpmW; John *de Stapulford* 1369 IpmNt; William *Stapulford* 1437–8 IpmNt. From Stapleford (Cambs, Ches, Essex, Herts, Leics, Lincs, Notts, Wilts).

Stapleton, Stapylton: Randulf *de Stapeltuna* 1166 P (Y); John, Robert *de Stapilton*' 1327 SRLei; William *Stapulton* 1460 IpmNt. From Stapleton (Cumb, Glos, Hereford, Leics, Salop, Som, NR, WRYorks).

Stark, Starks: Rannulf, William *Stark* 1222 Cur (Sf), 1314 FFEss. OE *stearc* 'firm, unyielding; harsh, severe'.

Starkey, Starkie: Richard *Starky* 1260 AssCh; Lawrence *Starky* 1446 AD v (Ch). A diminutive of STARK. cf. 'Starky, stiff, dry. Westmorland' (Halliwell).

Starkman: William *Starckeman, Starcman* 1279 RH (C). 'Strong, stern man.' cf. STARK.

Starling, Sterling: *Starlingus, Starlinc* 1066 DB (Sf); Willelmus *filius Sterling* 1133–60 Rams (Hu); Jordan, Wimund *Starling* 1166 P (C), 1203 Cur (Sf); Richard *Sterling* 1230 P (Herts). A nickname from the bird, OE *stærling* 'starling', used also occasionally as a personal name.

Starman: Margeria *Starremon* 1327 SRWo. 'Servant of *Star*.'

Starr: Leuenot *Sterre* 1066 DB (Db); Simon *Sterre* 1130 P (Nf); William *Sturre, Sterre* 1221 AssGl; John *Sterre, Starre* 1305–6 LLB B. OE *steorra*, ME *sterre* 'star', used, like the ON *Stjarna*, as a nickname, but also, occasionally, as a personal name: *Sterre* 1066 DB (Ha). Occasionally a sign-name: Richard *ate Sterre* 1322 LLB E.

Start, Starte, Stert, Sturt: Roger *de Lesturte*, Tomas *de Sterte* 1168, 1197 P (D); Walter *de la Sterte* 1225 AssSo; Richard *de Stirt* 1279 RH (Hu); John *Sterte* 1317 AssK; John *ate Sturte* 1332 SRSr. 'From residence near a promontory, tongue of land or a hill-spur' (OE *steort* 'tail'), as at Start (Devon).

Startifant, Sturdevant, Sturtevant, Sturtivant: John, Richard, Thomas *Stirtava(u)nt* 1404 Pat (Y), 1413, 1447 FrY; Alan *Stertevaunt* 1445 GildY; John *Sturdyvaunt* 1570 Bardsley. 'Start forward', ME *sterten* and AFr *avaunt*, a nickname for a messenger or pursuivant. cf. forms of *Startup* and John *Startout* 1381 ArchC 4, Robert *Styrtover* 1320 Shef (Y).

Startup: Stephen *Sturthup* 1190 P (W); Geoffrey

Sturchup 1219 Cur (R); William *Stercup* 1275 RH (Nf); Nicholas *Stirtupp* 1359 LLB G; Geoffrey *Startup* 1541 NorwW (Sf). 'Start up', probably with a meaning similar to that of *Startifant*, from OE *styrtan*, **steortan* 'to leap, jump' and *upp*. *Startup* was the original form of *upstart* and also the name of a kind of boot worn by rustics. These may both have contributed to the surname, but neither is recorded before the 16th century.

Statham, Stathum: Richard *de Stathum* 1413 DbCh; John, Henry *Stathum* 1450 IpmNt, 1488 Cl (La). From Statham (Ches).

Staunton: *v.* STANTON

Stay: Henry *le Stay* 1255 RH (W); Adam, Benedict *Stay* 1275 SRWo, 1332 SRCu. ME *staye* 'support, prop', used in the 16th century of persons.

Staziker: *v.* STIRZAKER

Stead, Stede, Steed, Steede, Steeds: (i) Vchtred *Stede* 1180 P (D); Henry *le Stede* 1281 Eynsham (O). OE *stēda* 'stud-horse, stallion'. As a surname, probably 'a man of mettle, of high spirit'. (ii) Richard *de Stede* 1276 AssLa; Roberd *del Stede* 1336 Calv (Y). OE *stede* of varied meanings; in ME used of 'a property or estate in land, a farm' (1338 NED). 'A farmer or farm-worker.'

Steadman, Stedman, Steedman, Stedmond: Roger *Stedeman* 1275 RH (Hu); John *Stedemon* 1275 SRWo; Henry *le Stedeman* 1285 *Ass* (Ess); Robert *le Stedman, le Stedeman* 1323 AssSt. The first element of this compound may be ME *stede* in either sense found for STEAD, (i) a man responsible for the care of the war-horses or a mounted warrior, (ii) a farmer or farm-worker.

Steady, Steddy: William *Stedy* 1327 SRSx. ME *stedy(e)*, *steadie* 'immovable, steadfast, firm' (1530 NED).

Stear(s): *v.* STEER

Stearman, Sterman: William *Stereman* 1202 AssL; Simon *Sterman* 1296 SRSx. OE *stēormann* 'pilot, master of a ship', or OE *stēor* 'steer' and *mann*, 'bullock-herd'.

Stearn(s): *v.* STERN

Steavenson: *v.* STEPHENSON

Steckles: *v.* STILE

Stedman: *v.* STEADMAN

Steede: *v.* STEAD

Steedman: *v.* STEADMAN

Steel, Steele, Steels: Walter, Robert *Stel* 1206 Oseney (O), 1278 AssLa; Jordan *le Stel* 1324 FFEss; Robert *Steel* 1327 SRSx. OE *stȳle, stēle* 'steel', probably for one hard, reliable as steel. cf. the common phrase 'true as steel' (a1300 NED).

Steeper: Alice Relicta *le Stepere*, Robert *le Stupere* 1327 SRSx. A derivative of ME *stepe* (OE *stīepan*) 'to steep', one who steeps flax, cloth, etc., probably a bleacher.

Steer, Steere, Steers, Stear, Stears: Geoffrey *Ster* 1209 P (Wo); Robert *le Steer* 1296 SRSx. OE *stēor* 'a steer'.

Steff: Robert *Steff* 1524 SRSf. ME *stef* 'firm, unyielding, strong'.

Steffan, Steffen, Steffens: *v.* STEPHEN

Steggall(s), Steggals, Steggel, Steggles: v. STILE

Stein, Steyn, Steyne, Stain, Staine, Staines, Stains, Stayne, Staynes: *Stain, Stein, Sten* 1066 DB (Y, Ch, Sa); *Steyne* de Holton 1246 AssLa; Galfridus *filius Steyne* 1275 SRWo; Alfricus *Stein* 1155–66 Holme (Nf); Richard *Steyn* 1275 SRWo. ON *Steinn*, ODa *Sten*. The modern *Stein* is often of late German origin (OHG *stein* 'stone'). v. STAINES.

Stekel: v. STILE

Stephen, Stephens, Steffan, Steffen, Steffens, Steven, Stevens, Stiven: *Stefanus* 1066 DB; *Stephanus* capellanus 1134–40 Holme (Nf); *Steffan(us)* 1142–53 DC (L), 1200 Cur (O); Robert *Stephen* 1260 AssCh; Agnes *Stiven* 1279 RH (Bk); Roger *Stefne* 1283 Oseney (O); Alice *Stevenes, Stephenes* 1279 RH (Hu), 1346 ColchCt; John *Steuene* 1296 SRSx; Sibilla *ate Stevenes* 1332 SRSr. Greek Στεφανᾶς from στέφανος 'crown', a name found already in OE, but only as a monk's name. It became common after the Conquest.

Stephenson, Stephinson, Steavenson, Steevenson, Stevenson, Stevinson, Steverson: Adam *Steveneson* 1327 *SR* (Ess); John *Stephenson* 1395 Whitby (Y); Katherin *Steverson* 1656 Bardsley. 'Son of Stephen.'

Sterling: v. STARLING

Sterman: v. STEARMAN

Stern, Sterne, Sterns, Stearn, Stearne, Stearns: Henry, William *Sterne* 1279 RH (C), 1289 FFC. OE *styrne* 'severe, strict; uncompromising, austere'.

Stert: v. START

Steuart: v. STEWARD

Steven, Stevens: v. STEPHEN

Stevenson, Stevinson: v. STEPHENSON

Stew, Stewer: *Stew* is a rare surname, metonymic for (William *le*) *Steweman* 1327 SRSf, which itself is probably identical in meaning with (William) *Steur* (i.e. *Stewer*) 1279 RH (Bk). The first element is probably (certainly in the country) ME *stewe* 'fish-pond' (c1386 NED), from OFr *estui*. cf. 'Cuidam valetto custodienti *le Stewe* manerii Episcopi' (139. NED). Or, possibly, from OFr *estuve* 'a heated room used for hot air or vapour baths' (1390 NED). Hence, either 'keeper of the fish-ponds' or 'attendant in charge of public baths'.

Steward, Stewart, Steuart, Stuart: Rogere *se Stiwerd* 1100–30 OEByn (D); Alwinus *Stiward* 1148 Winton (Ha); Reginald *le Stiward* 1205 ChR (Do); Martin *Steuhard* 1275 RH (Nf); Phelippe *Styward* 1296 Black (Roxburgh); Henry *Steward* 1327 MEOT (L). OE *stīweard, stigweard* 'steward'. The common derivation 'keeper of the pig-sties' has no authority. *Stiჳ* is of uncertain meaning; the compound probably denotes a 'keeper of the house' (NED). The word had various meanings: 'an official who controls the domestic affairs of a household' (c1000 NED); 'an officer of the royal household' (a955). After the Conquest it was used as the English equivalent of OFr *seneschal*, of 'the steward of a manor' (1303) and of 'the manager of an estate' (a1386). The (Lord High)

Steward of Scotland was the first officer of the Scottish King in early times; he had control of the royal household, great administrative powers, and the privilege of leading the army into battle. The office, described as *senescallatus Scotiae* in a charter of 1158, fell in to the crown upon the accession of Robert the Steward as Robert II, whence the name of the royal house of Stuart. According to Black, the spelling *Stuart* was a French spelling adopted by Mary, Queen of Scots, but he himself records the form in 1429. The final *t* is Scottish, *Stewart* occurring c1370–88 (Black) and in 1432 (NED), *Steuart* in 1504 (Black). Both in Scotland and in England the surname derives from the lesser offices. In Scotland the term was used of a magistrate originally appointed by the king to administer crown lands forming a stewartry (1432), but there, as in England, every bishop, earl and manor had a steward, and the surname is no proof of royal descent as James VI (who retained the old spelling) emphasized when he said that all Stewarts were not 'sib' to the King.

Stewardson, Stewartson: Osbertus *filius Stiwardi* 1148 Winton (Ha); William *le fiz le Stywarde* of the counte of Berewyk 1296 Black; Richard *Stewardson* 1710 Bardsley. 'Son of the steward.'

Steyne: v. STEIN

Steynor: v. STAINER

Stezeker: v. STIRZAKER

Stick: Gilbert *Stikke* 1190 P (Y); Wido *Stik*' 1204 P (Nf). OE *sticca* 'a rod or staff of wood', 'a slender branch', probably a nickname for a tall, slender man.

Stickels, Stickells, Stickles: Richard, Stephen *Stikel* 1194 Cur (Sf), 1327 SRC. OE *sticol* 'steep, rough, difficult', used later (1615) for 'rough, bristly, stickle-haired'. v. also STILE.

Stickney: Alan *de Stikenay* 1202 AssL; Richard *de Stykeneye* 1336 CorLo; William *Stykenay* 1380 AssWa. From Stickney (Lincs).

Stiddolph, Stidolph: John *Stithulf*, Richard *Stidolf* 1313 *Ass* (K); Richard *Stydolff* 1525 SRSx; Bryan *Stiddole* 1564 ArchC xxi. OE *Stīðwulf* 'hard-wolf'.

Stigand, Stigant, Stiggants, Stiggins: *Stigand, Stigan* 1066 DB; *Stigandus* presbiter 1126–7 Holme (Nf); Radulfus *filius Stigant*' 1222 AssWa; William *Stigaunt* 1296 SRSx; Matthew *Stigan* 1419 LLB I; Anne *Stigans* 1706 Bardsley; Mary *Stiggins* 1747 ib. ON *Stigandr*, also used in Normandy. v. also STYAN.

Stile, Stiles, Style, Styles, Steggall, Steggalls, Steggals, Steggel, Steggell, Steggle, Steggles, Steckel, Steckles, Stekel, Stickells, Stickels, Stickles, Stiggles, Stikel, Stygal, Stygall: Reginald *atte Stighel* 1227 AssBeds; William *de Stile* 1229 Pat (So); Richard *del Stigele* ib.; Osmund *Atthe Stihele* 1234 MELS (So); Robert *de la Stiele* 1275 SRWo; Elyas *atte Stigle* Ed 1 MELS (Sr); William *ate Stegele* 1296 SRSx; Roger *Attestichell* 1301 SRY; John *del Steghel* 1327 Wak (Y); Isabella *Stiles* 1337 ColchCt; Edmond *Stegyll*, Margery *Stekyll*, William *Stykyll*, William *Steykell*, Richard

Stegold 1524 SRSf; John *Steckles* 1674 HTSf. 'Dweller by the stile or steep ascent', OE *stigol*. The normal development is to *Stile*, but in surnames, *stigele* became *stigle* and the continuant *g* became a stopped *g*, hence *Stiggle*. As often, *gl* interchanged with *cl*, hence *Stickle*. ME *stegele* is from OE **steogol* and similarly developed to *Steggle* and *Steckle*.

Stileman, Stillman: Robert *Stegelman* 1270 HPD (Ess); John *Stighelman* 1327 SRSx; John *Stileman* 1327 SR (Ess). Identical in meaning with STILE, STILL. cf. STYLER.

Still, Stille: (i) Aluuinus *Stilla* 1066 DB (Ha); Lefwinus *Stille* 1166 P (Sx); Richard *le Stille* 1275 SRWo. OE *stille* 'still, quiet'. (ii) John *atte Stille* 1327 SRWo, 1332 SRWa; Reginald *atte Stylle* 1333 MELS (So). This may be for STILE, with a shortened vowel, but there seems to have been an OE *stiell, still* 'place for catching fish' or 'trap for wild animals', found in Stildon (Worcs). Hence, a name for a fisherman or trapper. *v.* MELS 200.

Stiller: Identical in meaning with STILL (ii).

Stillman: *v.* STILEMAN, STILLER

Stimpson, Stimson, Stinson: Edward *Stynson* 1539 Bardsley (Nb); Daniel *Stimpson* 1674 HTSf. 'Son of *Stephen*.'

Stirk: William *Sturc, Stirc* 1202 AssL; Hugh *Stirc* 1208 P (Sf); Richard *Styrke* 1275 Wak (Y); Henry *Sterck* 1279 RH (C). OE *styrc* 'bullock'.

Stirrup, Stirrop, Sturrup: Rannulf *de Stirap* 1200 P (Nt); John *Stirapp* 1268 AssSo; Simon *Stirop* 1327 SRSx. From Styrrup (Notts). The Sussex and Somerset examples, without the preposition, suggest that this was also, at times, a name for a stirrup-maker.

Stirzaker, Sturzaker, Staziker, Stezaker: William *de Steresacre* 1332 SRLa; Thomas *Styrsaker* 1620 Oxon (Leic); Robert *Sturzaker* 1664 Bardsley (La). From Stirzacre (Lancs).

Stitch, Stych, Styche, Stitcher: Philip *Sticher* 1235 Fees (W); William *Steche* 1296 SRSx; John *Stiche* 1327 SRSf. *Steche, Stiche* are probably for *atte steche, atte stiche*, from OE *stycce* 'piece of land' found in Cambridgeshire and Essex field-names, and in Essex dialect meaning 'a ploughing land'. Hence, probably, a man who owned or cultivated a 'stitch' of land.

Stittle, Stuttle: Wluuin *Stettel* 1095 Bury (Sf); Ralph *Stuttel* 1179 P (Nth); John *Stettel* 1319 SR (Ess). Probably, as suggested by Tengvik, an OE **styttel*, a diminutive formation from the Germanic stem **stu(t)-* 'to knock, strike against, push'. cf. dial *stot* 'a stupid, clumsy fellow', a likely nickname.

Stiven: *v.* STEPHEN

Stoakes, Stoaks: *v.* STOKES

Stoate: *v.* STOTT

Stobart, Stobbart: *v.* STUBBERT

Stobbe, Stobbs: *v.* STUBBE

Stock, Stocks, Stok: John *de la Stokke* 1225 AssSo; Roesia *atte Stocke* 1275 SRWo; William *atte Stokkes* 1310 LLB D (Herts); Rose *atte*

Stocke(s) 1316, 1325 FFEss. 'Dweller by the stump(s)' .or, in the singular, perhaps also 'by a foot-bridge', OE *stocc* 'stock, trunk or stump of a tree'.

Stockdale, Stockdill, Stogdale: Alan *de Stokdale* 1332 SRCu; William *de Stokdale* 1379 PTY. From Stockdale (Yorks, Cumb).

Stocken: Robert *Stokyn* 1327 SRSf. 'Dweller by the stumps', from the weak plural of *stocc*. cf. STOCK and Stocken in Inwardleigh (Devon). *v.* PN D 151.

Stocker: Richard, Elena *le Stocker* 1275 SRWo, 1276 RH (Bk). Identical in meaning with *atte stocke*. *v.* STOCK.

Stockfish: Roger *Stokfisshe* 1342 LLB F. Synonymous with Luke *le Stockfysmongere* 1293 AD ii (Mx). 'Seller of stockfish.'

Stockford: Robert *de Stokeford* 1246 AssLa. 'Dweller by a ford marked by a stump' (OE *stocc, ford*).

Stockill: Tomas *de Stochill'* 1212 Cur (Y); Baldewin *de Stokeld* 1222 ib. From Stockeld in Spofforth (Yorks).

Stockings: Edmund *del Stocking* 1279 RH (Bk). 'Dweller on ground cleared of stubbs' (OE **stoccing*).

Stockle, Stockleigh, Stockley, Stokeley, Stokely, Stokle: Pagan *de Stockleye* 1279 RH (O); Robert *de Stokele* 1296 SRSx. From Stockleigh or Stokeley, common place-names.

Stockman: Emma *Stokeman* 1279 RH (O); Roger *Stokman* 1327 SRC. Identical with *atte stocke*. *v.* STOCK, STOCKER.

Stocky: William *de Stochey* 1276 RH (L). From residence near an enclosure made with trunks and stumps (OE *stocc, (ge)hæg)*, as at Stockey in Meeth (Devon).

Stodart, Stoddard, Stoddart, Stodhart, Studart, Studdard, Studdeard, Studdert: Vlfus *Stodhyrda* 1195 P (Cu); Geoffrey *Stodhurd'* 1219 Cur (Nth); John *the Stodhirde* 1286 AssCh; Richard *le Stodehard* 1332 MEOT (Y); Thomas *Stoderd* 1481 FrY; John *Stodard* 1482 ib. OE *stōd* 'stud (of horses)' and *hierde* 'herd', 'servant in charge of a stud', 'horse-keeper' (1458 NED).

Stoffer, Stopher, Stopper: John *Stopper* 1471 GildY; Gyelles *Stofer* 1568 SRSf. A pet-form of *Christopher*.

Stogdale: *v.* STOCKDALE

Stogdon: Richard *de Stockdon'* 1274 RH (So); Robert *de Stokedon* 1281 PN D 415. From Stockadon (Devon) or residence by a 'hill with tree-stumps on it' (*stocc, dūn*).

Stokeley, Stokely, Stokle: *v.* STOCKLE

Stoker: Hugh *le Stoker* 1227 AssBeds. 'One who lived at Stoke', in this instance, Stoke Goldington (Bucks).

Stokes, Stooke, Stookes, Stoakes, Stoaks: Ricerus *de Stochas* 1084 GeldR (So); Cnut *de Stoch'* 1166 P (Db); William *Stoc* 1185 Templars (Wa); Ailwin *de Stokes* 1195 P (Nth). From Stoke (Som, Derby, Warwicks, Northants) or one of the other Stokes. Old forms vary between singular and plural.

Stokoe: Adam *de Stochowe* 1332 SRCu. From Stockhow (Cumb).

Stolerman: Robert *Stalwrthman* 1297 SRY. 'Sturdy, courageous man.' cf. STALLWOOD and STOLLERY.

Stollard: *v.* STALLARD

Stoller: Richard *le Stolere* 1343 LoPleas. A derivative of ME *stole* 'stole'. A maker or seller of stoles.

Stollery: Mrs, Michael *Stollery* 1674 HTSf, 1763 SfPR. Probably a dialectal pronunciation of STALLWORTHY, found in Suffolk in the 13th century.

Stolworthy: *v.* STALLWORTHY

Stonard: *v.* STANNARD

Stone, Stones: Robert *Ston* 1212 Cur (O); Roger *del ston* 1277 Ely (Sf); Robert *atte Stone* 1296 SRSx; Elias *atte Stonis* 1327 SRSf; John *in le Stones* 1332 SRSt; William *del stones* 1348 DbAS 36. 'Dweller by the stone(s) or rock(s)' or among the rocks. Walter *de Stanes* c1130 StCh came from Stone (Staffs) and Richard *de Stone* 1275 SRWo from Stone (Worcs). *v.* also ASTON.

Stoneage: Richard *de Stonhach* 1327 SR (Ess). From residence near a stone gate (OE *stān, hæcc*).

Stonebridge: Walter *de Stanbrugg* 1296 SRSx. 'Dweller by a stone bridge.'

Stoneham: *v.* STONHAM

Stonehewer, Stonier, Stanier, Stanyer: Walter *Stanhewer* 13th Kirkstall (Y); Thomas *Stonhewar* 1279 RH (O); John *Stonehewer* or *Stonier* 1605 Bardsley (Ch); Nathaniell *Stanyar* 1689 ib. OE *stān* and a derivative of *hēawan* 'to hew'. 'Stone-cutter, quarrier of stone.'

Stonehouse: Alexander *de Stonhuse* 1257 ArchC iii; Ranulf *del Stonhouse* 1332 SRSt; Henry *atte Stonhouse* 1359 MELS (Sr). From Stonehouse (Devon, Glos) or from residence at a stone house.

Stoneman: Richard *Staneman* 1327 SR (Ess). 'Dweller by the stone', or 'worker in stone', stone-mason. cf. STONEHEWER.

Stonestreet, Stanistreet, Stanistrete: Salomon *de Stonstret'* 1275 RH (K); Stephen *de Stonstred* 1276 RH (Berks); Elias *de Stonstrete* 1279 FFEss; Richard *atte Stanstrete* 1293 PN Sx 8. OE *stānstræt* 'a paved road', usually Roman. The Essex reference is to the Roman road to Colchester and that from Sussex to Stane Street.

Stoney: Amica *de Staneya* 1328 WhC (La) From residence near some gravelly low-lying land (OE *stān, ēg*).

Stonham, Stoneham: John *de Stanham* 1205 Pl (Sf); Roger *de Stonham* 1333 FFEss; John *Stoneham* 1525 SRSx. From Stonham (Suffolk), or Stoneham (Hants).

Stonhard, Stonner: *v.* STANNARD

Stonhill, Stonnill: *v.* STANHILL

Stonier: *v.* STONEHEWER

Stonor, Stoner, Stoners: John *de Stonore* 1323 CorNth; John *Stonere* 1376 *Ass* (Ess); Thomas *Stonor* 1472–3 FFSr. From Stonor (Oxon).

Stooke(s): *v.* STOKES

Stopford, Stopforth: Robert *de Stokeport* 1204 P (La); Thomas *Stoppforth* 1379 PTY; Henry *Stopford* 1669 FrY. The local pronunciation of Stockport (Ches).

Stopher: *v.* STOFFER

Stoppard, Stopard: For STOPFORD.

Stopper: John *Stopper* 1471 GildY. May be for either STOFFER or STOPFORD.

Storah: *v.* STORER

Stordy: *v.* STURDEE

Storer, Storah, Storrar, Storror, Storrow: William *le Estorur* 1309 Guisb (Y); Thomas *le Storer* 1332 SRCu; Adam *le Storour* 1357 AssSt; John *Storrer* 1501 GildY; William *Sturror* 1534 Black; Bessie *Storrar* 1732 ib. A derivative of ME *storen* 'to store', from OFr *estorer* 'to build, establish, furnish, stock', or of the corresponding noun ME *stor*, OFr *estor* 'store'. 'Storer', perhaps 'keeper or overseer of the provisions for a household' (1540 NED), or, as suggested by Bardsley, 'wool-storer, warehouseman'. In Scotland, the tenant of a sheep-farm was called a 'storemaster' and the *storour* had charge of the flocks and herds. For *Storah, Storrow*, cf. FARRAR and FARROW.

Storey, Storie, Story, Storrie, Storry: *Stori, Estori* 1066 DB; *Storicus de Wycham* 1132–60 Miller (C); Reginaldus *filius Story* 1219 AssY; Alexander *Story* 1248 FFEss; William *Stori* 1281 Black (Dundee). ON *Stóri*.

Stork: Osbert *Storc* 1198 P (K); Hugo *Stork* 1229 Pat (L); Robert *le Stork'* 1280 AssSo. OE *storc* 'stork', a nickname for a man with long legs.

Storm, Stormes, Storms: William, John *Storm* 1206 Cur (Nf), 1297 MinAcctCo (Y). OE *storm* 'storm'. cf. TEMPEST.

Storr: Geoffrey, John *Stor* 1200 P (Nf), 1290 LLB A. ON *stórr* 'big'.

Storrar, Storror, Storrow: *v.* STORER

Storrie, Storry: *v.* STOREY

Storrs: Matthew *de Stordes*, Robert *de Storthes*, Henry *del Storres* 1275, 1284, 1316 Wak (Y); Anthony *Storres* 1564 ShefA. 'Dweller by the brushwood or young plantation' (ON *storð*), as at Storrs (La) and High Storrs (Sheffield).

Story: *v.* STOREY

Stote: *v.* STOTT

Stothard, Stothart, Stothert, Stuttard: William *Stothard* 1279 RH (C); John *le Stothirde* 1297 SRY; Thomas *le Stothurd* 1306 AssSt; John *Stotard* 1317 AssK; Thomas *le Stotherd* 1327 SRSa. OE *stott* 'an inferior kind of horse', in ME also 'steer, bullock', and *hierde*, 'keeper of horses or bullocks' or 'oxherd'.

Stott, Stote, Stoat: Gamel *Stot* 1166 P (Y); John *Stotte* 1296 SRSx; Elena *la Stott* 1312 ColchCt. ME *stott* 'bullock'. cf. Agnes *Stotwylde* 1436 NorwW, perhaps 'wild as a young bullock'.

Stout, Stoute, Stoutt, Stutt: (i) Osbert *Stute, Stutte* 1190–1 P (Y); William *Stutte, Stute, le Estut, Stut* 1219 AssL, 1221 AssWo; William *Estoute* 1327 SRSx; Adam *Stout* 1373 ColchCt.

OE *stūt* 'gnat' or ME *stout*, from OFr *estolt*, *estout* 'stout, bold'. (ii) Henry *atte Stoute* 1330 PN D 652. Henry lived at Stout Fm in Yarcombe (Devon). 'Dweller by the rounded hill', OE **stūt*.

Stow, Stowe: Wlnoþus *de Stoue* c975 LibEl (C); Osbert *de Stowa* 1190 P (C); William *de la Stowe* 1315 MELS (Wo). From one of the many Stows. In Worcestershire, OE *stōw* 'place, holy place' was still in use in ME, and here the surname is probably 'dweller by the monastery or church'. *v.* MELS 203.

Stoyle, Stoyles: William *Stoile* 1194 P (Db); Eliot *Stoyle* 1210 Cur (K). ME *stoyle*, OFr *estoile* 'star'.

Strachan, Straghan, Strahan, Straughan: Waldevus *de Stratheihan* c1200 Black; David *Straughin* 1512 ib. From Strachan (Kincardineshire).

Strafford: Athelstan *de Straford* 1210 Cur (Bk). A variant of STRATFORD.

Straight: Godwin *Streit* 1203 FFL; Richard *Streht* Hy 3 AD i (Wo). ME *streȝt* 'not crooked, upright', probably 'erect'.

Strainge: *v.* STRANGE

Straker: Robert *le Straker* 1246 AssLa; Robert *Stracour* 1332 SRCu; William *Strakour* 1327 SRY. A derivative of ME *strake*, from OE *strācian* 'to stroke', related to OE *strīcan*, hence a variant of *Striker*. *v.* STRIKE.

Stranders: Ralph *Stronder*, John *atte*, *del Stronde* 1327 SRSf, SR (Ess). 'Dweller by the strand or shore', OE *strand*.

Strang: *v.* STRONG

Strange, Strainge, L'Estrange, Lestrange: John *Lestrange*, *Leestrange*, 1192 P (Nf), 1195 FFNf; Ralph *le Estrange* 1199 CurR (Sf); Hugh *le Strange* 1221 AssSa; Fulco *Strange* 1221 ElyA (C). ME *strange*, OFr *estrange* 'foreign', stranger, newcomer.

Strangeway, Strangeways, Strangways, Strangwick: James *Strangwishe*, *Strangwych*, *Strangwesh*, c1450, 1467, 1489 GildY; Anna *Strangwish* 1501 ib.; Richard *Strangeways* 1513 ib.; Martin *Strangways* 1527 ib. From Strangeways (Lancs).

Strangman, Strongman: *Strangman* c1095 Bury (Sf); Robert, John *Strangman* 1327 SRSf, SR (Ess). OE **Strangmann* 'strong, bold man'.

Stratford: Robert *de Stratford* 1086 DB (Sf). From one of the Stratfords.

Stratton: Richard *de Stratton* 1199 Pl (Do); Peter *de Stratton'* 1228 Cur (Beds); John *Stratton* 1366 IpmGl. From one or other of the many places of this name. Mainly southern.

Straughan: *v.* STRACHAN

Streake, Streek: Godwin, Walter *Streke* 1176 P (Sr), 1275 SRWo. OE *stræc, strec* 'strong, violent'.

Stream, Streamer: Henry *ate Streme* 1279 RH (O). 'Dweller by the stream.'

Streat: *v.* STREET

Streater: *v.* STREETER

Streek: *v.* STREAKE

Street, Streete, Streets, Streat: Modbert *de Strete* c1100–30 OEByn (D); Roger *Stret* 1197 P

(Nf); William *de la Stret'* 1228 Cl (D); Richard *del Strete* 1275 AssSo; Adam *of the Strete* 1284 AssLa; Reginald *atte Strete* 1309 LLB D. OE *strǣt* 'street, Roman road'. From Street (Hereford, Kent, Som), all of which are on or near Roman roads, or local, from residence in the village street as opposed, say, to the village green, or in a hamlet, called in some parts of the country a street.

Streeten, Streetin: Roger *de la Stratend* 1261–72 MELS (Sr), *de la Stretende* 1262 ib. (Sx); John *Strethende* 1296 SRSx; Robert *ate Stretende* 1297 MinAcctCo. 'Dweller at the end of the street.' cf. STREET.

Streeter, Streater: John *Streter* 1332 SRSx. Identical in meaning with *atte Strete*. *v.* STREET.

Streit: Roger *Streit* 1367 ColchCt. ME *streit*, AFr *estreit* 'narrow, strict'.

Stretch: Richard *Estrech'*, *le Strech'* 1176 P (Wo), 1221 AssWo; Adam *Strecche* 1210 P (Ha). OE *stræc, strec* 'strong, violent'.

Stretton, Stretten: Hervey *de Strettona* c1165 StCh; Hugh, Robert *de Stretton'* 1230 Cur (Nt), 1327 SRLei; John *Stretton* 1421 IpmY. From one or other of the many places of this name. Usually northern or midland.

Stribling: *v.* STRIPLING

Strickland: Vchtred *de Stirclanda* 1193 P (We); William *de Strikeland* 1278 IpmWe; Walter *Strykland* 1442 AssLo. From Strickland (Westmorland).

Strike, Striker: Nicholas *Stryke* 1296 SRSx; Reginald *le Strikere* 1297 Coram (L); Thomas *Strikere* 1360 FFSf. One of the clauses of Magna Carta provided that there should be one measure of corn, namely the London quarter. Local custom, however, was stronger than national law and there was a constant struggle between law and custom over the bushel and quarter. By statute the quarter should contain 8 bushels, each of 8 gallons, 'rased' or 'striked', that is to say, filled and levelled with the brim of the measure by passing a flat stick, or 'strike', over it. By custom, however, the quarter consisted of 8 'heaped' bushels, which were equivalent to 9 'striked'; and when this was prohibited the corn-dealers got round this prohibition by a measure of 9 striked bushels, which they called a 'fat' or 'vat' (METrade 43–47). The official responsible for the accuracy of the measure was clearly called a 'striker' and was sometimes named from the instrument he used.

String: William, Henry *Streng* 1177 P (Sa), 1275 RH (Sf). Metonymic for STRINGER.

Stringer: Walter *Stringere* 1194 Cur (W); Roger *le Strenger* 1293 MESO (Y). Derivative of OE *streng* 'string, cord', maker of strings for bows, a stringer (1420 NED), a common Yorkshire name.

Stringfellow: William *Strengfellow* 1286 AssCh; John *le Strengfelagh* 1308 Wak (Y); John *Stryngfelowe* 1489 Calv (Y). ME *streng* and OE *fēolaga*, ON *félagi* 'partner, fellow'. cf. the rare OE *strenge* 'severe'; *strenghefully* 'with might or power' 13.. NED. But *streng* may be for *strang* 'strong', with *e* on the analogy of the comparative *strengra* and OE *strengu*, ME *strenge* 'strength'.

Stripling, Strippling, Stribling, Stribbling: Symon *Stripling* 1259 RamsCt (Hu); William *Strupelynge* 1296 SRSx. ME *stryplynge* 'a youth' (1398 NED).

Strode, Strood, Stroud: Aluina *de Strodes* 1206 FFK; Thomas *de la Strode*, William *Strodde* 1230 P (D); William *atte Strode* 1275 SRWo; Edytha *atte Stroude* 1327 SRSo. 'Dweller by the marshy ground' (OE *strōd*) as at Strood (Kent) or Stroud (Glos).

Strong, Stronge, Strang: Richard *Stronge* 1185 Templars (Wa); Ralph *le Esstrang* 1228 FFSf; William *le Stronge* 1276 AssSo; Adam *Strang* 1379 PTY. OE *strang*, ME *strong* 'strong'. *Strang* was preserved in the north.

Strongitharm: John *Strongharme* 1379 FrLeic; Roger *Strongeitharme* 1581 Bardsley (Ch); Richard *Stronge in Arme* 1597 ib. Self-explanatory.

Strongman: *v.* STRANGMAN

Stroud: *v.* STRODE

Strumanger, Struminger: Thomas *le Strumonger* 1285 Oseney (O); Richard *straumongere* 1294 MEOT (Herts). OE *strēaw* and *mangere*, 'dealer in straw'.

Stuart: *v.* STEWARD

Stubbe, Stubbs, Stobbe, Stobbs: (i) Ælfeah *Stybb* c1000 OEByn; Richard *Stubbe* 1185 Templars (Y); William *Stob* 1332 SRSx. OE *stybb* 'stub', a nickname for one of short, stumpy stature. (ii) Geoffrey *de Stubbes* 1199 P (Nf); Robert *del Stobbes* 1288 AssCh; Thomas *de la Stubbe* 1296 SRSx; Richard *ate Stubbe* 1327 ib. 'Dweller by the tree-stump(s)', OE *stubb*.

Stubber: Jordan *Stubbere* 1181–91 StP (Lo); William *le Stubber* 1327 SRSx; William *Stubber* 1393 FFEss. A derivative of ME *stubben* 'to dig up by the roots', OE *stubb* 'tree-stump'. Hence 'one who grubs up roots or removes stumps from the ground'.

Stubbert, Stobbart, Stobart: *Stubart* 1066 DB (Sf); *Stubhard* Pape c1095 Bury (Sf); Simon *filius Stubbard'* 1203 Cur (Nf); Symon *Stubard* 1275 RH (Nf); Richard *Stobard* 1336 ColchCt. OE *Stubheard, a late formation.

Stubbing, Stubbings, Stubbins: (i) William, Astin *Stubbing'* 1191 P (Nf), 1219 AssY; Richard *Stubin* 1279 RH (O). OE *stybbing 'the stumpy one'. *v.* STUBBE. (ii) Richard *del Stubbyng'* 1297 Min-AcctCo. 'Dweller by the cleared land', ME *stubbing*.

Stubley, Stubbeley, Stubbley: William *de Stublegh* 1239–40 FFEss; William *de Stubleye* 1313 FFEss; John *Stubliegh* 1385 FFEss. From an unidentified minor place, presumably in Essex.

Studd, Studds: Alnod *Stud* 1066 DB; William *Studd* 1296 SRSx; Peter *Stud* 1334–5 SRK; John *Studde* 1540 FFEss. Probably a nickname, and Tengvik (OEByn 367) suggests OE *stūt* 'gnat', with the *d* due to AN influence. A personal name is also possible, cf. OE *Stūt*, ON *Stútr*, while Walter *de la Stud'* 1231 Cur (Sr) may have taken his name from OE *styde*, a by-form of *stede* 'site of a building, a farm'.

Studdard, Studdeard, Studdert: *v.* STODART

Studdy: Hamo *de Stodhag'* 1210 Cur (Y); Roger *Stody* 1275 SRWo. From Studdah in Fingal (Yorks), Stodday (Lancs), Stody (Norfolk), pronounced *Studdy*, or residence near, or employment at an enclosure for horses (OE *stōd*, (*ge*)*hæg*).

Studman: Walter, Adam *Stodman* 1297 MinAcctCo, 1332 SRCu. OE *stōd, mann* 'one employed at the stud'.

Stukeley, Stukely: Nicholas *de Stiuecle* 1198 Pl (Hu); Geoffrey *de Stiuecleg'* 1224 FFO; Thomas *Stukele* 1296 SRSx; George *Stukeley* 1642 PrD. Usually from Stukeley (Hunts), *Stivecle* DB, but occasionally from Stewkley (Bucks), *Stiuecelea* 1183.

Stumbles: Gervase *atte Stumble* 1296 SRSx; Juliana *Stumbel* 1311 ColchCt. 'Dweller by the tree-stump' (OE **stumbel*). *v.* MELS 205 and cf. Richard *Stombelere* 1327 SR (Ess). *v.* BRIDGER and p. xv.

Stump: Martin, William *Stumpe* 1332 SRSx; Henry *Stompe, Stoompe* 1373 ColchCt. 'Dweller by the stump' (ME *atte stumpe*).

Stunt: Simon *Stunt* 1230 Pat. OE *stunt* 'foolish'.

Sturdee, Sturdy, Stordy: Richard *Estordet, Estordit* 1084 GeldR (W); Hugo *Sturdy* 1219 AssY; *Sturdi* 1230 P (Y); Geoffrey *Sturdy, Sturdi* 1220 Oseney, Oriel (O). OFr *estordet, estordit*, identical with *estourdi, estordi, esturdi* 'reckless, violent'; in ME 'impetuously brave, fierce in combat' (1297 NED).

Sturdevant: *v.* STARTIFANT

Sturge, Sturges, Sturgess, Sturgis, Turgoose: Hugo *filius Turgisi* 1086 DB (Sa); *Turgis* Hy 2 DC (L); *Thurgis* filius *Owani* 1221 AssWa; Henry *Turgis* 1210 P (W); Adam *Thurgis* 1279 RH (Beds); John *Sturgys* 1353 FFC; Joan *Sturge* 1379 ColchCt; Richard *Sturges* 1481 LLB L; John *Turgos* 1524 SRSf. ON *Þorgils*, ODa, OSw *Thorgisl*. 'Thor's hostage.' cf. SPASHETT and Scaldhurst, earlier *Caldhous* (PN Ess 180).

Sturgeon: William *Sturjon* 1281 Ipm (Cu); Richard *Sturioun* (*Storioun*) 1327 SR (Ess); William *Sturgeon* 1380 LLB H. A nickname from the fish, OFr *esturgeon*.

Sturman: (i) Hugolinus, Stefanus *Stirman* 1066 DB (Berks, Ha, Wa); Turchil *Stirman Regis* E(dwardi) 1066 DB (Wa); Matildis uxor *Sturmanni* 1179 P (Sf). ODa *styreman* 'steersman', probably also 'captain, master of a ship'. Edricus *Stirman Regis Edwardi* (1066 DB), called also *Rector navis*, was the commander of the sea and land forces of the Bishop of Worcester in the service of Edward the Confessor (PNDB). The term was also used as a personal name and has, no doubt, been confused with STARMAN. (ii) William, Robert *Sturmyn* 1327 SRC, SRSf; John, Thomas *Stormyn* 1327 SRSf. This is probably **Sturmin*, a diminutive in *-in* of *Sturmi*. *v.* STURMEY.

Sturmey: *Sturmidus de Cotenham* 1086 InqEl (C); *Sturmi* Hy 2 DC (L); *Sturmy de Straton'* 1201 Cur (So); Richard *Estormid, Estormit* 1084 GeldR (W); Richard *Sturmid, Sturmi* 1086 DB (Sr, Ha); Ralph *Turmit* 1086 DB (Nf); John,

Richard *Esturmit* 1130 P (W, Sf); Henry *Esturmi* 1158 P (W); Hugo *Sturmi* 1192 P (Berks); Roger *Esturmy*, le *Esturmi*, le *Sturmy* 1236, 1242 Fees (Sf); Richard *Stormy* 1296 SRSx. We have clearly two different origins here, (i) a personal-name, OFr **Estourmi*, OG *Sturmi*, and (ii) OFr *estormi*, 'étourdi, troublé, accablé' (Godefroy). cf. STURDEE.

Sturrock: Robert *Stourok* 1275 RH (K); Walter *de Stonrok* 1283 LLB A; John *Stonrok* 1327 SRSx; Roger *ate Staurokk'* 1332 SRSr. 'Dweller by the high rock' (OE *stānrocc*), as at Stonyrock in Effingham (Surrey), the home of Henry *de la Stanrok* in 1241 (PN Sr 103) or at Starrock Green in Chipstead (Rocius *de Stonrocke* 1265 ib. 291).

Sturrup: *v.* STIRRUP

Sturt: *v.* START

Sturtevant, Sturtivant: *v.* STARTIFANT

Sturzaker: *v.* STIRZAKER

Stutfield: Rotbert *de Stutteuile* 1106 ASC E; Ralph *Stutville* 1260 AssC. From Estouteville or Étoutteville (Seine-Inférieure).

Stutt: *v.* STOUT

Stuttard: *v.* STOTHARD

Stutter, Stutters: Thomas *Stotere* 1327 SRSf. A derivative of ME *stut(te)*, *stoten* 'to stutter'. 'Stutterer.'

Stuttle: *v.* STITTLE

Styan, Styance, Styants: Robertus *filius Stiand* 1230 P (Wa); Nicholas *Stiant* 1275 RH (W); John *Stion* 1712 FrY. An anglicizing of ON *Stigandr*. *v.* STIGAND.

Styche: *v.* STITCH

Styer: William *Styers* 1674 HTSf. 'One employed at the stye', a pig-herd (OE *stig(u)* 'stye') or 'dweller by the path' (OE *stīg* 'path'). cf. Roger *ate Stye* 1297 MinAcctCo.

Stygall: *v.* STILE

Styler: William *le stygheler* 1332 SRSr; Roger *Stylere* 1428 FA (Sx). Equivalent to STILEMAN.

Styles: *v.* STILE

Suart: *v.* SEWARD

Such, Sutch, Souch, Zouch, Chuck, Chucks: Alan *de Lachuche*, *la Zuche*, *de la Zuche* 1172, 1177, 1198 P (Nth, Sx); Roger *la Zuche*, *de la Suche*, *de la Soche* 1212 Fees (D), 1275 RH (D); Alan *La Sutche* 1243 AssSo; Roger *Suche* 1275 RH (W); Walter *le Chuck* 1296 SRSx; William *la Zouche*, *de la Souche* 1316 FA (Wa, Sx); Roger *Souche* 1316 FA (Lei). OFr *souche* 'tree-stump', identical in meaning with the English STUMP. The name may have been brought from some small French place named La Souche. cf. Ashby de la Zouch (Leics), held by Roger de la Zuche in 1200 (FF). *Chuck* is from the Norman-Picard form *chouque*.

Sucker: Thomas *le Sukkere* 1277 Ely (Sf); William *Souker* 1301 SRY. A derivative of OE *sūcan* 'to suck', a sucker, probably, as suggested by Fransson, 'a blood-letter'.

Suckling: John *Sokeling* 1195 P (Berks); Richard *Sukeling* 1253 Oseney (O); Mabilia *Sucling* 1283 SRSf. A double diminutive from OE *sūcan* 'to suck'. 'Suckling', a nickname.

Sudbury, Sudberry, Sudbery: Hugh *de Suthberia* 1159 P; John *de Sudbury* 1359 IpmW; Henry *Sudbury* 1367 AssLo. From Sudbury (Derby, Middlesex, Suffolk).

Suddaby: *v.* SOTHEBY

Suddell, Sudell: Robert *de Sudale*, *de Suthdale* 1201–2 FFNf. 'Dweller in the south dale' (OE *sūð, dæl*).

Sudran, Sudron: *v.* SOTHERAN

Suett: *Siuuat(e)* 1066 DB (L, O); Gilbertus *filius Siwat'* 1180–1218 Rams (Hu); *Sygwat* Radbode 1275 RH (Nf); Gilbert *Siwate* 13th Rams (Hu); Geoffrey *Sewhat* (*Suat*) 1300 LoCt; John, Simon *Suet* 1327 SRDb; Richard *Sewet* 1568 SRSf. ON *Sighvatr*, OSw *Sighwat*. *Siuuate* reflects ON **Sighvati*.

Suffield, Suffell, Suffill: William *de Sudfeld'* 1191 P (Nf); Nicholas *de Sudfeld* 1208 P (Y); Roger *de Suffeld'* 1225 Cur (Nf). From Suffield (Norfolk, NRYorks).

Suffolk: Alexander, Edmund *de Suffolk* 1254–5 FFEss, 1301 CorLo; John *de Suthfolke* 1317 Glast (So). 'The man from Suffolk.'

Sugden, Sugdon: Adam *de Suggedone* 1327 SRSa; William *de Sugden* 1362 FFY; Richard *Sugden* 1672 HTY. From Sugden (WRYorks).

Sugg: Wadnod, Richard *Sugge* 1185 P (Ha), 1196–1237 Colch (Sf). OE *sucga*, ME *sugge* 'a bird', perhaps for *hegessugge* 'hedge-sparrow'.

Suggate, Suggett, Suggitt: *v.* SOUTHGATE

Sullivan: *v.* O'SULLIVAN

Sultan: *v.* SOWDEN

Sumeray, Sumray, Sumrie: Roger *de Sumeri* 1086 DB (Ess); Adam *de Sumeri* 1160 P (C); Walter *Somery* 1296 SRSx. From Sommery (Seine-Inférieure).

Summarsell: *v.* SUMMERSALL

Summer, Summers, Sommer, Sommers, Somer, Somers: Adam, Geoffrey *Sumer* 1203, 1205 P (Ess, O); William *Somer* 1275 SRWo, 1295 Barnwell (C); Isabella *Somerys* 1327 SRSo. A personal-name **Sumor* is the first element of Somersall (Db), Somersham (Sf), and, possibly, of Somersham (Hu), but it is unrecorded and there is no evidence for the use of such a personal name in DB or later. Christmas, Noel, Pentecost, etc., are specific times suitable for the commemoration of a birth, but that can hardly be said of a season like summer. These earlier explanations must, therefore, be rejected. The surname is probably identical with the Scottish SIMMER. In Scots, *somer* is 'a sumpter', applied to men and horses alike. Dauzat explains the French *Sommier* 'bete de sommer' as 'a muleteer'. The English name is probably also from OFr *somier* 'sumpter'. Alice *at Someres* 1327 SRSx must be a parallel to *Vickers* and *Parsons*, 'servant at the sumpter's'.

Summerlad, Sommerlat: *Sumerlet*, *Summerled(e)* 1066 DB (D, Sf, Hu, L); Adam *filius Sumerlad'* 1198 P (Y); Richard, Robert *Sumerlede* 1184 Gage, 1188 BuryS (Sf). ON *Sumarliðr*, *Sumarliði* 'summer warrior'. The personal-name was common in Scotland where it became Gaelic *Somhairle* and was corrupted by the chroniclers to *Sorli Marlady*, etc., whence the Scottish surnames *Sorley* and *M'Sorley*. *v.* Black.

Summerland: Adam *filius Sumerland* 1200 P (Y). An early corruption of SUMMERLAD.

Summersall, Summersell, Summarsell: Jacobus *de Sumereshal'* 1200 Cur (Herts); William *de Somersale* 1316 AssSt. From Somersall (Derby), or from *Somersale*, the old name of Hyde Hall in Sandon (PN Herts 165).

Summerscale, Summerscales, Summersgill, Summerskill, Somerscales: John *de Somerscale(s)* 1379 PTY; John *Summersgill* 1803 Bardsley. 'Herdsman at the summer-huts' (ON *sumar, skáli*).

Summersett: *v.* SOMERSET

Summerville: *v.* SOMERVELL

Sumner, Sumpner, Somner, Simner, Simnor: Robert *le Sumonur* 1199 Cur (Lei); Matthew *le Sumener* 1230 Pat (K); William *le Sumnir* 1279 AssSo; John *Somnour* 1327 SRC; William *Sumpnour* 1420 MEOT (La). AFr *somenour, sumenour*, OFr *somoneor, semoneor* 'summoner', a petty officer who cites and warns persons to appear in court (c1325 NED). For *Simner*, cf. SIMMER and SUMMER.

Sumpter, Sunter: Roger *le Summeter* 1206 Cur (Bk); William *le Sumeter* 1221 AssGl, AssWo; William *Sompter*, Alan *Sumpter* 1301 SRY. OFr *sometier, sommetier* 'driver of a pack-horse' (c1320 NED).

Sumray, Sumrie: *v.* SUMERAY

Sunman: *Suneman* 1066 DB (Sf, Y); Estmundus *filius Suneman* 1202 FFNf; Hugo *Suneman* 1200 P (Nf); William, Roger *Soneman* 1275, 1279 RH (Sf, C). Forssner and von Feilitzen take this to be OG *Suneman*. Late compounds of *-mann* are common in the eastern counties and *Sunnmann*, *Sunngifu* (f), and *Sunnwine*, all found in the same area, are probably native compounds of OE *Sunna* found in Sonning (Berks). cf. Robert *Sungyve* 1279 RH (C), *Sunuuinus* 1066 DB (Sf), Simon *Sonewyne* 1326 SRSf.

Sunter: *v.* SUMPTER

Surgenor, Surgeoner: William Rydale, *surgener* 1422 FrY; John *Sudgener* 1580 LaWills; Robert *Suggener* or *Sojourner* 1676 LaWills. A late, extended form of AFr *surgien* 'surgeon'. The surname-forms are late and dialectal, showing loss of r. The 1676 *Sojourner* is probably a dialectal pronunciation, but such a surname is possible. cf. Walter *Soiournaunt* 1377 AddCh (Ess).

Surgeon: Thomas *le Surigien* 1255 *Ass* (Ess); Robert *le Surgien* 1279 RH (C). AFr *surgien*, *sur(r)igien* 'surgeon' (13.. NED).

Surgerman: 'Servant of the surgeon', from OFr *surgier*, a rare by-form of *surgien* 'surgeon'. cf. Thomas Warde, *surgeour* 1487 FrY.

Surgison: *v.* SARGEANTSON

Surkett: *v.* CIRCUITT

Surr: *v.* SIRE

Surrell: *v.* SIRDIFIELD

Surrey, Surry: John *de Surreye* 1274 RH (O).

'The man from Surrey', cf. Henry, Roger *le Surreis* 1208 Pl (Y), 1231 Cur (He).

Surridge, Surrage: (i) Robert *Surrais* 1143–7 DC (L); Geoffrey *le Surreys* 1219 AssY. OFr *surreis* 'southerner'. *v.* also SEARCH. (ii) Ambrose *Surradge*, 1580 DWills; Robert *Surridge* 1609 ib.; Edward *Surredge* 1625 ib. From Surridge in Morebath (Devon).

Surtees: Randulf *de Super Teise* 1174 P (Nb); Ricardus *super Teisam* 1195 P (Nb); Ralph *de Supertay* 1230 P (Nb); Ralph *sur teyse* 1243 AssDu; Nicholas *de Surteys* 1315 Riev (Y). The forms vary between 'dweller by the Tees' and 'dweller at a place called Surtees'. cf. William *Overswale* 1301 SRY.

Susan: *Susanna* 1194 CurR (Sf); *Susanna Agnell'* 1206 Cur (Berks); William *Susann'* 1279 RH (O); Eustace *Susanne* 1327 SRSf. Hebrew *Shushannah* 'lily'. Not a common medieval name.

Sussams: Philip *Susson* 1327 SRSf; John *Sussoun* ib.; Samuel *Sussum* 1674 HTSf. *Susan*, with a short vowel and the common change of final *n* to *m*.

Sussands: John *Sussaunt* 1524 SRSf. *Susan*, with shortened vowel and an excrescent *t* or *d*.

Sutch: *v.* SUCH

Sutcliff, Sutcliffe: Hugo *de Suthclif* 1274 Wak (Y); Elyzabeth *Sutlyff* 1566 RothwellPR (Y). 'Dweller by the south cliff', a common Yorkshire name.

Suter: *v.* SOUTAR

Sutherby: *v.* SOTHEBY

Sutherin, Suthern(s), Suthren: *v.* SOTHERAN

Sutherland, Sutherlan, Southerland: David *de Sothirlandae* 1332 Black; Richard *Sutherlond* 1342 LoPleas; Alexander *Sutherland* 1441 Black. 'The man from Sutherland.'

Sutor: *v.* SOUTAR

Suttle, Suttill: Adam *le Sutel* 1275 RH (Lo); Reginald *Sutel* 1279 RH (O). AFr *sotil* 'subtle, clever, cunning'. *v.* also SOOTHILL.

Sutton: Ketel *de Sudtone, Suttune* 1086 DB (L); Alnod *Suttuna* 1086 InqEl (C). From Sutton (Cambs, Lincs, Kent, Suff, Som). *v.* also SINTON.

Swaffer, Swoffer: Robert *Swoffer, Swoffa* 1518 CantW, KentW; John *Swaffer* 1523 CantW; Robert *Swafford* 1549 ib. From Swatfield Bridge in Willesborough (Kent), *Swatford* 1254.

Swain, Swaine, Swayn, Swayne: (i) *Suein, Suen, Suuain, Suan, Suuan* 1066 DB; Eduuardus *filius Suani* 1066 DB (Mx, Ess); *Swein* de Hecham 1175–86 Holme (Nf); Robertus *filius Swain* 1219 AssY; Osgot *Sveyn* 1045 ASWills (C); Robert *Suein* 1166 P (Y); Walter *Swayn* 1295 FFSf. ON *Sveinn*, ODa, OSw *Sven*, often anglicized as *Swan*. cf. *Suanus carpentarius*, called also *Swein* carpentarius 1221 AssWa, and *v.* SWAN. (ii) Walter *le Swein* 1221 AssWo; James *le Swayn* 1300 LLB C. ON *sveinn* 'boy, servant', used also of a swineherd, a peasant.

Swainson: Thomas *Swaynson* 1332 SRCu. 'Son of *Sveinn* or of the swain.'

Swallow: (i) William *Sualewe, Swalewe* 1205 Cur (Y), 1275 SRWo. OE *swealwe* 'a swallow'. (ii)

Thomas *de Sualewe* 1175 P (L). From Swallow (Lincs).

Swan, Swann: (i) *Suannus* faber 1177 P (Cu); *Suan'* filius Arkill' 1219 AssY; Hugo *Suan* 1176 P (Sf); John *Swann'* 1221 AssSa; Gilbert *Swan* 1260 AssC; Thomas *le Swan*, John *le Swon* 1327 SRSf; Walter *le Swon*, Stephen *le Swan* 1296 SRSx. With the article, this may be either OE *swān* 'herdsman, swineherd, peasant', which became ME *swon*, or a nickname from OE *swan, swon* 'swan'. Without the article, these cannot be distinguished from OE *Swan*, an anglicizing of ON *Sveinn*. cf. SWAIN. (ii) Godfrey *atte Swan* 1344 LoPleas; Thomas *atte Swan* 1364 LLB G. From the sign of the Swan.

Swannack: *v.* SWANNICK

Swannell, Swonnell: *Swanild(a)* 1201 AssSo, 1221 AssSa; *Swanhild* de Herteford 1227 AssBk; John *Swonild* 1247 AssBeds, 1277 *Ely* (C); Ralph *Swanyld* 1332 SRSt. From the ON woman's name *Svanhildr*.

Swannick, Swannack: John, William *Swaneke* 1279 RH (C). Probably 'swan-neck'. cf. Edgyue *Suanneshals* 1066–86 OEByn. The surname is, no doubt, usually from Swanwick (Derby, Hants).

Swanton: Ralph *de Suaneton* 1204 P (K); Walter *de Suanton* 1283 SRSf; John *Swanton* 1373 AssLo. From Swanton (Kent, Norfolk).

Swart: Suenus, Mannius *Suart* 1066 DB (Sf); Walter *Swart* 1219 AssY; John *le Swart* 1285 LLB A. ON *svartr*, OE *sweart* 'swarthy'.

Swatman: *v.* SWEATMAN

Swatridge, Swattridge: Adam, William *Swetrich* 1309 SRBeds. OE **Swētrīc* 'sweet-ruler'.

Swears: (i) Ralph, Hugh *Swere* 1208 FFEss, 1225 AssSo. OE *swēora* 'neck', a nickname. (ii) Robert *atte Swer'* 1327 SRSx. 'Dweller by the neck of land', as at The Swares or Swear Fm (Sussex).

Sweatman, Sweetman, Swetman, Swatman: *Suetman* 1066 DB (Nf); *Suetman* Kempe 1169 P (Bk); *Swetmannus* ate Optone 1327 SRSx; Eche *Suetman* 1134–40 Holme (Nf); Robert *Sweteman* 1222 FFSf; Thomas *Swatman* 1524 SRSf. OE *Swētmann* 'sweet man'.

Sweet, Sweett: *Suet, Suot* 1066 DB (D), Winton (Ha); Æluric *Suete* filius c1095 Bury (Sf); *Swet* carbonel 1292 SRLo; Wimund *Svote* 1179–94 Seals (Beds); Adam *Swet* 1211 Cur (Wo); Richard *Swote* 1313 LLB B; William *le Swete* 1327 SRSx. OE *Swēt, Swēta* (m), *Swēte* (f) 'sweet', or a nickname, OE *swēte, swōt* 'sweet'.

Sweetapple: Henry *Suetappil* 1259 CtSt; Ralph *Swetappul* 1309 SRBeds. Apparently a nickname.

Sweeting: *Sueting* Cadica 1135 Oseney (O); *Sweting* de Hunebir' 1225 AssSo; Ralph *Suetinge* 1185 Templars (Herts); John *Sweting'* 1250 Fees (W). OE *Swēting*.

Sweetlove: *Swetelove* 1279 RH (C); William *Sueteluue* 1197 P (Y); Margeria *Swetelove* 1279 RH (C). OE **Swētlufu* (f) 'sweet-love'.

Swetman: *v.* SWEATMAN

Sweetnam, Swetenham, Swettenham: Richard

de Swetenham 1278 AssSt. From Swettenham (Ches).

Sweetser, Sweetsur, Sweetzer, Switsur, Switzer: Robert *Swetesire* 1355 Cl (Beds); Richard *Swetesyr* 1467 RochW; Denys *Swetesyre* 1498 RochW; Richard *Sweytsyer, Sweetser* 1553 ib., 1584 Bardsley. 'Sweet sire.' *v.* SIRE.

Swepstone, Swepson: Ralph *de Suepiston* 1199 FrLeic. From Swepstone (Leics).

Swetenham: *v.* SWEETNAM

Swetman: *v.* SWEATMAN

Swiers: *v.* SWIRE

Swift: *Suift* 1166 P (Nf); Nicholaus filius *Swift* 1222 Cur (Sf); William *Swift* 1167 P (Ha), 1219 AssY. OE *swift* 'swift, fleet', used also as a personal-name.

Swinburn, Swinburne, Swinbourn, Swinbourne: John *de Swynburn* 1256 AssNb; Robert *de Swynebourne* 1325 IpmGl; Robert *Swynbourn* 1382 FFEss; Widow *Swingbourne* 1662 HTEss. From Swinburn (Northumb), or 'dweller by the pig brook'.

Swinerd, Swinnard: Adam *Swynherde* 1327 SRSx; Walter *le Swynhurde* 1327 SRWo; Robert *le Swynerde* 1332 MEOT (Nf). Late OE *swīnhyrde* 'swineherd'.

Swinford: Geoffrey *de Suinford* 1190 P (Lei); William *de Suyneford* 1250 FFL; Roger *de Swyneford* 1332 SRWa. From Swinford (Berks, Leics), Kingswinford (Staffs), or Old Swinford (Worcs).

Swinnerton, Swynnerton: Ralph *de Suinerton* 1185 P (Sf); Robert *de Swinnerton'* 1221 AssSa; Roger *de Swynnerton* 1295 AssSt, 1322 LLB E. From Swynnerton (Staffs).

Swinyard: John *de Swynyard* 1332 SRLa. 'Worker at the swine-enclosure', OE *swīn, geard*.

Swire, Swires, Swiers, Swyer: Geoffrey *le Swyer* 1275 RH (Nt); John *Swyer* 1297 SRY. A northern form of SQUIRE.

Switsur, Switzer: *v.* SWEETSER

Swoffer: *v.* SWAFFER

Swonnell: *v.* SWANNELL

Sword, Swords, Soards, Soord: Robert *Suerd* 1185 P (Berks); Peter *Swerd* 1297 Wak (Y). OE *sweord* 'sword', used of a sword-maker. *v.* SWORDER.

Sworder: Walter *le Sorder* 1324 AD vi (Sx); Richard *Swordere* 1354 PN Ess 483; John *Swerdere* ib. A derivative of OE *sweord* 'sword', a maker of swords.

Swyer: *v.* SWIRE

Sy-: *v.* SI-

Sydenham, Syddenham, Sidenham, Siddenham: Ascelin *de Sidenham* 1202 AssNth; Walter, John *de Sydenham* 1284 FFO, 1327 SRSo; Richard *Sydenham* 1384 AssL. From Sydenham (Devon, Oxon, Som).

Sykes, Sikes, Sich, Sitch, Seach: Ralph *de Sich* 1166 P (Nf); Roger *del Sik* 1212 Cur (Nf); Robert *Sitche* 1255 RH (Sa); Richard *del Siche* 1298 AssSt; Richard *del Sikes* 1309 Wak (Y); John *atte Siche* 1327 SRWo; Richard *in le Syche* 1332 SRSt. From residence near a small stream or streams, especially one flowing through flat or marshy ground (OE *sīc*); also 'a gully, dip or hollow'. This became ME *siche* in the south and midlands, *sik(e)* in the north. cf. *ditch* and *dike*. *Sykes* (which is plural) is common in Yorkshire where it may also be from ON *sik*.

T

Tabah: v. TABER

Tabard, Tabbitt: Thomas *Tabart*, Peter *Tabard* 1275 RH (L, K). ME *tabard*, OFr *tabart*, *tabard* 'a sleeveless coat', formerly worn by ploughmen and noblemen and not restricted, as now, to heralds. Also from a sign-name: John *atte Tabard* 1371 LoPleas.

Tabberer, Tabborah: v. TABERER

Tabberner: v. TABERNER

Taber, Tabor, Tabah: Suein *Tabor* 1185 P (W); Adam *Tabur* 1204 P (Sa). OFr *tabur*, *tabour* 'drum, tabor', by metonymy for *Taberer*.

Taberer, Tabberer, Tabborah, Tabrar: Peter *Taburer* 1222 Cur (Nf); Peter *le Taburur* 1279 AssNb; Bernard *le Taborer* 1280 *Ass* (Ha). A derivative of ME *tab(e)re* 'to play on the tabor' or from OFr *tabur*, *tabour* 'tabour'; 'one who plays the tabor, a drummer' (c1400 NED).

Tabern: Metonymic for TABERNER.

Taberner, Tabberner, Tabiner, Tabner: Benedict *Taberner* 1274 RH (D); Robert *le Taburner* 1301 SRY. A derivative of ME *tabourne* or OFr *tabourner* 'to drum'. 'Drummer.' cf. TABERER.

Tabois, Ta'bois: v. TALLBOY

Tabor: v. TABER

Tabrar: v. TABERER

Tafner: v. TAVERNER

Taft: John *de Taft* 1340 AssC. An unrounded form of TOFT.

Tagart, Taggard, Taggart, Taggert: v. MC-TAGGART.

Tague: v. KEIG

Tailyour: v. TAYLOR

Tait, Teyte: Ralph *Tait* 1185 Templars (Y); Robert *Teyt* 1279 RH (O); Thomas *Tayte* 1301 SRY. ON *teitr* 'cheerful, gay'.

Talbert: John *Talbard* 1327 SRSf. A rare name, identical with the French *Talbert*. v. TALBOT.

Talbot, Talbott, Talbut, Talbutt, Taulbut: *Talebotus* prior 1121–38 Bury (Sf); *Talebod* de Neweham 1146–8 Seals (Ess); *Talebot* 1185 Templars (K), 1283 FFSf; Geoffrey, Richard *Talebot* 1086 DB (Ess, Beds); Gilbert, Andrew *Talebot* 1190, 1196 P (He, Do); William *Taillebot* 1202 AssL; Richard *Thalebot* 1225 AssSo; William *Taleboth* 1229 FFEss; Gilbert *Talbot* 1332 SRSx; John *Talbut* 1332 SRCu. Harrison explains this name as 'bandit', from OFr *talebot* which Moisy takes as a nickname for robbers who blacked their faces to avoid recognition, *talebot* meaning 'lampblack,

pot-black' in the dialect of Normandy. Tengvik associates the name with OFr *talbot* 'a wooden billet hung round the neck of animals to prevent them from straying'. Miss Withycombe, comparing *Telfer*, suggests a compound of *tailler* 'to cut' and *botte* 'faggot'. The 1202 form *Taillebot* lends some support to this, but it is a solitary form and early forms for *Telfer* and *Tallboy* usually have *Taille-*. We are undoubtedly concerned with a personal-name, not uncommon in the 12th and 13th centuries, the first theme of which is found also in the French *Talabert*, *Talbert* (OG *Talaberht*; cf. TALBERT), *Talamon* (OG *Talamund*). v. also TALLON. This Dauzat derives from an obscure root *dala*. Hence, OG *Dalabod*, *Talabod*, OFr *Talebot*.

Talboys: v. TALLBOY

Talfourd: v. TELFER

Tallamach, Tallemach: v. TALMADGE

Tallboy, Tallboys, Talboys, Tabois, Ta'bois: Ralph *Tailgebosc*, *Taillebosc*, *Tallbosc* 1086 DB (Herts); Yvo *Taileboys* 1133–60 Rams (Hu); Reginald *Tailebois*, *Tallebos*, *Tallebys*, *Taullebois* 1203–21 Cur (Herts); Robert *Tayleboys* alias *Taleboys* 1257 Ipm (Nb). OFr *taillebosc*, from *tailler* 'to cut' and *bosc* 'wood', 'cut wood', a name for a wood-cutter. cf. CUTBUSH. Two forms, if correct, suggest a place-name: Roger *de Tallebois* 1161 P (Herts), Robert *de Talbois* 1279 AssNb. *Taille* and *Taillis* 'copse' are French place-names and Harrison notes Taillebois (Orne).

Tallon: Henry *Talon*, *Talun* c1160 DC (L); Hugh, Geoffrey *Talun* 1180 P (Y), 1187 Oseney (O); Johanna *Taloun* 1327 SRSf. Probably, as suggested by Dauzat for the French *Talon*, the cas-régime of OG *Talo*, rather than OFr *talon* 'heel', 'claw', cf. TALBOT.

Talmadge, Talmage, Tallamach, Tallemach, Tammage, Tollemache: Hugo *Talamasche* 1130 P (O); Robert *Talemasche* 1150 Eynsham (O); William *Talmach'* 1297 MinAcctCo; William *Talmege* 1512 FFHu; Elizabeth *Talmage* 1524 SRSf. A nickname from OFr *talemache* 'knapsack'.

Tamlin, Tamlyn, Tambling, Tamplin: Peter *Tamelyn* 1327 SRSf. A double diminutive of *Tam* (Tom). cf. TOMLIN.

Tancred: *Tancredus* filius Bernardi, *Tancredus* de Witton 1252 Rams (Hu); John *Tankred* 1389 Crowland (C). OG *Tancrad* 'thought-counsel'.

Taney, Tawney: Hasculfus *de Tania* 1195 P

(Ess); John *Tawny* 1674 HTSf. From Saint-Aubin-du-Thenney or Saint-Jean-du-Thenney (Eure). *v.* ANF.

Tanguy, Tangye: *v.* TINGAY

Tankard: *Tankardus* Flandrensis 1175 P (Nf); Radulfus *filius Tancard* 1185 Templars (Y); William *Tankard* 1190 P (O); John *Tancart* 1202 AssL. OG *Tancard* 'thought-hard'. The surname may also be metonymic for a maker of tankards: John *le Tanckardmaker* 1298 LoCt.

Tanner: Henry *Taneur, le Tanur* 1166–7 P (Nf); Lemmer *le Tannur* c1175 Whitby (Y); William *le Tanner* 1256 AssNb. Usually OFr *taneor, tanour*; also OE *tannere* 'tanner'.

Taper: Robert, John *Taper* 1327 *SR* (Ess), 1332 SRSx. Metonymic for a maker of tapers: William (*le) Tapermaker* 1340–1 Oriel (O).

Tapner: Gregory *le Tapiner* 1272 MESO (Ha); Henry *le Tapenyr* 1327 SRSx. OFr *taponner* 'maker of chalons and burel'. *v.* BURREL, CHALLENER.

Tapp, Tappe: John, Roger *Tappe* 1194 P (Do), 1247 AssBeds, 1327 SRWo. OE **Tæppa*, unrecorded, but the first element of Taplow (Bucks), Tapners (Kent), Tappington (Kent) and Tapton (Derby). *v.* TAPPIN.

Tapper: Ulfuine *Teperesune* c1095 Bury (Sf); John, Robert *le Tapper* 1279 RH (C), 1332 SRLa. OE *tæppere* 'tapper (of casks), beer-seller, tavern-keeper'.

Tappin, Tapping: Ralph, Geoffrey *Tapping* 1220, 1235 Fees (Berks, Nth); Robert *Tappyng, Tepping* 1221 AssWa. OE **Tæpping* 'son of *Tæppa*'. *v.* TAPP.

Tapster: (i) Elisota *Tapester* 1379 NottBR; Alicia *Tapstere* 1384 AssWa. OE *tæppestere*, feminine of *tæppere*, a woman who sells ale, hostess. cf. TAPPER. (ii) Ralph, Thomas *le Tapicer* 1282 AD ii (Mx), 1306 LoCt. AFr *tapicer* 'maker of figured cloth or tapestry' (c1386 NED). As *tapiner* became *tapner*, so *tapicer* probably became *tapser* and, with intrusive *t*, *tapster*.

Tarbard, Tarbath, Tarbat, Tarbert, Tarbet, Tarbitt, Tarbutt: *v.* TURBARD

Tarbin, Tarbun: *v.* THURBAN

Tardew, Tardif: William, Geoffrey *Tardif* 1115 Winton (Ha), 1260 AssC; Hugh *Tardy* 13th WhC (La); Henry *Tardi* Ed 1 NottBR. OFr *tardif*, Fr *tardieu* 'slow, sluggish', the origin of *tardy*.

Tarleton, Tarlton: Maien *de Torleton'* 1204 P (Gl); Gilbert *de Tarleton* 1332 SRLa; Magota *de Tarlton* 1379 PTY. From Tarleton (Lancs, Glos).

Tarn: Hugo *del Tern* 1332 SRCu. 'Dweller by the tarn', ME *terne* 'small lake, pool'.

Tarrant: Reginald *de Tarenta* 1190 DC (L); John *de Tarent* 1212 Cur (Mx); Ralph *Taraunt* 1296 SRSx. From Tarrant (Dorset).

Tarrier: Geoffrey *le terrier, le terrer* 1193–4 P (Ess, Sx). ME *terrere, taryer*, Fr (*chien) terrier* 'a hunting dog' (c1440 NED).

Tarry: *v.* TERREY

Tarves, Tarvis: Nicholas *Talewaz* 1199 FFEss; Robert *Talvace* 1296 Wak (Y); Thomas *Taleuas* 1327 SRSf; William *Turphas, Turface* 1416, 1424

Petre (Ess); Robert *Talface* 1520 NorwCt; Margaret *Talves* 1524 SRSf. A maker or a seller of, or one armed with, a talevas, described by Cotgrave as 'a large, massive, and olde fashioned targuet, having in the bottom of it a pike, whereby, when need was, it was stuck in the ground'.

Tasch, Tash: *v.* ASH

Tasker: John *le Tasker* 1279 AssNb; Hugh *Tasker*, Benedict *le Taskur* 1279 RH (Bk). A derivative of ME *taske* 'task, assessment', in ME texts 'one who threshes corn with a flail as task-work or piece-work' (1375 NED).

Tatam, Tatem, Tatum, Tatham: William *de Tateham* 1208 Pl (Y); William, Robert *de Tatham* 1230 P (La), 1379 PTY; John *Tattum, Tatam* 1665 HTO, 1693 DKR. From Tatham (Lancs).

Tate: Uluric *Tates* c1095 Bury (Sf); Nicholas, Richard *Tate* 1279 RH (C), 1345 ColchCt. *Tates* is from OE **Tāt*, the strong form of *Tāta*, found in several place-names, with a diminutive in *-el*: Hugh, John *Tatel* 1195 P (Sf), 1373 ColchCt.

Tatman: Hugh, John *Tateman* 1195 P (Y), 1327 SRY. Either 'servant of *Tate*' or an unrecorded OE **Tātmann*.

Tattersall, Tattershall, Tattershaw, Tattersill, Tettersell, Tetsall: Hugo *de Tateshal'* 1191 P (L); Joan *de Tatersale* 1301 SRY. From Tattershall (Lincs).

Taulbut: *v.* TALBOT

Taverner, Tavernor, Tavener, Tavenner, Tavenor, Taviner, Tavner, Tafner, Tavender: William *le Tauerner, Tauernier* 1175, 1177 P (Y); William *le Taverner* 1268 Ipm (W); John *Tavender* 1674 HTSf. AFr *taverner*, OFr *tavernier* 'tavern-keeper'.

Tawney: *v.* TANEY

Tawyer: Ralph *le Tawyere* 1275 RH (W); Martin *le Tauier* 1300 LoCt; Henry *Tawar* 1381 PTY. A derivative of OE *tāwian* 'to taw', a tawyer, one who prepares white leather.

Taycell: *v.* TEASEL

Taylor, Tayler, Tailyour: Walter *Taylur* c1180 ArchC vi; William *le Taillur* 1182 P (So); John *le talliur* 1202 AssL. AFr *taillour*, OFr *tailleor, tailleur* 'tailor' (1296 NED).

Taylorson, Taylerson: Hugh *le Taylleressone* 1280 AssSo; Thomas *le Taillourson* 1324 Wak (Y). 'The tailor's son.'

Tazelaar, Tesler, Tessler: Geoffrey *Taseler* (*Taslere*) 1230 P (Ess); Matilda *la Taselere* 1301 ParlR (Ess); Richard *le Tesler* 1332 SRSr. A derivative of OE *tæsel* 'teasel', one who teasels cloth (14.. NED). The teaseler drew up from the body of the cloth all the loose fibres with teasels, the dried heads of the 'fuller's thistle' (MedInd 225).

Teague: *v.* KEIG

Teal, Teale, Teall: Ralph, Robert *Tele* 1201 P (Nt), 1275 SRWo; German *le Tele* 1327 *SR* (Ess). A nickname from the water-fowl, ME *tele*.

Tear, Teare: M'*Teare* 1504, *Teare* 1599 Moore. A Manx contraction of MACINTYRE.

Tearall: *v.* TIRRELL

Teasdale, Teesdale: Walter *de Tesedale* 1235–6

AssDu; Mariota *de Tesdale* 1332 SRCu; Thomas *Tesdall* 1525 SRSx. From Teesdale.

Teasel, Taycell: Metonymic for TAZELAAR.

Tebb, Tebbs: *Tebbe* de Wifardebi 1177 P (Y); *Tebbe* filius Toke 1208 FFL; Adam, John *Tebbe* 1316 FA (Lei), 1327 SRC; John *Tebbes* 1524 SRSf. A pet-form of *Tebbold*. *v.* THEOBALD.

Tebbell, Tebble: Either *Tebb-el*, a diminutive of *Tebb* (cf. TIBBLE), or a weakening of *Tebald*. *v.* THEOBALD.

Tebbet, Tebbett, Tebbit, Tebboth, Tebbutt: *v.* THEOBALD.

Tebrich, Thebridge: Robert *Tedbrith, Thedbryt* 1275 RH (Sf), 1296 SRSx. OE *Þēodbeorht* 'people-bright', rare in OE, but the forms suggest a native origin.

Tee: Robert *atte Ee* 1351 AssSt. 'Dweller by the stream', OE *ēa*.

Tegart: Stephen *Teghurde* 1396 Ct (Ha). 'Shepherd', from OE **tegga* 'young sheep'. cf. CALVERT.

Tegg, Tigg: Hugo *Tig* 1211 Cur (Sr); Henry *Teg* 1278 AssLa; Thomas *Tegge, Tigge* 1327 SRSo. 'Young sheep', probably metonymic for TEGART.

Telfer, Telford, Taillefer, Talfourd, Tilford, Til-fourd, Tolver, Tulliver: *Taillefer* de Scaccario 1214 Cur (Mx); *Taillefer* de Fraxineto 1221 AssWo; Dunning *Tailifer* a1103 OEByn (D); Humphrey *Tallifer* 1195 P (He); Richard *Taillefer* 1225 AssSo; Stephen *Tayleford* 1381 *SR* (Ess); John *Talyver, Tollfeyre* 1524 SRSf; William *Tylford* 1615 PN Ess 194; William *Tollever* 1674 HTSf; George *Telford* 1685 FrY; George *Tealfer* 1696 Bardsley (Cu). OFr *taille fer* 'cut iron', 'iron-cleaver', used as a personal-name, an original nickname for a man who could cleave clean through the iron armour of his foe.

Tellow: Nicholas *at(t)e Telgh* 1297 PN Sx 401, 1327 SRSx; Henry *Telowe* 1292 IpmGl. 'Dweller by the young oak', as at Sweetwillow Shaw (Sussex), from OE **telg, telga, telge* 'branch, twig', *v.* MELS 209.

Tellwright: Simon *le Tywelwrighte* 1280 MESO (Ha). OE *tigelwyrhta* 'tile-wright', tile-maker, brickmaker. cf. TILER, TILLMAN.

Tempany: Henry *Tynnepanne* 1254–67 Rams (Hu); Richard, William *Timpon* 1279 RH (C); Nicholas *Tympanye* 1402 FA (W). OFr *tympan* (Lat *tympanum*) 'a drum, timbrel or tambourine', later *tympany*. 'Praise him with tympany and tabret' (1535 NED). Metonymic for a drummer.

Tempest: Roger *Tempeste* 1168 P (Y), 1209 P (Y); Richard *Tempest* 1222 Cur (Y). ME *tempest*, OFr *tempeste* 'a violent storm' (c1250 NED), 'agitation, perturbation' (c1315).

Templar, Templer: Johannes *Miles templi* 1150–5 DC (L); Gilbert *Templer* 12th DC (L); Robert *le Templer* 1220 Cur (O). ME *templer*, (c1290 NED). AFr *templer*, OFr *templier* 'a member of a military and religious organization consisting of knights, chaplains and men-at-arms' founded c1118 chiefly for the protection of the Holy Sepulchre and of pilgrims to the Holy Land; suppressed in 1312. The Knights Templar were so called because of their occupation of a building on or near the site of the Temple of Solomon in Jerusalem. In later examples, probably identical in meaning with TEMPLEMAN.

Temple: Hugo *of þe temple* a1131 (*s.a.* 1128) ASC E; Paganus *de Templo* 1141 Oseney (O); Matilda *du Temple* 1273 RH (O); John *del Temple* 1360 AD vi (Lei); William *Temple* 1380 LoPleas. OE *templ*, ME, OFr *temple* 'temple'. Hugo Paganus, founder of the Templars was called Hugo of the Temple. *v.* TEMPLAR. Not all those called Temple or Templar can claim an association with Jerusalem. Between '1728 and 1755 no less than 104 foundlings baptized at the Temple [in London] were surnamed Temple or Templar, which will explain the frequency with which the name appears in the *London Directory*' (Ewen 270).

Templeman: William, Reginald *Templeman* 1240 FFY, 1260 FFC; Ambrose *le Templeman* 1279 RH (C). 'Servant of the Templars', 'one who lived on one of their manors'. The surname was not uncommon in Cambridgeshire where the Templars had manors at Isleham and Duxford, still called The Temple and Temple Fm respectively. The real name of Ricardus *serviens Templariorum*, employed in some capacity at the West Hanningfield manor of the Templars in 1277, was, no doubt, Richard *Templeman*, a variation of that of John *de Templo*, connected with the same neighbourhood in 1248 (PN Ess 252).

Tench: Alan, William *Tenche* 1193 P (L), 1221 AssWa. OFr *tenche* 'a tench', a fat and sleek fish.

Tennyson, Tenneson, Tennison, Tenison: John *Tennysone, Tenison* 1361 CorY, 1632 RamptonPR; Edward *Tennyson* 1691 FrYar. Usually explained as a variant of DENISON. Although no firm proof of this is forthcoming, there is clear evidence for the interchange of initial *t* and *d*, both early and late. *Tunstall* and *Tunnicliff* survive by the side of *Dunstall* and *Dunnicliff*. Tavistock is found as *Davistock* 1220 Cur, Peter *Tyson* or *Dysun* occurs in a Canterbury will of 1528, while Robert *Dredegold* must have been a *Treadgold* or *Threadgold*. *Dandridge* is from Tandridge (Sr), and cf. also John *Dendelyoun* 1313 SRWa and Richard *Taunteloun* 1327 *SR* (Ess), both for 'dandelion', *Tanefeld* and *Danefeld* 1086 for Tanfield (NRY), *Dyddenhamm* 956 and *Tideham* 1086 for Tidenham (Gl), and *Dreamanuuyrða* 824 for Trimworth (K). In view also of such pairs as *Dandy* and *Tandy*, *Dancock* and *Tancock* (Andrew), *Dannett* and *Tannett* (Daniel), the equivalence of *Tennyson* and *Denison* may be accepted.

Tengue: *v.* TINGAY

Tennant, Tennent, Tennents: Richard *Tenand* 1332 SRCu; Robert *Tenaunt* 1332 SRLa. OFr *tenant* 'tenant', a holder or possessor of a tenement.

Tenner: Robert *le Tennore* 1255 RH (Sa); Richard *le Tenur* 1275 SRWo; Henry *Tenere* 1377 AssEss. OFr *teneor, teneur, tenor* 'tenant'.

Ternent: William *le Turneaunt* 1223 Cur (Y); Richard *Turnaunt* 1486 ERO. Present participle of

OFr *turner* 'to turn', a variant of TURNER. cf. Fr *Tournant* (Dauzat).

Terrall, Terrell, Terrill: *v.* TIRRELL

Terrey, Terry, Terris, Tarry, Todrick, Torrey, Torrie, Torry: *Theodricus, Tedric(us), Teodericus* 1086 DB; *Willelmus filius Teorri* 1114–30 Rams (Lo); *Theodericus* 1124–30 Rams (Beds); *Terri* Vsuarius 1166 P (Nf); *Terricus* de Mudiford 1177 P (D); *Ricardus filius Thedrici* 1185 Templars (Wa); *Theoricus* de Werdesford' 1213 Cur (Do); Jordanus *frater Tedric'* 1219 AssY; *Tyrri* de Athelartone 13th Ronton (St); Ralph *Teri* 1199 FrLeic; Warinus *þedrich* 1221 ElyA (Sf); John *Terry* 1221 AssWa; Thomas *Therry* 1243 AssSo; Hugo *Tyry, Tyeri, Terry* c1250 Rams (Beds); Alice *Tedrich* 1276 RH (Berks); John *Thudrich* 1279 RH (O); Henry, William *Torry* 1276, 1279 RH (Do, Bk); William *Tarri* 1279 RH (O); Richard *Tarry (Thary)* 1327 SR (Ess); John *Therrich* 1327 SRSf. OFr *Thierri, Tierri, Terri,* OG *Theudoric* 'people-rule', a common name on the continent. OE *Þēodrīc* is well-evidenced in OE and may be the source of *Thedrich, Thudrich, Therrich.* Many of the early ME bearers of the name were Flemish or German merchants, frequently described as *Teutonicus, Alemannus* or *Flandrensis.* The name was at times confused with *Theodore.* Both *Terricus* de Treiagol and *Theoricus* de Wycheford 1221 Cur (Co, Wa) are alternatively called *Theodorus.*

Tesh: *v.* ASH

Tesler, Tessler: *v.* TAZELAAR

Testar, Tester: Roger, Hugh *Testard* 1135 Oseney (O), 1172 DC (L); Gilbert *Testar* Hy 2 DC (L); William *Testart* 1230 P (Sr); Thomas *Tester* 1551 SxWills. OFr *testard,* a pejorative of *teste* 'head', 'big head'. Fairly common.

Tetsall: *v.* TATTERSALL

Tett: Robertus, Ricardus *filius Tette* 1166 P (Nf), 1180 P (Y); John *Tette* 1275 SRWo. OE **Tetta,* found in several place-names, the masculine form of *Tette.*

Tettersell: *v.* TATTERSALL

Tew: (i) Hugo *de Tiw* 1130 P (O). From Tew (Oxon). (ii) Hugh *le Tyw, le Tuy* 1286–8 AssCh. Welsh *tew* 'fat, plump'.

Tewer, Tewers: Nicholas *le Teware* 1275 SRWo; John *Tewer* 1327 SRY. A derivative of ME *tewe* 'to taw'. *v.* TAWYER.

Tey: Walter *de Teye* 1294 FFEss. From Great, Little or Marks Tey (Essex); John *del Teie* 1221 ElyA (Sf). 'Dweller by the enclosure or common pasture' (OE *tēag*).

Teyte: *v.* TAIT

Thacker, Thakore: Richard *the Thaker* 1316 Wak (Y); Roger *le Thacchere, le Thakkere* 1339 Crowland (C). A derivative of OE *þacian* 'to thatch' or ON *þak* 'thatch'; 'thatcher' (1420 NED). cf. THATCHER and THEAKER.

Thackeray, Thackara, Thackra, Thackrah, Thackray, Thackwray: John *de Thakwra* 1379 PTY; John *Thackerowe* 1548 RothwellPR (Y); Anne *Thackarawe* 1566 ib.; James *Thackerey* 1602 FrY; Thomas *Thackwrey* 1613 ib. 'Dweller by the

nook where reeds for thatching grew', ON *þak, (v)rá,* as at Thackray Wood in Blindcrake (Cumb).

Thackway: Adam *de Thakthuait,* John *de Thaktwait* 1332 SRCu. 'Dweller by the land where thatching-reeds grew', as at Thackthwaite (Cumb, NRYorks).

Thain, Thaine, Thayne: Robertus *filius Thein,* Robert *Tein* 1166 P (Nf); Geoffrey *le þein* 1199 P (Nth); Adam *þein* 1221 ElyA (Sf); William *le Theyn* 1243 AssSo. OE *þegen, þegn* 'thane', a tenant by military service.

Tharp: *v.* THORP

Thatcher: (i) Reginald *le Thechare* 1273 RH (O); Robert *Thechere* 1327 SRSx. (ii) John *le Thacchere* 1275 SRWo; John *Thatcher* 1327 SRDb. A derivative of OE *þæccan* 'to cover', later 'to thatch', 'a thatcher' (c1440 NED). The modern form is from (ii), which is apparently Anglian. The Saxon *Thetcher* has been absorbed by this. cf. THACKER, THAXTER and THEAKER.

Thaxter: Elena *la Thakestere* 1295 MESO (Nf). A feminine form of THACKER (c1440 NED). cf. BAXTER. Apparently peculiar to Norfolk where it is still found.

Theadom: *v.* THEEDAM

Theaker: Walterus *filius Thecker* 1199 MESO (St); William *le Theker(e)* 1273 RH (Nf), 1297 SRY; Anabilla *thekker'* 1327 MESO (L). A derivative of ON *þekja* 'to cover'; 'one who roofs buildings' (14.. NED). The craftsmen of the York mystery plays included the *Tille-thekers* 'men who covered roofs with tiles'. cf. also Thomas *Ledtheker* 1305 MESO (Y), who used lead. cf. THACKER and THATCHER.

Thebridge: *v.* TEBRICH

Thede, Theed: Goduuine *Thede filius* c1095 Bury (Sf); Willelmus *filius Thede* 1166 P (Nf); *Thieda* de Westweniz 1198 FF (Nf); *Theda* mater Herlewini 1207 Cur (Nf); Alan *þede* 1277 Ely (Sf); Nicholas *Thede* 1279 RH (C). OE **Þēoda,* a short form of names in *Þēod-.* Alan, son of *Thede,* held land called *Theduluesmere* in Burstall (Suffolk) temp. Henry III (AD iii). cf. Geoffrey *Thedolf* 1276 RH (Bk), John *Thedwyne* 1317 AssK, and *v.* TEBRICH. Also occasionally from OE **Þēode* (f). cf. *Theberga* vidua c1250 Rams (Hu), Richard *Thedware* 1252 ib., Gerbaga *Thedlef* 1327 SRSf.

Theedam, Theedom, Theadam: Richard, William *Thedam* 1308 Cl (Nf), 1319 SRLo; Richard, Gerard *Thedom* 1317 AssK, 1327 SR (Ess). ME *þeodam, þeedom* 'thriving, prosperity'.

Theobald, Theobalds, Tebbet, Tebbett, Tebbit, Tebbitt, Tebboth, Tebbut, Tebbutt, Tibald, Tiball, Tibballs, Tibbatts, Tidbald, Tidball, Tidboald, Tudball: *Teobald, Tedbaldus, Tetbald, Tebaldus* 1086 DB; *Theobaldus* 1161–77 Rams (Hu); *Thebaldus, Tebbaldus* de Valeines 1206 Cur (Sf, C); *Tibaldus* Walteri 1212 RBE; *Tybaud* de Valeines 1212 RBE; Tomas *Teobald'* 1199 P (Gl); Hugo *Tebaud* 1202 P (L); William *Theobald* 1250 FFSf; Simon *Tebalde* 1255 Rams (Hu); Stephen *Thebaud* 1275 RH (Bk); Rustikill *Thedbald* 1277 LLB B; Thomas *Tedbald* 1279 RH (C); Margery *Tebbolt* ib. (C);

John *Tebold, Tebbel* 1296 SRSx; Philip *Tubald, Tubbald* 1332 SRSx; John *Tedbot* 1338 FFSf; Geoffrey *Tebbaut* 14th AD ii (Nth); William *Tebott* 1405 FrY; Herbert *Tebbell*, William *Tebball*, John *Tebbet* 1674 HTSf; John *Tibbatts* 1802 Bardsley. OFr *Theobald, Teobaud, Thiebaut, Tibaut*, OG *Theudobald, Thiotbald*, 'people-bold', a common continental name. The modern surname *Theobald* is a learned form. The vernacular pronunciation in the 16th and 17th centuries was *Tibbald*, even when the spelling was *Theobald*. *Tebboth* is from an AN spelling in which the *th* was pronounced *t*. *v.* also TEBB, TEBBELL, TIBB, TIBBETS, TIBBLE.

Thew, Thewes, Thow: Gilbert, William *Thewe* 1190 P (Y), 1196 P (Nt); Johanna *Thow* 1348 DbAS 36. OE *þēow* 'a slave, bondsman, thrall'.

Thewles, Thewless, Thewlis, Thouless, Thowless: John, William *Theules* 1327 Wak (Y); Thomas *Thewelesse* 1379 PTY; William *Thowlas, Thowless* 1464, 1493 Black. OE *þēawlēas* 'ill-mannered', from OE *þēaw* 'custom, usage; manner of behaving or acting; a personal quality (mental or moral)' and *lēas*, 'destitute of morals or virtue; vicious, immoral' (a1327 NED). *Thowless* is a Scottish form though the phonology is unexplained; 'wanton, dissolute' (1375 NED).

Thick, Thicks: John *le Thike* 1243 AssSo. OE *þicce*, ME *thikke* 'thick-set, stout'.

Thicknesse: Richard *de Thyknes* 1295 AssSt. From Thickness (Staffs).

Thin, Thyne, Thynne: Thomas *Thin* 1218 AssL; Gilbert *Thynne* 1269 AssNb. OE *þynne* 'thin, lean, slender'.

Thirkell: *v.* THURKELL

Thirkettle: *v.* THURKETTLE

Thirkhill, Thirkill, Thirtle: *v.* THURKELL

Thistlethwaite: Miles *Thissilthwate* 1581 FrY. The Penrith Thistlethwaites derive from a lost *Thistelthueyt* in the Forest of Inglewood (1285 Ipm). The name may also have arisen elsewhere.

Thistleton, Thiselton: Symon, Adam *de Thistelton* 1250 FFL, 1286 IpmY; William *Thistylton* 1480 IpmNt. From Thistleton (Lancs), or 'dweller at the farm where thistles abound'.

Thistlewood: Stephen *de Thysteleswortthe* 1327 SRSx; George *Thistlewood* 1643 FrY; John *Thustlewood* 1678 SRSf. From Thistleworth Fm in West Grinstead (Sussex) or some similar enclosure overgrown with thistles.

Thoburn: *v.* THURBAN

Thom, Thoms: John *Thomme* 1311 ColchCt; John *Thoms* 1327 SRSo. A pet-form of *Thomas*. In Scotland, *Thoms* is an anglicizing of *Mac-Thomas*.

Thomas, Tomas: *Thomas* 1086 DB; Walter *Thomas* 1275 RH (W); Hugo *Tomas* 1317 AssK. An Aramaic name meaning 'twin'. Before the Conquest, *Thomas* is found only as the name of a priest. After the Conquest it became one of the most popular christian names.

Thomason, Thomasson, Thomerson: Adam *Thomassone* 1327 SRDb. 'Son of *Thomas*.'

Thomazin: *Thomaysin* 1301 SRY; Walter *Thomasyn* 1327 *SR* (Ess). *Thomas-in*, a diminutive of *Thomas*. Both *Thomasinus* and *Thomasina* are found in 1346 (FA). The modern surname is rare, having been almost completely absorbed by *Thomason, Thomerson, Thomson* and *Tomson*.

Thomerson: *v.* THOMASON and THOMAZIN

Thomley: *v.* TOMLEY

Thomline: *v.* TOMLIN

Thomlinson: *v.* TOMLINSON

Thommen: *v.* TUMMAN

Thompsett, Thomsett, Tompsett, Tomsett: Peter *Thomasset* 1792 Bardsley; Charlotte *Thomsett* 1801 ib. *Thomas-et*, a diminutive of *Thomas*. The formation must be old, but examples are late.

Thompson, Thomson, Tompson, Tomsen, Tomson: John *Thomson* 1318 Black (Carrick); John *Thompson* 1349 Whitby (Y); John *Thomesson* 'Scot' 1375 LoPleas; Ralph *Thommyssone* 1381 SRSf; John *Tommesson* 1382 AssC; William *Tomsone* 1395 EA (NS) ii (C); Alexander *McThomas* alias *Thomsoune* 1590 Black; John *Tompson, Tomson* 1591 ShefA. 'Son of *Tom*', i.e. Thomas. *Thomson* is the Scottish form, that with the intrusive *p* being English.

Thompstone: William *de Tomestona* 1175 P (Nf); Geoffrey *de Thomestune* 13th Lewes (Nf). From Thompson (Norfolk).

Thonger: Henry *Thonger* 1428 FA (W). 'A maker of thongs' (OE *þwang*).

Thorburn: *v.* THURBAN

Thorkell: *v.* THURKELL

Thorman: *v.* THURMAN

Thorn, Thorne, Thornes, Thorns: William *Thorn* 1206 Cur (Sx); Magge *de Thornes* 1275 Wak (Y); William *del þorn* 1277 Ely (Sf); Richard *atte Thorn* 1296 SRSx. 'Dweller by the thorn-bush(es)' (OE *þorn*), or from Thorne (Som, WRYorks).

Thornberry, Thornbery, Thornber, Thornborough, Thornborrow, Thornburgh, Thornburrow, Thornbury: Markerus *de Torneberga* 1176 P (Bk); Robert *de Thorneberg'* 1208 Cur (Y); Hugh *de Thornburgh* 1327 SRY. From Thornborough (Bucks), Thornbrough (Northumb, NR, WR Yorks), or Thornbury (Devon, Glos, Hereford).

Thorndike, Thorndyke, Thorndick: Simon *Thornedike*, John *ThornediTch* 1674 HTSf. 'Dweller by the thorny ditch.'

Thornett, Thornitt: Thomas *de Thornheved* 1332 SRCu. 'Dweller by the thorn-covered headland.'

Thornhill: John *de Tornhull'* 1212 P (Y); Walter *de Thornhulle* 1327 SRSo; John *Thornhill'* 1379 PTY. From Thornhill (Derby, Dorset, Wilts, WRYorks).

Thornton: Beatrice *de Thornton'* 1202 FFY; Ralph *de Thorntone* 1312 LLB D; Henry *Thornton* 1362–4 FrC. From one or other of the many places of this name.

Thorogood, Thoroughgood, Thorougood, Thorowgood, Thorrowgood: Stephen *Thorghugod* 1301 ELPN, John *Thourgod* 1330 ib.; Walter *Thorougod* 1306 LLB B; William *Thorowgood* 1674 HTSf. Ekwall explains this as 'thorough-good', but perhaps contracted from ME *þurhūt gōd* (ELPN). This, of course, is a possible explanation, but it is curious that clear examples are so late and so few, whilst those of *Thurgood* are both earlier and more numerous. *Thorghugod* is not a complete proof of this etymology. It may stand for *Thurgood*. cf. Matilda *þorustan* 1279 RH (Beds), Walter *Thorouston* 1327 SRC, i.e. *Thurstan*, Richard *Thurubern* (C) for *Thorbern*, and William *Throwketyll* 1524 SRSf for *Thurkettle*, where we are certainly concerned only with personal names. Note, too, that three of these are earlier than the earliest example of *Thorghugod*. Many of our Thorogoods are probably Thurgoods though some Thurgoods may be Thorogoods .*v.* THURGOOD.

Thorold, Thorrold, Thourault, Turral, Turrall, Torode: *Turold* 1066 DB (L); *Turoldus* ib. (Nf, W); Azor *filius Turaldi* 1066 DB (So); *Toroldus, Thoroldus, Turoldus capellanus* 1121–61 Holme (Nf); *Toroudus, Toroldus presbiter* 1143–7 DC (L); Robertus *filius Thoradi* 1185 Templars (Y); William *Turolde* 1190 P (Gl); Simon *Turold*' (*Turoll*') 1220 Cur (Ess); Henry *Turaud* 1258 Oseney (O); Robert *Thorald* 1261 ib.; Edmund *Thorold* 1279 RH (C); Symon *Turrad* 1279 ib. (Hu); Walter *Turald* 1296 SRSx. ON *Þóraldr, Þorváldr,* ODa, OSw *Thorald* 'Thor-ruler', found also in Normandy. The initial *T* is due to the Anglo-Norman pronunciation of *Th*-. *Torald* became *Toraud, Toroud,* giving the modern *Torode*.

Thorp, Thorpe, Tharp: William *de Torp* 1158 P (Nb); Robert *de Thorp* 1287 AssCh; William *in le Thorp* 1327 SRDb; Jak *del Thorp* 1332 SRCu. From one of the numerous places named Thorp(e) or from residence in a hamlet or outlying dairy-farm (OE *þorp*). *v.* also THROP.

Thory, Tory: *Thori, Tori, Thuri, Thure, Turi* 1066 DB; Hugo *filius Thory* 1218 AssL; John *Thori* c1140 ELPN; Reginald *Thory* 1221 Cur (Nth). ON *Þórir,* ODa *Thorir, Thori.* A Danish personal name, found chiefly in the eastern counties and not found in Normandy. *Tory* is due to Anglo-Norman pronunciation in England.

Thoules, Thowless: *v.* THEWLES

Thow: *v.* THEW

Thoyts: *v.* THWAITE

Thrale, Thrall: John *Thral* 1309 SRBeds; Richard *le Threl* 1332 SRSx. OE *þræl,* from ON *þrǽll* 'a villein, serf, bondman'.

Thrasher, Thresher: Richard *þrescere* 1221 *ElyA* (Sf); Geoffrey *le Thressher* 1319 FFEss. A derivative of OE *þerscan, þrescan, þryscan* 'to thresh'. 'A thresher.'

Threader, Thredder: Thomas *Thredere* 1365 LoPleas; William *Treder* 1379 PTY. A derivative of OE *þræd* 'thread'. 'One employed to keep the shuttles threaded in weaving.'

Threadgold, Threadgould, Threadkell, Threadgill, Thridgould, Treadgold, Tredgold: *Tredegold* 1166 P (Sr); Reginald, Agnes *Tredegold*' 1199 MemR (W), 1202 AssL; Edmund *Thredgall* 1674 HTSf; Daniel *Thredkill,* Widow *Thredkell* ib.; John

Thridgale 1681 SfPR. 'Thread gold', a name for an embroiderer.

Thredder: *v.* THREADER

Threlfall, Trelfall: William *de Threliffal* 1246 AssLa. From Threlfall (Lancs).

Thresh: *v.* THRUSH

Thresher: *v.* THRASHER

Thrift: William *Thrift* 1315 Wak (Y). A name, presumably, for one possessed of this virtue. *v.* also FIRTH.

Thring: Robert *de Thring* 1275 RH (K). From Tring (Herts).

Thripp: A form of *Throp* or *Thorp* which does not seem to have survived as an independent place-name but is found in the unstressed position in Eastrip (Som), Westrip (Glos) and Williamstrip (Glos).

Throp, Throup, Thrupp: Ralph *de Trop, de Thorp, de Throp* 1263 Ipm (Nth); Adam *de la Thropp*' 1275 RH (W); Edward *Thrupp* 1618 ArchC 49. From Throop (Hants), Throope (Wilts), Thrup (Oxon), or Thrupp (Berks, Glos, Northants). A metathesized form of THORP.

Throssell, Thrussell, Thrustle: Roger *Throsle* 1282 AssCh; Richard *Throstel* 1297 SRY. OE *þros(t)le* 'throstle'. A nickname from the bird.

Throup: *v.* THROP

Thrower, Trower: Simon *le Throwere* 1293 AD i (Nf); Alice *la þraweres* 1301 ParlR (Ess); Thomas *le Throwere* (*Trowere*) 1327 SR (Ess). A derivative of OE *þrāwan* 'to throw', probably 'thread-thrower', one who converts raw silk into silk thread. It might also mean 'turner' or 'potter', though these trades gave rise to many other common surnames.

Thrupp: *v.* THROP

Thrush, Thresh: William *Thresse, Thrusse* c1204 Clerkenwell, 1230 P (Lo); Clement *Thresshe* 1524 SRSf. OE *þrysce* 'a thrush'.

Thrussell, Thrustle: *v.* THROSSELL

Thruston: Andrew *Thurston,* John *Thryston* 1524 SRSf. A metathesized form of THURSTAN.

Thum: Geoffrey *Thumb* 1232 Pat (L). Perhaps a nickname, 'a Tom Thumb', or from some peculiarity, or perhaps loss, of a thumb. cf. William *Thumbeles* 1260 AssC 'thumb-less'.

Thurban, Thurbon, Thurburn, Thorburn, Thoubboron, Thoburn, Turbin, Tarbun, Tarbin: *Thurbernus, Turbern, Torbern* 1066 DB; Thomas *filius Thurberni, Turberni* 1153–86 Holme (Nf); *Thurbarnus filius Ailiue* 1197 FF (Sf); Richard *Turbern* 1198 FF (Nf); William *Thurbern* 1221 AssWa; Richard *Thurubern* 1277 Ely (Nf); Richard *þorebarn,* William *Thorebern* 1279 RH (O); William *Thourubern* 1295 Barnwell (C); Walter *Thurbarn* 1327 SR (Ess); — *Thurbin,* Thomas *Thurbon* 1674 HTSf. ON *Þorbiǫrn,* ODa, OSw *Thorbiorn* 'Thor-bear', anglicized as *þurbeorn* 'Thor-warrior'. *Turbin* preserves an Anglo-Norman pronunciation of *Th* and may represent a diminutive, *Turb-in.* cf. Robert son of *Turbyn* 1227 AssLa, Unwinus *filius Turbini* Hy 3 Colch (Ess).

Thurgar, Thurger, Thurgur: *Turgar* 1066 DB

(Wo, He, Nth); *Thurgarus* 1066 ICC (C); *Turger filius Ade* 1230 P (L); *Paganus Thurgar* 1279 RH (Beds); Hugo *Thurger*, Matilda *Thorgor* 1327 SRSf. ON *Þorgeirr*, ODa, OSw *Thorger* 'Thor-spear', found also in Normandy.

Thurgate: *v.* THURGOOD

Thurgell: *v.* THURKELL

Thurgood, Thorgood, Thurgate: Hunfridus *filius Turgoti* 1183 P (St); Magnus *filius Thurgot* 1219 AssL; *Thurgod* de Fynnynghersh 1327 SRSx; Adam *Turgod*' 1207 ChR (Do); William *Þurgod* 1275 SRWo; William *Thorgot* 1297 SRY; Thomas *Torgod* (*Torgot*) 1298 LLB B; Adam *Thorgod* 1327 SRSo. ON *Þorgautr*, ODa, OSw *Thorgot* 'Thor-Geat'. *v.* also THOROGOOD.

Thurkell, Thurtell, Thurtle, Thorkell, Thirkell, Thirkill, Thirkhill, Thirtle, Turkel, Turkil, Turtill, Turtle, Tuttle, Thurgell, Turgell, Turgill, Toghill: *Turkil* 1066 DB (Sf); *Turchil* ib. (Nf), c1095 Bury (Sf); *Thorchill, Thurchill* 1066 InqEl (Herts); *Thirkillus* 12th Gilb (L); *Turkil* Palmer 1177 P (Nt); Robert *Turkil* 1190 P (Wo); John *thurkil* 1224–46 Bart (Lo); William *Thorekil* 1279 RH (O); Adam *Turkild* 1283 SRSf; John *Thurkeld*, Alan *Thurkild* 1327 SRSf; John *Togel* 1327 *SR* (Ess); Richard *Turtill*, John *Thyrthyll* 1524 SRSf; Richard *Thyrkle* 1544 NorwW (Nf); John *Tuttell* 1568 SRSf; John *Tirtle*, Henry *Turtle* 1674 HTSf; William *Tuttle* 1674 HTSf. ON *Þorkell*, ODa *Thorkil*, a contracted form of ON *Þorketill*, very common in England and often used in Normandy. *v.* THURKETTLE.

Thurkettle, Thurkittle, Thirkettle: *Turketel* 1066 DB (Nf, Sf); *Thurketel* c1095 Bury (Sf); Johannes *filius Turketilli* 1214 Cur (Nf); Robert *Turketil* 1182 P (O); Richard *Turchetel* 1198 FF (Nf); John *Thurketell, Therketell* 1524 SRSf; William *Throwketyll* ib. Anglo-Scand *Þurcytel*, from ON *Þorketill* 'Thor's (sacrificial) cauldron'. Less common than the shortened *Þorkell*. *v* THURKELL.

Thurlow, Thurloe: John *de Thrillowe* 1278 RH (C), 1327 SRSf; Antony *Thurlowe* 1524 SRSf. From Thurlow (Suffolk), *Thrillauue* c1095.

Thurman, Thurmand, Thorman: *Turmund* 1066 DB (Do, So); Adam *Thuremund* 1248 Ass (Ha); Henry, Walter *Þurmond* 1279 RH (O). ODa, OSw *Þormund* 'Thor's protection'. This is a rare personal name. More common is ON *Þormóþr*, ODa *Thormoth*, OSw *Thormodh* 'Thor's wrath': *Thurmot, Turmod* 1066 DB; *Þurmod* 1221 ElyA (Sf); Hubert *Thurmod* 1212 RBE (Sf); Alan, Hugh *Thormod* 1275 RH (Nf). The second theme *-mod* has probably been assimilated to the more common element *-mund*.

Thurrell: *v.* TURRILL

Thurstan, Thurstans, Thurston, Thursting, Tustain, Tustian, Tustin, Tusting, Tutin, Tuton, Tuting, Dusting: *Turstan* (Y), *Turstinus* (St), *Tursten* (Y), *Tostin* (He), *Turtin* (Sa) 1066 DB; *Turstin* (*Thursten*) 1086 ICC (C); *Thurstanus, Turstan* c1095 Bury (Sf); *Turstin*' 1177 P (Nf); *Tutan* Hy 2 DC (L); *Turstanus, Tostenus* Bodin 1180–1200 DC (L); *Turston* 1188 BuryS (Sf); *Tosten*' Basset 1190–4

Seals (Bk); *Thurstan* le Brok 1296 SRSx; *Tustanus cocus, Tostin* coc 14th AD' iv (Nth); Wlmer *Þurstan* 1221 ElyA (Sf); John *Turstein* 1250 Fees (So); William *Thurstan, Thursteyn* 1278 AssSo; Matilda *Þorustan* 1279 RH (Beds); William *Dusteyn* 1282 Ipm (Nf); William *Thurston* 1297 MinAcctCo (W); William *Thursten* 1354 Oriel (O); John *Tuteing* 1641 FrY; John *Tueton* 1653 RothwellPR (Y); John *Tutin* 1692 FrY. ON *Þorsteinn*, ODa *Thorsten* 'Thor's stone', anglicized as OE *Þurstān*. Common in Normandy as *Turstinus, Turstenus*, where it became Fr *Toustin, Toustain*. This, in England, became *Tustin*(*g*), *Tutin*(*g*). *Thurston* may also be local in origin: Osward *de Turstun*' 1121–48 Bury (Sf); Herueus *de Thurston* 1221 ElyA (Sf). From Thurston (Suffolk).

Thurtell, Thurtle: *v.* THURKELL

Thwaite, Thwaites, Thwaits, Thwaytes, Twaite, Twaites, Twaits, Tweats, Thoytes: Ralph *del Thweit* 1206 P (Nf); Ralph *de Thweit* (*Twaeit*) 1221 Cur (Nf); Alan *del Twayt* 1301 SRY; Robert *del Twaytes* 1379 PTY; William *Twaytes* 1492 BuryW (Sf); Matthew *Thwayts* son of James *Twayts* 1618 Oseney (O). From Thwaite (Norfolk, Suffolk), or from residence near a forest clearing, a piece of land fenced off and enclosed, or low meadows. ON *þveit* 'a meadow, piece of land'.

Thyne, Thynne: *v.* THIN

Tibb, Tibbs: *Tibbe, Tybbe* 1286, 1290 AssCh; William, Richard *Tibbe* 1327 SRWo, SRY. In the 13th century *Tibbe* was used as a pet-name for both men and women, from *Isabel* or *Tibald* (*Theobald*). The latter interchanged with *Tebbe*. Tibb's Fm (PN Sx 517) owes its name to Nicholas *Tebbe* (1327 SRSx).

Tibbets, Tibbett, Tibbetts, Tibbits, Tibbitt, Tibbitts, Tibbatts, Tibbott, Tibbotts: John *Tybote* 1327 SRWo; Stephen *Tybet* 1332 SRSt; James *Tibbett* 1674 HTSf. *Tib-et, Tib-ot* may be diminutives of *Tibb*, from *Tibaud* (*v.* THEOBALD) or of *Isabel.* cf. *Tibota* Foliot 1279 RH (O). *Tibbott*, like *Tibbatts*, may derive directly from *Tibold* or *Tibaud*.

Tibbins: Thomas *Tibben* 1332 SRWa. *v.* TIBB, GEFFEN.

Tibble, Tibbles: Ulketellus *Tibel* 1203 Cur (Nf); William *Tybel* 1309 SRBeds. A diminutive of *Tibb*. It may also be a late weakening of *Tibald* (Theobald).

Tichborne, Tichbourne, Tichbon, Tichband: Walter *de Ticheburne* 1235 *FF* (Ha). From Tichborne (Hants).

Tickel, Tickell, Tickle: William *de Tikehill* 1175 P (Y); Roger *de Tikell* 1327 SRDb. From Tickhill (WRYorks).

Tidbald, Tidball, Tidboald: *v.* THEOBALD

Tiddeman, Tidiman, Tidman, Tydeman, Titman, Tittman: William *tedingman, teðingman* 1193, 1197 P (W); John *Tytheman* 1327 SRSf; John *Tytman* 1524 SRSf. OE *tēoðingmann* 'the chief man of a tithing (originally ten householders), headborough'. For the development, cf. William

Tythynglomb 1333 LLB E, Agnes *Tidilamb* 1364 LoPleas.

Tiddswell, Tideswell, Tidswell, Tidsall: Warin *de Tideswell* 1206 P (Nth); Henry *de Tiddeswelle* 1336 AssSt. From Tideswell (Derby). Locally pronounced *Tidza.*

Tiffany, Tiffen, Tiffin: *Tephania* Hy 2 Gilb (L); *Theophania, Teffania, Theffanie* (identical) 1206 Cur (K); *Tiphina* le Justiser 1322 AD vi (D); *Tiffania* 1323 AD iii (Nf); *Tiffan, Teffan* 1379 PTY; Gilbert *Tyffayne* 1288 RamsCt (Nf); Cristina *Typhayn* 1327 SRSo; William *Tyffen* 1524 SRSf; Nicholas *Tiffin* 1674 HTSf. Late Latin *Theophania,* from Greek θεοφάνια 'the manifestation of God', another name for the Epiphany. In French this became *Tiphaine* and occasionally *Tiphine* and was given to girls born on Epiphany Day.

Tigar: *Tigerus* 1086 DB (Sf); John *Tygre* 1319 FFEss; Nicholas *Tygre* 1327 SRWo. OFr *Tigier,* OG *Thiodger* 'people-spear'.

Tigg: *v.* TEGG

Tighe, Tigue: *v.* KEIG

Tilcock, Tillcock: William *Tilkoke* 1556 Oxon. *Till* (Matilda) plus *cock.*

Tildesley, Tildsley, Tillsley, Tilsley, Tilzey, Tydsley, Tyldesley: Hugo *de Tildesle* 1212 Fees (La). From Tyldesley (Lancs), with varied simplifications of the difficult consonantal combination *ldsl.*

Tiler, Tyler, Tylor: (i) Roger *le Tuiler* 1185 Templars (Lo); Alard *le Tuilur* 1198–1212 Bart (Lo); Richard *le Tiwelur* 1205 P (L); Nicol *tyulur* 1230 P (L); Hamo *le Tewler* 1276 LLB B; John *le Tuler* 1281 ib. OFr *tieuleor; tieulier, tiewelier, tuiweliere, tiuelier, tuilier.* 'Tiler, tile-maker.' This French form, which is common, is earlier than the corresponding English one but does not seem to have survived and is not given in NED. (ii) Simon *le Tyeler'* 1286 MESO (Nf); Stephen *Le Tygeler'* 1288 ib. (Sx); Richard *le Tyghelere,* Simon *le Teylur'* 1296 SRSx; William *le Tielere* (*le Tiller'*) 1327 SR (Ess). A derivative of OE *tigule, tigele* 'a tile' or of the ME verb *tile* formed from this. 'Tiler.' (iii) Robert *le Tiler* 1222 Cur (Ess); Geoffrey *le Tylere* 1279 RH (Hu); Alan *le Tyliere* 1327 SRSf. NED has *tile* 'tile' once c1300 and *tyle* for both the noun and the verb from c1375 onwards, but it is doubtful whether the form had developed as early as 1222. Some of these forms with a single *l* may belong to TILLER.

Tiley, Tily, Tyley: *v.* TILLEY

Till, Tille, Tills: *Tilla* 1246 AssLa; *Tille* 1325 Wak (Y), 1332 SRCu; William *Tyl* 1327 SRWo; John, Richard *Tille* 1327 SRSx. A pet-form of *Matilda.*

Tiller, Tillier, Tillyer, Tilyer: John *le Tillere* 1299 LLB C; William *le Tiller* 1327 SRWo. ME *tiliere, tilyer,* a derivative of OE *tilian* 'to till' and taking the place of OE *tilia* (*v.* TILLEY), 'one who tills the soil, husbandman, farmer or farm labourer' (c1250 NED). Some of the forms under TILER (iii) may belong here.

Tillett, Tillott: *Tillot* Hobwyfe 1379 PTY; Cecilia, George *Tillote* 1279 RH (O), 1303 FA (Sf); John *Tillet* 1674 HTSf. *Till-ot,* a diminutive of *Till* (Matilda).

Tilley, Tillie, Tilly, Tiley, Tily, Tylee, Tyley: (i) Ralph *de Tilio* 1086 DB (D); Oto *de Tilli* 1185 Templars (Y); Wulwordus *Tillie* (*de Tilie*) 1230 P (K). From Tilly-sur-Seulles (Calvados) or Tilly (Eure). (ii) John, Matilda *Tilly* 1274 RH (So), 1277 *Ely* (Sf); Simon *Tyly* 1296 SRSx; William *le tylie* 1332 SRSr. OE *tilia,* ME *tilie,* from OE *tilian* 'to till', 'husbandman'. cf. TILLER. This may also be a diminutive of *Till* (Matilda).

Tilling: John *Tylling,* William *Tulling* 1279 RH (O); William *Tyllyng* 1280 AssSo; Richard *Tulling* 1327 SRSx. *Tilling* may be an unrecorded OE **Tilling* 'son of *Tilli*'; but the alternative *Tulling* suggests OE **Tylling* 'son of **Tylli*', an unrecorded mutated form of OE *Tulla.* The *Tulling* who was a witness at Exeter c1100 (Searle) bore a Devonshire form of the name.

Tillinghast: Ralph *de Tellingherst* 1230 P (Sx). From Tillinghurst (Sussex).

Tillman: Alexander, Alan *Tileman* 1204 P (Gl), 1260 AssC; Adam *Tilleman* 1301 SRY. Either OE **tilman* 'husbandman, farmer', identical in meaning with TILLER, or early examples of *tile-man* 'maker of tiles', *tyleman* 1479–81 NED, *tyll mane* 1609 ib. *v.* also TILER.

Tillotson: William *Tillotson* 1379 PTY. 'Son of *Tillot.*' *v.* TILLETT.

Tillott: *v.* TILLETT

Tillsley: *v.* TILDESLEY

Tilly: *v.* TILLEY

Tillyer: *v.* TILLER

Tilsley: *v.* TILDESLEY

Tilson: George *Tylson* 1609 FrY. 'Son of *Till*' (Matilda).

Tily: *v.* TILLEY

Tilyer: *v.* TILLER

Tilzey: *v.* TILDESLEY

Timberlake, Timblick: John *de Tymberlake* 1281 AssSt. From a lost Timberlake in Bayton, Worcestershire (PN Wo 40).

Timmerman: Margeria *Tymberman* 1327 SRSf. 'A dealer in timber' (1429 NED).

Timms, Tims, Timme, Timm, Tymms, Tymm, Tym: William *filius Tymme* 1285 AssCh; Alicia *Timme* 1327 SRWo; William *Tymmes* 1332 SRWa. OE **Tima,* OG *Thiemmo.* Hardly, as suggested by Bardsley and Harrison, from *Timothy,* since that name does not appear in England until after the Reformation.

Timperon: Adam *de Tymperon* 1332 SRCu. From Tymparon Hall in Dacre (Cumb).

Tindal, Tindale, Tindal, Tindall, Tindell, Tindill Tindle, Tyndale, Tyndall: Adam *de Tindal'* 1165 P (Nb); Roger *Tindale* 1332 SRCu; John *Tyndall* 1395 Whitby (Y). From Tynedale, the valley of the Tyne, or from Tindale (Cumb).

Tinegate: Thomas *Tynegate* 1332 SRCu.

Tingay, Tingey, Tengue, Tanguy, Tangye: Rogerus *filius Teingi* 1130 P (C); *Tinghi* 1182

Gilb (L); *Tengi* de angulo 1219 AssL; Ralph *Tenghy* 12th Lichfield (St); Richard *Tengi* 1202 AssL; Alexander *Tingy*, William *Tengy* 1260 AssC. *Tanguy, Tanneguy*, a common name in Brittany, from St Tanguy, one of the entourage of St Pol of Leon, found also in Cornwall. cf. Breton *Tanchi* 859–65, *Tangi* 1086 (Loth). The first element is Bret *tân* 'fire', the second may be *ci* 'dog'. In the 12th and 13th centuries the name is found in England in districts where Bretons are known to have settled, usually as *Tengi*, occasionally as *Tingi*.

Tingle, Tingler: Alan *Tingel* 1209 P (C); John *Tyngil* 1275 RH (Nf). ME *tingle, tyngyl* 'a very small kind of nail' (1288 NED), usually *tingle-nail*, used by metonymy for *Tingler*, a maker of these. cf. William *Tingenail* 1205 Cur (Nf) and HORSNAIL.

Tinker: Laurence *tinekere* 1244–46 Bart (Lo); Robert *le Tinker* 1243 AssSo. 'One who mends pots, kettles, etc.', 'a tinker'. The surname is not confined to the south as Bardsley thought. Examples have been noted between 1275 and 1292 in Yorks, Lancs, Lincs, Norfolk and Cheshire.

Tinkler: Roger *le Tinkelere* 1268 MESO (Y); Thomas *le Tinclere* 1279 AssNb. A formation based on *tinker*. 'A worker in metal, tinker' (c1175 NED). Characteristically northern, noted only in Yorks, Lancs, Cumberland and Northumberland.

Tiplady: Johanna *Tippelevedy* 1301 SRY; John *Typlady*, Henry *Tipelady* 1490, 1494 GildY. cf. TOPLADY, TOPLASS, both probably names for a libertine. cf. *Othello* i, 1.

Tipler: Robert *le Tipelere* 1250 MESO (Nf); William *Tipeler* 1275 RH (L). ME *tipeler* 'a seller of ale, tapster' (1396 NED).

Tipp: *Tipp*' filius Harding 1204 Cur (L); William *Tip* 1279 RH (C). A variant of *Tibb*, a pet-form of *Theobald*. *v.* TIPPING.

Tippell, Tipple, Tipples: Albreda *Tepple* 1185 Templars (Wa); (tenementum) *Tipel* 1275 RH (Nf); John *Typull* 1524 SRSf; Edmund *Tipall*, Robert *Tiple*, Robert *Tipell* 1674 HTSf. *Tipp-el*, a diminutive of *Tipp* (or *Tebb, Tepp*), or a contracted form of *Theobald*.

Tipper: William *Tipere* 1176 P (Hu); William (*le*) *Tipper* 1214 Cur (Wa). A derivative of ME *typpe* 'to furnish with a tip', 'a maker or fitter on of metal tips', probably of arrow-heads.

Tippett, Tippetts: Wimer *Tippet*' c1250 Rams (Hu); Hugh *Typet, Tepet* 1297 Wak (Y). *Tipp-et*, a diminutive of TIPP.

Tipping: Robert *Tipping*' 1301 SRY; Thomas *Typpyng* 1381 PTY. *Tipping* would appear to be OE *Tipping 'son of *Tippa', an unrecorded name found in place-names, which may be an occasional source of TIPP.

Tippins: Seman *Typoun* 1327 SRSf; Robert *Typpyn* 1524 SRSf. *Typoun* is *Tip-un*, a diminutive of *Tipp* (Theobald). *Typpyn* may be the same name, or *Tip-in*, also a diminutive of *Tipp*, or a weakening of *Tipping*.

Tipple(s): *v.* TIPPELL

Tipson: Richard *Tibson* 1326 Wak (Y); William *Tybessone* 1327 SRDb. 'Son of *Tibb*.'

Tiptaft, Tiptoft, Tiptod: Robert *de Typetot* 1275 FFEss; Elyas *Tybetot* 1327 SRSf; John *Typtofte* 1524 SRSf; Nathaniel *Tiptot*, William *Tiptod* 1674 HTSf. From some Norman place Tibetot.

Tirrell, Terrall, Terrell, Terrill, Tearall, Tyrell, Tyrrell: Walter *Tirel* 1086 DB (Ess); Rocelinus, Simon *Tirel* 1127 AC (Gl), 1194 Cur (W); Hugo, Eudo *Tirell* 1153 Seals (Ess), 1195 P (Wo); Henry *Terel* 1275 SRWo; William *Terryll* 1568 SRSf. The common association with Anglo-Scandinavian *Turold* is impossible. Probably, as suggested by Tengvik, a derivative of OFr *tirer* 'to draw' in the same sense as Fr *Tirand* which Dauzat explains as 'one who pulls on the reins', hence 'obstinate, stubborn'.

Tisser, Tissier: Nicholas *Tisser* 1327 SRC; John *Tyssur*' 1327 MESO (L). OFr *tisseur* 'weaver'. *Tissier* is a Guernsey name.

Titch(e)ner: *v.* TWITCHEN

Titler, Tytler: Richard *le Titteler*, Symon *le Titteler*, Symon *le Tuteler* 1275 RH (Sf). A derivative of ME *title*, 'a tell-tale, gossip'. *Tuteler* may be from ME *tutel* 'whisper'. Or we may have ME *titlere* 'hound'.

Titman: *v.* TIDDEMAN

Tobey, Toby, Tobias: *Tobias* prior c1142–50 PN Ess 261 (first prior of Thoby Priory); *Tobias* Ric 1 Gilb (L); Simon, William *Toby* 1271 RamsCt (C), 1275 RH (C). Hebrew *Tobiah* 'Jehovah is good'. *Tobias* is the learned, Greek form, *Toby* the vernacular.

Tod, Todd: Hugo, Arding *Tod* 1168–75 Holme (Nf), 1225 Oseney (O); Richard *Todd* 1231 Pat (Nb); Richard *le Todde* 1275 SRWo. ME *tod(de)* 'fox', chiefly, but not solely, northern.

Todhunter: Thomas *Todhunter* 1332 SRCu. 'Foxhunter'. Still a Cumberland surname.

Todman: Juliana *Todman* 1275 SRWo. This form cannot derive from Toddenham (Glos) as suggested by Bardsley and Harrison. It is a compound of *tod* 'fox' and *man*, probably a southern equivalent of TODHUNTER.

Todrick: *v.* TERREY

Toe, Toes: For *at* (*h*)*oe*. *v.* HOW, ATTO.

Tofield: *v.* TOVELL

Toft, Tofts: Elyas *del Toft* 1197 P (Nth); Robert *de Toft* 1279 RH (Beds); Gilbert *de Toftes* 1327 SRSf. 'Dweller at the croft(s) or homestead(s)' as at Toft (Cambs, Norfolk, Warwicks). cf. TAFT.

Toghill: *v.* THURKELL

Toke: *v.* TOOK

Tole, Toole: (i) William *filius Tole* 1130 P (Ess); Hugh, Peter *Tole* 1297 MinAcctCo, 1327 *SR* (Ess). OE *Tola*, ON *Toli*. (ii) In Ireland for *Ó Tuathail*, from *tuathal* 'people-mighty'.

Tolefree: *v.* TOLLFREE

Toley: *v.* TOOLEY

Toll, Tolles, Towle, Towll: (i) *Tolle* le grangier 1218 AssL; Nicholas, Richard *Tolle* 1275 RH (W), 1296 SRSx. OE *Toll, found in Tollesbury and Tolleshunt (Essex), or Anglo-Scand *Toll, a pet-form of ON *Þorleifr*, found in Thurleston (Leics, Warwicks) and Tollerton (Notts), or of ON *Þorleikr*, found in Thurloxton (Som). (ii) Robert *atte Tolle*, Roger *Tolle* 1327 SRWo. Probably an early example of the Kent to Hampshire dialectal *toll* 'a clump of trees' (1644 NED).

Tolladay, Tollady, Tolleday, Tolliday: Thomas *Towlewardie* 1574 SfPR; Thomas, Mary *Towlardy* 1664, 1668 ib.; Isaacke *Towlworthy* 1672 ib.; Thomas *Tilladay* 1674 HTSf. Suffolk pronunciations of *stalworthy*, with loss of initial *S*. cf. STALLWORTHY, STOLERMAN, STOLLERY, STALLWOOD.

Tollemache: *v.* TALMADGE

Toller, Toler, Towler: (i) Robert *Toller'* 1199 P (L); William, John *le Tollere* 1251 AssY, 1255 *Ass* (Ess); William, Richard *Towler* 1624 HorringerPR (Sf), 1639 RothwellPR (Y). OE *tollere* 'tax-gatherer'. (ii) Robert *de Tolra* 1179 P (Do). From Toller (Dorset).

Tollfree, Tolfree, Tolefree, Turfery, Turfrey, Tuffery, Tuffrey: *Turfredus* 1049 PNDB 392 (Rouen); *Toruert, Toruerd* 1066 DB; Godric *Turuerde filius* c1095 Bury (Sf); *Toruard Cappe* 1203 FFL; John *Torfray* 1279 RH (O); Robert, Henry *Tolfry*, William *Tholfry* 1296 SRSx; John *Tolfrut* 1297 MinAcctCo; Mary *Tufferey* 1765 *ERO*. ON *Þorfrøðr*, OSw *Thorfridh*.

Tollworthy: a variant of STALLWORTHY. cf. TOLLADAY.

Tolman, Tolmon, Toleman: Hereward *Tholeman* 1219 AssL; William *Tolman* 1327 SRSo. OE *toll* and *mann*, 'tollman, a collector of tolls'.

Tolson: *v.* TOWNSON

Tolver: *v.* TELFER

Tom, Tomes, Toms: William *Tom* 1245 HPD (Ess); Edmund *Tommys* 1524 SRSf. A pet-form of *Thomas*.

Tomalin: *v.* TOMLIN

Toman: *v.* TUMMAN

Tomas: *v.* THOMAS

Tombleson: Wylliam *Thomlesson* 1524 SRSf. From TOMLINSON, with intrusive *b*.

Tomblin, Tombling: *v.* TOMLIN

Tombs, Toombes, Toombs: Robert *Toume*, Walter *Tomes* 1327 SRWo; Thomas *Tombes* 1701 Bardsley. Identical with TOMS, with late intrusive *b*.

Tomkin, Tomkins, Tomkies, Tomkys, Tompkin, Tompkins: William *Thomekyn* 1323 Eynesham (O); William *Tumkyns* 1327 SRSt; Geoffrey *Tomkynes* 1332 SRWa; Richard *Tompkyn* 1566 Bardsley. 'Little Tom.'

Tomkinson, Tompkinson: John *Tomkynson* 1393 SaltAS (OS) ix. 'Son of *Tomkin*.'

Tomley, Thomley: John *Tompele* 1279 RH (C). From Thomley (Oxon).

Tomlin, Tomline, Tomlins, Tomalin, Tomblin, Tombling, Tomblings, Thomline: *Thomelinus* Herys 1380 Black; Robert *Thomelyn* 1327 SRC; John *Thomeling* 1327 SRSx; John *Tomelyn* 1327 SRSo. A double diminutive of *Tom* or *Thom* (Thomas), *Tom-el-in*.

Tomlinson, Thomlinson: Henry *Thomlinson*, Richard *Tomlynson* 1379 PTY. 'Son of *Tomlin*.' *v.* TOWNSON.

Tommis: Identical with TOM.

Tompkin, Tompkins: *v.* TOMKIN

Tompkinson: *v.* TOMKINSON

Tompsett, Tomsett: *v.* THOMPSETT

Tompson, Tomsen, Tomson: *v.* THOMPSON

Toms: *v.* TOM

Tonbridge, Tunbridge: Richard *de Tonebrige* 1086 DB (K); John *atte Tunbregg* 1345 MELS (Sr). Usually, certainly in Kent where the surname still survives, from Tonbridge (Kent); or from residence near a bridge by the *tūn* or village. Salom' *de Tunbrygge* (1274 RH) lived at Two Bridge, the bridge near the *Town* Quarter of Writtle, whilst Robert *de Tonebrugge* (1323 *For*) lived at the field still known as Tunbridge in Stapleford Abbots. *v.* PN Ess 279, 604.

Tone: *v.* TOWN

Toner: Irish *Ó Tomhrair* 'descendant of *Tomhrar*'. In England the surname is early: Hugh *Tunere* 1242 Fees (W); Andrew *le toner* 1327 Pinchbeck (Sf). 'Dweller by the farm or village', equivalent to *atte tune*. *v.* TOWN.

Toney: Richard *Tony* 1275 SRWo; William *Toni* 1279 RH (Beds). A pet-form of *Antony*.

Tong, Tonge, Tongs, Tongue: (i) Wluricus *Tunge* 1188 BuryS (Sf); Nicholas, Richard *Tonge* 1279 RH (Bk), 1297 MinAcctCo (O). The frequency of early forms without a preposition suggests a nick-name from OE *tunge* 'tongue', a chatter-box, scold. (ii) Richard *de Tanga, de Tong* c1200–10 Calv (Y); Elias *de Tong* 13th WhC (La). From Tong (Salop, WRYorks) or Tonge (Kent, Lancs, Leics), varying between OE *twang, tang* 'tongs' and *tunge* 'tongue of land'. (iii) William *in la Tunge* 1248 FFSx; James *a Tonge* 1545 ArchC 42. 'Dweller in the tongue of land' (OE *tunge*).

Tonnell, Tunnell: Ralph, William *Tonild* 1279 RH (C); Henry *Thonild* 1327 SRC. OE *Tūnhild* (f), unrecorded, but both themes are common.

Tooby: *v.* TOBEY

Toogood, Towgood, Tugwood: Richard, Robert *Togod* 1200 P (L), 1221 *ElyA* (C), 1264 Oriel (O); Roger *Togod, Togot* 1207 Cur (Nth); Agnes, Stephen *Tougod* 1297 MinAcctCo, 1327 SRSx; Stephen *Togoud* 1332 SRSx; Margerie *Toogood* 1473 Rad (C); Mary *Tugwood* 1761 BishamPR (Berks): Hilton *Toogood, Twogood, Tugwood* 1763, 1765 ib. This name cannot be associated with *Thurgood* and *Thorogood* as suggested by Bardsley and Harrison. These names regularly retain the *r*, of which there is no trace in *Toogood*. As Weekley suggests, the surname is really an adjectival nick-name 'too good'. cf. Scots 'unco guid', Hamon *Toproud* 1287 AssCh 'too proud', Adam *Overprud* 1222 AssLa, and TRAPNELL.

Took, Tooke, Toke, Tuke: *Toc* 1066 DB (Y); Rogerus *filius Toke* 1214 Cur (Nth); Wrange *Tocha* 1166 P (Nf); Henry *Thoche* 12th DC (L); Robert, William *Toke* 1200 P (Sf), 1211 Cur (Nth); Robert *Touk* 1325 AssSt; Wylliam *Took*

1524 SRSf. Anglo-Scand *Tōka, Tōke* (ON *Tóki*).
v. TOOKEY.

Tookey, Tuckey: *Tochi, Toke, Toche, Toca, Tuka* 1066 DB; Ormus, Rogerus *filius Toki* 1183 Boldon (Du). 1206 Cur (R); William, John *Toki* 1200 P (Sf), c1248 Bec (Bk); Thomas *Tookye* 1599 Oxon (Lei); Joane *Tuckey* 1624 Bardsley. ON *Tóki*, ODa *Toki, Tuki*, OSw *Toke, Tuke*.

Toole: v. TOLE

Tooley, Toley: *Toli, Thole, Tholi* 1066 DB; Reginaldus *filius Toli, Tuly* 1214 Cur (L); Richard *Toly* c1150 StThomas (St); Peter *Toli* 1155 P (Nt); David *Toolye* 1631 Bardsley. ON *Tóli*.

Toomb(e)s: v. TOMBS

Toon(e): v. TOWN

Toop, Toope: *Topi, Tope* 1066 DB (Herts, L); Ulf *Tope sune* ib. (L); Aldene *Tope* ib. (L); Robert *Topi* 1200 P (Nf); Alan, John *Tupe* 1202 P (Y), 1307 Wak (Y). ODa *Topi*.

Tooth: Hugo *cum dentibus* c1102–11 ELPN; Robert *Tothe* 1219 AssY; Thomas *Toth* 1275 RH (Nth). OE *tōð* 'tooth', a nickname for one with a prominent tooth or teeth.

Toothill, Tootal, Tootell, Tootill, Tootle, Tothill, Tottle, Tuthill, Tutill: Gilbert *de Totehille* 1185 Templars (Wa). 'Dweller by the look-out hill' (OE *tōt-hyll*), as at Toot Hill (Essex), Tothill (Lincs, Middlesex), Tootle Height (Lancs), or Tuttle Hill (Warwicks). v. THURKELL

Toovey: v. TOVEE

Toplady: John *Taplady* 1400 AD vi (Db). cf. TIPLADY.

Toplass, Toplis, Topliss: Robert *Topples* 1596 Shef. cf. TIPLADY.

Topliffe: Herueus *de Toppecliue* 1219 AssY; John *Topplyffe* 1491 GildY. From Topcliff (NRYorks).

Topp, Topps: Herueius *filius Toppe* 1200 P (L); Robert *Toppe* 1196 P (Gl); Roger *Top* 1208 Cur (Nf). ON *Toppr*.

Topper: Walter *le Toppare* 1275 SRWo; Robert *le Toppere* 1327 AD i (W). A derivative of ME *toppe* 'a tuft or handful of hair, wool, fibre, etc., especially the portion of flax or tow put on the distaff'. A topper was probably the one who put the 'toppe' on the distaff.

Torbett, Torbitt: v. TURBARD

Torch: Alueue *Torce* c1095 Bury (Sf); Robert *Torche* Ed 1 Battle (Sx). OFr *torce* 'torch', perhaps for a torch-bearer.

Toril: Robert, Ralph *Torel* c1150 DC (Lei), 1185 Templars (Herts). A diminutive of OFr *tor* 'bull'.

Torode: v. THOROLD

Torr, Torra, Torre: (i) Robert *de Torra* 1182 P (Co); Martin *de la Torre* 1242 Fees (D); Walter *atte Torre* 1296 SRSx. 'Dweller by the rocky peak or hill' (OE *torr*). (ii) John, Gilbert *le Tor* 1240 Oriel (O), 1276 LLB A. OFr *tor* 'bull'.

Torr(e)y, Torrie: v. TERREY

Tortise, Tortiss: Hubert *Turtuse* 1200 Cur (Sf); Gilbert *Tortouse* 1327 SR (Ess). ME *tortuse* 'tortoise', a type of slowness.

Tory: v. THORY

Tosh: v. MCINTOSH

Toshach, Toshack: Simon *Tuschech* 1219–37 Black; Finlay *Tosscheach* 1516 ib. EGael *toisech*, Gaelic *toiseach* 'chief, leader'.

Tothill: v. TOOTHILL

Totman, Tottman: Robert *Toteman* 1202 P (Ess). OE *tōt-mann* 'look-out man', 'watchman'.

Tott: Iweinus *Tottes* 1219 AssL; Gilbert *Tot* 1275 RH (Sf). ME *totte* 'simpleton, fool'.

Tottle: v. TOOTHILL

Tough, Tow, Towe, Towes: Robert, Gilbert *Towe* 1275 RH (L, Ha); Alicia *la Towe* 1275 SRWo; Nicholas *le Toghe* 1275 RH (K); John *Towes* 1685 FrY. OE *tōh*, ME *togh, tow(e)* 'vigorous, steadfast, stubborn'.

Toulson: v. TOWNSON

Tours, Towers: Picoth *de Turs* c1150 DC (L); Robert *de Tours* 1297 MinAcctCo. From Tours (Indre-et-Loire).

Tout: Richard, William *Tut* 1219 AssY, 1296 SRSx; Simon, Richard *Tute* 1275 RH (Nf); Cissota *Toute* 1307 Wak (Y). OE *tūte*, ME *toute* 'buttocks, rump'. Also used topographically, of a smooth, rounded hillock: John *de la Toute* 1316 AssK.

Tovee, Tovey, Toovey, Tuvey: *Toui* 1066 DB; *Toue fox de Salebi* Hy 2 DC (L); *Toui Hering'* 1177 P (Nf); Richard, William *Toui* 1197 P (Nf), 1200 P (Ha). ON *Tófi*, ODa *Tovi*, a diminutive of *Þioðvaldr* 'nation ruler', a name brought to this country by Tovi the Proud, a follower of Cnut.

Tovell, Tofield, Tuffield, Tuffill: *Touillda* 1066 DB (Ess); *Touilt* 1086 DB (Sf); Willelmus *filius Touild'* 1175 P (Sf); *Touild'* 1201 Cur (Nf); Stephen *Tovild* 1473 NorwW (Sf); John *Tovell* 1491 ib.; Alice *Tovyld* 1506 ib.; Robert *Toveld*, William *Tuffeld* 1524 SRSf. A rare surname from a rare Scandinavian personal name of an unusual type, ON *Tófa-Hildr* (f), 'Hildr the daughter of Tófi', found chiefly in Suffolk, occasionally in Essex and Norfolk.

Toward: Margery *Toward* 1275 RH (Nf). ME *toward* 'compliant, docile'.

Tow(e), Towes: v. TOUGH

Tower: (i) Elyas *de Toure* 1202 P (So); William *de la Tur* 1260 AssC; Theobald *atte Tur* 1296 SRSx. 'Dweller by the tower', OE *tūr* or OFr *tour* 'tower'. (ii) Gilbert *le Tower'* 1255 RH (W); Thomas *le Touere* 1275 RH (Ha); William *le Towyere, le Tawyere* 1280 MESO (Ha). A derivative of OE *tāwian* 'to taw'. v. TAWYER and MESO 122.

Towers: v. TOURS

Towgood: v. TOOGOOD

Towl(e): v. TOLL

Towler: v. TOLLER

Towlson: v. TOWNSON

Town, Towne, Townes, Towns, Tone, Toon, Toone, Tune: Wistric *Oftun* c1095 Bury (Sf); Peter *de la Tune* a1219 Seals (Sr); Arnold *Inthetune* 1243 AssSo; John *de la Tone* 1275 RH (Sf); Peter *Abopetoune*, Richard *above the toune* 1275 SRWo; Nicholas *Tone* 1279 RH (C); Mabel *atte Tune*

1296 SRSx; John *Douninthetoune* 1327 SRWo; Alan *de Toune*, William *dil Toun* 1327 SRSf; Henry *Town* 1428 FA (D); John *Townes* 1524 SRSf. OE *tūn* originally denoted a 'fence' or 'enclosure' but at an early date came to mean 'enclosure round a house', 'homestead', 'village', 'town'. In these surnames, originally preceded by a preposition, the reference is to 'one who lived in, at, above or down in the *tūn*' which must here mean 'the village' as in *Townend* and *Townsend*.

Townend, Townen, Townsend, Townshend: (i) Richard *atte Tounende* 1297 MinAcctCo; Adam *Attetounhend*' 1297 SRY. (ii) Wulfric *at te tunesende* 1192 P (Sf); Godmannus *atte Tounsende* 1284 RamsCt (Hu); William *atte Townesend* 1327 SRWo. 'Dweller (i) at the town-end, (ii) at the town's end', a genitival compound always the more common, *town* having the meaning 'village' as in TOWN.

Towner: Hugh *le Tolnur* 1221 AssWo. OE *tolnere* 'tax-gatherer'. cf. TOLLER.

Towning: Nicholas *Tounyng*' 1327 SRWo. OE **tūning* 'dweller in the village'.

Townley, Townly, Towneley: Richard *de Tunleie* 1214 FFSf; Robert *de Tounlegh* 1287 IpmLa; Laurence *of Tounlay* alias Laurence of Lehg 1401 AssLa; Richard *Towneley* de Towneley 1622 PrGR. From Towneley (Lancs), or 'dweller by the farm clearing'.

Towns(h)end: *v.* TOWNEND

Townson, Tolson, Toulson, Towlson: Christopher *Towson, Tolson* 1553, 1593 Ipsw (Sf); Edmund *Tollenson, Townson* 1571 LaWills; Robert *Tolneson, Townson* 1580 ib.; Richard *Towlson, Tounson* 1587 ib.; Jenet *Tomlinson, Towenson* 1588 ib.; Catherine *Toinson, Towenson* 1591 ib. Colloquial pronunciations of *Tomlinson*, particularly common in North Lancashire.

Toy, Toye: Aluric *Toi* 1066 Winton; Aldwin *Toie* 1184 P (D); Wydo, Alan *Toye* 1274 RH (Sf). Presumably a nickname, the meaning and origin of which remain obscure, *v.* Tengvik 372. It was evidently used also as a personal name, cf. Godfrey *filius Toye* 1200 ChR (L).

Tozer: John *le Tosere*, William *le Thosere* 1249 MESO (Sx), 1280 AssSo; John *Tosere* 1333 PN D 519. A derivative of OE **tāsian* 'to toze, tease', a side-form of OE *tǣsan* 'to tease'. cf. William *le Tesere* 1275 AssSo. 'A comber or carder of wool.'

Tracey, Tracy: Henry *Traci* 1139 Templars (O); Henry *de Traci* 1148 Winton (Ha); Oliver *de Trazi* 1166 P (D). The Tracies were undertenants in the department of La Manche (ANF). The surname derives from Tracy-Bocage or Tracy-sur-Mer (Calvados).

Trad(e)well: *v.* TREADWELL

Train: (i) Warin *Traine* 1181 P (Nb); Robert *Trayne* 1243 AssDu. ME *trayne*, OFr *traine* 'guile, trickery', 'a trap or snare for catching wild animals', metonymic for a trapper, hunter. (ii) Richard *Trane* 1301 SRY; Thomas *Tran* 1455 Black; William *Trayne* 1557 ib. A northern and Scottish form of ON *trani* 'crane'. (iii) In Devon-

shire, from Train in Wembury or Traine in Modbury, the homes respectively of Thomas *atte Trewen* (1311) and John Tirry *atte Trewen* (1370), 'at the trees' (PN D 261, 281). *v.* TREE.

Trainer, Trainor, Treanor, Traynor: Robert *Treiner, Trainer* 1243 AssDu, 1379 PTY. A derivative of ME *trayne* 'to lay a train or snare, to set a trap', a trapper.

Tranter, Trenter: Terri *Trauetarius* 1148 Winton (Ha); Philip *Trenter*' 1221 Cur (Ess); Hugo *le Trauenter* 1292 MESO (Ess); Mark *le Traveter* 1306 AD iii (Co); Simon *le Traunter* 1332 SRWa. MedLat *travetarius* 'carrier, hawker'. *v.* tranter (NED).

Trapnell: William *Tropisnel* 1183 P (Nf); Walter, William *Tropinel(l)* 1195 P (W), 1201 AssSo; Robert *Tropnell* 1497 RochW; Anne *Trapnell* 1662 SfPR. OFr *trop isnel* 'too swift'.

Trapp, Trappe: John, Henry *Trappe* 1230 P (Wo), c1250 Rams (Hu). OE *træppe, trappe* 'trap, gin, snare', no doubt for a trapper of animals.

Travell, Travil: (i) William *le traueillie* 1196 P (Nb); Malger *le Travaile, le Travaillie, le Travallie* 1205–7 Cur (L); (ii) Ralph, Robert *Trauel* 1185 Templars (L), 1203 P (Bk); Thomas *Trauail* 1202 AssL; William *Trauayl* 1296 SRSx. The past part. of OFr *travaillier, traveillier* 'to afflict, vex, trouble', corresponding to ME *traveled, travailed* 'wearied in body and mind, troubled, harassed' (c1420 NED), alternating with ME, OFr *travail* 'exertion, trouble, hardship, suffering' (c1250 NED).

Travers, Traves, Travis, Traviss: Robert *Trauers, Traues, trauerse* Hy 2 DC (L); Walter *Travers* 1172 Gilb (L); Margareta *Travas* 1433 GildY; Ann *Travis* or *Travers* 1578 Bardsley; Cordell *Traverse* son of Phillip *Travesse* 1640 ib. ME *travers*, later *travas, traves, travis*, corresponds to two OFr nouns, *travers* (m) and *traverse* (f), 'the act of passing through a gate or crossing a river, bridge, etc.', used of a toll paid on passing the boundary of a town or lordship (*toll-traverse* 1567 NED). In 1285 (QW) the Bishop of Norwich claimed that he and his predecessors were accustomed to take a certain *Travers* at South Elmham (Suffolk) from foreign merchants crossing a certain bridge with merchandise towards Beccles, Yarmouth and Bungay for the upkeep of the bridge. The same custom existed elsewhere in Suffolk and Norfolk, and continued at Hull as late as 1852. The surname, which was common and widespread, probably refers to one who possessed this custom or to one who collected the toll.

Traynor: *v.* TRAINER

Treacher: Walter *le Trichur* 1243 AssSo; Robert *Trechour* 1301 SRY. OFr *trecheor, tricheor* 'deceiver, cheat'.

Treadaway: *v.* TRETHEWEY

Treadgold: *v.* THREADGOLD

Treadwell, Tredwell, Tretwell, Tradewell, Tradwell: Seeman, Thomas *Treddewel* c1248 Bec (Sf). 'Tread well.' cf. Symon *Tredeven* 1275 SRWo, John *Tredebas* 1327 SRC.

Treanor: *v.* TRAINER

Treasure: Ansgod *Tresor*, Clement *treisor* 1148 Winton (Ha); Adgar *Treissor'* 1199 FFEss; Laurence *Tresor*, *Thresor* 1207, 1230 P (Ha); Nicholas *le Tresor* 1243 AssSo. OFr *tresor*, ME *tresor*, *treysour*, *thresur* 'wealth, riches' (1154 NED). Metonymic for 'treasurer'. cf. Henricus *Thesaurius* 1066 Winton (Ha), Nicholas *de la Tresorie* 1325 FFEss.

Tredgett, Tredjett, Trudgett: William *de* (sic) *Treget* 1176 P (He); Robert, Roger *Treget* 1188 P (He), 1327 SRSf; John *Tredgett*, Richard *Tridgitt* 1674 HTSf; — *Trudgett* 1674 HTSf. OFr *tresgiet*, *treget*, ME *treget*, *trigit* 'jugglery, trickery, deceit' (a1300 NED), metonymic for a juggler. cf. Robert *le Tregettur* 1203 AssSt, Symon *le Tregetor* 1279 RH (C), ME *tregetour*, *trigettur*, 'a juggler, mountebank' (a1300 NED).

Tredgold: v. THREADGOLD

Tredinnick, Treddinick: Ralph *de Tredenek'* 1297 MinAcctCo. From Tredinnick (Cornwall).

Tree, Treece, Trees, Treen, Trewin: Henry *en le Tres* 1327 SRDb; John *del Trees* 1379 PTY. 'Dweller by the tree(s).' *Treen*, the weak plural form, survives in Trewyn (PN D 148). cf. TRAIN (iii).

Trefusis: James *Trefusis* 1359 Putnam (Co). From Trefusis (Cornwall).

Tregellas, Tregelles, Tregillus: Nicholas *de Tregellest* 1297 MinAcctCo. From Tregelles (Cornwall).

Trelfall: v. THRELFALL

Treloar: Gregory *de Trelouargh'* 1297 Coram. From Treloar (Cornwall).

Tremayne, Tremain, Tremaine, Treman: Nicholas *Tremeayne*, *Tremayn* 1562 Pat (Co); Andrew *Tremayne* 1576 SRW; John *Tremaine* 1642 PrD. From Tremaine (Cornwall).

Tremelling: William *Tremillin* 1255 RH (St). From Tremellen (Cornwall).

Tremenheere: Thomas *Tremenhir* 1359 Putnam (Co). From Tremenheere (Cornwall).

Tremlett, Trimlett: Walter *de Tribus Minetis* 1130 P (D); Joslen *Treismunettes* 1194 P (D); Richard *de Treminettes* 1204 Pl (St); Richard *Treminet* 1275 RH (D); John *Trymlett* 1525 SRSx; Matthew, Thomas *Tremlett* 1642 PrD. From Les Trois Minettes (Calvados).

Trenchard: Ralph *Trencart*, *Trenchard* 1086 DB (So); Robert *Trenchart* 1166 P (Ha). A derivative in -*ard* of OFr *trenchier* 'to cut'. Bardsley suggests 'swordsman'. It might be occupational: cf. Walter *Trenchebof* 1214 Cur (Mx) 'cut ox', butcher.

Trendall, Trendell, Trindall: Ernald *Trendel* 1177 P (Sf); John *atte Trandle* 1327 SRSx. 'Dweller by the circle', OE *trendel*, used of woods, wells, hills, earthworks, etc. of circular shape.

Trenow: Clement *Trenowe* 1297 MinAcctCo. From Treknow in Tintagel (Cornwall).

Trenowath, Trenoweth, Trenouth: Ranulf *de Trenewyth* c1210 Fees (Co). From Trenoweth (Cornwall).

Trenter: v. TRANTER

Treseder, Tresidder, Tressider: William *de Tre-*

soder 1297 MinAcctCo. From Tresidder (Cornwall).

Tresilian: Robert *Tresilian* 1379 AD iii (Co). From Tresillian (Cornwall).

Trethewey, Trethewy, Treadaway: Andrew *de Tredewi* c1210 Fees (Co); Henry *de Trethewy* 1297 MinAcctCo. From Trethewey (Cornwall).

Trett: Baldwin *le Tret* 1194 P (Do). ME *tret* 'neat, graceful, handsome', used of the face, nose and neck.

Tretwell: v. TREADWELL

Treveal: William *de Treuael* 1297 MinAcctCo. From Treveal (Cornwall).

Trevellick: John *de Treuellek* 1297 MinAcctCo. From Trevillick (Cornwall).

Trew: v. TRUE

Trewin: v. TREE

Tricker: Gilbert *Trykere* 1260 FFEss; Adam *le Trikur* 1275 Wak (Y). A derivative of ME *trik*, OFr *trique*, Norman-Picard form of *triche* 'trick'. 'Cheat, deceiver.'

Trickett: Ralph *Trichet* 1130 P (Mx); Robert *Triket* 1198 Cur (Bk). A Norman-Picard form of Fr *Trichet*, *Trichot* which Dauzat takes as hypocoristics of *Trichard*, Norman-Picard *Tricard* 'cheat, deceiver'.

Trickey: A surname from Trickey (Devon) existed in 1238 (PN D 620).

Trigg, Trigge, Triggs: *Trig* 1185 Templars (Y); William *Trig* 1202 AssL, 1240 Rams (Nf); William *Trigges* 1279 RH (C); Ralph *Trigge* 1332 SRLa. ON *tryggr* 'true, faithful, trustworthy', also used as a personal-name.

Trillo: Philip *de Trillowe* 1279 RH (C). From Thurlow (Suffolk).

Trimlett: v. TREMLETT

Trimmer: William *le Trymmare* 1327 MESO (Ha). A derivative of *trim* vb. v. NED. 'One who trims', the exact sense being uncertain as the verb has not been found in ME.

Trindall: v. TRENDALL

Trinder: Hugo *le Trinder* 1275 RH (Nf); John *le Trendare* 1278 AssSo. A derivative of OE *trendan* 'to turn round, roll'. As ME *trend* means 'to twist, plait' and *tryndelle* is a spindle, the surname probably denotes a braider.

Tripe: Herbert *Tripe* 1185 Templars (K); Robert *Tripes* 1302 SRY. ME *tripe*, *tripis*, OFr *tripe* 'tripe', metonymic for a tripe-seller. cf. Fr *Tripier*.

Tripp: Gilbert, Hugh *Trip* 1275 RH (W), 1312 LLB D; Robert *Tryppe* 1296 SRSx. Either a variant of TRIPE (OFr *trippe*) or metonymic for TRIPPER.

Tripper: William *le Trippere* 1293 AssSt. ME *trippere* 'dancer' (c1380 NED).

Trippett: Ralph, Peter *Tripet* 1204 Cur (Beds), 1256 AssNb; William *Tripat* 1327 *SR* (Ess). ME *tripet*, *trepett*, OFr *tripot* 'an evil scheme, malicious trick'. *Trypet* alternates with *treget* c1330 (NED). cf. TREDGETT.

Trist, Trister: Peter *ate Treste* 1279 RH (Bk); Richard *Trist* 1332 SRCu; William *Trystour* 1394

LLB H. ME *triste, tryster, tristur,* OFr *triste, tristre* 'an appointed station in hunting', denoting, probably, the man in charge of the hounds and the preparations for the hunt.

Tristram, Trustram: *Tristram* Cementarius 1204 Cur; *Tristram* Merewyne 1296 SRSx; Henry, Leonard, Richard *Tristram* 1207 Pl (Ess), 1296 SRSx, 1334 SRK; Richard *Trustram* 1577 Musters (Nf). Celtic *Drystan,* from *drest, drust* 'tumult, din'. It appears as a christian name in England from the end of the 12th century, usually in the form *Tristram.*

Troath: *v.* TROTH

Trobridge: *v.* TROWBRIDGE

Trollop, Trollope: John, Andrew *Trollop* 1427 AD iii (Du), 1461 Past; Androwe *Trowlopp,* Thomas *Trollopp* 1525 SRSx; John *Trollope* 1577 Musters (Nf). From Troughburn (Northumb), formerly *Trolhop* 'troll-valley.'

Tromans: *v.* TRUEMAN

Tronson: *v.* TRUNCHION

Troop, Troops, Troup, Troupe, Trupp: John *de Trope* 1275 SRWo. A variant of THROP.

Troth, Troath: Roger *Troth* 1327 SRSf. ME *trouþe, trothe* 'faithfulness, loyalty'.

Trotman: Richard *Troteman* 1224 Cur (Ess); Robert *Trotteman* 1281 Ipm (Sx). Synonymous with TROTTER.

Trott: Walter, Robert *Trot* 1206 P (Sr), Cur (Bk); William *le Trot* 1327 SRSx. A verbal substantive from 'to trot' in the sense of TROTTER. Or, perhaps, AFr *trote* 'old woman, hag', though usually *trate* in ME.

Trotter: Robert *trotar* 1148 Winton (Ha); Adam *le Troter* 1219 AssY. OFr *trotier* 'a trotter, messenger'.

Troubridge: *v.* TROWBRIDGE

Trouncer: Gilbert *le trunchier* 1192 P (Lo); Henry *le Truncer* 1315 Wak (Y). A derivative of OFr *tronche* 'club, cudgel'. A maker or seller of cudgels.

Trounson: *v.* TRUNCHION

Troup(e): *v.* TROOP

Trout, Troutt, Trowt, Trute: William *Trute, Troute* 1202 AssL, 1327 SRSf. OE *trūht* 'trout'.

Trow: *v.* TRUE

Trowbridge, Troubridge, Trobridge, Trubridge: Walter *de Trobrigge* 1184 P (Gl); William *de Trewebrugg'* 1275 SRWo. From Trowbridge (Wilts).

Trowell, Trowill, Trowles: Richard *de Trowell'* 1204 P (Nt); Edmund *Trowlles* 1524 SRSf. From Trowell (Notts).

Trower: *v.* THROWER

Trowman: *v.* TRUEMAN

Trowt: *v.* TROUT

Troy: Elyas *de Troie* 1200 P (Bk); Copyn *de Troys* 1276 LLB A. From Troyes (Aube).

Troyt, Troyte: Robertus *filius Troite* 1159 P (Cu); Robert *Troite* 1166 ib.; Richard *Troyte* 1230 ib. OIr **Troit.* cf. Ir *troid* 'quarrel' (Smith).

Trubridge: *v.* TROWBRIDGE

Truce: Juliana *in Trewes* 1279 RH (Beds). 'Dweller among the trees.' cf. TRUE (ii).

Trudgett: *v.* TREDGETT

True, Trew, Trow: (i) Rannulfus *Truue (Triue)* 1180 P (Wa); Ralph *Truwe* 1185 Templars (K); Roger *Trowe* 1200 Cur (W); William *Trewe* 1301 SRY; Henry *le Trewe* 1327 AD i (W). OE *trēowe,* ME *trew(e), trow(e)* 'faithful, loyal, trustworthy'. (ii) Hugo *de la Truwe, de la Trowe* 1250 Fees (So); Laurence *atte Trowe* 1332 SRSx. OE *trēow,* ME *treow, trew, trow* 'tree', from residence near some prominent tree or from one of the places in Devon named Tree, Trew, True or Trow. (iii) Roger *de Trow* 1207 Cur (W); Jacobus *de Trewe, de Trowe* 1219, 1222 Pat (W). From Trow Fm and Down (Wilts), from OE *trog* 'trough'. This becomes *Trow. v.* PN W 200.

Truebody: Roger *Trewebodi* 1277 AssSo; William *Treubody* 1301 ArchC ix. 'True, faithful man.'

Truelove, Trolove: Roger *Trewelove* 1275 RH (Sa); Robert *Treuweloue* 1296 SRSx; John *Truloue* 1384 AssWa. OE *trēowe* and *lufu* 'faithful love' in the sense 'faithful lover, sweetheart, beloved' (c1385 NED).

Trueman, Truman, Trewman, Troman, Tromans, Trowman: Richard *Treweman* c1215 StGreg (K); William *Trueman* 1279 RH (O); Robert *Trowman* 1327 SRSf. 'Faithful, trusty man' (1297 NED).

Truett: *v.* TYRWHITT

Trumble, Trumbull: Alan *Tumbald, Thrumball* 1313, 1316 Wak (Y); Peter, Reginald *Thrumbald* 1315 ib., 1327 SRSf; Alice *Thrumbald, Trumbald* 1316–17 Wak (Y); Elizabeth *Trumble* 1568 SRSf; Ralph *Trumball* 1696 DKR 41 (Berks). OE **Trumbeald* 'strong-bold'. cf. OE *Trumbeorht, Trumwine,* and Robert *Trumwine* 1236 Fees (St). *v.* TURNBULL.

Trump: Patrick, Nicholas *Trumpe* 1275 Ipm (Cu), 1279 RH (C). Metonymic for *Trumper.*

Trumper: Adam *Trumpur* 1253 AD iv (Ess); William *Trompour* 1320 LLB E; John *le Trumpour* 1327 SRY. OFr *trompeor, trompour, trumpeur* 'trumpeter'.

Trunchion, Tronson, Trounson: William *Trunchun* 1209 FrLeic; Thomas *Trunson* 1327 SRC. OFr *truncun, tronchon* 'truncheon, club', metonymic for a maker or seller of cudgels. Or, perhaps, for an official who carried a truncheon.

Trupp: *v.* TROOP

Truscott: Michael *de Trescote* 1272 AssSt. From Trescott (Staffs).

Trushell: *v.* TRUSSEL

Trusher: William *Trussehare* 1206 Cur (Wo). 'Carry off the hare', a nickname, probably for a poacher. cf. TRUSLOVE.

Truslove, Trusler, Trussler: Henry *de* (sic) *Trusseluue* 1221 AssWa; Nicholas, Adam *Trusselove* 1296 SRSx, 1302 SRY; Thomas *Truslowe* 1524 SR (W). OFr *trousser, trusser* 'to truss, bind, carry off' and AFr *love* 'wolf'; 'bind wolf', a wolf-hunter. cf. BINDLOES and Walkelin *Trussevilain* 1171 Riev (Y),

Truss: Robert, John *Trusse* 1202 FFSf, 1275

SRWo. OFr *trousse* 'bundle, package'. *v.* TRUSS-MAN.

Trussel, Trussell, Trushell: Robert *Trusel* 1195 P (Lei); Godfrey *Trussel* 1204 P (Y); Richard *Trussell* 1221 AssWa; William *Troussel* 1285 FA (St). OFr *troussel* 'packet', in ME also 'the puncheon or mould used in the stamping of coins'. A maker or user of 'trussels'.

Trussman: John *Trusseman* 1327 SRSx. Probably a baggage-man, porter. *v.* TRUSS.

Trustram: *v.* TRISTRAM

Trute: *v.* TROUT

Try, Trye: Thomas *Trie* 1274 RH (Sa); Juliana *Trye* 1301 SRY. ME *trie, triȝe* 'excellent, good'.

Tubb, Tubbs, Tubby: *Tubi, Tube* 1066 DB (Bk, Wa); Reginaldus *filius Tobbe* 1166 P (Y); Laurencius *filius Tubb* 1230 ib.; Alan *Tubbi* 1206 Cur (Nf); John *Tub* 1212–23 Bart (Mx); Roger, William *Tubbe* 1243 AssSo, 1296 AssNb. ON, ODa *Tubbi*, OSw *Tubbe*.

Tubman: Robert *Tubman* 1430 FrY. A derivative of ME *tubbe*, a maker of tubs, cooper.

Tuck: *Tukke* faber 1101–7 Holme (Nf); Radulfus *filius Tokke* 1175 P (Y); Symon *filius Thocche* a1187 DC (L); Johannes *filius Tuch* c1250 Rams (C); Besi *Tuk* 1051 KCD 795 (L); Henry *Thoche* 12th DC (L); Robert *Tucke* 1202 FF (Nf). Tengvik derives (Besi) *Tuk* from ODa **Tuk*, a strong form of *Tuki*, which is possible, but the frequent occurrence of the personal name in the 12th and 13th centuries suggests that we have an Anglo-Scand. **Tukka*, a pet-form of ON *Þorketill*.

Tucker: Baldwin *Tuckere* 1236 Battle (Sx); Wolward *le Tukare* 1243 AssSo; Thomas *le Touchere* 1293 Pinchbeck (Sf); Hugo *le Tukker'* 1297 MinAcctCo (Co); Richard *le Touker* 1327 SRSo. A derivative of OE *tūcian* 'to torment', later 'to tuck, to full', 'a tucker, fuller'. *v.* FULLER. Occasionally a nickname for courage (Fr *tout cœur*): Geoffrey *Tutquor, Totquer* 1217 Pat (K), Hy 3 Colch (Ess).

Tuckerman, Tuckermann: Richard *Tuckerman* 1647 DWills. 'The tuckerman', a tucker, fuller.

Tuckey: *v.* TOOKEY

Tudball: *v.* THEOBALD

Tuddenham: John *de Tudeham* 1191 P (Sf). From Tuddenham (Norfolk, Suffolk).

Tudman: John *Tudnham*, Thomas *Tudnam*, William *Tudman* 1524 SRSf. For TUDDENHAM. cf. DEBENHAM.

Tudor: *Tudor* 1221 AssSa; David *ap Tudir* 1287 AssCh; *Tudur* ap Llywelyn 1391 Chirk; Christian *Tudor* 1327–9 FrC; John *Tewdre* 1334–5 SRK. The Welsh form of *Theodore*.

Tuer: *v.* TEWER

Tuffery, Tuffrey: *v.* TOLLFREE

Tuffield, Tuffill: *v.* TOVELL

Tugwood: *v.* TOOGOOD

Tulliver: *v.* TELFER

Tumber: John *Tumbur* 1276 MEOT (O); Henry *le Tombere* 1327 ib. (Ha). OE *tumbere* or OFr *tombeor, tumbeur* 'tumbler, dancer'.

Tumman, Tummon, Thommen, Toman: (i) Ralph, Adam *Tuneman* 1279 RH (Beds), 1296 SRSx; Pagan *Toneman* 1327 SR (Ess); Nicholas *Tounman* 1365 LoPleas; Thomas *Tonman* 1379 PTY. OE *tūnmann* 'villager'. (ii) Nicholas *Thomasman* 1301 SRY; William *Thomeman* 1379 PTY. Cf. Johannes *Tomman* Cisson 1379 PTY, i.e. 'John, servant of Tom Cisson'. Rarer than (i) and, no doubt, the origin of the Yorkshire *Tummon*. cf. ADDYMAN, MATTHEWMAN.

Tunbridge: *v.* TONBRIDGE

Tune: *v.* TOWN

Tunn: Hugo *filius Tunne* 1204 P (Y); Robert *Tun* 1218 AssL; Robert, Reginald *Tunne* 1279 RH (O), 1311 RamsCt (Hu). *Tunne* is OE *Tunna* (Redin), a pet-form of such names as OE *Tūnrǣd, Tūnwulf* and *Tūnrīc*. cf. Robertus *filius Tunrici* 1182–1200 BuryS (Sf). The surname may also be metonymic for a maker of tuns. cf. Robert *le Tunnewrytte* 1279 AssNb and *v.* TUNNAH.

Tunnah: (i) William *le Tunnere* 1280 MESO (Ha). A derivative of OE *tunne* 'a tun', a maker of tuns. (ii) Hugh, William *le Tundur* 1275 RH (Nf), 1296 SRSx. AFr *tundour*, OFr *tondeur* 'shearman'. For the development, cf. *Lunnon* from *London* and *Farrah* for *Farrer*.

Tunnard: Augustin *Tunherd* 1279 RH (C); Robert *le Tunherd* 1327 SRC. OE **tūn-hierde* 'guardian of the village or town animals'. Johannes *filius Tunherd* 1327 SRC may mean 'son of the town-herd' but we may have an unrecorded OE **Tūnheard*. cf. *Tonhardus* 1066–87 Bury (Sf).

Tunnell: *v.* TONNELL

Tunney: *Tunne* 1066 DB (L); Gillibertus *filius Tunny* 1219 AssY; Simon *Tunnie* 1327 AssSt; Adam *Tunnyson* 1332 SRCu. ODa *Tunni*, OSw *Tunne*.

Tunnicliff, Tunnicliffe, Dunnicliff, Dunnicliffe: Henry *de Tunwaleclif* 1246 AssLa. From Tonacliffe (Lancs).

Tunsley: Robert *de Tundesle* 1214 Cur (Sr). From Townslow (Surrey).

Tunstall, Tunstill, Dunstall: Reginald *de Tunstal* 1185 P (Y). From Tunstall (ER, NRYorks, Suffolk, etc.).

Tupper: Robert *Tupper* 1314 Wak (Y). At York in 1365 men were employed in beating and ramming (*tupant'*) 'the earth and mud, strengthened with straw, with rammers (*tuppis*) and great hammers' (Building 85). As the rams were called *tups*, these workmen may well have been named *tuppers*. The surname may also be a late form of *tup-herd* (ME *tup* 'ram'): Robert *Tophird* 1327 SRY, William *Tuphird* 1379 PTY.

Turbard, Turbet, Turbett, Turbott, Turbutt, Torbett, Torbitt, Tarbard, Tarbert, Tarbath, Tarbat, Tarbet, Tarbitt, Tarbutt: *Turbert, Torbertus* 1066 DB; *Thurbert* 1066 InqEl (Sf); *Turbertus* c1160–70 NthCh (Beds); Alanus, Gaufridus *Torberti* 1212 Cur (Berks); John *Turbut* 1221 Cur (Herts); William *Turbert* 1248 Fees (Ess); John *Turberd* 1274 RH (Ess); Thomas *Torebat* 1279 RH (C); Eudo *Turbot* 1327 *SR* (Ess). There is no OE or Scand personal name which fits these forms.

We are concerned with a hybrid *Þorbert, Þurbert* in which the first theme is Scand *Þor-, Þur-,* and the second OG *-bert*. The name was probably formed on the Continent and is identical with the Norman *Turbert* found in *Turbertivilla*, probably Thouberville (Eure). Hence the Norman initial *T* and the frequent loss of the second *r*. Only one example of the name is found in England before the Conquest but it is common in DB and continued in use until at least the 13th century. It is sometimes confused with *Þorbiǫrn*. v. THURBAN.

Turbefield, Turberfield, Turberville: Ralph *de Tuberilli* 1115 Winton (Ha); Robert *de Turbertuulla* 1121 AC (He); Hugo *de Turbervilla* 1123 AC (He); William *de Truble villa*, c1125–30 EngFeud, *de Turbertiuilla* 1130 P (Do); Maud *de Turbervill, de Trubleuile* 1269, 1279 AssSo. From Thouberville (Eure). v. PNDB 391, n. 8.

Turbett, Turbott: v. TURBARD
Turbin: v. THURBAN
Turfery, Turfrey: v. TOLLFREE
Turgel, Turgill: v. THURKELL
Turgoose: v. STURGE

Turk: *Turch, Turcus* 1066 DB (C); *Turche* c1150 DC (L); *Turkus fugitivus* 1172 P (Sx); Ricardus *filius Torke* 1188 P (Y); Ricardus *filius Turk'* 1205 ChR (K); Eadwin *Turcus* (*le Turch, Tercus*) c1140 ELPN; William *Turc, le Turc* 1193, 1196 P (Gl); Robert *Turk* 1296 SRSx. The DB *Turch* is explained by von Feilitzen as ON *Þorkell*, with AN loss of *-el*. It seems clear that it was also used as a pet-form of this Scandinavian name. Most of the surnames appear to be nicknames from OFr *turc* 'Turk', a word which NED suggests was introduced into England during the third crusade (1187–92). It is found as a nickname in London half a century earlier.

Turkel, Turkil: v. THURKELL
Turkentine, Turketine: Robertus *filius Turketin* c1150 DC (L); Nathaniel *Turquentine* 1654 Shotley PR (Sf); Mr *Turkenton* 1674 HTSf; Hannah *Turkeytine* 1817 Rushbrook PR (Sf). A double diminutive of *Turk*, from ON *Þorkell*, *Turk-et-in*. cf. Nicholas *Turkot* 1317 AssK.

Turnbull, Turnbill: Willelmus *dictus Turnebule* 1314 Black; William *Turbolle* 1327 SRSf; Walter *Tornebole* c1354 Black; Richard *Turnebull'* 1379 PTY; David *Trumbull* or *Turnbull* 1495 Bardsley. There can be no doubt that this much-discussed surname is a nickname 'turn bull', indicative of strength or bravery. The name appears to be northern, particularly Scottish, but early examples are not common. Black's derivation from *Trumbald* cannot be correct. The early forms of *Trumble* are quite distinct from those of *Turnbull* and there is no proof that any of the 15th-century Scottish Trumbles were Turnbulls. The Fife families of Trimbill, Trombill and Trumble may well have owed their name, as Black suggests, to the same place from which Robert de Tremblee (1296) came. OE *Trumbeald* developed naturally to *Trumball*, also spelled *Trumbull*. It is much more likely that this should be corrupted to *Turnbull* than that

Turnbull should become an unintelligible *Trumbull, Trumble*. The nickname origin of the surname is proved by Ewen himself (despite his antipathy to nicknames) in his reference to a Yorkshire horse named *Turnebull* (1358) and is confirmed by the modern French *Tournebœuf* which Dauzat explains as a name for a drover.

Turner, Turnor: (i) Warner *le Turnur* 1180 P (Lo); Ralph *le tornur, tornator, le turner* 1191–2 P (Lei). OFr *tornour, tourneour* 'turner, one who turns or fashions objects of wood, metal, bone, etc., on a lathe' (c1400 NED). This is, no doubt, the common source of this occupational surname. Its frequency is due to the variety of objects that could be turned and to the use of the word in other senses. Lat *tornator* meant 'turnspit' (1308) as well as 'turner' (1327 MLWL). cf. 'Turnowre, *Tornator*' PromptParv, and 'Turnare, or he that turnythe a spete or other lyke, *versor*' ib., *tornerers* 'translaters' 1387 NED and v. DISHER. Nor can we exclude OFr *tornoieor, tournoieur* 'one who takes part in a tourney or tournament' (Lat *torneator* 'jouster' 1220 MLWL; ME *tourn(e)our* 1303 NED). cf. JUSTER. (ii) Bernard, Robert *Turnehare* 1224 Cur (St), 1301 SRY. 'Turn hare', one so speedy that he could outstrip and turn the hare. As a surname, the second element would be unstressed and became *Turner*. cf. CATCHER.

Turney, Tournay: Goisfridus *Tornai* 1086 DB (L); Thomas *de Turnay* 1192 P (Lo). From Tournai, Tournay or Tourny, all in Normandy. The DB baron came from Tournai (Calvados).

Turnpenney, Turnpenny: Ralf *Turnepeny* 1227 AssBk; John *Tornepeny* 1269 AssSt. A nickname from the phrase 'to turn a penny' (1546 NED) in the sense 'a person who is intent on a profit' (1824 ib.).

Turp: Robert *de Turp* 1177, 1230 P (Cu); Adam *Tourpp* 1332 SRCu. A metathesized form of TROOP, for THORP.

Turpie: John *Turpy* 1607 Black (Fife). A Scottish diminutive of *Turpin*.

Turpin: *Torfin, Turfin* 1066 DB (Y); *Turfinus filius Torfini* 1130 P (Y); *Turpin* Hy 2 DC (L); *Turpinus* 1180 P (Ha); *Torphinus* 1196 P (Y), c1227 Fees (Nb); *Turfin* 1202 P (Nb); Gaufridus *filius Thorphini* 1204 Cur (Y); *Thorpinus filius Simonis* 1230 P (D); William, Richard *Turpin* 1187, 1196 P (Ha, Y); Thomas *Thurpin* 1230 P (Y); Simon *Turpyn, Tropyn* 1317 AssK. The above forms make it clear that *Turpin* derives from ON *Þorfinnr*, from *Þórr*, the god, and the ethnic name *Finnr*. The French *Turpin, Tourpin* is derived by Dauzat and Michaëlsson from *Turpinus*, a derivative of Lat *turpis* 'disgraceful, base', a name adopted by the early Christians as a token of humility, which came into vogue again, its meaning forgotten, through the influence of the *Chanson de Roland*, where the 8th-century archbishop of Rheims appears as *Turpin*. Forcellini has no example of *Turpinus*. *Þorfinnr* is found in Normandy where the earliest examples of *Turpin* occur and the modern surname is common. The English and the French surnames must have the same origin.

Turpitt: Stacia *del Torſpet*, William *Turpet* 1327 SRSf. 'Dweller by or worker at a turf-pit' (OE *turf* and *pytt*).

Turral, Turrall: v. THOROLD

Turreff, Turriff: (i) *Turgiua* feneratrix 1169 P (Gl); *Thurrieua* de Cestrehunte 1197 FF (Herts); William *Thuryff* 1404 DbCh. An unrecorded Anglo-Scandinavian hybrid *Þórgifu* (f), from ON *Þórr* 'Thor' and OE *g(i)efu, gifu* 'gift'. (ii) David *Turreff* 1682 Black (Aberdeen). From Turreff (Aberdeenshire).

Turrill: *Durilda* 1066 DB (Sf); Claricia *Þourild*, Walter *Þurild* 1279 RH (O); John *Torild* 1308 Wak (Y). ON *Þórhildr*, ODa *Thorild*, a rare woman's name.

Turtill: v. THURKELL

Turtle: Robert *Turtell'* 1176 P (Nth); Walter *Turtel* 1214 Cur (K); Henry *Turtle* 1327 *SR* (Ess). A nickname from the turtle-dove, ME *turtel, turtle*, OE *turtle* (f), *turtla* (m). Or this may sometimes be from Fr *tourtel*, a diminutive from Lat *tortus* 'crooked'. Most commonly no doubt, the modern surname is due to a late assimilation of *kl* to *tl* in *Turkle*. v. THURKELL.

Turvill, Turville, Turvell: Geoffrey *de Tureuilla* 1130 P (Bk); Maurice *de Turuill'* 1206 Pl (Ha); Robert *de Turevill'* 1280 FFY; John *Turuyll* 1332 SRWa. From Turville-la-campagne (Eure). The name can have no connexion with Turville (Bucks) since the original *-feld* in this name was not replaced by *-ville* until the 19th century.

Tustain, Tustian, Tustin, Tusting: v. THURSTAN
Tutchener, Tutchings: v. TWITCHEN
Tuthill, Tutill: v. TOOTHILL
Tutin, Tuting, Tuton: v. THURSTAN
Tuttle: v. THURKELL, TOOTHILL, TURTLE
Tuttlebee, Tuttleby: Roger *de Turkelby, de Thirkelby* 1241 Eynsham, 1257 Riev (Y). From Thirkelby (ER, NRYorks). For *Tuttle-*, cf. THURKELL.
Tuvey: v. TOVEE
Twaite, Twaits: v. THWAITE
Tweedale, Tweddell, Tweddle, Tweedle: Robert *de Twedhall'* 1279 AssNb; John *de Tweddale* 1376 Black. 'Man from the valley of the Tweed.'
Twell, Twells: Hugh *Twell* 1566 ShefA; Godfrie *Twelles* 1606 RushbrookPR (Sf). An aphetic form of ATTWELL.
Twiceaday, Twisaday: Thomas *Twyssaday, Twyseaday* 1485 Pat (K), 1487 Cl (Lo); Richard *Twyssoday* 1496 GildY; Thomas *Twysaday, Twysdey* or *Twysadey* 1509 LP (Lo); Harry *Twisedaie* 1548 Bardsley (La); Edward *Twiceaday* 1661 LaWills. This is almost certainly a popular perversion of *Tuesday*, for someone born on that day, cf. twysday c1275, Twesdaie 1587 NED, and John *Tewyssnothe*, Denyce *Twesnott*, Robert *Twysnoth* 1493, 1508, 1541 CantW, Thomas *Twisnodde* 1558 Pat, all from Tuesnoad (Kent).
Twigg, Twigge: John *Twyg* 1296 AssCh. Northern OE *twigge* 'a slender shoot'.
Twin, Twinn: Nicholas *Twin* 1279 RH (C). OE *(ge)twinn* 'twin'. cf. GEMMELL.

Twine: Edmund *Twyne* 1422 FFHu. OE *twīn* 'thread, string'. Metonymic for TWINER or (Agnes) *Twynmaker* 1367 ColchCt.
Twiner: Adam *Tweyner* 1327 SRC; John *Twyner* 1429 LLB K. A derivative of ME *twīnen* 'to twine', one who twines or twists thread.
Twisaday: v. TWICEADAY
Twissell: v. TWIZEL
Twitchen, Twitching, Twitchings, Tutchings, Tutchener, Titchener, Tichner: Thomas *de la Twichene* 1275 SRWo; Gilbert *ate Thuychene* 1297 MinAcctCo; Richard *Twichener* 1432 LLB K. 'Dweller at the place where two roads meet', OE *twicen(e)*, particularly common in Devon as Twitchen (once as Tuchenor), with forms: *Nitheretochene* 1330, *Tuchyn* 1577, *Towchyn* 1650, *Twitching* 1679, *Titchin* 1809 (PN D 90, 353, 42, 57).
Twite: (i) Lambert *del Tuuit* c1190 Gilb (L); Hugh *de Twyt* 1219 AssY; Ymanye *de Thuyt* 1274 RH (Nf). OE *þwīt* or ON *þvīt*, a variant of *þveit*, surviving in Twit (Lincs). v. THWAITE. (ii) Richard *Twit* 1275 SRWo; William, Robert *Twyt* 1296 SRSx; John *Twyt* 1315 Wak (Y). A species of linnet called the Mountain Linnet or Twite-finch (1562 NED), found in the hilly and moorland districts of the north. In winter they migrate south and haunt the coast and 'enliven the marshes with their twittering song' (NED). In the 18th century they were sold as singing birds.
Twizel, Twissell: Richard *Twisle* 1196 P (Du); Richard *de Twysel* 1272 AssSt. From residence near the fork of a river or land in such a fork (OE *twisla*), or from Twizel Castle or Twizell (Northumb). Magota *atte Twisele* in 1379 lived at Twissell's Mill (PN Sx 467). cf. also Tweazle Wood (ib. 470).
Twysden: John *de Twysdenne* 1334 SRK; John, Richard *Twysden* 1447 CtH, 1525 SRSx. From Twysden in Goudhurst (Kent).
Tyas, Tyes: Everard *le Tieis* 1170–90 Seals (Herts); Fulbrich *Tyes* 1236–7 Clerkenwell (Lo). OFr *tieis* 'German'.
Tydeman: v. TIDDEMAN
Tydsley: v. TILDESLEY
Tye: Hugo *de la Tye* 1230 P (D); Richard *ater Tye* 1296 SRSx. 'Dweller by a common or enclosure' (OE *tēag*). cf. TEY.
Tyldesley: v. TILDESLEY
Tylee, Tyley: v. TILLEY
Tyler, Tylor: v. TILER
Tym, Tymm, Tymms: v. TIMMS
Tyndale, Tyndall: v. TINDAL
Tyrell, Tyrrell: v. TIRRELL
Tyrie: v. TERREY
Tyrwhitt, Truett: John *de Tyrwyt* 1256 AssNb; William *Tyrwhit* 1383 IpmGl; William *Truwhet* 1515 GildY. From Trewhitt (Northumb), *Tirwit* 1150–62.
Tyson: Gilbert *Tison* 1086 DB (Nt); Adam *Tisun* 1130 P (Y). OFr *tison* 'firebrand'.
Tytler: v. TITLER

U

Ubank: v. EWBANK

Ufford: Robert *de Vffewurda* 1179 P (Nth); Turstan *de Vfford'* 1199 P (Ha); Thomas *Ufford* 1391 FFEss. From Ufford (Northants, Suffolk).

Ughtred: v. OUGHTRED

Ugo: v. HUGH

Ullett, Ulliott: v. WOOLVETT

Ullman, Ullmann, Ulman, Ulmann: John *le Ulemon* 1275 SRWo; Richard *Olmon* 1297 SRY. ME *oli*, *oyle*, *uile*, OFr *oile*, *uille* 'oil' and ME *man*. 'A maker or seller of oil.' Now often for German *Ullmann*.

Ullmer: v. WOOLMER

Ullrich: v. WOOLRICH

Ullyatt, Ullyett, Ullyott: v. WOOLVETT

Ulph: *Vlf*, *Ulfus*, *Olf(us)* 1066 DB; *Ulf* c1095 Bury (Sf); Alwinus *Wlf* c1125 Bury (Sf); Ædwin', Robert *Vlf* 1166 P (Nf), 1279 RH (Hu). ON *Úlfr*, ODa, OSw *Ulf* 'wolf'.

Ulrich, Ulrik: v. WOOLRICH

Ulyate, Ulyatt, Ulyett: v. WOOLVETT

Uman: v. HUMAN

Umfreville: Gilbert *de Vnfranuilla* 1166 P (Nb). From Umfreville (La Manche).

Umpelby, Umpleby, Umplebye: William *de Anlauby* 1289 Pat. A Leeds and Bradford name, deriving from Anlaby (Hull), DB *Umlouebi*.

Uncle, Uncles, Ungles, Ungless: (i) William *Uncle* Hy 2 Gilb (L); Eustace *le Uncle* c1200 ArchC vi; William *le Huncle* 1243 AssSo. ME *uncle*, OFr *oncle* 'uncle'. (ii) *Ulfketel*, *Ulketel*, *Vlchetel* 1066 DB; *Vlchel*, *Vlchil* ib.; *Unchel* de Mersca 1170–85 YCh; *Ulketel* 1186–8 BuryS (Sf); *Vlfketellus* presbiter 1189–98 ib.; *Ulfkillus* 1208 Cur (Wa); Willelmus *filius Ulkilli* 1242 Fees (Nb); Robert *Hulfketell* 1199 SIA iv; Robert *Huneketel* 1214 FFK; William *Unketel* 1274 RH (So); Symon, Thomas *Ulfketel* 1275 RH (Sf); John *Unkyl* 1445 NorwW (Sf); Henry *Ulketyll* 1460 ib. Thomas *Unketyll* 1500 ib. (Nf); Myghell *Uncketyll*, John, William *Unkyll* 1524 SRSf; Christofer *Ungle* 1568 SRSf. The DB *Hunchil* (Y) is explained by von Feilitzen as ON **Húnkell* or **Hundkell*, or if the *H* is inorganic, as identical with Anglo-Scandinavian *Unketel*. In *le Huncle* the *H* is undoubtedly inorganic as it is in *Hulfketell*. The Suffolk examples make it clear we are concerned with only one name, ON *Úlfketel*, *Úlfkell* 'wolf-cauldron', which is common in that county where we also have the mutated **Ylfketill* in Ilketshall. *Ulfketell* and

Ulfkell became *Ulketel*, *Ulkell*, and then by dissimilation of *l—l* to *n—l*, *Unketell* and *Unkell*.

Underdown: Wulfwinus *Vnderdune* 1185 Templars (K); Theobald *de Vnderdoune* 1316 FFK. 'Dweller at the foot of the hill' (OE *dūn*) or at a place called Underdown.

Underhill, Undrell: Henry *Underhulle* 1275 SRWo; Geoffrey *Undrehille* 13th Rams (Hu); Robert *de Underhull* 1268 AssSo. 'One who lived at the foot of a hill' or at a place called Underhill, as in Devon.

Underwater: Walter *under Water* 1219 Fees (La). 'Dweller south of the stream.' cf. Undermillbeck (We), '(place) below, i.e. south of Millbeck'.

Underwood: William *de Underwode* 1188 BuryS (Sf); William *Underwude* de Clokton' 1219 AssY; William *Under the Wode* 1332 SRSt. Either one who lived below a wood on a hillside, or within a wood (lit. 'below the trees of the wood'), or at a place so named, as Underwood (Derby, Notts).

Undrell: v. UNDERHILL

Ungle(s): v. UNCLE

Unicume: v. HONEYCOMB

Unthank: John *de Unthanc* 1242 Fees (Nb); Alan *de Unthanke* 1332 SRCu. From one of the places named Unthank in Cumberland, Northumberland or the North Riding of Yorkshire. OE *unþances* 'without leave', dweller at a squatter's farm.

Unwin, Hunwin: *Hunuuinus*, *Onouuinus* 1066 DB (C, Do); *Vnwine*, *Hunwine* de Batha 1166–7 P (Nf); Hugo *filius Unwini* 1221 AssWo; Rannulf *Vnwine* 1195 P (Nf); William *Unwin* 1221 AssSa; Gilbert *Unwine* 1228 Cl (K); Walter *þonwyne* 1275 SRWo; Reginald *Hunwyn* 1275 RH (C); Edmund *Hunwine* 1283 SRSf; John *Hunwyne*, *Onewyne* 1295, 1301 ParlR (Ess); Thomas *Unwyn* alias *Onyon* 1559 PN Ess 428. OE *Hūnwine* 'young bear-friend', with loss of the initial *H* would tend to be confused with OE *unwine* 'unfriend, enemy' which is certainly a common source of the surname. *þonwyne* is for *the onwyne*. There may have been some contribution from OE *Unwine*. The story of *Unwen* 'son born beyond hope', with those of Hengest and Horsa, was current till so long after the Norman Conquest that it was possible for these heroes to be classed with Waltheof (Chambers, *Widsith* 254). There has also been some confusion with ONIANS.

Upcher: v. UPSHER

Uphill: (i) Roger *de Vphull'* 1199 P (Co). From Uphill (Devon). (ii) Henry *Uppenhull* 1255 RH

359

(W); John *Uphulle* 1268 AssSo; William *Vppehelle* 1320 FFK. OE *uppan hylle* '(Dweller) up on the hill'.

Upjohn: Roger *ap-John* 1638 Bardsley (Ch); Richard *Upjohn* 1778 DWills. Welsh *ap John* 'Son of John'.

Uppington: (i) Adam *de Uppinton'* 1275 SRWo. From Uppington (Salop). (ii) Richard, Geoffrey *Uppinton'* 1275, 1327 SRWo; Nicholas *Up-in-the-ton* of Waterfal 1318 AssSt. OE *upp in tūne* '(Dweller) up in the village'.

Uprichard: Robert *Upprichard* 1637 Bardsley. Welsh *ap Richard* 'son of Richard'. cf. PRITCHARD.

Upright: William *Uprict* 1210 Cur (Beds); Symon *Upriht* 1279 RH (C); Walter *Upright* 1307 FFEss. OE *ūpriht* 'erect'.

Upsher, Upcher: John *Upchar* 1420 AD i (Ess); George *Upsher* 1674 HTSf. From Upshire (Essex).

Upson, Upsom: Probably for UPSTON.

Upston, Upstone: Roger *de Ubbeston'* 1279 RH (Sf); John *Upston* 1524 SRSf. From Ubbeston (Suffolk).

Upton: Ethestan *on Optune* 972 OEByn (Nth); Richard *de Vpton'* 1162 P (Nth); Swetmann *atte Uppeton* 1332 SRSx. From one of the numerous Uptons.

Urban, Urben: *Vrbanus* de Herlingdon' 1197 P (Bk); William *Urban* 1275 RH (Herts). *Urban*, Latin *urbanus* 'of the city', the name of a 3rd-century saint and seven popes, used occasionally as a christian name in the Middle Ages.

Urlin, Urling, Urlwin: *v.* HURLIN

Urquhart: Adam *Urquhart* 1358 Black; Alexander *of Hurcharde* 1381 ib.; Charles *Urquhart* 1669–1734 ib. From the barony of Urquhart (Inverness).

Urry, Urie: *v.* HURRY

Ursell: *Ursellus* de Busco 1200 Cur (Y); William *Vrsel* 1163 P (Beds). *Ursel*, a diminutive of Latin *ursus* 'bear'.

Urvine: *v.* IRVIN

Urwin: *v.* ERWIN

Ury: *v.* HURRY

Usborne: *v.* OSBORN

Usher, Ussher, Husher, Lusher: Richard *Ussier* Hy 3 Colch (Ess); William *le Usser*, *Lussier* 1243 AssSo; Geoffrey *le Uscher* 1300 LLB C; Richard *Lusscher* 1319 SRBeds; Adam *Husser* 1332 SRCu; John *Huscher* 1506 GildY. OFr (*le*) *ussier, huissier*, AFr *usser*, ME *usher* 'usher, door-keeper' (NED c1380).

Usherwood: *v.* ISHERWOOD

Usmar: *v.* OSMER

Ussell, Uzzell: Matthew *Oisel* 1168 P (Nb); Geoffrey *Oysel* 1262 For (Ess); Margeria *Ussell*, John *Ossell* 1327 SRWo. OFr *oisel* 'bird'. cf. OSLAR.

Ussher: *v.* USHER

Utteridge, Utridge: *v.* OUTRIDGE

Utting, Uttin: Willelmus *filius Uttingi* 1183 Boldon (Du); *Utting'* 1219 AssY; Coket *Uttingus* 1183 Boldon (Du); Tomas *Vtting* 1191 P (Y); Anthony *Uttinge*, Goody *Utten* 1674 HTSf. OE **Utting*, a derivative of *Utta*.

Uwins: *v.* EWAN

Uzzell: *v.* USSELL

V

Vacher, Vacha, Vatcher: Simon *le Vacher* 1219 AssY; Hugh *le Vachir* 1227 AssSt. OFr *vachier* 'cowherd'.

Vagg(s): *v.* FAGG

Vail(e): *v.* VALE

Vaillant: *v.* VALIANT

Vaines, Veigne, Vein: Richard *de Vein* (*Veym*) 1221 AssGl. From Vains (La Manche). *v.* ANF.

Vairo: *v.* VARROW

Vaisey, Vaizey, Vasey, Veasey, Veasy, Veazey, Vesey, Vezey, Veysey, Voisey, Voizey, Voysey, Voyzey, Facey, Faizey, Fasey, Feacey, Feasey, Feazey, Feesey, Foizey, Phaisey, Phasey, Phazey, Pheasey, Pheazey, Pheysey, Lenfestey: Robertus *Invesiatus, Lascivus* 1086 DB (Ess); Robert *Lenveiset* 1131 Riev (Y); Thomas *le Envaiset* c1150 ib.; Jordan *Veiset, le Envaise* 12th ib.; William *le Enveise* (*Lenvesie*) 1220 Cur (Nf); Adam *le Veyse* 1270 AssSo; Robert *le Enueysi* 1277 ib.; Alice *Vesy* 1296 SRSx; Peter *le voyse* 1327 SRC; Thomas *Fecy* 1327 SRSo; Beatrice *a Vesy* 1332 SRSx; William *Veysy* 1357 Crowland (C); Nicholas *Vaysi* 1386 AD iv; Robert *Feysy* 1395 NottBR; John *le Vesie* 1420 DKR 41; John *Vasey* 1456 NorwW (Sf); John *Veysey,* or *Vesey,* or *Voysye,* or *Pheysy* 1512 Oxon; Maud *Fyseye* 1541 W'stowWills (Ess); Christian *Facy* 1671 DWills; Philip *Veasy* 1674 HTSf. In spite of Weekley's correct explanation of *Vaisey,* Tengvik has repeated Bardsley's confusion of the name with *Vessey.* True, there has been a late and occasional confusion between these surnames, as in the 1524 Subsidy Roll for Suffolk where we find *Vessy* side by side with *Vasy, Veysy* and *Vaysy,* but all the above surnames undoubtedly derive from AFr *enveisé,* OFr *envoisié* 'playful', latinized in DB as *invesiatus* (cf. MedLat *invasus* 'possessed by a demon') and paralleled by *lascivus* 'wanton'. As with FANT, the first syllable was lost, the meaning of the remaining *Veyse* was forgotten and the initial *V* frequently regarded as a dialectal pronunciation of *F,* hence *Feasey,* etc., and, with the spelling change of *Ph* for *F, Phaisey,* etc. The surname is common in all its forms except *Lenfestey* which is rare and preserves the fuller form with an intrusive medial *t.*

Valance: *v.* VALLANCE

Vale, Vail, Vaile: Wido *de la Val* 1190 P (Nth); Robert *del Val* 1221 AssWa; Walter *ate Vale* 1327 SRSx; John *Vale* 1382 AssC; Nicholas *Vayle* 1623

RothwellPR (Y). 'Dweller in the valley', ME *val*(*e*), OFr *val. v.* also VEAL, VEIL.

Valentin, Valentine, Valintine, Vallentin, Vallentine, Vallintine: *Valentinus* 1198 Cur (W), 1276 RH (C); *Valentyn* le Warner 1327 SRC; Matilda *Valentyn* 1251 Rams (Hu); William *Valentin* 1260 AssC. Lat *Valentinus,* a derivative of *valens* 'strong, healthy', the name of a 3rd-century Roman saint and martyr. Found in England from the end of the 12th century.

Valet(t): *v.* VALLET

Valiant, Vaillant: Hugo *le Vaillant* 1185 P (Y); Gilbert *le Valiand* 1207 Cur (Do); Gilbert *Valiant* 1212 Cur (So). OFr *vaillant* 'courageous, sturdy'.

Valin, Valins: *v.* VALLIN

Vallance, Vallans, Valance: Reiner *de Valenc'* 1158 P (Lo); Almerus (Eymerus) *de Valencia, de Valence, de Valenz* 1303–46 FA (Sf). From Valence (Drôme).

Vallentin, Vallentine: *v.* VALENTIN

Vallet, Valet, Valett: Walter *Vadlet* 1198 P (Sx); Robert *Valet* 1221 Cur (Gl); Richard *le Vallet* 1243 AssSo. OFr *valet, vallet* 'man-servant'.

Valley: Richard *atte Valeye* 1346 LLB F. 'Dweller in the valley.'

Vallin, Vallins, Vallings, Valin, Valins: Petrus *de Valoinges* 1086 DB (C); Robert *de Valeynes* 1155–68 Holme (Nf); Robert *de Valuynes* 1238–42 StGreg (K); John *de Ualin'* a1237 ib. From Valognes (La Manche).

Vallintine: *v.* VALENTIN

Vallis: Sibil *de Valeyse* 1275 RH (Sf); James *Valloyes, Valleys* 1601–2 Bardsley. From the old province of Valois in the Ile-de-France.

Van, Vance: *v.* FANN

Vandervelde, Vandervell: Henry *Vandelveld* (denization) 1550 Pat. Dutch *van der veld* 'of the field'.

Vane(s): *v.* FANE

Vann(e), Vanns: *v.* FANN

Vannah, Vanner: *v.* FANNER

Vant: *v.* FANT

Vantage: William, Adam *Vauntage* 1319 SRLo, 1327 SRSo. ME *vantage* 'advantage, profit, gain'.

Varah: *v.* VARROW

Varden, Vardon: *v.* VERDEN

Varder, Verdier: Walter *le Verder* 1279 RH (O); Richard *le Verdour* 1327 SRSa. AFr *verder, verdour,* OFr *verdier, verdeur* 'verderer', a judicial officer of a royal forest (1502 NED).

Vare: *v.* FARE

Varey: *v.* VARROW

Varley, Verley, Virley: This may be a southern form of *Farleigh*: Thomas *de Varley* 1316 FA (Sf). Both Varley and Varleys (Devon), earlier *Fernlegh*, gave rise to surnames in the 14th century. The surname cannot derive, as has been suggested, from Virley (Essex) which is not so called before the 16th century. It was originally *Salcota*, later *Salcote Verly*, from its Domesday lord Robert *de Verli*, who came from Verly (Aisne), whence the surnames of Hugo *de Verli* 1219 AssL, and Thomas *Virley* 1275 RH (Sf). *v.* PN Ess 323, OEByn. Hugh *de Verleio* (1166 RBE) is said to have come from Vesly (La Manche). *v.* ANF.

Varlow: *v.* FARLOW

Varnals: *v.* FARNALL

Varndell: *v.* FARNDALE

Varnes: *v.* FERN

Varney: *v.* VERNAY

Varnham, Varnam: *v.* FARNHAM

Varnish: *v.* FURNACE

Varnon: *v.* VERNON

Varns: *v.* FERN

Varran: *v.* FARREN

Varrow, Varah, Varey, Vary, Vairo: John *Vary* 1663 FrY; Humfrey and Frederick, sons of Charles and Mary *Varow* bapt. 1754 HorringerPR (Sf); Humfrey and Frederick *Varoh* infants bur. 1755 ib.; Charles *Varo* 1760 ib.; Mary *Varo* 1843 ib.; Mary *Varer* bur. 1795 ib.; Mary *Varer* mar. 1819 ib.; Lucy *Varer* m. 1837 ib. This is clearly a late development of *Farrow*, due to an unetymological substitution of initial *V* for *F*. *v.* FARRAR.

Varty: *v.* VERITY

Varwell: *v.* FAREWELL

Vary: *v.* VARROW

Vasey: *v.* VAISEY

Vass, Vasse: *Vasse* le Poynur 1275 RH (C). OFr *vasse*, Lat *vassus* 'servant, vassal'. Like *Vassal*, occasionally used as a personal name.

Vassall: *Vassallus* de Aunfoilliis 1221 Cur (R); Hugo *Vassall'* 1202 P (Gl); Henry *Vassal* 1221 AssWo. ME, OFr *vassal* 'vassal, servant, dependant'. Occasionally used as a personal-name.

Vassar: Thomas *Vasour* 1327 *SR* (Ess); John *Vasour* 1332 MEOT (Nf). OFr *vasseor, vasseur* 'vassal'.

Vassie: Walter *de Vasci* 1203 P (D). From Vassy (Calvados).

Vatcher: *v.* VACHER

Vaughan, Vaugham: Grifit *Vehan* 1222–64 Seals (Brecon); Rys *Vychan* 1248 Harrison; William *Vachan* 1275 RH (Sa); Gronou *Vahan* 1285 Ch (Radnor); Jeuan *Vachann, Vaghann* 1391 Chirk; Mr *Vaughan* 1674 HTSf. Welsh *fychan*, mutation of *bychan* 'small, little'.

Vaus, Vause, Vaux: (i) Robert *de Vals, de Valibus, de Vaux* (Ess), *de Wals* (Nf) 1086 DB; Robert *de Wals, de Vallibus* 1134–40, 1188 Holme (Nf); Ralph *de Vaus* 1185 Templars (Y); Richard *de Vause* 12th DC (Lei). From Vaux, a common French place-name, plural of *val*, Lat *vallis* 'val-

ley'. The occasional initial *W* survives in Wasse's Fm in Terling, from Nicholas *Vaux* (1522 PN Ess 298) and so may have contributed to *Wass*. We also find an unvoicing of *V* to *F* in Fowe's Fm in Belchamp Otton and Fox Hall in Shopland, both from a *de Vaux* (PN Ess 410, 201) and this may survive as *Fow*. It is an interesting speculation whether this is the clue to the unexplained surname of Daniel Defoe (b. 1661). It is said that he did not add the *De* to his family name of *Foe* until he had reached manhood. In 1524 SRSf we find Edmund *Foo*, James *a Foo* and Robert *a Fowe*. The *a* may be a substitution of an English preposition for the French *de*, or the *d* may have been absorbed in pronunciation by the *t* of Robert. These names, like Fowe's Fm, may derive from *de Vaux* and *Defoe* may have the same origin. Daniel may have been following some family tradition in insisting on the *De*. (ii) A number of surnames have *le* instead of *de*: Agnes *le Vaus* 1275 SRWo, Nicol' *le Vaus* 1296 SRSx; Alexander, Robert, John *le Vaus* 1327 SRSf. There is only one doubtful example of late OE *fals* 'false'. The frequency of the word in 12th-century English and later is due to OFr *fals, faus*. This French word would retain its initial *f* in the south where the above surnames are found but the ME form of OE *fals* would become *vals*. Examples are rare but NED gives a few, including some from the verb (from OFr *falser*): a1225: *ualse* 'mendacious', *ualse* (vb.), *valsinde* (pres. part.); 1340: *uales* moneye, *ualse* lettres, *ualsehedes* 'falsehoods', *ualsnesse* 'falseness', *ualsere* 'falsifier'. Thus *le vaus* probably owes its *v* to OE *fals* and its *au* to OFr *faus*, though the French *f* might have been voiced occasionally in the south. cf. FANT, FIDLER (ii), and the forms of VIVIAN.

Vavasour, Vavasseur: William *Vavassur* 1166 RBE (Y); Gilbert *le Vauassur* 1167 P (Nf); John *le Vavaseur* 1288 LLB A. OFr *vavas(s)our, vavasseur*, Lat *vassus vassorum* 'vassal of vassals' (NED 13..). A feudal tenant ranking immediately below a baron. The surname is common in the 12th and 13th centuries. The status of the vavassor varied with time and place. In England at the time of Domesday the vavassors were men of very moderate estate. By the 12th century the whole of military society was divided into two great classes, barons and vavassors. *v.* EngFeud 16–23.

Vawser: Nicholas *Vausour* 1379 PTY. A syncopated form of VAVASOUR.

Vayne: *v.* FANE

Veail: *v.* VEIL

Veal, Veale, Veall, Veel: (i) Richard *le Vele* 1270 AssSo; William *Vel* 1276 FFSf; Thomas *le Veel* 1296 SRSx. OFr *veel* 'calf'. (ii) Reginald *Leviel* 1173 P (Lo); Geoffrey *Viele* 1206 Cur (Sx); William *le Viel* 1218 AssL. AFr *viel*, OFr *vieil* 'old', or OFr *viel* 'calf'. Without the article, *Viel* is indistinguishable from VIAL. There has also been confusion with VALE: Martin *Veal, Vale* 1774, 1780 WStowPR (Sf).

Vear(e): *v.* VERE

Vearncombe: *v.* FARNCOMBE

Veasey: v. VAISEY

Veck, Vick: Henry le Eueske 1218 AssL; Richard Veke c1248 Bec (W); Robert Vesk 1275 SRWo; Robert le Veck 1279 RH (C); Richard le Veske 1296 SRSx. OFr le eveske 'the bishop' became leveske which was wrongly taken for le vesk. This became Vesk and later Veck, Vick. The full form survives as LEVICK. cf. BISHOP.

Veel: v. VEAL

Veigne: v. VAINES

Veil, Veail, Vail: Roger de Ueille 1127–34 Holme (Nf); Richard la Veille 1175–86 ib.; Richard la Veyle 1242 FFEss; Geoffrey de Veel 1256 AssSo; Robert le Veyle 1260 AssY; Thomas le Veyl 1276 AssSo; Hubert la Veylle 1277 FFEss. This must be OFr de la veille 'of the watch', 'watchman', with common loss of de as in early forms of BATTLE and WARE. There has been confusion with VALE and VEAL.

Vein: v. VAINES

Velden: v. FIELDEN

Venables: William de Venables c1200 WhC (La). From Venables (Eure).

Vender: Peter le Vendier 1206 P (K); William le Vendur Ed 1 NottBR. AFr vendour, OFr vendeor, *vendier 'seller, dealer'.

Venes, Veness, Venis, Venise, Venus: Robert de Venuiz 1130 P (Ha); William de Venuz,' de Venoiz 1197 P, 1205 ChR (Ha); Robert de Veniz 1203 Cur (Ha); William de Venus 1230 P (Wa). From Venoix (Calvados). v. ANF.

Venn: v. FENN

Vennall, Vennel, Vennell: Reginald de la Venele 1240 FFEss; Michael in la Venele 1279 RH (Beds). 'Dweller in the alley', Fr venelle 'small street, alley'.

Venner, Venour, Fenner: Walter le Veneur 1195 P (C); David, William le Venur 1219 AssY, Cur (Sx); Adam le venour 1297 MinAcctCo (Herts). OFr veneor, veneur 'hunter, huntsman'. A common surname in early records. In view of the existence of Fanner and Vanner, one would have expected Fenner and Venner also to mean 'marsh-dweller', from OE fenn. but the only evidence noted is that of Lower who states that Fenn Place in Worth, Sussex, had owners called from it Atte Fenne, who in the time of Henry VI changed their name to Fenner, whilst a Kentish branch wrote themselves Fenour. As Fenner is common and still found in Kent and Sussex, where Bridger, Brooker, etc., are frequent, this seems probable.

Vennicker: 'Dweller at the dairy-farm in the marsh.' cf. FENWICK.

Venters, Ventress, Ventriss: Francis Ventreys 1600 FFHu; Edward Ventres 1642 SfPR; Mrs Ventris 1674 HTSf. 'The venturous', from ME aventurous.

Venton, Ventom: From Venton (Devon), Venton 1301 PN D 255.

Ventre, Ventur, Venture: William Aventur 1279 RH (Hu); William le Ventre 1327 SRSx. ME aventure 'chance, hazard', in the same sense as VENTERS and VENTURA.

Ventura: John le Ventrer 1273 RH (Nt). 'The adventurer, venturesome.'

Venus: v. VENES

Verden, Verdin, Verdon, Verduin, Varden, Vardon: Bertrannus de Verduno 1086 DB (Bk); Iue de Verdun 1101–7 Holme (Nf); William de Verduin 1196 Cur (Lei). From Verdun (La Manche). v. ANF. Possibly also from Verdun (Eure).

Verdier: v. VARDER

Vere, Vear, Veare: Alberic de Ver 1086 DB (Ess); Roger, Walter de Ver 1121–35 Bury, 1208 FFY; Gilbert de Veer 1303 LLB C; Robert Veer 1403 IpmY. From Ver (La Manche, Calvados).

Vergin(e), Vergo: v. VIRGIN

Verity, Varty: Adam, Richard (le) Verite 1275 SRWo, 1296 SRSx; Thomas Verty 1379 PTY. Fr vérité 'truth'.

Verley: v. VARLEY

Vern(e): v. FERN

Vernall: v. FARNALL

Vernay, Verney, Verny, Varney: Robert de Vernai 1221 AssGl. From a French place Vernay, probably chiefly Saint-Paul-de-Vernay (Calvados).

Vernon, Vernum, Varnon: Richard de Vernon 1086 DB (Ch); William de Vernun 1130 P (Wt). From Vernon (Eure). v. ANF.

Verrier, Verriour: Roger Verer c1100 MedEA (Nf); Fulko le Verrier 1185 P (W); Walter le verrour 1313 FrY. AFr verrer, OFr verrier, verrieur 'worker in glass, glazier' (1415 NED).

Vesey: v. VAISEY

Vessell: Metonymic for VESSELO.

Vesselo: William, John le Vesseler 1296 SRSx, 1327 SRSf. A derivative of ME vessele, AFr, OFr vessel(e) 'vessell'. A maker or seller of household vessels.

Vessey: Robert de Veci 1086 DB (Nth); William de Vescy 1166 RBE (Ess). From Vessey (La Manche). v. OEByn.

Veysey, Vezey: v. VAISEY

Vezin: v. VOICIN

Vial, Vials, Viall, Vialls, Viel, Vidal, Vidall, Vital, Vitall: Vitalis, Vitel, Fitel 1066 DB; Vithele abbode 1076 ASC E; Fiþele abbode 1077 ASC D; Uiðel æt Culumtune 11th PNDB 406 (D); Vitalis de Colintone 1086 DB (D); Viel Luuet c1150 DC (L); Adam filius Viell Hy 2 Whitby (Y); Radulfus Vitalis 1086 DB (D); Estanus Fitele 1175–86 Holme (Nf); Richard Viel 1194 P (D); John Vitele 1207 P (Sx); Henry Vyel 1275 SRWo; Thomas Vytele 1296 SRSx; Thomas Vyall 1524 SRSf. Vitalis, OFr Vitel, Viel, the name of some ten saints (Latin vitalis 'pertaining to life, vital'), became common in England after the Conquest both in its learned form Vitalis and in the northern French form Viel. The absence of early forms of Vidal suggests that this was a later immigrant from Languedoc. Black gives no example of the name from Scotland. Viel also survives as VEAL. Vital may also be attributive from ME vital in the sense 'full of vitality': Adam, Matilda le Vytele 1327 SRSx.

Vian: Ralph de Viana 1184 P (K); Hugh de

Vyen(na) 1286–8 AssSt. Probably from Vienne (Calvados), *Viana* 1198.

Viant: William *Viand'* 1161 P (O); Emma *Viaunde* 1324 Bart. OFr *viande* 'meat, food', no doubt for a seller of foodstuffs.

Vicar, Vicker: Richard *Vicar* 1251 AssSo; Thomas *le Vicayr* 1279 RH (O); Stephen *le Vyker* 1313 FFEss. AFr *vikere, vicare, vicaire* 'vicar', one acting as parish priest in place of the parson or rector. (c1325 NED).

Vicarage, Vickerage, Vickridge, Vickress: Hugh *Vicaries* 1332 LLB E; John *Vicarish* 1547 Bardsley; Alice *Vicaridge* 1665 ib.; Anne *Vickris* 1706 DKR 41 (So). 'Servant of the *Vicary*', with the dialectal change of final *s* to *sh* as in *Parish* for *Paris*.

Vicarey, Vicari, Vicary, Viccari, Viccary, Vickary, Vickery: Henry *le Vicarie* 1249 MEOT (Sx); William *Vikery* 1319 SRLo. An adaptation of Lat *vicārius* 'vicar' (1303 NED).

Vicars, Viccars, Vickars, Vickers: (i) William *del Vikers* 1327 SRSt; William *de Vykeres* 1332 SRSt; Henry *Attevickers* 1327 SRDb; Joan *Atvicars* 1400 YWills. '(Servant) at the vicar's.' (ii) Margery *le Vikers* 1332 SRWa; Anne *Vickars* 1592 RothwellPR (Y). 'The vicar's servant.' Occasionally, perhaps, also for 'the vicar's son': Gilebertus *filius vicarii* c1248 Bec (O).

Vick: *v.* VECK

Vickerman: William *Vikarman* 1379 PTY. 'The vicar's servant.' cf. Richard *le Wycarisman* 1275 RH (C) and Isabella *Vikerwoman* 1379 PTY.

Vickress, Vickridge: *v.* VICARAGE

Vidal(l): *v.* VIAL

Videan, Vidgen, Vidgeon: *v.* VIVIAN

Vidler: *v.* FIDLER

Viel: *v.* VEAL, VIAL

Vieler, Viola: Robert *Vielur* 1210 P (Ha); Adam *le Vielur* 1212 Fees (La); Brun *le Vilur* 1242 Fees (Nb); Richard *le Vyolour* 1311 LLB B. AFr *violour*, OFr *violeur* 'player on the viol, fiddler' (1551 NED).

Vigar, Viggor, Vigor, Vigour: Richard *Vigur* 1224 Pat; Peter *Viger* 1284 LLB A. OFr *vigor, vigur* 'vigour, liveliness', by metonymy for one displaying this quality.

Vigars, Vigers, Viggars, Viggers, Vigors, Vigours, Vigrass, Vigurs, Vigus: Walter *le Vigrus* 1221 AssWo; Henry *Vigrus* 1256 AssSo; Hugh *Vigeros* 1275 SRWo; William *Vigerus* 1279 RH (O); William *Vigerous* 1305 LLB B; Lewis *Vigures* 1598 Oxon (D); Samuel *Vigars* 1746 Bardsley. AFr *vigrus*, OFr *vigoro(u)s* 'hardy, lusty, strong'.

Vigeon: *v.* VIVIAN

Vigne, Vignes: *v.* VINE

Vigrass, Vigus: *v.* VIGARS

Villain, Villin, Vilain: Ernald *Vilein* 1167 P (Nf); Robert *Vilain* 1188 Eynsham (O); Roger *le Vilain* 1196 Cur (Nth). AFr *villein, vilein* 'serf, bondman, servile tenant', an occupier or cultivator entirely subject to a lord or attached to a manor (1303 NED).

Villar, Villars, Villers, Villiers, Villis: William *de Vilers* c1130 StCh; William *de Viliers* 1185 Templars (Y); Nicholas *de Vylirs* 1327 SRSx. From Viller(s) or Villier(s), both common French place-names. Roger *de Vilers* (1166 RBE), of Dorset, came from Villiers-le-Sec (Calvados). *v.* ANF.

Villy: Vnfridus *de Villi* 1190 P (Y); Robert *de Vili, de Villi* 1208–9 Cur (Db). From Villy-Bocage (Calvados). *v.* ANF.

Vince: Antony *Vince* 1674 HTSf. A short form of *Vincent*.

Vincent, Vincett, Vinsen, Vinson, Vinsun: *Vincencius* 1206 Cur (Nf); *Vincentius filius Wuluiet* 1222 AssWa; *Vincent'* de Wyke 1296 SRSx; William, Agatha *Vincent* 1230 Oseney (O), 1296 SRSx; Abram *Vincent*, Anthony *Vinson* 1674 HTSf; Thomas *Vincen* 1776 Bardsley. Lat *Vincentius*, from *vincens* 'conquering', the name of a 3rd-century martyr. Introduced into England about 1200. *Vinson*, etc., are due to loss of the final *t*, *Vincett* to assimilation of *nt* to *tt*.

Vinck: *v.* FINCH

Vine, Vines, Le Vine, Vigne, Vignes: Robert *de Vigne* 1236 Fees (So); Henry *de la Vine* 1283 LLB A; Roger *atte Vine* 1297 LLB B; Richard *atte Vygne*, brewer 1311 LLB D; Richard *Vygn* 1327 SRSo. OFr *vigne* 'vine'. The surname probably means 'worker at a vineyard'. cf. VINER. Vine-growing was of some importance in England in the Middle Ages. There are still places named Vineyards in Essex and Cambridgeshire. *v.* WINYARD. Or the meaning may be 'one living by some prominent vine'. In towns it may denote a wine-seller 'at the sign of the vine'.

Vinen: Walter *le vyngnon* 1333 MEOT (So). OFr *vignon, vingnon, viegnon* 'vine-dresser, vine-grower'.

Viner, Vyner: Robert *le Vinnur, le Vinior, le Vinur* 1207, 1211 Cur (Hu); Symon *le Vignur* 1221 ElyA (Sf); William *le Vinyour* 1279 RH (Hu); Walter *le Vynour* 1309 LLB B; John *Vyner* 1407 FFSx. OFr *vignour, vigneur, vigneour*, AFr *viner* 'vine-grower, vine-dresser' (1390 NED).

Vinick: *v.* FENWICK

Vink: *v.* FINCH

Vinsen, Vinson, Vinsun: *v.* VINCENT

Vinter, Vintor: Saulfus *uineter* 1170 Oseney (O); Baldwin *le Vineter* 1221 Cur (Sr); John *le vynter* 1327 SRSf. AFr *viniter, vineter, vinter* 'vintner, wine-merchant' (1297 NED).

Vintiner: Robert *le uintner* c1179 Bart; Richard *le Vyntener* 1327 MESO (La). An alteration of *vineter* (c1430 NED), 'wine-merchant'.

Viola: *v.* VIELER

Vipan, Vipond, Vipont, Vippond: Robert *de Viezponte, de Vezpunt* 1159, 1178 P (D); Roger *de Vipont* 13th WhC (La); Thomas *Vipond* 1772 Bardsley. From Vieuxpont (Calvados).

Virgin, Vergin, Vergine, Virgo, Virgoe, Vergo: Simon *Virg'* 1275 RH (K); Isabella *Virgo* 1428 FA (Wa); William *Virgyn* 1581 Bardsley; John *Vergine* 1610 ib. Probably, as Bardsley suggests, a name given to one who had played the part of the Virgin Mary in some miracle play.

Virley: *v.* VARLEY

Vise, Vize, Vyse: Robert *atte Vise* 1327 SRSx; John *de la Vise* 1330 PN D 128. 'Dweller by the boundary' (OFr *devise*), as at Viza in Ashwater (Devon), Vyse Wood in Morthoe (Devon), or from Devizes (Wilts), formerly *The Devise, Vises* and *The Vyse* (PN W 243).

Visick: *v.* PHYSICK

Vital(l): *v.* VIAL

Vivian, Vivians, Vivien, Vyvyan, Videan, Vidgen, Vidgeon, Vigeon, Fiddian, Fidgen, Fidgeon, Phethean, Phythian: Johannes *filius Viuian* 1175 P (K); *Vivianus* de Cattele c1200 Gilb (L); *Fithian alias Vivian* 1514 ODCN; Henry *Vivien* 1235 Stone (St); William *Phythien* c1250 Rams (C); William *Phivien* 1271 Rams (Herts); John *Vivyan* 1275 RH (Ha); John *Fiuian* 1279 RH (O); Roger *Fidian*, Robert *Fithion* 1279 RH (C); John *Vyvyan* 1296 SRSx; Agatha *Fydion* 1310 FFSf; Roger *Fythien* 1327 SRSf; John *Fifian* 1327 SRSo; David *Fyuyen* 1332 SRSx; William *Fetheon*' 1379 AssC; Joan *Fithyan* 1406 LLB I; Laurence *ffedyan* 1493 SIA xii; James *Vydean, Vydyan* 1513, 1548 ArchC 33, 34; John *Fiffeon, Phiffion, Pfiffian, Phithien, Fitheon* 1604–38 ER 55 (Ess); Thomas *Phydian, Fython, Pythian, Pitheon* 1712–34 ib. Fr *Vivian, Vivien* (m), Lat *Vivianus*, a derivative of *vivus* 'living', the name of a 5th-century martyr not uncommon in England from the 12th century. Its pronunciation appears to have caused difficulty and it is found in a bewildering variety of forms, not all of which have survived. In the south, the *v* was regarded as the normal southern pronunciation of *f* and was replaced by it. As the child says *fum* for *thumb*, and *fevver* for *feather*, and the dialect-speaker *favver* for *father*, *Fivian* became *Fithian*, and this, with the common interchange of intervocalic *th* and *d*, gave *Fidian*. The initial *Ph* is merely scribal. As *Goodier* becomes *Goodger* and *Indian* is often colloquially *Injun*, so *Fidian* became *Fidgeon* and *Vidian*, *Vidgen*. The normal *Vivian* is much more common than appears from the above forms.

Vizard: *v.* WISHART

Vize: *v.* VISE

Vizer, Vizor: John *le Visur* 1273 RH (Wo). OFr *viseur* 'observer, overlooker'.

Voak: *v.* FOLK

Voicin, Vezin: William *Veisin* 1192 P (Gl); William *le Veysin* 1279 RH (O). AFr *veisin*, OFr *voicin* 'neighbour'.

Voisey: *v.* VAISEY

Vokes: *v.* FOLK

Volant, Volante: Robert *le volant* 1221 ElyA (Sf); Henry *(le) Volaunt* 1221 AssGl. Present participle of OFr *voler* 'to fly', 'flying, nimble, agile'.

Volk(e), Volkes: *v.* FOLK

Volker: *v.* FULCHER

Voller(s): *v.* FULLER

Voss: *v.* FOSS

Voules, Vowells, Vowles: *v.* FOWLE

Vowler: *v.* FOWLER

Voyle: Dauid *Voil* 1332 Chirk; George *Voyell* 1586 Oxon (Pembroke); William *Voile* 1609 ib. (He). A mutated form of Welsh *moel* 'bald'. cf. *pen-foel* 'bald-headed'.

Voysey: *v.* VAISEY

Vreede: *v.* FIRTH

Vroome: *v.* FROME

Vyner: *v.* VINER

Vyse: *v.* VISE

Vyvyan: *v.* VIVIAN

W

Wace, Waison, Wase, Wash, Wason, Wass, Wasson, Wayson, Gaish, Gasche, Gash, Gashion, Gason, Gass, Gasson, Gaze: Teðion *filius Wasso* c1000 OEByn (Co); *Wazo, Gazo* 1086 DB; Robertus *filius Wazonis* 1087 DM (K); Herebertus *filius Watscon'* 1148 Winton (Ha); *Wace* armiger (seal: *Wazo*) c1150-60 DC (L); *Waszo* cocus . . . ipsi *Wasconi* 1170 P (Gl); Reginaldus *filius Wasce* 1177 P (W); *Wazo, Wace* de Norton' 1195-6 P (Y, Nth); *Gace* de Gisorz 1225 ClR; William *Wase* 1194 Cur (Ess); Wido *Wasun* 1195 P (So); William *Was* 1210 Cur (C); William *Wace, Waze, Wasce* 1220 Cur, 1235 Fees (O); John *Gace, Wace* 1224-5 Pat (W); John *Gace, Gasce* 1230 P, Cl (Ha, K); Godesman *Gase* 1232 Pat (L); Richard *Wason* 1273 Ipm (So); Simon *Gason* 1498 ArchC 34; James *Gasse* 1568 SRSf; Leonard *Waice* or *Wace* 1568 Oxon; Sarah *Gasson* 1773 Bardsley. The first form is from OCymr **Wasso*, OCornish *Wasō*, which may sometimes survive, but the surnames are usually from OFr *Gace*, OG *Waz(z)o*, Frisian *Watso*, hypocoristics of OG names in *Wad-* or *Warin-*. *Wace*, etc., are Northern, *Gace*, etc., Central French. The forms with *-on* are OFr accusatives. cf. WASTLING.

Wacey, Wasey, Wassey: *Wascius* Cokus 1187 P (Gl); Robertus *filius Wacey* 1275 RH (L); *Gaceus* de Broughton 1322 FrY. *Wascius* Cokus is identical with *Waszo* cocus above, a latinization of *Wazo*. This might possibly survive as *Wacey*, which might also derive from OG **Waswig*, cf. *Wasuuic* 1086 DB (Gl).

Wacher: *v.* WATCHER
Wachman: *v.* WATCHMAN
Wackley: *v.* WAKELEY
Wackrill, Wakerell: *Wakerilda* c1130 ELPN, 1211 Cur (Mx); *Wekerild* 1185 Templars (K); Justinus *filius Wakerild* 1229 Pat (Sx); William, Osbert, Agnes *Wakerild* 1188 BuryS (Sf), 1319 FFK, 1327 SR (Ess); William *Whaykrylle* 1374 Putnam (Mx). OE **Wacerhild* (f) 'watchful war' (cf. OG *Wagarhilt*) or, in view of the Kent form, OE **Wæcerhild*.
Waddelow: *v.* WADDILOVE
Waddie: *v.* WALTHEW
Waddilove, Waddilow, Waddelow, Wadlow: William, John *Wadylove* 1260 AssY, 1321 AD iv (L); Ralph *Wadiluue* 13th FeuDu; John, William *Wadeinlove* 1279 RH (Hu); Thomas *Wadyloue*, Robert *Wadyloef*, Adam *Wadinlof* 1379 PTY;

Thomas *Wadloffe* 1564 Bardsley; Susannah *Wadlow* 1684 ib. '*Waddilove*', says Weekley, 'is a phrase-name which seems very out of place in the thirteenth century. . . . In fact *wade in love* is so unlike anything medieval that I am inclined to guess that the first element may belong to ME *weden*, to rage, and that the name may mean rather "furious wolf". . . . cf. Walter *Wodelof* (*Pat. R*), from the related ME *wode*, mad.' The names are rather from Anglo-Scand *Wealdþēof* which is commonly *Waldeve* or *Waldive* in ME. With a metathesis of *ld* to *dl*, these give *Wadleve, Wadlive*. Other forms given under *Walthew*, would similarly give *Wadleuf* or *Wadeluf* (Waltheuf), *Wadlief* or *Wadilef* (Waldief), and, by association with the common names in *-lēof* or *-lufu*, would be written *Wadilove*, etc. *Wadeinlove* should, no doubt, be read *Wadeuiloue*, an eccentric form combining *Wadeleue* and *Wadiloue*. Weekley's *Wodelof* probably also belongs here, showing the otherwise unrecorded development of *Waldeof* to *Woldeof*, with metathesis to *Wodelof*.

Waddington, Wadington: Ogis de *Wadintona* 1169 P (L); Walter *de Wadington* 1276 AssLa; Richard *Wadyngton* 1519 FFEss. From Waddington (Lincs, Surrey, WRYorks).

Wadds: *Wadde* forestar 1332 SRCu. A short form of some common name, probably *Waltheof*. cf. WALTHEW.

Waddy: *v.* WALTHEW

Wade, Waide: (i) *Wada, Wade, Wado* 1066 DB; *Wade* de Langad' 1176 P (Sa); *Wade* le fol 1297 MinAcctCo; Godwin, Gilbert *Wade* 1166 P (Ess), 1190 BuryS (Sf). OE *Wada*, from *wadan* 'to go', or OG *Wado*. The persistence of the personal-name may be due, in part, to the tale of Wade, originally a sea-giant, dreaded and honoured by the coast tribes of the North Sea and the Baltic. 'In England the memory of Wade lived longer than that of any of the old heroes of song, Weland only excepted' (*v.* Chambers, *Widsith* 95-100). (ii) Ordmar *de la Wade* 1189 P (Nf); Richard *del Wade* 1327 SRSf. 'Dweller by the ford', OE *(ge)wæd*.

Wademan, Wadman, Wodeman: (i) Symon *le Wademan* 1296 MESO (Nf); Richard de Norham, *waddeman* 1375 FrY; William *Wadman* 1417 MESO (Y). OE *wād* 'woad' and *mann*, identical in meaning with WADER. (ii) John *Wodeman* 1296 SRSx. This spelling, common in ME, is indistinguishable in form from *wodeman* 'woodman'. That

ME *wōdman* from OE **wādmann* existed is proved by the modern *Wadman* and *Wader* (ii) b.

Wader, Waider, Weider: (i) William *le Waisdier* 1185 P (Y); Erkenbald *Wesdier, le Waisder, le Weisdier, le Waisdier* 1191–8 P (Y); Alan *le Wader, le Weider* p1197, 1227–37 Clerkenwell (Lo); Reiner *le Waider* 1202 AssL. OFr *wesdier, quesdier, waisdier* 'dyer with or seller of woad', a blue dyestuff obtained from the plant, in great demand in the Middle Ages. (ii) (*a*) Thorald de Cawston *le Wader* 1290 MESO (Nf), *le Weyder* 1293 ib.; Robert, Walter *le Wadere* 1296 SRSx; John *le Wadder* 1332 SRLa, SRCu. A derivative of OE *wād* 'woad', 'woad-merchant' (1415 NED). This English form is more common today, but rarer in ME than the French *Waider*. (*b*) Simon *le Wodier* 1206 Cur (K); Andr' *le Wodere* 1275 MESO (Sx). As with *Wodeman*, this form is indistinguishable from ME *wodere* 'woodman'. ME *wōdere* 'woad-merchant' certainly existed; Robert *le Woder* de Merthone is identical with Robert de Merthone, *wayder* (1276 LLB B). OE **wādere* became ME *wōdere* and should give a modern *Woader* or *Woder*. The identity of spelling may have led to confusion of the two names and the absorption of the less common *Woder* by the more frequent and more readily understood *Wooder*.

Wadeson, Waidson: Tobias *Waidson* 1614 Bardsley; Thomas *Wadeson* 1697 LaWills. 'Son of *Wade*.' cf. William *Wadecok* 1327 *SR* (Ess).

Wadey, Wadie: v. WALTHEW

Wadlow: John *de Wadelaw* 1212 Cur (Beds). From a lost place *Wadlow* in Toddington (Beds).

Wadman: v. WADEMAN

Wadsworth, Wordsworth: Adam *de Waddeswrth* 1275 Wak. From Wadsworth (WRYorks). Bardsley notes that at Silkstone the surname appears as *Waddysworth* (1556), *Wardsworth* (1656), *Wadsworth* (1666) and *Wordsworth* (1668 seq.).

Wady: v. WALTHEW

Wafer: (i) Simon *le Wafre, le Wafrer* 1212 Fees (He), *le Wafrer* 1221 AssSa, *le Wafre* 1222 AssWa (He); Ralph *le Waverer* c1227 Fees (Y), *le Wafrur* 1250 ib. (Y). AFr *wafre* 'wafer', alternating with AFr *wafrer, *wafrour* 'waferer, maker or seller of wafers or thin cakes' (1362 NED). The waferers seem to have been chiefly concerned with the provision of the eucharistic bread but also sold sweet, spiced cakes, the 'wafers piping hot' which Absolon the clerk gave to Alison. (ii) Ricardus *filius Waifier* 1180 P (W); Richard *Waifer* 1242 Fees (W); Ranus *Wayfer* 1267 AssSo. OG *Waifar, Waifer*, OFr *Gaifier*, a less common source than (i).

Waghorn, Waghorne: Roger *Waggehorn* 1332 PN K 185; Peter *Waghorne* 1357 Black (Dumbarton). 'Wag horn', a name for a hornblower or trumpeter.

Wagstaff, Wagstaffe: William *Waggestaf* 1219 Cur (Lei); Robert *Waggestaff* 1279 RH (O); William *Waggestave* 1301 SRY. 'Wag staff', perhaps a name for a beadle. cf. WAPLE and Walter *Waggespere* 1227 AssLa, Richard *Wagetail* 1187 P (St), and v. SHAKESPEAR.

Waide: v. WADE
Waider: v. WADER
Waidson: v. WADESON
Waigh: v. WAY
Waight(s): v. WAIT
Wailes: v. WALES

Wain, Waine, Waines, Wayne: John, Richard *Wayn* 1319 FFEss, 1386 LoPleas. Metonymic for WAINER, WAINMAN or WAINEWRIGHT, or 'dweller at the sign of the wain': John *Attewayne* 1327 SRDb.

Wainer: Henry *le Wayner* 1381 LoPleas. A derivative of OE *wægn, wægen* 'wain, wagon'; 'driver of a wain, wagoner' (a1500 NED).

Wainewright, Wainright, Wainwright, Wainwrigt: Ailmar *Wanwrecthe* 1237 HPD (Ess); Adam *the Waynwrith* 1285 Wak (Y); Alan *le Waynwright* 1332 SRLa. OE *wægnwyrhta* 'wainwright, wagon-builder'.

Wainman, Wenman, Whenman: John *Waynman* 1297 SRY; John *Weneman* 1327 *SR* (Ess). OE *wægn, wæn* 'wagon' and *mann*; 'wagoner' (1392 NED).

Waison: v. WACE
Waistcoat: v. WESTCOTT

Wait, Waite, Waites, Waits, Wates, Wayt, Wayte, Waytes, Waight, Waighte, Weight, Weait, Whait, Whaite, Whaites, Whaits, Whate: (i) Ailward *Waite* 1170–87 ELPN; Roger *le Wayte* 1221 ElyA (Sf); Hugh *le Weyt* 1251 AssSt; Roger *le Wate* 1296 SRSx; Adam *le Whaite* 1349 LLB G; Richard *Waight, Weight* 1595, 1610 Bardsley. ONFr *waite*, OFr *guaite, gaite* 'watchman', either in a fortified place or a town. The town waits combined the functions of watchmen and musicians (EngLife). For *guaite*, v. GAIT. *Wait* may also be a late form of WHEAT. cf. *Whaytley* for *Whatley* 1539 PN Wa 18. v. also WHITE. (ii) Roger *la Waite* 1197 FF (Wa); Ralph *laweite* 12th DC (Nt); John *la Wayte* 1243 AssSo. For *de la waite* 'of the watch', with frequent loss of *de* as in early forms of BATTLE, VEIL, and WARR. Robert *la Waite* 1207 P (Ess) is also called *de la Waite* (1206 P), whilst Ralph *la Waite* 1202 Cur (Ha) is identical with Radulfus *Vigil* 'the watchman'.

Waithman: Richard *Weythman, Waitman* 1223 Cur (We); Robert *Waythman* 1437 FrY; Jean, Thomas *Wayman* or *Waithman* 1612–13 LaWills. ON *veiðimaðr, veiðimann* 'hunter'. This may also survive as *Wayman*.

Wake: Hugo *Vigil* 1133 StCh; Hugo *Wac* 1153 ib.; Hugo *Wach* 1176 P (L); William *le Wacce* 1185 Templars (Y); Henry *le Wake* 1298 LLB C. Clearly a nickname, translated by Lat *vigil* 'watchful, alert'. The most common early form is *Wac*, found chiefly in Staffs, Lincs, Leics and Yorks, where a Scandinavian origin is possible, probably ON *vakr* 'watchful'.

Wakeham, Wakem, Whackum: Henry *de Wakeham* 1296 SRSx; William *Wakeham* alias *Wakam* 1715 DKR 41 (Co). From Wakeham in Aveton Gifford (Devon) or Wakeham in Terwick (Sussex).

Wakehurst: Alice *de Wekehurst* 1221 Cur (Sx).

From Wakehurst Place in Ardingly (Sussex).

Wakelam: v. WAKELIN

Wakeley, Wakely, Wakley, Wackley: Roger *Wakeley* 1332 SRSt. From Wakeley (Herts).

Wakelin, Wakeling, Wakling, Wakelam, Walklin, Walkling, Walklyn: *Walcelin* 1086 DB; Ricardus *filius Walkelini* 1119 Bury (Sf); *Wauchelinus* Maminot 1157 Templars (Lo); *Walclinus* de Normentun Hy 2 DC (L); *Wakelinus* de Roking' 1221 Cur (Wa); John *Wakelin* 1221 Cur (Lo); Nicholas *Walklin* 1225 AssSo; John *Wakelam* 1544 FFSt. From *Walchelin*, a Norman-French double diminutive of OG *Walho* or *Walico*.

Wakem: v. WAKEHAM

Wakeman: William *Wakeman* 1200 Oseney (O); Richard *le Wakeman* 1225–50 Dublin. ME *wake* 'watch, vigil' and *man*, 'watchman' (c1200 NED). *Wakeman* was the title of the chief magistrate of the borough of Ripon until 1604 when it was changed to mayor. He was the head of the body of wakemen whose duty was to blow a cow's horn every night at nine o'clock. If between then and sunrise any burglary took place, it was made good at the public charge.

Wakenshaw: v. WALKINGSHAW

Waker: William *Waker* 1230 P (Berks); Richard *le Waker* 1327 SRSx. OE *wacor*, ME *waker* 'watchful, vigilant'.

Wakerell: v. WACKRILL

Wakley: v. WAKELEY

Walbanck, Walbancke, Walbank, Wallbank, Wallbanks: Adam *de Wallebonk* 1332 SRLa; Thomas *Walbanke* 1489 GildY. *Wall-* is the West Midland form of *well*, hence 'dweller on the bank(s) of the stream'.

Walbey: v. WALBY

Walbourn, Walbourne, Walburn: *Walebrun* c1155 DC (L); Robert *Walebrun* 1296 SRSx; John *Walebron* 1327 SRSx. OFr *Walebron* (Langlois).

Walbrook, Walbrooke: Albin *de Walebroc* 1197 Clerkenwell (Lo). From Walbrook (London).

Walburn: v. WALBOURN

Walby, Walbey, Wauldby, Waudby: (i) Tomas *de Waldebi* 1190 P (Y); Peter de *Walebi* 1193 P (L). From Wauldby (ERYorks), DB *Walbi* 'village on the wold'. (ii) William *de Walby* 1332 SRCu. From Walby (Cumb), 'village by the Roman Wall'.

Walch: v. WALSH

Walcot, Walcott: Stephen *de Walecote* 1199 FFO; Warin *de Walcote* 1259 Ronton; John *Walcot'* 1379 CorO. From Walcot (Lincs, Northants, Oxon, Salop, Wilts, Warwicks), Walcote (Leics), or Walcott (Norfolk, Worcs).

Wald, Walde, Waud, Weald, Weild, Weld, Wolde, Would, Woulds: William *de Welde* 1121–48 Bury (Sf); Gilbert *del Wald'* 1206 Cur (Bk); Hugh *in þe Wold* 1279 RH (O); John *Weld* 1279 RH (C); Thomas *de la Waude* 1279 RH (Bk); John *at þe Welde* 1316 MELS (Sx); Richard *of ye Wolde* 1327 Pinchbeck (Sf); John *atte Wolde* 1327 SR (Ess); John *Woulde* 1568 SRSf. 'Dweller in the forest or by the woodland.' West Saxon *weald* survives as Weald (Essex, Kent, Hants, Oxon, Sussex), Wield (Hants), and in surnames also as Weld and Weild. Anglian *wald*, later *wold*, survives in Old (Northants) and The Wolds, and in surnames also as Wald(e), Waud, Wold(e) and Would(s).

Walder: Adam *Waldere* 1226 FFBk; Robert *Walder* 1296 SRSx; John *Wolder* 1558 SxWills. A derivative of OE *wald*. 'Forest-dweller.'

Waldie: v. WALTHEW

Walding, Welding: Willelmus *filius Walding* 1171 P (Y); *Walding* c1248 Bec (Bk); Roger, Henry *Walding* 1193 P (Wo), 1210 P (Gl); Henry *Wolding* 1275 SRWo. OE **Wealding*, a derivative of *Weald-* in *Wealdhelm*, etc. There has been some confusion with OG *Waldin*. *Wadin* or *Waldin* Crede (1191, 1195 P) is also called *Waldingus* 1195 P (Wa). The surname may also be descriptive, from OE **wealding*, a derivative of *weald*, 'forest-dweller'. v. GAUDIN.

Waldman: William *Waldeman* 1329 Rams (C); Thomas *Waldman* 1349 MESO (Y). OE *wald* (Anglian) and *mann*, 'dweller in the forest'.

Waldo: v. WALTHEW

Waldram, Waldren, Waldron, Waldrum, Waleran, Walrond: Iohannes *filius Waleranni, Galerami* 1086 DB (Ess); *Waleran* t Stephen DC (L); *Walran* Hy 2 ib. (Lei); *Walerannus, Galerannus, Walerandus* de Crikelade 1182, 1191, 1200 Oseney (O); John *Waleram, Walerand* 1196–8, 1218–20 Clerkenwell (Lo); Richard *Walram* 1262 FFEss; Robert *Waldrond* 1275 SRWo; Matilda *Walrond* 1275 RH (W); Roysa *Walraunt* 1297 MinAcctCo; William *Galeram* 1332 SRSx. OG *Walahram, Waleran*, OFr *Galeran(t)*. v. also WALLRAVEN.

Waldwyn: v. WALWIN

Waldy: v. WALTHEW

Wale: (i) *Walo* 1086 DB (Sx); *Walo, Wale* 1219 AssY; Robert, Lewin *Wale*, 1169 P (Y), 1221 ElyA (Sf); Hugo *le Wale* 1220 Cur (Wo); Richard *le Wale* 1250 Fees (Ha). *le Wale* is from ME *wale*, a general laudatory expression, 'excellent, noble, goodly', from ME *wale* 'act of choosing, choice', used as in 'men of wale' (a1300 NED), 'men of merit'. The simple *Wale* may be from this or from OG *Walo*, OFr *Gal, Galon*, which has also given *Gale* and *Gallon*. The nominative survives as *Gales* and *Wales*. (ii) Richard *de Wale* 1196 P (Nth); Philip *atte Wale* 1296 SRSx. 'Dweller by the ridge' (OE *walu* 'ridge, bank').

Wales, Wailes: (i) Ricardus *filius Wales (Walis)* 1175 P (Bk), *filius Wales* 1188 P (Bk), *filius Wale* 1208 Fees (Nth); *Wales (Waleis)* de Possbroc 1203 Cur (Sf). The cas-sujet of OFr *Galon*, OG *Walo*, probably from *walh* 'foreign', which has been associated with *waleis* (v. WALLIS) and is one source of GALES. (ii) William *le Wales* 1275 RH (L). Identical with WALLIS. (iii) Amicia, Cecilia *de Wales* 1327 SRSf, 1379 PTY; John *Wailes* 1587 LaWills; James *Wales* 1612 ib. Amicia may have come from Wales and her surname may be a variant of *Wallis*. But she may have come from Yorkshire, as certainly did Cecilia, who lived at Wales, near Sheffield.

Walford: William *de Waleford'* 1221 AssWa; Henry *de Walford* 1279 IpmGl; Gilbert *Walford* 1327 SRSo. From Walford (Dorset, Hereford, Salop), or Walford Hall (Warwicks).

Walker: Richard *le Walkere* c1248 Bec (Wa); Robert *le Walker* 1260 AssY. OE *wealcere* 'fuller'. *v.* FULLER.

Walkingshaw, Walkinshaw, Wakenshaw: Robert *Walkyngschaw* 1551 Black; Constantine *Walkin-schaw* 1562 ib.; — *Wakinshaw* 1658 ib. From the lands of Walkinshaw (Renfrewshire), *Walkein-schaw* c1235 ib.

Walklate, Walklett: William, John *Walkelate* 1353 LLB G, 1365 LoPleas; George *Walklot* 1511 Black (Edinburgh). Black unconsciously gives the clue to this surname when he refers to a *domus Wauklet* in a confirmation of the foundation charter of Holy Trinity, Edinburgh. This must be 'the house of Wauklet', i.e. *Walk-el-et*, a double diminutive of OG *Walho, Walico.* cf. *Walkelin s.n.* WAKELIN. *Walkelot* seems also to have existed.

Walklin, Walkling, Walklyn: *v.* WAKELIN

Walkman: A variant of WAKEMAN 'watchman'. cf. 'Angels ben called walkmen and wardeyns for they warne men of perylles that may fall' (1398 NED).

Wall, Walle, Walls: Robert *de la Walle* 1195 P (Ess); Robert *del Wal* 1213 Cur (St); Alexander *super le Wal* 1279 RH (Hu); Walter *Opethewalle* 1312 ColchCt; John *Bithwalle* 1321 LLB E; Robert *atte Walle* 1327 SRWo; Agnes *Walle* 1327 SRSf. From residence near some wall (OE *weall*). In Essex the reference is probably to the sea-walls of Rochford Hundred, in Oxford, London and Colchester to the town wall, in Northumberland to the Roman Wall. Wall (Staffs) is on the site of a Roman station. In the West Midlands, *walle* is a dialectal form of *welle* and here the reference may be to a stream. cf. WALLER (ii).

Wallace, Wallas: *v.* WALLIS

Wallaker: *v.* WALLENGER

Wallbank(s): *v.* WALBANCK

Wallenger, Wallinger, Wallaker, Walliker: *Warengerus* 1086 DB (Nf, Sf); *Garengerus* ib. (Ess, Sf); *Waringarus* Frost 1202 FFNf; *Walingerus* filius Hugonis 1221 AssSa; Roger *Wareng'* 1086 DB (Sf); Thomas *Warenger* 1482 LLB B; Robert *Walenger* 1524 SRSf; John *Walycar* 1575 *ERO* (Ess). OG *Warengar, Guarenger.*

Waller, Wallers: (i) John *le Walur* Hy 2 DC (Nt); William *Waliere* 1185 Templars (K); Adam *le Walere* 1280 MESO (Ha); Nicholas *le Walour* 1327 SRSf. OFr *galure, galier, gallier, guallier* 'a coxcombe, spark' or 'a man of pleasant temper'. This survives as *Gallear, Galler, Gallier, Galliers, Gallyer*, from the Central French form; *Waller* is from the NE French form. (ii) Henry *le Waller'* 1279 RH (C); John *le Wallere* 1312 LLB C. This name is common in this form and is usually a derivative of ME *walle* 'to furnish with walls'; 'a builder of walls' (c1440 NED). ME *walle* is also a dialectal form of *welle*, found in place-names from Herefordshire to Lancashire and from Worcester-

shire to Cambridge and Suffolk. Here it may also mean 'dweller by a stream': William *le Waller* 1327 SRSf. *v.* WELLER: or, in Cheshire, Worcs and Staffs, 'salt-weller', 'salt-boiler' (1600 NED), John *le Waller'* 1221 AssWo.

Walles: *v.* WALLIS

Wallet, Wallett: *Wallauiet, Walhauiet, Welleuiet* 1221 AssGl; *Wallet* 1249-86 Black; *Walettus* de Bygestrode 1296 SRSx; Thomas *Waleth* 1296 SRSx; William *Walot* 1327 SRDb; Alexander *Wallet* 1679 Black. Clearly a personal-name, perhaps an *-et* diminutive of Anglo-Scandinavian *Walþēof.* cf. WALTHEW.

Walley: *v.* WHALLEY

Walliker: *v.* WALLENGER

Wallis, Wallice, Walles, Wallace, Wallas: Osbert *Waleis* 1156-85 Seals (Wa); Robert *Waliscus, Waleis* 1166, 1169 P (Nf); Eudo *le Waleis* c1200 DC (L); Richard *le Waleis, le Walles* 1225, 1244 Oseney (O); Maddock *le Waleys* 1283 AssSt; Alice *Walas* 1379 PTY; William *Wallis* 1463 LLB L. AFr *Waleis, Walais* 'Welshman, Celt'. In the border counties of Warwicks, Worcs and Staffs, we clearly have reference to Welshmen. In Norfolk and Lincs, the Celts were probably Bretons, many of whom settled in the Eastern counties after the Conquest. *Wallace* is a Scottish form. Here it means a Briton of the kingdom of Strathclyde where we find Richard *Walensis* or *Waleis* between 1165 and 1173. *Walace* is found in 1432 and *Wallas* in 1497 (Black).

Wallman, Walman: Ailwin, John *Waleman* 1166 P (Hu), 1279 RH (C). These forms mean 'servant of *Wale*'. *v.* WALE. The modern form may also be an assimilated form of *Waldeman* (*v.* WALDMAN), or equivalent to *atte Wall*: Ralph *Walleman* 1332 SRCu. *v.* WALL.

Wallraven: *Walrauen, Welrauen* 1066 DB (L); *Walrafnus* de Muirteus 1275 RH (C); John *Wal-raven* 1275 RH (Sf); Agnes *Walreuen* 1275 SRWo. A rare name, from *Wælhræfn*, an anglicizing of OG *Walahram.* This is not Scandinavian as sometimes suggested but was probably introduced into England by Franks and other Germans who came over with the Scandinavian settlers (PNDB 409). After the Conquest it was reintroduced in its later OG and Romance form *Waleram* which survives in WALDRAM.

Wallwin: *v.* WALWIN

Walman: *v.* WALLMAN

Walmesley, Walmisley, Walmsley, Wamsley, Warmsley, Waumsley: Roger *de Walmeresleghe* 1332 SRLa; John *Wamesley* 1549 FrLeic; Henry *Walmesley* 1582 PrGR. From Walmersley (Lancs).

Walpole, Wolpole, Waple, Waples: Godfrey *de Walpoll'* 1198 Pl (Nf); Henry *de Walepol* 1230 Cur (K); William *Walpol* 1356 FFEss; Andrewe *Walpole*, Thomas *Wapyle* 1524 SRSf; Hillary *Wapolle* 1557 Bardsley. From Walpole (Norfolk, Suffolk).

Walrond: *v.* WALDRAM

Walsh, Walshe, Walch: Rose *la Walesche* 1277 AssSo; John *le Walsche, le Walche* 1327 SRSf; John *Walshe, Walche* 1360, 1376 Black (Roxburgh). ME *walsche*, OE *wælisc* 'foreigner'. cf. WELSH.

Walshman, Walsman: Walter *Walseman* 1279 RH (C); John *Walsheman* 1303 LoCt; Walter *Walcheman* 1327 SRY; William *Walisshman* 1367 AD iii (K). 'Welshman.' cf. WALSH. John *Walshman*, tailor 1324 Cor (Lo) is probably identical with John *le Walshe*, tailor 1340 LLB F.

Walter, Walters, Fitzwalter, Fitzwater, Gaulter: *Walterus episcopus* 1066 DB; *Robertus filius Walterii, Galterii* 1086 DB; *Galterus* le Lingedraper 1210 Oseney (O); Petrus *Walterus* 1182 Bury (Sf); Petrus *Walteri* 1191 P (Sf); Geoffrey *Walter* 1296 SRSx; William *Walters* 1327 SRSt; Johan *fitz Waulter* 1350 AssEss. OG *Walter* 'mighty army'. The name was introduced into England in the reign of the Confessor and, after the Conquest, soon became one of the most popular christian names, usually as *Walter* or *Wauter*, the latter representing the actual pronunciation. *v.* WATER.

Waltham, Whatham: John *de Waltham* 1119–27 Colch (Ess); Geoffrey *de Waltham* 1190 P (L). From one of the numerous Walthams.

Walthew, Waltho, Waldie, Waldo, Waldy, Watthews, Watthey, Waddie, Waddy, Wadey, Wadie, Wady, Wealthy, Wildee, Wildey, Wildy, Wilthew: *Waltef, Walteu, Walteif, Waldeuus* 1066 DB; *Wallef* filius Arnabol c1153–65 Black (Kelso); *Willelmus filius Walthef* Hy 2 DC (L); *Waldeuius* filius Wesescop 1176 P (Nb); *Willelmus filius Waldeu'* 1192 P (Y); Henricus *filius Waldief* 1200 P (Ha); *Waldef* filius *Waldef* 1212 Cur (Cu); *Walyf* de Derby Ed 3 Rydware (St); Robert *Wlthef* Hy 2 DC (L); Adam *Walthef'* 1219 AssY; Hugo *Waldef* 1275 SRWo; Alexander *Waltheuf, Walthew* 1297 Wak (Y); Hugh *Waddy* 1316 Wak (Y); Adam *Waldi* 1400 Black (Aberdeen); Thomas *Watho* 1539 ib. (Kelso); James *Waddie* 1543 ib. (Edinburgh); John *Waddo* 1567 ib. (Kelso); Robert *Wadie* 1689 ib. Anglo-Scand *Wælþeof*, ON *Valþiófr*, familiar as *Waltheof*. *Waddy*, etc., are due to the common development of *Wald-* to *Waud-* and *Wad-*. Similarly, *Watthey* is from *Wautheu*. Most of our forms are from the north, where *Wæl-* became *Wal-*. In the south, this would become *Wel-*, and later, *Wil-*, hence *Wealthy*, *Wilthew*, *Wildey*, etc. *v.* also WADDILOVE.

Walton, Walten, Wauton: Geoffrey, Osmund *de Waltona* 1189 Sol; Richard *de Walton* 1253 ForNth; Alan *Walton* 1352 IpmW. From one or other of the many places of this name.

Walwin, Walwyn, Wallwin, Waldwyn: *Walduinus* 1066 DB (Sf); *Wealdwine* Wm 2 Searle; *Welwin* 1205 Cur (Ess); Mable *Welwyne* 1327 *SR* (Ess). The DB *Walduinus* is derived by von Feilitzen from OG *Waldwin*, a possible explanation, but the existence of an OE **Wealdwine* 'power-friend' is proved by the later *We(a)l-* forms. The surname may also derive from *Walweyn*. *v.* GAVIN.

Wamsley: *v.* WALMESLEY

Wanless, Wanlass, Wanliss, Wanlace, Wandless, Wandloss: Simon *Wanles* 1451 Black (Montrose);

Robert *Wanless* 1538 ib. (Linlithgow); Robert *Wandles* 1638 ib. ME *wanles* 'hopeless, luckless'.

Wann: Warner, Robert *Wan* 1297 SRY, 1327 SRSf. OE *wann* 'wan, pale'.

Wansey: Hugo *de Wanceio* 1086 DB (Sf); Roger *de Wanci* 1146–8 Seals (Ess). From Wanchy (Seine-Inférieure). *v.* ANF.

Want, Whant: (i) Edwin *Wante* 1207 Cur (Nf); Benedict *le Want* 1327 SRSx. ME *want* 'mole'. (ii) James *atte Wante* 1332 SRSx. 'Dweller by the cross-roads', ME *want*, a dialect form of WENT.

Wantling: *Wentiliana* 1208 Cur (Sa); *Wantliana* 1221 AssSa; *Wenthelen* 1411 Fine (Glam); Albreda *Wentelien'* 1221 AssWa; Thomas *Wantlyn* 1674 HTSf. Welsh *Gwenllian* (f) 'fair-flaxen', the name of the daughter of a Prince of Powys (c1180) and the subject of a song 'Gwenllian's Repose' composed in 1236.

Waple: Everard, William *Wagepol(e)* 1169 P (W), 1206 Cur (Sf); Thomas *Waghepol'* 1219 AssY; Geoffrey *Waupol, Wagpoll* 1271 LeicBR. 'Wag pole', synonymous with WAGSTAFF. *Wagpoll* suggests an alternative 'wag head'. cf. William *Wauberd* 1295 Barnwell (C), John *Wagheberd* 1297 MinAcctCo. 'wag beard' *v.* also WALPOLE.

Waraker: *v.* WARWICKER

Warboy, Warboys, Worboys: (i) William *de Wardeboys* 1261 FFEss. From Warboys (Hunts). (ii) Richard, Silvester, William *Wardebois* 1207 P (St), 1227 AssBeds, 1219 AssY; John *Gardeboys* 1280 LLB A. The last form, and the wide distribution of forms without a preposition, show we have also a nickname 'guard wood' for a forester (OFr *garder, warder* and *bois*).

Warburton, Warbleton: Mabilia *de Warberton'* 1212 P (Ess, Herts); William *de Warbilton* 1278 RH (C); Geoffrey *de Werberton'* 1325 WhC; John *Warberton* or *Warbulton* 1413–14 FFSr. From Warburton (Ches), or Warbleton (Sussex), *Warburton* 1211, *Warbelton* 1273.

Ward, Warde, Wards: (i) William, John *Warde* 1194 P (Y), 1257 MEOT (Sx); Thomas, Simon *le Warde* 1279 RH (Beds, O); Alice *le Wardes* 1352 *ERO*. OE *weard* 'watchman, guard'. (ii) William *de la Warda* 1176 P (Lei), *de la Warde* 1203 P (Db); Robert *del Warde* 1285 AssSt; Peter *ate Warde* 1332 MELS (Sr). This may go back to an OE **wearde, *wearda* 'beacon', but is more probably OE *weard* 'watching, guarding', with the same meaning as (i) above, '(man) of the watch', 'watchman'. We may, however, sometimes be concerned with ME *werd, ward* 'marsh', found in Essex, Kent and Herts, hence 'marshman'. cf. WARDMAN and *v.* MELS 220.

Wardale, Wardall, Wardell: *v.* WARDILL

Warden: (i) Wluric *Uuerdenus* 1066 DB (Herts); Walter *Wardein* 1279 RH (O); John *le Wardeyn* 1289 Barnwell (C). AFr *wardein*, OFr *gardein* 'one who guards, warden', perhaps a gate-keeper, porter or sentinel (a1225 NED). (ii) Symon *de Waredon'* 1232 Clerkenwell (K); Elyas *de Wardon'* 1297 MinAcctCo (R). From Warden (Beds, Durham, Kent, Northumb, Northants).

Wardill, Wardle, Wardale, Wardall, Wardel, Wardell: (i) William *de Werdale* 1216, *de Werdall* c1217 FeuDu; William *Wardell* 1539 ib. From Weardale (Durham), which may also have developed to *Wardill*. (ii) Thomas *de Wardhill* 1218 AssLa; Alexander *de Wardhull* c1238 WhC (La), *de Werdul* 13th ib.; Richard *de Wardle* 1275 RH (L). From Wardle (Ches, Lancs), both earlier *weardhyll 'watch hill'.

Wardman, Wordman: John *Werdeman*, *Wirdman* 1351 AssEss, 1374 Pat (Ess); Christopher *Wardeman* 1491 GildY. The Essex name is 'marshman' (ME *werde*). The surname may also mean 'watchman'. cf. WARD.

Wardrobe, Wardrop, Wardrope, Wardrupp, Whatrup: Robert *de Warderob* c1210 Black; Joscelin *de la Warderob(e)* 1219, 1220 Cur (Bk); Thomas *de Garderoba* 1286 Wak (Y); John *atte Warderobe* 1327 SRSx; Thomas *Warderope* 1334 LLB E; William *Waddrope* 1608 Black. ONFr *warderobe*, OFr *garderobe*, from *warder*, *garder* 'to watch' and *robe*. An official of the wardrobe, identical in meaning with WARDROPER.

Wardroper, Wardropper, Waredraper: William *Warderober* 1275 RH (K); William *Wardroper* 1301 SRY; Thomas *Garderober*, *(le) Wardrober* 1351 AssEss; Thomas *Wardroppare* 1465 Black. ONFr *warderobier*, OFr *garderobier* 'an official of the household in charge of the robes, wearing-apparel, etc.' (a1400 NED).

Ware, Wares: (i) Peter *le Ware* 1218 ChR (Gl), 1297 MinAcctCo (D). OE *wær*, ME *war(e)* 'wary, astute, prudent'. This nickname certainly existed but examples are rare. (ii) Anschil *de Waras* 1066 DB (Herts), *de Wara*, *de Wares* 1086 ib.; Aschi *Wara* 1066 DB (Herts); John *de Ware* 1276 LLB B. From Ware (Herts). (iii) William *de la War'* 1194 Cur (Sr); William *ater Ware* 1296 SRSx; Richard *atte Ware* 1327 SR (Ess); Nicholas *Betheware* 1369 LLB G. From residence near or employment at a weir or dam (OE *wær*), one who looked after a fishing-weir.

Wareing, Waring, Warin, Warring, Wearing, Wharin, FitzWarin: Robertus *filius Warini* (*Warin*) 1086 InqEl (C); Gislebertus *filius Garini* 1086 DB (Ess); *Warinus* filius Toruerdi 1142 NthCh (L); Willelmus *filius Warin*, *Gwarini* Hy 2 DC (L); Robert, Gilbert *Warin'* 1198 Cur (Y), c1209 Fees (Du); John *Waryng* 1275 SRWo; Roger *Warenge* 1478 LLB L; John *Warren* alias *Waryng* 1512 Oxon; William *Wairin* 1665 RothwellPR (Y); Thomas *Warring* 1674 HTSf. AFr *Warin*, OFr *Guarin*, *Guérin*, from OG *Warin*, a very common Norman personal name. This has been confused with WARREN.

Warlock, Werlock, Worlock: Nicholas *Warloc* 1279 RH (C); Simon *(le) Warlok* 1290–1 Crowland (C); John *Werlok* 1327 SRC. OE *wærloga* 'traitor, enemy, devil', not noted as a surname, came to be applied especially to the Devil, sorcerers (with particular reference to the power of assuming inhuman shapes) and monsters. The normal development would be to *warlow*. In Scotland we find *warloche* and *warlok*, used of wizards. As these forms do not appear before the 16th century, NED discounts association with ON *varðlokkur* 'incantations'. *Warloc* has now been noted in the 13th century on Cambridgeshire manors of Crowland Abbey, a district subject to Scandinavian influence.

Warman, Warmen: (i) Robertus *filius Waremanni* 1208 P (So); Henry, Richard *Wareman* 1214 Cur (Nth), 1263 ArchC iii; William *Warman* 1338 LLB F. OE *waru* 'articles of merchandise, goods (for sale)' and *mann*. *Wareman* probably meant a chapman. (ii) *Warmundus* 1199 MemR (Sr); John *Waremund* 1275 RH (Berks); Isabella *Wermund* 1279 RH (C). OE *Wærmund* 'faith-protector'.

Warme: Matilda, Henry *Warme* 1279 RH (O). OE *wearm* 'warm', probably in the sense 'zealous, keen'.

Warmington: Þurfeorð æt *Wermingtune* 972 OEByn (Nth); William *de Warmintona* 1185 Templars; Richard *Warmyngton* 1376 AD i (Sr). From Warmington (Northants, Warwicks).

Warmoll: *v.* WORMALD

Warmsley: *v.* WALMESLEY

Warne, Warnes, Warn, Wearn, Wearne: Jervase, John *de Werne* 1273 RH (So); John, William *Warne* 1524–5, 1545 SRW. From Wearne (Som), or Warne in Marytavy (Devon).

Warneford, Warnford: Wulfric æt *Wernæforda* c1050 OEByn (Ha); Ralph *de Warneford* 1296 SRSx; John *Warneforde* 1545 SRW. From Warnford (Hants).

Warner: (i) *Warnerus* de Lusoriis 1140 Eyns (O); *Garnerus*, *Gwarnerius*, *Warnerus* de Campania c1160 DC (L); *Warner* (*Garner*) de Waxtunesham 1221 Cur (Nf); *Wariner* le Botiler 1275 RH (Bk); Robert *Warnier* 1196 P (Do); Geoffrey *Warner* 1203 Cur (Sr). ONFr *Warnier*, OFr *Guarnier*, *Garnier*, from OG *Warinhar(i)*, a common Norman personal name. (ii) Peter *le Warner* 1214 Cur (Y). A contracted form of OFr *warrennier* 'warrener'. *v.* WARRENER, GARNER.

Warnett: *v.* GARNET

Warr, Warre: Herebertus *la Guerre* 1179 P (Do); John *la Werre*, *la Guerre* 1187, 1195 P (Gl); Tomas *la Werre*, *la Guerre*, *de la Warre* 1196, 1199 P (So, Gl); Peter *le Werre*, *de Warre* 1199, 1203 P (Gl); George *Warre* 1468 LLB L. OFr *werre*, *guerre* 'war', originally *de la werre*, *de la guerre* 'of the war', a warrior. cf. Fr *Guerre*, *Laguerre*. Geoffrey *le Werreur* is also called *le Werre* (1221 AssWa). For the common loss of the preposition, cf. BATTLE, VEIL.

Warrack: *v.* WARRICK

Warren, Warran, Warrand, Warrant: William *de Warene*, *de Warenne*, *de Garenna* 1086 DB; Hamelinus *de Warrena* 1187 Gilb (L); William *de Warenne* 1285 FFEss. From La Varenne (Seine-Inférieure). There is no reason to suppose that this also means 'at the warren' as stated by Bardsley. There are no examples with *atte*. The surname has been confused with *Wareing*.

Warrender: Thomas *Warendier* Hy 3 Colch

(Sf); John *Warrender* 1327 *SR* (Ess); William *le Warender* 1332 SRLa. A form of WARRENER with intrusive *d*, found already in OFr *garendier* (Godefroy).

Warrener, Warriner, Warner: William *le Wariner* 1198 FF (K); Adam *le Warner* 1218 FFSt; John *le Warner*, *le Warener*, *le Wariner*, *le Warenner* 1280 AssSo; William *le Warrener* 1317 AD iii (W). NE OFr *warrennier*, central OFr *garennier* 'warrener', an officer employed to watch over game in a park or preserve (1297 NED). *v.* also WARNER, which has an alternative origin.

Warrick, Warrack: Walter, Roger *Warrock* 1271 ForSt, 1285 *Ass* (Ess). In building, the lashings for scaffolds were tightened by driving in wedges called *warrocks*. cf., at Westminster in 1324, 'for 6 pieces of timber for *warrokis* for binding the scaffolds' and 'for half a hundred of talwode of *ash* for *warrokes* for making scaffolds' (Building 320). The surname is probably metonymic for a maker of warrocks or a builder of scaffolds. It has been assimilated to *Warwick* with which it has been confused.

Warricker: *v.* WARWICKER

Warring: *v.* WAREING

Warrington: Richard *de Warynton'* 1316–17 FFWa; Agnes *de Werynton* 1354 Putnam (Ch). From Warrington (Bucks, Lancs).

Warrior, Warrier, Wharrier: Herbert, Jordan *le Werreur* 1202 AssL, 1230 P (He); Thomas *le Werreor* 1324 LoPleas. NE OFr *werreieor*, *werrieur* 'warrior'. cf. WARR.

Warriss, Warry: *v.* WERRY

Warter: Robert *de Warter* 1219 AssY. From Warter (ERYorks).

Warters, Worters: Roger *Warters* 1637 EA (NS) ii (Sf). For *Waters*

Warton: Ruffus *de Wertona* c1175 Seals (Nf); Adam, John *de Warton* 1246 AssLa, 1332 SRWa; Peter *Warton* 1527 FFEss. From Warton (Lancs, Northumb, Warwicks). *v.* also WHARTON with which there may have been some confusion.

Warwick, Warrick, Wharrick: Turchil *de Waruuic* 1086 DB (Wa); Richard *de Warewic* a1196 Black (Glasgow). From Warwick. Turchil owed his surname to his office of sheriff of Warwickshire. Less commonly, but particularly in Dumfries and Kirkcudbright, from Warwick (Cumb).

Warwicker, Warricker, Waraker, Woracker, Woraker, Woricker: *Warwicker* is an alteration of *Warricker* through the influence of *Warwick*. The surname denotes a maker of 'warrocks' or a builder of scaffolds. *v.* WARRICK.

Wasey: *v.* WACEY

Wash: *v.* WACE

Washbourn, Washbourne, Washburn, Washburne: William *de Wasseburn'* 1204 Pl (Wo); John *Washburn'* c1280 SRWo; William *de Wasshebourn* 1333 FFY. From Washbourne (Devon, Glos), or Washburn (WRYorks).

Washbrook, Washbrooke: John *de Wassebroc'* 1202 Pl (Sf); Margaret *Wasshebrook* 1374 ColchCt;

Caleb *Wasbrook* 1628 Musters (Sr). From Washbrook (Suffolk).

Washer: Henry *le Wassere* 1293 MESO (Y); Alan *le Wascere* 1295 ib. (Nf). A derivative of OE *wæscan* 'to wash', 'washer'. cf. LAVENDER.

Washington: Ralph *de Wassingeton* 1327 SRSx; Robert *de Wasshington* 1395 IpmLa; John *Wasshyngton* 1401 AssLa. From Washington (Durham, Sussex).

Washtell: *v.* WASTALL

Waskett: Elyas *Wasket* 1274 RH (Ess); John *Wasket* 1351 AssEss. Probably a diminutive of *Wask*, the Norman form of OFr *Gasc* 'Gascon'. cf. Fr *Gasquet*. The same development appears in Adam *Waskin* 1276 RH (Db), for *Gaskin*.

Waslin: *v.* WASTLING

Wasnidge: *v.* WASTNAGE

Wasp, Waspe: William *Waps* 1202–16 StP (Lo); Richard *Wasp* 1203 P (Sr); Roger *le Waps* 1296 SRSx. A nickname from OE *wæps* 'wasp'.

Wason, Wass: *v.* WACE

Wassall, Wassell: *v.* WASTALL

Wasselin: *v.* WASTLING

Wassey: *v.* WACEY

Wasson: *v.* WACE

Wastall, Wastell, Washtell, Waistell, Wassall, Wassell, Gastall: (i) Ralph *Wastel* 1182–1211 BuryS (Sf), 1279 RH (O); Thomas *Wassall* 1674 HTSf. OFr *wastel*, north-eastern form of *g(u)astel*, modFr *gâteau*, 'a cake or bread made of the finest flour' (c1300 NED). A common medieval name, metonymic for (John) *Wasteler* 1327 MESO (L) or (Robert) *Wastelmonger* 1317 MEOT (O), maker or seller of *wastels*. *Gastall* is rare. (ii) Nicholas *de Wasthull'* 1221 AssWo. From Wast Hills in Alvechurch (Worcs).

Wastenay: *v.* WASTNAGE

Wastling, Waslin, Wasselin: *Wacelinus* clericus Hy 2 DC (L); *Wascelinus* de Brunham c1200 DC (L); William *Wacelin*, *Waselin* c1150, 1157 Gilb (L); Thomas *Wazelin* 1162 P (Y); Samson *Wascelin'* 1176 P (Ha); Adam *Wastelyn* 1327 SRSf; Peter *Waslinge* 1581 FrY. OG *Wazelin*, *Wa(s)celin*, OFr *Gacelin*, *Gaselin*, a double diminutive of OG *Wazo*.

Wastnage, Wastnidge, Wasnidge, Wastenay, Westnage, Westnedge, Westnidge, Westney: Robert *de Wastenays* c1165 StCh; William *Wastineis* 1177 P (St); William *de Westenay* 1191 P (L); Robert *de Westeneis* 1203 P (L); William *Wastneys* 1249 AD i (Lei); Ralph *le Wasteneys* 1281 AssCh. From le Gâtinais, formerly Gastinois, a district south of Paris and east of Orleans.

Watcher, Wacher: Johan *Wachere* 1237 ELPN; Elys *le Wacher* 1279 RH (C). A derivative of OE *wæcce* 'watch, vigil'. A watchman.

Watchman: Robert *Wachman* 1513 Black; James *Watchman* 1564 ib. 'Watchman'.

Watcyns: *v.* WATKIN

Wate(s): *v.* WAIT

Water, Waters: (i) *Waterus* de Cantelupo c1135 DC (L); *Walterus*, *Waterus* filius Herberti Hy 2 DC (L); *Water* Dey 1479 BuryW (Sf); John

Watter 1214 Cur (Wa); Richard *Wauter*, Roger *Water* 1275 SRWo; Hugh *Water* 1279 AssNb; Alice *Waters* 1327 SRSf; John *Wauters* 1348 AD i (Wa); Thomas *Watter* 1509 GildY. *Water* was the normal medieval pronunciation of *Walter*. Theobald *Walter* is also called Theobaldus *filius Walteri*, Theobaldus *Walteri*, Tebaut *Water* 1212–36 Fees (La). (ii) William *de la Watere* 1245 FFC; Thomas *del Water* 1246 AssLa; William *atte Watere* 1296 SRSx. 'Dweller by the water or stream.' cf. ATTWATER, BYWATER.

Waterer, Watrer: Richard *Waterer* 1443 MEOT (Sx). A derivative of OE *wæterian* 'to water, irrigate, lead (cattle) to water'.

Waterfield: Hugo *of Walteruile* 1137 ASC E; Guefridus *de Walteriuill* c1142 Seals (He); Ralph *de Walteruill'* 1190 P (L); Ascelina *de Watervill'* 1205 Cur (L); Roger *Wateruile* 1327 SRC; John *Waterfield* 1601 Oxon. From Vatierville (Seine-Inférieure).

Waterhouse: Adam *del Waterhous* 1308 Wak (Y). 'Dweller at a house by the water' or, possibly, at a moated house.

Waterkeyn: John *Waterkyn* 1301 LLB C. 'Little Walter.' *v.* WATKIN.

Waterman: (i) Adam *Walterman* 1260 AssY; Geoffrey *Walterman* 1275 RH (Sx). 'Servant of Walter', which would inevitably become *Waterman*. *v.* WALTER, WATER. (ii) Wilke *Waterman* 1196 FrLeic; William *le Waterman* 1249 Oseney (O). 'Waterman', i.e. waterbearer, water-carrier. cf. William *Waterladar'* 1197 P (Wa) 'water-carrier', one who carts water for sale; Richard *Waterberere* 1381 LoPleas, one who carries water from a spring, etc. for domestic use. 'Boatman' is also a possible sense.

Waterson, Watterson: John *Wauterson* 1379 PTY; William *Watterson* 1507 GildY; Thomas *Waterson* 1674 HTSf. 'Son of *Walter*.' *v.* WATER.

Wath, Wathe, Wathes, Waythe: Ioseph *de Waða* 1177 (P) (L); Walter *del Wathe* 1301 SRY. From Wath (NRYorks, WRYorks), Wade (Suffolk), Waithe (L), DB *Wada*, or from residence by a ford, ON *vað*.

Watkin, Watking, Watkins, Watkeys, Watkis, Watkiss, Watcyns, Whatkins: Adam *filius Walterkini* 1200 Oseney (O); *Watkin* 1252 Bardsley; *Watkynge* Llooyde 1623 ib. (Gl); John *Watkyns* 1327 SRSf; John *Wattkyn* 1552 ShefA; Thomas *Watkys* 1662 PrGR. *Wat-kin*, a diminutive of *Walter*.

Watkinson: John *Watkynson* 1485 GildY. 'Son of *Watkin*.'

Watler, Whattler: Thomas *Watelere* 1377 AssEss. 'Wattler.' *v.* DAUBER.

Watley: *v.* WHATELEY

Watling: *v.* WHATLIN

Watman: *v.* WHATMAN

Watmough, Watmore, Watmuff, Whatmaugh, Whatmough, Whatmoor, Whatmore, Whatmuff: Robert *Waltersmaghe* 1305 Black; Robert *Watmaghe* 1379 PTY; Hugh *Watmoughe* 1581 Oxon (Y); Hugo *Watmouth* 1599 Bardsley (Y): William *Watmer* 1718 DKR 41 (Wo). The first element is

Wat, a pet form of *Walter*; the second is ME *maugh*, *mough* which may be from ON *mágr* 'brother-, father- or son-in-law', OE *māga* 'relative, son', OE *māge* 'female relative', or OE *magu* 'child, son, servant'. The usual explanation of the compound is 'Wat's brother-in-law', but there seems no special reason for selecting this particular relative, except that *maugh* or *mauf* has this meaning in dialect. The variation between *Mago Healfdenes* and *sunu Healfdenes* (BT) suggests that the meaning may well be 'Wat's son', but this is unsuitable for William *Barnmaw* 1273 RH (Y) where the reference must be to some other relative of the child. This type of name was not uncommon in Yorkshire and Lancashire and survives also in HICKMOTT, HITCHMOUGH and HUDSMITH. cf. Geoffrey *Cokesmahc* 1183 Boldon; Henry *Ravesmaughe* 1296 CalSc; William *Matheumogh* 1327 SRDb; Adam *Duncanmaugh*, Thomas *Nicholmagh*, William *Raynaldmagh* 1332 SRCu; Adam *Dyemogh*, William *Robertmogh*, John *Wilkemogh* 1332 SRLa; John *Godesmagh* 1351 FrY; John *Elysmagh*, Richard *Gepmouth*, John *Tailliourmoghe* 1379 PTY. -*moor*, -*more* are more or less phonetic spellings of -*maw*.

Watrer: *v.* WATERER

Watsham: Osbert *de Wachesham* c1190 BuryS (Sf). From Wattisham (Suffolk).

Watson: Richard *Watson* 1324 Wak (Y); Thomas *Watteson* 1327 SRWo; William *Wattesson*, *Wattysson* 1409, 1430 Crowland (C). 'Son of *Wat*.'

Watt, Wattis, Watts: *Watte* 1292 AssCh, 1306 Wak (Y); *Wat* of Carnegy 1446 Black; Paganus *Wat* 1176 P (D); William *Watte* 1317 AssK; William *Wattes* 1279 RH (O); Roger *Wattys* 1381 SRSf. A pet-form of *Walter* or *Water*. cf. Matilda *Walte* 1278 Oseney (O).

Watters: *v.* WATER

Watterson: *v.* WATERSON

Watthews, Watthey: *v.* WALTHEW

Waud: *v.* WALD

Waudby: *v.* WALBY

Waugh: Robert, Thomas *Walgh(e)* 1296 Black (Roxburgh, Peebles); William *Wahh* 1379 PTY; William *Waugh* 1436 Black; Edward *Wauch* 1526 ib. Neither Black's derivation from *Wauchope* nor Harrison's from *waugh* 'wall' can be accepted. The only evidence for a place-name is David *de Waughe* 1296 Black (Lanarks) and this may be an error for *le Waughe*. The places along the Roman Wall are from OE *weall*, not from *wāg*: Walby, Walton, Wallhead, Wallsend. The surname is common on both sides of the Scottish border and is probably OE (Anglian) *walh* 'foreigner', a name given by the Anglians to Strathclyde Celts, parallel to *Gall* given by Highlanders to Lowlanders.

Wauldby: *v.* WALBY

Waule: May be for WALL or WALD.

Waumsley: *v.* WALMESLEY

Wauton: *v.* WALTON

Wavell, Weavill, Wevell, Wevill: William *de*

Waluile 1086 DB (D); Robert *de Wavill'* 1220 Cur (L); Henry *de Wayvill, de Wavill* 1268 AssSo; Richard *de Weavile*, Henry *de Wevile* 1276 RH (Beds); Jannes *de Weuyle* 1296 SRSx; Thomas *de Weyuile* 1327 ib.; John *Wauel* 1376 ColchCt. From Vauville (La Manche).

Wax: Ralph *Wax* 1279 RH (O). Metonymic for *Waxman.*

Waxman: Adam *Wexman* 1185 P (Wo), OE *weax* 'wax' and *mann.* 'Seller of wax.' cf. Robert *le Waxmongere* 1310 MESO (Nf).

Way, Waye, Waigh, Weigh, Wey, Whay: Roger *de Waie* 1194 P (Do); William *Waye* 1236 Fees (Do); Richard *de la Weye* 1249 Fees (D); John *ate Wey* 1279 RH (C). From Waye (Devon, Dorset) or from residence near a road or path (OE *weg*).

Waybrow: *v.* WYBER

Waylatt, Waylett: Peter *Atteweilete* 1275 RH (Sf); Gundreda *atte Weylete* 1280 Bart (Ess); Robert *Weylate* 1327 *SR* (Ess). 'Dweller by the cross-roads' (OE *weg-gelǣte*).

Wayler: *v.* WHEELER

Wayman: *v.* WAITHMAN, WYMAN

Waymark: *v.* WYMARK

Waymont: *v.* WYMAN

Wayne: *v.* WAIN

Wayre, Weyer: Henry *ate Wayhore* 1296 SRSx. 'Dweller by the bathing-pond or stream', ME *weyour*, AFr *wayour*, OFr *gayoir.*

Wayson: *v.* WACE

Wayt(e), Waytes: *v.* WAIT

Waythe: *v.* WATH

Weald: *v.* WALD

Wealthy: *v.* WALTHEW

Wear, Weare, Wears, Weir, Were, Where: Peter *de la Were* 1242 Fees (He); John *atte Wer* 1332 SRSx. OE *wer* 'weir, dam, fish-trap'. 'Dweller by a dam' or 'keeper of the fishing-weir', fisherman.

Wearing: *v.* WAREING

Wearn(e): *v.* WARNE

Weate: *v.* WHEAT

Weather, Weathers: Almer *Wether, Weder* 1180–2 P (K); William, John *le Wether* 1327 *SR* (Ess), 1332 SRSx. OE *weðer* 'wether, sheep'.

Weatherall, Weatherell, Weatherhill, Weatherill, Weatherilt, Weatheritt: *v.* WETHERALD

Weatherby: *v.* WETHERBEE

Weatherhead: *v.* WETHERHEAD

Weathrall: *v.* WETHERALD

Weaver, Weavers, Weafer, Wheaver: (i) John *le Weuere*, William *Weuere* 1296 SRSx. A derivative of OE *wefan* 'to weave', 'a weaver'. (ii) Simon *de Wevere* 1259 AssCh. From Weaver Hall (Ches).

Weavill: *v.* WAVELL

Webb, Webbe: Alger *se Webba* c1100–30 OEByn (D); Jernagan, Osbert, Wigor *Webbe* 1221 *ElyA* (Sf); Elyas *le Webbe* 1255 Oseney (O); Alice *la Webbe*, *Webbes* 1337 ColchCt. OE *webba* (m) or *webbe* (f), 'weaver'.

Webber: John *le Webber* 1255 FFEss; Hugo *le Webbere* 1327 SRSf. A derivative of OE *web* 'web', 'weaver' (c1440 NED).

Webster: John *le Webestere* 1275 RH (Nf);

William *le Webbester* 1284 AssLa. OE *webbestre* 'female weaver', though usually used of men. *v.* WEBB.

Wederell: *v.* WETHERALD

Weech, Week(e)s: *v.* WICH

Weems: *v.* WEMYSS

Weet: *v.* WHEAT

Weetch: *v.* WICH

Weetman: *v.* WHATMAN

Weigall, Weighell, Weighill, Wiggall: Katerina *de Wyghehale* 1379 PTY. From Wighill (WRYorks).

Weigh: *v.* WAY

Weight: *v.* WIGHT

Weightman: *v.* WIGHTMAN

Weild: *v.* WALD

Weir: *v.* WEAR

Welbelove, Wellbeloved: *v.* WELLBELOVE

Welbourn, Welbourne, Welbon, Welburn, Wellborne, Wellburn: Ailmer *de Welleburnia* 1185 Templars (L). From Welborne (Norfolk), Welbourn (Lincs) or Welburn (NRYorks).

Welby, Wellby: Thomas *de Wellebi* 1202 P (L); Henry *de Welleby* 1332 SRWa; Geoffrey *Welby* 1395 AssL. From Welby (Leics, Lincs).

Welch: *v.* WELSH

Welchman: *v.* WELSHMAN

Welcome, Welcomme, Wellcome, Wellicome, Willicombe: (i) Hynulfus *de Welecumb'* 1221 AssWa; William *de Wellecumb'* 1275 AssSo. From Welcombe (Devon) or Welcombe in Stratford (Warwicks). (ii) Picotus *Wilicom* 1279 RH (C); Roger *Welcum* Ed 3 Rydware (St). OE *wilcume* 'welcome'. (iii) Ralph *Welikempt* 1275 SRWo; Lovekyn *Welikembd* 1285 *Ass* (Ess); Edmund *Welkemt* 1332 SRWa. 'Well-kempt, well-combed', past part. of OE *cemban* 'to comb'. The original reference would be to well-kept hair or a well-trimmed beard, later to one of elegant appearance. The nickname was not uncommon and *Welkemt* would easily become *Welcome.*

Weld: *v.* WALD

Welding: *v.* WALDING

Weldon, Welden, Wellden, Welldon: William *de Welledon'* 1197 P (Nth); Henry *de Weldon* 1327 SRWo; William *Weldon* 1468 IpmNt. From Weldon (Northants), or 'dweller by a hill near a stream'.

Weldrick, Wildrake: Adam *de Queldrik* 1272 FrY. From Wheldrake (ERYorks).

Weldsmith: *v.* WILDSMITH

Welfare, Welfear: Simon *Welfare* 1275 RH (Nf). OE **wel-faru* 'well faring'. cf. FAREWELL.

Welfitt: William *Welifed* 1195 P (D); John *le Welyfed* 14th AD iii (Sx); William *Wellefed* 1379 PTY; William *Welfed* 1411 Finchale; Jeremiah *Welfitt* 1664 FrY. 'The well-fed', a nickname not uncommon and widely distributed. *Welfitt* might also be for WELFORD.

Welford: Ralph *de Welleford'* 1190 P (Gl); Geoffrey *de Welleforde* 1313 Balliol (O). From Welford (Berks, Glos, Northants).

Welham, Wellam, Wellum: John *de Weleham*

1276 RH (Lei); Adam *de Wellome* 1363 FrY; Peter *Wellam* 1483 FrY. From Welham (Leics, Notts, ERYorks). *Welham*, *Wellam* and *Wellom* are common variants (1560–1617) in the Horringer Parish Register (Suffolk).

Wellbelove, Wellbeloved, Wellbelow, Wellbeluff, Welbelove, Welbeloved: Richard *Wellbyloved* 1327 SRWo. Self-explanatory.

Wellborne, Wellbourn: *v.* WELBOURN

Wellby: *v.* WELBY

Wellcome: *v.* WELCOME

Wellden, Welldon: *v.* WELDON

Wellemin: *v.* GILLMAN

Weller, Wheller: Richard *le Weller* 1272 FFSx, Gregory *Wellor* 1332 SRCu. A derivative of OE *wiellan*, *wellan* 'to boil', a salt-boiler. May also mean 'dweller by the spring or stream'. *v.* WELLS.

Wellerman: *v.* GILLMAN

Wellesley, Wellersley, Wellsley: Christiana *de Welleslegh'* 1220 Cur (So); William *de Wellesleye* 1252 IpmSo; Robert *Wellesleghe* 1327 SRSo. From Wellesley in Wells (So).

Welliam: *v.* WILLIAMS

Wellicome: *v.* WELCOME

Wellisch, Wellish: *v.* WELSH

Wellman, Welman: Simon *le Welleman* 1308 MESO (Nf); John *Welman* 1327 *SR* (Ess). 'Dweller by a well or stream' (OE *wella*). *v.* also GILLMAN.

Wells, Wels: Toke *de Welles* 1177 P (Nf); Roger *Attewell'* 1200 Cur (Sx); Isabella *Welles* 1312 ColchCt. From Wells next the Sea (Norfolk) or Wells (Som), or from residence near a group of springs (OE *wella*). The singular *atte*, *del*, *de la Welle* is very common in medieval sources and survives in ATTWELL 'dweller by a spring or stream' but the modern *Well* seems to have been completely absorbed by *Wells*.

Wellsley: *v.* WELLESLEY

Wellsman: *v* WELSHMAN

Wellstead, Wellsteed, Welsted, Wellstood, Welstead, Welsted, Willstead, Willsteed: (i) Robert *de Wellested* 1305 LLB C. If the form is correct, this is 'dweller by the site of the well' and is unidentified. (ii) Walter *atte Wellesheuede*, *atte Willeshefde* 1327, 1333 MELS (So). From Wellshead near Exford (Som). The variety of modern forms suggests that the name was not uncommon, 'dweller at the upper end of the stream', from OE *hēafod* 'head' and *wella*, preserving also the Somerset dialect *will* 'well'.

Wellum: *v.* WELHAM

Welman: *v.* WELLMAN

Welsh, Welch, Wellisch, Wellish: Simon *Welsche* 1279 RH (Beds); Margery *Wellis* 1327 SR (Ess); Roger *Welch* 1334 ColchCt. ME *welshe*, OE *wēalisc*, *wēlisc*, 'foreign, Welsh', cf. WALSH.

Welshman, Welchman, Wellsman, Welsman: Davye *Welchman* 1544 Bardsley; John *Welsheman* 1564 ib. 'Welshman'. cf. WALSHMAN.

Welstead, Welsted: *v.* WELLSTEAD

Welton: William *de Welletun* c1155 Gilb; Isabella *de Welton* 1296 SRSx; Thomas *Welton*

1411–12 FFSr. From Welton (Cumb, Lincs, Northants, Northumb, Som, ERYorks).

Wemyss, Weems, Wemes: Michael *de Wemys* 1261 Black; David *Wemyss* 1286 ib.; David *de Wemes* 1314 ib. From the lands of Wemyss (Fife).

Wenborn, Wenbourne, Wenban, Wenbon: Gilbert *de Waneburne* 1296 SRSx; John *Wenbourne* 1410 CtH; Katherine *Wenborn* 1510 *Ct*. Thomas *Wenborne* 1772 SalehurstPR (Sx) signed the marriage register as *Wenban*. From Wenbon's Farm in Wadhurst (Sussex).

Wende: William *Wende* 1275 RH (Nf); Roger *atte Wend* 1297 SRY. 'Dweller by the bend', OE *wende*.

Wender: Robert *Wender* 1332 SRCu. 'Dweller by a bend.' *v.* WENDE.

Wendover: Richard *de Wendovr'* 1214 Cur (Bk); John *de Wendovre* 1341 FFEss; Nicholas *Wendover* 1470 FFEss. From Wendover (Bucks).

Wenham: William, Hawise *de Wenham* 1194 P (Sr), 1327 SRSo; Robert *Wenam* 1525 SRSx. From Wenham (Suffolk, Sussex).

Wenlock: William *de Wenlac* 1203 Pl (Sa); John *de Wenlak* 1323 IpmGl; William *Wenlocke* 1421 IpmNt. From Wenlock (Salop).

Wenman: *v.* WAINMAN

Wenn: John *atte Wenne* 1316 SRSo; Walter *atte Wen* 1327 SRSf. OE *wenn* 'wen, wart', used topographically of a hill or barrow and, as a surname, of a dweller by such.

Wennell, Whennell: Gilbert *Weynild* 1327 SRSf. OE **Wynhild* (f) 'joy-war'.

Wensley, Wensly: Jordan *de Wandesleye* 1204 AssY; Walter *de Wendeslay* 1339 FFY; John *Wensley* or *Wenslowe* 1509 LP (Y). From Wensley (Derby, NRYorks).

Went, Whent: Henry *de la, ate Wente* 1275 RH (Sf); Stephen *ad le Wente* 1279 RH (C); John *Wente* 1327 SRC. 'Dweller by the cross-road', ME *went(e)*.

Wentworth: Robert *de Wintewrth'* 1219 AssY; William *de Wynteworth* 1303 IpmY; Richard *Wenteworth* 1422 IpmNt. From Wentworth (Cambs, WRYorks), both *Winteworde* DB.

Were: *v.* WEAR

Werlock: *v.* WARLOCK

Werman: For WARMAN or, possibly, WORKMAN.

Werren, Werring: Richard *Weryn* 1332 SRSx. OG *Werin*, *Guerin*, more commonly found as *Warin*. *v.* WAREING. cf. *Warinus*, *Werinus* (identical) LVD.

Werry, Warry, Warriss: *Guericus*, *Gueri* 1086 DB (Nf, Lo); *Werri* de Marinis 1166 RBE (Y); *Werreis* de Pilledona 1179 P (Do); *Werricus*, *Warricus*, *Werrei*, *Werreys* de Cadamo 1219–20 Cur (Sf); Nicholas, Geppe *Werri* 1206 P (C), 1228 FeuDu; John *Warry* 1260 AssC. OG **Werric*, OFr *Guerri*.

Werth: *v.* WORTH

Wesbroom: *v.* WESTBROOM

Wesby: *v.* WESTBY

Wescomb(e): *v.* WESTCOMBE

Wescot(t): *v.* WESTCOTT

Weske: v. VECK

Wesker: Robert *Westker* 1275 RH (Nf). 'Dweller by the west fen', from ME *kerr* 'bog, fen', ON *kjarr* 'brushwood'. v. also WISHART.

Weskett: v. WESTCOTT

Wesley, Westley, Westly: Wlmar *de Westle* c1095 Bury; Adam *de Westeleg'* 1242 Fees (La); Richard *de Westleye* 1332 SRWa; William *Westly*, Robert *Wesly* 1674 HTSf. From Westleigh (Devon, Lancs), Westley Waterless (Cambs), or Westley (Suffolk).

Wesson: v. WESTON

West: Maurice *de West* 1152–70 Colch (Ess); Goche *West* 1197 P (Nf); William *del West* 1262 For (Ess); Robert *bi Westen* de Copford 13th Colch (Ess); John *Bywest* de Welde LLB D; John *in le West* 1379 PTY. 'Man from the west' or 'dweller to the west' of a certain place.

Westaby: v. WESTOBY

Westacott: v. WESTCOTT

Westbrook, Westbrooke, Westbrock: Reginald *de Westbroc* 1255 FFK; John *de Westbroke* 1327 SRC; Edmund *Westbrook* 1440 FFEss. From Westbrook (Berks, Devon, Kent, Wight).

Westbroom, Wesbroom: Æilmer *de Westbrom* c1095 Bury (Sf). From a lost place in Woolpit (Sf).

Westby, Westbey, Wesby: William *de Westebi* 1219 AssL. From Westby (Lancs, Lincs, WRYorks). v. also WESTOBY.

Westcoate: v. WESTCOTT

Westcombe, Wescomb, Wescombe: (i) Henry *de Westecomb* 1333 PN D 436. From one of the three Westcombes in Devon. (ii) Thomas *atte Westcompe* 1327 SRSx. 'Dweller by the west field', OE *camp*.

Westcott, Westcoate, Westacott, Westicott, Waistcoat, Wescot, Wescott, Weskett: Turbertus *de Westcota* 1170 P (Berks); Robert *de Westecote* 1221 AssSt; Robert *atte Westcote* 1327 SRSx. From Westcot (Berks), Westcote (Glos, Hants, Warwicks), Westcott (Bucks, Surrey, Devon), Westacott (Devon), or from residence at the west cottage.

Wester: Laurence *le Westre* 1327 SRSx. 'The westerner.' OE **wester*.

Westerby: From Westerby (Leics) or for WESTOBY.

Western, Westren, Westron: Geoffrey *le Westerne* c1172–80 DC (L); Richard *le Westerne*, *le Westerneys* 1286 ForSt; Adam, Richard *le Westren* 1296, 1307 Wak (Y); Alan *Westerne* 1327 SRSf. OE *westerne* 'western', the man from the west.

Westgate: William *de Westgat'* 1199 Cur (Sr). From Westgate (Durham, Kent, Northumb, Wilts). Peter *de Westgate* of Canterbury (1198 P) no doubt lived near the west gate of the city.

Westhead: Robert *del Westheved* 1313 FFLa. From Westhead (Lancs) or one who lived near the west headland (OE *hēafod*).

Westhorp, Westhorpe: Hugh *de Westorp* 1194 P (Db). From Westhorpe (Suffolk). cf. WESTROP.

Westicott: v. WESTCOTT

Westie: Andrew *de Westheie* 1185 Templars (Ess); Coleman *de Westhaie* c1188 BuryS (Sf);

Peter *de Weysthagh* 1296 SRSx. From Westhay (Northants) or from residence near some western enclosure (OE *(ge)hæg*).

Westington: William *a Westethun, de Westetoune* 1296, 1332 SRSx; Ralph *Biwestetoun* 1327 SRSx; William *Westetoun* 1332 SRSx. This was a common type of surname in Sussex, found in some 22 parishes between 1296 and 1332. Occasionally *west in tūne*, the man who lived 'west in the *tūn*', but usually from residence at a place so called, *Westi(n)ton, Westeton*, which occasionally became *Weston*. v. SINTON.

Westlake, Weslake: Martin *de Westlak'* 1211 Cur (St). From residence 'west of the streamlet'. Richard *Bywestelake* lived at Westlake (Devon) in 1333 (PN D 274).

Westley, Westly: v. WESLEY

Westmacott, Westmancoat: Elena *de Westmecote* 1327 SRWo. From Westmancote (Worcs).

Westman: Herebertus *filius Westman*, Herebert *Westman* 1148 Winton (Ha); Elyas *Westman* 1200 P (Ha). ON *Vestmaðr* 'man from the west', especially from Ireland, as a personal name.

Westmore: Isabell' *de Westemere* 1332 SRSx. 'Dweller by the west mere.'

Westmoreland, Westmorland, Westmarland: Richard *de Westmerland* 1242 AssDu; William *de Westmarlonde* 1375 SRWo; John *Westmerland'* 1379 PTY. 'The man from Westmorland.'

Westnage, Westnedge, Westnidge, Westney: v. WASTNAGE

Westoby, Westaby: Tomas *Westibi* 1203 P (Y); Ernebertus *Westiby* 1208 FFL; Peter *Westinby* 1297 SRY; John *Westerbe* 1500 GildY; John *Westobie* 1607 FrY; William *Westaby* 1630 YWills. Scand *vestr í bý* (the man who lived) 'west in the village'. *Westinby* is partly anglicized. v. also SOTHEBY, EASTERBY, DUNNABY, and NORDABY. *Northinby* 1297 SRY, Robert *Northibi* 1301 SRY, John *Northobe* 1535 GildY, Nicholas *Northaby* 1617 FrY, which does not seem to have survived. For a similar English formation, v. SINTON.

Weston: (i) Godwinus *de Westuna* 1086 DB (Hu); Adestan *de Westuna* 1086 InqEl (C). From one of the numerous Westons. (ii) Adam *de la Weston* 1275 SRWo; William *Weston* 1296 SRSx; Alan *ate Weston* 1327 SRSx. 'Dweller at the west farm.' (iii) Robert *Biweston* 1200 P (Ess). OE *(be) westan tūne* (one who lived) 'to the west of the village'. v. WESTINGTON.

Westover: John *de Westouer* 1296 SRSx; John *Westhouer*, Richard *Westouer* 1327, 1332 ib. From Westover (Som, Wight), Westovers in Twineham (Sussex).

Westrap: v. WESTROP

Westray: v. WESTRICH. Also from Westray (Cumb): Roger *de Westwra* 1292 PN Cu 384.

Westren: v. WESTERN

Westrich, Westray: Richard *le Westrais* 1206 AssL; William *le Westreys* 1219 Cur (Nth); Philip *Westrays (le Westreis)* 1230 P (Wa); John *Westrey* 1372 ColchCt. OFr *westreis* 'the westerner'.

Westron: v. WESTERN

Westrop, Westrope, Westropp, Westrap, Westrup: Gilbert *de Westrop* 1297 MinAcctCo (W); Martha *Westhrope* 1599 SfPR; Frances *Westroppe* 1624 ib. A metathesized form of WESTHORP, surviving in Westrop (Wilts).

Westward: Robert *a Westeward* 1279 RH (O). Dweller 'to the westward'.

Westwood: Robert *de Westwod*' 1207 Pl (K); Alan *de Westwude* 1221 AssGl; John *Westwod*' 1371 CorEss. From Westwood (Kent, Wilts, Warwicks, Worcs), or 'dweller by the west wood'.

Wetherald, Wetherall, Wetherell, Wetheril, Wetherill, Wetherilt, Weatherall, Weatherell, Weatherill, Weatherilt, Weatheritt, Weatherhill, Weathrall, Wederell: Richard *de Wederhal* 1332 SRCu; William *Wethereld, Wetherald, Wetherold* 1429–33 Bacon (Sf); Elizabeth *Wetherill* 1648 Bardsley. From Wetheral (Cumb).

Wetherbee, Wetherby, Weatherby, Witherby: Ivo *de Werreby* 1219 AssY; Richard de *Wetherby* 1302 LLB B. From Wetherby (WRYorks).

Wetherhead, Wethered, Weatherhead: Thomas dictus *Wethyrhyrde* c1200 Black; Augustin *Wetherherde* 1214 FFK; John *le Wetherhirde* 1297 SRY; Henry *Weydurherd, Wedirhed* 1476 DbCh; George *Weddirheid* 1532 Black; Thomas *Weatherheade* 1634 LaWills. OE *weðer* 'wether, sheep, ram' and *hierde* 'shepherd'.

Wetheril(l), Wetherilt: *v.* WETHERALD

Wetter, Wetters: John *atte Wetere, Atwater* 1328 ArchC 33; Thomas *Wettas* 1524 SRSf. 'Dweller by the water.'

Wetwan: Richard *de Wetewang*' 1219 AssY. From Wetwang (ERYorks).

Wevell, Wevill: *v.* WAVELL

Wey: *v.* WAY

Weyer: *v.* WAYRE

Weyman, Weymont: *v.* WYMAN

Whackum: *v.* WAKEHAM

Whaite(s): *v.* WAIT

Whale, Whales, Whall: Hugh *le Whal*' 1249 FFEss; John *Whale* 1568 SRSf. OE *hwæl*, ME *whal* 'whale', used of any large fish including the walrus, grampus and the porpoise. The original sense was 'roller' and the name may refer to gait or to size and weight.

Whaler: *v.* WHEELER

Whaley: *v.* WHALLEY

Whalley, de Whalley, Whaley, Walley: Adam *de Walleg*' 1185 P (La); Robert *de Walley* 1230 P (Nt). From Whalley (Lancs) or Whaley (Derby).

Wham: Nicol *atte Wamme* 1296 SRSx; John *atte Whamme* 1327 ib. 'Dweller in the corner, angle or small valley' (OE *hwamm*).

Whamond: *v.* WYMAN

Whant: *v.* WANT

Wharf, Wharfe: Alan *ate Warf* 1320 LLB E. 'Worker at a wharf' (OE *hwerf*). cf. John *le Wharfager* 1322 LLB E.

Wharin: *v.* WAREING

Wharrick: *v.* WARWICK

Wharrier: *v.* WARRIOR

Wharton: Richard *de Wharton* 1324 IpmNt; Alexander, Thomas *Wharton* 1481 Past, 1672 HTY. From Wharton (Ches, Lincs, Westmorland). *v.* also WARTON.

Whate: *v.* WAIT, WHEAT

Whateley, Whately, Whatley, Wheatleigh, Wheatley, Wheatly, Watley: Lambert *de Watileia* 1084 GeldR (So); Martin *de Watelega* 1130 P (Nt); Roger *de Wetelea* 1182 P (St); Peter *de Watteleg*' 1196 P (Y); Elyas *de Hwatele* 1219 AssY; Peter *de Watteleg*' 1221 AssWa; Henry *de Whateleia* Hy 3 Colch (Ess); Walter *de Whetele* 1273 RH (Nt); Reginald *de Watele*, Robert *Watteleghe* 1296 SRSx. From Whateley (Warwicks), Whatley (Som), Wheatley (Essex, Lancs, Notts, Oxon, WRYorks), or Wattlehill Fm in Ewhurst (Sussex), all 'wheat-lea'. cf. WHITELEY.

Whatham: *v.* WALTHAM

Whatkins: *v.* WATKIN

Whatlin, Whatling, Watling: *Whatlingus, Watlin*' portarius, *Wathling* janitor 12th FeuDu; Edmund *Watlyng* 1524 SRSf. OE **Hwætling* 'son of Hwætel', a diminutive of names in *Hwæt-* or a derivative of OE *hwæt* 'active, bold, brave'. The unrecorded **Hwætel* is the first element of Whatlington (Sussex).

Whatman, Wheatman, Watman: *Wateman, Wetman* 1066 DB (Do, He); Algar *filius Watman* 1168 P (D); *Wheteman* atte Brok 1359 LLB G; John *Watemon* 1264 Eynsham (O); Hugo *Weteman* 1279 RH (O); Richard *Whateman* (*Wateman*) 1327 SR (Ess); OE *Hwætmann* 'bold, brave man'. cf. WHATLIN.

Whatmaugh, Whatmough, Whatmuff: *v.* WATMOUGH

Whatmoor, Whatmore, Watmore: William *de Wetemor*' 1274 RH (Sa). From Whatmoor (Salop). Or for WATMOUGH.

Whatrup: *v.* WARDROBE

Whattler: *v.* WATLER

Whay: *v.* WAY

Whayman, Whaymand, Whaymond: *v.* WYMAN

Whealler: *v.* WHEELER

Wheal(s): *v.* WHEEL

Wheat, Wheate, Whate, Weate, Weet: Bernard *Hwette, Wete* c1157, 1180 Holme (Nf); Hugh, John *le Wete* 1249, 1327 PN Ess 483; Henry *Whete* 1440 ShefA; William *Whett, Wheate* 1484, 1563 ib. OE *hwæt* 'active, bold, brave'.

Wheatcroft, Whitcroft: Adam *de Wetecroft* 1191 P (Y); Richard *de Whatecrofth* 1327 SRSf; Thomas *de Whatecroft* son of Adam *Whetecroft* 1339 AssSt. 'Dweller by a croft where wheat was grown.' cf. Wheatcroft Fm in Cullompton (Devon), *Whitecroft* 1809 PN D 562.

Wheater: *v.* WHITER

Wheatfill: Ailmer *de Hwatefelde* 1121–38 Bury (Sf). From Whatfield (Suffolk), 'wheat-field'. Possibly also from Wheatfield (Oxon), 'white field'.

Wheatland: Richard *Whetlond* 1327 SRSx. 'Dweller by the wheat-land.' In Devon, Wheatland is from a family (*atte*) *Whytelond* 1281, 1333 PN D 375, 331, 'white land'.

Wheatleigh, Wheatley, Wheatly: v. WHATELEY

Wheatman: v. WHATMAN

Wheaver: v. WEAVER

Wheeker: v. WICKER

Wheel, Wheele, Wheels, Wheal, Wheale, Wheals: Isabella del Wele 1297 MinAcctCo (Y); Hugh atte Wheole 1327 SRSo. One who lived near or was in charge of a water-wheel (OE hwēol 'wheel'). cf. WHEELHOUSE.

Wheeldon, Wheelden, Wheildon, Whieldon, Wheldon, Wildon: Hugo de Hweldon' 1279 RH (O); Peter de Whilden 1281 Pat (Bk). From Whielden Lane in Amersham (Bucks) 'curving valley' (PN Bk 212). Or from Wheeldon in North Huish (Devon), Whyledon 1520, Wheldon 1614 (PN D 304).

Wheeler, Wheeller, Wheler, Whealler, Wailer, Wayler, Whaler: Roger le Weweler 1249 MESO (Sx); John le Whelare 1275 SRWo; Hugh le Welere 1279 RH (C); Thomas le Wegheler 1284 FFSx; Stephen le Whelere 1317 FFEss; John le Wheghler 1327 SRSx; Gilbert le Whygler 1351 AD i (Sr). A derivative of OE hweogol, hweowol, hwēol 'wheel', 'wheel-maker, wheelwright' (1497 NED). Wailer, Wayler, both rare, are from Wegheler; Whaler, also rare, is from Wheghler, with spelling assimilated to that of the more common word.

Wheelhouse: William de Whelehous 1379 PTY; Martin Whelas 1617 FrY; Joseph Wheelhouse 1702 FrY. From residence near or employment at a wheelhouse, often, no doubt, near a dammed-up stream where the cutler ground his knives on a wheel driven by water. The name is especially a West Riding one. Sometimes equated with Wheeler: James Wheelar, inholder, son of John Wheelas alias Wheelar, flax-dresser 1740 FrY.

Wheelwright: Brihtric Hueluurihte c1095 Bury (Sf); Hugo le Wellewriche 1256 AssNb; Walter Welwryhte 1274 RH (Ess); Henry le welwrite 1297 MinAcctCo; Richard Whelwright 1305 MESO (Y); Robert le Whilwright 1349 DbCh. OE hwēol 'wheel' and wyrhta 'wright', maker of wheels and wheeled vehicles (1281 NED).

Wheildon, Wheldon: v. WHEELDON

Wheler: v. WHEELER

Wheller: v. WELLER

Whenman: v. WAINMAN

Whennell: v. WENNELL

Whent: v. WENT

Where: v. WEAR

Whesker: For Wesker or Whisker. v. WISHART.

Whetman: v. WHATMAN

Whetter: Richard le Wetthere 1332 SRSr. A derivative of OE hwettan 'to whet, sharpen', a sharpener of tools.

Wheybrew: v. WYBER

Whicher: v. WHITCHER

Whick: v. WICH

Whicker: v. WICKER

Whickman: v. WICKMAN

Whieldon: v. WHEELDON

Whight: v. WIGHT

Whild(e): v. WILD

Whilesmith: v. WILDSMITH

Whillis: v. WILLIS

Whinnerah, Whineray, Whinrae, Whinray, Winnery, Winrow: Elizabeth Whinnery 1568 SRSf; John Whinray 1584 Bardsley (La); Hugo Whynrowe 1622 PrGR; John Whinerall 1682 ib. Probably from Whinneray in Gosforth (Cumb).

Whinney: John de Whinhow 1332 SRCu. 'Dweller on the whin-covered hill', perhaps Winnow in Thursby (Cumb), Whinney, Whynna 1589, or from Whinnah in Lamplugh or a Cumberland place named Whinny.

Whinyates: v. WINGATE

Whiscard, Whisker: v. WISHART

Whissell: (i) William Wystle 1247 AssBeds; Richard Whistel 1297 MinAcctCo (Y). OE hwistle 'pipe, flute', metonymic for WHISTLER. (ii) Simon Whytsall 1275 RH (Sx); John, William, Nicholas Whitsaul(e) 1279 RH (C). OE hwīt 'white' and sāwol 'soul'. The reason for the nickname is not clear. cf. GODSAL.

Whisson, Wisson: Gilbert de Wiscand, de Wissand, de Witsand 1086 DB (Sf); William de Wisant c1180 Bury (Sf); William de Whitsand 1197 P (Y); William Whitsond 1242 Fees (W); William de Wytsonde 1296 SRSx. From Wissant (Pas-de-Calais). Some of the forms may have a different origin. cf. Thomas de la Witesand 1236 MELS (Sr). 'Dweller by the white sand.'

Whistance, Wistance: Cissota de Wistones 1309 Wak (Y). 'Dweller by the white stones.' From Whitestones (NRYorks).

Whistlecraft, Whistlecroft: Thomas Wyslylcroft (sic) 1524 SRSf. Probably 'dweller at the croft in the river-fork' (OE twisla), ME at twiselcroft becoming at wiselcroft.

Whistler, Wissler: Osbert le Wistler 1243 AssSo; John Whiseller, Nat. Whisler 1674 HTSf. OE hwistlere 'piper, fluter'. In 1279 AssSo the scribe has altered William le Wyzelere to le Vylur 'fiddler'. v. VIELER.

Whistondale: Wytstayndale occurs in 1290 (PN NRY 204) for Whitestones in Hawnby (NRYorks). cf. WHISTANCE.

Whitaker, Whiteaker, Whittaker, Whitticase, Widdaker: (i) Richard de Wetacra 1177 P (Nf); Furmentinus de Whetacre 1254 ArchC xii; Walter Weat Aker 1296 SRSx; John de Wheteacre 1327 SRSf. From Wheatacre (Norfolk) or Whiteacre in Waltham (Kent), both 'wheat-field'. (ii) Simon de Wit Acra 1180 P (Wa); Robert de Witacra 1189 P (Nth); Richard de Whitacre 1336 WhC (La); Henry Wyteacre 1379 PTY. From Whitacre (Warwicks) or High Whitaker (Lancs), 'white field'.

Whitamore: v. WHITEMORE

Whitbourn, Whitbourne, Whiteborn: (i) Thomas de Wytebourne 1327 SRSo. From Whitbourne (Hereford). (ii) Robert Wytebarne 1301 SRY; William Whitbarn 1438 LLB K. OE hwīt and bearn 'fair child'. cf. Richard Whiteboye 1277 AssSo, Roger Wyitfelawe 1264 AD iii (Beds).

Whitbread, Whitebread: (i) Roger *Wythbred* 1254–67 Rams (Hu), father of Richard *Witbred* 1267–85 ib.; William *Wytbred* 1275 SRWo; Robert *Witbred* 1279 RH (O); Robert *Whytbred* 1327 SRSf; Robert *Whytebrede* 1436 FFHu. OE *hwīt* and *brēad* 'white bread', used of a seller of white, i.e. the best bread, made of wheat. (ii) William *Watebred* 1221 ElyA (Ess); John *Wetebred* 1239 FrLeic; Robert *Whetbred* 1327 SRSx; John *Whatebred* 1327 SR (Ess). OE *hwǣte* and *brēad* 'wheat-bread'. For the development to *Whitbread*, cf. WHITAKER. (iii) William *Witberd* 1221 ElyA (Sf); Walter *Wyteberd* 1297 MinAcctCo; Adam *Whitberd* 1327 SRSx; John *Whiteberd* 1503 RochW. OE *hwīt* and *beard* 'white beard'.

Whitcher, Whicher, Witcher: William, Richard *Wicher* 1176 P (Bk), 1279 RH (Beds); Robert *le Wiccher* 1288 MESO (Sx); Richard *Whychere* 1327 SRSx; Robert *le Whicchere* 1333 MESO (Ha). A derivative of OE *hwicce* 'chest', a maker of chests. The early loss of the *h* is proved by the synonymous William *le Wyccewrichte* (1256 FFSo) who, no doubt, followed the same occupation as Richard *Le Wycher* 1305 MESO (So). As OE *wīc* became both *wike*, and *wiche* in ME, the surname may also mean 'dweller at a place called *Wich* (or *Wick*)' or 'dairy-farmer', as is proved by Peter *le Wycher* and John *Wych* (1327 SRWo) who were both assessed in the parish of Hambury juxta Wych. In view of the common interchange of *Wh* and *W*, this may also have become *Whi(t)cher*. Or, we may have 'dweller by the wych-elm enclosure', as at Witcha Fm in Ramsbury (Wilts), the home of Richard *atte Wycheheye* in 1332 (PN W 290).

Whitcomb, Whitcombe, Witcomb, Witcombe: William *de Whitecumbe* 1201 P (So); Isoda *Wytecoumbe*, Robert *de Wythecoumb* 1332 SRSx. The first example is from Whitcombe (Som). As a place-name, Whitcombe 'wide or withy valley' is found in Dorset, Wilts and the Isle of Wight, and in Devon as 'wheat valley'. Witcombe 'wide or withy valley' occurs in Devon, Gloucester and Somerset. The surname may derive from any of these or from a lost place in Sussex and is sometimes identical in meaning with WIDDECOMBE.

Whitcroft: *v.* WHEATCROFT

White, Whitt, Whyte, Witt, Witte, Witts: (i) *Whita* 1066 DB (Sf); *Wit* filius Willelmi 1198 FFNf; Þurcil *Hwita*, *Wite*, *Wita* 1038, 1066 OEByn (He); Ordgar *se Wite* c1070 ib. (So); Alestanus *hwit* 1066 Winton (Ha); Alwin *Wit* 1066, 1086 DB (Ha); Uuiaett *Hwite* c1097–1107 Black; Lewinus *Wite* c1114 Burton (St); Berwaldus *le White* Hy 2 DC (L); Hugo *Wit* 1190 BuryS (Sf); Walter *le Whyte* 1284 LLB A; William *le Wytt* 1327 SRY; John *le Whytt* 1327 SRSo. Occasionally this is from OE *Hwīta*, a short form of names in *Hwīt-*, but is more often a nickname from OE *hwīt* 'white', with reference to fair hair or complexion, a well-established name before the Conquest and very common thereafter. (ii) Ralf *de Wyıe* 1279 AssSo; John *atte Wyte* 1296 SRSx.

'Dweller by a bend or curve' in a river or road (OE *wiht), the source of Great Whyte (Hunts). *v.* WIGHT. *White* also appears to be a development of *wait*. cf. White (Devon), the home of Adam *atte Wayte* in 1330. This is explained in PN D 108 as 'ambush', 'place where one lies in wait'. It is more likely to denote 'a place where one watches', 'a look-out post'. cf. WAIT.

Whiteaker: *v.* WHITAKER

Whitear: *v.* WHITTIER

Whiteaway: *v.* WHITEWAY

Whitebread: *v.* WHITBREAD

Whitefield, Whitfield: Leonard *de Witefelde* 1154 Eynsham; William, John *de Whitefeld* 1230 P (So), 1338 CorLo; Richard *Whytefeld* 1396 IpmGl. From Whitefield (Glos, Lancs, Wight), Whitfield (Derby, Kent, Northants, Northumb), or 'dweller by the white field'.

Whitefoot: Ulfuine *Huitfot* c1095 Bury (Sf); John *Weytefot* 1327 SRC; Robert *Whitfott* 1311 ColchCt. A nickname. OE *hwītfōt* 'white foot'.

Whitehair: *v.* WHITTIER

Whitehand: Robert *Withand* 1181 P (Nt); Richard *Whithand* 1204 P (Nf); Robert *Wytehand* SRY. A nickname. 'White hand.'

Whitehart: *v.* WHITTARD

Whitehead, Whytehead: John *Whithaued* 1219 Cur (Lei); Roger *Witheved* 1279 RH (Hu); William *Hwitheued* 1317 AssK; William *Whithefd* 1332 SRSx; Robert *Whithede* 1338 ShefA (Y). OE *hwīt*, *hēafod* 'white head', i.e. whitehaired or fairhaired. Occasionally from *hwīt*, *hōd* 'white hood': Agnes *Wythod* 1279 RH (O). Also occasionally local, from residence at the 'white head' of a field or hill; Henry *de Whiteheved* 1297 MinAcctCo.

Whiteheard, Whiteheart: *v.* WHITTARD

Whitehorn, Whitehorne, Whithorn: Martin *Withorn* 1275 RH (Sf); Thomas *Whithorn* 1327 SRSx. Clearly a nickname, perhaps one with a splendid trumpet or drinking-horn (OE *hwīt* 'white, fair, splendid' and *horn*).

Whitehouse, Whithouse, Whitters: (i) Stephen *atte Whitehous* 1327 SRSo. 'Dweller at the white (stone) house.' Whittas Park in Torpenhow (Cumb) is *Whitt house* in 1777 (PN Cu 326). (ii) William *Whitehals* 1369 FrY; Robert *Whithawse* 1551 ib.; Marmaducus *Whithaus* 1598 ib.; Anthonius *Whitus* 1615 ib. 'White neck.' cf. WHITTLES, SHORTHOSE.

Whiteing: *v.* WHITING

Whitelam, Whitelum, Whitlam, Whitlum: Alice *Whitlambe* 1379 PTY; Richard *Whitelam* 1488 GildY. 'White lamb', a nickname.

Whitelark: *v.* WHITELOCK

Whitelaw, Whitlaw, Whytelaw, Whytlaw: John *de Wytelowe* 1296 Black (Edinburgh); John *Whitelaw* 1430 ib. From Whitelaw (Morebattle, Bowden).

Whitelegg, Whitelegge: Agnes *Whytlegge* 1584 Bardsley. This cannot be identical with *Whiteley* as suggested by Bardsley, Harrison and Weekley. *-leg(ge)* is a common medieval form of *-ley* but never gives a modern *-leg* in place-names. The surname must be a nickname 'white leg'. cf. the ON nickname *Hvítbeinn* 'white leg', WHITEFOOT, WHITEHAND, WHITEHEAD, WHITESIDE and Robert *Wytfleis* 1223 Pat (Y); William *Witteflese* 1326 FeuDu 'white flesh'.

Whiteley, Whitely, Whitla, Whitley, Whittla, Whittley, Witley: William *de Witteleia* 1125 StCh; R. *de Witelay* 1190 P (Y); Hilda *de Whitelai* 1200 P (Nt); Henry *de Hwittele* 1221 AssWa; Richard *de Whiteleg* 1246 AssLa; John *del Wyteley* 13th Shef (Y). From Whitleigh (Berks) or Whitley (Ches, Northumb, Wilts, Warwicks, WRYorks). The place-name is common and all these are 'white *lēah*'; it is found in minor names as Whiteley (Devon) and Whiteley Woods (Sheffield) and in many that have not survived. Occasionally it is 'wheat *lēah*'. *Whetelegh* (1333 PN D 344) is a surname derived from Whitley in Molland (Devon). Edith *de Wheteley* was probably of the same family as Thomas *de Whitteley* 1316 Wak (Y). cf. WHITAKER and WHATELEY.

Whitell: *v.* WHITTLE

Whitelock, Whitelocke, Whitlock, Whitelark: (i) *Witlac* 1066 DB (L), *Wislak* ib. (Ha); *Willak* 1086 DB (Ha); *Withlac* de molend' 1202 P (Ha); *Wihtlac* de Longo Vado 1207 FineR (Ha); Emma *filia Witlok* 1279 RH (Hu); Toke *Wictlok* 1208 Cur (Nf); John *Witloc* 1243 AssSo; William *Whytlok* 1285 FFHu; John *Wyhtlok* (*Wytlok*) 1327 *SR* (Ess); John *Whytlak* 1524 SRSf; James *Whitlake* 1568 SRSf. Sometimes from OE *Wihtlāc* 'elf-play', but also a nickname from OE *hwīt* and *locc* 'white lock, white hair'. The Suffolk river Lark is either a back-formation from Lackford or was originally called *lacu* 'stream'. *Whitelark* may be due to a similar dialectal pronunciation of the 1524 *Whytlak*. cf. WOODLAKE. (ii) William *atte Whytelak* 1327 SRSo. 'Dweller by the white stream' (OE *lacu*).

Whitelum: *v.* WHITELAM

Whiteman, Whitman, Wittman: *Quithmanus* 1121–38 Bury (Sf); *Witeman* fugitiuus 1170 P (Gl); William *Witman* 1230 P (K); Richard *Wyteman* 1243 AssSt; Stephen *Whytman* 1243 AssSo; Michael *Whiteman* 1310 ColchCt; OE *Hwītmann*.

Whitemore, Whitamore, Whitmer, Whitmore, Whittamore, Whittemore, Whittimore, Wittamore: John *de Witemore* 1199 AssSt; Adam *de Whitemor* 1249 PN D 353; Gilbert *de Whitemere* 1275 SRWo. From Whitmore (Staffs), Whitmoor (Devon) or residence near a white moor or mere. *Whittamore*, etc. are Devonshire forms which do not seem to survive as place-names.

Whitenow: (i) Thomas *Wytynow* 1327 SRSo. 'White enough.' (ii) John *Whiteknafe* 1379 PTY. 'White, fair boy', or 'servant of White'. cf. GOODENOUGH. (iii) 'Dweller by the white knoll', as at Whiteknowe in Nicholforest (Cumb).

Whiteoak: *v.* WHITTOCK

Whiter, Whitter, Whitta, Wheater: John *Witer* 1181–6 Clerkenwell (Ess); Henry *le Witere, le Wytter'* 1221 AssWa; Andrew *le Whytere* 1310 ColchCt; Thomas *le Whittere* 1320 MESO (So). A derivative of OE *hwītian* 'to make white', 'white-

washer'. 'The Keep of the Tower of London was known as the White Tower from its being resplendent with whitewash'. Corfe Castle was all whitewashed outside. (Building 157). For *Wheater*, cf. WHITAKER.

Whiteside, Whitesides: Robert *Wytside* 1230 P (Wa); John *Witside* 1250 Fees (Ha); Richard *Whitside* 1279 RH (C). A nickname 'white side' (OE *hwīt* and *sīde* 'side, flank').

Whitesmith: Richard, William *le Wytesmith* 1260 Cl (O), 1279 RH (C); John *le Wytesmyt, le Whitesmyth* 1313, 1332 SRWa. OE *hwīt* and *smið* 'white-smith', a tin-smith (1302 NED).

Whiteson: *v.* WHITSON

Whiteway, Whiteaway: William *Wyttewey, Whitewe* 1296, 1327 SRSx. From Whiteway House, Whiteway Barton (Devon), where the surname was *Whythaweye* in 1335 (PN D 491, 479), or from residence near a white road (OE *hwīt, weg*).

Whitewhite: Thomas *de Whitthuait* 1332 SRCu. 'Dweller by the white clearing' (OE *hwīt*, ON *þveit*).

Whitewick, Whittick, Wittick: Euarard *de Whitwic, de Witic*, 1208 AssY, Cur (Y). From Whitwick (Lei), pronounced *Wittick*.

Whitewright: *v.* WHITTERIDGE

Whitey, Whitie, Whittey, Whitty: (i) John *Witege* 1186 Eynsham (O); Richard *Whiteye* 1276 RH (L). Either a nickname 'white eye' (OE *hwīt, ēage*) or OE *wītega* 'wise man, prophet, soothsayer'. (ii) Nicholas *de la Wytheg* 1279 RH (O); Bartholomew *atte Withegh* 1332 SRSx; Edmund *de Whitehey* 1351 AssEss. 'Dweller by the white enclosure' (OE *hwīt*, (*ge*)*hæg*). *v.* also WITTY, with which there has, no doubt, been confusion.

Whitfield: *v.* WHITEFIELD

Whithair, Whithear: *v.* WHITTIER

Witham: *v.* WITHAM

Whithorn: *v.* WHITEHORN

Whithouse: *v.* WHITEHOUSE

Whitie: *v.* WHITEY

Whiting, Whiteing, Whitting, Witting: Simundus *filius Witing* a1150 DC (L); Roger *Witenc* 1084 GeldR (So); John *Hwiteng, Witinge* 1128–34 Colch (Ess); William *Witting* 1194 Cur (Bk); William *Whiting* 1197 P (Bk); Giffard *Whytteng* 1230 P (So); Walter *le Witing* 1268 AssSo; Thomas, Matilda *Hwytyng* 1327 SRSx. OE *Hwīting*, a patronymic from OE *Hwīta* 'Hwīta's son', a personal name still in use in the 12th century. Also, and probably more commonly, an original nickname from OE *hwīta* 'the white one'.

Whitla: *v.* WHITELEY

Whitlam: *v.* WHITELAM

Whitlaw: *v.* WHITELAW

Whitley: *v.* WHITELEY

Whitling: (i) *Witling* de Inskip 1261 AssLa; William *Wytling* 1327 SRSf; John *Whitling* 1332 SRLa; Cecilia *Whytling* 1345 ColchCt. OE **Wihtling*, known only from the above example, but probably also the personal-name which lies behind Whitlingham (Norfolk). This Ekwall derives from OE *Wihthelm*, a compound not evidenced in the early forms: *Wislingeham* DB, *Wicthlingham* 1206 DEPN. OE *Wihtlāc* may well have had a short form **Wihtla*, from which was formed **Wihtling* 'son of Wihtla'. Or *Wihtling* may have been regarded as a pet-form of *Wihtlāc*. cf. the interchange of *Brihtling* and *Brihtric* in Brightlingsea (PN Ess 331). But, as forms are few and late, and show no sign of OE *-ht-*, we may have OE **Hwītling*, similarly formed from *Hwīta*. (ii) Walter *de Whittling'* 1221 AssWo. From Whitlinge (Worcs). *v.* WICKLING.

Whitlock: *v.* WHITELOCK

Whitlum: *v.* WHITELAM

Whitman: *v.* WHITEMAN

Whitmarsh: Henry *de Wytemers* 1245 FFEss. 'Dweller by the white marsh', as at Whitemarsh Fm in Sedgehill or Witmarsh Bottom in West Dean (Wilts). *v.* PN W 192, 378.

Whitmee, Whitney: Henry *Whitemay* 1255 RH (Sa); William *Wytemey* 1279 RH (O). ME *may* 'young man or maid'. The surname may mean 'fair youth' or may be a derogatory nickname 'fair maid'.

Whitmer, Whitmore: *v.* WHITEMORE

Whitney: William *de Wittenheia* 1210–11 PWi; John *de Whyteneye* 1327 SRSf; Emanuel *Whitney* 1642 PrD. From Whitney (Hereford), Whitney Wood in Stevenage (Herts), or 'dweller by or on the white island'.

Whitrick, Whitridge: *v.* WHITTERIDGE

Whitson, Whitsun, Whiteson: Nicholas *Witesone* Ed 1 Battle (Sx); Walter *Hwyttesone* 1318 AD iv (Sa); John *Whitsone* 1327 SRSx; William *Quhitsoun* 1369 Black (Perth). 'Son of *White* or *Whitt*.' Occasionally this may be a simplified pronunciation of *Whitston* 'white stone'. cf. Whitson Fm (PN D 243).

Whitt: *v.* WHITE

Whitta: *v.* WHITER

Whittaker: *v.* WHITAKER

Whittam: *v.* WITHAM

Whittamore: *v.* WHITEMORE

Whittard, Whitehart, Whiteheart, Whiteheard, Witard: *Wiþardus* de Foro 1185 Templars (Ess); Thomas *Wytard* 1275 SRWo; William *Whitherd*, Gilbert *Whitard* 1327 SRSx. Perhaps OE *Wihtheard* 'elf-brave', of which only one pre-Conquest example is known (in 825). cf. also *terra Wichardi* 1190 BuryS (Sf). Or OE* *Hwītheard*.

Whittear: *v.* WHITTIER

Whittek: *v.* WHITTOCK

Whittell: *v.* WHITTLE

Whittemore: *v.* WHITEMORE

Whitter: *v.* WHITER

Whitteridge, Whittrick, Whitrick, Whitridge, Whitewright, Witherick, Witrick, Witterick, Wittrick, Wittridge, Widrich: (i) *Wihtric* (Sf), *Wictric*, *Witric* (Sa), *Wistricus* (St), *Wistrinc* (Ha) 1066 DB; John, William *Wickrik* 1276 RH (Berks); William *Wyterik* 1279 RH (C); Roger *Wythrich* 1327 SRSf; Simon *Wheterich* 1327 SRC; Henry *Wyhtrich* (*Whytrich*) 1327 *SR* (Ess). OE *Wihtrīc* 'sprite-ruler'. (ii) Robert *de Wyterik'* 1249 Cl (Cu);

Robert *de Whiterig* 1332 SRCu. From Wheatridge (Northumb), and perhaps occasionally from one of the three places named Whitrigg in Cumberland; though the latter are from ON *hryggr*, forms in *-rik* are found.

Whitters: *v.* WHITEHOUSE

Whittey: *v.* WHITEY

Whitticase: For *Whittakers*: Thomas *Whitacres* 1526 FrY.

Whittick: *v.* WHITEWICK

Whitticom: *v.* WIDDECOMBE

Whittier, Whittear, Whitear, Whitehair, Whithair, Whithear: Ralf *Wittauuere* 12th AD ii (Nth); Norman *Wittowiere* 1224–46 Bart (Lo); Thomas *le Wytewere* 1279 RH (C); Eustace *le Wittowere* 1279 RH (Hu); William *le Wyttawyere* 1285 *Ass* (Ess); William *le Whythawere* 1309 SRBeds; John *Whitouer* 1364 LLB G; Grace *Whityer* 1634 Bardsley. 'White-leather dresser', one who taws skins into whiteleather (1284 NED), from OE *hwīt* 'white' and ME *tawyere, towyere, tewere*, from WS *tāwian*, Anglian **tēwian* 'to taw'. *v.* MESO.

Whittimore: *v.* WHITEMORE

Whitting: *v.* WHITING

Whittingham, Whittenham, Wittenham: Vhtred *de Witingeham* 1163 P; Gilbert, Oliver *de Whitingham* c1214 Black, 1279 AssNb; Thomas *de Whytenham* 1339 CorLo; Adam *Whityngham* 1401 AssLa. From Whittingham (Lancs, Northumb), Whittinghame (East Lothian), or Wittenham (Berks).

Whittington, Whitington: Peter *de Witinton'* 1201 Pl (Co); John *de Whityngton'* 1327 SRLei; Richard *Whityngton* 1420–1 FFWa. From Whittington (Derby, Glos, Lancs, Northumb, Salop, Staffs, Warwicks, Worcs).

Whittla: *v.* WHITELEY

Whittle, Whittell, Whitell: Robert *de Withull* 1242 Fees (La); John *Whittle* 1581 Bardsley (Ch); Anthonius *Whitell* 1608 FrY; Christopherus *Whithill* son of Anthonius *Whithill* 1637 ib. From Whittle (Lancs, Northumb), Whittle-le-Woods (Lancs), or from residence near a white hill. Whittles Fm in Mapledurham (Oxon) is *Whitelewe* 1493 (PN O), 'white hill', from OE *hlǣw*. Also 'dweller by a clear spring or stream': Whittles Hall in Springfield (Essex) was the home of Hasculph *de Whitewell* 1346 Cl. Whitwell (Cambs) is pronounced *Wittle*.

Whittles: Richard *Wythals* son of Ralph *Wythals* 1316 AD ii (Nf). A nickname, 'white neck', OE *hwīt, hals*. *v.* WHITEHOUSE.

Whittley: *v.* WHITELEY

Whittock, Whittuck, Whytock, Whittek: John *Wyttok* 1327 SRSo; William *Whittoc* 1334 AD ii (Wt); Joseph *Whiteoak* 1704 FrY. OE *Hwit(t)uc*, a diminutive of *Hwīt*.

Whittome: *v.* WITHAM

Whittrick: *v.* WHITTERIDGE

Whittuck: *v.* WHITTOCK

Whitty: *v.* WHITEY

Whitworth: Elyas *de Witewurde* 1194 P (Sr); John *de Whiteworth* 1336 FFY; Leonard *Whytworth* 1539 CorNt. From Whitworth (Durham, Lancs).

Wholehouse: v. WOOLHOUSE
Whorall: v. WORRAL
Why(e): v. GUY
Whyard: v. WYARD
Whyatt: v. WYATT
Whyberd, Whybird: v. WYBERD
Whyborn: v. WYBORN
Whybra, Whybray, Whybrew, Whybro, Whybrow: v. WYBER
Whyman, Whymant: v. WYMAN
Whymark: v. WYMARK
Whysall: Roger *de Wisho* 1199 P (Nt). From Wysall (Notts).
Whyte: v. WHITE
Whytehead: v. WHITEHEAD
Whytelaw, Whytlaw: v. WHITELAW
Whytok: v. WHITTOCK
Wiatt: v. WYATT
Wiberg: v. WYBER
Wiblin: Jordan *Wibelin* 1203 P (L); Godfrey *Wybelyn* 1327 SRSx. A Norman double diminutive of *Wibbe.* cf. Willelmus *filius Wibbe* 1231 Pat (Nb), Richard *Wybbe* 1381 AssWa. OE *Wibba* is probably the first element of Wibtoft (Warwicks). cf. *(to) wibban beorge* 959 BCS 1045.

Wibrew, Wibroe, Wibrow: v. WYBER
Wich, Wych, Weech, Weetch, Wick, Wicke, Wickes, Wicks, Wix, Wike, Wyke, Wykes, Weekes, Weeks, Whick: Alueredus *de Uuica* 1084 GeldR (So); Goscelin *del Wich* 1184 P (Wo); Jordan *de la Wike* 1194 Cur (Gl); Robert *de la Wyk* 1248 FFEss; Nicholas *Attewyche* 1270 AssSo; William *Wiche* c1280 *ERO* (Ess); Thomas *Wiches* 1302 ib.; Roger *atte Wykes* 1327 SRSo; Thomas *atte Whic* 1327 SRSx; William *Wyxe* ib.; John *Weekes* 1571 Bardsley. OE *wīc*, primarily 'dwelling-place, abode', then 'village, hamlet, town', was later used of a dairy-farm, as in Cowick, Gatwick (goat-farm), Oxwick, Shapwick (sheep-farm), Butterwick, Chiswick (cheese-farm), and in this sense the simple *wick* was very common in the 13th and 14th centuries and survived in common use in Essex as late as 1729 when we read of 'a wick or dairy of 20 cows' at St Osyth. The surname may derive from Wix (Essex) or any of the many places named Wick, Wyke or Week (a south-western, particularly Devon, form), or it may denote a dweller near or a worker at a dairy-farm. The final *-s* is a plural form. cf. WICKEN. There seem to be no certain examples of the palatalized form (*Wich*) surviving in the uncompounded place-name but the form certainly existed and may survive as a surname. Camden refers to 'making cheese of ewes' milk in their little dairy houses or huts [in Canvey Island] built for that purpose, which they call Wiches'. *Wich*, *Wych*, *Weech* and *Weetch*, may also, and, probably usually, mean 'dweller by the wych-elm' (OE *wice*), as at Weach Barton (Devon) and Wychstreet in Woking (Surrey).

Wicken, Wickens, Wickins: Thomas *de le Wikin* 1275 RH (Nf); Henry *de Wikin* 1279 RH (Bk); Geoffrey *Wykin* 1327 *SR* (Ess). From Wicken (Cambs, Northants), Wicken Bonhunt (Essex), or 'dweller or worker at the dairy-farms', ME *atte wiken.* cf. WICH. Both the Essex and Cambridgeshire places are found as *Wykyng* in the 16th century which may be one source of *Wicking.*

Wickenden: Martin *de Wiggindenn* c1200 ArchC vi 210; John *de Wykendene* 1337 LLB F. From a lost place in Cowden (Kent), now represented by Polefields, first recorded in a charter of 1044 as *Wingindene* and in one of 1081 as *Wigendene* (KPN 324) and last mentioned as *Wykenden* in a list of church marks of 1542, but in that of 1663 as *Polefields*, long occupied by the Wickenden family; 'ould mother wickenden of powlfields' was buried in 1626. Prosperous landholders in Cowden, in the 16th century they were so numerous that their surname required a further attribute: Wickenden de Ludwells, Thomas Wykinden de Cowden Streate (1558), Thomas Wickenden de Bechinwoode (1571), Thomas Wickenden de la hole (1589). v. Ewing. The surname is still found in Tonbridge, on the Kent–Sussex border, and in Essex.

Wicker, Wickers, Wheeker, Whicker: Walter *le Wykere* 1225 AssSo; Henry *Wyker* Hy 3 Gilb (L); Thomas *Whicker* 1581 Oxon (D). 'Dweller or worker at the dairy-farm' (OE *wīc*). cf. WICH.

Wicket, Wickett, Wicketts: v. WIGGETT

Wickfield: Nigel *de Wikefeld'* 1211 Cur (Berks). 'Dweller by the field near the dairy-farm.' OE *wīc, feld.* cf. *Wykfeld* 1253 Ch (St).

Wickham, Wykeham: Wulfric *æt Wicham* 955 OEByn; Robert *de Wikam* 1218 FFO; William *de Wykeham* 1305 IpmY; Walter *Wykham* 1400 IpmGl. From one or other of the many places of this name, or from Wickhambreux (Kent), Wickhambrook (Suffolk), Wycomb (Leics), Wycombe (Bucks), or Wykeham (Lincs, NRYorks).

Wicking, Wickings: (i) *Wiching* (Wa), *Wikingus* (Sf), *Wichin* (D) 1066 DB; *Wiching* c1095 Bury (Sf, C). ON *Víkingr*, ODa, OSw *Viking*. Or OE *wīcing* 'pirate'. (ii) Richard *Wykyng* 1456 Ewing; Thomas *Wekyn, Wikyng* 1505–10 ib.; Thomas *Wycken* 1588 ib. From Wickens in Cowden (Kent) where the surname appears as *de Wyking'* in 1248 (KPN 324, n. 2).

Wickins: v. WICKEN

Wickling: William *de Wyklinge* 1275 SRWo. From Whitlinge in Hartlebury (Worcs) where William was assessed. v. WHITLING.

Wicklow: Richard *de Wikelaw'* 1212 Cur (Sf). From a lost *Wicklow*, the meeting-place of the Suffolk franchise of the Bishop of Ely.

Wickman, Whickman: Herbertus *filius Wycmanni* 1140–53 Holme (Nf); Vxor *Wichmanni* 1170 P (Nf); William *Wikeman* 1209 P (Nf); Alan *Wichman* 1275 RH (Sf); Richard *Wycman* 1275 RH (Nf). OE *wīc* and *mann* 'dairy-farm man'. cf. WICKER. For its use as a personal-name, cf. *Ewicman* 1066 DB (Nf), probably **eowu-wīcman* 'worker at the ewe-farm'.

Widdaker: v. WHITAKER
Widdas: v. WIDDOWES

Widdecombe, Widdicombe, Withacombe, Withecombe, Withycombe, Whitticom: Geoffrey *de Widecumbe* 1196 P (So); Hugh *Widecombe* alias *Withecomb* 1700 DKR 41 (D). From Widdacombe, Widdecombe, Widdicombe (Devon), or Withycombe (Devon, Somerset), all 'withy valley'.

Widders, Widdess: *v.* WIDDOWES

Widderson, Widdeson, Widdison: *v.* WIDDOWSON

Widdiwiss: *v.* WOODIWISS

Widdowes, Widdows, Widdas, Widders, Widdess: (i) Alice *Wedue* 1279 RH (C); Agnes *le Wydu*, Peter *le Wydoue* 1297 SRY; John *le Wydewe* 1327 SRSf. OE *widuwe, widewe* 'widow'. In ME, and perhaps also in OE, the word could have the sense 'widower'. (ii) William *Widders* 1576 FrLeic; Edward *Widdhouse* 1586 FrY; Thomas *Widdowes* 1619 ib.; John *Widhouse* 1681 ib.; George *Woodhouse* son of John *Widhouse* 1732 ib. A variant of WOODHOUSE, from OE *widu* 'wood', though the forms are late. As *Widdowson* exists, *Widdowes*, no doubt, sometimes means 'the widow's son', but the final -*s* has probably often been added to *Widdow* through association with *Widhouse*.

Widdowson, Widderson, Widdeson, Widdison, Widowson: Richard *Wyduesone* 1309 SRBeds; Peter, John *la Wydewesone* 1326 FFEss, 1327 SRDb; William *le Wydusone* 1332 SRSt. 'The widow's son.'

Widger: *Wihtgarus, Witgarus, Withgarus, Wisgar* 1066 DB (Sf); *Wyhtgarus presbiter* 1198 Colch (Ess); Ordric *Wihgar* c1095 Bury (Sf); Adam *Wydger* 1327 SRWo. OE *Wihtgār* 'elf-spear'.

Widrich: *v.* WHITTERIDGE

Wigan: Adam *de Wigain* 1209 P (La). From Wigan (Lancs).

Wigan, Wigand, Wigens, Wigin, Wiggans, Wiggin, Wiggins: *Wighen* 1086 ICC, DB (C); *Radulfus filius Wigein* 1163 P (Lei); *Wygan le Breton* 1252 FFEss; William *Wygeyn* 1275 RH (Nf); John *Wygen* 1297 MinAcctCo (Co); James *Wiggans, Wiggins* 1752, 1756 FrY. An OFr personal name of Breton origin, OBret *Uuicon, Guegon* (Loth), introduced into England at the Conquest.

Wigfall, Wigfull: Henry *de Wigfall*, John *Wigfall* 1379 PTY. From Wigfall (WRYorks).

Wigg, Wiggs: Ailmar *Wigga* c1130 ELPN; Walter *Wigge* 1204 P (Ess). Probably a nickname from OE *wicga* 'beetle'. In later examples, perhaps also metonymic for WIGGER.

Wiggall: *v.* WEIGALL

Wiggans: *v.* WIGAN

Wigger: (i) *Wiger filius Roberti* 1210 Cur (L); *Wigor'* Buuebroc, *Wigorus* Webbe 1221 *ElyA* (Sf); Roger *Wygor* ib. ON *Vigarr* or OE **Wiggār* (cf. PNDB 413). In 13th-century Suffolk, *Wigor* was a not uncommon peasant's name. The surname may also derive from OG *Wigger*. (ii) William *le Wygger* 1332 MESO (Ess). A derivative of ME *wygge*, MLG, MDu *wigge* 'wedge, wedge-shaped cake', a maker or seller of buns or cakes. cf. Matilda *la Wyggestr'* 1296 SRSx.

Wiggett, Wicket, Wickett, Wicketts: *Wigot*, *Wigod* 1066 DB; Willelmus *filius Wigot* 1212 Cur (L); John *Wiket, Wiget* 1180, 1182 P (Wo); William *Wigot* 1185 Templars (Wa); John *Wigod* 1255 RH (Sa); Walter *Wyket* 1284 FFSf. ODa, OSw *Vigot* (PNDB). Early examples of *Wiket* are not common.

Wiggin(s): *v.* WIGAN

Wigglesworth, Wiglesworth, Wigelsworth: Geoffrey *de Wicleswrthe* 1202 FFY; William *de Wyglesworth* 1379 PTY; Henrie *Wigglesworth* 1629 FrY. From Wigglesworth (WRYorks).

Wight, Weight, Whight: Roger *Wicht* 1176 P (Gl); Richard *Wiht* 1200 P (Beds); Hugh *Wyght* 1222 Cur (Beds); William *le Wyhte* 1275 RH (Sx); Thomas *Whight* 1291 Black. ME *wiht, wight* 'agile, strong', from ON *víg-t*. Nicholas *de Wight* (1332 SRLo) probably came from the Isle of Wight. *v.* also WHITE.

Wightman, Weightman: *Wyctman de Freton* 1248 FFEss; William *Wihtman* 1227 AssBeds; William *Wightman* 1332 SRCu; Roger *Wightman* son of John *Whightman*, milloner 1639 FrY; Henry *Weightman* son of John *Weightman*, milner 1654 FrY. OE **Wihtmann* 'elf-man', or a nickname, 'brave, strong man', from ME *wiht* (*v.* WIGHT) and *man*.

Wigin: *v.* WIGAN

Wigman: Alexander *Wigman* 1275 RH (Nth); Geoffrey *Wyg(e)man* RH (Y). Either 'dairy-farm man' (*v.* WICKMAN) or 'cake-man' (*v.* WIGG). cf. CHEESEMAN.

Wike: *v.* WICH

Wilber: *v.* WILDBORE

Wilberforce, Wilberfosse: William *de Wilburfoss* temp. Stephen Whitby (Y). From Wilberfoss (ERYorks).

Wilbert: Henry *Wylbert* 1279 RH (Hu). OE *Wilbeorht* 'will-bright', an early but uncommon OE name, which is not recorded in DB or later. It must have remained in use, probably among the peasants.

Wilby, Wilbye, Wilbe, Wilbee: Robert *de Willeby* a1161 YCh; Adam *de Wilebi* 1208 P (R); Robert *Wilby* 1372 FFEss. From Wilby (Norfolk, Northants, Suffolk).

Wilcock, Wilcocke, Wilcocks, Wilcox, Willcock, Willcocks, Willcox: *Wilcok* 1246 AssLa; *Wilcoc* 1286 AssCh; *Wylecok* Hervy 1275 RH (Lo); William *Wylecok* 1254 AssSo; John *Wilcokes* 1316 Wak (Y); Godfrey *Willecok* 1327 SRSf. *Wilcoc*, a pet-name for *William*.

Wilcockson, Wilcoxson: William *Wilcokson* 1332 SRCu. 'Son of *Wilcock*.'

Wild, Wilde, Whild, Whilde, Wyld, Wylde, Wyldes, Wylds: (i) Uluricus *Wilde* 1066 DB (L); William *le Wilde* 1177 P (Lei); Henry *le Wylde* 1236 FFEss. OE *wilde* 'wild, violent'. (ii) William *de Wilde* 1200 P (Sx); Walter *de la Wylde* 1256 RamsCt (Hu); William *atte Wylde* 1347 LLB F. 'Dweller by the waste, uncultivated land' from OE *wilde* 'wild, waste', used as a noun. The above forms are much too early to be regarded as due to the development of *weald* to *wild*.

Wildash: v. WILDISH

Wildblood, Wildeblood: Roger, William *Wylde-blod* 1366 SRLa, 1381 SaltAS (OS) xiv. A nick-name for an untamed spirit or a rake. Nicknames formed with a compound of *wild-* were common. cf. Richard *Wildecat* 1176 P (Wo), William *Wilde-bef* 1327 SRSx, William *Wildecnave* 1327 SRWo, Roger *Wildehog* 1246 FFK, Robert *Wildprest* 13th Guisb, Stephen *Wyldraven* 1300 ib.

Wildbore, Wildeboer, Wyldbore, Wilber: William *Wyldebar* 1242 AssLa; William *Wyldebor* 1307 Wak (Y); John *Wylbor* 1379 PTY. A nick-name, 'wild-boar' from OE *bār*.

Wildee: v. WALTHEW

Wilder, Wilders: William *Wilder, Wyldere* 1327 SRDb. Probably OE *wildēor* 'wild animal'.

Wildey: v. WALTHEW

Wildgoose, Wildgose, Wildgust, Willgoss: Henry *Wildegos* 1201 Cur (Sa); Osbert *Wildgos* 1206 Cur (Sf); John *Wylegous* 1379 PTY. A nickname 'wild goose'. cf. William *Wildefuhel* 1185 Templars (Y), Nicholas *Wyldefoul* 1288 RamsCt (Hu). 'Wild bird.'

Wilding, Willding: *Wildingus* Prepositus 1224 Cur (He); Adam *Wilding* 1207 Cur (Nf), 1286 AssCh; John *Wylding* 1332 SRCu. OE **Wilding*, a derivative of *wilde*, 'the wild one', both as a personal name and a nickname. As Adekyn *Wylding* (1285 AssCh) was the son of Alice *Wildegos*, the nickname may have been regarded as synonymous with *wild-goose*. The modern sur-name may also be a late development of *Wheeldon* or *Wheldon*. Wilding's Copse in Aldbourne (Wilts) was *Wheleding, Whelden* in 1561 (PN W 293).

Wildish, Wildash: Simon *le Wealdessh* 1316 FFK; Robert *de* (sic) *Weldysh* 1317 FFK. OE **wealdisc* 'belonging to the Weald'; the inhabit-ants of the Weald were called Wealdish men. The name survives in Kent farms: Wildage Fm in Elham (from John *Weldisse* 1292, John *Wealdissh*' 1327); Welldishes Fm in Linton (William *Woldishe* 1542); Upper and Lower Woolwich in Rolvenden (Robert *de Waldeys, de Weldysh*' 1278, 1317, William *Weldisshe* 1327). v. PN K 434, 139, 355.

Wildman: William *Wyldman* 1379 PTY. 'The wild man.'

Wildon: v. WHEELDON

Wildrake: v. WELDRICK

Wildridge, Willdridge, Willrich: Hugo *filius Wilrici* 1203 Cur (Nth); *Wildricus* Mæl 1205 Cur (He); Henry *Wildriche* 1568 SRSf. OE *Wilrīc* 'will-powerful', a rare name, only two OE ex-amples being known.

Wildsmith, Wilesmith, Weldsmith, Whilesmith: Euota *Welsmyth*' 1319 *SR* (Ess); Ivo *le Welsmyth* 1327 *SR* (Ess); Anne *Wilesmith* 1787 Bardsley. This surname has been variously explained as a corruption of *weld-smith*, a forger in iron, weald-smith, and the smith in the wild, none of which is satisfactory, nor is Bardsley's association of the name with wool. *Welsmyth* is from OE **hwēol-smið* 'wheel-smith', a maker of wheels, especially the iron parts. cf. WHEELWRIGHT. The vowel

was raised to [ī] (*Wheelsmith*), then shortened to *Willsmith*, which, with an intrusive *d*, became *Wildsmith*. ME *W(h)īlsmith* developed normally to *W(h)ilesmith*. cf. *Whygler* for *Wheeler*, *Whil-wright* for *Wheelwright*, and the development of *weald* to *wild*.

Wildy: v. WALTHEW

Wiles, Wyles: (i) William *de la Wile* 1185 P (Do); Osbert *de Wila* 1204 P (Sa); Adam *de la Wile* 1221 AssWo; Walter, Thomas *atte Wyle* 1296 SRSx, 1317 AD iii (Wa). From Wild (Berks), Monkton Wyld (Dorset), or Wylam (Northumb), all of which Ekwall (DEPN) derives from late OE *wīl* 'trick', used of some such mechanical device as a windmill or a trap. Löfvenberg (MELS) notes ME *wyle* 'a wicker trap for catching fish, especially eels' (1256 NED), and the frequency of the name suggests that this may have been a common mean-ing. (ii) Robert *le Wile* 1195 FFNf; John *Wiles* 1202 AssL; John, Robert *Wyles* 1251 AssY, 1327 SRLei. This, too, is probably from late OE *wīl* 'trick', and the almost invariable plural suggests that it is metonymic for a trapper, one in charge of the fishing traps, though it could be metaphorical, 'a man of many wiles'. For the type of name, cf. TRAPP, WRENCH.

Wiley, Wylie, Wyley, Wyly: John *de Wili, de Wylegh* 1201 P (W), 1230 Cur (Wa); William *de Wyly* 1299 IpmW; Simon *Wylegh* 1327 SRSx; Richard *Wyleye* 1390 FFEss. From Willey (Ches, Devon, Hereford, Salop, Warwicks), Wylye (Wilts), or Wyly in East Hoathly, Whiligh in Ticehurst (Sussex).

Wilford, Willford: Roger *de Willeford* 1199–1200 FFSf; Gervase *de Wylford* 1360 IpmNt; Thomas *Wilforde* 1576 SRW. From Wilford (Notts, Suffolk).

Wilfred: *Wilfrei* miles 1055 FeuDu; Robert *Wilfrith* c1280 SRWo. OE *Wilfrið* 'will-peace'.

Wilgress: v. WILLGRASS

Wilk, Wilke, Wilkes, Wilks, Wilck: *Wylke de Chyrchele* 1246 AssLa; *Wilke* 1286 AssCh; Roger *Wylk* 1279 RH (Beds); John *Wilkys* 1327 SRWo. *Wilke* may be a shortening of *Willock*. cf. DILKE.

Wilkerson: v. WILKINSON

Wilkie: David *Wilke* 1495 Black (Fife); William *Wilkie* 1529 ib.; John *Wilky* 1580 ib. A distinctively Scottish double diminutive of *William*. v. WILLIAMS.

Wilkin, Wilkins, Wilkens, Wilkings: *Wilechin* 1166 P (Nb); *Wilekinus* 1191 P (Ha), 1207 Cur (Nth); Richard, William *Wilekin* 1180 P (Ha), 1220 Cur (Lo); Roger *Wylkyns* 1327 SRSt. *Wilkin*, a diminutive of *Will*. William de Ros 1201 Cur (K) and William Chubbe 1230 P (Lo) are both also called *Wilekin*.

Wilkinson, Wilkerson: Roger *Wyleconsesone* 1332 SRSx; Thomas *Wilkynson* 1332 SRCu. 'Son of *Wilkin*.'

Wilkshire: v. WILTSHIRE

Will, Wille, Willes, Wills, Wyllys: (i) *Wille* Walt' 1207 Cur (Nf); *Wille* Bret 1212 Cur (L); Robert, William *Wille* 1279 RH (C), 1323 AssSt; Cecily *Willes* 1279 AD v (W). *Will*, a short form of *William*. (ii) John *atte Wylle* 1296 SRSx; Walter *de la Wille* 1297 MinAcctCo. 'Dweller by the spring or stream.' *v.* WELLS.

Willament, Willment: *v.* GILLMAN

Willard, Wyllarde: *Wielardus* 1086 DB (Ess); *Willardus* de Wridlint' 1121–48 Bury (Sf); *Hwylardus* de Wytherendenn c1180 ArchC vi; *Wilardus* uinitor 1192 P (Y); William, Geoffrey *Wilard* 1166, 1190 P (Nf, Wo); Nicholas *Wyþelard* 1279 RH (O); Nicholas *Wylard* 1296 SRSx; Richard *Withelard* (*Wythelard*) 1327 *SR* (Ess). OG *Widelard*. Occasionally, perhaps, OE *Wilheard. v.* WILLET.

Willcock, Willcox: *v.* WILCOCK

Willday, Willdey: *v.* WALTHEW

Willding: *v.* WILDING

Willdridge: *v.* WILDRIDGE

Willer, Willers: William *le Willer* 1327 SRSx; John *le Wylyare* 1327 MEOT (Ha); William *le Wyliere* 1332 ib.; Robert *le Wyliar* 1332 SRSx. A derivative of OE *wilige* 'basket', a basket-maker.

Willeson: *v.* WILSON

Willet, Willets, Willats, Willett, Willetts, Willitt, Willott: *Wil(l)ot* de Foxwist 1286 AssCh; Matill', Symon *Wylot* c1248 Bec, 1269 FFSf; Thomas *Wilet* 1277 AssSo; William *Wyllet, Wyllot* (identical) 1327, 1332 SRSx; Stephen *Wilotes* 1327 SRWo; Thomas *Willard* alias *Willett* 1582 FFHu. *Wilot, Wilet*, diminutives of *Will* (William). Also a late development of WILLARD, and, occasionally, a variant of WAYLATT: Aspelon *atte Wylet* 1240 FFEss.

Willford: *v.* WILFORD

Willgoss: *v.* WILDGOOSE

Willgrass, Willgress, Willgross, Wilgress: Gilbert *Wildegris* Hy 2 DC (Nt); William *Wyıdgryce* 1511 NorwW (Nf). 'Wild pig' (ON *gríss*).

Williams, Willems, Welliam, Fitzwilliam, Fitzwilliams: Robertus *filius Willelmi* 1086 DB; Richard *Willam* 1279 RH (O); John *Wylyam* 1296 SRSx; Rauf *le fuiz William* 1299 Whitby (Y); Henry *Fitz William* 1300 LoCt; Ralph *Willem, Willeam* 1304, 1315 AD vi (K); Thomas *Willames* 1307 AssSt; Robert *Williames* 1309 ib.; Thomas *William* 1327 SRSf. OG *Willihelm, Willelm*, the Norman form of Fr *Guillaume* (*v.* GILLMAN), after the Conquest the most popular christian name until superseded by *John*.

Williamson: Arnald *Williamssone* 1360 ColchCt; Roger *Williamson* 1386 NottBR. 'Son of *William*.'

Willicombe: *v.* WELCOME

Williman, Williment, Willimont: *v.* GILLMAN

Willis, Wyllys, Whillis: Walter *Willys* 1327 SRSt; Roger *Wyllys* 1438 LLB K; Richard *Willys* 1517 FFEss. Forms of WILL retaining the vowel of the genitive ending.

Willisher: *v.* WILTSHIRE

Willison: *v.* WILSON

Willman, Wilman: Symon, Adam *Willeman* 1279 RH (C), 1379 PTY. 'Servant of *Will*.' *v.* also GILLMAN.

Willmin: *v.* GILLMAN

Willmore: *v.* WILMORE

Willmot, Willmott, Willmett, Willmetts, Willimott, Wilmot, Wilmott, Wilmut: *Willimot* Ric 1 Cur (L); *Wylimot* 1306 Wak (Y); Walter *Wilimot* 1252 Rams (Hu); Henry *Wilmot* 1279 RH (C); Thomas *Wilmet* 1317 AssK. A hypocoristic of *Willelm* (William). cf. OFr *Guillemot*.

Willock, Willocks, Willox: Rannulfus *filius Willoc* 1219 AssL; William *Willoc* 1221 AssWo. OE *Willoc* (rare).

Willott: *v.* WILLET

Willoughby: Robert *de Wilgebi* 1175–84 YCh; William *de Wylugby* 1301 FFY; Thomas *Willoughby* 1449 FFEss. From Willoughby (Leics, Lincs, Notts, Warwicks).

Willows: Robert *in le Willewys* 1290 Crowland (C); John *in le Welwes* 1327 SRC. 'Dweller among the willows', OE *wylig, welig*.

Willrich: *v.* WILDRIDGE

Willshaw, Willshear, Willshire: *v.* WILTSHIRE

Willstead, Willsteed: *v.* WELLSTEAD

Wilmer, Wilmers: William, Simon *Wilmer* 1296 Wak (Y), 1327 SRC; John *Wilmer* 1374–5 AssL. OE *Wilmǣr* 'will-famous'. *v.* also WILMORE

Wilmore, Willmore: William *de Wiltemore* 1221 AssWo; Thomas *de la Wildemore* 1275 MELS (Wo); William *de Wyldemor* 1327 SRSt; John *atte Wildemor'* 1327 MELS (Wo). From Wildmore (Lincs), Wildmore in Belbroughton (Worcs), or 'dweller by the waste fen'.

Wilsham: Robert *de Wylesham, de Wylsham* 1296, 1332 SRSx lived at Wilson's Cross in Ashburnham (Sussex). There is also a Wilsham in Devon, *Willmersham* 1426.

Wilshaw, Wilsher, Wilshere, Wilshire: *v.* WILTSHIRE

Wilson, Willeson, Willison, Willson: Robert *Willeson* 1324 Wak (Y); Robert *Wilson* 1341 Kirkstall (Y); John *Willison* 1366 SRLa. 'Son of *Will*', i.e. William. Surnames derived from Wilson (Devon, Leics) may have contributed to the frequency of this name.

Wiltcher: *v.* WILTSHIRE

Wilthew: *v.* WALTHEW

Wilton: Gerald *de Wiltune* 1066 DB (W); Hugh, Walter *de Wilton* 1162 P, 1273 IpmW; John *Wilton* 1390 FFEss. From Wilton (Cumb, Hereford, Norfolk, Som, Wilts, ER, NRYorks).

Wiltshire, Wiltshear, Wiltsher, Wiltshier, Wiltshaw, Wilcher, Wilshaw, Wilsher, Wilshere, Wilshire, Wilkshire, Willisher, Willshaw, Willshear, Willsher, Willshere, Willshire: Hunfr' *de Wilechier*, *de Wilecher* 1157, 1162 P (Sx); Nicholas *de Wiltesir'* 1207 Cur (W); Robert *Wylchar* 1275 SRWo; John *Wilteshire* 1298 *Ct* (Ha); William *Wylkeshire* 1440 LLB K; Richard *Wylshyre* 1456 Oriel (O); Thomas *Wylshere* 1483 FFC; Nathaniel *Wilksheire* 1674 HTSf; William *Willshaw* 1758 FrY. From Wiltshire.

Wimbolt: *v.* WINBOLT

Wimmer, Wimmers: John *filius Winemeri* 1187 P (K); Hamo *filius Wymer'* 1219 AssY; William *Wymer* 1230 Cur (St); Richard, Roger *Winemer*

1279 RH (C); Henry *Wymer* 1301 CorNth. OE
*Winemǣr 'friend-famous'.

Wimpenny: *v.* WINPENNY

Wimple: cf. John *le Wymppelwebbe* 1325 AD ii
(Herts); Simon (*le*) *Wimpler* 1183–4 P (Nth).
Wimple is OE *wimpel* 'veil' and is metonymic for a
weaver or maker of wimples.

Winbolt, Wimbolt, Winbow: *Winebaldus* 1195 P
(Nth); *Winebold*' 1197 P (Y); John *Winebald* 1210
P (Nf); Geoffrey *Wynebaud* 1229 Cl (W). OE
Winebeald 'friend-bold'.

Wincer: *v.* WINDSOR

Winch, Wynch, Wink, Winks: (i) William *de la
Winche* 1275 SRWo; Stephen *atte Wynke* 1327
SRSo; Thomas *atte Wynche* 1332 SRWo. OE
wince 'winch, pulley' later developed the meanings
'well-wheel' and 'well'. In place-names it has been
taken to mean 'a sharp bend in a river or valley'.
Hence, 'dweller by the well from which the water
is drawn by a winch' or 'dweller in a bend'. (ii)
Walter *Winch* 1184 P (C); William *Wynk* 1312
FFSf; William *le Wynch* 1327 SRSx. A nickname
from the lapwing, recorded as OE *hlēapewince*,
from its leaping, twisted flight.

Winchcombe, Winchecombe: Vincent *de Winche-
cumbe* 1207 Pl (O); Richard *de Wynchecoumbe*,
John *Wynchecombe* 1351, 1382 AssLo. From
Winchcombe (Glos).

Winchester: Odo *de Wincestre* 1086 DB (Ha);
William *de Wyncestre* 1286 IpmY; John *Wyn-
chestre* 1360 IpmGl. From Winchester (Hants).

Wind, Wynde: (i) Walter *Winde* 1197 P (Ess);
Geoffrey *Wynd* 1230 P (Hu); Clement *le Wynd*
1327 *SR* (Ess). OE *wind*, a nickname for one speedy
as the wind. cf. Richard *Wyndswyft* 1301 SRY. (ii)
John *de Wynd* 1268 Whitby (Y); William *de la
Wynde* 1275 RH (Sx); Roger *atte Wynde* 1285 *Ass*
(Ess); John *in ye Wyndde* 1297 SRY. 'Dweller by
the winding path or ascent', OE (*ge*)*wind*.

Windebank, Windibank: Henry *de Wyndibonk*
c1300 WhC (La); Robert *del Wyndybankes* 1315
Wak (Y). 'Dweller on the windy hill.'

Windell, Windle: Alan *de Windhull*', *de Windul*
1201 P, 1242 Fees (La); Walter *del Wyndhel* 1327
SRSf; Richard *atte Wyndhull* 1327 *SR* (Ess).
'Dweller on the windy hill', as at Windhill
(WRYorks) or Windle (Lancs).

Winder: Richard, John *le Winder*(*e*) 1275, 1276
RH (L, D). A derivative of OE *windan* 'to wind',
probably a winder of wool.

Winders, Windes: *v.* WINDUS

Windham, Wyndham: Thomas *de Wymundeham*,
de Wymondham 1261–2 FFEss, 1305 LoCt; Robert
de Wyndeham 1327 SRSx; Ralph *Wyndeham* 1332
SRSx. From Wymondham (Leics, Norfolk).

Windmill, Winmill: Isabella *atte Wyndmylle* 1366
Oseney (O). 'Dweller or worker at a windmill.'

Windows: *v.* WINDUS

Windridge: *Wenric* 1066 DB (Gl); Goduine
Uuenric c1095 Bury (Sf); Margrett *Wyndrych* 1524
SRSf. OE *Wynrīc* 'joyful-ruler'.

Windsor, Wincer, Winser, Winsor, Winzer:
Godfrey *de Windelesor* 1066 Winton (Ha); Regi-

nald *de Windesor*' 1130 P (Bk). From Windsor
(Berks) or Little Windsor and Broadwindsor
(Dorset).

Windus, Windows, Winders, Windes: William *de
Wyndhows* 1379 PTY; Thomas *Wyndhouse* 1431
FrY; William *Wyndowes* 1458 ib.; William *Wyndes*
1530 ib.; the last three, all weavers. 'Worker at the
winding-house' (for threads, yarn, etc.). cf.
WINDER.

Wine, Wines, Wyne, Wynes, Wyness: Osketel
Wine 1199 P (Sf); Thomas *le Wyne* 1296 SRSx.
OE *wine* 'friend'.

Winfarthing: Thomas *de Wynneferthyn* 1279 RH
(C). From Winfarthing (Norfolk).

Winfield, Wingfield: Nicholas *de Wynefeld*' 1228
Cur (Beds); Richard *de Winfeld* 1274 RH (Nb);
John *de Wingefeld* 1343 FFY; Robert *Wyngefeld*
1465 Past. From Wingfield (Beds, Derby, Suffolk),
the first two *Winfeld* c1200, *Winefeld* DB.

Wingar, Winger: *Winegar* 1182–1211 BuryS
(Sf); Henry *Wyngar* 1251 Rams (Hu); William
Wyneger 1327 SRSf. OE *Winegār* 'friend-spear',
found as the name of an East Anglian moneyer
and in an 11th-century place-name.

Wingard: *v.* WINYARD

**Wingate, Wingett, Whinyates, Wynniatt, Wyn-
yates:** Aldret *de Windegate* c1145–65 Seals (Nb);
Henry *de Wingate* 1204 P (K); David *de Windyates*
1332 SRCu. 'Dweller in a windy pass' (OE **wind-
geat* 'gate for the wind'), as at Wingate (Devon,
Durham), Wingates (Northumb), and Winnats
(Derby).

Winger: *v.* WINGAR

Wingfield: *v.* WINFIELD

Wingood: *Winegod* 1066 DB (W), 1208 ChR;
Geoffrey *Winegod* 1221 *ElyA* (Hu); William
Wynegod 1276 RH (Berks). OG *Winegot*.

Wink: *v.* WINCH

Winman: *Wineman de Wanetun*' 1166 P (Nt);
Walter *Wineman, Wyneman* 1225 Pat (W), 1250
Fees (Nth); William *Wynemon* 1274 RH (Sa). OE
Winemann 'friend-man'.

Winmill: *v.* WINDMILL

Winn, Wynn, Wynne, Wynnes: Walter *Win* 1198
P (Ess); William *Wine* 1202 AssL; Robert *le Win*
1293 Fees (Db). OE *wine* 'friend'. Also a personal-
name. OE **Wine*, a short form of names like *Winebeald*, etc. *v.* WINE.

Winnery, Winrow: *v.* WHINNERAH

Winney, Winny: *Wengeue* uidua 1205 FFSf;
Robert *Wyneue*, Benedict *Wynyeue* 1327 SRSf;
John *Wyneue*, Thomas *Wynyff* 1478, 1479 SIA
xii; John *Wenef, Wyny*, Robert *Wyndyff* 1524
SRSf; Nicholas *Wynnye* 1577 Musters (Nf). OE
*Wyngeofu (f) 'joy-battle'.

Winpenny, Wimpenny: Richard *Winepeni* 1219
SaG; William *Wynpeny* 1379 PTY; John *Winpenny*
1642 PrD. 'Win penny', a nickname for one of
acquisitive habits'. cf. John *Wynnegold* 1327 SRSf,
1365 LoPleas.

Winser, Winsor: *v.* WINDSOR

Winslow, Winsloe: William *de Wynselowe* 1332
SRWa; William *Wynselawe, Wynselowe* 1370, 1372

FFEss; Robert *Wynslowe* 1525 SRSx. From Winslow (Bucks).

Winstanley, Winnstanley: Roger *de Winstanesleg'* 1212 Fees (La); Hugh *de Wynstanlegh*, *de Wynstanley* 1387 IpmLa, 1401 AssLa. From Winstanley (Lancs).

Winston, Winstone: (i) Burewold *filius Wnstani* 1066 DB; Ælfwine *filius UUenstani* 1087–98 Bury; Amice *Wynston* 1303 IpmW. OE *Wynstān* 'joystone'. (ii) Emma, Robert *de Wineston* 1205 Pl (Sf); Robert *de Wynnestone* 1298 IpmGl; Adam *de Winstone* 1317 AssK. From Winston (Durham, Suffolk, Wight), Winston in Brixton (Devon), or Winstone (Glos). (iii) In Wales used as a translation of Welsh *Trewin* 'house of *Wyn*', cf. Drogo *de Wynston*, lord of the manor of *Trewyn* 1623 Morris.

Winter, Winters, Wintour, Wynter, Wynters: *Winter* c1113 Burton (St); William, Roger *Winter* 1185 Templars (Wa), 1195 P (Berks). OE *Winter*, *Wintra*, or OG *Wintar*. Or a nickname. Medieval houses often had their walls painted with scenes from biblical history, romances, etc., or allegorical subjects such as the Wheel of Fortune or the representation of Winter 'with a sad and miserable face', which Henry III had painted over the fireplace in one of his rooms (EngLife 94).

Winterborn, Winterborne, Winterbourn, Winterbourne, Winterburn: Henry *de Winterburna* 1175 P (Do, So); James *de Winterburn'* 1230 Cur (O); John *de Wynterbourne* 1341 IpmW; William *Wynterbourne* 1372 IpmGl. From Winterborne (Dorset), Winterbourne (Berks, Wilts), or Winterburn (WRYorks).

Winterman: John *Wynterman* 1312 LLB D. 'Servant of *Winter*', or a nickname for one cold and cheerless as winter.

Winterscale, Wintersgill: William *Wynterskale* 1584 FrLeic; Robert *Winterskill* 1721 FrY; George *Wintersgill* 1739 ib. From Winterscale 'winter hut' (ON *skáli*) in Rathmell, or Winterscales in Garsdale or Ingleton (WRYorks).

Winterton: Tochus *de Wintretune* 1066 DB (Nf); Osmund *de Winterton'* 1204 Pl (L); William *Wynterton* 1379 PTY. From Winterton (Lincs, Norfolk).

Winton, Wynton: William *de Winton'* 1202 FFY; Nicholas *de Wynton'* 1277 FFEss; Richard *Wynton* 1525 SRSx. From Winton (Hants, Lancs, Westmorland, NRYorks).

Winyard, Wingard, Wynyard: Sarra *de Winiard'* 1212 Cur (Berks); Juliana *de la Wingarde* 1275 SRWo; William *ate Wyneard* 1327 SRSo. 'Worker in the vineyard' (OE *wīngeard*).

Wiper, Wypers: William *Wiper* 1202 Cur (Sx). An occupational name. The meaning is obscure but there is obviously no support for Weekley's derivation from Ypres.

Wirth: *v.* WORTH

Wiscard: *v.* WISHART

Wisdom: Durand *Wisdom* 1198 P (Ess); Gilbert *Wysdom* 1243 AssSo. OE *wīsdōm* 'wisdom, learning'. Lower derives this from an estate in Cornwood (Devon). This is Wisdome, so named in 1618,

and, possibly, earlier *Wymesdone* (PN D 271). Wisedom Fm in Drewsteignton is *Wisdoms* in 1464 (ib. 434), and is probably named from an owner called *Wisdom*. All the forms of the surname point clearly to the abstract noun.

Wise, Wyse: Johann *se Wisa* 11th OEByn; Ædwin *Wise* 1176 P (D); Roger *le Wis* 1203 P (Sx). OE *wīs* 'wise'.

Wiseman: *Wisman'* 1166 P (C); Lewin, Alexander *Wisman* 1154 Bury (Sf), 1202 AssL. OE *wīs* and *mann* 'the wise, discreet man', clearly used as a personal name. As an attribute, the meaning need not always be literal. Meanings recorded only later may have existed much earlier. The word is used ironically, applied to a fool, as in the 'wise men of Gotham'. Cf. also 'Yonge *Wyseman* othyrwyse callyd *Foole*' (1471 NED). It was also used of a man skilled in the hidden arts, as magic, witchcraft and the like, 'magician, wizard' (1382 Wycliff).

Wish: Godric *Wisce* 1087 OEByn; Hugo *Wisc* 1199 P (Nf); John *de la Wisse* 1261 PN Sx 418; William *atte Wyshe* de la Rye 1305 LLB B. From residence near a damp meadow or marsh (OE *wisc*).

Wishart, Wiskar, Wisker, Wesker, Whiscard, Whisker, Wysard, Vizard: *Wischardus* Leidet 1176 P (Beds); *Guichard* de Charrun 1270 Ipm (Nb); Walter *Wiscard*, *Wishard* 1162, 1169 P (Sr); Rannulf *Wichard'* 1212 Cur (Ess). ONFr *Wisc-(h)ard*, OFr *Guisc(h)ard*, *Guiscart*, from ON *vizkr* 'wise' and the French suffix *-(h)ard*.

Wissler: *v.* WHISTLER

Wisson: *v.* WHISSON

Wistance: *v.* WHISTANCE

Wiswall: Henry *de Wysewell* 1246 AssLa. From Wiswell (Lancs).

Witard: *v.* WHITTARD

Witchell: Perhaps OE *hwīt* and *cild* 'fair child': Alan *Wytechild*, *Whitechill* 1221 AssWo; Richard *Whitchild* 1322 FrLeic. Or from a place, as Witchells in Shirwell (Devon), *Wichehole* 1423 PN D 68.

Witcher: *v.* WHITCHER

Witcomb(e): *v.* WHITCOMB

Withacombe: *v.* WIDDECOMBE

Witham, Withams, Wittams, Whitham, Whittam, Whittome: Warin *de Whyteham* Ed 1 FFEss; Peter *de Wytham* 1295 FFEss; John *Witham* 1327 SR (Ess). From Witham (Essex, Devon, Lincs, Som).

Withecombe: *v.* WIDDECOMBE

Wither, Withers: (i) *Wither*, *Wider* 1066 DB (Nf, L); *Wyther* cognomento Turnel 1134–40 Holme (Nf); Richerus *filius Wither* 1153–68 ib.; William *Wither* c1160 Gilb (L); Robert *Wiðer* 1176 P (St); Geoffrey *Wider* 1192 P (Gl). ON *Viðarr*, ODa *Withar*. (ii) John *Wythiar'* 1327 SRSx; Thomas *le Wythier* 1332 ib. 'Dweller by the willow' (OE *wīþig*). cf. WITHEY.

Witherby: For WETHERBEE.

Witherick: *v.* WHITTERIDGE

Witheridge: Ralph *de Wyþerug'* 1279 RH (O).

From Witheridge Hill in Rotherfield Greys (Oxon). Also from Witheridge (Devon).

Witherington, Withrington: Hwylardus *de Wytherendenn* c1180 ArchC vi; Crystina *de Wytheryndenn* 1296 SRSx. From Witherenden in Ticehurst (Sussex).

Withey, Withy: Adam *de la Wythye* 1241 Abbr (So); Richard *atte Widege*, Robert *Widie* 1279 RH (O). 'Dweller by the willow' (OE *wīþig*). cf. WITHER. (ii) John *de Wythye* and Alan *atte Wythye* (1296, 1332 SRSx) lived at Withy Fm in Danehill (Sussex).

Withycombe: *v.* WIDDECOMBE
Witley: *v.* WHITELEY
Witrick: *v.* WHITTERIDGE
Witt, Witte, Witts: *v.* WHITE
Wittaker: *v.* WHITAKER
Wittamore: *v.* WHITEMORE
Wittams: *v.* WITHAM
Wittenham: *v.* WHITTINGHAM
Witterick: *v.* WHITTERIDGE
Wittey: *v.* WITTY
Wittick: *v.* WHITEWICK
Witting: *v.* WHITING
Wittman: *v.* WHITEMAN
Wittrick, Wittridge: *v.* WHITTERIDGE
Witty, Wittey: Robert *Witie*, *Wity* 1221 AssWo; Symon *Wittie* 13th Riev (Y). OE *wit(t)ig* 'sagacious, wise', also in ME 'witty'. cf. Willelmus *Fascetus* (*Facetus*) 1200 Cur (Nf). *v.* also WHITEY.
Wix: *v.* WICH
Woby: Probably for *Waudby*. *v.* WALBY.
Wod, Wode: *v.* WOOD
Wodhams: *v.* WOODHAM
Wodehouse: *v.* WOODHOUSE
Wodeman: *v.* WADEMAN
Woffenden, Woffinden, Woffindin: *v.* WOLFENDEN
Woffitt: *v.* WOOLVETT

Wogan: John *Wogan* 1292 QW (Cu); John *Wougan* 1297 MinAcctCo (Y). An anglicizing of Welsh *Gwgan*, a name found in the *Mabinogion*, a diminutive of *gwg* 'a scowl, frown'.

Wolbold: *Wlbald*, *Wlbolt* 1066 DB (Sf); *Ulbold*, *Hulboldus* c1130 ELPN; Robert *filius Wulfbalt* 1177 P (Sf); *Wulbald* 1275 RH (K); Walter *Woulbould*, John *Wolbol* 1327 SRSo. OE *Wulfbeald* 'wolf-bold', found only in the 10th and 11th centuries in OE. The surname is rare. Catherine *Woolball* was a benefactor of Walthamstow (Essex) in 1786.

Wolde: *v.* WALD
Woledge: *v.* WOOLWICH, WORLEDGE

Wolf, Wolfe, Wolfes, Woolf, Woolfe, Wulff, Woof, Wooff: Robert *Wulf* 1166 P (L); John *le Wolf* 1279 RH (Beds). A nickname from the wolf (OE *wulf*), often latinized as *Lupus* and found in the French forms *Lou* and *Love*. *v.* LOW, LOVE. The derivation from OE *Wulf* is very doubtful. This personal name is late and not common in OE and Redin doubts if any of the examples are really native. ON *Úlfr* was not uncommon and has survived. *v.* ULPH. But *Wolf* as a surname is very

seldom without the article *le* in the 13th and 14th centuries. The frequency of the surname, and some of its forms, are due to recent immigrants from Germany.

Wolfarth: *v.* WOOLLARD
Wolfendale: Richard *Woofendall*, *Woffendale* 1675 RothwellPR (Y). Perhaps a dialectal pronunciation of *Wolfenden*, a name not uncommon in Leeds and Bradford.
Wolfenden, Woolfenden, Woffenden, Woffendon, Woffinden, Woffindin, Wooffinden: James *Wolfenden* 1614 Bardsley. From Wolfenden in Newchurch-in-Rossendale (Lancs), earlier *Wolfhamdene*.
Wolfin: *v.* WOOLVEN
Wolfit: *v.* WOOLVETT
Wolfner: *v.* WOOLNER
Wolford, Wolforth, Wolfoot: *v.* WOOLLARD
Wolfram: *Vluerona* uxor Vlf 1130 P (L); Ralph *filius Wlfrun* 1209 Pl (Nf); John *Wulfrun* 1230 Cur (Sr); Thomas *Woulfran* 1297 MinAcctCo (O); Alice *Wolfroun* 1332 SRSr. OE *Wulfrūn* (f).
Wolfryd: *v.* WOOLFREY
Woll: *v.* WOOLL
Wollan: *v.* WOOLLAND
Wollard: *v.* WOOLLARD
Wollas: *v.* WOOLHOUSE
Wolledge: *v.* WOOLWICH, WORLEDGE
Wollen: *v.* WOOLLAND
Woller: *v.* WOOLLER
Wollerton: *v.* WOOLERTON
Wollett: *v.* WOOLVETT
Wolley: *v.* WOOLLEY
Wollman, Wolman: *v.* WOOLMAN
Wollmer: *v.* WOOLMER
Wolpole: *v.* WALPOLE
Wolrich, Wolrige: *v.* WOOLRICH
Wolseley, Wolsley, Woosley: William *de Wulfsieslega* 1177 P (St); Robert *de Wolsleg* 1285 FA (St). From Wolseley (Staffs).
Wolsey: *v.* WOOLSEY
Wolstencroft, Wolstoncroft, Woolstencroft, Worsencroft, Worstencroft, Wosencroft, Wozencroft: Thomas *Wustyncrofte*, John *Wustencroft* 1524 SRSf; James *Wolsoncroft* 1584 Bardsley; Thomas *Worsencroft* 1610 ib.; William *Woolstencroft* 1613 ib.; John *Wossencroft* 1635 ib. From Wolstancroft (Lancs).
Wolstenholme, Wolstanholme, Wolstenhulme, Woolstenhulme, Worstenholme, Wostenholm, Wusteman, Woosnam, Woosman, Worsman: Andrew *de Wolstanesholm* 13th WhC (La). From Wolstenholme in Rochdale (Lancs).
Wolston: *v.* WOOLSTON
Wolters: *v.* WALTER
Wolton: *v.* WOOLTON
Wolveridge: *v.* WOOLRICH
Wolverton: *v.* WOOLVERTON
Wolvey: (i) Robert *de Wlueia* 1200 P (Wa); Maurice *ate Wolfaghe* 1327 SRSx; Roger *Wolfey* 1327 *SR* (Ess). From Wolvey (Warwicks), or 'man in charge of the enclosure to protect flocks from wolves' (OE *wulfhaga*), or 'wolf-trapper'. (ii)

Robertus *filius Wulfiue* 1193 P (Nf); Willelmus *filius Wulveve* 1279 RH (C); Hardwin *Wuluiue* 1205 P (Nf); Isabella *Wolfueue* 1327 SRSf. OE *Wulfgifu* (f) 'wolf-gift'. *v.* WOOLWAY.

Wombwell, Wombell, Woombell, Woombill, Woomble, Womwell: Reiner *de Wambewell'* 1219 AssY; William *Wombell* 1666 FrY. From Wombwell (WRYorks).

Wood, Woodd, Woode, Woods, Wod, Wode: (i) Walter *de la Wode* 1242 Fees (He); John *del Wode* 1274 Wak (Y); John *Atewode* 1274 RH (Ess); John *I the Wode*, Gilbert *a la Wode* 1275 SRWo; Elias *in le Wode* 1279 RH (C); Alexander *of the Wode* 1285 AssLa; John *at the Wode* 1293 Fees (D); William *Bythewode* 1296 SRSx; Richard *dilwod* 1327 Pinchbeck (Sf). From residence in or near a wood. (ii) Adam *le Wode* 1221 AssWo; Richard *Wod* 1230 P (So); William *le Wod* 1275 RH (Do). OE *wōd*, ME *wod(e)*, wood 'frenzied, wild'. Much less common than the local origin. cf. Shakespeare's 'And heere am I, and *wood* within this wood'.

Woodall: *v.* WOODHALL

Woodard, Huddart: (i) *Wudardus* de Rosshebrok 1148–56 Bury (Sf); Johannes *filius Wdardi* 1166 RBE (Nb), *filius Wudardi* 1168 P (W); Willelmus *filius Vdard'* 1181 P (Cu); *Udardus* de Karelton 1214 Cur (Nt); Walterus *filius Wodard* 1227 Pat (Sf); Walter *Wudard* 1221 AssWa; William *Hudard* Hy 3 Colch (Sf); John *Wodard* 1279 RH (C). OE **Wuduheard*, unrecorded in OE, but regularly formed of the themes *wudu* 'wood' and *heard* 'hard'. (ii) Richard *le Wodehirde* 1275 RH (Nf); Robert *le Wodehirde* 1325 FFSf. OE *wudu* 'wood' and *hierde* 'herd', one who tends animals feeding in a wood; probably a swineherd.

Woodcock, Woodcocks: William *Wdecoch'* 1175 P (Nf); Roger *Wudecoc* 1176 P (Herts); William *Widecoc* 1200 FFEss; Nicholas *Wodecok* 1288 AssCh. A nickname from the bird, OE *wuducocc* 'woodcock', later used to mean 'a fool, simpleton, dupe'. The frequency of this surname is probably partly due to the absorption of a local surname *Woodcot*: Richard *de Wdecote* 1198 FF (O); Adam *de Wudecota* 1193 P (Sa); Henry, Thomas *at(t)e Wodecote* 1327 SRSx, 1332 SRWo, from Woodcote (Hants, Oxon, Salop, Surrey, Warwicks), Woodcott (Ches, Hants), or from residence at a cottage in or near a wood.

Woodcraft, Woodcroft: Ascelinus *de Wudecroft* 1162 P (Nth). 'Dweller at a croft by a wood' (OE *wudu, croft*).

Wooddin: *v.* WOODING

Wooddisse: *v.* WOODHOUSE, WOODIWISS

Woodell: A weakening of *Woodhall, Woodhill* or *Woodwell*: Michael *Woodhill* 1693 FrY; William *Woodwill* son of Michael *Woodell* 1721 ib.; William *Woodell* son of William *Woodell* 1755 ib.; all cordwainers.

Woodend, Woodsend: Clarcia *de la Wodeande* 1260 FFEss; Adam *de Wodeshende* 1273 RH (Do); Robert *de la Wode ende* 1275 SRWo. 'Dweller at the end of the wood'. cf. TOWNEND.

Wooder: Andrew, Geoffrey *le Wodere* 1275 RH (Sx), 1280 AssSo. OE *wudere* 'wood-man, wood-carrier'. *v.* also WADER.

Wooders: *v.* WOODHOUSE

Woodey: (i) Thomas *de la Wdhaye* 1275 RH (L); Robert *atte Wodeheye* 1333 MELS (So). 'Dweller by the enclosure in the wood', OE *wudu, (ge)hæg.* (ii) Roger *Wody* 1255 RH (Sa); Geoffrey *Wody* 1275 RH (Nth); Richard *le Wodye* 1296 SRSx; John *Woodye* 1568 SRSf. This seems to have been more common in ME than (i) and is apparently ME **wody*, a derivative of ME *wod*, wood, from OE *wōd* 'frenzied, wild', formed on the analogy of *moody, mighty.* cf. WOOD.

Woodfall: Gilbert *de Wudefalde* 1193 P (Ess); Richard *de Wodefalle* 1285 AssLa 'Dweller by a fold in the wood' as at Woodfalls (Wilts), *Wude-folde* 1258 PN W 398, or at a place where trees have fallen, as at Woodfall Hall (Lancs), *Wudefal* a1230 PN La 109.

Woodford, Woodforde, Woodfords: (i) Daniel *de Wudeford'* 1196 P (O); Geoffrey *de Wodeford* 1327 SRSo; William *Wodeford* 1423 FFEss. From Woodford (Ches, Cornwall, Essex, Northants, Wilts). (ii) Jordan *de Wodford* c1170 Black; Robert *de Wodforde, de Vodford* 1296, c1330 ib. From Woodford in St. Boswells (Roxburgh).

Woodfull: *Wudefugel* 1195 P (Y), 1196 P (Nth); Avice, Robert *Wodefoul* 1279 RH (Bk), 1311 RamsCt (Hu). OE *wudu-fugol* 'a bird of the woods', perhaps a nickname, but certainly used as a personal-name like *Sǣfugul.* *v.* SAFFELL.

Woodgate, Woodgates, Woodget, Woodgett, Woodjetts, Woodyatt: William *de Wudegat'* 1199 Cur (Do); Walter *de Wodiate* 1208 Cur (Do); Aluric *de la Wdegate* 1222 DBStP (Ess); Martin *atte Wodegate* 1296 SRSx; William *Wodiet* 1328 AD i (Bk); John *atte Wodeyate* 1332 SRWa. From Woodyates (Dorset) or residence by the gate to the wood (OE *wudu, geat*). *Woodgett* shows the same development of *di* as in *soldier.*

Woodger: *v.* WOODIER

Woodgett: *v.* WOODGATE

Woodhall, Woodall: Peter *de Wudehale* 1193 P (L); Jordan *de la Wodehalle* c1265 Calv (Y); John *del Wodhall* 1332 SRCu; Alice *atte Wode-halle* 1332 MELS (Sr). 'Dweller (or servant) at the hall in the wood.'

Woodham, Woodhams, Wodhams: Alexander *de Wudeham* 1170 P (Ess); Thomas *ate Wodehamme* 1332 SRSr; Thomas *Wodeham* 1351 AssEss. From Woodham (Essex, Surrey), **Wuduhām* 'village in the wood', or 'dweller at the enclosure in the wood', **Wuduhamm.*

Woodhatch: Robert *atte Wodehacche* 1369 MELS (Sr). 'Dweller by, or keeper of the gate to the wood', OE *wudu, hæcc*, as at Woodhatch (Essex, Surrey).

Woodhead: Edward *de Wodheved* 1243 AssSo; Christiana *del Wodeheved* 1316 Wak (Y); Isabel *Wodhed* 1440 ShefA (Y). 'Dweller at the head or top of the wood' (OE *hēafod*), as at Woodhead (Devon, WRYorks).

Woodhouse, Wodehouse, Woodus, Wooders, Wooddisse: Helias *de Wudehus* 1170 P (Nt); Richard *del Wodehus* 1275 RH (Sf); Geoffrey *Wodehus* 1276 RH (Y); Roger *ate Wodehose*, Thomas *Wodehose* 1332 SRSr; Walter *atte Wodehous* 1332 SRSt; Thomas *Wodehouse* or *Wodesse* 1509 Ewen. 'Dweller at the house in the wood.' Woodhouse Fm in Upper Arley (Worcs) is *Woddus* 1387 PN Wo 33. *v.* WIDDOWES.

Woodier, Woodyear, Woodyer, Woodger: Robert *le Wodehyewere* 1301 ParlR (Ess); Walter *le Wodehewer* 1309 SRBeds; Richard *Woodyere* 1605 Oxon; John *Woodger* 1663 Bardsley. OE *wuduhēawere* 'hewer of wood, wood-cutter'. For *Woodger*, cf. WOODGATE, GOODGER.

Wooding, Woodings, Wooddin, Woodin, Wooden: William *Woding* 1247 AssBeds; Richard *atte Woding* 1294 MELS (Wo); Abram *Woodinge*, Daniel *Wooden* 1674 HTSf. 'Dweller at a place where wood has been cut', OE **wudung* 'cutting of wood'. The first example, without a preposition, though not without parallels at this date, may be a nickname from OE **wōding*, from *wōd* 'mad', 'the mad one'.

Woodiwiss, Wooddisse, Widdiwiss: Robert *de* (sic) *Wudewuse* 1251 AssY. OE *wuduwāsa* 'faun, satyr'. cf. 'Wodewese (woodwose). *Silvanus, satirus*' PromptParv.

Woodjetts: *v.* WOODGATE

Woodlake: Turstin *filius Wudelach'* 1180 P (W); Goduine *Udelac* c1095 Bury (Sf); John *Wdeloch* 1225–50 Dublin. OE **Wudulāc*, an addition to the rare compounds of *Wudu-*. Roger *Wudeloc* 1245 Ct (Ha) gave name to Woodlark Fm in Bighton (Hants).

Woodland, Woodlands: Henry *de Wudeland'* 1195 P (L); William *Wudeland'* 1214 Cur (Sx); Thomas *atte Wodelond* 1327 SRSo. 'Dweller by the woodland.'

Woodley, Woodleigh: Ælfnoð *æt Wudeleage* 1008–12 OEByn (D); Osbert *de Wudeleg'* 1199 P (D); Walter *de Wodeleye* 1332 SRWo; Richard *Wodle* 1384 IpmGl. From Woodleigh (Devon), or 'dweller at a glade in the wood'.

Woodman: *Vdeman, Odeman* 1066 DB; *Wudemann* 1066–75 ASWrits; *Wdemannus* Hy 2 AD i (Nth); Hugo *Wudeman* 1166 P (Y); John *Wodeman* 1213 Cur (Do); Nicholas *le Wodeman* 1294 AssSt. OE *Wudumann*, from **wudumann* 'woodman', also used as an occupational name.

Woodriff, Woodriffe: This surname is probably from OE *wudurife* 'woodruff'. *v.* WOODROFF. It is just possible it may be for *wood-reeve*: Philip *Wodereve* 1253 AssSo (1579 NED). This is rare and no modern example has been noted, although Harrison gives *Woodreefe, Woodreeve* and *Woodreve*.

Woodroff, Woodroffe, Woodroof, Woodroofe, Woodrooffe, Woodrough, Woodruff, Woodruffe, Woodrup: *Wuderoua* 1170 P (Wa); Hugo *Wderoue* 1185 Templars (L); Robert *Woderove* 1225 AssSo; John *Woderofe* 1419 DbAS 36. OE *wudurofe* 'woodruff'. cf. 'Woderove, herbe. *Hasta regia,*

hastula, ligiscus.' It was formerly a custom for women to carry woodruff, because of its sweet smell, with their prayer-books to church. 'The woodruff is also called *sweet woodruff* because of its strongly sweet-scented leaves. This may account for the nickname. It may have been given to a person who used perfumes, or the nicknames may be ironical' (ELPN 172). The usual etymology from 'wood-reeve' finds no support in the above forms.

Woodrow: William *Woderowe* 1260 AssC; Juliana *de Woderoue*, William, Matilda *Woderoue* 1296 SRSx. The last three were assessed in the same parish. OE *wudu* 'wood' and *rāw* 'row', probably from residence in a row of cottages in a wood. Also probably from Woodrow (Wilts, Worcs).

Woodsend: *v.* WOODEND

Woodside: Robert *del Wodsid* 1332 SRCu. 'Dweller by the wood-side.'

Woodus: *v.* WOODHOUSE

Woodward: Sewhal *le wudeward* 1208 P (Ha); Ralph *de* (sic) *Wodeward* 1230 P (Herts); Robert *Wodeward* 1296 SRSx. OE *wuduweard* 'forester'. Henry the reeve (*prepositus*) is also called *le wudeward'* 1221 AssWa.

Woodyatt: *v.* WOODGATE

Woodyear, Woodyer: *v.* WOODIER

Woof(f): *v.* WOLF

Wooffinden: *v.* WOLFENDEN

Wooland: *v.* WOOLLAND

Woolard: *v.* WOOLLARD

Woolas(s): *v.* WOOLHOUSE

Woolaway: *v.* WOOLWAY

Woolbar: Probably a corruption of WOLBOLD.

Woolbridge: *v.* WOOLL

Wooldridge: *v.* WOOLRICH

Wooler: *v.* WOOLLER

Woolerton, Wollerton, Woolloton: Robert *de Wuluriton'* 1221 AssSa. From Wollerton (Salop).

Wooles: *v.* WOOLL

Wooley: *v.* WOOLLEY

Woolf(e): *v.* WOLF

Woolfall: John *de la Wulfhal* 1242 FFLa; Robert *de Wolfalle* 1332 SRLa. From Wolfall Hall in Huyton (Lancs) or Wolf Hall in Grafton (Wilts).

Woolfenden: *v.* WOLFENDEN

Woolfield: Richard *Wolfild* 1334 SRK. OE *Wulfhild* (f) 'wolf-war', recorded four times in the 10th and 11th centuries but, though rare, must have survived the Conquest.

Woolfit: *v.* WOOLVETT

Woolford(e), Woolfoot: *v.* WOOLLARD

Woolfrey, Woolfries, Wolfryd: *Vlfert, Vluert* 1066 DB (D, So); Thomas *Wulfrith* 1260 AssC; William *Wlfrið* 1279 RH (C); John *Wolfrith*, Matilda *Woulfryth* 1297 MinAcctCo. OE *Wulfrið* 'wolf-peace'.

Woolgar, Woolger: *Wlgar, Vlgar* 1066 DB; *Wlfgarus de Cokesale* 1252 Colch (Ess); Brixi *Wulgar* 1188 P (Nf); Teobald *Wolgar* c1250 Rams (C). OE *Wulfgār* 'wolf-spear'.

Woolham: *v.* WOOLLAND

Woolhouse, Woolas, Woolass, Wollas, Wholehouse: Malyn *del Wllehus* 1277 Wak (Y); Ralph *del Wolehouse* 1301 SRY; John *Wllehous, Wollehous* 1377 ColchCt. 'Worker at the wool-(ware) house' (OE *wull, hūs*).

Woolich, Woolidge: v. WOOLWICH, WORLEDGE

Wooll, Woolls, Wooles, Woll: John *de Wolle* 1296 SRSx; Henry *atte Wolle* 1327 SRSx; Thomas, Alan *atte Wulle* 1327 SRSo, 1332 SRSr. 'Dweller by the spring or stream.' In the southwest, particularly in Dorset, OE *wielle, wyll* became ME *wull, woll*, instead of *well*, and this survives in Wool and in Wool Bridge in East Stoke which gave rise to a surname *Wullebrigg* in 1244 (PN Do 145). The same development has been noted in Somerset, West Sussex and West Surrey.

Woollage: v. WOOLWICH, WORLEDGE

Woollam(s): v. WOOLLAND

Woolland, Woollan, Woollon, Woollons, Woollen, Wooland, Woolen, Wollan, Wollen, Woollam, Woollams, Woolham: Samuel *Woolons* 1637 FrY; John *Woolland* 1674 HTSf. 'Dweller by the curved or crooked land(s)' (OE *wōh, land*). cf. Woollensbrook (PN Herts 212): *la Wowelond* 1235, *Wowlondes* 1466, *Woolans brook* 1689, *Woollens* c1840; Woolens Copse in Damerham, *Wolonde* (1518 PN W 402); *Woulond* 1230 PN C 335; and v. also Woolland (PN Do 192). This is a type of placename likely to be common and accounts for all the forms. The final *n*, as often, became *m*, giving *Woollam*, and this was re-spelled *Woolham* on the analogy of names in *-ham*. No such place as *Woolham* is known. The occasional *-s* is from the plural, *-lands*.

Woollard, Woolard, Woolatt, Wollard, Woolward, Wolfarth, Wolford, Wolforth, Woolford, Woolforde, Woolfoot: (i) *Wluuard, Vluuard* 1066 DB; *Wluerdus* Legredere 1188 BuryS (Sf); Robertus *filius Wolfward* 1212 Fees (Sr); *Wulford* atte Heghelonde 1275 RH (K); Martin *Wlward* 1199 FFC; Richard *Wulward* 1206 P (Hu); Matilda *Woleward* 1275 SRWo; Robert *Wlfard, Wulvard* 1279 RH (O, C); Ralph *Wolford* 1317 AssK; John *Woolat* 1674 HTSf. OE *Wulfweard* 'wolf-ward'. (ii) Robert *de Wlfward* 1210 P (Wa); Engerram *de Wolward*' 1212 Cur (Wa). From Wolford (Warwicks).

Wooler, Wooler, Woller: William *le Woller*' 1319 *SR* (Ess); John *Woller* 1327 SRSo. A derivative of OE *wull* 'wool', a dresser, weaver or seller of wool. cf. Thomas *le Wollestere* 1297 Wak (Y), where we have the feminine form. In John *Wollore* 1430 FrY, the name derives from Wooler (Northumb), *Wulloure* 1187 DEPN.

Woollet, Woollett: v. WOOLVETT

Woolley, Wooley, Wolley: *Hugo de Wuluele* 1219 AssY; Ralph *de Wullueleye* 1230 P (Berks); Roger *de Wolvele* 1279 RH (O); Nicholas *de Wolveleye* 1280 AssSt; Bate *de Wolflay* 1308 Wak (Y); Robert *de Woluelie* 1327 SRSx; John *de Wolley* 1332 SRSt. From Woolley (Berks, Devon, Hunts, Wilts, WRYorks) or Woolfly Fm in Henfield (Sussex), all 'wolves' wood', or lost places of

the same name, or from Wooley in Slaley (Northumb), *Ulflawe* 1296 'wolf-hill', or from Woolley (Som), *Wilege* DB 'clearing by a stream'. cf. WOOLL.

Woollon(s): v. WOOLLAND

Woolloton: v. WOOLVERTON

Woollston: v. WOOLSTON

Woollven, Woollvern, Woollvin: v. WOOLVEN

Woolman, Wolman, Wollman: William *Wolleman* 1351 AssEss; Richard *Woolman* 1674 HTSf. OE *wull* 'wool' and *mann*, a dealer in wool, a wool-merchant (1390 NED).

Woolmer, Woolmore, Wollmer, Ullmer: (i) *Wlmer, Vlfmer, Wlmar* 1066 DB; *Ulmer Æltredes* c1095 Bury (Sf); *Wlfmerus* filius Sirici 1101–7 Holme (Nf); *Wulmarus* Lamb 1230 P (Nf); William *Wulmare* 1260 AssC; Reginald *Wlmer* 1263 Rams (Hu). OE *Wulfmær* 'wolf-famous'. (ii) Richard *de Wulvemor*, Robert *de Wullemore* 1246 AssLa. This is from a lost *Wolmoor* in Ormskirk (Lancs) 'wolves' moor'. The surname may also derive from Woolmer Forest (Hants), Wolmer Fm in Ogbourne St George (Wilts), or Woolmore Fm in Melksham (Wilts), all 'wolves' pool'.

Woolner, Woolnoth, Woolnough, Wolfner: *Wlnod, Vlnoth, Vlnoht* 1066 DB; Godwine *Hulnodi filius* c1095 Bury (Sf); *Wulnoth* Koc 1296 SRSx; William *Wulnoð* 1221 ElyA (Sf); Ranolph *Wollenoth* 1284 RamsCt (Hu); Robert *Wolthnoth* 1327 SRSf; Thomas *Wolnoth* 1348 FFSf; William *Vlnawgh* son of Mawt *Vlnaugh*, William *Wulnow*, Richard *Wulnaw* 1524 SRSf; Edmund *Wolner* 1524 SRSf; Margaret *Woollnoth* 1525 SIA xii; John *Woolnough*, Francis *Woolnoe*, Henry *Woolner* 1674 HTSf. OE *Wulfnōð* 'wolf-boldness', a personal name which, though not common, remained in use until the beginning of the 14th century. As with *Elnough*, from *Æðelnōð*, the form *Woolnough* probably reflects the dialectal sound change of *ð* to *f*. v. OEByn 170. The *-er* of *Woolner* and *Wolfner* represents the pronunciation of unaccented *-nough*. cf. ALLNATT.

Woolrich, Woolrych, Wooldridge, Woolridge, Wolrich, Wolrige, Wolryche, Wolveridge, Woolveridge, Woolwright, Ullrich, Ulrich, Ulrik: *Wlfric, Vlfric* 1066 DB; *Uluric* Stanilde filius c1095 Bury (Sf); *Wlricus* filius Actman 1198 Cur (K); William *Wulfric* 1212 Cur (Berks); William *Wlwrith* 1242 Rams (C); Ralph *Wolfrich* 1250 Fees (Sr); Robert *Wolfrick, Wolurich* 1279 RH (O); Robert *Wulrich* 1286 AssSt; Robert *Wolvrych* 1296 SRSx; Richard *Wolrich* 1307 AssSt; Ralph *Wolverych* 1318 AD vi (Berks); Robert *Wolryge* 1332 SRSt; John *Woldrych* 1524 SRSf; John *Wooldridge* 1663 SfPR. OE *Wulfrīc* 'wolf-powerful', a personal name fairly common after the Conquest.

Woolsey, Wolsey, Woosey: (i) Leofwine *Wulfsiges sunu* a1038 OEByn (Ha); *Wlsi, Vlsi* 1066 DB; *Willelmus* filius *Wulsi* (*Wlfsi*) 1166 P (Nf); William *Wulsy* 1219 AssY; Richard *Wolsy* 1313 FFEss; Robert *Wulcy, Wolcye* 1524 SRSf. OE *Wulfsige* 'wolf-victory'. The personal name was common in Suffolk where it gave rise to the surname of Cardinal Wolsey. (ii) Roger *Wulfesege*, *Wulfes æge* 1168, 1171 P (Ha); Waldevus *Wulfesega* 1176 P (Nb). A nickname, 'wolf's eye', which may have contributed to the frequency of the surname.

Woolstencroft: *v.* WOLSTENCROFT

Woolstenhulme: *v.* WOLSTENHOLME

Woolston, Woolstone, Woollston, Wolston: (i) *Vlfstan, Wlstan, Vlstan* 1066 DB; Ordric *Uulfstani filius* c1095 Bury (Sf); *Wlston* 1188 BuryS (Sf); Gilbert *Wlstan* 1199 P (L); Ralph *Wolstan* 1212 Cur (Nf). OE *Wulfstān* 'wolf-stone'. (ii) Hugelot *de Wolueston'* 1131 FeuDu; William *de Wolstone* 1279 RH (Bk). The surname may also be local in origin, from several places of varied origin: Wolston (Warwicks), *Ulvricetone* DB; Woolston (Devon), *Ulsiston* DB; (Lancs), *Wolueston* 1242; (Hants), *Oluestune* DB; Woolston in North Cadbury (Som), *Wolston* 1316; Woolston in Bicknoller (Som), *Wolwardeston* 1225; Woolston Hall in Chigwell (Essex), *Ulfelmestuna* DB; Woolstone (Bucks), *Wlsiestone* DB; or Wolviston (Durham), locally pronounced *Wooston*.

Woolterton, Wooltorton: Walter *de Wulterton'* 1220 Cur (Nf). From Wolterton (Norfolk).

Woolton, Wolton: John *de Wulton'* 1180 P (Lei); John *de Woleton* 1241 FFK; Thomas *de Wolton* 1382 IpmGl. From Woolton (Lancs).

Woolven, Woollven, Woollvern, Woollvin, Wolfin, Woollen, Woollin, Woollings, Woollon, Woollons: *Wluuine, Vlfuuinus, Vluuin* 1066 DB; Lefstan *Ulfuini filius* c1095 Bury (Sf); *Wlfwinus Holepot* 1182–1211 BuryS (Sf); *Wolvin* Cote 1340 Husting; Nicholas *Wolwin* c1236 Seals (W); William *Wulwyne* 1296 SRSx; John *Wolvyne* 1328 LLB E; Richard *Woluen* 1381 PTY. OE *Wulfwine* 'wolf-friend'.

Woolveridge: *v.* WOOLRICH

Woolverton, Wolverton: Of varied local origin. Nicholas *de Wulferton'* 1166 P (Nf), from Wolferton (Norfolk); Tomas *de Wulfrinton'* 1190 P (Sa), from Wollerton (Salop); Vivian *de Wluerton'* 1200 P (Bk), from Wolverton (Bucks); Alina *de Wulwardinton'* 1221 AssWa, from Wolverton (Warwicks); Richard *de Wulfrinton'* 1221 AssWo, from Wolverton (Worcs); or from Wolverton (Hants) or Woolverton (Som).

Woolvett, Woolfit, Woollatt, Woollet, Woollett, Wolfit, Wollett, Ullett, Ulliott, Ullyatt, Ullyett, Ullyott, Ulyate, Ulyatt, Ulyett, Woffitt: *Wluiet, Wluiat, Vlfiet, Vluiet* 1066 DB; *Wlfgiet* 1066 InqEl; Goduuin *Ulfgeti filius* c1095 Bury (Sf); *Vlfgiet Moder* 1162 P (Nth); *Wulfiet Mus* 1176 P (Nt); *Wulfet de Branwic'*, Thoroldus *filius Wulfat* 1219 AssY; Johannes *filius Wulfoti* 1223 Pat (Y); Leuricus *Wlfuiet*, Eudo *Wluiet* 1199 P (L, Nf); Robert *Woluyet* 1306 FFEss; Robert *Woluet* 1315 AD iv (Ess); Margaria *Woliet* 1351 AssEss; John *Wlyet* 1367 AD iv (Ess); Widow *Ullet* 1674 HTSf. OE *Wulfgēat* 'wolf-Geat'.

Woolving: *Wlueing* 1227 AssBk. OE *Wulfing* 'son of *Wulf(a)*'.

Woolward: *v.* WOOLLARD

Woolway, Woolaway: *Wluui, Wlui* 1066 DB;

Ricardus *filius Ulfui* c1095 Bury (Sf); Willelmus *filius Wlwi* 1202 P (Bk); Robert *Wulfwi* 1190 P (Lei); Lucas *Wulwy* 1230 Pat; William *Wolwy* 1275 SRWo; Symon *Wolvy, Wolwy* 1279 RH (C). OE *Wulfwīg* 'wolf-war'. This might also have contributed to WOLVEY.

Woolwich, Woolich, Woolidge, Woollage, Woledge, Wolledge: From Woolwich (Kent) 'wool-farm'. Also from Wollage Green and Woolwich Wood in Womenswold (Kent) where the surname was *de Wolfech'*, *de Wulfhecch* 1313 PN K 540, OE *wulf-hæcce*, probably denoting a wolf-pit, wolf-trap. *v.* also WORLEDGE.

Woolwright: *v.* WOOLRICH

Woombell, Woombill, Woomble: *v.* WOMBWELL

Woor, Woore: Nicholas *le Wowere* 1275 RH (Sf); Emma *Woweres* 1279 RH (O); Adam *le Wogher'* 1327 SRSx. OE *wōgere* 'wooer, suitor'.

Woosey: *v.* WOOLSEY

Woosley: *v.* WOLSELEY

Woosman, Woosnam: *v.* WOLSTENHOLME

Wooster: *v.* WORCESTER

Wooton, Wootton, Wootten, Wotton: Wagen *de Wotton* c1048 OEByn (Wa); Robert *de Wodeton'* 1242 Fees (Sa); John *de Wutton* 1256 AssNb; John *ate Wodeton* 1275 RH (Mx); Gilbert *de la Wotton* 1316 MELS (Wo). From one of the many places named Wootton or Wotton, or from residence at a farm by a wood (OE **wudu-tūn*).

Wora(c)ker: *v.* WARWICKER

Worboys: *v.* WARBOY

Worcester, Worster, Wooster, Wostear: Ralph *de Wircestr'* 1180 P (C); William *de Worcester* 1290 AssSt; Reynold *Woster* 1567 Bardsley; Alice *Wooster* 1658 ib. From Worcester.

Wordman: *v.* WARDMAN

Wordsworth: *v.* WADSWORTH

Woricker: *v.* WARWICKER

Work, Worke: Richard *del Worke* c1260 ERO (Ess); Simon *Werk* 1279 RH (Bk); Nicholas *del Werk* 1357 Whitby. OE *(ge)weorc* 'work, fortification'. A name, probably, for one working on fortifications or for a man employed in some capacity at a fort.

Worker: Richard *le Wercare* 1332 MEOT (Sr). A derivative of OE *wyrcan, weorcan* 'to work'. One who works or does work of any kind (13.. NED). A rare surname.

Workman: Adwordus *Wercman* 1214 StGreg (K); William *le Werkman* 1236 FFSx; Gilbert *le Worcman* 1279 RH (O). OE *weorcmann* 'workman'. In addition to this meaning, PromptParv has: 'Werkemanne, þat cann werke wythe bothe handys a-lyke. *Ambidexter*', which might well have given rise to a nickname.

Worledge, Worlidge, Worlledge, Worllege, Woledge, Wolledge, Woolidge, Woollage: John *Woorliche* 1468 SIA xii; John *Worlych, Wurlych* 1524 SRSf; Richard *Worleche* 1536 SIA xii; John *Worlich* 1551 SfPR; William *Worlege* 1568 SRSf; Maria *Worledge* 1671 SfPR; Philip *Worledge*, Robert *Wolladge*, William *Woollagge*,—*Woolage*,

— *Worlike* 1674 HTSf; William *Wooledge* 1827 SfPR. Forms are late, but this is probably OE *weorþlīc* 'worthy, noble, distinguished'. cf. LOVELY, and *v.* WOOLWICH.

Worlock: *v.* WARLOCK

Worm, Worms: Water *Wormes* 1275 RH (D); John *le Werm*, William *le Wurm* 1296 SRSx. OE *wyrm* 'snake, dragon'.

Wormald, Wormhall, Wormal, Wormell, Warmoll, Wormull: Alexander *de Wormwall* 1379 PTY; Robert *Wormall, Wormell* 1592, 1598 RothwellPR (Y); Samuel *Wormald* 1748 FrY. From Wormald (WRYorks), or Wormhill (Derby).

Worral, Worrall, Worrell, Worrill, Whorall: Roger *de Wyrhal'* 1219 AssY; Richard *de Wyrall* 1351 ShefA; Alan *de Worrell* 1388 IpmNt; William *Worrall* 1517 ShefA; Joseph *Worrell* 1705 FrY. From Wirral (Ches), or Worrall (WRYorks).

Worsdale, Worsdall, Worsdell: John *de Wiresdale* 1332 SRLa; Anne *Worsdall* 1667 Bardsley. From Wyresdale (Lancs).

Worsell, Worssell, Woursell, Wurzal: Peter *de Wirkeshal'* 1219 AssY; John *Worsell* 1439 FrY. From Worsall (NRYorks), *Wercesel* DB.

Worsencroft: *v.* WOLSTENCROFT

Worship: John *Worchipe* 1327 SRSf; Robert *Worshipe* 1327 SRSx; John *Worschep* 1332 SRCu. OE *weorþscipe* 'worship, honour, dignity'.

Worsick: *v.* WORSWICK

Worsley, Worslay: Geoffrey *de Wyrkesle* 1246 AssLa; Robert *de Worvesle* 1275 SRWo; Richard *Worseley* 1396 AssL; James *Wursley* 1548 CorNt. From Worsley (Lancs), *Werkesleia* 1196, or Worsley (Worcs), *Worvesleg* c1180.

Worsman: *v.* WOLSTENHOLME
Worssell: *v.* WORSELL
Worstencroft: *v.* WOLSTENCROFT
Worstenholme: *v.* WOLSTENHOLME
Worster: *v.* WORCESTER

Worswick, Worsick: Anne *Worswick* 1670 LaWills; Alexander *Worsick* 1731 ib. From Urswick (Lancs).

Wort, Worts, Wortt: Æluuric *Uuort* c1095 Bury (Sf); Henry *Wortes* 1524 SRSf. OE *wyrt*, ME *wort* 'plant, vegetable'. Metonymic for WORTMAN.

Worters: *v.* WARTERS

Worth, Werth: John *de Wurde* 1195 P (K); Hawisia *de la Wurth* 1204 FFSo; Elyas *de la Worth'* 1243 AssSo; William *de Werthe* 1275 RH (Sx); Richard *atte Werthe* 1296 SRSx; William *atte Worthe* 1327 SRSx. OE *worð* (*wyrð*) 'enclosure, homestead'. From Worth (Ches, Devon, Kent, Sussex), Worth Matravers (Dorset), Highworth (Wilts) or Littleworth (Berks), both *Wurda* 1196 P, or from residence or employment at an outlying farm.

Wortham: Adam *de Wrtham* 1188 BuryS (Sf). From Wortham (Suffolk).

Worthen: Richard *de Worthin* 1274 RH (Sa); Richard *atte Worthyne* 1316 MELS (Wo). From Worthen (Salop), Worthing (Norfolk), or from residence at an enclosure or homestead, OE *worþign*, a term particularly common in the West Midlands. It sometimes becomes *Wortham*: William *atte Wurthen* lived at Wortham (Devon) in 1330 (PN D 212).

Worthing: (i) Robert *de Worthinge* 1276 RH (Beds). From Worthing (Sussex), probably the usual source; or a variant of WORTHEN. (ii) *Worthing'* Medicus, *Honorius* Medicus 1203 Cur (Nf); *Worthingus* 1206 Cur (Beds); *Urthing, Wrthing* de Marisco 1240 ER 61; John *Worthang'* 1219 Cur (Sx). An OE personal-name *Wurð* has been postulated to explain the place-names Worsthorne (Lancs), Worston Lancs), Worthing (Sussex) and Worthington (Lancs, Leics). In the form *Weorð*, it has now been noted twice in 12th-century London: *Werth* Hy 1 ELPN, *Werd* 1111–38 ib.; in addition, three examples of an unrecorded compound *Weorðgifu* (f) are now known: Æilric *Uuordgiue filius* c1095 Bury (Sf); Ricardus *filius Wrthiue* 1212 Cur (Beds); Ricardus *nepos Wrtheve* 1222 DBStP (Ess). *Weorð* is from OE *weorð*, late OE *wurð* 'worthy'. From this a derivative *Weorðing* was formed, of which the above are the only known examples.

Worthington: Snarri *de Wurðintona* 1169 P (L); William *de Wurthington* 1246 AssLa; John *Worthyngton* 1439 IpmNt. From Worthington (Lancs, Leics).

Worthy: Godwine *æt Worðige* 1001 ASC (Ha); Chiping' *de Ordia* 1066 Winton (Ha); Geoffrey *de la Worthy* 1293 Fees (D). From Worthy (Hants, Devon).

Wortman: Simon *Wurtman* 1297 MinAcctCo. 'Seller of vegetables', OE *wyrt* and *mann*.

Wosencroft: *v.* WOLSTENCROFT
Wostear: *v.* WORCESTER
Wostenholm: *v.* WOLSTENHOLME
Wotton: *v.* WOOTON
Would(s): *v.* WALD

Wouldhave: John *Waldhaue* 1396 FrY. Possibly a corruption of *Waldeve*. cf. WADDILOVE, WALTHEW.

Woursell: *v.* WORSELL
Wozencroft: *v.* WOLSTENCROFT

Wragg, Wragge: *Wrag* 1193 P (Nth); William *Wraggi* 1192 P (Wo); William, John *Wrag* 1221 AssWa, 1323 AD i (L). ODa *Wraghi*.

Wraight, Wrate: *v.* WRIGHT

Wraith: John *Wrayth* son of Thomas *Wrath* 1587 FrY. OE *wrāð* 'angry, fierce'. A northern form of WROTH.

Wray: *v.* WREY, WROE
Wreath, Wrede: *v.* WRIDE

Wreghitt: Richard *Wreggett* 1653 FrY. From Wreggets in Wheldrake (ERYorks), *Wragate* 13th PN ERY 271.

Wreight: *v.* WRIGHT

Wren, Wrenn: Wlsy, William *Wrenne* 1275 RH (Nf), 1317 AssK; Ralph *Wranne* 1296 SRSx. A nickname from the wren, OE *wrenna, wrænna*.

Wrench, Wrinch: Alnodus *Wrench* 1176 P (D); Edwin *Wrench* 1199 P (Nf). ME *wrench*, OE *wrenc* 'wile, trick, artifice'.

Wrey: (i) Robert *de Wrey* 1275 RH (D). From Wray Barton (Devon). (ii) Stephen *le Wrey* 1313 PN D 212. 'The twisted, crooked', from ME *wry(e)* 'awry', from OE *wrīgian* 'to turn'.

Wride, Wreath, Wrede: Roger *Wrid* 1199 P (Sf); John *Wrid'* 1219 AssL; Elyas *le Wrede* 1274 RH (Ess); Hugh *Wride* 1279 RH (O); Roberd *Wrethe* 1522 BuryW (Sf). OE **wride* 'twist, turn', from OE *wrīþan* 'to twist', was used topographically of a winding stream. cf. Wryde (PN C 282). The term may also have been applied to a 'twisting' man, the colloquial 'slippery customer'. In ME the *i* was sometimes lowered to *e*, as in *Wrethefeld* 1318. Hence *Wrethe* and *Wreath*.

Wridgway: For RIDGEWAY.

Wrigglesworth, Wriglesworth, Rigglesford, Riggulsford: John *de Writhelfford* 1379 FrY; Robert *Wriglesforth* 1591 RothwellPR (Y); William *Wriglesworth* 1605 ib. From Woodlesford (WRYorks), *Wridelesford* 12th, *Wudelesford* 1425, *Wriglesforth* 1596, *Wriglesworth* 1620 (PN WR-Yorks ii,141).

Wright, Wrighte, Wraight, Wraighte, Wrate, Wreight: Patere *le Writh* 1214 FFSx; Robert *le Wrichte* 1255 FFEss; Robert *Wricht* 1274 RH (Sa); Richard *le Wreȝte* 1317 AssK; Hugh *le Wreghte* 1327 SRSx; Thomas *le Wrighte* 1327 SRDb; Walter *le Wrytte* 1327 SRSf; Amiscia *la Wrihtes* 1333 ColchCt; Thomas *Wrayte* 1547 RochW. OE *wyrhta, wryhta* 'carpenter, joiner'.

Wrightson: Robert *Wryghtson* 1379 PTY, 'Son of the wright'.

Wrigley, Rigley: William *de Wriggeley* 1327 SRDb. From Wrigley Head (Lancs).

Wrinch: *v.* WRENCH

Writer: Adam *le Wrytar* 1275 SRWo. OE *wrītere* 'writer, copier of manuscripts'. The writers of London formed two separate crafts in 1422: the writers of the ordinary book-hand, 'textscriveyns', and the writers of the court-hands (LoPleas 199).

Wrixon: Adam *Wrygson* 1379 PTY. ME *wright* had a variety of forms, and names like *Aldrich* often vary between *-rich* and *-rick*. Hence, probably for *Wrightson*, through such forms as *Wrichtson, Wrichson, Wrickson, Wrigson*.

Wroath: *v.* WROTH

Wroe, Wray: Tomas *de Wra* 1196 P (Y); Richard *del Wro* 1210 Cur (Nf); Ralph *in le Wra* 1260 AssY; John *in ye Wro* 1366 ShefA. ON *vrá* 'nook, corner, remote or isolated place'. In the north it became Wray (Lancs) and Wrea, Wreay (Cumb). At Wrayside (Cumb) in 1285 lived Henry *del Wra*. Farther south this became ME *wro* which does not seem to have survived as a place-name. Both *wra* and *wro* were common in Yorks where both *Wray* and *Wroe* are still found. Here and in Norfolk they must derive from unidentified remote spots.

Wrong: (i) Osbert *Wrange* 1182 P (D); Ailnoth *Wrang* 1202 P (Sr); John *Wrong* 1275 RH (Sf); William *le Wronge* 1317 AssK. Late OE *wrang* of Scand origin, 'crooked'. (ii) Robert *ate Wrong*

1327 SRC; Richard *atte Wronge* 1348 FFC. OE *wrang* is found as a compound in place-names meaning 'crooked'. Here it is used as a substantive for a crooked, irregularly shaped piece of land.

Wronger, Wronker: Equivalent to *atte Wronge*.

Wroot: (i) John, William *Wrote* 1200 P (Ha), 1296 SRSx. A nickname from OE *wrōt* 'snout'. (ii) Algar *Wroth*, Walter *Wrot* 1202 AssL. These Lincs names must be early examples of the loss of the preposition and derive from Wroot (Lincs), formerly an island or a spur of land thought to resemble a pig's snout.

Wroth, Wroath: W. *Wrothe* c1210 ELPN; Walter *le Wrothe* 1221 AssSa. OE *wrāð* 'angry, fierce'.

Wulff: *v.* WOLF

Wurzal: *v.* WORSELL

Wusteman: *v.* WOLSTENHOLME

Wyard, Wyartt, Whyard: *Wiardus* de Nichole Hy 2 Gilb (L); Henry *Wiard, Wihard* 1188, 1193 P (Ha); Edmund *Wyard* 1230 P (Ess). OE *Wīgheard* 'war-brave'. This surname has, no doubt, frequently become WYATT. Wyatt's Lane in Walthamstow (Ess) owes its name to the family of Walter and Richard *Wiard* (1223–52 PN Ess 106), the latter of whom is also called Richard son of *Wyard* 1223–52 AD i.

Wyatt, Wiatt, Whyatt, Guyat, Guyatt, Gyatt, Guyot, Giot: *Wiot* de Acham 1192 P (L); *Wioth* de Cratella Hy 2 DC (Nt); *Gwiot* 1203 Cur (Gl); *Wyot* 1219 AssY; William *Wyot* 1274 RH (Sa); Robert *Wiot* 1279 RH (Beds); Thomas *Guyot* 1295 FFEss; Henry *Guyot* 1327 SRSo. A diminutive in *-ot* of OFr *Guy*, OG *Wido*. Occasionally we have a diminutive in *-et*: Richard *Guiet* 1141–51 Colch (Ess), Elias *Wyete* 1296 SRSx. *Giot* de Kemesinge 1317 AssK is also called *Guydo* Formage. Occasionally, *Wiot* is a diminutive of *William*: *Wiotus* or *Guillotus* 1175 P (Berks). The form *Wyatt* really represents *Wyard*. *Wyott* does not survive but seems to have become *Wyatt* commonly in the 16th century: John *Wyot* 1575 Oxon (D), William *Wyatt* 1576 ib. (D). The Norman *Wyatt* is much more common both in ME and today than the French *Guyatt*. On the other hand, *Guy* is the regular modern form of *Wido*. *Giot* survives in Jersey.

Wyber, Wyberg, Wybergh, Wybrew, Wybrow, Waybrow, Wheybrew, Whybra, Whybray, Whybrew, Whybro, Whybrow, Wiber, Wiberg, Wibrew, Wibroe, Wibrow: *Wyburgh* (f) 1182–1211 BuryS (Sf); Osbertus *filius Wiburge* 1219 Cur (Lei); *Wybur'* 1279 RH (O); Roger *Wybir'* 1279 RH (O); Margeria *Wyburgh'* 1327 SRC; Thomas *Wybourgwe* 1327 SRSf. OE *Wīgburh* 'war-fortress', a woman's name recorded once in 901 and then not until the 12th century. In view of the variety and frequency of the surnames it must have been more common than the records suggest.

Wyberd, Wyburd, Whyberd, Whybird: *Wibert* 1066 DB (Y); *Guibertus* 1086 DB (Ess); Rodbertus *filius Wiberti* 1121–48 Bury (Sf); *Wibertus* 1214 Cur (K); Robert, Amicia *Wyberd* 1327, 1332

SRSx; Bartholomew *Wyberd* 1327 SRSf. OE *Wīgbeorht* 'war-bright' or OFr *Wibert*, *Guibert* from OG *Wigbert*. Both are probably represented.

Wyborn, Wybourn, Wyburn, Wybron, Whyborn: *Wibern* de Keistret' 1212 Cur (K); Ralph *Wybern* 1241 FFEss; Richard *Wyborn*' 1275 SRWo. OE *Wīgbeorn* 'war-hero', late and rare in OE and not common later.

Wybrew, Wybrow: *v.* WYBER

Wyburn: *v.* WYBORN

Wych: *v.* WICH

Wye: Hugh *de Wy* 1275 RH (K). From Wye (Kent). *v.* also GUY.

Wyke(s): *v.* WICH

Wykeham: *v.* WICKHAM

Wyld(e), Wyld(e)s: *v.* WILD

Wyldbore: *v.* WILDBORE

Wyles, Wyley: *v.* WILES, WILEY

Wyllys: *v.* WILLIS

Wyly: *v.* WILEY

Wyman, Wymann, Wymans, Weyman, Weymont, Wayman, Waymont, Whayman, Whaymand, Whaymond, Whaymont, Whyman, Whymant, Whamond: *Wimundus* 1066 DB (Nf); *Wymund* ater Walle 1296 SRSx; Robert *Wymund*, *Wimund* 1275 SRWo, 1279 RH (C); Alan *Wymand* 1275 SRWo; Robert *Waymon* 1275 SRWo; Peter, Robert *Weymund* 1279 RH (C); William *Wayman* 1357 AD ii (D); Robert *Whayemonde* 1568 SRSf. OE *Wīgmund* 'war-protection'. In Lincs, Leics and Norfolk the personal name may be ON *Vígmundr*, ODa, OSw *Vimund*.

Wymark, Waymark: Robertus *filius Wimarc* 1066 DB (Ess); *Wimarca* (f) Hy 2 DC (L); *Wimarc* (f) 1219 AssY; Robert *Wimarc* 1066 DB (Ess), 1199 P (Nf). OBret *Wiuhomarch*, both masculine and feminine. *v.* also WYMER.

Wymer: *Wimerus* 1066, 1086 DB (Sf); *Wymerus* de Westwyc 1153–66 Holme (Nf); Eche *filius Wymeri*, Eche *Wimer* c1160, 1186–1210 ib.; Willelmus *filius Wimari*, William *Wymer*' 1212, 1236 Fees (St); Adam *Wymer* 1327 SRSf. OE *Wīgmǣr* 'battle-famous' or OG *Wigmar*. Forms like *Wiomar*, *Wiomer* 1208 Cur (C), *Wyomer*' 1219 AssY are not uncommon in districts where Bretons are known to have been numerous and there has been confusion with OBret *Wiuhomarch* 'worthy to have a horse' which was originally masculine. This confusion is found already in 1086. *Wihumar*' dapifer comitis Alani, called also *Wiemar*'; *Wihemar*' 1086 ICC (C) appears in DB as *Wihomarc*. A similar assimilation to a more common ending *-ard* took place in France where OFr *Guiomarch* became *Guyomard*.

Wyn, Wynne: *v.* GWINN

Wynch: *v.* WINCH

Wynde: *v.* WIND

Wyndham: *v.* WINDHAM

Wyne(s), Wyness: *v.* WINE

Wynn(e), Wynnes: *v.* WINN

Wynniatt: *v.* WINGATE

Wynter(s): WINTER

Wynton: *v.* WINTON

Wynyard: *v.* WINYARD

Wynyates: *v.* WINGATE

Wyon, Wyons, Guyon: Robertus *filius Guiun*, *Gwiun* 1203, 1209 P (Y); *Wyon*, *Wyun* 1246 AssLa; William *Wyonn*, Nicholas *Gyan* 1327 AssSo. Either the cas-régime of GUY, *Guyon*, usually in the Norman form *Wyon*, or a diminutive in *-un* of GUY. Rare surnames.

Wyvill, Wyville: Hugo *de Wituile*, *de Widuile* 1086 DB; William *de Wituilla*, *de Wiuilla* Hy 2 DC (L). From Gouville (Eure), earlier *Wivilla*. *v.* OEByn.

Y

Yalland, Yelland, Yolland: John *de la Yaldelonde* 1275 RH (D). 'Dweller by the old cultivated land'. Common place-names in Devonshire, with surnames *de la Yalelande* 1238, *Attenoldelonde* 1244, *de la Yoldelonde* 1270, *Yollelonde* 1281, *Yeallelond* 1333 (PN D).

Yapp: Richard *Yap, Yape* 1200 P (Nt), 1297 SRY. A nickname from OE *gēap* 'bent'.

Yard, Yarde: Thomas *de la Yurda* 1225 AssSo; Robert *atte Yerde* 1309 LLB D. OE *gerd, gyrd* 'virgate, thirty acres', probably denoting a holder of a yardland.

Yardley, Yeardley: Richard *de Gerdelai* 1199 Pl (Nth); William *de Erdeleg'* 1229 Cur (Herts); Adam *de Jerdeleye* c1280 SRWo; Robert *Yerdeleye* 1372 IpmGl; John *Yardeley* 1499 FFEss. From Yardley (Essex, Northants, Worcs), or Yarley (Som), *Gyrdleg* 1065.

Yarker, Yorker: John *le Yarker, Yurker* 1327 SRC; John *Yarkar* 1379 PTY. A derivative of ME *yerk* 'to draw stitches tight, to twitch, as a shoemaker in sewing' (c1430 NED), a shoemaker.

Yate, Yates, Yeates, Yeats, Yetts: Hereward *de Jette* 1198 P (Gl); Philip *del Yate* 1260 AssCh; Roger *atte Yat* 1268 AssSo; John *atte Yete* 1327 SRSo; Robert *atte Yates* 1344 FrNorw. From Yate (Glos), or 'dweller by a gate', or 'gate-keeper' (OE *geat*). *v.* GATE.

Yatman, Yeatman, Yetman: John *Yateman* 1603 Bardsley; Ann *Yeatman* 1758 ib.; David *Yetman* 1775 ib. *v.* YATE.

Yea, Yeo: Geoffrey *de la Ya* 1242 Fees (D); Alexander *de Ya* 1257 AssSo; Viel *de la Yo* 1260 MELS (So); Richard *atte ȝeo*, Adam *atte ȝaa* 1333 ib.; Robert *atte Yea* 1340 ib. (So); Hugo *de la Yeo* 1333 PN D 287; Nicholas *Yeo, Yoo* 1439 LLB K. From residence near a stream; OE *ēa* in Somerset and Devon became ME *eā, ya, yo*, which survives in various places named Yeo. *v.* ATYEO, REA, NYE.

Yealland: Adam *de Yeland* 1230 P (La). From Yealand (Lancs).

Yeaman: *v.* YEOMAN
Yeardley: *v.* YARDLEY
Yeates: *v.* YATE
Yeatman: *v.* YATMAN
Yelland: *v.* YALLAND
Yeman: *v.* YEOMAN
Yeo: *v.* YEA

Yeoman, Yeomans, Yeaman, Yeman: William *Zeman* 1296 SRSx; John *Yemon* 1332 SRLa; Thomas *le Yomon* 1381 SRSt. ME *ȝoman, ȝeman* 'servant or attendant in a noble house, ranking between a sergeant and a groom or between a squire and a page'.

Yeoward, Yeowart: *v.* EWART
Yeowell, Yeuell: *v.* YOULE
Yetman: *v.* YATMAN
Yetts: *v.* YATE
Yewen: *v.* EWAN
Yoell: *v.* YOULE
Yolland: *v.* YALLAND
Yong(e): *v.* YOUNG

Yonwin: *Iunguine* c1095 Bury (Sf); Robertus *filius Iunguini* 1182 Oseney (O); *Yungwin'* de Tedford 1177 P (Sf); Simon *Yongwyne* 1327 SRSf; Roger *Youngwyne* 1327 SR (Ess). OE **Geongwine* 'young friend'.

York, Yorke: Ernisius *de Eboraco* a1160 YCh; John *de York* 1324 CorLo; Thomas *York* 1522 CorNt. From York.

Yorkshire, Yorksher, Yorksheer: John *de Euirwikescire* 1260 AssCh; William *Yorkescher* 1379 PTY. 'The man from Yorkshire.'

Youatt: *v.* EWART
Youens, Youings: *v.* EWAN

Youlden, Youldon: 'Dweller on the old hill', as at Youlden and Youldon (Devon), with the same development as in Yalland. *v.* PN D.

Youle, Youles, Youll, Youel, Youels, Yoell, Yeowell, Yeuell, Youhill, Yuell, Yule, Yuile, Yuill, Yuille: William *Yol* 1199 P (L); William *Yoel* 1297 Wak (Y); Robert *Youle* 1379 PTY. OE *geōl*, ON *jól* 'Yule, Christmas', a name for one born at that time.

Young, Younge, Youngs, Yong, Yonge: Wilferð *seo Iunga* 744 ASC E; Richard *le Yunge* 12th Lichfield (St); Walter *Yonge* 1296 SRSx. OE *geong* 'young', a name often used, no doubt, to distinguish a younger from an older man.

Younger: Edmund *Yonger* 1379 PTY. 'The younger.' cf. Alanus *Junior* 1201 Cur. John *Yongehere* 1364 LoPleas was a Fleming and his surname is MDu *jonghheer* 'young nobleman', an earlier example of which is probably: William *Yunghare* 1297 Wak (Y).

Younghusband: Richard *le Yongehosebonde* 1275 SRWo; Robert *þe yengehusbonde* 1277 *Ely* (Sf); Robert *le Yungehusebonde* 1298 AssSt. 'Young farmer' (late OE *hūsbonda*).

Youngman, Younkman: Roger *Yungeman* 1235 FFEss; William *le Yongeman* 1302 Clerkenwell (Lo). 'Young servant.'

Youngmay: Martin *le Yungemey* 1275 RH (Sx). 'Young lad, servant.' OE *mǣg*.

Youngson: Peter *Yungeson* 1268 AssSo. 'Young son.'

Younson: John *Ewynsone* 1296 Black; William *Yewnsoun* 1603 ib. 'Son of *Ewan*.'

Yuell, Yuill, Yule: *v.* YOULE

Z

Zeal, Zeale: *v.* SEAL
Zealey, Zealley: *v.* SEALEY
Zell, Zelle: *v.* SELL

Zeller: *v.* SELLAR
Zelley: *v.* SEALEY
Zouch: *v.* SUCH